Samuel Johnson's

DICTIONARY

Samuel Johnson's

DICTIONARY

Selections from the 1755 work
that defined the English language

EDITED BY JACK LYNCH

LEVENGER
PRESS

Delray Beach, Florida

This edition published 2004
By BCA
In association with Levenger Press

CN 131177

First published in Great Britain in
Hardback in 2004 by
Atlantic Books, an imprint of
Grove Atlantic Ltd.

Printed in The Netherlands by Krips BV

CONTENTS

*Animals • Art and Theatre • Books and Writing • Cant Words •
Clothes and Jewelry • Food and Drink • Games and Sports •
Inkhorn Terms • Insults • Law and Crime • Learning and
Education • Literature, Language, Grammar and Rhetoric • Low
and Bad Words • Ludicrous Words • Mathematics • Medicine and
Health • Money and Business • Music and Dance • Philosophy and
Psychology • Plants • Politics and Government • Religion • Science
• Sex and the Sexes • Social Rank • Superstition and the
Supernatural • Transportation • Warfare • World Cultures*

Belly-timber?

Words have a way of begetting words. At Levenger, we first came upon Samuel Johnson's *Dictionary* while publishing an earlier book, *Words That Make a Difference*. Johnson's work, we discovered, was still a bible among lexicographers.

But the real discovery began when we started reading what was known for a century and a half simply as The Dictionary. *Scholy...answer-jobber...hobit...yux*: what were these words and their meanings? It was as if we had unearthed a lost language, and that language was English.

belly-timber Food; materials to support the belly.

Johnson takes us back to the mid-eighteenth-century way of defining the world, one in which the Industrial Revolution had barely begun and the American Revolution was not in the lexicon. But *electricity, evolution, suburb* and *vermicelli* were. A lively back-door chronicle of history, Johnson's dictionary serves as a Rosetta stone of what English used to mean, an invaluable marker of how our language has—and hasn't—changed. (Fancy *sneaker* being something you drank from, *terrific* being awful, *awful* being awesome and *let* meaning just the opposite of what it does today. Meanwhile, we've let *slubberdegullion, curtain-lecture* and a legion of other satisfying words all but vanish from our vernacular.)

Johnson shone a light on our language that no other lexicographer had before. He showed us the words in context, citing passages from the works of Shakespeare (who had no dictionary to consult), Bacon, Swift, Pope, Milton and a host of other writers. Occasionally even the great lexicographer had to throw up his hands (*skilt*: "I know not either the etymology or meaning"). Other times, he waxed indignant against interlopers such as *finesse* ("an unnecessary word, creeping into the language").

The result is a fascinating read, a serious and scholarly work—and a word treasury you can have fun with. If you're looking for new names for your friends that will send them to the dictionary to find what you meant by *fopdoodle*, this is your secret and authoritative source.

Jack Lynch, our steadfast editor and an estimable Johnson scholar, believes that every age needs an edition of Samuel Johnson's work. We hope ours does justice to the man who, by his great deed of 1755, defined the very word dictionary.

— Steven Leveen, President
Levenger

ACKNOWLEDGMENTS

Johnson published his *Dictionary* "with frigid tranquillity," having written it "without one Act of assistance, one word of encouragement, or one smile of favour." My experience in editing it has been much more pleasant, thanks to the assistance, encouragement and favor of many friends and colleagues. The bibliography records some of my debts, but I owe more personal thanks to those who helped to shape this book, including Lisa Berglund, Brycchan Carey, Paul Fussell, Kristine Haugen, Rachel Kennedy, Natasha McEnroe, David McKay, Alan T. McKenzie, John Scanlan, Lana Schwebel, Paul Tankard and David Venturo.

Several *Dictionary* experts—Robert DeMaria Jr., Anne McDermott, Graham Nicholls and Allen Reddick—were uncommonly generous in offering advice, even sharing the still-unpublished results of their research. I am doubtless responsible for "a few wild blunders, and risible absurdities" of my own, but they have saved me from some of the more egregious ones.

It has been a real pleasure to collaborate with Mim Harrison and Jeff Simon of Levenger Press and the design team in Levenger Studios: Lee Passarella, Danielle Furci, Dawn Hyden, Shari Blyn and Vicki Ehrenman. I am most grateful to Steve and Lori Leveen for their support of this edition. A special thanks to Professor John Guson, an early champion of a Levenger Press edition.

I also owe thanks to the staffs of the Firestone Library at Princeton University, the Dana Library of Rutgers University, the Van Pelt Library of the University of Pennsylvania and the New York Public Library.

INTRODUCTION TO THIS EDITION

The myth is wrong: Johnson's was *not* the first English dictionary. Dozens of them had appeared in the century and a half before *A Dictionary of the English Language* was published in 1755.

It's certainly not the newest dictionary, in an age when novelty sells books. You'll find no trendy buzzwords in Johnson, who had barely heard of the steam engine, to say nothing of the search engine.

It's not the most comprehensive dictionary. The *Oxford English Dictionary*, its great successor, contains more than ten times as many words. Even in Johnson's own day, Nathan Bailey's *Dictionarium Britannicum* had almost fifty percent more entries.

Nor is it the most accurate dictionary. There are any number of blunders, from absurd etymologies ("May not *spider* be *spy dor*, the insect that watches the *dor*?") to inaccurate definitions (*pastern*, "the knee of an horse") to frank admissions of ignorance (*stammel*, "Of this word I know not the meaning").

Why, then, should anyone care about a dictionary published a quarter of a millennium ago? For several good reasons.

Though not the first English dictionary, it was the first standard dictionary. Until the *Oxford English Dictionary* was completed in 1928, English readers who turned to *the* dictionary turned to Johnson. His book went through countless abridgments, expansions, revisions and adaptations over the years, and dictionaries calling themselves Johnson's were still appearing in the 1870s. It was Johnson's *Dictionary* that Coleridge complained about in *Biographia Literaria*, that Dickens mentioned in "Mrs. Lirriper's Legacy" and that Robert Browning read from cover to cover to "qualify" himself to be a poet. It was Johnson's "Dixonary" that Becky Sharp threw out of the carriage window in Thackeray's *Vanity Fair*. It was *the* dictionary for Wordsworth, Keats, Shelley, Austen, the Brontës, Arnold, Trollope and George Eliot.

Though devoid of the latest coinages, it provides a record of a fascinating age. It was the dawn of the Industrial Revolution and the time of Ben Franklin's experiments with electricity. Britain's Empire was expanding as its colonies in America were beginning to show signs of discontent. Johnson's *Dictionary* is a portrait of that rapidly changing world.

Though not the most comprehensive dictionary, it was the most faithful record of the language people used. Most dictionaries paid scant attention to everyday words, and instead swelled their word counts with thousands of so-called inkhorn terms—mostly Latin or Greek words with English suffixes that dictionary makers invented. Johnson put more energy than any of his predecessors into the common words, the ones that appeared in the works of the best

Most dictionaries paid scant attention to everyday words, and instead swelled their word counts with thousands of so-called inkhorn terms—mostly Latin or Greek words with English suffixes that dictionary makers invented. Johnson put more energy than any of his predecessors into the common words, the ones that appeared in the works of the best English writers.

English writers. His book also included more than 100,000 quotations from these authors—the first English dictionary to do so. It therefore serves not only as a dictionary but also as an encyclopedia, an anthology of English literature and a dictionary of quotations.

Johnson's is the only English dictionary that can be called a great work of literature. Most reference books are interesting only as long as they're current; Johnson remains fascinating long after his definitions have been superseded. No dictionary is better suited to browsing or even reading straight through.

Though not the most accurate dictionary available today, it is the work of a singularly powerful mind, and it shows Johnson's incisive intelligence and wide reading on every page. Johnson was one of the most important writers of the eighteenth century, a period still often called "the age of Johnson," and his age continues to speak to ours. He is the most quoted prose author in the English language (he merits ten pages of quips and *bons mots* in the most recent *Oxford Dictionary of Quotations*), and many of his works have never gone out of print. The *Dictionary* is the longest work by one of the greatest authors in our language, and it deserves to be read for that reason alone.

But its most important claim on our attention is that Johnson's is the only English dictionary that can be called a great work of literature. Most reference books are interesting only as long as they're current; Johnson remains fascinating long after his definitions have been superseded. No dictionary is better suited to browsing or even reading straight through. Coleridge didn't think much of it "as a *dictionary*" but he found it "a most instructive and entertaining *book*." Lord Macaulay, never one of Johnson's supporters, called it "the first dictionary which could be read with pleasure. The definitions show so much acuteness of thought and command of language, and the passages quoted from poets, divines and philosophers are so skillfully selected, that a leisure hour may always be very agreeably spent in turning over the pages."

Earlier Dictionaries

Dictionaries go back thousands of years, to word lists assembled by translators in ancient Sumer. Greek scholars at Alexandria compiled lexicons to aid their reading of Homer, and medieval scribes worked on Latin glossaries in their study of the Bible. The first modern dictionaries began appearing in Europe during the Renaissance. By the seventeenth century, lexicography was far advanced on the Continent, as the monumental dictionaries of the Accademia della Crusca and the Académie Française attest.

England lagged behind Italy and France. The earliest English dictionaries were bilingual: *The Dictionary of Syr Thomas Eliot Knight* (1538), the first English work to be called a dictionary, translated Latin into English; John Withals's *Shorte Dictionarie for Yonge Begynners* (1553) went from English to Latin. But the English language was undergoing rapid change in the sixteenth century, and English speakers began to feel the inconvenience of not understanding the whole of their native language. In *The First Part of the Elementarie, which Entreateth Chefelie of the Right Writing of Our English Tung* (1582), Richard Mulcaster therefore proposed a new kind of book, an English-to-English dictionary. "It were a thinge verie praiseworthie in my opinion," he wrote, "if som one well learned and as laborious a man, wold gather all the words which we use in our *English* tung...into one dictionarie.... The want thereof, is the onelie cause why, that verie manie men, being excellentlie well learned in foren speche, can hardlie discern what theie have at home."

Robert Cawdrey was the first to answer the call with *A Table Alphabeticall*, published in 1604. It was a short work, with only around twenty-five hundred entries, and it didn't look much like a modern dictionary. His definitions were usually little more than synonyms, such as "*Baud*, whore.... *Magistrate*, governour.... *Maladie*, disease." And although Cawdrey attacked the "strange ynkhorne termes" so beloved by scholars in his day, his book was filled with these obscure words—*neotericke, obnubilate, pervicacie*. His interest in abstruse words comes through in his title, in all its seventeenth-century splendor: *A Table Alphabeticall, Conteyning and Teaching the True Writing, and Understanding of Hard Usuall English Words, Borrowed from the Hebrew, Greeke, Latine, or French, &c. with the Interpretation thereof by Plaine English Words, Gathered for the Benefit & Helpe of Ladies, Gentlemen, or Any Other Unskilfull Persons, whereby They May the More Easilie and Better Understand Many Hard English Wordes, which They Shall Heare or Read in Scriptures, Sermons, or Elsewhere, and Also Be Made Able to Use the Same Aptly Themselves.*

Attacks on inkhorn terms were *de rigueur* among lexicographers, but most seventeenth-century dictionaries were, like Cawdrey's, mere lists of difficult terminology, or "hard words," that made no pretense of being comprehensive records of the language. In *The English Dictionarie; or, An Interpreter of Hard English Words* (1623), for instance, Henry Cockeram offered a kind of Inkhorn-English, English-Inkhorn dictionary. The first section lets readers translate "the choicest words themselves now in use" like *aconick* and *adpugne* into more familiar terms like *poisonous* and *to fight against*; the second section translates "the Vulgar words" like *feasting* and *fit* into "a more refined and elegant speech," like *obsonation* and *idoneous*. In *Glossographia* (1656), Thomas Blount accused hard-word users of preferring "the novelty or affected elegance of the phrase to the nerves and importance of the sence," but his dictionary provided little else. Early English lexicographers, write DeWitt Starnes and Gertrude Noyes, "vied with each other in their claims to the longest lists of the hardest, oddest, and most specialized words."

As the decades went by, though, dictionaries became more expansive. *A New English Dictionary* (1702) by J. K.—probably John Kersey— advertised itself as "A Compleat Collection Of the Most Proper and Significant Words, Commonly used in the Language." Kersey's definitions are skimpy, and sometimes hardly definitions at all ("*Ake*, as, my head akes," or "An *Apron*, for a Woman, &c."). But most of his twenty-eight thousand entries had never appeared in an English dictionary before. Johnson's most important predecessor, Nathan Bailey, continued the tradition in *An Universal Etymological English*

Robert Cawdrey was the first to answer the call with A Table Alphabeticall, *published in 1604. It was a short work, and it didn't look much like a modern dictionary. His definitions were usually little more than synonyms. And although Cawdrey attacked the "strange ynkhorne termes" so beloved by scholars in his day, his book was filled with these obscure words— neotericke, obnubilate, pervicacie.*

Dictionary (1721) and the *Dictionarium Britannicum* (1730). The latter, with its improved etymologies, distinguished senses and large word list (forty-eight thousand in the first edition and sixty thousand in the second), was the most useful dictionary before Johnson's. Lexicographers were finally paying attention to real words.

And yet, with all these dictionaries vying to regulate the language, none was wholly satisfactory. As the philosopher David Hume lamented in 1741, "The Elegance and Propriety of Stile have been very much neglected among us. We have no Dictionary of our Language, and scarce a tolerable Grammar." People were convinced English was degenerating and in need of regulation. Rapid change was worrisome: if the language kept mutating, modern English would soon be as unintelligible as Middle English had become. "And such as *Chaucer* is, shall *Dryden* be," wrote Alexander Pope, who considered compiling his own dictionary to arrest the decay. John Dryden, Daniel Defoe, Jonathan Swift and many others hoped for an English Academy, something like the Académie Française, which could rule definitively on what was appropriate and what was not. It was time for a standard dictionary to settle all the disputes.

As the philosopher David Hume lamented in 1741, "We have no Dictionary of our Language, and scarce a tolerable Grammar." People were convinced English was degenerating and in need of regulation. Rapid change was worrisome: if the language kept mutating, modern English would soon be as unintelligible as Middle English had become.

Enter Samuel Johnson

Johnson was born in Lichfield, in the English West Midlands, on 7 September 1709. (After England adopted the Gregorian calendar in 1752—see the note on *December* at the back of this edition— he observed his birthday on 18 September.) The son of a bookseller, he grew up reading widely and voraciously: poems, plays, romances, histories, sermons, philosophical treatises; English, French, Latin, Greek. When he held a book, James Boswell wrote, he "seemed to read it ravenously, as if he devoured it, which was to all appearance his method of studying. 'He knows how to read better than any one (said Mrs. Knowles); he gets at the substance of a book directly; he tears out the heart of it.'"

He was therefore well prepared when he went to Pembroke College Oxford in October 1728, dreaming of becoming a renowned Neo-Latin scholar and poet. But it was not to be. A lack of funds forced him to return home, without a degree, in just a year. After a brief term as undermaster at Market Bosworth Grammar School, he set up his own school at Edial, near his hometown, but it never prospered. (One of his few pupils there was David Garrick, who went on to become the greatest actor of the century.) And so he headed for the metropolis.

Eighteenth-century London was booming, the commercial and intellectual center of the country. Johnson arrived in 1737 with his half-finished verse tragedy, *Irene* (pronounced *eye-REE-nee*), hoping to score a success on the London stage. Still entertaining visions of a scholarly reputation, he proposed an edition of the Renaissance Latin poet Politian (Angelo Poliziano) and a translation of a *History of the*

Council of Trent. But the market for such things was small, and few publishers were willing to take a chance on an unknown provincial without a university degree. He was forced to immerse himself in the Grub Street culture of the 1730s: hack writers turning out political pamphlets, translations, poems and biographies for low wages. (His definition of *grubstreet*, with its "small histories, dictionaries, and temporary poems," shows he counted himself among these writers of "mean productions.")

These are the years before his meeting with James Boswell, his most famous biographer. Boswell was not yet born when Johnson arrived in London; he was fourteen when the *Dictionary* appeared, and the two did not meet until 16 May 1763, when Boswell was twenty-two and Johnson fifty-three. The day-to-day details are therefore sketchy. We know he was a regular contributor to *The Gentleman's Magazine*, reporting (illegally) on the debates in Parliament and, for a while, practically editing the magazine. His works from this period include political satires, an annotated catalogue of a scholarly library, translations and biographies. His first major poem, *London*, was published anonymously in May 1738, prompting Alexander Pope, England's most famous poet, to remark that the unknown author "will soon be *déterré* [brought to light]." But years passed and his reputation remained buried.

The turning point came in 1746, when Johnson was approached by a consortium of booksellers, who in the eighteenth century also functioned as publishers. They asked him to prepare an English dictionary. He agreed, and later admitted he "had long thought of it." He spelled out his goals in "A Short Scheme for the Compiling of a New Dictionary of the English Language," and signed the contract on 18 June 1746. (The revised version of this "Short Scheme," published in 1747 as *The Plan of a Dictionary of the English Language*, appears in this edition as an appendix.)

Johnson announced his determination to complete the dictionary single-handedly in three years. Many were incredulous: the Académie Française, after all, with its staff of forty distinguished scholars, spent forty years on a dictionary of a similar scope. Johnson was confident he could do better, observing that "This is the proportion. Let me see; forty times forty is sixteen hundred. As three to sixteen hundred, so is the proportion of an Englishman to a Frenchman."

The boast sounds absurd, but he wasn't far wrong. As it happens, he took nine years.

The turning point came in 1746, when a consortium of booksellers asked him to prepare an English dictionary. Johnson announced his determination to complete the dictionary single-handedly in three years. As it happens, he took nine years.

Composition

They were nine years of hard work and application. His first task was to find a means of support. The booksellers offered him £1,575— perhaps £100,000 or $150,000 in today's money, though it is notoriously difficult to find equivalents. This would have to sustain him and his assistants through years of work.

It would be unusual for an eighteenth-century writer to rely only on payments from booksellers. Patronage was then the usual mode of publication for such works: an author approached a wealthy nobleman and requested financial support in exchange for a flattering dedication. Philip Dormer Stanhope, the Fourth Earl of Chesterfield, was one of the most distinguished politicians, diplomats and patrons of the day, so Johnson was hopeful when he addressed his *Plan* to him. But Chesterfield received the young unknown coldly. He apparently gave him £10 but offered none of the support a writer expected from a patron. Johnson resolved to go it alone.

By 1746 he had moved into 17 Gough Square, where he lived while working on the *Dictionary*. (The house—Johnson's only London house that still stands—is now open to the public as a museum.) He furnished the place with several large tables and hired a half-dozen amanuenses, or scribes, to copy the passages he indicated—"a rag-tag group of predominantly Scottish ne'er-do-wells," in the words of Allen Reddick, who offers the best description of Johnson's working methods.

Convinced that "the chief glory of every people arises from its authors," he read the works of hundreds of English writers. When he found a passage he wanted to include, he made a vertical pencil mark before and after it; he then underscored the word he wanted to define and wrote its initial letter in the margin. His amanuenses would copy out the marked passages and cross out the marginal letters.

It was in this house that Johnson worked his way through the mountains of books he quotes so copiously in the *Dictionary*. Convinced that "the chief glory of every people arises from its authors," he read the works of hundreds of English writers. He often used borrowed books, and some of those who lent volumes from their libraries were not pleased when he lost some and damaged many. But several of these books survive, and they let us see how he worked. When he found a passage he wanted to include, he made a vertical pencil mark before and after it; he then underscored the word he wanted to define and wrote its initial letter in the margin. When he finished with the book, he handed it over to his amanuenses, who would copy out the marked passages and cross out the marginal letters.

Once the words and quotations were collected, Johnson began the demanding work of writing definitions and assembling the materials into a usable form. This was more difficult than he expected, and as his ideas for the book kept changing, he faced endless problems. He collected too many quotations and had to weed them out. The manuscript was too messy for the printers to read; it had to be copied out again at considerable expense. And in 1750, after more than three years, Johnson realized his methods were not working: he had made a false start, and had to stop to reconsider his plans from scratch. The booksellers, frustrated by the delays, pressured him to finish the work.

All the while he was busy with other projects. His best poem, *The Vanity of Human Wishes*, came out in 1749. David Garrick's company at Drury Lane finally acted his old play *Irene* in the same year (it was received respectfully, but could hardly be called a hit). *The Rambler*, a series of twice-weekly essays, ran from 1750 through 1752; the essays fill three fat volumes in a modern edition.

He was also plagued by personal hardships, foremost among them the death of his wife, Tetty, on 17 March 1752. His grief and weariness come through at the end of the *Preface*: "I have protracted my work till most of those whom I wished to please, have sunk into the grave, and success and miscarriage are empty sounds: I therefore dismiss it with frigid tranquillity, having little to fear or hope from censure or from praise."

The Plan and Preface

Most of the *Preface*, though, has none of this melancholy tone. It is one of Johnson's finest productions, a forceful description of the theory that guided him and the problems that confronted him in compiling his most influential work.

It is instructive to compare his early theoretical statements in the *Plan* with the more mature thoughts expressed in the *Preface*, to see how eight years' experience had changed his mind. Most important is how his attitude toward "fixing the language" altered. We have seen that many wanted a prescriptive dictionary, one that would pronounce magisterially on what was right or wrong. Johnson evidently had this sort of work in mind in 1747, when he wrote of "a dictionary by which the pronunciation of our language may be fixed, and its attainment facilitated; by which its purity may be preserved, its use ascertained, and its duration lengthened."

But after eight years of work on the *Dictionary*, his attitudes had shifted: he became less prescriptive and more descriptive, concerned with the language not as he imagined it should be but as it was actually written. Other countries, he said, formed academies "to guard the avenues of their languages, to retain fugitives, and repulse intruders; but their vigilance and activity have hitherto been vain; sounds are too volatile and subtle for legal restraints; to enchain syllables, and to lash the wind, are equally the undertakings of pride."

Donald J. Greene put it plainly: "The habit of talking about Johnson's lexicography as 'normative' or 'dictatorial' or 'authoritarian' is completely wrong." This is clear in the *Preface*, where he repeatedly refuses to accept the emperor's crown. Some wanted him to keep new words out of the language, but Johnson insisted that any civilized people would always need new words and expressions. "The language most likely to continue long without alteration," he wrote, "would be that of a nation raised a little, and but a little, above barbarity.... Every increase of knowledge, whether real or fancied, will produce new words." Others worried about obsolescence, but not Johnson: "*Swift*, in his petty treatise on the *English* language, allows that new words must sometimes be introduced, but proposes that none should be suffered to become obsolete. But what makes a word obsolete, more than general agreement to forbear it?"

This "general agreement" is what regulates the language, not the whims of some arbitrary dictator. As Reddick writes, "Johnson's

It is instructive to compare his early theoretical statements in the Plan *with the more mature thoughts expressed in the* Preface, *to see how eight years' experience had changed his mind. Most important is how his attitude toward "fixing the language" altered. He became less prescriptive and more descriptive, concerned with the language not as he imagined it should be but as it was actually written.*

The same spirit that led him to base his definitions on "general agreement" also led him "to collect the words of our language" through "the perusal of our writers"—that is, to collect the vocabulary actually in use. Almost every word is supported by a major English author. This is what makes a word a word: not a lexicographer's fancy, but the practice of the best writers in the language.

Dictionary was the first to attempt...to determine its meanings according to word usage as it was encountered in the works of the authors in the language." He sometimes tried to influence usage in small ways, as when he promoted Browne's word *pictorial* as "A word not adopted by other writers, but elegant and useful," and downgraded *writative* as "A word of Pope's coining: not to be imitated." He even confessed to making up a few. When he used the words *peregrinity* and *depeditation* in conversation, Boswell asked whether they were "real words." Johnson, Boswell tells us, "laughed and owned he had made the word[s]; and that he had not made above three or four in the Dictionary."

But these episodes are the exception, not the rule, and he was usually adamant that usage should be determined by consensus, not by fiat. To those who called for an English academy, Johnson replied, "I, who can never wish to see dependance multiplied, hope the spirit of *English* liberty will hinder or destroy" any such idea. The economist Adam Smith wished he had been a little more imperious: "We cannot help wishing, that the author...had oftener passed his own censure upon those words which are not of approved use." Johnson had anticipated his criticism, and insisted in his *Preface* that a lexicographer should "not form, but register the language."

The Word List

Johnson's *Dictionary* contains 42,773 entries, more than some eighteenth-century dictionaries, less than others. But the words are different in character from those of many other works. The same spirit that led him to base his definitions on "general agreement" also led him "to collect the words of our language" through "the perusal of our writers"—that is, to collect the vocabulary actually in use. Almost every word is supported by a major English author.

This is what makes a word a word: not a lexicographer's fancy, but the practice of the best writers in the language. *Fustilarian* and *scroyle* he found only in Shakespeare: that was enough, and he included them. He wasn't fond of *spick and span*, and conceded that "This word I should not have expected to have found authorised by a polite writer." But he did find it in Butler, Burnet and Swift, so in it went. One scholar estimates that, by using this method, he defined about eighty percent of the vocabulary used in his day.

However wide his reading and meticulous his record-keeping, though, there was no way he could have encountered every word in the language—one lifetime isn't enough for that. To fill the gaps, he went through earlier dictionaries, especially Edward Phillips's *New World of Words* (1658), Robert Ainsworth's *Thesaurus Linguæ Latinæ Compendiarius* (1736) and Bailey's *Dictionarium Britannicum* (1736). They contained many words he could find nowhere else, and he decided to include at least some of them. He provided no quotations, merely a note, "Dict." or "D.," to show they came from other dictionaries. These inkhorn words—the first few pages include *abaft*, *abannition*, *aberuncate*, *ablepsy*, *abligurition*, *abnormous*, *absinthiated*, *acephalous* and *acervose*—are sometimes amusing, but Johnson knew that few of them were ever in circulation. Indeed, "I am not always certain that they are read in any book but the works of lexicographers," who often coined new English words to fatten their books. "Of such I have omitted many, because I had never read them; and many I have inserted, because they may perhaps exist, though they have escaped my notice."

He did exercise some discretion: not every word belongs in a dictionary. He was concerned with the written rather than the spoken language, since "the boundless chaos of a living speech" was too difficult to record. He omitted many "terms of art," or specialized jargon, because he "could not visit caverns to learn the miner's language, nor take a voyage to perfect my skill in the dialect of navigation." And he drew the line at obscenity. An early biographer tells the story of "two ladies" who "very much commended the omission of all *naughty* words. 'What, my dears! then you have been looking for them?' said the moralist. The ladies, confused at being thus caught, dropped the subject." But if the *Dictionary* has no outright obscenities, Johnson was by no means squeamish. Words such as *piss*, *fart*, *arse*, *snot*, *puke* and *turd* show he was unafraid of vulgarity. A few words are euphemized: *priapism*, for instance, is merely "a preternatural tension," whereas today's less finicky *American Heritage Dictionary* defines it as "persistent, usually painful erection of the penis, especially as a consequence of disease." But such examples are uncommon, and he generally gives a candid description of the state of the language in his day.

Modern readers must be careful about drawing inappropriate conclusions from the word list. For example, the *Dictionary* contains a large misogynist vocabulary, as a glance at this edition's Index of Piquant Terms under "Sex and the Sexes" will show. But Johnson was anything but a misogynist himself: few in his day did more to support women writers and intellectuals. As Howard Weinbrot has often pointed out, this is a *Dictionary of the English Language*, not a *Dictionary of Johnson's Language*. *Doxy*, *hoiden* and *strumpet* appeared in Shakespeare, Swift and Dryden, and therefore they belonged in a dictionary. It is likewise risky business to draw conclusions about Johnson's political or philosophical positions from the words he includes and authors he quotes. Once again he is trying to register, not to shape, the language.

Definitions

"That part of my work on which I expect malignity most frequently to fasten," Johnson wrote in his *Preface*, "is the *Explanation*" or definition. His expectation was right, and the sport of catching his blunders began early. He was unfazed. "A few of his definitions," said Boswell, "must

He did exercise some discretion: not every word belongs in a dictionary. He was concerned with the written rather than the spoken language, since "the boundless chaos of a living speech" was too difficult to record. He omitted many "terms of art," or specialized jargon. And he drew the line at obscenity. But if the Dictionary *has no outright obscenities, Johnson was by no means squeamish.*

be admitted to be erroneous.... A lady once asked him how he came to define Pastern the knee of a horse. [It is actually the part of the foot between the fetlock and the hoof.] Instead of making an elaborate defence, as she expected, he at once answered, 'Ignorance, Madam, pure ignorance.'" He missed on *strappado* as well: not "chastisement by blows," but a kind of torture in which the victim's hands were tied to a pulley behind his back.

These very few mistaken entries have unjustly become more famous than the tens of thousands of perfectly sound ones, which show Johnson's intelligence at its most penetrating. Writing definitions is arduous work, as Johnson knew:

> To interpret a language by itself is very difficult; many words cannot be explained by synonimes, because the idea signified by them has not more than one appellation; nor by paraphrase, because simple ideas cannot be described.... To explain, requires the use of terms less abstruse than that which is to be explained, and such terms cannot always be found.

The most common words in the language are often the most difficult to define; verbs like *set* and *go* (not included in this edition) have dozens of meanings. And when we combine them with prepositions or adverbs, the problem becomes even more complex. "We modify the signification of many verbs," Johnson writes, "by a particle subjoined; as to *come off*, to escape by a fetch; to *fall on*, to attack; to *fall off*, to apostatize; *to break off*, to stop abruptly," and so on. Some of these phrasal verbs "appear wildly irregular, being so far distant from the sense of the simple words, that no sagacity will be able to trace the steps by which they arrived at the present use. These I have noted with great care."

This "great care" is obvious when we compare Johnson with his predecessors, for no English lexicographer had ever done anything comparable to his meticulous discrimination of meanings. Even Bailey, who gave the common words more attention than most, dispensed with *take* in a mere 362 words. Johnson's entries for *take*, with 133 numbered senses and 363 quotations, run to more than eight thousand words. (*Take* is not included in this edition, where it would require a full fifteen pages.) Few words have as many meanings as *set* and *take*, but *civil* with twelve numbered senses, *spirit* with nineteen and *heart* with twenty show his attention to some of the most difficult problems in lexicography.

We have grown accustomed to dictionaries written by faceless committees and may be surprised to catch a glimpse of humanity when entries are opinionated or ignorant. This was a one-man production, and Johnson was forthright when words baffled him. *Skilt*, for instance, is "A word used by Cleaveland, of which I know not either the etymology or meaning." He thought some words didn't belong in the language, among them *ruse* ("A French word neither elegant nor necessary"), *thro'* ("Contracted by barbarians from *through*") and *shabby*

We have grown accustomed to dictionaries written by faceless committees and may be surprised to catch a glimpse of humanity when entries are opinionated or ignorant. This was a one-man production, and Johnson was forthright when words baffled him.

("A word that has crept into conversation and low writing; but ought not to be admitted into the language"). Nor did he shrink from offering the occasional editorial comment. A *geomancer*, for example, is "a cheat who pretends to foretell futurity," and *newfangled* is "Formed with vain or foolish love of novelty."

Here again, as with his mistakes, these opinionated entries get more than their fair share of attention. Johnson occasionally plays the tyrant, but most of the *Dictionary* is a sober and modest affair. For all the brouhaha generated by his definitions of *excise*, *tory*, *whig* and *oats*, personal biases rarely show through. This is clear in a comparison of Johnson's definition of *Talmud* with one from Blount's *Glossographia* (1656). For Johnson, Talmud is simply "The book containing the Jewish traditions, the rabbinical constitutions and explications of the law." For Blount, it is "a superstitious and blasphemous Book containing the body of the Jewish Law, composed by their *Rabbins*." Johnson was content merely to report on the words, with none of Blount's vitriol.

Etymologies

Few have been as harsh as Lord Macaulay, who called Johnson "a wretched etymologist," but the etymologies have long been recognized as the weakest part of the book. To be fair, Johnson wasn't much better or worse at tracing word histories than his contemporaries. He was fluent in Greek, Latin and French; his proficiency in the Germanic languages was somewhat less sound; and his knowledge of Arabic and Hebrew was limited at best. He therefore relied extensively on the etymological dictionaries of Stephen Skinner, Francis Junius, Richard Verstegan and Edward Lye, usually borrowing from them uncritically, but sometimes pausing to criticize them. A footnote in the *Preface*, for instance, ridicules the "etymological extravagance" of Junius, and in his entry on *oak* he shows Junius and Skinner at their most confused. When his sources let him down, he sometimes hazarded his own guesses, usually without much success.

More important than any individual derivation, though, is his attitude toward derivation itself. Johnson knew better than most of his contemporaries that meanings are not determined by etymologies. For Bailey, etymology was the key to meaning; he even defined *etymology* as "a Part of Grammar, shewing the Original of Words, in order to fix their true Meaning and Signification." For Johnson, a word's "true Meaning and Signification" come not from its root, but from the writers who used it. As Greene put it, "Words in themselves are meaningless sounds and marks. 'Meaning' becomes attached to them when they are used, in context, by human beings."

More important than any individual derivation is his attitude toward derivation itself. Johnson knew better than most of his contemporaries that meanings are not determined by etymologies. For Johnson, a word's "true Meaning and Signification" come not from its root, but from the writers who used it.

Quotations

The quotations made Johnson's book not only the largest dictionary of its day, but also one of the most substantial anthologies of English literature ever published. Johnson praised Shakespeare as the best guide to the language of "common life" and quoted from all thirty-six of his plays.

Those human beings and that context were provided by the hundreds of authors and thousands of quotations Johnson read and transcribed.

Users of modern dictionaries are sometimes surprised when they open Johnson's: the definitions, the usual business of a dictionary, account for only a small fraction of the book. The bulk of the *Dictionary* comes from the quotations, about 114,000 of them, that illustrate the words more precisely than any definition could.

The idea of including quotations in a dictionary wasn't entirely original—it was common in Greek and Latin lexicons, and the Accademia della Crusca had already done it in Italian—but no English lexicographer had ever tried anything remotely comparable. The quotations made Johnson's book not only the largest dictionary of its day, but also one of the most substantial anthologies of English literature ever published. And although Noah Webster fretted about Johnson's "injudicious selection of authorities," Johnson drew from hundreds of the most important English authors, from the thirteenth-century Bishop Grosseteste to his own friends and contemporaries.

At the head of the pack was Shakespeare, who achieved his position at the center of the English literary canon only during Johnson's lifetime. The year of Johnson's birth, 1709, saw the first scholarly edition of Shakespeare's works and the first biography, both by the playwright Nicholas Rowe. Rowe's was the first of many increasingly learned editions published throughout the century, including contributions by Alexander Pope and Johnson himself; after completing the *Dictionary*, his next major project was an extensively annotated edition of Shakespeare, which appeared in eight volumes in 1765. Johnson praised Shakespeare as the best guide to the language of "common life" and quoted from all thirty-six of his plays (*Two Noble Kinsmen* and *Pericles, Prince of Tyre* were not considered part of the canon).

Other major authors of the sixteenth, seventeenth and eighteenth centuries contribute most of the other quotations. Sir Philip Sidney, Francis Bacon, John Milton, John Dryden, Joseph Addison, Jonathan Swift and Alexander Pope are quoted thousands of times, and Johnson knew works such as *Paradise Lost*, *The Spectator* and *The Rape of the Lock* so well that he could recite large parts of them by heart. He lived with these works and authors throughout his life; his last major project was a series of literary biographies, commonly known as *Lives of the English Poets*, which included biographies of Milton, Dryden, Addison, Swift and Pope.

Not all the quotations, though, come from traditionally literary works such as poems, plays and fiction. Religion was at the center of Johnson's life, and Christian writers like Richard Hooker, Richard Allestree, John Tillotson and Robert South loom large. The Bible, in the Authorized (King James) Version of 1611, illustrates words such as *god*, *faith*, *love*, *hell*, *judgment* and *hope*. And Johnson surveys the whole circle of knowledge—the literal translation of *encyclopedia*—by drawing on writers in surprisingly diverse fields. Philosophers like John Locke and Joseph Glanvill, scientists like Sir Isaac Newton and Robert Boyle, scholars like Richard Bentley and Henry Felton, legal writers like John Ayliffe and John Cowell, statesmen like the Earl of Clarendon and Sir William Temple, and physicians like John Arbuthnot and John Quincy—all these authorities contribute hundreds of quotations and turn the *Dictionary* into a unique hybrid: part dictionary, part encyclopedia, part textbook. Robert DeMaria Jr. has argued that the book as a whole "carries an important moral message...chiefly by presenting quotations that, besides illustrating the meanings of words, teach fundamental points of morality."

Johnson turned to different authors for different kinds of words. His *Preface* identifies Hooker as the best source for "the language of theology," Bacon for "the terms of natural knowledge," Raleigh for "the phrases of policy, war, and navigation," Spenser and Sidney for "the dialect of poetry and fiction" and Shakespeare for "the diction of common life." He found "low" and "cant" words in Samuel Butler, whose mock epic *Hudibras* provides entries like *blockhead*, *fopdoodle* and *jiggumbob*, and Roger L'Estrange, who serves up *huggermugger* and *twittletwattle*.

Often he drew words from their most important users. To illustrate *property* ("right of possession"), he quotes Locke twice; it was Locke who, in *Two Treatises of Government*, formulated the most influential theory of property rights. Locke also illustrates *idea*, *memory* and *mental* because his *Essay concerning Humane Understanding* was the definitive treatise of the age on the workings of the mind. To illustrate *prism*, *spectrum* and *refraction*, who better than Sir Isaac Newton, who first described the separation of light? The chemist Robert Boyle shows up under *laboratory* and *hermetical*, the naturalist John Ray under *animal* and *plant*, and the statesman Sir William Temple under *monarch* and *democracy*. The poets offer examples of the poetic vocabulary: Milton appears under *genius* and *poet*, Dryden under *epic* and *passion*, Pope under *imagination* and *critick*. *Compass* is illustrated by John Donne's famous image of lovers as "stiff twin compasses." Pope and Swift, the best-known satirists of eighteenth-century England, appear under *ridicule*.

Johnson set some limits on the authors who provided the quotations. He was convinced that "From the authours which rose in the time of *Elizabeth*, a speech might be formed adequate to all the purposes of use and elegance"; he was therefore "cautious lest my zeal for antiquity might drive me into times too remote, and croud my book with words now no longer understood." He rarely consulted authors before Sir Philip Sidney in the late sixteenth century, though he made the occasional exception for Chaucer and Sir Thomas More. At the other end of the period, he tried to draw as many quotations as possible from before 1660: "I have studiously endeavoured to collect examples and authorities from the writers before the restoration, whose works I

Often he drew words from their most important users. To illustrate property *("right of possession"), he quotes Locke twice; it was Locke who, in* Two Treatises of Government, *formulated the most influential theory of property rights. To illustrate* prism, spectrum *and* refraction, *who better than Sir Isaac Newton, who first described the separation of light?*

regard as *the wells of English undefiled*, as the pure sources of genuine diction." (I discuss this linguistic golden age in *The Age of Elizabeth in the Age of Johnson*.)

Johnson's original plan was "to admit no testimony of living authours," but he didn't always follow that plan either. He sometimes quoted contemporaries "when some performance of uncommon excellence excited my veneration, when my memory supplied me, from late books, with an example that was wanting, or when my heart, in the tenderness of friendship, solicited admission for a favourite name." It was apparently the tenderness of friendship that prompted him to quote Alexander Macbean, one of his amanuenses, under *scale* 7. He often turned to the novels of his friend Samuel Richardson. Johnson even quoted his own works dozens of times, sometimes by name, sometimes as "Anonymous."

There are also a few pointed exclusions. He famously barred the philosopher Thomas Hobbes from the *Dictionary*. " 'I scorned, sir, to quote him at all,' " wrote his biographer Thomas Tyers, " " 'because I did not like his principles.' " And although he quoted Milton's poetry thousands of times, he hardly touched Milton's prose works. *Paradise Lost* and *Samson Agonistes* are enduring masterpieces, but *The Second Defense*, advocating the murder of King Charles I, and *An Essay on Divorce*, with its heterodox opinions on marriage, did not belong.

He famously barred the philosopher Thomas Hobbes from the Dictionary *"because I did not like his principles." And although he quoted Milton's poetry thousands of times, he hardly touched Milton's prose works. The Second Defense, advocating the murder of King Charles I, and An Essay on Divorce, with its heterodox opinions on marriage, did not belong.*

Publication

After nearly a decade of labor, the *Dictionary* was nearing completion in late 1754. Expectation ran high. Oxford, his old university, conferred on Johnson the honorary degree of Master of Arts, just in time for him to advertise it on the title page. In November and December 1754, a pair of anonymous essays appeared in *The World*, a monthly magazine published by Robert Dodsley. A few weeks later, they were reprinted with the name of their author: the same Lord Chesterfield who had snubbed Johnson more than seven years earlier. This time his tone was different:

> I think the public in general, and the republic of letters in particular, greatly obliged to Mr. Johnson, for having undertaken and executed so great and desirable a work…. Our language is at present in a state of anarchy…. The time for discrimination seems to be now come. Toleration, adoption and naturalization have run their lengths. Good order and authority are now necessary…. I hereby declare that I make a total surrender of all my rights and privileges in the English language, as a free-born British subject, to the said Mr. Johnson, during the term of his dictatorship. Nay more; I will not only obey him, like an old Roman, as my dictator, but, like a modern Roman, I will implicitly believe him as my pope, and hold him to be infallible while in the chair.

This unctuous praise did not please Johnson. We have already seen that he didn't want to be anyone's dictator, let alone pope—an idea he probably found blasphemous. More to the point, he remembered that Chesterfield had brushed him off when he was just beginning. Now that the work promised to be a hit, Chesterfield was puffing it in the press in the hopes of securing the dedication. As Johnson complained to Garrick, "I have sailed a long and painful voyage round the world of the English language; and does he now send out two cock-boats to tow me into the harbour?" The sour taste left in his mouth by Chesterfield's rejection obviously influenced Johnson's famous definition of *patron*: "Commonly a wretch who supports with insolence, and is paid with flattery." It also led him to revise his *Vanity of Human Wishes*. Where the original version of 1749 included the "garret" (attic) among the evils that afflicted the young writer, after his experiences with Chesterfield he "dismissed the word *garret* from the sad group," said Boswell, producing the revised version of 1755:

> There mark what ills the scholar's life assail,
> Toil, envy, want, the patron, and the jail.

Johnson had gone it alone and wanted to make that clear. On 7 February 1755, he replied with one of the most devastating poison-pen letters ever written, presented here in full:

My Lord: February 1755

I have been lately informed by the Proprietor of The World that two Papers in which my Dictionary is recommended to the Public were written by your Lordship. To be so distinguished is an honour which, being very little accustomed to favours from the Great, I know not well how to receive, or in what terms to acknowledge.

When upon some slight encouragement I first visited your Lordship I was overpowered like the rest of Mankind by the enchantment of your adress, and could not forbear to wish that I might boast myself Le Vainqueur du Vainqueur de la Terre [the conqueror of the conqueror of the earth], that I might obtain that regard for which I saw the world contending, but I found my attendance so little incouraged, that neither pride nor modesty would suffer me to continue it. When I had once addressed your Lordship in public, I had exhausted all the Art of pleasing which a retired and uncourtly Scholar can possess. I had done all that I could, and no Man is well pleased to have his all neglected, be it ever so little.

Seven years, My lord have now past since I waited in your outward Rooms or was repulsed from your Door, during which time I have been pushing on my work through difficulties of which it is useless to complain, and have brought it at last to the verge of Publication without one Act of assistance, one word of encouragement, or one smile of favour. Such treatment I did not expect, for I never had a Patron before.

The sour taste left in his mouth by Chesterfield's rejection obviously influenced Johnson's famous definition of patron: "Commonly a wretch who supports with insolence, and is paid with flattery." He replied to Chesterfield's essay with one of the most devastating poison-pen letters ever written.

A Dictionary of the
English Language
*finally appeared
in two large folio
volumes on 15 April
1755; two thousand
copies were printed.
Noah Webster,
America's first major
lexicographer, prepared
the ground for his
own work by finding
his competitor's*
Dictionary *"extremely
imperfect and full
of error."*

The Shepherd in Virgil grew at last acquainted with Love, and found him a Native of the Rocks. Is not a Patron, My Lord, one who looks with unconcern on a Man struggling for Life in the water and when he has reached ground encumbers him with help. The notice which you have been pleased to take of my Labours, had it been early, had been kind; but it has been delayed till I am indifferent and cannot enjoy it, till I am solitary and cannot impart it, till I am known, and do not want it.

I hope it is no very cinical asperity not to confess obligation where no benefit has been received, or to be unwilling that the Public should consider me as owing that to a Patron, which Providence has enabled me to do for myself.

Having carried on my work thus far with so little obligation to any favourer of Learning I shall not be disappointed though I should conclude it, if less be possible, with less, for I have been long wakened from that Dream of hope, in which I once boasted myself with so much exultation, My lord, Your Lordship's Most humble, most obedient servant,

S.J.

In his study of Johnson and authorship, Alvin Kernan calls this remarkable letter "the Magna Carta of the modern author, the public announcement that the days of courtly letters were at last ended." This may be an exaggeration, but even Chesterfield, who must have been stung by it, left the letter "upon his table, where any body might see it," admitting, "This man has great powers."

A Dictionary of the English Language finally appeared in two large folio volumes on 15 April 1755; two thousand copies were printed. Of course there were carping voices. The linguistic theorist John Horne Tooke, for instance, detested Johnson's politics, and wrote venomously, "His Dictionary is the most imperfect and faulty, and the least valuable of any of his productions…. His *Grammar* and *History* and Dictionary of what *he calls* the English language, are in all respects…most truly contemptible performances." Johnson, he grumbled, "possessed not one single requisite for the undertaking." Horne Tooke's linguistic theories were eccentric, even crackpot; but a more competent dictionary maker had similar reservations. Noah Webster, America's first major lexicographer, prepared the ground for his own work by finding his competitor's *Dictionary* "extremely imperfect and full of error." Johnson's History of the English Language showed he was "very imperfectly acquainted with the subject," and Webster found the *Grammar* "wretchedly imperfect." "Not a single page of Johnson's *Dictionary*," he griped, "is correct."

Many singled out the inkhorn terms, forgetting that Johnson included fewer of them than any previous lexicographer. Sometimes his definitions were too dense, such as *network* ("Any thing reticulated or decussated, at equal distances, with interstices between the intersections") or *cough* ("A convulsion of the lungs, vellicated by some sharp serosity"). Horne Tooke complained that "Nearly one third of this Dictionary is as much the language of the Hottentots as of the English." Webster agreed in censuring the "multitude of words that do not belong to the language," listing *advesperate, abstrude, epicosity* and *morigerous*. In 1767, Archibald Campbell satirized Johnson's fondness for Latinate words in *Lexiphanes*, where a pompous blowhard called "Mr. J——n" boasts of "my oraculous dictionary" in terms like this:

> Deject then exaggeratory obloquy below the horizon of your prospects, without the servility of adulation afford openness of ears, sedulity of thought, and stability of attention. But above all expulse hereditary aggregates and agglomerated asperities which may obumbrate your intellectual luminaries with the clouds of obscurity, or obthurate the porches of your intelligence with the adscititious excrement of critical malevolence.

But over time the negative voices were drowned out: most considered the *Dictionary* a triumph. Adam Smith (who later wrote *The Wealth of Nations*) praised the *Dictionary* and its author in *The Edinburgh Review*: "The merit of its author appears very extraordinary…. [Johnson has] made a very full collection of all the different meanings of each English word, justified by examples from authors of good reputation." Johnson's friend and former student David Garrick celebrated the completion of the *Dictionary* with this poem:

> Talk of war with a Briton, he'll boldly advance,
> That one English soldier will beat ten of France;
> Would we alter the boast from the sword to the pen,
> Our odds are still greater, still greater our men:
> In the deep mines of science though Frenchmen may toil,
> Can their strength be compar'd to Locke, Newton, and Boyle?
> Let them rally their heroes, send forth all their pow'rs,
> Their verse-men and prose-men; then match them with ours:
> First Shakespeare and Milton, like Gods in the fight,
> Have put their whole drama and epic to flight;
> In satires, epistles, and odes, would they cope,
> Their numbers retreat before Dryden and Pope;
> And Johnson, well-arm'd like a hero of yore,
> Has beat forty French, and will beat forty more.

Sales were slow at first. This is not surprising in light of the Dictionary's *cost: £4 10s, several months' wages for an unskilled laborer. The following year, Johnson produced an abridgment. This more affordable edition sold briskly. Dictionaries, once confined to scholars' libraries, now began to be a standard fixture in every literate home.*

Sales were slow at first. This is not surprising in light of the *Dictionary's* cost: the two volumes sold for £4 10s, several months' wages for an unskilled laborer. In June, the booksellers tried to improve sales by offering it in 165 weekly parts, at sixpence each, again with little success. But in the following year, Johnson produced an abridgment in two smaller octavo volumes, without the quotations that filled the original (though some writers' names remained to "authorize" the definitions). This more affordable edition sold briskly, going through more than one thousand copies a year for the next thirty years. Dictionaries, once confined to scholars' libraries, now began to be a standard fixture in every literate home.

Revisions and Reprints

*Nearly every early
American library
owned a copy of the
Dictionary, and
Thomas Jefferson
included it in a list
of essential reading
for one of his friends.
The framers of the
U.S. Constitution
depended on Johnson's
work. Indeed, his
authority may have
been too great,
especially coming
from a staunch
supporter of Britain
during the American
Revolution.*

Johnson's interest in the language did not end there. After writing another series of periodical essays (*The Idler*) and a short work of fiction (*Rasselas*), he edited Shakespeare's works, applying his unmatched knowledge of the history of the language to the difficult passages in the plays. (Many of his notes from 1765 are still reprinted in editions of Shakespeare to this day.) And he continued to work on the *Dictionary* itself. As Reddick noted, "Johnson's attention to the details of the text of the *Dictionary*...was virtually obsessive; and in fact, Johnson revised no other of his works even half as thoroughly or as frequently." The most significant product of this obsession was the fourth edition of 1773, a thorough revision with many hundreds of new quotations. Even after his death, the *Dictionary* continued to thrive, as revised editions appeared bearing his name: "Johnson's" was synonymous with "authoritative." When Henry Tilney questions Catherine Morland's use of a word in Jane Austen's *Northanger Abbey*, Eleanor warns, "You had better change it as soon as you can, or we shall be overpowered with Johnson."

That authority extended across the Atlantic to Britain's colonies. Nearly every early American library owned a copy of the *Dictionary*, and Thomas Jefferson included it in a list of essential reading for one of his friends. The framers of the U.S. Constitution depended on Johnson's work. Indeed, his authority may have been too great, especially coming from a staunch supporter of Britain during the American Revolution. As H. L. Mencken wrote, Johnson's "implacable hatred of all things American was well known to the citizens of the new republic," prompting Noah Webster to write an American dictionary of English.

The work underwent many revisions over the decades and remained the standard English dictionary well into the nineteenth century. The London editions were sold around the world, and soon new editions and abridgments were published in Dublin (1758), Edinburgh (1797), Philadelphia (1805) and even Heidelberg (1828). Henry Todd's popular London edition of 1818 introduced the book to a new generation. When, in 1857, the Philological Society of London described the need for a new dictionary, they considered simply giving Johnson's a thorough revision. They ultimately decided that this was unworkable and began afresh. After seventy years, a team of dozens of full-time lexicographers and hundreds of volunteers from around the world finally produced the dictionary that superseded Johnson's: *A New English Dictionary on Historical Principles*, better known today as the *Oxford English Dictionary*. But even the O.E.D. contains more than seventeen hundred definitions lifted straight from Johnson and attributed to "J." Many other dictionaries are less scrupulous, filching definitions without credit even today.

Johnson knew his book was flawed. "A perfect performance of any kind is not to be expected," he wrote late in life, "and certainly not a perfect dictionary." And he was modest enough to admit that "Dictionaries are like watches, the worst is better than none, and the best cannot be expected to go quite true." But he knew he had succeeded in his *Dictionary of the English Language*. When Boswell said of the *Dictionary*, "You did not know what you were undertaking," he replied, "Yes, Sir, I knew very well what I was undertaking,—and very well how to do it,—and have done it very well."

About this Edition

This Levenger Press edition is a selection from the first edition of the *Dictionary*, published in 1755. I have worked mostly from a copy in the Department of Rare Books and Special Collections at Princeton University Library.

The complete text of the *Preface* appears before the dictionary entries; the *Plan of a Dictionary of the English Language* is printed as an appendix. Johnson's *Grammar* and *History of the Language* have been omitted: the former is a derivative and perfunctory effort; the latter consists mostly of long quotations from English authors with little commentary. The two are of almost no interest to the general reader (and of little interest even to the specialist).

The selection of entries comes from a personal sense of what's most worth reading, but a few policies have guided my choice of words. I have tried to include:

- All of the widely quoted entries, including *oats*, *lexicographer*, *tory* and *network*

- Words that have changed meaning in interesting ways, including *nice*, *enthusiasm*, *philosophy* and *pencil*

- A selection of Johnson's self-quotations, including *dissipate*, *lord*, *pimp* and *prowl*, and words that resonate in Johnson's writings, including *rambler*, *idler*, *adventurer*, *vanity*, *hope*, *fear* and *happiness*

- Words that appear in the works Johnson used in preparing the *Dictionary*. What does *Hamlet*'s "hoist on his own petard" mean? What are the "umbrageous grots" in Milton's *Paradise Lost*, and what is the "vile caitiff" in Spenser's *Faerie Queene*? Belinda, the heroine of Pope's *Rape of the Lock*, "part[s] her time 'twixt reading and bohea." What is she doing?

- Words that appear in the literature of Johnson's own day and shortly afterwards. If Jane Austen's readers wanted definitions of *pride*, *prejudice*, *sense* and *sensibility*, what would they have found? What was a *militia* when the U.S. Constitution was written? In 1817, John Keats called a long poem "a test of invention which I take to be the polar star of poetry, as fancy is the sails, and imagination the rudder." What would these words have called to mind?

A team of dozens of full-time lexicographers and hundreds of volunteers from around the world finally produced the dictionary that superseded Johnson's: A New English Dictionary on Historical Principles, better known today as the Oxford English Dictionary. But even the O.E.D. contains more than seventeen hundred definitions lifted straight from Johnson and attributed to "J."

- Entries that open a window onto the age of Johnson, including words on social rank (*bootcatcher, levee, linkboy*), fashion (*bodice, mantua, smicket*), games (*cricket, ombre, quadrille*), modes of transportation (*chair, equipage, wherry*), politics (*parliament, tory, whig*), law (*entail, impeach, spunginghouse*), literature (*novel, metaphor, poem*), the book trade (*folio, compositor, typography*), art (*beauty, crayon, japan*), philosophy (*dialectick, intelligence, imagination*), science (*electricity, airpump, milky-way*) and medicine (*calenture, humour, ague*)

The entries are uncut, and include the etymologies, definitions, usage notes and quotations. Following Johnson's own advice to Boswell that "An authour's language is a characteristical part of his composition," I have not modernized the spelling or capitalization, leaving them as they appeared in 1755. They rarely pose real problems for modern readers and they give a better sense of the language in the age of Johnson.

The entries are uncut, and include the etymologies, definitions, usage notes and quotations. (When a word form has several main entries, though, such as when it is both a noun and a verb, I usually included only one.) Following Johnson's own advice to Boswell that "An authour's language is a characteristical part of his composition," I have not modernized the spelling or capitalization, leaving them as they appeared in 1755. They rarely pose real problems for modern readers— after a moment's reflection, it becomes clear that the "flower" in the definition of *sausage* would be spelled "flour" today—and they give a better sense of the language in the age of Johnson. Johnson's errors of fact—his mistaken definitions, false etymologies and inaccurate quotations—also remain intact. (I discuss some of the more important errors in the Notes.)

I have, however, cleaned up a few things that make the *Dictionary* tough going for today's readers. Entry words are printed in lowercase, not capitals, with accents on the stressed letters instead of apostrophes after them: not "PRE'JUDICE" but "préjudice." The long *s* (which looks to modern eyes too much like an *f*) is replaced with the familiar short *s*. The eighteenth-century usage of italics is regularized. Saxon (Old English) and Greek words are printed in modern typefaces, without accents, and the quotations are printed in italics.

In Johnson's day, *I* and *J* were considered the same letter for purposes of alphabetization, as were *U* and *V*. This means *jack* comes before *icon* in the original *Dictionary* (they could just as well be *iack* and *jcon*) and *savage* before *saucebox* (because *saua* comes before *sauc*). Since this makes it frustrating to find words, I have put the entries in modern alphabetical order. I have also corrected the obvious typographical errors, whenever they seem to be the printer's or amanuenses' rather than Johnson's. Inconsistent spellings are allowed to stand, but outright errors are silently changed. This is sometimes a judgment call, and I have often consulted the *Dictionary*'s fourth edition to see whether the errors were corrected during Johnson's lifetime.

'The Vexation of Expunging'

After he had collected his materials, Johnson realized that "the bulk of [his] volumes would fright away the student," and he faced "the vexation of expunging" many quotations. In expunging still more of

Johnson's "accumulation of elegance and wisdom," I, too, have been vexed by the need to omit many fascinating entries.

What remains, I hope, is a fair representation of the original, one that gives modern readers some insights into the book, its author and his age. No abridgment can do justice to Johnson's *Dictionary*, but I have tried to acquaint readers of the twenty-first century with one of the richest and most engaging books of the eighteenth.

HOW TO READ JOHNSON'S DICTIONARY

This edition of the *Dictionary* is faithful to Johnson's in providing full entries, including the part of speech, the etymology, every definition and all the quotations for each selected word.

This sample entry will help acquaint your eye with the *Dictionary*.

> **élegant** adj. [*elegans*, Latin]
>
> 1. Pleasing with minuter beauties.
>
> *Trifles themselves are elegant in him.* Pope.
>
> *There may'st thou find some elegant retreat.* London.
>
> 2. Nice; not coarse; not gross.
>
> *Polite with candour, elegant with ease.* Pope.

- The word being defined is in dark blue, with an accent on the stressed syllable: **élegant.**

  If the word being defined appears in italics, as *abracadabra* does, it indicates that Johnson considered it a foreign term rather than a fully naturalized English word.

- The part of speech follows: adj.

- The etymology is in brackets: [*elegans*, Latin].

  Occasionally Johnson referred to other entries in the *Dictionary*, indicating the cross-references in italics, as he did here with *fico*:

  > **to fig** v.a. [See *fico.*]

  (It hasn't always been possible in this edition to include all the words he cross-references.)

- The definition comes next:

  > 1. Pleasing with minuter beauties.

  When words had more than one sense, Johnson numbered the definitions.

  Some of the defined words are preceded by a particle or an article, as in *to* clapperclaw, *the* chickenpox. This was common in dictionaries of the seventeenth and eighteenth centuries.

- Quotations under each definition are in italics:

  > *Trifles themselves are elegant in him.*

- The attribution for the quotation is in blue: Pope.

- The symbol † refers to the editor's Notes in the back of the book (the only exception being Johnson's footnotes in the Preface and the Plan).

Frequently Found Abbreviations

Parts of Speech		*Etymologies*	
adj.	adjective	**Dut.**	Dutch
adv.	adverb	**Fr.**	French
interj.	interjection	**Germ.**	German
n.s.	noun substantive	**Gr.**	Greek
prep.	preposition	**Lat.**	Latin
pret.	preterite (past tense)	**Sax.**	Saxon (Old English)
v.a.	verb active (transitive)		
v.n.	verb neuter (intransitive)		

Glossary of Usage Terms

bad	A general term of disapproval
barbarous	Impure or unsuited to the language
cant	The jargon of any group
country	Either rustic or ignorant
low	Informal; not suited to dignified writing
low Latin	Post-classical or medieval Latin
ludicrous	Funny, not serious
rustick	Like "country": either rural or ignorant
scarce English	Not naturalized in the language
unauthorized	Not supported by an authority

PREFACE

IT is the fate of those who toil at the lower employments of life, to be rather driven by the fear of evil, than attracted by the prospect of good; to be exposed to censure, without hope of praise; to be disgraced by miscarriage, or punished for neglect, where success would have been without applause, and diligence without reward.

Among these unhappy mortals is the writer of dictionaries; whom mankind have considered, not as the pupil, but the slave of science, the pionier of literature, doomed only to remove rubbish and clear obstructions from the paths of Learning and Genius, who press forward to conquest and glory, without bestowing a smile on the humble drudge that facilitates their progress. Every other authour may aspire to praise; the lexicographer can only hope to escape reproach, and even this negative recompence has been yet granted to very few.

I have, notwithstanding this discouragement, attempted a dictionary of the *English* language, which, while it was employed in the cultivation of every species of literature, has itself been hitherto neglected, suffered to spread, under the direction of chance, into wild exuberance, resigned to the tyranny of time and fashion, and exposed to the corruptions of ignorance, and caprices of innovation.

When I took the first survey of my undertaking, I found our speech copious without order, and energetick without rules: wherever I turned my view, there was perplexity to be disentangled, and confusion to be regulated; choice was to be made out of boundless variety, without any established principle of selection; adulterations were to be detected, without a settled test of purity; and modes of expression to be rejected or received, without the suffrages of any writers of classical reputation or acknowledged authority.

Having therefore no assistance but from general grammar, I applied myself to the perusal of our writers; and noting whatever might be of use to ascertain or illustrate any word or phrase, accumulated in time the materials of a dictionary, which, by degrees, I reduced to method, establishing to myself, in the progress of the work, such rules as experience and analogy suggested to me; experience, which practice and observation were continually increasing; and analogy, which, though in some words obscure, was evident in others.

I have...attempted a dictionary of the English *language, which, while it was employed in the cultivation of every species of literature, has itself been hitherto neglected, suffered to spread, under the direction of chance, into wild exuberance, resigned to the tyranny of time and fashion, and exposed to the corruptions of ignorance, and caprices of innovation.*

Every language has its anomalies, which, though inconvenient, and in themselves once unnecessary, must be tolerated among the imperfections of human things....

In adjusting the ORTHOGRAPHY, which has been to this time unsettled and fortuitous, I found it necessary to distinguish those irregularities that are inherent in our tongue, and perhaps coeval with it, from others which the ignorance or negligence of later writers has produced. Every language has its anomalies, which, though inconvenient, and in themselves once unnecessary, must be tolerated among the imperfections of human things, and which require only to be registred; that they may not be increased, and ascertained, that they may not be confounded: but every language has likewise its improprieties and absurdities, which it is the duty of the lexicographer to correct or proscribe.

As language was at its beginning merely oral, all words of necessary or common use were spoken before they were written; and while they were unfixed by any visible signs, must have been spoken with great diversity, as we now observe those who cannot read to catch sounds imperfectly, and utter them negligently. When this wild and barbarous jargon was first reduced to an alphabet, every penman endeavoured to express, as he could, the sounds which he was accustomed to pronounce or to receive, and vitiated in writing such words as were already vitiated in speech. The powers of the letters, when they were applied to a new language, must have been vague and unsettled, and therefore different hands would exhibit the same sound by different combinations.

From this uncertain pronunciation arise in a great part the various dialects of the same country, which will always be observed to grow fewer, and less different, as books are multiplied; and from this arbitrary representation of sounds by letters, proceeds that diversity of spelling observable in the *Saxon* remains, and I suppose in the first books of every nation, which perplexes or destroys analogy, and produces anomalous formations, which, being once incorporated, can never be afterward dismissed or reformed.

Of this kind are the derivatives *length* from *long*, *strength* from *strong*, *darling* from *dear*, *breadth* from *broad*, from *dry*, *drought*, and from *high*, *height*, which *Milton*, in zeal for analogy, writes *highth*; *Quid te exempta juvat spinis de pluribus una*; to change all would be too much, and to change one is nothing.

This uncertainty is most frequent in the vowels, which are so capriciously pronounced, and so differently modified, by accident or affectation, not only in every province, but in every mouth, that to them, as is well known to etymologists, little regard is to be shewn in the deduction of one language from another.

Such defects are not errours in orthography, but spots of barbarity impressed so deep in the *English* language, that criticism can never wash them away; these, therefore, must be permitted to remain untouched: but many words have likewise been altered by accident, or depraved by ignorance, as the pronunciation of the vulgar has been weakly followed; and some still continue to be variously written, as authours differ in their care or skill: of these it was proper to enquire the true orthography, which I have always considered as depending on their derivation, and have therefore referred them to their original languages: thus I write *enchant, enchantment, enchanter*, after the *French*, and *incantation* after the *Latin*; thus *entire* is chosen rather than *intire*, because it passed to us not from the *Latin integer*, but from the *French entier*.

Of many words it is difficult to say whether they were immediately received from the *Latin* or the *French*, since at the time when we had dominions in *France*, we had *Latin* service in our churches. It is, however, my opinion, that the *French* generally supplied us; for we have few *Latin* words, among the terms of domestick use, which are not *French*; but many *French*, which are very remote from *Latin*.

Even in words of which the derivation is apparent, I have been often obliged to sacrifice uniformity to custom; thus I write, in compliance with a numberless majority, *convey* and *inveigh, deceit* and *receipt, fancy* and *phantom*; sometimes the derivative varies from the primitive, as *explain* and *explanation, repeat* and *repetition*.

Some combinations of letters having the same power are used indifferently without any discoverable reason of choice, as in *choak, choke; soap, sope; fewel, fuel*, and many others; which I have sometimes inserted twice, that those who search for them under either form, may not search in vain.

In examining the orthography of any doubtful word, the mode of spelling by which it is inserted in the series of the dictionary, is to be considered as that to which I give, perhaps not often rashly, the preference. I have left, in the examples, to every authour his own practice unmolested, that the reader may balance suffrages, and judge between us: but this question is not always to be determined by reputed or by real learning; some men, intent upon greater things, have thought little on sounds and derivations; some, knowing in the ancient tongues, have neglected those in which our words are commonly to be sought. Thus *Hammond* writes *fecibleness* for *feasibleness*, because I suppose he imagined it derived immediately from the *Latin*; and some words, such as *dependant, dependent; dependance, dependence*, vary their final syllable, as one or other language is present to the writer.

In this part of the work, where caprice has long wantoned without controul, and vanity sought praise by petty reformation, I have endeavoured to proceed with a scholar's reverence for antiquity, and a grammarian's regard to the genius of our tongue. I have attempted few alterations, and among those few, perhaps the greater part is from the modern to the ancient practice; and I hope I may be allowed to recommend to those, whose thoughts have been, perhaps, employed too anxiously on verbal singularities, not to disturb, upon narrow views, or for minute propriety, the orthography of their fathers. It has been

In this part of the work, where caprice has long wantoned without controul, and vanity sought praise by petty reformation, I have endeavoured to proceed with a scholar's reverence for antiquity, and a grammarian's regard to the genius of our tongue.

I am not yet so lost in lexicography, as to forget that words are the daughters of earth, and that things are the sons of heaven. Language is only the instrument of science, and words are but the signs of ideas: I wish, however, that the instrument might be less apt to decay, and that signs might be permanent, like the things which they denote.

asserted, that for the law to be *known*, is of more importance than to be *right*. Change, says *Hooker*, is not made without inconvenience, even from worse to better. There is in constancy and stability a general and lasting advantage, which will always overbalance the slow improvements of gradual correction. Much less ought our written language to comply with the corruptions of oral utterance, or copy that which every variation of time or place makes different from itself, and imitate those changes, which will again be changed, while imitation is employed in observing them.

This recommendation of steadiness and uniformity does not proceed from an opinion, that particular combinations of letters have much influence on human happiness; or that truth may not be successfully taught by modes of spelling fanciful and erroneous: I am not yet so lost in lexicography, as to forget that *words are the daughters of earth, and that things are the sons of heaven.* Language is only the instrument of science, and words are but the signs of ideas: I wish, however, that the instrument might be less apt to decay, and that signs might be permanent, like the things which they denote.

In settling the orthography, I have not wholly neglected the pronunciation, which I have directed, by printing an accent upon the acute or elevated syllable. It will sometimes be found, that the accent is placed by the authour quoted, on a different syllable from that marked in the alphabetical series; it is then to be understood, that custom has varied, or that the authour has, in my opinion, pronounced wrong. Short directions are sometimes given where the sound of letters is irregular; and if they are sometimes omitted, defect in such minute observations will be more easily excused, than superfluity.

In the investigation both of the orthography and signification of words, their ETYMOLOGY was necessarily to be considered, and they were therefore to be divided into primitives and derivatives. A primitive word, is that which can be traced no further to any *English* root; thus *circumspect, circumvent, circumstance, delude, concave,* and *complicate,* though compounds in the *Latin,* are to us primitives. Derivatives, are all those that can be referred to any word in *English* of greater simplicity.

The derivatives I have referred to their primitives, with an accuracy sometimes needless; for who does not see that *remoteness* comes from *remote, lovely* from *love, concavity* from *concave,* and *demonstrative* from *demonstrate*? but this grammatical exuberance the scheme of my work did not allow me to repress. It is of great importance in examining the general fabrick of a language, to trace one word from another, by noting the usual modes of derivation and inflection; and uniformity must be preserved in systematical works, though sometimes at the expence of particular propriety.

Among other derivatives I have been careful to insert and elucidate the anomalous plurals of nouns and preterites of verbs, which in the *Teutonick* dialects are very frequent, and, though familiar to those who have always used them, interrupt and embarrass the learners of our language.

The two languages from which our primitives have been derived are the *Roman* and *Teutonick*: under the *Roman* I comprehend the *French* and provincial tongues; and under the *Teutonick* range the *Saxon*, *German*, and all their kindred dialects. Most of our polysyllables are *Roman*, and our words of one syllable are very often *Teutonick*.

In assigning the *Roman* original, it has perhaps sometimes happened that I have mentioned only the *Latin*, when the word was borrowed from the *French*; and considering myself as employed only in the illustration of my own language, I have not been very careful to observe whether the *Latin* word be pure or barbarous, or the *French* elegant or obsolete.

For the *Teutonick* etymologies I am commonly indebted to *Junius* and *Skinner*, the only names which I have forborn to quote when I copied their books; not that I might appropriate their labours or usurp their honours, but that I might spare a perpetual repetition by one general acknowledgment. Of these, whom I ought not to mention but with the reverence due to instructors and benefactors, *Junius* appears to have excelled in extent of learning, and *Skinner* in rectitude of understanding. *Junius* was accurately skilled in all the northern languages, *Skinner* probably examined the ancient and remoter dialects only by occasional inspection into dictionaries; but the learning of *Junius* is often of no other use than to show him a track by which he may deviate from his purpose, to which *Skinner* always presses forward by the shortest way. *Skinner* is often ignorant, but never ridiculous: *Junius* is always full of knowledge; but his variety distracts his judgment, and his learning is very frequently disgraced by his absurdities.

The votaries of the northern muses will not perhaps easily restrain their indignation, when they find the name of *Junius* thus degraded by a disadvantageous comparison; but whatever reverence is due to his diligence, or his attainments, it can be no criminal degree of censoriousness to charge that etymologist with want of judgment, who can seriously derive *dream* from *drama*, because *life is a drama, and a drama is a dream*; and who declares with a tone of defiance, that no man can fail to derive *moan* from μονος, *monos*, who considers that grief naturally loves to be *alone*.[†]

Skinner is often ignorant, but never ridiculous: Junius is always full of knowledge; but his variety distracts his judgment, and his learning is very frequently disgraced by his absurdities.

Our knowledge of the northern literature is so scanty, that of words undoubtedly *Teutonick* the original is not always to be found in any ancient language; and I have therefore inserted *Dutch* or *German* substitutes, which I consider not as radical but parallel, not as the parents, but sisters of the *English*.

The words which are represented as thus related by descent or cognation, do not always agree in sense; for it is incident to words, as to their authours, to degenerate from their ancestors, and to change their manners when they change their country. It is sufficient, in etymological enquiries, if the senses of kindred words be found such as may easily pass into each other, or such as may both be referred to one general idea.

The etymology, so far as it is yet known, was easily found in the volumes where it is particularly and professedly delivered; and, by proper attention to the rules of derivation, the orthography was soon adjusted. But to COLLECT the WORDS of our language was a task of greater difficulty: the deficiency of dictionaries was immediately apparent; and when they were exhausted, what was yet wanting must be sought by fortuitous and unguided excursions into books, and gleaned as industry should find, or chance should offer it, in the boundless chaos of a living speech. My search, however, has been either skilful or lucky; for I have much augmented the vocabulary.

As my design was a dictionary, common or appellative, I have omitted all words which have relation to proper names; such as *Arian*, *Socinian*, *Calvinist*, *Benedictine*, *Mahometan*; but have retained those of a more general nature, as *Heathen*, *Pagan*.

Of the terms of art I have received such as could be found either in books of science or technical dictionaries; and have often inserted, from philosophical writers, words which are supported perhaps only by a single authority, and which being not admitted into general use, stand yet as candidates or probationers, and must depend for their adoption on the suffrage of futurity.

The words which our authours have introduced by their knowledge of foreign languages, or ignorance of their own, by vanity or wantonness, by compliance with fashion, or lust of innovation, I have registred as they occurred, though commonly only to censure them, and warn others against the folly of naturalizing useless foreigners to the injury of the natives.

I have not rejected any by design, merely because they were unnecessary or exuberant; but have received those which by different writers have been differently formed, as *viscid*, and *viscidity*, *viscous*, and *viscosity*.

Compounded or double words I have seldom noted, except when they obtain a signification different from that which the components have

To collect the words of our language was a task of greater difficulty: the deficiency of dictionaries was immediately apparent; and when they were exhausted, what was yet wanting must be sought by fortuitous and unguided excursions into books, and gleaned as industry should find, or chance should offer it, in the boundless chaos of a living speech.

in their simple state. Thus *highwayman*, *woodman*, and *horsecourser*, require an explication; but of *thieflike* or *coachdriver* no notice was needed, because the primitives contain the meaning of the compounds.

Words arbitrarily formed by a constant and settled analogy, like diminutive adjectives in *ish*, as *greenish*, *bluish*, adverbs in *ly*, as *dully*, *openly*, substantives in *ness*, as *vileness*, *faultiness*, were less diligently sought, and many sometimes have been omitted, when I had no authority that invited me to insert them; not that they are not genuine and regular offsprings of *English* roots, but because their relation to the primitive being always the same, their signification cannot be mistaken.

The verbal nouns in *ing*, such as the *keeping* of the *castle*, the *leading* of the *army*, are always neglected, or placed only to illustrate the sense of the verb, except when they signify things as well as actions, and have therefore a plural number, as *dwelling*, *living*, or have an absolute and abstract signification, as *colouring*, *painting*, *learning*.

The participles are likewise omitted, unless, by signifying rather qualities than action, they take the nature of adjectives; as a *thinking* man, a man of prudence; a *pacing* horse, a horse that can pace: these I have ventured to call *participial adjectives*. But neither are these always inserted, because they are commonly to be understood, without any danger of mistake, by consulting the verb.

Obsolete words are admitted, when they are found in authours not obsolete, or when they have any force or beauty that may deserve revival.

As composition is one of the chief characteristicks of a language, I have endeavoured to make some reparation for the universal negligence of my predecessors, by inserting great numbers of compounded words, as may be found under *after*, *fore*, *new*, *night*, *fair*, and many more. These, numerous as they are, might be multiplied, but that use and curiosity are here satisfied, and the frame of our language and modes of our combination amply discovered.

Of some forms of composition, such as that by which *re* is prefixed to note *repetition*, and *un* to signify *contrariety* or *privation*, all the examples cannot be accumulated, because the use of these particles, if not wholly arbitrary, is so little limited, that they are hourly affixed to new words as occasion requires, or is imagined to require them.

There is another kind of composition more frequent in our language than perhaps in any other, from which arises to foreigners the greatest difficulty. We modify the signification of many verbs by a particle subjoined; as to *come off*, to escape by a fetch; to *fall on*, to attack; to *fall off*, to apostatize; *to break off*, to stop abruptly; to *bear out*, to justify; to *fall in*, to comply; to *give over*, to cease; to *set off*, to embellish; to *set in*, to begin a continual tenour; to *set out*, to begin a course or journey; to *take off*, to copy; with innumerable expressions of the same kind, of

As composition is one of the chief characteristicks of a language, I have endeavoured to make some reparation for the universal negligence of my predecessors, by inserting great numbers of compounded words, as may be found under after, fore, new, night, fair, and many more.

That part of my work on which I expect malignity most frequently to fasten, is the Explanation; *in which I cannot hope to satisfy those, who are perhaps not inclined to be pleased, since I have not always been able to satisfy myself.*

which some appear wildly irregular, being so far distant from the sense of the simple words, that no sagacity will be able to trace the steps by which they arrived at the present use. These I have noted with great care; and though I cannot flatter myself that the collection is complete, I believe I have so far assisted the students of our language, that this kind of phraseology will be no longer insuperable; and the combinations of verbs and particles, by chance omitted, will be easily explained by comparison with those that may be found.

Many words yet stand supported only by the name of *Bailey, Ainsworth, Philips*, or the contracted *Dict.* for *Dictionaries* subjoined: of these I am not always certain that they are read in any book but the works of lexicographers. Of such I have omitted many, because I had never read them; and many I have inserted, because they may perhaps exist, though they have escaped my notice: they are, however, to be yet considered as resting only upon the credit of former dictionaries. Others, which I considered as useful, or know to be proper, though I could not at present support them by authorities, I have suffered to stand upon my own attestation, claiming the same privilege with my predecessors of being sometimes credited without proof.

The words, thus selected and disposed, are grammatically considered: they are referred to the different parts of speech; traced, when they are irregularly inflected, through their various terminations; and illustrated by observations, not indeed of great or striking importance, separately considered, but necessary to the elucidation of our language, and hitherto neglected or forgotten by *English* grammarians.

That part of my work on which I expect malignity most frequently to fasten, is the *Explanation*; in which I cannot hope to satisfy those, who are perhaps not inclined to be pleased, since I have not always been able to satisfy myself. To interpret a language by itself is very difficult; many words cannot be explained by synonimes, because the idea signified by them has not more than one appellation; nor by paraphrase, because simple ideas cannot be described. When the nature of things is unknown, or the notion unsettled and indefinite, and various in various minds, the words by which such notions are conveyed, or such things denoted, will be ambiguous and perplexed. And such is the fate of hapless lexicography, that not only darkness, but light, impedes and distresses it; things may be not only too little, but too much known, to be happily illustrated. To explain, requires the use of terms less abstruse than that which is to be explained, and such terms cannot always be found; for as nothing can be proved but by supposing something intuitively known, and evident without proof, so nothing can be defined but by the use of words too plain to admit a definition.

Other words there are, of which the sense is too subtle and evanescent to be fixed in a paraphrase; such are all those which are by the grammarians termed *expletives*, and, in dead languages, are suffered to pass for empty sounds, of no other use than to fill a verse, or to modulate a period, but which are easily perceived in living tongues to have power and emphasis, though it be sometimes such as no other form of expression can convey.

My labour has likewise been much increased by a class of verbs too frequent in the *English* language, of which the signification is so loose and general, the use so vague and indeterminate, and the senses detorted so widely from the first idea, that it is hard to trace them through the maze of variation, to catch them on the brink of utter inanity, to circumscribe them by any limitations, or interpret them by any words of distinct and settled meaning: such are *bear, break, come, cast, full, get, give, do, put, set, go, run, make, take, turn, throw*. If of these the whole power is not accurately delivered, it must be remembered, that while our language is yet living, and variable by the caprice of every one that speaks it, these words are hourly shifting their relations, and can no more be ascertained in a dictionary, than a grove, in the agitation of a storm, can be accurately delineated from its picture in the water.

The particles are among all nations applied with so great latitude, that they are not easily reducible under any regular scheme of explication: this difficulty is not less, nor perhaps greater, in *English*, than in other languages. I have laboured them with diligence, I hope with success; such at least as can be expected in a task, which no man, however learned or sagacious, has yet been able to perform.

Some words there are which I cannot explain, because I do not understand them; these might have been omitted very often with little inconvenience, but I would not so far indulge my vanity as to decline this confession: for when *Tully* owns himself ignorant whether *lessus*, in the twelve tables, means a *funeral song*, or *mourning garment*; and *Aristotle* doubts whether ουρευς, in the Iliad, signifies a *mule*, or *muleteer*, I may freely, without shame, leave some obscurities to happier industry, or future information.

The rigour of interpretative lexicography requires that *the explanation, and the word explained, should be always reciprocal*; this I have always endeavoured, but could not always attain. Words are seldom exactly synonimous; a new term was not introduced, but because the former was thought inadequate: names, therefore, have often many ideas, but few ideas have many names. It was then necessary to use the proximate word, for the deficiency of single terms can very seldom be supplied by circumlocution; nor is the inconvenience great of such mutilated interpretations, because the sense may easily be collected entire from the examples.

Some words there are which I cannot explain, because I do not understand them; these might have been omitted very often with little inconvenience, but I would not so far indulge my vanity as to decline this confession....

In every word of extensive use, it was requisite to mark the progress of its meaning, and show by what gradations of intermediate sense it has passed from its primitive to its remote and accidental signification; so that every foregoing explanation should tend to that which follows, and the series be regularly concatenated from the first notion to the last.

These complaints of difficulty will, by those that have never considered words beyond their popular use, be thought only the jargon of a man willing to magnify his labours, and procure veneration to his studies by involution and obscurity. But every art is obscure to those that have not learned it....

This is specious, but not always practicable; kindred senses may be so interwoven, that the perplexity cannot be disentangled, nor any reason be assigned why one should be ranged before the other. When the radical idea branches out into parallel ramifications, how can a consecutive series be formed of senses in their nature collateral? The shades of meaning sometimes pass imperceptibly into each other; so that though on one side they apparently differ, yet it is impossible to mark the point of contact. Ideas of the same race, though not exactly alike, are sometimes so little different, that no words can express the dissimilitude, though the mind easily perceives it, when they are exhibited together; and sometimes there is such a confusion of acceptations, that discernment is wearied, and distinction puzzled, and perseverance herself hurries to an end, by crouding together what she cannot separate.

These complaints of difficulty will, by those that have never considered words beyond their popular use, be thought only the jargon of a man willing to magnify his labours, and procure veneration to his studies by involution and obscurity. But every art is obscure to those that have not learned it: this uncertainty of terms, and commixture of ideas, is well known to those who have joined philosophy with grammar; and if I have not expressed them very clearly, it must be remembered that I am speaking of that which words are insufficient to explain.

The original sense of words is often driven out of use by their metaphorical acceptations, yet must be inserted for the sake of a regular origination. Thus I know not whether *ardour* is used for *material heat*, or whether *flagrant*, in *English*, ever signifies the same with *burning*; yet such are the primitive ideas of these words, which are therefore set first, though without examples, that the figurative senses may be commodiously deduced.

Such is the exuberance of signification which many words have obtained, that it was scarcely possible to collect all their senses; sometimes the meaning of derivatives must be sought in the mother term, and sometimes deficient explanations of the primitive may be supplied in the train of derivation. In any case of doubt or difficulty, it will be always proper to examine all the words of the same race; for some words are slightly passed over to avoid repetition, some admitted easier and clearer explanation than others, and all will be better understood, as they are considered in greater variety of structures and relations.

All the interpretations of words are not written with the same skill, or the same happiness: things equally easy in themselves, are not all equally easy to any single mind. Every writer of a long work commits errours, where there appears neither ambiguity to mislead, nor obscurity to confound him; and in a search like this, many felicities of expression will be casually overlooked, many convenient parallels will be forgotten, and many particulars will admit improvement from a mind utterly unequal to the whole performance.

But many seeming faults are to be imputed rather to the nature of the undertaking, than the negligence of the performer. Thus some explanations are unavoidably reciprocal or circular, as *hind, the female of the stag; stag, the male of the hind:* sometimes easier words are changed into harder, as *burial* into *sepulture* or *interment, drier* into *desiccative, dryness* into *siccity* or *aridity, fit* into *paroxysm;* for the easiest word, whatever it be, can never be translated into one more easy. But easiness and difficulty are merely relative, and if the present prevalence of our language should invite foreigners to this dictionary, many will be assisted by those words which now seem only to increase or produce obscurity. For this reason I have endeavoured frequently to join a *Teutonick* and *Roman* interpretation, as to CHEER to *gladden,* or *exhilarate,* that every learner of *English* may be assisted by his own tongue.

The solution of all difficulties, and the supply of all defects, must be sought in the examples, subjoined to the various senses of each word, and ranged according to the time of their authours.

When first I collected these authorities, I was desirous that every quotation should be useful to some other end than the illustration of a word; I therefore extracted from philosophers principles of science; from historians remarkable facts; from chymists complete processes; from divines striking exhortations; and from poets beautiful descriptions. Such is design, while it is yet at a distance from execution. When the time called upon me to range this accumulation of elegance and wisdom into an alphabetical series, I soon discovered that the bulk of my volumes would fright away the student, and was forced to depart from my scheme of including all that was pleasing or useful in *English* literature, and reduce my transcripts very often to clusters of words, in which scarcely any meaning is retained; thus to the weariness of copying, I was condemned to add the vexation of expunging. Some passages I have yet spared, which may relieve the labour of verbal searches, and intersperse with verdure and flowers the dusty desarts of barren philology.

When first I collected these authorities, I was desirous that every quotation should be useful to some other end than the illustration of a word; I therefore extracted from philosophers principles of science; from historians remarkable facts; from chymists complete processes; from divines striking exhortations; and from poets beautiful descriptions. Such is design, while it is yet at a distance from execution.

If the language of theology were extracted from Hooker *and the translation of the Bible; the terms of natural knowledge from* Bacon; *the phrases of policy, war, and navigation from* Raleigh; *the dialect of poetry and fiction from* Spenser *and* Sidney; *and the diction of common life from* Shakespeare, *few ideas would be lost to mankind....*

The examples, thus mutilated, are no longer to be considered as conveying the sentiments or doctrine of their authours; the word for the sake of which they are inserted, with all its appendant clauses, has been carefully preserved; but it may sometimes happen, by hasty detruncation, that the general tendency of the sentence may be changed: the divine may desert his tenets, or the philosopher his system.

Some of the examples have been taken from writers who were never mentioned as masters of elegance or models of stile; but words must be sought where they are used; and in what pages, eminent for purity, can terms of manufacture or agriculture be found? Many quotations serve no other purpose, than that of proving the bare existence of words, and are therefore selected with less scrupulousness than those which are to teach their structures and relations.

My purpose was to admit no testimony of living authours, that I might not be misled by partiality, and that none of my cotemporaries might have reason to complain; nor have I departed from this resolution, but when some performance of uncommon excellence excited my veneration, when my memory supplied me, from late books, with an example that was wanting, or when my heart, in the tenderness of friendship, solicited admission for a favourite name.

So far have I been from any care to grace my pages with modern decorations, that I have studiously endeavoured to collect examples and authorities from the writers before the restoration, whose works I regard as *the wells of English undefiled*, as the pure sources of genuine diction. Our language, for almost a century, has, by the concurrence of many causes, been gradually departing from its original *Teutonick* character, and deviating towards a *Gallick* structure and phraseology, from which it ought to be our endeavour to recal it, by making our ancient volumes the ground-work of stile, admitting among the additions of later times, only such as may supply real deficiencies, such as are readily adopted by the genius of our tongue, and incorporate easily with our native idioms.

But as every language has a time of rudeness antecedent to perfection, as well as of false refinement and declension, I have been cautious lest my zeal for antiquity might drive me into times too remote, and croud my book with words now no longer understood. I have fixed *Sidney's* work for the boundary, beyond which I make few excursions. From the authours which rose in the time of *Elizabeth*, a speech might be formed adequate to all the purposes of use and elegance. If the language of theology were extracted from *Hooker* and the translation of the Bible; the terms of natural knowledge from *Bacon*; the phrases of policy, war, and navigation from *Raleigh*; the dialect of poetry and fiction from *Spenser* and *Sidney*; and the diction of common life from *Shakespeare*, few ideas would be lost to mankind, for want of *English* words, in which they might be expressed.

It is not sufficient that a word is found, unless it be so combined as that its meaning is apparently determined by the tract and tenour of the sentence; such passages I have therefore chosen, and when it happened that any authour gave a definition of a term, or such an explanation as is equivalent to a definition, I have placed his authority as a supplement to my own, without regard to the chronological order, that is otherwise observed.

Some words, indeed, stand unsupported by any authority, but they are commonly derivative nouns or adverbs, formed from their primitives by regular and constant analogy, or names of things seldom occurring in books, or words of which I have reason to doubt the existence.

There is more danger of censure from the multiplicity than paucity of examples; authorities will sometimes seem to have been accumulated without necessity or use, and perhaps some will be found, which might, without loss, have been omitted. But a work of this kind is not hastily to be charged with superfluities: those quotations which to careless or unskilful perusers appear only to repeat the same sense, will often exhibit, to a more accurate examiner, diversities of signification, or, at least, afford different shades of the same meaning: one will shew the word applied to persons, another to things; one will express an ill, another a good, and a third a neutral sense; one will prove the expression genuine from an ancient authour; another will shew it elegant from a modern: a doubtful authority is corroborated by another of more credit; an ambiguous sentence is ascertained by a passage clear and determinate; the word, how often soever repeated, appears with new associates and in different combinations, and every quotation contributes something to the stability or enlargement of the language.

When words are used equivocally, I receive them in either sense; when they are metaphorical, I adopt them in their primitive acceptation.

I have sometimes, though rarely, yielded to the temptation of exhibiting a genealogy of sentiments, by shewing how one authour copied the thoughts and diction of another: such quotations are indeed little more than repetitions, which might justly be censured, did they not gratify the mind, by affording a kind of intellectual history.

The various syntactical structures occurring in the examples have been carefully noted; the licence or negligence with which many words have been hitherto used, has made our stile capricious and indeterminate; when the different combinations of the same word are exhibited together, the preference is readily given to propriety, and I have often endeavoured to direct the choice.

Thus have I laboured to settle the orthography, display the analogy, regulate the structures, and ascertain the signification of English words, to perform all the parts of a faithful lexicographer: but I have not always executed my own scheme, or satisfied my own expectations. The work, whatever proofs of diligence and attention it may exhibit, is yet capable of many improvements....

When first I engaged in this work, I resolved to leave neither words nor things unexamined, and pleased myself with a prospect of the hours which I should revel away in feasts of literature, the obscure recesses of northern learning, which I should enter and ransack, the treasures with which I expected every search into those neglected mines to reward my labour, and the triumph with which I should display my acquisitions to mankind.....But these were the dreams of a poet doomed at last to wake a lexicographer.

Thus have I laboured to settle the orthography, display the analogy, regulate the structures, and ascertain the signification of *English* words, to perform all the parts of a faithful lexicographer: but I have not always executed my own scheme, or satisfied my own expectations. The work, whatever proofs of diligence and attention it may exhibit, is yet capable of many improvements: the orthography which I recommend is still controvertible, the etymology which I adopt is uncertain, and perhaps frequently erroneous; the explanations are sometimes too much contracted, and sometimes too much diffused, the significations are distinguished rather with subtilty than skill, and the attention is harrassed with unnecessary minuteness.

The examples are too often injudiciously truncated, and perhaps sometimes, I hope very rarely, alleged in a mistaken sense; for in making this collection I trusted more to memory, than, in a state of disquiet and embarrassment, memory can contain, and purposed to supply at the review what was left incomplete in the first transcription.

Many terms appropriated to particular occupations, though necessary and significant, are undoubtedly omitted; and of the words most studiously considered and exemplified, many senses have escaped observation.

Yet these failures, however frequent, may admit extenuation and apology. To have attempted much is always laudable, even when the enterprize is above the strength that undertakes it: To rest below his own aim is incident to every one whose fancy is active, and whose views are comprehensive; nor is any man satisfied with himself because he has done much, but because he can conceive little. When first I engaged in this work, I resolved to leave neither words nor things unexamined, and pleased myself with a prospect of the hours which I should revel away in feasts of literature, the obscure recesses of northern learning, which I should enter and ransack, the treasures with which I expected every search into those neglected mines to reward my labour, and the triumph with which I should display my acquisitions to mankind. When I had thus enquired into the original of words, I resolved to show likewise my attention to things; to pierce deep into every science, to enquire the nature of every substance of which I inserted the name, to limit every idea by a definition strictly logical, and exhibit every production of art or nature in an accurate description, that my book might be in place of all other dictionaries whether appellative or technical. But these were the dreams of a poet doomed at last to wake a lexicographer. I soon found that it is too late to look for instruments, when the work calls for execution, and that whatever abilities I had brought to my task, with those I must finally perform it. To deliberate whenever I doubted, to enquire whenever I was ignorant, would have protracted the undertaking without end, and, perhaps, without much improvement; for I did not find by my first experiments, that what I had not of my own was easily to be obtained: I saw that one enquiry only gave occasion to another, that book referred to book, that to search was not always to find, and to find was not always to be informed; and that thus to persue perfection, was, like the first inhabitants of Arcadia, to chace the sun, which, when they had reached the hill where he seemed to rest, was still beheld at the same distance from them.

I then contracted my design, determining to confide in myself, and no longer to solicit auxiliaries, which produced more incumbrance than assistance: by this I obtained at least one advantage, that I set limits to my work, which would in time be finished, though not completed.

Despondency has never so far prevailed as to depress me to negligence; some faults will at last appear to be the effects of anxious diligence and persevering activity. The nice and subtle ramifications of meaning were not easily avoided by a mind intent upon accuracy, and convinced of the necessity of disentangling combinations, and separating similitudes. Many of the distinctions which to common readers appear useless and idle, will be found real and important by men versed in the school philosophy, without which no dictionary ever shall be accurately compiled, or skilfully examined.

Some senses however there are, which, though not the same, are yet so nearly allied, that they are often confounded. Most men think indistinctly, and therefore cannot speak with exactness; and consequently some examples might be indifferently put to either signification: this uncertainty is not to be imputed to me, who do not form, but register the language; who do not teach men how they should think, but relate how they have hitherto expressed their thoughts.

The imperfect sense of some examples I lamented, but could not remedy, and hope they will be compensated by innumerable passages selected with propriety, and preserved with exactness; some shining with sparks of imagination, and some replete with treasures of wisdom.

The orthography and etymology, though imperfect, are not imperfect for want of care, but because care will not always be successful, and recollection or information come too late for use.

That many terms of art and manufacture are omitted, must be frankly acknowledged; but for this defect I may boldly allege that it was unavoidable: I could not visit caverns to learn the miner's language, nor take a voyage to perfect my skill in the dialect of navigation, nor visit the warehouses of merchants, and shops of artificers, to gain the names of wares, tools and operations, of which no mention is found in books; what favourable accident, or easy enquiry brought within my reach, has not been neglected; but it had been a hopeless labour to glean up words, by courting living information, and contesting with the sullenness of one, and the roughness of another.

To furnish the academicians *della Crusca* with words of this kind, a series of comedies called *la Fiera*, or *the Fair*, was professedly written by *Buonaroti*; but I had no such assistant, and therefore was content to

The imperfect sense of some examples I lamented, but could not remedy, and hope they will be compensated by innumerable passages selected with propriety, and preserved with exactness; some shining with sparks of imagination, and some replete with treasures of wisdom.

want what they must have wanted likewise, had they not luckily been so supplied.

Nor are all words which are not found in the vocabulary, to be lamented as omissions. Of the laborious and mercantile part of the people, the diction is in a great measure casual and mutable; many of their terms are formed for some temporary or local convenience, and though current at certain times and places, are in others utterly unknown. This fugitive cant, which is always in a state of increase or decay, cannot be regarded as any part of the durable materials of a language, and therefore must be suffered to perish with other things unworthy of preservation.

Care will sometimes betray to the appearance of negligence. He that is catching opportunities which seldom occur, will suffer those to pass by unreguarded, which he expects hourly to return; he that is searching for rare and remote things, will neglect those that are obvious and familiar: thus many of the most common and cursory words have been inserted with little illustration, because in gathering the authorities, I forbore to copy those which I thought likely to occur whenever they were wanted. It is remarkable that, in reviewing my collection, I found the word SEA unexemplified.

Thus it happens, that in things difficult there is danger from ignorance, and in things easy from confidence; the mind, afraid of greatness, and disdainful of littleness, hastily withdraws herself from painful searches, and passes with scornful rapidity over tasks not adequate to her powers, sometimes too secure for caution, and again too anxious for vigorous effort; sometimes idle in a plain path, and sometimes distracted in labyrinths, and dissipated by different intentions.

A large work is difficult because it is large, even though all its parts might singly be performed with facility; where there are many things to be done, each must be allowed its share of time and labour, in the proportion only which it bears to the whole; nor can it be expected, that the stones which form the dome of a temple, should be squared and polished like the diamond of a ring.

Of the event of this work, for which, having laboured it with so much application, I cannot but have some degree of parental fondness, it is natural to form conjectures. Those who have been persuaded to think well of my design, require that it should fix our language, and put a stop to those alterations which time and chance have hitherto been suffered to make in it without opposition. With this consequence I will confess that I flattered myself for a while; but now begin to fear that I have indulged expectation which neither reason nor experience can justify. When we see men grow old and die at a certain time one after another, from century to century, we laugh at the elixir that promises to prolong life to a thousand years; and with equal justice may the lexicographer be derided, who being able to produce no example of a nation that has preserved their words and phrases from mutability, shall imagine that his dictionary can embalm his language, and secure it from corruption and decay, that it is in his power to change sublunary nature, or clear the world at once from folly, vanity, and affectation.

With this hope, however, academies have been instituted, to guard the avenues of their languages, to retain fugitives, and repulse intruders; but their vigilance and activity have hitherto been vain; sounds are too volatile and subtile for legal restraints; to enchain syllables, and to lash the wind, are equally the undertakings of pride, unwilling to measure its desires by its strength. The *French* language has visibly changed under the inspection of the academy; the stile of *Amelot*'s translation of father *Paul* is observed by *Le Courayer* to be *un peu passé*; and no *Italian* will maintain, that the diction of any modern writer is not perceptibly different from that of *Boccace*, *Machiavel*, or *Caro*.

Total and sudden transformations of a language seldom happen; conquests and migrations are now very rare: but there are other causes of change, which, though slow in their operation, and invisible in their progress, are perhaps as much superiour to human resistance, as the revolutions of the sky, or intumescence of the tide. Commerce, however necessary, however lucrative, as it depraves the manners, corrupts the language; they that have frequent intercourse with strangers, to whom they endeavour to accommodate themselves, must in time learn a mingled dialect, like the jargon which serves the traffickers on the *Mediterranean* and *Indian* coasts. This will not always be confined to the exchange, the warehouse, or the port, but will be communicated by degrees to other ranks of the people, and be at last incorporated with the current speech.

There are likewise internal causes equally forcible. The language most likely to continue long without alteration, would be that of a nation raised a little, and but a little, above barbarity, secluded from strangers, and totally employed in procuring the conveniencies of life; either without books, or, like some of the *Mahometan* countries, with very few: men thus busied and unlearned, having only such words as common use requires, would perhaps long continue to express the same notions by the same signs. But no such constancy can be expected in a people polished by arts, and classed by subordination, where one part of the community is sustained and accommodated by the labour of the other. Those who have much leisure to think, will always be enlarging the stock of ideas, and every increase of knowledge, whether real or fancied, will produce new words, or combinations of words. When the mind is unchained from necessity, it will range after convenience; when it is left at large in the fields of speculation, it will shift opinions; as any custom is disused, the words that expressed it must perish with it; as any opinion grows popular, it will innovate speech in the same

When we see men grow old and die at a certain time one after another, from century to century, we laugh at the elixir that promises to prolong life to a thousand years; and with equal justice may the lexicographer be derided, who being able to produce no example of a nation that has preserved their words and phrases from mutability, shall imagine that his dictionary can embalm his language....

proportion as it alters practice.

If an academy should be established for the cultivation of our stile, which I, who can never wish to see dependance multiplied, hope the spirit of English liberty will hinder or destroy, let them...endeavour, with all their influence, to stop the licence of translatours, whose idleness and ignorance, if it be suffered to proceed, will reduce us to babble a dialect of France.

As by the cultivation of various sciences, a language is amplified, it will be more furnished with words deflected from their original sense; the geometrician will talk of a courtier's zenith, or the excentrick virtue of a wild hero, and the physician of sanguine expectations and phlegmatick delays. Copiousness of speech will give opportunities to capricious choice, by which some words will be preferred, and others degraded; vicissitudes of fashion will enforce the use of new, or extend the signification of known terms. The tropes of poetry will make hourly encroachments, and the metaphorical will become the current sense: pronunciation will be varied by levity or ignorance, and the pen must at length comply with the tongue; illiterate writers will at one time or other, by publick infatuation, rise into renown, who, not knowing the original import of words, will use them with colloquial licentiousness, confound distinction, and forget propriety. As politeness increases, some expressions will be considered as too gross and vulgar for the delicate, others as too formal and ceremonious for the gay and airy; new phrases are therefore adopted, which must, for the same reasons, be in time dismissed. *Swift*, in his petty treatise on the *English* language, allows that new words must sometimes be introduced, but proposes that none should be suffered to become obsolete. But what makes a word obsolete, more than general agreement to forbear it? and how shall it be continued, when it conveys an offensive idea, or recalled again into the mouths of mankind, when it has once by disuse become unfamiliar, and by unfamiliarity unpleasing.

There is another cause of alteration more prevalent than any other, which yet in the present state of the world cannot be obviated. A mixture of two languages will produce a third distinct from both, and they will always be mixed, where the chief part of education, and the most conspicuous accomplishment, is skill in ancient or in foreign tongues. He that has long cultivated another language, will find its words and combinations croud upon his memory; and haste or negligence, refinement or affectation, will obtrude borrowed terms and exotick expressions.

The great pest of speech is frequency of translation. No book was ever turned from one language into another, without imparting something of its native idiom; this is the most mischievous and comprehensive innovation; single words may enter by thousands, and the fabrick of the tongue continue the same, but new phraseology changes much at once; it alters not the single stones of the building, but the order of the columns. If an academy should be established for the cultivation of our stile, which I, who can never wish to see dependance multiplied, hope the spirit of *English* liberty will hinder or destroy, let them, instead of compiling grammars and dictionaries, endeavour, with all their influence, to stop the licence of translatours, whose idleness and ignorance, if it be suffered to proceed, will reduce us to babble a dialect of *France*.

If the changes that we fear be thus irresistible, what remains but to acquiesce with silence, as in the other insurmountable distresses of humanity? it remains that we retard what we cannot repel, that we palliate what we cannot cure. Life may be lengthened by care, though death cannot be ultimately defeated: tongues, like governments, have a natural tendency to degeneration; we have long preserved our constitution, let us make some struggles for our language.

In hope of giving longevity to that which its own nature forbids to be immortal, I have devoted this book, the labour of years, to the honour of my country, that we may no longer yield the palm of philology to the nations of the continent. The chief glory of every people arises from its authours: whether I shall add any thing by my own writings to the reputation of *English* literature, must be left to time: much of my life has been lost under the pressures of disease; much has been trifled away; and much has always been spent in provision for the day that was passing over me; but I shall not think my employment useless or ignoble, if by my assistance foreign nations, and distant ages, gain access to the propagators of knowledge, and understand the teachers of truth; if my labours afford light to the repositories of science, and add celebrity to *Bacon*, to *Hooker*, to *Milton*, and to *Boyle*.

When I am animated by this wish, I look with pleasure on my book, however defective, and deliver it to the world with the spirit of a man that has endeavoured well. That it will immediately become popular I have not promised to myself: a few wild blunders, and risible absurdities, from which no work of such multiplicity was ever free, may for a time furnish folly with laughter, and harden ignorance in contempt; but useful diligence will at last prevail, and there never can be wanting some who distinguish desert; who will consider that no dictionary of a living tongue ever can be perfect, since while it is hastening to publication, some words are budding, and some falling away; that a whole life cannot be spent upon syntax and etymology, and that even a whole life would not be sufficient; that he, whose design includes whatever language can express, must often speak of what he does not understand; that a writer will sometimes be hurried by eagerness to the end, and sometimes faint with weariness under a task, which *Scaliger* compares to the labours of the anvil and the mine; that what is obvious is not always known, and what is known is not always present; that sudden fits of inadvertency will surprize vigilance, slight avocations will seduce attention, and casual eclipses of the mind will darken learning; and that the writer shall often in vain trace his memory at the moment of need, for that which yesterday he knew

I look with pleasure on my book, however defective, and deliver it to the world with the spirit of a man that has endeavoured well. That it will immediately become popular I have not promised to myself: a few wild blunders, and risible absurdities, from which no work of such multiplicity was ever free, may for a time furnish folly with laughter...but useful diligence will at last prevail....

with intuitive readiness, and which will come uncalled into his thoughts to-morrow.

In this work, when it shall be found that much is omitted, let it not be forgotten that much likewise is performed; and though no book was ever spared out of tenderness to the authour, and the world is little solicitous to know whence proceeded the faults of that which it condemns; yet it may gratify curiosity to inform it, that the *English Dictionary* was written with little assistance of the learned, and without any patronage of the great; not in the soft obscurities of retirement, or under the shelter of academick bowers, but amidst inconvenience and distraction, in sickness and in sorrow: and it may repress the triumph of malignant criticism to observe, that if our language is not here fully displayed, I have only failed in an attempt which no human powers have hitherto completed. If the lexicons of ancient tongues, now immutably fixed, and comprised in a few volumes, be yet, after the toil of successive ages, inadequate and delusive; if the aggregated knowledge, and co-operating diligence of the *Italian* academicians, did not secure them from the censure of *Beni*; if the embodied criticks of *France*, when fifty years had been spent upon their work, were obliged to change its oeconomy, and give their second edition another form, I may surely be contented without the praise of perfection, which, if I could obtain, in this gloom of solitude, what would it avail me? I have protracted my work till most of those whom I wished to please, have sunk into the grave, and success and miscarriage are empty sounds: I therefore dismiss it with frigid tranquillity, having little to fear or hope from censure or from praise.

---

† That I may not appear to have spoken too irreverently of *Junius*, I have here subjoined a few Specimens of his etymological extravagance.

BANISH, *religare, ex banno vel territorio exigere*, in *exilium agere*. G. *bannir*. It. *bandire, bandeggiare*. H. *bandir*. B. bannen. Ævi medii scriptores bannire dicebant. V. Spelm. in Bannum & in Banleuga. Quoniam verò regionum urbiumq; limites arduis plerumq; montibus, altis fluminibus, longis deniq; flexuosisq; angustissimarum viarum amfractibus includebantur, fieri potest id genus limites *ban* dici ab eo quod Βαννᾰται & Βαννᾰτροι Tarentinis olim, sicuti tradit Hesychius, vocabantur αι λοξοι και μη ιθυτενεις οδοι, "obliquæ ac minimè in rectum tendentes viæ." Ac fortasse quoque huc facit quod Βαvους, eodem Hesychio teste, dicebant ορη στραγγυλη, montes arduous.

EMPTY, emtie, *vacuus, inanis*. A. S. *Æmtig*. Nescio an sint ab εμεω vel εμεταω. Vomo, evomo, vomitu evacuo. Videtur interim etymologiam hanc non obscurè firmare codex Rush. Matt. xii. 22. ubi antiquè scriptum invenimus *gemoeted hit emetig*. "Invenit eam vacantem."

HILL, *mons, collis*. A. S. *hyll*. Quod videri potest abscissum ex χολωνη vel χολωνος. Collis, tumulus, locus in plano editior. Hom. Il. b. v. 811, εστι δε τις προπαροιθε πολεος αιπεια, χολωνη. Ubi authori brevium scholiorum χολωνη exp. τοπος εις υψος ανηκων, γεωλοφος εξοχη.

NAP, *to take a nap. Dormire, condormiscere.* Cym. heppian. A. S. *hnæppan.* Quod postremum videri potest desumptum ex κνεφας, obscuritas, tenebræ: nihil enim æque solet conciliare somnum, quàm caliginosa profundæ notis obscuritas.

STAMMERER, Balbus, blæsus. Goth. STAMMS. A. S. *stamer, stamur.* D. stam. B. stameler. Su. stamma. Isl. stamr. Sunt à στωμυλειν vel στωμυλλειν, nimiâ loquacitate alios offendere; quod impeditè loquentes libentissimè garrire soleant; vel quod aliis nimii semper videantur, etiam parcissimè loquentes.

A, the first letter of the European alphabets, has, in the English language, three different sounds, which may be termed the broad, open, and slender.

The broad sound, resembling that of the German *a*, is found in many of our monosyllables, as *all*, *wall*, *malt*, *salt*; in which *a* is pronounced as *au* in *cause*, or *aw* in *law*. Many of these words were anciently written with *au*, as *sault*, *waulk*; which happens to be still retained in *fault*. This was probably the ancient sound of the Saxons, since it is almost uniformly preserved in the rustick pronunciation, and the northern dialects, as *maun* for *man*, *haund* for *hand*.

A open, not unlike the *a* of the Italians, is found in *father*, *rather*, and more obscurely in *fancy*, *fast*, &c.

A slender or close, is the peculiar *a* of the English language, resembling the sound of the French *e* masculine, or diphthong *ai* in *païs*, or perhaps a middle sound between them, or between the *a* and *e*; to this the Arabic *a* is said nearly to approach. Of this sound we have examples in the words *place*, *face*, *waste*, and all those that terminate in *ation*, as, *relation*, *nation*, *generation*.

A is short, as, *glass*, *grass*; or long, as, *glaze*, *graze*: it is marked long, generally, by an *e* final, *plane*, or by an *i* added, as, *plain*.

A, in abbreviations, stands for *artium,* or arts; as, A.B. bachelor of arts, *artium baccalaureus;* A.M. master of arts, *artium magister;* or, *anno;* as, A.D. *anno domini.*

abáft adv. [of *abaftan,* Sax. Behind.] From the fore-part of the ship, towards the stern. Dict.

abannítion n.s. [Lat. *abannitio.*] A banishment for one or two years, among the ancients, for manslaughter. Dict.

abba n.s. [Heb. אב] A Syriac word, which signifies father.

ábbey-lubber n.s. See *lubber.* A slothful loiterer in a religious house, under pretence of retirement and austerity.

This is no Father Dominic, no huge overgrown abbeylubber; this is but a diminutive sucking friar. Dryd. Sp. Fr.

a, b, c

1. Is taken for the alphabet; as, he has not learned his a, b, c.

2. Sometimes for the little book by which the elements of reading are taught.

abecedárian n.s. [from the names of a, b, c, the three first letters of the alphabet.] He that teaches or learns the alphabet, or first rudiments of literature.

This word is used by Wood in his *Athenæ Oxonienses,* where mentioning Farnaby the critic, he relates, that, in some part of his life, he was reduced to follow the trade of an abecedarian by his misfortunes.

to aberúncate v.a. [*averunco,* Lat.] To pull up by the roots; to extirpate utterly. Dict.

to abláctate v.a. [*ablacto,* Lat.] To wean from the breast.

áblepsy n.s. [αβλεψια, Gr.] Want of sight, natural blindness; also unadvisedness. Dict.

abligurition n.s. [*abliguritio,* Lat.] A prodigal spending on meat and drink. Dict.

abnórmous adj. [*abnormis,* Lat. out of rule.] Irregular, mishapen. Dict.

aborígines n.s. [Lat.] The earliest inhabitants of a country; those of whom no original is to be traced; as the Welsh in Britain.

above-board In open sight; without artifice or trick. A figurative expression, borrowed from gamesters, who, when they put their hands under the table, are changing their cards. It is used only in familiar language.

It is the part also of an honest man to deal above-board; and without tricks. L'Estrange.

Though there have not been wanting such heretofore, as have practised these unworthy arts (for as much as there have been villains in all places, and all ages) yet now-a-days they are owned above-board.
South's Sermons.

above-ground An expression used to signify, that a man is alive; not in the grave.

abracadábra A superstitious charm against agues.

abrídgment n.s. [*abregement,* Fr.]

1. The contraction of a larger work into a small compass.

Surely this commandment containeth the law and the prophets; and, in this one word, is the abridgment of all volumes of scripture. Hooker, b. ii. § 5.

   Myself have play'd
The int'rim, by remembring you 'tis past;
Then brook abridgment, and your eyes advance
After your thought, straight back again to
France? Shakespeare's Henry V.

Idolatry is certainly the first-born of folly, the great and leading paradox; nay, the very abridgment and sum total of all absurdities. South's Sermons.

2. A diminution in general.

All trying, by a love of littleness,
To make abridgments, and to draw to less,
Even that nothing which at first we were. Donne.

3. Restraint, or abridgment of liberty.

The constant desire of happiness, and the constraint it puts upon us, no body, I think, accounts an abridgment of liberty, or at least

an abridgment of liberty, to be complained of.
Locke.

absínthiated part. [from *absinthium*, Lat. wormwood.] Imbittered, impregnated with wormwood. Dict.

ábsonous adj. [*absonus*, Lat. ill-sounding.] Absurd, contrary to reason.

To suppose an uniter of a middle constitution, that should partake of some of the qualities of both, is unwarranted by any of our faculties; yea, most absonous, to our reason. Glanville's Scepsis Scientifica, c. 4.

to abstérge v.a. [*abstergo*, Lat.] To cleanse by wiping; to wipe.

abstórted adj. [*abstortus*, Lat.] Forced away, wrung from another by violence.

académick n.s. [from *academy*.] A student of an university.

A young academic shall dwell upon a journal that treats of trade in a dictatorial style, and shall be lavish in the praise of the author; while, at the same time, persons well skilled in those different subjects, hear the tattle with contempt. Watts's Improvement of the Mind, p. i. c. 5.

ácademy n.s. [anciently, and properly, with the accent on first syllable, now frequently on the second. *Academia*, Lat. from *Academus* of Athens, whose house was turned into a school, from whom the *Groves of Academe* in Milton.]†

1. An assembly or society of men, uniting for the promotion of some art.

Our court shall be a little academy,
Still and contemplative in living arts.
Shak. Love's Lab. Lost.

2. The place where sciences are taught.

Amongst the academies, which were composed by the rare genius of those great men, these four are reckoned as the principal; namely, the Athenian school, that of Sicyon, that of Rhodes, and that of Corinth.
Dryden's Dufresnoy.

3. An university.

4. A place of education, in contradistinction to the universities or public schools.

áccidence n.s. [a corruption of *accidents*, from *accidentia*, Lat.] The little book containing the first rudiments of grammar, and explaining the properties of the eight parts of speech.

I do confess I do want eloquence,
And never yet did learn mine accidence.
Taylor the Water-poet.

áccident n.s. [*accidens*, Lat.]

1. The property or quality of any being, which may be separated from it, at least in thought.

If she were but the body's accident,
And her sole being did in it subsist,
As white in snow, she might herself absent,
And in the body's substance not be miss'd.
Sir John Davies.

An accidental mode, or an accident, is such a mode as is not necessary to the being of a thing; for the subject may be without it, and yet remain of the same nature that it was before; or it is that mode which may be separated or abolished from its subject.
Watts's Logick.

2. In grammar, the property of a word.

The learning of a language is nothing else but the informing of ourselves, what composures of letters are, by consent and institution, to signify such certain notions of things, with their modalities and accidents. Holder's Elements of Speech.

3. That which happens unforeseen; casualty, chance.

General laws are like general rules in physick, according whereunto, as no wise man will desire himself to be cured, if there be joined with his disease some special accident, in regard whereof, that whereby others in the same infirmity, but without the like accident, recover health, would be, to him, either hurtful, or, at the least, unprofitable.
Hooker, b. v. § 9.

The flood, and other accidents of time, made it one common field and pasture with the land of Eden. Raleigh's Hist. World.

Thus we rejoic'd, but soon our joy is turn'd Into perplexity, and new amaze; For whither is he gone? What accident Hath rapt him from us? Paradise Regained, b. i.

And trivial accidents shall be forborn, That others may have time to take their turn. Dryd. Fables.

The reformation owed nothing to the good intentions of king Henry. He was only an instrument of it (as the logicians speak) by accident. Swift's Miscellanies.

acclívous adj. [*acclivus*, Lat.] Rising with a slope.

accubátion n.s. [from *accubo*, to lye down to, Lat.] The antient posture of leaning at meals.

It will appear, that accubation, or lying down at meals, was a gesture used by very many nations. Brown.

acéphalous adj. [ακεφαλος, Gr.] Without a head. Dict.

acérvose adj. Full of heaps. Dict.

ácme n.s. [ακμη, Gr.] The height of any thing; more especially used to denote the height of a distemper, which is divided into four periods. 1. The *arche*, the beginning or first attack. 2. *Anabasis*, the growth. 3. *Acme*, the height. And, 4. *Paracme*, which is the declension of the distemper. Quincy.

an acróstick n.s. [from ακρος and στιχος, Gr.] A poem in which the first letter of every line being taken, makes up the name of the person or thing on which the poem is written.

actitátion n.s. [from *actito*, Lat.] Action quick and frequent. Dict.

acúleate adj. [*aculeatus*, Lat.] That which has a point or sting; prickly; that which terminates in a sharp point.

adágio n.s. [Italian.] A term used by musicians, to mark a slow time.

ádamant n.s. [*adamas*, Lat. from α and δαμνω, Gr. that is insuperable, infrangible.]

1. A stone, imagined by writers, of impenetrable hardness.

So great a fear my name amongst them spread, That they suppos'd I could rend bars of steel, And spurn in pieces posts of adamant. Shakesp.

Satan, with vast and haughty strides advanc'd, Came tow'ring, arm'd in adamant, and gold. Milton.

Eternal Deities, Who rule the world with absolute decrees, And write whatever time shall bring to pass, With pens of adamant, on plates of brass. Dryd.

2. The diamond.

Hardness, wherein some stones exceed all other bodies, and among them the adamant all other stones, being exalted to that degree thereof, that art in vain endeavours to counterfeit it, the factitious stones of chymists, in imitation, being easily detected by an ordinary lapidist. Ray on the Creation.

3. Adamant is taken for the loadstone.

Let him change his lodging from one end and part of the town to another, which is a great adamant of acquaintance. Bacon's Essays.

You draw me, you hard-hearted adamant! But yet you draw not iron; for my heart Is true as steel. Shakespeare.

to addict v.a. [*addico*, Lat.]

1. To devote, to dedicate, in a good sense; which is rarely used.

Ye know the house of Stephanus, that they have addicted themselves to the ministry of the saints. 1 Cor. xvi. 15.

2. It is commonly taken in a bad sense; as, he addicted himself to vice.

to áddle v.a. [from *addle*, adj.] To make addle; to corrupt; to make barren.

This is also evidenced in eggs, whereof the sound one sinks, and such as are addled swim; as do also those that are termed hypanemiæ, *or wind-eggs.* Brown's Vulgar Errours.

to addúlce v.a. [*addoucir*, Fr. *dulcis*, Lat.]
To sweeten; a word not now in use.

*Thus did the French embassadors, with great
shew of their king's affection, and many
sugared words, seek to addulce all matters
between the two kings.* Bacon's Henry VII.

adépt n.s. [from *adeptus*, Lat. that is *adeptus
artem.*] He that is completely skilled in all
the secrets of his art. It is, in its original
signification, appropriated to the chymists,
but is now extended to other artists.

*The preservation of chastity is easy to true
adepts.* Pope.

adiáphory n.s. [αδιαφορια, Gr.]
Neutrality; indifference.

ádipous adj. [*adiposus*, Lat.] Fat. Dict.

an adjútrix n.s. [Lat.] She who helps. Dict.

adscitítious adj. [*adscititius*, Lat.] That
which is taken in to complete something else,
though originally extrinsick; supplemental;
additional.

to adúlter v.a. [*adulterer*, Fr. *adultero*, Lat.]
To commit adultery with another: a word
not classical.

    *His chaste wife
He adulters still: his thoughts lye with a whore.*
Ben. Johns.

adúlterine n.s. [*adulterine*, Fr. *adulterinus*,
Lat.] A child born of an adulteress: a term
of canon law.

to adúmbrate v.a. [*adumbro*, Lat.]
To shadow out; to give a slight likeness;
to exhibit a faint resemblance, like that
which shadows afford of the bodies which
they represent.

*Heaven is designed for our reward, as well
as rescue; and therefore is adumbrated by all
those positive excellencies, which can endear
or recommend.* Decay of Piety.

advénturer n.s. [*adventurier*, Fr.] He that
seeks occasions of hazard; he that puts
himself in the hands of chance.

*He is a great adventurer, said he,
That hath his sword through hard assay forgone,
And now hath vow'd, till he avenged be
Of that despight, never to wear none.*
Fairy Queen, b. ii.

*The kings of England did not make the
conquest of Ireland their own work; it was
begun by particular adventurers, and other
voluntaries, who came to seek their fortunes
in Ireland.* Sir John Davies on Ireland.

*In this action, highly commendable, he
intended to hazard his own action, that
so the more easily he might win adventurers,
who else were like to be less forward.*
Sir W. Raleigh's Ess.

*Had it not been for the British, which the late
wars drew over, and of adventurers or soldiers
seated here, the country had, by the last war,
and plague, been left, in a manner, destitute.*
Temple's Miscellanies.

*Their wealthy trade from pirate's rapine free,
Our merchants shall no more advent'rers be.*
Dryden.

advertísement, or **advértisement** n.s.
[*advertissement*, Fr.]

1. Instruction; admonition.

    *—'Tis all men's office to speak patience
To those, that wring under the load of sorrow;
But no man's virtue nor sufficiency,
To be so moral, when he shall endure
The like himself: therefore give me no counsel;
My griefs are louder than advertisement.*
Shakespeare's Much ado about Nothing.

2. Intelligence; information.

*Then, as a cunning prince that useth spies,
If they return no news, doth nothing know;
But if they make advertisement of lies,
The prince's counsel all awry do go.*
Sir John Davies.

*He had received advertisement, that the
party, which was sent for his relief from
London, had received some brush in
Somersetshire, which would much retard
their march.* Clarendon.

*The drum and trumpet, by their several
sounds, serve for many kinds of*

advertisements, in military affairs: the bells serve to proclaim a scare-fire; and, in some places, water-breaches; the departure of a man, woman, or child; time of divine service; the hour of the day; day of the month. Holder.

3. Notice of any thing published in a paper of intelligence.

AE, or **Æ.** A diphthong of very frequent use in the Latin language, which seems not properly to have any place in the English; since the *æ* of the Saxons has been long out of use, being changed to *e* simple, to which, in words frequently occurring, the *æ* of the Romans is, in the same manner, altered, as in *equator, equinoctial,* and even in *Eneas.*

Ægyptíacum n.s. An ointment consisting only of honey, verdigrease and vinegar. Quincy.

aérial adj. [*aërius,* Lat.]

1. Belonging to the air, as consisting of it.

The thunder, when to roll
With terrour through the dark aerial hall.
Paradise Lost.

From all that can with fins or feathers fly,
Thro' the aerial or the wat'ry sky. Prior.

I gathered the thickness of the air, or aerial interval, of the glasses at that ring. Newton's Opticks.

Vegetables abound more with aerial particles, than animal substances. Arbuthnot on Aliments.

2. Produced by the air.

The gifts of heav'n my foll'wing song pursues, Aerial honey, and ambrosial dews. Dryd. Virg. Georg.

3. Inhabiting the air.

Where those immortal shapes
Of bright aerial spirits live inspher'd,
In regions mild, of calm and serene air.
Paradise Regained.

Aerial animals may be subdivided into birds and flies. Locke.

4. Placed in the air.

Here subterranean works and cities see, There towns aerial on the waving tree. Pope's Essay on Man.

5. High; elevated in situation, and therefore in the air.

A spacious city stood, with firmest walls, Sure mounded, and with numerous
   turrets crown'd,
Aerial spires, and citadels, the seat
Of kings and heroes resolute in war. Philips.

áeromancy n.s. [αηρ and μαντις, Gr.] The art of divining by the air. Dict.

afflátus n.s. [Lat.] Communication of the power of prophecy. Dict.

to affórd v.a. [*affourrer, affourrager,* Fr.]

1. To yield or produce; as, the soil affords grain; the trees afford fruits. This seems to be the primitive signification.

2. To grant, or confer any thing; generally in a good sense, and sometimes in a bad, not properly.

So soon as Maurmon there arrived, the door To him did open, and afforded way. Fairy Queen.

This is the consolation of all good men, unto whom his ubiquity affordeth continual comfort and security; and this is the affliction of hell, to whom it affordeth despair and remediless calamity. Brown's Vulgar Errours, b. i. c. 2.

3. To be able to sell. It is used always with reference to some certain price; as, *I can afford this for less than the other.*

They fill their magazines in times of the greatest plenty, that so they may afford cheaper, and increase the public revenue at a small expence of its members. Addison on Italy.

4. To be able to bear expences; as, traders can afford more finery in peace than war.

The same errours run through all families, where there is wealth enough to afford that their sons may be good for nothing. Swift on Modern Education.

áfterages n.s. [from *after* and *ages*.] Successive times; posterity. This word has no singular.

Not the whole land, which the Chusites should, or might in future time, conquer; seeing, in afterages, they became lords of many nations. Raleigh's History of the World.

Nor to philosophers is praise deny'd,
Whose wise instructions afterages guide.
Sir J. Denham.

What an opinion will afterages entertain of their religion, who bid fair for a gibbet, by endeavouring to bring in a superstition, which their forefathers perished in flames to keep out. Addison's Freeholder, Nº 1.

áfterclap n.s. [from *after* and *clap*.] Unexpected events happening after an affair is supposed to be at an end.

For the next morrow's meed they closely went,
For fear of afterclaps to prevent.
Spens. Hub. Tale.

It is commonly taken in an ill sense.

ága n.s. The title of a Turkish military officer.

ágalaxy n.s. [from α and γαλα, Gr.] Want of milk. Dict.

age n.s. [*age*, Fr. anciently *age*, or *aage*; it is deduced by Menage, from *ætatium*, of *ætas*; by Junius, from *aa*, which, in the Teutonic dialects, signified long duration.]

1. Any period of time attributed to something as the whole, or part, of its duration: in this sense, we say, the age of man, the several ages of the world, the golden or iron age.

One man in his time plays many parts,
His life being seven ages. Shakespeare.

And Jacob lived in the land of Egypt seventeen years; so the whole age of Jacob was an hundred forty and seven years. Genesis, xlvii. 28.

2. A succession or generation of men.

Hence, lastly, springs care of posterities,
For things their kind would everlasting make.
Hence is it, that old men do plant young trees,

The fruit whereof another age shall take.
Sir J. Davies.

   Next, to the Son,
Destin'd Restorer of mankind, by whom
New heav'n, and earth, shall to the ages rise,
Or down from heav'n descend. Milton's Paradise Lost.

   No declining age
E'er felt the raptures of poetic rage.
Roscommon.

3. The time in which any particular man, or race of men, lived, or shall live; as, the age of heroes.

4. The space of a hundred years; a secular period; a century.

5. The latter part of life; old-age; oldness.

You see how full of change his age is: the observation we have made of it hath not been little; he always loved our sister most, and with what poor judgment he hath now cast her off. Shakespeare's King Lear.

Boys must not have th' ambitious care of men,
Nor men the weak anxieties of age.
Roscommon.

And on this forehead, where your verse has said,
The loves delighted, and the graces play'd;
Insulting age will trace his cruel way,
And leave sad marks of his destructive sway.
Prior.

6. Maturity; ripeness; full strength of life.

A solemn admission of proselytes, all that either, being of age, desire that admission for themselves, or that, in infancy, are by others presented to that charity of the church. Hammond.

We thought our sires, not with their own content,
Had, ere we came to age, our portion spent.
Dryd.

7. In law.

In a man, the age of fourteen years is the age of discretion; and twenty-one years is the full age: In a woman, at seven years of age, the lord her father may distrain his tenants for aid to marry her; at the age of nine years, she is dowable; at twelve years, she is able finally to ratify and confirm her former consent given to matrimony; at fourteen, she is enabled to receive her land into her own hands, and shall be out of ward at the death of her ancestor; at sixteen, she shall be out of ward, though, at the death of her ancestor, she was within the age of fourteen years; at twenty-one, she is able to alienate her lands and tenements. At the age of fourteen, a stripling is enabled to choose his own guardian; at the age of fourteen, a man may consent to marriage. Cowell.

to ággravate v.a. [*aggravo*, Lat.]

1. To make heavy; used only in a metaphorical sense; as, to aggravate an accusation, or a punishment.

A grove hard by, sprung up with this their change,
His will who reigns above! to aggravate
Their penance, laden with fruit, like that
Which grew in paradise, the bait of Eve
Us'd by the tempter. Milton's Paradise Lost, b. x.

Ambitious Turnus in the press appears,
And aggravating crimes augment their fears. Dryd. Æneid.

2. To make any thing worse, by the addition of some particular circumstance, not essential.

This offence, in itself so heinous, was yet in him aggravated by the motive thereof, which was not malice or discontent, but an aspiring mind to the papacy. Bacon's Henry VII.

ágminal adj. [from *agmen*, Lat.] Belonging to a troop. Dict.

agnátion n.s. [from *agnatus*, Lat.] Descent from the same father, in a direct male line, distinct from cognation, or consanguinity, which includes descendants from females.

agnominátion n.s. [*agnominatio*, Lat.] Allusion of one word to another, by resemblance of sound.

The British continueth yet in Wales, and some villages of Cornwall, intermingled with provincial Latin, being very significative, *copious, and pleasantly running upon agnominations, although harsh in aspirations.* Camden.

agnus castus n.s. [Lat.] The name of the tree commonly called the Chaste Tree, from an imaginary virtue of preserving chastity.

Of laurel some, of woodbine many more,
And wreathes of agnus castus others bore. Dryden.

agonístes n.s. [αγωνιστης, Gr.] A prize-fighter; one that contends at any public solemnity for a prize. Milton has so stiled his tragedy, because Sampson was called out to divert the Philistines with feats of strength.

agrámmatist n.s. [α, *priv.* and γραμμα, Gr.] An illiterate man. Dict.

agréstick, or **agréstical** adj. [from *agrestis*, Lat.] Having relation to the country; rude; rustick. Dict.

águe n.s. [*aigu*, Fr. *acute.*] An intermitting fever, with cold fits succeeded by hot. The cold fit is, in popular language, more particularly called the ague, and the hot the fever.

Our castle's strength
Will laugh a siege to scorn. Here let them lie,
Till famine and the ague eat them up. Shakesp. Macbeth.

Though
He feels the heats of youth, and colds of age,
Yet neither tempers nor corrects the other;
As if there were an ague in his nature,
That still inclines to one extreme. Denham's Sophy.

air n.s. [*air*, Fr. *aër*, Lat.]

1. The element encompassing the terraqueous globe.

If I were to tell what I mean by the word air, I may say, it is that fine matter which we breathe in and breathe out continually; or it is that thin fluid body, in which the birds fly, a little above the earth; or it is that invisible matter, which fills all places near the earth, or which immediately encompasses the globe of earth and water. Watts's Logick.

2. The state of the air; or the air considered with regard to health.

There be many good and healthful airs, that do appear by habitation and other proofs, that differ not in smell from other airs. Bacon's Natural History, Nº 904.

3. Air in motion; a small gentle wind.

Fresh gales, and gentle airs,
Whisper'd it to the woods, and from their wings
Flung rose, flung odours from the spicy shrub
Disporting! Milton's Paradise Lost,
b. viii. l. 515.

But safe repose, without an air of breath,
Dwells here, and a dumb quiet next to death.
Dryden.

Let vernal airs through trembling osiers play,
And Albion's cliffs resound the rural lay.
Pope's Pastorals.

4. Blast.

All the stor'd vengeancies of heaven fall
On her ingrateful top! strike her young bones,
You taking airs, with lameness.
Shakesp. King Lear.

5. Any thing light or uncertain; that is as light as air.

O momentary grace of mortal men,
Which we more hunt for than the grace of God!
Who builds his hope in air of your fair looks,
Lives like a drunken sailor on a mast,
Ready, with ev'ry nod, to tumble down
Into the fatal bowels of the deep.
Shakesp. Rich. III.

6. The open weather; air unconfined.

The garden was inclos'd within the square,
Where young Emilia took the morning air.
Dryd. Fables.

7. Vent; utterance; emission into the air.

I would have ask'd you, if I durst for shame,
If still you lov'd? you gave it air before me.
But ah! why were we not both of a sex?
For then we might have lov'd without
a crime. Dryd. D. Seb.

8. Publication; exposure to the publick view and knowledge.

I am sorry to find it has taken air, that I have some hand in these papers. Pope's Letters.

9. Intelligence; information.

It grew also from the airs, which the princes and states abroad received from their ambassadors and agents here; which were attending the court in great number. Bacon's Henry VII.

10. Poetry; a song.

And the repeated air
Of sad Electra's poet, had the pow'r
To save th' Athenian walls from ruin bare.
Parad. Regain.

11. Musick, whether light or serious.

This musick crept by me upon the waters,
Allaying both their fury and my passion,
With its sweet air. Shakespeare's Tempest.

Call in some musick; I have heard, soft airs
Can charm our senses, and expel our cares.
Denh. Sophy.

The same airs, which some entertain with most delightful transports, to others are importune. Glanville's Scepsis Scient.

Since we have such a treasury of words, so proper for the airs of musick, I wonder that persons should give so little attention. Addison, Spectator, Nº 406.

Born on the swelling notes, our souls aspire,
While solemn airs improve the sacred fire;
And angels lean from heav'n to hear!
Pope's St. Cæcilia.

—When the soul is sunk with cares,
Exalts her in enliv'ning airs. Pope's Cæcilia.

12. The mien, or manner, of the person.

Her graceful innocence, her ev'ry air,
Of gesture, or least action, over-aw'd
His malice. Milton's Paradise Lost,
b. ix. l. 459.

For the air of youth
Hopeful and chearful, in thy blood shall reign
A melancholy damp of cold and dry,
To weigh thy spirits down; and last consume
The balm of life. Milt. Par. Lost, b. xi. l. 452.

But, having the life before us, besides the experience of all they knew, it is no wonder to hit some airs and features, which they have missed. Dryden on Dramatick Poetry.

There is something wonderfully divine in the airs of this picture. Addison on Italy.

Yet should the Graces all thy figures place,
And breathe an air divine on ev'ry face.
Pope.

13. An affected or laboured manner or gesture; as, a lofty air, a gay air.

Whom Ancus follows, with a fawning air;
But vain within, and proudly popular.
Dryd. Æn. vi.

There are of these sort of beauties, which last but for a moment; as, the different airs of an assembly, upon the sight of an unexpected and uncommon object, some particularity of a violent passion, some graceful action, a smile, a glance of an eye, a disdainful look, a look of gravity, and a thousand other such like things.
Dryden's Dufresnoy.

Their whole lives were employed in intrigues of state, and they naturally give themselves airs of kings and princes, of which the ministers of other nations are only the representatives. Addison's Remarks on Italy.

    To curl their waving hairs,
Assist their blushes, and inspire their airs.
Pope.

He assumes and affects an entire set of very different airs; he conceives himself a being of a superiour nature. Swift.

14. Appearance.

As it was communicated with the air of a secret, it soon found its way into the world.
Pope's Ded. to Rape of the Lock.

15. [In horsemanship.] Airs denote the artificial or practised motions of a managed horse. Chambers.

áirling n.s. [from *air*, for gayety.] A young, light, thoughtless, gay person.

Some more there be, slight airlings, will be won With dogs, and horses, and perhaps a whore.
B. John. Catil.

áirpump n.s. [from *air* and *pump*.] A machine by whose means the air is exhausted out of proper vessels. The principle on which it is built, is the elasticity of the air; as that on which the waterpump is founded, is on the gravity of the air. The invention of this curious instrument is ascribed to Otto de Guerick, consul of Magdebourg, who exhibited his first publick experiments before the emperour and the states of Germany, in 1654. But his machine laboured under several defects, in the force necessary to work it, which was very great, and the progress very slow; besides, it was to be kept under water, and allowed of no change of subjects for experiments. However, Mr. Boyle, with the assistance of Dr. Hooke, removed several of these inconveniencies; though, still, the working of this pump was laborious, by reason of the pressure of the atmosphere at every exsuction, after a vacuum was nearly obtained. This labour has been since removed by Mr. Hawksbee; who, by adding a second barrel and piston, to rise as the other fell, and fall as it rose, made the pressure of the atmosphere on the descending one, of as much service as it was of disservice in the ascending one. Vream made a further improvement in Hawksbee's air-pump, by reducing the alternate motion of the hand and winch to a circular one. Chambers.

For the air that, in exhausted receivers of airpumps, is exhaled from minerals, and flesh, and fruits, and liquours, is as true and genuine as to elasticity and density, or rarefaction, as that we respire in; and yet this factitious air is so far from being fit to be breathed in, that it kills animals in a moment, even sooner than the very absence of all air, or a vacuum itself.
Bentley's Sermons.

alamóde adv. [*à la mode*, Fr.] According to the fashion: a low word. It is used likewise by shopkeepers for a kind of thin silken manufacture.

alb n.s. [*album*, Lat.] A surplice; a white linen vestment worn by priests.

álcahest n.s. An Arabick word, to express an universal dissolvent, which was pretended to by Paracelsus and Helmont. Quincy.

álchymy n.s. [of *al*, Arab. and χημα.]

1. The more sublime and occult part of chymistry, which proposes, for its object, the transmutation of metals, and other important operations.

There is nothing more dangerous than this licentious and deluding art, which changeth the meaning of words, as alchymy doth, or would do, the substance of metals, maketh of any thing what it listeth, and bringeth, in the end, all truth to nothing. Hooker, b. v. § 58.

O he sits high in all the people's hearts;
And that which would appear offence in us,
His countenance, like richest alchymy,
Will change to virtue, and to worthiness.
Shakesp. J. Cæsar.

Princes do but play us; compared to this,
All honours mimick, all wealth alchymy.
Donne.

2. A kind of mixed metal used for spoons, and kitchen utensils.

The golden colour may be some mixture of orpiment, such as they use to brass in the yellow alchymy. Bacon.

White alchymy is made of pan-brass one pound, and arsenicum three ounces; or alchymy is made of copper and auripigmentum. Bacon's Physical Remains.

They bid cry,
With trumpets regal sound, the great result:
Tow'rds the four winds, four speedy cherubim
Put to their mouths the sounding alchymy,
By herald's voice explain'd. Milton's Paradise Lost, b. ii.

álcohol n.s. An Arabick term used by chymists for a high rectified dephlegmated spirit of wine, or for any thing reduced into an impalpable powder. Quincy.

If the same salt shall be reduced into alcohol, as the chymists speak, or an impalpable powder, the particles and intercepted spaces will be extremely lessened. Boyle.

Sal volatile oleosum will coagulate the serum on account of the alcahol, or rectified spirit which it contains. Arbuthnot.

Álcoran n.s. [*al* and *koran*, Arab.] The book of the Mahometan precepts, and credenda.

If this would satisfy the conscience, we might not only take the present covenant, but subscribe to the council of Trent; yea, and to the Turkish alcoran; and swear to maintain and defend either of them. Sanderson against the Covenant.

áleberry n.s. [from *ale* and *berry*.] A beverage made by boiling ale with spice and sugar, and sops of bread: a word only used in conversation.

áleconner n.s. [from *ale* and *con*.] An officer in the city of London, whose business is to inspect the measures of publick houses. Four of them are chosen or rechosen annually by the common-hall of the city; and whatever might be their use formerly, their places are now regarded only as sinecures for decayed citizens.

alexándrine n.s. A kind of verse borrowed from the French, first used in a poem called *Alexander*. They consist, among the French, of twelve and thirteen syllables, in alternate couplets; and, among us, of twelve.

Our numbers should, for the most part, be lyrical. For variety, or rather where the majesty of thought requires it, they may be stretched to the English heroick of five feet, and to the French Alexandrine of six. Dryd.

Then, at the last, an only couplet fraught
With some unmeaning thing they call a thought,
A needless Alexandrine ends the song,
That, like a wounded snake, drags it slow
*   length along.* Pope's Essay on Criticism.

álgebra n.s. [an Arabick word of uncertain etymology; derived, by some, from *Geber* the philosopher; by some, from *gefr*, parchment; by others, from *algehista*, a bone-setter; by Menage, from *algiatarat*, the restitution of things broken.] This is a peculiar kind of arithmetick, which takes the quantity sought, whether it be a number or a line, or any other quantity, as if it were granted, and, by means of one or more quantities given, proceeds by consequence, till the quantity at first only supposed to be known, or at least some power thereof, is found to be equal to some quantity or quantities which are known, and consequently itself is known. The origin of this art is very obscure. It was in use, however, among the Arabs, long before it came into this part of the world; and they are supposed to have borrowed it from the Persians, and the Persians from the Indians. The first Greek author of algebra was Diophantus, who, about the year 800, wrote thirteen books. In 1494, Lucas Pacciolus, or Lucas de Burgos, a cordelier, printed a treatise of algebra, in Italian, at Venice. He says, that algebra came originally from the Arabs, and never mentions Diophantus; which makes it probable, that that authour was not yet known in Europe; whose method was very different from that of the Arabs, observed by Pacciolus and his first European followers. His algebra goes no farther than simple and quadratick equations; and only some of the others advanced to the solution of cubick equations. After several improvements by Vieta, Oughtred, Harriot, Descartes, Sir Isaac Newton brought this art to the height at which it still continues. Trevoux. Chambers.

It would surely require no very profound skill in algebra, to reduce the difference of ninepence in thirty shillings. Swift.

álgid adj. [*algidus*, Lat.] Cold; chill. Dict.

álgorism, **álgorithm** n.s. Arabick words, which are used to imply the six operations of arithmetick, or the science of numbers. Dict.

álias adv. A Latin word, signifying

otherwise; often used in the trials of criminals, whose danger has obliged them to change their names; as, Simpson alias Smith, alias Baker; that is, otherwise Smith, otherwise Baker.

alíferous adj. [from *ala* and *fero*, Lat.] Having wings. D.

álimony n.s. [*alimonia*, Lat.] Alimony signifies that legal proportion of the husband's estate, which, by the sentence of the ecclesiastical court, is allowed to the wife for her maintenance, upon the account of any separation from him, provided it be not caused by her elopement or adultery. Ayliffe's Parergon.

Before they settled hands and hearts,
Till alimony or death them parts. Hudibras, p. iii. c. iii.

álkahest n.s. A word used first by Paracelsus, and adopted by his followers, to signify an universal dissolvent, or liquour, which has the power of resolving all things into their first principles.

állegory n.s. [αλληγορια.] A figurative discourse, in which something other is intended, than is contained in the words literally taken; as, wealth is the daughter of diligence, and the parent of authority.

Neither must we draw out our allegory too long, lest either we make ourselves obscure, or fall into affectation, which is childish. Ben. Johnson's Discovery.

This word nympha meant nothing else but, by allegory, the vegetative humour or moisture that quickeneth and giveth life to trees and flowers, whereby they grow. Peacham.

allégro n.s. A word, denoting one of the six distinctions of time. It expresses a sprightly motion, the quickest of all, except Presto. It originally means gay, as in Milton.†

all fours n.s. [from *all* and *four*.] A low game at cards, played by two; so named from the four particulars by which it is reckoned, and which, joined in the hand of either of the parties, are said to make all fours.

alligátor n.s. [See *crocodile*.] The crocodile.

This name is chiefly used for the crocodile of America, between which, and that of Africa, naturalists have laid down this difference, that one moves the upper, and the other the lower jaw; but this is now known to be chimerical, the lower jaw being equally moved by both.

In his needy shop a tortoise hung,
An alligator stuff'd, and other skins
Of ill-shap'd fishes. Shakesp. Romeo and Juliet.

Aloft in rows large poppy-heads were strung,
And here a scaly alligator hung. Garth's Dispensary.

to allów v.a. [*allouer*, Fr. from *allaudare*.]

1. To admit; as, to *allow* a position; not to contradict; not to oppose.

The principles, which all mankind allow for true, are innate; those, that men of right reason admit, are the principles allowed by all mankind. Locke.

The pow'r of musick all our hearts allow;
And what Timotheus was, is Dryden now. Pope's Ess. Crit.

As to what is alleged, that some of the Presbyterians declared openly against the king's murder, I allow it to be true. Swift.

2. To grant; to yield; to own any one's title to.

We will not, in civility, allow too much sincerity to the professions of most men; but think their actions to be interpreters of their thoughts. Locke.

I will help you to enough of them, and shall be ready to allow the pope as little power here as you please. Swift.

3. To grant licence to; to permit.

Let's follow the old earl, and get the beldam
To lead him where he would; his roguish madness
Allows itself to any thing. Shakespeare's King Lear.

But as we were allowed of God to be put in trust with the gospel, even so we speak, not as pleasing men, but God, which trieth our hearts. 1. Thess. ii. 4.

They referred all laws, that were to be passed in Ireland, to be considered, corrected and allowed first by the state of England. Sir John Davies on Ireland.

4. To give a sanction to; to authorize.

There is no slander in an allow'd fool. Shakesp. Tw. Night.

5. To give to; to pay to.

Ungrateful then! if we no tears allow
To him that gave us peace and empire too. Waller.

6. To appoint for; to set out to a certain use; as, he *allowed* his son the third part of his income.

7. To make abatement, or provision; or to settle any thing, with some concessions or cautions, regarding something else.

If we consider the different occasions of ancient and modern medals, we shall find they both agree in recording the great actions and successes in war; allowing still for the different ways of making it, and the circumstances that attended it. Addison.

allubéscency n.s. [*allubescentia*, Lat.] Willingness; content. Dict.

allúvious adj. [from *alluvion*.] That which is carried by water to another place, and lodged upon something else.

álogy n.s. [αλογος.] Unreasonableness; absurdity. Dict.

altíloquence n.s. [*altus* and *loquor*, Lat.] High speech; pompous language.

altívolant adj. [*altivolans*, Lat. from *altus* and *volo*.] High flying. Dict.

A.M. Stands for *artium magister*, or master of arts; the second degree of our universities, which, in some foreign countries, is called doctor of philosophy.

amanuénsis n.s. [Lat.] A person who writes what another dictates.

amáritude n.s. [*amaritudo*, Lat.] Bitterness.

What amaritude or acrimony is deprehended in choler, it acquires from a commixture of melancholy, or external malign bodies. Harvey on Consumptions.

amatórculist n.s. [*amatorculus*, Lat.] A little insignificant lover; a pretender to affection. Dict.

to amáze v.a. [from *a* and *maze*, perplexity.]

1. To confuse with terrour.

Yea, I will make many people amazed at thee, and their kings shall be horribly afraid for thee, when I shall brandish my sword before them, and they shall tremble at every moment; every man for his own life in the day of the fall. Ezek. xxxii. 10.

2. To put into confusion with wonder.

Go, heav'nly pair, and with your dazling virtues,
Your courage, truth, your innocence and love,
Amaze and charm mankind. Smith's Phædr. and Hippol.

3. To put into perplexity.

That cannot choose but amaze him. If he be not amazed, he will be mocked; if he be amazed, he will every way be mocked. Shakespeare's Merry Wives of Windsor.

Ámazon n.s. [α and μαζος.] The Amazons were a race of women famous for valour, who inhabited Caucasus; they are so called from their cutting off their breasts, to use their weapons better. A warlike woman; a virago.

Stay, stay thy hands, thou art an amazon,
And fightest with the sword. Shakesp. Henry VI.

ambáges n.s. [Lat.] A circuit of words; a circumlocutory form of speech; a multiplicity of words; an indirect manner of expression.

They gave those complex ideas names, that they might the more easily record and discourse of things they were daily conversant in, without long ambages and circumlocutions; and that the things, they were continually to give and receive information about, might be the easier and quicker understood. Locke.

ambidéxter n.s. [Lat.]

1. A man who has equally the use of both his hands.

Rodiginus, undertaking to give a reason of ambidexters, and left-handed men, delivereth a third opinion. Brown's Vul. Err.

2. A man who is equally ready to act on either side, in party disputes. This sense is ludicrous.

amén adv. [A word of which the original has given rise to many conjectures. Scaliger writes, that it is Arabick; and the Rabbies make it the compound of the initials of three words, signifying *the Lord is a faithful king*; but the word seems merely Hebrew, אמן, which, with a long train of derivatives, signifies firmness, certainty, fidelity.] A term used in devotions, by which, at the end of a prayer, we mean, so be it, at the end of a creed, so it is.

One cried, God bless us! and, Amen! the other,
As they had seen me with these hangman's hands.
Listening their fear, I could not say Amen,
When they did say God bless us.
Shakesp. Macbeth.

Blessed be the Lord God of Israel, from everlasting and to everlasting, Amen and amen. Psalm xli. 13.

amnícolist n.s. [*amnicola*, Lat.] Inhabiting near a river. D.

ámorist n.s. [from *amour*.] An inamorato; a galant; a man professing love.

Female beauties are as fickle in their faces as their minds; though casualties should spare them, age brings in a necessity of decay; leaving doters upon red and white, perplexed by incertainty both of the continuance of their mistress's kindness, and her beauty, both which are necessary to the amorist's joys and quiet. Boyle.

amóur n.s. [*amour*, Fr. *amor*, Lat.] An affair of gallantry; an intrigue: generally used of vicious love. The ou sounds like oo in poor.

No man is of so general and diffusive a lust, as to prosecute his amours all the world over; and let it burn never so outrageously, yet the impure flame will either die of itself,

or consume the body that harbours it.
South's Sermons.

The restless youth search'd all the world around;
But how can Jove in his amours be found?
Addison's Ovid's Metam.

amphibólogy n.s. [αμφιβολογια.]
Discourse of uncertain meaning. It is
distinguished from equivocation, which
means the double signification of a single
word; as, *noli regem occidere, timere bonum
est*, is amphibology; *captare lepores*, meaning
by *lepores*, either hares or jests, is
equivocation.†

*Now the fallacies, whereby men deceive
others, and are deceived themselves, the
ancients have divided into verbal and real; of
the verbal, and such as conclude from mistakes
of the word, there are but two worthy our
notation; the fallacy of equivocation and
amphibology.* Brown's Vulgar Errours.

*In defining obvious appearances, we are to use
what is most plain and easy; that the mind be
not misled by amphibologies; or ill conceived
notions, into fallacious deductions.* Glanville's
Scepsis Scientifica.

amphisbæna n.s. [Lat. αμφισβαινη.] A
serpent supposed to have two heads.

*That the amphisbæna, that is, a smaller kind
of serpent, which moveth forward and
backward, hath two heads, or one at either
extreme, was affirmed by Nicander, and
others.* Brown's Vulgar Errours; b. iii.

*Scorpion, and asp, and amphisbæna dire,
Cerastes horn'd, hydrus, and ellops drear,
And dipsas.* Milton's Paradise Lost, b. x.

ámulet n.s. [*amulette*, Fr. *amuletum*, Lat.]
An appended remedy, or preservative: a
thing hung about the neck, or any other
part of the body, for preventing or curing of
some particular diseases.†

*That spirits are corporeal, seems at first view
a conceit derogative unto himself; yet herein
he establisheth the doctrine of lustrations,
amulets, and charms.* Brown's Vulgar Errours.

*They do not certainly know the falsity
of what they report; and their ignorance*

*must serve you as an amulet against the guilt
both of deceit and malice.* Government of
the Tongue.

amygdaline adj. [*amygdala*, Lat.] Relating
to almonds; resembling almonds.

ána n.s. Books so called from the last
syllables of their titles; as, *Scaligerana,
Thuaniana;* they are loose thoughts, or
casual hints, dropped by eminent men, and
collected by their friends.†

anacámptick adj. [ανακαμπτω.]
Reflecting, or reflected: an anacamptick
sound, an echo; an anacamptick hill, a hill
that produces an echo.

anáchronism n.s. [from ανα and χρονος.]
An errour in computing time, by which
events are misplaced with regard to each
other. It seems properly to signify an errour
by which an event is placed too early; but is
generally used for any errour in chronology.

*This leads me to the defence of the famous
anachronism, in making Æneas and Dido
cotemporaries: for it is certain, that the hero
lived almost two hundred years before the
building of Carthage.* Dryden's Virgil,
Dedicat.

anagógical adj. [*anagogique*, Fr.]
Mysterious; elevated; religiously exalted.
Dict.

ánagram n.s. [ανα and γραμμα.] A
conceit arising from the letters of a name
transposed; as this, of *W,i,l,l,i,a,m, N,o,y*,
attorney-general to Charles I. a very
laborious man, *I moyl in law*.

*Though all her parts be not in th' usual place,
She hath yet the anagrams of a good face:
If we might put the letters but one way,
In that lean dearth of words, what could
   we say?* Donne.

*Thy genius calls thee not to purchase fame
In keen iambicks, but mild anagram.*
Dryden.

análogy n.s. [αναλογια.]

1. Resemblance between things with
   regard to some circumstances or effects;

as, *learning* is said to *enlighten* the mind; that is, it is to the mind what light is to the eye, by enabling it to discover that which was hidden before.

From God it hath proceeded, that the church hath evermore held a prescript form of common prayer, although not in all things every where the same, yet, for the most part, retaining the same analogy. Hooker, b. v. § 25.

What I here observe of extraordinary revelation and prophecy, will, by analogy and due proportion, extend even to those communications of God's will, that are requisite to salvation. South.

2. When the thing to which the analogy is supposed, happens to be mentioned, *analogy* has after it the particles *to* or *with;* when both the things are mentioned after *analogy*, the particle *between* or *betwixt* is used.

If the body politick have any analogy to the natural, an act of oblivion were necessary in a hot distemper'd state. Dryd. Pref. to Absalom and Achitop.

By analogy with all other liquours and concretions, the form of the chaos, whether liquid or concrete, could not be the same with that of the present earth. Burnet's Theory of the Earth.

If we make him express the customs of our country, rather than of Rome, it is either when there was some analogy betwixt the customs, or to make him more easy to vulgar understanding. Dryden's Juvenal, Dedication.

3. By grammarians, it is used to signify the agreement of several words in one common mode; as, from love is formed loved, from hate, hated, from grieve, grieved.

análysis n.s. [αναλυσις.]

1. A separation of a compound body into the several parts of which it consists.

There is an account of dew falling, in some places, in the form of butter, or grease, which grows extremely fetid; so that the analysis of the dew of any place, may, perhaps, be the best method of finding such contents of the soil as are within the reach of the sun. Arbuthnot.

2. A consideration of any thing in parts, so as that one particular is first considered, then another.

Analysis consists in making experiments and observations, and in drawing general conclusions from them by induction, and admitting of no objections against the conclusions, but such as are taken from experiments, or other certain truths. Newton's Opticks.

3. A solution of any thing, whether corporeal or mental, to its first elements; as, of a sentence to the single words; of a compound word, to the particles and words which form it; of a tune, to single notes; of an argument, to simple propositions.

We cannot know any thing of nature, but by an analysis of its true initial causes; till we know the first springs of natural motions, we are still but ignorants. Glanville's Scepsis Scientif.

ánarch n.s. See *anarchy*. An authour of confusion.

Him thus the anarch old,
With fault'ring speech, and visage incompos'd,
Answer'd. Milton's Paradise Lost, b. ii.

ánarchy n.s. [αναρχια.] Want of government; a state in which every man is unaccountable; a state without magistracy.

Where eldest night
And chaos, ancestors of nature, hold
Eternal anarchy, amidst the noise
Of endless wars, and by confusion stand.
Paradise Lost.

Arbitrary power is but the first natural step from anarchy, or the savage life; the adjusting power and freedom being an effect and consequence of maturer thinking. Swift.

anatiferous adj. [from *anas* and *fero*, Lat.] Producing ducks.

*If there be anatiferous trees, whose corruption
breaks forth into barnacles; yet, if they
corrupt, they degenerate into maggots, which
produce not them again.* Brown's Vulgar
Errours.

anátomy n.s. [ανατομια]

1. The art of dissecting the body.

*It is therefore in the anatomy of the mind, as
in that of the body; more good will accrue to
mankind, by attending to the large, open, and
perceptible parts, than by studying too much
such finer nerves and vessels, as will for ever
escape our observation.* Pope's Essay on
Man, Pref.

2. The doctrine of the structure of the
body, learned by dissection.

*Let the muscles be well inserted and bound
together, according to the knowledge of them
which is given us by anatomy.* Dryden's
Dufresnoy.

3. The act of dividing any thing, whether
corporeal or intellectual.

*When a moneyed man hath divided his chests,
he seemeth to himself richer than he was;
therefore, a way to amplify any thing, is to
break it, and to make anatomy of it in several
parts.* Bacon's Essays.

4. The body stripped of its integuments;
a skeleton.

*O that my tongue were in the thunder's mouth,
Then with a passion I would shake the world,
And rouze from sleep that fell anatomy,
Which cannot hear a feeble lady's voice.*
Shakesp. K. John.

5. By way of irony or ridicule, a thin
meagre person.

*They brought one Pinch, a hungry lean-fac'd
villain,
A meer anatomy, a mountebank,
A thread-bare juggler, and a fortune-teller,
A needy hollow-ey'd, sharp-looking wretch,
A living dead man.* Shakespeare's Comedy
of Errours.

áncient adj. [*ancien*, Fr. *antiquus*, Lat.]

1. Old; that happened long since; of old

time; not modern. Ancient and old are
distinguished; old relates to the duration
of the thing itself, as, an old coat, a coat
much worn; and ancient, to time in
general, as, an ancient dress, a habit
used in former times. But this is not
always observed; for we mention old
customs; but though old be sometimes
opposed to modern, ancient is seldom
opposed to new.

*Ancient tenure is that whereby all the
manours belonging to the crown, in St.
Edward's or William the Conquerour's days,
did hold. The number and names of which
manours, as all others belonging to common
persons, he caused to be written in a book,
after a survey made of them, now remaining
in the exchequer, and called doomsday book;
and such as by that book appeared to have
belonged to the crown at that time, are called
ancient demesnes.* Cowell.

2. Old; that has been of long duration.

*With the ancient is wisdom, and in length
of days understanding.* Job, xii. 12.

*Thales affirms, that God comprehended all
things, and that God was of all things the
most ancient, because he never had any
beginning.* Raleigh's History of the World.

*Industry
Gave the tall ancient forest too his axe.*
Thomson's Summer.

3. Past; former.

*I see thy fury: if I longer stay,
We shall begin our ancient bickerings.*
Shakesp. Henry VI.

áncient n.s. [from *ancient, adj.*] Those that
lived in old time were called ancients,
opposed to the moderns.

*And though the ancients thus their rules invade,
As kings dispense with laws themselves
    have made;
Moderns, beware! or if you must offend
Against the precept, ne'er transgress its end.*
Pop. Ess. on Crit.

áncient n.s. The bearer of a flag, as was
Ancient Pistol; whence in present use, ensign.[†]

andrótomy n.s. [from αvηρ and τεμvω.] The practice of cutting human bodies. Dict.

ánecdote n.s. [αvεκδoτov.] Something yet unpublished; secret history.

Some modern anecdotes aver,
He nodded in his elbow-chair. Prior.

anfráctuose, anfráctuous adj. [from *anfractus,* Lat.] Winding; mazy; full of turnings and winding passages.

Behind the drum are several vaults and anfractuose cavities in the ear-bone, so to intend the least sound imaginable, that the sense might be affected with it; as we see in subterraneous caves and vaults, how the sound is redoubled. Ray.

ángel shot n.s. [from *angel* and *shot.*] Chain shot, being a cannon bullet cut in two, and the halves being joined together by a chain. Dict.

ánglicism n.s. [from *Anglus,* Lat.] A form of speech peculiar to the English language; an English idiom.

anhelóse adj. [*anhelus,* Lat.] Out of breath; panting; labouring of being out of breath. Dict.

aníleness, anílity n.s. [*anilitas,* Lat.] The state of being an old woman; the old age of women.

animadvérsion n.s. [*animadversio,* Lat.]

1. Reproof; severe censure; blame.

He dismissed their commissioners with severe and sharp animadversions. Clarendon, b. viii.

2. Punishment. When the object of animadversion is mentioned, it has the particle *on* or *upon* before it.

When a bill is debating in parliament, it is usual to have the controversy handled by pamphlets on both sides; without the least animadversion upon the authours. Swift.

3. In law.

An ecclesiastical censure, and an ecclesiastical animadversion, are different things; for a censure has a relation to a spiritual punishment, but an animadversion has only a respect to a temporal one; as, degradation, and the delivering the person over to the secular court. Ayliffe's Parergon Juris Canonici.

ánimal n.s. [*animal,* Lat.]

1. A living creature corporeal, distinct, on the one side, from pure spirit, on the other, from mere matter.

Animals are such beings, which, besides the power of growing, and producing their like, as plants and vegetables have, are endowed also with sensation and spontaneous motion. Mr. Ray gives two schemes of tables of them.

Animals are either
Sanguineous, that is, such as have blood, which breathe either by
  Lungs, having either
    Two ventricles in their heart, and those either
      Viviparous,
        Aquatick, as the whale kind,
        Terrestrial, as quadrupeds;
      Oviparous, as birds.
    But one ventricle in the heart, as frogs, tortoises, and serpents.
  Gills, as all sanguineous fishes, except the whale kind.
Exsanguineous, or without blood, which may be divided into
  Greater, and those either,
    Naked,
      Terrestrial, as naked snails.
      Aquatick, as the poulp, cuttle-fish, &c.
    Covered with a tegument, either
      Crustaceous, as lobsters and crab-fish.
      Testaceous, either
        Univalve, as limpets;
        Bivalve, as oysters, muscles, cockles;
        Turbinate, as periwinkles, snails, &c.
  Lesser, as insects of all sorts.

Viviparous hairy animals, or quadrupeds, are either

Hoofed, which are either
  Whole-footed or hoofed, as the horse
  and ass;
Cloven-footed, having the hoof
divided into
  Two principal parts, called bisulca, either
    Such as chew not the cud, as swine;
    Ruminant, or such as chew the cud;
    divided into
      Such as have perpetual and
      hollow horns.
        Beef-kind,
        Sheep-kind,
        Goat-kind.
      Such as have solid, branched and
      deciduous horns, as the deer-kind.
  Four parts, or quadrisulca, as the
  rhinoceros and hippopotamus.
Clawed or **digitate**, having the foot
divided into
  Two parts or toes, having two nails,
  as the camel kind;
  Many toes or claws; either
    Undivided, as the elephant;
    Divided, which have either
      Broad nails, and an human shape,
      as apes;
      Narrower, and more pointed nails,
      which, in respect of their teeth, are
      divided into such as have
        Many fore-teeth, or cutters in
        each jaw;
          The greater, which have
          A shorter snout and rounder
          head, as the cat-kind;
          A longer snout and head, as
          the dog-kind.
          The lesser, the vermin or
          weazel kind.
        Only two large and remarkable
        fore-teeth, all which are
        phytivorous, and are called the
        hare kind. Ray.

Vegetables are proper enough to repair
animals, as being near of the same specifick
gravity with the animal juices, and as
consisting of the same parts with animal
substances, spirit, water, salt, oil, earth; all

which are contained in the sap they derive
from the earth. Arbuthnot on Aliments.

Some of the animated substances have various
organical or instrumental parts, fitted for
a variety of motions from place to place, and
a spring of life within themselves, as beasts,
birds, fishes, and insects; these are called
animals. Other animated substances are called
vegetables, which have within themselves the
principles of another sort of life and growth,
and of various productions of leaves and fruit,
such as we see in plants, herbs, and trees.
Watts's Logick.

2. By way of contempt, we say of a stupid
man, that he is a stupid animal.

ánimal adj. [*animalis*, Lat.]

1. That which belongs or relates
to animals.

There are other things in the world of spirits,
wherein our ideas are very dark and confused;
such as their union with animal nature,
the way of their acting on material beings,
and their converse with each other.
Watts's Logick.

2. Animal functions, distinguished from
natural and vital, are the lower powers
of the mind, as, the will, memory, and
imagination.

3. Animal life is opposed, on one side,
to intellectual, and, on the other, to
vegetable.

4. Animal is used in opposition to spiritual
or rational; as, the animal nature.

animálcule n.s. [*animalculum*, Lat.] A
small animal; particularly those which are
in their first and smallest state.

We are to know, that they all come of the seed
of animalcules of their own kind, that were
before laid there. Ray.

anno domini [Lat.] In the year of our Lord;
as, *anno domini*, or *A.D.* 1751; that is, in the
seventeen hundred and fifty first year from
the birth of our Saviour.

annotátor n.s. [Lat.] A writer of notes, or
annotations; a scholiast; a commentator.

I have not that respect for the annotators, which they generally meet with in the world. Felton on the Classicks.

ánomy n.s. [α *priv.* and νομος.] Breach of law.

If sin be good, and just, and lawful, it is no more evil, it is no sin, no anomy. Bramham against Hobbes.

anoréxy n.s. [ανορηξια.] Inappetency, or loathing of food. Quincy.

ánswerable adj. [from *answer.*]

1. That to which a reply may be made; that which may be answered; as, the argument, though subtle, is yet answerable.

2. Obliged to give an account, or stand the trial of an accusation.

Every chief of every kindred or family should be answerable, and bound to bring forth every one of that kindred, at all times to be justified, when he should be required, or charged with any treason, felony, &c. Spenser's State of Ireland.

Will any man argue, that if a physician should manifestly prescribe poison to all his patients, he cannot be justly punished, but is answerable only to God? Swift.

He cannot think ambition more justly laid to their charge, than to other men; because that would be to make church government answerable for the errours of human nature. Swift.

3. Correspondent.

It was but such a likeness as an imperfect glass doth give, answerable enough in some features and colours, but erring in others. Sidney.

The daughters of Atlas were ladies, who, accompanying such as came to be registered among the worthies, brought forth children answerable in quality to those that begot them. Raleigh's History of the World.

4. Proportionate.

*Only add
Deeds to thy knowledge answerable; add faith,*

*Add virtue, patience, temperance; add love
By name to come call'd charity, the soul
Of all the rest.* Milton's Paradise Lost, b. xii.

5. Suitable; suited.

The following, by certain estates of men, answerable to that which a great person himself professeth, as of soldiers to him that hath been employed in the wars, hath been a thing well taken even in monarchies. Bacon's Essays.

*If answerable style I can obtain
Of my celestial patroness, who deigns
Her mighty visitation unimplor'd.* Milt. Parad. Lost, b. ix.

6. Equal.

There be no kings whose means are answerable unto other mens desires. Raleigh's History of the World.

7. Relative; correlative.

That, to every petition for things needful, there should be some answerable sentence of thanks provided particularly to follow, is not requisite. Hooker, b. v. § 43.

ánswer-jobber n.s. [from *answer* and *jobber.*] He that makes a trade of writing answers.

What disgusts me from having any thing to do with answer-jobbers, is, that they have no conscience. Swift.

antaphrodítick adj. [from αντι, against, and Αφροδιτη, Venus.] That which is efficacious against the venereal disease.

ántepast n.s. [from *ante,* before, and *pastum,* to feed.] A foretaste; something taken before the proper time.

Were we to expect our bliss only in the satiating our appetites, it might be reasonable, by frequent antepasts, to excite our gust for that profuse perpetual meal. Decay of Piety.

anthelmínthick adj. [αντι, against, and ελμινθος, a worm.] That which kills worms.

Anthelminthicks, or contrary to worms, are things which are known by experience to kill them, as oils, or honey taken upon an empty stomach. Arbuthnot on Diet.

anthólogy n.s. [ανθολογια, from ανθος, a flower, and λεγω, to gather.]

1. A collection of flowers.

2. A collection of devotions in the Greek church.

3. A collection of poems.

anthrax n.s. [ανθραξ, a burning coal.] A scab or blotch that is made by a corrosive humour, which burns the skin, and occasions sharp pricking pains, a carbuncle. Quincy.

anthropólogy n.s. [from ανθρωπος, man, and λεγω, to discourse.] The doctrine of anatomy; the doctrine of the form and structure of the body of man.

anthropóphagi n.s. It has no singular. [ανθρωπος, man, and φαγω, to eat.] Man-eaters; cannibals; those that live upon human flesh.

The cannibals that each other eat,
The anthropophagi, and men whose heads
Do grow beneath their shoulders.
Shakesp. Othello.

ántick adj. [probably from *antiquus*, ancient, as things out of use appear old.] Odd; ridiculously wild; buffoon in gesticulation.

    What! dares the slave
Come hither cover'd with an antick face,
And fleer and scorn at our solemnity?
Shakesp. Rom. & Jul.

Of all our antick sights, and pageantry,
Which English idiots run in crouds to see.
Dryden.

The prize was to be conferred upon the
whistler, that could go through his tune
without laughing, though provoked by the
antick postures of a merry Andrew, who was
to play tricks. Addison, Spectator, Nº 179.

ántinomy n.s. [from αντι and νομος.] A contradiction between two laws, or two articles of the same law.

antípodes n.s. It has no singular. [from αντι, against, and ποδες, feet.] Those people who, living on the other side of the globe, have their feet directly opposite to ours.

We should hold day with the antipodes,
If you would walk in absence of the sun.
Shakespeare's Merchant of Venice.

So shines the sun, tho' hence remov'd, as clear
When his beams warm th' antipodes, as here.
Waller.

ántiquary n.s. [*antiquarius*, Lat.] A man studious of antiquity; a collector of ancient things.

All those arts, rarities, and inventions, are
but the relicts of an intellect defaced with sin.
We admire it now, only as antiquaries do a
piece of old coin, for the stamp it once bore.
South's Sermons.

With sharpen'd sight pale antiquaries pore,
Th' inscription value, but the rust adore.
Pope.

The rude Latin of the monks is still very
intelligible; had their records been delivered
in the vulgar tongue, they could not now be
understood, unless by antiquaries. Swift.

antíquity n.s. [*antiquitas*, Lat.]

1. Old times; time past long ago.

I mention Aristotle, Polybius, and Cicero,
the greatest philosopher, the most impartial
historian, and the most consummate
statesman of all antiquity. Addison,
Freeholder, Nº 51.

2. The people of old times; the ancients.

That such pillars were raised by Seth, all
antiquity has avowed. Raleigh's History
of the World.

3. The works or remains of old times.

As for the observation of Machiavel,
traducing Gregory the Great, that he did
what in him lay, to extinguish all heathen
antiquities: I do not find that those zeals last
long; as it appeared in the succession of
Sabinian, who did revive the former
antiquities. Bacon's Essays.

4. Old age: a ludicrous sense.

Is not your voice broken? your wind short?
your chin double? your wit single? and every
part about you blasted with antiquity? and
will you yet call yourself young?
Shakespeare's Henry IV.

5. Ancientness; as, this ring is valuable for
   its antiquity.

antístrophe n.s. [αντιστροφη, from αντι,
the contrary way, and στροφη, turning.] In
an ode supposed to be sung in parts, the
second stanza of every three, or sometimes
every second stanza; so called because the
dance turns about.

antíthesis n.s. in the plural *antitheses.*
[αντιθεσις, placing in opposition.]
Opposition of words or sentiments;
contrast; as in these lines:

Though gentle, yet not dull,
Strong without rage, without o'erflowing, full.
Denham.†

I see a chief, who leads my chosen sons,
All arm'd with points, antitheses, and puns.
Pope's Dunciad.

ántler n.s. [*andouillier*, Fr.] Properly the
first branches of a stag's horns; but,
popularly and generally, any of his
branches.

Grown old, they grow less branched, and first
lose their brow antlers, or lowest furcations
next to the head. Brown's Vulgar Errours,
b. iii. c. 9.

A well grown stag, whose antlers rise
High o'er his front, his beams invade the skies.
Dryden.

Bright Diana
Brought hunted wild goats heads, and
branching antlers
Of stags, the fruit and honour of her toil.
Prior.

ape n.s. [*ape*, Icelandish.]

1. A kind of monkey remarkable for
   imitating what he sees.

I will be more newfangled than an ape,
more giddy in my desires than a monkey.
Shakesp. As you like it.

Writers report, that the heart of an ape worn
near the heart, comforteth the heart, and
increaseth audacity. It is true, that the ape is
a merry and bold beast. Bacon's Natural
History.

With glittering gold and sparkling gems
  they shine,
But apes and monkeys are the gods within.
Granville.

2. An imitator; used generally in the
   bad sense.

Julio Romano, who, had he himself eternity,
and could put breath into his work, would
beguile nature of her custom: so perfectly he
is her ape. Shakesp. Winter's Tale.

aphrodisíacal, aphrodisíack adj. [from
Αφροδιτη, Venus.] Relating to the
venereal disease.

apítpat adv. [a word formed from the
motion.] With quick palpitation.

O there he comes—Ay, my Hector of Troy,
welcome my bully, my back; agad my heart
has gone apitpat for you. Congreve's Old
Batchelor.

apócalypse n.s. [from αποκαλυπτω.]
Revelation; discovery: a word used only of
the sacred writings.

O for that warning voice, which he who saw
Th' apocalypse heard cry in heav'n aloud.
Milton's Par. Lost.

With this throne, of the glory of the Father,
compare the throne of the Son of God, as
seen in the apocalypse. Burnet's Theory
of the Earth.

apócrypha n.s. [from αποκρυπτω, to put
out of sight.] Books whose authours are not
known. It is used for the books appended to
the sacred writings, which, being of
doubtful authours, are less regarded.

We hold not the apocrypha for sacred, as we do
the holy scripture, but for human compositions.
Hooker, b. v.

ápophthegm n.s. [αποφθεγμα.] A
remarkable saying; a valuable maxim
uttered on some sudden occasion.

We may magnify the apophthegms, or reputed replies of wisdom, whereof many are to be seen in Laertius and Lycosthenes. Brown's Vulgar Errours, b. i. c. 6.

I had a mind to collect and digest such observations and apophthegms, as tend to the proof of that great assertion, All is vanity. Prior's Pref. to Solomon.

ápoplexy n.s. [ἀποπληξις.] A sudden deprivation of all internal and external sensation, and of all motion, unless of the heart and thorax. The cause is generally a repletion, and indicates evacuation, joined with stimuli. Quincy.

Apoplexy is a sudden abolition of all the senses, external and internal, and of all voluntary motion, by the stoppage of the flux and reflux of the animal spirits through the nerves destined for those motions. Arbuthnot on Diet.

Peace is a very apoplexy, lethargy, mulled, deaf, sleepy, insensible. Shakesp. Coriolanus.

A fever may take away my reason, or memory, and an apoplexy leave neither sense nor understanding. Locke.

apória n.s. [ἀπορια.] Is a figure in rhetorick, by which the speaker shews, that he doubts where to begin for the multitude of matter, or what to say in some strange and ambiguous thing; and doth, as it were, argue the case with himself. Thus Cicero says, *Whether he took them from his fellows more impudently, gave them to a harlot more lasciviously, removed them from the Roman people more wickedly, or altered them more presumptuously, I cannot well declare.* Smith's Rhetorick.

áppetence, áppetency n.s. [*appetentia*, Lat.] Carnal desire; sensual desire.

Bred only and completed to the taste
Of lustful appetence; to sing, to dance,
To dress, to troule the tongue, and roll the eye.
Milton's Paradise Lost, b. xi. l. 619.

to appropínquate v.a. [*appropinquo*, Lat.] To draw nigh unto; to approach.

ápricate v.n. [*apricor*, Lat.] To bask in the sun. Dict.

aqua fortis [Latin.] A corrosive liquor made by distilling purified nitre with calcined vitriol, or rectified oil of vitriol in a strong heat: the liquor, which rises in fumes red as blood, being collected, is the spirit of nitre or aqua fortis; which serves as a menstruum for dissolving of silver, and all other metals, except gold. But if sea salt, or *sal ammoniack*, be added to *aqua fortis*, it commences *aqua regia*, and will then dissolve no metal but gold. *Aqua fortis* is commonly held to have been invented about the year 1300; though others will have it to have been known in the time of Moses. It is serviceable to refiners, in separating silver from gold and copper; to the workers in mosaick, for staining and colouring their woods; to dyers, in their colours, particularly scarlet; and to other artists, for colouring bone and ivory. With *aqua fortis* bookbinders marble the covers of books, and diamond cutters separate diamonds from metalline powders. It is also used in etching copper or brass plates. Chambers.

The dissolving of silver in aqua fortis, *and gold in* aqua regia, *and not vice versâ, would not be difficult to know.* Locke.

aqua mirabilis [Latin.] The wonderful water, is prepared of cloves, galangals, cubebs, mace, cardomums, nutmegs, ginger, and spirit of wine, digested twenty four hours, then distilled. It is a good and agreeable cordial.

aqua-vitæ [Latin.] It is commonly understood of what is otherwise called brandy, or spirit of wine, either simple or prepared with aromaticks. But some appropriate the term brandy to what is procured from wine, or the grape; *aqua-vitæ*, to that drawn after the same manner from malt. Chambers.

I will rather trust a Fleming with my butter, parson Hugh the Welchman with my cheese, an Irishman with my aqua vitæ *bottle, or a thief to walk with my ambling gelding, than my wife with herself.* Shakesp. Merry Wives of Windsor.

A.R. *anno regni;* that is, the year of the reign: as, *A.R. G.R.* 20. *Anno regni Georgii regis vigesimo,* in the twentieth year of the reign of king George.

archaiólogy n.s. [from αρχαιος, ancient, and λογος, a discourse.] A discourse on antiquity.

árchaism n.s. [αρχαισμος] An ancient phrase, or mode of expression.

I shall never use archaisms, like Milton. Watts.

architécture n.s. [*architectura*, Lat.]

1. The art or science of building.

Architecture is divided into civil architecture, called by way of eminence architecture; military architecture, or fortification; and naval architecture, which, besides building of ships and vessels, includes also ports, moles, docks, &c. Some think the Tyrians were the first improvers of architecture; but others contend, that the rules of this art were delivered by God himself to Solomon, from whom the Tyrians had their instruction, which they afterwards communicated to the Egyptians; these to the Grecians, and these again to the Romans. Under Augustus, architecture arrived to its greatest glory; but it afterwards dwindled by degrees, and at last fell with the western empire, in the fifth century, when the Visigoths destroyed all the most beautiful monuments of antiquity; and a new manner of building took its rise, called the Gothick, coarse, artless, and massive. Of the same kind was the Arabesk, Moorisk or Moorish architecture, brought from the South by the Moors and Saracens. The architects of the thirteenth, fourteenth, and fifteenth centuries, who had some knowledge of sculpture, seemed to make perfection consist altogether in the delicacy and multitude of ornaments, which they frequently bestowed on their buildings without any conduct or taste. In the two last centuries, the architects of Italy and France were wholly bent upon retrieving the primitive simplicity and beauty of ancient architecture, in which they did not fail of success. This art is divided into five orders; the Tuscan, Dorick, Ionick, Corinthian, and Composite; which took their rise from the different proportions that the different kinds of buildings rendered necessary, according to the bulk, strength, delicacy, richness, or simplicity required. Chambers.

Our fathers next in architecture skill'd,
Cities for use, and forts for safety build:
Then palaces and lofty domes arose,
These for devotion, and for pleasure those.
Blackm. Creat.

2. The effect or performance of the science of building.

The formation of the first earth being a piece of divine architecture, ascribed to a particular providence. Burnet's Theory.

arenátion n.s. [from *arena*, Lat. sand.] Is used by some physicians for a sort of dry bath, when the patient sits with his feet upon hot sand. Dict.

argilláceous adj. [from *argil*.] Clayey; partaking of the nature of argil; consisting of argil, or potter's clay.

ária n.s. [Ital. in musick.] An air, song, or tune.

aristócracy n.s. [αριστος, greatest, and κρατεω, to govern.] That form of government which places the supreme power in the nobles, without a king, and exclusively of the people.

The aristocracy of Venice hath admitted so many abuses through the degeneracy of the nobles, that the period of its duration seems to approach. Swift.

arithmetick n.s. [αριθμος, number, and μετρεω, to measure.] The science of numbers; the art of computation. We have very little intelligence about the origin and invention of arithmetick; but probably it must have taken its rise from the introduction of commerce, and consequently be of Tyrian invention. From Asia it passed into Egypt, where it was greatly cultivated. From thence it was transmitted to the Greeks, who conveyed it to the Romans with additional improvements. But, from some treatises of the ancients remaining on this subject, it appears that their arithmetick was much inferiour to that of the moderns. Chambers.

On fair ground I could beat forty of them;
But now 'tis odds beyond arithmetick.
Shakesp. Coriolanus.

The christian religion, according to the Apostle's arithmetick, hath but these three parts of it; sobriety, justice, religion. Taylor.

armígerous adj. [from *armiger*, Lat. an armour-bearer.] Bearing arms.

armísonous adj. [*armisonus*, Lat.] Rustling with armour.

arms n.s. without the singular number. [*arma*, Lat.]

1. Weapons of offence, or armour of defence.

   Those arms which Mars before
Had giv'n the vanquish'd, now the victor bore. Pope's Iliad.

2. A state of hostility.

Sir Edward Courtney, and the haughty prelate,
With many more confed'rates, are in arms.
Shakes. R. III.

3. War in general.

Arms and the man I sing. Dryd. Virgil.

Him Paris follow'd to the dire alarms,
Both breathing slaughter, both resolv'd in arms. Pope's Iliad.

4. Action; the act of taking arms.

Up rose the victor angels, and to arms
The matin trumpet sung. Milton's Paradise Lost, b. vi.

5. The ensigns armorial of a family.

aróynt adv. [a word of uncertain etymology, but very ancient use.] Be gone; away: a word of expulsion, or avoiding.

Saint Withold footed thrice the wold,

He met the night-mare, and her name told,
Bid her alight, and her troth plight,
And aroynt thee, witch, aroynt thee right.
Shak. King Lear.

arrísion n.s. [*arrisio*, Lat.] A smiling upon. Dict.

to arróde v.a. [*arrodo*, Lat.] To gnaw or nibble. Dict.

arse n.s. [*earse*, Sax.] The buttocks, or hind part of an animal.

to hang an arse A vulgar phrase, signifying to be tardy, sluggish, or dilatory.

For Hudibras wore but one spur,
As wisely knowing, could he stir
To active trot one side of's horse,
The other would not hang an arse. Hudibras, cant. i.

art n.s. [*arte*, Fr. *ars*, Lat.]

1. The power of doing something not taught by nature and instinct; as, to walk is natural, to dance is an art.

Art is properly an habitual knowledge of certain rules and maxims, by which a man is governed and directed in his actions. South.

Blest with each grace of nature and of art. Pope.

Ev'n copious Dryden wanted, or forgot,
The last and greatest art, the art to blot. Pope.

2. A science; as, the liberal *arts*.

Arts that respect the mind were ever reputed nobler than those that serve the body. Ben. Johnson's Discovery.

3. A trade.

This observation is afforded us by the art of making sugar. Boyle.

4. Artfulness; skill; dexterity.

The art of our necessities is strange,
That can make vile things precious.
Shak. King Lear.

5. Cunning.

6. Speculation.

I have as much of this in art as you;

But yet my nature could not bear it so.
Shakesp. J. Cæsar.

artificial adj. [*artificiel*, Fr.]

1. Made by art; not natural.

Basilius used the artificial day of torches
to lighten the sports their inventions could
contrive. Sidney, b. i.

The curtains closely drawn the light to skreen,
As if he had contriv'd to lie unseen:
Thus cover'd with an artificial night,
Sleep did his office. Dryden's Fables.

There is no natural motion perpetual; yet
it doth not hinder but that it is possible to
contrive such an artificial revolution.
Wilkins's Dædalus.

2. Fictitious; not genuine.

Why, I can smile, and murder while I smile,
And cry, content, to that which grieves my heart,
And wet my cheeks with artificial tears.
Shakesp. Hen. VI.

3. Artful; contrived with skill.

These seem to be the more artificial, as those of
a single person the more natural governments,
orders, and institutions. Temple.

artificial numbers, are the same with logarithms.

ártist n.s. [*artiste*, Fr.]

1. The professor of an art, generally of an art manual.

How to build ships, and dreadful ordnance cast,
Instruct the artists, and reward their haste.
Waller.

Rich with the spoils of many a conquer'd land,
All arts and artists Theseus could command,
Who sold for hire, or wrought for better fame:
The master painters and the carvers came.
Dryden's Fables.

When I made this, an artist undertook to
imitate it; but using another way, fell much
short. Newton's Opticks.

2. A skilful man; not a novice.

If any one thinks himself an artist at this, let
him number up the parts of his child's body.
Locke.

ártless adj. [from *art* and *less*.]

1. Unskilful; sometimes with the particle *of*.

The high-shoo'd plowman, should he quit
the land,
Artless of stars, and of the moving sand.
Dryden's Pers.

2. Without fraud; as, an artless maid.

3. Contrived without skill; as, an artless tale.

to ártuate v.a. [*artuatus*, Lat.] To tear limb from limb. D.

to ascertáin v.a. [*acertener*, Fr.]

1. To make certain; to fix; to establish.

The divine law both ascertaineth the truth,
and supplieth unto us the want of other laws.
Hooker, b. i.

Money differs from uncoined silver in this,
that the quantity of silver in each piece is
ascertained by the stamp. Locke.

2. To make confident; to take away doubt; often with *of*.

If it be on right judgment of myself, it may
give me the other certainty, that is, ascertain
me that I am in the number of God's children.
Hammond's Practical Catechism.

This makes us act with a repose of mind and
wonderful tranquillity, because it ascertains
us of the goodness of our work. Dryden's
Dufresnoy.

áscii n.s. It has no singular. [from α, without, and σκια, a shadow.] Those people who, at certain times of the year, have no shadow at noon; such are the inhabitants of the torrid zone, because they have the sun twice a year vertical to them. Dict.

to asséver, to asséverate v.a. [*assevero*, Lat.] To affirm with great solemnity, as upon oath.

ásshead n.s. [from *ass* and *head*.] One slow of apprehension; a blockhead.

Will you help an asshead, and a coxcomb,
and a knave, a thin-faced knave, a gull.
Shakesp. Hamlet.

astrígerous adj. [*astriger*, Lat.] Adorned with stars. Dict.

astrólogy n.s. [*astrologia*, Lat.] The practice of foretelling things by the the knowledge of the stars; an art now generally exploded, as without reason.

I know it hath been the opinion of the learned, who think of the art of astrology, that the stars do not force the actions or wills of men. Swift.

astrónomy n.s. [αστρονομια, from αστρον, a star, and νομος, a law, or rule.] A mixed mathematical science teaching the knowledge of the celestial bodies, their magnitudes, motions, distances, periods, eclipses, and order. The origin of astronomy is uncertain; but from Egypt it travelled into Greece, where Pythagoras was the first European who taught that the earth and planets turn round the sun, which stands immoveable in the center; as he himself had been instructed by the Egyptian priests. From the time of Pythagoras, astronomy sunk into neglect, till it was revived by the Ptolemys, kings of Egypt, and the Saracens, after their conquest of that country, having acquired some knowledge of it, brought it from Africa to Spain, and again restored this science to Europe, where it has since received very considerable improvements. Chambers.

To this must be added the understanding of the globes, and the principles of geometry and astronomy. Cowley.

átheist n.s. [αθεος, without God.] One that denies the existence of God.

To these, that sober race of men, whose lives Religious, titled them the sons of God, Shall yield up all their virtue, all their fame, Ignobly! to the trains, and to the smiles Of these fair atheists. Milton's Paradise Lost, b. xi.

Though he were really a speculative atheist, yet if he would but proceed rationally, he could not however be a practical atheist, nor live without God in this world. South.

Atheist, use thine eyes, And having view'd the order of the skies, Think, if thou canst, that matter blindly hurl'd,

Without a guide, should frame this wond'rous world. Creech.

No atheist, as such, can be a true friend, an affectionate relation, or a loyal subject. Bentley's Sermons.

athlétick adj. [from *athleta*, Lat. αθλητης, a wrestler.]

1. Belonging to wrestling.

2. Strong of body; vigorous; lusty; robust.

Seldom shall one see in rich families that athletick soundness and vigour of constitution, which is seen in cottages, where nature is cook, and necessity caterer. South.

Science distinguishes a man of honour from one of those athletick brutes, whom undeservedly we call heroes. Dryden.

átom n.s. [*atomus*, Lat. ατομος.]

1. Such a small particle as cannot be physically divided: and these are the first rudiments, or the component parts of all bodies. Quin.

Innumerable minute bodies are called atoms, because, by reason of their perfect solidity, they were really indivisible. Ray.

See plastick nature working to this end, The single atoms each to other tend, Attract, attracted to, the next in place, Form'd and impell'd its neighbour to embrace. Pope.

2. Any thing extremely small.

It is as easy to count atoms, as to resolve the propositions of a lover. Shakesp. As you like it.

to attáint v.a. [*attenter*, Fr.]

1. To attaint is particularly used for such as are found guilty of some crime or offence, and especially of felony or treason. A man is attainted two ways, by appearance, or by process. Attainder by appearance is by confession, battle, or verdict. Confession is double; one at the bar before the judges, when the prisoner, upon his indictment read, being asked guilty or not guilty, answers guilty, never putting himself upon the

verdict of the jury. The other is before the coroner in sanctuary, where he, upon his confession, was in former times constrained to abjure the realm; which kind is called attainder by abjuration. Attainder by battle is, when the party appealed, and choosing to try the truth by combat rather than by jury, is vanquished. Attainder by verdict is, when the prisoner at the bar, answering to the indictment not guilty, hath an inquest of life and death passing upon him, and is by the verdict pronounced guilty. Attainder by process is, where a party flies, and is not found till five times called publickly in the county, and at last outlawed upon his default. Cowel.

Were it not an endless trouble, that no traitor or felon should be attainted, but a parliament must be called. Spenser on Ireland.

I must offend before I be attainted. Shakesp. Hen. VI.

2. To taint; to corrupt.

My tender youth was never yet attaint With any passion of inflaming love. Shakesp. Henry VI.

auríferous adj. [*aurifer*, Lat.] That which produces gold.

Rocks rich in gems, and mountains big with mines, Whence many a bursting stream auriferous plays. Thomson.

aurioátion n.s. [*auriga*, Lat.] The act or practice of driving carriages. Dict.

áuthor n.s. [*auctor*, Lat.]

1. The first beginner or mover of any thing; he to whom any thing owes its original.

That law, the author and observer whereof is one only God, to be blessed for ever. Hooker, b. i.

The author of that which causeth another thing to be, is author of that thing also which thereby is caused. Hooker, b. iii.

I'll never Be such a gosling to obey instinct; but stand As if a man was author of himself, And knew no other kin. Shakesp. Coriolanus.

Thou art my father, thou my author, thou My being gav'st me; whom should I obey, But thee? Milton's Paradise Lost, b. ii.

But Faunus came from Picus, Picus drew His birth from Saturn, if records be true. Thus king Latinus, in the third degree, Had Saturn author of his family. Dryden, Æneid vii.

If the worship of false Gods had not blinded the heathen, instead of teaching to worship the sun, and dead heroes, they would have taught us to worship our true Author and benefactor, as their ancestors did under the government of Noah and his sons, before they corrupted themselves. Newton's Opticks.

2. The efficient; he that effects or produces any thing.

That which is the strength of their amity, shall prove the immediate author of their variance. Shakesp. Antony and Cleopat.

Now while the tortur'd savage turns around, And flings about his foam, impatient of the wound; The wound's great author close at hand provokes His rage. Dryden's Fables.

From his loins New authors of dissention spring; from him Two branches, that in hosting long contend For sov'reign sway. Philips.

3. The first writer of any thing; distinct from the translator or compiler.

To stand upon every point in particulars, belongeth to the first author of the story. 2 Macc. ii. 30.

An author has the choice of his own thoughts and words, which a translator has not. Dryden.

4. A writer in general.

Yet their own authors faithfully affirm, That the land Salike lies in Germany. Shakesp. Henry V.

autógraphy n.s. [αυτογραφον, from αυτος, and γραφω, to write.] A particular person's own writing; or the original of a treatise, in opposition to a copy.

automátical adj. [from *automaton.*] Belonging to an automaton; having the power of moving themselves.

áutopsy n.s. [αυτοψια.] Ocular demonstration; seeing a thing one's self. Quincy.

In those that have forked tails, autopsy convinceth us, that it hath this use. Ray on the Creation.

avást adv. [from *basta*, Ital. it is enough.] Enough; cease. A word used among seamen.

Áve Mary n.s. [from the first words of the salutation to the Blessed Virgin, *Ave Maria.*] A form of worship repeated by the Romanists in honour of the Virgin Mary.

All his mind is bent on holiness,
To number Ave Maries on his beads.
Shakesp. Henry VI.

áwful adj. [from *awe* and *full.*]

1. That which strikes with awe, or fills with reverence.

So awful, that with honour thou may'st love
Thy mate; who sees, when thou art seen least
   wise. Milt. Par. Lost, b. viii. l. 577.

I approach thee thus, and gaze
Insatiate; I thus single; nor have fear'd
Thy awful brow, more awful thus retir'd,
Fairest resemblance of thy Maker fair!
Milton's Paradise Lost, b. ix.

2. Worshipful; in authority; invested with dignity. This sense is obsolete.

Know then, that some of us are gentlemen,
Such as the fury of ungovern'd youth
Thrust from the company of awful men.
Shakesp. Two Gentlemen of Verona.

3. Struck with awe; timorous; scrupulous. This sense occurs but rarely.

It is not nature and strict reason, but a weak and awful reverence for antiquity, and the vogue of fallible men. Watts's Improvement of the Mind.

axíllar, áxillary adj. [from *axilla*, Lat.] Belonging to the armpit.

In the same manner is the axillary artery distributed unto the hand; below the cubit, it divideth unto two parts. Brown's Vulgar Errours.

B

B, the second letter of the English alphabet, is pronounced as in most other European languages, by pressing the whole length of the lips together, and forcing them open with a strong breath. It has a near affinity with the other labial letters, and is confounded by the Germans with *P*, and by the Gascons with *V*; from which an epigrammatist remarks, that *bibere* and *vivere* are in Gascony the same. The Spaniards, in most words, use *B* or *V* indifferently.

babóon n.s. [*babouin*, Fr. It is supposed by Skinner to be the augmentation of *babe*, and to import a *great babe*.] A monkey of the largest kind.

You had looked through the grate like a geminy of baboons. Shakesp. Merry Wives of Windsor.

He cast every human feature out of his countenance, and became a baboon. Addison. Spect. N° 174.

báccated adj. [*baccatus*, Lat.] Beset with pearls; having many berries. Dict.

bacchanálian n.s. [from *bacchanalia*, Lat.] A riotous person; a drunkard.

baccívorous adj. [from *bacca*, a berry, and *voro*, to devour, Lat.] A devourer of berries. Dict.

báckbiter n.s. [from *backbite*.] A privy calumniator; a censurer of the absent.

No body is bound to look upon his backbiter, or his underminer, his betrayer, or his oppressor, as his friend. South.

báckfriend n.s. [from *back* and *friend*.] A friend backwards; that is, an enemy in secret.

Set the restless importunities of talebearers and backfriends against fair words and professions. L'Estrange.

Far is our church from encroaching upon the civil power; as some who are backfriends to both, would maliciously insinuate. South.

backgámmon n.s. [from *bach gammon*, Welch, a little battle.] A play or game at tables, with box and dice.

In what esteem are you with the vicar of the parish? can you play with him at backgammon? Swift.

badger legged adj. [from *badger* and *legged*.] Having legs of an unequal length, as the badger is supposed to have.

His body crooked all over, big-bellied, badger legged, and his complexion swarthy. L'Estrange.

bágatelle n.s. [*bagatelle*, Fr.] A trifle; a thing of no importance.

Heaps of hair rings and cypher'd seals; Rich trifles, serious bagatelles. Prior.

bággage n.s. [from *bag*, *bagage*, Fr.]

1. The furniture and utensils of an army.

The army was an hundred and seventy thousand footmen, and twelve thousand horsemen, beside the baggage. Judith, vii. 2.

Riches are the baggage of virtue; they cannot be spared, nor left behind, but they hinder the march. Bacon.

They were probably always in readiness, and carried among the baggage of the army. Addison's Remarks on Italy.

2. The goods that are to be carried away, as bag and baggage.

Dolabella designed, when his affairs grew desperate in Egypt, to pack up bag and baggage, and sail for Italy. Arbuth. on Coins.

3. A worthless woman; in French *bagaste*; so called, because such women follow camps.

A spark of indignation did rise in her, not to suffer such a baggage to win away any thing of hers. Sidney.

When this baggage meets with a man who has vanity to credit relations, she turns him to account. Spectat. N° 205.

bágnio n.s. [*bagno*, Ital. a bath.] A house for bathing, sweating, and otherwise cleansing the body.

I have known two instances of malignant fevers produced by the hot air of a bagnio. Arbuthnot on Air.

to balbúcinate v.n. [from *balbutio*, Lat.] To stammer in speaking. Dict.

bálderdash n.s. [probably of *bald*, Sax. bold, and *dash*, to mingle.] Any thing jumbled together without judgment; rude mixture; a confused discourse.

to bálderdash v.a. [from the noun.] To mix or adulterate any liquor.

bállad n.s. [*balade*, Fr.] A song.

Ballad once signified a solemn and sacred song, as well as trivial, when Solomon's Song was called the ballad of ballads; but now it is applied to nothing but trifling verse. Watts.

An' I have not ballads made on you all, and sung to filthy tunes, may a cup of sack be my poison. Shakesp. Henry IV.

Like the sweet ballad, this amusing lay
Too long detains the lover on his way.
Gay's Trivia.

ballétte n.s. [*ballette*, Fr.] A dance in which some history is represented.

ballotátion n.s. [from *ballot*.] The act of voting by ballot.

The election is intricate and curious,
consisting of ten several ballotations. Wotton.

balneátion n.s. [from *balneum*, Lat. a bath.] The act of bathing.

As the head may be disturbed by the skin, it may the same way be relieved, as is observable in balneations, and fomentations of that part. Brown's Vulgar Errours, b. ii. c. 6.

to bambóozle v.a. [a cant word not used in pure or in grave writings.] To deceive; to impose upon; to confound.

After Nick had bamboozled about the money, John called for counters. Arbuthnot's John Bull.

bánnian n.s. A man's undress, or morning-gown; such as is worn by the Bannians in the East Indies.

bánnock n.s. A kind of oaten or pease meal cake, mixed with water, and baked upon an iron plate over the fire; used in the northern counties, and in Scotland.

bar shot n.s. Two half bullets joined together by an iron bar; used in sea engagements for cutting down the masts and rigging.

barbárian n.s. [*barbarus*, Lat. It seems to have signified at first only foreign, or a foreigner; but, in time, implied some degree of wildness or cruelty.]

1. A man uncivilized; untaught; a savage.

Proud Greece, all nations else barbarians held,
Boasting, her learning all the world excell'd.
Denham.

There were not different gods among the Greeks and barbarians. Stillingfleet's Defence of Disc. on Romish Idolatry.

But with descending show'rs of brimstone fir'd,
The wild barbarian in the storm expir'd.
Addison.

2. A foreigner.

I would they were barbarians, as they are,
Though in Rome litter'd.
Shakesp. Coriolanus.

3. A brutal monster; a man without pity: a term of reproach.

   Thou fell barbarian!
What had he done? what could provoke thy madness
To assassinate so great, so brave a man! A. Philips D. Mot.

bárbarism n.s. [*barbarismus*, Lat.]

1. A form of speech contrary to the purity and exactness of any language.

The language is as near approaching to it, as our modern barbarism will allow; which is all that can be expected from any now extant. Dryden's Juvenal, Dedication.

2. Ignorance of arts; want of learning.

I have for barbarism spoke more
Than for that angel knowledge you can say.
Shakesp. Love's Labour Lost.

The genius of Raphael having succeeded to the times of barbarism and ignorance, the knowledge of painting is now arrived to perfection. Dryd. Dufresnoy, Preface.

3. Brutality; savageness of manners; incivility.

Moderation ought to be had in tempering and managing the Irish, to bring them from their delight of licentious barbarism unto the love of goodness and civility. Spenser's State of Irel.

Divers great monarchies have risen from barbarism to civility, and fallen again to ruin. Sir J. Davies on Ireland.

4. Cruelty; barbarity; unpitying hardness of heart.

They must per force have melted,
And barbarism itself have pity'd him.
Shakesp. Richard II.

to bárbecue v.a. A term used in the West-Indies for dressing a hog whole; which, being split to the backbone, is laid flat upon a large gridiron, raised about two foot above a charcoal fire, with which it is surrounded.

Oldfield, with more than harpy throat endu'd,
Cries, send me, gods, a whole hog barbecu'd.
Pope.

barber-chirurgeon n.s. A man who joins the practice of surgery to the barber's trade; such as were all surgeons formerly, but now it is used only for a low practiser of surgery.

He put himself into barber-chirurgeons hands,
who, by unfit applications, rarified the
tumour. Wiseman's Surgery.

bard n.s. [*bardd*, Welch.] A poet.

There is amongst the Irish a kind of people
called bards, which are to them instead of
poets; whose profession is to set forth the
praises or dispraises of men in their poems or
rhimes; the which are had in high regard and
estimation among them. Spenser on Ireland.

And many bards that to the trembling chord,
Can tune their timely voices cunningly.
Fairy Queen, b. i.

The bard who first adorn'd our native tongue,
Tun'd to his British lyre this ancient song,
Which Homer might without a blush rehearse.
Dryden.

báron n.s. [The etymology of this word is very uncertain. *Baro*, among the Romans, signified a brave warriour, or a brutal man; and, from the first of these significations, Menage derives *baron*, as a term of military dignity. Others suppose it originally to signify only a man; in which sense *baron*, or *varon*, is still used by the Spaniards; and, to confirm this conjecture, our law yet uses *baron* and *femme*, husband and wife. Others deduce it from *ber*, an old Gaulish word, signifying commander; others from the

Hebrew נברי, of the same import. Some think it a contraction of *par homme*, or *peer*, which seems least probable.]

1. A degree of nobility next to a viscount. It may be probably thought, that anciently, in England, all those were called barons, that had such signiories as we now call court barons. And it is said, that, after the conquest, all such came to the parliament, and sat as nobles in the upper house. But when, by experience, it appeared, that the parliament was too much crouded with such multitudes, it became a custom, that none should come, but such as the king, for their extraordinary wisdom or quality, thought good to call by writ; which writ ran *hac vice tantum*.[†] After that, men, seeing that this state of nobility was but casual, and depending merely on the prince's pleasure, obtained of the king letters patent of this dignity to them and their heirs male: and these were called barons by letters patent, or by creation; whose posterity are now those barons that are called lords of the parliament; of which kind the king may create more at his pleasure. It is nevertheless thought, that there are yet barons by writ, as well as barons by letters patent, and that they may be discerned by their titles; the barons by writ being those, that to the title of lord have their own surnames annexed; whereas the barons by letters patent, are named by their baronies. These barons which were first by writ, may now justly also be called barons by prescription; for that they have continued barons, in themselves and their ancestors, beyond the memory of man. There are also barons by tenure, as the bishops of the land, who, by virtue of baronies annexed to their bishopricks, have always had place in the upper house of parliament, and are called lords spiritual.

2. Baron is an officer, as barons of the exchequer to the king: of these the

principal is called lord chief baron, and the three others are his assistants, between the king and his subjects, in causes of justice, belonging to the exchequer.

3. There are also barons of the cinque ports; two to each of the seven towns, Hastings, Winchelsea, Rye, Rumney, Hithe, Dover, and Sandwich, that have places in the lower house of parliament. Cowel.

They that bear
The cloth of state above, are four barons
Of the cinque ports. Shakesp. Henry VIII.

4. Baron is used for the husband in relation to his wife. Cowel.

5. A baron of beef is when the two sirloins are not cut asunder, but joined together by the end of the backbone. Dict.

base-born adj. Born out of wedlock.

But see thy base-born child, thy babe of shame,
Who, left by thee, upon our parish came. Gay.

basháw n.s. [sometimes written *bassa*.] A title of honour and command among the Turks; the viceroy of a province; the general of an army.

The Turks made an expedition into Persia;
and because of the straits of the mountains, the
bashaw consulted which way they should get
in. Bacon's Apophthegms.

bástard n.s. [*bastardd*, Welch, of low birth; *bastarde*, Fr.]

1. Bastard, according to the civil and canon law, is a person born of a woman out of wedlock, or not married; so that, according to order of law, his father is not known. Ayliffe.

Him to the Lydian king Lycimnia bare,
And sent her boasted bastard to the war.
Dryden.

2. Any thing spurious or false.

It lies on you to speak to th' people;
Not by your own instruction, but with words
But rooted in your tongue; bastards and syllables
Of no allowance to your bosom's truth.
Shakesp. Coriolanus.

bat n.s. [the etymology unknown.] An animal having the body of a mouse and the wings of a bird; not with feathers, but with a sort of skin which is extended. It lays no eggs, but brings forth its young alive, and suckles them. It never grows tame, feeds upon flies, insects, and fatty substances, such as candles, oil, and cheese; and appears only in the summer evenings, when the weather is fine. Calmet.

When owls do cry,
On the bat's back I do fly. Shakesp. Tempest.

But then grew reason dark; that fair star no more
Could the fair forms of good and truth discern;
Bats they became who eagles were before;
And this they got by their desire to learn.
Sir J. Davies.

Some animals are placed in the middle
betwixt two kinds, as bats, which have
something of birds and beasts. Locke.

Where swallows in the winter season keep,
And how the drowsy bat and dormouse sleep.
Gay.

báting, or **abáting** prep. [from *bate*, or *abate*. This word, though a participle in itself, seems often used as a preposition.] Except.

The king, your brother, could not choose
*   an advocate,*
Whom I would sooner hear on any subject,
Bating that only one, his love, than you.
Rowe's R. Conv.

If we consider children, we have little reason
to think, that they bring many ideas with
them, bating, perhaps, some faint ideas of
hunger and thirst. Locke.

bawd n.s. [*baude*, old Fr.] A procurer, or procuress; one that introduces men and women to each other, for the promotion of debauchery.

If your worship will take order for the drabs
and the knaves, you need not to fear the
bawds. Shakesp. Measure for Meas.

This commodity,
This bawd, this broker, this all changing word,
Hath drawn him from his own determin'd
*   aid.* Sh. K. John.

Our author calls colouring lena sororis, *the bawd of her sister design; she dresses her up, she paints her, she procures for the design, and makes lovers for her.* Dryden's Dufresnoy.

báwdy-house n.s. A house where traffick is made by wickedness and debauchery.

Has the pope lately shut up the bawdy-houses, or does he continue to lay a tax upon sin? Dennis.

bead n.s. [*beade*, prayer, Saxon.]

1. Small globes or balls of glass or pearl, or other substance, strung upon a thread, and used by the Romanists to count their prayers; from whence the phrase to tell beads, or to be at one's beads, is to be at prayer.

That aged dame, the lady of the place, Who all this while was busy at her beads. Fairy Q. b. i.

Thy voice I seem in every hymn to hear, With ev'ry bead I drop too soft a tear. Pope's El. to Abel.

2. Little balls worn about the neck for ornament.

With scarfs and fans, and double change of brav'ry, With amber bracelets, beads, and all such knav'ry. Shakesp. Taming of a Shrew.

3. Any globular bodies.

Thy spirit within thee hath been so at war, That beads of sweat have stood upon thy brow. Sh. H. IV.

Several yellow lumps of amber, almost like beads, with one side flat, had fastened themselves to the bottom. Boyle.

to beard v.a. [from *beard*.]

1. To take or pluck by the beard, in contempt or anger.

No man so potent breathes upon the ground, But I will beard him. Shakesp. Henry IV. p. i.

2. To oppose to the face; to set at open defiance.

He, whensoever he should swerve from duty, may be able to beard him. Spenser's State of Ireland.

The design of utterly extirpating monarchy and episcopacy, the presbyterians alone begun, continued, and would have ended, if they had not been bearded by that new party, with whom they could not agree about dividing the spoil. Swift.

bear-garden adj. A word used in familiar or low phrase for rude or turbulent; as, a bear-garden fellow; that is, a man rude enough to be a proper frequenter of the bear-garden. Bear-garden sport, is used for gross inelegant entertainment.

beau n.s. [*beau*, Fr. It is sounded like *bo*, and has often the French plural *beaux*.] A man of dress; a man whose great care is to deck his person.

What, will not beaux attempt to please the fair? Dryden.

The water nymphs are too unkind To Vill'roy; are the land nymphs so? And fly they all, at once combin'd To shame a general, and a beau? Prior.

You will become the delight of nine ladies in ten, and the envy of ninety-nine beaux in a hundred. Swift's Direct. to Footm.

beaúty n.s. [*beauté*, Fr.]

1. That assemblage of graces, or proportion of parts, which pleases the eye.

Beauty consists of a certain composition of colour and figure, causing delight in the beholder. Locke.

Your beauty was the cause of that effect, Your beauty, that did haunt me in my sleep.—— ——If I thought that, I tell thee, homicide, These nails should rend that beauty from my cheeks. Shakesp. Richard III.

Beauty is best in in a body that hath rather dignity of presence than beauty of aspect. The beautiful prove accomplished, but not of great spirit, and study for the most part rather behaviour than virtue. Bacon.

The best part of beauty is that which a picture cannot express. Bacon's Ornament. Ration. Nº 64.

Of the beauty of the eye I shall say little, leaving that to poets and orators; that it is a very pleasant and lovely object to behold, if we consider the figure, colours, splendour of it, is the least I can say. Ray on Creation.

He view'd their twining branches with delight, And prais'd the beauty of the pleasing sight. Pope.

2. A particular grace, feature, or ornament.

The ancient pieces are beautiful, because they resemble the beauties of nature; and nature will ever be beautiful, which resembles those beauties of antiquity. Dryden's Dufresnoy.

Wherever you place a patch, you destroy a beauty. Addison.

3. Any thing more eminently excellent than the rest of that with which it is united.

This gave me an occasion of looking backward on some beauties of my author in his former books. Dryd. Fab. Pref.

With incredible pains have I endeavoured to copy the several beauties of the ancient and modern historians. Arbuthnot.

4. A beautiful person.

Remember that Pellean conquerour, A youth, how all the beauties of the east He slightly view'd, and slightly overpass'd. Paradise Lost.

What can thy ends, malicious beauty, be? Can he, who kill'd thy brother, live for thee? Dryden.

béchicks n.s. [βηχικα, of βηξ, a cough.] Medicines proper for relieving coughs. Dict.

bédlam n.s. [corrupted from *Bethlehem*, the name of a religious house in London, converted afterwards into an hospital for the mad and lunatick.]

1. A madhouse; a place appointed for the cure of lunacy.

2. A madman; a lunatick.

Let's follow the old earl, and get the bedlam To lead him where he would; his roguish madness Allows itself to any thing. Shakesp. King Lear.

bédpresser n.s. [from *bed* and *press*.] A heavy lazy fellow.

This sanguine coward, this bedpresser, this horseback-breaker, this huge hill of flesh. Shakesp. Henry IV. p. i.

to béetle v.n. [from the noun.] To jut out; to hang over.

What if it tempt you tow'rd the flood, my lord? Or to the dreadful summit of the cliff, That beetles o'er his base into the sea. Shakesp. Hamlet.

> *Or where the hawk, High in the beetling cliff, his airy builds.* Thomson's Spring.

to befóul v.a. [from *be* and *foul*.] To make foul; to soil; to dirt.

béglerbeg n.s. [Turkish.] The chief governour of a province among the Turks.

to belábour v.a. [from *be* and *labour*.] To beat; to thump: a word in low speech.

What several madnesses in men appear: Orestes runs from fancy'd furies here; Ajax belabours there an harmless ox, And thinks that Agamemnon feels the knocks. Dryden, jun.

He sees virago Nell belabour, With his own staff, his peaceful neighbour. Swift.

belch n.s. [from the verb.]

1. The act of eructation.

2. A cant term for malt liquour.

A sudden reformation would follow, among all sorts of people; porters would no longer be drunk with belch. Dennis.

beldám n.s. [*belle dame*, which, in old French, signified probably an old woman, as *belle age*, old age.]

1. An old woman; generally a term of contempt, marking the last degree of old age, with all its faults and miseries.

Then sing of secret things that came to pass,
When beldam nature in her cradle was.
Milton.

2. A hag.

Why, how now, Hecat, you look angerly?—
—Have I not reason, beldams, as you are?
Saucy and overbold? Shakesp. Macbeth.

The resty sieve wagg'd ne'er the more;
I wept for woe, the testy beldam swore.
Dryden.

belles lettres n.s. [Fr.] Polite literature. It has no singular.

The exactness of the other, is to admit of
something like discourse, especially in what
regards the belles lettres. Tatler.

béllibone n.s. [from *bellus*, beautiful, and *bonus*, good, Lat. *belle & bonne*, Fr.] A woman excelling both in beauty and goodness. A word now out of use.

Pan may be proud, that ever he begot
Such a bellibone,
And Syrinx rejoice, that ever was her lot
To bear such a one. Spenser's Pastorals.

bellípotent adj. [*bellipotens*, Lat.] Puissant; mighty in war. Dict.

béllybound adj. [from *belly* and *bound*.] Diseased, so as to be costive, and shrunk in the belly.

béllygod n.s. [from *belly* and *god*.] A glutton; one who makes a god of his belly.

What infinite waste they made this way, the
only story of Apicus, a famous bellygod, may
suffice to shew. Hakewell on Providence.

bélly-timber n.s. [from *belly* and *timber*.] Food; materials to support the belly.

Where belly-timber, above ground
Or under, was not to be found.
Hudibras, cant. i.

The strength of every other member
Is founded on your belly-timber. Prior.

belswágger n.s. A cant word for a whoremaster.

You are a charitable belswagger; my wife cried
out fire, and you called out for engines.
Dryden's Spanish Friar.

benign disease, is when all the usual symptoms appear in the small pox, or any acute disease, favourably, and without any irregularities, or unexpected changes. Quincy.

to bepíss v.a. [from *piss*.] To wet with urine.

One caused, at a feast, a bagpipe to be played,
which made the knight bepiss himself,
to the great diversion of all then present,
as well as confusion of himself.
Derham's Physico-Theol.

bétty n.s. [probably a cant word, without etymology.] An instrument to break open doors.

Record the stratagems, the arduous exploits,
and the nocturnal scalades of needy heroes,
describing the powerful betty, or the artful
picklock. Arbuthnot's History of J. Bull.

bibácious adj. [*bibax*, Lat.] Much addicted to drinking. D.

bibácity n.s. [*bibacitas*, Lat.] The quality of drinking much.

Bíble n.s. [from βιβλιον, a book; called, by way of excellence, *The Book*.] The sacred volume in which are contained the revelations of God.

If we pass from the apostolic to the next ages
of the church, the primitive christians looked
on their bibles as their most important
treasure. Government of the Tongue, § 3.

We must take heed how we accustom ourselves
to a slight and irreverent use of the name of
God, and of the phrases and expressions of the
holy bible, which ought not to be applied upon
every slight occasion. Tillotson, sermon i.

In questions of natural religion, we should
confirm and improve, or connect our
reasonings, by the divine assistance of the
bible. Watts's Logick.

bígot n.s. [The etymology of this word is unknown; but it is supposed, by Camden and others, to take its rise from some occasional phrase.] A man devoted to a certain party; prejudiced in favour of certain opinions; a blind zealot. It is used often

with *to* before the object of zeal; as, a bigot
to the Cartesian tenets.

Religious spite, and pious spleen bred first
This quarrel, which so long the bigots nurst.
Tate. Juvenal.

In philosophy and religion, the bigots of all
parties are generally the most positive.
Watts's Improvement of the Mind.

bílbo n.s. [corrupted from *Bilboa*, where the
best weapons are made.] A rapier; a sword.

To be compassed like a good bilbo, in the
circumference of a peck, hilt to point, heel
to head. Shakesp. M. W. of Windsor.

bílingsgate n.s. [A cant word, borrowed
from *Bilingsgate* in London, a place where
there is always a croud of low people, and
frequent brawls and foul language.]
Ribaldry; foul language.

There stript, fair rhet'rick languish'd on
  the ground,
And shameful bilingsgate her robes adorn.
Dunciad, b. iv.

bílliards n.s. without a singular. [*billard*, Fr.
of which that language has no etymology;
and therefore they probably derived from
England both the play and the name; which
is corrupted from *balyards*; yards or sticks
with which a ball is driven along a table.
Thus Spenser:

  Balyards much unfit,
And shuttlecocks misseeming manly wit.
Hubb. Tale.] A game at which a ball is
forced against another on a table.

Let it alone; let's to billiards.
Shakesp. Antony and Cleop.

Even nose and cheek, withal,
Smooth as is the billiard ball.
Ben. Johnson's Underwoods.

Some are forced to bound or fly upwards,
almost like ivory balls meeting on a billiard
table. Boyle.

When the ball obeys the stroke of a billiard
stick, it is not any action of the ball, but bare
passion. Locke.

bínary arithmetick A method of
computation proposed by Mr. Leibnitz, in
which, in lieu of the ten figures in the
common arithmetick, and the progression
from ten to ten, he has only two figures, and
uses the simple progression from two to
two. This method appears to be the same
with that used by the Chinese four
thousand years ago. Chambers.

bínocle n.s. [from *binus* and *oculus*.] A kind
of dioptrick telescope, fitted so with two
tubes joining together in one, as that a
distant object may be seen with both eyes
together. Harris.

biógrapher n.s. [βιος and γραφω.] A
writer of lives; a relator not of the history of
nations, but of the actions of particular
persons.

Our Grubstreet biographers watch for the
death of a great man, like so many
undertakers, on purpose to make a penny
of him. Addison, Freeholder, Nº 35.

bíshop n.s. A cant word for a mixture of
wine, oranges, and sugar.

  Fine oranges,
Well roasted, with sugar and wine in a cup,
They'll make a sweet bishop, when gentle folks
  sup. Swift.

bísson adj. [derived by Skinner from *by* and
sin.] Blind.

But who, oh! who hath seen the mobled queen,
Run barefoot up and down, threat'ning
  the flames
With bisson rheum. Shakesp. Hamlet.

What harm can your bisson conspectuities
glean out of this character.
Shakesp. Coriolanus.

bitch n.s. [*bitge*, Saxon.]

1. The female of the canine kind; as the
  wolf, the dog, the fox, the otter.

And at his feet a bitch wolf suck did yield
To two young babes. Spens. Vision of
Bellay.

I have been credibly informed, that a bitch
will nurse, play with, and be fond of young
foxes, as much as, and in place of her puppies.
Locke.

2. A name of reproach for a woman.

John had not run a madding so long, had it not been for an extravagant bitch of a wife. Arbuthnot's History of J. Bull.

black adj. [*blac*, Saxon.]

1. Of the colour of night.

In the twilight in the evening, in the black and dark night. Prov. vii. 9.

By Aristotle it seems to be implied, in these problems which enquire why the sun makes man black, and not the fire, why it whitens wax, yet blacks the skin. Brown's Vulgar Errours.

2. Dark.

The heaven was black with clouds and wind, and there was a great rain. 1 Kings, xviii. 45.

3. Cloudy of countenance; sullen.

She hath abated me of half my train; Look'd black upon me. Shakesp. King Lear.

4. Horrible; wicked; atrocious.

Either my country never must be freed, Or I consenting to so black a deed. Dryden's Indian Emp.

5. Dismal; mournful.

A dire induction am I witness to; And will to France, hoping, the consequence, Will prove as bitter, black, and tragical. Shakesp. Rich. III.

6. Black and blue. The colour of a bruise; a stripe.

Mistress Ford, good heart, is beaten black and blue, that you cannot see a white spot about her. Merry Wives of Windsor.

And, wing'd with speed and fury, flew To rescue knight from black and blue. Hudibras, cant. ii.

black-mail n.s. A certain rate of money, corn, cattle, or other consideration, paid to men allied with robbers, to be by them protected from the danger of such as usually rob or steal. Cowel.

blátant adj. [*blatttant*, Fr.] Bellowing as a calf.

You learn'd this language from the blatant beast. Dryden.

blatterátion n.s. [*blateratio*, Lat.] Noise; senseless roar.

blíndman's buff n.s. A play in which some one is to have his eyes covered, and hunt out the rest of the company.

Disguis'd in all the mask of night, We left our champion on his flight: At blindman's buff to grope his way, In equal fear of night and day. Hudibras, p. iii. c. ii.

He imagines I shut my eyes again; but surely he fancies I play at blindman's buff with him; for he thinks I never have my eyes open. Stillingfleet's Defence of Disc. on Romish Idolatry.

blóbberlip n.s. [from *blob*, or *blobber*, and *lip*.] A thick lip.

They make a wit of their insipid friend, His blobberlips and beetlebrows commend. Dryden's Juvenal.

blóckhead n.s. [from *block* and *head*.] A stupid fellow; a dolt; a man without parts.

Your wit will not so soon out as another man's will; it is strongly wedged up in a blockhead. Shakesp. Coriolanus.

We idly sit like stupid blockheads, Our hands committed to our pockets. Hudibras, p. iii. c. ii.

A blockhead rubs his thoughtless skull, And thanks his stars he was not born a fool. Pope.

to blood-let v.a. [from *blood* and *let*.] To bleed; to open a vein medicinally.

The chyle is not perfectly assimilated into blood, by its circulation through the lungs, as is known by experiments of blood-letting. Arbuthnot on Aliments.

blowze n.s. A ruddy fat-faced wench.

blúnderbuss n.s. [from *blunder*.] A gun that is charged with many bullets, so that, without any exact aim, there is a chance of hitting the mark.

There are blunderbusses in every loop-hole,
that go off of their own accord, at the
squeaking of a fiddle. Dryden.

blúnderhead n.s. [from *blunder* and *head.*]
A stupid fellow.

At the rate of this thick-skulled blunderhead,
every plowjobber shall take upon him to read
upon divinity. L'Estrange.

bódice n.s. [from *bodies.*] Stays; a waistcoat
quilted with whalebone, worn by women.

Her bodice halfway she unlac'd,
About his arms she slily cast
The silken band, and held him fast. Prior.

This consideration should keep ignorant
nurses and bodice makers from meddling.
Locke on Education, § 11.

bódkin n.s. [*boddiken,* or small body,
Skinner.]

1. An instrument with a small blade and
   sharp point, used to bore holes.

Each of them had bodkins in their hands,
wherewith continually they pricked him.
Sidney's Arcadia.

2. An instrument to draw a thread or
   ribbond through a loop.

Or plung'd in lakes of bitter washes lie,
Or wedg'd whole ages in a bodkin's eye.
Pope's R. of the L.

3. An instrument to dress the hair.

   You took constant care
The bodkin, comb, and essence to prepare:
For this your locks in paper-durance bound.
Pope.

bóghouse n.s. [from *bog* and *house.*] A
house of office.†

bohéa n.s. [an Indian word.] A species of
tea, of higher colour, and more astringent
taste, than green tea.

Coarse pewter, appearing to consist chiefly of
lead, is part of the bales in which bohea tea
was brought from China. Woodw.

As some frail cup of China's fairest mold,
The tumults of the boiling bohea braves,
And holds secure the coffee's sable waves.
Tickell.

She went from op'ra, park, assembly, play,
To morning walks, and pray'rs three hours a day;
To part her time 'twixt reading and bohea,
To muse, and spill her solitary tea. Pope.

bómbast n.s. [This word seems to be
derived from *Bombastius,* one of the names
of Paracelsus; a man remarkable for
sounding professions, and unintelligible
language.] Fustian; big words, without
meaning.

Not pedants motley tongue, soldiers bombast,
Mountebanks drug-tongue, nor the terms of law,
Are strong enough preparatives to draw
Me to hear this. Donne.

Are all the flights of heroick poetry to be
concluded bombast, unnatural, and mere
madness, because they are not affected with
their excellencies? Dryden's State of
Innocence, Preface.

bombycinous adj. [*bombycinus,* Lat.]
Silken; made of silk. D.

bona roba n.s. [Ital. a fine gown.] A whore.

We knew where the bona robas were.
Shakesp. Henry IV.

bóoby n.s. [a word of no certain etymology;
Henshaw thinks it a corruption of *bull-beef*
ridiculously; Skinner imagines it to be
derived from *bobo,* foolish, Span. Junius
finds *bowbard* to be an old Scottish word for
a coward, a contemptible fellow; from
which he naturally deduces *booby;* but the
original of *bowbard* is not known.] A dull,
heavy, stupid fellow; a lubber.

But one exception to this fact we find,
That booby Phaon only was unkind,
An ill-bred boatman, rough as waves and
   wind. Prior.

Young master next must rise to fill him wine,
And starve himself to see the booby dine.
King.

book n.s. [*boc,* Sax. supposed from *boc,* a
beech; because they wrote on beechen
boards, as *liber* in Latin, from the rind of
a tree.]

1. A volume in which we read or write.

See a book of prayer in his hand;
True ornaments to know a holy man.
Shakesp. Richard III.

Receive the sentence of the law for sins,
Such as by God's book are adjudg'd to death.
Shakesp. Henry VI.

But in the coffin that had the books, they were
found as fresh as if they had been but newly
written; being written on parchment, and
covered over with watch candles of wax.
Bacon.

Books are a sort of dumb teachers; they cannot
answer sudden questions, or explain present
doubts: this is properly the work of a living
instructor. Watts.

2. A particular part of a work.

The first book we divide into sections;
whereof the first is these chapters past.
Burnet's Theory of the Earth.

3. The register in which a trader keeps an
account of his debts.

This life
Is nobler than attending for a check;
Prouder, than rustling in unpaid for silk:
Such gain the cap of him that makes them fine,
Yet keeps his book uncross'd.
Shakesp. Cymbeline.

4. In books. In kind remembrance.

I was so much in his books, that, at his
decease, he left me the lamp by which he used
to write his lucubrations. Addison.

5. Without book. By memory; by
repetition; without reading.

Sermons read they abhor in the church; but
sermons without book, sermons which spend
their life in their birth, and may have publick
audience but once. Hooker, b. v. § 21.

bóokful adj. [from *book* and *full.*] Full of
notions gleaned from books; crouded with
undigested knowledge.

The bookful blockhead, ignorantly read,
With loads of learned lumber in his head,
With his own tongue still edifies his ears,
And always list'ning to himself appears.
Pope's Ess. on Crit.

bóokish adj. [from *book.*] Given to books;
acquainted only with books. It is generally
used contemptuously.

I'll make him yield the crown,
Whose bookish rule hath pull'd fair England
down. Shakesp. Henry VI. p. ii.

I'm not bookish, yet I can read waiting
gentlewomen in the 'scape. Shakesp.
Winter's Tale.

Xantippe follows the example of her
namesake; being married to a bookish man,
who has no knowledge of the world.
Spectator, Nº 482.

bóokworm n.s. [from *book* and *worm.*]

1. A worm or mite that eats holes in
books, chiefly when damp.

My lion, like a moth or bookworm, feeds upon
nothing but paper, and I shall beg of them to
diet him with wholesome and substantial
food. Guardian, Nº 114.

2. A student too closely given to books;
a reader without judgment.

Among those venerable galleries and solitary
scenes of the university, I wanted but a black
gown, and a salary, to be as mere a bookworm
as any there. Pope's Letters.

bóotcatcher n.s. [from *boot* and *catch.*] The
person whose business at an inn is to pull
off the boots of passengers.

The ostler and the bootcatcher ought to
partake. Swift.

boráchio n.s. [*borracho,* Span.] A drunkard.

How you stink of wine! D' ye think my niece
will ever endure such a borachio! you're an
absolute borachio. Congreve's Way of
the World.

bóree n.s. A kind of dance.

Dick could neatly dance a jig,
But Tom was best at borees. Swift.

bósky adj. [*bosque,* Fr.] Woody.

And with each end of thy blue bow do'st crown
My bosky acres, and my unshrub'd down.
Shakesp. Tempest.

I know each land, and every alley green,
Dingle, or bushy dell, of this wild wood,
And every bosky bourn from side to side.
Milton.

bótryoid adj. [βοτρυοιδης.] Having the form of a bunch of grapes.

The outside is thick set with botryoid efflorescencies, or small knobs, yellow, bluish, and purple; all of a shining metallick hue.
Woodward of Fossils.

bóusy adj. [from *bouse.*] Drunken.

The guests upon the day appointed came,
Each bousy farmer, with his simp'ring dame.
King.

With a long legend of romantick things,
Which in his cups the bousy poet sings.
Dryden's Juv. Sat. x.

bówels n.s. [*boyaux,* Fr.]

1. Intestines; the vessels and organs within the body.

He smote him therewith in the fifth rib, and shed out his bowels. 2 Sam. xx. 10.

2. The inner parts of any thing.

Had we no quarrel else to Rome, but that
Thou art thence banish'd, we would muster all
From twelve to seventy; and pouring war
Into the bowels of ungrateful Rome,
Like a bold flood appear.
Shakesp. Coriolanus.

His soldiers spying his undaunted spirit,
A Talbot! Talbot! cried out amain,
And rush'd into the bowels of the battle.
Shakesp. Henry VI.

As he saw drops of water distilling from the rock, by following the veins, he has made himself two or three fountains in the bowels of the mountain. Addison on Italy.

3. Tenderness; compassion.

He had no other consideration of money, than for the support of his lustre; and whilst he could do that, he cared not for money; having no bowels in the point of running in debt, or borrowing all he could. Clarendon.

4. This word seldom has a singular, except in writers of anatomy.

bóxer n.s. [from *box.*] A man who fights with his fist.

brach n.s. [*braque,* Fr.] A bitch hound.

Truth's a dog must to kennel; he must be whipped out, when the lady brach may stand by the fire, and stink. Shakesp.

brachygraphy n.s. [βραχυς, short, and γραφω, to write.] The art or practice of writing in a short compass.

All the certainty of those high pretenders, bating what they have of the first principles, and the word of God, may be circumscribed by as small a circle as the creed, when brachygraphy had confined it within the compass of a penny. Glanville.

brain n.s. [*brægen,* Sax. *breyne,* Dutch.]

1. That collection of vessels and organs in the head, from which sense and motion arise.

The brain is divided into cerebrum and cerebellum. Cerebrum is that part of the brain, which possesses all the upper and forepart of the cranium, being separated from the cerebellum by the second process of the dura mater, under which the cerebellum is situated. The substance of the brain is distinguished into outer and inner; the former is called corticalis, cinerea, or glandulosa; the latter, medullaris, alba, or nervea. Cheselden.

If I be served such another trick, I'll have my brains ta'en out, and buttered, and give them to a dog for a new year's gift. Shakesp. Merry Wives of Windsor.

That man proportionably hath the largest brain, I did, I confess, somewhat doubt, and conceived it might have failed in birds, especially such as having little bodies, have yet large cranies, and seem to contain much brain, as snipes and woodcocks; but, upon trial, I find it very true. Brown's Vulgar Errours.

2. That part in which the understanding is placed; therefore taken for the understanding.

The force they are under is a real force, and that of their fate but an imaginary conceived one; the one but in their brains, the other on their shoulders. Hammond's Fundamentals.

A man is first a geometrician in his brain,
before he be such in his hand. Hale's Origin
of Mankind.

3. Sometimes the affections.

My son Edgar! had he a hand to write
this, a heart and brain to breed it in?
Shakesp. King Lear.

to brain v.a. [from the noun.] To dash out
the brains; to kill by beating out the brains.

Why, as I told thee, 'tis a custom with him i'
th' afternoon to sleep; there thou may'st brain
him. Shakesp. Tempest.

> *Outlaws of nature,*
Fit to be shot and brain'd, without a process,
To stop infection; that's their proper death.
Dryden.

Next seiz'd two wretches more, and
> *headlong cast,*
Brain'd on the rock, his second dire repast.
Pope's Odyssey.

brait n.s. A term used by jewellers for
a rough diamond. D.

brake n.s. [of uncertain etymology.] A
thicket of brambles, or of thorns.

A dog of this town used daily to fetch meat,
and to carry the same unto a blind mastiff,
that lay in a brake without the town.
Carew's Survey of Cornwal.

If I'm traduc'd by tongues, which neither know
My faculties nor person; let me say,
'Tis but the fate of place, and the rough brake
That virtue must go through. Shakesp.
Henry VIII.

In every bush and brake, where hap may find
The serpent sleeping. Milton's Par. Lost,
b. ix. l. 160.

Full little thought of him the gentle knight,
Who, flying death, had there conceal'd his flight;
In brakes and brambles hid, and shunning
mortal sight. Dryden's Fables.

brávo n.s. [*bravo*, Ital.] A man who
murders for hire.

For boldness, like the bravoes and banditti, is
seldom employed, but upon desperate services.
Government of the Tongue.

No bravoes here profess the bloody trade,
Nor is the church the murd'rer's refuge made.
Gay's Trivia.

bréeches n.s. [*bræc*, Sax. from *bracca*, an old
Gaulish word; so that Skinner imagines the
name of the part covered with breeches, to
be derived from that of the garment. In this
sense it has no singular.]

1. The garment worn by men over the
   lower part of the body.

Petrachio is coming in a new hat and an old
jerkin, and a pair of old breeches, thrice
turned. Shakesp. Taming the Shrew.

Rough satires, sly remarks, ill-natur'd speeches,
Are always aim'd at poets that wear breeches.
Prior.

Give him a single coat to make, he'd do 't;
A vest, or breeches, singly; but the brute
Cou'd ne'er contrive all three to make a suit.
King's Art of Cookery.

2. To wear the breeches, is, to usurp the
   authority of the husbands.

The wife of Xanthus was proud and
domineering, as if her fortune, and her
extraction, had entitled her to the breeches.
L'Estrange.

bréviary n.s. [*breviaire*, Fr. *breviarium*, Lat.]

1. An abridgment; an epitome; a
   compendium.

Cresconius, an African bishop, has given
us an abridgment, or breviary thereof.
Ayliffe's Parergon.

2. The book containing the daily service of
   the church of Rome.

brevíer n.s. A particular size of letter used
in printing; so called, probably, from being
originally used in printing a breviary; as,

> Nor love thy life, nor hate, but
>> what thou liv'st,
> Live well, how long or short,
>> permit to heav'n. Milton.

Brídewell n.s. [The palace built by St.
Bride's, or *Bridget's well*, was turned into
a workhouse.] A house of correction.

*He would contribute more to reformation
than all the workhouses and Bridewells in
Europe.* Spectator, Nº 157.

brílliant n.s. A diamond of the finest cut,
formed into angles, so as to refract the light,
and shine more.

*In deference to his virtues, I forbear
To shew you what the rest in orders were;
This brilliant is so spotless and so bright,
He needs not foil, but shines by his own
    proper light.* Dryd.

brínded adj. [*brin*, Fr. a branch.] Streaked;
tabby; marked with branches.

Thrice the brinded cat hath mew'd.
Shakesp. Macbeth.

*She tam'd the brinded lioness,
And spotted mountain pard.* Milton.

*My brinded heifer to the stake I lay;
Two thriving calves she suckles twice a day.*
Dryden.

brogue n.s. [*brog*, Irish.]

1. A kind of shoe.

    *I thought he slept; and put
My clouted brogues from off my feet,
    whose rudeness
Answer'd my steps too loud.*
Shakesp. Cymbeline.

*Sometimes it is given out, that we must either
take three halfpence, or eat our brogues.* Swift.

2. A cant word for a corrupt dialect, or
    manner of pronunciation.

brontólogy n.s. [βροντη and λογια.] A
dissertation upon thunder. Dict.

bróthel, bróthelhouse n.s. [*bordel*, Fr.]
A house of lewd entertainment; a
bawdyhouse.

    *Perchance
I saw him enter such a house of sale,
Videlicet, a brothel.* Shakesp. Hamlet.

*Then courts of kings were held in high renown,
Ere made the common brothels of the town:
There, virgins honourable vows receiv'd,
But chaste as maids in monasteries liv'd.*
Dryden's W. of B.

*From its old ruins brothelhouses rise,
Scenes of lewd loves, and of polluted joys.*
Dryden's Mackfl.

*The libertine retires to the stews, and to the
brothel.* Rogers.

to bruit v.a. [from the noun.] To report; to
noise abroad; to rumour. Neither the verb
nor the noun are now much in use.

    *His death,
Being bruited once, took fire and heat away
From the best temper'd courage in his troops.*
Shak. Hen. V.

*It was bruited, that I meant nothing less than
to go to Guiana.* Raleigh's Essays.

bub n.s. [a cant word.] Strong malt liquour.

*Or if it be his fate to meet
With folks who have more wealth than wit,
He loves cheap port, and double bub,
And settles in the humdrum club.* Prior.

to búbble v.a. To cheat: a cant word.

*He tells me, with great passion, that she has
bubbled him out of his youth; and that she
has drilled him on to five and fifty.*
Addison, Spectator, Nº 89.

*Charles Mather could not bubble a young
beau better with a toy.* Arbuthnot's Hist.
of J. Bull.

búbby n.s. A woman's breast.

*Foh! say they, to see a handsome, brisk,
genteel, young fellow, so much governed by
a doating old woman; why don't you go and
suck the bubby?* Arbuthnot's John Bull.

bucaníers n.s. A cant word for the
privateers, or pirates, of America.

búffleheaded adj. [from *buffle* and *head*.]
A man with a large head, like a buffalo;
dull; stupid; foolish.

bug n.s. A stinking insect bred in old
houshold stuff. In the following passage,
wings are erroneously ascribed to it.

*Yet let me flap this bug with gilded wings,
This painted child of dirt, which stinks and
    stings.* Pope.

búlimy n.s. [βουλιμια, from βους, an ox, and λιμος, hunger.] An enormous appetite, attended with fainting, and coldness of the extremities. Dict.

bum n.s. [*bomme*, Dutch.]

1. The buttocks; the part on which we sit.

The wisest aunt telling the saddest tale,
Sometime for threefoot stool mistaketh me,
Then slip I from her bum, down topples she.
Shakesp.

This said, he gently rais'd the knight,
And set him on his bum upright. Hudibras.

From dusty shops neglected authours come,
Martyrs of pies, and relicks of the bum.
Dryden's Mackfl.

The learned Sydenham does not doubt,
But profound thought will bring the gout;
And that with bum on couch we lie,
Because our reason's soar'd too high. W—n.†

2. It is used, in composition, for any thing mean or low, as *bumbailiff.*

búmpkin n.s. [This word is of uncertain etymology; Henshaw derives it from *pumpkin,* a kind of worthless gourd, or melon. This seems harsh. *Bump* is used amongst us for a knob, or lump; may not bumpkin be much the same with clodpate, loggerhead, block, and blockhead.] An awkward heavy rustick; a country lout.

The poor bumpkin, that had never seen nor heard of such delights before, blessed herself at the change of her condition.
L'Estrange's Fables.

A heavy bumpkin, taught with daily care,
Can never dance three steps with a becoming air. Dryden.

In his white cloak the magistrate appears,
The country bumpkin the same liv'ry wears.
Dryden.

It was a favour to admit them to breeding; they might be ignorant bumpkins and clowns, if they pleased. Locke.

búngler n.s. [*bwngler,* Welch; *q. bôn y glér,* i.e. the last or lowest of the profession. Davies.] A bad workman; a clumsy performer; a man without skill.

Painters, at the first, were such bunglers, and so rude, that, when they drew a cow or a hog, they were fain to write over the head what it was; otherwise the beholder knew not what to make of it. Peacham on Drawing.

Hard features every bungler can command;
To draw true beauty shews a master's hand.
Dryden.

A bungler thus, who scarce the nail can hit,
With driving wrong will make the pannel
split. Swift.

búrbot n.s. A fish full of prickles. Dict.

búrden n.s. [*byrðen,* Sax. and therefore properly written *burthen.* It is supposed to come from *burdo,* Lat. a male, as *onus* from ονος, an ass.]

1. A load; something to be carried.

Camels have their provender
Only for bearing burdens, and sore blows
For sinking under them.
Shakesp. Coriolanus.

It is of use in lading of ships, and may help to shew what burden in the several kinds they will bear. Bacon's Phys. Rem.

2. Something grievous or wearisome.

Couldst thou support
That burden, heavier than the earth to bear?
Par. Lost, b. x.

None of the things they are to learn, should ever be made a burden to them, or imposed on them as a task. Locke.

Deaf, giddy, helpless, left alone,
To all my friends a burden grown. Swift.

3. A birth: now obsolete.

Thou hadst a wife once, called Æmilia,
That bore thee at a burden two fair sons.
Shakesp.

4. The verse repeated in a song.

At ev'ry close she made, th' attending throng
Reply'd, and bore the burden of the song.
Dryden's Fab.

burlésque adj. [Fr. from *burlare,* Ital. to jest.] Jocular; tending to raise laughter, by unnatural or unsuitable language or images.

Homer, in his character of Vulcan and Thersites, in his story of Mars and Venus, in his behaviour of Irus, and in other passages, has been observed to have lapsed into the burlesque character, and to have departed from that serious air, which seems essential to the magnificence of an epick poem. Addison, Spectator, Nº 279.

to burlésque v.a. [from the adjective.] To turn to ridicule.

Would Homer apply the epithet divine to a modern swineherd? if not, it is an evidence, that Eumeus was a man of consequence; otherwise Homer would burlesque his own poetry. Broome's Notes on the Odyssey.

búsiness n.s. [from *busy*.]

1. Employment; multiplicity of affairs.

Must business thee from hence remove? Oh! that's the worst disease of love. Donne.

2. An affair. In this sense it has the plural.

Bestow
Your needful counsel to our businesses, Which crave the instant use.
Shakesp. King Lear.

3. The subject of business; the affair or object that engages the care.

You are so much the business of our souls, that while you are in sight, we can neither look nor think on any else; there are no eyes for other beauties. Dryden.

The great business of the senses, being to take notice of what hurts or advantages the body. Locke.

4. Serious engagement, in opposition to trivial transactions.

I never knew one, who made it his business to lash the faults of other writers, that was not guilty of greater himself. Addis.

He had business enough upon his hands, and was only a poet by accident. Prior's Preface.

When diversion is made the business and study of life, though the actions chosen be in themselves innocent, the excess will render them criminal. Rogers.

5. Right of action.

What business has a tortoise among the clouds? L'Estrange.

6. A point; a matter of question; something to be examined or considered.

Fitness to govern, is a perplexed business; some men, some nations, excel in the one ability, some in the other. Bacon.

7. Something to be transacted.

They were far from the Zidonians, and had no business with any one. Judges, xviii. 7.

8. Something required to be done.

To those people that dwell under or near the equator, this spring would be most pestilent; as for those countries that are nearer the poles, in which number are our own, and the most considerable nations of the world, a perpetual spring will not do their business; they must have longer days, a nearer approach of the sun. Bentley.

9. To do one's business. To kill, destroy, or ruin him.

to buss v.a. [from the noun.] To kiss; to salute with the lips.

Yonder walls, that partly front your town, Yond towers, whose wanton tops do buss the clouds, Must kiss their feet. Shakesp. Troilus and Cressida.

Go to them with this bonnet in thy hand, Thy knee bussing the stones; for, in such business, Action is eloquence. Shakesp. Coriolanus.

C

C, the third letter of the alphabet, has two sounds; one like *k*, as, *call, clock, craft, coal, companion, cuneiform*; the other as *s*, as, *Cæsar, cessation, cinder*. It sounds like *k* before *a*, *o*, *u*, or a consonant; and like *s*, before *e*, *i*, and *y*.

cabál n.s. [*cabale*, Fr. קבלה tradition.]

1. The secret science of the Hebrew rabbins.

2. A body of men united in some close design. A cabal differs from a party, as few from many.

She often interposed her royal authority, to break the cabals which were forming against her first ministers. Addison.

3. Intrigue.

When each, by curs'd cabals of women, strove, To draw th' indulgent king to partial love. Dryden's Aureng.

cábaret n.s. [French.] A tavern.

Suppose this servant passing by some cabaret, or tennis-court, where his comrades were drinking or playing, should stay with them, and drink or play away his money. Bramhall against Hobbes.

to cábbage v.a. [a cant word among taylors.] To steal in cutting clothes.

Your taylor, instead of shreads, cabbages whole yards of cloth. Arbuthnot's History of J. Bull.

cachéxy n.s. [καχεξια.] A general word to express a great variety of symptoms; most commonly it denotes such a distemperature of the humours, as hinders nutrition, and weakens the vital and animal functions, proceeding from weakness of the fibres, and an abuse of the non-naturals, and often from severe acute distempers. Arbuthnot on Diet.

cachinnátion n.s. [*cachinnatio*, Lat.] A loud laughter. D.

cáckerel n.s. A fish, said to make those who eat it laxative.

cacóphony n.s. [κακοφωνια.] A bad sound of words.

to cacúminate v.a. [*cacumino*, Lat.] To make sharp or pyramidal. Dict.

cade n.s. [It is deduced, by Skinner, from *cadeler*, Fr. an old word, which signifies to breed up tenderly.] Tame; soft; delicate; as

a cade lamb, a lamb bred at home.

cádent adj. [*cadens*, Lat.] Falling down.

cádger n.s. A huckster; one who brings butter, eggs, and poultry, from the country to market.

cádi n.s. A magistrate among the Turks, whose office seems to answer to that of a justice of peace.

cæsúra n.s. [Lat.] A figure in poetry, by which a short syllable after a complete foot is made long.

cáisson n.s. [French.] A chest of bombs or powder, laid in the enemy's way, to be fired at their approach.

cáitiff n.s. [*cattivo*, Ital. a slave; whence it came to signify a bad man, with some implication of meanness; as knave in English, and *fur* in Latin; so certainly does slavery destroy virtue.

Ημισυ της αρετης αποαινυται δουλιον ημαρ. Homer.†

A slave and a scoundrel are signified by the same words in many languages.] A mean villain; a despicable knave.

Vile caitiff, vassal of dread and despair, Unworthy of the common breathed air; Why livest thou, dead dog, a longer day, And dost not unto death thyself prepare? Fairy Queen, b. ii.

'Tis not impossible But one, the wicked'st caitiff on the ground, May seem as shy, as grave, as just, as absolute, As Angelo. Shakesp. Measure for Measure.

The wretched caitiff, all alone, As he believ'd, began to moan, And tell his story to himself. Hudibras, p. iii. c. iii.

to cajóle v.a. [*cageoller*, Fr.] To flatter; to sooth; to coax: a low word.

Thought he, 'tis no mean part of civil State-prudence, to cajole the devil. Hudibras, cant. ii. p. iii.

The one affronts him, while the other cajoles and pities him; takes up his quarrel, shakes his head at it, clasps his hand upon his breast, and then protests and protests. L'Estrange.

calásh n.s. [*caleche*, Fr.] A small carriage of pleasure.

*Daniel, a sprightly swain, that us'd to slash
The vig'rous steeds, that drew his lord's calash.*
King's Mully of Mountown.

The ancients used calashes, the figures of several of them being to be seen on ancient monuments. They are very simple, light, and drove by the traveller himself. Arbuthnot on Coins.

cálceated adj. [*calceatus*, Lat.] Shod; fitted with shoes.

calculátor n.s. [from *calculate*.] A computer; a reckoner.

cálculus n.s. [Latin.] The stone in the bladder.

calefáctive adj. [from *calefacio*, Lat.] That which makes any thing hot; heating.

cálends n.s. [*calendæ*, Lat. It has no singular.] The first day of every month among the Romans.

cálenture n.s. [from *caleo*, Lat.] A distemper peculiar to sailors, in hot climates; wherein they imagine the sea to be green fields, and will throw themselves into it, if not restrained. Quincy.

*And for that lethargy was there no cure,
But to be cast into a calenture.* Denham.

*So, by a calenture misled,
The mariner with rapture sees,
On the smooth ocean's azure bed,
Enamell'd fields, and verdant trees;
With eager haste, he longs to rove
In that fantastick scene, and thinks
It must be some enchanted grove;
And in he leaps, and down he sinks.* Swift.

cálid adj. [*calidus*, Lat.] Hot; burning; fervent.

cálif, cáliph n.s. [*khalifa*, Arab. an heir or successor.] A title assumed by the successors of Mahomet among the Saracens, who were vested with absolute power in affairs, both religious and civil.

calíginous adj. [*caliginosus*, Lat.] Obscure; dim; full of darkness.

cállat, cállet n.s. A trull.

*He call'd her whore; a beggar, in his drink,
Could not have laid such terms upon his
   callet.* Shakesp.

to calúmniate v.a. To slander.

One trade or art, even those that should be the most liberal, shall make it their business to disdain and calumniate another. Sprat.

camélopard n.s. [from *camelus* and *pardus*, Lat.] An Abyssinian animal, taller than an elephant, but not so thick. He is so named, because he has a neck and head like a camel; he is spotted like a pard, but his spots are white upon a red ground. The Italians call him *giaraffa*. Trevoux.

camisádo n.s. [*camisa*, a shirt, Ital. *camisium*, low Lat.] An attack made by soldiers in the dark; on which occasion they put their shirts outward, to be seen by each other.

They had appointed the same night, whose darkness would have encreased the fear, to have given a camisado upon the English. Hayward.

canáry n.s. [from the Canary islands.] Wine brought from the Canaries; sack.

I will to my honest knight Falstaff, and drink canary with him.—I think I shall drink in pipe wine first with him; I'll make him dance. Shakesp. Merry Wives of Windsor.

cáncer n.s. [*cancer*, Lat.]

1. A crabfish.

2. The sign of the summer solstice.

*When now no more th' alternate twins are sir'd,
And Cancer reddens with the solar blaze,
Short is the doubtful empire of the night.*
Thomson.

3. A virulent swelling, or sore, not to
   be cured.

Any of these three may degenerate into a schirrus, and that schirrus into a cancer. Wiseman.

As when a cancer on the body feeds,
And gradual death from limb to limb proceeds;
So does the chilness to each vital part,
Spread by degrees, and creeps into the heart.
Addison's Ovid.

cáncrine adj. [from *cancer*.] Having the qualities of a crab.

cándid adj. [*candidus*, Lat.]

1. White. This sense is very rare.

The box receives all black: but, pour'd
  from thence,
The stones came candid forth, the hue of
  innocence. Dryd.

2. Without malice; without deceit; fair; open; ingenuous.

The import of the discourse will, for the most part, if there be no designed fallacy, sufficiently lead candid and intelligent readers into the true meaning of it. Locke.

A candid judge will read each piece of wit, With the same spirit that its authour writ. Pope.

to cándify v.a. [*candifico*, Lat.] To make white; to whiten. Dict.

cánnibal n.s. An anthropophagite; a man-eater.

The cannibals themselves eat no man's flesh, of those that die of themselves, but of such as are slain. Bacon's Nat. Hist.

They were little better than cannibals, who do hunt one another; and he that hath most strength and swiftness, doth eat and devour all his fellows. Davies on Ireland.

  It was my bent to speak,
Of the cannibals that each other eat;
The anthropophagi, and men whose heads
Did grow beneath their shoulders.
Shakesp. Othello.

The captive cannibal, opprest with chains, Yet braves his foes, reviles, provokes, disdains; Of nature fierce, untameable, and proud, He bids defiance to the gaping croud; And spent at last, and speechless as he lies, With firy glances mocks their rage, and dies. Granville.

If an eleventh commandment had been given, Thou shalt not eat human flesh; would not these cannibals have esteemed it more difficult than all the rest? Bentley.

cánon n.s. [κανων.]

1. A rule; a law.

The truth is, they are rules and canons of that law, which is written in all mens hearts; the church had for ever, no less than now, stood bound to observe them, whether the apostle had mentioned them, or no. Hooker, b. iii. § 4.

His books are almost the very canon to judge both doctrine and discipline by. Hooker, Pref.

Religious canons, civil laws are cruel, Then what should war be? Shakesp. Timon.

Canons in logick are such as these: every part of a division, singly taken, must contain less than the whole; and a definition must be peculiar and proper to the thing defined. Watts's Logick.

2. The laws made by ecclesiastical councils.

Canon law is that law, which is made and ordained in a general council, or provincial synod of the church. Ayliffe.

These were looked on as lapsed persons, and great severities of penance were prescribed them, as appears by the canons of Ancyra, and many others. Stillingfleet.

3. The books of Holy Scripture; or the great rule.

Canon also denotes those books of Scripture, which are received as inspired and canonical, to distinguish them from either profane, apocryphal, or disputed books. Thus we say, that Genesis is part of the sacred canon of the Scripture. Ayliffe.

4. A dignitary in cathedral churches.

For deans and canons, or prebends, of cathedral churches, in their first institution, they were of great use in the church; they were to be of counsel with the bishop for his revenue, and for his government in causes ecclesiastical. Bacon.

Swift much admires the place and air,
And longs to be a canon there.
A canon! that's a place too mean:
No, doctor, you shall be a dean,
Two dozen canons round your stall,
And you the tyrant o'er them all. Swift.

5. Canons Regular. Such as are placed in monasteries. Ayliffe.

6. Canons Secular. Lay canons, who have been, as a mark of honour, admitted into some chapters.

7. [Among chirurgeons.] An instrument used in sewing up wounds. Dict.

8. A large sort of printing letter, probably so called from being first used in printing a book of canons; or perhaps from its size, and therefore properly written cannon.

cant n.s. [probably from *cantus*, Lat. implying the odd tone of voice used by vagrants; but imagined by some to be corrupted from *quaint*.]

1. A corrupt dialect used by beggars and vagabonds.

2. A particular form of speaking peculiar to some certain class or body of men.

I write not always in the proper terms of navigation, land service, or in the cant of any profession. Dryden.

If we would trace out the original of that flagrant and avowed impiety, which has prevailed among us for some years, we should find, that it owes its rise to that cant and hypocrisy, which had taken possession of the people's minds in the times of the great rebellion. Addison, Freeholder, Nº 37.

Astrologers, with an old paltry cant, and a few pot-hooks for planets, to amuse the vulgar, have too long been suffered to abuse the world. Swift's Predictions for the Year 1701.

A few general rules, with a certain cant of words, has sometimes set up an illiterate heavy writer, for a most judicious and formidable critick. Addison, Spectator, Nº 291.

3. A whining pretension to goodness, in formal and affected terms.

Of promise prodigal, while pow'r you want,
And preaching in the self-denying cant.
Dryden's Aurengz.

4. Barbarous jargon.

The affectation of some late authours, to introduce and multiply cant words, is the most ruinous corruption in any language. Swift.

5. Auction.

Numbers of these tenants, or their descendants, are now offering to sell their leases by cant, even those which were for lives. Swift.

to cant v.n. [from the noun.] To talk in the jargon of particular professions, or in any kind of formal affected language, or with a peculiar and studied tone of voice.

Men cant endlessly about materia and forma; hunt chimeras by rules of art, or dress up ignorance in words of bulk or sound, which may stop up the mouth of enquiry. Glanville's Scepsis Scientifica.

That uncouth affected garb of speech, or canting language rather, if I may so call it, which they have of late taken up, is the signal distinction and characteristical note of that, which, in that their new language, they call the godly party. Sanderson.

The busy, subtile serpents of the law,
Did first my mind from true obedience draw;
While I did limits to the king prescribe,
And took for oracles that canting tribe.
Roscommon.

Unskill'd in schemes by planets to foreshow,
Like canting rascals, how the wars will go.
Dryden's Juven.

cantata n.s. [Ital.] A song.

cantátion n.s. [from *canto*, Lat.] The act of singing.

cáper n.s. [from *caper*, Latin, a goat.] A leap; a jump; a skip.

We that are true lovers, run into strange capers; but as all is mortal in nature, so is

all nature in love mortal in folly. Shakesp.
As you like it.

*Flimnap, the treasurer, is allowed to cut a
caper on the strait rope, at least an inch higher
than any other lord in the whole empire.*
Swift's Gulliver's Travels.

captátion n.s. [from *capto*, Lat.] The
practice of catching favour or applause;
courtship; flattery.

*I am content my heart should be discovered,
without any of those dresses, or popular
captations, which some men use in their
speeches.* King Charles.

capuchín n.s. A female garment, consisting
of a cloak and hood, made in imitation of
the dress of capuchin monks; whence its
name is derived.

cardíacal, cárdiack adj. [καρδια, the
heart.] Cordial; having the quality of
invigorating.

cárious adj. [*cariosus*, Lat.] Rotten.

*I discovered the blood to arise by a carious
tooth.* Wiseman.

cárnival n.s. [*carnaval*, Fr.] The feast held
in the popish countries before Lent.

*The whole year is but one mad carnival, and
we are voluptuous not so much upon desire or
appetite, as by way of exploit and bravery.*
Decay of Piety.

cárroty adj. [from *carrot*.] Spoken of red
hair, on account of its resemblance in colour
to carrots.

cartóon n.s. [*cartone*, Ital.] A painting or
drawing upon large paper.

*It is with a vulgar idea that the world beholds
the cartoons of Raphael, and every one feels
his share of pleasure and entertainment.*
Watts's Logick.

cáseous adj. [*caseus*, Lat.] Resembling
cheese; cheesy.

*Its fibrous parts are from the caseous parts of
the chyle.* Floyer on Humours.

cástanet n.s. [*castaneta*, Sp.] Small shells of

ivory, or hard wood, which dancers rattle in
their hands.

*If there had been words enow between them,
to have expressed provocation, they had gone
together by the ears like a pair of castanets.*
Congreve's Way of the World.

cástellain n.s. [*castellano*, Span.] The
captain, governour, or constable of a castle.

cat n.s. [*katz*, Teuton. *chat*, Fr.] A
domestick animal that catches mice,
commonly reckoned by naturalists the
lowest order of the leonine species.

   'Twas you incens'd the rabble:
Cats, that can judge as fitly of his worth,
As I can of those mysteries, which heav'n
Will not have earth to know. Shakesp.
Coriolanus.

Thrice the brinded cat hath mew'd. Shakesp.
Macbeth.

*A cat, as she beholds the light, draws the ball
of her eye small and long, being covered over
with a green skin, and dilates it at pleasure.*
Peacham on Drawing.

cátaphract n.s. [*cataphracta*, Lat.] A
horseman in complete armour.

On each side went armed guards,
Both horse and foot before him and behind,
Archers and slingers, cataphracts and spears.
Milt. Agonist.

catástrophe n.s. [καταστροφη.]

1. The change or revolution, which
   produces the conclusion or final event of
   a dramatick piece.

*Pat!—He comes like the catastrophe of the old
comedy.* Shakesp. King Lear.

*That philosopher declares for tragedies, whose
catastrophes are unhappy, with relation to the
principal characters.* Dennis.

2. A final event; a conclusion generally
   unhappy.

*Here was a mighty revolution, the most
horrible and portentuous catastrophe that
nature ever yet saw; an elegant and habitable
earth quite shattered.* Woodward's Nat. Hist.

cátcal n.s. [from *cat* and *call*.] A squeaking instrument, used in the playhouse to condemn plays.

A young lady, at the theatre, conceived a passion for a notorious rake that headed a party of catcals. Spectator, N° 602.

Three catcals be the bribe
Of him, whose chatt'ring shames the monkey
   tribe. Pope.

cátchword n.s. [from *catch* and *word*. With printers.] The word at the corner of the page under the last line, which is repeated at the top of the next page.

caterpíllar n.s. [This word Skinner and Minshew are inclined to derive from *chatte peluse*, a weasel; it seems easily deducible from *cates*, food, and *piller*, Fr. to rob; the animal that eats up the fruits of the earth.] A worm which, when it gets wings, is sustained by leaves and fruits.

The caterpillar breedeth of dew and leaves; for we see infinite caterpillars breed upon trees and hedges, by which the leaves of the trees or hedges are consumed. Bacon.

Auster is drawn with a pot pouring forth water, with which descend grasshoppers, caterpillars, and creatures bred by moisture. Peacham on Drawing.

cates n.s. [of uncertain etymology; Skinner imagines it may be corrupted from *delicate;* which is not likely, because Junius observes, that the Dutch have *kater* in the same sense with our *cater*. It has no singular.] Viands; food; dish of meat; generally employed to signify nice and luxurious food.

The fair acceptance, Sir, creates
The entertainment perfect, not the cates.
Ben Johnson.

O wasteful riot, never well content
With low priz'd fare; hunger ambitious
Of cates by land and sea far fetcht and sent.
Raleigh.

Alas, how simple to these cates,
Was that crude apple, that diverted Eve!
Par. Lost, b. ii.

They by th' alluring odour drawn, in haste
Fly to the dulcet cates, and crouding sip
Their palatable bane. Philips.

With costly cates she stain'd her frugal board,
Then with ill-gotten wealth she bought a
   lord. Arbuthnot.

cathéter n.s. [καθετηρ.] A hollow and somewhat crooked instrument, to thrust into the bladder, to assist in bringing away the urine, when the passage is stopped by a stone or gravel.

A large clyster, suddenly injected, hath frequently forced the urine out of the bladder; but if it fail, a catheter must help you. Wiseman's Surgery.

cátholick adj. [*catholique*, Fr. καθολικος.] Universal or general.

1. The church of Jesus Christ is called catholick, because it extends throughout the world, and is not limited by time.

2. Some truths are said to be catholick, because they are received by all the faithful.

3. Catholick is often set in opposition to heretick or sectary, and to schismatick.

4. Catholick, or canonical epistles, are seven in number; that of St. James, two of St. Peter, three of St. John, and that of St. Jude. They are called catholick, because they are directed to all the faithful, and not to any particular church; and canonical, because they contain excellent rules of faith and morality. Calmet.

Doubtless the success of those your great and catholick endeavours will promote the empire of man over nature, and bring plentiful accession of glory to your nation. Glanville's Scepsis.

Those systems undertake to give an account of the formation of the universe, by mechanical hypotheses of matter, moved either uncertainly, or according to some catholick laws. Ray.

cátsup n.s. A kind of pickle, made from mushrooms.

And, for our home-bred British cheer,
Botargo, catsup, and cavier. Swift.

cáudebeck n.s. A sort of light hats, so called from a town in France where they were first made. Phillips's World of Words.

cáudle n.s. [*chaudeau*, Fr.] A mixture of wine and other ingredients, given to women in childbed, and sick persons.

Ye shall have a hempen caudle then, and the help of a hatchet. Shakesp. Henry VI. p. ii.

He had good broths, caudle, and such like; and I believe he did drink some wine. Wiseman's Surgery.

cécity n.s. [*cæcitas*, Lat.] Blindness; privation of sight.

They are not blind, nor yet distinctly see; there is in them no cecity, yet more than a cecutiency; they have sight enough to discern the light, though not perhaps to distinguish objects or colours. Brown's Vulgar Errours.

cénatory adj. [from *ceno*, to sup, Lat.] Relating to supper.

The Romans washed, were anointed, and wore a cenatory garment; and the same was practised by the Jews. Brown's Vulgar Errours.

cénsor n.s. [*censor*, Lat.]

1. An officer of Rome, who had the power of correcting manners.

2. One who is given to censure and exprobation.

Ill-natur'd censors of the present age,
And fond of all the follies of the past. Roscommon.

The most severe censor cannot but be pleased with the prodigality of his wit, though, at the same time, he could have wished, that the master of it had been a better manager. Dryd.

cénto n.s. [*cento*, Lat.] A composition formed by joining scrapes from other authours.

It is quilted, as it were, out of shreds of divers poets, such as scholars call a cento. Camden's Remains.

If any man think the poem a cento, our poet will but have done the same in jest which Boileau did in earnest. Advertisement to Pope's Dunciad.

centuriátor n.s. [from *century*.] A name given to historians, who distinguish times by centuries; which is generally the method of ecclesiastical history.

The centuriators of Magdeburg were the first that discovered this grand imposture. Ayliffe's Parergon.

céphalalgy n.s. [κεφαλαλγια.] The headach. Dict.

cerulífick adj. [from *ceruleous*.] Having the power to produce a blue colour.

The several species of rays, as the rubifick, cerulifick, and others are separated one from another. Grew's Cosmol. Sacra.

cerúmen n.s. [Latin.] The wax or excrement of the ear.

Cesárian adj. [from *Cæsar*.] The Cesarian section is cutting a child out of the womb either dead or alive, when it cannot otherwise be delivered. Which circumstance, it is said, first gave the name of *Cæsar* to the Roman family so called. Quincy.

CH has, in words purely English, or fully naturalized, the sound of tch; a peculiar pronunciation, which it is hard to describe in words. In some words derived from the French, it has the sound of sh, as chaise; and, in some derived from the Greek, the sound of k, as cholerick.

chair n.s. [*chair*, Fr.]

1. A moveable seat.

Whether thou choose Cervantes' serious air,
Or laugh and shake in Rab'lais' easy chair,
Or praise the court, or magnify mankind,
Or thy griev'd country's copper chains unbind. Pope.

If a chair be defined a seat for a single person, with a back belonging to it, then a stool is a seat for a single person, without a back. Watts's Logick.

2. A seat of justice, or of authority.

He makes for England, here to claim the
   crown.—
—Is the chair empty? Is the sword unsway'd?
Is the king dead? Shakesp. Richard III.

If thou be that princely eagle's bird,
Show thy descent by gazing 'gainst the sun;
For chair and dukedom, throne and
   kingdom, say;
Either that's thine, or else thou wert not his.
Shakesp. Henry VI. p. iii.

   The honour'd gods
Keep Rome in safety, and the chairs of justice
Supply with worthy men. Shakesp.
Coriolanus.

The committee of the commons appointed Mr.
Pym to take the chair. Clarendon.

   Her grace sat down to rest a while,
In a rich chair of state. Shakesp. Henry
VIII.

In this high temple, on a chair of state,
The seat of audience, old Latinus sate.
Dryden's Æneid.

3. A vehicle born by men; a sedan.

Think what an equipage thou hast in air,
And view with scorn two pages and a chair.
Pope.

cháirman n.s. [from *chair* and *man*.]

1. The president of an assembly.

In these assemblies generally one person is
chosen chairman or moderator, to keep the
several speakers to the rules of order. Watts's
Improvement of the Mind.

2. One whose trade it is to carry a chair.

One elbows him, one justles in the shole,
A rafter breaks his head, or chairman's pole.
Dryden.

   Troy chairmen bore the wooden steed,
Pregnant with Greeks, impatient to be freed;
Those bully Greeks, who, as the moderns do,
Instead of paying chairmen, run them
   through. Swift.

chalcógraphy n.s. [χαλκογραφια.]
Engraving in brass.

cháncery n.s. [from *chancellor;* probably *chancellery;* then shortened.] The court of equity and conscience, moderating the rigour of other courts, that are tied to the letter of the law; whereof the lord chancellor of England is the chief judge, or the lord keeper of the great seal. Cowel.

The contumacy and contempt of the party
must be signified in the court of chancery, by
the bishops letters under the seal episcopal.
Ayliffe's Parergon.

cháncre n.s. [*chancre*, Fr.] An ulcer usually arising from venereal maladies.

It is possible he was not well cured, and would
have relapsed with a chancre. Wiseman.

chángeling n.s. [from *change;* the word arises from an odd superstitious opinion, that the fairies steal away children, and put others that are ugly and stupid in their places.]

1. A child left or taken in the place of
   another.

And her base elfin breed there for thee left;
Such, men do changelings call, so chang'd
   by fairies theft. Spenser's Fairy Queen,
b. i. c. x. stanz. 65.

   She, as her attendant, hath
A lovely boy stol'n from an Indian king;
She never had so sweet a changeling.
Shakesp. Midsummer Night's Dream.

2. An ideot; a fool; a natural.

Changelings and fools of heav'n, and
   thence shut out,
Wildly we roam in discontent about.
Dryden's Tyrr. Love.

Would any one be a changeling, because he is
less determined by wise considerations than
a wise man? Locke.

3. One apt to change; a waverer.

   'Twas not long
Before from world to world they swung;
As they had turn'd from side to side,
And as they changelings liv'd, they died.
Hudibras.

chá́racter n.s. [*character*, Lat. χαρακτηρ.]

1. A mark; a stamp; a representation.

In outward also her resembling less
His image, who made both; and less expressing
The character of that dominion giv'n
O'er other creatures. Paradise Lost,
b. viii. l. 542.

2. A letter used in writing or printing.

But his neat cookery!—
He cut our roots in characters. Shakesp.
Cymbeline.

The purpose is perspicuous even as substance,
Whose grossness little characters sum up.
Shakesp. Troilus and Cressida.

It were much to be wished, that there were
throughout the world but one sort of character
for each letter, to express it to the eye; and that
exactly proportioned to the natural alphabet
formed in the mouth. Holder's Elements
of Speech.

3. The hand or manner of writing.

I found the letter thrown in at the casement of
my closet.
—You know the character to be your brother's.
Shak. King Lear.

4. A representation of any man as to his
personal qualities.

Each drew fair characters, yet none
Of these they feign'd, excels their own.
Denham.

5. An account of any thing as good or bad.

This subterraneous passage is much mended,
since Seneca gave so bad a character of it.
Addison on Italy.

6. The person with his assemblage of
qualities.

In a tragedy, or epick poem, the hero of the
piece must be advanced foremost to the view
of the reader or spectator; he must outshine the
rest of all the characters; he must appear the
prince of them, like the sun in the Copernican
system, encompassed with the less noble
planets. Dryden's Dufresnoy.

Homer has excelled all the heroick poets that
ever wrote, in the multitude and variety of
his characters; every god that is admitted into
his poem, acts a part which would have been
suitable to no other deity. Addison,
Spectator, Nº 273.

7. Personal qualities; particular constitution
of the mind.

Nothing so true as what you once let fall,
Most women have no characters at all. Pope.

8. Adventitious qualities impressed by
a post or office.

The chief honour of the magistrate consists in
maintaining the dignity of his character by
suitable actions. Atterbury.

chaste adj. [*chaste*, Fr. *castus*, Lat.]

1. Pure from all commerce of sexes; as
a chaste virgin.

2. With respect to language; pure;
uncorrupt; not mixed with barbarous
phrases.

3. Without obscenity.

Among words which signify the same
principal ideas, some are clean and decent,
others unclean; some chaste, others obscene.
Watts's Logick.

4. True to the marriage bed.

Love your children, be discreet, chaste, keepers
at home. Titus, ii. 5.

cheese n.s. [*caseus*, Lat. *cyse*, Saxon.] A kind
of food made by pressing the curd of
coagulated milk, and suffering the mass
to dry.

I will rather trust a Fleming with my butter,
parson Hugh the Welchman with my cheese,
than my wife with herself. Shakesp. Merry
Wives of Windsor.

chéésecake n.s. [from *cheese* and *cake*.] A
cake made of soft curds, sugar and butter.

Effeminate he sat, and quiet;
Strange product of a cheesecake diet. Prior.

Where many a man at variance with his wife,
With soft'ning mead and cheesecake ends the
strife. King's Art of Cookery.

chess n.s. [*echec*, Fr.] A nice and abstruse

game, in which two sets of men are moved in opposition to each other.

This game the Persian magi did invent,
The force of Eastern wisdom to express;
From thence to busy Europeans sent,
And styl'd by modern Lombards pensive chess.
Denham.

So have I seen a king on chess,
(His rooks and knights withdrawn,
His queen and bishops in distress)
Shifting about, grow less and less,
With here and there a pawn. Dryden.

chicánery n.s. [*chicanerie*, Fr.] Sophistry; mean arts of wrangle.

His anger at his ill success, caused him to destroy the greatest part of these reports; and only to preserve such as discovered most of the chicanery and futility of the practice.
Arbuthnot and Pope's Mart. Scrib.

the chíckenpox n.s. An exanthematous distemper, so called from its being of no very great danger.

chíliad n.s. [from χιλιας.] A thousand; a collection or sum containing a thousand.

We make cycles and periods of years; as decads, centuries, chiliads, &c. for the use of computation in history. Holder.

chiliáedron n.s. [from χιλια.] A figure of a thousand sides.

chiméra n.s. [*Chimæra*, Lat.] A vain and wild fancy, as remote from reality as the existence of the poetical chimera, a monster feigned to have the head of a lion, the belly of a goat, and the tail of a dragon.

In short, the force of dreams is of a piece,
Chimeras all; and more absurd, or less.
Dryden's Fables.

No body joins the voice of a sheep with the shape of a horse, to be the complex ideas of any real substances, unless he has a mind to fill his head with chimeras, and his discourse with unintelligible words. Locke.

chína n.s. [from *China*, the country where it is made.] China ware; porcelain; a species of vessels made in China, dimly transparent, partaking of the qualities of earth and glass. They are made by mingling two kinds of earth, of which one easily vitrifies; the other resists a very strong heat: when the vitrifiable earth is melted into glass, they are completely burnt.

Spleen, vapours, or small pox, above them all,
And mistress of herself, tho' china fall.
Pope's Epist. ii.

After supper, carry your plate and china together in the same basket.
Swift's Directions to the Butler.

chirágrical adj. [*chiragra*, Lat.] Having the gout in the hand; subject to the gout in the hand.

Chiragrical persons do suffer in the finger as well as in the rest, and sometimes first of all.
Brown's Vulgar Errors, b. iv. c. 5.

chirúrgeon n.s. [χειρουργος, from χειρ, the hand, and εργον, work.] One that cures ailments, not by internal medicines, but outward applications. It is now generally pronounced, and by many written, *surgeon*.

When a man's wounds cease to smart, only because he has lost his feeling, they are nevertheless mortal, for his not seeing his need of a chirurgeon. South's Sermons.

chítchat n.s. [corrupted by reduplication from *chat*.] Prattle; idle prate; idle talk. A word only used in ludicrous conversation.

I am a member of a female society, who call ourselves the chitchat club. Spectat. Nº 560.

chítterlings n.s. without singular. [from *schyterlingh*, Dut. Minshew; from *kutteln*, Germ. Skinner.] The guts; the bowels. Skinner.

chívalrous adj. [from *chivalry*.] Relating to chivalry, or errant knighthood; knightly; warlike; adventurous; daring. A word now out of use.

And noble minds of yore allied were
In brave pursuit of chivalrous emprise.
Fairy Queen, b. i.

chócolate n.s. [*chocolate*, Span.]

1. The nut of the cacao-tree.

The tree hath a rose flower, of a great number of petals, from whose empalement arises the pointal, being a tube cut into many parts, which becomes a fruit shaped somewhat like a cucumber, and deeply furrowed, in which are contained several seeds, collected into an oblong heap, and slit down, somewhat like almonds. It is a native of America, and is found in great plenty in several places between the Tropicks, and grows wild. See *cocoa.* Miller.

2. The cake or mass, made by grinding the kernel of the cacaonut with other substances, to be dissolved in hot water.

The Spaniards were the first who brought chocolate into use in Europe, to promote the consumption of their cacaonuts, achiot, and other drugs, which their West Indies furnish, and which enter the composition of chocolate. Chambers.

3. The liquor, made by a solution of chocolate in hot water.

Chocolate is certainly much the best of these three exotick liquors: its oil seems to be both rich, alimentary, and anodyne. Arbuthnot on Aliments.

In fumes of burning chocolate shall glow, And tremble at the sea that froths below! Pope.

chócolate-house n.s. [*chocolate* and *house.*] A house where company is entertained with chocolate.

Ever since that time, Lisander has been twice a day at the chocolate-house. Tatler, N° 54.

chóky adj. [from *choke.*] That which has the power of suffocation.

chóler n.s. [*cholera*, Lat. from χολη.]

1. The bile.

Marcilius Ficimus increases these proportions, adding two more of pure choler. Wotton on Education.

There would be a main defect, if such a feeding animal, and so subject unto diseases from bilious causes, should want a proper

conveyance for choler. Brown's Vulgar Errours.

2. The humour, which, by its super-abundance, is supposed to produce irascibility.

It engenders choler, planteth anger; And better 'twere that both of us did fast, Since, of ourselves, ourselves are cholerick, Than feed it with such over-roasted flesh. Sh. Tam. of Shrew.

3. Anger; rage.

Put him to choler straight: he hath been used Ever to conquer, and to have his word Of contradiction. Shakesp. Coriolanus.

He, methinks, is no great scholar, Who can mistake desire for choler. Prior.

chop-house n.s. [*chop* and *house.*] A mean house of entertainment, where provision ready dressed is sold.

I lost my place at the chop-house, where every man eats in publick a mess of broth, or chop of meat, in silence. Spectat.

Christian n.s. [*Christianus,* Lat.] A professor of the religion of Christ.

We christians have certainly the best and the holiest, the wisest and most reasonable religion in the world. Tillotson.

Christian-name n.s. The name given at the font, distinct from the Gentilitious name, or surname.

chrónogram n.s. [χρονος, time, and γραφω, to write.] An inscription including the date of any action. Of this kind the following is an example:

Gloria lausque Deo, *sæ*CL*or*VM *in sæc*V*la sunt.*[†]

A chronogrammatical verse, which includes not only this year 1660, but numerical letters enough to reach above a thousand years further, until the year 2867. Howel's Parley.

chronóloger n.s. [χρονος, time, and λογος, doctrine] He that studies or explains the science of computing past time, or of ranging past events according to their proper years.

Chronologers differ among themselves about most great epocha's. Holder on Time.

a chronómeter n.s. [χρονος and μετρον.] An instrument for the exact mensuration of time.

According to observation made with a pendulum chronometer, a bullet, at its first discharge, flies five hundred and ten yards in five half seconds. Derham's Physico-Theology.

chúffily adv. [from *chuffy.*] Surlily; stomachfully.

John answered chuffily. Clarissa.

chum n.s. [*chom,* Armorick, to live together.] A chamber fellow; a term used in the universities.

church n.s. [*circe,* Sax. κυριακη.]

1. The collective body of christians, usually termed the catholick church.

The church being a supernatural society, doth differ from natural societies in this; that the persons unto whom we associate ourselves in the one, are men, simply considered as men; but they to whom we be joined in the other, are God, angels, and holy men. Hooker, b. i. p. 45.

2. The body of christians adhering to one particular opinion, or form of worship.

The church is a religious assembly, or the large fair building where they meet; and sometimes the same word means a synod of bishops, or of presbyters; and in some places it is the pope and a general council. Watts's Logick.

3. The place which christians consecrate to the worship of God.

That churches were consecrated unto none but the Lord only, the very general name chiefly doth sufficiently shew: church doth signify no other thing than the Lord's house. Hook.

Tho' you unty the winds, and let them fight Against the churches. Shakesp. Macbeth.

4. It is used frequently in conjunction with other words; as church-member, the member of a church; church-power, spiritual or ecclesiastical authority.

churl n.s. [*ceorl,* Sax. *carl,* in German, is *strong,* rusticks being always observed to be strong bodied.]

1. A rustick; a countryman; a labouret.

One of the baser sort, which they call churls, being reproved for his oath, answered confidently, that his lord commanded him. Spenser's State of Ireland.

*Churl, upon thy eyes I throw
All the pow'r this charm doth owe.*
Shak. Mids. Night's Dr.

*From this light cause th' infernal maid prepares
The country churls to mischief, hate, and wars.* Dryd. Æn.

2. A rude, surly, ill-bred man.

A churl's courtesy rarely comes, but either for gain or falshood. Sidney, b. ii.

3. A miser; a niggard; a selfish or greedy wretch.

*Poison, I see, hath been his timeless end!
O churl, drink all, and leave no friendly drop
To help me after.* Shakesp. Romeo and Juliet.

chymist n.s. See *chymistry.* A professor of chymistry; a philosopher by fire.

*The starving chymist, in his golden views
Supremely blest.* Pope's Essay on Man, Epist. ii.

chymistry n.s. [derived by some from χυμος, juice, or χυω, to melt; by others from an oriental word, *kema,* black. According to the etymology, it is written with *y* or *e.*] An art whereby sensible bodies contained in vessels, or capable of being contained therein, are so changed, by means of certain instruments, and principally fire, that their several powers and virtues are thereby discovered, with a view to philosophy, or medicine. Boerhaave.

Operations of chymistry fall short of vital force: no chymist can make milk or blood of grass. Arbuthnot on Aliment.

cibárious adj. [*cibarius,* Lat. from *cibus,* food.] Relating to food; useful for food; edible.

ciliary adj. [*cilium*, Lat.] Belonging to the eyelids.

The ciliary processes, or rather the ligaments, observed in the inside of the sclerotick tunicles of the eye, do serve instead of a muscle, by the contraction, to alter the figure of the eye. Ray on Creation.

cipher n.s. [*chifre*, Fr. *zifra*, Ital. *cifra*, low Lat. from an oriental root.]

1. An arithmetical character, by which some number is noted; a figure.

2. An arithmetical mark, which, standing for nothing itself, increases the value of the other figures.

Mine were the very cipher of a function,
To find the faults, whose fine stands in record,
And let go by the actor. Shakesp. Measure for Measure.

If the people be somewhat in the election, you cannot make them nulls or ciphers in the privation or translation. Bac.

As, in accounts, ciphers and figures pass for real sums, so names pass for things. South's Sermons.

3. An intertexture of letters engraved usually on boxes or plate.

Troy flam'd in burnish'd gold; and o'er the throne,
Arms and the man in golden ciphers shone. Pop. Temp. of F.

Some mingling stir the melted tar, and some Deep on the new-shorn vagrant's heaving side, To stamp the master's cipher, ready stand. Thoms. Summer.

4. A character in general.

In succeeding times this wisdom began to be written in ciphers and characters, and letters bearing the form of creatures. Raleigh's History of the World.

5. A secret or occult manner of writing, or the key to it.

This book, as long liv'd as the elements,
In cipher writ, or new made idioms. Donne.

He was pleased to command me to stay at London, to send and receive all his letters; and

I was furnished with mine several ciphers, in order to it. Denham's Dedication.

circumforáneous adj. [*circumforaneus*, Lat.] Wandering from house to house. As a circumforaneous fidler; one that plays at doors.

cit n.s. [contracted from *citizen*.] An inhabitant of a city, in an ill sense. A pert low townsman; a pragmatical trader.

We bring you now to show what different things, The cits or clowns are from the courts of kings. Johnson.

Study your race, or the soil of your family will dwindle into cits or squires, or run up into wits or madmen. Tatler.

Barnard, thou art a cit, with all thy worth; But Bug and D—l, their honours, and so forth. Pop. Hor.[†]

cítizen n.s. [*civis*, Lat. *citoyen*, French.]

1. A freeman of a city; not a foreigner; not a slave.

All inhabitants within these walls are not properly citizens, but only such as are called freemen. Raleigh's Hist. World.

2. A townsman; a man of trade; not a gentleman.

When he speaks not like a citizen,
You find him like a soldier. Shakespeare's Coriolanus.

3. An inhabitant; a dweller in any place.

Far from noisy Rome, secure, he lives; And one more citizen to Sibyl gives. Dryden's Juvenal.

cívil adj. [*civilis*, Latin.]

1. Relating to the community; political; relating to the city or government.

God gave them laws of civil regimen, and would not permit their commonweal to be governed by any other laws than his own. Hooker, b. iii. N⁰ 11.

Part such as appertain To civil justice; part, religious rites Of sacrifice. Milton's Paradise Lost, b. xii. l. 231.

But there is another unity, which would be most advantageous to our country; and that is your endeavour after a civil, a political union in the whole nation. Sprat's Sermon.

2. Relating to any man as a member of a community.

Break not your promise, unless it be unlawful or impossible; either out of your natural, or out of your civil power. Taylor.

3. Not in anarchy; not wild; not without rule or government.

For rudest minds with harmony were caught, And civil life was by the muses taught. Roscommon.

4. Not foreign; intestine.

From a civil war, God of his mercy defend us, as that which is most desperate of all others. Bacon to Villers.

5. Not ecclesiastical; as, the ecclesiastical courts are controlled by the civil.

6. Not natural; as, a person banished or outlawed is said to suffer civil, though not natural death.

7. Not military; as, the civil magistrates authority is obstructed by war.

8. Not criminal; as, This is a civil process, not a criminal prosecution.

9. Civilised; not barbarous.

England was very rude and barbarous; for it is but even the other day since England grew civil. Spenser on Ireland.

10. Complaisant; civilised; gentle; well bred; elegant of manners; not rude; not brutal; not coarse.

I heard a mermaid, on a dolphin's back, Uttering such dulcet and harmonious breath, That the rude sea grew civil at her song. Shakespeare.

He was civil and well natured, never refusing to teach another. Dryden's Dufresnoy.

And fall these sayings from that gentle tongue, Where civil speech and soft persuasion hung. Prior.

11. Grave; sober; not gay or shewy.

Thus night oft see me in thy pale career, 'Till civil suited morn appear. Milton's Poems.

12. Relating to the ancient consular or imperial government; as, civil law.

No woman had it, but a civil doctor. Shak. Merch. of Ven.

civílian n.s. [*civilis*, Lat.] One that professes the knowledge of the old Roman law, and of general equity.

The professors of that law, called civilians, because the civil law is their guide, should not be discountenanced nor discouraged. Bacon's Advice to Villers.

A depending kingdom is a term of art, unknown to all ancient civilians, and writers upon government. Swift.

to cívilize v.a. [from *civil.*] To reclaim from savageness and brutality; to instruct in the arts of regular life.

We send the graces and the muses forth, To civilize and to instruct the North. Waller.

Musæus first, then Orpheus civilize Mankind, and gave the world their deities. Denham.

Amongst those who are counted the civilized part of mankind, this original law of nature still takes place. Locke.

Osiris, or the Bacchus of the antients, is reported to have civilized the Indians, and reigned amongst them fifty-two years. Arbuthnot on Coins.

to clappercláw v.a. [from *clap* and *claw.*] To tonguebeat; to scold.

Now they are clapperclawing one another, I'll go look on. Shakespeare's Troilus and Cressida.

They've always been at daggers-drawing, And one another clapperclawing. Hudibras, part ii. canto 2.

clássical, clássick adj. [*classicus*, Latin]

1. Relating to antique authors; relating to literature.

Poetick fields encompass me around,
And still I seem to tread on classick ground.
Addison.

With them the genius of classick learning
dwelleth, and from them it is derived.
Felton on the Classicks.

2. Of the first order or rank.

From this standard the value of the Roman
weights and coins are deduced: in the settling
of which I have followed Mr. Greaves, who
may be justly reckoned a classical author on
this subject. Arbuthnot on Coins.

clássick n.s. [*classicus*, Lat.] An author of
the first rank: usually taken for ancient
authors.

clícker n.s. [from *click*.] A low word for the
servant of a salesman, who stands at the
door to invite customers.

climactérick, climactérical adj. [from
climacter.] Containing a certain number of
years, at the end of which some great
change is supposed to befal the body.

Certain observable years are supposed to
be attended with some considerable
change in the body; as the seventh year;
the twenty-first, made up of three times
seven; the forty-ninth, made up of seven
times seven; the sixty-third, being nine
times seven; and the eighty-first, which is
nine times nine: which two last are called
the grand climactericks.

The numbers seven and nine, multiplied into
themselves, do make up sixty-three, commonly
esteemed the great climacterical of our lives.
Brown's Vulgar Errours, b. iv. c. 12.

Your lordship being now arrived at your great
climacterique, yet give no proof of the least
decay of your excellent judgment and
comprehension. Dryden.

My mother is something better, tho', at her
advanced age, every day is a climacterick.
Pope.

clinch n.s. [from the verb.]

1. A word used in a double meaning;
   a pun; an ambiguity; a duplicity of

meaning, with an identity of expression.

Such as they are, I hope they will prove,
without a clinch, luciferous searching after
the nature of light. Boyle.

Pure clinches the suburbian muse affords,
And Panton waging harmless war with
  words. Dryden.

Here one poor word a hundred clinches makes.
Pope.

2. That part of the cable which is fastened
   to the ring of the anchor.

clódpate n.s. [*clod* and *pate*.] A stupid
fellow; a dolt; a thickscull.

clótpoll n.s. [from *clot* and *poll*.]

1. Thickskull; blockhead.

What says the fellow, there? call the clotpoll
back. Shakes.

2. Head, in scorn.

I have sent Clotens clotpoll down the stream,
In embassy to his mother. Shakespeare's
Cymbeline.

clown n.s. [imagined by Skinner and Junius
to be contracted from *colonus*. It seems rather
a Saxon word, corrupted from *lown; loen,*
Dut. a word nearly of the same import.]

1. A rustick; a country fellow; a churl.

He came out with all his clowns, horst upon
cart-jades. Sidney, b. ii.

The clowns, a boist'rous, rude, ungovern'd crew,
With furious haste to the loud summons flew.
Dryden's Æn.

2. A coarse ill-bred man.

In youth a coxcomb, and in age a clown.
Spectator.

A country squire, represented with no other
vice but that of being a clown, and having the
provincial accent. Swift.

club n.s. [*clwppa*, Welsh; *kluppel*, Dutch.]

1. A heavy stick; a staff intended for
   offence.

He strove his combred club to quit
Out of the earth. Spenser's Fairy Queen,
b. i. cant. 8.

As he pulled off his helmet, a butcher slew him with the stroak of a club. Hayward.

Arm'd with a knotty club another came. Dryden's Æn.

2. The name of one of the suits of cards.

The clubs black tyrant first her victim died, Spite of his haughty mien and barb'rous pride. Pope.

3. [From *cleofan*, to divide. Skinner.] The shot or dividend of a reckoning, paid by the company in just proportions.

A fuddling couple sold ale: their humour was to drink drunk, upon their own liquor: they laid down their club, and this they called forcing a trade. L'Estrange.

4. An assembly of good fellows, meeting under certain conditions.†

What right has any man to meet in factious clubs to vilify the government? Dryden's Medal. Dedication.

5. Concurrence; contribution; joint charge.

He's bound to vouch them for his own, Tho' got b' implicite generation, And general club of all the nation. Hudibras, p. ii. cant. 1.

cóctile adj. [*coctilis*, Lat.] Made by baking, as a brick.

codílle n.s. [*codille*, Fr. *codillo*, Span.] A term at ombre, when the game is won against the player.

She sees, and trembles at th' approaching ill, Just in the jaws of ruin, and codille. Pope's Rape of the Lock.

cóffee n.s. [It is originally Arabick, pronounced *caheu* by the Turks, and *cahuah* by the Arabs.] The tree is a species of Arabick *jessamine*, which see. It is found to succeed as well in the Caribbee islands as in their native place of growth: but whether the coffee produced in the West Indies will prove as good as that from Mocha in Arabia Felix, time will discover. The berry brought from the Levant is most esteemed; and the berry, when ripe, is found as hard as horn. Miller.

Coffee also denotes a drink prepared from the berries, very familiar in Europe for these eighty years, and among the turks for one hundred and fifty. Some refer the invention of coffee to the Persians; from whom it was learned, in the fifteenth century, by a mufti of Aden, a city near the mouth of the Red Sea, where it soon came in vogue, and passed from thence to Mecca, and from Arabia Felix to Cairo. From Egypt the use of coffee advanced to Syria and Constantinople. Thevenot, the traveller, was the first who brought it into France; and a Greek servant, called Pasqua, brought into England by Mr. Daniel Edwards, a Turky merchant, in 1652, to make his coffee, first set up the profession of coffeeman, and introduced the drink among us; though some say Dr. Harvey had used it before. Chambers.†

They have in Turky a drink called coffee, made of a berry of the same name, as black as soot, and of a strong scent, but not aromatical; which they take, beaten into powder, in water, as hot as they can drink it. This drink comforteth the brain and heart, and helpeth digestion. Bacon.

To part her time 'twixt reading and bohea, Or o'er cold coffee trifle with the spoon. Pope.

cóffeehouse n.s. [*coffee* and *house*.] A house of entertainment where coffee is sold, and the guests are supplied with news papers.

At ten, from coffeehouse or play, Returning, finishes the day. Prior.

It is a point they do not concern themselves about, farther than perhaps as a subject in a coffeehouse. Swift.

cóllege n.s. [*collegium*, Latin.]

1. A community; a number of persons living by some common rules.

On barbed steeds they rode in proud array, Thick as the college of the bees in May. Dryden.

2. A society of men set apart for learning or religion.

He is return'd with his opinions, which
Have satisfied the king for his divorce,
Gather'd from all the famous colleges
Almost in Christendom. Shakespeare's
Henry VIII.

I would the college of the cardinals
Would chuse him pope, and carry him to
   Rome. Sh. H. VI.

This order or society is sometimes called
Solomon's house, and sometimes the college of
the six days work. Bacon.

3. The house in which the collegians reside.

Huldah the prophetess dwelt in Jerusalem in
the college. 2 Kings xxii. 14.

4. A college in foreign universities is
   a lecture read in publick.

to cólour v.n. To blush. A low word, only
used in conversation.

cómedy n.s. [*comedia*, Lat.] A dramatick
representation of the lighter faults of
mankind.

   Your honour's players
Are come to play a pleasant comedy. Shak.
Tam. of the Shrew.

A long, exact, and serious comedy,
In every scene some moral let it teach,
And, if it can, at once both please and preach.
Pope.

cómmerce n.s. [*commercium*, Latin. It was
anciently accented on the last syllable.]
Intercourse; exchange of one thing for
another; interchange of any thing; trade;
traffick.

Places of publick resort being thus provided,
our repair thither is especially for mutual
conference, and, as it were, commerce to be had
between God and us. Hooker, b. v. s. 17.

   How could communities,
Degrees in schools, and brotherhoods in cities,
Peaceful commerce from dividable shores,
But by degree stand in authentick place?
Sh. Troil. and Cress.

Instructed ships shall sail to quick commerce,
By which remotest regions are ally'd;
Which makes one city of the universe,

Where some may gain, and all may be
   supply'd. Dryden.

These people had not any commerce with the
other known parts of the world. Tillotson.

In any country, that hath commerce with the
rest of the world, it is almost impossible now
to be without the use of silver coin. Locke.

comminátion n.s. [*comminatio*, Latin.]

1. A threat; a denunciation of punishment,
   or of vengeance.

Some parts of knowledge God has thought fit
to seclude from us, to fence them not only by
precept and commination, but with difficulty
and impossibilities. Decay of Piety.

2. The recital of God's threatenings on
   stated days.

commonwéal, commonwéalth n.s. [from
common and *weal*, or *wealth*.]

1. A polity; an established form of civil life.

Two foundations bear up publick societies;
the one inclination, whereby all men desire
sociable life; the other an order agreed upon,
touching the manner of their union in living
together: the latter is that which we call the
law of a commonweal. Hooker.

It was impossible to make a commonweal
in Ireland, without settling of all the estates
and possessions throughout the kingdom.
Davies on Ireland.

A continual parliament would but keep the
commonweal in tune, by preserving laws in
their vigour. King Charles.

There is no body in the commonwealth of
learning who does not profess himself a lover
of truth. Locke.

2. The publick; the general body of
   the people.

   Such a prince,
So kind a father of the commonweal.
Shakesp. Henry VI.

Their sons are well tutored by you: you are
a good member of the commonwealth.
Shakespeare's Love's Labour Lost.

3. A government in which the supreme power is lodged in the people; a republick.

Did he, or do yet any of them, imagine
The gods would sleep to such a Stygian practice,
Against that commonwealth which they have
    founded. Johnson.

Commonwealths were nothing more, in their original, but free cities; though sometimes, by force of orders and discipline, they have extended themselves into mighty dominions. Temple.

to commúnicate v.n.

1. To partake of the blessed sacrament.

The primitive Christians communicated every day. Taylor.

2. To have something in common with another; as, the houses communicate, there is a passage between them common to both, by which either may be entered from the other.

The whole body is nothing but a system of such canals, which all communicate with one another, mediately or immediately. Arbuthnot on Aliments.

to commúte v.n. To attone; to bargain for exemption.

Those institutions which God designed for means to further men in holiness, they look upon as a privilege to serve instead of it, and to commute for it. South's Sermons.

cómpass n.s. [from the verb.]

1. Circle; round.

This day I breathed first; time is come round;
And where I did begin, there shall I end:
My life is run its compass. Shakesp.
Julius Cæsar.

2. Extent; reach; grasp.

O, Juliet, I already know thy grief;
It strains me past the compass of my wits.
Shakespeare.

That which is out of the compass of any man's power, is to that man impossible. South's Sermons.

How few there are may be justly bewailed, the compass of them extending but from the time of Hippocrates to that of Marcus Antoninus. Temple.

Animals in their generation are wiser than the sons of men; but their wisdom is confined to a few particulars, and lies in a very narrow compass. Addison's Spectator, Nᵒ 120.

This author hath tried the force and compass of our language with much success. Swift.

3. Space; room; limits.

No less than the compass of twelve books is taken up in these. Pope's Essay on Homer's Battles.

The English are good confederates in an enterprize which may be dispatched in a short compass of time. Addis. Freeholder.

You have heard what hath been here done for the poor by the five hospitals and the workhouse, within the compass of one year, and towards the end of a long, expensive war. Atterb.

4. Enclosure; circumference.

    And their mount Palatine,
Th' imperial palace, compass huge, and high
The structure. Milton's Paradise Regained, b. iv. l. 50.

Old Rome from such a race deriv'd her birth,
Which now on sev'n high hills triumphant reigns,
And in that compass all the world contains. Dryd. Virg Geor.

5. A departure from the right line; an indirect advance; as, to fetch a compass round the camp.

6. Moderate space; moderation; due limits.

Certain it is, that in two hundred years before (I speak within compass) no such commission had been executed in either of these provinces. Davies on Ireland.

Nothing is likelier to keep a man within compass than the having constantly before his eyes the state of his affairs, in a regular course of account. Locke.

7. The power of the voice to express the notes of musick.

You would sound me from my lowest note to the top of my compass. Shakespeare's Hamlet.

From harmony, from heavenly harmony,
This universal frame began:
From harmony to harmony,
Through all the compass of the notes it ran,
The diapason closing full in man. Dryden.

8. [This is rarely used in the singular.] The instrument with which circles are drawn.

If they be two, they are two so,
As stiff twin compasses are two:
Thy soul, the fixt foot, makes no show
To move; but doth, if th' other do. Donne.

In his hand
He took the golden compasses, prepar'd
In God's eternal store, to circumscribe
This universe, and all created things.
Milton's Parad. Lost.

To fix one foot of their compass wherever they think fit, and extend the other to such terrible lengths, without describing any circumference at all, is to leave us and themselves in a very uncertain state. Swift on Dissentions in Athens and Rome.

9. The instrument composed of a needle and card, whereby mariners steer.

The breath of religion fills the sails, profit is the compass by which factious men steer their course. King Charles.

Rude as their ships was navigation then;
No useful compass or meridian known:
Coasting, they kept the land within their ken,
And knew no North but when the pole-star shone. Dryden.

With equal force the tempest blows by turns,
From ev'ry corner of the seamen's compass.
Row's J. Shore.

He that first discovered the use of the compass, did more for the supplying and increase of useful commodities than those who built workhouses. Locke.

cómplex adj. [*complexus*, Latin] Composite; of many parts; not simple; including many particulars.

Ideas made up of several simple ones, I call complex; such as beauty, gratitude, a man, the universe; which though complicated of various simple ideas, or complex ideas made up of simple ones, yet are considered each by itself as one. Locke.

A secondary essential mode, called a property, sometimes goes toward making up the essence of a complex being. Watts.

With such perfection fram'd,
Is this complex stupendous scheme of things.
Thoms. Spring.

compósitor n.s. [from *compose.*] He that ranges and adjusts the types in printing; distinguished from the pressman, who makes the impression upon paper.

compúter n.s. [from *compute.*] Reckoner; accountant; calculator.

The kalendars of these computers, and the accounts of these days, are different. Brown's Vulgar Errours, b. vi. c. 4.

I have known some such ill computers, as to imagine the many millions in stocks so much real wealth. Swift.

concéit n.s. [*concept*, French; *conceptus*, Latin.]

1. Conception; thought; idea; image in the mind.

Here the very shepherds have their fancies lifted to so high conceits, as the learned of other nations are content both to borrow their names and imitate their cunning. Sidney.

Impossible it was, that ever their will should change or incline to remit any part of their duty, without some object having force to avert their conceit from God. Hooker, b. i.

His grace looks chearfully and smooth this morning:
There's some conceit, or other, likes him well,
When that he bids good-morrow with such spirit. Shakesp.

In laughing there ever precedeth a conceit of somewhat ridiculous, and therefore it is proper to man. Bacon's Nat. Hist.

2. Understanding; readiness of apprehension.

How often, alas! did her eyes say unto me, that they loved? and yet, I not looking for such a matter, had not my conceit open to understand them. Sidney, b. ii.

The first kind of things appointed by laws humane, containeth whatsoever is good or evil, is notwithstanding more secret than that it can be discerned by every man's present conceit, without some deeper discourse and judgment. Hooker, b. i.

I shall be found of a quick conceit in judgment, and shall be admired. Wisd. viii. 11.

3. Opinion, generally in a sense of contempt; fancy; imagination; fantastical notion.

*I know not how conceit may rob
The treasury of life, when life itself
Yields to the theft.* Shakespeare's King Lear.

Strong conceit, like a new principle, carries all easily with it, when yet above common sense. Locke.

*Malbranche has an odd conceit,
As ever enter'd Frenchman's pate.* Prior.

4. Opinion in a neutral sense.

Seest thou a man wise in his own conceit? There is more hope of a fool than of him. Prov. xxvi. 12.

*I shall not fail t' approve the fair conceit
The king hath of you.* Shakespeare's Henry VIII.

5. A pleasant fancy.

His wit is as thick as Tewksbury mustard: there is no more conceit in him than is in a mallet. Shakesp. Henry IV. p. ii.

While he was on his way to the gibbet, a freak took him in the head to go off with a conceit. L'Estrange.

6. Sentiment, as distinguished from imagery.

*Some to conceit alone their works confine,
And glitt'ring thoughts struck out at ev'ry line.* Pope.

7. Fondness; favourable opinion; opinionative pride.

Since by a little studying in learning, and great conceit of himself, he has lost his religion; may he find it again by harder study under humbler truth. Bentley.

8. Out of conceit with. No longer fond of.

Not that I dare assume to myself to have put him out of conceit with it, by having convinced him of the fantasticalness of it. Tillotson, Preface.

What hath chiefly put me out of conceit with this moving manner, is the frequent disappointment. Swift.

to concéive v.a. [*concevoir*, Fr. *concipere*, Latin.]

1. To admit into the womb.

I was shapen in iniquity, and in sin did my mother conceive me. Psalm li. 5.

2. To form in the mind; to imagine.

Nebuchadnezzar hath conceived a purpose against you. Jer.

3. To comprehend; to understand. He conceives the whole system.

*This kiss, if it durst speak,
Would stretch thy spirits up into the air:
Conceive, and fare thee well.* Shakespeare's King Lear.

4. To think; to be of opinion.

If you compare my gentlemen with Sir John, you will hardly conceive him to have been bred in the same climate. Sw.

concínnity n.s. [from *concinnitas*, Latin.] Decency; fitness.

to condescénd v.n. [*condescendre*, Fr. from *descendo*, Latin.]

1. To depart from the privileges of superiority by a voluntary submission; to

sink willingly to equal terms with inferiours; to sooth by familiarity.

This method carries a very humble and condescending air, when he that instructs seems to be the enquirer. Watts.

2. To consent to do more than mere justice can require.

   Spain's mighty monarch,
In gracious clemency does condescend,
On these conditions, to become your friend.
Dryd. Ind. Em.

He did not primarily intend to appoint this way; but condescended to it as most accommodate to their present state. Tillotson, Sermon 5.

3. To stoop; to bend; to yield; to submit; to become subject.

Can they think me so broken, so debas'd
With corporal servitude, that my mind ever
Will condescend to such absurd commands?
Milton.

   Nor shall my resolution
Disarm itself, nor condescend to parly
With foolish hopes. Denham's Sophy.

condígn adj. [*condignus*, Latin.] Worthy of a person; suitable; deserved; merited: it is always used of something deserved by crimes.

Unless it were a bloody murtherer,
I never gave them condign punishment.
Shakesp. Henry VI.

Consider who is your friend, he that would have brought him to condign punishment, or he that has saved him. Arbuthn.

to cónfect v.a. [*confectus*, Latin.] To make up into sweetmeats; to preserve with sugar. It seems now corrupted into *comfit*.

confórmist n.s. [from *conform*.] One that complies with the worship of the church of England; not a dissenter.

confóundedly adv. [from *confounded*.] Hatefully; shamefully: a low or ludicrous word.

You are confoundedly given to squirting up and down, and chattering. L'Estrange.

Thy speculations begin to smell confoundedly of woods and meadows. Addison's Spectator, Nº 131.

conglaciátion n.s. [from *conglaciate*.] The state of being changed, or act of changing into ice.

If crystal be a stone, it is concreted by a mineral spirit and lapidifical principles; for, while it remained in a fluid body, it was a subject very unfit for proper conglaciation. Brown.

connoisséur n.s. [French.] A judge; a critick: it is often used of a pretended critick.

Your lesson learnt, you'll be secure
To get the name of connoisseur. Swift.

consérvative adj. [from *conservo*, Latin.] Having the power of opposing diminution or injury.

The spherical figure, as to all heavenly bodies, so it agreeth to light, as the most perfect and conservative of all others. Peacham.

consopiátion n.s. [from *consopio*, Latin.] The act of laying to sleep.

One of his maxims is, that a total abstinence from intemperance is no more philosophy than a total consopiation of the senses is repose. Digby to Pope.

constitútion n.s. [from *constitute*.]

1. The act of constituting; enacting; deputing; establishing; producing.

2. State of being; particular texture of parts; natural qualities.

This is more beneficial to us than any other constitution. Bentley's Sermons.

This light being trajected through the parallel prisms, if it suffered any change by the refraction of one, it lost that impression by the contrary refraction of the other; and so, being restored to its pristine constitution, became of the same condition as at first. Newton's Opt.

3. Corporeal frame.

Amongst many bad effects of this oily constitution, there is one advantage; such who arrive to age, are not subject to stricture of fibres. Arbuthnot on Aliments.

4. Temper of body, with respect to health or disease.

If such men happen, by their native constitutions, to fall into the gout, either they mind it not at all, having no leisure to be sick, or they use it like a dog. Temple.

Beauty is nothing else but a just accord and mutual harmony of the members, animated by a healthful constitution. Dryden's Dufresnoy.

5. Temper of mind.

Dametas, according to the constitution of a dull head, thinks no better way to shew himself wise than by suspecting every thing in his way. Sidney.

Some dear friend dead; else nothing in the world Could turn so much the constitution Of any constant man. Shakespeare's Merchant of Venice.

He defended himself with undaunted courage, and less passion than was expected from his constitution. Clarendon.

6. Established form of government; system of laws and customs.

The Norman conqu'ring all by might, Mixing our customs, and the form of right, With foreign constitutions he had brought. Daniel's Civ. War.

7. Particular law; established usage; establishment; institution.

We lawfully may observe the positive constitutions of our own churches. Hooker, b. iv. sect. 5.

Constitution, properly speaking in the sense of the civil law, is that law which is made and ordained by some king or emperor; yet the canonists, by adding the word sacred to it, make it to signify the same as an ecclesiastical canon. Ayliffe.

cónstuprate v.a. [*constupro*, Lat.] To violate; to debauch; to defile.

consúmer n.s. [from *consume*.] One that spends, wastes, or destroys any thing.

Money may be considered as in the hands of the consumer, or of the merchant who buys the commodity, when made to export. Locke.

conterráneous adj. [*conterraneus*, Lat.] Of the same country. Dict.

contráct n.s. [from the verb. Anciently accented on the first.]

1. An act whereby two parties are brought together; a bargain; a compact.

The agreement upon orders, by mutual contract, with the consent to execute them by common strength, they make the rise of all civil governments. Temple.

Shall Ward draw contracts with a statesman's skill?
Or Japhet pocket, like his grace, a will? Pope.

2. An act whereby a man and woman are betrothed to one another.

Touch'd you the bastardy of Edward's children?—
—I did, with his contract with lady Lucy, And his contract by deputy in France. Shakes. Richard III.

3. A writing in which the terms of a bargain are included.

cóny n.s. [*kanin*, Germ. *connil* or *connin*, Fr. *cuniculus*, Latin.] A rabit; an animal that burroughs in the ground.

With a short-legg'd hen, Lemons and wine for sauce; to these a cony Is not to be despair'd of, for our money. Ben. Johns. Epig.

The husbandman suffers by hares and conys, which eat the corn, trees. Mortimer's Husbandry.

to cónycatch v.n. To catch a cony, is, in the old cant of thieves, to cheat; to bite; to trick.

I have matter in my head against you, and against your conycatching rascals. Shakesp. Merry Wives of Windsor.

coquétte n.s. [*coquette*, Fr. from *coquart*, a prattler.] A gay, airy girl; a girl who endeavours to attract notice.

The light coquettes in sylphs aloft repair,
And sport and flutter in the fields of air.
Pope's Ra. of Lock.

A coquette and a tinder-box are sparkled.
Arbuthn. and Pope.

córdial n.s. [from *cor*, the heart, Latin.]

1. A medicine that increases the force of the heart, or quickens the circulation.

2. Any medicine that increases strength.

A cordial, properly speaking, is not always
what increaseth the force of the heart; for, by
increasing that, the animal may be weakened,
as in inflammatory diseases. Whatever
increaseth the natural or animal strength, the
force of moving the fluids and muscles, is a
cordial: these are such substances as bring the
serum of the blood into the properest condition
for circulation and nutrition; as broths made
of animal substances, milk, ripe fruits, and
whatever is endued with a wholsome but not
pungent taste. Arbuthnot on Aliments.

3. Any thing that comforts, gladdens, and exhilerates.

Then with some cordials seek for to appease
The inward languor of my wounded heart,
And then my body shall have shortly ease;
But such sweet cordials pass physicians art.
Spenser.

Comfort, like cordials after death, comes late.
Dryden.

Your warrior offspring that upheld the crown,
The scarlet honour of your peaceful gown,
Are the most pleasing objects I can find,
Charms to my sight, and cordials to my mind.
Dryden.

to cornúte v.a. [*cornutus*, Latin.] To bestow horns; to cuckold.

córsair n.s. [French.] A pirate; one who professes to seize merchants.

cótquean n.s. [probably from *coquin*, French.] A man who busies himself with women's affairs.

Look to the bak'd meats, good Angelica;
Spare not for cost.—
—Go, go, you cotquean, go;

Get you to bed. Shakespeare's Romeo and Juliet.

A stateswoman is as ridiculous a creature as a
cotquean: each of the sexes should keep within
its particular bounds. Addison's Freeholder, Nº 38.

You have given us a lively picture of husbands
hen-peck'd; but you have never touched upon
one of the quite different character, and who
goes by the name of cotquean. Add. Spect.

cough n.s. [*kuch*, Dutch.] A convulsion of the lungs, vellicated by some sharp serosity. It is pronounced *coff*.

In consumptions of the lungs, when nature
cannot expel the cough, men fall into fluxes of
the belly, and then they die. Bacon's Natural History, Nº 63.

For his dear sake long restless nights you bore,
While rattling coughs his heaving vessels tore.
Smith.

cóuntenance n.s. [*contenance*, French.]

1. The form of the face; the system of the features.

So spake our sire, and by his count'nance seem'd
Entering on studious thoughts abstruse.
Milton's Parad. Lost.

To whom, with count'nance calm, and
soul sedate,
Thus Turnus. Dryden's Æn.

2. Air; look.

Well, Suffolk, yet thou shalt not see me blush,
Nor change my countenance for this arrest:
A heart unspotted is not easily daunted.
Shakesp. Henry VI.

3. Calmness of look; composure of face.

She smil'd severe; nor with a troubled look;
Or trembling hand, the fun'ral present took;
Ev'n kept her count'nance, when the lid remov'd,
Disclos'd the heart unfortunately lov'd.
Dryden's Fables.

The two maxims of any great man at court
are, always to keep his countenance, and never
to keep his word. Swift.

4. Confidence of mien; aspect of assurance.

The night beginning to persuade some retiring place, the gentlewoman, even out of countenance before she began her speech, invited me to lodge that night with her father. Sidney.

We will not make your countenance to fall by the answer ye shall receive. Bacon's New Atlantis.

Their best friends were out of countenance, because they found that the imputations, which their enemies had laid upon them, were well grounded. Clarendon, b. viii.

Your examples will meet it at every turn, and put it out of countenance in every place; even in private corners it will soon lose confidence. Sprat's Sermons.

If the outward profession of religion and virtue were once in practice and countenance at court, a good treatment of the clergy would be the necessary consequence. Swift.

If those preachers would look about, they would find one part of their congregation out of countenance, and the other asleep. Swift.

It is a kind of ill manners to offer objections to a fine woman, and a man would be out of countenance that should gain the superiority in such a contest: a coquette logician may be rallied, but not contradicted. Addison's Freeholder, Nº 32.

It puts the learned in countenance, and gives them a place among the fashionable part of mankind. Addison's Freeholder.

5. Affection or ill will, as it appears upon the face.

Yet the stout fairy, mongst the middest crowd, Thought all their glory vain in knightly view, And that great princess too, exceeding proud, That to strange knight no better countenance allow'd. Fa. Q.

The king hath on him such a countenance, As he had lost some province, and a region Lov'd, as he loves himself. Shakespeare's Winter's Tale.

6. Patronage; appearance of favour; appearance on any side; support.

The church of Christ, which held that profession which had not the publick allowance and countenance of authority, could not so long use the exercise of Christian religion but in private. Hooker, b. v. sect. 11.

His majesty maintained an army here, to give strength and countenance to the civil magistrate. Davies on Ireland.

Now then, we'll use His countenance for the battle; which being done, Let her who would be rid of him, devise His speedy taking off. Shakespeare's King Lear.

This is the magistrate's peculiar province, to give countenance to piety and virtue, and to rebuke vice and profaneness. Atterb.

7. Superficial appearance; show; resemblance.

The election being done, he made countenance of great discontent thereat. Ascham's Schoolmaster.

Oh, you blessed ministers above! Keep me in patience, and with ripen'd time Unfold the evil, which is here wrapt up In countenance. Shakespeare's Measure for Measure.

Bianca's love Made me exchange my state with Tranio, While he did bear my countenance in the town. Shakespeare.

coupée n.s. [French.] A motion in dancing, when one leg is a little bent and suspended from the ground, and with the other a motion is made forwards. Chambers.

couple-beggar n.s. [*couple* and *beggar.*] One that makes it his business to marry beggars to each other.

No couple-beggar in the land, E'er join'd such numbers hand in hand. Swift.

cow-leech n.s. [*cow* and *leech.*] One who professes to cure distempered cows.

cóxcomb n.s. [*cock* and *comb*, corrupted from *cock's comb.*]

1. The top of the head.

As the cockney did to the eels, when she put them i' the pasty alive; she rapt them o' th' coxcombs with a stick, and cried down, wantons, down. Shakespeare's King Lear.

2. The comb resembling that of a cock, which licensed fools wore formerly in their caps.

There take my coxcomb: why, this fellow has banished two of his daughters, and did the third a blessing against his will: if thou follow him, thou must needs wear my coxcomb. Shakes.

3. A fop; a superficial pretender to knowledge or accomplishments.

I sent to her,
By this same coxcomb that we have i' th' wind,
Tokens and letters, which she did resend.
Shakespeare.

I scorn, quoth she, thou coxcomb silly,
Quarter or council from a foe. Hudibras,
p. i. cant. iii.

It is a vanity common in the world, for every pretending coxcomb to make himself one of the party still with his betters. L' Estrange,
Fable 135.

They overflowed with smart repartees, and were only distinguished from the intended wits by being called coxcombs, though they deserved not so scandalous a name. Dryd. Dufres.

Some are bewilder'd in the maze of schools,
And some made coxcombs, nature meant but fools. Pope.

cózener n.s. [from *cozen*.] A cheater; a defrauder.

Indeed, sir, there are cozeners abroad, and therefore it behoves men to be wary. Shakespeare's Winter's Tale.

crack-brained adj. [*crack* and *brained*.] Crazy; without right reason.

We have sent you an answer to the ill-grounded sophisms of those crack-brained fellows. Arbuth. and Pope's Mart. Scrib.

crack-hemp n.s. [*crack* and *hemp*.] A wretch fated to the gallows; a crack-rope. Furcifer.†

Come hither, crack-hemp.
—I hope I may chuse, sir.
—Come hither, you rogue:
What, have you forgot me? Shakes. Taming of the Shrew.

crack-rope n.s. [from *crack* and *rope*.] A fellow that deserves hanging.

crámbo n.s. [a cant word, probably without etymology.] A play at which one gives a word, to which another finds a rhyme; a rhyme.

So Mævius, when he drain'd his skull
To celebrate some suburb trull,
His similes in order set,
And ev'ry crambo he could get. Swift.

crápulence n.s. [*crapula*, a surfeit, Latin.] Drunkenness; sickness by intemperance. Dict.

cráver n.s. [from *crave*.] A weak-hearted spiritless fellow. It is used in *Clarissa*.

cráyon n.s. [*crayon*, French.]

1. A kind of pencil; a roll of paste to draw lines with.

Let no day pass over you without drawing a line; that is to say, without working, without giving some strokes of the pencil or the crayon. Dryden's Dufresnoy.

2. A drawing or design done with a pencil or crayon.

crébritude n.s. [from *creber*, frequent, Latin.] Frequentness. Dict.

to crépitate v.n. [*crepito*, Latin.] To make a small crackling noise.

cretáted adj. [*cretatus*, Latin.] Rubbed with chalk. Dict.

críbbage n.s. A game at cards.

cricket n.s. [*krekel*, from *kreken*, to make a noise, Dutch.]

1. An insect that squeaks or chirps about ovens and fireplaces.

Didst thou not hear a noise?—
—I heard the owl scream, and the crickets cry. Shakes. Macb.

Far from all resort of mirth,

Save the cricket on the hearth. Milton.

The solemn death-watch click'd the hour she dy'd,
And shrilling crickets in the chimney cry'd.
Gay's Pastorals.

2. [from *cryce*, Saxon, a stick.] A sport, at which the contenders drive a ball with sticks in opposition to each other.

The judge, to dance, his brother serjeant call;
The senator at cricket urge the ball.
Pope's Dunciad, b. iv.

3. [from *kriechen*, Germ. to creep.] A low seat or stool.

críncum n.s. [a cant word.] A cramp; a contraction; whimsy.

For jealousy is but a kind
Of clap and crincum of the mind. Hudibras, p. iii. cant. 1.

crinígerous adj. [*criniger*, Latin.] Hairy; overgrown with hair. Dict.

crísis n.s. [κρισις.]

1. The point in which the disease kills, or changes to the better.

Wise leeches will not vain receipts obtrude;
Deaf to complaints, they wait upon the ill,
'Till some safe crisis authorize their skill.
Dryden.

2. The point of time at which any affair comes to the height.

This hour's the very crisis of your fate;
Your good or ill, your infamy or fame,
And all the colour of your life depends
On this important now. Dryden's Spanish Fryar.

The undertaking, which I am now laying down, was entered upon in the very crisis of the late rebellion, when it was the duty of every Briton to contribute his utmost assistance to the government, in a manner suitable to his station and abilities. Addison's Freeholder, Nº 55.

crispísulcant adj. [*crispisulcans*, Latin.] Waved, or undulating; as lightning is represented. Dict.

crítical adj. [from *critick*.]

1. Exact; nicely judicious; accurate; diligent.

It is submitted to the judgment of more critical ears, to direct and determine what is graceful and what is not. Holder.

Virgil was so critical in the rites of religion, that he would never have brought in such prayers as these, if they had not been agreeable to the Roman customs. Stillingfleet.

2. Relating to criticism; as, he wrote a critical dissertation on the last play.

3. Captious; inclined to find fault.

What wouldst thou write of me, if thou
*   shouldst praise me?—*
—O, gentle lady, do not put me to 't;
For I am nothing, if not critical.
Shakespeare's Othello.

4. [from *crisis*.] Comprising the time at which a great event is determined.

The moon is supposed to be measured by sevens, and the critical or decretory days to be dependent on that number. Brown's Vulgar Errours, b. iv. c. 12.

Opportunity is in respect to time, in some sense, as time is in respect to eternity: it is the small moment, the exact point, the critical minute, on which every good work so much depends. Sprat's Sermons.

The people cannot but resent to see their apprehensions of the power of France, in so critical a juncture, wholly laid aside. Swift.

to críticise v.n. [from *critick*.]

1. To play the critick; to judge; to write remarks upon any performance of literature; to point out faults and beauties.

They who can criticise so weakly, as to imagine I have done my worst, may be convinced, at their own cost, that I can write severely with more ease than I can gently. Dryden.

Know well each ancient's proper character,
Without all this at once before your eyes,
Cavil you may, but never criticise.
Pope's Essay on Criticism.

2. To animadvert upon as faulty.

Nor would I have his father look so narrowly into these accounts, as to take occasion from thence to criticise on his expences. Locke.

críticism n.s. [from *critick*.]

1. Criticism, as it was first instituted by Aristotle, was meant a standard of judging well. Dryden's Innocence, Pref.

2. Remark; animadversion; critical observations.

There is not a Greek or Latin critick who has not shewn, even in the stile of his criticisms, that he was a master of all the eloquence and delicacy of his native tongue. Addis. Spect.

crítick n.s. [κριτικος.]

1. A man skilled in the art of judging of literature; a man able to distinguish the faults and beauties of writing.

This settles truer ideas in men's minds of several things, whereof we read the names in ancient authors, than all the large and laborious arguments of criticks. Locke.

Criticks I saw, that other names deface, And fix their own with labour in their place. Pope.

Where an author has many beauties consistent with virtue, piety, and truth, let not little criticks exalt themselves, and shower down their ill-nature. Watts.

2. A censurer; a man apt to find fault.

My chief design, next to seeing you, is to be a severe critick on you and your neighbour. Swift.

crítick n.s.

1. A critical examination; critical remarks; animadversions.

I should be glad if I could persuade him to continue his good offices, and write such another critick on any thing of mine. Dryden.

I should as soon expect to see a critique on the poesy of a ring, as on the inscription of a medal. Addison on Medals.

2. Science of criticism.

If ideas and words were distinctly weighed, and duly considered, they would afford us another sort of logick and critick than what we have been hitherto acquainted with. Locke.

What is every year of a wise man's life, but a censure and critique on the past? Pope.

Not that my quill to criticks was confin'd, My verse gave ampler lessons to mankind. Pope.

crócodile n.s. [from κροκος, saffron, and δειλων, fearing.] An amphibious voracious animal, in shape resembling a lizard, and found in Egypt and the Indies. It is covered with very hard scales, which cannot, without great difficulty, be pierced; except under the belly, where the skin is tender. It has a wide throat, with several rows of teeth, sharp and separated, which enter one another. Though its four legs are very short, it runs with great swiftness; but does not easily turn itself. It is long lived, and is said to grow continually to its death, but this is not probable. Some are fifteen or eighteen cubits long. Its sight is very piercing upon the ground, but in the water it sees but dimly; and it is said to spend the four winter months under water. When its bowels are taken out, or it is wounded, it smells very agreeably. Crocodiles lay their eggs, resembling goose-eggs, sometimes amounting to sixty, on the sand near the waterside, covering them with the sand, that the heat of the sun may contribute to hatch them. The Ichneumon, or Indian rat, which is as large as a tame cat, is said to break the crocodile's eggs whenever it finds them; and also, that it gets into the very belly of this creature, while it is asleep with its throat open, gnaws its entrails, and kills it. Calmet.

Glo'ster's show
Beguiles him; as the mournful crocodile, With sorrow, snares relenting passengers. Shakesp. Hen. VI.

Crocodiles were thought to be peculiar unto the Nile. Brown.

Cæsar will weep, the crocodile will weep. Dryden.

Enticing crocodiles, whose tears are death; Syrens, that murder with enchanting breath. Granville.

Crocodile is also a little animal, otherwise called stinx, very much like the lizard, or small crocodile. It lives by land and water; has four short small legs, a very sharp muzzle, and a short small tail. It is pretty enough to look at, being covered all over with little scales of the colour of silver, intermixt with brown, and of a gold colour upon the back. It always remains little, and is found in Egypt near the Red Sea, in Lybia, and in the Indies. Trevoux.

cróssrow n.s. [*cross* and *row*.] Alphabet; so named because a cross is placed at the beginning, to shew that the end of learning is piety.

He hearkens after prophecies and dreams, And from the crossrow plucks the letter G; And says a wizard told him, that by G His issue disinherited should be. Shakespeare's Richard III.

crówder n.s. [from crowd.] A fiddler.

Chevy-chase sung by a blind crowder. Sidney.

crúentate adj. [*cruentatus*, Latin.] Smeared with blood.

Atomical aporrheas pass from the cruentate cloth or weapon to the wound. Glanv. Sceps. c. 24.

cryptógraphy n.s. [κρυπτω and γραφω.]

1. The act of writing secret characters.

2. Secret characters; cyphers.

cryptólogy n.s. [κρυπτω and λογος.] Ænigmatical language.

cubátion n.s. [*cubatio*, Lat.] The act of lying down. Dict.

cúckingstool n.s. An engine invented for the punishment of scolds and unquiet women, which, in ancient times, was called tumbrel. Cowel.

These mounted on a chair-curale, Which moderns call a cucking-stool, March proudly to the river's side. Hudibras, p. ii. cant. 2.

cúdden, cúddy n.s. [without etymology.] A clown; a stupid rustick; a low dolt: a low bad word.

The slavering cudden, propp'd upon his staff, Stood ready gaping with a grinning laugh. Dryden.

to cúddle v.n. [a low word, I believe, without etymology.] To lye close; to squat.

Have you mark'd a partridge quake, Viewing the tow'ring faulcon nigh? She cuddles low behind the brake; Nor would she stay, nor dares she fly. Prior.

cúlly n.s. [*coglione*, Ital. a fool.] A man deceived or imposed upon; as, by sharpers or a strumpet.

Why should you, whose mother wits Are furnish'd with all perquisits, B' allow'd to put all tricks upon Our cully sex, and we use none? Hudibras, p. iii.

Yet the rich cullies may their boasting spare: They purchase but sophisticated ware. Dryden.

He takes it in mighty dudgeon, because I won't let him make me over by deed as his lawful cully. Arbuthnot.

to cup v.a. [from the noun.]

1. To supply with cups: this sense is obsolete.

Plumpy Bacchus, with pink eyne, In thy vats our cares be drown'd: With thy grapes our hairs be crown'd! Cup us, 'till the world go round. Shakesp. Ant. and Cleopatra.

2. To fix a glass-bell or cucurbite upon the skin, to draw the blood in scarification.

The clotted blood lies heavy on his heart, Corrupts, and there remains in spite of art: Nor breathing veins, nor cupping will prevail; All outward remedies and inward fail. Dryden's Fables.

You have quartered all the foul language upon me, that could be raked out of the air of Billingsgate, without knowing who I am; or whether I deserve to be cupped and scarified at this rate. Spectator, Nº 595.

Blistering, cupping, and bleeding are seldom of use but to the idle and intemperate. Addison's Spectator, Nº 195.

Him the damn'd doctors and his friends immur'd;
They bled, they cupp'd, they purg'd; in short
*   they cur'd.* Pope.

cúrfew n.s. [*couvre feu*, French.] An evening-peal, by which the conqueror willed, that every man should rake up his fire, and put out his light; so that in many places at this day, where a bell is customarily rung towards bed time, it is said to ring curfew. Cowel.

*   You whose pastime*
Is to make midnight mushrooms, that rejoice
To hear the solemn curfew. Shakespeare's Tempest.

Oft on a plat of rising ground,
I hear the far off curfew sound,
Over some wide-water'd shoar,
Swinging slow with sullen roar. Milton.

2. A cover for a fire; a fireplate.

But now for pans, pots, curfews, counters and the like, the beauty will not be so much respected, so as the compound stuff is like to pass. Bacon's Phys. Rem.

curmúdgeon n.s. [It is a vitious manner of pronouncing *cœur mechant*, Fr. an unknown correspondent.]† An avaritious churlish fellow; a miser; a niggard; a churl; a griper.

And when he has it in his claws,
He'll not be hide-bound to the cause;

Nor shalt thou find him a curmudgeon,
If thou dispatch it without grudging.
Hudibras, p. iii. c. 2.

Both their wine and their victuals these
*   curmudgeon lubbards*
Lock up from my sight, in cellars and
*   cupboards.* Swift.

A man's way of living is commended, because he will give any rate for it; and a man will give any rate rather than pass for a poor wretch, or a penurious curmudgeon. Locke.

curtain-lecture n.s. [from *curtain* and *lecture*.] A reproof given by a wife to her husband in bed.

What endless brawls by wives are bred!
The curtain-lecture makes a mournful bed.
Dryden's Juven.

She ought to exert the authority of the curtain-lecture, and, if she finds him of a rebellious disposition, to tame him. Addis.

cyclopædía n.s. [κυκλος and παιδεια.] A circle of knowledge; a course of the sciences.

cynánthropy n.s. [κυων κυνος, and ανθρωπος.] A species of madness in which men have the qualities of dogs.

cynick n.s. [κυνικος.] A philosopher of the snarling or currish sort; a follower of Diogenes; a rude man; a snarler; a misanthrope.

How vilely doth this cynick rhime?—
Get you hence, sirrah; saucy fellow, hence.
Shakespeare.

czar n.s. [A Sclavonian word, written more properly *tzar*.] The title of the emperour of Russia.

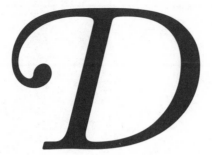

D, is a consonant nearly approaching in sound to *T*, but formed by a stronger appulse of the tongue to the upper part of the mouth. The sound of *D* in *English* is uniform, and it is never mute.

da capo [Ital.] A term in musick, which signifying from the head or the beginning, means that the first part of the tune should be repeated at the conclusion.

dad, dáddy n.s. [The child's way of expressing father. It is remarkable, that, in all parts of the world, the word for father, as first taught to children, is compounded of *a* and *t*, or the kindred letter *d* differently placed; as *tad*, Welsh; αττα, Greek; *atta*, Gothick; *tata*, Latin. *Mammas atque tatas habet Afra*, Mart.]† Father.

I was never so bethumpt with words,
Since first I call'd my brother's father dad.
Shakes. K. John.

His loving mother left him to my care;
Fine child, as like his dad as he could stare!
Gay.

dáffodil, daffodílly, daffodowndílly n.s. [Supposed by Skinner to be corrupted from *asphodelus*.] This plant hath a lily-flower, consisting of one leaf, which is bell-shaped, and cut into six segments, which incircle its middle like a crown; but the empalement, which commonly rises out of a membranous vagina, turns to an oblong or roundish fruit, which is triangular, and gapes in three parts; is divided into three cells, and full of roundish seeds. Miller.

Strew me the green ground with
*   daffodowndillies,*
And cowslips, and kingcups, and loved lilies.
Spenser.

Bid Amaranthus all his beauty shed,
And daffodillies fill their cups with tears,
To strew the laureate herse where Lycid lies.
Milton.

The daughters of the flood have search'd the mead
For violets pale, and cropp'd the poppy's head:
The short narcissus, and fair daffodil,
Pancies to please the sight, and cassia sweet
*   to smell.* Dryden.

dáisy n.s. [*dægeseage*, day's eye. Chaucer.] A Spring-flower.

It hath a perennial root: the stalks are naked, and never branch out: the cup of the flower is scaly and simple, divided into many segments to the foot-stalk. The flowers are radiated; and the heads, after the petals are fallen off, resemble obtuse cones. Miller.

When daisies pied, and violets blue,
And lady smocks all over white,
*   And cuckow buds of yellow hue,*
Do paint the meadows much bedight.
Shakespeare.

Then sing by turns, by turns the muses sing,
Now hawthorns blossom, now the daisies spring;
Now leaves the trees, and flow'rs adorn
*   the ground:*
Begin, the vales shall ev'ry note rebound.
Pope's Spring.

This will find thee picking of daisies, or smelling to a lock of hay. Addison's Spectator, Nº 131.

Fair-handed Spring unbosoms every grace;
The daisy, primrose, violet, darkly blaze.
Thomson's Spring.

dálliance n.s. [from *dally*.]

1. Interchange of caresses; acts of fondness.

Look thou be true: do not give dalliance
Too much the rein: the strongest oaths are straw
To th' fire i' th' blood. Shakespeare's Tempest.

Nor gentle purpose, nor endearing smiles
Wanted; nor youthful dalliance, as beseems
Fair couple, link'd in happy nuptial league,
Alone as they. Milton's Paradise Lost, b. iv. l. 332.

*   I'll head my people;*
Then think of dalliance when the danger's o'er:
My warlike spirits work now another way,
And my soul's tun'd to trumpets. Dryden's Don Sebastian.

2. Conjugal conversation.

The giant, self-dismayed with the sound,
Where he with his Duessa dalliance found,
In haste came rushing forth from inner bow'r.
Fairy Queen.

That, not mystick, where the sapient king
Held dalliance with his fair Egyptian spouse.
Milt. Par. Lost.

Since thou claim'st me for thy sire,
And my fair son here show'st me, the
    dear pledge
Of dalliance had with thee in heav'n, and joys
Then sweet, now sad to mention.
Milton's Paradise Lost.

3. Delay; procrastination.

Nay, come, I pray you, sir, give me the chain;
Both wind and tide stay for this gentleman;
And I, to blame, have held him here too
    long.—
—Good lord, you use this dalliance to excuse
Your breach of promise. Shakesp. Comedy
of Errours.

dam n.s. [from *dame*, which formerly
signified mother. *Had Nero never been an*
emperour, shulde never his dame have be
slaine. Chaucer.]

1. The mother: used of beasts, or other
   animals not human.

The dam runs lowing up and down,
Looking the way her harmless young one went,
And can do nought but wail her darling loss.
Shak. H. VI.

Mother, says a sick kite, give over
lamentations, and let me have your prayers:
alas, my child, says the dam, which of the gods
shall I go to? L'Estrange, Fab. 17.

They bring but one morsel of meat at a time,
and have not fewer, it may be, than seven or
eight young in the nest together, which, at the
return of their dams, do all at once, with
equal greediness, hold up their heads and gape.
Ray.

2. A human mother: in contempt or
   detestation.

   This brat is none of mine;
It is the issue of Polixena:
Hence with it, and, together with the dam,
Commit them to the fire. Shakespeare's
Winter's Tale.

dan n.s. [from *dominus*, as now *don* in
Spanish, and *donna*, Italian, from *domina*.]
The old term of honour for men; as we now
say master.

This whimpled, whining, purblind,
   wayward boy,
This signor Junio's giant dwarf, dan Cupid.
Shakespeare.

Dick, if this story pleaseth thee,
Pray thank dan Pope, who told it me.
Prior's Alma.

to dance v.n. [*danser*, Fr. *dançar*, Span. as
some think from *tanza*, Arabick, a dance; as
Junius, who loves to derive from Greek,
thinks, from δονησις.]

1. To move in measure; to move with
   steps correspondent to the sound of
   instruments.

What say you to young Mr. Fenton? He
capers, he dances, he has eyes of youth, he
writes verses. Sh. Mer. W. of Winds.

to dance attendance v.a. To wait with
suppleness and obsequiousness.

Men are sooner weary to dance attendance at
the gates of foreign lords, than to tarry the
good leisure of their own magistrates.
Raleigh's Essays.

   It upbraids you
To let your father's friend, for three long months,
Thus dance attendance for a word of audience.
Dryd. Cleom.

dándiprat n.s. [*dandin*, French.] A little
fellow; an urchin: a word used sometimes in
fondness, sometimes in contempt.

dapátical adj. [from *dapaticus*, Latin.]
Sumptuous in cheer. Bailey.

dárkling [a participle, as it seems, from
darkle, which yet I have never found.] Being
in the dark; being without light: a word
merely poetical.

O, wilt thou darkling leave me? do not so.
Shakespeare.

   Darkling stands
The varying shore o' th' world. Shakesp.
Ant. and Cleopatra.

   The wakeful bird
Sings darkling, and, in shadiest covert hid,
Tunes her nocturnal note. Milton's Paradise
Lost, b. iii.

Darkling they mourn their fate, whom
   Circe's pow'r,
With words and wicked herbs, from human kind
Had alter'd, and in brutal shapes confin'd.
Dryden's Æn.

dealbátion n.s. [*dealbatio*, Lat.] The act of bleaching or whitening; rendering things white, which were not so before: a word which is now almost grown into disuse.

All seed is white in viviparous animals, and such as have preparing vessels, wherein it receives a manifold dealbation. Brown's Vulgar Errours, b. vi. c. 10.

death n.s. [*deaþ*, Saxon.]

1. The extinction of life; the departure of the soul from the body.

He is the mediator of the New Testament, that by means of death, for the redemption of the transgressions, they which are called might receive the promise of eternal inheritance. Heb. ix. 15.

They say there is divinity in odd numbers, either in nativity or death. Shakes. Merry Wives of Windsor.

   Death, a necessary end,
Will come, when it will come. Shakesp. Julius Cæsar.

   He must his acts reveal,
From the first moment of his vital breath,
To his last hour of unrepenting death.
Dryden's Æn. b. 6.

2. Mortality; destruction.

   How did you dare
To trade and traffick with Macbeth,
In riddles and affairs of death?
Shakespeare's Macbeth.

3. The state of the dead.

   In swinish sleep
Their drenched natures lie, as in a death.
Shakes. Macbeth.

4. The manner of dying.

Thou shalt die the deaths of them that are slain in the midst of the seas. Ez. xxviii. 8.

5. The image of mortality represented by a skeleton.

I had rather be married to a death's head, with a bone in his mouth, than to either of these. Shakes. Merch. of Venice.

If I gaze now, 'tis but to see
What manner of death's head 'twill be,
   When it is free
From that fresh upper skin;
The gazer's joy, and sin. Suckling.

6. Murder, the act of destroying life unlawfully.

As in manifesting the sweet influence of his mercy, on the severe stroke of his justice; so in this, not to suffer a man of death to live. Bacon, Essay 14.

7. Cause of death.

They cried out, and said, O thou man of God, there is death in the pot. 2 Kings, iv. 40.

He caught his death the last county-sessions, where he would go to see justice done to a poor widow woman. Addis. Spectat.

8. Destroyer.

All the endeavours Achilles used to meet with Hector, and be the death of him, is the intrigue which comprehends the battle of the last day. Pope's View of Epic Poetry.

9. [In poetry.] The instrument of death.

   Deaths invisible come wing'd with fire;
They hear a dreadful noise, and straight
   expire. Dry. In. Em.

Sounded at once the bow; and swiftly flies
The feather'd death, and hisses through the
   skies. Dryd. Æn.

Oft, as in airy rings they skim the Heath,
The clam'rous plovers feel the leaden death.
Pope.

10. [In theology.] Damnation; eternal torments.

We pray that God will keep us from all sin and wickedness, from our ghostly enemy, and from everlasting death. Church Catechism.

déathsman n.s. [*death* and *man*.] Executioner; hangman; headsman; he that executes the sentence of death.

He's dead; I'm only sorry
He had no other deathsman. Shakespeare's
King Lear.

As deathsmen you have rid this sweet young
prince. Shak.

to deáurate v.a. [*deauro*, Latin.] To gild, or
cover with gold. Dict.

debacchátion n.s. [*debacchatio*, Latin.] A
raging; a madness. Dict.

to debárb adj. [from *de* and *barba*, Latin.]
To deprive of his beard. Dict.

debullítion n.s. [*debullitio*, Lat.] A
bubbling or seething over. Dict.

decacúminated adj. [*decacuminatus*, Latin.]
Having the top cut off. Dict.

Decémber n.s. [*december*, Latin.] The last
month of the year; but named *december*,
or the tenth month, when the year began
in March.†

Men are April when they woo, and
December when they wed. Shakespeare's
As you like it.

   What should we speak of,
When we are old as you? When we shall hear
The rain and wind beat dark December.
Shakesp. Cymbeline.

decémpedal adj. [from *decempeda*, Latin.]
Ten feet in length. Dict.

décimal adj. [*decimus*, Latin.] Numbered by
ten; multiplied by ten.

In the way we take now to name numbers by
millions of millions of millions, it is hard to go
beyond eighteen, or, at most, four and twenty
decimal progressions, without confusion.
Locke.

decollátion n.s. [*decollatio*, Lat] The act of
beheading.

He, by a decollation of all hope, annihilated
his mercy: this, by an immoderancy thereof,
destroyed his justice. Brown.

decórum n.s. [Latin.] Decency; behaviour
contrary to licentiousness, contrary to
levity; seemliness.

   If your master
Would have a queen his beggar, you must
   tell him,
That majesty, to keep decorum, must
No less beg than a kingdom. Shakespeare's
Ant. and Cleop.

I am far from suspecting simplicity, which is
bold to trespass in points of decorum. Wotton.

Beyond the fix'd and settled rules
Of vice and virtue in the schools,
The better sort should set before 'em
A grace, a manner, a decorum. Prior.

Gentlemen of the army should be, at least,
obliged to external decorum: a profligate life
and character should not be a means of
advancement. Swift.

He kept with princes due decorum;
Yet never stood in awe before 'em. Swift.

decrepitátion n.s. [from *decrepitate*.] The
crackling noise which salt makes, when put
over the fire in a crucible. Quincy.

decurtátion n.s. [*decurtatio*, Latin.] The act
of cutting short, or shortening.

dedicátion n.s. [*dedicatio*, Latin.]

1. The act of dedicating to any being
   or purpose; consecration; solemn
   appropriation.

It cannot be laid to many mens charge, that
they have been so curious as to trouble bishops
with placing the first stone in the churches; or
so scrupulous as, after the erection of them, to
make any great ado for their dedication.
Hooker, b. v. s. 12.

Among publick solemnities there is none so
glorious as that under the reign of king
Solomon, at the dedication of the temple.
Addison's Freeholder, Nº 49.

2. A servile address to a patron.

Proud as Apollo on his forked hill,
Sat full blown Bufo, puff'd by ev'ry quill;
Fed by soft dedication all day long,
Horace and he went hand in hand in song.
Pope, Epist. xi.

to défecate v.a. [*defæco*, Latin.]

1. To purge liquors from lees or foulness; to purify; to cleanse.

I practised a way to defecate the dark and muddy oil of amber. Boyle's History of Firmness.

The blood is not sufficiently defecated or clarified, but remains muddy. Harvey on Consumptions.

 Provide a brazen tube
Inflext; self-taught and voluntary flies
The defecated liquor, through the vent
Ascending; then, by downward tract convey'd,
Spouts into subject vessels, lovely clear.
Philips.

2. To purify from any extraneous or noxious mixture; to clear; to brighten.

We defecate the notion from materiality, and abstract quantity, place, and all kind of corporeity from it. Glanv. Sceps.

We are puzzled with contradictions, which are no absurdities to defecate faculties. Glanv. Sceps. c. 13.

deflúxion n.s. [*defluxio*, Latin.] A defluxion; a flowing down of humours.

We see that taking cold moveth looseness, by contraction of the skin and outward parts; and so doth cold likewise cause rheums and defluxions from the head. Bacon's Natural History.

deglutítion n.s. [*deglutition*, Fr. from *deglutio*, Lat.] The act or power of swallowing.

When the deglutition is totally abolished, the patient may be nourished by clysters. Arbuthnot on Diet.

déicide n.s. [from *deus* and *cædo*, Latin.] The murder of God; the act of killing God. It is only used in speaking of the death of our blessed Saviour.

Explain how perfection suffer'd pain,
Almighty languish'd, and Eternal dy'd;
How by her patient victor death was slain,
And earth profan'd, yet bless'd with deicide!
Prior.

deíparous adj. [*deiparus*, Latin.] That brings forth a god; the epithet applied to the blessed Virgin. Dict.

déism n.s. [*deisme*, French] The opinion of those that only acknowledge one God, without the reception of any revealed religion.

Deism, or the principles of natural worship, are only the faint remnants or dying flames of revealed religion in the posterity of Noah. Dryden's Pref. to Rel. Laici.

déist n.s. [*deiste*, French.] A man who follows no particular religion, but only acknowledges the existence of God, without any other article of faith.

The discourse is in the second epistle of St. Peter, the third chapter, where certain deists, as they seem to have been, laughed at the prophecy of the day of judgment. Burnet.

to delírate v.n. [*deliro*, Latin.] To dote; to rave; to talk or act idly. Dict.

démocracy n.s. [δημοκρατια.] One of the three forms of government; that in which the sovereign power is neither lodged in one man, nor in the nobles, but in the collective body of the people.

While many of the servants, by industry and virtue, arrive at riches and esteem, then the nature of the government inclines to a democracy. Temple.

The majority having the whole power of the community, may employ all that power in making laws, and executing those laws; and there the form of the government is a perfect democracy. Locke.

demonócracy n.s. [δαιμων and κρατεω.] The power of the devil. Dict.

demonólogy n.s. [δαιμων and λογος.] Discourse of the nature of devils. Thus king James entitled his book concerning witches.

dendrólogy n.s. [δενδρον and λογος.] The natural history of trees.

déntifrice n.s. [*dens* and *frico*, Latin.] A powder made to scour the teeth.

Is this grey powder a good dentifrice? Ben. Johns Catil.

The shells of all sorts of shell-fish, being burnt, obtain a caustick nature: most of them, so ordered and powdered, make excellent dentifrices. Grew's Musæum.

deosculátion n.s. [*deosculatio*, Latin.] The act of kissing.

We have an enumeration of the several acts of worship required to be performed to images, viz. processions, genuflections, thurifications and deosculations. Stillingfleet.

to depúcelate v.a. [*depuceler*, French.] To deflower; to bereave of virginity. Dict.

dérvis n.s. [*dervis*, French.] A Turkish priest.

Even there, where Christ vouchsaf'd to teach, Their dervises dare an impostor preach. Sandys.

The dervis at first made some scruple of violating his promise to the dying brachman; but told him, at last, that he could conceal nothing from so excellent a prince. Spectator.

déscant n.s. [*discanto*, Italian.]

1. A song or tune composed in parts.

   Nay, now you are too flat,
And mar the concord with too harsh a descant. Shakespeare.

   The wakeful nightingale
All night long her amorous descant sung. Milton's Par. Lost.

2. A discourse; a disputation; a disquisition branched out into several divisions or heads. It is commonly used as a word of censure, or contempt.

Look you get a prayer-book in your hand, And stand between two churchmen, good
   my lord;
For on that ground I'll build a holy descant. Shak. Rich. III.

Such kindness would supplant our unkind reportings, and severe descants upon our brethren. Government of the Tongue.

desídiose adj. [*desidiosus*, Latin.] Idle; lazy; heavy. Dict.

despumátion n.s. [from *despumate*.] The

act of throwing off excrementitious parts in scum or foam.

desquamátion n.s. [from *squama*, Latin.] The act of scaling foul bones.

deuce n.s. [*deux*, French.]

1. Two: A word used in games.

You are a gentleman and a gamester; then, I am sure, you know how much the gross sum of deuce ace amounts to. Shak.

2. The devil. See *deuse*.

deuse n.s. [more properly than *deuce*, Junius, from *Dusius*, the name of a certain species of evil spirits.] The devil: a ludicrous word.

'Twas the prettiest prologue, as he wrote it; Well, the deuce take me if I ha'n't forgot it. Congreve.

deuterógamy n.s. [δευτερος and γαμος.] A second marriage. Dict.

dévil n.s. [*dioful*, Saxon; *diabolus*, Latin. It is more properly written *divel*.]

1. A fallen angel; the tempter and spiritual enemy of mankind.

   Are you a man?
—Ay, and a bold one, that dare look on that Which might appal the devil. Shakespeare's Macbeth.

2. A wicked man or woman.

   See thyself, devil:
Proper deformity seems not in the fiend So horrid as in woman. Shakespeare's King Lear.

3. A ludicrous term for mischief.

A war of profit mitigates the evil; But to be tax'd, and beaten, is the devil. Granville.

4. A kind of expletive, expressing wonder or vexation.

The things, we know, are neither rich nor rare; But wonder how the devil they got there! Pope, Epist. ii.

5. A kind of ludicrous negative in an adverbial sense.

The devil was well, the devil a monk was he.
A Proverb.

dévilkin n.s. [from *devil.*] A little devil.
Clarissa.

devotée n.s. [*devot*, French.] One erroneously or superstitiously religious; a bigot.

devótionalist n.s. [from *devotion.*] A man zealous without knowledge; superstitiously devout.

diabétes n.s. [διαβαιτης.] A morbid copiousness of urine; a fatal colliquation by the urinary passages.

An increase of that secretion may accompany the general colliquations; as in fluxes, hectick sweats and coughs, diabetes, and other consumptions. Derham's Physico-Theology.

dialéctick n.s. [διαλεκτικη.] Logick; the act of reasoning.

diamond n.s. [*diamant*, French; *adamas*, Latin.] The diamond, the most valuable and hardest of all the gems, is, when pure, perfectly clear and pellucid as the purest water; and is eminently distinguished from all other substances by its vivid splendour, and the brightness of its reflexions. It is extremely various in shape and size, being found in the greatest quantity very small, and the larger ones extremely seldom met with. The largest ever known is that in the possession of the great Mogul, which weighs two hundred and seventy-nine carats, and is computed to be worth seven hundred and seventy-nine thousand two hundred and forty-four pounds. The diamond bears the force of the strongest fires, except the concentrated solar rays, without hurt; and even that infinitely fiercest of all fires does it no injury, unless directed to its weaker parts. It bears a glass-house fire for many days, and, if taken carefully out, and suffered to cool by degrees, is found as bright and beautiful as before; but if taken hastily out, it will sometimes crack, and even split into two or three pieces. The places where we have diamonds are the East Indies and the Brasils; and though they are usually found clear and colourless, yet they are sometimes slightly tinged with the colours of the other gems, by the mixture of some metalline particles. Hill on Fossils.

This diamond was my mother's: take it, heart;
But keep it 'till you woo another wife.
Shakesp. Cymbeline.

Give me the ring of mine you had at dinner;
Or, for the diamond, the chain you promised.
Shakespeare.

I see how thine eye would emulate the diamond: thou hast the right arched bent of the brow. Shak. Mer. Wives of Winds.

The diamond is preferable and vastly superior to all others in lustre and beauty; as also in hardness, which renders it more durable and lasting, and therefore much more valuable, than any other stone. Woodward's Mett. Foss.

The diamond is by mighty monarchs worn,
Fair as the star that ushers in the morn.
Blackm. Creation.

The lively diamond drinks thy purest rays,
Collected light, compact. Thomson's
Summer, l. 140.

díaper n.s. [*diapre*, French, of uncertain etymology.]

1. Linen cloth woven in flowers, and other figures.

Not any damsel, which her vaunteth most
In skilful knitting of soft silken twine;
Nor any weaver, which his work doth boast
In diaper, in damask, or in lyne,
Might in their diverse cunning ever dare
With this so curious net-work to compare.
Spenser.

2. A napkin; a towel.

Let one attend him with a silver bason
Full of rose-water, and bestrew'd with flowers;
Another bear the ewer, a third a diaper.
Shakespeare.

diatónick [of διατονος.] The ordinary sort of musick which proceeds by different tones, either in ascending or descending. It contains only the two greater and lesser tones, and the greater semi-tone. Harris.

díbble n.s. [from *dipfel*, Dutch, a sharp point, Skinner; from *dabble*, Junius.] A small spade; a pointed instrument with which the gardeners make holes for planting.

díbstone n.s. A little stone which children throw at another stone.

I have seen little girls exercise whole hours together, and take abundance of pains to be expert at dibstones, as they call it. Locke.

dicácity n.s. [*dicacitas*, Lat.] Pertness; sauciness. Dict.

díckens A kind of adverbial exclamation, importing, as it seems, much the same with the devil; but I know not whence derived.

Where had you this pretty weathercock?
—I cannot tell what the dickens his name is my husband had him of. Shakesp. Merry Wives of Windsor.

What a dickens does he mean by a trivial sum? But han't you found it, sir? Congreve's Old Batchelor.

díctionary n.s. [*dictionarium*, Latin.] A book containing the words of any language in alphabetical order, with explanations of their meaning; a lexicon; a vocabulary; a word-book.

Some have delivered the polity of spirits, and left an account that they stand in awe of charms, spells, and conjurations; that they are afraid of letters and characters, notes and dashes, which, set together, do signify nothing; and not only in the dictionary of man, but in the subtler vocabulary of Satan. Brown's Vulgar Errours, b. i. c. 10.

Is it such a horrible fault to translate simulacra *images? I see what a good thing it is to have a good catholick dictionary.* Still.

An army, or a parliament, is a collection of men; a dictionary, or nomenclature, is a collection of words. Watts.

to dídder v.a. [*diddern*, Teut. *zittern*, Germ.] To quake with cold; to shiver. A provincial word. Skinner.

to díet v.a. [from the noun.]

1. To feed by the rules of medicine.

She diets him with fasting every day,
The swelling of his wounds to mitigate,
And made him pray both early and eke late.
Fairy Queen.

Shew a while like fearful war,
To diet rank minds sick of happiness,
And purge th' obstructions, which begin to stop
Our very veins of life. Shakespeare's Henry IV. p. ii.

He was not taken well; he had not din'd:
The veins unfill'd, our blood is cold; and then
We powt upon the morning, are unapt
To give or to forgive; but when we've stuff'd
These pipes, and these conveyances of blood,
With wine and feeding, we have suppler souls
Than in our priestlike fasts; therefore I'll
    watch him
'Till he be dieted to my request. Shakesp. Coriolanus.

I will attend my husband, be his nurse,
Diet his sickness; for it is my office.
Shakesp. Com. of Err.

*   Henceforth my early care*
Shall 'tend thee, and the fertile burden ease
'Till dieted by thee, I grow mature
In knowledge as the gods, who all things
    know. Milt. P. L.

We have lived upon expedients, of which no country had less occasion: we have dieted a healthy body into a consumption, by plying it with physick instead of food. Swift.

2. To give food to.

I'm partly led to diet my revenge,
For that I do suspect the lusty Moor
Hath leapt into my seat. Shakespeare's Othello.

3. To board; to supply with diet.

differéntial method is applied to the doctrine of infinitesimals, or infinitely small quantities, called the arithmetick of fluxions; about the invention of which there has been a contest between Leibnitz and Sir Isaac Newton. It consists in descending from whole quantities to their infinitely small differences, and comparing together these infinitely small differences, of what kind soever they be: and from thence it takes the name of the differential calculus, or analysis of infinitesimals. Harris.†

digladiátion n.s. [*digladiatio,* Latin.] A combat with swords; any quarrel or contest.

Aristotle seems purposely to intend the cherishing of controversial digladiations, by his own affection of an intricate obscurity. Glanv. Sceps. c. 19.

díphthong n.s. [διφθογγος.] A coalition of two vowels to form one sound; as *vain, leaf, Cæsar.*

We see how many disputes the simple and ambiguous nature of vowels created among grammarians, and how it has begot the mistake concerning diphthongs: all that are properly so are syllables, and not diphthongs, as is intended to be signified by that word. Holder's Elements of Speech.

Make a diphthong of the second eta *and* iota, *instead of their being two syllables, and the objection is gone.* Notes on the Iliad.

diplóma n.s. [διπλωμα.] A letter or writing conferring some privilege, so called because they used formerly to be written on waxed tables, and folded together.

dirt-pie n.s. [*dirt* and *pie.*] Forms moulded by children of clay, in imitation of pastry.

Thou set'st thy heart upon that which has newly left off making of dirt-pies, and is but preparing itself for a greensickness. Suckling.

to disannúl v.a. [*dis* and *annul.* This word is formed contrary to analogy by those who not knowing the meaning of the word annul, intended to form a negative sense by the needless use of the negative particle. It ought therefore to be rejected as ungrammatical and barbarous.] To annul; to deprive of authority; to vacate; to make null; to make void; to nullify.

The Jews ordinances for us to resume, were to check our Lord himself, which hath disannulled them. Hooker, b. iv. § 11.

That gave him power of disannulling of laws, and disposing of mens fortunes and estates, and the like points of absolute power, being in themselves harsh and odious. Bacon, Hen. VII.

  To be in both worlds full,
Is more than God was, who was hungry here:
Wouldst thou his laws of fasting disannul? Herbert.

Wilt thou my judgments disannul? Defame My equal rule, to clear thyself of blame? Sandys.

dísard n.s. [*disi disig,* Saxon, a fool, Skinner; *diseur,* French, Junius.] A prattler; a boasting talker. This word is inserted both by Skinner and Junius; but I do not remember it.

disáster n.s. [*desastre,* French.]

1. The blast or stroke of an unfavourable planet.

Stars shone with trains of fire, dews of blood fall; Disasters veil'd the sun; and the moist star, Upon whose influence Neptune's empire stands, Was sick almost to doomsday with eclipse. Shakesp. Hamlet.

2. Misfortune; grief; mishap; misery; calamity.

This day black omens threat the brightest fair, That e'er deserv'd a watchful spirit's care, Some dire disaster, or by force or slight; But what, or where, the fates have wrapt in night. Pope.

discalceátion n.s. [from *dicalceated.*] The act of pulling off the shoes.

The custom of discalceation, or putting off their shoes at meals, is conceived to have been done, as by that means keeping their beds clean. Brown's Vulgar Errours, b. v. c. 6.

to discáse v.a. [*dis* and *case.*] To strip; to undress.

Fetch me the hat and rapier in my cell: I will discase me, and myself present. Shakesp. Tempest.

discipline n.s. [*disciplina*, Latin.]

1. Education; instruction; the act of cultivating the mind; the act of forming the manners.

The cold of the northern parts is that which, without aid of discipline, doth make the bodies hardest, and the courage warmest. Bacon, Essay 59.

They who want that sense of discipline, hearing, are also by consequence deprived of speech. Holder's Elements of Speech.

It must be confessed, it is by the assistance of the eye and the ear especially, which are called the senses of discipline, that our minds are furnished with various parts of knowledge. Watts.

2. Rule of government; order; method of government.

They hold, that from the very apostles time 'till this present age, wherein yourselves imagine ye have found out a right pattern of sound discipline, there never was any time safe to be followed. Hooker, Preface.

As we are to believe for ever the articles of evangelical doctrine, so the precepts of discipline we are, in like sort, bound for ever to observe. Hooker, b. iii. s. 10.

While we do admire
This virtue and this moral discipline,
Let's be no stoicks. Shakespeare.

3. Military regulation.

This opens all your victories in Scotland, Your discipline in war, wisdom in peace. Shakesp. Rich. III.

4. A state of subjection.

The most perfect among us, who have their passions in the best discipline, are yet obliged to be constantly on their guard. Rogers, Sermon 13.

5. Any thing taught; art; science.

Art may be said to overcome and advance nature in these mechanical disciplines, which, in this respect, are much to be preferred. Wilkins's Math. Magick.

6. Punishment; chastisement; correction.

A lively cobler kicked and spurred while his wife was carrying him, and had scarce passed a day without giving her the discipline of the strap. Addison's Spectator, Nº 499.

discord n.s. [*discordia*, Latin.]

1. Disagreement; opposition; mutual anger; reciprocal oppugnancy.

See what a scourge is laid upon your hate,
That heav'n finds means to kill your joys
*   with love!*
And I, for winking at your discords too,
Have lost a brace of kinsmen. Shakesp. Rom. and Jul.

Take but degree away, untune that string, And hark what discord follows; each thing meets In meer oppugnancy. Shakesp. Troil. and Cress.

He is a false witness that speaketh lies, and that soweth discord among brethren. Prov. vi. 19.

2. Difference, or contrariety of qualities.

Discord, like that of music's various parts,
Discord that makes the harmony of hearts;
Discord that only this dispute shall bring,
Who best shall love the duke and serve the
*   king.* Dryd. Ep.

All nature is but art unknown to thee;
All chance, direction which thou canst not see;
All discord, harmony not understood;
All partial evil, universal good.
Pope's Essay on Man.

3. [In music.] Sounds not of themselves pleasing, but necessary to be mixed with others.

It is sound alone that doth immediately and incorporeally affect most; this is most manifest in music, and concords and discords in music: for all sounds, whether they be sharp or flat, if they be sweet, have a roundness and equality; and if they be harsh, are unequal: for a discord itself is but a harshness of divers sounds meeting. Bacon's N. Hist. Part I. p. 400.

It is the lark that sings so out of tune, Straining harsh discords and unpleasing sharps. Shakesp.

*How doth music amaze us, when of discords
she maketh the sweetest harmony?* Peacham.

to discóver v.a. [*descouvrir*, French; *dis*
and *cover*.]

1. To shew; to disclose; to bring to light.

*Go draw aside the curtains, and discover
The several caskets to this noble prince.*
Sh. Merch. of Ven.

*He discovereth deep things out of darkness,
and bringeth out to light the shadow of death.*
Job xii. 22.

2. To make known.

*We will pass over unto those men, and we
will discover ourselves unto them.* Isa. xiv. 8.

3. To find out; to espy.

*He shall never by any alteration in me
discover my knowledge of his mistake.*
Pope's Letters.

dishabílle n.s. Undress; loose dress.

*A woman, who would preserve a lover's
respect to her person, will be careful of her
appearance before him when in dishabille.*
Clarissa.

to disjóint v.a. [*dis* and *joint*.]

1. To put out of joint.

*Be all their ligaments at once unbound,
And their disjointed bones to powder ground.*
Sandys's Paraph.

*Yet what could swords or poison, racks or flame,
But mangle and disjoint the brittle frame,
More fatal Henry's words; they murder
    Emma's fame.* Pr.

2. To break at junctures; to separate at the
part where there is a cement.

Mould'ring arches, and disjointed columns.
Irene.

3. To break in pieces; to dilaniate.

   *Rotation must disperse in air,
All things which on the rapid orb appear;
And if no power that motion should controul,
It must disjoint and dissipate the whole.*
Blackmore.

*Should a barbarous Indian, who had never
seen a palace or a ship, view the separate and
disjointed parts, he would be able to form but
a very lame and dark idea of either of those
excellent and useful inventions.* Watts's
Improvm. of the Mind.

4. To carve a fowl.

5. To make incoherent; to break the
relation between the parts.

*The constancy of your wit was not wont
to bring forth such disjointed speeches.*
Sidney, b. ii.

*But now her grief has wrought her into frenzy,
The images her troubled fancy forms
Are incoherent, wild; her words disjointed.*
Smith.

to dislímb v.a. [*dis* and *limb*.] To dilaniate;
to tear limb from limb. Dict.

to dislímn v.a. [*dis* and *limn*.] To unpaint;
to strike out of a picture.

*That which is now a horse, even with a thought
The rack dislimns, and makes it indistinct
As water is in water.* Shakespeare's Ant.
and Cleop.

to dissémble v.n. To play the hypocrite.

*Ye dissembled in your hearts when ye sent me
unto the Lord your God, saying, pray for us.*
Jer. xlii. 20.

*I would dissemble with my nature, where
My fortunes, and my friends, at stake, requir'd
I should do so in honour.* Shakespeare's
Coriolanus.

*I am curtail'd of this fair proportion,
Cheated of feature by dissembling nature,
Deform'd, unfinish'd.* Shakesp. Richard III.

*Thy function too will varnish o'er our arts,
And sanctify dissembling.* Rowe's Ambitious
Stepmother.

to díssipate v.a. [*dissipatus*, Latin.]

1. To scatter every way; to disperse.

*The heat at length grows so great, that it
again dissipates and bears off those very
corpuscles which before it brought.*
Woodward's Natural History.

The circling mountains eddy in,
From the bare wild, the dissipated storm.
Thomson's Autumn.

2. To scatter the attention.

This slavery to his passions produced a life
irregular and dissipated. Savage's Life.†

3. To spend a fortune.

   The wherry that contains
Of dissipated wealth the poor remains.
London.

distaff n.s. [*distæf*, Saxon.]

1. The staff from which the flax is drawn
   in spinning.

In sum, proud Boreas never ruled fleet,
Who Neptune's web on danger's distaff spins,
With greater power than she did make
   them wend
Each way, as she that ages praise did bend.
Sidney.

Weave thou to end this web which I begin;
I will the distaff hold, come thou and spin.
Fairfax, b. iv.

Ran Coll our dog, and Talbot with the band,
And Malkin with her distaff in her hand.
Dryden.

2. It is used as an emblem of the
   female sex.

In my civil government some say the
crosier, some say the distaff was too busy.
Howel's England's Tears.

   See my royal master murder'd,
His crown usurp'd, a distaff in the throne.
Dryden.

distémper n.s. [*dis* and *temper.*]

1. A disproportionate mixture of parts;
   want of a due temper of ingredients.

2. A disease; a malady; the peccant
   predominance of some humour;
   properly a slight illness; indisposition.

They heighten distempers to diseases.
Suckling.

It argues sickness and distemper in the mind,
as well as in the body, when a man is
continually turning and tossing. South.

3. Want of due temperature.

It was a reasonable conjecture, that those
countries which were situated directly under
the tropick, were of a distemper
uninhabitable. Raleigh's History of
the World.

4. Bad constitution of the mind;
   predominance of any passion or
   appetite.

If little faults, proceeding on distemper,
Shall not be wink'd at, how shall we
   stretch our eye
At capital crimes? Shakespeare's Henry V.

5. Want of due ballance between
   contraries.

The true temper of empire is a thing rare, and
hard to keep; for both temper and distemper
consist of contraries. Bac.

6. Ill humour of mind; depravity of
   inclination.

I was not forgetful of those sparks, which some
mens distempers formerly studied to kindle in
parliament. King Charles.

7. Tumultuous disorder.

Still as you rise, the state exalted too,
Finds no distemper while 'tis chang'd by you.
Waller.

8. Disorder; uneasiness.

   There is a sickness,
Which puts some of us in distemper; but
I cannot name the disease, and it is caught
Of you that yet are well. Shakespeare's
Winter's Tale.

distráction n.s. [*distractio*, Latin.]

1. Tendency to different parts; separation.

   While he was yet in Rome
His power went out in such distractions as
Beguil'd all spies. Shakespeare's Anthony
and Cleopatra.

2. Confusion; state in which the attention
   is called different ways.

Never was known a night of such distraction;
Noise so confus'd and dreadful; jostling crowds,
That run, and knew not whither. Dryden's
Spanish Fryar.

What may we not hope from him in a time of quiet and tranquillity, since, during the late distractions, he has done so much for the advantage of our trade? Addison's Freeholder.

3. Perturbation of mind; violence of some painful passion.

The distraction of the children, who saw both their parents expiring together, would have melted the hardest heart. Tatler.

4. Madness; frantickness; loss of the wits.

Madam, this is a meer distraction: You turn the good we offer into envy. Shakesp. H. VIII.

So to mad Pentheus double Thebes appears, And furies howl in his distemper'd ears: Orestes so, with like distraction tost, Is made to fly his mother's angry ghost. Waller.

Commiserate all those who labour under a settled distraction, and who are shut out from all the pleasures and advantages of human commerce. Atterbury's Sermons.

5. Disturbance; tumult; difference of sentiments.

The two armies lay quiet near each other, without improving the confusion and distraction which the king's forces were too much inclined to. Clarendon, b. viii.

dithyrámbick n.s. [*dithyrambus*, Latin.]

1. A song in honour of Bacchus; in which anciently, and now among the Italians, the distraction of ebriety is imitated.

2. Any poem written with wildness and enthusiasm.

Pindar does new words and figures roll Down his impetuous dithyrambick tide. Cowley.

diván n.s. [An Arabick or Turkish word.]

1. The council of the Oriental princes.

2. Any council assembled: used commonly in a sense of dislike.

Forth rush'd in haste the great consulting peers, Rais'd from the dark divan, and with like joy

Congratulant approach'd him. Milton's Paradise Lost, b. x.

Swift to the queen the herald Medon ran, Who heard the consult of the dire divan. Pope's Odyssey.

divérsion n.s. [from *divert.*]

1. The act of turning any thing off from its course.

Cutting off the tops, and pulling off the buds, work retention of the sap for a time, and diversion of it to the sprouts that were not forward. Bacon's Natural History.

2. The cause by which any thing is turned from its proper course or tendency.

Fortunes, honour, friends, Are mere diversions from love's proper object, Which only is itself. Denham's Sophy.

3. Sport; something that unbends the mind by turning it off from care. Diversion seems to be something lighter than amusement, and less forcible than pleasure.

You for those ends whole days in council sit, And the diversions of your youth forget. Waller.

In the book of games and diversions the reader's mind may be supposed to be relaxed. Addison's Spectator.

Such productions of wit and humour as expose vice and folly, furnish useful diversions to readers. Addison's Freeholder.

4. [In war.] The act or purpose of drawing the enemy off from some design, by threatening or attacking a distant part.

divíne n.s.

1. A minister of the gospel; a priest; a clergyman.

Claudio must die to-morrow: let him be furnished with divines, and have all charitable preparation. Sh. Meas. for Meas.

Give Martius leave to proceed in his discourse; for he spoke like a divine in armour. Bacon's Holy War.

A divine has nothing to say to the wisest congregation, which he may not express in a manner to be understood by the meanest among them. Swift.

2. A man skilled in divinity; a theologian.

Th' eternal cause in their immortal lines Was taught, and poets were the first divines. Denham.

divísor n.s. [*divisor*, Latin.] The number given, by which the dividend is divided; the number which sheweth how many parts the dividend is to be divided into.

to dízen v.a. [This word seems corrupted from *dight*.] To dress; to deck; to rig out. A low word.

Your ladyship lifts up the sash to be seen; For sure I had dizen'd you out like a queen. Swift.

dízzard n.s. [from *dizzy*.] A blockhead; a fool. Dict.

dóctor n.s. [*doctor*, Latin.]

1. One that has taken the highest degree in the faculties of divinity, law, or physick. In some universities they have doctors of musick. In its original import it means a man so well versed in his faculty, as to be qualified to teach it.

No woman had it, but a civil doctor, Who did refuse three thousand ducats of me, And begg'd the ring. Shakespeare's Merchant of Venice.

Then stood there up one in the council, a pharisee, named Gamaliel, a doctor of laws. Acts v. 34.

2. A man skilled in any profession.

Then subtle doctors scriptures made their pride, Casuists, like cocks, struck out each other's eyes. Denham.

Each proselyte would vote his doctor best, With absolute exclusion to the rest. Dryd. Hind and Panth.

3. A physician; one who undertakes the cure of diseases.†

By med'cine life may be prolong'd, yet death Will seize the doctor too. Shakespeare's Cymbeline.

How does your patient, doctor? —Not so sick, my lord, As she is troubl'd with thick coming fancies. Shakesp. Macb.

Children will not take those medicines from the doctor's hand, which they will from a nurse or mother. Gov. of Tongue.

To 'pothecaries let the learn'd prescribe, That men may die without a double bribe: Let them, but under their superiors, kill, When doctors first have sign'd the bloody bill. Dryden.

He that can cure by recreation, and make pleasure the vehicle of health, is a doctor at it in good earnest. Collier.

In truth, nine parts in ten of those who recovered, owed their lives to the strength of nature and a good constitution, while such a one happened to be the doctor. Swift.

4. Any able or learned man.

The simplest person, that can but apprehend and speak sense, is as much judge of it as the greatest doctor in the school. Digby of Bodies.

dóctrine n.s. [*doctrina*, Latin.]

1. The principles or positions of any sect or master; that which is taught.

To make new articles of faith and doctrine, no man thinketh it lawful: new laws of government, what church or commonwealth is there which maketh not either at one time or other? Hooker, b. iii. s. 10.

Ye are the sons of clergy, who bring all their doctrines fairly to the light, and invite men with freedom to examine them. Atterbury's Sermons.

That great principle in natural philosophy is the doctrine of gravitation, or mutual tendency of all bodies toward each other. Watts's Improvement of the Mind.

2. The act of teaching.

He said unto them in his doctrine. Mark iv. 2.

dodecatemórion n.s. [δωδεκατεμοριον.] The twelfth part.

'Tis dodecatemorion thus describ'd:
Thrice ten degrees, which every sign contains,
Let twelve exhaust, that not one part remains;
It follows streight, that every twelfth confines
Two whole, and one half portion of the signs.
Creech.

dog n.s. [*dogghe*, Dutch.]

1. A domestick animal remarkably various in his species; comprising the mastiff, the spaniel, the buldog, the greyhound, the hound, the terrier, the cur, with many others. The larger sort are used as a guard; the less for sports.

Such smiling rogues as these sooth every passion!
Renege, affirm, and turn their halcyon beaks
With ev'ry gale and vary of their masters,
As knowing nought, like dogs, but following.
Shak. K. Lear.

Why should we not think a watch and pistol as distinct species one from another, as a horse and a dog. Locke.

The clamour roars of men and boys, and dogs,
Ere the soft fearful people, to the flood
Commit their woolly sides. Thomson's Spring, l. 375.

2. A constellation called Sirius, or Canicula, rising and setting with the sun during the canicular days, or dog days.

Among the southern constellations two there are who bear the name of the dog; the one in sixteen degrees latitude, containing on the left thigh a star of the first magnitude, usually called Procyon, or Anticanus. Brown's Vulgar Errours, b. iv.

It parts the twins and crab, the dog divides,
And Argo's keel that broke the frothy tides.
Creech.

3. A reproachful name for a man.

I never heard a passion so confus'd,
So strange, outrageous, and so variable,
As the dog Jew did utter in the streets.
Shak. Mer. of Venice.

Beware of dogs, beware of evil workers.
Phil. iii. 2.

4. To give or send to the dogs; to throw away. To go to the dogs; to be ruined, destroyed, or devoured.

Had whole Colepeper's wealth been hops and hogs,
Could he himself have sent it to the dogs?
Pope's Epistles.

5. It is used as the term for the male of several species; as, the dog fox, the dog otter.

If ever I thank any man, I'll thank you; but that they call compliments is like the encounter of two dog apes. Shakesp.

6. *Dog* is a particle added to any thing to mark meanness, or degeneracy, or worthlessness; as dog rose.

to dog v.a. [from the noun.] To hunt as a dog, insidiously and indefatigably.

I have dogg'd him like his murtherer. Shakes. Twelfth Night.

His taken labours bid him me forgive;
I, his despiteful Juno, sent him forth
From courtly friends, with camping foes to live,
Where death and danger dog the heels of worth. Shakesp.

*   Sorrow dogging sin,*
Afflictions sorted. Herbert.

These spiritual joys are dogged by no such sad sequels as are the products of those titillations, that reach no higher than fancy and the senses. Glanv. Sceps. Pref.

I have been pursued, dogged, and way-laid through several nations, and even now scarce think myself secure. Pope.

Hate dogs their rise, and insult mocks their fall. Vanity of Human Wishes.

dogmátical, dogmátick adj. [from *dogma*.] Authoritative; magisterial; positive; in the manner of a philosopher laying down the first principles of a sect.

The dim and bounded intellect of man seldom prosperously adventures to be dogmatical about things that approach to infinite, whether in vastness or littleness. Boyle.

I laid by my natural diffidence and scepticism for a while, to take up that dogmatical way, which is so much his character. Dryden.

Learning gives us a discovery of our ignorance, and keeps us from being peremptory and dogmatical in our determinations. Collier on Pride.

Criticks write in a positive dogmatick way, without either language, genius, or imagination. Spectator.

One of these authors is indeed so grave, sententious, dogmatical a rogue, that there is no enduring him. Swift.

dógweary adj. [*dog* and *weary.*] Tired as a dog; excessively weary.

Oh, master, master, I have watch'd so long,
That I'm dogweary. Shakesp. Taming of the Shrew.

dóllar n.s. [*daler*, Dutch.] A Dutch and German coin of different value, from about two shillings and sixpence to four and sixpence.

He disburs'd, at St. Colmeskill isle,
Ten thousand dollars for our gen'ral use.
Shakesp. Macbeth.

dolt n.s. [*dol*, Teutonick.] A heavy stupid fellow; a blockhead; a thickscul; a loggerhead.

Let dolts in haste some altar fair erect
To those high powers, which idlely sit above.
Sidney, b. ii.

Thou hast not half that power to do me harm,
As I have to be hurt: oh, gull! oh, dolt!
As ignorant as dirt! Shakespeare's Othello.

Like men condemn'd to thunder-bolts,
Who, ere the blow, become mere dolts;
They neither have the hearts to stay,
Nor wit enough to run away. Hudibras, p. iii. cant. 2.

Wood's adult'rate copper,
Which, as he scatter'd, we, like dolts,
Mistook at first for thunder-bolts. Swift.

doméstical, doméstick adj. [*domesticus*, Latin.]

1. Belonging to the house; not relating to things publick.

The necessities of man had at the first no other helps and supplies than domestical; such as that which the prophet implyeth, saying, can a mother forget her child? Hooker.

The practical knowledge of the domestick duties is the principal glory of a woman. Clarissa.

2. Private; done at home; not open.

In this their domestical celebration of the Passover, they divided supper into two courses. Hooker, b. iii.

Beholding thus, O, happy as a queen!
We cry; but shift the gaudy, flattering scene,
View her at home in her domestick light,
For thither she must come, at least at night.
Granville.

3. Inhabiting the house; not wild.

The faithful prudent husband is an honest, tractable, and domestick animal. Addison's Spectator, N° 128.

4. Not foreign; intestine.

Domestical evils, for that we think we can master them at all times, are often permitted to run on forward, 'till it be too late to recall them. Hooker, Dedication.

Equality of two domestick pow'rs
Breeds scrupulous faction. Shakespeare's Anth. and Cleopatra.

Combine together 'gainst the enemy;
For these domestick and particular broils
Are not the question here. Shakespeare's King Lear.

Next to the sin of those who began that rebellion, theirs must needs be who hindered the speedy suppressing of it, by domestick dissentions. King Charles.

Such they were, who might presume t' have done Much for the king and honour of the state;
Having the chiefest actions undergone,
Both foreign and domestical of late. Daniel's Civil War.

domínion n.s. [*dominium*, Latin.]

1. Sovereign authority; unlimited power.

They on the earth
Dominion exercise, and in the air,
Chiefly on man. Milton's Par. Lost.

He gave us only over beast, fish, fowl,
Dominion absolute; that right we hold
By his donation: but man over man
He made not lord. Milton.

Blest use of pow'r, O virtuous pride in kings!
And like his bounty, whence dominion
springs. Tickell.

2. Power; right of possession or use, without being accountable.

He could not have private dominion over
that, which was under the private dominion
of another. Locke.

3. Territory; region; subject; district.

The donations of bishopricks were a flower of
the crown, which the kings of England did
ever retain in all their dominions, when the
pope's usurped authority was at the highest.
Davies on Ireland.

4. Predominance; ascendant.

Objects placed foremost ought to be more
finished than those cast behind, and to have
dominion over things confused and transient.
Dryden's Dufresnoy.

5. An order of angels.

By him were all things created, visible and
invisible, whether they be thrones or
dominions, or principalities or powers.
Col. i. 16.

don n.s. [*dominus*, Latin.] The Spanish title for a gentleman; as, don Quixote.

dónjon n.s. [now corrupted to *dungeon*, from *domnionum*, low Latin, according to Menage.] The highest and strongest tower of the castle, in which prisoners were kept; as in Chaucer.

The grete toure, that was so thicke and strong,
Which of the castle was the chief dongeon,
Wherein the knightes were in prison,

Was evin joynant to the garden-wall,
Ther as this Emely had her playeing.
Chaucer.

dóodle n.s. [a cant word, perhaps corrupted from *do little*, Faineant.] A trifler; an idler.

dóomsday n.s. [*doom* and *day*.]

1. The day of final and universal judgment; the last, the great day.

Men, wives, and children stare, cry out, and run,
As it were doomsday. Shakespeare's Julius Cæsar.

They may serve for any theme, and never be
out of date until doomsday. Brown's Vulgar Errours, b. i. c. 6.

Our souls, not yet prepar'd for upper light,
'Till doomsday wander in the shades of night:
This only holiday of all the year,
We privileg'd in sunshine may appear.
Dryden.

2. The day of sentence or condemnation.

All-souls day is my body's doomsday.
Shakespeare's R. III.

dótard n.s. [from *dote*.] A man whose age has impaired his intellects; a man in his second childhood; called in some provinces a twichild.

Dotard, said he, let be thy deep advise,
Seems that through many years thy wits thee fail,
And that weak old hath left thee nothing wise,
Else never should thy judgement be so frail.
Fairy Queen.

The sickly dotard wants a wife,
To draw off his last dregs of life. Prior.

to dote v.n. [*doten*, Dutch; *radoter*, French.]

1. To have the intellect impaired by age or passion; to be delirious.

Unless the fear of death make me dote,
I see my son. Shakesp. Com. of Err.

A sword is upon the liars, and they shall dote:
a sword is upon her mighty men, and they
shall be dismayed. Jer. l. 36.

Time has made you dote, and vainly tell
Of arms imagin'd, in your lonely cell:
Go, be the temple and the gods your care;

Permit to men the thought of peace and war.
Dryd. Æn.

*When an old woman begins to dote, and grow
chargeable to a parish, she is turned into a
witch, and fills the country with extravagant
fancies.* Addison's Spectator, Nº 117.

2. To be in love to extremity.

*He was striken with great affection towards
me, which since is grown to such a doting
love, that, 'till I was fain to get this place,
sometimes to retire in freely: I was even
choked with his tediousness.* Sidney.

*I have long loved her, and bestowed much on
her, followed her with a doting observance.*
Shak. M. Wives of Winds.

double-dealer n.s. [*double* and *dealer*.] A
deceitful, subtle, insidious fellow; one who
acts two parts at the same time; one who
says one thing and thinks another.

*Double-dealers may pass muster for a while;
but all parties wash their hands of them in
the conclusion.* L'Estrange.

dóublet n.s. [from *double*.]

1. The inner garment of a man; the
waistcoat: so called from being double
for warmth.

*What a pretty thing a man is, when he goes
in his doublet and hose, and leaves off his wit.*
Sh. Much Ado about Nothing.

*His doublet was of sturdy buff,
And though not sword yet cudgel proof.*
Hudibras, p. i.

*It is common enough to see a countryman
in the doublet and breeches of his great
grandfather.* Addison's Italy.

*They do but mimick ancient wits at best,
As apes our grandsires, in their doublets drest.*
Pope's Criticism.

2. Two; a pair.

*Those doublets on the sides of his tail seem to
add strength to the muscles which move the
tail-fins.* Grew's Musæum.

doublón n.s. [French.] A Spanish coin
containing the value of two pistoles.

to doubt v.n. [*doubter*, French; *dubito*,
Latin.]

1. To question; to be in uncertainty.

*Even in matters divine, concerning some
things, we may lawfully doubt and suspend
our judgment, inclining neither to one side or
other; as, namely, touching the time of the fall
both of man and angels.* Hooker, b. ii. s. 7.

*Let no man, while he lives here in the world,
doubt whether there is any hell or no, and
thereupon live so, as if absolutely there were
none.* South's Sermons.

*I doubt not to make it appear to be a
monstrous folly to deride these things.*
Tillotson's Sermons.

*Can we conclude upon Luther's instability,
because in a single notion, no way
fundamental, an enemy writes that he had
some doubtings?* Atterbury.

2. To question any event, fearing
the worst.

*Doubting things go ill, often hurt more
Than to be sure they do.* Shakespeare's
Cymbeline.

3. Sometimes with *of* in both the
foregoing senses.

*Solyman said he had hitherto made war
against divers nations, and always had the
victory, whereof he doubted not now also.*
Knolles's History of the Turks.

*Have I not manag'd my contrivance well,
To try your love, and make you doubt of
mine?* Dryden.

4. To fear; to be apprehensive.

*I doubt there's deep resentment in his mind,
For the late slight his honour suffer'd there.*
Otway's Orph.

*If there were no fault in the title, I doubt
there are too many in the body of the work.*
Baker on Learning.

*This is enough for a project, without any
name; I doubt more than will be reduced into
practice.* Swift.

5. To suspect; to have suspicion.

The king did all his courage bend
Against those four which now before him were,
Doubting not who behind him doth attend.
Daniel's C. War.

6. To hesitate; to be in suspense.

At first the tender blades of grass appear,
And buds that yet the blast of Eurus fear,
Stand at the door of life, and doubt to clothe
the year. Dry.

dówager n.s. [*douairiere*, French.]

1. A widow with a jointure.

She lingers my desires,
Like to a stepdame or a dowager,
Long wintering on a young man's revenue.
Shakespeare.

Widows have a greater interest in property
than either maids or wives; so that it is
as unnatural for a dowager as a freeholder
to be an enemy to our constitution.
Addis. Freehold.

2. The title given to ladies who survive
their husbands.

Catharine no more
Shall be call'd queen; but princess dowager,
And widow to prince Arthur. Shakespeare's
Henry VIII.

dówdy n.s. An aukward, ill-dressed,
inelegant woman.

Laura, to his lady, was but a kitchen wench;
Dido, a dowdy; Cleopatra, a gipsy; Helen and
Hero, slidings and harlots. Shakespeare's
Romeo and Juliet.

The bedlam train of lovers use
T' inhance the value, and the faults excuse;
And therefore 'tis no wonder if we see
They doat on dowdies and deformity.
Dryden.

No houswifry the dowdy creature knew;
To sum up all, her tongue confess'd the shrew.
Gay's Past.

dówer, dówery n.s. [*douaire*, French.]

1. That which the wife bringeth to her
husband in marriage.

His wife brought in dow'r Cilicia's crown,
And in herself a greater dow'r alone. Dryden.

His only daughter in a stranger's pow'r;
For very want, he could not pay a dow'r.
Pope's Epistles.

2. That which the widow possesses.

His patrimonial territories of Flanders were
partly in dower to his mother-in-law, and
partly not serviceable, in respect of the late
rebellions. Bacon's Henry VII.

3. The gifts of a husband for a wife.

Ask me never so much dowery and gift, and I
will give according as ye shall say unto me; but
give me the damsel to wife. Gen. xxxiv. 12.

4. Endowment; gift.

What spreading virtue, what a sparkling fire;
How great, how plentiful, how rich a dow'r,
Do'st thou within this dying flesh inspire!
Davies.

dóxy n.s. A whore; a loose wench.

When daffadils begin to pure,
With heigh! the doxy over the dale.
Shakes. Winter's Tale.

drab n.s. [*drabbe*, Saxon, lees.] A whore;
a strumpet.

That I, the son of a dear father murder'd,
Must, like a whore, unpack my heart
with words,
And fall a cursing, like a very drab!
Shakesp. Hamlet.

If your worship will take order for the drabs
and the knaves, you need not to fear the
bawds. Shakespeare.

Babe,
Ditch-deliver'd by a drab. Shakespeare's
Macbeth.

Curs'd be the wretch so venal, and so vain,
Paltry and proud as drabs in Drury-lane.
Pope.

dracunculus n.s. [Latin.] A worm bred in
the hot countries, which grows to many
yards length between the skin and flesh.

dráffy adj. [from *draff*.] Worthless; dreggy.

drágon n.s. [*draco*, Latin; *dragon*, French.]

1. A kind of winged serpent, perhaps
imaginary, much celebrated in the
romances of the middle age.

I go alone,
Like to a lonely dragon, that his fen
Makes fear'd and talk'd of more than seen.
Shak. Coriolan.

Swift, swift, you dragons of the night! that
dawning
May bear the raven's eye. Shakespeare's
Cymbeline.

And you, ye dragons! of the scaly race,
Whom glittering gold and shining armours grace;
In other nations harmless are you found,
Their guardian genii and protectors own'd.
Rowe.

On spiry volumes there a dragon rides;
Here, from our strict embrace, a stream he
glides. Pope.

2. A fierce violent man or woman.

3. A constellation near the North pole.

dráma n.s. [δραμα.] A poem accommodated to action; a poem in which the action is not related, but represented; and in which therefore such rules are to be observed as make the representation probable.

Many rules of imitating nature Aristotle
drew from Homer, which he fitted to the
drama; furnishing himself also with
observations from the theatre, when it
flourished under Eschylus, Euripides, and
Sophocles. Dryden's Æn. Dedicat.

dream n.s. [*droom*, Dutch.] This word is derived by Meric Casaubon, with more ingenuity than truth, from δραμα του βιου, the comedy of life; dreams being, as plays are, a representation of something which does not really happen. This conceit Junius has enlarged by quoting an epigram.

Σληνη πας ο βιος και παιγνιον η
μιαθε παιζειν,
Την σπουδην μεταθεις, η φερε τας
οδυνας. Anthol.[†]

1. A phantasm of sleep; the thoughts of a sleeping man.

We eat our meat in fear, and sleep
In the affliction of those terrible dreams

That shake us nightly. Shakespeare's
Macbeth.

In dreams they fearful precipices tread;
Or, shipwreck'd, labour to some distant shore.
Dryden.

Glorious dreams stand ready to restore
The pleasing shapes of all you saw before.
Dryden.

2. An idle fancy; a wild conceit; a groundless suspicion.

Let him keep
A hundred knights; yes, that on ev'ry dream,
Each buz, each fancy, each complaint, dislike,
He may enguard his dotage. Shakespeare's
King Lear.

drínkmoney n.s. [*drink* and *money*.] Money given to buy liquor.

Peg's servants were always asking for
drinkmoney. Arbuthnot.

drop serene n.s. [*gutta serena*, Latin.] A disease of the eye, proceeding from an inspissation of the humour.

So thick a drop serene hath quench'd their orbs,
Or dim suffusion veil'd! Milton's Paradise
Lost, b. iii.

drópsy n.s. [*hydrops*, Latin; whence anciently hydropisy, thence dropisy, dropsy.] A collection of water in the body, from too lax a tone of the solids, whereby digestion is weakened, and all the parts stuffed. Quincy.[†]

An anasarca, a species of dropsy, is an
extravasation of water lodged in the cells
of the membrana adiposa. Sharp.

Drúid n.s. [*derio*, oaks, and *hud*, incantation; which may be as ancient as the Grecian δρυς. *Perron; darrach*, oak, Erse.] The priests and philosophers of the antient Britons.

dúcat n.s. [from *duke*.] A coin struck by dukes: in silver valued at about four shillings and six pence; in gold at nine shillings and six pence.

I cannot instantly raise up the gross
Of full three thousand ducats. Shakesp.
Merchant of Venice.

There was one that died in debt: it was reported, where his creditors were, that he was dead: one said, he hath carried five hundred ducats of mine into the other world. Bacon.

duénna n.s. [Spanish.] An old woman kept to guard a younger.

I felt the ardour of my passion increase as the season advanced, 'till in the month of July I could no longer contain: I bribed her duenna, was admitted to the bath, saw her undressed, and the wonder displayed. Arbuthnot and Pope.

dug n.s. [*deggia*, to give suck, Islandick.]

1. A pap; a nipple; a teat: spoken of beasts, or in malice or contempt of human beings.

Of her there bred
A thousand young ones, which she daily fed,
Sucking upon her poisonous dugs; each one
Of sundry shape, yet all ill favoured.
Fairy Queen, b. i.

They are first fed and nourished with the milk of a strange dug. Raleigh's History of the World.

Then shines the goat, whose brutish dugs supply'd
The infant Jove, and nurst his growing pride.
Creech.

2. It seems to have been used formerly of the breast without reproach.

It was a faithless squire that was the source
Of all my sorrow, and of these sad tears;
With whom, from tender dug of common nourse,
At once I was up brought. Fairy Queen,
b. ii. cant. 4.

As mild and gentle as the cradle-babe,
Dying with mother's dug between its lips.
Shakes. Hen. VI.

duke n.s. [*duc*, French; *dux*, Latin.] One of the highest order of nobility in England; in rank a nobleman next to the royal family.

The duke of Cornwal, and Regan his dutchess,
will be here with him this night.
Shakespeare's King Lear.

Aurmarle, Surrey, and Exeter must lose
The names of dukes, their titles, dignities,

And whatsoever profits thereby rise. Daniel's C. War.

dúlcet adj. [*dulcis*, Latin.]

1. Sweet to the taste; luscious.

From sweet kernels press'd,
She tempers dulcet creams; nor these to hold
Wants she fit vessels pure. Milton's Paradise Lost, b. v.

2. Sweet to the ear; harmonious; melodious.

I sat upon a promontory,
And heard a mermaid, on a dolphin's back,
Uttering such dulcet and harmonious breath,
That the rude sea grew civil at her song.
Shakespeare.

A fabrick huge
Rose like an exhalation, with the sound
Of dulcet symphonies, and voices sweet. Milt. Parad. Lost.

dull adj. [*dwl*, Welsh; *dole*, Saxon; *dol*, mad, Dutch.]

1. Stupid; doltish; blockish; unapprehensive; indocile; slow of understanding.

Such is their evil hap to play upon dull spirited men. Hooker.

He that hath learned no wit by nature, nor art, may complain of gross breeding, or comes of a very dull kindred. Shak.

Sometimes this perception, in some kind of bodies, is far more subtile than the sense; so that the sense is but a dull thing in comparison of it. Bacon's Natural History.

Every man, even the dullest, is thinking more than the most eloquent can teach him how to utter. Dryden.

2. Blunt; obtuse.

Meeting with time, Slack thing, said I,
Thy scythe is dull; whet it, for shame.
Herbert.

3. Unready; awkward.

Gynecia a great while stood still, with a kind of dull amazement looking stedfastly upon her.
Sidney.

O help thou my weak wit, and sharpen my dull tongue. Fairy Queen, b. i. stanz. 2.

Memory is so necessary to all conditions of life, that we are not to fear it should grow dull for want of exercise, if exercise would make it stronger. Locke.

4. Hebetated; not quick.

This people's heart is waxed gross, and their ears are dull of hearing. Math. xiii. 15.

5. Sad; melancholy.

6. Sluggish; heavy; slow of motion.

Thenceforth the waters waxed dull and slow, And all that drunk thereof did faint and feeble grow. F. Q.

7. Gross; cloggy; vile.

She excels each mortal thing Upon the dull earth dwelling. Shak. Two Gent. of Verona.

8. Not exhilarating; not delightful; as, to make dictionaries is dull work.

9. Not bright; as, the mirror is dull, the fire is dull.

I'll not be made a soft and dull ey'd fool, To shake the head, relent, and sigh, and yield To Christian intercessors. Shakespeare's Merch. of Venice.

10. Drowsy; sleepy.

to dúmbfound v.a. [from *dumb.*] To confuse; to strike dumb. A low phrase.

They had like to have dumbfounded the justice; but his clerk came in to his assistance. Spectator, Nº 616.

dúmpling n.s. [from *dump*, heaviness.] A sort of pudding.

You prate too long, like a book-learn'd sot, 'Till pudding and dumpling burn to pot. Dryden.

dunce n.s. [A word of uncertain etymology; perhaps from *dum*, the Dutch stupid.] A dullard; a dolt; a thickskul; a stupid indocile animal.

Dunce at the best; in streets but scarce allow'd, To tickle, on thy straw, the stupid crowd. Dryden's Virgil.

Was Epiphanius so great a dunce to imagine a thing, indifferent in itself, should be directly opposite to the law of God? Stillingfleet.

I never knew this town without dunces of figure, who had credit enough to give rise to some new word. Swift.

dwarf n.s. [*dweorf*, Sax. *dwerg*, Dutch; *sherg*, Scottish.]

1. A man below the common size of men.

Get you gone, you dwarf! You minimus, of hind'ring knot-grass made. Shakespeare.

Such dwarfs were some kind of apes. Brown's Vulg. Err.

They but now who seem'd In bigness to surpass earth's giant sons, Now less than smallest dwarfs in narrow room Throng numberless. Milton's Paradise Lost, b. i. l. 779.

2. Any animal or plant below its natural bulk.

It is a delicate plantation of trees, all well-grown, fair, and smooth: one dwarf was knotty and crooked, and the rest had it in derision. L'Estrange.

Saw off the head of the stock in a smooth place; and for dwarf trees, graft them within four fingers of the ground. Mortimer's Art of Husbandry.

3. An attendant on a lady or knight in romances.

The champion stout, Eftstoones dismounted from his courser brave, And to the dwarf a-while his needless spear he gave. F. Qu.

4. It is used often by botanists in composition; as, dwarf elder, dwarf honeysuckle.

dyspépsy n.s. [δυσπεψια.] A difficulty of digestion, or bad fermentation in the stomach or guts. Dict.

dyspnóea n.s. [δυσπνοια.] A difficulty of breathing; straitness of breath.

dysury n.s. [δυσουρια.] A difficulty in making urine.

It doth end in a dysentery, pains of the hæmorrhoids, inflammations of any of the lower parts, diabetes, a continual pissing, or a hot dysury, difficulty of making water. Harvey.

E, has two sounds; long, as *scene*, and short, as *men*. *E* is the most frequent vowel in the English language; for it not only is used like the rest in the beginning or end of words, but has the peculiar quality of lengthening the foregoing vowel, as *can*, *cane*; *man*, *mane*; *gap*, *gape*; *glad*, *glade*; *bred*, *brede*; *chin*, *chine*; *whip*, *wipe*; *thin*, *thine*; *nod*, *node*; *tun*, *tune*; *plum*, *plume*. Yet it sometimes occurs final, where yet the foregoing vowel is not lengthened; as *gone*, *knowledge*, *edge*, *give*. Anciently almost every word ended with *e*; as for *can*, *canne*; for *year*, *yeare*; for *great*, *greate*; for *need*, *neede*; for *flock*, *flocke*. It is probable that this *e* final had at first a soft sound, like the female *e* of the French; and that afterwards it was in poetry either mute or vocal, as the verse required, 'till at last it became universally silent.

eame n.s. [*eam*, Saxon; *eom*, Dutch] Uncle: a word still used in the wilder parts of Staffordshire.

Daughter, says she, fly, fly; behold, thy dame
Foreshows the treason of thy wretched eame!
Fairfax.

earl n.s. [*eorl*, Saxon; *eoryl*, Erse.] A title of nobility, anciently the highest of this nation, now the third.

    Thanes and kinsmen,
Henceforth be earls, the first that ever Scotland
For such an honour nam'd. Shakespeare's Macbeth.

earthling n.s. [from *earth*.] An inhabitant of the earth; a mortal; a poor frail creature.

To earthlings, the footstool of God, that stage
which he raised for a small time, seemeth
magnificent. Drummond.

earthquake n.s. [*earth* and *quake*.] Tremor or convulsion of the earth.

This subterranean heat or fire being in any part of the earth stopt, by some accidental glut or obstruction in the passages through which it used to ascend, and being preternaturally assembled in greater quantity into one place, causes a great rarefaction and intumescence of the water of the abyss, putting it into very great commotions; and making the like effort upon the earth, expanded upon the face of the abyss, occasions that agitation and concussion which we call an earthquake. Woodward's Natural History.

These tumults were like an earthquake, shaking the very foundations of all, than which nothing in the world hath more of horrour. King Charles.

Was it his youth, his valour, or success,
These might perhaps be found in other men:
'Twas that respect, that awful homage paid me;
That fearful love which trembled in his eyes,
And with a silent earthquake shook his soul.
Dryd. Sp. Fryar.

The country, by reason of its vast caverns and subterraneous fires, has been miserably torn by earthquakes, so that the whole face of it is quite changed. Addison's Remarks on Italy.

eath adj. [eað, Saxon.] Easy; not difficult. An old word.

Where ease abounds, it's eath to do amiss.
Fairy Queen.

What works not beauty, man's relenting mind
Is eath to move with plaints and shews of
   woe. Fairfax, b. iv.

The way was strait and eath. Fairfax.

ebríety n.s. [*ebrietas*, Latin.] Drunkenness; intoxication by strong liquors.

Bitter almonds, as an antidote against ebriety, hath commonly failed. Brown's Vulgar Errours, b. ii. c. 6.

echináte, echináted adj. [from *echinus*, Latin.] Bristled like an hedgehog; set with prickles.

An echinated pyrites in shape approaches the echinated crystalline balls. Woodward on Fossils.

ecléctick adj. [εκλεκτικος.] Selecting; chusing at will.

Cicero gives an account of the opinions of philosophers; but was of the eclectick sect, and chose out of each such positions as came nearest truth. Watts's Improvement of the Mind.

éclogue n.s. [εκλογη.] A pastoral poem so called, because Virgil called his pastorals eclogues.

What exclaiming praises Basilius gave this eclogue any man may guess, that knows love is better than spectacles to make every thing seem great. Sidney.

It is not sufficient that the sentences be brief, the whole eclogue should be so too. Pope.

ecónomy n.s. [οικονομια. This word is often written, from its derivation, *œconomy*; but *œ* being no diphthong in English, it is placed here with the authorities for different orthography.]

1. The management of a family; the government of a houshold.

By St. Paul's economy the heir differs nothing from a servant, while he is in his minority; so a servant should differ nothing from a child in the substantial part. Taylor's Rule of living holy.

2. Frugality; discretion of expence; laudable parsimony.

Particular sums are not laid out to the greatest advantage in his economy; but are sometimes suffered to run waste, while he is only careful of the main. Dryden's State of Innocence, Preface.

I have no other notion of economy, than that it is the parent of liberty and ease. Swift to Lord Bolingbroke.

3. Disposition of things; regulation.

All the divine and infinitely wise ways of economy that God could use towards a rational creature, oblige mankind to that course of living which is most agreeable to our nature. Hamm.

4. The disposition or arrangement of any work.

In the Greek poets, as also in Plautus, we shall see the economy and disposition of poems better observed than in Terence. Ben. Johnson's Discoveries.

If this economy must be observed in the minutest parts of an epick poem, what soul, though sent into the world with great advantages of nature, cultivated with the liberal arts and sciences, can be sufficient to inform the body of so great a work? Dryden's Dedication to the Æn.

5. System of motions; distribution of every thing active or passive to its proper place.

  These the strainers aid,
That, by a constant separation made,
They may a due economy maintain,
Exclude the noxious parts, the good retain.
Blackm. Creat.

écstasy n.s. [εκστασις.]

1. Any passion by which the thoughts are absorbed, and in which the mind is for a time lost.

  Follow them swiftly,
And hinder them from what this ecstasy

May now provoke them to. Shakespeare's Tempest.

  'T may be
No longer joy there, but an ecstasy. Suckling.

Whether what we call ecstasy be not dreaming with our eyes open, I leave to be examined. Locke.

2. Excessive joy; rapture.

O, love, be moderate! Allay thy ecstasy! Shakespeare.

The religious pleasure of a well disposed mind moves gently, and therefore constantly: it does not affect by rapture and ecstasy; but is like the pleasure of health, still and sober. South's Sermons.

  Each delighted, and delighting, gives
The pleasing ecstasy which each receives.
Prior.

A pleasure, which no language can express;
An ecstasy, that mothers only feel,
Plays round my heart. Phillips's Distrest Mother.

3. Enthusiasm; excessive elevation of the mind.

He lov'd me well, and oft would beg me sing;
Which when I did, he on the tender grass
Would sit, and hearken even to ecstasy.
Milton.

4. Excessive grief or anxiety. This is not now used.

Sighs and groans, and shrieks that rend the air,
Are made, not mark'd; where violent
  sorrow seems
A modern ecstasy. Shakespeare's Macbeth.

  Better be with the dead,
Than on the torture of the mind to lie
In restless ecstasy. Shakespeare's Macbeth.

5. Madness; distraction. This sense is not now in use.

Now see that noble and most sovereign reason,
Like sweet bells jangled out of tune, and harsh,
That unmatch'd form, and feature of
  blown youth,
Blasted with ecstasy. Shakespeare's Hamlet.

éctype n.s. [εκτυπον.] A copy.

The complex ideas of substances are ectypes, copies, but not perfect ones, not adequate. Locke.

edácious adj. [*edax*, Latin.] Eating; voracious; devouring; predatory; ravenous; rapacious; greedy.

éditor n.s. [*editor*, Latin.] Publisher; he that revises or prepares any work for publication.

When a different reading gives us a different sense, or a new elegance in an author, the editor does very well in taking notice of it. Addison's Spectator, N° 450.

This nonsense got into all the editions by a mistake of the stage editors. Pope's Notes on Shakesp. Henry V.

to éducate v.a. [*educo*, Latin.] To breed; to bring up; to instruct youth.

Their young succession all their cares employ;
They breed, they brood, instruct and educate,
And make provision for the future state.
Dryd. Virg. Georg.

Education is worse, in proportion to the grandeur of the parents: if the whole world were under one monarch, the heir of that monarch would be the worst educated mortal since the creation. Swift on Modern Education.

educátion n.s. [from *educate*.] Formation of manners in youth; the manner of breeding youth; nurture.

Education and instruction are the means, the one by use, the other by precept, to make our natural faculty of reason both the better and the sooner to judge rightly between truth and error, good and evil. Hooker, b. i. s. 6.

All nations have agreed in the necessity of a strict education, which consisted in the observance of moral duties. Swift.

to edúlcorate v.n. [from *dulcis*, Latin.] To sweeten.

to efféminate v.a. [*effemino*, Latin.] To make womanish; to weaken; to emasculate; to unman.

When one is sure it will not corrupt or effeminate childrens minds, and make them fond of trifles, I think all things should be contrived to their satisfaction. Locke.

to effígiate v.a. [*effigio*, Latin.] To form in semblance; to image.

efflúvia, efflúvium n.s. [from *effluo*, Latin.] Those small particles which are continually flying off from bodies; the subtilty and fineness of which appears from their being able, a long time together, to produce very sensible effects, without any sensible diminution of the body from whence they arise. Quincy.

If the earth were an electrick body, and the air but the effluvium thereof, we might perhaps believe that from attraction, and by effluxion, bodies tended to the earth. Brown's Vulgar Errours, b. ii. c. 2.

Neither the earth's diurnal revolution upon its axis, nor any magnetick effluvia of the earth, nor the air, or atmosphere which environs the earth, can produce gravity. Woodward.

If these effluvia, which do upward tend,
Because less heavy than the air, ascend;
Why do they ever from their height retreat,
And why return to seek their central seat?
Blackm. Creat.

effóssion n.s. [*effosumo*, Latin.] The act of digging up from the ground; deterration.

He set apart annual sums for the recovery of manuscripts, the effossion of coins, and the procuring of mummies. Arbuthn.

éftsoons adv. [*eft* and *soon*.] Soon afterwards; in a short time; again. An obsolete word.

He in their stead eftsoons placed Englishmen, who possessed all their lands. Spenser's State of Ireland.

Eftsoons the nymphs, which now had flowers their fill,
Run all in haste to see that silver brood.
Spenser's Epithalam.

The Germans deadly hated the Turks, whereof it was to be thought that new wars would eftsoons ensue. Knolles's History.

Eftsoons, O sweetheart kind, my love repay,
And all the year shall then be holiday. Gay's
Pastorals.

égotism n.s. [from *ego*, Latin.] The fault
committed in writing by the frequent
repetition of the word ego, or I; too
frequent mention of a man's self, in writing
or conversation.

The most violent egotism which I have met
with, in the course of my reading, is that of
cardinal Wolsey's; ego & rex meus, I and my
king. Spectator, Nº 562.

egrégious adj. [*egregius*, Latin.]

1. Eminent; remarkable; extraordinary.

He might be able to adorn this present age,
and furnish history with the records of
egregious exploits, both of art and valour.
More's Antidote against Atheism.

　　One to empire born;
Egregious prince! whose manly childhood shew'd
His mingled parents, and portended joy
Unspeakable. Phillips.

2. Eminently bad; remarkably vicious. This
is the usual sense.

We may be bold to conclude, that these last
times, for insolence, pride and egregious
contempt of all good order, are the worst.
Hooker, Preface.

　　Ah me, most credulous fool!
Egregious murtherer! Shakespeare's
Cymbeline.

And hence th' egregious wizzard shall foredoom
The fate of Louis, and the fall of Rome. Pope.

eisel n.s. [*eosil*, Saxon.] Vinegar; verjuice;
any acid.

Woo 't drink up eisel, eat a crocodile?
I'll do 't. Shakespeare's Hamlet.

ejáculation n.s. [from *ejaculate*.]

1. A short prayer darted out occasionally,
without solemn retirement.

In your dressing let there be ejaculations fitted
to the several actions of dressing; as at
washing your hands, pray God to cleanse your
soul from sin. Taylor's Guide to Devotion.

2. The act of darting or throwing out.

There seemeth to be acknowledged, in the act
of envy, an ejaculation or irradiation of the
eye. Bacon's Essays.

There is to be observed, in those dissolutions
which will not easily incorporate, what the
effects are; as the ebullition, the precipitation
to the bottom, the ejaculation towards the top,
the suspension in the midst, and the like.
Bacon.

eléctre n.s. [*electrum*, Latin.]

1. Amber; which, having the quality when
warmed by friction of attracting bodies,
gave to one species of attraction the
name of electricity, and to the bodies
that so attract the epithet electrick.

2. A mixed metal.

Change silver plate or vessel into the
compound stuff, being a kind of silver electre,
and turn the rest into coin. Bacon.

electrícity n.s. [from *electrick*. See *electre*.] A
property in some bodies, whereby, when
rubbed so as to grow warm, they draw little
bits of paper, or such like substances, to
them. Quincy.

Such was the account given a few years ago
of electricity; but the industry of the present
age, first excited by the experiments of
Gray, has discovered in electricity a
multitude of philosophical wonders. Bodies
electrified by a sphere of glass, turned
nimbly round, not only emit flame, but may
be fitted with such a quantity of the
electrical vapour, as, if discharged at once
upon a human body, would endanger life.
The force of this vapour has hitherto
appeared instantaneous, persons at both
ends of a long chain seeming to be struck
at once. The philosophers are now
endeavouring to intercept the strokes
of lightning.[†]

eleemósynary adj. [ελεημοσυνη.]

1. Living upon alms; depending upon
charity.

It is little better than an absurdity, that the cause should be an eleemosynary for its subsistence to its effects, as a nature posteriour to and dependent on itself. Glanv. Sceps. c. 18.

2. Given in charity.

élegant adj. [*elegans*, Latin]

1. Pleasing with minuter beauties.

Trifles themselves are elegant in him. Pope.

There may'st thou find some elegant retreat. London.

2. Nice; not coarse; not gross.

Polite with candour, elegant with ease. Pope.

élegy n.s. [*elegus*, Latin.]

1. A mournful song.

He hangs odes upon hawthorns, and elegies upon brambles, all forsooth deifying the name of Rosalind. Shak. As you like it.

2. A funeral song.

So on meanders banks, when death is nigh, The mournful swan sings her own elegy. Dryden.

3. A short poem without points or turns.

élement n.s. [*elementum*, Latin.]

1. The first or constituent principle of any thing.

If nature should intermit her course, those principal and mother elements of the world, whereof all things in this lower world are made, should lose the qualities which now they have. Hooker, b. i. §. 3.

A man may rationally retain doubts concerning the number of those ingredients of bodies, which some call elements, and others principles. Boyle's Phys. Consider.

Simple substances are either spirits, which have no manner of composition, or the first principles of bodies, usually called elements, of which other bodies are compounded. Watts.

2. The four elements, usually so called, are earth, fire, air, water, of which our world is composed.†

The king is but a man: the violet smells to him as it doth to me; and the element shews to him as it doth to me. Shakes.

My dearest sister, fare thee well; The elements be kind to thee, and make Thy spirits all of comfort. Shakes. Anth. and Cleopatra.

The king, Contending with the fretful elements, Bids the wind blow the earth into the sea, Or swell the curled waters. Shakespeare's King Lear.

The heavens and the earth will pass away, and the elements melt with fervent heat. Peter.

Here be four of you were able to make a good world; for you are as differing as the four elements. Bacon's Hol. War.

He from his flaming ship his children sent, To perish in a milder element. Waller.

3. The proper habitation or sphere of any thing: as water of fish.

We are simple men; we do not know she works by charms, by spells, and such dawbry as is beyond our element. Shakesp.

Our torments may, in length of time, Became our elements. Milton's Paradise Lost, b. ii. l. 275.

They shew that they are out of their element, and that logick is none of their talent. Baker's Reflections on Learning.

4. An ingredient; a constituent part.

Who set the body and the limbs Of this great sport together, as you guess? —One sure that promises no element In such a business. Shakespeare's Henry VIII.

5. The letters of any language.

6. The lowest or first rudiments of literature or science.

With religion it fareth as with other sciences; the first delivery of the elements thereof must, for like consideration, be framed according to the weak and slender capacity of young beginners. Hooker, b. v. s. 18.

*Every parish should keep a petty schoolmaster,
which should bring up children in the first
elements of letters.* Spenser on Irel.

*We, when we were children, were in bondage
under the elements of the world.* Gal. iv. 3.

*There is nothing more pernicious to a youth,
in the elements of painting, than an ignorant
master.* Dryden's Dufresn.

elephantíasis n.s. [*elephantiasis*, Latin.] A
species of leprosy, so called from covering
the skin with incrustations like those on the
hide of an elephant.

elíxir n.s. [Arabick.]

1. A medicine made by strong infusion,
   where the ingredients are almost
   dissolved in the menstruum, and give it
   a thicker consistence than a tincture.
   Quincy.

*For when no healing art prevail'd,
When cordials and elixirs fail'd,
On your pale cheek he dropp'd the show'r,
Reviv'd you like a dying flow'r.* Waller.

2. The liquor, or whatever it be, with
   which chymists hope to transmute
   metals to gold.

*No chymist yet the elixir got,
But glorifies his pregnant pot,
If by the way to him befal
Some odoriferous thing, or medicinal.* Donne.

3. The extract or quintessence of
   any thing.

*In the soul, when the supreme faculties move
regularly, the inferior passions and affections
following, there arises a serenity infinitely
beyond the highest quintessence and elixir of
worldly delight.* South's Sermons.

4. Any cordial; or invigorating substance.

*What wonder then, if fields and regions here
Breathe forth elixir pure!* Milton's Paradise
Lost, b. iii.

elk n.s. [*ælc*, Saxon] The elk is a large and
stately animal of the stag kind. The neck is
short and slender; the ears nine inches in
length, and four in breath. The colour of its
coat in Winter is greyish, in Summer it is

paler; generally three inches in length, and
equalling horsehair in thickness. The upper
lip of the elk is large. The articulations of its
legs are close, and the ligaments hard, so
that its joints are less pliable than those of
other animals. The horns of the male elk are
short and thick near the head, where it by
degrees expands into a great breadth, with
several prominences in its edges. Elks live
in herds, and are very timorous. The hoof of
the left hinder foot only, has been famous
for the cure of epilepsies; but it is probable,
that the hoof of any other animal will do as
well. Hill's Mat. Med.

*And, scarce his head
Rais'd o'er the heapy wreath, the branching elk
Lies slumb'ring sullen in the white abyss.*
Thomson's Winter.

ell n.s. [*eln*, Saxon.]

1. A measure containing forty-five inches,
   or a yard and a quarter.

*They are said to make yearly forty thousand
pieces of linnen cloath, reckoning two hundred
ells to the piece.* Addison.

2. It is taken proverbially for a long
   measure.

*Acquit thee bravely, play the man;
Look not on pleasures as they come, but go:
Defer not the last virtue; life's poor span
Make not an ell by trifling in thy woe.*
Herbert.

elm n.s. [*ulmus*, Latin; *elm*, Saxon.]

1. The name of a tree. The flower consists
   of one leaf, striped like a bell, having
   many stamina in the center: from the
   bottom arises the pointal, which
   becomes a membranaceous or leafy fruit,
   almost heart-shaped; in the middle of
   which is placed a pear-shaped seed-
   vessel, containing one seed of the same
   shape. The species are, the common
   rough-leaved elm; the witch hazel, or
   broad-leaved elm, by some called the
   British elm; the smooth-leaved or witch
   elm. It is generally believed neither of
   them were originally natives of this
   country; but they have propagated

themselves by seeds and suckers in such plenty as hardly to be rooted out, where they have had long possession; especially in hedgerows, where there is harbour for their roots, which will send forth various twigs. They are very proper to place in hedgerows upon the borders of fields, where they will thrive better than when planted in a wood or close plantation, and their shade will not be very injurious to whatever grows under them. They are also proper to plant at a distance from a garden, or building, to break the violence of winds; for they may be trained up in form of an hedge, keeping them cut every year, to the height of forty or fifty feet: but they should not be planted too near a garden where fruit-trees or other plants are placed, because the roots of the elm run superficially near the top of the ground, and will intermix with the roots of other trees, and deprive them of nourishment. Miller.

The rural seat,
Whose lofty elms and venerable oaks
Invite the rook, who high amid the boughs,
In early Spring, his airy city builds.
Thomson's Spring.

2. It was used to support vines, to which the poets allude.

Thou art an elm, my husband; I a vine,
Whose weakness married to thy stronger state,
Makes me with thy strength to communicate.
Shakespeare.

elúmbated adj. [*elumbis*, Lat.] Weakened in the loins. Dict.

to emásculate v.a. [*emasculo*, Latin.]

1. To castrate; to deprive of virility.

When it is found how many ews, suppose twenty, one ram will serve, we may geld nineteen, or thereabouts; for if you emasculate but ten, you shall, by promiscuous copulation, hinder the increase. Graunt's Bills of Mortality.

2. To effeminate; to weaken; to vitiate by unmanly softness.

From wars and from affairs of state abstain;
Women emasculate a monarch's reign.
Dryden's Aurengzebe.

Dangerous principles not only impose upon our understandings, but emasculate our spirits, and spoil our temper. Collier on Pride.

émblem n.s. [εμβλημα.]

1. Inlay; enamel; any thing inserted into the body of another.

2. An occult representation; an allusive picture; a typical designation.

She had all the royal makings of a queen,
The rod, and bird of peace, and all such emblems,
Laid nobly on her. Shakespeare's Henry VIII.

If you draw your beast in an emblem, shew a landscape of the country natural to the beast. Peacham on Drawing.

Gentle Thames,
Thy mighty master's emblem, in whose face
Sate meekness, heighten'd with majestick grace. Denham.

He is indeed a proper emblem of knowledge and action, being all head and paws. Addison's Guardian, Nº 114.

émbolism n.s. [εμβολισμος.]

1. Intercalation; insertion of days or years to produce regularity and equation of time.

The civil constitutions of the year were after different manners in several nations; some using the sun's year, but in divers fashions; and some following the moon, finding out embolisms or equations, even to the addition of whole months, to make all as even as they could. Holder on Time.

2. The time inserted; intercalatory time.

emíction n.s. [from *emiclum*, Latin.] Urine; what is voided by the urinary passages.

Gravel and stone grind away the flesh, and effuse the blood apparent in a sanguine emiction. Harvey on Consumptions.

émmet n.s. [*æmette*, Saxon.] An ant; a pismire.

When cedars to the ground fall down by the
    weight of an emmet,
Or when a rich ruby's just price be the worth
    of a walnut. Sidney, b. i.

emótion n.s. [*emotion*, French.] Disturbance of mind; vehemence of passion, or pleasing or painful.

I will appeal to any man, who has read this poet, whether he finds not the natural emotion of the same passion in himself, which the poet describes in his feigned persons? Dryden.

Those rocks and oaks that such emotion felt, Were rural maids whom Orpheus taught to melt. Granv.

empásm n.s. [εμπασσω.] A powder to correct the bad scent of the body.

émpire n.s. [*empire*, French; *imperium*, Latin.]

1. Imperial power; supreme dominion; sovereign command.

Assert, ye fair ones, who in judgment sit, Your ancient empire over love and wit. Rowe.

2. The region over which dominion is extended.

A nation extended over vast tracts of land, and numbers of people, arrives in time at the ancient name of kingdom, or modern of empire. Temple.

    Sextus Pompeius
Hath given the dare to Cæsar, and commands The empire of the sea. Shakesp. Ant. and Cleopatra.

3. Command over any thing.

empíric n.s. [εμπειρικος.] A trier or experimenter; such persons as have no true education in, or knowledge of physical practice, but venture upon hearsay and observation only. Quincy.

The name of Hippocrates was more effectual to persuade such men as Galen, than to move a silly empirick. Hooker.

That every plant might receive a name, according unto the diseases it cureth, was the wish of Paracelsus; a way more likely to multiply empiricks than herbalists. Brown.

Such an aversion and contempt for all manner of innovators, as physicians are apt to have for empiricks, or lawyers for pettifoggers. Swift.

empírical, émpirick adj. [from the noun.]

1. Versed in experiments.

    By fire
Of sooty coal, the empirick alchymist Can turn, or holds it possible to turn, Metals of drossiest ore to perfect gold. Milton's Parad. Lost.

2. Known only by experience; practised only by rote, without rational grounds.

The most sovereign prescription in Galen is but empirick to this preservative. Shakespeare's Coriolanus.

    In extremes, bold counsels are the best; Like empirick remedies, they last are try'd, And by th' event condemn'd or justify'd. Dryden's Aurengz.

empíricism n.s. [from *empirick*.] Dependence on experience without knowledge or art; quackery.

émption n.s. [*emptio*, Latin.] The act of purchasing; a purchase.

There is a dispute among the lawyers, whether Glaucus his exchanging his golden armour with the brazen one of Tydides, was emption or commutation. Arbuthnot on Coins.

empyreal adj. [εμπυρος.] Formed of the element of fire; refined beyond aerial; pertaining to the highest and purest region of heaven. Tickell accents it on the penult.

    Now went forth the morn, Such as in highest heav'n, array'd in gold Empyreal. Milton's Paradise Lost, b. vi. l. 13.

Go, soar with Plato to th' empyreal sphere, To the first good, first perfect, and first fair. Pope.

But empyreal forms, howe'er in sight
Gash'd and dismember'd, easily unite. Tickell.

empyréan n.s. [εμπυρος.] The highest heaven where the pure element of fire is supposed to subsist.

Almighty Father from above,
From the pure empyrean, where he sits
High thron'd above all height, bent down
his eye. Milton.

Under his burning wheel
The stedfast empyrean shook throughout,
All but the throne itself of God. Milton's Paradise Lost.

The empyrean rung
With hallelujahs. Milton's Paradise Lost, b. vii. l. 633.

empyrósis n.s. [εμπυρεω.] Conflagration; general fire.

The former opinion that held these cataclysms and empyroses universal, was such as held that it put a total consummation unto things in this lower world, especially that of conflagration. Hale's Origin of Mankind.

to emúlge v.a. [*emulgeo*, Latin.] To milk out.

enatátion n.s. [*enato*, Latin.] The act of swimming out; escape by swimming. Dict.

encéinte n.s. [French.] Inclosure; ground inclosed with a fortification. A military term not yet naturalised.

to enchánt v.a. [*enchanter*, French.]

1. To give efficacy to any thing by songs of sorcery.

And now about the cauldron sing,
Like elves and fairies in a ring,
Enchanting all that you put in.
Shakespeare's Macbeth.

These powerful drops thrice on the threshold pour,
And bathe with this enchanted juice her door;
That door where no admittance now is found,
But where my soul is ever hov'ring round.
Granville.

2. To subdue by charms or spells.

Arcadia was the charmed circle, where all his spirits for ever should be enchanted. Sidney, b. ii.

One whom the musick of his own vain tongue
Doth ravish, like enchanting harmony.
Sh. Love's Lab. Lost.

John thinks them all enchanted: he enquires if Nick had not given them some intoxicating potion. Arbuthnot's J. Bull.

3. To delight in a high degree.

Too dear I priz'd a fair enchanting face;
Beauty unchaste is beauty in disgrace.
Pope's Odyssey, b. viii.

enchántress n.s. [*enchanteress*, French.]

1. A sorceress; a woman versed in magical arts.

Fell banning hag! Enchantress, hold thy tongue. Shakes.

I have it by certain tradition, that it was given to the first who wore it by an enchantress. Tatler, Nº 52.

2. A woman whose beauty or excellencies give irresistible influence.

From this enchantress all these ills are come;
You are not safe 'till you pronounce her doom.
Dryden.

Oft with th' enchantress of his soul he talks,
Sometimes in crowds distress'd. Thomson's Spring, l. 1050.

encómium n.s. [ενκωμιον.] Panegyrick; praise; elogy.

How eagerly do some men propagate every little encomium their parasites make of them. Government of the Tongue, s. 9.

A vile encomium doubly ridicules;
There's nothing blackens like the ink of fools.
Pope.

encyclopédia,   encyclopédy   n.s. [ενκυκλοπαιδεια.] The circle of sciences; the round of learning.

Every science borrows from all the rest, and we cannot attain any single one without the encyclopædy. Glanv. Sceps, c. 25.

This art may justly claim a place in the encyclopædia, especially such as serves for a model of education for an able politician. Arbuthnot's History of John Bull.

to énecate v.a. [*eneco*, Latin.] To kill; to destroy.

Some plagues partake of such a pernicious degree of malignity, that, in the manner of a most presentaneous poison, they enecate in two or three hours, suddenly corrupting or extinguishing the vital spirits. Harvey on the Plague.

enfóuldred adj. [from *foudre*, French.] Mixed with lightning.

Heart cannot think what outrage and what cries, With foul enfouldred smoak and flashing fire, The hell-bred beast threw forth unto the skies. Fairy Queen.

éngine n.s. [*engin*, French; *ingegno*, Italian.]

1. Any mechanical complication, in which various movements and parts concur to one effect.

2. A military machine.

This is our engine, towers that overthrows; Our spear that hurts, our sword that wounds our foes. Fairf.

3. Any instrument.

The sword, the arrow, the gun, with many terrible engines of death, will be well employed. Raleigh's Essays.

He takes the scissars, and extends The little engine on his fingers ends. Pope's Rape of the Lock.

4. Any instrument to throw water upon burning houses.

Some cut the pipes, and some the Engines play; And some, more bold, mount ladders to the fire. Dryden.

5. Any means used to bring to pass, or to effect. Usually in an ill sense.

Prayer must be divine and heavenly, which the devil with all his engines so violently opposeth. Duppa's Rules for Devotion.

6. An agent for another. In contempt.

They had th' especial engines been, to rear His fortunes up into the state they were. Daniel.

Énglish adj. [*engles*, Saxon.] Belonging to England; thence English is the language of England.

He hath neither Latin, French, nor Italian; and you may come into the court, and swear that I have a poor pennyworth in the English. Shakespeare's Merchant of Venice.

Of English talc, the coarser sort is called plaister, or parget; the finer, spoad. Woodward.

to Énglish v.a. [from the noun.] To translate into English.

We find not a word in the text can properly be rendered anise, *which is what the Latins call* anethum, *and properly Englished* dill. Brown's Vulgar Errours, b. vii. c. 7.

enígmatist n.s. [from *enigma*.] One who deals in obscure and ambiguous matters; maker of riddles.

That I may deal more ingenuously with my reader than the abovementioned enigmatist has done, I shall present him with a key to my riddle; which, upon application, he will find exactly fitted to all the words of it. Addison's Whig Exam.

to enjóin v.a. [*enjoindre*, French.] To direct; to order; to prescribe. It is more authoritative than *direct*, and less imperious than *command*.

To satisfy the good old man, I would bend under any heavy weight That he'll enjoin me to. Shakes. Much Ado about Nothing.

Monks and philosophers, and such as do continually enjoin themselves. Bacon's Natural History, Nᵒ 292.

It endeavours to secure every man's interest, by enjoining that truth and fidelity be inviolably preserved. Tillots. Sermons.

to enlíghten v.a. [from *light.*]

1. To illuminate; to supply with light.

As one sun shineth to the whole world, so there is no faith but this one published, the brightness whereof must enlighten all that come to the knowledge of the truth. Hooker, b. v. s. 46.

2. To instruct; to furnish with encrease of knowledge.

This doctrine is so agreeable to reason, that we meet with it in the writings of the enlightened heathens. Spectator.

'Tis he who enlightens our understanding, corrects our wills, and enables us to subdue our affections to the law of God. Rog.

3. To cheer; to exhilarate; to gladden.

4. To supply with sight; to quicken in the faculty of vision.

Love never fails to master what he finds;
The fool enlightens, and the wise he blinds.
Dryden.

enneátical adj. [εννεα.] Enneatical days, are every ninth day of a sickness; and enneatical years, every ninth year of one's life.

en passant adv. [French.] By the way.

to entáil v.a. [*tailler*, to cut; *entailler*, French.]

1. To settle the descent of any estate so that it cannot be by any subsequent possessor bequeathed at pleasure.

    I here entail
The crown to thee and to thine heirs for ever.
Shak. H. VI.

Had Richard unconstrain'd resign'd the throne,
A king can give no more than is his own:
The title stood entail'd, had Richard had
    a son. Dryden.

2. To fix unalienably upon any person or thing.

None ever had a privilege of infallibility entailed to all he said. Digby on Bodies.

The intemperate and unjust transmit their bodily infirmities and diseases to their children, and entail a secret curse upon their estates. Tillotson, Sermon 4.

3. To cut. Obsolete.

The mortal steel dispiteously entail'd,
Deep in their flesh, quite through the iron walls,
That a large purple stream adown their
    giambeux falls. F.Q.

entertáinment n.s. [from *entertain*.]

1. Conversation.

2. Treatment at the table; convivial provision.

Arrived there, the little house they fill,
Ne look for entertainment where none was;
Rest is their feast, and all things at their will;
The noblest mind the best contentment has.
Fairy Queen.

With British bounty in his ship he feasts
Th' Hesperian princes, his amazed guests,
To find that watry wilderness exceed
The entertainment of their great Madrid.
Waller.

3. Hospitable reception.

4. Reception; admission.

It is not easy to imagine how it should at first gain entertainment, but much more difficult to conceive how it should be universally propagated. Tillotson, Sermon 1.

5. The state of being in pay as soldiers or servants.

Have you an army ready, say you?
—A most royal one. The centurions and their charges distinctly billeted, already in the entertainment, and to be on foot at an hour's warning. Shakespeare's Coriolanus.

6. Payment of soldiers or servants. Now obsolete.

The entertainment of the general, upon his first arrival, was but six shillings and eight pence. Davies on Ireland.

The captains did covenant with the king to serve him with certain numbers of men, for certain wages and entertainments. Davies on Ireland.

7. Amusement; diversion.

Because he that knoweth least is fittest to ask questions, it is more reason, for the entertainment of the time, that he ask me questions than that I ask you. Bacon's New Atlantis.

Passions ought to be our servants, and not our masters; to give us some agitation for entertainment, but never to throw reason out of its seat. Temple.

8. Dramatick performance; the lower comedy.

A great number of dramatick entertainments are not comedies, but five act farces. Gay's Pref. to What d'ye Call it.

enthúsiasm n.s. [ενθουσιασμος.]

1. A vain belief of private revelation; a vain confidence of divine favour or communication.

Enthusiasm is founded neither on reason nor divine revelation, but rises from the conceits of a warmed or overweening brain. Locke.

2. Heat of imagination; violence of passion; confidence of opinion.

3. Elevation of fancy; exaltation of ideas.

Imaging is, in itself, the very height and life of poetry, which, by a kind of enthusiasm, or extraordinary emotion of soul, makes it seem to us that we behold those things which the poet paints. Dryden's Juv. Preface.

enthusiástical, **enthusiástick** adj. [ενθουσιαστικος.]

1. Persuaded of some communication with the Deity.

He pretended not to any seraphick enthusiastical raptures, or inimitable unaccountable transports of devotion. Calamy.

2. Vehemently hot in any cause.

3. Elevated in fancy; exalted in ideas.

It commonly happens in an enthusiastick or prophetick style, that, by reason of the eagerness of the fancy, it doth not always follow the even thread of discourse. Burnet.

*At last, sublim'd
To rapture and enthusiastick heat,
We feel the present Deity.* Thomson's Spring, l. 895.

to enúbilate v.a. [*e* and *nubile*, Latin.] To clear from clouds. Dict.

to enúcleate v.a. [*enucleo*, Latin.] To solve; to clear; to disentangle. Dict.

epáct n.s. [επακτη.] A number, whereby we note the excess of the common solar year above the lunar, and thereby may find out the age of the moon every year. For the solar year consisting of 365 days, the lunar but of 354, the lunations every year get eleven days before the solar year; and thereby, in 19 years, the moon completes 20 times 12 lunations, or gets up one whole solar year; and having finished that circuit, begins again with the sun, and so from 19 to 19 years. For the first year afterwards the moon will go before the sun but 11 days; the second year 22 days; the third 33 days: but 30 being an entire lunation, cast that away, and the remainder 3 shall be that year's epact; and so on, adding yearly 11 days. To find the epact, having the prime or golden number given, you have this rule:

Divide by three; for each one left add ten; Thirty reject: the prime makes epact then. Harris.

As the cycle of the moon seems to shew the epacts, and that of the sun the dominical letter, throughout all their variations; so this Dionysian period serves to shew these two cycles both together, and how they proceed or vary all along, 'till at last they accomplish their period, and both together take their beginning again, after every 532d year. Holder on Time.

ephémera n.s. [εφημερη.]

1. A fever that terminates in one day.

2. An insect that lives only one day.

épic adj. [*epicus*, Latin; επος.] Narrative; comprising narrations, not acted, but rehearsed. It is usually supposed to be heroick, or to contain one great action atchieved by a hero.

Holmes, whose name shall live in epic song, While music numbers, or while verse has feet. Dryden.

The epic poem is more for the manners, and the tragedy for the passions. Dryden.

From morality they formed that kind of poem and fable which we call epic. Pope's View of Epic Poems.

epicúrism n.s. [from *epicure*.] Luxury; sensual enjoyment; gross pleasure.

Here you do keep a hundred knights and squires;
Men so disorder'd, so debauch'd and bold,
That this our court, infected with their manners,
Shews like a riotous inn; epicurism and lust
Make it a tavern or a brothel. Shakespeare's King Lear.

There is not half so much epicurism in any of their most studied luxuries, as a bleeding fame at their mercy. Government of the Tongue, s. 6.

Some good men have ventured to call munificence, the greatest sensuality, a piece of epicurism. Calamy's Sermons.

epidérmis n.s. [ἐπιδερμις.] The scarf-skin of a man's body.

epigrám n.s. [*epigramma*, Latin.] A short poem terminating in a point.

A college of witcrackers cannot flout me out of my humour: do'st thou think I care for a satire or an epigram? Shak.

What can be more witty than the epigram of Moore upon the name of Nicolaus, an ignorant physician, that had been the death of thousands? Peacham of Poetry.

I writ
An epigram that boasts more truth than wit. Gay.

épilepsy n.s. [ἐπιλεψις.] An convulsion, or convulsive motion of the whole body, or of some of its parts, with a loss of sense. A convulsive motion happens when the blood, or nervous fluid, runs into any parts with so great violence, that the mind cannot restrain them from attraction. Quincy.

My lord is fell into an epilepsy:
This is the second fit. Shak. Othello.

Melancholy distempers are deduced from spirits drawn from that cacochymia; the phrenitis from cholerick spirits, and the epilepsy from fumes. Floyer on the Humours.

épisode n.s. [ἐπισωδη.] An incidental narrative, or digression in a poem, separable from the main subject, yet rising naturally from it.

The poem, which we have now under our consideration, hath no other episodes than such as naturally arise from the subject. Addison's Spectator.

epithalámium n.s. [ἐπι θαλαμος.] A nuptial song; a compliment upon marriage.

I presume to invite you to these sacred nuptials: the epithalamium sung by a crowned muse. Sandys's Paraphrase.

The forty-fifth psalm is an epithalamium to Christ and the church, or to the lamb and his spouse. Burnet.

epítome n.s. [ἐπιτομη.] Abridgment; abbreviature; compendious abstract; compendium.

This is a poor epitome of your's,
Which, by th' interpretation of full time,
May shew like all yourself. Shakespeare's Coriolanus.

Epitomes are helpful to the memory, and of good private use; but set forth for publick monuments, accuse the industrious writers of delivering much impertinency. Wotton.

I think it would be well, if there were a short and plain epitome made, containing the chief and most material heads. Locke on Education.

Such abstracts and epitomes may be reviewed in their proper places. Watts's Improvement of the Mind.

époch, épocha n.s. [ἐποχη.] The time at which a new computation is begun; the time from which dates are numbered.

Moses distinctly sets down this account, computing by certain intervals, memorable æras and epochas, or terms of time. Brown's Vulgar Errours, b. vi. c. 1.

These are the practices of the world, since the year sixty; the grand epoch of falsehood, as well as debauchery. South.

Some lazy ages, lost in sleep and ease,
No action leave to busy chronicles;
Such whose supine felicity but makes
In story chasms, in epochas mistakes. Dryden.

Their several epochas or beginnings, as from the creation of the world, from the flood, from the first olympiad, from the building of Rome, or from any remarkable passage or accident, give us a pleasant prospect into the histories of antiquity and of former ages. Holder on Time.

Time is always reckoned from some known parts of this sensible world, and from some certain epochs marked out to us by the motions observeable in it. Locke.

Time, by necessity compel'd, shall go Through scenes of war, and epochas of woe. Prior.

epopée n.s. [εποποιια.] An epick or heroick poem.

Tragedy borrows from the epopee, and that which borrows is of less dignity, because it has not of its own. Dryd. Virgil.

epulátion n.s. [*epulatio*, Latin.] Banquet; feast.

Contented with bread and water, when he would dine with Jove, and pretended to epulation, he desired no other addition than a piece of cheese. Brown's Vulgar Errours, b. vii. c. 17.

equation [In algebra.] Is an expression of the same quantity in two dissimilar terms, but of equal value; as 3 *s.*=36 *d.* Dict.

equátor n.s. [*æquator*, Latin.] On the earth, or equinoctial in the heavens, is a great circle, whose poles are the poles of the world. It divides the globe into two equal parts, the northern and southern hemispheres. It passes through the east and west points of the horizon; and at the meridian is raised as much above the horizon as is the complement of the latitude of the place. Whenever the sun comes to this circle, it makes equal days and nights all round the globe, because he then rises due east and sets due west, which he doth at no other time of the year. Harris.

By reason of the convexity of the earth, the eye of man, under the equator, cannot discover both the poles; neither would the eye, under the poles, discover the sun in the equator. Brown's Vulgar Errours, b. vi. c. 5.

On the other side the equator there is much land still remaining undiscovered. Ray on the Creation.

Rocks rich in gems, and mountains big with mines, That on the high equator ridgy rise, Whence many a bursting stream auriferous plays. Thomson.

équipage n.s. [*equipage*, French.]

1. Furniture for a horseman.

2. Carriage of state; vehicle.

Winged spirits, and chariots wing'd, From th' armory of God; where stand of old Myriads, between two brazen mountains lodg'd Against a solemn day, harness'd at hand, Celestial equipage! Milton's Paradise Lost, b. vii. l. 203.

3. Attendance; retinue.

Think what an equipage thou hast in air, And view with scorn two pages and a chair. Pope.

4. Accoutrements; furniture.

Soon as thy dreadful trump begins to sound, The god of war, with his fierce equipage, Thou do'st awake, sleep never he so sound. Fairy Queen.

I will not lend thee a penny.— I will retort the sum in equipage. Shakespeare's Merry Wives of Windsor.

éremite n.s. [*eremita*, Latin; ερημος.] One who lives in a wilderness; one who lives in solitude; an hermit; a solitary.

Antonius the eremite findeth a fifth commodity not inferior to any of these four. Raleigh's History of the World.

And many more too long, Embryoes and idiots, eremites and friars, White, black, and grey, with all their trumpery. Milton.

ereptátion n.s. [*erepto*, Latin.] A creeping forth. Bail.

eréption n.s. [*ereptio*, Latin.] A snatching or taking away by force. Bail.

erístical adj. [ερις.] Controversial; relating to dispute; containing controversies.

erke n.s. [*earg*, Saxon.] Idle; lazy; slothful. An old word.

For men therein should hem delite;
And of that dede be not erke,
But oft sithes haunt that werke. Chaucer.

erránt adj. [*errans*, Latin; *errant*, French.]

1. Wandering; roving; rambling. Particularly applied to an order of knights much celebrated in romances, who roved about the world in search of adventures.

There are just seven planets, or errant stars,
in the lower orbs of heaven; but it is now
demonstrable unto sense, that there are many
more. Brown's Vulgar Errours, b. iv. c. 12.

Chief of domestick knights and errant,
Either for chartel or for warrant. Hudibras.

2. Vile; abandoned; completely bad. See *arrant*.

Any way, so thou wilt do it, good impertinence:
Thy company, if I slept not very well
A-nights, would make me an errant fool with
questions. Johnson's Catiline.

erráta n.s. [Latin.] The faults of the printer inserted in the beginning or end of the book.

If he meet with faults, besides those that
the errata take notice of, he will consider the
weakness of the author's eyes. Boyle.

érrhine n.s. [ερρινα.] Snuffed up the nose; occasioning sneezing.

We see sage or betony bruised, sneezing
powder, and other powders or liquors, which
the physicians call errhines, put into the nose
to draw phlegm and water from the head.
Bacon's Natural History, Nº 38.

erubéscent adj. [*erubescens*, Latin.] Reddish; somewhat red; inclining to redness.

eructátion n.s. [from *eruct.*]

1. The act of belching.

2. Belch; the matter vented from the stomach.

The signs of the functions of the stomach being
depraved, are eructations, either with the taste
of the aliment, acid, inodorous, or fetid.
Arbuthnot.

3. Any sudden burst of wind or matter.

Thermæ, are hot springs, or fiery eructations;
such as burst forth of the earth during
earthquakes. Woodward's Nat. Hist.

escárgatoire n.s. [French.] A nursery of snails.

At the Capuchins I saw escargatoires, which
I took the more notice of, because I do not
remember to have met with any thing of the
same kind in other countries. It is a square
place boarded in, and filled with a vast
quantity of large snails that are esteemed
excellent food, when they are well dressed.
Add.

eschútcheon n.s. The shield of the family; the picture of the ensigns armorial.

Eschutcheon is a French word, from the Latin
scutum, *leather; and hence cometh our*
English word buckler, lere *in the old Saxon*
signifying leather, and buck *or* bock *a buck or*
stag; of whose skins, quilted close together with
horn or hard wood, the ancient Britons made
their shields. Peacham.

There be now, for martial encouragement,
some degrees and orders of chivalry, and some
remembrance perhaps upon the eschutcheon.
Bacon's Essays.

We will pass over the eschutcheons of the tribes
of Israel, as they are usually described in the
maps of Canaan. Brown.

escrítoir n.s. [French.] A box with all the implements necessary for writing.

ésculent adj. [*esculentus*, Latin.] Good for food; eatable.

I knew a man that would fast five days; but
the same man used to have continually a great
wisp of herbs that he smelled on, and some
esculent herbs of strong scent, as garlick.
Bacon.

to essáy v.a. [*essayer*, French.]

1. To attempt; to try; to endeavour.

While I this unexampled task essay,
Pass awful gulphs, and beat my painful way,
Celestial dove, divine assistance bring.
Blackmore's Creation.

No conquest she, but o'er herself desir'd;
No arts essay'd, but not to be admir'd.
Pope, Epistle 5.

2. To make experiment of.

3. To try the value and purity of metals.

The standard in our mint being now settled,
the rules and methods of essaying suited to it
should remain unvariable. Locke.

éssay n.s. [from the verb. The accent is used on either syllable.]

1. Attempt; endeavour.

Fruitless our hopes, though pious our essays;
Your's to preserve a friend, and mine to praise.
Smith.

2. A loose sally of the mind; an irregular
indigested piece; not a regular and
orderly composition.

My essays, of all my other works, have been
most current. Bac.

Yet modestly he does his work survey,
And calls his finish'd poem an essay.
Poem to Roscommon.

3. A trial; an experiment.

He wrote this but as an essay, or taste of my
virtue. Shak.

Repetitions wear us into a liking of what
possibly, in the first essay, displeased us.
Locke.

4. First taste of any thing; first experiment.

Translating the first of Homer's Iliads,
I intended as an essay to the whole work.
Dryden's Fables, Preface.

estivátion n.s. [*æstivatio*, Latin.] The act of passing the Summer.

A grotto is a place of shade, or estivation.
Bacon's Essays.

éstrich n.s. [commonly written *ostrich*.]
The largest of birds.

To be furious,
Is to be frighted out of fear; and, in that mood,
The dove will peck the estridge. Shak. Anth.
and Cleopatra.

The peacock, not at thy command, assumes
His glorious train; nor estrich her rare plumes.
Sandys.

ésurient adj. [*esuriens*, Latin.] Hungry; voracious. Dict.

etc. A contraction of the two Latin words
et cætera, which signifies and so on; and
the rest; and others of the like kind.

etch n.s. A country word, of which I know
not the meaning.†

When they sow their etch crops, they sprinkle
a pound or two of clover on an acre.
Mortimer's Husbandry.

Where you find dunging of land makes it
rank, lay dung upon the etch, and sow it with
barley. Mortimer's Husbandry.

éther n.s. [*æther*, Latin; αιθηρ.]

1. An element more fine and subtle than
air; air refined or sublimed.

If any one should suppose that ether, like our
air, may contain particles which endeavour
to recede from one another; for I do not know
what this ether is; and that its particles are
exceedingly smaller than those of air, or even
than those of light, the exceeding smallness of
its particles may contribute to the greatness of
the force, by which those particles may recede
from one another. Newton's Opt.

The parts of other bodies are held together by
the eternal pressure of the ether, and can have
no other conceivable cause of their cohesion
and union. Locke.

2. The matter of the highest regions above.

There fields of light and liquid ether flow,
Purg'd from the pond'rous dregs of earth
    below. Dryden.

éthicks n.s. without the singular. [ηθικη.]
The doctrine of morality; a system of
morality.

For of all moral virtues, she was all
That ethicks speak of virtues cardinal.
Donne.

*I will never set politicks against ethicks;
especially for that true ethicks are but as
a handmaid to divinity and religion.*
Bacon's War with Spain.

*Persius professes the stoick philosophy; the most
noble, generous, and beneficial amongst all the
sects who have given rules of ethicks.*
Dryden's Juvenal, Dedicat.

*If the atheists would live up to the ethicks of
Epicurus himself, they would make few or no
proselytes from the Christian religion.*
Bentley's Sermons.

éthnick adj. [εθνικος.] Heathen; Pagan;
not Jewish; not Christian.

*Such contumely as the ethnick world durst
not offer him, is the peculiar insolence of
degenerated Christians.* Gov. of Tongue.

*I shall begin with the agreement of profane,
whether Jewish or ethnick, with the Sacred
Writings.* Grew's Cosm. Sac.

etymólogy n.s. [*etymologia*, Lat. ετυμος
and λογος.]

1. The descent or derivation of a word
   from its original; the deduction of
   formations from the radical word; the
   analysis of compound words into
   primitives.

*Consumption is generally taken for any
universal diminution and colliquation of the
body, which acception its etymology implies.*
Harvey on Consumptions.

*When words are restrained, by common usage,
to a particular sense, to run up to etymology,
and construe them by dictionary, is wretchedly
ridiculous.* Collier's View of the Stage.

*Pelvis is used by comick writers for a looking-
glass, by which means the etymology of the
word is visible, and* pelvidera *will signify
a lady who looks in her glass.* Addison's
Spectator.

*If the meaning of a word could be learned by
its derivation or etymology, yet the original
derivation of words is oftentimes very dark.*
Watts's Logick.

2. The part of grammar which delivers the
   inflections of nouns and verbs.

eúcharist n.s. [ευχαριστια.] The act of
giving thanks; the sacramental act in which
the death of our Redeemer is commemorated
with a thankful remembrance; the sacrament
of the Lord's supper.

*Himself did better like of common bread to be
used in the eucharist.* Hooker, Preface.

*Some receive the sacrament as a means to
procure great graces and blessings, others as
an eucharist and an office of thanksgiving for
what they have received.* Taylor.

to eúnuchate v.a. To make an eunuch.

*It were an impossible act to eunuchate or
castrate themselves.* Brown's Vulgar Errours,
b. viii. c. 4.

euthanásia, euthánasy n.s. [ευθανασια.]
An easy death.

*A recovery, in my case, and at my age, is
impossible: the kindest wish of my friends
is euthanasia.* Arbuthnot.

to evénterate v.a. [*eventero*, Latin.] To rip
up; to open by ripping the belly.

*In a bear, which the hunters eventerated, or
opened, I beheld the young ones with all their
parts distinct.* Brown.

évil n.s. [generally contracted to *ill*.]

1. Wickedness; a crime.

   *Not in the legions
Of horrid hell can come a devil more damn'd
In evils to top Macbeth.* Shakespeare's
Macbeth.

2. Injury; mischief.

*Whoso rewardeth evil for good, evil shall not
depart from his house.* Prov. xvii. 13.

*Let thine enemies, and they that seek evil to
my Lord, be as Nabal.* 1 Sa. xxv. 26.

3. Malignity; corruption.

The heart of the sons of men is full of evil.
Eccles. ix. 3.

4. Misfortune; calamity.

*Shall we receive good at the hand of God, and
shall we not receive evil.* Job ii. 10.

A prudent man foreseeth the evil, and hideth himself. Prov.

If we will stand boggling at imaginary evils, let us never blame a horse for starting at a shadow. L'Estrange.

Evil is what is apt to produce or increase any pain, or diminish any pleasure in us; or else to procure us any evil, or deprive us of any good. Locke.

5. Malady; disease: as, the king's evil.

At his touch,
Such sanctity hath heaven given his hand,
They presently amend.
—*What's the disease he means?*
—*'Tis call'd the evil.* Shakespeare's Macbeth.

evolútion n.s. [*evolutus*, Latin.]

1. The act of unrolling or unfolding.

2. The series of things unrolled or unfolded.

The whole evolution of ages, from everlasting to everlasting, is so collectedly and presentifickly represented to God at once, as if all things which ever were, are, or shall be, were at this very instant, and so always, really present and existent before him. More's Divine Dialogues.

3. [In geometry.] The equable evolution of the periphery of a circle, or any other curve, is such a gradual approach of the circumference to rectitude, as that all its parts do meet together, and equally evolve or unbend; so that the same line becomes successively a less arch of a reciprocally greater circle, 'till at last they turn into a strait line. In the Philos. Transactions, N° 260. you have a new quadratrix to the circle, found by this means. Harris.

4. [In tacticks.] The motion made by a body of men in changing their posture, or form of drawing up, either to make good the ground they are upon, or to possess themselves of another; that so they may attack the enemy, or receive his onset more advantageously. And

these evolutions are doubling of ranks or files, countermarches, and wheelings. Harris.

This spontaneous coagulation of the little saline bodies was preceded by almost innumerable evolutions, which were so various, that the little bodies came to obvert to each other those parts by which they might be best fastened together. Boyle.

5. Evolution of Powers [in algebra]. Extracting of roots from any given power, being the reverse of involution. Harr.

exánimous adj. [*exanimis*, Latin.] Lifeless; dead; killed.

to excárnate v.a. [*ex* and *carnes*, Latin.] To clear from flesh.

The spleen is most curiously excarnated, and the vessels filled with wax, whereby its fibres and vessels are very well seen. Grew's Musæum.

excíse n.s. [*accijs*, Dutch; *excisum*, Latin.] A hateful tax levied upon commodities, and adjudged not by the common judges of property, but wretches hired by those to whom excise is paid.[†]

The people should pay a ratable tax for their sheep, and an excise for every thing which they should eat. Hayward.

Ambitious now to take excise
Of a more fragrant paradise. Cleaveland.

Excise,
With hundred rows of teeth, the shark exceeds,
And on all trades like Cassawar she feeds. Marvel.

Can hire large houses, and oppress the poor,
By farm'd excise. Dryden's Juvenal, Sat. 3.

to excógitate v.a. [*excogito*, Latin.] To invent; to strike out by thinking.

If the wit of man had been to contrive this organ for himself, what could he have possibly excogitated more accurate? More's Antidote against Atheism.

The tradition of the origination of mankind seems to be universal; but the particular

*methods of that origination, excogitated
by the heathen, were particular.* Hale's
Orig. of Mank.

*We shall find them to be little else than
excogitated and invented models, not much
arising from the true image of the things
themselves.* Hale's Origin of Mankind.

to excómmunicate v.a. [*excommunico*, low
Latin.] To eject from the communion of the
visible church by an ecclesiastical censure;
to interdict from the participation of holy
mysteries.

*Thou shalt stand curst and excommunicate;
And blessed shall he be, that doth revolt
From his allegiance to an heretick.* Shakesp.
King John.

*What if they shall excommunicate me, hath
the doctrine of meekness any salve for me
then?* Hammond's Pract. Catech.

*The office is performed by the parish-priest
at interment, but not unto persons
excommunicated.* Ayliffe's Parergon.

excubátion n.s. [*excubatio*, Latin.] The act
of watching all night. Dict.

exécrable adj. [*execrabilis*, Latin.] Hateful;
detestable; accursed; abominable.

*For us to change that which he hath
established, they hold it execrable pride and
presumption.* Hooker, b. iii. s. 10.

*Of the visible church of Jesus Christ those may
be, in respect of their outward profession; who,
in regard of their inward disposition, are most
worthily both hateful in the sight of God
himself, and in the eyes of the sounder parts
of the visible church most execrable.*
Hooker, b. iii. §. 1.

*Give sentence on this execrable wretch,
That hath been breeder of these dire events.*
Shak. Tit. And.

*When execrable Troy in ashes lay,
Through fires, and swords, and seas,
   they forc'd their way.* Dryden's Æn.
b. vii. l. 408.

exegésis n.s. [εξηγησις.] An explanation.

exemptítious adj. [from *exemptus*, Latin.]
Separable; that which may be taken from
another.

*If motion were loose or exemptitious from
matter, I could be convinced that it had
extension of its own.* More.

éxercise n.s. [*exercitium*, Latin.]

1. Labour of the body; labour considered
as conducive to the cure or prevention
of diseases.

*Men ought to beware that they use not
exercise and a spare diet both; but if much
exercise, a plentiful diet; if sparing diet, little
exercise.* Bacon's Natural History, N° 298.

*The wise for cure on exercise depend;
God never made his work for man to mend.*
Dryden.

*He is exact in prescribing the exercises of his
patients, ordering some of them to walk eighty
stadia in a day, which is about nine English
miles.* Arbuthnot on Coins.

   *The purest exercise of health,
The kind refresher of the Summer heats.*
Thomson's Summer.

2. Something done for amusement.

*As a watchful king, he would not neglect his
safety, thinking nevertheless to perform all
things rather as an exercise than as a labour.*
Bacon's Henry VII.

3. Habitual action by which the body is
formed to gracefulness, air, and agility.

*He was strong of body, and so much the
stronger as he, by a well disciplined
exercise, taught it both to do and to suffer.*
Sidney, b. ii.

*The French apply themselves more universally
to their exercises than any nation: one seldom
sees a young gentleman that does not fence,
dance, and ride.* Addison.

4. Preparatory practice in order to skill: as,
the exercise of soldiers.

5. Use; actual application of any thing.

*The sceptre of spiritual regimen over us in this
present world, is at the length to be yielded up
into the hands of the Father which gave it;
that is, the use and exercise thereof shall cease,
there being no longer on earth any militant
church to govern.* Hooker, b. v. s. 54.

6. Practice; outward performance.

The same prince refused even those of the church of England, who followed their master to St. Germain's, the publick exercise of their religion. Addison on Italy.

7. Employment.

The learning of the situation and boundaries of kingdoms, being only an exercise of the eyes and memory, a child with pleasure will learn them. Locke.

Children, by the exercise of their senses about objects that affect them in the womb, receive some few ideas before they are born. Locke.

Exercise is very alluring and entertaining to the understanding, while its reasoning powers are employed without labour. Watts.

8. Task; that which one is appointed to perform.

Patience is more oft the exercise
Of saints, the trial of their fortitude
Making them each his own deliverer,
And victor over all
That tyranny or fortune can inflict.
Milton's Agonistes.

9. Act of divine worship whether publick or private.

   Good sir John,
I'm in your debt for your last exercise;
Come the next Sabbath, and I will content
   you. Shakesp.

exigúous adj. [*exiguus*, Latin.] Small; diminutive; little.

Their subtile parts and exiguous dose are consumed and evaporated in less than two hours time. Harvey.

exímious adj. [*eximius*, Latin.] Famous; eminent; conspicuous; excellent. Dict.

to exíst v.n. [existo, Latin.] To be; to have a being.

It is as easy to conceive that an infinite Almighty Power might produce a thing out of nothing, and make that to exist de novo, which did not exist before; as to conceive the world to have had no beginning, but to have existed from eternity. South's Sermons.

It seems reasonable to enquire, how such a multitude comes to make but one idea, since that combination does not always exist together in nature. Locke.

One year is past; a different scene!
No farther mention of the dean:
Who now, alas, no more is mist
Than if he never did exist. Swift.

exómphalos n.s. [εξ and ομφαλος.] A navel rupture.

exóssated adj. [*exossatus*, Latin.] Deprived of bones. Dict.

exótick adj. [εξωτικος.] Foreign; not produced in our own country; not domestick.

Some learned men treat of the nature of letters as of some remote exotick thing, whereof we had no knowledge but by fabulous relations. Holder's Elements of Speech.

Continue fresh hot-beds to entertain such exotick plants as arrive not to their perfection without them. Evelyn's Kalendar.

to expátiate v.n. [*expatior*, Latin.]

1. To range at large; to rove without any prescribed limits.

Religion contracts the circle of our pleasures, but leaves it wide enough for her votaries to expatiate in. Addison's Spectat.

He looks in heav'n with more than mortal eyes,
Bids his free soul expatiate in the skies;
Amidst her kindred stars familiar roam,
Survey the region, and confess her home.
Pope.

Expatiate free o'er all this scene of man;
A mighty maze! but not without a plan.
Pope's Ess. on Man.

With wonder seiz'd, we view the
   pleasing ground,
And walk delighted, and expatiate round.
Pope's Odyssey.

2. To enlarge upon in language.

They had a custom of offering the tongues to Mercury, because they believed him the giver of eloquence: Dacier expatiates upon this custom. Notes on Pope's Odyssey, b. iii.

3. To let loose; to allow to range. This sense is very improper.

Make choice of a subject, which, being of itself capable of all that colours and the elegance of design can possibly give, shall afterwards afford art an ample field of matter wherein to expatiate itself. Dryden's Dufresnoy.

expériment n.s. [*experimentum*, Latin.] Trial of any thing; something done in order to discover an uncertain or unknown effect.

That which sheweth them to be wise, is the gathering of principles out of their own particular experiments; and the framing of our particular experiments, according to the rule of their principles, shall make us such as they are. Hooker, b. v.

It is good also not to try experiments in states, except the necessity be urgent, or the utility evident. Bacon.

Adam! by sad experiment I know,
How little weight with thee my words can find,
Found so erroneous. Milton's Paradise Lost, b. x.

'Till his fall it was ignorant of nothing but of sin; or, at least, it rested in the notion without the smart of the experiment. South's Sermons.

When we are searching out the nature or properties of any being by various methods of trial, this sort of observation is called experiment. Watts's Improvement of the Mind.

expirátion n.s. [from *expire.*]

1. That act of respiration which thrusts the air out of the lungs, and contracts the cavity of the breast. Quincy.

In all expiration the motion is outwards, and therefore rather driveth away the voice than draweth it. Bacon's Nat. History.

Of an inflammation of the diaphragm, the symptoms are a violent fever, and a most exquisite pain increases upon inspiration; by which it is distinguished from a pleurisy, in which the greatest pain is in expiration. Arbuthnot on Diet.

2. The last emission of breath; death.

We have heard him breathe the groan of expiration. Rambler.

3. Evaporation; act of fuming out.

4. Vapour; matter expired.

Words of this sort resemble the wind in fury and impetuousness, in transientness and sudden expiration. Decay of Piety.

Close air is warmer than open air, as the cause of cold is an expiration from the earth, which in open places is stronger. Bacon's Natural History, Nº 866.

5. The cessation of any thing to which life is figuratively ascribed.

To satisfy ourselves of its expiration we darkened the room, and in vain endeavoured to discover any spark of fire. Boyle.

6. The conclusion of any limited time.

If 'till the expiration of your month,
You will return and sojourn with my sister,
Dismissing half your train, come there to me. Shak. K. Lear.

This he did in a fortnight after the expiration of the treaty of Uxbridge. Clarendon, b. viii.

to expúgn v.a. [*expugno*, Latin.] To conquer; to take by assault.

expúrgatory adj. [*expurgatorius*, Latin.] Employed in purging away what is noxious: as, the expurgatory index of the Romanists directs the abolition or expunction of passages admitted by any authors contrary to popery.

There wants expurgatory animadversions, whereby we might strike out great numbers of hidden qualities; and having once a conceded list, we might with more safety attempt their reasons. Brown's Vulgar Errours, b. ii. c. 7.

éxscript n.s. [*exscriptum*, Latin.] A copy; a writing copied from another.

expuítion n.s. [*expuo*, Latin.] A discharge of saliva by spitting. Quincy.

exsudátion n.s. [from *exudo*, Latin.] A sweating out; an extillation; an emission.

They seemed to be made by an exsudation, or extillation of some petrifying juices out of the rocky earth. Derham.

extradíctionary adj. [*extra* and *dictio*, Latin.] Not consisting in words but realities.

Of these extradictionary and real fallacies, Aristotle and logicians make six; but we observe men are commonly deceived by four thereof. Brown's Vulgar Errours, b. i. c. 4.

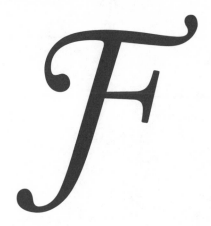

F, a consonant generally reckoned by authors, and admitted by *Scaliger*, among the semi-vowels, and according to that opinion distinguished in the enumeration of the alphabet by a name beginning with a vowel, yet has so far the nature of a mute, that it is easily pronounced before a liquid in the same syllable. It has in English an invariable sound, formed by compression of the whole lips and a forcible breath. Its kindred letter is *V*, which, in the Islandick alphabet, is only distinguished from it by a point in the body of the letter.

fabáceous adj. [*fabaceus*, Latin] Having the nature of a bean. Dict.

fáble n.s. [*fable*, French; *fabula*, Latin.]

1. A feigned story intended to enforce some moral precept.

Jotham's fable of the bees is the oldest extant, and as beautiful as any made since. Addison's Spectator.

2. A fiction in general.

Triptolemus, so sung the nine,
Strew'd plenty from his cart divine;
But, spite of all those fable makers,
He never sow'd on Almaign acres. Dryden.

3. A vitious or foolish fiction.

But refuse profane and old wives fables. 1 Tim. iv. 7.

4. The series or contexture of events which constitute a poem epick or dramatick.

The moral is the first business of the poet: this being formed, he contrives such a design or fable as may be most suitable to the moral. Dryden's Dufresnoy.

The first thing to be considered in an epick poem is the fable, which is perfect or imperfect, according as the action, which it relates, is more or less so. Addison's Spectator.

5. A lye. This sense is merely familiar.

to fáble v.n. [from the noun.]

1. To feign; to write not truth but fiction.

That Saturn's sons receiv'd the three-fold reign
Of heav'n, of ocean, and deep hell beneath,
Old poets mention, fabling. Prior.

Vain now the tales which fabling poets tell,
That wav'ring conquest still desires to rove!
In Marlbro's camp the goddess knows to dwell. Prior.

2. To tell falsehoods; to lye.

He fables not: I hear the enemy. Shakesp. Henry VI.

fábrick n.s. [*fabrica*, Latin.]

1. A building; an edifice.

There must be an exquisite care to place the columns, set in several stories, most precisely
one over another, that so the solid may answer to the solid, and the vacuities to the vacuities, as well for beauty as strength of the fabrick.* Wotton.

2. Any system or compages of matter; any body formed by the conjunction of dissimilar parts.

Still will ye think it strange,
That all the parts of this great fabrick change;
Quit their old station and primeval frame. Prior.

fábulous adj. [*fabulosus*, Latin.] Feigned; full of fables, or invented tales.

A person terrified with the imagination of spectres, is more reasonable than one who thinks the appearance of spirits fabulous and groundless. Addison's Spectator, Nº 110.

facínorous adj. [*facinora*, Latin.] Wicked; atrocious; detestably bad.

fáction n.s. [*faction*, French; *factio*, Latin.]

1. A party in a state.

The queen is valued thirty thousand strong;
If she hath time to breathe, be well assur'd
Her faction will be full as strong as ours. Shakes. Henry VI.

He has been known to commit outrages,
And cherish factions. Shakespeare's Timon.

Their hatred went so far, that by one of Simon's faction murders were committed. 2 Mac. iv. 9.

By the weight of reason I should counterpoise the overbalancings of any factions. King Charles.

2. Tumult; discord; dissension.

They remained at Newbery in great faction among themselves. Clarendon.

factítious adj. [*factitius*, Latin.] Made by art, in opposition to what is made by nature.

In the making and distilling of soap, by one degree of fire the salt, the water, and the oil or grease, whereof that factitious concrete is made up, being boiled up together, are easily brought to incorporate. Boyle.

Hardness wherein some stones exceed all other bodies, and among them the adamant all other stones, being exalted to that degree that art in vain endeavours to counterfeit it; the factitious stones of chymists, in imitation, being easily detected by an ordinary lapidist. Ray on the Creation.

fáctory n.s. [from *factor.*]

1. A house or district inhabited by traders in a distant country.

2. The traders embodied in one place.

factótum n.s. [*fac totum*, Latin. It is used likewise in burlesque French.] A servant employed alike in all kinds of business: as Scrub in the *Stratagem.*[†]

fácture n.s. [French.] The act or manner of making any thing.

fáculty n.s. [*faculté*, French; *facultas*, Latin.]

1. The power of doing any thing; ability whether corporal or intellectual.

There is no kind of faculty or power in man, or any creature, which can rightly perform the functions allotted to it without perpetual aid and concurrence of that supreme cause of all things. Hooker, b. i. s. 8.

*Orators may grieve; for in their sides,
Rather than heads, their faculty abides.*
Denham.

Reason in man supplies the defect of other faculties wherein we are inferior to beasts, and what we cannot compass by force we bring about by stratagem. L'Estrange.

2. Powers of the mind, imagination, reason, memory.

*For well I understand in the prime end
Of nature, her the inferior; in the mind
And inward faculties, which most excel.*
Milt. Parad. Lost.

In the ordinary way of speaking, the understanding and will are two faculties of the mind. Locke.

Neither did our Saviour think it necessary to explain to us the nature of God, because it would be impossible, without bestowing on us

other faculties than we possess at present. Swift.

3. [In physick.] A power or ability to perform any action natural, vital, and animal: by the first they understand that by which the body is nourished and augmented, or another like it generated: the vital faculty is that by which life is preserved, and the ordinary functions of the body performed; and the animal faculty is what conducts the operations of the mind. Quincy.

4. A knack; habitual excellence; dexterity.

He had none of those faculties, which the other had, of reconciling men to him. Clarendon, b. viii.

A sober man would have wondered how our author found out monarchical absolute power in that text, had he not had an exceeding good faculty to find it himself where he could not shew it others. Locke.

He had an excellent faculty in preaching, if he were not too refined. Swift.

5. Quality; disposition or habit of good or ill.

*I'm traduc'd by tongues which neither know
My faculties nor person, yet will be
The chronicles of my doing.* Shakespeare's Henry VIII.

6. Power; authority.

   *This Duncan
Hath born his faculties so meek, hath been
So clear in his great office, that his virtues
Will plead like angels.* Shakespeare's Macbeth.

7. Privilege; right to do any thing.

Law hath set down to what persons, in what causes, with what circumstances, almost every faculty or favour shall be granted. Hooker, b. v.

8. Faculty, in an university, denotes the masters and professors of the several sciences: as, a meeting of the faculty or faculties.

facúnd adj. [*facundus*, Latin.] Eloquent. Dict.

to fáddle v.n. [corrupted from *To fiddle*, or toy with the fingers.] To trifle; to toy; to play.

to fag v.a. [*fatigo*, Latin.] To grow weary; to faint with weariness.

Creighton witheld his force 'till the Italian begun to fag, and then brought him to the ground. Mackenzie's Lives.

fain adv. [from the adjective.] Gladly; very desirously; according to earnest wishes.

Now I would give a thousand furlongs of sea for an acre of barren ground: I would fain die a dry death. Shakespeare.

Why would'st thou urge me to confess a flame I long have stifled, and would fain conceal. Addison's Cato.

Fain wou'd I Raphael's godlike art rehearse, And show th' immortal labours in my verse. Addison.

The plebeians would fain have a law enacted to lay all mens rights and privileges upon the same level. Swift.

fáintling adj. [from *faint*.] Timorous; feebleminded. A burlesque or low word.

There's no having patience, thou art such a faintling silly creature. Arbuthnot's History of John Bull.

faith n.s. [*foi*, French; *fede*, Italian; *fides*, Latin.]

1. Belief of the revealed truths of religion.[†]

The name of faith being properly and strictly taken, it must needs have reference unto some uttered word, as the object of belief. Hooker, b. ii. b. 4.

Faith, if it have not works, is dead. Jam. ii. 17.

Vision in the next life is the perfecting of that faith in this life, or that faith here is turned into vision there, as hope into enjoying. Hammond's Pract. Catech.

Then faith shall fail, and holy hope shall die; One lost in certainty, and one in joy. Prior.

2. The system of revealed truths held by the Christian church; the credenda.

Felix heard Paul concerning the faith. Acts xxiv. 24.

This is the catholick faith. Common Prayer.

3. Trust in God.

Faith is an entire dependence upon the truth, the power, the justice, and the mercy of God; which dependence will certainly incline us to obey him in all things. Swift.

4. Tenet held.

Which to believe of her, Must be a faith, that reason, without miracle, Should never plant in me. Shakespeare's King Lear.

5. Trust in the honesty or veracity of another.

6. Fidelity; unshaken adherence.

Her failing, while her faith to me remains, I should conceal, and not expose to blame By my complaint. Milton's Paradise Lost, b. x. l. 129.

7. Honour; social considence.

For you alone I broke my faith with injur'd Palamon. Dryd. Knight's Tale.

8. Sincerity; honesty; veracity.

Sir, in good faith, in meer verity. Shakes. King Lear.

They are a very froward generation, children in whom is no faith. Deutr. xxxii. 20.

9. Promise given.

I have been forsworn, In breaking faith with Julia whom I lov'd. Shakespeare.

fálchion n.s. [*ensis falcatus;* in French *fauchon.*] A short crooked sword; a cymeter.

I've seen the day, with my good biting falchion, I would have made them skip: I am old now. Sh. K. Lear.

Old falchions are new temper'd in the fires; The sounding trumpet ev'ry soul inspires. Dryden's Æn.

What sighs and tears Hath Eugene caused! how many widows curse His cleaving falchion! Phillips.

fállingsickness n.s. [*fall* and *sickness*.] The epilepsy; a disease in which the patient is without any warning deprived at once of his senses, and falls down.

Did Cæsar swoon?—He fell down in the market-place, and foam'd at mouth, and was speechless.—He hath the falling-sickness. Shakespeare's Julius Cæsar.

The dogfisher is good against the fallingsickness. Walton.

to fámble v.a. [*famler*, Danish] To hesitate in the speech. This word I find only in Skinner.

fame n.s. [*fama*, Latin; φαμα, Dorick.]

1. Celebrity; renown.

The house to be builded for the Lord must be exceeding magnifical, of fame and of glory throughout all countries. 1 Chro. xxii. 5.

The desire of fame will not suffer endowments to lie useless. Addison's Spectator.

What is this fame, for which we thoughts employ, The owner's wife, which other men enjoy? Pope.

2. Report; rumour.

We have heard the fame of him, and all that he did in Egypt. Jos. ix. 9.

I shall shew what are true fames. Bacon.

famósity n.s. [from *famous.*] Renown; celebrity. Dict.

fanáticism n.s. [from *fanatick.*] Enthusiasm; religious frenzy.

A church whose doctrines are derived from the clear fountains of the Scriptures, whose polity and discipline are formed upon the most uncorrupted models of antiquity, which has stood unshaken by the most furious assaults of popery on the one hand, and fanaticism on the other; has triumphed over all the arguments of its enemies, and has nothing now to contend with but their slanders and calumnies. Rogers's Sermons.

fanátick n.s. [from the adjective.] An enthusiast; a man mad with wild notions of religion.

The double armature of St. Peter is a more destructive engine than the tumultary weapon snatcht up by a fanatick. Decay of Piety.

fáncy n.s. [contracted from *phantasy, phantasia*, Latin; φαντασια.]

1. Imagination; the power by which the mind forms to itself images and representations of things, persons, or scenes of being.

Shakespeare, fancy's sweetest child! Milton.

   In the soul
Are many lesser faculties, that serve
Reason as chief: among these fancy next
Her office holds; of all external things,
Which the five watchful senses represent,
She forms imaginations, airy shapes,
Which reason joining, or disjoining, frames
All what we affirm, or what deny, and call
Our knowledge, or opinion. Milton's Paradise Lost, b. v.

Though no evidence affects the fancy so strongly as that of sense, yet there is other evidence, which gives as full satisfaction and as clear a conviction to our reason. Atterbury.

Love is by fancy led about,
From hope to fear, from joy to doubt:
  Whom we now a goddess call,
Divinity grac'd in every feature,
Strait's a deform'd, a perjur'd creature;
  Love and hate are fancy all. Granville.

2. An opinion bred rather by the imagination than the reason.

Mens private fancies must give place to the higher judgment of that church which is in authority over them. Hooker.

A person of a full and ample fortune, who was not disturbed by any fancies in religion. Clarendon, b. viii.

I have always had a fancy, that learning might be made a play and recreation to children. Locke.

3. Taste; idea; conception of things.

The little chapel called the Salutation is very neat, and built with a pretty fancy. Addison on Italy.

4. Image; conception; thought.

How now, my lord, why do you keep alone;
Of sorriest fancies your companions making,
Using those thoughts which should indeed
    have died
With them they think on? Shakespeare's
Macbeth.

5. Inclination; liking; fondness.

Tell me where is fancy bred,
Or in the heart, or in the head?
How begot, how nourished?
It is engender'd in the eyes,
With gazing fed, and fancy dies
In the cradle where it lies. Shakes.
Merchant of Venice.

His fancy lay extremely to travelling.
L'Estrange.

For you, fair Hermia, look you arm yourself,
To fit your fancies to your father's will;
Or else the law of Athens yields you up
To death, or to a vow of single life.
Shakespeare.

A resemblance in humour or opinion, a fancy
for the same business or diversion, is
oftentimes a ground of affection. Collier
of Friendship.

6. Caprice; humour; whim.

True worth shall gain me, that it may be said
Desert, not fancy, once a woman led.
Dryden's Ind. Emp.

The sultan of Egypt kept a good
correspondence with the Jacobites towards
the head of the Nile, for fear they should take
a fancy to turn the course of that river.
Arbuthnot.

7. Frolick; idle scheme; vagary.

One that was just entring upon a long
journey, took up a fancy of putting a trick
upon Mercury. L'Estrange.

8. Something that pleases or entertains.

The altering of the scent, colour, or taste of
fruit, by infusing, mixing, or cutting into the
bark or root of the tree, herb, or flower, any
coloured, aromatical, or medicinal substance,
are but fancies: the cause is, for that those

things have passed their period, and nourish
not. Bacon's Nat. History.

London-pride is a pretty fancy, and does well
for borders. Mortimer's Husbandry.

fáncysick adj. [*fancy* and *sick.*] One whose
imagination is unsound; one whose
distemper is in his own mind.

'Tis not necessity, but opinion, that makes
men miserable; and when we come once to be
fancysick, there's no cure for it. L'Estrange.

fantástical, fantástick adj. [*fantastique,* Fr.
from *fantasy.*]

1. Irrational; bred only in the imagination.

The delight that a man takes from another's
sin, can be nothing else but a fantastical,
preternatural complacency, arising from that
which he really has no feeling of. South.

2. Subsisting only in the fancy; imaginary.

   Present feats
Are less than horrible imaginings:
My thought, whose murther yet is but fantastical,
Shakes so my single state of man, that function
Is smother'd in surmise; and nothing is,
But what is not. Shakespeare's Macbeth.

Men are so possessed with their own fancies,
that they take them for oracles; and are
arrived to some extraordinary revelations of
truth, when indeed they do but dream dreams,
and amuse themselves with the fantastick
ideas of a busy imagination. Decay of Piety.

3. Unreal; apparent only; having the nature
of phantoms which only assume visible
forms occasionally.

Are ye fantastical, or that indeed
Which outwardly ye shew? Shakespeare's
Macbeth.

4. Capricious; humourous; unsteady;
irregular.

Nor happiness can I, nor misery feel,
From any turn of her fantastick wheel. Prior.

5. Whimsical; fanciful; indulgent to one's
own imagination.

They put such words in the mouths of one of
these fantastical mind-infected people, that
children and musicians call lovers. Sidney.

I'll knit it up in silken strings,
With twenty odd conceited true love knots:
To be fantastick, may become a youth
Of greater time than I. Shakes. Two
Gentlemen of Verona.

Duumvir is provided with an imperious,
expensive and fantastick mistress; to whom he
retires from the conversation of a discreet and
affectionate wife. Tatler.

We are apt to think your medallists a little
fantastical in the different prices they set upon
their coins, without any regard to the metal of
which they are composed. Addison.

fap adj. Fuddled; drunk. It seems to have
been a cant word in the time of Shakespeare.

The gentleman had drunk himself out of his
five senses; and being fap, sir, was, as they say,
cashiered. Shakespeare.

farce n.s. [from the verb; or from *farcer*,
French, to mock.] A dramatick
representation written without regularity,
and stuffed with wild and ludicrous
conceits.

There is yet a lower sort of poetry and
painting, which is out of nature; for a farce is
that in poetry which grotesque is in a picture:
the persons and actions of a farce are all
unnatural, and the manners false; that is,
inconsistent with the characters of mankind:
grotesque painting is the just resemblance of
this. Dryden's Dufresnoy.

What should be great, you turn to farce. Prior.

They object against it as a farce, because the
irregularity of the plot should answer to the
extravagance of the characters, which they say
this piece wants, and therefore is no farce.
Gay.

fárcy n.s. [*farcina*, Italian; *farcin*, French.]
The leprosy of horses. It is probably curable
by antimony.

fárdel ns. [*fardello*, Italian; *fardeau*, Fr.] A
bundle; a little pack.

Let us to the king: there is that in this fardel
will make him scratch his beard.
Shakespeare's Winter's Tale.

Who would fardels bear,
To groan and sweat under a weary life?
Shakesp. Hamlet.

farináceous adj. [from *farina*, Latin.]
Mealy; tasting like meal or flower of corn.

The properest food of the vegetable kingdom
for mankind, is taken from the farinaceous or
mealy seeds of some culmiferous plants; as oats,
barley, wheat, rice, rye, maize, panick, and
millet. Arbuthnot on Aliments.

farrágo n.s. [Latin.] A mass formed
confusedly of several ingredients; a medley.

fart n.s. [*fert*, Saxon.] Wind from behind.

Love is the fart
Of every heart;
It pains a man when 'tis kept close;
And others doth offend, when 'tis let loose.
Suckling.

to fart v.a. [from the noun.] To break wind
behind.

As when we a gun discharge,
Although the bore be ne'er so large,
Before the flame from muzzle burst,
Just at the breech it flashes first;
So from my lord his passion broke,
He farted first, and then he spoke. Swift.

fásces n.s. [Latin.] Rods anciently carried
before the consuls as a mark of their
authority.

The duke beheld, like Scipio, with disdain,
That Carthage, which he ruin'd, rise once more;
And shook aloft the fasces of the main,
To fright those slaves with what they felt
* before.* Dryden.

to fáscinate v.a. [*fascino*, Latin.] To
bewitch; to enchant; to influence in some
wicked and secret manner.

There be none of the affections which have
been noted to fascinate or bewitch, but love
and envy. Bacon, Essay 9.

Such a fascinating sin this is, as allows men
no liberty of consideration. Decay of Piety.

fáscinous adj. [*fascinum*, Latin.] Caused or
acting by witchcraft, or enchantment.

I shall not discuss the possibility of fascinous diseases, farther than refer to experiment. Harvey on Consumptions.

fáshion n.s. [*façon*, French; *facies*, Latin.]

1. Form; make; state of any thing with regard to its outward appearance.

They pretend themselves grieved at our solemnities in erecting churches, at their form and fashion, at the stateliness of them and costliness, and at the opinion which we have of them. Hooker, b. v. s. 17.

The fashion of his countenance was altered. Luke ix. 29.

Stand these poor people's friend.
—I will,
Or let me lose the fashion of a man. Shakes. Henry VIII.

2. The make or cut of cloaths.

I'll be at charges for a looking-glass,
And entertain a score or two of taylors,
To study fashions to adorn my body. Shakes. Richard III.

You, sir, I entertain for one of my hundred; only, I do not like the fashion of your garments. Shakesp. King Lear.

3. Manner; sort; way.

For that I love your daughter
In such a righteous fashion as I do,
Perforce against all checks, rebukes, and manners,
I must advance. Shakespeare's Merry Wives of Windsor.

Pluck Casca by the sleeve,
And he will, after his sour fashion, tell you
What hath proceeded. Shakespeare's Julius Cæsar.

The commissioners either pulled down or defaced all images in churches; and that in such unseasonable and unseasoned fashion, as if it had been done in hostility against them. Hayw.

4. Custom operating upon dress, or any domestick ornaments.

Here's the note
How much your chain weighs to the utmost carat,

The fineness of the gold, the chargeful fashion. Shakespeare.

5. Custom; general practice.

Zelmane again, with great admiration, begun to speak of him; asking whether it were the fashion or no, in Arcadia, that shepherds should perform such valorous enterprizes. Sidn.

Though the truth of this hath been universally acknowledged, yet because the fashion of the age is to call every thing into question, it will be requisite to satisfy mens reason about it. Tillotson, Sermon 3.

Why truly, wife, it was not easily reconciled to the common method; but then it was the fashion to do such things. Arbuthnot's History of John Bull.

6. Manner imitated from another; way established by precedent.

Sorrow so royally in you appears,
That I will deeply put the fashion on,
And wear it in my heart. Shakespeare.

7. General approbation; mode.

A young gentleman accommodates himself to the innocent diversions in fashion. Locke.

His panegyricks were bestowed only on such persons as he had familiarly known, and only at such times as others cease to praise, when out of power, or out of fashion. Pope.

8. Rank; condition above the vulgar. It is used in a sense below that of quality.

It is strange that men of fashion, and gentlemen, should so grosly belie their own knowledge. Raleigh.

9. Any thing worn.

Now, by this maiden blossom in my hand,
I scorn thee, and thy fashion, peevish boy. Shak. Hen. VI.

10. The farcy; a distemper in horses; the horses leprosy. A barbarous word.

His horse is possest with the glanders, infected with the fashions, and full of windgalls. Shak. Taming of the Shrew.

fáshionist n.s. [from *fashion*.] A follower of the mode; a fop; a coxcomb. Dict.

fástuous adj. [*fastuosus*, Latin; *fastueux-se*, Fr.] Proud; haughty. Dict.

fáther n.s. [*fæðer*, Saxon; *aaher*, Erse. This word is found likewise in the Persian language.]

1. He by whom the son or daughter is begotten.

Father is a notion superinduced to the substance, or man, and refers only to an act of that thing called man, whereby he contributed to the generation of one of his own kind. Locke.

Son of Bensalem, thy father saith it; the man by whom thou hast breath and life speaketh the word. Bacon.

   He shall forget
Father and mother, and to his wife adhere. Milt. Pa. Lost.

2. The first ancestor.

   It was said
It should not stand in thy posterity;
But that myself should be the root and father
Of many kings. Shakespeare's Macbeth.

Abraham is the father of us all. Rom. iv. 16.

3. The appellation of an old man.

A poor blind man was accounted cunning in prognosticating weather: Epsom, a lawyer, said in scorn, Tell me, father, when doth the sun change? The old man answered, when such a wicked lawyer as you goeth to heaven. Camden.

4. The title of any man reverend for age, learning, and piety.

You shall find one well accompanied
With reverend fathers and well learned ˌ
   bishops. Sh. R. III.

5. One who has given original to any thing good or bad.

Jubal was the father of all such as handle the harp and organ. Gen. iv. 21.

6. The ecclesiastical writers of the first centuries.

Men may talk of the fathers, and magnify the fathers, and seem to make the authority of the fathers next to infallible; and yet none expose them more to contempt than they which give such answers as these. Stillingfleet.

7. One who acts with paternal care and tenderness.

I was a father to the poor. Job xxix. 16.

He hath made me a father to Pharaoh, and lord of all his house. Gen. xlv. 8.

8. The title of a popish confessor, particularly of a Jesuit.

   Formal in apparel,
In gait and countenance surely like a father. Shakespeare.

There was in this place a father of a convent, who was very much renowned for his piety and exemplary life; and as it is usual, under any great affliction, to apply themselves to the most eminent confessors, our beautiful votary took the opportunity of confessing herself to this celebrated father. Add.

9. The title of a senator of old Rome.

From hence the race of Alban fathers come,
And the long glories of majestick Rome. Dryden's Virgil.

10. The appellation of the first person of the adorable Trinity.

The eternal son of God esteemed it his meat and drink to do the will of his Father, and for his obedience alone obtained the greatest glory. Taylor's Rule of living holy.

11. The compellation of God as Creator.

We have one Father, even God. John viii. 41.

Almighty and most merciful Father. Common Prayer.

fatídical adj. [*fatidicus*, Latin; *fatidique*, French.] Prophetick; having the power to foretell future events.

The oak, of all other trees only fatidical, told them what a fearful unfortunate business this would prove. Howel.

fatíferous adj. [*fatifer*, Latin.] Deadly; mortal; destructive. Dict.

fátigable adj. [*fatigo*, Lat.] Easily wearied; susceptible of weariness.

fátwitted adj. [*fat* and *wit.*] Heavy; dull; stupid.

Thou art so fatwitted with drinking old sack, and unbuttoning thee after supper, and sleeping upon benches in the afternoon, that thou hast forgotten. Shakes. Henry IV.

fáutress n.s. [*fautrix*, Latin; *fautrice*, Fr.] A woman that favours, or shows countenance.

*It made him pray, and prove
Minerva's aid his fautress still.*
Chapman's Iliads.

He comes from banishment to the fautress of liberty, from the barbarous to the polite. Garth's Dedicat. to Ovid.

fávourite n.s. [*favori*, *favorite*, French; *favorita*, Ital.]

1. A person or thing beloved; one regarded with favour; any thing in which pleasure is taken; that which is regarded with particular approbation or affection.

Every particular master in criticism has his favourite passages in an author. Addison's Spectator, No 202.

So fathers speak, persuasive speech and mild! Their sage experience to the fav'rite child. Pope's Odyssey.

2. One chosen as a companion by his superiour; a mean wretch whose whole business is by any means to please.

All favours and punishments passed by him, all offices and places of importance were distributed to his favourites. Sidney.

I was a Thessalian gentleman, who, by mischance, having killed a favourite of the prince of that country, was pursued so cruelly, that in no place but by favour or corruption they would obtain my destruction. Sidney, b. I.

The great man down, you mark, his fav'rite flies; The poor advanc'd, makes friends of enemies. Shak. Haml.

Bid her steal into the plashed bower, Where honeysuckles, ripen'd by the sun,

Forbid the sun to enter; like to favourites, Made proud by princes, that advance their pride Against that power that bred it. Shakespeare.

Nothing is more vigilant, nothing more jealous than a favourite, especially towards the waining time, and suspect of satiety. Wotton.

This man was very capable of being a great favourite to a great king. Clarendon.

What fav'rites gain, and what the nation owes, Fly the forgetful world. Pope.

fáxed adj. [from *fæx*, Saxon, hair.] Hairy. Now obsolete.

They could call a comet a faxed star, which is all one with stella crinita, *or* cometa. Camden's Remains.

to feague v.a. [Gower uses To feige, for to censure; *fegen*, German, to sweep; *fyken*, Dutch, to strike.] To whip; to chastise; to beat. In Scottish *feake*, to slutter; to be idly or officiously busy.

fear n.s. [*fearan*, Sax. to fear; *vaer*, Dut. *feakle*, Erse.]

1. Dread; horrour; painful apprehension of danger.

Fear is an uneasiness of the mind, upon the thought of future evil likely to befal us. Locke.

Trembling fear still to and fro did fly, And found no place where safe she shrowd him might. F. Q.

For fear was upon them, because of the people of those countries. Ezra iii. 3.

What then remains? Are we depriv'd of will? Must we not wish, for fear of wishing ill? Dryden's Juv.

Fear, in general, is that passion of our nature whereby we are excited to provide for our security upon the approach of evil. Rogers, Sermon 1.

2. Awe; dejection of mind at the presence of any person or thing.

And the fear of you, and the dread of you, shall be upon every beast. Gen. ix. 2.

3. Anxiety; solicitude.

The greatest and principal fear was for the holy temple. 2 Mac. xv. 18.

4. That which causes fear.

   Antony, stay not by his side:
Thy demon, that's the spirit that keeps thee, is
Noble, courageous, high, unmatchable,
Where Cæsar's is not; but near him, thy angel
Becomes a fear, as being o'erpower'd.
Shak. Ant. and Cleop.

5. The object of fear.

Except the God of Abraham and the fear of Isaac had been with me. Gen. xxxi. 42.

6. Something hung up to scare deer by its colour or noise.

He who fleeth from the noise of the fear shall fall into the pit, and he that cometh up out of the midst of the pit shall be taken in the snare. Is. xxiv. 18.

féateous adj. [from *feat.*] Neat; dexterous. Obsolete.

to febrícitate v.n. [*febricitor*, Latin.] To be in a fever. Dict.

febrifúge n.s. [*febris* and *fugo*, Latin; *febrifuge*, Fr.] Any medicine serviceable in a fever. Quincy.

Bitters, like choler, are the best sanguifiers, and also the best febrifuges. Floyer on the Humours.

féculent adj. [*fæculentus*, Lat. *feculent*, French.] Foul; dreggy; excrementitious.

But both his hands, most filthy feculent,
Above the water were on high extent,
And fain'd to wash themselves incessantly,
Yet nothing cleaner were for such intent.
Fairy Queen.

We may affirm them to be to the body as the light of a candle to the gross and feculent snuff, which as it is not pent up in it, so neither doth it partake of its stench and impurity. Glanv. Apology.

féline adj. [*felinus*, Latin.] Like a cat; pertaining to a cat.

Even as in the beaver; from which he differs principally in his teeth, which are canine, and in his tail, which is feline, or a long taper. Grew's Musæum.

fellífluous adj. [*fel* and *fluo*, Latin.] Flowing with gall. Dict.

féllmonger n.s. [from *fell.*] A dealer in hides.

felo-de-se n.s. [In law.] He that committeth felony by murdering himself.

félony n.s. [*felonie*, Fr. *felonia*, low Latin, from *felon.*] A crime denounced capital by the law; an enormous crime.

I will make it felony to drink small beer. Shakes. Henry VI.

felúcca n.s. [*feleu*, Fr. *felkon*, Arab.] A small open boat with six oars. Dict.

fémale n.s. [*femelle*, French; *femella*, Latin.] A she; one of the sex which brings young.

God created man in his own image, male and female created he them. Gen. i. 27.

   Man, more divine,
Lord of the wide world, and wide wat'ry seas,
Indu'd with intellectual sense and soul,
Are masters to their females, and their lords.
Shakespeare.

femINálity n.s. [from *fæmina*, Latin.] Female nature.

If in the minority of natural vigour the parts of feminality take place, upon the increase or growth thereof the masculine appears. Brown's Vulgar Errours, b. iii. c. 17.

ferácity n.s. [*feracitas*, Lat.] Fruitfulness; fertility. Dict.

feriátion n.s. [*feriatio*, Lat.] The act of keeping holiday; cessation from work.

As though there were any feriation in nature, this season is commonly termed the physicians vacation. Brown's Vulg. Err.

férity n.s. [*feritas*, Latin.] Barbarity; cruelty; wildness; savageness.

He reduced him from the most abject and stupid ferity to his senses, and to sober reason. Woodward's Natural History.

to férry v.a. [*faran*, to pass, Saxon; *fahr*, German, a passage. Skinner imagines that this whole family of words may be deduced from the Latin *veho*. I do not love Latin originals; but if such must be sought, may not these words be more naturally derived from *ferri*, to be carried?] To carry over in a boat.

Cymocles heard and saw,
He loudly call'd to such as were aboard,
The little bark unto the shore to draw,
And him to ferry over that deep ford.
Fairy Queen, b. ii.

férula n.s. [*ferule*, Fr. from *ferula*, giant fennel, Lat.] An instrument of correction with which young scholars are beaten on the hand: so named because anciently the stalks of fennel were used for this purpose.

These differ as much as the rod and ferula.
Shaw's Gramm.

fescue n.s. [*veese*, Dutch; *festu*, French.] A small wire by which those who teach to read point out the letters.

Teach him an alphabet upon his fingers,
making the points of his fingers of his left
hand both on the inside to signify some letter,
when any of them is pointed at by the
forefinger of the right hand, or by any kind
of fescue. Holder.

Teach them how manly passions ought to move;
For such as cannot think, can never love;
And since they needs will judge the poet's art,
Point 'em with fescues to each shining part.
Dryden.

féstinate adj. [*festinatus*, Latin.] Hasty; hurried. A word not in use.

Advise the duke, where you are going, to
a most festinate preparation: we are bound
to the like. Shakes. King Lear.

féuterer n.s. A dogkeeper: perhaps the cleaner of the kennel.

fib n.s. [A cant word among children.] A lye; a falsehood.

Destroy his fib or sophistry; in vain,
The creature's at his dirty work again.
Pope's Epistles.

I so often lie,
Scarce Harvey's self has told more fibs than I.
Pope.

fibre n.s. [*fibre*, Fr. *fibra*, Latin.]

1. A small thread or string; the first constituent parts of bodies.

Now sliding streams the thirsty plants renew,
And feed their fibres with reviving dew.
Pope.

2. A fibre, in physick, is an animal thread, of which there are different kinds: some are soft, flexible, and a little elastick; and these are either hollow, like small pipes, or spongious and full of little cells, as the nervous and fleshy fibres: others are more solid, flexible, and with a strong elasticity or spring, as the membranous and cartilaginous fibres: and a third sort are hard and flexible, as the fibres of the bones. Now of all those some are very sensible, and others destitute of all sense: some so very small as not to be easily perceived; and others, on the contrary, so big as to be plainly seen; and most of them, when examined with a microscope, appear to be composed of still smaller fibres: these fibres first constitute the substance of the bones, cartilages, ligaments, membranes, nerves, veins, arteries and muscles. And again, by the various texture and different combination of some or all of those parts, the more compound organs are framed; such as the lungs, stomach, liver, legs and arms, the sum of all which make up the body. Quincy.

My heart sinks in me while I hear him speak,
And every slacken'd fibre drops its hold,
Like nature letting down the springs of life:
The name of father awes me still.
Dryd. Spanish Fryar.

fíco n.s. [Italian.] An act of contempt done with the fingers, expressing a *fig for you.*

Having once recovered his fortress, he then
gives the fico to all that his adversaries can by
siege, force, or famine attempt against him.
Carew's Survey of Cornwal.

fiction n.s. [*fictio*, Latin; *fiction*, French.]

1. The act of feigning or inventing.

If the presence of God in the image, by a mere fiction of the mind, be a sufficient ground to worship that image, is not God's real presence in every creature a far better ground to worship it! Stillingfleet.

Fiction is of the essence of poetry, as well as of painting: there is a resemblance in one of human bodies, things, and actions, which are not real; and in the other of a true story by a fiction. Dryden's Dufresnoy.

2. The thing feigned or invented.

>　*If through mine ears pierce any consolations,*
> *By wise discourse, sweet tunes, or poets fictions;*
>　*If ought I cease these hideous exclamations,*
> *While that my soul, she, she lives in afflictions.*
> Sidney.

So also was the fiction of those golden apples kept by a dragon, taken from the serpent, which tempted Evah. Raleigh.

3. A falsehood; a lye.

fiddlefaddle n.s. [A cant word.] Trifles.

She said that their grandfather had a horse shot at Edgehill, and their uncle was at the siege of Buda; with abundance of fiddlefaddle of the same nature. Spectator, N° 299.

to fig v.a. See *fico*.

1. To insult with fico's or contemptuous motions of the fingers.

When Pistol lies, do this, and fig me like The bragging Spaniard. Shakespeare's Henry IV.

2. To put something useless into one's head. Low cant.

Away to the sow she goes, and figs her in the crown with another story. L'Estrange.

figulate adj. [from *figulus*, Latin.] Made of potters clay.

figurative adj. [*figurative*, Fr. from *figura*, Latin.]

1. Representing something else; typical; representative.

This, they will say, was figurative, and served by God's appointment but for a time, to shadow out the true everlasting glory of a more divine sanctity; where into Christ being long since entered, it seemeth that all these curious exornations should rather cease. Hooker, b. v. s. 15.

2. Changed by rhetorical figures from the primitive meaning; not literal.

How often have we been railed at for understanding words in a figurative sense, which cannot be literally understood without overthrowing the plainest evidence of sense and reason. Stillingfleet's Def. of Disc. on Rom. Idol.

This is a figurative expression, where the words are used in a different sense from what they signify in their first ordinary intention. Rogers, Sermon 14.

3. Full of figures; full of rhetorical exornations; full of changes from the original sense.

Sublime subjects ought to be adorned with the sublimest and with the most figurative expressions. Dryden's Juvenal, Pref.

figure n.s. [*figura*, Latin.]

1. The form of any thing as terminated by the outline.

Flowers have all exquisite figures, and the flower numbers are chiefly five and four; as in primroses, briar-roses, single muskroses, single pinks and gilliflowers, &c. which have five leaves; lilies, flower-de-luces, borage, buglass, &c. which have four leaves. Bacon's Natural History.

Men find green clay that is soft as long as it is in the water, so that one may print on it all kind of figures, and give it what shape one pleases. Boyle.

Figures are properly modifications of bodies; for pure space is not any where terminated, nor can be: whether there be or be not body in it, it is uniformly continued. Locke.

2. Shape; form; semblance.

He hath borne himself beyond the promise of his age, doing in the figure of a lamb the feats of a lion. Shakespeare.

3. Person; external form; appearance graceful or inelegant, mean or grand.

The blue German shall the Tigris drink,
E'er I, forsaking gratitude and truth,
Forget the figure of that godlike youth.
Dryden's Virgil.

I was charmed with the gracefulness of his figure and delivery, as well as with his discourses. Addison's Spectator.

A good figure, or person, in man or woman, gives credit at first sight to the choice of either. Clarissa.

4. Distinguished appearance; eminence; remarkable character.

While fortune favour'd, while his arms support
The cause, and rul'd the counsels of the court,
I made some figure there; nor was my name
Obscure, nor I without my share of fame.
Dryden's Æn.

The speech, I believe, was not so much designed by the knight to inform the court, as to give him a figure in my eye, and keep up his credit in the country.
Addison's Spectator.

Not a woman shall be unexplained that makes a figure either as a maid, a wife, or a widow. Addison's Guardian.

Whether or no they have done well to set you up for making another kind of figure, time will witness. Addison.

Many princes made very ill figures upon the throne, who before were the favourites of the people. Addison's Freeholder.

5. A statue; an image; something formed in resemblance of somewhat else.

The several statues, which seemed at a distance to be made of the whitest marble, were nothing else but so many figures in snow. Addison's Freeholder.

6. Representations in painting; persons exhibited in colours.

In the principal figures of a picture the painter is to employ the sinews of his art; for in them consists the principal beauty of his work. Dryden's Dufresnoy.

My favourite books and pictures sell;
Kindly throw in a little figure,
And set the price upon the bigger. Prior.

7. Arrangement; disposition; modification.

The figure of a syllogism is the proper disposition of the middle term with the parts of the question. Watts's Logick.

8. A character denoting a number.

Hearts, tongues, figures, scribes, bards,
*   poets cannot*
Think, speak, cast, write, sing, number
His love to Anthony. Shakespeare's Ant. and Cleopatra.

He that seeketh to be eminent amongst able men, hath a great task; but that is ever good for the publick: but he that plots to be the only figure among cyphers, is the decay of a whole age. Bacon's Essays.

As in accounts cyphers and figures pass for real sums, so in human affairs words pass for things themselves. South's Serm.

9. The horoscope; the diagram of the aspects of the astrological houses.

We do not know what's brought to pass under the profession of fortunetelling: she works by charms, by spells, by the figure, and dawbry beyond our element. Shakespeare.

He set a figure to discover
If you were fled to Rye or Dover.
Hudibras, p. iii. cant. 1.

Figure flingers and star-gazers pretend to foretell the fortunes of kingdoms, and have no foresight in what concerns themselves. L'Estrange, Fable 94.

10. [In theology.] Type representative.

Who was the figure of him that is to come. Romans.

11. [In rhetorick.] Any mode of speaking in which words are detorted from their literal and primitive sense. In strict

acceptation, the change of a word is a trope, and any affection of a sentence a figure; but they are generally confounded by the exactest writers.

Silken terms precise,
Three pil'd hyperboles, spruce affectation,
Figures pedantical, these Summer flies
Have blown me full of maggot ostentation.
Shakespeare.

Here is a strange figure invented against the plain and natural sense of the words; for by praying to bestow, must be understood only praying to pray. Stillingfleet.

They have been taught rhetorick, but yet never taught to express themselves in the language they are always to use; as if the names of the figures that embellished the discourse of those, who understood the art of speaking, were the very art and skill of speaking well. Locke.

12. [In grammar.] Any deviation from the rules of analogy or syntax.

figure-flinger n.s. [*figure* and *fling*.] A pretender to astrology and prediction.

Quacks, figure-flingers, pettifoggers, and republican plotters cannot well live without it. Collier of Confidence.

fin n.s. [*fin*, Saxon; *vin*, Dutch.] The wing of a fish; the limb by which he balances his body, and moves in the water.

He that depends
Upon your favours, swims with fins of lead,
And hews down oaks with rushes.
Shakespeare's Othello.

Their fins consist of a number of gristly bones, long and slender, like pins and needles.
More's Antid. against Atheism.

Thus at half-ebb a rowling sea
Returns, and wins upon the shore;
The watry herd, affrighted at the roar,
Rest on their fins awhile, and stay,
Then backward take their wond'ring way.
Dryden.

Still at his oar th' industrious Libys plies;
But as he plies, each busy arm shrinks in,

And by degrees is fashion'd to a fin.
Addis. Ovid's Metam.

findy adj. [*fyndig*, Saxon.] Plump; weighty; firm; solid. Thus the proverb,

A cold May and a windy,
Makes the barn fat and findy.

means that it stores the barn with plump and firm grain. Jun.

finésse n.s. [French.] Artifice; stratagem: an unnecessary word which is creeping into the language.

A circumstance not much to be stood upon, in case it were not upon some finess. Hayward.

finical adj. [from *fine*.] Nice; foppish; pretending to superfluous elegance.

A whorson, glassgazing, superserviceable, finical rogue. Shakespeare's King Lear.

I cannot hear a finical fop romancing, how the king took him aside at such a time; what the queen said to him at another.
L'Estrange, Fable 34.

firebránd n.s. [*fire* and *brand*.]

1. A piece of wood kindled.

I have eased my father-in-law of a firebrand, to set my own house in a flame. L'Estrange.

2. An incendiary; one who inflames factions; one who causes mischief.

Troy must not be, nor goodly Ilion stand;
Our firebrand brother, Paris, burns us all.
Shakespeare.

He sent Surrey with a competent power against the rebels, who fought with the principal band of them, and defeated them, and took alive John Chamber, their firebrand.
Bacon.

fireman n.s. [*fire* and *man*.]

1. One who is employed to extinguish burning houses.

The fireman sweats beneath his crooked arms;
A leathern casque his vent'rous head defends,
Boldly he climbs where thickest smoke ascends.
Gay.

2. A man of violent passions.

I had last night the fate to drink a bottle with two of these firemen. Tatler, Nº 61.

firework n.s. [*fire* and *work.*] Shows of fire; pyrotechnical performances.

The king would have me present the princess with some delightful ostentation, or pageant, or antick, or firework. Shak.

We represent also ordnance, and new mixtures of gunpowder, wildfires burning in water and unquenchable; and also fireworks of all variety. Bacon's New Atlantis.

The ancients were imperfect in the doctrine of meteors, by their ignorance of gunpowder and fireworks. Brown.

In fireworks give him leave to vent his spite; Those are the only serpents he can write. Dryden.

Our companion proposed a subject for a firework, which he thought would be very amusing. Addison's Guardian.

Their fireworks are made up in paper. Tatler, Nº 88.

Fitz n.s. [Norman, from *fils*, a son, Fr.] A son. Only used in law and genealogy: as Fitzherbert, the son of Herbert; Fitzthomas, the son of Thomas; Fitzroy, the son of the king. It is commonly used of illegitimate children.

fizgig n.s. A kind of dart or harpoon with which seamen strike fish.

flábile adj. [*flabilis*, Latin.] Blown about by the wind; subject to be blown. Dict.

flágelet n.s. [*flageolet*, French.] A small flute; a small instrument of wind musick.

Play us a lesson on your flagelet. More's Divine Dialogues.

flagítious adj. [from *flagitius*, Latin.] Wicked; villainous; atrocious.

No villany or flagitious action was ever yet committed, but, upon a due enquiry into the causes of it, it will be found that a lye was first or last the principal engine to effect it. South.

There's no working upon a flagitious and perverse nature by kindness and discipline. L'Estrange.

First, those flagitious times, Pregnant with unknown crimes, Conspire to violate the nuptial bed. Roscommon.

Perjury is a crime of so flagitious a nature, we cannot be too careful in avoiding every approach towards it. Addison.

But if in noble minds some dregs remain, Not yet purg'd off, of spleen and sour disdain, Discharge that rage on more provoking crimes, Nor fear a dearth in these flagitious times. Pope.

flam n.s. [A cant word of no certain etymology.] A false-hood; a lye; an illusory pretext.

A flam more senseless than the rog'ry Of old aruspicy and aug'ry. Hudibras, p. ii. cant. 3.

'Till these men can prove the things, ordered by our church, to be either intrinsically unlawful or indecent, all pretences or pleas of conscience to the contrary are nothing but cant and cheat, flam and delusion. South's Sermons.

What are most of the histories of the world but lyes? Lyes immortalized and consigned over as a perpetual abuse and flam upon posterity. South's Sermons.

flámbeau n.s. [French.] A lighted torch.

The king seiz'd a flambeau with zeal to destroy. Dryden.

As the attendants carried each of them a flambeau in their hands, the sultan, after having ordered all the lights to be put out, gave the word to enter the house, find out the criminal, and put him to death. Addison's Guardian.

flammívomous adj. [*flamma* and *vomo*, Latin.] Vomiting out flame. Dict.

flápdragon n.s.

1. A play in which they catch raisins out of burning brandy, and, extinguishing them by closing the mouth, eat them.

2. The thing eaten at flapdragon.

He plays at quoits well, and eats conger and fennel, and drinks candles ends for flapdragons, and rides the wild mare with the boys. Shakespeare's Henry IV. p. ii.

flásher n.s. [from *flash*.] A man of more appearance of wit than reality.

flátuous adj. [from *flatus*, Latin.] Windy; full of wind.

Rhubarb in the stomach, in a small quantity, doth digest and overcome, being not flatuous nor loathsome; and so sendeth it to the mesentery veins, and, being opening, it helpeth down urine. Bacon's Natural History, N° 44.

fleam n.s. [corrupted from φλεβοτομον, the instrument used in phlebotomy.] An instrument used to bleed cattle, which is placed on the vein, and then driven by a blow.

fleer n.s. [from the verb.]

1. Mockery expressed either in words or looks.

   Encave yourself,
And mark the fleers, the gibes, and notable scorns,
That dwell in ev'ry region of his face.
Shakesp. Othello.

2. A deceitful grin of civility.

If a man will but observe such persons exactly, he shall generally spy such false lines, and such a sly treacherous fleer upon their face, that he shall be sure to have a cast of their eye to warn him, before they give him a cast of their nature to betray him. South's Sermons.

fléshmonger n.s. [from *flesh*.] One who deals in flesh; a pimp.

Was the duke a fleshmonger, a fool, and a coward, as you then reported him? Shakespeare's Measure for Measure.

flexánimous adj. [*flexanimus*, Latin.] Having power to change the disposition of the mind. Dict.

flipp n.s. [A cant word.] A liquor much used in ships, made by mixing beer with spirits and sugar.

The tarpawlin and swabber is lolling at Madagascar, with some drunken sunburnt whore, over a can of flip. Dennis.

flirt n.s. [from the verb.]

1. A quick elastick motion.

In unfurling the fan are several little flirts and vibrations, as also gradual and deliberate openings. Addison's Spectator.

Before you pass th' imaginary sights
While the spread fan o'ershades your closing eyes,
Then give one flirt, and all the vision flies.
Pope.

2. A sudden trick.

Have licence to play,
At the hedge a flirt,
For a sheet or a shirt. Ben. Johnson's Gypsies.

3. A pert young hussey.

Scurvy knave, I am none of his flirt gills;
I am none of his skains mates. Shakesp. Romeo and Juliet.

Several young flirts about town had a design to cast us out of the fashionable world. Addison's Guardian, N° 109.

flíttermouse n.s. The bat.

flook n.s. [*pflug*, a plow, German.] The broad part of the anchor which takes hold of the ground.

flósculous adj. [*flosculus*, Latin.] Composed of flowers; having the nature or form of flowers.

The outward part is a thick and carnous covering, and the second a dry and flosculous coat. Brown's Vulgar Errours.

flúmmery n.s. A kind of food made by coagulation of wheatflower or oatmeal.

Milk and flummery are very fit for children. Locke.

fluviátick adj. [*fluviaticus*, Latin.] Belonging to rivers.

flux n.s. [*fluxus*, Latin; *flux*, French.]

1. The act of flowing; passage.

The most simple and primary motion of fire is a flux, in a direct line from the centre of the fuel to its circumference. Digby on Bodies.

By the perpetual flux of the liquids, a great part of them is thrown out of the body. Arbuthnot.

2. The state of passing away and giving place to others.

The heat of the sun in animals whose parts are successive, and in a continual flux, can produce a deep and perfect gloss of blackness. Brown's Vulgar Errours, b. vi. c. 10.

What the stated rate of interest should be, in the constant change of affairs, and flux of money, is hard to determine. Locke.

In the constituent matter of one body, turning naturally to another like body, the stock or fund can never be exhausted, nor the flux and alteration sensible. Woodward.

Languages, like our bodies, are in a perpetual flux, and stand in need of recruits to supply the place of those words that are continually falling through disuse. Felton on the Class.

3. Any flow or issue of matter.

Quinces stop fluxes of blood. Arbuthnot on Diet.

4. Dysentery; disease in which the bowels are excoriated and bleed; bloody flux.

    Eat eastern spice, secure
From burning fluxes and hot calenture. Hallifax.

5. Excrement; that which falls from bodies.

Civet is the very uncleanly flux of a cat. Shakespeare.

6. Concourse; confluence.

Left and abandon'd of his velvet friends;
'Tis right, quoth he; thus misery doth part
The flux of company. Shakesp. As you like it.

7. The state of being melted.

8. That which mingled with a body makes it melt.

flúxion n.s. [*fluxio*, Latin.]

1. The act of flowing.

2. The matter that flows.

3. [In mathematicks.] The arithmetick or analysis of infinitely small variable quantities; or it is the method of finding an infinite small or infinitely small quantity, which, being taken an infinite number of times, becomes equal to a quantity given. Harris.

A penetration into the abstruse difficulties and depths of modern algebra and fluxions, are not worth the labour of those who design the learned professions as the business of life. Watts.

fœtus n.s. [Latin.] The child in the womb after it is perfectly formed: but before, it is called embryo. Quincy.

A fœtus, in the mother's womb, differs not much from the state of a vegetable. Locke.

foh interject. [from *fah*, Saxon, an enemy.] An interjection of abhorrence: as if one should at sight of any thing hated cry out *a foe!*

Not to affect many proposed matches
Of her own clime, complection and degree,
Whereto we see in all things nature tends,
Foh! one may smell in such a will most rank,
Foul disproportions, thoughts unnatural. Shakes. Othello.

fólio n.s. [*in folio*, Latin.] A large book, of which the pages are formed by a sheet of paper once doubled.

Plumbinus and Plumeo made less progress in knowledge, though they had read over more folio's. Watts's Improvement.

fond n.s. [*fonn*, Scottish. A word of which I have found no satisfactory etymology. To *fonne* is in Chaucer to doat, to be foolish.]

1. Foolish; silly; indiscreet; imprudent; injudicious.

This we know that the Grecians or Gentiles did account foolishness; but that they ever did think it a fond or unlikely way to seek men's conversion by sermons, we have not heard. Hooker, b. v. s. 22.

*He was beaten out of all love of learning by
a fond schoolmaster.* Ascham.

> *Tell these sad women,*
> *'Tis fond to wail inevitable strokes,*
> *As 'tis to laugh at them.* Shakespeare's
> Coriolanus.

Grant I may never prove so fond
To trust man on his oath or bond.
Shakespeare's Timon.

I am weaker than a woman's tear,
Tamer than sleep, fonder than ignorance.
Shakespeare.

Fond thoughts may fall into some idle brain;
But one belief of all, is ever wise. Davies.

> *Thou see'st*
> *How subtly to detain thee I devise,*
> *Inviting thee to hear while I relate;*
> *Fond! were it not in hope of thy reply.*
> Milt. Paradise Lost.

> *So fond are mortal men,*
> *Fall'n into wrath divine,*
> *As their own ruin on themselves t' invite.*
> Milton's Agonistes.

'Twas not revenge for griev'd Apollo's wrong
Those ass's ears on Midas' temples hung;
But fond repentance of his happy wish.
Waller.

But reason with your fond religion fights;
For many gods are many infinites.
Dryden's Tyran. Love.

*This is fond, because it is the way to cheat
thyself.* Tillotson.

2. Trifling; valued by folly.

Not with fond shekles of the tested gold,
Or stones, whose rate are either rich or poor
As fancy values them. Shakespeare's Meas.
for Measure.

3. Foolishly tender; injudiciously
   indulgent.

I'm a foolish fond wife. Addison.

Like Venus I'll shine,
Be fond and be fine. Addison.

4. Pleased in too great a degree; foolishly
   delighted.

*Fame is in itself a real good, if we may believe
Cicero who was perhaps too fond of it.*
Dryden's Juvenal, Dedication.

I, fond of my well-chosen seat,
My pictures, medals, books complete. Prior.

*Some are so fond to know a great deal at once,
and love to talk of things with freedom and
boldness before they thoroughly understand
them.* Watts's Improvem. of the Mind.

fool n.s. [*ffol*, Welsh; *fol*, Islandick; *fol*,
French.]

1. One whom nature has denied reason;
   a natural; an idiot.

Do'st thou call me fool, boy?
*—All thy other titles thou hast given away
that thou wast born with.* Shakespeare's
King Lear.

The fool multitude, that chuse by show,
Not learning more than the fond eye doth teach,
Which pry not to the interior. Shak.
Merchant of Venice.

*It may be asked, whether the eldest son, being
a fool, shall inherit paternal power before the
younger, a wise man.* Locke.

He thanks his stars he was not born a fool.
Pope.

2. [In Scripture.] A wicked man.

*The fool hath said in his heart there is no
God.* Ps. xiv. 1.

3. A term of indignity and reproach.

*To be thought knowing, you must first put the
fool upon all mankind.* Dryden's Juvenal,
Preface.

4. One who counterfeits folly; a buffoon;
   a jester.

*Where's my knave, my fool? Go you, and call
my fool hither.* Shakespeare's King Lear.

*I scorn, although their drudge, to be their fool
or jester.* Milt.

*If this disguise sit not naturally on so grave a
person, yet it may become him better than that
fool's coat.* Denham.

5. To play the fool. To play pranks like
   a hired jester; to jest; to make sport.

*I returning where I left his armour, found
another instead thereof, and armed myself
therein to play the fool.* Sidney.

6. To play the fool. To act like one void of
common understanding.

*Well, thus we play the fools with the time,
And the spirits of the wise sit in the clouds
And mock us.* Shakespeare's Henry IV. p. ii.

*Is it worth the name of freedom to be at
liberty to play the fool, and draw shame and
misery upon a man's self?* Locke.

7. To make a fool. To disappoint; to defeat.

*'Twere as good a deed as to drink when a
man's a-hungry, to challenge him to the field,
and then to break promise with him, and
make a fool of him.* Shakes. Twelfth Night.

fóotball n.s. [*foot* and *ball*.] A ball
commonly made of a blown bladder cased
with leather, driven by the foot.

*Am I so round with you as you with me,
That like a football you do spurn me thus?*
Shakespeare.

*Such a Winter-piece should be beautified with
all manner of works and exercises of Winter;
as footballs, felling of wood, and sliding upon
the ice.* Peacham.

*As when a sort of lusty shepherds try
Their force at football, care of victory
Makes them salute so rudely, breast to breast,
That their encounter seems too rough for jest.*
Waller.

*One rolls along a football to his foes,
One with a broken truncheon deals his blows.*
Dryden.

*He was sensible the common football was
a very imperfect imitation of that exercise.*
Arbuthnot and Pope's Mart. Scribl.

fóotlicker n.s. [*foot* and *lick*.] A slave;
an humble fawner; one who licks the foot.

*Do that good mischief which may make
    this island
Thine own for ever; and I, thy Caliban,
For ay thy footlicker.* Shakespeare's Tempest.

fóotpad n.s. [*foot* and *pad*.] A highwayman
that robs on foot, not on horseback.

fop n.s. [A word probably made by chance,
and therefore without etymology.] A
simpleton; a coxcomb; a man of small
understanding and much ostentation; a
pretender; a man fond of show, dress, and
flutter; an impertinent.

*A whole tribe of fops,
Got 'tween asleep and wake.* Shakespeare's
King Lear.

*When such a positive abandon'd fop,
Among his numerous absurdities,
Stumbles upon some tolerable line,
I fret to see them in such company.*
Roscommon.

*The leopard's beauty, without the fox's wit,
is no better than a fop in a gay coat.*
L'Estrange.

*In a dull stream, which moving slow,
You hardly see the current flow;
When a small breeze obstructs the course,
It whirls about for want of force,
And in its narrow circle gathers
Nothing but chaff, and straws, and feathers:
The current of a female mind
Stops thus, and turns with ev'ry wind;
Thus whirling round, together draws
Fools, fops, and rakes, for chaff and straws.*
Swift.

fópdoodle n.s. [*fop* and *doodle*.] A fool; an
insignificant wretch.

*Where sturdy butchers broke your noodle,
And handled you like a fopdoodle.*
Hudibras, p. ii.

fórehead n.s. [*fore* and *head*.]

1. That part of the face which reaches
from the eyes upward to the hair.

*The breast of Hecuba,
When she did suckle Hector, look'd not lovelier
Than Hector's forehead, when it spit forth blood
At Grecian swords contending.* Shakespeare's
Coriolanus.

*Some angel copy'd, while I slept, each grace,
And molded ev'ry feature from my face:
Such majesty does from her forehead rise,
Her cheeks such blushes cast, such rays her eyes.*
Dryden.

2. Impudence; confidence; assurance;
audaciousness; audacity.

*A man of confidence presseth forward upon
every appearance of advantage, and thinks
nothing above his management or his merit:
where his force is too feeble, he prevails by dint
of impudence; these men of forehead are
magnificent in promises, and infallible in
their prescriptions.* Collier.

*I would fain know to what branch of the
legislature they can have the forehead to
apply.* Swift's Presbyterian Plea.

to forfénd v.a. To prevent; to forbid.
Hanmer.

fórgery n.s. [from *forge.*]

1. The crime of falsification.

*Has your king married the lady Gray?
And now, to sooth your forgery and his,
Sends me a paper to persuade me patience.*
Shakes. Hen. VI.

*Nothing could have been easier than for the
Jews, the enemies of Jesus Christ, to have
disproved these facts, had they been false,
to have shewn their falshood, and to
have convicted them of forgery.*
Stephens's Sermons.

*A forgery, in setting a false name to a
writing, which may prejudice another's
fortune, the law punishes with the loss of ears;
but has inflicted no adequate penalty for doing
the same thing in print, though books sold
under a false name are so many forgeries.*
Swift.

2. Smith's work; fabrication; the act of
the forge.

*He ran on embattl'd armies clad in iron,
And weaponless himself,
Made arms ridiculous, useless the forgery
Of brazen shield and spear, the hammer'd cuirass,
Chalybean temper'd steel, and frock of mail
Adamantean proof.* Milton's Agonistes,
l. 129.

fórmal adj. [*formel*, French; *formalis*, Latin.]

1. Ceremonious; solemn; precise; exact to
affectation.

*The justice,
In fair round belly, with good capon lin'd,
With eyes severe, and beard of formal cut,
Full of wise saws and modern instances,
And so he plays his part.* Shakespeare's
As you like it.

*Formal in apparel,
In gait and countenance surely like a father.*
Shakespeare.

*Ceremonies especially be not to be omitted to
strangers and formal natures; but the exalting
them above the mean is not only tedious, but
doth diminish the credit of him that speaks.*
Bacon, Essay 53.

2. Done according to established rules and
methods; not irregular; not sudden; not
extemporaneous.

*There is not any positive law of men, whether
it be general or particular, received by formal
express consent, as in councils; or by secret
approbation, as in customs it cometh to pass,
but the same may be taken away, if occasion
serve.* Hooker, b. iv. s. 14.

*As there are formal and written leagues,
respective to certain enemies; so there is a
natural and tacit consideration amongst all
men against the common enemy of human
society, so as there needs no intimation or
denunciation of the war; but all these
formalities the law of nature supplies, as
in the case of pyrates.* Bacon's Holy War.

3. Regular; methodical.

*The formal stars do travel so,
As we their names and courses know;
And he that on their changes looks,
Would think them govern'd by our books.*
Waller.

4. External; having the appearance but not
the essence.

*Of formal duty, make no more thy boast;
Thou disobey'st where it concerns me most.*
Dryd. Aureng.

5. Depending upon establishment
or custom.

*Still in constraint your suffering sex remains,
Or bound in formal or in real chains.* Pope.

6. Having the power of making any thing what it is; constituent; essential.

Of letters the material part is breath and voice: the formal is constituted by the motions and figure of the organs of speech affecting breath with a peculiar sound, by which each letter is discriminated. Holder's Elements of Speech.

Bellarmine agrees in making the formal act of adoration to be subjection to a superior; but withal he makes the mere apprehension of excellency to include the formal reason of it: whereas mere excellency, without superiority, doth not require any subjection, but only estimation. Stillingfleet.

The very life and vital motion, and the formal essence and nature of man, is wholly owing to the power of God. Bentl.

7. Retaining its proper and essential characteristick.

Thou shou'dst come like a fury cover'd with snakes,
Not like a formal man. Shakesp. Ant. and Cleopatra.

   I will not let him stir,
'Till I have us'd th' approved means I have;
With wholsome syrups, drugs, and holy prayers,
To make of him a formal man again.
Shakesp. Com. of Err.

fórmalist n.s. [*formaliste*, French, from *form.*] One who practises external ceremony; one who prefers appearance to reality; one who seems what he is not.

It is a ridiculous thing, and fit for a satyr to persons of judgment, to see what shifts formalists have, and what prospectives to make superficies to seem a body that hath depth and bulk. Bacon, Essay 27.

A grave, stanch, skilfully managed face, set upon a grasping aspiring mind, having got many a sly formalist the reputation of a primitive and severe piety. South's Sermons.

to fórnicate v.a. [from *fornix*, Latin.] To commit lewdness.

It is a new way to fornicate at a distance. Brown's Vul. Err.

fortificátion n.s. [*fortification*, French, from *fortify.*]

1. The science of military architecture.

Fortification is an art shewing how to fortify a place with ramparts, parapets, moats, and other bulwarks; to the end that a small number of men within may be able to defend themselves, for a considerable time, against the assaults of a numerous army without; so that the enemy, in attacking them, must of necessity suffer great loss. It is either regular or irregular; and, with respect to time, may be distinguished into durable and temporary. Harris.

The Phœacians, tho' an unwarlike nation, yet understood the art of fortification. Notes on the Odyssey.

2. A place built for strength.

Excellent devices were used to make even their sports profitable; images, battles, and fortifications being then delivered to their memory, which, after stronger judgments, might dispense some advantage. Sidney, b. ii.

fórtnight n.s. [contracted from *fourteen nights, feowretyne night* Saxon. It was the custom of the ancient northern nations to count time by nights: thus we say, this day seven-night. So Tacitus, *Non dierum numerum ut nos, sed noctium computant.*]† The space of two weeks.

She would give her a lesson for walking so late, that should make her keep within doors for one fortnight. Sidney, b. ii.

Hanging in a deep well, somewhat above the water, for some fortnights space, is an excellent means of making drink fresh and quick. Bacon's Natural History.

About a fortnight before I had finished it, his majesty's declaration for liberty of conscience came abroad. Dryden.

He often had it in his head, but never, with much apprehension, 'till about a fortnight before. Swift.

fórtuneteller n.s. [*fortune* and *teller.*] One who cheats common people by pretending to the knowledge of futurity.

They brought one Pinch, a hungry lean-fac'd villain,
A thread-bare juggler, and a fortuneteller. Shakespeare.

A Welchman being at a sessions-house, and seeing the prisoners hold up hands at the bar, related to some of his acquaintance that the judges were good fortunetellers; for if they did but look upon their hand, they could certainly tell whether they should live or die. Bacon's Apophthegms.

Hast thou given credit to vain predictions of men, to dreams or fortunetellers, or gone about to know any secret things by lot? Duppa's Rules for Devotion.

There needs no more than impudence on one side, and a superstitious credulity on the other, to the setting up of a fortuneteller. L'Estrange, Fable 94.

 Long ago a fortuneteller
Exactly said what now befell her. Swift.

fóssil adj. [*fossilis*, Latin; *fossile*, French.] That which is dug out of the earth.

The fossil shells are many of them of the same kinds with those that now appear upon the neighbouring shores; and the rest such as may be presumed to be at the bottom of the adjacent seas. Woodward's Natural History.

Fossil or rock salt, and sal gemm, differ not in nature from each other; nor from the common salt of salt springs, or that of the sea, when pure. Woodward's Natural History.

It is of a middle nature, between fossil and animal, being produced from animal excrements, intermixed with vegetable salts. Arbuthnot on Aliments.

to foupe v.a. To drive with sudden impetuosity. A word out of use.

We pronounce, by the confession of strangers, as smoothly and moderately as any of the northern nations, who foupe their words out of the throat with fat and full spirits. Camden.

fóutra n.s. [from *foutre*, French.] A fig; a scoff; an act of contempt.

A foutra for the world, and worldlings base. Shak. H. IV.

fráischeur n.s. [French.] Freshness; coolness. A word foolishly innovated by Dryden.

Hither in Summer-ev'nings you repair,
To taste the fraischeur of the purer air. Dryden.

fraise n.s. [French, the caul of an animal.] A pancake with bacon in it.

frank n.s. [from the adjective.]

1. A place to feed hogs in; a sty: so called from liberality of food.

Where sups here? Doth the old boar feed in the old frank? Shakespeare's Henry IV.

2. A letter which pays no postage.

You'll have immediately, by several franks, my epistle to lord Cobham. Pope to Swift.

3. A French coin.

fráughtage n.s. [from *fraught*.] Lading; cargo. A bad word.

 Our fraughtage, sir,
I have convey'd aboard. Shakes. Comedy of Errours.

freak n.s. [*frech*, German, saucy, petulant; *fræc*, Saxon, fugitive.]

1. A sudden and causeless change of place.

2. A sudden fancy; a humour; a whim; a capricious prank.

O! but I fear the fickle freaks, quoth she,
Of fortune, and the odds of arms in field. Fairy Queen.

When that freak has taken possession of a fantastical head, the distemper is incurable. L'Estrange, Fable 100.

She is so restless and peevish that she quarrels with all about her, and sometimes in a freak will instantly change her habitation. Spectator, N° 427.

To vex me more, he took a freak
To slit my tongue, and make me speak. Swift.

to fream v.n. [*fremere*, Lat. *fremir*, French.] To growl or grunt as a boar. Bailey.

freethinker n.s. [*free* and *think*.] A libertine; a contemner of religion.

Atheist is an old-fashion'd word: I'm a freethinker, child. Addison's Drummer.

Of what use is freedom of thought, if it will not produce freedom of action, which is the sole end, how remote soever in appearance, of all objections against Christianity? And therefore the freethinkers consider it as an edifice, wherein all the parts have such a mutual dependance on each other, that if you pull out one single nail, the whole fabrick must fall to the ground. Swift's Argument against abolishing Christianity.

fren n.s. A worthless woman. An old word wholly forgotten.

But now from me his madding mind is start,
And wooes the widow's daughter of the glen;
And now fair Rosalind hath bred his smart,
So now his friend is changed for a fren.
Spenser's Past.

to Frénchify v.a. [from *French*.] To infect with the manner of France; to make a coxcomb.

They misliked nothing more in king Edward the Confessor than that he was Frenchified; and accounted the desire of foreign language then to be a foretoken of bringing in foreign powers, which indeed happened. Camden's Remains.

   Has he familiarly dislik'd
Your yellow starch, or said your doublet
Was not exactly Frenchified. Shakespeare's As you like it.

fríbbler n.s. [from the verb.] A trifler.

A fribbler is one who professes rapture for the woman, and dreads her consent. Spectator, Nº 288.

fricassée n.s. [French.] A dish made by cutting chickens or other small things in pieces, and dressing them with strong sauce.

Oh, how would Homer praise their dancing dogs,
Their stinking cheese, and fricacy of frogs!
He'd raise no fables, sing no flagrant lye,
Of boys with custard choak'd at Newberry.
King.

frigorífick adj. [*frigorificus, frigus* and *facio*, Lat.] Causing cold. A word used in science.

Frigorifick atoms or particles mean those nitrous salts which float in the air in cold weather, and occasion freezing. Quincy.

frípperer n.s. [from *frippier*, French.] One who deals in old things vamped up.

fríppery n.s. [*fripperie*, French; *fripperia*, Italian.]

1. The place where old cloaths are sold.

Oh, oh, monster, we know what belongs to a frippery. Shakespeare's Tempest.

Lurana is a frippery of bankrupts, who fly thither from Druina to play their after-game. Howel's Vocal Forrest.

2. Old cloaths; cast dresses; tattered rags.

  Poor poet ape, that would be thought
    our chief,
Whose works are e'en the frippery of wit;
  From brocage is become so bold a thief,
As we, the robb'd, leave rage, and pity it.
Ben. Johnson.

The fighting-place now seamens rage supply,
And all the tackling is a frippery. Donne.

Ragfair is a place near the Tower of London, where old cloaths and frippery are sold.
Notes to Pope's Dunciad.

frísky adj. [*frisque*, French, from *frisk*.] Gay; airy. A low word.

frúctiferous adj. [*fructifer*, Latin.] Bearing fruit. Ains.

fruménty n.s. [*frumentum*, corn, Latin.] Food made of wheat boiled in milk.

to frump v.a. To mock; to browbeat. Skinner. Ainsw.

fub n.s. A plump chubby boy. Ainsworth.

fúcated adj. [*fucatus*, Latin.]

1. Painted; disguised with paint.

2. Disguised by false show.

to fúddle v.a. [Of unknown etymology.] To make drunk.

Earnest brimming bowls
Leave every soul the table floating round,
And pavement faithless to the fuddled feet.
Thoms. Autumn.

to fúddle v.n. To drink to excess.

Men, we see, will be whoring and fuddling
on still. L'Estr.

fugh interj. [perhaps from φευ.] An
expression of abhorrence.

A very filthy fellow: how odiously he smells
of his country garlick! fugh, how he stinks of
Spain! Dryd. Don Sebastian.

fúlgid adj. [*fulgidus*, Latin.] Shining;
glittering; dazzling.

fulgurátion n.s. [*fulguratio*, Latin.] The act
of lightening.

fúlham n.s. A cant word for false dice.
Hanmer.

Let vultures gripe thy guts, for gourd and
Fulham's hold,
And high and low beguile the rich and poor.
Shakespeare.

fúlminant adj. [*fulminant*, Fr. *fulminans*,
Latin.] Thundering; making a noise like
thunder.

fúlsome adj. [from *fulle*, Saxon, foul.]

1. Nauseous; offensive.

The skilful shepherd peel'd me certain wands;
And in the doing of the deed of kind,
He stuck them up before the fulsome ewes.
Shakespeare.

He that brings fulsome objects to my view,
With nauseous images my fancy fills,
And all goes down like oxymel of squills.
Roscommon.

Now half the youth of Europe are in arms,
How fulsome must it be to stay behind,
And die of rank diseases here at home?
Otway's Orphan.

2. Of a rank odious smell.

White satyrion is of a dainty smell, and bean-
flowers: again, if the plant puts forth white
flowers only, and those not thin or dry, they
are commonly of rank and fulsome smell.
Bacon's Natural History, Nº 507.

3. Tending to obscenity.

A certain epigram, which is ascribed to the
emperor, is more fulsome than any passage
I have met with in our poet. Dryden.

fumétte n.s. [French.] A word introduced
by cooks, and the pupils of cooks, for the
stink of meat.

A haunch of ven'son made her sweat,
Unless it had the right fumette. Swift.

fun n.s. [A low cant word.] Sport; high
merriment; frolicksome delight.

Don't mind me, though, for all my fun and jokes,
You bards may find us bloods good-natur'd
folks. Moore.

fungósity n.s. [from *fungus*.] Unsolid
excrescence. Dict.

funk n.s. A stink. A low word.

furácious adj. [*furax*, Latin.] Thievish;
inclined to steal. Dict.

fúrbelow n.s. [*fur* and *below*.] Fur sewed on
the lower part of the garment; an ornament
of dress.

Nay, oft in dreams invention we bestow
To change a flounce, or add a furbelow. Pope.

fúry n.s. [*furor*, Latin; *fureur*, French.]

1. Madness.

2. Rage; passion of anger; tumult of mind
approaching to madness.

I do oppose my patience to his fury; and am arm'd
To suffer with a quietness of spirit
The very tyranny and rage of his. Shakesp.
Mer. of Venice.

He hath given me to know the natures of
living creatures, and the furies of wild beasts.
Wisd. vii. 20.

3. Enthusiasm; exaltation of fancy.

Taking up the lute, her wit began to be with
a divine fury inspired; and her voice would,
in so beloved an occasion, second her wit.
Sidney, b. ii.

A sybil, that had number'd in the world
The sun to course two hundred compasses,
In her prophetick fury sew'd the work.
Shakesp. Othello.

Greater than human kind she seem'd to look,
And with an accent more than mortal spoke;
Her staring eyes with sparkling fury roll,
When all the god came rushing on her soul.
Dryden's Æn.

4. [From *furia*, Latin] One of the deities
   of vengeance, and thence a stormy,
   turbulent, violent, raging woman.

The sight of any of the house of York,
Is as a fury to torment my soul.
Shakesp. Henry VI. p. iii.

It was the most proper place for a fury to
make her exit; and I believe every reader's
imagination is pleased, when he sees the angry
goddess thus sinking in a tempest, and plunging
herself into hell, amidst such a scene of horror
and confusion. Addison's Remarks on Italy.

fuscátion n.s. [*fuscus*, Latin.] The act of
darkening or obscuring. Dict.

fústian n.s. [*futaine*, French, from *fuste*,
a tree, because cotton grows on trees.]

1. A kind of cloth made of linen and
   cotton, and perhaps now of cotton only.

Is supper ready, the house trimm'd, the
serving-men in their new fustian and their
white stockings? Shakespeare.

2. A high swelling kind of writing made
   up of heterogeneous parts, or of words
   and ideas ill associated; bombast.

Nor will you raise in me combustion,
By dint of high heroick fustian. Hudibras,
p. ii. cant. 1.

What fustian have I heard these gentlemen
find out in Mr. Cowley's odes! In general,
I will say, that nothing can appear more
beautiful to me than the strength of those
images which they condemn. Dryden.

I am much deceived if this be not abominable
fustian; that is, thoughts and words ill sorted,
and without the least relation to each other.
Dryden's Spanish Fryar, Dedication.

Chance thoughts, when govern'd by the close,
Oft rise to fustian, or descend to prose.
Smith.

to fústigate v.a. [*fustigo*, Latin.] To beat
with a stick; to cane. Dict.

fústilarian n.s. [from *fusty.*] A low fellow;
a stinkard; a scoundrel. A word used by
Shakespeare only.

Away, you scullion, you rampallian, you
fustilarian: I'll tickle your catastrophe.
Shakespeare's Henry IV. p. ii.

to fuzz v.n. [without etymology.] To fly out
in small particles.

fúzzball n.s. [*fuzz* and *ball.*] A kind of
fungus, which, when pressed, bursts and
scatters dust in the eyes.

G

G has two sounds, one from the Greek Γ, and the Latin, which is called that of the hard *G*, because it is formed by a pressure somewhat hard of the forepart of the tongue against the upper gum. This sound *G* retains before *a, o, u, l, r*; as, *gate, go, gull.* The other sound, called that of the soft *G*, resembles that of *J*, and is commonly, though not always, found before *e, i*; as, *gem, gibbet.* Before *n*, at the end of a word, *g* is commonly melted away; as in the French, from which these words are commonly derived: thus, for *benign, malign, condign*, we pronounce *benine, maline, condine.* It is often silent in the middle of words before *h*; as, *might.* The Saxon *G, g,* seems to have had generally the sound of *y* consonant; whence *gate* is by rusticks still pronounced *yate.*

gábel n.s. [*gabelle*, French; *gabello*, Italian; *gafel*, Saxon, a tribute.] An excise; a tax.

The gabels of Naples are very high on oil, wine, and tobacco. Addison's Remarks on Italy.

gábion n.s. [French.] A wicker basket which is filled with earth to make a fortification or intrenchment.

His battery was defended all along with gabions, and casks filled with sand. Knolles's History of the Turks.

gáffer n.s. [*gafere*, companion, Saxon.] A word of respect now obsolete, or applied only in contempt to a mean person.

For gaffer Treadwell told us by the bye, Excessive sorrow is exceeding dry. Gay's Pastorals.

galáge n.s. A shepherd's clog.

My heart-blood is well nigh frorne, I feel; And my galage grown fast to my heel. Spenser's Pastorals.

galáxy n.s. [γαλαξια; *galaxie*, Fr.] The milky way; a stream of light in the sky.

A broad and ample road, whose dust is gold, And pavement stars, as stars to thee appear, Seen in the galaxy. Milton's Paradise Lost, b. vii.

A brown, for which heaven would disband The galaxy, and stars be tann'd. Cleaveland.

Men doubt, because they stand so thick i' th' sky, If those be stars that paint the galaxy. Cowley.

We dare not undertake to shew what advantage is brought to us by those innumerable stars in the galaxy. Bentley's Serm.

galerículate adj. [from *galerus*, Latin.] Covered as with a hat.

gállant n.s. [from the adjective.]

1. A gay, sprightly, airy, splendid man.

The new proclamation. —What is 't for? —The reformation of our travell'd gallants, That fill the court with quarrels, talk, and taylors. Shakesp.

The gallants and lusty youths of Naples came and offered themselves unto Vastius. Knolles's History of the Turks.

The gallants, to protect the lady's right, Their fauchions brandish'd at the grisly spright. Dryden.

Gallants, look to 't, you say there are no sprights; But I'll come dance about your beds at nights. Dryden.

2. A whoremaster, who caresses women to debauch them.

One, worn to pieces with age, shews himself a young gallant. Shakespeare's Merry Wives of Windsor.

The next carried a handsome young fellow upon her back: she had left the good man at home, and brought away her gallant. Addison's Spectator.

3. A wooer; one who courts a woman for marriage. In the two latter senses it has commonly the accent on the last syllable.

gálliard n.s. [*gaillard*, French; imagined to be derived from the Gaulish *ard*, genius, and *gay*.]

1. A gay, brisk, lively man; a fine fellow.

Selden is a galliard by himself. Cleaveland.

2. An active, nimble, spritely dance. It is in both senses now obsolete.

I did think by the excellent constitution of thy leg, it was form'd under the star of a galliard. Shakesp. Twelfth Night.

   There's nought in France That can be with a nimble galliard won: You cannot revel into dukedoms there. Shakesp. Henry V.

If there be any that would take up all the time, let him find means to take them off, and bring others on; as musicians use to do with those that dance too long galliards. Bacon.

The tripla's and changing of times have an agreement with the changes of motion; as when galliard time and measure time are in the medley of one dance. Bacon's Natural History.

gálliardise n.s. [French.] Merriment; exuberant gaiety.

At my nativity my ascendant was the watry sign of Scorpius: I was born in the planetary hour of Saturn, and I think I have a piece of that leaden planet in me: I am no way facetious, nor disposed for the mirth and galliardise of company. Brown's Rel. Med.

Gállicism n.s. [*gallicisme*, French, from *gallicus*, Latin.] A mode of speech peculiar to the French language: such as, he *figured* in controvery; he *held* this conduct; he *held* the same language that another had *held* before: with many other expressions to be found in the pages of Bolinbroke.

In English I would have Gallicisms avoided, that we may keep to our own language, and not follow the French mode in our speech. Felton on the Classicks.

gálligaskins n.s. [*Caligæ Gallo-Vasconum*. Skinner.] Large open hose.†

*My galligaskins, that have long withstood
The Winter's fury, and encroaching frosts,
By time subdu'd, what will not time subdue,
An horrid chasm disclose.* Phillips.

gallimátia n.s. [*galimathias*, French.] Nonsense; talk without meaning.

gallimaúfry n.s. [*galimafrée*, French.]

1. A hoch-poch, or hash of several sorts of broken meat; a medley. Hanmer.

*They have made of our English tongue
a gallimaufry, or hodge-podge of all other speeches.* Spenser.

2. Any inconsistent or ridiculous medley.

They have a dance, which the wenches say is a gallimaufry of gambols, because they are not in 't. Shakesp. Winter's Tale.

The painter who, under pretence of diverting the eyes, would fill his picture with such varieties as alter the truth of history, would make a ridiculous piece of painting, and a mere gallimaufry of his work. Dryden's Dufresnoy.

3. It is used by Shakespeare ludicrously of a woman.

*Sir John affects thy wife.
—Why, sir, my wife is not young.
—He wooes both high and low, both rich and poor;
He loves thy gallimaufry, friend.*
Shakespeare.

gallóon n.s. [*galon*, French.] A kind of close lace, made of gold or silver, or of silk alone.

to gállow v.a. [*agælwan*, to fright, Saxon.] To terrify; to fright.

*The wrathful skies
Gallow the very wand'rers of the dark,
And make them keep their caves.*
Shakespeare's King Lear.

gállowtree n.s. [*gallows* and *tree*.] The tree of terrour; the tree of execution.

*He hung their conquer'd arms, for more defame,
On gallowtrees, in honour of his dearest dame.*
Fai. Queen.

*A Scot, when from the gallowtree got loose,
Drops into Styx, and turns a soland goose.*
Cleaveland.

gámbler n.s. [A cant word, I suppose, for *game* or *gamester*.] A knave whose practice it is to invite the unwary to game and cheat them.

gámester n.s. [from *game*.]

1. One who is vitiously addicted to play.

Keep a gamester from the dice, and a good student from his book, and it is wonderful. Shak. Merry Wives of Windsor.

A gamester, the greater master he is in his art, the worse man he is. Bacon.

*Gamesters for whole patrimonies play;
The steward brings the deeds, which must convey
The whole estate.* Dryden's Juvenal, Sat. 1.

Could we look into the mind of a common gamester, we should see it full of nothing but trumps and mattadores: her slumbers are haunted with kings, queens and knaves. Addison.

*All the superfluous whims relate,
That fill a female gamester's pate;
What agony of soul she feels
To see a knave's inverted heels.* Swift.

2. One who is engaged at play.

When lenity and cruelty play for kingdoms,
The gentler gamester is the soonest winner.
Shakes. Hen. V.

A man may think, if he will, that two eyes see
no more than one; or that a gamester seeth
always more than a looker-on: but, when all
is done, the help of good counsel is that which
setteth business strait. Bacon, Essay 28.

3. A merry frolicksome person.

You're a merry gamester,
My lord Sands. Shakesp. Henry VIII.

4. A prostitute.

She's impudent, my lord,
And was a common gamester to the camp.
Shakespeare.

gámmer n.s. [Of uncertain etymology;
perhaps from *grand mere*, and therefore
used commonly to old women.] The
compellation of a woman corresponding
to gaffer.

gámut n.s. [*gama*, Italian.] The scale of
musical notes.

Madam, before you touch the instrument,
To learn the order of my fingering,
I must begin with rudiments of art,
To teach you gamut in a briefer sort.
Shakespeare.

When by the gamut some musicians make
A perfect song, others will undertake,
By the same gamut chang'd, to equal it:
Things simply good can never be unfit.
Donne.

Long has a race of heroes fill'd the stage,
That rant by note, and through the gamut rage;
In songs and airs express their martial fire,
Combat in trills, and in a feuge expire.
Addison.

to ganch v.a. [*ganciare*, from *gancio*, a hook,
Italian; *ganche*, French.] To drop from a
high place upon hooks by way of
punishment: a practice in Turkey, to which
Smith alludes in his *Pocockius*.†

Cohors catenis qua pia stridulis
Gemunt onusti, vel sude trans sinum

Luctantur actâ, pendulive
Sanguineis luctantur in unæs. Musæ Angl.

gaol n.s. [*geol*, Welsh; *geole*, French.] A
prison; a place of confinement. It is always
pronounced and too often written *jail*, and
sometimes *goal*.

Then am I the prisoner, and his bed my gaol.
Sh. K. Lear.

Have I been ever free, and must my house
Be my retentive enemy, my gaol?
Shakespeare's Timon.

If we mean to thrive and do good, break open
the gaols, and let out the prisoners.
Shakespeare's Henry VI. p. ii.

gáp-toothed adj. [*gap* and *tooth*.] Having
interstices between the teeth.

The reeve, miller, and cook, are distinguished
from each other as much as the mincing lady
prioress and the broad-speaking gap-toothed
wife of Bath. Dryden's Fables, Preface.

gare n.s. Coarse wool growing on the legs
of sheep. Dict.

to gargaríze v.a. [γαργαριζω; *gargariser*,
French.] To wash the mouth with
medicated liquors.

Vinegar, put to the nostrils, or gargarized,
doth ease the hiccough; for that it is
astringent, and inhibiteth the motion of
the spirit. Bacon's Natural History.

This being relaxed, may make a shaking
of the larynx; as when we gargarize.
Holder's Elements of Speech.

gárlick n.s. [*gar*, Saxon, a lance, and *leek*,
the leek that shoots up in blades. Skinner.]
It has a bulbous root, consisting of many
small tubercles included in its coats: the
leaves are plain: the flowers consist of six
leaves, formed into a corymbus on the top
of the stalk; and are succeeded by subrotund
fruit, divided into three cells, which contain
roundish seeds. Miller.

Garlick is of an extremely strong, and to most
people a disagreeable smell, and of an acrid
and pungent taste. It is an extremely active
and penetrating medicine, as may be proved

by applying plaisters of garlick to the soles of the feet, which will in a very little time give a strong smell to the breath. Issues will smell strongly of garlick three or four hours after a person has eaten it; and given to fowls, it communicates its taste strongly to their flesh, and in some degree to their eggs. Bruised, and laid on any tender part of the skin, it corrodes it, and raises blisters. Some are very fond of it in food; and a little of it is not only agreeable this way, but assists digestion, and strengthens the stomach. Hill.

Garlick has, of all our plants, the greatest strength, affords most nourishment, and supplies most spirits to those who eat little flesh. Temple.

'Tis mortal sin an onion to devour;
Each clove of garlick is a sacred pow'r:
Religious nations sure, and blest abodes,
Where ev'ry orchard is o'er-run with gods.
Tate's Juven.

garlickeáter n.s. [*garlick* and *eat*.] A mean fellow.

You've made good work,
You and your apron men, that stood so much
Upon the voice of occupation, and
The breath of garlickeaters. Shakespeare's Coriolanus.

gárnish n.s. [from the verb.]

1. Ornament; decoration; embellishment.

So are you, sweet,
Ev'n in the lovely garnish of a boy.
Shak. Merch. of Venice.

Matter and figure they produce;
For garnish this, and that for use;
They seek to feed and please their guests.
Prior.

2. Things strewed round a dish.

3. [In gaols.] Fetters.

4. *Pensiuncula carceraria;* an acknowledgment in money when first a prisoner goes into a gaol. Ainsworth.[†]

gas n.s. [A word invented by the chymists.] It is used by Van Helmont, and seems designed to signify, in general, a spirit not capable of being coagulated: but he uses it loosely in many senses, and very unintelligibly and inconsistently. Har.

gasconáde n.s. [French, from *Gascon*, a nation eminent for boasting.] A boast; a bravado.

Was it a gasconade to please me, that you said your fortune was increased to one hundred a year since I left you? Swift.

gastrótomy n.s. [γαστηρ and τετομα.] The act of cutting open the belly.

gávot n.s. [*gavotte*, French.] A kind of dance.

The disposition in a fiddle to play tunes in preludes, sarabands, jigs and gavots, are real qualities in the instrument. Arbuthnot and Pope's Mart. Scriblerus.

gáwntree n.s. [Scottish.] A wooden frame on which beer-casks are set when tunned.

gay adj. [*gay*, French.]

1. Airy; chearful; merry; frolick.

Smooth flow the waves, the zephyrs gently play;
Belinda smil'd, and all the world was gay.
Pope.

Ev'n rival wits did Voiture's fate deplore,
And the gay mourn'd, who never mourn'd
   before. Pope.

2. Fine; showy.

A virgin that loves to go gay. Bar. vi. 9.

geck n.s. [*geac*, a cuckow; *geck*, German, a fool; *gawk*, Scottish.] A bubble easily imposed upon. Hanmer.

Why did you suffer Jachimo to taint his noble heart and brain with needless jealousy, and to become the geck and scorn o' th' other's villany? Shakespeare's Cymbeline.

Why have you suffer'd me to be imprison'd,
And made the most notorious geck and gull
That e'er invention plaid on? Shakesp. Twelfth Night.

gee A term used by waggoners to their horses when they would have them go faster.

gélid adj. [*gelidus*, Latin.] Extremely cold.

From the deep ooze and gelid cavern rous'd,
They flounce. Thomson's Spring.

gemélliparous adj. [*gemelli* and *pario*, Latin.] Bearing twins. Dict.

to géminate v.a. [*gemino*, Latin.] To double. Dict.

gemmósity n.s. [from *gem.*] The quality of being a jewel. Dict.

génder n.s. [*genus*, Latin; *gendre*, French.]

1. A kind; a sort.

Our bodies are our gardens, to the which our
wills are gardeners; so that if we will supply it
with one gender of herbs, or distract it with
many, the power and corrigible authority of
this lies in our will. Shakespeare's Othello.

    The other motive,
Why to a publick court I might not go,
Is the great love the general gender bear me.
Shak. Hamlet.

2. A sex.

3. [In grammar.] A denomination given to nouns, from their being joined with an adjective in this or that termination. Clark.

Cubitus, sometimes cubitum *in the neutral*
gender, signifies the lower part of the arm on
which we lean. Arbuthnot.

Ulysses speaks of Nausicaa, yet immediately
changes the words into the masculine gender.
Notes on the Odyssey.

génerous adj. [*generosus*, Latin; *genereux*, French.]

1. Not of mean birth; of good extraction.

2. Noble of mind; magnanimous; open of heart.

His gen'rous spouse, Theano, heav'nly fair,
Nurs'd the young stranger. Pope.

3. Liberal; munificent.

4. Strong; vigorous.

Having in a digestive furnace drawn off the
ardent spirit from some good sack, the phlegm,
even in this generous wine, was copious. Boyle.

genethlíacks n.s. [from γενεθλη.] The science of calculating nativities, or predicting the future events of life from the stars predominant at the birth.

genéva n.s. [A corruption of *genevre*, French, a juniperberry.] We used to keep a distilled spirituous water of juniper in the shops; but the making of it became the business of the distiller, who sold it under the name of geneva. At present only a better kind is distilled from the juniper-berry: what is commonly sold is made with no better an ingredient than oil of turpentine, put into the still, with a little common salt, and the coarsest spirit they have, which is drawn off much below proof strength, and is consequently a liquor that one would wonder any people could accustom themselves to drink with pleasure. Hill's Mat. Medica.†

geniculátion n.s. [*geniculatio*, Latin.] Knottiness; the quality in plants of having knots or joints.

génio n.s. [*genio*, Italian; *genius*, Latin.] A man of a particular turn of mind.

Some genio's are not capable of pure affection;
and a man is born with talents for it as much
as for poetry, or any other science.
Tatler, N° 53.

génitals n.s. [*genitalis*, Lat.] Parts belonging to generation.

Ham is conceived to be Jupiter, who was the
youngest son, who is said to have cut off the
genitals of his father. Brown.

génius n.s. [Latin; *genie*, French.]

1. The protecting or ruling power of men, places, or things.

    There is none but he
Whose being I do fear: and, under him,
My genius is rebuk'd; as it is said
Antony's was by Cæsar. Shakespeare's
Macbeth.

The genius and the mortal instruments
Are then in council; and the state of man,
Like to a little kingdom, suffers then.
Shakes. Jul. Cæsar.

And as I awake, sweet musick breathe,
Sent by some spirit to mortals good,
Or th' unseen genius of the wood. Milton.

And the tame demon that should guard
   my throne,
Shrinks at a genius greater than his own.
Dryden.

To your glad genius sacrifice this day;
Let common meats respectfully give way.
Dryden.

2. A man endowed with superiour
   faculties.

There is no little writer of Pindarick who
is not mentioned as a prodigious genius.
Addison.

3. Mental power or faculties.

The state and order does proclaim
The genius of that royal dame. Waller.

4. Disposition of nature by which any
   one is qualified for some peculiar
   employment.

A happy genius is the gist of nature.
Dryden's Dufresnoy.

Your majesty's sagacity, and happy genius for
natural history, is a better preparation for
enquiries of this kind than all the dead
learning of the schools. Burnet's Theory,
Preface.

One science only will one genius fit;
So vast is art, so narrow human wit.
Pope on Criticism.

The Romans, though they had no great genius
for trade, yet were not entirely neglectful of it.
Arbuthnot on Coins.

5. Nature; disposition.

Studious to please the genius of the times,
With periods, points and tropes he slurs his
   crimes. Dryd.

Another genius and disposition improper for
philosophical contemplations is not so much
from the narrowness of their spirit and
understanding, as because they will not
take time to extend them. Burnet's Theory
of the Earth, Preface.

He tames the genius of the stubborn plain.
Pope.

géntile n.s. [*gentilis*, Latin.]

1. One of an uncovenanted nation; one
   who knows not the true God.

Tribulation and anguish upon every soul that
doeth evil, of the Jew first, and also of the
gentile. Rom. ii. 2.

Gentiles or infidels, in those actions, upon both
the spiritual and temporal good, have been in
one pursuit conjoined. Bacon.

2. A person of rank. Obsolete.

Fine Basil desireth it may be her lot
To grow, as a gilliflower, trim in a pot;
That ladies and gentiles, for whom ye do serve,
May help him as needeth, poor life to preserve.
Tusser.

géntle adj. [*gentilis*, Latin.]

1. Well born; well descended; ancient,
   though not noble.

They entering and killing all of the gentle and
rich faction, for honesty sake broke open all
prisons. Sidney.

These are the studies wherein our noble and
gentle youth ought to bestow their time.
Milton on Education.

Of gentle blood, part shed in honour's cause,
Each parent sprung. Pope.

2. Soft; bland; mild; tame; meek;
   peaceable.

I am one of those gentle ones that will use the
devil himself with curtesy. Shakespeare's
Twelfth Night.

   Her voice was ever soft,
Gentle and low; an excellent thing in woman.
Shakespeare.

As gentle, and as jocund, as to jest,
Go I to fight. Shakespeare's Richard II.

A virtuous and a good man, reverend in
conversation, and gentle in condition.
2 Mac. xv. 12.

The gentlest heart on earth is prov'd unkind.
Fairfax.

Your change was wise; for, had she been deny'd,
A swift revenge had follow'd from her pride:
You from my gentle nature had no fears;
All my revenge is only in my tears.
Dryden's Ind. Emp.

He had such a gentle method of reproving
their faults, that they were not so much afraid
as ashamed to repeat them. Atter.

3. Soothing; pacifick.

And though this sense first gentle musick found,
Her proper object is the speech of men.
Davies.

géntry n.s. [*gentlery, gentry,* from *gentle.*]

1. Birth; condition.

You are certainly a gentleman,
Clerk-like experienc'd, which no less adorns
Our gentry than our parents' noble name,
In whose success we are gentle. Shakesp.
Winter's Tale.

2. Class of people above the vulgar; those
   between the vulgar and the nobility.

They slaughtered many of the gentry, for
whom no sex or age could be accepted for
excuse. Sidney.

Let states, that aim at greatness, take heed
how their nobility and gentry multiply too
fast. Bacon's Ornam. Ration.

How chearfully the hawkers cry
A satire, and the gentry buy. Swift.

3. A term of civility real or ironical.

The many-colour'd gentry there above,
By turns are rul'd by tumult and by love.
Prior.

4. Civility; complaisance. Obsolete.

Shew us so much gentry and good-will,
As to extend your time with us a-while.
Shakesp. Hamlet.

geógraphy n.s. [γη and γραφω; *geographie,*
Fr.] Geography in a strict sense, signifies
the knowledge of the circles of the earthly
globe, and the situation of the various parts
of the earth. When it is taken in a little
larger sense, it includes the knowledge of
the seas also; and in the largest sense of all,

it extends to the various customs, habits,
and governments of nations. Watts.

Olympus is extolled by the Greeks as attaining
unto heaven; but geography makes slight
account hereof, when they discourse of Andes
or Teneriff. Brown's Vulgar Errours, b. vi.

According to ancient fables the Argonauts
sailed up the Danube, and from thence passed
into the Adriatick, carrying their ships upon
their shoulders: a mark of great ignorance in
geography. Arbuthnot on Coins.

geólogy n.s. [γη and λογος.] The doctrine
of the earth; the knowledge of the state and
nature of the earth.

géomancer n.s. [γη and μαντια.] A
fortuneteller; a caster of figures; a cheat who
pretends to foretell futurity by other means
than the astrologer.

Fortunetellers, jugglers, geomancers, and the
incantatory impostors, though commonly men
of inferior rank, daily delude the vulgar.
Brown's Vulgar Errours, b. i.

géometry n.s. [γεωμετρια; *geometrie,*
French.] Originally signifies the art of
measuring the earth, or any distances or
dimensions on or within it: but it is now
used for the science of quantity, extension,
or magnitude abstractedly considered,
without any regard to matter.

Geometry very probably had its first rise in
Egypt, where the Nile annually overflowing
the country, and covering it with mud,
obliged men to distinguish their lands one
from another, by the consideration of their
figure; and after which, 'tis probable, to be
able also to measure the quantity of it, and
to know how to plot it, and lay it out again
in its just dimensions, figure and proportion:
after which, it is likely, a farther
contemplation of those draughts and figures
helped them to discover many excellent and
wonderful properties belonging to them;
which speculations were continually
improving, and are still to this day. Geometry
is usually divided into speculative and
practical; the former of which contemplates
and treats of the properties of continued

quantity abstractedly; and the latter applies these speculations and theorems to use and practice, and to the benefit and advantage of mankind. Harris.

In the muscles alone there seems to be more geometry than in all the artificial engines in the world. Ray on the Creation.

Him also for my censor I disdain,
Who thinks all science, as all virtue, vain;
Who counts geometry and numbers toys,
And with his foot the sacred dust destroys.
Dryd. Pers. Sat.

geórgick n.s. [γεωργικον; *georgiques*, Fr.] Some part of the science of husbandry put into a pleasing dress, and set off with all the beauties and embellishments of poetry. Addison.

ghérkin n.s. [from *gurcke*, German, a cucumber.] A pickled cucumber. Skinner.

gíant n.s. [*geant*, French; *gigas*, Latin.] A man of size above the ordinary rate of men; a man unnaturally large. It is observable, that the idea of a giant is always associated with pride, brutality, and wickedness.

Now does he feel his axle
Hang loose about him, like a giant's robe
Upon a dwarfish thief. Shakespeare's Macbeth.

Gates of monarchs
Are arch'd so high that giants may jet through,
And keep their impious turbands on, without
Good-morrow to the sun. Shakespeare's Cymbeline.

Woman's gentle brain
Could not drop forth such giant rude invention;
Such Ethiop words. Shakesp. As you like it.

Fierce faces threat'ning wars,
Giants of mighty bone, and bold emprise!
Milt. Pa. Lost.

Those giants, those mighty men, and men of renown, far exceeded the proportion, nature, and strength of those giants remembered by Moses of his own time. Raleigh's History.

The giant brothers, in their camp, have found
I was not forc'd with ease to quit my ground.
Dryden's Æn.

By weary steps and slow
The groping giant with a trunk of pine
Explor'd his way. Addison.

Neptune, by pray'r repentant, rarely won,
Afflicts the chief t' avenge his giant son,
Great Polypheme, of more than mortal might.
Pope.

gíbberish n.s. [Derived by Skinner from *gaber*, French, to cheat; by others conjectured to be formed by corruption from *jabber*. But as it was anciently written *gebrish*, it is probably derived from the chymical cant, and originally implied the jargon of *Geber* and his tribe.] Cant; the private language of rogues and gipsies; words without meaning.

Some, if they happen to hear an old word, albeit very natural and significant, cry out straitway, that we speak no English, but gibberish. Spenser.

Some of both sexes writing down a number of letters, just as it came into their heads; upon reading this gibberish, that which the men had wrote sounded like High Dutch, and the other by the women like Italian. Swift.

gíbbet n.s. [*gibet*, French.]

1. A gallows; the post on which malefactors are hanged, or on which their carcases are exposed.

When was there ever cursed atheist brought
Unto the gibbet, but he did adore
That blessed pow'r which he had set at
*   nought?* Davies.

You scandal to the stock of verse, a race
Able to bring the gibbet in disgrace.
Cleaveland.

Haman suffered death himself upon the very gibbet that he had provided for another. L'Estrange.

Papers of universal approbation, lay such principles to the whole body of the Tories, as, if they were true, our next business should be to erect gibbets in every parish, and hang them out of the way. Swift.

2. Any traverse beams.

gíbcat n.s. [*gib* and *cat*.] An old worn-out cat.

I am as melancholy as a gibcat, or a lugg'd bear. Shakesp.

to gíggle v.n. [*gichgelen*, Dutch.] To laugh idly; to titter; to grin with merry levity. It is retained in Scotland.

gíglet n.s. [*geagl*, Saxon; *geyl*, Dutch; *gillet*, Scottish, is still retained.] A wanton; a lascivious girl. Now out of use.

Young Talbot was not born
To be the pillage of a giglet wench.
Shakesp. Henry VI.

The fam'd Cassibelan was once at point,
Oh giglet fortune! to master Cæsar's sword.
Shak. Cymbel.

Away with those giglets too, and with the other confederate companion. Shakespeare's Measure for Measure.

gímcrack n.s. [Supposed by Skinner to be ludicrously formed from *gin*, derived from *engine*.] A slight or trivial mechanism.

For though these gimcracks were away,
However, more reduc'd and plain,
The watch would still a watch remain;
But if the horal orbit ceases,
The whole stands still, or breaks to pieces.
Prior.

What's the meaning of all these trangrams and gimcracks? What, in the name of wonder, are you going about, jumping over my master's hedges, and running your lines cross his grounds? Arbuthnot's Hist. of J. Bull.

gin n.s. [from *engine*.]

1. A trap; a snare.

As the day begins,
With twenty gins we will the small birds take,
And pastime make. Sidney, b. i.

Which two, through treason and deceitful gin,
Hath slain sir Mordant. Fairy Queen, b. ii.

So strives the woodcock with the gin;
So doth the cony struggle in the net.
Shakesp. Henry VI.

Be it by gins, by snares, by subtilty.
Shakes. Hen. VI.

If those, who have but sense, can shun
The engines that have them annoy'd;
Little for me had reason done,
If I could not thy gins avoid.
Ben. Johnson's Forest.

  I know thy trains,
Though dearly to my cost, thy gins and toils;
No more on me have pow'r, their force is
   null'd. Milton.

He made a planetary gin,
Which rats would run their own heads in,
And come on purpose to be taken,
Without th' expence of cheese and bacon.
Hudibras, p. ii.

Keep from flaying scourge thy skin,
And ankle free from iron gin. Hudibras,
p. i. cant. 2.

2. Any thing moved with screws, as an engine of torture.

Typhæus' joints were stretched on a gin.
Fairy Queen.

3. A pump worked by rotatory sails.

A bituminous plate, alternately yellow and black, formed by water driveling on the outside of the gin pump of Mostyn coalpits.
Woodward on Fossils.

4. [Contracted from *geneva*, which see.] The spirit drawn by distillation from juniper berries.

This calls the church to deprecate our sin,
And hurls the thunder of our laws on gin.
Pope, Dial. 1.

Thee shall each alehouse, thee each
  gillhouse mourn,
And answ'ring gin shops sourer sighs return.
Pope's Dunciad.

gíngerbread n.s. [*ginger* and *bread*.] A kind of farinaceous sweetmeat made of dough, like that of bread or biscuit, sweetened with treacle, and flavoured with ginger and some other aromatick seeds. It is sometimes gilt.

An' I had but one penny in the world, thou should'st have it to buy gingerbread.
Shakespeare's Love's Labour Lost.

Her currans there and gooseberries were spread,
With the enticing gold of gingerbread. King's
Cookery.

'Tis a loss you are not here, to partake of three
weeks frost, and eat gingerbread in a booth by
a fire upon the Thames. Swift.

ginseng n.s. [I suppose Chinese.] A root
brought lately into Europe. It never grows
to any great size, and is of a brownish colour
on the outside, and somewhat yellowish
within; and so pure and fine, that it seems
almost transparent. It is of a very agreeable
and aromatick smell, though not very
strong. Its taste is acrid and aromatick, and
has somewhat bitter in it. We have it from
China; and there is of it in the same
latitudes in America. The Chinese value
this root so highly, that it sells with them
for three times its weight in silver. The
Asiaticks in general think the ginseng
almost an universal medicine. The virtues
most generally believed to be in it are those
of a restorative, and a cordial. The
European physicians esteem it a good
medicine in convulsions, vertigoes, and all
nervous complaints; and recommend it as
one of the best restoratives known. Hill.

to gip v.a. To take out the guts of herrings.
Bailey.

gipsy n.s. [Corrupted from *Egyptian;* for
when they first appeared in Europe they
declared, and perhaps truly, that they were
driven from Egypt by the Turks. They are
now mingled with all nations.]

1. A vagabond who pretends to foretell
   futurity, commonly by palmestry or
   physiognomy.

The butler, though he is sure to lose a knife, a
fork, or a spoon every time his fortune is told
him, shuts himself up in the pantry with an
old gipsy for above half an hour. Addison.

A frantick gipsey now, the house he haunts,
And in wild phrases speaks dissembled wants.
Prior.

I, near yon stile, three sallow gypsies met;
Upon my hand they cast a poring look,
Bid me beware, and thrice their heads they
   shook. Gay.

In this still labyrinth around her lie
Spells, philters, globes, and spheres of palmistry;
A sigil in this hand the gipsy bears,
In th' other a prophetick sieve and sheers.
Garth's Dispensat.

2. A reproachful name for a dark
   complexion.

Laura, to his lady, was but a kitchen-wench;
Dido a dowdy; Cleopatra a gipsy; Helen and
Hero hildings and harlots. Shakespeare's
Romeo and Juliet.

3. A name of slight reproach to a woman.

The widow play'd the gypsy, and so did her
confidant too, in pretending to believe her.
L'Estrange.

A slave I am to Clara's eyes:
The gipsy knows her pow'r, and flies. Prior.

girdle n.s. [*gyrdel*, Saxon.]

1. Any thing drawn round the waist, and
   tied or buckled.

There will I make thee beds of roses,
With a thousand fragrant posies;
A cap of flowers, and a girdle,
Embroider'd all with leaves of myrtle.
Shakespeare.[†]

Many conceive there is somewhat amiss, until
they put on their girdle. Brown's Vulgar
Errours, b. v. c. 21.

On him his mantle, girdle, sword and bow,
On him his heart and soul he did bestow.
Cowley.

2. Enclosure; circumference.

Suppose within the girdle of these walls
Are now confin'd two mighty monarchies.
Shakes. Hen. V.

3. The equator; the torrid zone.

Great breezes in great circles, such as are
under the girdle of the world, do refrigerate.
Bacon.

girl n.s. [About the etymology of this word
there is much question: Meric Casaubon, as
is his custom, derives it from κορη, of the
same signification; Minshew from *garrula,*
Latin, a prattler, or *girella,* Italian, a

weathercock; Junius thinks that it comes from *herlodes*, Welsh, from which, says he, *harlot* is very easily deduced. Skinner imagines that the Saxons, who used *ceorl* for a man, might likewise have *ceorla* for a woman, though no such word is now found. Dr. Hickes derives it most probably from the Islandick *karlinna*, a woman.] A young woman, or female child.

In those unfledg'd days was my wife a girl. Shakespeare.

And let it not displease thee, good Bianca;
For I will love thee ne'er the less, my girl. Shakespeare.

A weather-beaten lover, but once known,
Is sport for every girl to practise on. Donne.

Tragedy should blush as much to stoop
To the low mimick follies of a farce,
As a grave matron would to dance with girls. Roscommon.

A boy, like thee, would make a kingly line;
But oh, a girl, like her, must be divine! Dryden.

glábrity n.s. [from *glaber*, Latin.] Smoothness; baldness. Dict.

glácis n.s. [French.] In fortification, a sloping bank. It is more especially taken for that which rangeth from the parapet of the covered way to the level on the side of the field. Harris.

to glaire v.a. [*glairer*, French; from the noun.] To smear with the white of an egg. This word is still used by the bookbinders.

glássgazing adj. [*glass* and *gazing*] Finical; often contemplating himself in a mirrour.

A whorson, glassgazing, superserviceable, finical rogue. Shakespeare's King Lear.

glaucóma n.s. [γλαυκωμα; *glaucome*, French.] A fault in the eye, which changes the crystalline humour into a greyish colour, without detriment of sight, and therein differs from what is commonly understood by suffusion. Quincy.

The glaucoma is no other disease than the cataract. Sharp.

glebe n.s. [*gleba*, Latin.]

1. Turf; soil; ground.

Fertile of corn the glebe, of oil and wine,
With herds the pastures throng'd, with flocks the hills. Milt.

Mark well the flow'ring almonds in the wood;
If od'rous blooms the bearing branches load,
The glebe will answer to the sylvan reign,
Great heats will follow, and large crops of grain. Dryden.

*   Sleeping vegetables lie,*
'Till the glad summons of a genial ray
Unbinds the glebe, and calls them out to day. Garth.

2. The land possessed as part of the revenue of an ecclesiastical benefice.

The ordinary living or revenue of a parsonage is of three sorts: the one in land, commonly called the glebe; another in tythe, which is a set part of our goods rendered to God; the third, in other offerings bestowed upon God and his church by the people. Spelman.

A trespass done on a parson's glebe land, which is a freehold, cannot be tried in a spiritual court. Ayliffe's Parergon.

Many parishes have not an inch of glebe. Swift.

glében adj. [from *glebe.*] Turfy; perhaps in the following passage fat or fruitful, if it has indeed any meaning.

Pernicious flatt'ry! thy malignant seeds
In an ill hour, and by a fatal hand
Sadly diffus'd o'er virtue's gleby land,
With rising pride amidst the corn appear,
And choke the hopes and harvest of the year. Prior.

gleek n.s. [*gligge*, Saxon.] Musick; or musician.

What will you give us?—No money, but the gleek: I will give you the minstrel. Shakesp. Romeo and Juliet.

to glib v.a. [from the adjective.] To castrate.

I'll geld them all: fourteen they shall not see,
To bring false generations; they are coheirs,
And I had rather glib myself than they
Should not produce fair issue. Shakesp.
Winter's Tale.

glike n.s. [*glig*, Saxon.] See *gleek*. A sneer;
a scoff; a flout. Not now in use.

Now where's the bastard's braves, and Charles
his glikes? Shakespeare's Henry VI. p. i.

to gloat v.n. [This word I conceive to be
ignorantly written for *gloar*.] To cast side
glances as a timorous lover.

Teach every grace to smile in your behalf,
And her deluding eyes to gloat for you.
Rowe's Ja. Shore.

gloss n.s. [γλωσσα; *glose*, French.]

1. A scholium; a comment.

They never hear sentence, which mentioneth
the word or scripture, but forthwith their
glosses upon it are the word preached, the
scripture explained, or delivered unto us in
sermons. Hooker, b. v. s. 22.

If then all souls, both good and bad, do teach,
With gen'ral voice, that souls can never die;
'Tis not man's flatt'ring gloss, but nature's speech,
Which, like God's oracles, can never lie.
Davies.

Some mutter at certain passages therein, by
putting ill glosses upon the text, and taking
with the left hand what I offer with the right.
Howel.

All this, without a gloss or comment,
He could unriddle in a moment. Hudibras,
p. i. cant. 1.

In many places he has perverted my meaning
by his glosses, and interpreted my words into
blasphemy and bawdry, of which they were
not guilty. Dryden's Fables, Preface.

They give the scandal, and the wise discern;
Their glosses teach an age too apt to learn.
Dryden.

Explaining the text in short glosses, was
Accursius's method. Baker's Reflections
on Learning.

Indentures, cov'nants, articles they draw,
Large as the fields themselves, and larger far
Than civil codes with all their glosses are.
Pope.

2. An interpretation artfully specious;
a specious representation.

Poor painters oft with silly poets join,
To fill the world with strange but vain conceit;
One brings the stuff, the other stamps the coin,
Which breeds nought else but glosses of deceit.
Sidney, b. ii.

It is no part of my secret meaning to draw you
hereby into hatred, or to set upon the face of
this cause any fairer gloss than the naked
truth doth afford. Hooker, Preface.

   He seems with forged quaint conceit
To set a gloss upon his bad intent.
Shakespeare's Henry VI.

   The common gloss
Of theologians. Milton.

3. Superficial lustre.

His iron coat, all over grown with rust,
Was underneath enveloped with gold,
Whose glistering gloss dark'ned with filthy
dust. Fai. Queen.

   You are a sectary,
That's the plain truth: your painted
   gloss discovers,
To men that understand you, words and
   weakness. Shakes.

Golden opinions from all sorts of people,
Which would be worn now in their newest
   gloss. Shakesp.

The doubt will be whether it will polish so
well; for steel glosses are more resplendent than
the like plates of brass, and so is the glittering
of a blade. Bacon's Phys. Rem.

   Weeds that the wind did toss
The virgins wore: the youths, woven coats,
   that cast a faint dim gloss,
Like that of oil. Chapman's Iliads, b. xviii.

It was the colour of devotion, giving a
lustre to reverence, and a gloss to humility.
South's Sermons.

Groves, fields, and meadows, are at any season pleasant to look upon; but never so much as in the opening of the Spring, when they are all new and fresh, with their first gloss upon them. Addison's Spectator, N⁰ 412.

glóssary n.s. [*glossarium*, Latin; *glossaire*, French.] A dictionary of obscure or antiquated words.

According to Varro, the most learned of the Romans, when delubrum *was applied to a place, it signified such a one,* in quo dei simulachrum dedicatum est; *and also in the old glossaries.* Stillingfleet.†

I could add another word to the glossary. Baker.

to glout v.n. [A low word of which I find no etymology.] To pout; to look sullen. It is still used in Scotland.

She lurks in midst of all her den, and streaks From out a ghastly whirlpool all her necks, Where, glowting round her rock, to fish she falls. Chapman.

Glouting with sullen sight, the fury shook Her clotted locks, and blasted with each look. Garth.

to gloze v.n. [*glesan*, Saxon.]

1. To flatter; to wheedle; to insinuate; to fawn.

Man will hearken to his glozing lies, And easily transgress. Milton's Paradise Lost, b. iii.

So gloz'd the tempter, and his proem tun'd: Into the heart of Eve his words made way. Milt. Par. Lost.

A false glozing parasite would call his foolhardiness valour, and then he may go on boldly, because blindly, and by mistaking himself for a lion, come to perish like an ass. South.

Now for a glozing speech, Fair protestations, specious marks of friendship. Phillips.

2. To comment. This should be *gloss.*

Which Salique land the French unjustly gloze To be the realm of France. Shakespeare's Henry V.

glum adj. [A low cant word formed by corrupting *gloom.*] Sullen; stubbornly grave.

Some, when they hear a story, look glum, and cry, Well, what then? Guardian.

gnómonicks n.s. [γνομονικη.] A science which makes a part of the mathematicks: it teaches to find the just proportion of shadows for the construction of all kinds of sun and moon dials, and for knowing what o'clock it is by means thereof; as also of a gnomon or stile, that throws off the shadow for this purpose. Trevoux.

goat n.s. [*gat*, Saxon and Scottish.] A ruminant animal that seems a middle species between deer and sheep.

Gall of goat, and slips of yew. Shakesp. Macbeth.

You may draw naked boys riding and playing with their paper-mills or bubble-shells upon goats, eagles, or dolphins. Peacham on Drawing.

The little bear that rock'd the mighty Jove, The swan whose borrow'd shape conceal'd his love, Are grac'd with light; the nursing goat's repaid With heaven, and duty rais'd the pious maid. Creech.

gob n.s. [*gobe*, French.] A small quantity. A low word.

Do'st think I have so little wit as to part with such a gob of money? L'Estrange.

góblin n.s. [French; *gobelina*, which Spenser has once retained, writing it in three syllables. This word some derive from the *Gibellines* a faction in Italy; so that *elfe* and *goblin* is *Guelph* and *Gibelline*, because the children of either party were terrified by their nurses with the name of the other: but it appears that *elfe* is Welsh, and much older than those factions. *Eilss Uylhon* are phantoms of the night, and the Germans likewise have long had spirits among them named *Goboldi*, from which *gobelin* might be derived.]

1. An evil spirit; a walking spirit; a frightful phantom.

Angels and ministers of grace defend us!
Be thou a spirit of health, or goblin damn'd,
Bring with thee airs from heav'n, or blasts
   from hell? Shak.

To whom the goblin, full of wrath, reply'd,
Art thou that traytor angel? Milton's
Paradise Lost, b. ii.

Always, whilst he is young be sure to preserve
his tender mind from all impressions and
notions of spirits and goblins, or any fearful
apprehensions in the dark. Locke.

2. A fairy; an elf.

His son was Elfinel, who overcame
The wicked gobbelines in bloody field;
But Elfant was of most renowned fame,
Who of all crystal did Panthea build.
Fairy Queen, b. ii.

Go, charge my goblins that they grind their joints
With dry convulsions; shorten up their sinews
With aged cramps. Shakespeare's Tempest.

Mean time the village rouzes up the fire,
While well attested, and as well believ'd,
Heard solemn goes the goblin story round.
Thomson's Winter.

go-cart n.s. [*go* and *cart.*] A machine in
which children are inclosed to teach them
to walk, and which they push forward
without danger of falling.

   Young children, who are try'd in
Go-carts, to keep their steps from sliding,
When members knit, and legs grow stronger,
Make use of such machine no longer. Prior.

god n.s. [*god*, Saxon, which likewise
signifies *good.* The same word passes in both
senses with only accidental variations
through all the Teutonick dialects.]

1. The Supreme Being.

God is a spirit, and they that worship him
must worship him in spirit and in truth.
John iv. 24.

   God above
Deal between thee and me: for ever now
I put myself to thy direction. Shakespeare's
Macbeth.

The Supreme Being, whom we call God, is

necessary, self-existent, eternal, immense,
omnipotent, omniscient, and best being;
and therefore also a being who is and ought
to be esteemed most sacred or holy.
Grew's Cosmol. Sacr. b. i.

2. A false god; an idol.

He that sacrificeth unto any god, save unto
the Lord only, he shall be utterly destroyed.
Exod. xxii. 20.

As flies to wanton boys are we to the gods,
They kill us for their sport. Shakespeare's
King Lear.

Strong god of arms, whose iron sceptre sways
The freezing North, and Hyperborean seas,
And Scythian colds, and Thracia's Winter coast,
Where stand thy steeds, and thou art honour'd
   most. Dryd.

3. Any person or thing deified or too much
honoured.

Whose end is destruction, whose god is their
belly. Phil. iii.

   I am not Licio,
Nor a musician as I seem to be;
But one that scorns to live in this disguise,
For such a one as leaves a gentleman,
And makes a god of such a cullion.
Shakespeare.

gódling n.s. [from *god.*] A little divinity;
a diminutive god.

Thy puny godlings of inferior race,
Whose humble statues are content with brass.
Dryd. Juven.

gold n.s. [*gold*, Saxon; *golud*, riches, Welsh.
It is called gold in our English tongue
either of *geel*, as Scaliger says, which is in
Dutch to shine; or of another Dutch word,
which is *gelten*, and signifies in Latin *valere*,
in English to be of price or value: hence
cometh their ordinary word *gelt*, for money.
Peacham on Drawing.]

1. Gold is the heaviest, the most dense, the
most simple, the most ductile, and most
fixed of all bodies; not to be injured
either by air or fire, and seeming
incorruptible. It is soluble by means of

sea-salt; but is injured by no other salt, and is most easily of all metals amalgamated with silver. Gold is frequently found native, and very rarely in a state of ore. It never constitutes a peculiar ore, but is found most frequently among ore of silver. Native gold is seldom found pure, but has almost constantly silver with it, and very frequently copper. Gold dust, or native gold, in small masses, is mixed among the sand of rivers in many parts of the world. It is found, in the greatest abundance, bedded in masses of hard stone, often at the depth of a hundred and fifty fathoms in the mines of Peru. Pure gold is so fixed, that Boerhaave informs us of an ounce of it set in the eye of a glass furnace for two months, without losing a single grain. Hill on Fossils.

Gold hath these natures: greatness of weight, closeness of parts, fixation, pliantness or softness, immunity from rust, and the colour or tincture of yellow. Bacon's Nat. History.

Ah! Buckingham, now do I ply the touch,
To try if thou be current gold indeed.
Shakes. Rich. III.

We commonly take shape and colour for so presumptive ideas of several species, that, in a good picture, we readily say this is gold, and that a silver goblet, only by the different figures and colours represented to the eye by the pencil. Locke.

The gold fraught vessel, which mad
tempests beat,
He sees now vainly make to his retreat.
Dryd. Tyran. Love.

2. Money.

For me, the gold of France did not seduce,
Although I did admit it as a motive
The sooner to effect what I intended.
Shakesp. Henry V.

Thou, that so stoutly hast resisted me,
Give me thy gold, if thou hast any gold;
For I have bought it with an hundred blows.
Shakes. H. VI.

If I want gold, steal but a beggar's dog,
And give it Timon, why, the dog coins gold.
Shakespeare.

3. It is used for any thing pleasing or valuable. So among the ancients χρυση αφροδιτη; and *animamq; moresque aureos educit in astra.* Horace.[†]

The king's a bawcock, and a heart of gold,
A lad of life, an imp of fame. Shakespeare's Henry V.

góndola n.s. [*gondole*, French.] A boat much used in Venice; a small boat.

He saw did swim
Along the shore, as swift as glance of eye,
A little gondelay, bedecked trim
With boughs and arbours woven cunningly.
Fairy Queen.

In a gondola were seen together Lorenzo and his amorous Jessica. Shakespeare's Merchant of Venice.

As with gondola's and men, his
Good excellence the duke of Venice
Sails out, and gives the gulph a ring. Prior.

gonorrhoéa n.s. [γονος and ρεω.] A morbid running of venereal hurts.

Rauty mummy or stone mummy grows on the tops of high rocks: they powder and boil it in milk, and then give it to stop gonorrhœas. Woodward on Fossils.

goódy n.s. [corrupted from *good wife.*] A low term of civility used to mean persons.

Soft, goody sheep, then said the fox, not so;
Unto the king so rash ye may not go.
Hubberd's Tale.

Swarm'd on a rotten stick the bees I spy'd,
Which erst I saw when goody Dobson dy'd.
Gay's Pastorals.

Plain goody would no longer down;
'Twas madam in her grogram gown. Swift.

górbelly n.s. [from *gor*, dung, and *belly*, according to Skinner and Junius. It may perhaps come from *gor*, Welsh, beyond, too much; or, as seems to me more likely, may be contracted from *gormand*, or *gormand's belly*, the belly of a glutton.] A big paunch; a swelling belly. A term of reproach for a fat man.

górmand n.s. [*gourmand*, French.] A greedy eater; a ravenous luxurious feeder.

góspel n.s. [*godes spel*, or God's or good tidings; ευαγγελιον; *soskkel*, *skeal suach*, happy tidings, Erse.]

1. God's word; the holy book of the Christian revelation.

Thus may the gospel to the rising sun
Be spread, and flourish where it first begun.
Waller.

How is a good Christian animated and cheered by a stedfast belief of the promises of the gospel! Bentley's Sermons.

2. Divinity; theology.

góspeller n.s. [from *gospel*.] A name of the followers of Wicklif, who first attempted a reformation from popery, given them by the Papists in reproach, from their professing to follow and preach only the gospel.

These gospellers have had their golden days,
Have troden down our holy Roman faith.
Rowe's J. Shore.

góssip n.s. [from *god* and *syb*, relation, affinity, Saxon.]

1. One who answers for the child in baptism.

Go to a gossip's feast and gaude with me,
After so long grief such nativity:
—With all my heart, I'll gossip at this feast.
Shakespeare.

At the christening of George duke of Clarence, who was born in the castle of Dublin, he made both the earl of Kildare and the earl of Ormond his gossips. Davies on Ireland.

2. A tippling companion.

And sometimes lurk I in a gossip's bowl,
In very likeness of a roasted crab,
And when she drinks against her lips I bob.
Shakespeare.

3. One who runs about tattling like women at a lying-in.

To do the office of a neighbour,
And be a gossip at his labour. Hudibras, p. ii. cant. 1.

   'Tis sung in ev'ry street,
The common chat of gossips when they meet.
Dryden.

góujeres n.s. [from *gouje*, French, a camp trull.] The French disease. Hanmer.†

gout n.s. [*goutte*, French.]

1. The arthritis; a periodical disease attended with great pain.†

The gout is a disease which may affect any membranous part, but commonly those which are at the greatest distance from the heart or the brain, where the motion of the fluids is the slowest, the resistance, friction, and stricture of the solid parts the greatest, and the sensation of pain, by the dilaceration of the nervous fibres, extreme. Arbuthnot on Diet.

One that's sick o' th' gout, had rather
Groan so in perplexity than be cur'd
By th' sure physician death. Shakespeare's Cymbeline.

This very rev'rend lecher, quite worn out
With rheumatisms, and crippled with his gout,
Forgets what he in youthful times has done,
And swinges his own vices in his son.
Dryden's Juvenal.

2. A drop. [*goutte*, French; *gutta*, Latin.] *Gut* for *drop* is still used in Scotland by physicians.

   I see thee still,
And on the blade o' th' dudgeon gouts of blood,
Which was not so before. Shakespeare's Macbeth.

gout n.s. [French.] A taste. An affected cant word.

The method which he has published will make these catalogues exceeding useful, and serve for a direction to any one that has a gout for the like studies. Woodward on Fossils.

góvernment n.s. [*gouvernement*, French.]

1. Form of a community with respect to the disposition of the supreme authority.

There seem to be but two general kinds of government in the world: the one exercised according to the arbitrary commands and will of some single person; and the other according to certain orders or laws introduced by agreement or custom, and not to be changed without the consent of many. Temple.

2. An establishment of legal authority.

*There they shall found
Their government, and their great senate chuse
Through the twelve tribes, to rule by laws ordain'd.* Milton.

*While he survives, in concord and content
The commons live, by no divisions rent;
But the great monarch's death dissolves the government.* Dryd.

Every one knows, who has considered the nature of government, that there must be in each particular form of it an absolute unlimited power. Addison.

Where any one person or body of men seize into their hands the power in the last resort, there is properly no longer a government, but what Aristotle and his followers call the abuse or corruption of one. Swift.

3. Administration of publick affairs.

*Safety and equal government are things
Which subjects make as happy as their kings.* Waller.

4. Regularity of behaviour.

*You needs must learn, lord, to amend this fault;
Though sometimes it shews greatness, courage, blood,
Yet oftentimes it doth present harsh rage,
Defect of manners, want of government,
Pride, haughtiness, opinion and disdain.* Shakes. Hen. IV.

*'Tis government that makes them seem divine;
The want thereof makes thee abominable.* Shakes. H. VI.

5. Manageableness; compliance; obsequiousness.

*Thy eyes windows fall,
Like death, when he shuts up the day of life;
Each part depriv'd of supple government,*

Shall stiff and stark, and cold appear, like death. Shakesp.

6. Management of the limbs or body. Obsolete.

*Their god
Shot many a dart at me with fierce intent;
But I them warded all with wary government.* Fairy Queen.

7. [In grammar.] Influence with regard to construction.

to grábble v.n. [probably corrupted from *grapple.*] To grope; to feel eagerly with the hands.

My blood chills about my heart at the thought of these rogues, with their bloody hands grabbling in my guts, and pulling out my very entrails. Arbuthnot's Hist. of John Bull.

grácile adj. [*gracilis*, Latin.] Slender; small. Dict.

grácilent n.s. [*gracilentus*, Latin.] Lean. Dict.

graduátion n.s. [*graduation*, French, from *graduate.*]

1. Regular progression by succession of degrees.

The graduation of the parts of the universe is likewise necessary to the perfection of the whole. Grew's Cosmol. Sacra.

Of greater repugnancy unto reason is that which he delivers concerning its graduation, that heated in fire, and often extinguished in oyl of mars or iron, the loadstone acquires an ability to extract a nail fastened in a wall. Brown's Vu. Err.

2. The act of conferring academical degrees.

gramíneous adj. [*gramineus*, Latin.] Grassy. Gramineous plants are such as have a long leaf without a footstalk.

grámmar n.s. [*grammaire*, French; *grammatica*, Latin; γραμματικη.]

1. The science of speaking correctly; the art which teaches the relations of words to each other.

We make a countryman dumb, whom we will not allow to speak but by the rules of grammar. Dryden's Dufresnoy.

Men, speaking language according to the grammar rules of that language, do yet speak improperly of things. Locke.

2. Propriety or justness of speech; speech according to grammar.

Varium & mutabile semper femina, is the sharpest satire that ever was made on woman; for the adjectives are neuter, and animal must be understood to make them grammar. Dryden.†

3. The book that treats of the various relations of words to one another.

grámmar school n.s. A school in which the learned languages are grammatically taught.

Thou hast most traitorously corrupted the youth of the realm in erecting a grammar school. Shakespeare's Hen. VI.

The ordinary way of learning Latin in a grammar school I cannot encourage. Locke.

grammaticáster n.s. [Latin.] A mean verbal pedant; a low grammarian.

I have not vexed their language with the doubts, the remarks, and eternal triflings of the French grammaticasters. Rymer's Tragedies of the last Age.

grandévity n.s. [from *grandævus*, Latin.] Great age; length of life. Dict.

grándinous adj. [*grande*, Latin.] Full of hail; consisting of hail. Dict.

gránnam n.s. [for *grandam*.] Grandmother. Only used in burlesque works.

Oft my kind grannam told me, Tim, take warning. Gay.

grátefulness n.s. [from *grateful*.]

1. Gratitude; duty to benefactors. Now obsolete.

A Laconian knight, having sometime served him with more gratefulness than good courage defended him. Sidney.

Blessings beforehand, ties of gratefulness, The sound of glory ringing in our ears. Herbert.

2. Quality of being acceptable; pleasantness.

grátis adv. [Latin.] For nothing; without a recompence.

The people cry you mock'd them; and, of late, When corn was given them gratis, you repin'd. Shakesp.

They sold themselves; but thou, like a kind fellow, gav'st thyself away gratis, and I thank thee for thee. Shakespeare.

Kindred are no welcome clients, where relation gives them a title to have advice gratis. L'Estrange.

I scorned to take my degree at Utrecht or Leyden, though offered it gratis by those universities. Arbuthnot's John Bull.

gravídity n.s. [*gravidus*, Latin.] Pregnancy; state of being with child.

Women, obstructed, have not always the forementioned symptoms: in those the signs of gravidity and obstructions are hard to be distinguished in the beginning. Arbuthnot on Diet.

grávity n.s. [*gravitas*, Latin; *gravité*, French.]

1. Weight; heaviness; tendency to the centre.

That quality by which all heavy bodies tend towards the centre of the earth, accelerating their motion the nearer they approach towards it, true philosophy has shewn to be unsolveable by any hypothesis, and resolved it into the immediate will of the Creator. Of all bodies, considered within the confines of any fluid, there is a twofold gravity, true and absolute, and apparent, vulgar or comparative: absolute gravity is the whole force by which any body tends downwards; but the relative or vulgar is the excess of gravity in one body above the specifick gravity of the fluid, whereby it tends downwards more than the ambient fluid doth. Quincy.

Bodies do swim or sink in different liquors, according to the tenacity or gravity of those liquors which are to support them. Brown's Vulgar Errours, b. vii. c. 15.

Though this increase of density may at great distances be exceeding slow, yet if the elastick tone of this medium be exceeding great, it may suffice to impel bodies from the denser parts of the medium towards the rarer, with all that power which we call gravity. Newton's Opt.

2. Atrociousness; weight of guilt.

No man could ever have thought this reasonable, that had intended thereby only to punish the injury committed, according to the gravity of the fact. Hooker, b. i. s. 10.

3. Seriousness; solemnity.

There is not a white hair on your face but should have his effect of gravity. Shakespeare's Henry IV. p.i.

Our youths and wildness shall no whit appear, But all be buried in his gravity. Shakespeare's Jul. Cæsar.

For the advocates and council that plead, patience and gravity of hearing is an essential part of justice. Bacon, Essay 57.

Great Cato there, for gravity renown'd. Dryden's Æn.

The emperors often jested on their rivals or predecessors, but their mints still maintained their gravity. Addison.

grávy n.s. The serous juice that runs from flesh not much dried by the fire.

They usually boil and roast their meat until it falls almost off from the bones; but we love it half raw, with the blood trickling down from it, delicately terming it the gravy, which in truth looks more like an ichorous or raw bloody matter. Harvey on Consumptions.

There may be a stronger broth made of vegetables than of any gravy soup. Arbuthnot on Aliments.

gréatbellied adj. [*great* and *belly*.] Pregnant; teeming.

Greatbellied women, That had not half a week to go, like rams In the old time of war, would shake the press, And make 'em reel from before 'em. Shakesp. Henry VIII.

A greatbellied woman, walking through the city in the daytime, had her child struck out of her womb, and carried half a furlong from her. Wilkins's Math. Magick.

greaves n.s. [from *gréves*, French.] Armour for the legs; a sort of boots. It wants the singular number.

He had greaves of brass upon his legs. 1 Sa. xvii. 6.

A shield make for him, and a helm, fair greaves, and curets such As may renown thy workmanship, and honour him as much. Chapman's Iliads, b. xviii.

Grécism n.s. [*græcismus*, Latin.] An idiom of the Greek language.

green adj. [*grun*, German; *groen*, Dutch.]

1. Having a colour formed commonly by compounding blue and yellow; of the colour of the leaves of trees or herbs. The green colour is said to be most favourable to the sight.

The general colour of plants is green, which is a colour that no flower is of: there is a greenish primrose, but it is pale, and scarce a green. Bacon's Natural History.

Groves for ever green. Pope.

2. Pale; sickly: from whence we call the maid's disease the *green* sickness, or *chlorosis.* Like it is Sappho's χλωροτερη ποιας.†

Was the hope drunk Wherein you drest yourself? Hath it slept since? And wakes it now to look so green and pale At what it did so freely? Shakespeare's Macbeth.

There's never any of these demure boys come to any proof: they fall into a kind of male green sickness. Shak. Henry IV.

'Till the green sickness and love's force betray'd To death's remorseless arms th' unhappy maid. Garth.

3. Flourishing; fresh; undecayed: from trees in Spring.

4. New; fresh: as, a green wound.

The door is open, sir; there lies your way:
You may be jogging while your boots are
green. Shakesp.

Griefs are green;
And all thy friends, which thou must make
thy friends,
Have but their stings and teeth newly ta'en
out. Sh. H. IV.

In a vault,
Where bloody Tybalt, yet but green in earth,
Lies festering in his blood. Shakes. Romeo
and Juliet.

A man that studieth revenge keeps his own
wounds green, which otherwise would heal
and do well. Bacon, Essay 4.

5. Not dry.

If a spark of error have thus far prevailed,
falling even where the wood was green, and
farthest off from any inclination unto furious
attempts; must not the peril thereof be greater
in men, whose minds are of themselves as
dry fewel, apt beforehand unto tumults?
Hooker, Dedication.

Of fragility the cause is an impotency to be
extended, and therefore stone is more fragil
than metal, and so dry wood is more fragil
than green. Bacon's Natural History.

If you but consider a piece of green wood
burning in a chimney, you will readily
discern, in the disbanded parts of it, the four
elements. Boyle.

The green do often heat the ripe, and the ripe,
so heated, give fire to the green. Mortimer's
Husbandry.

6. Not roasted; half raw.

Under this head we may rank those words
which signify different ideas, by a sort of an
unaccountable far-fetched analogy, or distant
resemblance, that fancy has introduced
between one thing and another; as when we
say the meat is green, when it is half roasted.
Watts's Logick.

7. Unripe; immature; young; because fruits
are green before they are ripe.

My sallad days,
When I was green in judgment, cold in blood!
Shakesp.

O charming youth, in the first op'ning page;
So many graces in so green an age. Dryden.

You'll find a difference
Between the promise of his greener days,
And these he masters now. Shakesp. Henry V.

If you would fat green geese, shut them up
when they are about a month old. Mortimer's
Husbandry.

Stubble geese at Michaelmas are seen
Upon the spit, next May produces green.
King's Cookery.

grégal adj. [*grex, gregis*, Lat.] Belonging to
a flock. Dict.

gregárious adj. [*gregarius*, Latin.] Going in
flocks or herds, like sheep or partridges.

No birds of prey are gregarious. Ray on the
Creation.

grémial adj. [*gremium*, Lat.] Pertaining to
the lap. Dict.

grenáde n.s. [from *pomum granatum*,
Latin.] A little hollow globe or ball of iron,
or other metal, about two inches and a half
in diameter, which, being filled with fine
powder, is set on fire by means of a small
fusee fastened to the touch-hole: as soon as
it is kindled, the case flies into many
shatters, much to the damage of all that
stand near. These granades serve to fire
close and narrow passages, and are often
thrown with the hand among the soldiers to
disorder their ranks, more especially in
those posts where they stand thickest; as in
trenches, redoubts, and lodgments. Harr.

grócer n.s. [This should be written *grosser*,
from *gross*, a large quantity; a *grocer*
originally being one who dealt by
wholesale; or from *grossus*, a fig, which their
present state seems to favour.] A grocer is
a man who buys and sells tea, sugar and
plumbs and spices for gain. Watts's Logick.

But still the offspring of your brain shall prove
The grocer's care, and brave the rage of Jove.
Garth.

grot n.s. [*grotte*, French; *grotta*, Italian.] A cave; a cavern for coolness and pleasure.

In the remotest wood and lonely grot,
Certain to meet that worst of evils, thought.
Prior.

Awful see the Egerian grot. Pope.

grotésque adj. [*grotesque*, French; *grottesco*, Italian.] Distorted of figure; unnatural; wildly formed.

The champaign head
Of a steep wilderness, whose hairy sides
With thicket overgrown, grotesque and wild,
Access deny'd. Milton's Paradise Lost, b. iv.

There is yet a lower sort of poetry and
painting, which is out of nature; for a farce is
that in poetry which grotesque is in a picture:
the persons and actions of a farce are all
unnatural, and the manners false, that is,
inconsisting with the characters of mankind:
grotesque painting is the just resemblance of
this. Dryden's Dufresnoy.

An hideous figure of their foes they drew,
Nor lines, nor looks, nor shades, nor colours true,
And this grotesque design expos'd to publick
*   view.* Dryden.

Palladian walls, Venetian doors,
Grotesco roofs, and stucco floors. Pope's Sat. of Horace.

grúbstreet n.s. Originally the name of a street in Moorfields in London, much inhabited by writers of small histories, dictionaries, and temporary poems; whence any mean production is called grubstreet.

Χαιρ' Ιθακη μετ' αεθλα, μετ' αλγε
    πικρα
Ασπασιως τεον ουδας ικανομαι.†

The first part, though calculated only for the
meridian of grubstreet, was yet taken notice
of by the better sort. Arbuthn.

I'd sooner ballads write, and grubstreet lays.
Gay.

gruel n.s. [*gruau*, *gruelle*, French.] Food made by boiling oatmeal in water; any kind of mixture made by boiling ingredients in water.

Finger of birth-strangl'd babe,
Ditch-deliver'd by a drab;
Make the gruel thick and slab. Shakespeare's Macbeth.

Was ever Tartar fierce or cruel
Upon the strength of water gruel? Prior.

Gruel made of grain, broths, malt-drink not
much hopped, posset-drinks, and in general
whatever relaxeth. Arbuthnot.

grum adj. [contracted from *grumble*.] Sour; surly; severe. A low word.

Nic looked sour and grum, and would not
open his mouth. Arbuthnot's History of John Bull.

gry n.s. [γρυ.] Any thing of little value: as, the paring of the nails. Dict.

to guggle v.n. [*gorgoliare*, Italian.] To sound as water running with intermissions out of a narrow mouthed vessel.

guínea n.s. [from *Guinea*, a country in Africa abounding with gold.] A gold coin valued at one and twenty shillings.

By the word gold I must be understood to
design a particular piece of matter; that is,
the last guinea that was coined. Locke.

guíneapig n.s. A small animal with a pig's snout.

guitár n.s. [*ghitara*, Italian; *guiterre*, French.] A stringed instrument of musick.

Sallads and eggs, and lighter fare,
Tune the Italian spark's guitar. Prior.

gulósity n.s. [*gulosus*, Latin.] Greediness; gluttony; voracity.

They are very temperate, seldom offending
in ebriety, or excess of drink; nor erring in
gulosity, or superfluity of meats. Brown's Vulgar Errours, b. iv. c. 10.

gun n.s. [Of this word there is no satisfactory etymology. Mr. Lye observes that *gun* in Iceland signifies *battle;* but when guns came into use we had no commerce with Iceland.] The general name for firearms; the instrument from which shot is discharged by fire.

These dread curses, like the sun 'gainst glass,
Or like an overcharged gun, recoil
And turn upon thyself. Shakespeare's Henry
VI. p. ii.

The emperor, smiling, said that never emperor
was yet slain with a gun. Knolles's History
of the Turks.

The bullet flying, makes the gun recoil.
Cleaveland.

In vain the dart or glitt'ring sword we shun,
Condemn'd to perish by the slaught'ring gun.
Granville.

gúnpowder n.s. [*gun* and *powder.*] The
powder put into guns to be fired. It consists
of about twenty parts of nitre, three parts of
sulphur, and three of charcoal. The
proportions are not exactly kept.

Gunpowder consisteth of three ingredients,
saltpetre, smallcoal, and brimstone. Brown's
Vulgar Errours, b. ii.

Burning by gunpowder frequently happens at
sea. Wiseman.

gustátion n.s. [*gusto*, Latin.] The act
of tasting.

In it the gullet and conveying parts are only
seated, which partake of the nerves of
gustation, or appertaining unto sapor.
Brown's Vulgar Errours, b. vii.

gústo n.s. [Italian.]

1. The relish of any thing; the power by
   which any thing excites sensations in
   the palate.

Pleasant gustos gratify the appetite of the
luxurious. Derh.

2. Intellectual taste; liking.

In reading what I have written, let them
bring no particular gusto along with them.
Dryden.

gut n.s. [*kutteln*, German.]

1. The long pipe reaching with many
   convolutions from the stomach to
   the vent.

This lord wears his wit in his belly, and
his guts in his head. Shakespeare's Troilus
and Cressida.

Reveng'd I will be, as sure as his guts are
made of puddings. Shakespeare's Merry
Wives of Windsor.

A viol should have a lay of wire-strings
below, close to the belly, and then the strings
of guts mounted upon a bridge, that by this
means the upper strings stricken should make
the lower resound. Bacon's Natural History.

The intestines or guts may be inflamed by any
acrid or poisonous substance taken inwardly.
Arbuthnot on Diet.

2. The stomach; the receptacle of food:
   proverbially.

And cramm'd them 'till their guts did ake,
With cawdle, custard, and plum-cake.
Hudibras, p. ii.

With false weights their servants guts they cheat,
And pinch their own to cover the deceit.
Dryden's Juvenal.

3. Gluttony; love of gormandising.

Apicius, thou did'st on thy guts bestow
Full ninety millions; yet, when this was spent,
Ten millions still remain'd to thee; which thou,
Fearing to suffer thirst and famishment,
In poison'd potion drank'st. Hakewill on
Providence.

to gúttle v.a. [from *gut.*] To feed
luxuriously; to gormandise. A low word.

His jolly brother, opposite in sense,
Laughs at his thrift; and, lavish of expence,
Quaffs, crams, and guttles in his own defence.
Dryden.

gymnástick   adj.   [γυμναστικος;
gymnastique, French.] Pertaining to athletick
exercises; consisting of leaping, wrestling,
running, throwing the dart, or quoit.

The Cretans wisely forbid their servants
gymnasticks as well as arms; and yet your
modern footmen exercise themselves daily,
whilst their enervated lords are softly lolling
in their chariots. Arbuthnot and Pope's
Mart. Scribterus.

gymnospérmous adj. [γυμνος and
σπερμα.] Having the seeds naked.

gynecocracy n.s. [γυναικοκρατια;
gynecocratie, French.] Petticoat government;
female power.

H is in English, as in other languages, a note of aspiration, sounded only by a strong emission of the breath, without any conformation of the organs of speech, and is therefore by many grammarians accounted no letter. The *h* in English is scarcely ever mute at the beginning of a word, or where it immediately precedes a vowel; as *house*, *behaviour*: where it is followed by a consonant it has no sound, according to the present pronunciation: but anciently, as now in Scotland, it made the syllable guttural; as *right*, *bought*.

habilitátion n.s. [from *habilitate*.] Qualification.

The things formerly spoken of, are but habilitations towards arms; and what is habilitation without intention and act? Bacon, Essay 30.

hábit n.s. [*habitus*, Latin.]

1. State of any thing: as, habit of body.

2. Dress; accoutrement.

I shifted
Into a madman's rags, t' assume a semblance
The very dogs disdain'd; and in this habit
Met I my father. Shakespeare's King Lear.

If you have any justice, any pity;
If ye be any thing, but churchmen's habits.
Shakespeare.

Both the poets being dressed in the same English habit, story compared with story, judgment may be made betwixt them. Dryden's Fables, Preface.

The scenes are old, the habits are the same We wore last year. Dryden's Indian Emperor.

There are among the statues several of Venus, in different habits. Addison on Italy.

The clergy are the only set of men who wear a distinct habit from others. Swift.

3. Habit is a power or ability in man of doing any thing, when it has been acquired by frequent doing the same thing. Locke.

He hath a better bad habit of frowning than the count Palatine. Shakesp. Merchant of Venice.

4. Custom; inveterate use.

This is the last fatal step but one, which is, by frequent repetition of the sinful act, to continue and persist in it, 'till at length it settles into a fixed confirmed habit of sin; which being properly that which the apostle calls the finishing of sin, ends certainly in death; death not only as to merit, but also as to actual infliction. South's Sermons.

No civil broils have since his death arose,
But faction now by habit does obey;

And wars have that respect for his repose,
As winds for halcyons when they breed at sea.
Dryden.

The force of education is so great, that we may mould the minds and manners of the young into what shape we please, and give the impressions of such habits as shall ever afterwards remain. Atterbury's Sermons.

hábnab adv. [*hap ne hap*, or *nap*; as *would ne would, will ne will*; that is, *let it happen or not*.] At random; at the mercy of chance; without any rule or certainty of effect.

He circles draws and squares,
With cyphers, astral characters;
Then looks 'em o'er to understand 'em,
Although set down habnab at random.
Hudibras, p. ii.

háckney n.s. [*hacnai*, Welsh; *hackeneye*, Teuton. *haquenée*, French.]

1. A pacing horse.

2. A hired horse; hired horses being usually taught to pace, or recommended as good pacers.

Light and lewd persons were as easily suborned to make an affidavit for money, as post-horses and hackneys are taken to hire. Bacon's Off. of Alienation.

Who, mounted on a broom, the nag
And hackney of a Lapland hag,
In quest of you came hither post,
Within an hour, I'm sure, at most.
Hudibras, p. iii.

3. A hireling; a prostitute.

Three kingdoms rung
With his accumulative and hackney tongue.
Roscommon.

That is no more than every lover
Does from his hackney lady suffer. Hudibras.

Shall each spurgall'd hackney of the day,
Or each new pension'd sycophant, pretend
To break my windows. Pope, Dial. 2.

4. Any thing let out for hire.

A wit can study in the streets;
Not quite so well, however, as one mought;

*A hackney coach may chance to spoil
   a thought.* Pope.

5. Much used; common.

*These notions young students in physick
derive from their hackney authors.* Harvey
on Consumptions.

hággess n.s. [from *hog* or *hack.*] A mass of
meat, generally pork chopped, and inclosed
in a membrane. In Scotland it is commonly
made in a sheep's maw of the entrails of the
same animal, cut small, with suet and spices.

to hággle v.n. To be tedious in a bargain; to
be long in coming to the price.

hágiographer n.s. [αγιος and γραφω.] A
holy writer. The Jews divide the Holy
Scriptures of the Old Testament, into the
law, the prophets, and the hagiographers.

half-scholar n.s. Imperfectly learned.

*We have many half-scholars now-a-days, and
there is much confusion and inconsistency in
the notions and opinions of some persons.*
Watts's Improvement of the Mind.

half-wit n.s. [*half* and *wit.*] A blockhead;
a foolish fellow.

*Half-wits are fleas, so little and so light,
We scarce could know they live, but that they
   bite.* Dryden.

hálituous adj. [*halitus*, Latin.] Vaporous;
fumous.

*We speak of the atmosphere as of a peculiar
thin and halituous liquor, much lighter than
spirit of wine.* Boyle.

hallelújah n.s. [הללויה] *Praise ye the Lord.*
A song of thanksgiving.

*   Then shall thy saints
Unfained hallelujahs to Thee sing,
Hymns of high praise.* Milton's Paradise
Lost, b. vi.

*Singing those devout hymns and heavenly
anthems, in which the church militant seems
ambitious to emulate the triumphant, and
echo back the solemn praises and hallelujahs
of the celestial choirs.* Boyle.

hallucinátion n.s. [*hallucinatio*, Latin.]
Errour; blunder; mistake; folly.

*A wasting of flesh, without cause, is frequently
termed a bewitched disease; but questionless a
meer hallucination of the vulgar.* Harvey on
Consumptions.

*This must have been the hallucination of the
transcriber, who probably mistook the dash of
the I for a T.* Addis. Spect.

hámated adj. [*hamatus*, Latin.] Hooked; set
with hooks.

to hámble v.a. [from *ham.*] To cut the
sinews of the thigh; to hamstring.

hame n.s. [*hama*, Saxon.] The collar by
which a horse draws in a waggon.

hándwriting n.s. [*hand* and *writing.*] A cast
or form of writing peculiar to each hand.

*That you beat me at the mart, I have your
   hand to show;
If the skin were parchment, and the blows you
   gave me ink,
Your own handwriting would tell you what
   I think.* Shak.

*To no other cause than the wise providence
of God can be referred the diversity of
handwritings.* Cockburn.

hándydandy n.s. A play in which children
change hands and places.

*See how yond justice rails upon yond simple
thief! Hark in thine ear: change places, and,
handydandy, which is the justice, which is the
thief.* Shakespeare's King Lear.

*Neither cross and pile, nor ducks and drakes,
are quite so ancient as handydandy.* Arbuthn.
and Pope's Mart. Scrib.

háppiness n.s. [from *happy.*]

1. Felicity; state in which the desires
   are satisfied.

*Happiness is that estate whereby we attain,
so far as possibly may be attained, the full
possession of that which simply for itself is
to be desired, and containeth in it after an
eminent sort the contentation of our desires,
the highest degree of all our perfection.*
Hooker, b. i.

Oh! happiness of sweet retir'd content,
To be at once secure and innocent. Denham.

The various and contrary choices that men
make in the world, argue that the same thing
is not good to every man alike: this variety of
pursuits shews, that every one does not place
his happiness in the same thing. Locke.

2. Good luck; good fortune.

3. Fortuitous elegance; unstudied grace.

Certain graces and happinesses, peculiar to
every language, give life and energy to the
words. Denham.

Some beauties yet no precepts can declare;
For there's a happiness as well as care. Pope
on Criticism.

háqueton n.s. A piece of armour. Spenser.

hárdware n.s. [*hard* and *ware*.]
Manufactures of metal.

hárlequin n.s. [This name is said to have
been given by Francis of France to a busy
buffoon, in ridicule of his enemy *Charles le*
quint. Menage derives it more probably
from a famous comedian that frequented
M. Harlay's house, whom his friends called
Harlequino, little Harley. Trev.] A buffoon
who plays tricks to divert the populace; a
Jack-pudding; a zani.

The joy of a king for a victory must not be like
that of a harlequin upon a letter from his
mistress. Dryden.

The man in graver tragick known,
Though his best part long since was done,
   Still on the stage desires to tarry;
And he who play'd the harlequin,
After the jest still loads the scene,
   Unwilling to retire, though weary. Prior.

hárlot n.s. [*herlodes,* Welsh, a girl. Others
for *horelet,* a little whore. Others from the
name of the mother of William the
Conqueror. *Hurlet* is used in Chaucer for
a low male drudge.] A whore; a strumpet.

Away, my disposition, and possess me with
Some harlot's spirit. Shakesp. Coriolanus.

They help thee by such aids as geese and
harlots. Ben. Johns.

The barbarous harlots crowd the publick place;
Go, fools, and purchase an unclean embrace.
Dryd. Juven.

hármony n.s. [αρμονια; *harmonie,*
French.]

1. The just adaptation of one part
to another.

The pleasures of the eye and ear are but
the effects of equality, good proportion, or
correspondence; so that equality and
correspondence are the causes of harmony.
Bacon.

   The harmony of things,
As well as that of sounds, from discord springs.
Denham.

Sure infinite wisdom must accomplish all its
works with consummate harmony, proportion,
and regularity. Cheyne.

2. Just proportion of sound; musical
concord.

Harmony is a compound idea, made up of
different sounds united. Watts's Logick.

3. Concord; correspondent sentiment.

   In us both one soul,
Harmony to behold in wedded pair!
More grateful than harmonious sounds to
   th' ear. Milton.

I no sooner in my heart divin'd,
My heart, which by a secret harmony
Still moves with thine, join'd in connexion
   sweet! Milton.

hárpsicord n.s. A musical instrument.

harridán n.s. [corrupted from *haridelle,*
a worn-out worthless horse.] A decayed
strumpet.

She just endur'd the Winter she began,
And in four months a batter'd harridan;
Now nothing's left, but wither'd, pale,
   and shrunk,
To bawd for others, and go shares with punk.
Swift.

hárrow interj. An exclamation of sudden
distress. Now out of use.

hártshorn n.s. Hartshorn is a drug that comes into use as many ways, and under as many forms, as any one in the whole *materia medica*. What is used here are the whole horns of the common male deer, which fall off every year. This species is the fallow deer; but some tell us, that the medicinal hartshorn should be that of the true hart or stag, called the red deer. The salt of hartshorn is a great sudorifick, and the spirit has all the virtues of volatile alkalies: it is used to bring people out of faintings by its pungency, holding it under the nose, and pouring down some drops of it in water. Hill's Mat. Med.

Ramose concretions of the volatile salts are observable upon the glass of the receiver, whilst the spirits of vipers and hartshorn are drawn. Woodward on Fossils.

hásty-pudding n.s. A pudding made of milk and flower, boiled quick together; as also of oatmeal and water boiled together.

Sure hasty-pudding is thy chiefest dish,
With bullock's liver, or some stinking fish.
Dorset.

hátchet-face n.s. An ugly face; such, I suppose, as might be hewn out of a block by a hatchet.

An ape his own dear image will embrace;
An ugly beau adores a hatchet-face. Dryden.

háutboy n.s. [*haut* and *bois*.] A wind instrument.[†]

I saw it, and told John of Gaunt he beat his own name; for you might have truss'd him and all his apparel into an eelskin: the case of a treble hautboy was a mansion for him, a court; and now hath he land and beeves. Shakes. Henry IV.

Now give the hautboys breath; he comes, he comes. Dry.

hávock interj. [from the noun.] A word of encouragement to slaughter.

Why stand these royal fronts amazed thus?
Cry havock, kings! Shakesp. King John.

Até by his side,
Cries havock! and lets loose the dogs of war.
Shakespeare.

to haw v.n. [Perhaps corrupted from *hawk* or *hack*.] To speak slowly with frequent intermission and hesitation.

'Tis a great way; but yet, after a little humming and hawing upon 't, he agreed to undertake the job. L'Estrange.

héadgargle n.s. [*head* and *gargle*.] A disease, I suppose, in cattle.

For the headgargle give powder of fenugreek. Mortimer.

heart n.s. [*heort*, Saxon; *hertz*, German.]

1. The muscle which by its contraction and dilation propels the blood through the course of circulation, and is therefore considered as the source of vital motion. It is supposed in popular language to be the seat sometimes of courage, sometimes of affection.

He with providence and courage so passed over all, that the mother took such spiteful grief at it, that her heart brake withal, and she died. Sidney.

Thou wouldst have left thy dearest heart blood there,
Rather than made that savage duke thine heir,
And disinherited thine only son. Shakes. Henry VI.

Snakes, in my heart blood warm'd, that sting my heart. Shakespeare's Richard II.

Our battle is more full of names than your's,
Our men more perfect in the use of arms,
Our armour all as strong, our cause the best;
Then reason wills our hearts should be as good. Shak. H. IV.

I thank you for my venison, master Shallow.
—Master Page, much good do it your good heart. Shakesp.

But since the brain doth lodge the pow'rs of sense,
How makes it in the heart those passions spring?
The mutual love, the kind intelligence
'Twixt heart and brain, this sympathy doth bring. Davies.

We all set our hearts at rest, since whatever comes from above is for the best. L'Estrange.

The only true zeal is that which is guided by a good light in the head, and that which consists of good and innocent affections in the heart. Spratt's Sermons.

Prest with heart corroding grief and years,
To the gay court a rural shed prefers.
Pope's Odessy.

2. The chief part; the vital part.

Barley being steeped in water, and turned upon a dry floor, will sprout half an inch; and, if it be let alone, much more, until the heart be out. Bacon's Natural History.

3. The inner part of any thing.

Some Englishmen did with great danger pass by water into the heart of the country. Abbot's Description of the World.

The king's forces are employed in appeasing disorders more near the heart of the kingdom. Hayward.

Generally the inside or heart of trees is harder than the outward parts. Boyle.

Here in the heart of all the town I'll stay,
And timely succour, where it wants, convey.
Dryden.

If the foundations be bad, provide good piles made of heart of oak, such as will reach ground. Moxon's Mech. Exer.

4. Person; character. Used with respect to courage or kindness.

The king's a bawcock, and a heart of gold,
A lad of life, an imp of fame. Shakespeare's Henry V.

Hey, my hearts; cheerly, my hearts. Shakesp. Tempest.

What says my heart of elder? Ha! is he dead, bully-stale? Is he dead? Shakes. Merry Wives of Windsor.

5. Courage; spirit.

If it please you to make his fortune known, as I have done Erona's, I will after take heart again to go on with his falsehood. Sidney, b. ii.

There did other like unhappy accidents happen out of England, which gave heart and good opportunity to them to regain their old possessions. Spenser on Ireland.

Wide was the wound; and a large
*   lukewarm flood,*
Red as the rose, thence gushed grievously,
That when the painim spy'd the streaming blood,
Gave him great heart and hope of victory.
Fairy Queen.

Eve, recov'ring heart, reply'd. Milton.

Having left that city well provided, and in good heart, his majesty removed with his little army to Bewdley. Clarendon.

Finding that it did them no hurt, they took heart upon 't, went up to 't, and viewed it. L'Estrange's Fables.

The expelled nations take heart, and when they fly from one country invade another. Temple.

6. Seat of love.

Ah! what avails it me the flocks to keep,
Who lost my heart while I preserv'd my sheep?
Pope.

7. Affection; inclination.

Joab perceived that the king's heart was towards Absalom. 2 Sa. xiv. 1.

Means how to feel, and learn each other's heart,
By th' abbot's skill of Westminster is found.
Daniel.

*   Nor set thy heart,*
Thus over-fond, on that which is not thine.
Milton.

'Tis well to be tender; but to set the heart too much upon any thing, is what we cannot justify. L'Estrange.

A friend makes me a feast, and sets all before me; but I set my heart upon one dish alone, and if that happen to be thrown down, I scorn all the rest. Temple.

Then mixing pow'rful herbs with magick art,
She chang'd his form who could not change his
*   heart.* Dryd.

What did I not, her stubborn heart to gain?
But all my vows were answer'd with disdain.
Dryden.

8. Memory.

Whatsoever was attained to, concerning God
and his working in nature, the same was
delivered over by heart and tradition from
wise men to a posterity equally zealous.
Raleigh.

We call the committing of a thing to memory
the getting it by heart; for it is the memory
that must transmit it to the heart; and it is
in vain to expect that the heart should keep
its hold of any truth, when the memory has
let it go. South.

Shall I in London act this idle part?
Composing songs for fools to get by heart.
Pope.

9. Good-will; ardour of zeal. To take to
heart any thing, is to be zealous or
solicitous or ardent about it.

If he take not their causes to heart, how should
there be but in them frozen coldness, when his
affections seem benumbed, from whom theirs
should take fire? Hooker.

If he would take the business to heart, and
deal in it effectually, it would succeed well.
Bacon's Henry VII.

The lady marchioness of Hertford engaged
her husband to take this business to heart.
Clarendon, b. viii.

Amongst those, who took it most to heart, sir
John Stawel was the chief. Clarendon, b. viii.

Every prudent and honest man would join
himself to that side which had the good of
their country most at heart. Addis.

Learned men have been now a long time
searching after the happy country from which
our first parents were exiled: if they can
find it, with all my heart. Woodward's
Nat. History.

I would not be sorry to find the Presbyterians
mistaken in this point, which they have most
at heart. Swift.

What I have most at heart is, that some

method should be thought on for ascertaining
and fixing our language. Swift.

10. Passions; anxiety; concern.

Set your heart at rest;
The fairy land buys not the child of me.
Shakespeare.

11. Secret thoughts; recesses of the mind.

Michal saw king David leaping and dancing
before the Lord, and she despised him in her
heart. 2 Sa. vi. 16.

The next generation will in tongue and heart,
and every way else, become English; so as
there will be no difference or distinction, but
the Irish sea, betwixt us. Davies on Ireland.

Thou sawest the contradiction between my
heart and hand. King Charles.

Would you have him open his heart to you,
and ask your advice, you must begin to do
so with him first. Locke.

Men, some to pleasure, some to business take;
But every woman is, at heart, a rake.
Pope, Epistle ii.

12. Disposition of mind.

Doing all things with so pretty a grace, that
it seemed ignorance could not make him do
amiss, because he had a heart to do well.
Sidney.

13. The heart is considered as the seat of
tenderness: a hard heart therefore is
cruelty.

I've seen thee stern, and thou hast oft beheld
Heart hardening spectacles. Shakesp.
Coriolanus.

Such iron hearts we are, and such
The base barbarity of human kind. Rowe's
Jane Shore.

14. To find in the heart. To be not wholly
averse.

For my breaking the laws of friendship with
you, I could find in my heart to ask you
pardon for it, but that your now handling of
me gives me reason to confirm my former
dealing. Sidney.

15. Secret meaning; hidden intention.

I will on with my speech in your praise,
And then shew you the heart of my message.
Shakespeare.

16. Conscience; sense of good or ill.

Every man's heart and conscience doth in good
or evil, even secretly committed, and known to
none but itself, either like or disallow itself.
Hooker, b. i. s. 9.

17. Strength; power.

Try whether leaves of trees, swept together,
with some chalk and dung mixed, to give
them more heart, would not make a good
compost. Bacon's Natural History.

He keeps a sabbath of alternate years,
That the spent earth may gather heart again,
And, better'd by cessation, bear the grain.
Dryden's Georg.

Care must be taken not to plow ground out
of heart, because if 'tis in heart, it may be
improved by marl again. Mortimer.

18. Utmost degree.

   This gay charm,
Whose eye beck'd forth my wars, and call'd
   thee home,
Whose bosom was my crownet, my chief end,
Like a right gipsy, hath, at fast and loose,
Beguil'd me to the very heart of loss.
Shakespeare.

19. Life. *For my heart seems sometimes*
   to signify, *if life was at stake;* and
   sometimes *for tenderness.*

I bid the rascal knock upon your gate,
And could not get him for my heart to do it.
Shakespeare.

   I gave it to a youth,
A prating boy, that begg'd it as a fee:
I could not for my heart deny it him.
Shakes. Mer. of Venice.

Profoundly skill'd in the black art,
As English Merlin for his heart.
Hudibras, p. i.

20. It is much used in composition for
   mind, or affection.

heart-breaker n.s. A cant name for a
woman's curls, supposed to break the heart
of all her lovers.

Like Sampson's heartbreakers, it grew
In time to make a nation rue. Hudibras, p. i.

heart-burning n.s. [*heart* and *burn*.]

1. Pain at the stomach, commonly from an
   acrid humour.

Fine clean chalk is one of the most noble
absorbents, and powerfully corrects and
subdues the acrid humours in the stomach:
this property renders it very serviceable in
the cardialgia, or heart-burning. Woodward
on Fossils.

2. Discontent; secret enmity.

In great changes, when right of inheritance is
broke, there will remain much heart-burning
and discontent among the meaner people.
Swift to Pope.

héathen n.s. [*heyden*, German.] The
gentiles; the pagans; the nations
unacquainted with the covenant of grace.

Deliver us from the heathen, that we may
give thanks to thy holy name.
1 Chro. xvi. 35.

If the opinions of others, whom we think well
of, be a ground of assent, men have reason to
be heathens in Japan, mahometans in Turkey,
papists in Spain, and protestants in England.
Locke.

In a paper of morality, I consider how I may
recommend the particular virtues I treat of,
by the precepts or examples of the ancient
heathens. Addison's Spectator.

héaven n.s. [*heofon*, which seems to be
derived from *heofd*, the places over head,
Saxon.]

1. The regions above; the expanse of
   the sky.

A station like the herald Mercury,
New lighted on a heaven kissing hill.
Shakes. Hamlet.

   Thy race in time to come
Shall spread the conquests of imperial Rome;
Rome, whose ascending tow'rs shall
   heav'n invade,
Involving earth and ocean in her shade.
Dryden's Æn.

*The words are taken more properly for the air
and ether than for the heavens, as the best
Hebrecians understand them.* Raleigh's
History of the World.

*This act, with shouts heav'n high, the
  friendly band
Applaud.* Dryden's Fables.

2. The habitation of God, good angels,
 and pure souls departed.

 *It is a knell
That summons thee to heaven, or to hell.*
Shakes. Macbeth.

 *These, the late
Heav'n banish'd host, left desert utmost hell.*
Milton.

 *All yet left of that revolted rout,
Heav'n fall'n, in station stood, or just array,
Sublime with expectation.* Milton's Paradise
Lost, b. x.

3. The supreme power; the sovereign
 of heaven.

Now heav'n help him! Shakespeare's
King Lear.

 *The will
And high permission of all-ruling heav'n
Left him at large.* Milton.

*The prophets were taught to know the will of
God, and thereby instruct the people, and
enabled to prophesy, as a testimony of their
being sent by heaven.* Temple.

4. The pagan gods; the celestials.

 *Our brows
No more obey the heavens than our courtiers.*
Shak. Cymbel.

 *Take physick, pomp;
Expose thyself to feel what wretches feel,
That thou may'st shake the superflux to them,
And show the heavens more just.* Shakes.
King Lear.

 *They can judge as fitly of his worth,
As I can of those mysteries which heaven
Will not have earth to know.* Shakespeare's
Coriolanus.

*Heav'ns! what a spring was in his arm,
  to throw!
How high he held his shield, and rose at
  ev'ry blow.* Dryd.

5. Elevation; sublimity.

*O, for a muse of fire, that would ascend
The brightest heav'n of invention.* Shakesp.
Henry V. Prol.

6. It is often used in composition.

hébdomad n.s. [*hebdomas*, Latin.] A week;
a space of seven days.

*Computing by the medical month, the first
hebdomad or septenary consists of six days,
seventeen hours and a half.* Brown.

to hebétate v.a. [*hebeto*, Latin; *hebeter*,
French.] To dull; to blunt; to stupify.

*The eye, especially if hebetated, might cause
the same perception.* Harvey on
Consumptions.

*Beef may confer a robustness on the limbs
of my son, but will hebetate and clog his
intellectuals.* Arb. and Pope's M. Scrib.

Hébraism n.s. [*hebraisme*, French;
hebraismus, Latin.] A Hebrew idiom.

*Milton has infused a great many Latinisms,
as well as Græcisms, and sometimes
Hebraisms, into his poem.* Spectator.

hécatomb n.s. [*hecatombe*, French;
εκατομβη.] A sacrifice of an hundred
cattle.

 *In rich mens homes
I bid kill some beasts, but no hecatombs;
None starve, none surfeit so.* Donne.

*One of these three is a whole hecatomb,
And therefore only one of them shall die.*
Dryden.

*Her triumphant sons in war succeed,
And slaughter'd hecatombs around 'em bleed.*
Addison.

héctor n.s. [from the name of Hector,
the great Homeric warriour.] A bully;
a blustering, turbulent, pervicacious,
noisy fellow.

Those usurping hectors, who pretend to
honour without religion, think the charge of
a lye a blot not to be washed out but by blood.
South's Sermons.

We'll take one cooling cup of nectar,
And drink to this celestial hector. Prior.

hederáceous adj. [*hederaceus*, Lat.]
Producing ivy. Dict.

hedge-pig n.s. [*hedge* and *pig*.] A young
hedge-hog.

Thrice the brinded cat hath mew'd,
Thrice and once the hedge-pig whin'd.
Shakes. Macbeth.

Hégira n.s. [Arabick.] A term in
chronology, signifying the epocha, or
account of time, used by the Arabians and
Turks, who begin their computation from
the day that Mahomet was forced to make
his escape from the city of Mecca, which
happened on Friday July 16, A.D. 622,
under the reign of the emperor Heracleus.
Harris.

hélioscope *n. s.* [*helioscope*, Fr. ηλιος and
σκοπεω.] A sort of telescope fitted so as to
look on the body of the sun, without
offence to the eyes. Harris.

héliotrope n.s. [ηλιος and τρεπω;
heliotrope, French; *heliotropium*, Latin.] A
plant that turns towards the sun; but more
particularly the turnsol, or sun-flower.

'Tis a common observation of flatterers, that
they are like the heliotrope; they open only
towards the sun, but shut and contract
themselves at night, and in cloudy weather.
Government of the Tongue.

hell n.s. [*helle*, Saxon.]

1. The place of the devil and wicked souls.

  For it is a knell
That summons thee to heaven, or to hell.
Shakes. Macbeth.

If a man were a porter of hell gates, he should
have old turning the key. Shakespeare's
Macbeth.

  Let none admire
That riches grow in hell; that soil may best
Deserve the precious bane. Milton.

Hell's black tyrant trembled to behold
The glorious light he forfeited of old. Cowley.

2. The place of separate souls, whether
  good or bad.

I will go down to my son mourning to hell.
Gen. vi. 35.

He descended into hell. Apostles Creed.

3. Temporal death.

The pains of hell came about me; the snares of
death overtook me. Psalm xviii. 4.

4. The place at a running play to which
  those who are caught are carried.

Then couples three be straight allotted there;
They of both ends the middle two do fly;
The two that in mid-place, hell called were,
Must strive with waiting foot, and
* watching eye,*
To catch of them, and them to hell to bear,
That they, as well as they, hell may supply.
Sidney.

5. The place into which the taylor throws
  his shreds.

This trusty squire, he had, as well
As the bold Trojan knight, seen hell;
Not with a counterfeited pass
Of golden bough, but true gold lace.
Hudibras, p. i.

In Covent-garden did a taylor dwell,
Who might deserve a place in his own hell.
King's Cookery.

6. The infernal powers.

Much danger first, much did he sustain,
While Saul and hell crost his strong fate
* in vain.* Cowley.

7. It is used in composition by the old
  writers more than by the modern.

Héllenism n.s. [ελληνισμος.] An idiom of
the Greek. Ainsworth.

helmínthick adj. [from ελμινθος.]
Relating to worms. Dict.

helter-skelter adv. [As Skinner fancies,
from *heolster sceado*, the darkness of hell;
hell, says he, being a place of confusion.] In
a hurry; without order; tumultuously.

Sir John, I am thy Pistol, and thy friend;
And helter-skelter have I rode to England,
And tidings do I bring. Shakespeare's Henry V.

He had no sooner turned his back but they
were at it helter-skelter, throwing books at one
another's heads. L'Estrange.

hémorrhoids n.s. [αιμορροιδες; *hemorrhoids*, French.] The piles; the emrods.

I got the hemorrhoids. Swift.

heptacápsular adj. [επτα and *capsula*.] Having seven cavities or cells.

herbéscent adj. [*herbescens*, Latin.] Growing into herbs.

héresiarch n.s. [*heresiarque*, French; αιρεσις and αρχη.] A leader in heresy; the head of a herd of hereticks.

The pope declared him not only an heretick, but an heresiarch. Stillingfleet.

héresy n.s. [*heresie*, French; *hæresis*, Latin; αιρεσις.] An opinion of private men different from that of the catholick and orthodox church.

Heresy prevaileth only by a counterfeit shew of reason, whereby notwithstanding it becometh invincible, unless it be convicted of fraud by manifest remonstrance clearly true, and unable to be withstood. Hooker, b. iii.

As for speculative heresies, they work mightily upon mens wits; yet they do not produce any great alterations in states. Bacon, Essay 59.

Let the truth of that religion I profess be represented to her judgment, not in the odious disguises of levity, schism, heresy, novelty, cruelty, and disloyalty. King Charles.

hermáphrodite n.s. [*hermaphrodite*, French, from ερμης and αφροδιτη.] An animal uniting two sexes.

Man and wife make but one right
Canonical hermaphrodite. Cleaveland.

Monstrosity could not incapacitate from marriage, witness hermaphrodites. Arbuthn. and Pope's Mart. Scrib.

hermétical, hermétick adj. [from *Hermes*, or Mercury, the imagined inventer of chymistry; *hermetique*, French.] Chymical.

An hermetical seal, or to seal any thing hermetically, is to heat the neck of a glass 'till it is just ready to melt, and then with a pair of hot pincers to twist it close together. Quincy.

The tube was closed at one end with diachylon, instead of an hermetical seal. Boyle.

héro n.s. [*heros*, Latin; ηρως.]

1. A man eminent for bravery.

In which were held, by sad decease,
Heroes and heroesses. Chapman's Odyssey.

I sing of heroes and of kings,
In mighty numbers mighty things. Cowley.

Heroes in animated marble frown. Pope.

In this view he ceases to be an hero, and his return is no longer a virtue. Pope's Odyssey, Notes.

These are thy honours, not that here thy bust
Is mix'd with heroes, or with kings thy dust. Pope.

   Heroes, kings,
Joy thy wish'd approach to see. Welsted.

2. A man of the highest class in any respect.

hérpes n.s. [ερπις.] A cutaneous inflammation of two kinds: miliaris, or pistularis, which is like millet-seed upon the skin; and exedens, which is more corrosive and penetrating, so as to form little ulcers, if not timely taken care of. Quincy.

A farther progress towards acrimony maketh a herpes; and, if the access of acrimony be very great, it maketh an herpes exedens. Wiseman's Surgery.

héterodox adj. [*heterodoxe*, French; ετερος and δοξα.] Deviating from the established opinion; not orthodox.

Partiality may be observed in some to vulgar, in others to heterodox tenets. Locke.

hexástick n.s. [εξ and στιχος.] A poem of six lines.

hiccius doccius n.s. [corrupted, I fancy, from *hic est doctus*, this *or* here is the learned man. Used by jugglers of themselves.] A cant word for a juggler; one that plays fast and loose.

An old dull sot, who told the clock
For many years at Bridewell dock,
At Westminster and Hicks's hall,
And hiccius doccius play'd in all;
Where, in all governments and times,
H' had been both friend and foe to crimes.
Hudibras, p. iii.

to híccough v.n. [from the noun.] To sob with convulsion of the stomach.

hide and seek n.s. A play in which some hide themselves, and another seeks them.

The boys and girls would venture to come and play at hide and seek in my hair. Gulliver's Travels.

híerarchy n.s. [*hierarchie*, French, from *hierarch*.]

1. A sacred government; rank or subordination of holy beings.

Out of the hierarchies of angels sheen,
The gentle Gabriel call'd he from the rest.
Fairfax, b. i.

He rounds the air, and breaks the hymnick notes
In birds, heav'n's choristers, organick throats;
Which, if they did not die, might seem to be
A tenth rank in the heavenly hierarchy.
Donne.

These the supreme king
Exalted to such pow'r, and gave to rule,
Each in his hierarchy, the orders bright.
Milton's Par. Lost.

Jehova, from the summit of the sky,
Environ'd with his winged hierarchy,
The world survey'd. Sandys.

The blessedest of mortal wights, now questionless the highest saint in the celestial hierarchy, began to be so importuned, that a great part of the divine liturgy was addressed solely to her. Howel's Vocal Forest.

2. Ecclesiastical establishment.

The presbytery had more sympathy with the discipline of Scotland than the hierarchy of England. Bacon.

While the old levitical hierarchy continued, it was part of the ministerial office to slay the sacrifices. South.

Consider what I have written, from regard for the church established under the hierarchy of bishops. Swift.

hieroglyph, hieroglyphick n.s. [*hieroglyphe*, French; ιερος, sacred, and γλυφω, to carve.]

1. An emblem; a figure by which a word was implied. Hieroglyphicks were used before the alphabet was invented.[†]

This hieroglyphick of the Egyptians was erected for parental affection, manifested in the protection of her young ones, when her nest was set on fire. Brown's Vulgar Errours.

A lamp amongst the Egyptians is the hieroglyphick of life. Wilkins's Dædalus.

The first writing they used was only the single pictures and gravings of the things they would represent, which way of expression was afterwards called hieroglyphick. Woodward.

Between the statues obelisks were plac'd,
And the learn'd walls with hieroglyphicks grac'd. Pope.

2. The art of writing in picture.

No brute can endure the taste of strong liquor, and consequently it is against all the rules of hieroglyph to assign those animals as patrons of punch. Swift.

híerophant n.s. [ιεροφαντης.] One who teaches rules of religion; a priest.

Herein the wantonness of poets, and the crafts of their heathenish priests and hierophants, abundantly gratified the fancies of the people. Hales's Origin of Mankind.

to híggle v.n. [of uncertain etymology; probably corrupted from *haggle*.]

1. To chaffer; to be penurious in a bargain.

*In good offices and due retributions we may
not be pinching and niggardly: it argues an
ignoble mind, where we have wronged, to
higgle and dodge in the amends.* Hale.

   Base thou art!
To higgle thus for a few blows,
To gain thy knight an op'lent spouse.
Hudibras, p. ii.

*Why all this higgling with thy friend about
such a paultry sum? Does this become the
generosity of the noble and rich John Bull?*
Arbuthnot's History of John Bull.

2. To go selling provisions from door to
door. This seems the original meaning.

higgledy-piggeldy adv. A cant word,
corrupted from *higgle*, which denotes any
confused mass, as higglers carry a huddle of
provisions together.

high-flier n.s. One that carries his opinions
to extravagance.

*She openly professeth herself to be a high-flier;
and it is not improbable she may also be a
papist at heart.* Swift.

high-víced Enormously wicked.

*Be as a planetary plague, when Jove
Will o'er some high-vic'd city hang his poison
In the sick air.* Shakespeare's Timon of
Athens.

híghwayman n.s. [*highway* and *man.*] A
robber that plunders on the publick roads.

*'Tis like the friendship of pickpockets and
highwaymen, that observe strict justice among
themselves.* Bentley's Sermons.

*A remedy like that of giving my money to an
highwayman before he attempts to take it by
force, to prevent the sin of robbery.* Swift.

hip, hippish adj. A corruption of
hypochondriack. Ainsworth.

hippópotamus n.s. [ιππος and ποταμος.]
The river horse. An animal found in the
Nile.

híreling n.s. [from *hire.*]

1. One who serves for wages.

*The hireling longs to see the shades ascend,
That with the tedious day his toil might end,
And he his pay receive.* Sandys.

*In the framing of Hiero's ship there were three
hundred carpenters employed for a year,
besides many other hirelings for carriages.*
Wilkins's Dædalus.

*'Tis frequent here to see a freeborn son
On the left hand of a rich hireling run.*
Dryd. Juvenal.

2. A mercenary; a prostitute.

*Now she shades thy evening walk with bays,
No hireling she, no prostitute to praise.* Pope.

history n.s. [ιστορια; *historia,* Latin;
histoire, French.]

1. A narration of events and facts delivered
with dignity.

*Justly Cæsar scorns the poet's lays;
It is to history he trusts for praise.* Pope.

2. Narration; relation.

The history part lay within a little room.
Wiseman's Surgery.

*What histories of toil could I declare?
But still long-weary'd nature wants repair.*
Pope's Odyssey.

3. The knowledge of facts and events.

*History, so far as it relates to the affairs
of the Bible, is necessary to divines.*
Watts's Improvement of the Mind.

histriónical, histriónick adj. [from *histrio,*
Latin; *histrion,* Fr.] Befitting the stage;
suitable to a player; becoming a buffoon;
theatrical.

hóary adj. [*har, harung,* Saxon.] See *hoar.*

1. White; whitish.

*Thus she rested on her arm reclin'd,
The hoary willows waving with the wind.*
Addison.

2. White or grey with age.

*A comely palmer, clad in black attire,
Of ripest years, and hairs all hoary grey.*
Spenser.

*Solyman, marvelling at the courage and
majesty of the hoary old prince in his so great
extremity, dismissed him, and sent him again
into the city.* Knolles's History of the Turks.

Has then my hoary head deserv'd no better?
Rowe.

Then in full age, and hoary holiness,
Retire, great preacher, to thy promis'd bliss.
Prior.

3. White with frost.

Through this distemperature we see
The seasons alter; hoary headed frosts
Fall in the fresh lap of the crimson rose.
Shakespeare.

4. Mouldy; mossy; rusty.

There was brought out of the city into the
camp very coarse, hoary, moulded bread.
Knolles's History of the Turks.

hóbit n.s. A small mortar to shoot little bombs.

hocus pocus [The original of this word is referred by Tillotson to a form of the Romish church. Junius derives it from *hocced*, Welsh, a cheat, and *poke* or *pocus*, a bag, jugglers using a bag for conveyance. It is corrupted from some words that had once a meaning, and which perhaps cannot be discovered.]† A juggle; a cheat.

This gift of hocus pocussing, and of disguising matters, is surprising. L'Estrange.

hod n.s. [corrupted perhaps in contempt from *hood*, a hod being carried on the head.] A kind of trough in which a labourer carries mortar to the masons.

A fork and a hook to be tampering in clay,
A lath, hammer, trowel, a hod or a tray.
Tuss. Husband.

hodge-podge n.s. [*hach poch, hochepot*, quasi *hachis en pot*, French.] A medley of ingredients boiled together.

They have made our English tongue a gallimaufrey, or hodge-podge of all other speeches. Spenser.

It produces excellent corn, whereof the Turks make their trachana and bouhourt, a certain hodge-podge of sundry ingredients. Sandys's Travels.

hodiérnal adj. [*hodiernus*, Latin.] Of to-day.

hóiden n.s. [*hoeden*, Welsh; *fœmina levioris famæ*, Latin.] An ill-taught awkward country girl.

to hóiden v.n. [from the noun.] To romp indecently.

Some of them would get a scratch; but we always discovered, upon examining, that they had been hoidening with the young apprentices. Swift.

hólland n.s. Fine linen made in Holland.

Some for the pride of Turkish courts design'd,
For folded turbants finest holland bear.
Dryden.

hólocaust n.s. [ολος and καιω.] A burnt sacrifice; a sacrifice of which the whole was consumed by fire, and nothing retained by the offerer.

Isaac carried the wood for the sacrifice, which being an holocaust, or burnt offering, to be consumed unto ashes, we cannot well conceive a burthen for a boy. Brown's Vulg. Err.

Let the eye behold no evil thing, and it is made a sacrifice; let the tongue speak no filthy word, and it becomes an oblation; let the hand do no unlawful action, and you render it a holocaust. Ray on the Creation.

Eumenes cut a piece from every part of the victim, and by this he made it an holocaust, or an entire sacrifice. Broome.

hólograph n.s. [ολος and γραφω.] This word is used in the Scottish law to denote a deed written altogether by the granter's own hand.

hóly adj. [*halig*, Saxon; *heyligh*, Dutch, from *hal*, healthy, or in a state of salvation.]

1. Good; pious; religious.

See where his grace stands 'tween two clergymen!
And see a book of prayer in his hand,
True ornaments to know a holy man.
Shakesp. Rich. III.

   Doubtless
With joy he will embrace you; for he's honourable,
And, doubling that, most holy. Shakes.
Cymbeline.

2. Hallowed; consecrated to divine use.

State, holy or unhallow'd, what of that?
Shak. Hen. VI.

Bare was his hoary head; one holy hand
Held forth his laurel crown, and one his
   sceptre. Dryden.

3. Pure; immaculate.

Common sense could tell them, that the good
God could not be pleased with any thing cruel;
nor the most holy God with any thing filthy
and unclean. South's Sermons.

4. Sacred.

An evil soul producing holy witness,
Is like a villain with a smiling cheek.
Shak. Merch. of Ven.

He has deserv'd it, were it carbuncled
Like holy Phœbus' car. Shakespeare's
Ant. and Cleopatra.

homónymous adj. [*homonyme*, Fr.
ομωνυμος.] Denominating different
things; equivocal; ambiguous.

As words signifying the same thing are called
synonymous, so equivocal words, or those
which signify several things, are called
homonymous, or ambiguous; and when
persons use such ambiguous words, with a
design to deceive, it is called equivocation.
Watts's Logick.

hóney-moon n.s. [*honey* and *moon*.] The
first month after marriage, when there is
nothing but tenderness and pleasure.

A man should keep his finery for the latter
season of marriage, and not begin to dress 'till
the honey-moon is over. Addis.

hónour n.s. [*honeur*, French; *honor*, Latin.]

1. Dignity; high rank.

2. Reputation; fame.

A man is an ill husband of his honour, that
entereth into any action, the failing wherein
may disgrace him more than the carrying of it
through can honour him. Bacon's Essays.

3. The title of a man of rank.

   Return unto thy lord,
Bid him not fear the separated councils:

His honour and myself are at the one;
And at the other is my good friend Catesby.
Shakes. R. III.

4. Subject of praise.

   Thou happy father,
Think that the clearest gods, who make
   them honours
Of man's impossibilities, have preserv'd thee.
Shakesp.

5. Nobleness of mind; scorn of meanness;
   magnanimity.

Now shall I see thy love; what motive may
Be stronger with thee than the name of wife?
—That which upholdeth him, that thee upholds,
His honour. Oh, thine honour, Lewis; thine
   honour. Shak.

If by honour is meant any thing distinct
from conscience, 'tis no more than a regard
to the censure and esteem of the world.
Rogers's Sermons.

6. Reverence; due veneration.

   They take thee for their mother,
And every day do honour to thy grave.
Shakes. Cymbeline.

   There, my lord,
The high promotion of his grace of Canterbury,
Who holds his state at door, 'mongst pursuivants.
—Ha! 'tis he, indeed!
Is this the honour they do one another?
Shakesp. Hen. VIII.

This is a duty in the fifth commandment,
required towards our prince and our parent,
under the name of honour; a respect, which, in
the notion of it, implies a mixture of love and
fear, and, in the object, equally supposes
goodness and power. Rogers's Sermons.

7. Chastity.

   Be she honour flaw'd,
I have three daughters, the eldest is eleven;
If this prove true, they'll pay for 't.
Shak. Winter's Tale.

She dwells so securely on the excellency of her
honour, that the folly of my soul dares not
prevent itself: she is too bright to be looked
against. Shakesp. Merry Wives of Windsor.

8. Dignity of mien.

Two of far nobler shape, erect and tall,
Godlike erect! with native honour clad,
In naked majesty, seem'd lords of all.
Milton's Parad Lost.

9. Glory; boast.

A late eminent person, the honour of his
profession for integrity and learning. Burnet's
Theory of the Earth.

10. Publick mark of respect.

He saw his friends, who whelm'd beneath
  the waves,
Their fun'ral honours claim'd, and ask'd their
  quiet graves. Dryden's Æn. b. vi.

Such discourses, on such mournful occasions as
these, were instituted not so much in honour
of the dead, as for the use of the living.
Atterbury's Sermons.

Numbers engage their lives and labours, some
to heap together a little dirt that shall bury
them in the end; others to gain an honour,
that, at best, can be celebrated but by an
inconsiderable part of the world, and is envied
and calumniated by more than 'tis truly
given. Wake's Preparation for Death.

11. Privileges of rank or birth.

Henry the seventh, truly pitying
My father's loss, like a most royal prince,
Restor'd to me my honours; and, from ruins,
Made my name once more noble. Shakesp.
Henry VIII.

12. Civilities paid.

Then here a slave, or if you will a lord,
To do the honours, and to give the word.
Pope's Horace.

13. Ornament; decoration.

The sire then shook the honours of his head,
And from his brows damps of oblivion shed.
Dryden.

My hand to thee, my honour on my promise.
Shakesp.

hope n.s. [*hopa*, Saxon; *hope*, Dutch.]

1. Expectation of some good; an
   expectation indulged with pleasure.

There is hope of a tree, if cut down, that it
will sprout again. Job xiv. 7.

Hope is that pleasure in the mind which every
one finds in himself, upon the thought of a
profitable future enjoyment of a thing, which
is apt to delight him. Locke.

When in heav'n she shall his essence see,
This is her sov'reign good, and perfect bliss;
Her longing, wishings, hopes, all finish'd be;
Her joys are full, her motions rest in this.
Davies.

Sweet hope! kind cheat! fair fallacy! by thee
We are not where or what we be;
But what and where we would be: thus art thou
Our absent presence, and our future now.
Crashaw.

Faith is opposed to infidelity, and hope to
despair. Taylor.

He sought them both, but wish'd his hap
  might find
Eve separate: he wish'd, but not with hope
Of what so seldom chanc'd: when to his wish,
Beyond his hope, Eve separate he spies.
Milton's Parad. Lost.

   The Trojan dames
To Pallas' fane in long procession go,
In hopes to reconcile their heav'nly foe.
Dryden's Virg. Æn.

Why not comfort myself with the hope of what
may be, as torment myself with the fear on 't?
L'Estrange.

To encourage our hopes it gives us the highest
assurance of most lasting happiness, in case of
obedience. Tillotson.

The deceased really lived like one that had his
hope in another life; a life which he hath now
entered upon, having exchanged hope for
sight, desire for enjoyment. Atterbury.

Young men look rather to the past age than
the present, and therefore the future may have
some hopes of them. Swift.

2. Confidence in a future event, or in the
   future conduct of any body.

It is good, being put to death by men, to look
for hope from God, to be raised up again by
him. 2 Mac. vii. 14.

Blessed is he who is not fallen from his hope in the Lord. Ecclus. xiv. 2.

    I had hope of France,
Ev'n as I have of fertile England's soil.
Shakes. Henry VI.

3. That which gives hope; that on which the hopes are fixed, as an agent by which something desired may be effected.

I might see from far some forty truncheoneers draw to her succour, which were the hope of the Strand, where she was quarter'd. Shakespeare's Henry VIII.

4. The object of hope.

Thy mother felt more than a mother's pain,
And yet brought forth less than a mother's hope;
To wit, an indigested deform'd lump. Shakes. Henry VI.

She was his care, his hope, and his delight,
Most in his thought, and ever in his sight.
Dryden.

to hope v.n. [from the noun.]

1. To live in expectation of some good.

Hope for good success, according to the efficacy of the causes and the instrument; and let the husbandman hope for a good harvest. Taylor's Rule of living holy.

    My muse, by storms long tost,
Is thrown upon your hospitable coast;
And finds more favour by her ill success,
Than she could hope for by her happiness.
Dryden.

Who knows what adverse fortune may befall!
Arm well your mind, hope little, and fear all.
Dryden.

2. To place confidence in futurity.

He shall strengthen your heart, all ye that hope in the Lord. Ps. xxxi. 24.

hóral adj. [from *hora*, Latin.] Relating to the hour.

Howe'er reduc'd and plain,
The watch would still a watch remain;
But if the horal orbit ceases,
The whole stands still, or breaks to pieces.
Prior.

hórologe, hórology n.s. [*horologium*, Latin.] Any instrument that tells the hour: as a clock; a watch; an hourglass.

'Tis evermore the prologue to his sleep;
He'll watch the horologe a double set,
If drink rock not his cradle. Shakespeare's Othello.

Before the days of Jerome there were horologies, that measured the hours not only by drops of water in glasses, called clepsydra, but also by sand in glasses, called clepsammia. Brown.

hóroscope n.s. [*horoscope*, French; ωροσκοπος.] The configuration of the planets at the hour of birth.

How unlikely is it, that the many almost numberless conjunctions of stars, which occur in the progress of a man's life, should not match and countervail that one horoscope or conjunction which is found at his birth? Drummond.

A proportion of the horoscope unto the seventh house, or opposite signs every seventh year, oppresseth living natures. Bro.

Him born beneath a boding horoscope,
His sire, the blear-ey'd Vulcan of a shop,
From Mars his forge sent to Minerva's school.
Dryd. Juven.

The Greek names this the horoscope;
This governs life, and this marks out our parts,
Our humours, manners, qualities and arts.
Creech's Manil.

They understood the planets and the zodiack by instinct, and fell to drawing schemes of their own horoscopes in the same dust they sprung out of. Bentley's Sermons.

horrísonous adj. [*horrisonus*, Latin.] Sounding dreadfully. Dict.

hórtatory adj. [from *hortor*, Latin.] Encouraging; animating; advising to any thing: used of precepts, not of persons; a hortatory speech, not a hortatory speaker.

hóspital n.s. [*hospital*, French; *hospitalis*, Latin.]

1. A place built for the reception of the sick, or support of the poor.

They who were so careful to bestow them in a college when they were young, would be so good as to provide for them in some hospital when they are old. Wotton.

I am about to build an hospital, which I will endow handsomely for twelve old husbandmen. Addison's Spectator.

2. A place for shelter or entertainment.

They spy'd a goodly castle, plac'd
Foreby a river in a pleasant dale,
Which chusing for that evening's hospital,
They thither march'd. Fairy Queen, b. ii.

hotcóckles n.s. [*hautes coquilles*, French.] A play in which one covers his eyes, and guesses who strikes him.

The chytindra is certainly not our hotcockles; for that was by pinching, not by striking. Arbuthn. and Pope's Mar. Scribl.

As at hotcockles once I laid me down,
And felt the weighty hand of many a clown,
Buxoma gave a gentle tap, and I
Quick rose, and read soft mischief in her eye. Gay's Past.

hóthouse n.s. [*hot* and *house*.]

1. A bagnio; a place to sweat and cup in.

Now she professes a hothouse, which,
I think, is a very ill house too. Shak.
Measure for Measure.

2. A brothel.

Where lately harbour'd many a famous whore,
A purging bill, now fix'd upon the door,
Tells you it is a hothouse; so it may,
And still be a whorehouse: th' are synonyma. Ben. Johnson.

hóusewife n.s. [*house* and *wife*. This is now frequently written *huswife*, or *hussy*.]

1. The mistress of a family.

You will think it unfit for a good housewife to stir in or to busy herself about her housewifry. Spenser on Ireland.

I have room enough, but the kind and hearty housewife is dead. Pope to Swift.

2. A female œconomist.

Fitting is a mantle for a bad man, and surely for a bad housewife it is no less convenient; for some of them, that be wandering women, it is half a wardrobe. Spenser on Ireland.

Let us sit and mock the good housewife, fortune, from her wheel, that her gifts may henceforth be disposed equally. Shak.

Farmers in degree,
He a good husband, a good housewife she. Dryden.

Early housewives leave the bed,
When living embers on the hearth are spread. Dryden.

The fairest among the daughters of Britain shew themselves good stateswomen as well as good housewives. Addis. Freehold.

3. One skilled in female business.

He was bred up under the tuition of a tender mother, 'till she made him as good an housewife as herself: he could preserve apricocks, and make jellies. Addison's Spectator.

húggermugger n.s. [corrupted perhaps from *hug er morcker*, or hug in the dark. *Morcker* in Danish is darkness, whence our *murky*. It is written by Sir Thomas More, *hoker moker. Hoker*, in Chaucer, is peevish, crossgrained, of which *moker* may be only a ludicrous reduplication. *Hooke* is likewise in German *a corner*, and *moky* is in English *dark*. I know not how to determine.] Secrecy; bye-place.†

Now hold in huggermugger in their hand,
And all the rest do rob of goods and land. Hubberd's Tale.

But if I can but find them out,
Where e'er th' in huggermugger lurk,
I'll make them rue their handy-work. Hudibras, p. i.

There's a distinction betwixt what's done openly and bare-faced, and a thing that's done in huggermugger, under a seal of secrecy and concealment. L'Estrange's Fables.

húmanist n.s. [*humaniste*, French.] A philologer; a grammarian.

húmblebee n.s. [*hum* and *bee*.] A buzzing wild bee.

The honeybags steal from the humblebees,
And for night-tapers crop their waxen thighs.
Shakespeare.

This puts us in mind once again of the
humblebees and the tinderboxes. Atterbury.

humicubátion n.s. [*humi* and *cubo*, Latin.] The act of lying on the ground.

Fasting and sackcloth, and ashes and tears,
and humicubations, used to be companions
of repentance. Bramhall.

húmmer n.s. [from *hum*.] An applauder. Ainsworth.

húmorist n.s. [*humoristo*, Italian; *humoriste*, French.]

1. One who conducts himself by his own fancy; one who gratifies his own humour.

The wit sinks imperceptibly into an humorist.
Spectator.

The notion of a humorist is one that is greatly
pleased, or greatly displeased, with little
things; his actions seldom directed by the
reason and nature of things. Watts's Logick.

This humorist keeps to himself much more
than he wants, and gives a vast refuse
of his superfluities to purchase heaven.
Addison's Spectator.

2. One who has violent and peculiar passions.

By a wise and timous inquisition the peccant
humours and humorists must be discovered
and purged, or cut off: mercy, in such a case,
in a king, is true cruelty. Bacon to Villiers.

húmorous adj. [from *humour*.]

1. Full of grotesque or odd images.

Some of the commentators tell us, that Marsya
was a lawyer who had lost his cause; others
that this passage alludes to the story of the
satire Marsyas, who contended with Apollo,
which I think is more humorous. Addison
on Italy.

Thy humorous vein, thy pleasing folly,
Lies all neglected, all forgot;

And pensive, wav'ring, melancholy,
Thou dread'st and hop'st thou know'st not
  what. Prior.

2. Capricious; irregular; without any rule but the present whim.

I am known to be a humorous patrician; said
to be something imperfect, in favouring the
first complaint; hasty and tinder-like, upon
too trivial motion. Shakesp. Coriolanus.

Thou fortune's champion, that do'st never fight
But when her humorous ladyship is by,
To teach thee safety. Shakesp. King John.

He's humorous as Winter, and as sudden
As flaws congeal'd in the spring of day.
Shakesp. Hen. IV.

O, you awake then: come away,
Times be short, are made for play;
The humorous moon too will not stay:
What doth make you thus delay?
Ben. Johnson.

Vast is his courage, boundless is his mind,
Rough as a storm, and humorous as the wind.
Dryden.

He that would learn to pass a just sentence
on persons and things, must take heed of a
fanciful temper of mind, and an humorous
conduct in his affairs. Watts's Logick.

3. Pleasant; jocular. Ainsworth.

húmour n.s. [*humeur*, French; *humor*, Latin.]

1. Moisture.

The aqueous humour of the eye will not
freeze, which is very admirable, seeing it hath
the perspicuity and fluidity of common water.
Ray on the Creation.

2. The different kind of moisture in man's body, reckoned by the old physicians to be phlegm, blood, choler, and melancholy, which, as they predominated, were supposed to determine the temper of mind.

Believe not these suggestions, which proceed
From anguish of the mind, and humours black,
That mingle with thy fancy. Milton's
Agonistes.

3. General turn or temper of mind.

As there is no humour, to which impudent poverty cannot make itself serviceable; so were there enow of those of desperate ambition, who would build their houses upon others ruin. Sidney, b. ii.

There came with her a young lord, led hither with the humour of youth, which ever thinks that good whose goodness he sees not. Sidney.

King James, as he was a prince of great judgment, so he was a prince of a marvellous pleasant humour: as he was going through Lusen by Greenwich, he asked what town it was; they said Lusen. He asked, a good while after, what town is this we are now in? They said still it was Lusen: said the king, I will be king of Lusen. Bacon's Apophthegms.

Examine how your humour is inclin'd,
And which the ruling passion of your mind. Roscommon.

They, who were acquainted with him, know his humour to be such, that he would never constrain himself. Dryden.

In cases where it is necessary to make examples, it is the humour of the multitude to forget the crime, and to remember the punishment. Addison's Freeholder.

Good humour only teaches charms to last,
Still makes new conquests, and maintains
    the past. Pope.

4. Present disposition.

It is the curse of kings to be attended
By slaves, that take their humours for a warrant
To break into the blood-house of life. Shakesp. K. John.

Another thought her nobler humour fed. Fairfax, b. ii.

Their humours are not to be won,
But when they are impos'd upon. Hudibras, p. iii.

    Tempt not his heavy hand;
But one submissive word which you let fall,
Will make him in good humour with us all. Dryden.

5. Grotesque imagery; jocularity; merriment.

6. Diseased or morbid disposition.

He was a man frank and generous; when well, denied himself nothing that he had a mind to eat or drink, which gave him a body full of humours, and made his fits of the gout frequent and violent. Temple.

7. Petulance; peevishness.

Is my friend all perfection, all virtue and discretion? Has he not humours to be endured, as well as kindnesses to be enjoyed? South's Sermons.

8. A trick; a practice.

I like not the humour of lying: he hath wronged me in some humours: I should have born the humour'd letter to her. Shakespeare's Merry Wives of Windsor.

9. Caprice; whim; predominant inclination.

In private, men are more bold in their own humours; and in consort, men are more obnoxious to others humours; therefore it is good to take both. Bacon's Essays.

húngerstarved adj. [*hunger* and *starved.*] Starved with hunger; pinched by want of food.

All my followers to th' eager foe
Turn back, and fly like ships before the wind,
Or lambs pursu'd by hungerstarved wolves. Shakesp. H. VI.

O'ertake me, if thou can'st; I scorn thy strength:
Go, go, chear up thy hungerstarved men. Shakesp. H. VI.

As to some holy house th' afflicted came,
Th' hungerstarv'd, the naked, and the lame,
Want and diseases, fled before her name. Dryden.

hunks n.s. [*hunskur*, sordid, Islandick.] A covetous sordid wretch; a miser; a curmudgeon.

The old hunks was well served, to be tricked out of a whole hog for the securing of his puddings. L'Estrange.

She has a husband, a jealous, covetous, old hunks. Dryden.

Irus has given all the intimations of being a close hunks, worth money. Addison's Spectator.

húrly, húrlyburly n.s. [I have been told that this word owes its original to two neighbouring families named *Hurly* and *Burly*, or *Hurleigh* and *Burleigh*, which filled their part of the kingdom with contests and violence. If this account be rejected, the word must be derived from *hurl*, *hurly*, and *burly*, a ludicrous reduplication. *Hurlade*, French; *hurlubrelu*, inconsiderately.] Tumult; commotion; bustle.

Winds take the ruffian billows by the top, That with the hurley death itself awakes. Shakesp. H. IV.

   Poor discontents,
Which gape and rub the elbow at the news Of hurlyburly innovation. Shakes. Henry IV. p. i.

Methinks, I see this hurly all on foot. Shakesp. K. John.

All places were filled with tumult and hurlyburly, every man measured the danger by his own fear; and such a pitiful cry was in every place, as in cities presently to be besieged. Knolles.

húsband n.s. [*hossband*, master, Danish, from *house* and *bonda*, Runick, a master.]

1. The correlative to wife; a man married to a woman.

Thy husband is thy lord, thy life, thy keeper, Thy head, thy sovereign. Shakesp. Taming of the Shrew.

Why, woman, your husband is in his old lunes again: he so takes on yonder with my husband, and so rails against all married mankind. Shakesp. Merry Wives of Windsor.

This careful husband had been long away, Whom his chaste wife and little children mourn. Dryden.

The contract and ceremony of marriage is the occasion of the denomination or relation of husband. Locke.

2. The male of animals.

Ev'n though a snowy ram thou shalt behold, Prefer him not in haste, for husband to thy fold. Dryden.

3. An œconomist; a man that knows and practises the methods of frugality and profit. Its signification is always modified by some epithet implying bad or good.

Edward I. shewed himself a right good husband; owner of a lordship ill husbanded. Davies on Ireland.

I was considering the shortness of life, and what ill husbands we are of so tender a fortune. Collier on Fame.

4. A tiller of the ground; a farmer.

Husband's work is laborious and hard. Hubberd's Tale.

I heard a great husband say, that it was a common error to think that chalk helpeth arable grounds. Bacon's Nat. History.

   In those fields
The painful husband plowing up his ground, Shall find all fret with rust, both pikes and shields. Hakewill.

   If continu'd rain
The lab'ring husband in his house restrain, Let him forecast his work. Dryden's Georgicks.

húshmoney n.s. [*hush* and *money*.] A bribe to hinder information; pay to secure silence.

A dext'rous steward, when his tricks are sound, Hushmoney sends to all the neighbours round; His master, unsuspicious of his pranks, Pays all the cost, and gives the villain thanks. Swift.

hússy n.s. [corrupted from *housewife*: taken in an ill sense.] A sorry or bad woman; a worthless wench. It is often used ludicrously in slight disapprobation.

Get you in, hussy, go: now will I personate this hopeful young jade. Southern's Innocent Adultery.

húswifery n.s. [from *huswife.*]

1. Management good or bad.

Good huswifery trieth
To rise with the cock;
Ill huswifery lyeth
'Till nine of the clock. Tusser.

2. Management of rural business committed to women.

If cheeses in dairie have Argus his eyes,
Tell Cisley the fault in her huswifery lies.
Tuss Husbandry.

hydraulicks n.s. [υδωρ, water, and αυλος, a pipe.] The science of conveying water through pipes or conduits.

hydrocéle n.s. [υδροκηλη; *hydrocele,* Fr.] A watery rupture.

hydrógrapher n.s. [υδωρ and γραφω; *hydrographe,* Fr.] One who draws maps of the sea.

It may be drawn from the writings of our hydrographer. Boyle.

hydromancy n.s. [υδωρ and μαντια; *hydromantie,* Fr.] Prediction by water.

Divination was invented by the Persians: there are four kinds of divination; hydromancy, pyromancy, aeromancy, and geomancy. Ayliffe's Parergon.

hydromel n.s. [υδωρ and μελι; *hydromel,* Fr.] Honey and water.

Hydromel is a drink prepared of honey, being one of the most pleasant and universal drinks the northern part of Europe affords, as well as one of the most ancient. Mortimer's Husb.

In fevers the aliments prescribed by Hippocrates were ptisans and cream of barley; hydromel, that is, honey and water, when there was no tendency to a delirium. Arbuthnot.

hyen, hyéna n.s. [*hyene,* French; *hyæna,* Latin.] An animal like a wolf, said fabulously to imitate human voices.

I will weep when you are disposed to be merry; I will laugh like a hyen, when you are inclined to sleep. Shakespeare.

A wonder more amazing would we find;
The hyena shews it, of a double kind:
Varying the sexes in alternate years,
In one begets, and in another bears.
Dryden's Fables.

The hyena was indeed well joined with the bever, as having also a bag in those parts, if thereby we understand the hyena odorata, or civet cat. Brown's Vulgar Errours.

The keen hyena, fellest of the fell. Thomson's Summer.

hyper n.s. [A word barbarously curtailed by Prior from *hypercritick.*] A hypercritick; one more critical than necessity requires. Prior did not know the meaning of the word.

Criticks I read on other men,
And hypers upon them again. Prior.

hyphen n.s. [υφεν.] A note of conjunction: as, *vir-tue, ever-living.*

hypochondríacal, hypochondríack adj. [*hypocondriaque,* French, from *hypochondres.*]

1. Melancholy; disordered in the imagination.

Socrates laid down his life in attestation of that most fundamental truth, the belief of one God; and yet he's not recorded either as fool or hypochondriack. Decay of Piety.

2. Producing melancholy.

Cold sweats are many times mortal, and always suspected; as in great fears, and hypochondriacal passions, being a relaxation or forsaking of the spirits. Bacon's Nat. History.

hypnótick n.s. [υπνος.] Any medicine that induces sleep.

hypotenúse n.s. [*hypotenuse,* Fr. υποτενουσα.] The line that subtends the right angle of a right-angled triangle; the subtense.

The square of the hypotenuse in a right-angled triangle, is equal to the squares of the two other sides. Locke.

hystérical, hystérick adj. [*hysterique,* French; υστερικος.]

1. Troubled with fits; disordered in the regions of the womb.

In hysterick women the rarity of symptoms doth oft strike such an astonishment into spectators, that they report them possessed with the devil. Harvey on Consumptions.

Many hysterical women are sensible of wind passing from the womb. Floyer on the Humours.

2. Proceeding from disorders in the womb.

Parent of vapours, and of female wit,
Who gave th' hysterick or poetick fit.
Pope's Ra. of the Lock.

This terrible scene made too violent an impression upon a woman in her condition, and threw her into a strong hysterick fit. Arbuthn. and Pope's Mart. Scribl.

I

I, is in English considered both as a vowel and consonant; though, since the vowel and consonant differ in their form as well as sound, they may be more properly accounted two letters.

I vowel has a long sound, as *fine*, *thine*, which is usually marked by an *e* final; and a short sound, as *fin*, *thin*. Prefixed to *e* it makes a diphthong of the same sound with the soft *i*, or double *e*, *ee:* thus *field*, *yield*, are spoken as *feeld*, *yeeld*; except *friend*, which is spoken *frend*. Subjoined to *a* or *e* it makes them long, as *fail*, *neigh*; and to *o* makes a mingled sound, which approaches more nearly to the true notion of a diphthong, or sound composed of the sounds of two vowels, than any other combination of vowels in the English language, as *oil*, *coin*. The sound of *i* before another *i*, and at the end of a word, is always expressed by *y*.

J consonant has invariably the same sound with that of *g* in *giant*; as *jade*, *jet*, *jilt*, *jolt*, *just*.

iámbick n.s. [*iambique*, French; *iambicus*, Latin.] Verses composed of iambick feet, or a short and long syllable alternately: used originaly in satire, therefore taken for satire.

In thy felonious heart though venom lies,
It does but touch thy Irish pen, and dies:
Thy genius calls thee not to purchase fame
In keen iambicks, but mild anagram.
Dryden.

ichnéumon n.s. [ιχνευμων.] A small animal that breaks the eggs of the crocodile.

ícon n.s. [εικων.] A picture or representation.

Boysardus, in his tract of divination, hath set forth the icons of these ten, yet added two others. Brown's Vulg. Err.

Some of our own nation, and many Netherlanders, whose names and icons are published, have deserved good commendation. Hakewill on Providence.

icónoclast n.s. [*iconoclaste*, French; εικονοκλαστης.] A breaker of images.

idéa n.s. [*idée*, French; ιδεα.] Mental imagination.

Whatsoever the mind perceives in itself, or is the immediate object of perception, thought, or understanding, that I call idea. Locke.

The form under which these things appear to the mind, or the result of our apprehension, is called an idea. Watts.

Happy you that may to the saint, your only idea,
Although simply attir'd, your manly affection utter. Sidney.

Our Saviour himself, being to set down the perfect idea of that which we are to pray and wish for on earth, did not teach to pray or wish for more than only that here it might be with us, as with them it is in heaven. Hooker, b. i.

Her sweet idea wander'd through his thoughts. Fairfax.

I did infer your lineaments,
Being the right idea of your father,
Both in your form and nobleness of mind. Shakesp. R. III.

How good, how fair,
Answering his great idea! Milton's Paradise Lost, b. vii.

If Chaucer by the best idea wrought,
The fairest nymph before his eyes he set. Dryden.

idéal adj. [from *idea*.] Mental; intellectual; not perceived by the senses.

There is a two-fold knowledge of material things; one real, when the thing, and the real impression thereof on our senses, is perceived; the other ideal, when the image or idea of a thing, absent in itself, is represented to and considered on the imagination. Cheyne's Phil. Prin.

idiócrasy n.s. [*idiocrase*, French; ιδιος and κρασις.] Peculiarity of constitution.

idiosyncrasy n.s. [*idiosynacrase*, Fr. ιδιος, συν, and κρασις.] A peculiar temper or disposition not common to another. Qui.

Whether quails, from any idiosyncrasy or peculiarity of constitution, do innocuously feed upon hellebore, or rather sometimes but medicinally use the same. Brown's Vulg. Errours.

The understanding also hath its idiosyncrasies, as well as other faculties. Glanv. Sceps. c. 15.

ídiot n.s. [*idiote*, Fr. *idiota*, Latin; ιδιωτης.] A fool; a natural; a changeling; one without the powers of reason.

Life is a tale,
Told by an idiot, full of sound and fury,
Signifying nothing. Shakespeare's Macbeth.

What else doth he herein, than by a kind of circumlocution tell his humble suppliants that he holds them idiots, or base wretches, not able to get relief? Raleigh's Essays.

By idle boys and idiots vilify'd,
Who me and my calamities deride. Sandys.

Many idiots will believe that they see what they only hear. Dennis.

ídiotism n.s. [*idiotisme*, French; ιδιωτισμος.]

1. Peculiarity of expression; mode of expression peculiar to a language.

Scholars sometimes in common speech, or writing, in their native language, give terminations and idiotisms suitable to their native language unto words newly invented. Hale.

2. Folly; natural imbecillity of mind.

idle adj. [*idel*, Saxon.]

1. Lazy; averse from labour.

For shame, so much to do, and yet idle. Bull.

2. Not busy; at leisure.

For often have you writ to her; and she in modesty,
Or else for want of idle time, could not again reply. Shak.

3. Unactive; not employed.

No war or battle's sound
Was heard the world around,
The idle spear and shield were high up hung. Milton.

Children generally hate to be idle; all the care then is, that their busy humour should be constantly employed in something of use to them. Locke.

Supposing, among a multitude embarked in the same vessel, there are several that, in the fury of a tempest, will rather perish than work for their preservation; would it not be madness in the rest to stand idle, and rather chuse to sink than do more than comes to their share? Addison.

4. Useless; vain; ineffectual.

They astonish'd, all resistance lost,
All courage; down their idle weapons dropp'd. Milton.

And threatning France, plac'd like a painted Jove,
Held idle thunder in his lifted hand. Dryden.

    Where was then
The power that guards the sacred lives of kings?
Why slept the lightning and the thunderbolts,
Or bent their idle rage on fields and trees,
When vengeance call'd 'em here? Dryden's Spanish Fryar.

5. Worthless; barren; not productive of good.

Suffice it then, thou money god, quoth he,
That all thine idle offers I refuse;
All that I need I have: what needeth me
To covet more than I have cause to use? Fairy Queen.

Of antres vast, and desarts idle,
It was my hent to speak. Shakespeare's Othello.

    The murmuring surge,
That on th' unnumber'd idle pebbles chafes,
Cannot be heard so high. Shakesp. King Lear.

    He was met even now,
Crown'd with rank fumiter and furrow-weeds,
Darnel, and all the idle weeds that grow
In our sustaining corn. Shakesp. King Lear.

6. Trifling; of no importance: as, an idle story.

This answer is both idle in regard of us, and also repugnant to themselves. Hooker.

They are not, in our estimation, idle reproofs, when the authors of needless innovations are opposed with such negatives, as that of Leo: how are these new devices brought in, which our fathers never knew? Hooker, b. ii.

His friend smil'd scornful, and, with proud contempt,
Rejects as idle what his fellow dreamt. Dryden.

An idle reason lessens the weight of the good ones you gave before. Swift.

How ill he wishes to recall the precious hours he has spent in trifles, and loitered away in idle unprofitable diversions. Rogers's Sermons.

idler n.s. [from *idle*.] A lazy person; a sluggard.

Many of these poor fishermen and idlers, that are commonly presented to his majesty's ships, are so ignorant in sea-service as that they know not the name of a rope. Raleigh.

Thou sluggish idler, dilatory slave. Irene.

idóneous adj. [*idoneus*, Latin.] Fit; proper; convenient; adequate.

You entangle, and so fix their saline part,
by making them corrode some idoneous body.
Boyle.

An ecclesiastical benefice is sometimes void
de jure & facto, *and then it ought to be*
conferred on an idoneous person. Ayliffe.[†]

ídyl n.s. [εἰδύλλιον; *idyllium,* Latin.] A
small short poem.

ígnis fatuus n.s. [Latin.] Will with the
wisp; Jack with the lanthorn.

Vapours arising from putrified waters are
usually called ignes fatui. Newton's Opt.

ignívomous adj. [*ignivomus,* Latin.]
Vomiting fire.

Vulcanos and ignivomous mountains are some
of the most terrible shocks of the globe.
Derham's Physico-Theology.

ignorámus n.s. [Latin.]

1. Ignoramus is a word properly used by
   the grand inquest impannelled in the
   inquisition of causes criminal and
   publick; and written upon the bill,
   whereby any crime is offered to their
   consideration, when they mislike their
   evidence as defective, or too weak to
   make good the presentment: the effect
   of which word so written is, that all
   farther inquiry upon that party, for that
   fault, is thereby stopped, and he
   delivered without farther answer. Cowel.

2. A foolish fellow; a vain uninstructed
   pretender. A low word.

Tell an ignoramus, in place and power, that
he has a wit and an understanding above all
the world, and he shall readily admit the
commendation. South's Sermons.

to ignóre v.a. [*ignorer,* French; *ignoro,*
Latin.] Not to know; to be ignorant of. This
word Boyle endeavoured to introduce; but
it has not been received.

I ignored not the stricter interpretation, given
by modern criticks to divers texts, by me
alleged. Boyle.

Philosophy would solidly be established, if men
would more carefully distinguish those things

that they know from those that they ignore.
Boyle.

ignóscible adj. [*ignoscibilis,* Latin.] Capable
of pardon. Dict.

illáchrymable adj. [*illachrymabilis,* Latin.]
Incapable of weeping. Dict.

to illáqueate v.a. [*illaqueo,* Latin.] To
entangle; to entrap; to ensnare.

I am illaquated, but not truly captivated into
an assent to your conclusion. More's Divine
Dialogues.

illíterate adj. [*illiteratus,* Latin.]
Unlettered;   untaught;   unlearned;
unenlightened by science.

The duke was illiterate, yet had learned
at court to supply his own defects, by the
drawing unto him of the best instruments
of experience. Wotton.

Th' illiterate writer, empirick like, applies
To minds diseas'd unsafe chance remedies:
The learn'd in schools, where knowledge
*   first began,*
Studies with care th' anatomy of man;
Sees virtue, vice, and passions in their cause,
And fame from science, not from fortune
draws. Dryden.

In the first ages of Christianity not only the
learned and the wise, but the ignorant and
illiterate embraced torments and death.
Tillotson's Sermons.

illnáture n.s. [*ill* and *nature.*] Habitual
malevolence; want of humanity.

Illnature inclines a man to those actions that
thwart and sour and disturb conversation,
and consists of a proneness to do ill turns,
attended with a secret joy upon the sight of
any mischief that befals another, and of an
utter insensibility of any kindness done him.
South's Sermons.

illuminátor n.s. [from *illuminate.*]

1. One who gives light.

2. One whose business it is to decorate
   books with pictures at the beginning
   of chapters.

Illuminators of manuscripts borrowed their title from the illumination which a bright genius giveth to his work. Felton.

imágination n.s. [*imaginatio*, Latin; *imagination*, French, from *imagine*.]

1. Fancy; the power of forming ideal pictures; the power of representing things absent to one's self or others.

Imagination I understand to be the representation of an individual thought. Imagination is of three kinds: joined with belief of that which is to come; joined with memory of that which is past; and of things present, or as if they were present: for I comprehend in this imagination feigned and at pleasure, as if one should imagine such a man to be in the vestments of a pope, or to have wings. Bacon.

Our simple apprehension of corporal objects, if present, is sense; if absent, imagination: when we would perceive a material object, our fancies present us with its idea. Glanv. Sceps.

O whither shall I run, or which way fly The sight of this so horrid spectacle, Which erst my eyes beheld, and yet behold! For dire imagination still pursues me. Milton's Agonistes.

His imaginations were often as just as they were bold and strong. Dennis.

Where beams of warm imagination play, The memory's soft figures melt away. Pope.

2. Conception; image in the mind; idea.

Sometimes despair darkens all her imaginations; sometimes the active passion of love cheers and clears her invention. Sidn.

Princes have but their titles for their glories, An outward honour for an inward toil; And, for unfelt imaginations, They often feel a world of restless cares. Shakesp. R. III.

Better I were distract, So should my thoughts be sever'd from my griefs; And woes, by wrong imaginations, lose The knowledge of themselves. Shakesp. King Lear.

We are apt to think that space, in itself, is actually boundless; to which imagination, the idea of space, of itself leads us. Locke.

3. Contrivance; scheme.

Thou hast seen all their vengeance, and all their imaginations against me. Lam. iii. 60.

immáne adj. [*immanis*, Latin.] Vast; prodigiously great.

immarcéssible adj. [*in* and *marcesco*, Latin.] Unfading. Dict.

immóment adj. [*in* and *moment*.] Trifling; of no importance or value. A barbarous word.

I some lady-trifles have reserv'd, Immoment toys, things of such dignity As we greet modern friends withal. Shakesp. Ant. and Cleop.

to impéach v.a. [*empecher*, French.]

1. To hinder; to impede. This sense is little in use.

Each door he opened without any breach; There was no bar to stop, nor foe him to impeach. Fairy Queen.

These ungracious practices of his sons did impeach his journey to the Holy Land, and vexed him all the days of his life. Davies.

If they will impeach the purposes of an army, which they have no reason to think themselves able to resist, they put themselves out of all expectation of mercy. Hayward.

A defluxion on my throat impeached my utterance. Howel.

2. To accuse by publick authority.

They were both impeached by a house of commons. Addison.

Great dissentions were kindled between the nobles and commons on account of Coriolanus, whom the latter had impeached. Swift.

impénnous adj. [*in* and *penna*, Latin.] Wanting wings.

It is generally received an earwigg hath no wings, and is reckoned amongst impennous insects; but he that shall with a needle put aside the short and sheathy cases on their back, may draw forth two wings, larger than in many flies. Brown.

impértinence, impértinency n.s. [*impertinence*, French; from *impertinent*.]

1. That which is of no present weight; that which has no relation to the matter in hand.

Some tho' they lead a single life, yet their thoughts do end with themselves, and account future times impertinencies. Bac.

2. Folly; rambling thought.

O, matter and impertinency mixt,
Reason and madness! Shakesp. King Lear.

3. Troublesomeness; intrusion.

It will be said I handle an art no way suitable to my employments or fortune, and so stand charged with intrusion and impertinency. Wotton's Architecture.

We should avoid the vexation and impertinence of pedants, who affect to talk in a language not to be understood. Swift.

4. Trifle; thing of no value.

I envy your felicity, delivered from the gilded impertinencies of life, to enjoy the moments of a solid contentment. Evelyn.

Nothing is more easy than to represent as impertinencies any parts of learning, that have no immediate relation to the happiness or convenience of mankind. Addison.

There are many subtle impertinencies learnt in the schools, and many painful trifles, even among the mathematical theorems and problems. Watts's Improvement of the Mind.

impetíginous adj. [from *impetigo*, Latin.] Scurfy; covered with small scabs.

to impígnorate v.a. [*in* and *pignus*, Latin.] To pawn; to pledge.

to impínguate v.a. [*in* and *pinguis*, Lat.] To fatten; to make fat.

Frictions also do more fill and impinguate the body than exercise; for that in frictions the inward parts are at rest. Bacon.

impléx adj. [*implexus*, Latin.] Intricate; entangled; complicated.

Every poem is either simple or implex: it is called simple when there is no change of fortune in it; implex, when the fortune of the chief actor changes from bad to good, or from good to bad. Spectator.

impósture n.s. [*imposture*, Fr. *impostura*, Latin.] Cheat; fraud; supposititiousness; cheat committed by giving to persons or things a false character.

That the soul and angels have nothing to do with grosser locality is generally opinioned; but who is it that retains not a great part of the imposture, by allowing them a definitive ubi, which is still but imagination? Glanv. Sceps.†

Open to them so many of the interior secrets of this mysterious art, without imposture or invidious reserve. Evelyn.

We know how successful the late usurper was, while his army believed him real in his zeal against kingship; but when they found out the imposture, upon his aspiring to the same himself, he was presently deserted, and never able to crown his usurped greatness with that title. South.

    Form new legends,
And fill the world with follies and impostures. Irene.

imprecátion n.s. [*imprecatio*, Lat. *imprecation*, Fr. from *imprecate*.] Curse; prayer by which any evil is wished.

My mother shall the horrid furies raise
With imprecations. Chapman's Odyssey.

Sir John Hotham, uncursed by any language or imprecation of mine, not long after paid his own and his eldest son's heads. King Charles.

With imprecations thus he fill'd the air,
And angry Neptune heard th' unrighteous pray'r. Pope.

ináne adj. [*inanis*, Latin.] Empty; void.

We sometimes speak of place in the great inane, beyond the confines of the world. Locke.

ináppetency n.s. [*in* and *appetentia*, Latin.] Want of stomach or appetite.

to incárnadine v.a. [*incarnadine*, Fr. *incarnadino*, pale red, Italian.] To dye red. This word I find only once.

Will all great Neptune's ocean wash this blood
Clean from my hand? No, this my hand
*   will rather*
The multitudinous sea incarnardine,
Making the green one red. Shakespeare's Macbeth.

incéndiary n.s. [*incendiarius*, from *incendo*, Latin; *incendiaire*, French.]

1. One who sets houses or towns on fire in malice or for robbery.

2. One who inflames factions, or promotes quarrels.

Nor could any order be obtained impartially
to examine impudent incendiaries.
King Charles.

Incendiaries of figure and distinction, who are
the inventers and publishers of gross falshoods,
cannot be regarded but with the utmost
detestation. Addison.

Several cities of Greece drove them out as
incendiaries, and pests of commonweals.
Bentley's Sermons.

incéptor n.s. [Latin.] A beginner; one who is in his rudiments.

incerátion n.s. [*incero*, Latin.] The act of covering with wax. Dict.

incóg adv. [corrupted by mutilation from *incognito*, Latin.] Unknown; in private.

But if you're rough, and use him like a dog,
Depend upon it, he'll remain incog. Addison.

incóntinent adj. [*incontinens*, Lat. *in* and *continent*.]

1. Unchaste; indulging unlawful pleasure.

In these degrees have they made a pair of
stairs to marriage, which they will climb
incontinent, or else be incontinent before
marriage. Shakes. As you like it.

Men shall be lovers of their own selves, false
accusers, incontinent, fierce. 2 Tim. iii. 3.

2. Shunning delay; immediate. This is a meaning now obsolete.

They ran towards the far rebounded noise,
To weet what wight so loudly did lament;
Unto the place they came incontinent.
Fairy Queen.

Come, mourn with me for what I do lament,
And put on sullen black incontinent.
Shakesp. Rich. II.

He says he will return incontinent.
Shak. Othello.

incóny adj. [perhaps from *in* and *conn*, to know.]

1. Unlearned; artless.

2. In Scotland it denotes mischievously unlucky: as, he's an incony fellow. This seems to be the meaning in Shakespeare.

O' my troth, most sweet jests, most incony
*   vulgar wit,*
When it comes so smoothly off. Shakespeare.

to íncrepate v.a. [*increpo*, Latin.] To chide; to reprehend.

íncubus n.s. [Latin; *incube*, Fr.] The night-mare.

The incubus is an inflation of the membranes
of the stomach, which hinders the motion of
the diaphragma, lungs, pulse, and motion,
with a sense of a weight oppressing the breast.
Floyer on the Humours.

indepéndence,   indepéndency n.s. [*independance*, Fr. *in* and *dependence*.] Freedom; exemption from reliance or control; state over which none has power.

Dreams may give us some idea of the great
excellency of a human soul, and some
intimations of its independency on matter.
Addison's Spectator.

Let fortune do her worst, whatever she makes
us lose, as long as she never makes us lose our
honesty and our independence. Pope.

indígenous adj. [*indigéne*, Fr. *indigena*, Latin.] Native to a country; originally produced or born in a region.

Negroes were all transported from Africa, and
are not indigenous or proper natives of
America. Brown's Vulg. Err.

It is wonderful to observe one creature, that is, mankind, indigenous to so many different climates. Arbuthnot.

indigitátion n.s. [from *indigitate.*] The act of pointing out or showing.

Which things I conceive no obscure indigitation of providence. More against Atheism.

indiscérptible adj. [*in* and *discerptible.*] Not to be separated; incapable of being broken or destroyed by dissolution of parts.

inescátion n.s. [*in* and *esca,* Lat.] The act of baiting. Dict.

ínfancy n.s. [*infantia,* Latin.]

1. The first part of life. Usually extended by naturalists to seven years.

Dare we affirm it was ever his meaning, that unto their salvation, who even from their tender infancy never knew any other faith or religion than only Christian, no kind of teaching can be available, saving that which was so needful for the first universal conversion of Gentiles, hating Christianity? Hooker.

   Pirithous came t' attend
This worthy Theseus, his familiar friend:
Their love in early infancy began,
And rose as childhood ripen'd into man.
Dryden.

The insensible impressions on our tender infancies have very important and lasting consequences. Locke.

2. Civil infancy, extended by the English law to one and twenty years.

3. First age of any thing; beginning; original; commencement.

In Spain our springs, like old mens children, be Decay'd and wither'd from their infancy. Dryd. Ind. Emp.

The difference between the riches of Roman citizens in the infancy and in the grandeur of Rome, will appear by comparing the first valuation of estates with the estates afterwards possessed. Arbuthnot on Coins.

infánticide n.s. [*infanticide,* Fr. *infanticidium,* Lat.] The slaughter of the infants by Herod.

infáusting n.s. [from *infaustus,* Lat.] The act of making unlucky. An odd and inelegant word.

As the king did in some part remove the envy from himself, so he did not observe that he did withal bring a kind of malediction and infausting upon the marriage, as an ill prognostick. Bacon's Henry VII.

ínfidel n.s. [*infidelle,* Fr. *infidelis,* Latin.] An unbeliever; a miscreant; a pagan; one who rejects Christianity.

Exhorting her, if she did marry, yet not to join herself to an infidel, as in those times some widows christian had done, for the advancement of their estate in this world. Hooker.

infúndibuliform n.s. [*infundibulum* and *forma,* Lat.] Of the shape of a funnel or tundish.

infuscátion n.s. [*infuscatus,* Latin.] The act of darkening or blackening.

ingannátion n.s. [*ingannare,* Italian.] Cheat; fraud; deception; juggle; delusion; imposture; trick; slight. A word neither used nor necessary.

Whoever shall resign their reasons, either from the root of deceit in themselves, or inability to resist such trivial ingannations from others, are within the line of vulgarity. Brown.

to ingéminate v.a. [*ingemino,* Latin.] To double; to repeat.

He would often ingeminate the word peace, peace. Clarendon.

to ingúrgitate v.a. [*ingurgito,* Latin.] To swallow down. Dict.

inkhórn n.s. [*ink* and *horn.*] A portable case for the instruments of writing, commonly made of horn.

Bid him bring his pen and inkhorn to the jail; we are now to examine those men. Shakesp. Much ado about Nothing.

Ere that we will suffer such a prince
To be disgrac'd by an inkhorn mate,
We, and our wives and children, all will fight.
Shakesp.

What is more frequent than to say, a silver
inkhorn. Grew.

ínly adv. Internally; within; secretly; in the heart.

Her heart with joy unwonted inly swell'd,
As feeling wond'rous comfort in her weaker
    eld. Fa. Qu.

    I've inly wept,
Or should have spoke ere this. Shakespeare's
Tempest.

Whereat he inly rag'd, and as they talk'd,
Smote him into the midriff with a stone,
That beat out life. Milton's Par. Lost, b. xi.

    The stubborn only to destroy
These growing thoughts, my mother
    soon perceiving
By words at times cast forth, inly rejoic'd,
And said to me apart. Milton's Par.
Reg. b. i.

The soldiers shout around with gen'rous rage;
He prais'd their ardor: inly pleas'd to see
His host. Dryden's Knight's Tale.

inópinate adj. [*inopinatus*, Lat. *inopiné*, Fr.]
Not expected.

insánable adj. [*insanabilis*, Latin.]
Incurable; irremediable.

insect n.s. [*insecta*, Latin.]

1. Insects may be considered together as
   one great tribe of animals: they are
   called insects from a separation in the
   middle of their bodies, whereby they
   are cut into two parts, which are joined
   together by a small ligature, as we see
   in wasps and common flies. Locke.

Beast, bird, insect, or worm, durst enter none.
Milton.

2. Any thing small or contemptible.

In ancient times the sacred plough employ'd
The kings, and awful fathers of mankind;
And some with whom compar'd, your
    insect tribes

Are but the beings of a Summer's day,
Have held the scale of empire.
Thomson's Spring.

inseminátion n.s. [*insemination*, Fr.
insemino, Lat.] The act of scattering seed
on ground.

to inspíre v.a.

1. To breathe into; to infuse into the mind;
   to impress upon the fancy.

I have been troubled in my sleep this night;
But dawning day new comfort hath inspir'd.
Shakespeare.

He knew not his Maker, and he that inspired
into him an active soul, and breathed in a
living spirit. Wisd. xv. 11.

    Then to the heart inspir'd
Vernal delight. Milton.

2. To animate by supernatural infusion.

    Nor th' inspir'd
Castalian spring. Milton.

Erato, thy poet's mind inspire,
And fill his soul with thy celestial fire.
Dryd. Æn.

The letters are often read to the young
religious, to inspire with sentiments of virtue.
Addison.

3. To draw in with the breath.

By means of sulphurous coal smoaks the lungs
are stifled and oppressed, whereby they are
forced to inspire and expire the air with
difficulty, in comparison of the facility of
inspiring and expiring the air in the country.
Harvey.

His baleful breath inspiring as he glides;
Now like a chain around her neck he rides.
Dryden.

to inspíssate v.a. [*in* and *spissus*, Lat.] To
thicken; to make thick.

Sugar doth inspissate the spirits of the wine,
and maketh them not so easy to resolve into
vapour. Bacon's Nat. Hist.

This oil farther inspissated by evaporation,
turns by degrees into balm. Arbuthnot
on Aliments.

instaurátion n.s. [*instauration*, French; *instauratio*, Lat.] Restoration; reparation; renewal.

instillátion n.s. [*instillatio*, Lat. from *instil.*]

1. The act of pouring in by drops.

2. The act of infusing slowly into the mind.

3. The thing infused.

They imbitter the cup of life by insensible instillations. Rambler.

instíncted adj. [*instinctus*, Lat.] Impressed as an animating power. This, neither musical nor proper, was perhaps introduced by Bentley.

What native unextinguishable beauty must be impressed and instincted through the whole, which the defedation of so many parts by a bad printer and a worse editor could not hinder from shining forth. Bentley's Preface to Milton.

institútion n.s. [*institution*, Fr. *institutio*, Latin.]

1. Act of establishing.

2. Establishment; settlement.

The institution of God's law is described as being established by solemn injunction. Hooker.

It became him by whom all things are, to be the way of salvation to all, that the institution and restitution of the world might be both wrought with one hand. Hooker, b. v.

This unlimited power placed fundamentally in the body of a people, is what legislators have endeavoured, in their several schemes or institutions of government, to deposit in such hands as would preserve the people. Swift.

3. Positive law.

The holiness of the first fruits and the lump is an holiness, merely of institution, outward and nominal; whereas the holiness of the root is an holiness of nature, inherent and real. Atterbury's Sermons.

The law and institution founded by Moses was to establish religion, and to make mercy and peace known to the whole earth. Forbes.

4. Education.

After baptism, when it is in infancy received, succeeds instruction and institution in the nature and several branches of that vow, which was made at the font, in a short intelligible manner. Hammond's Fundamentals.

It is a necessary piece of providence in the institution of our children, to train them up to somewhat in their youth, that may honestly entertain them in their age. L'Estrange.

His learning was not the effect of precept or institution. Bentley.

insúlse adj. [*insulsus*, Lat.] Dull; insipid; heavy. Dict.

insusurrátion n.s. [*insusurro*, Latin.] The act of whispering.

intelléctual adj. [*intellectuel*, French; *intellectualis*, low Latin.]

1. Relating to the understanding; belonging to the mind; transacted by the understanding.

Religion teaches us to present to God our bodies as well as our souls: if the body serves the soul in actions natural and civil, and intellectual, it must not be eased in the only offices of religion. Taylor.

2. Mental; comprising the faculty of understanding; belonging to the mind.

Logick is to teach us the right use of our reason, or intellectual powers. Watts.

3. Ideal; perceived by the intellect, not the senses.

In a dark vision's intellectual scene, Beneath a bow'r for sorrow made, The melancholy Cowley lay. Cowley.

A train of phantoms in wild order rose, And, join'd, this intellectual scene compose. Pope.

4. Having the power of understanding.

Anaxagoras and Plato term the maker of the world an intellectual worker. Hooker.

    Who would lose, Though full of pain, this intellectual being, Those thoughts that wander through eternity,

To perish rather, swallow'd up and lost,
In the wide womb of uncreated night,
Devoid of sense and motion? Milton's
Parad. Lost.

5. Proposed as the object not of the senses
but intellect: as, Cudworth names his
book the intellectual system of the
universe.

intélligence, intélligency n.s. [*intelligence*,
French; *intelligentia*, Latin.]

1. Commerce of information; notice;
mutual communication; account of
things distant or secret.

It was perceived there had not been in the
catholicks, either at Armenia or at Seleucia,
so much foresight as to provide that true
intelligence might pass between them of
what was done. Hooker, b. v.

A mankind witch! hence with her, out of door!
A most intelligency bawd! Shakespeare.

He furnished his employed men liberally with
money, to draw on and reward intelligences;
giving them also in charge to advertise
continually what they found. Bacon's H. VII.

The advertisements of neighbour princes are
always to be regarded, for that they receive
intelligence from better authors than persons
of inferior note. Hayward.

Let all the passages
Be well secur'd, that no intelligence
May pass between the prince and them.
Denham's Sophy.

Those tales had been sung to lull children
asleep, before ever Berosus set up his
intelligence office at Coos. Bentley.

2. Commerce of acquaintance; terms on
which men live one with another.

Factious followers are worse to be liked, which
follow not upon affection to him with whom
they range themselves; whereupon commonly
ensueth that ill intelligence that we see
between great personages. Bacon.

He lived rather in a fair intelligence than any
friendship with the favourites. Clarendon.

3. Spirit; unbodied mind.

How fully hast thou satisfied me, pure
Intelligence of heav'n, angel! Milt.
Parad. Lost.

There are divers ranks of created beings
intermediate between the glorious God and
man, as the glorious angels and created
intelligences. Hale.

They hoped to get the favour of the houses,
and by the favour of the houses they hoped for
that of the intelligencies, and by their favour
for that of the supreme God. Stillingfleet.

The regularity of motion, visible in the great
variety and curiosity of bodies, is a
demonstration that the whole mass of matter
is under the conduct of a mighty intelligence.
Collier.

Satan, appearing like a cherub to Uriel, the
intelligence of the sun circumvented him even
in his own province. Dryden.

4. Understanding; skill.

Heaps of huge words, up hoarded hideously,
They think to be chief praise of poetry;
And thereby wanting due intelligence,
Have marr'd the face of goodly poesie.
Spenser.

intelligéncer n.s. [from *intelligence*.] One
who sends or conveys news; one who gives
notice of private or distant transactions; one
who carries messages between parties.

His eyes, being his diligent intelligencers,
could carry unto him no other news but
discomfortable. Sidney.

Who hath not heard it spoken
How deep you were within the books of heav'n?
To us, th' imagin'd voice of heav'n itself;
The very opener and intelligencer
Between the grace and sanctities of heav'n,
And our dull workings. Shakes. Henry IV.

If they had instructions to that purpose, they
might be the best intelligencers to the king of
the true state of his whole kingdom. Bacon.

They are the best sort of intelligencers; for they
have a way into the inmost closets of princes.
Howel.

They have news-gatherers and intelligencers, who make them acquainted with the conversation of the whole kingdom. Spectator.

intércalar, intércalary adj. [*intercalaire*, Fr. *intercalaris*, Latin.] Inserted out of the common order to preserve the equation of time, as the twenty-ninth of February in a leap-year is an intercalary day.

íntercourse n.s. [*entrecours*, French.]

1. Commerce; exchange.

This sweet intercourse
Of looks, and smiles; for smiles from reason flow,
To brute deny'd, and are of love the food.
Milton.

2. Communication.

The choice of the place requireth many circumstances, as the situation near the sea, for the commodiousness of an intercourse with England. Bacon.

What an honour is it that God should admit us into such a participation of himself? That he should give us minds capable of such an intercourse with the Supreme Mind? Atterbury.

intermúndane adj. [*inter* and *mundus*, Latin.] Subsisting between worlds, or between orb and orb.

The vast distances between these great bodies are called intermundane spaces; in which though there may be some fluid, yet it is so thin and subtile, that it is as much as nothing. Locke.

internúncio n.s. [*internuncius*, Latin.] Messenger between two parties.

to intérpret v.a. [*interpreter*, French; *interpretor*, Lat.] To explain; to translate; to decipher; to give a solution; to clear by exposition; to expound.

One, but painted thus,
Would be interpreted a thing perplex'd
Beyond self-explication. Shakes. Cymbeline.

You should be women,
And yet your beards forbid me to interpret
That you are so. Shakesp. Macbeth.

He hanged the chief baker, as Joseph had interpreted to them. Gen. xl. 22.

Pharaoh told them his dream; but there was none that could interpret them unto him. Gen. xli. 8.

An excellent spirit, knowledge, and understanding, interpreting of dreams, and shewing of hard sentences, and dissolving of doubts, were found in the same Daniel. Dan. v. 12.

Hear his sighs, though mute!
Unskilful with what words to pray, let me
Interpret for him. Milton's Paradise Lost, b. xi.

to intímidate v.a. [*intimider*, French; *in* and *timidus*, Lat.] To make fearful; to dastardize; to make cowardly.

Now guilt once harbour'd in the conscious breast, Intimidates the brave, degrades the great. Irene.

invéntion n.s. [*invention*, French; *inventio*, Latin.]

1. Fiction.

O for a muse of fire, that would ascend
The brightest heaven of invention!
Shakes. H. V. Prol.

By improving what was writ before,
Invention labours less, but judgment more.
Roscommon.

Invention is a kind of muse, which, being possessed of the other advantages common to her sisters, and being warmed by the fire of Apollo, is raised higher than the rest. Dryden.

The chief excellence of Virgil is judgment, of Homer is invention. Pope.

2. Discovery.

Nature hath provided several glandules to separate this juice from the blood, and no less than four pair of channels to convey it into the mouth, which are of a late invention, and called ductus salivales. Ray on the Creation.

3. Excogitation; act of producing something new.

Mine is th' invention of the charming lyre;
Sweet notes and heav'nly numbers I inspire.
Dryden.

4. Forgery.

We hear our bloody cousins, not confessing
Their cruel parricide, filling their hearers
With strange invention. Shakesp. Macbeth.

    If thou can'st accuse,
Do it without invention suddenly.
Shakesp. Henry VI.

5. The thing invented.

The garden, a place not fairer in natural
ornaments than artificial inventions. Sidney.

Th' invention all admir'd; and each how he
To be th' inventor miss'd, so easy it seem'd
Once found, which yet unfound most would
    have thought
Impossible. Milton's Parad. Lost.

to irk v.a. [*yrk*, work, Islandick.] This word
is used only impersonally, it irks me; *mihi*
pœnae est, it gives me pain; or, I am weary of
it. Thus the authors of the Accidence say,
tædet, it irketh.

Come, shall we go and kill us venison?
And yet it irks me, the poor dappled fools
Should, in their own confines, with forked heads,
Have their round haunches gor'd.
Shakespeare.

It irks his heart he cannot be reveng'd.
Shakes. H. VI.

ironwood n.s. A kind of wood extremely
hard, and so ponderous as to sink in water.
It grows in America. Rob. Cruso.

irony n.s. [*ironie*, Fr. ειρωνεια.] A mode of
speech in which the meaning is contrary to
the words; as, Bolingbroke was a holy man.†

So grave a body, upon so solemn an occasion,
should not deal in irony, or explain their
meaning by contraries. Swift.

irrefrágable adj. [*irrefragabilis*, school
Latin; *irrefragable*, Fr.] Not to be confuted;
superior to argumental opposition.

Strong and irrefragable the evidences of
Christianity must be: they who resisted them
would resist every thing. Atterbury.

The danger of introducing unexperienced
men was urged as an irrefragable reason for
working by slow degrees. Swift.

irrísion n.s. [*irrisio*, Lat. *irrision*, French.]
The act of laughing at another.

This person, by his indiscreet and unnatural
irrision, and exposing of his father, incurs his
indignation and curse. Woodward's Natural
History.

íschury n.s. [ισχουρια, ισχω and ουρον,
urine; *ischurie*, Fr. *ischuria*, Latin.] A
stoppage of urine, whether by gravel or
other cause.

ish [*isc*, Saxon.]

1. A termination added to an adjective
to express diminution, a small degree,
or incipient state of any quality: as,
bluish, tending to blue; brightish,
somewhat bright.

2. It is likewise sometimes the termination
of a gentile or possessive adjective: as,
Swedish, Danish; the Danish territories,
or territories of the Danes.

3. It likewise notes participation of the
qualities of the substantive to which it is
added: as fool, foolish; man, mannish;
rogue, roguish.

ísland n.s. [*insula*, Latin; *isola*, Italian;
ealand, Erse. It is pronounced *iland*.] A
tract of land surrounded by water.

He will carry this island home in his pocket,
and give it his son for an apple.
—And sowing the kernels of it in the sea,
bring forth more islands. Shakespeare's
Tempest.

Within a long recess there lies a bay,
An island shades it from the rolling sea,
And forms a port. Dryden.

Some safer world in depth of woods embrac'd,
Some happier island in the wat'ry waste.
Johnson.†

Island of bliss! amid' the subject seas.
Thomson.

ísthmus n.s. [*isthmus*, Latin.] A neck of
land joining the peninsula to the continent.

There is a castle strongly seated on a high rock,
which joineth by an isthmus to the land, and
is impregnably fortified. Sandys's Travels.

The north side of the Assyrian empire
stretcheth northward to that isthmus between
the Euxine and the Caspian seas. Brerewood
on Languages.

O life, thou nothing's younger brother!
Thou weak built isthmus, that do'st proudly rise
Up betwixt two eternities,
Yet can'st not wave nor wind sustain;
But broken and o'erwhelm'd the ocean
    meets again. Cowley.

Our church of England stands as Corinth
between two seas, and there are some busy in
cutting the isthmus, to let in both at once upon
it. Stillingfleet.

Cleomenes thinking it more adviseable to
fortify, not the isthmus, but the mountains,
put his design in execution. Creech.

Plac'd on this isthmus of a middle state,
A being darkly wise, and rudely great. Pope.

it pronoun. [*hit*, Saxon.]

1. The neutral demonstrative. Used in
   speaking of things.

Nothing can give that to another which it
hath not itself. Bramh. against Hobbs.

Will our great anger learn to stoop so low?
I know it cannot. Cowley.

Tell me, O tell, what kind of thing is wit,
Thou who master art of it. Cowley.

His son, it may be, dreads no harm;
But kindly waits his father's coming home.
Flatman.

The time will come, it will, when you shall know
The rage of love. Dryden.

How can I speak? or how, sir, can you hear?
Imagine that which you would most deplore,
And that which I would speak, is it or more.
Dryden.

A mind so furnished, what reason has it to
acquiesce in its conclusions! Locke.

The glory which encompassed them covered
the place, and darted its rays with so much

strength, that the whole fabrick began to melt.
Addison's Freeholder.

If we find a greater good in the present
constitution, than would have accrued either
from the total privation of it, or from other
frames and structures, we may then
reasonably conclude, that the present
constitution proceeded from an intelligent
and good being, that formed it that particular
way out of choice. Bentley's Sermons.

2. It is used absolutely for the state of
   a person or affair.

How is it with our general?
—Even so
As with a man by his own alms impoison'd,
And with his charity slain. Shakespeare's
Coriolanus.

3. It is used for the thing; the matter;
   the affair.

    It's come to pass,
That tractable obedience is a slave
To each incensed will. Shakesp. Henry VIII.

4. It is sometimes expressed by *'t*.

He rallied, and again fell to 't;
For catching foe by nearer foot,
He lifted with such might and strength,
As would have hurl'd him thrice his length.
Hudibras.

The design, it seems, is to avoid the dreadful
imputation of pedantry. Swift.

5. It is used ludicrously after neutral verbs,
   to give an emphasis.

If Abraham brought all with him, it is not
probable that he meant to walk it back again
for his pleasure. Raleigh.

The Lacedemonians, at the straights of
Thermopylæ, when their arms failed them,
fought it out with their nails and teeth.
Dryden.

I have often seen people lavish it profusely in
tricking up their children, and yet starve their
minds. Locke.

A mole courses it not on the ground, like
the rat or mouse, but lives under the earth.
Addison's Spectator.

Whether the charmer sinner it, or saint it,
If folly grows romantick, I must paint it.
Pope.

6. Sometimes applied familiarly,
   ludicrously, or rudely to persons.

    Let us after him,
Whose care is gone before to bid us welcome:
It is a peerless kinsman. Shakespeare's
Macbeth.

Do, child, go to it grandam, child:
Give grandam kingdom, and its grandam will
Give it up him. Shakesp. King John.

7. It is sometimes used of the first or
   second person, sometimes of more. This
   mode of speech, though used by good
   authors, and supported by the *il y a* of
   the French, has yet an appearance of
   barbarism.

    Who was't came by?
—*'Tis two or three, my lord, that bring you word*
Macduff is fled to England. Shakes. Macbeth.

    City,
'Tis I, that made thy widows. Shakesp.
Coriolanus.

'Tis these that early taint the female soul.
Pope.

jack n.s. [Probably by mistake from *Jaques*,
which in French is James.]

1. The diminutive of John. Used as
   a general term of contempt for saucy
   or paltry fellows.

    I am in estimation:
You will perceive that a Jack gardant cannot
Office me from my son Coriolanus.
Shakespeare.

    I have in my mind
A thousand raw tricks of these bragging Jacks,
Which I will practise. Shakes. Merchant
of Venice.

Every Jack slave hath his belly-full of
fighting, and I must go up and down like
a cock that nobody can match. Shakesp.

2. The name of instruments which supply
   the place of a boy, as an instrument to
   pull off boots.

Foot-boys, who had frequently the common
name of jack given them, were kept to turn
the spit, or to pull off their masters boots; but
when instruments were invented for both
those services, they were both called jacks.
Watts's Logick.

3. An engine which turns the spit.

The excellencies of a good jack are, that the
jack frame be forged and filed square; that the
wheels be perpendicularly and strongly fixed
on the squares of the spindles; that the teeth
be evenly cut, and well smoothed; and that
the teeth of the worm-wheel fall evenly into
the groove of the worm. Moxon.

The ordinary jacks, used for roasting of meat,
commonly consist but of three wheels.
Wilkins's Math. Magick.

Clocks and jacks, though the screws and teeth
be never so smooth, yet, if not oiled, will
hardly move. Ray.

A cookmaid, by the fall of a jack weight
upon her head, was beaten down.
Wiseman's Surgery.

Some strain in rhyme; the muses on their racks
Scream, like the winding of ten thousand
    jacks. Pope.

4. A young pike.

No fish will thrive in a pond where roach
or gudgeons are, except jacks. Mortimer's
Husbandry.

5. [*Jacque*, French.] A coat of mail.

The residue were on foot, well furnished with
jack and skull, pike, dagger, bucklers made of
board, and slicing swords, broad, thin, and
of an excellent temper. Hayward.

6. A cup of waxed leather.

Dead wine, that stinks of the borrachio, sup
From a foul jack, or greasy mapple cup.
Dryden's Pers.

7. A small bowl thrown out for a mark to
   the bowlers.

'Tis as if one should say, that a bowl equally
poised, and thrown upon a plain
bowling-green, will run necessarily in a direct

motion; but if it be made with a byass, that may decline it a little from a straight line, it may acquire a liberty of will, and so run spontaneously to the jack. Bentley's Sermons.

8. A part of the musical instrument called a virginal.

In a virginal, as soon as ever the jack falleth, and toucheth the string, the sound ceaseth. Bacon's Natural History.

9. The male of animals.

A jack ass, for a stallion, was bought for three thousand two hundred and twenty-nine pounds three shillings and four pence. Arbuthnot on Coins.

10. A support to saw wood on. Ainsworth.

11. The colours or ensign of a ship. Ainsworth.

12. A cunning fellow who can turn to any thing.

Jack of all trades, show and sound;
An inverse burse, an exchange under ground. Cleaveland.

jackalént n.s. [*Jack in Lent,* a poor starven fellow.] A simple sheepish fellow.

You little jackalent, have you been true to us?
—Ay, I'll be sworn. Shakesp. Merry Wives of Windsor.

jack pudding n.s. [*jack* and *pudding.*] A zani; a merry Andrew.

Every jack pudding will be ridiculing palpable weaknesses which they ought to cover. L'Estrange.

A buffoon is called by every nation by the name of the dish they like best: in French jean pottage, *and in English* jack pudding. Guardian.

Jack pudding, in his party-colour'd jacket,
Tosses the glove, and jokes at ev'ry packet. Gay.

jactitátion n.s. [*jactito,* Latin.] Tossing; motion; restlessness; heaving.

If the patient be surprised with jactitation, or great oppression about the stomach, expect no relief from cordials. Harv.

jáilbird n.s. [*jail* and *bird.*] One who has been in a jail.

jakes n.s. [Of uncertain etymology.] A house of office.†

I will tread this unbolted villain into mortar, and daub the walls of jakes with him. Shakespeare's King Lear.

Their sordid avarice rakes
In excrements, and hires the very jakes. Dryden's Juvenal.

Some have fished the very jakes for papers left there by men of wit. Swift.

jánizary n.s. [A Turkish word.] One of the guards of the Turkish king.

His grand visier, presuming to invest
The chief imperial city of the West,
With the first charge compel'd in haste to rise;
The standards lost, and janizaries slain,
Render the hopes he gave his master vain. Waller.

japán n.s. [from *Japan* in Asia, where figured work was originally done.] Work varnished and raised in gold and colours.

The poor girl had broken a large japan glass, of great value, with a stroke of her brush. Swift.

járgon n.s. [*jargon,* French; *gerigonça,* Spanish.] Unintelligible talk; gabble; gibberish.

Nothing is clearer than mathematical demonstration, yet let one, who is altogether ignorant in mathematicks, hear it, and he will hold it to be plain fustian or jargon. Bramhall.

From this last toil again what knowledge flows?
Just as much, perhaps, as shows
That all his predecessor's rules
Were empty cant, all jargon of the schools. Prior.

During the usurpation an infusion of enthusiastick jargon prevailed in every writing. Swift.

jeer n.s. [from the verb.] Scoff; taunt; biting jest; flout; jibe; mock.

Midas, expos'd to all their jeers,
Had lost his art, and kept his ears. Swift.

They tipt the forehead in a jeer,
As who should say—she wants it here;
She may be handsome, young and rich;
But none will burn her for a witch. Swift.

jégget n.s. A kind of sausage. Ainsworth.

Jehóvah n.s. [יהוה] The proper name of God in the Hebrew language.

jejúne adj. [*jejunus*, Latin.]

1. Wanting; empty; vacant.

Gold is the only substance which hath nothing in it volatile, and yet melteth without much difficulty: the melting sheweth that it is not jejune, or scarce in spirit. Bacon.

2. Hungry; not saturated.

In gross and turbid streams there might be contained nutriment, and not jejune or limpid water. Brown's Vulgar Err.

3. Dry; unaffecting.

You may look upon an inquiry made up of meer narratives, as somewhat jejune. Boyle.

to jig v.n. [from the noun.] To dance carelesly; to dance. Expressed in contempt.

As for the jigging part and figures of dances,
I count that little. Locke.

jíggumbob n.s. [A cant word.] A trinket; a knick-knack; a slight contrivance in machinery.

He rifled all his pokes and fobs
Of gimcracks, whims, and jiggumbobs.
Hudibras, p. iii.

jilt n.s. [*gilia*, Islandick, to intrap in an amour. Mr. Lye. Perhaps from *giglot*, by contraction; or *gillet*, or *gillot*, the diminutive of *gill*, the ludicrous name for a woman. 'Tis also called *jillet* in Scotland.]

1. A woman who gives her lover hopes, and deceives him.

Avoid both courts and camps,
Where dilatory fortune plays the jilt
With the brave, noble, honest, gallant man,
To throw herself away on fools.
Otway's Orphan.

2. A name of contempt for a woman.

When love was all an easy monarch's care,
Jilts rul'd the state, and statesmen farces writ.
Pope.

jobbernówl n.s. [most probably from *jobbe*, Flemish, dull, and *nowl*, *knol*, Saxon, a head.] Loggerhead; blockhead.

And like the world, men's jobbernowls
Turn round upon their ears, the poles.
Hudibras, p. iii.

jógger n.s. [from *jog*.] One who moves heavily and dully.

They, with their fellow joggers of the plough.
Dryden.

jóinture n.s. [*jointure*, French.] Estate settled on a wife to be enjoyed after her husband's decease.

The jointure that your king must make,
With her dow'ry shall be counterpois'd.
Shakesp.

The old countess of Desmond, who lived in 1589, and many years since, was married in Edward the fourth's time, and held her jointure from all the earls of Desmond since then. Raleigh's Hist. of the World.

There's a civil question us'd of late,
Where lies my jointure, where your own estate? Dryden.

What's property? You see it alter,
Or, in a mortgage, prove a lawyer's share,
Or, in a jointure, vanish from the heir. Pope.

jólthead n.s. [I know not whence derived.] A great head; a dolt; a blockhead.

Fie on thee, jolthead, thou can'st not read.
Shakespeare.

Had he been a dwarf, he had scarce been a reasonable creature; for he must then have either had a jolthead, and so there would not have been body and blood enough to supply his brain with spirits; or he must have had a small head, and so there would not have been brain enough for his business. Grew.

jóurneyman n.s. [*journée*, a day's work, Fr. and *man*.] A hired workman.

They were called journeymen that wrought with others by the day, though now by statute it be extended to those likewise that convenant to work in their occupation with another by the year. Cowel.

Players have so strutted and bellowed, that I have thought some of nature's journeymen had made men, and not made them well.
Shakespeare's Hamlet.

I intend to work for the court myself, and will have journeymen under me to furnish the rest of the nation. Addison.

Says Frog to Bull, this old rogue will take the management of the young lord's business into his hands: in that case what must become of us and our families? We must starve or turn journeymen to old Lewis Baboon.
Arbuthnot's John Bull.

to judáize v.n. [*judaiser*, Fr. *judaizo*, low Latin.] To conform to the manner of the Jews.

Paul judaiz'd with Jews, was all to all.
Sandys.

júdgment n.s. [*jugement*, French]

1. The power of discerning the relations between one term or one proposition and another.

O judgment! thou art fled to brutish beasts, And men have lost their reason. Shak. Julius Cæsar.

The faculty, which God has given man to supply the want of certain knowledge, is judgment, whereby the mind takes any proposition to be true or false, without perceiving a demonstrative evidence in the proofs. Locke.

Judgment is that whereby we join ideas together by affirmation or negation; so, this tree is high. Watts.

2. Doom; the right or power of passing judgment.

If my suspect be false, forgive me, God; For judgment only doth belong to thee.
Shakes. H. VI.

3. The act of exercising judicature.

They gave judgment upon him.
2 Kings xxv. 6.

When thou, O Lord, shalt stand disclos'd In majesty severe, And sit in judgment on my soul, O how shall I appear. Addison's Spectator.

4. Determination; decision.

Where distinctions or identities are purely material, the judgment is made by the imagination, otherwise by the understanding.
Glanv. Sceps.

We shall make a certain judgment what kind of dissolution that earth was capable of.
Burnet's Theory of the Earth.

Reason ought to accompany the exercise of our senses, whenever we would form a just judgment of things proposed to our inquiry.
Watts.

5. The quality of distinguishing propriety and impropriety; criticism.

Judgment, a cool and slow faculty, attends not a man in the rapture of poetical composition.
Dennis.

'Tis with our judgments as our watches, none Go just alike; yet each believes his own. Pope.

6. Opinion; notion.

I see mens judgments are A parcel of their fortunes, and things outward Draw the inward quality after them, To suffer all alike. Shakes. Ant. and Cleopatra.

When she did think my master lov'd her well, She, in my judgment, was as fair as you.
Shakespeare.

7. Sentence against a criminal.

When he was brought again to th' bar, to hear His knell rung out, his judgment, he was stirr'd With agony. Shakesp. Henry VIII.

The chief priests informed me, desiring to have judgment against him. Acts xxv. 15.

On Adam last this judgment he pronounc'd.
Milton.

8. Condemnation. This is a theological use.

*The judgment was by one to condemnation;
but the free gift is of many offences unto
justification.* Rom. v. 16.

*The precepts, promises, and threatenings of the
Gospel will rise up in judgment against us,
and the articles of our faith will be so many
articles of accusation.* Tillotson.

9. Punishment inflicted by providence,
with reference to some particular crime.

*This judgment of the heavens that makes
us tremble,
Touches us not with pity.* Shakes. King Lear.

*We cannot be guilty of greater
uncharitableness, than to interpret afflictions
as punishments and judgments: it aggravates
the evil to him who suffers, when he looks
upon himself as the mark of divine vengeance.*
Addison's Spectator.

10. Distribution of justice.

*The Jews made insurrection against Paul, and
brought him to the judgment seat.*
Acts xviii. 12.

*Your dishonour
Mangles true judgment, and bereaves the state
Of that integrity which should become it.*
Shakes. Coriol.

*In judgments between rich and poor, consider
not what the poor man needs, but what is his
own.* Taylor.

*A bold and wise petitioner goes strait to the
throne and judgment seat of the monarch.*
Arbuthn. and Pope's Mart. Scrib.

11. Judiciary laws; statutes.

*If ye hearken to these judgments, and keep and
do them, the Lord thy God shall keep unto
thee the covenant.* Deutr.

12. The last doom.

*The dreadful judgment day
So dreadful will not be as was his sight.*
Shakes. Hen. VI.

to júggle v.n. [*jougler* or *jongler*, Fr. *jocari*,
Lat.]

1. To play tricks by slight of hand; to show
false appearances of extraordinary
performances.

*The ancient miracle of Memnon's statue seems
to be a juggling of the Ethiopian priests.*
Digby on Bodies.

2. To practise artifice or imposture.

*Be these juggling fiends no more believ'd,
That palter with us in a double sense.*
Shakesp. Macbeth.

*Is 't possible the spells of France should juggle
Men into such strange mockeries?* Shakesp.
Henry VIII.

*They ne'er forswore themselves, nor lied,
Disdain'd to stay for friends consents;
Nor juggl'd about settlements.* Hudibras,
p. iii.

júnto n.s. [Italian.] A cabal; a kind of
men combined in any secret design.

*Would men have spent toilsome days and
watchful nights in the laborious quest of
knowledge preparative to this work, at length
come and dance attendance for approbation
upon a junto of petty tyrants, acted by party
and prejudice, who denied fitness from
learning, and grace from morality.* South.

*From this time began an intrigue between his
majesty and a junto of ministers, which had
like to have ended in my destruction.*
Gulliver's Travels.

juppón n.s. [*juppon*, French.] A short
close coat.

*Some wore a breast-plate and a light juppon,
Their horses cloath'd with rich caparison.*
Dryden.

júrist n.s. [*juriste*, Fr. *jura*, Lat.] A civil
lawyer; a man who professes the science of
the law; a civilian.

*This is not to be measured by the principles of
jurists.* Bac.

júry n.s. [*jurata*, Lat. *juré*, Fr.] Jury, a
company of men, as twenty-four or twelve,
sworn to deliver a truth upon such evidence
as shall be delivered them touching the
matter in question. There be three manners
of trials in England: one by parliament,
another by battle, and the third by assise or
jury. The trial by assise, be the action civil or

criminal, publick or private, personal or real, is referred for the fact to a jury, and as they find it, so passeth the judgment. This jury is used not only in circuits of justices errant, but also in other courts, and matters of office, as, if the escheatour make inquisition in any thing touching his office, he doth it by a jury of inquest: if the coroner inquire how a subject found dead came to his end, he useth an inquest: the justices of peace in their quarter-sessions, the sheriff in his county and turn, the bailiff of a hundred, the steward of a court-leet or court-baron, if they inquire of any offence, or decide any cause between party and party, they do it by the same manner: so that where it is said, that all things be triable by parliament, battle, or assize; assize, in this place, is taken for a jury or inquest, empanelled upon any cause in a court where this kind of trial is used. This jury, though it appertain to most courts of the common law, yet it is most notorious in the half year courts of the justices errants, commonly called the great assizes, and in the quarter-sessions, and in them it is most ordinarily called a jury, and that in civil causes; whereas in other courts it is often termed an inquest. In the general assize, there are usually many juries, because there be store of causes, both civil and criminal, commonly to be tried, whereof one is called the grand jury, and the rest petit juries. The grand jury consists ordinarily of twenty-four grave and substantial gentlemen, or some of them yeomen, chosen indifferently out of the whole shire by the sheriff, to consider of all bills of indictment preferred to the court; which they do either approve by writing upon them these words, *billa vera*, or disallow by writing *ignoramus*. Such as they do approve, if they touch life and death, are farther referred to another jury to be considered of, because the case is of such importance; but others of lighter moment are, upon their allowance, without more work, fined by the bench, except the party traverse the indictment, or challenge it for insufficiency,

or remove the cause to a higher court by *certiorari*; in which two former cases it is referred to another jury, and in the latter transmitted to the higher. Those that pass upon civil causes real, are all, or so many as can conveniently be had, of the same hundred, where the land or tenement in question doth lie, and four at the least; and they, upon due examination, bring in their verdict either for the demandant or tenant: according unto which, judgment passeth afterward in the court where the cause first began; and the reason hereof is, because these justices of assize are, in this case, for the ease of the countries only to take the verdict of the jury by the virtue of the writ called *nisi prius*, and so return it to the court where the cause is depending. Cowell.

The jury, passing on the prisoner's life,
May in the sworn twelve have a thief or two
Guiltier than him they try. Shakesp.
Meas. for Measure.

How innocent I was,
His noble jury and foul cause can witness.
Shakesp. H. VIII.

Clodius was acquitted by a corrupt jury, that
had palpably taken shares of money before
they gave up their verdict. Bac.

júryman n.s. [*jury* and *man*.] One who is impannelled on a jury.

The hungry judges soon the sentence sign,
And wretches hang that jurymen may dine.
Pope.

No judge was known, upon or off the bench,
to use the least insinuation, that might affect
the interests of any one single juryman, much
less of a whole jury. Swift's Miscel.

jústice n.s. [*justice*, French; *justitia*, Latin.]

1. The virtue by which we give to every man what is his due.

O that I were judge, I would do justice.
2 Sam. xv. 4.

The king-becoming graces,
As justice, verity, temp'rance, stableness,
I have no relish of them. Shakesp. Macbeth.

*The nature and office of justice being to
dispose the mind to a constant and perpetual
readiness to render to every man his due, it is
evident, that if gratitude be a part of justice,
it must be conversant about something that is
due to another.* Loc.

2. Vindicative retribution; punishment.

*This shews you are above
You justices, that these our nether crimes
So speedily can venge.* Shakesp. King Lear.

He executed the justice of the Lord. Deut.
xxxiii. 21.

Lest justice overtake us. Is. lix. 9.

*Examples of justice must be made, for terror
to some; examples of mercy, for comfort to
others: the one procures fear, and the other love.*
Bacon's Advice to Villiers.

3. Right; assertion of right.

*Draw thy sword,
That if my speech offend a noble heart,
Thy arm may do thee justice.* Shakesp.
King Lear.

4. [*Justiciarius,* Lat.] One deputed by the
king to do right by way of judgment.
Cowel.

*And thou, Esdras, ordain judges and justices,
that they may judge in all Syria.* 1 Esdr.
viii. 23.

5. Justice of the King's Bench. [*justiciarius
de Banquo Regis.*] Is a lord by his office,
and the chief of the rest; wherefore he
is also called *capitalis justiciarius Angliæ.*
His office especially is to hear and
determine all pleas of the crown; that
is, such as concern offences committed
against the crown, dignity, and peace of
the king; as treasons, felonies, mayhems,
and such like: but it is come to pass,
that he with his assistants heareth all
personal actions, and real also, if they
be incident to any personal action
depending before them. Cowel.

*Give that whipster his errand,
He'll take my lord chief justice' warrant.*
Prior.

6. Justice of the Common Pleas.
[*justiciarius Communium Placitorum.*] Is
a lord by his office, and is called *dominus
justiciarius communium placitorum.* He
with his assistants originally did hear
and determine all causes at the common
law; that is, all civil causes between
common persons, as well personal as
real; for which cause it was called the
court of common pleas, in opposition
to the pleas of the crown, or the king's
pleas, which are special, and
appertaining to him only. Cowel.

7. Justice of the Forest. [*justiciarius
Forestæ.*] Is a lord by his office, and
hath the hearing and determining of
all offences within the king's forest,
committed against venison or vert: of
these there be two, whereof the one
hath jurisdiction over all the forests on
this side Trent, and the other of all
beyond. Cowel.

8. Justices of Assise. [*justiciarii ad capiendas
Assisas.*] Are such as were wont, by
special commission, to be sent into this
or that country to take assises; the
ground of which polity was the ease of
the subjects: for whereas these actions
pass always by jury, so many men might
not, without great hinderance, be
brought to London; and therefore
justices, for this purpose, were by
commission particularly authorised and
sent down to them. Cowel.

9. Justices in Eyre. [*justiciarii itinerantes.*]
Are so termed of the French *erre, iter.*
The use of these, in ancient time, was to
send them with commission into divers
counties, to hear such causes especially
as were termed the pleas of the crown,
and therefore I must imagine they were
sent abroad for the ease of the subjects,
who must else have been hurried to the
king's bench, if the cause were too high
for the country court. They differed
from the justices of Oyer and Terminer,
because they were sent upon some one
or few especial cases, and to one place;

whereas the justices in eyre were sent through the provinces and countries of the land, with more indefinite and general commission. Cowel.

10. Justices of Gaol Delivery. [*justiciarii ad Gaolas deliberandas.*] Are such as are sent with commission to hear and determine all causes appertaining to such as for any offence are cast into gaol, part of whose authority is to punish such as let to mainprise those prisoners, that by law be not bailable. These by likelihood, in ancient time, were sent to countries upon several occasions; but afterward justices of assise were likewise authorised to this. Cowel.

11. Justices of Nisi Prius are all one now-a-days with justices of assise; for it is a common adjournment of a cause, in the common pleas, to put it off to such a day: *nisi prius justiciarii venerint ad eas partes ad capiendas assisas*; and upon this clause of adjournment they are called justices of *nisi prius*, as well as justices of assise, by reason of the writ or action that they have to deal in. Cowel.

12. Justices of Peace. [*justiciarii ad Pacem.*] Are they that are appointed by the king's commission, with others, to attend the peace of the country where they dwell; of whom some, upon especial respect, are made of the quorum, because some business of importance may not be dealt in without the presence of them, or one of them. Cowel.

The justice,
In fair round belly with good capon lin'd,
With eyes severe, and beard of formal cut,
Full of wise saws and modern instances,
And so he plays his part. Shakes. As you like it.

Thou hast appointed justices of the peace to call poor men before them, about matters they were not able to answer. Shakespeare's Henry VI.

The justices of peace are of great use: anciently they were conservators of the peace; these are the same, saving that several acts of parliament have enlarged their jurisdiction. Bacon's Advice to Villiers.

I sing no harm
To officer, juggler, or justice of peace. Donne.

K

K. A letter borrowed by the English from the Greek alphabet. It has before all the vowels one invariable sound: as, *keen, ken, kill;* but is not much in use, except after *c* at the end of words: as, *knock, clock, crack, back, brick, stick, pluck, check,* which were written anciently with *e* final: as, *clocke, checke, tricke.* It is also in use between a vowel and the silent *e* final: as, *cloke, broke, brake, pike, duke, eke.* It likewise ends a word after a diphthong: as, *look, break, shock, beek.* The English never use *c* at the end of a word. *K* is silent in the present pronunciation before *n*: as, *knife, knee, knell.*

to keck v.n. [*kecken*, Dutch.] To heave the stomach; to reach at vomiting.

All those diets do dry up humours and rheums, which they first attenuate, and while the humour is attenuated it troubleth the body a great deal more; and therefore patients must not keck at them at the first. Bacon's Nat. Hist. Nº 68.

The faction, is it not notorious?
Keck at the memory of glorious.
Swift's Miscel.

kéelfat n.s. [*cœlan*, Saxon, *to cool*, and *fat* or *vat*, a vessel.] Cooler; tub in which liquor is let to cool.

to kéelhale v.a. [*keel* and *hale*.] To punish in the seamens way, by dragging the criminal under water on one side of the ship and up again on the other.

to kemb v.a. [*cœmban*, Saxon; *kammen*, German: now written, perhaps less properly, *to comb*.] To separate or disentangle by a denticulated instrument.

Yet are the men more loose than they,
More kemb'd and bath'd, and rubb'd and trim'd,
More sleek. Benj. Johnson.

Thy head and hair are sleek;
And then thou kemb'st the tuzzes on thy cheek.
Dryden.

ken n.s. [from the verb.] View; reach of sight.

Lo! within a ken, our army lies. Shakesp. Henry IV.

When from the mountain top Pisanio
shew'd thee,
Thou wast within a ken. Shakesp. Cymbeline.

It was a hill
Of paradise the highest; from whose top
The hemisphere of earth, in clearest ken,
Stretch'd out to th' amplest reach of prospect,
lay. Milton.

He soon
Saw within ken a glorious angel stand.
Milton.

Rude, as their ships, was navigation then;
No useful compass or meridian known:
Coasting they kept the land within their ken,
And knew the North but when the pole-star
shone. Dryd.

When we consider the reasons we have to think, that what lies within our ken is but a small part of the universe, we shall discover an huge abyss of ignorance. Locke.

kern n.s. [an Irish word.] Irish foot soldier; an Irish boor.

Out of the fry of these rake-hell horseboys, growing up in knavery and villainy, are their kearn supplied. Spenser.

No sooner justice had with valour arm'd,
Compell'd these skipping kernes to trust
their heels,
But the Norweyan lord, surveying advantage,
Began a fresh assault. Shakespeare's Macbeth.

If in good plight these Northern kerns arrive,
Then does fortune promise fair.
Philips's Briton.

kíckshaw n.s. [This word is supposed, I think with truth, to be only a corruption of *quelque chose*, something; yet Milton seems to have understood it otherwise; for he writes it *kickshoe*, and seems to think it used in contempt of dancing.]

1. Something uncommon; fantastical; something ridiculous.

Shall we need the monsieurs of Paris to take our hopeful youth into their slight and prodigal custodies, and send them over back again transformed into mimicks, apes, and kickshoes? Milton.

2. A dish so changed by the cookery that it can scarcely be known.

Some pigeons, a couple of short-legged hens, a joint of mutton, and any pretty little tiny kickshaws. Shakes. H. IV.

In wit, as well as war, they give us vigour;
Cressy was lost by kickshaws and
soup-meagre. Fenton.

kicksy-wicksey n.s. [from *kick* and *wince*.]
A made word in ridicule and disdain of
a wife. Hanmer.

He wears his honour in a box, unseen,
That hugs his kicksy-wicksey here at home,
Spending his manly marrow in her arms.
Shakespeare.

kidney n.s. [Etymology unknown.]

1. These are two in number, one on each
   side: they have the same figure as
   kidneybeans: their length is four or five
   fingers, their breadth three, and their
   thickness two: the right is under the
   liver, and the left under the spleen.
   The use of the kidneys is to separate
   the urine from the blood, which, by
   the motion of the heart and arteries,
   is thrust into the emulgent branches,
   which carry it to the little glands, by
   which the serosity being separated, is
   received by the orifice of the little tubes,
   which go from the glands to the pelvis,
   and from thence it runs by the ureters
   into the bladder. Quincy.

A youth laboured under a complication of
diseases, from his mesentery and kidneys.
Wiseman's Surgery.

2. Race; kind: in ludicrous language.

Think of that, a man of my kidney; think
of that, that am as subject to heat as butter;
a man of continual dissolution and thaw.
Shakesp. Merry Wives of Windsor.

There are millions in the world of this man's
kidney, that take up the same resolution
without noise. L'Estrange.

kimbo adj. [*a schembo*, Italian.] Crooked;
bent; arched.

The kimbo handles seem with bears-foot carv'd,
And never yet to table have been serv'd.
Dryden's Virgil.

He observed them edging towards one another
to whisper; so that John was forced to sit with
his arms a kimbo, to keep them asunder.
Arbuthnot's History of John Bull.

kind n.s. [*cynne*, Saxon.]

1. Race; generical class. *Kind* in Teutonick
   English answers to *genus*, and *sort*
   to *species*; though this distinction, in
   popular language, is not always
   observed.

Thus far we have endeavoured in part to
open of what nature and force laws are,
according to their kinds. Hooker.

   As when the total kind
Of birds, in orderly array on wing,
Came summon'd over Eden, to receive
Their names of Thee. Milton's Parad.
Lost, b. vi.

   That both are animalia,
I grant; but not rationalia;
For though they do agree in kind,
Specifick difference we find. Hudibras, p. i.

God and nature do not principally concern
themselves in the preservation of particulars,
but of kinds and companies.
South's Sermons.

He with his wife were only left behind
Of perish'd man; they two were human kind.
Dryden.

I instance some acts of virtue common to
Heathens and Christians; but I suppose them
to be performed by Christians, after a more
sublime manner than ever they were among
the Heathens; and even when they do not
differ in kind from moral virtues, yet differ
in the degrees of perfection. Atterb.

He, with a hundred arts refin'd,
Shall stretch thy conquests over half the kind.
Pope.

2. Particular nature.

No human laws are exempt from faults, since
those that have been looked upon as most
perfect in their kind, have been found, upon
enquiry, to have so many. Baker.

3. Natural state.

He did, by edict, give the goods of all the
prisoners unto those that had taken them,
either to take them in kind, or compound
for them. Bacon's Henry VII.

The tax upon tillage was often levied in kind upon corn, and called decumæ, *or tithes.* Arbuthnot on Coins.

4. Nature; natural determination.

The skilful shepherd peel'd me certain wands,
And in the doing of the deed of kind,
He stuck them up before the fulsome ewes.
Shakespeare.

Some of you, on pure instinct of nature,
Are led by kind t' admire your fellow-creature.
Dryden.

5. Manner; way.

Send me your prisoners with the speediest means,
Or you shall hear in such a kind from me
As will displease you. Shakes. Henry IV.

This will encourage industrious improvements, because many will rather venture in that kind that take five in the hundred. Bacon's Essays.

6. Sort. It has a slight and unimportant sense.

Diogenes was asked, in a kind of scorn, what was the matter that philosophers haunted rich men, and not rich men philosophers? He answered, because the one knew what they wanted, the other did not. Bacon.

kine n.s. plur. from *cow.*

To milk the kine,
E'er the milk-maid fine
Hath open'd her eyne. Ben. Johnson.

A field I went, amid' the morning dew,
To milk my kine. Gay.

king n.s. [A contraction of the Teutonick word *cuning*, or *cyning*, the name of sovereign dignity. In the primitive tongue it signifies stout or valiant, the kings of most nations being, in the beginning, chosen by the people on account of their valour and strength. Verstegan.]

1. Monarch; supreme governour.

The great king of kings,
Hath in the table of his law commanded,
That thou shalt do no murder. Shakes. R. III.

A substitute shines brightly as a king,
Until a king be by; and then his state
Empties itself, as doth an inland brook
Into the main of waters. Shak. Merch. of Venice.

True hope is swift, and flies with
   swallows wings;
Kings it makes gods, and meaner
   creatures kings. Shakesp.

   The king becoming graces,
As justice, verity, temp'rance, stableness,
Bounty, persev'rance, mercy, lowliness,
Devotion, patience, courage, fortitude,
I have no relish of them. Shakespeare's Macbeth.

Thus states were form'd; the name of
   king unknown,
'Till common int'rest plac'd the sway in one;
'Twas virtue only, or in arts, or arms,
Diffusing blessings, or averting harms,
The same which in a sire the sons obey'd,
A prince the father of a people made. Pope.

2. It is taken by Bacon in the feminine: as prince also is.

Ferdinand and Isabella, kings of Spain, recovered the great and rich kingdom of Granada from the Moors. Bacon.

3. A card with the picture of a king.

   The king unseen
Lurk'd in her hand, and mourn'd his captive
   queen. Pope.

4. King at Arms, or of heralds, a principal officer at arms, that has the pre-eminence of the society; of whom there are three in number, viz. Garter, Norroy, and Clarencieux. Phillips.

A letter under his own hand was lately shewed me by sir William Dugdale, king at arms. Walton.

kingsévil n.s. [*king* and *evil.*] A scrofulous distemper, in which the glands are ulcerated, commonly believed to be cured by the touch of the king.[†]

Sore eyes are frequently a species of the kingsevil, and take their beginning from vicious humours inflaming the tunica adnata. Wiseman's Surgery.

kirk n.s. [*cyrce*, Saxon; κυριακκη.] An old word for a church, yet retained in Scotland.

Home they hasten the posts to dight,
And all the kirk pillars ere day-light,
With hawthorn buds, and sweet eglantine.
Spenser.

Nor is it all the nation hath these spots,
There is a church as well as kirk of Scots.
Cleaveland.

What one party thought to rivet by the Scots,
that the other contemns, despising the kirk
government and discipline of the Scots.
King Charles.

kitchenwench n.s. [*kitchen* and *wench*.] Scullion; maid employed to clean the instruments of cookery.

Laura to his lady was but a kitchenwench.
Shakespeare.

Roasting and boiling leave to the
kitchenwench. Swift.

kitten n.s. [*katteken*, Dutch.] A young cat.

That a mare will sooner drown than an horse
is not experienced, nor is the same observed
in the drowning of whelps and kittens.
Brown's Vulg. Err.

It was scratched in playing with a kitten.
Wiseman.

Helen was just slipt into bed;
Her eyebrows on the toilet lay,
Away the kitten with them fled,
As fees belonging to her prey. Prior.

to knápple v.n. [from *knap*] To break off with a sharp quick noise. Ainsworth.

knave n.s. [*cnapa*, Saxon.]

1. A boy; a male child.

2. A servant. Both these are obsolete.

For as the moon the eye doth please
With gentle beams not hurting sight,
Yet hath sir sun the greater praise,
Because from him doth come her light;
So if my man must praises have,
What then must I that keep the knave?
Sidney.

He eats and drinks with his domestick slaves;
A verier hind than any of his knaves. Dryden.

3. A petty rascal; a scoundrel; a dishonest fellow.

Most men rather brook their being reputed
knaves, than for their honesty be accounted
fools; knave, in the mean time, passing for
a name of credit. South's Sermons.

When both plaintiff and defendant happen to
be crafty knaves, there's equity against both.
L'Estrange.

An honest man may take a knave's advice;
But idiots only may be cozen'd twice. Dryden.

See all our fools aspiring to be knaves. Pope.

4. A card with a soldier painted on it.

For 'twill return, and turn t' account,
If we are brought in play upon 't,
Or but by casting knaves get in,
What pow'r can hinder us to win? Hudibras.

knight n.s. [*cniht*, Sax. *knecht*, Germ. a servant, or pupil.]

1. A man advanced to a certain degree of military rank. It was anciently the custom to knight every man of rank or fortune, that he might be qualified to give challenges, to fight in the lists, and to perform feats of arms. In England knighthood confers the title of sir: as, sir Thomas, sir Richard. When the name was not known, it was usual to say sir knight.

That same knight's own sword this is of yore,
Which Merlin made. Spenser.

Sir knight, if knight thou be,
Abandon this forestalled place. Spenser.

When every case in law is right,
No squire in debt, and no poor knight.
Shak. King Lear.

Pardon, goddess of the night,
Those that slew thy virgin knight;
For the which, with songs of woe,
Round about her tomb they go. Shakesp.

This knight; but yet why should I
* call him knight,*
To give impiety to this rev'rent stile.
Daniel's Civil War.

No squire with knight did better fit
In parts, in manners, and in wit. Hudibras.

2. Among us the order of gentlemen next to the nobility, except the baronets.

The knight intends to make his appearance. Addison.

3. A champion.

He suddenly unties the poke,
Which out of it sent such a smoke,
As ready was them all to choke,
  So grievous was the pother;
So that the knights each other lost,
And stood as still as any post. Drayton.

Did I for this my country bring
To help their knight against their king,
And raise the first sedition? Denham.

knight errant [*chevalier errant.*] A wandering knight; one who went about in quest of adventures.

Like a bold knight errant did proclaim
Combat to all, and bore away the dame. Denham.

The ancient errant knights
Won all their mistresses in fights;
They cut whole giants into fritters,
To put them into am'rous twitters. Hudibras.

knight of the post A hireling evidence.

There are knights of the post, and holy cheats enough, to swear the truth of the broadest contradictions, where pious frauds shall give them an extraordinary call. South's Sermons.

knówledge n.s. [from *know.*]

1. Certain perception; indubitable apprehension.

Knowledge, which is the highest degree of the speculative faculties, consists in the perception of the truth of affirmative or negative propositions. Locke.

2. Learning; illumination of the mind.

Ignorance is the curse of God,
Knowledge the wing wherewith we fly
to heav'n. Shakesp.

3. Skill in any thing.

Do but say to me what I should do,
That in your knowledge may by me be done,
And I am prest unto it. Shak. Merchant of Venice.

4. Acquaintance with any fact or person.

The dog straight fawned upon his master for old knowledge. Sidney.

That is not forgot,
Which ne'er I did remember; to my knowledge
I never in my life did look on him. Shakesp. Rich. II.

5. Cognisance; notice.

Why have I found grace in thine eyes, that thou shouldst take knowledge of me, seeing I am a stranger? Ruth ii. 10.

A state's anger should not take
Knowledge either of fools or women. Ben. Johnson's Catil.

6. Information; power of knowing.

I pulled off my headpiece, and humbly entreated her pardon, or knowledge why she was cruel. Sidney.

to knúbble v.a. [*knipler,* Danish.] To beat. Skinner.

knuff n.s. [perhaps corrupted from *knave,* or the same with *chuff.*] A lout. An old word preserved in a rhyme of prediction.

The country knuffs, Hob, Dick, and Hick,
With clubs and clouted shoon,
Shall fill up Dussendale
With slaughtered bodies soon. Hayward.

L, a liquid consonant, which preserves always the same sound in English. In the Saxon it was aspirated as *hlaf*, *loaf*; *hlæfdig*, *lady*.

At the end of a monosyllable it is always doubled; as, *shall*; *still*, *full*, except after a diphthong; as, *fail*; *feel*; *veal*; *cool*. In a word of more syllables it is written single; as, *channel*; *canal*; *tendril*. It is sometimes put before *e*, and sounded feebly after it; as *bible*; *title*.

la interject. [corrupted by an effeminate pronunciation from *lo*.] See; look; behold.

La you! if you speak ill of the devil,
How he takes it at heart. Shakes.
Twelfth Night.

to lábefy v.a. [*labefacio*, Latin.] To weaken; to impair. Dict.

lábent adj. [*labens*, Lat.] Sliding; gliding; slipping. Dict.

láboratory n.s. [*laboratoire*, French.] A chemist's workroom.

It would contribute to the history of colours,
if chemists would in their laboratory take a
heedful notice, and give us a faithful account,
of the colours observed in the steam of bodies,
either sublimed or distilled. Boyle on
Colours.

The flames of love will perform those miracles
they of the furnace boast of, would they employ
themselves in this laboratory. Decay of Piety.

lábra n.s. [Spanish.] A lip. Hanmer.

Word of denial in thy labras here;
Word of denial, froth and scum thou liest.
Shakespeare.

laced mutton An old word for a whore.

Ay, Sir, I, a lost mutton, gave your letter to
her a lac'd mutton, and she gave me nothing
for my labour. Shakes.

lácerate v.a. [*lacero*, Latin.] To tear; to rend; to separate by violence.

And my sons lacerate and rip up, viper
like, the womb that brought them forth.
Howel's England's Tears.

The heat breaks through the water, so as to
lacerate and lift up great bubbles too heavy
for the air to buoy up, and causeth boiling.
Derham's Physico-Theology.

Here lacerated friendship claims a tear. Va. of
human Wishes.

láchrymary adj. [*lachryma*, Latin.] Containing tears.

How many dresses are there for each
particular deity? what a variety of shapes
in the ancient urns, lamps, and lachrymary
vessels. Addison's Travels through Italy.

lacíniated adj. [from *lacinia*, Lat.] Adorned with fringes and borders.

láckbrain n.s. [*lack* and *brain*.] One that wants wit.

What a lackbrain is this? Our plot is as good
a plot as ever was laid. Shakespeare's
Henry IV. p. i.

láctary n.s. [*lactarium*, Latin.] A dairy house.

lády n.s. [*hlæfdig*, Saxon.]

1. A woman of high rank: the title of lady properly belongs to the wives of knights, of all degrees above them, and to the daughters of earls, and all of higher ranks.

I am much afraid, my lady, his mother, play'd
false with a smith. Shakespeare's Merch. of
Verona.†

I would thy husband were dead; I would
make thee my lady.
—I your lady, Sir John? alas, I should
be a pitiful lady. Shakes. Merry Wives
of Windsor.

I am sorry my relation to so deserving a lady,
should be any occasion of her danger and
affliction. K. Charles.

2. An illustrious or eminent woman.

O foolish fairy's son, what fury mad
Hath thee incens'd to haste thy doleful fate?
Were it not better I that lady had,
Than that thou hadst repented it too late?
Fairy Qu.

I love and hate her; for she's fair and royal,
And that she hath all courtly parts more exquisite
Than lady ladies; winning from each one
The best she hath, and she of all compounded
Out-sells them all. Shakespeare's
Cymbeline.

Before Homer's time this great lady was scarce
heard of. Ral.

May every lady an Evadne prove,
That shall divert me from Aspasia's love.
Waller.

   Shou'd I shun the dangers of the war,
With scorn the Trojans wou'd reward my pains,
And their proud ladies with their sweeping
   trains. Dryden.

*We find on medals the representations of
ladies, that have given occasion to whole
volumes on the account only of a face.*
Addison on ancient Medals.

*Of all these bounds, even from this line to this,
With shadowy forests, and with
    champaigns rich'd,
With plenteous rivers, and wide-skirted meads,
We make thee lady.* Shakespeare's King Lear.

3. A word of complaisance used of women.

*Say, good Cæsar,
That I some lady trifles have reserv'd,
Immoment toys, things of such dignity
As we greet modern friends withal.*
Shakes. Ant. and Cl.

*I hope I may speak of women without offence
to the ladies.* Guardian.

lády-like adj. [*lady* and *like.*] Soft;
delicate; elegant.

*Her tender constitution did declare,
Too lady-like a long fatigue to bear.* Dry.
Hind and Panth.

laird n.s. [*hlaford*, Saxon.] The lord of
a manor in the Scottish dialect.

*Shrive but their title, and their moneys poize,
A laird and twenty pence pronounc'd with noise,
When constru'd but for a plain yeoman go,
And a good sober two pence, and well so.*
Cleaveland.

lambs-wool n.s. [*lamb* and *wool.*] Ale
mixed with the pulp of roasted apples.

A cup of lambs-wool they drank to him there.
Song of the King and the Miller.

to lamm v.a. To beat soundly with a cudgel.
Dict.

Lámmas n.s. [This word is said by Bailey, I
know not on what authority, to be derived
from a custom, by which the tenants of the
archbishop of York were obliged, at the
time of mass, on the first of August, to
bring a lamb to the altar. In Scotland they
are said to wean lambs on this day. It may
else be corrupted from *lattermath.*] The first
of August.

*In 1578 was that famous lammas day, which
buried the reputation of Don John of Austria.*
Bacon.

lampóon n.s. [Bailey derives it from
lampons, a drunken song. It imports, *let us
drink*, from the old French *lamper*, and was
repeated at the end of each couplet at
carousals. Trev.] A personal satire; abuse;
censure written not to reform but to vex.

*They say my talent is satire; if so, it is a
fruitful age: they have sown the dragon's teeth
themselves, and it is but just they should reap
each other in lampoons.* Dryden.

Make satire a lampoon. Pope.

to láncinate v.a. [*lancino*, Latin.] To tear; to
rend; to lacerate.

lándfall n.s. [*land* and *fall.*] A sudden
translation of property in land by the death
of a rich man.

lándgrave n.s. [*land* and *grave*, a count,
German.] A German title of dominion.

lándjobber n.s. [*land* and *job.*] One who
buys and sells lands for other men.

*If your master be a minister of state, let him
be at home to none but his land-jobbers, or his
inventor of new funds.* Swift's Directions to
the Steward.

lánguage n.s. [*language*, French; *lingua*,
Latin.]

1. Human speech.

*We may define language, if we consider it
more materially, to be letters, forming and
producing words and sentences; but if we
consider it according to the design thereof, then
language is apt signs for communication of
thoughts.* Holder.

2. The tongue of one nation as distinct
   from others.

*O! good my lord, no Latin;
I am not such a truant since my coming,
As not to know the language I have liv'd in.*
Shakes.

*He not from Rome alone, but Greece,
Like Jason, brought the golden fleece;
To him that language, though to none
Of th' others, as his own was known.*
Denham.

3. Stile; manner of expression.

Though his language should not be refin'd,
It must not be obscure and impudent.
Roscommon.

Others for language all their care express,
And value books, as women, men, for dress:
Their praise is still—the stile is excellent,
The sense, they humbly take upon content.
Pope.

lánguet n.s. [*languette*, French.] Any thing cut in the form of a tongue.

lánigerous adj. [*laniger*, Latin.] Bearing wool.

lánsquenet n.s. [*lance* and *knecht*, Dutch.]

1. A common foot-soldier.

2. A game at cards.

lápicide n.s. [*lapicida*, Latin.] A stonecutter. Dict.

to lápidate v.a. [*lapido*, Latin.] To stone; to kill by stoning. Dict.

lárdon n.s. [French.] A bit of bacon.

lárum n.s. [from *alarum* or *alarm*.]

1. Alarm; noise noting danger.

Utterers of secrets he from thence debarr'd,
His larum bell might loud and wide be heard,
When cause requir'd, but never out of time,
Early and late it rung, at evening and at
    prime. Fa. Qu.

The peaking cornute her husband dwelling in
a continual larum of jealousy, comes to me in
the instant of our encounter. Shakespeare's Merry Wives of Windsor.

How far off lie these armies?
—Within a mile and half.
—Then shall we hear their larum, and
they ours. Shakes.

She is become formidable to all her neighbours,
as she puts every one to stand upon his guard,
and have a continual larum bell in his ears.
Howell's Vocal Forest.

2. An instrument that makes a noise at a certain hour.

Of this nature was that larum, which, though
it were but three inches big, yet would both
wake a man, and of itself light a candle for
him at any set hour. Wilkins.

I see men as lusty and strong that eat but two
meals a day, as others that have set their
stomachs, like larums, to call on them for four
or five. Locke on Education.

The young Æneas all at once let down,
Stunn'd with his giddy larum half the town.
Dunciad.

lascívient adj. [*lasciviens*, Lat.] Frolicksome; wantoning.

Látin adj. [*Latinus.*] Written or spoken in the language of the old Romans.

Augustus himself could not make a new Latin
word. Locke.

Látinism [*Latinisme*, French; *latinismus*, low Latin.] A Latin idiom; a mode of speech peculiar to the Latin.

Milton has made use of frequent
transpositions, Latinisms, antiquated words
and phrases, that he might the better deviate
from vulgar and ordinary expressions.
Addison's Rem.

Latínity n.s. [*Latinité*, French; *latinitas*, Latin.] Purity of Latin stile; the Latin tongue.

If Shakespeare was able to read Plautus with
ease, nothing in Latinity could be hard to
him. Dennis's Letters.

latitátion n.s. [from *latito*, Latin.] The state of lying concealed.

látitudinarian adj. [*latitudinaire*, French; *latitudinarius*, low Latin.] Not restrained; not confined; thinking or acting at large.

Latitudinarian love will be expensive, and
therefore I would be informed what is to be
gotten by it. Collier on Kindness.

látitudinarian n.s. One who departs from orthodoxy.†

láudanum n.s. [A cant word, from *laudo*, Latin.] A soporifick tincture.

lávatory n.s. [from *lavo*, Latin.] A wash; something in which parts diseased are washed.

Lavatories, to wash the temples, hands, wrists, and jugulars, do potently profligate, and keep off the venom. Harvey.

lavólta n.s. [*la volte*, French.] An old dance, in which was much turning and much capering. Hanmer.

    I cannot sing,
Nor heel the high lavolt; nor sweeten talk;
Nor play at subtle games. Shakes. Troilus and Cressida.

law n.s. [*laga*, Saxon; *loi*, French; *lawgh*, Erse.]

1. A rule of action.

Unhappy man! to break the pious laws
Of nature, pleading in his children's cause. Dryden.

2. A decree, edict, statute, or custom, publickly established as a rule of justice.

    He hath resisted law,
And therefore law shall scorn him further trial
Than the severity of publick power. Shakes. Coriolanus.

    Thou art a robber,
A law-breaker, a villain; yield thee, thief. Shakespeare.

Our nation would not give laws to the Irish, therefore now the Irish gave laws to them. Davies on Ireland.

One law is split into two. Baker Reflect. on Learning.

3. Judicial process.

When every case in law is right. Shakes. King Lear.

    Who has a breast so pure,
But some uncleanly apprehensions
Keep leets and law days, and in sessions sit,
With meditations lawful. Shakespeare's Othello.

Tom Touchy is a fellow famous for taking the law of every body: there is not one in the town where he lives that he has not sued at a quarter-sessions. Addison's Spectator.

4. Conformity to law; any thing lawful.

    In a rebellion,
When what's not meet, but what must be, was law,
Then were they chosen. Shakespeare's Coriolanus.

5. An established and constant mode or process; a fixed correspondence of cause and effect.

I dy'd, whilst in the womb he stay'd,
Attending Nature's law. Shakespeare's Cymbeline.

lawn n.s. [*land*, Danish; *lawn*, Welsh; *lande*, French.]

1. An open space between woods.

Betwixt them lawns, or level downs, and flocks,
Grazing the tender herb, were interpos'd. Milt. Pa. Lost.

His mountains were in a few years shaded with young trees, that gradually shot up into groves, woods, and forests, intermixed with walks, and lawns, and gardens. Addison's Spectator, N° 58.

Stern beasts in trains that by his truncheon fell,
Now grisly forms shoot o'er the lawns of hell. Pope.

Interspers'd in lawns and opening glades,
Thin trees arise that shun each other's shades. Pope.

2. [*Linon*, French.] Fine linen, remarkable for being used in the sleeves of bishops.

    Should'st thou bleed,
To stop the wounds my finest lawn I'd tear,
Wash them with tears, and wipe them with my hair. Prior.

From high life high characters are drawn,
A saint in crape is twice a saint in lawn. Pope.

What awe did the slow solemn knell inspire:
The duties by the lawn rob'd prelate pay'd,
And the last words, that dust to dust convey'd! Tickell.

láwyer n.s. [from *law*.] Professor of law; advocate; pleader.

It is like the breath of an unfeed lawyer,
you gave me nothing for it. Shakespeare's
King Lear.

Is the law evil, because some lawyers in their
office swerve from it? Whitgift.

I have entered into a work touching laws, in
a middle term, between the speculative and
reverend discourses of philosophers, and the
writings of lawyers. Bacon's Holy War.

The nymphs with scorn beheld their foes,
When the defendant's council rose;
And, what no lawyer ever lack'd,
With impudence own'd all the fact. Swift.

lay n.s. [*lay*, French. It is said originally to
signify sorrow or complaint, and then to
have been transferred to poems written to
express sorrow. It is derived by the French
from *lessus*, Latin, a funeral song; but it is
found likewise in the Teutonick dialect: *ley*,
leoδ, Saxon; *leey*, Danish.] A song; a poem.

To the maiden's sounding timbrels sung,
In well attuned notes, a joyous lay.
Spens. Fairy Queen.

Soon he slumber'd, fearing not be harm'd,
The whiles with a loud lay, she thus
*   him sweetly charm'd.* Spenser's Fairy
Queen, b. ii.

This is a most majestick vision, and
Harmonious charming lays. Shakespeare's
Tempest.

*   Nor then the solemn nightingale*
Ceas'd warbling, but all night tun'd her
*   soft lays.* Milton.

*   If Jove's will*
Have link'd that amorous power to thy soft lay,
Now timely sing. Milton.

He reach'd the nymph with his harmonious lay,
Whom all his charms could not incline to stay.
Waller.

On Ceres let him call, and Ceres praise,
With uncouth dances, and with country lays.
Dryd. Virg.

Ev'n gods incline their ravish'd ears,
And tune their own harmonious spheres
To his immortal lays. Dennis.

lázar n.s. [from *Lazarus* in the gospel.] One
deformed and nauseous with filthy and
pestilential diseases.

They ever after in most wretched case,
Like loathsome lazars, by the hedges lay.
Fairy Queen.

I'll be sworn and sworn upon 't, she never
shrowded any but lazars. Shakespeare's
Troil. and Cressida.

I am weary with drawing the deformities
of life, and lazars of the people, where every
figure of imperfection more resembles me.
Dryden's Aurengzebe.

*   Life he labours to refine*
Daily, nor of his little stock denies
Fit alms, to lazars, merciful, and meek. Philips.

lazar-house, lazarétto n.s. [*lazaret*, French;
lazzeretto, Italian; from *lazar*.] A house for
the reception of the diseased; an hospital.

*   A place*
Before his eyes appear'd, sad, noisome, dark,
A lazar-house it seem'd, where were laid
Numbers of all diseas'd. Milton's Paradise
Lost, b. xi.

leading-strings n.s. [*lead* and *string*.]
Strings by which children, when they learn
to walk, are held from falling.

Sound may serve such, ere they to sense
*   are grown,*
Like leading-strings, 'till they can walk alone.
Dryden.

Was he ever able to walk without leading-
strings, or swim without bladders, without
being discovered by his hobbling and his
sinking? Swift.

leaf n.s. plural leaves. [*leaf*, Saxon;
leaf, Dutch.]

1. The green deciduous parts of plants
and flowers.

This is the state of man; to-day he puts forth
The tender leaves of hopes, to-morrow
*   blossoms.* Shakes.

A man shall seldom fail of having cherries
borne by his graft the same year in which his

incision is made, if his graft have blossom buds; whereas if it were only leaf buds, it will not bear fruit till the second season. Boyle.

Those things which are removed to a distant view, ought to make but one mass; as the leaves on the trees, and the billows in the sea. Dryden's Dufresnoy.

2. A part of a book, containing two pages.

Happy ye leaves, when as those lilly hands Shall handle you. Spenser.

Peruse my leaves through ev'ry part, And think thou seest my owner's heart Scrawl'd o'er with trifles. Swift.

3. One side of a double door.

The two leaves of the one door were folding. I Kings.

4. Any thing foliated, or thinly beaten.

Eleven ounces two pence sterling ought to be of so pure silver, as is called leaf silver, and then the melter must add of other weight seventeen pence halfpenny farthing. Camden.

Leaf gold, that flies in the air as light as down, is as truly gold as that in an ingot. Digby on Bodies.

leap-frog n.s. [*leap* and *frog*.] A play of children, in which they imitate the jump of frogs.

If I could win a lady at leap-frog, I should quickly leap into a wife. Shakespeare's Henry V.

leap-year n.s. Leap-year or bissextile is every fourth year, and so called from its *leaping* a day more that year than in a common year: so that the common year hath 365 days, but the leap-year 366; and then February hath 29 days, which in common years hath but 28. To find the leap-year you have this rule:

> Divide by 4; what's left shall be
> For leap-year 0; for past 1, 2, 3.
> Harris.

That the sun consisteth of 365 days and almost six hours, wanting eleven minutes; which six hours omitted will, in process of *time, largely deprave the compute; and this is the occasion of the bissextile or leap-year.* Brown's Vulg. Err.

to learn v.a. [*leornian*, Saxon.]

1. To gain the knowledge or skill of.

Learn a parable of the fig-tree. Mat. xxiv. 32.

He, in a shorter time than was thought possible, learned both to speak and write the Arabian tongue. Knolles.

Learn, wretches! learn the motions of the mind, And the great moral end of humankind. Dryd. Persius.

You may rely upon my tender care, To keep him far from perils of ambition: All he can learn of me, will be to weep! A. Philips.

2. To teach. [It is observable, that in many of the European languages the same word signifies to learn and to teach; to gain or impart knowledge.]

> *He would learn*
> *The lion stoop to him in lowly-wise,*
> *A lesson hard.* Spenser's Fairy Queen, b. i.

You taught me language, and my profit on 't Is, I know not how to curse: the red plague rid you, For learning me your language. Shakesp. Tempest.†

A thousand more mischances than this one, Have learn'd me how to brook this patiently. Shakes.

> *Hast thou not learn'd me how*
> *To make perfumes?* Shakespeare's Cymbeline.

Ye might learn in us not to think of men above that which is written. 1 Cor. iv. 6.

learned adj. [from *learn*.]

1. Versed in science and literature.

It is indifferent to the matter in hand, which way the learned shall determine of it. Locke.

Some by old words to fame have made pretence: Such labour'd nothings, in so strange a style, Amaze th' unlearn'd, and make the learned smile. Pope.

The learned met with free approach,
Although they came not in a coach. Swift.

The best account is given of them by
their own authors: but I trust more to the
table of the learned bishop of Bath.
Arbuthnot on Coins.

2. Skilled; skilful; knowing.

Though train'd in arms, and learn'd in
martial arts,
Thou chusest not to conquer men but hearts.
Granville.

3. Skilled in scholastick knowledge.

Till a man can judge whether they be truths
or no, his understanding is but little
improved: and thus men of much reading are
greatly learned, but may be little knowing.
Locke.

learning n.s. [from *learn.*]

1. Literature; skill in languages or sciences;
   generally scholastick knowledge.

Learning hath its infancy, when it is almost
childish; then its youth, when luxuriant and
juvenile; then its strength of years, when solid;
and, lastly, its old age, when dry and exhaust.
Bacon's Essays.

To tongue or pudding thou hast no pretence,
Learning thy talent is, but mine is sense.
Prior.

As Moses was learned in all the wisdom of the
Egyptians, so it is manifest from this chapter,
that St. Paul was a great master in all the
learning of the Greeks. Bentley's Sermons.

2. Skill in any thing good or bad.

An art of contradiction by way of scorn, a
learning wherewith we were long sithence
forewarned; that the miserable times
whereunto we are fallen should abound.
Hooker.

lécher n.s. [Derived by Skinner from
luxure, old French: *luxuria* is used in the
middle ages in the same sense.] A
whoremaster.

I will now take the leacher; he's at my house;
he cannot 'scape me. Shakes. Merry Wives
of Windsor.

You, like a letcher, out of whorish loins
Are pleas'd to breed out your inheritors.
Shakespeare.

The lecher soon transforms his mistress; now
In Io's place appears a lovely cow. Dryden.

The sleepy leacher shuts his little eyes,
About his churning chaps the frothy bubbles
   rise. Dryden.

   She yields her charms
To that fair letcher, the strong god of arms.
Pope's Odys.

léction n.s. [*lectio,* Lat.] A reading; a variety
in copies.

Every critick has his own hypothesis: if the
common text be not favourable to his opinion,
a various lection shall be made authentick.
Watts's Logick.

lécture n.s. [*lecture,* French.]

1. A discourse pronounced upon
   any subject.

Mark him, while Dametas reads his rustick
lecture unto him, how to feed his beasts before
noon, and where to shade them in the extreme
heat. Sidney, b. ii.

   Wrangling pedant,
When in musick we have spent an hour,
Your lecture shall have leisure for as much.
Shakesp.

When letters from Cæsar were given
to Rusticus, he refused to open them till
the philosopher had done his lectures.
Taylor's Holy Living.

Virtue is the solid good, which tutors should
not only read lectures and talk of, but the
labour and art of education should furnish
the mind with, and fasten there. Locke.

Numidia will be blest by Cato's lectures.
Addison's Cato.

2. The act or practice of reading; perusal.

In the lecture of holy scripture, their
apprehensions are commonly confined unto
the literal sense of the text. Browne.

3. A magisterial reprimand.

léechcraft n.s. [*leech* and *craft*.] The art of healing.

We study speech, but others we persuade:
We leechcraft learn, but others cure with it.
Davies.

léeward adj. [*lee* and *weard*, Saxon.]

1. Towards the wind. See *lee*.†

The classicæ were called long ships, the
onerariæ round, because of their figure
approaching towards circular: this figure,
though proper for the stowage of goods, was
not the fittest for sailing, because of the great
quantity of leeward way, except when they
sailed full before the wind. Arbuth.

    Let no statesman dare,
A kingdom to a ship compare;
Lest he should call our commonweal
A vessel with a double keel;
Which just like ours, new rigg'd and man'd,
And got about a league from land,
By change of wind to leeward side,
The pilot knew not how to guide. Swift.

légend n.s. [*legenda*, Latin.]

1. A chronicle or register of the lives of saints.

Legends being grown in a manner to be
nothing else but heaps of frivolous and
scandalous vanities, they have been even with
disdain thrown out, the very nests which bred
them abhorring them. Hooker, b. v.

There are in Rome two sets of antiquities, the
christian and the heathen; the former, though
of a fresher date, are so embroiled with fable
and legend, that one receives but little
satisfaction. Addison's Remarks on Italy.

2. Any memorial or relation.

And in this legend all that glorious deed
Read, whilst you arm you; arm you whilst
    you read. Fairfax, b. i.

3. An incredible unauthentick narrative.

Who can show the legends, that record
More idle tales, or fables so absurd.
Blackmore.

It is the way and means of attaining to
heaven, that makes profane scorners so
willingly let go the expectation of it. It
is not the articles of the creed, but the duty
to God and their neighbour, that is such
an inconsistent incredible legend.
Bentley's Sermons.

4. Any inscription; particularly on medals or coins.

Compare the beauty and comprehensiveness
of legends on ancient coins. Addison on Medals.

légerdemain n.s. [contracted perhaps from *legereté de main*, French.] Slight of hand; juggle; power of deceiving the eye by nimble motion; trick; deception; knack.

He so light was at legerdemain,
That what he touch'd came not to light again.
Hubberd.

Of all the tricks and legerdemain by which
men impose upon their own souls, there is
none so common as the plea of a good
intention. South's Sermons.

legisláture n.s. [from *legislator*, Latin.] The power that makes laws.

Without the concurrent consent of all three
parts of the legislature, no law is or can be
made. Hale's Com. Law.

In the notion of a legislature is implied a
power to change, repeal, and suspend laws
in being, as well as to make new laws.
Addison's Freeholder, N° 16.

By the supreme magistrate is properly
understood the legislative power; but the
word magistrate seeming to denote a single
person, and to express the executive power,
it came to pass that the obedience due to the
legislature was, for want of considering
this easy distinction, misapplied to the
administration. Swift's Sentiments of a Ch. of England Man.

léman n.s. [Generally supposed to be *laimant*, the lover, French; but imagined by Junius, with almost equal probability, to be derived from *leef*, Dutch, or *leof*, Saxon, *beloved* and *man*. This etymology is strongly supported by the antient orthography, according to which it was written *leveman*.] A sweetheart; a gallant; or a mistress. Hanmer.

Hold for my sake, and do him not to dye;
But vanquish'd, thine eternal bondslave make,
And me thy worthy meed unto thy leman
    take. Fa. Qu.

A cup of wine,
That's brisk and fine,
And drink unto the leman mine.
Shakes. Henry IV.

lemonáde n.s. [from *lemon*.] Liquor made of water, sugar, and the juice of lemons.

Thou, and thy wife, and children, should walk in my gardens, buy toys, and drink lemonade. Arbuth. J. Bull.

lens n.s. A glass spherically convex on both sides, is usually called a *lens;* such as is a burning-glass, or spectacle-glass, or an object glass of a telescope. Newton's Opticks.

According to the difference of the lenses, I used various distances. Newton's Opticks.

léntiform adj. [*lens* and *forma*, Latin.] Having the form of a lens.

léntiginous adj. [from *lentigo*.] Scurfy; furfuraceous.

léporine adj. [*leporinus*, Lat.] Belonging to a hare; having the nature of a hare.

léprosy n.s. [*lepra*, Latin; *lepre*, French.] A loathsome distemper, which covers the body with a kind of white scales.

    Itches, blains,
Sow all the Athenian bosoms, and their crop
Be general leprosy. Shakesp. Timon of Athens.

It is a plague of leprosy. Lev. xiii. 3.

Between the malice of my enemies and other mens mistakes, I put as great a difference as between the itch of novelty and the leprosy of disloyalty. King Charles.

Authors, upon the first entrance of the pox, looked upon it so highly infectious, that they ran away from it as much as the Jews did from the leprosy. Wiseman's Surgery.

lérry [from *lere*.] A rating; a lecture. A rustick word.

let n.s. [from the verb.] Hindrance; obstacle; obstruction; impediment.

The secret lets and difficulties in public proceedings are innumerable and inevitable. Hooker, b. i.

Solyman without let presented his army before the city of Belgrade. Knolles's History of the Turks.

It had been done e'er this, had I been consul; We had had no stop, no let. Benj. Johnson's Catiline.

Just judge, two lets remove; that free from dread, I may before thy high tribunal plead. Sandys on Job.

To these internal dispositions to sin add the external opportunities and occasions concurring with them, and removing all lets and rubs out of the way, and making the path of destruction plain before the sinner's face; so that he may run his course freely. South.

léthe n.s. [λήθη.] Oblivion; a draught of oblivion.

The conquering wine hath steept our sense In soft and delicate lethe. Shakes. Ant. and Cleopatra.

Lethe, the river of oblivion, rolls Her wat'ry labyrinth, which who so drinks Forgets both joy and grief. Milton.

létter n.s. [*lettre*, French; *litera*, Latin.]

1. One of the elements of syllables.

A superscription was written over him in letters of Greek, Latin, and Hebrew. Luke xxiii. 38.

Thou whoreson Zed! thou unnecessary letter! Shakes.

2. A written message; an epistle.

They use to write it on the top of letters. Shakespeare.

    I have a letter from her Of such contents as you will wonder at. Shakespeare.

When a Spaniard would write a letter by him, the Indian would marvel how it should be possible, that he, to whom he came, should be able to know all things. Abbot.

The asses will do very well for trumpeters, and the hares will make excellent letter carriers. L'Estrange's Fables.

The stile of letters ought to be free, easy, and natural; as near approaching to familiar conversation as possible: the two best qualities in conversation are, good humour and good breeding; those letters are therefore certainly the best that shew the most of these two qualities. Walsh.

Mrs. P. B. has writ to me, and is one of the best letter writers I know; very good sense, civility, and friendship, without any stiffness or constraint. Swift.

3. The literal or expressed meaning.

Touching translations of holy scripture, we may not disallow of their painful travels herein, who strictly have tied themselves to the very original letter. Hooker, b. v.

In obedience to human laws, we must observe the letter of the law, without doing violence to the reason of the law, and the intention of the lawgiver. Taylor's holy living.

Those words of his must be understood not according to the bare rigour of the letter, but according to the allowances of expression. South's Sermons.

What! since the pretor did my fetters loose, And left me freely at my own dispose, May I not live without controul and awe, Excepting still the letter of the law? Dryden's Persius.

4. Letters without the singular: learning.

The Jews marvelled, saying, How knoweth this man letters, having never learned? John vii. 15.

5. Any thing to be read.

Good laws are at best but a dead letter. Addis. Freeholder.

6. Type with which books are printed.

The iron ladles that letter founders use to the casting of printing letters, are kept constantly in melting metal. Moxon.

léttered adj. [from *letter*.] Literate; educated to learning.

A martial man, not sweetened by a lettered education, is apt to have a tincture of sourness. Collier on Pride.

lévant adj. [*levant*, French.] Eastern.

    Thwart of those, as fierce Forth rush the levant, and the ponent winds, Eurus and Zephyr. Milton's Paradise Lost, b. x.

lévee n.s. [French.]

1. The time of rising.

2. The concourse of those who croud round a man of power in a morning.

The servile rout their careful Cæsar praise; Him they extol, they worship him alone, They croud his levees, and support his throne. Dryden.

Woud'st thou be first minister of state? To have thy levees crouded with resort, Of a depending, gaping, servile court. Dryden's Juvenal.

None of her Sylvan subjects made their court, Levees and couchees pass'd without resort. Dryden.

léveller n.s. [from *level*.]

1. One who makes any thing even.

2. One who destroys superiority; one who endeavours to bring all to the same state of equality.

You are an everlasting leveller; you won't allow encouragement to extraordinary merit. Collier on Pride.

leviathan n.s. [לִוְיָתָן.] A water animal mentioned in the book of Job. By some imagined the crocodile, but in poetry generally taken for the whale.

We may, as bootless, spend our vain command Upon th' enraged soldiers in their spoil, As send our precepts to th' leviathan, To come ashore. Shakespeare's Henry V.

Canst thou draw out leviathan with an hook?
Job.

More to embroil the deep; leviathan,
And his unwieldy train, in dreadful sport
Tempest the loosen'd brine.
Thomson's Winter.

lévite n.s. [*levita*, Latin, from *Levi*.]

1. One of the tribe of Levi; one born to the office of priesthood among the Jews.

In the Christian church, the office of deacons succeeded in the place of the levites among the Jews, who were as ministers and servants to the priests. Ayliffe's Parergon.

2. A priest: used in contempt.

lévity n.s. [*levitas*, Latin.]

1. Lightness; not heaviness: the quality by which any body has less weight than another.

He gave the form of levity to that which ascended; to that which descended, the form of gravity. Raleigh.

This bubble, by reason of its comparative levity to the fluidity that encloses it, would necessarily ascend to the top. Bentley's Sermons.

2. Inconstancy; changeableness.

They every day broached some new thing; which restless levity they did interpret to be their growing in spiritual perfection. Hooker.

Where wigs with wigs, with sword-knots sword-knots strive,
Beaus banish beaus, and coaches coaches drive,
This erring mortals levity may call. Pope.

3. Unsteadiness; laxity of mind.

I unbosom'd all my secrets to thee;
Not out of levity, but over-pow'r'd
By thy request. Milton's Agonistes.

4. Idle pleasure; vanity.

He never employed his omnipotence out of levity or ostentation, but as the necessities of men required. Calamy.

5. Trifling gaiety; want of seriousness.

Our graver business frowns at this levity. Shakespeare.

Hopton abhorred the licence, and the levities, with which he saw too many corrupted. Clarendon, b. viii.

That spirit of religion and seriousness vanished, and a spirit of levity and libertinism, infidelity and prophaneness, started up in the room of it. Atterbury's Sermons.

lewd adj. [*lœwede*, Saxon.]

1. Lay; not clerical. Obsolete.

For leuyd men this book I writ. Bishop Grosthead.

So these great clerks their little wisdom shew
To mock the lewd, as learn'd in this as they.
Davies.

2. Wicked; bad; naughty.

If some be admitted into the ministry, either void of learning, or lewd in life, are all the rest to be condemned? Whitgift.

Before they did oppress the people, only by colour of a lewd custom, they did afterwards use the same oppressions by warrant. Davies on Ireland.

3. Lustful; libidinous.

He is not lolling on a lewd love bed,
But on his knees at meditation. Shakespeare's Rich. III.

Then lewd Anchemolus he laid in dust,
Who stain'd his stepdam's bed with impious lust. Dryden.

léwdster n.s. [from *lewd*.] A lecher; one given to criminal pleasures.

Against such lewdsters, and their lechery,
Those that betray them do no treachery.
Shakespeare.

Léwis d'or n.s. [French.] A golden French coin, in value twelve livres, now settled at seventeen shillings. Dict.

lexicógrapher n.s. [λεξικον and γραφω; *lexicographe*, French.] A writer of dictionaries; a harmless drudge, that busies himself in tracing the original, and detailing the signification of words.

Commentators and lexicographers acquainted with the Syriac language, have given these hints in their writings on scripture. Watts's Improvement of the Mind.

léxicon n.s. [λεξικον.] A dictionary; a book teaching the signification of words.

Though a linguist should pride himself to have all the tongues that Babel cleft the world into, yet if he had not studied the solid things in them as well as the words and lexicons, yet he were nothing so much to be esteemed a learned man as any yeoman competently wise in his mother dialect only. Milton.

líbel n.s. [libellus, Latin; libelle, French.]

1. A satire; defamatory writing; a lampoon.

Are we reproached for the name of Christ? that ignominy serves but to advance our future glory; every such libel here becomes panegyrick there. Decay of Piety.

Good heav'n! that sots and knaves should
      be so vain,
To wish their vile resemblance may remain
And stand recorded, at their own request,
To future days, a libel or a jest. Dryden.

2. [In the civil law.] A declaration or charge in writing against a person in court.

líberal adj. [liberalis, Latin; liberal, French.]

1. Not mean; not low in birth; not low in mind.

2. Becoming a gentleman.

3. Munificent; generous; bountiful; not parcimonious.

Her name was Mercy, well known over all
To be both gracious and eke liberal.
Spens. Fa. Queen.

Sparing would shew a worse sin than
      ill doctrine.
Men of his way should be most liberal,
They're set here for examples. Shakesp.
Henry VIII.

      Needs must the pow'r
That made us, and for us this ample world,
Be infinitely good, and of his good
As liberal and free, as infinite. Milton.

There is no art better than to be liberal of praise and commendation to others, in that wherein a man's self hath any perfection. Bacon's Essays.

    The liberal are secure alone;
For what we frankly give, for ever is
    our own. Granville.

Several clergymen, otherwise little fond of obscure terms, are, in their sermons, very liberal of all those which they find in ecclesiastical writers, as if it were our duty to understand them. Swift.

líbertine n.s. [libertin, French.]

1. One unconfined; one at liberty.

    When he speaks,
The air, a charter'd libertine, is still;
And the mute wonder lurketh in men's ears,
To steal his sweet and honied sentences.
Shakesp. Hen. V.

2. One who lives without restraint or law.

Man, the lawless libertine, may rove
Free and unquestion'd. Rowe's Jane Shore.

Want of power is the only bound that a libertine puts to his views upon any of the sex. Clarissa.

3. One who pays no regard to the precepts of religion.

They say this town is full of couzenage,
As nimble jugglers, that deceive the eye;
Disguised cheaters, prating mountebanks,
And many such like libertines of sin.
Shakespeare.

That word may be applied to some few libertines in the audience. Collier's View of the Stage.

4. [In law; libertinus, Lat.] A freedman; or rather, the son of a freedman.

Some persons are forbidden to be accusers on the score of their sex, as women; others on the score of their age, as pupils and infants; others on the score of their conditions, as libertines against their patrons. Ayliffe's Parergon.

líberty n.s. [liberté, French; libertas, Latin.]

1. Freedom, as opposed to slavery.

*My master knows of your being here, and
hath threatened to put me into everlasting
liberty, if I tell you of it; for he swears, he'll
turn me away.* Shakespeare.

*O liberty! thou goddess, heav'nly bright!
Profuse of bliss, and pregnant with delight,
Eternal pleasures in thy presence reign.*
Addison.

2. Freedom, as opposed to necessity.

*Liberty is the power in any agent to do, or
forbear, any particular action, according to
the determination, or thought of the mind,
whereby either of them is preferred to the
other.* Locke.

*As it is in the motions of the body, so it is in
the thoughts of our minds: where any one is
such, that we have power to take it up, or lay
it by, according to the preference of the mind,
there we are at liberty.* Locke.

3. Privilege; exemption; immunity.

*His majesty gave not an intire country to
any, much less did he grant* jura regalia, *or
any extraordinary liberties.* Davies.†

4. Relaxation of restraint.

5. Leave; permission.

*I shall take the liberty to consider a third
ground, which, with some men, has the same
authority.* Locke.

líbral adj. [*libralis*, Latin.] Of a pound
weight. Dict.

librárian n.s. [*librarius*, Latin.]

1. One who has the care of a library.

2. One who transcribes or copies books.

*Charybdis thrice swallows, and thrice refunds,
the waves: this must be understood of regular
tides. There are indeed but two tides in a day,
but this is the error of the librarians.*
Broome's Notes on the Odyssey.

license n.s. [*licentia*, Latin; *licence*, French.]

1. Exorbitant liberty; contempt of legal
and necessary restraint.

*Some of the wiser seeing that a popular licence
is indeed the many-headed tyranny, prevailed
with the rest to make Musidorus their chief.*
Sidney.

*Taunt my faults
With such full licence, as both truth and malice
Have power to utter.* Shakesp. Ant. and
Cleopatra.

*They baul for freedom in their senseless moods,
And still revolt when truth would set them free;
Licence they mean, when they cry liberty.*
Milton.

*The privilege that ancient poets claim,
Now turn'd to license by too just a name.*
Roscommon.

*Though this be a state of liberty, yet it is not
a state of licence; though man, in that state,
have an uncontroulable liberty to dispose of
his person or possessions, yet he has not liberty
to destroy himself.* Locke.

2. A grant of permission.

*They sent some to bring them a licence from
the senate.* Judith xi. 14.

*Those few abstract names that the schools
forged, and put into the mouths of their
scholars, could never yet get admittance into
common use, or obtain the licence of publick
approbation.* Locke.

*We procured a licence of the duke of Parma
to enter the theatre and gallery.* Addison
on Italy.

3. Liberty; permission.

*It is not the manner of the Romans to deliver
any man to die, before that he which is
accused have the accusers face to face, and
have licence to answer for himself.* Acts.

licéntious n.s. [*licencieux*, French;
licentiosus, Latin.]

1. Unrestrained by law or morality.

*Later ages pride, like corn-fed steed,
Abus'd her plenty, and fat swoln encrease,
To all licentious lust, and gan exceed
The measure of her mean, and natural
first need.* Fa. Qu.

*How would it touch thee to the quick,
Should'st thou but hear I were licentious?
And that this body, consecrate to thee,
With ruffian lust should be contaminate.*
Shakespeare.

2. Presumptuous; unconfined.

The Tyber, whose licentious waves,
So often overflow'd the neighbouring fields,
Now runs a smooth and inoffensive course.
Roscommon.

lich n.s. [*lice*, Saxon.] A dead carcase;
whence *lichwake*, the time or act of
watching by the dead; *lichgate*, the gate
through which the dead are carried to the
grave; *Lichfield*, the field of the dead, a city
in Staffordshire, so named from martyred
christians. *Salve magna parens. Lichwake* is
still retained in Scotland in the same sense.†

licorice n.s. [γλυκυρριζα; *liquoricia*,
Italian; *glycyrrhzza*, Latin.] A root of
sweet taste.

Liquorice hath a papilionaceous flower; the
pointal which arises from the empalement
becomes a short pod, containing several
kidney-shaped seeds; the leaves are placed
by parts joined to the mid-rib, and are
terminated by an odd lobe. Miller.

Liquorice root is long and slender, externally
of a dusky reddish brown, but within of a
fine yellow, full of juice, void of smell, and
of a taste sweeter than sugar; it grows wild in
many parts of France, Italy, Spain, and
Germany. This root is excellent in coughs,
and all disorders of the lungs. The inspissated
juice of this root is brought to us from Spain
and Holland; from the first of which places
it obtained the name of Spanish juice.
Hill's Materia Medica.

lie n.s. [*lige*, Saxon.]

1. A criminal falshood.

> *My name's Macbeth.*
> *—The devil himself could not pronounce a title*
> *More hateful to mine ear.*
> *—No; nor more fearful.*
> *—Thou liest, abhorred tyrant; with my sword*
> *I'll prove the lie thou speak'st.* Shakespeare's
> Macbeth.

A lye is properly an outward signification of
something contrary to, or at least beside, the
inward sense of the mind; so that when one
thing is signified or expressed, and the same
thing not meant, or intended, that is properly
a lye. South.

Truth is the object of our understanding, as
good is of our will; and the understanding can
no more be delighted with a lye, than the will
can chuse an apparent evil. Dryden.

When I hear my neighbour speak that which
is not true, and I say to him, this is not true,
or this is false, I only convey to him the naked
idea of his error; this is the primary idea: but
if I say it is a lie, the word lie carries also a
secondary idea; for it implies both the falshood
of the speech, and my reproach and censure of
the speaker. Watts's Logick.

2. A charge of falshood.

That lie shall lye so heavy on my sword,
That it shall render vengeance and revenge;
Till thou the lie giver, and that lie, rest
In earth as quiet as thy father's skull.
Shakes. Rich. II.

It is a contradiction to suppose, that whole
nations of men should unanimously give the
lie to what, by the most invincible evidence,
every one of them knew to be true. Locke.

Men will give their own experience the lye,
rather than admit of any thing disagreeing
with these tenets. Locke.

3. A fiction.

The cock and fox, the fool and knave imply;
The truth is moral, though the tale a lie.
Dryden.

lief adv. Willingly.

If I could speak so wisely under an arrest, I
would send for certain of my creditors; and yet
to say the truth, I had as lief have the foppery
of freedom, as the morality of imprisonment.
Shakesp. Measure for Measure.

lifeguárd n.s. [*life* and *guard.*] The guard
of a king's person.

light n.s. [*leoht*, Saxon.]

1. That quality or action of the medium of
sight by which we see.

Light is propagated from luminous bodies in
time, and spends about seven or eight minutes
of an hour in passing from the sun to the
earth. Newton's Opticks.

2. Illumination of mind; instruction; knowledge.

Of those things which are for direction of all the parts of our life needful, and not impossible to be discerned by the light of nature itself, are there not many which few mens natural capacity hath been able to find out. Hooker, b. i.

Light may be taken from the experiment of the horsetooth ring, how that those things which assuage the strife of the spirits, do help diseases contrary to the intention desired. Bacon's Natural History, Nº 968.

I will place within them as a guide
My umpire conscience, whom if they will hear
Light after light well us'd they shall attain,
And to the end persisting safe arrive.
Milton's Par. Lost.

I opened Ariosto in Italian, and the very first two lines gave me light to all I could desire. Dryden.

If this internal light, or any proposition which we take for inspired, be conformable to the principles of reason, or to the word of God, which is attested revelation, reason warrants it. Locke.

The ordinary words of language, and our common use of them, would have given us light into the nature of our ideas, if considered with attention. Locke.

The books of Varro concerning navigation are lost, which no doubt would have given us great light in those matters. Arbuthnot on Coins.

3. The part of a picture which is drawn with bright colours, or in which the light is supposed to fall.

Never admit two equal lights in the same picture; but the greater light must strike forcibly on those places of the picture where the principal figures are; diminishing as it comes nearer the borders. Dryden's Dufresnoy.

4. Reach of knowledge; mental view.

Light, and understanding, and wisdom, like the wisdom of the gods, was found in him. Dan. v. 11.

We saw as it were thick clouds, which did put us in some hope of land, knowing how that part of the South sea was utterly unknown, and might have islands or continents that hitherto were not come to light. Bacon's Nat. Hist.

They have brought to light not a few profitable experiments. Bacon's Natural History.

5. Point of view; situation; direction in which the light falls.

Frequent consideration of a thing wears off the strangeness of it; and shews it in its several lights, and various ways of appearance, to the view of the mind. South.

It is impossible for a man of the greatest parts to consider any thing in its whole extent, and in all its variety of lights. Addison's Spectator, Nº 409.

An author who has not learned the art of ranging his thoughts, and setting them in proper lights, will lose himself in confusion. Addison's Spectator, Nº 291.

6. Explanation.

I have endeavoured, throughout this discourse, that every former part might give strength unto all that follow, and every latter bring some light unto all before. Hooker, b. i.

We should compare places of scripture treating of the same point: thus one part of the sacred text could not fail to give light unto another. Locke's Essay on St. Paul's Epistles.

7. Any thing that gives light; a pharos; a taper.

That light we see is burning in my hall;
How far that little candle throws his beams,
So shines a good deed in a naughty world. Shakespeare.

Then he called for a light, and sprang in, and fell down before Paul. Acts xvi. 29.

I have set thee to be a light of the Gentiles, for salvation unto the ends of the earth. Acts xiii. 47.

Let them be for signs,
For seasons, and for days, and circling years;
And let them be for lights, as I ordain
Their office in the firmament of heav'n,
To give light on the earth. Milton's Par. Lost.

I put as great difference between our new
lights and ancient truths, as between the sun
and an evanid meteor. Glanville's Scep.

Several lights will not be seen,
If there be nothing else between;
Men doubt because they stand so thick i' th' sky,
If those be stars that paint the galaxy. Cowley.

I will make some offers at their safety, by
fixing some marks like lights upon a coast,
by which their ships may avoid at least
known rocks. Temple.

He still must mourn
The sun, and moon, and ev'ry starry light,
Eclips'd to him, and lost in everlasting night.
Prior.

lightfingered adj. [*light* and *finger*.] Nimble
at conveyance; thievish.

lime tree, or **linden** n.s. [*lind*, Saxon.] The
linden tree.

The flower consists of several leaves, placed
orbicularly, in the form of a rose, having a
long narrow leaf growing to the footstalk of
each cluster of flowers, from whose cup rises
the pointal, which becomes testiculated, of one
capsule, containing an oblong seed. The timber
is used by carvers and turners. These trees
continue sound many years, and grow to
a considerable bulk. Sir Thomas Brown
mentions one, in Norfolk, sixteen yards in
circuit. Millar.

Go, gentle gales! and bear my sighs along.
For her the limes their pleasing shades deny,
For her the lilies hang their heads, and die.
Pope.

2. A species of lemon. [*lime*, French.]

Bear me, Pomona! to thy citron groves;
To where the lemon and the piercing lime,
With the deep orange glowing through the green,
Their lighter glories blend. Thomson's
Summer.

limitáneous adj. [from *limit*.] Belonging to
the bounds. Dictionary.

to limn v.a. [*enluminer*, French, to adorn
books with pictures.] To draw; to paint
any thing.

Mine eye doth his effigies witness,
Most truly limn'd, and living in your face.
Shakespeare.

Emblems limned in lively colours. Peacham.

How are the glories of the field spun, and
by what pencil are they limned in their
unaffected bravery? Glanville.

línctus n.s. [from *lingo*, Latin.] Medicine
licked up by the tongue.

língo n.s. [Portuguese.] Language; tongue;
speech. A low cant word.

I have thoughts to learn somewhat of your
lingo, before I cross the seas. Congreve's
Way of the World.

linguácious adj. [*linguax*, Latin.] Full of
tongue; loquacious; talkative.

línguist n.s. [from *lingua*.] A man skilful in
languages.

Though a linguist should pride himself to
have all the tongues that Babel cleft the world
into, yet, if he had not studied the solid things
in them, as well as the words and lexicons, he
were nothing so much to be esteemed a learned
man, as any yeoman or tradesman
competently wise in his mother dialect only.
Milton on Education.

Our linguist received extraordinary
rudiments towards a good education.
Addison's Spectator.

línkboy n.s. [*link* and *boy*.] A boy that
carries a torch to accommodate passengers
with light.

What a ridiculous thing it was, that the
continued shadow of the earth should be
broken by sudden miraculous disclusions
of light, to prevent the officiousness of the
linkboy. More's Divine Dialogues.

Though thou art tempted by the linkman's call,
Yet trust him not along the lonely wall. Gay.

In the black form of cinder wench she came.
O may no linkboy interrupt their love.
Gay's Trivia.

línseywoolsey adj. [*linen* and *wool.*] Made of linen and wool mixed. Vile; mean; of different and unsuitable parts.

A lawless linseywoolsie brother,
Half of one order, half another.
Hudibras, p. i.

Peel'd, patch'd and pyebald, linseywoolsey
brothers,
Grave mummers! sleeveless some, and shirtless
others. Pope's Dunciad, b. iii.

líon n.s. [*lion,* French; *leo,* Latin.] The fiercest and most magnanimous of fourfooted beasts.

King Richard's sirname was Cor-de-Lion, for
his lion-like courage. Camden's Remains.

Dismay'd not this
Our captains Macbeth and Banquo?
—Yes,
As sparrows, eagles, or the hare, the lion.
Shakespeare.

Be lion mettled; proud, and take no care
Who chafes, who frets, or where conspirers are;
Macbeth shall never vanquish'd be.
Shakes. Macbeth.

The sphinx, a famous monster in Egypt, had
the face of a virgin, and the body of a lion.
Peacham on Drawing.

They rejoice
Each with their kind, lion with lioness;
So fitly them in pairs thou hast combin'd.
Milt. Pa. Lost.

The lion for the honours of his skin,
The squeezing crab, and stinging scorpion shine
For aiding heaven, when giants dar'd to brave
The threat'ned stars. Creech's Manilius.

See lion hearted Richard,
Piously valiant, like a torrent swell'd
With wintry tempests, that disdains all mounds,
Breaking away impetuous, and involves
Within its sweep trees, houses, men, he press'd,
Amidst the thickest battle. Philips.

liplábour n.s. [*lip* and *labour.*] Action of the lips without concurrence of the mind; words without sentiments.

Fasting, when prayer is not directed to its
own purposes, is but liplabour. Taylor's Rule of holy living.

líquor n.s. [*liquor,* Latin; *liqueur,* French.]

1. Any thing liquid: it is commonly used of fluids inebriating, or impregnated with something, or made by decoction.

   Nor envy'd them the grape
   Whose heads that turbulent liquor fills with
   fumes. Milton.

Sin taken into the soul, is like a liquor poured
into a vessel; so much of it as it fills, it also
seasons. South's Sermons.

2. Strong drink; in familiar language.

to lisp v.n. [*hlisp,* Saxon.] To speak with too frequent appulses of the tongue to the teeth or palate, like children.

Come, I cannot cog, and say, thou art this and
that, like a many of these lisping hawthorn
buds, that come like women in mens apparel,
and smell like Bucklersbury in simpling time.
Shakespeare's Merry Wives of Windsor.

Scarce had she learnt to lisp a name
Of martyr, yet she thinks it shame
Life should so long play with that breath,
Which spent can buy so brave a death.
Crashaw.

They ramble not to learn the mode,
How to be drest, or how to lisp abroad.
Cleaveland.

Appulse partial, giving some passage to
breath, is made to the upper teeth, and
causes a lisping sound, the breath being
strained through the teeth. Holder's Elements of Speech.

As yet a child, nor yet a fool to fame,
I lisp'd in numbers, for the numbers came.
Pope.

to list v.n. [*lystan,* Saxon.] To chuse; to desire; to be disposed; to incline.

Let other men think of your devices as they list, in my judgment they be mere fansies. Whitgift.

Unto them that add to the word of God what them listeth, and make God's will submit unto their will, and break God's commandments for their own tradition's sake, unto them it seemeth not good. Hooker, b. ii.

They imagine, that laws which permit them not to do as they would, will endure them to speak as they list. Hooker.

*To fight in field, or to defend this wall,
Point what you list, I nought refuse at all.*
Fairy Queen.

*Now by my mother's son, and that's myself,
It shall be moon, or star, or what I list.*
Shakespeare.

*Kings, lords of times, and of occasions, may
Take their advantage when, and how, they
    list.* Daniel.

*When they list, into the womb
That bred them they return; and howl,
   and gnaw
My bowels, their repast.* Milton's
Paradise Lost.

líteral adj. [*literal*, French; *litera*, Latin.]

1. According to the primitive meaning, not figurative.

Through all the writings of the antient fathers, we see that the words, which were, do continue; the only difference is, that whereas before they had a literal, they now have a metaphorical use, and are as so many notes of remembrance unto us, that what they did signify in the letter, is accomplished in the truth. Hooker, b. iv.

A foundation, being primarily of use in architecture, hath no other literal notation but what belongs to it in relation to an house, or other building, nor figurative, but what is founded in that, and deduced from thence. Hammond.

2. Following the letter, or exact words.

The fittest for publick audience are such as, following a middle course between the rigour

of literal translations and the liberty of paraphrasts, do with greater shortness and plainness deliver the meaning. Hooker, b. v.

3. Consisting of letters; as, the literal notation of numbers was known to Europeans before the cyphers.

literáti n.s. [Italian.] The learned.

I shall consult some literati on the project sent me for the discovery of the longitude. Spectator, Nᵒ 581.

líterature n.s. [*literatura*, Latin.] Learning; skill in letters.

This kingdom hath been famous for good literature; and if preferment attend deservers, there will not want supplies. Bacon's Advice to Villiers.

When men of learning are acted by a knowledge of the world, they give a reputation to literature, and convince the world of its usefulness. Addison's Freeholder, Nᵒ 377.

lithógraphy n.s. [λιθος and γραφω.] The art or practice of engraving upon stones.

lithótomist n.s. [λιθος and τεμνω.] A chirurgeon who extracts the stone by opening the bladder.

líttoral v.a. [*littoris*, Latin.] Belonging to the shore.

lívery n.s. [from *livrer*, French.]

1. The act of giving or taking possession.

*You do wrongfully seize Hereford's right,
Call in his letters patents that he hath
By his attorneys general to sue
His livery, and deny his offered homage.*
Shakesp.

2. Release from wardship.

Had the two houses first sued out their livery, and once effectually redeemed themselves from the wardship of the tumults, I should then suspect my own judgment. K. Charles.

3. The writ by which possession is obtained.

4. The state of being kept at a certain rate.

What livery is, we by common use in England know well enough, namely, that it is an allowance of horse meat; as they commonly use the word stabling, as to keep horses at livery; the which word, I guess, is derived of livering or delivering forth their nightly food; so in great houses, the livery is said to be served up for all night, that is, their evening allowance for drink: and livery is also called the upper weed which a serving man wears; so called, I suppose, for that it was delivered and taken from him at pleasure: so it is apparent, that, by the word livery, is there meant horse meat, like as by the coigny is understood man's meat. Some say it is derived of coin, for that they used in their coignies not only to take meat but money; but I rather think it is derived of the Irish, the which is a common use amongst landlords of the Irish to have a common spending upon their tenants, who being commonly but tenants at will, they used to take of them what victuals they lift; for of victuals they were wont to make a small reckoning. Spenser on Ireland.

5. The cloaths given to servants.

My mind for weeds your virtue's livery wears. Sidney.

Perhaps they are by so much the more loth to forsake this argument, for that it hath, though nothing else, yet the name of scripture, to give it some kind of countenance more than the pretext of livery coats affordeth. Hooker.

I think, it is our way,
If we will keep in favour with the king,
To be her men, and wear her livery.
Shakesp. Rich. III.

Yet do our hearts wear Timon's livery,
That see I by our faces. Shakesp. Timon of Athens.

Ev'ry lady cloath'd in white,
And crown'd with oak and laurel ev'ry knight,
Are servants to the leaf, by liveries known
Of innocence. Dryden's Flower and Leaf.

On others int'rest her gay liv'ry flings,
Int'rest that waves on party-colour'd wings;
Turn'd to the sun she casts a thousand dyes,
And as she turns the colours fall or rise.
Dunciad.

If your dinner miscarries, you were teized by the footmen coming into the kitchen; and to prove it true, throw a ladleful of broth on one or two of their liveries. Swift.

6. A particular dress; a garb worn as a token or consequence of any thing.

Of fair Urania, fairer than a green,
Proudly bedeck'd in April's livery. Sidney.

Mistake me not for my complexion
The shadow'd livery of the burning sun,
To whom I am a neighbour, and near bred.
Shakesp.

At once came forth whatever creeps the ground,
Insect, or worm: those wav'd their limber fans,
For wings, and smallest lineaments exact,
In all the liveries deck'd of summer's pride,
With spots of gold and purple, azure, green.
Milton.

Now came still evening on, and twilight grey
Had in her sober livery all things clad.
Milt. Pa. Lost.

living n.s. [from *live*.]

1. Support, maintenance; fortune on which one lives.

The Arcadians fought as in unknown place, having no succour but in their hands; the Helots, as in their own place, fighting for their livings, wives, and children. Sidney.

All they did cast in of their abundance; but she of her want did cast in all that she had, even all her living. Mark.

2. Power of continuing life.

There is no living without trusting some body or other, in some cases. L'Estrange's Fables.

3. Livelihood.

For ourselves we may a living make.
Hubberd's Tale.

Then may I set the world on wheels, when she can spin for her living. Shakespeare.

Isaac and his wife, now dig for your life,
Or shortly you'll dig for your living.
Denham.

Actors must represent such things as they are capable to perform, and by which both they and the scribbler may get their living.
Dryden's Dufresnoy.

4. Benefice of a clergyman.

Some of our ministers having the livings of the country offered unto them, without pains, will, neither for any love of God, nor for all the good they may do, by winning souls to God, be drawn forth from their warm nests. Spenser.

The parson of the parish preaching against adultery, Mrs. Bull told her husband, that they would join to have him turned out of his living for using personal reflections. Arbuth.

lívre n.s. [French.] The sum by which the French reckon their money, equal nearly to our shilling.

lízard n.s. [*lisarde*, French; *lacertus*, Latin.] An animal resembling a serpent, with legs added to it.

There are several sorts of lizards; some in Arabia of a cubit long. In America they eat lizards; it is very probable likewise that they were eaten sometimes in Arabia and Judæa, since Moses ranks them among the unclean creatures. Calmet.

Thou'rt like a foul mis-shape stigmatic, Mark'd by the destinies to be avoided, As venomous toads, or lizards dreadful stings. Shakesp.

Adder's fork, and blind worm's sting, Lizard's leg, and owlet's wing. Shakespeare's Macbeth.

L.L.D. n.s. [*legum doctor*.] A doctor of the canon and civil laws.†

lob n.s.

1. Any one heavy, clumsy, or sluggish.

Farewel, thou lob of spirits, I'll be gone, Our queen and all her elves come here anon. Shakesp.

2. Lob's pound; a prison. Probably a prison for idlers, or sturdy beggars.

Crowdero, whom in irons bound, Thou basely threw'st into lob's pound. Hudibras.

3. A big worm.

For the trout the dew worm, which some also call the lob worm, and the brandling are the chief. Walton's Angler.

locomótive adj. [*locus* and *moveo*, Lat.] Changing place; having the power of removing or changing place.

I shall consider the motion, or locomotive faculty of animals. Derham's Physico-Theol.

In the night too oft he kicks, Or shows his locomotive tricks. Prior.

An animal cannot well be defined from any particular, organical part, nor from its locomotive faculty, for some adhere to rocks. Arbuthnot on Aliments.

lócust n.s. [*locusta*, Latin.] The Hebrews had several sorts of locusts, which are not known among us: the old historians and modern travellers remark, that locusts are very numerous in Africk, and many places of Asia; that sometimes they fell like a cloud upon the country, and eat up every thing they meet with. Moses describes four sorts of locusts. Since there was a prohibition against using locusts, it is not to be questioned but that these creatures were commonly eaten in Palestine, and the neighbouring countries. Calmet.

To-morrow will I bring the locusts into thy coast. Exod.

Air replete with the steams of animals, rotting, has produced pestilential fevers; such have likewise been raised by great quantities of dead locusts. Arbuthnot on Air.

lógarithms n.s. [*logarithme*, Fr. λογος and αριθμος.] Logarithms, which are the indexes of the ratio's of numbers one to another, were first invented by Napier lord Merchison, a Scottish baron, and afterwards completed by Mr. Briggs, Savilian professor at Oxford. They are a series of artificial numbers, contrived for the expedition of calculation, and proceeding in an arithmetical proportion, as the numbers they answer to do in a geometrical one: for instance,

0 1 2 3 4 5 6 7 8 9
1 2 4 8 16 32 64 128 256 512

Where the numbers above, beginning with (0), and arithmetically proportional, are called logarithms. The addition and subtraction of logarithms answers to the multiplication and division of the numbers they correspond with; and this saves an infinite deal of trouble. In like manner will the extraction of roots be performed, by dissecting the logarithms of any numbers for the square root, and trisecting them for the cube, and so on. Harris.

lóggats n.s. Loggats is the ancient name of a play or game, which is one of the unlawful games enumerated in the thirty-third statute of Henry VIII. It is the same which is now called kittlepins, in which boys often make use of bones instead of wooden pins, throwing at them with another bone instead of bowling. Hanmer.

Did these bones cost no more the breeding, but to play at loggats with them. Shakespeare's Hamlet.

lógick n.s. [*logique*, French; *logica*, Latin, from λογος.] The art of reasoning.

Logick is the art of using reason well in our inquiries after truth, and the communication of it to others. Watts's Logick.

Talk logick with acquaintance,
And practise rhetorick in your common talk.
Shakespeare.

By a logick that left no man any thing which he might call his own, they no more looked upon it as the case of one man, but the case of the kingdom. Clarendon.

Here foam'd rebellious logick, gagg'd and bound,
There stript fair rhetorick languish'd on the
ground. Pope.

lógomachy n.s. [λογομαχια.] A contention in words; a contention about words.

Forced terms of art did much puzzle sacred theology with distinctions, cavils, quiddities, and so transformed her to a meer kind of sophistry and logomachy. Howel.

lomp n.s. A kind of roundish fish.

loo n.s. A game at cards.

A secret indignation, that all those affections of the mind should be thus vilely thrown away upon a hand at loo. Addis.

In the fights of loo. Pope.

lóoby n.s. [Of this word the derivation is unsettled. Skinner mentions *lapp*, German, *foolish*; and Junius, *llabe*, a clown, Welsh, which seems to be the true original.] A lubber; a clumsy clown.

The vices trace
From the father's scoundrel race
Who could give the looby such airs?
Were they masons, were they butchers? Swift.

lord n.s. [*hlaford*, Saxon.]

1. Monarch; ruler; governour.

Man over man
He made not lord. Milton.

Of Athens he was lord. Dryden's Knight's Tale.

We have our author's only arguments to prove, that heirs are lords over their brethren.
Locke.

They call'd their lord Actæon to the game,
He shook his head in answer to the name.
Addison.

O'er love, o'er fear, extends his wide domain,
Unconquer'd lord of pleasure and of pain.
Va. of hu. Wishes.

2. Master; supreme person.

But now I was the lord
Of this fair mansion, master of my servants,
Queen o'er myself; and even now, but now,
This house, these servants, and this same myself
Are yours, my lord. Shakesp. Merchant of Venice.

3. A tyrant; an oppressive ruler.

Now being assembled into one company, rather without a lord than at liberty to accomplish their misery, they fall to division.
Hayward.

'Tis death to fight, but kingly to controul
Lord-like at ease, with arbitrary pow'r,
To peel the chiefs, the people to devour.
Dryden.

4. A husband.

I oft in bitterness of soul deplor'd
My absent daughter, and my dearer lord.
Pope's Odyssey.

5. One who is at the head of any business; an overseer.

Grant harvest lord more by a peny or two,
To call on his fellows the better to doo.
Tusser's Husb.

6. A nobleman.

Thou art a lord, and nothing but a lord.
Shakespeare.

7. A general name for a peer of England.

Nor were the crimes objected against him so
clear, as to give convincing satisfaction to the
major part of both houses, especially that of
the lords. King Charles.

8. A baron.

9. An honorary title applied to offices; as, lord chief justice, lord mayor, and lord chief baron.

lórdling n.s. A diminutive lord.

Traulus, of amphibious breed,
By the dam from lordlings sprung,
By the sire exhal'd from dung. Swift.

lósel n.s. [from *losian*, to perish.] A scoundrel; a sorry worthless fellow. A word now obsolete.

Such losels and scatterlings cannot easily,
by any sheriff, be gotten, when they are
challenged for any such fact. Spenser.

   A losel wand'ring by the way,
One that to bounty never cast his mind,
Ne thought of honour ever did assay
His baser breast. Fairy Queen, b. ii.

And losels lifted high, where I did look,
I mean to turn the next leaf of the book.
Hubberd's Tale.

Be not with work of losels wit defamed,
Ne let such verses poetry be named.
Hubberd's Tale.

By Cambridge a towne I do know,
Whose losses by lossels doth shew
More heere then is needful to tell.
Tusser's Husbandry.

   A gross hag!
And, losel, thou art worthy to be hang'd,
That wilt not stay her tongue. Shakesp.
Winter's Tale.

lóttery n.s. [*lotterie*, Fr. from *lot*.] A game of chance; a sortilege; distribution of prizes by chance; a play in which lots are drawn for prizes.

Let high-sighted tyranny range on,
Till each man drop by lottery. Shakesp.
Julius Cæsar.

The lottery that he hath devised in these three
chests of gold, silver, and lead, will never be
chosen by any but whom you shall rightly
love. Shakes. Merchant of Venice.

Every warriour may be said to be a soldier
of fortune, and the best commanders to
have a kind of lottery for their work.
South's Sermons.

Fortune, that with malicious joy
Does man, her slave, oppress,
Still various and unconstant still,
Promotes, degrades, delights in strife,
And makes a lottery of life.
Dryden's Horace.

to love v.a. [*lufian*, Saxon.]

1. To regard with passionate affection, as that of one sex to the other.

Good shepherd, tell this youth what 'tis to love.
—It is to be made all of sighs and tears;
It is to be made all of faith and service;
It is to be all made of fantasy,
All made of passion, and all made of wishes;
All adoration, duty, and obedience;
All humbleness, all patience, all impatience,
All purity, all trial, all observance.
Shakesp. As you like it.

I could not love I'm sure
One who in love were wise. Cowley.

The jealous man wishes himself a kind of
deity to the person he loves; he would be the
only employment of her thoughts. Addison's
Spectator, Nº 170.

2. To regard with the affection of a friend.

None but his brethren he, and sisters, knew,
Whom the kind youth prefer'd to me,
And much above myself I lov'd them too.
Cowley.

3. To regard with parental tenderness.

He that loveth me shall be loved of my father,
and I will love him, and will manifest myself
to him. John xiv. 21.

4. To be pleased with.

Fish used to salt water delight more in fresh:
we see that salmons and smelts love to get
into rivers, though against the stream.
Bacon's Nat. Hist. Nº 703.

Wit, eloquence, and poetry,
Arts which I lov'd. Cowley.

He lov'd my worthless rhimes. Cowley.

5. To regard with reverent unwillingness
to offend.

Love the Lord thy God with all thine heart.
Deut. vi. 5.

lóveknot n.s. [*love* and *knot*.] A
complicated figure, by which affection
interchanged is figured.

lóveletter n.s. [*love* and *letter*.] Letter of
courtship.

The children are educated in the different
notions of their parents: the sons follow
the father, while the daughters read
loveletters and romances to their mother.
Addison's Spect.

lóvesick adj. [*love* and *sick*.] Disordered
with love; languishing with amorous desire.

See, on the shoar inhabits purple spring,
Where nightingales their lovesick ditty sing.
Dryden.

To the dear mistress of my lovesick mind,
Her swain a pretty present has design'd.
Dryden's Virg.

Of the reliefs to ease a lovesick mind,
Flavia prescribes despair. Granville.

lóvetrick n.s. [*love* and *trick*.] Art of
expressing love.

Other disports than dancing jollities;
Other lovetricks than glancing with the eyes.
Donne.

lown n.s. [*liun*, Irish; *loen*, Dutch, a stupid
drone.] A scoundrel; a rascal.

King Stephen was a worthy peer,
His breeches cost him but a crown,
He thought them sixpence all too dear,
And therefore call'd the taylor lown.
Shakespeare.

to lowt v.a. This word seems in Shakespeare
to signify, to overpower.

I am lowted by a traitor villain,
And cannot help the noble chevalier.
Shakesp. Henry VI.

lúbber n.s. [of this word the best derivation
seems to be from *lubbed*, said by Junius to
signify in Danish *fat*.] A sturdy drone; an
idle, fat, bulky losel; a booby.

For tempest and showers deceiveth a many,
And ling'ring lubbers loose many a penie.
Tusser's Husb.

These chase the smaller shoals of fish from the
main sea into the havens, leaping up and
down, puffing like a fat lubber out of breath.
Carew's Survey of Cornwall.

They clap the lubber Ajax on the shoulder,
As if his feet were on brave Hector's breast,
And great Troy shrinking. Shakesp. Troil.
and Cressida.

A notable lubber thou reportest him to be.
Shakesp.

Tell how the drudging goblin sweat;
His shadowy flail hath thresh'd the corn,
That ten day labourers could not end;
Then lies him down the lubber fiend. Milton.

Venetians do not more uncouthly ride,
Than did your lubber state mankind bestride.
Dryden.

How can you name that superannuated
lubber? Congreve.

lucíferous adj. [*lucifer*, Latin.] Giving light;
affording means of discovery.

The experiment is in itself not ignoble, and
luciferous enough, as shewing a new way to
produce a volatile salt. Boyle.

lucrífick adj. [*lucrum* and *facio*, Latin.]
Producing gain. Dict.

lúctation n.s. [*luctor*, Latin.] Struggle;
effort; contest.

lucubrátion n.s. [*lucubratio*, Latin.] Study by candlelight; nocturnal study; any thing composed by night.

Thy lucubrations have been perused by several of our friends. Tatler, N° 78.

lúdicrous adj. [*ludicer*, Lat.] Burlesque; merry; sportive; exciting laughter.

Plutarch quotes this as an instance of Homer's judgment, in closing a ludicrous scene with decency and instruction. Notes on the Odyssey.

ludificátion n.s. [*ludificor*, Latin.] The act of mocking, or making sport with another. Dict.

lugúbrious adj. [*lugubre*, French; *lugubris*, Lat.] Mournful; sorrowful.

A demure, or rather a lugubrious look, a sad or whining tone, makes up the sum of many mens humiliations. Decay of Piety.

lumbágo n.s. [*lumbi*, Lat. the loins.]

Lumbago's are pains very troublesome about the loins, and small of the back, such as precede ague fits and fevers: they are most commonly from fullness and acrimony, in common with a disposition to yawnings, shudderings, and erratick pains in other parts, and go off with evacuation, generally by sweat, and other critical discharges of fevers. Quincy.

lúmber n.s. [*loma*, *geloma*, Saxon, housholdstuff; *lommering*, the dirt of an house, Dutch.] Any thing useless or cumbersome; any thing of more bulk than value.

The very bed was violated
By the coarse hands of filthy dungeon villains,
And thrown amongst the common lumber.
Otway.

One son at home
Concerns thee more than many guests to come.
If to some useful art he be not bred,
He grows mere lumber, and is worse than
     dead. Dryden.

Thy neighbour has remov'd his wretched store,
Few hands will rid the lumber of the poor.
Dryden's Juv.

If God intended not the precise use of every single atom, that atom had been no better than a piece of lumber. Grew.

The poring scholiasts mark;
Wits, who, like owls, see only in the dark;
A lumber-house of books in ev'ry head.
Pope's Dunciad.

lúmpish adj. [from *lump.*] Heavy; gross; dull; unactive; bulky.

Out of the earth was formed the flesh of man, and therefore heavy and lumpish. Raleigh's Hist. of the World.

Sylvia is lumpish, heavy, melancholy. Shakespeare.

Love is all spirit: fairies sooner may
Be taken tardy, when they night tricks play,
Than we; we are too dull and lumpish.
Suckling.

Little terrestrial particles swimming in it after the grossest were sunk down, which, by their heaviness and lumpish figure, made their way more speedily. Burnet.

How dull and how insensible a beast
Is man, who yet wou'd lord it o'er the rest?
Philosophers and poets vainly strove
In every age the lumpish mass to move.
Dryden.

lúnacy n.s. [from *luna*, the moon.] A kind of madness influenced by the moon; madness in general.

Love is merely madness, and deserves as well a dark house and a whip as madmen do; and the reason why they are not so punished and cured is, that the lunacy is so ordinary, that the whippers are in love too. Shakesp. As you like it.

Your kindred shun your house,
As beaten hence by your strange lunacy.
Shakespeare.

There is difference of lunacy: I had rather be mad with him, that, when he had nothing, thought all the ships that came into the haven his, than with you, who, when you have so much coming in, think you have nothing. Suckling.

lúnatick n.s. A madman.

The lunatick, the lover, and the poet,
Are of imagination all compact:
One sees more devils than vast hell can hold;
The madman. Shakesp. Midsummer
Night's Dream.

I dare ensure any man well in his wits, for
one in the thousand that he shall not die a
lunatick in Bedlam within these seven years;
because not above one in about one thousand
five hundred have done so. Graunt's Bills.

See the blind beggar dance, the cripple sing,
The sot a hero, lunatick a king. Pope.

The residue of the yearly profits shall be laid
out in purchasing a piece of land, and in
building thereon an hospital for the reception
of idiots and lunaticks. Swift.

lunch, lúncheon n.s. [Minshew derives it
from *louja*, Spanish; Skinner from *kleinken*,
a small piece. Teutonick. It probably comes
from *clutch* or *clunch*.] As much food as
one's hand can hold.

When hungry thou stood'st staring, like an oaf,
I slic'd the luncheon from the barley loaf;
With crumbled bread I thicken'd well the mess.
Gay.

lunt n.s. [*lonte*, Dutch.] The matchcord
with which guns are fired.

lusk adj. [*lusche*, French.] Idle; lazy;
worthless. Dict.

lusórious adj. [*lusorius*, Latin.] Used in
play; sportive.

Things more open to exception, yet unjustly
condemned as unlawful; such as the lusorious
lots, dancing and stageplays. Bishop
Sanderson.

lust n.s. [*lust*, Saxon; *lust*, Dutch.]

1. Carnal desire.

This our court, infected with their manners,
Shews like a riotous inn, Epicurism and lust
Make it more like a tavern or a brothel,
Than a grac'd palace. Shakespeare's
King Lear.

Lust, and rank thoughts. Shakespeare's
Cymbeline.

They are immoderately given to the lust of the
flesh, making no conscience to get bastards.
Abbot.

When a temptation of lust assaults thee, do
not resist it by disputing with it, but flie
from it, that is, think not at all of it. Taylor's
holy Living.

2. Any violent or irregular desire.

I will divide the spoil; my lust shall be
satisfied upon them. Exod. xv. 9.

The ungodly, for his own lust, doth persecute
the poor: let them be taken in the crafty
wiliness they imagined. Psal.

Virtue was represented by Hercules: he is
drawn offering to strike a dragon; by the
dragon are meant all manner of lusts.
Peacham on Drawing.

All weigh our acts, and whate'er seems unjust,
Impute not to necessity, but lust. Dryden's
Ind. Emp.

The lust of lucre. Pope.

3. Vigour; active power. Not used.

Trees will grow greater, and bear better fruit,
if you put salt, or lees of wine, or blood, to the
root: the cause may be, the increasing the lust
or spirit of the root. Bacon.

lústy adj. [*lustig*, Dutch.] Stout; vigorous;
healthy; able of body.

This lusty lady came from Persia late,
She with the Christians had encounter'd oft.
Fairy Qu.

If lusty love should go in quest of beauty,
Where should he find it fairer than in Blanch?
Shakesp.

We yet may see the old man in a morning,
Lusty as health, come ruddy to the field,
And there pursue the chase. Otway.

lutárious adj. [*lutarius*, Latin.] Living in
mud; of the colour of mud.

A scaly tortoise-shell, of the lutarious kind.
Grew.

luxúrious adj. [*luxurieux*, Fr. *luxuriosus*,
Latin.]

1. Delighting in the pleasures of the table.

2. Administring to luxury.

The luxurious board. Anon.†

3. Lustful; libidinous.

She knows the heat of a luxurious bed:
Her blush is guiltiness, not modesty.
Shakespeare.

   I grant him bloody,
Luxurious, avaricious, false, deceitful.
Shakespeare.

4. Voluptuous; enslaved to pleasure.

   Those whom last thou saw'st
In triumph, and luxurious wealth, are they
First seen in acts of prowess eminent,
And great exploits; but of true virtue void.
Milton.

Luxurious cities, where the noise
Of riot ascends above their loftiest tow'rs.
Milton.

5. Softening by pleasure.

Repel the Tuscan foes, their city seize,
Protect the Latians in luxurious ease. Dryden.

6. Luxuriant; exuberant.

   Till more hands
Aid us, the work under our labour grows

Luxurious by restraint. Milton's Par.
Lost, b. ix.

lycánthropy n.s. [*lycantropie*, French; λυκαν
and ανθρωπος.] A kind of madness, in
which men have the qualities of wild beasts.

He sees like a man in his sleep, and grows
as much the wiser as the man that dreamt of
a lycanthropy, and was for ever after wary
not to come near a river. Taylor.

lymphated adj. [*lymphatus*, Latin.] Mad.
Dict.

lyrical, lyrick adj. [*lyricus*, Latin; *lyrique*,
French.] Pertaining to an harp, or to odes or
poetry sung to an harp; singing to an harp.

   All his trophies hung and acts enroll'd
In copious legend, or sweet lyrick song.
Milton's Agonist.

Somewhat of the purity of English, somewhat
of more equal thoughts, somewhat of sweetness
in the numbers; in one word, somewhat of a
finer turn, and more lyrical verse, is yet
wanting. Dryden.

The lute neglected, and the lyrick muse,
Love taught my tears in sadder notes to flow,
And tun'd my heart to elegies of woe. Pope.

M has, in English, one unvaried sound, by compression of the lips; as, *mine*, *tame*, *camp*: it is never mute.

macaróon n.s. [*macarone*, Italian.]

1. A coarse, rude, low fellow; whence *macaronick* poetry, in which the language is purposely corrupted.

Like a big wife, at sight of lothed meat,
Ready to travail; so I sigh and sweat,
To hear this macaroon talk on in vain.
Donne.

2. [*Macaron*, French, from μακαρ.] A kind of sweet biscuit, made of flower, almonds, eggs, and sugar.

machíne n.s. [*machina*, Latin; *machine*, French. This word is pronounced *masheen*.]

1. Any complicated piece of workmanship.

We are led to conceive this great machine of the world to have been once in a state of greater simplicity, as to conceive a watch to have been once in its first materials. Burnet.

In a watch's fine machine,
The added movements which declare
How full the moon, how old the year,
Derive their secondary pow'r
From that which simply points the hour.
Prior.

2. An engine.

In the hollow side,
Selected numbers of their soldiers hide;
With inward arms the dire machine they load,
And iron bowels stuff the dark abode.
Dryden.

3. Supernatural agency in poems.

The marvellous fable includes whatever is supernatural, and especially the machines of the gods. Pope.

machínery n.s. [from *machine*.]

1. Enginery; complicated workmanship; self-moved engines.

2. The machinery signifies that part which the deities, angels, or demons, act in a poem. Pope's Rape of the Lock.

mácilent adj. [*macilentus*, Latin.] Lean.

mácrocosm n.s. [*macrocosme*, French; μακρος and κοσμος.] The whole world, or visible system, in opposition to the microcosm, or world of man.

mactátion n.s. [*mactatus*, Latin.] The act of killing for sacrifice.

to máculate v.a. [*maculo*, Lat.] To stain; to spot.

mádcap n.s. [*mad* and *cap*; either taking the *cap* for the head, or alluding to the caps put upon distracted persons by way of distinction.] A madman; a wild hotbrained fellow.

That last is Biron, the merry madcap lord;
Not a word with him but a jest.
Shakespeare.

Where is his son,
The nimble-footed madcap prince of Wales,
And his comrades, that daft the world aside,
And bid it pass. Shakespeare's Henry IV.

to mádefy v.a. [*madefio*, Latin.] To moisten; to make wet.

mádhouse n.s. [*mad* and *house*.] A house where madmen are cured or confined.

A fellow in a madhouse being asked how he came there? why, says he, the mad-folks abroad are too many for us, and so they have mastered all the sober people, and cooped them up here. L'Estrange.

mádness n.s. [from *mad*.]

1. Distraction; loss of understanding; perturbation of the faculties.

Why, woman, your husband is in his old lunes again: he so rails against all married mankind, so curses all Eve's daughters, and so buffets himself on the forehead, that any madness I ever yet beheld seemed but tameness and civility to this distemper. Shakesp. Merry Wives of Windsor.

There are degrees of madness as of folly, the disorderly jumbling ideas together, in some more, some less. Locke.

2. Fury; wildness; rage.

The power of God sets bounds to the raging of the sea, and restrains the madness of the people. King Charles.

He rav'd with all the madness of despair,
He roar'd, he beat his breast, and tore his hair.
Dryden.

to máffle v.n. To stammer. Ains.

magazíne n.s. [*magazine*, French, from the Arabick *machsan*, a treasure.]

1. A storehouse, commonly an arsenal or armoury, or repository of provisions.

If it should appear fit to bestow shipping in those harbours, it shall be very needful that there be a magazine of all necessary provisions and munitions. Raleigh's Essays.

Plain heroick magnitude of mind;
Their armories and magazines contemns.
Milton's Agonist.

Some o'er the publick magazines preside,
And some are sent new forage to provide.
Dryden's Virg.

Useful arms in magazines we place,
All rang'd in order, and disposed with grace.
Pope.

His head was so well stored a magazine, that nothing could be proposed which he was not master of. Locke.

2. Of late this word has signified a miscellaneous pamphlet, from a periodical miscellany named the *Gentleman's Magazine*, by Edward Cave.†

mage n.s. [*magus*, Latin.] A magician. Spenser.

mágick n.s. [*magia*, Latin.]

1. The art of putting in action the power of spirits: it was supposed that both good and bad spirits were subject to magick; yet magick was in general held unlawful; sorcery; enchantment.

She once being loost,
The noble ruin of her magick, Antony,
Claps on his sea-wing. Shakesp. Ant. and Cleopatra.

What charm, what magick, can over-rule the force of all these motives. Rogers.

2. The secret operations of natural powers.

The writers of natural magick do attribute much to the virtues that come from the parts of living creatures, as if they did infuse some immaterial virtue into the part severed.
Bacon's Nat. Hist.

magnálity n.s. [*magnalia*, Latin.] A great thing; something above the common rate. Not used.

Too greedy of magnalities, we make but favourable experiments concerning welcome truths. Brown's Vulgar Errours.

mágnet n.s. [*magnes*, Latin.] The lodestone; the stone that attracts iron.

Two magnets, heav'n and earth, allure to bliss,
The larger loadstone that, the nearer this.
Dryden.

It may be reasonable to ask, whether obeying the magnet be essential to iron? Locke.

maid, maíden n.s. [*mæden, mægden*, Saxon, *maegd*, Dutch.]

1. An unmarried woman; a virgin.

Your wives, your daughters,
Your matrons, and your maids, could not fill up
The cistern of my lust. Shakespeare's Macbeth.

This is a man old, wrinkl'd, faded, wither'd,
And not a maiden, as thou say'st he is.
Shakespeare.

I am not solely led
By nice direction of a maiden's eyes.
Shakespeare.

She employed the residue of her life to repairing of highways, building of bridges, and endowing of maidens. Carew.

Your deluded wife had been a maid;
Down on the bridal bed a maid she lay,
A maid she rose at the approaching day.
Dryden's Juv.

Let me die, she said,
Rather than lose the spotless name of maid.
Dryden.

2. A woman servant.

My maid Nerissa and myself, mean time,
Will live as maids and widows. Shakesp. Merch. of Venice.

Old Tancred visited his daughter's bow'r;
Her cheek, for such his custom was, he kiss'd,
Then bless'd her kneeling, and her maids
dismiss'd. Dryd.

Her closet and the gods share all her time,
Except when, only by some maids attended,
She seeks some shady solitary grove. Rowe.

A thousand maidens ply the purple loom,
To weave the bed, and deck the regal room.
Prior.

3. Female.

If she bear a maid child. Lev. xii. 5.

máidmarian n.s. [*puer ludius*, Latin.] A kind of dance, so called from a buffoon dressed like a man, who plays tricks to the populace.

A set of morrice-dancers danced a
maidmarian with a tabor and pipe. Temple.

máinprise n.s. [*main* and *pris*, French.] Delivery into the custody of a friend, upon security given for appearance; bail.

Sir William Bremingham was executed for
treason, though the earl of Desmond was
left to mainprize. Davies.

Give its poor entertainer quarter;
And, by discharge or mainprise, grant
Deliv'ry from this base restraint.
Hudibras, p. ii.

maize, or *Indian wheat* n.s. The whole maize plant has the appearance of a reed; the male flowers are produced at remote distances from the fruit on the same plant, growing generally in a spike upon the top of the stalk; the female flowers are produced from the wings of the leaves, and are surrounded by three or four leaves, which closely adhere to the fruit until it is ripe: this plant is propagated in England only as a curiosity, but in America it is the principal support of the inhabitants, and consequently propagated with great care. Miller.

Maize affords a very strong nourishment,
but more viscous than wheat. Arbuthnot
on Aliments.

málapert adj. [*mal* and *pert*.] Saucy; quick with impudence; sprightly without respect or decency.

Peace, master marquis, you are malapert;
Your fire-new stamp of honour is scarce
current. Shakesp.

If thou dar'st tempt me further, draw thy sword.
—What, what? nay, then, I must have an
ounce or two of this malapert blood from you.
Shakesp. Twelfth Night.

Are you growing malapert? Will you force
me make use of my authority? Dryden's
Spanish Fryar.

male adj. [*male*, French; *masculus*, Lat.] Of the sex that begets young; not female.

Which shall be heir of the two male twins,
who, by the dissection of the mother, were
laid open to the world? Locke.

You are the richest person in the
commonwealth; you have no male child;
your daughters are all married to wealthy
patricians. Swift's Examiner, N° 27.

maléfick, maléfique adj. [*maleficus*, Latin.] Mischievous; hurtful. Dict.

malváceous adj. [*malva*, Latin.] Relating to mallows.

malversátion n.s. [French.] Bad shifts; mean artifices; wicked and fraudulent tricks.

mam, mammá n.s. [*mamma*, Latin: this word is said to be found for the compellation of *mother* in all languages; and is therefore supposed to be the first syllables that a child pronounces.] The fond word for mother.

Poor Cupid sobbing scarce could speak;
Indeed, mamma, I did not know ye:
Alas! how easy my mistake?
I took you for your likeness Cloe. Prior.

Little masters and misses are great
impediments to servants; the remedy is to
bribe them, that they may not tell tales
to papa and mamma. Swift's Rules to
Servants.

mámmiform adj. [*mammiforme*, French; *mamma* and *forma*, Latin.] Having the shape of paps or dugs.

mámmon n.s. [Syriack.] Riches.

man n.s. [*man, mon,* Saxon.]

1. Human being.

The king is but a man as I am; the violet smells to him as it doth to me; the element shews to him as it doth to me, all his senses have but human conditions. Shakesp.

All the west bank of Nilus is possessed by an idolatrous, man-eating nation. Brerewood on Languages.

A creature of a more exalted kind
Was wanted yet, and then was man design'd,
Conscious of thought. Dryden's Ovid.

Nature in man capacious souls hath wrought,
And given them voice expressive of their thought;
In man the God descends, and joys to find
The narrow image of his greater mind.
Creech's Manilius.

A combination of the ideas of a certain figure, with the powers of motion, and reasoning joined to substance, make the ordinary idea of a man. Locke.

On human actions reason though you can,
It may be reason, but it is not man.
Pope's Epistles.

2. Not a woman.

Bring forth men children only!
For thy undaunted metal should compose
Nothing but males. Shakespeare's King Lear.

I had not so much of man in me,
But all my mother came into mine eyes,
And gave me up to tears. Shakespeare's Henry V.

Every man child shall be circumcised.
Gen. xvii. 10.

Ceneus, a woman once, and once a man,
But ending in the sex she first began.
Dryden's Æn.

A long time since the custom began, among people of quality, to keep men cooks of the French nation. Swift.

3. Not a boy.

The nurse's legends are for truths receiv'd,
And the man dreams but what the boy believ'd. Dryden.

4. A servant; an attendant; a dependant.

Now thanked be the great god Pan,
Which thus preserves my loved life,
Thanked be I that keep a man,
Who ended hath this bloody strife:
For if my man must praises have,
What then must I that keep the knave?
Sidney, b. i.

My brother's servants
Were then my fellows, now they are my men.
Shakesp.

Such gentlemen as are his majesty's own sworn servants should be preferred to the charge of his majesty's ships; choice being made of men of valour and capacity rather than to employ other mens men. Raleigh's Essays.

I and my man will presently go ride
Far as the Cornish mount. Cowley.

5. A word of familiarity bordering on contempt.

You may partake of any thing we say:
We speak no treason, man. Shakesp. Richard III.

6. It is used in a loose signification like the French *on*, one, any one.

This same young sober-blooded boy doth not love me, nor a man cannot make him laugh. Shakesp. Henry IV.

A man in an instant may discover the assertion to be impossible. More's Divine Dialogues.

He is a good-natured man, and will give as much as a man would desire. Stillingfleet.

By ten thousand of them a man shall not be able to advance one step in knowledge. Tillotson's Sermons.

Our thoughts will not be directed what objects to pursue, nor be taken off from those they have once fixed on; but run away with a man, in pursuit of those ideas they have in view. Locke.

A man would expect to find some antiquities; but all they have to show of this nature is an old rostrum of a Roman ship. Addison.

*A man might make a pretty landscape of his
own plantation.* Addison.

7. One of uncommon qualifications.

Manners maketh man. William of
Wickham.

*I dare do all that may become a man;
Who dares do more is none.
—What beast was 't then
That made you break this enterprise to me?
When you durst do it, then you were a man;
And, to be more than what you were, you would
Be so much more the man.* Shakespeare's
Macbeth.

*He tript me behind, being down, insulted, rail'd,
And put upon him such a deal of man,
That worthied him.* Shakespeare's
King Lear.

*Will reckons he should not have been the man
he is, had not he broke windows, and knocked
down constables, when he was a young fellow.*
Addison's Spect. N° 105.

8. A human being qualified in any
particular manner.

*Thou art but a youth, and he a man of war
from his youth.* 1 Sam. xvii. 33.

9. Individual.

*In matters of equity between man and man,
our Saviour has taught us to put my
neighbour in the place of myself, and myself
in the place of my neighbour.* Watts's Logick.

10. Not a beast.

*Thy face, bright Centaur, autumn's heats retain,
The softer season suiting to the man.* Creech's
Manilius.

11. Wealthy or independant person: to this
sense some refer the following passage
of Shakespeare, others to the sense
next foregoing.

*There would this monster make a man; any
strange beast there makes a man.*
Shakespeare's Tempest.

*What poor man would not carry a great
burthen of gold to be made a man for ever.*
Tillotson's Sermons.

12. When a person is not in his senses, we
say, he is not his own man. Ains.

13. A moveable piece at chess or draughts.

14. Man of war. A ship of war.

*A Flemish man of war lighted upon them,
and overmastered them.* Carew's Survey
of Cornwall.

mancipátion n.s. [from *mancipate.*]
Slavery; involuntary obligation.

mandarín n.s. A Chinese nobleman or
magistrate.

mándrake n.s. [*mandragoras,* Lat.
mandragôre, Fr.] The flower of the
mandrake consists of one leaf in the shape
of a bell, and is divided at the top into
several parts; the pointal afterwards
becomes a globular soft fruit, in which
are contained many kidney-shaped seeds:
the root of this plant is said to bear a
resemblace to the human form. The reports
of tying a dog to this plant, in order to root
it up, and prevent the certain death of the
person who dares to attempt such a deed,
and of the groans emitted by it when the
violence is offered, are equally fabulous.
Miller.

*Among other virtues, mandrake has been
falsely celebrated for rendering barren women
fruitful: it has a soporifick quality, and the
ancients used it when they wanted a narcotick
of the most powerful kind.* Hill's Mat. Med.

*Would curses kill, as doth the mandrake's groan,
I would invent as bitter searching terms,
As curst, as harsh, and horrible to hear.*
Shakespeare.

*Not poppy, nor mandragora,
Nor all the drowsy syrups of the world,
Shall ever med'cine thee to that sweet sleep.*
Shakespeare.

*And shrieks like mandrakes, torn out of the earth,
That living mortals, hearing them, run mad.*
Shakesp.

Give me of thy sons mandrakes.
Gen. xxx. 14.

*Go, and catch a falling star,
Get with child a mandrake root.* Donne.

to mánducate v.a. [*manduco*, Lat.] To chew; to eat.

manes n.s. [Latin.] Ghost; shade; that which remains of man after death.

Hail, O ye holy manes! hail again
Paternal ashes. Dryden's Virg.

mángo n.s. [*mangostan*, Fr.] A fruit of the isle of Java, brought to Europe pickled.

The fruit with the husk, when very young,
makes a good preserve, and is used to pickle
like mangoes. Mortimer.

What lord of old wou'd bid his cook prepare
Mangoes, potargo, champignons, cavare.
King.

mánly adj. [from *man*.] Manlike; becoming a man; firm; brave; stout; undaunted; undismayed.

As did Æneas old Anchises bear,
So I bear thee upon my manly shoulders.
Shakespeare.

Let's briefly put on manly readiness,
And meet i' th' hall together. Shakespeare's Macbeth.

I'll speak between the change of man and boy
With a reed voice; and turn two mincing steps
Into a manly stride. Shakesp. Merchant of Venice.

Serene and manly, harden'd to sustain
The load of life, and exercis'd in pain.
Dryden's Juv.

See great Marcellus! how inur'd in toils,
He moves with manly grace. Dryden's Æn.

mánnikin n.s. [*man* and *klein*, German.] A little man; a dwarf.

manse n.s. [*mansio*, Latin.] A parsonage house.

mantíger n.s. [*man* and *tiger*.] A large monkey or baboon.

Near these was placed, by the black prince of
Monomotapas's side, the glaring cat-a-
mountain, and the man-mimicking mantiger.
Arbuth. and Pope.

mántua n.s. [this is perhaps corrupted from *manteau*, Fr.] A lady's gown.

Not Cynthia, when her mantua's pinn'd awry,
E'er felt such rage, resentment, and despair,
As thou, sad virgin! for thy ravish'd hair.
Pope.

How naturally do you apply your hands to
each other's lappets, ruffles, and mantua's.
Swift.

manúbial adj. [*manubiæ*, Lat.] Belonging to spoil; taken in war. Dict.

to manumít v.a. [*manumitto*, Latin.] To release from slavery.

Help to manumit and release him from those
servile drudgeries to vice, under which those
remain who live without God. Government of the Tongue.

Thou wilt beneath the burthen bow,
And glad receive the manumitting blow
On thy shav'd slavish head. Dryden's Juvenal.

mánuscript n.s. [*manuscrit*, Fr. *manuscriptum*, Latin.] A book written, not printed.

A collection of rare manuscripts, exquisitely
written in Arabick, and sought in the most
remote parts by the diligence of Erpenius, the
most excellent linguist, were upon sale to the
jesuits. Wotton.

Her majesty has perused the manuscript of
this opera, and given it her approbation.
Dryden's Dedication to K. Arthur.

march n.s. [*marcher*, French.]

1. Movement; journey of soldiers.

These troops came to the army harrassed with
a long and wearisome march, and cast away
their arms and garments, and fought in their
shirts. Bacon's War with Spain.

Who should command, by his Almighty nod,
These chosen troops, unconscious of the road,
And unacquainted with th' appointed end,
Their marches to begin, and thither tend.
Blackmore.

Their march begins in military state. Van. of hu. Wishes.

2. Grave and solemn walk.

Waller was smooth, but Dryden taught to join
The varying verse, the full resounding line,
The long majestick march, and energy divine.
Pope.

3. Deliberate or laborious walk.

We came to the roots of the mountain, and had
a very troublesome march to gain the top of it.
Addison on Italy.

4. Signals to move.

The drums presently striking up a march,
they make no longer stay, but forward they
go directly towards Neostat. Knolles's
Hist. of the Turks.

5. Marches, without singular. [*marcu*,
   Gothick; *mearc*, Saxon; *marche*, French.]
   Borders; limits; confines.

   They of those marches
Shall be a wall sufficient to defend
Our inland from the pilferring borderers.
Shakespeare.

The English colonies were enforced to keep
continual guards upon the borders and
marches round them. Davies.

It is not fit that a king of an island should
have any marches or borders but the four seas.
Davies on Ireland.

to márinate v.a. [*mariner*, French.] To salt
fish, and then preserve them in oil or
vinegar.

Why am I styl'd a cook, if I'm so loath
To marinate my fish, or season broth.
King's Cookery.

máritated adj. [from *maritus*, Latin.]
Having a husband. Dict.

mármalade, mármalet n.s. [*marmelade*, Fr.
marmelo, Portuguese, a quince.] Marmalade
is the pulp of quinces boiled into a
consistence with sugar: it is subastringent,
and grateful to the stomach. Quincy.

marmórean adj. [*marmoreus*, Lat.] Made of
marble. Dict.

Martínmas n.s. [*martin* and *mass*.] The
feast of St. Martin; the eleventh of
November, commonly corrupted to
martilmass or *martlemass*.

Martilmas beefe doth bear good tacke,
When countrey-folke do dainties lacke.
Tusser's Husb.

mártyr n.s. [μαρτυρ; *martyr*, French.] One
who by his death bears witness to the truth.

Prayers and tears may serve a good man's
turn; if not to conquer as a soldier, yet to suffer
as a martyr. King Charles.†

Thus could not the mouths of worthy martyrs
be silenced. Brown.

Nearer heav'n his virtues shone more bright,
Like rising flames expanding in their height,
The martyr's glory crown'd the soldier's fight.
Dryden.

To be a martyr signifies only to witness the
truth of Christ; but the witnessing of the
truth was then so generally attended with
persecution, that martyrdom now signifies not
only to witness, but to witness by death.
South's Sermons.

The first martyr for Christianity was
encouraged, in his last moments, by a vision
of that divine person for whom he suffered.
Addison on the Christian Religion.

   Socrates,
Truth's early champion, martyr for his God.
Thomson.

mask n.s. [*masque*, French.]

1. A cover to disguise the face; a visor.

Now love pulled off his mask, and shewed his
face unto her, and told her plainly that she
was his prisoner. Sidney.

Since she did neglect her looking-glass,
And throw her sun-expelling mask away;
The air hath starv'd the roses in her cheeks,
And pitch'd the lily tincture of her face.
Shakespeare.

Could we suppose that a mask represented
never so naturally the general humour of a
character, it can never suit with the variety
of passions that are incident to every single
person in the whole course of a play. Addison
on Italy.

2. Any pretence or subterfuge.

Too plain thy nakedness of soul espy'd,
Why dost thou strive the conscious shame to hide,
By masks of eloquence, and veils of pride?
Prior.

3. A festive entertainment, in which the
company is masked.

Will you prepare for this masque to-night.
Shakespeare.

4. A revel; a piece of mummery;
a wild bustle.

They in the end agreed,
That at a masque and common revelling,
Which was ordain'd, they should perform
the deed. Daniel.

This thought might lead me through this
world's vain mask,
Content, though blind, had I no other guide.
Milton.

5. A dramatick performance, written in
a tragick stile without attention to rules
or probability.

Thus I have broken the ice to invention, for
the lively representation of floods and rivers
necessary for our painters and poets in their
pictures, poems, comedies, and masks.
Peacham.

matérialist n.s. [from *material*.] One who
denies spiritual substances.

He was bent upon making Memmius
a materialist. Dryd.

mathemáticks n.s. [μαθηματικη.] That
science which contemplates whatever is
capable of being numbered or measured;
and it is either pure or mixt: pure considers
abstracted quantity, without any relation to
matter; mixt is interwoven with physical
considerations. Harris.

The mathematicks and the metaphysicks
Fall to them, as you find your stomach serves
you. Shak.

See mystery to mathematicks fly. Pope.

mathésis n.s. [μαθησις.] The doctrine of
mathematicks.

Mad Mathesis alone was unconfin'd. Pope.

mátin n.s. Morning.

The glow-worm shews the mattin to be near,
And gins to pale his uneffectual fire.
Shakespeare.

mátrimony n.s. [*matrimonium*, Lat.]
Marriage; the nuptial state; the contract of
man and wife; nuptials.

If any know cause why this couple should
not be joined in holy matrimony, they are
to declare it. Common Prayer.

mátrix n.s. [Lat. *matrice*, Fr.] Womb; a
place where any thing is generated or
formed.

If they be not lodged in a convenient matrix,
they are not excited by the efficacy of the sun.
Brown's Vulgar Err.

máudlin adj. [*Maudlin* is the corrupt
appellation of *Magdelen*, who being drawn
by painters with swoln eyes, and disordered
look, a drunken countenance, seems to have
been so named from a ludicrous
resemblance to the picture of Magdelen.]
Drunk; fuddled.

And the kind maudling crowd melts in her
praise. Southern's Spartan Dame.

And largely, what she wants in words, supplies
With maudlin eloquence of trickling eyes.
Roscommon.

to máunder v.n. [*maudire*, French.] To
grumble; to murmur.

He made me many visits, maundring as if I
had done him a discourtesy in leaving such an
opening. Wiseman's Surgery.

mausóleum n.s. [Latin; *mausolée*, French. A
name which was first given to a stately
monument erected by his queen Artimesia
to her husband Mausolus, king of Caria.] A
pompous funeral monument.

M.D. *Medicinæ doctor*, doctor of physick.

méacock n.s. [*mes coq*, Skinner.] An
uxorious or effeminate man.

mead n.s. [*mædo*, Saxon; *meethe*, Dutch;
meth, German; *hydromeli*, Lat.] A kind of
drink made of water and honey.

Though not so solutive a drink as mead, yet it will be more grateful to the stomach. Bacon.

He sheers his over-burden'd sheep;
Or mead for cooling drink prepares,
Of virgin honey in the jars. Dryden.

mealy-mouthed adj. [imagined by Skinner to be corrupted from *mild-mouthed* or *mellow-mouthed*: but perhaps from the sore mouths of animals, that, when they are unable to comminute their grain, must be fed with meal.] Soft mouthed; unable to speak freely.

She was a fool to be mealy-mouthed where nature speaks so plain. L'Estrange.

mean adj. [*mæne*, Saxon.]

1. Wanting dignity; of low rank or birth.

She was stricken with most obstinate love to a young man but of mean parentage, in her father's court, named Antiphilus; so mean, as that he was but the son of her nurse, and by that means, without other desert, became known of her. Sidney, b. ii.

This fairest maid of fairer mind;
By fortune mean, in nature born a queen. Sidney.

Let pale-fac'd fear keep with the
*   mean-born man,*
And find no harbour in a royal heart. Shakesp. Henry VI.

True hope is swift, and flies with swallow wings;
Kings it makes gods, and meaner creatures,
*   kings.* Shak.

2. Low-minded; base; ungenerous; spiritless.

The shepherd knows not thunder from a tabor,
More than I know the sound of Marcius' tongue
From every meaner man. Shakespeare's Coriolanus.

Can you imagine I so mean could prove,
To save my life by changing of my love? Dryden.

We fast not to please men, nor to promote any mean, worldly interest. Smalridge's Sermons.

3. Contemptible; despicable.

The Roman legions, and great Cæsar found
Our fathers no mean foes. Philips.

I have sacrificed much of my own self-love, in preventing not only many mean things from seeing the light, but many which I thought tolerable. Pope.

4. Low in the degree of any property; low in worth; low in power.

Some things are good, yet in so mean a degree of goodness, that many are only not disproved nor disallowed of God for them. Hooker, b. ii.

The lands be not holden of her majesty in chief, but by a mean tenure in soccage, or by knight's service at the most. Bacon's Office of Alienation.

By this extortion he suddenly grew from a mean to a mighty estate, insomuch that his ancient inheritance being not one thousand marks yearly, he became able to dispend ten thousand pounds. Davies on Ireland.

To peaceful Rome new laws ordain;
Call'd from his mean abode a sceptre to
*   sustain.* Dryden.

5. [*Moyen*, French.] Middle; moderate; without excess.

He saw this gentleman, one of the properest and best-graced men that ever I saw, being of middle age and a mean stature. Sidney, b. ii.

Now read with them those organick arts which enable men to discourse and write, and according to the fittest style of lofty, mean, or lowly. Milton on Education.

6. Intervening; intermediate.

In the mean while the heaven was black with clouds and wind, and there was a great rain. 1 Kings xviii. 45.

There is French wheat, which is bearded, and requireth the best soil, recompensing the same with a profitable plenty; and not wheat, so termed because it is unbearded, is contented with a meaner earth, and contenting with a suitable gain. Carew on Cornwall.

mechánick n.s. A manufacturer; a low workman.

> *Do not bid me*
> *Dismiss my soldiers, or capitulate*
> *Again with Rome's mechanicks.* Shakesp.
> Coriolanus.

A third proves a very heavy philosopher, who possibly would have made a good mechanick, and have done well enough at the useful philosophy of the spade or the anvil. South.

mechánicks n.s. [*mechanica,* Latin.] Dr. Wallis defines mechanicks to be the geometry of motion, a mathematical science, which shews the effects of powers, or moving forces, so far as they are applied to engines, and demonstrates the laws of motion. Harris.

The rudiments of geography, with something of mechanicks, may be easily conveyed into the minds of acute young persons. Watts's Improvement of the Mind.

Salmoneus was a great proficient in mechanicks, and inventor of a vessel which imitated thunder. Broome.

médicine n.s. [*medicine,* Fr. *medicina,* Latin. It is generally pronounced as if only of two syllables, *med'cine.*] Physick; any remedy administered by a physician.

> *O, my dear father! restauration, hang*
> *Thy medicine on my lips; and let this kiss*
> *Repair those violent harms.* Shakesp.
> King Lear.

Let's make us medicines of our great revenge,
To cure this deadly grief. Sakespeare's
Macbeth.

A merry heart doth good like a medicine; but a broken spirit drieth the bones. Prov. xvii. 22.

I wish to die, yet dare not death endure;
Detest the medicine, yet desire the cure.
Dryden.

médly n.s. [from *meddle* for *mingle.*] A mixture; a miscellany; a mingled mass. It is commonly used with some degree of contempt.

Some imagined that the powder in the armory had taken fire; others, that troops of horsemen approached: in which medly of conceits they bare down one upon another, and jostled many into the tower ditch. Hayward.

Love is a medley of endearments, jars,
Suspicions, quarrels, reconcilements, wars;
Then peace again. Walsh.

They count their toilsome marches, long fatigues,
Unusual fastings, and will bear no more
This medley of philosophy and war.
Addison's Cato.

Mahomet began to knock down his fellow citizens, and to fill all Arabia with an unnatural medley of religion and bloodshed. Freeholder, Nº 50.

There are that a compounded fluid drain
From different mixtures: the blended streams,
Each mutually correcting each, create
A pleasurable medley. Philips.

meeting-house n.s. [*meeting* and *house.*] Place where Dissenters assemble to worship.†

His heart misgave him that the churches were so many meeting-houses; but I soon made him easy. Addison.

mégrim n.s. [from *Hemicrany, migrain, megrim,* ημικρανια.] Disorder of the head.†

In every megrim or vertigo there is an obtenebration joined with a semblance of turning round. Bacon's Nat. Hist.

There screen'd in shades from day's detested glare,
Spleen sighs for ever on her pensive bed,
Pain at her side, and megrim at her head.
Pope.

méiny n.s. [*menigu,* Saxon. See *many. Mesnie,* Fr.] A retinue; domestick servants.

They summon'd up their meiny; strait took horse;
Commanded me to follow, and attend.
Shakespeare.

melanchóly n.s. [*melancolie,* Fr. from μελας and χολη.]

1. A disease, supposed to proceed from a redundance of black bile; but it is better known to arise from too heavy and too

viscid blood: its cure is in evacuation, nervous medicines, and powerful stimuli. Quincy.

2. A kind of madness, in which the mind is always fixed on one object.†

I have neither the scholar's melancholy, which is emulation; nor the musician's, which is fantastical; nor the courtier's, which is proud; nor the soldier's, which is ambitious; nor the lawyer's, which is politick; nor the lady's, which is nice; nor the lover's, which is all these; but it is a melancholy of mine own, compounded of many simples, extracted from many objects, and, indeed, the sundry contemplation of my travels, in which my often rumination wraps me in a most humorous sadness. Shakesp. As you like it.

3. A gloomy, pensive, discontented temper.

He protested unto them, that he had only been to seek solitary places by an extreme melancholy that had possessed him. Sidney, b. ii.

All these gifts come from him; and if we murmur here, we may at the next melancholy be troubled that God did not make us angels. Taylor's holy Living.

This melancholy flatters, but unmans you; What is it else but penury of soul, A lazy frost, a numbness of the mind? Dryden.

melliferous adj. Productive of honey. Dict.

mélody n.s. [μελωδια.] Musick; harmony of sound.

The prophet David having singular knowledge not in poetry alone but in musick also, judged them both to be things most necessary for the house of God, left behind him for that purpose a number of divinely indited poems, and was farther the author of adding unto poetry melody in publick prayer, melody both vocal and instrumental, for the raising up of mens hearts, and the sweetening of their affections towards God. Hooker, b. v.

Singing and making melody in your hearts to the Lord. Eph. v. 19.

Why rather, sleep, liest thou in smoky cribs, And husht with buzzing night flies to thy slumber; Than in the perfum'd chambers of the great, And lull'd with sounds of sweetest melody. Shakespeare.

Lend me your songs, ye nightingales: Oh pour The mazy-running soul of melody Into my varied verse. Thomson's Spring, l. 570.

mémory n.s. [*memoire*, Fr. *memoria*, Latin.]

1. The power of retaining or recollecting things past; retention; reminiscence; recollection.

Memory is the power to revive again in our minds those ideas which after imprinting have disappeared, or have been laid aside out of sight. Locke.

The memory is perpetually looking back, when we have nothing present to entertain us: it is like those repositories in animals that are filled with stores of food, on which they may ruminate, when their present pasture fails. Addison's Spectator.

2. Exemption from oblivion.

That ever-living man of memory, Henry the Fifth! Shakesp. Henry VI.

3. Time of knowledge.

Thy request think now fulfill'd, that ask'd How first this world, and face of things, began, And what, before thy memory, was done. Milton.

4. Memorial; monumental record.

   Be better suited; These weeds are memories of those worser hours: I pr'ythee put them off. Shakesp. King Lear.

A swan in memory of Cycnus shines; The mourning sisters weep in wat'ry signs. Addison.

5. Reflection; attention. Not in use.

When Duncan is asleep, his two chamberlains Will I with wine and wassel so convince, That memory, the warder of the brain, Shall be a fume. Shakespeare's Macbeth.

menáge n.s. [French.] A collection of animals.

I saw here the largest menage that I met with any-where. Addison on Italy.

méndicant n.s. [*mendicant*, Fr.] A beggar; one of some begging fraternity in the Romish church.

ménsal adj. [*mensalis*, Lat.] Belonging to the table; transacted at table. A word yet scarcely naturalised.

Conversation either mental or mensal. Clarissa.

to ménsurate v.a. [from *mensura*, Latin.] To measure; to take the dimension of any thing.

méntal adj. [*mentale*, French; *mentis*, Lat.] Intellectual; existing in the mind.

> *What a mental power*
> *This eye shoots forth? How big imagination*
> *Moves in this lip? To the dumbness of the gesture*
> *One might interpret.* Shakesp. Timon of Athens.

> *So deep the pow'r of these ingredients pierc'd,*
> *Ev'n to the inmost seat of mental sight*
> *That Adam now enforc'd to close his eyes,*
> *Sunk down, and all his spirits became*
>   *entranc'd.* Milton.

The metaphor of taste would not have been so general, had there not been a very great conformity between the mental taste and that sensitive taste that affects the palate. Addison's Spect. Nº 409.

If the ideas be not innate, there was a time when the mind was without those principles; for where the ideas are not, there can be no knowledge, no assent, no mental or verbal propositions about them. Locke.

> *She kindly talk'd, at least three hours,*
> *Of plastick forms, and mental pow'rs.* Prior.

Those inward representations of spirit, thought, love, and hatred, are pure and mental ideas, belonging especially to the mind, and carry nothing of shape or sense in them. Watts's Logick.

merácious adj. [*meracus*, Latin.] Strong; racy.

mérchant n.s. [*marchand*, French.] One who trafficks to remote countries.

> *France hath flaw'd the league, and hath attach'd*
> *Our merchants goods at Bourdeaux.* Shakesp. Henry VIII.

The Lord hath given a commandment against the merchant city to destroy the strong holds thereof. Isa. xxiii. 11.

The most celebrated merchants in the world were situated in the island of Tyre. Addison's Freeholder, Nº 42.

mércurial adj. [*mercurialis*, Lat.]

1. Formed under the influence of mercury; active; sprightly.

> *I know the shape of 's leg: This is his hand,*
> *His foot mercurial, his martial thigh,*
> *The brawns of Hercules.* Shakesp. Cymbeline.

This youth was such a mercurial, as could make his own part, if at any time he chanced to be out. Bacon's Hen. VII.

Tully considered the dispositions of a sincere, more ignorant, and less mercurial nation, by dwelling on the pathetick part. Swift's Miscel.

2. Consisting of quicksilver.

mércury n.s. [*mercurius*, Latin.]

1. The chemist's name for quicksilver is mercury. Hill.

The gall of animals and mercury kill worms; and the water in which mercury is boiled has this effect. Arbuthnot.

2. Sprightly qualities.

> *Thus the mercury of man is fix'd,*
> *Strong grows the virtue with his nature mix'd;*
> *The dross cements what else were too refin'd,*
> *And in one int'rest body acts with mind.*
> Pope.

3. A news-paper. Ains.

4. It is now applied, in cant phrase, to the carriers of news and pamphlets.

meretrícious adj. [*meretricius, meretrix,* Latin.] Whorish; such as is practised by prostitutes; alluring by false show.

Our degenerate understandings having suffered a sad divorce from their dearest object, defile themselves with every meretricious semblance, that the variety of opinion presents them with. Glanville's Scep.

Not by affected, meretricious arts,
But strict harmonious symmetry of parts.
Roscommon.

merry-ándrew n.s. A buffoon; a zany; a jack-pudding.

He would be a statesman because he is a buffoon; as if there went no more to the making of a counsellor than the faculties of a merry-andrew or tumbler. L'Estrange.

The first who made the experiment was a merry-andrew. Spectator, Nº 599.

mérrythought n.s. [*merry* and *thought.*] A forked bone on the body of fowls; so called because boys and girls pull in play at the two sides, the longest part broken off betokening priority of marriage.

Let him not be breaking merrythoughts under the table with my cousin. Eachard's Contempt of the Clergy.

meséems, impersonal verb [*me* and *seems*, or *it seems to me*: for this word it is now too common to use *methinks* or *methought*, an ungrammatical word.] I think; it appears to me; methinks.

Alas, of ghosts I hear the gastly cries;
Yet there, meseems, I hear her singing loud.
Sidney.

Meseemed by my side a royal maid,
Her dainty limbs full softly down did lay.
Fairy Queen.

To that general subjection of the land meseems that the custom or tenure can be no bar nor impeachment. Spenser.

Messíah n.s. [from the Hebrew.] The Anointed; the Christ; the Saviour of the world; the Prince of peace.

Great and publick opposition the magistrates made against Jesus the man of Nazareth, when he appeared as the Messiah. Watts's Improvement of the Mind.

metagrámmatism n.s. [μετα and γραμμα.] Anagrammatism, or metagrammatism, is a dissolution of a name truly written into its letters, as its elements, and a new connexion of it by artificial transposition, without addition, subtraction, or change of any letter into different words, making some perfect sense applicable to the person named. Camden's Remains.

métaphor n.s. [*metaphore*, Fr. μεταφορα.] The application of a word to an use to which, in its original import, it cannot be put: as, he *bridles* his anger; he *deadens* the sound; the spring *awakes* the flowers. A metaphor is a simile comprized in a word; the spring putting in action the powers of vegetation, which were torpid in the winter, as the powers of a sleeping animal are excited by awaking him.

The work of tragedy is on the passions, and in a dialogue: both of them abhor strong metaphors, in which the epopœa delights. Dryden's Ded. to Virgil's Æneis.

metaphráse n.s. [μεταφρασις.] A mere verbal translation from one language into another.

This translation is not so loose as paraphrase, nor so close as metaphrase. Dryden.†

metaphysick, **metaphysicks** n.s. [*metaphysique*, Fr. μεταφυσικη.] Ontology; the doctrine of the general affections of substances existing.

The mathematicks and the metaphysicks,
Fall to them as you find your stomach serves
* you.* Shakesp.

Call her the metaphysicks of her sex,
And say she tortures wits, as quartans vex
Physicians. Cleaveland.

If sight be caused by intromission, or receiving in, the form of contrary species should be received confusedly together, which how absurd it is, Aristotle shews in his metaphysicks. Peacham on Drawing.

See physick beg the Stagyrite's defence!
See metaphysick call for aid on sense!
Pope's Dunciad.

The topicks of ontology or metaphysick,
are cause, effect, action, passion, identity,
opposition, subject, adjunct, and sign.
Watts's Logick.

metempsychósis n.s. [μετεμψυχωσις.]
The transmigration of souls from body
to body.

From the opinion of metempsychosis, or
transmigration of the souls of men into the
bodies of beasts, most suitable unto their
human condition, after his death Orpheus
the musician became a swan. Brown's
Vulgar Errours, b. iii.

méthodist n.s. [from *method.*]

1. A physician who practises by theory.

Our wariest physicians, not only chemists
but methodists, give it inwardly in several
constitutions and distempers. Boyle.

2. One of a new kind of puritans lately
   arisen, so called from their profession
   to live by rules and in constant method.†

metónymy n.s. [*metonymie*, Fr.
μετωνυμια.] A rhetorical figure, by which
one word is put for another, as the matter
for the materiate; *he died by steel*, that is, by
a sword.

They differ only as cause and effect, which by
a metonymy usual in all sorts of authors, are
frequently put one for another. Tillotson.

métre n.s. [*metrum*, Latin; μετρον.]
Speech confined to a certain number and
harmonick disposition of syllables; verse;
measure; numbers.

For the metre sake, some words be driven
awry which require a straighter placing in
plain prose. Ascham's Schoolmaster.

He taught his Romans in much better metre,
To laugh at fools. Pope.

mézzotinto n.s. [Italian.] A kind of graving,
so named as nearly resembling paint, the
word importing half-painted: it is done
by beating the whole into asperity with a

hammer, and then rubbing it down with a
stone to the resemblance intended.

míasm n.s. [from μιαινω, *inquino*, to
infect.] Such particles or atoms as are
supposed to arise from distempered,
putrefying, or poisonous bodies, and to
affect people at a distance.

The plague is a malignant fever, caused
through pestilential miasms insinuating into
the humoral and consistent parts of the body.
Harvey on Consumptions.

Micháelmass n.s. [*Michael* and *mass.*] The
feast of the archangel Michael, celebrated
on the twenty-ninth of September.

They compounded to furnish ten oxen after
Michaelmass for thirty pounds price. Carew.

míckle adj. [*micel*, Saxon.] Much; great.
Obsolete. In Scotland it is pronounced
muckle.

This reade is rife that oftentime
Great cumbers fall unsoft:
In humble dales is footing fast,
The trode is not so tickle,
And though one fall through heedless haste,
Yet is his miss not mickle. Spenser's
Pastorals.

Many a little makes a mickle.
Camden's Remains.

If I to-day die with Frenchmens rage,
To-morrow I shall die with mickle age.
Shakesp. Henry VI.

O, mickle is the pow'rful grace, that lies
In plants, herbs, stones, and their true
   qualities. Shakesp.

All this tract that fronts the falling sun,
A noble peer, of mickle trust and power,
Has in his charge. Milton.

míscroscope n.s. [μικρος and σκοπεω;
microscope, Fr.] An optick instrument,
contrived various ways to give to the eye a
large appearance of many objects which
could not otherwise be seen.

If the eye were so acute as to rival the finest
microscopes, and to discern the smallest hair
upon the leg of a gnat, it would be a curse,

*and not a blessing, to us; it would make all
things appear rugged and deformed; the most
finely polished crystal would be uneven and
rough; the sight of our own selves would
affright us; the smoothest skin would be beset
all over with ragged scales and bristly hairs.*
Bentley.

*The critick eye, that microscope of wit,
Sees hairs and pores, examines bit by bit.*
Dunciad, b. iv.

mien n.s. [*mine*, French.] Air; look; manner.

*In her alone that owns this book is seen
Clorinda's spirit, and her lofty mien.* Waller.

*What can have more the figure and mien
of a ruin than craggs, rocks, and cliffs.*
Burnet's Theory of the Earth.

*One, in whom an outward mien appear'd,
And turn superior to the vulgar herd.* Prior.

*What winning graces, what majestick mien,
She moves a goddess, and she looks a queen.*
Pope.

mighty adv. In a great degree. Not to be
used but in very low language.

*Lord of his new hypothesis he reigns:
He reigns; How long? Till some usurper rise,
And he too mighty thoughtful, mighty wise:
Studies new lines.* Prior.

militia n.s. [Latin.] The trainbands; the
standing force of a nation.

*Let any prince think soberly of his forces,
except his militia be good and valiant soldiers.*
Bacon's Essays, Nº 30.

*The militia was so settled by law, that
a sudden army could be drawn together.*
Clarendon.

*Unnumbered spirits round thee fly,
The light militia of the lower sky.*
Pope's Rape of the Lock.

milksop n.s. [*milk* and *sop*.] A soft, mild,
effeminate, feeble-minded man.

*Of a most notorious thief, which lived all his
life-time of spoils, one of their bards in his
praise will say, that he was none of the idle
milksops that was brought up by the fire-side,*

*but that most of his days he spent in arms, and
that he did never eat his meat before he had
won it with his sword.* Spenser on Ireland.

*A milksop, one that never in his life
Felt so much cold as over shoes in snow.*
Shak. Rich. III.

*We have as good passions as yourself; and a
woman was never designed to be a milksop.*
Addison's Spect.

*But give him port and potent sack;
From milksop he starts up mohack.* Prior.

milky-way n.s. [*milky* and *way*.] The galaxy.

*The milky-way, or via lactea, is a broad
white path or track, encompassing the whole
heavens, and extending itself in some places
with a double path, but for the most part with
a single one. Some of the ancients, as Aristotle,
imagined that this path consisted only of a
certain exhalation hanging in the air; but, by
the telescopical observations of this age, it hath
been discovered to consist of an innumerable
quantity of fixed stars, different in situation
and magnitude, from the confused mixture of
whose light its whole colour is supposed to be
occasioned. It passes through the constellations
of Cassiopeia, Cygnus, Aquila, Perseus,
Andromeda, part of Ophiucus and Gemini, in
the northern hemisphere; and in the southern
it takes in part of Scorpio, Sagittarius,
Centaurus, the Argo Navis and the Ara. The
galaxy hath usually been the region in which
new stars have appeared; as that in
Cassiopeia, which was seen in A.D. 1572;
that in the breast of the Swan, and another in
the knee of Serpentarius; which have appeared
for a while, and then become invisible again.*
Harris.

*Nor need we with a prying eye survey
The distant skies to find the milky-way:
It forcibly intrudes upon our sight.*
Creech's Manilius.

*How many stars there must be, a naked eye
may give us some faint glimpse, but much
more a good telescope, directed towards that
region of the sky called the milky-way.*
Cheyne.

millénnium n.s. [Latin.] A thousand years; generally taken for the thousand years, during which, according to an ancient tradition in the church, grounded on a doubtful text in the Apocalypse, our blessed Saviour shall reign with the faithful upon earth after the resurrection, before the final completion of beatitude.[†]

We must give a full account of that state called the millennium. Burnet's Theory of the Earth.

míllion n.s. [*million*, Fr. *milliogne*, Italian.]

1. The number of an hundred myriads, or ten hundred thousand.

Within thine eyes sat twenty thousand deaths,
In thy hands clutch'd as many millions, in
Thy lying tongue both numbers.
Shakespeare.

2. A proverbial name for any very great number.

That the three angles of a triangle are equal to two right ones, is a truth more evident than many of those propositions that go for principles; and yet there are millions who know not this at all. Locke.

There are millions of truths that a man is not concerned to know. Locke.

She found the polish'd glass, whose small convex
Enlarges to ten millions of degrees
The mite, invisible else. Philips.

Midst thy own flock, great shepherd, be receiv'd;
And glad all heav'n with millions thou hast
*   sav'd.* Prior.

mímick n.s. [*mimicus*, Latin.]

1. A ludicrous imitator; a buffoon who copies another's act or manner so as to excite laughter.

Like poor Andrew I advance,
False mimick of my master's dance:
Around the cord a while I sprawl,
And thence, though slow, in earnest fall.
Prior.

2. A mean or servile imitator.

Of France the mimick, and of Spain the prey.
Anon.[†]

mimógrapher n.s. [*mimus* and γραφω.] A writer of farces. Dict.

minácious adj. [*minax*, Lat.] Full of threats.

mínim n.s. [from *minimus*, Lat.]

1. A small being; a dwarf.[†]

  Not all
Minims of nature; some of serpent-kind,
Wond'rous in length, and corpulence, involv'd
Their snaky folds, and added wings. Milton's Par. Lost.

2. This word is applied, in the northern counties, to a small sort of fish, which they pronounce *mennim*. See *minnow*.

to mínorate v.a. [from *minor*, Lat.] To lessen; to diminish. A word not yet admitted into the language.

This it doth not only by the advantageous assistance of a tube, but by shewing in what degrees distance minorates the object. Glanville's Sceps.

mínuet n.s. [*menuet*, French.] A stately regular dance.

The tender creature could not see his fate,
With whom she'd danc'd a minuet so late. Stepney.

John Trot has the assurance to set up for a minuet dancer. Spectator, N° 308.

mínum n.s.

1. [With printers.] A small sort of printing letter.

2. [With musicians.] A note of slow time, two of which make a semibrief, as two crotchets make a minum; two quavers a crotchet, and two semiquavers a quaver. Bailey.

Oh, he's the courageous captain of compliments; he fights as you sing pricksongs, keeps time, distance, and proportion; rests his minum, one, two, and the third in your bosom. Shakespeare's Romeo and Juliet.

minx n.s. [contracted, I suppose, from *minnock*.] A young, pert, wanton girl.

Lewd minx!
Come, go with me apart. Shakespeare.

Some torches bore, some links,
Before the proud virago minx.
Hudibras, p. ii.

She, when but yet a tender minx, began
To hold the door, but now sets up for man.
Dryden.

míracle n.s. [*miracle*, Fr. *miraculum*, Latin.]

1. A wonder; something above human
   power.

Nothing almost sees miracles
But misery. Shakespeare's King Lear.

Virtuous and holy, chosen from above,
To work exceeding miracles on earth.
Shakesp. Henry VI.

Be not offended, nature's miracle,
Thou art allotted to be ta'en by me.
Shakesp. Henry VI.

2. [In theology.] An effect above human or
   natural power, performed in attestation
   of some truth.

The miracles of our Lord are peculiarly
eminent above the lying wonders of demons,
in that they were not made out of vain
ostentation of power, and to raise unprofitable
amazement; but for the real benefit and
advantage of men, by feeding the hungry,
healing all sorts of diseases, ejecting of devils,
and reviving the dead. Bentley's Sermons.

mírksome n.s. [*morck*, dark, Danish. In
the derivatives of this set, no regular
orthography is observed: it is common to
write *murky*, to which the rest ought to
conform.] Dark; obscure.

Through mirksome air her ready way she
makes. F. Qu.

mis, an inseparable particle used in
composition to mark an ill sense, or
depravation of the meaning: as, *chance*, luck;
mischance, ill luck; *computation*, reckoning;
miscomputation, false reckoning; *to like*, to
be pleased; *to mislike*, to be offended; from
mes in Teutonick and French, used in the
same sense. Of this it is difficult to give all
the examples; but those that follow will
sufficiently explain it.

mísanthrope,   misánthropos   n.s.
[*misanthrope*, French; μισανθρωπος.] A
hater of mankind.

I am misanthropos, and hate mankind.
Shakespeare.

Alas, poor dean! his only scope
Was to be held a misanthrope;
This into gen'ral odium drew him.
Swift's Miscel.

misdeméanor n.s. [*mis* and *demean.*]
Offence; ill behaviour; something less than
an atrocious crime.

The house of commons have only power to
censure the members of their own house, in
point of election or misdemeanors, in or
towards that house. Bacon.

It is no real disgrace to the church merely to
lose her privileges, but to forfeit them by her
fault or misdemeanor. South.

These could never have touched the head, or
stopped the source of these unhappy
misdemeanors, for which the punishment was
sent. Woodward's Nat. Hist. p. ii.

míshmash n.s. Ains. A low word. A mingle
or hotchpotch.

misógamist n.s. [μισω and γαμος.] A
marriage hater.

misógyny n.s. [μισω and γυνη.] Hatred of
women.

to mispél v.a. [*mis* and *spell.*] To spell
wrong.

She became a profest enemy to the arts and
sciences, and scarce ever wrote a letter to him
without wilfully mispelling his name.
Spectator, Nº 635.

míssile adj. [*missilis*, Lat.] Thrown by the
hand; striking at distance.

We bend the bow, or wing the missile dart.
Pope.

místress n.s. [*maistresse, maitresse*, French.]

1. A woman who governs: correlative to
   subject or to servant.

Here stood he in the dark, his sharp sword out,
Mumbling of wicked charms, conj'ring the moon
To stand 's auspicious mistress. Shakesp.
King Lear.

Let us prepare
Some welcome for the mistress of the house.
Shakespeare.

    Like the lily,
That once was mistress of the field and flourish'd,
I'll hang my head and perish. Shakesp.
Henry VIII.

He'll make your Paris louvre shake for it,
Were it the mistress court of mighty Europe.
Shakespeare.

I will not charm my tongue; I'm bound to speak;
My mistress here lies murther'd in her bed.
Shakesp. Othello.

The late queen's gentlewoman! a knight's
    daughter!
To be her mistress' mistress! the queen's queen.
Shakesp.

Rome now is mistress of the whole world, sea
and land, to either pole. Benj. Johnson's
Catiline.

Wonder not, sov'reign mistress! if perhaps
Thou can'st, who art sole wonder; much less arm
Thy looks, the heav'n of mildness, with
    disdain. Milton.

Those who assert the lunar orb presides
O'er humid bodies, and the ocean guides;
Whose waves obsequious ebb, or swelling run
With the declining or encreasing moon;
With reason seem her empire to maintain
As mistress of the rivers and the main.
Blackmore.

What a miserable spectacle, for a nation
that had been mistress at sea so long!
Arbuthnot on Coins.

2. A woman who possesses faculties
uninjured.

There had she enjoyed herself while she was
mistress of herself, and had no other thoughts
but such as might arise out of quiet senses.
Sidney, b. ii.

Ages to come, that shall your bounty hear,
Will think you mistress of the Indies were;
Though streighter bounds your fortune
    did confine,
In your large heart was found a wealthy
    mine. Waller.

3. A woman skilled in any thing.

A letter desires all young wives to make
themselves mistresses of Wingate's
Arithmetick. Addison's Spect. Nº 92.

4. A woman teacher.

Erect publick schools, provided with the best
and ablest masters and mistresses. Swift.

5. A woman beloved and courted.

They would not suffer the prince to confer
with, or very rarely to see, his mistress, whom
they pretended he should forthwith marry.
Clarendon.

Nice honour still engages to requite
False mistresses and proud with slight
    for slight. Granville.

6. A term of contemptuous address.

    Look you, pale mistress,
Do you perceive the ghastness of her eye?
Shakespeare.

7. A whore; a concubine.

míttimus [Latin.] A warrant by which a
justice commits an offender to prison.

mnemónicks n.s. [μνημονικη.] The act of
memory.

móbby n.s. An American drink made of
potatoes.

to móble v.a. [sometimes written *mable*,
perhaps by a ludicrous allusion to the
French *je m' habille*.] To dress grossly or
inelegantly.

But who, oh! hath seen the mobled queen,
Run barefoot up and down. Shakesp.
Hamlet.

módern n.s. [*moderne*, Fr. from *modernus*,
low Latin, supposed a casual corruption of
hodiernus. Vel potius ab adverbio mado,
modernus, ut a die diurnus. Ains.]†

1. Late; recent; not ancient; not antique.

Some of the ancient, and likewise divers of
the modern writers, that have laboured in
natural magick, have noted a sympathy
between the sun and certain herbs. Bacon.

The glorious parallels then downward bring
To modern wonders, and to Britain's king.
Prior.

2. In Shakespeare, vulgar; mean; common.

Trifles, such as we present modern friends
withal. Shakesp.

The justice
With eyes severe and beard of formal cut,
Full of wise saws and modern instances.
Shakespeare.

We have our philosophical persons to make
modern and familiar things supernatural and
causeless. Shakespeare.

módernism n.s. [from *modern*.] Deviation
from the ancient and classical manner. A
word invented by Swift.

Scribblers send us over their trash in prose and
verse, with abominable curtailings and quaint
modernisms. Swift.

móderns n.s. Those who have lived lately,
opposed to the ancients.[†]

There are moderns who, with a slight
variation, adopt the opinion of Plato.
Boyle on Colours.

Some by old words to fame have made pretence;
Ancients in phrase, mere moderns in their
sense! Pope.

modesty-piece n.s. A narrow lace which
runs along the upper part of the stays
before, being a part of the tucker, is called
the modestypiece. Addison's Guard.
Nº 118.

módish adj. [from *mode*.] Fashionable;
formed according to the reigning custom.

But you, perhaps, expect a modish feast,
With am'rous songs, and wanton dances
grac'd. Dryd.

Hypocrisy, at the fashionable end of the town,
is very different from hypocrisy in the city; the
modish hypocrite endeavours to appear more
vitious than he really is, the other kind of
hypocrite more virtuous. Addison's Spect.
Nº 399.

to módulate v.a. [*modulor*, Latin.] To form
sound to a certain key, or to certain notes.

The nose, lips, teeth, palate, jaw, tongue,
weasan, lungs, muscles of the chest,
diaphragm, and muscles of the belly, all
serve to make or modulate the sound.
Grew's Cosmol.

Could any person so modulate her voice as
to deceive so many. Broome's Notes on
the Odyssey.

Echo propagates around
Each charm of modulated sound. Anon.[†]

móhock n.s. The name of a cruel nation of
America given to ruffians who infested, or
rather were imagined to infest, the streets
of London.

From milk-sop he starts up mohock. Prior.

Who has not trembled at the mohock's name?
Gay.

Thou hast fallen upon me with the rage of
a mad dog, or a mohock. Dennis.

moídered adj. Crazed. Ains.

móidore n.s. [*moede*, Fr.] A Portugal coin,
rated at one pound seven shillings.

móky adj. Dark: as, *moky* weather. Ains. It
seems a corruption of murky: and in some
places they call it muggy, dusky.

mome n.s. A dull, stupid blockhead, a
stock, a post: this owes its original to the
French word *momon*, which signifies the
gaming at dice in masquerade, the custom
and rule of which is, that a strict silence is
to be observed; whatsoever sum one stakes
another covers, but not a word is to be
spoken; from hence also comes our word
mum for silence. Hanmer.

Mome, malthorse, capon, coxcomb, idiot, patch!
Either get thee from the door, or sit down
at the hatch. Shakespeare's Comedy
of Errours.

mónachal adj. [*monacal*, Fr. *monachalis*,
Lat. μοναχος.] Monastick; relating to
monks, or conventual orders.

mónarch n.s. [*monarch*, Fr. μοναρχος.]

1. A governor invested with absolute authority; a king.

I was
A morsel for a monarch. Shakesp. Ant. and Cleopatra.

Your brother kings and monarchs of the earth
Do all expect that you should rouse yourself.
Shakespeare.

The father of a family or nation, that uses
his servants like children, and advises with
them in what concerns the commonweal,
and thereby is willingly obeyed by them, is
what the schools mean by a monarch.
Temple's Miscel.

2. One superior to the rest of the same kind.

The monarch oak, the patriarch of the trees,
Three centuries he grows, and three he stays
Supreme in state, and in three more decays.
Dryden.

With ease distinguish'd is the regal race,
One monarch wears an open, honest face;
Shap'd to his size, and godlike to behold,
His royal body shines with specks of gold.
Dryden's Virg.

Return'd with dire remorseless sway,
The monarch savage rends the trembling prey.
Pope's Odys.

3. President.

Come, thou monarch of the vine,
Plumpy Bacchus, with pink eyne,
In thy vats our cares be drown'd.
Shakesp. Ant. and Cleop.

móney n.s. [*monnoye*, French; *moneta*, Latin. It has properly no plural except when money is taken for a single piece; but monies was formerly used for sums.] Metal coined for the purposes of commerce.[†]

Importune him for monies; be not ceast
With slight denial. Shakesp. Timon of Athens.

The jealous wittolly knave hath masses of money. Shakesp.

You need my help, and you say,
Shylock, we would have monies.
Shakespeare.

I will give thee the worth of it in money.
1 Kings xxi. 2.

Wives the readiest helps
To betray heady husbands, rob the easy,
And lend the monies on return of lust.
Benj. Johnson.

Money differs from uncoined silver, in that
the quantity of silver in each piece of money
is ascertained by the stamp it bears, which is
a publick voucher. Locke.

My discourse to the hen-peck'd has produced
many correspondents; such a discourse is of
general use, and every married man's money.
Addison's Spect. No 482.

People are not obliged to receive any monies,
except of their own coinage by a publick mint.
Swift.

Those hucksterers or money jobbers will be
found necessary, if this brass money is made
current in the exchequer. Swift.

mónkery n.s. [from *monk.*] The monastick life.

Neither do I meddle with their evangelical
perfection of vows, nor the dangerous
servitude of their rash and impotent votaries,
nor the inconveniences of their monkery.
Hall.

mónkey n.s. [*monikin*, a little man.]

1. An ape; a baboon; a jackanapes. An animal bearing some resemblance of man.

One of them shewed me a ring that he had of
your daughter for a monkey: Tubal, it was
my turquoise; I would not have given it for
a wilderness of monkeys. Shakespeare.

More new-fangled than an ape; more giddy
in my desires than a monkey. Shakesp.
As you like it.

Other creatures, as well as monkeys, destroy
their young ones by senseless fondness. Locke
on Education.

With glittering gold and sparkling gems
   they shine,
But apes and monkeys are the gods within.
Granville.

2. A word of contempt, or slight kindness.

This is the monkey's own giving out; she is
persuaded I will marry her. Shakespeare's
Othello.

Poor monkey! how wilt thou do for a father?
Shakesp.

mónody n.s. [μονωδια; *monodie*, Fr.] A
poem sung by one person not in dialogue.

monógamist n.s. [μονος and γαμος;
monogame, Fr.] One who disallows second
marriages.

mónogram n.s. [μονος and γραμμα;
monogramme, Fr.] A cypher; a character
compounded of several letters.

mónomachy n.s. [μονομαχια; μονος and
μαχη.] A duel; a single combat.

monópoly n.s. [μονοπωλια; *monopole*, Fr.
μονος and πωλεω.] The exclusive privilege
of selling any thing.

Dost thou call me fool, boy?
—All thy other titles hast thou given away;
that thou wast born with.
—Lords and great men will not let me; if
I had a monopoly on 't they would have
part on 't. Shakesp. King Lear.

One of the most oppressive monopolies
imaginable; all others can concern only
something without us, but this fastens upon
our nature, yea upon our reason. Go. of
the Tongue.

Shakespeare rather writ happily than
knowingly and justly; and Johnson, who by
studying Horace, had been acquainted with
the rules, yet seemed to envy to posterity that
knowledge, and to make a monopoly of his
learning. Dryden's Juv.

monóstich   n.s.   [μονοστιχον.]   A
composition of one verse.

mónsieur n.s. [French.] A term of reproach
for a Frenchman.

A Frenchman his companion;
An eminent monsieur, that, it seems, much loves
A Gallian girl. Shakespeare's Cymbeline.

mónster n.s. [*monstre*, Fr. *monstrum*, Latin.]

1. Something out of the common order
   of nature.

It ought to be determined whether monsters
be really a distinct species; we find, that some
of these monstrous productions have none of
those qualities that accompany the essence of
that species from whence they derive. Locke.

2. Something horrible for deformity,
   wickedness, or mischief.

If she live long,
And, in the end, meet the old course of death,
Women will all turn monsters. Shakesp.
King Lear.

All human virtue
Finds envy never conquer'd but by death:
The great Alcides ev'ry labour past,
Had still this monster to subdue at last. Pope.

mónstrous adv. Exceedingly; very much.
A cant term.

Oil of vitriol and petroleum, a dram of each,
turn into a mouldy substance, there residing
a fair cloud in the bottom, and a monstrous
thick oil on the top. Bacon.

She was easily put off the hooks, and
monstrous hard to be pleased again.
L'Estrange.

Add, that the rich have still a gibe in store,
And will be monstrous witty on the poor.
Dryden's Juv.

moon-calf n.s. [*moon* and *calf.*]

1. A monster; a false conception: supposed
   perhaps anciently to be produced by the
   influence of the moon.

How cam'st thou to be the siege of this moon-
calf. Shak.

2. A dolt; a stupid fellow.

The potion works not on the part design'd,
But turns his brain, and stupifies his mind;
The sotted moon-calf gapes. Dryden's
Juvenal.

móonstruck adj. [*moon* and *struck.*] Lunatick; affected by the moon.

Demoniack phrensy, moaping melancholy,
And moonstruck madness. Milton's Par. Lost, b. xi.

moose n.s. The large American deer; the biggest of the species of deer.

to mope v.n. [Of this word I cannot find a probable etymology.] To be stupid; to drowse; to be in a constant daydream; to be spiritless, unactive and inattentive; to be stupid and delirious.

What a wretched and peevish fellow is this
king of England, to mope with his fat-brain'd
followers. Shakespeare.

Eyes without feeling, feeling without sight,
Ears without hands or eyes, smelling sans all,
Or but a sickly part of one true sense
Could not so mope. Shakespeare's Hamlet.

Ev'n in a dream, were we divided from them,
And were brought moping hither. Shakesp. Tempest.

Intestine stone, and ulcer, cholick pangs,
Demoniack phrensy, moping melancholy,
And moon-struck madness. Milton's Par. Lost, b. xi.

The busy craftsman and o'erlabour'd hind,
Forget the travel of the day in sleep;
Care only wakes, and moping pensiveness;
With meagre discontented looks they sit,
And watch the wasting of the midnight taper.
Rowe.

móppet, mópsey n.s. [perhaps from *mop.*] A puppet made of rags, as a mop is made; a fondling name for a girl.

Our sovereign lady: made for a queen?
With a globe in one hand, and a sceptre
  in t' other?
A very pretty moppet! Dryden's Spanish Fryar.

mópus n.s. [A cant word from *mope.*] A drone; a dreamer.

I'm grown a mere mopus; no company comes
But a rabble of tenants. Swift's Miscel.

móral adj. [*moral,* Fr. *moralis,* Latin.]

1. Relating to the practice of men towards each other, as it may be virtuous or criminal; good or bad.

Keep at the least within the compass of moral
actions, which have in them vice or virtue.
Hooker, b. ii.

Laws and ordinances positive he
distinguisheth from the laws of the two tables,
which were moral. Hooker, b. iii.

In moral actions divine law helpeth
exceedingly the law of reason to guide man's
life, but in supernatural it alone guideth.
Hooker, b. i.

Now, brandish'd weapons glitt'ring in
  their hands,
Mankind is broken loose from moral bands;
No rights of hospitality remain,
The guest, by him who harbour'd him,
  is slain. Dryden.

2. Reasoning or instructing with regard to vice and virtue.

France spreads his banners in our noiseless land,
With plumed helm thy slayer begins his threats,
Whilst thou, a moral fool, sit'st still and criest.
Shakesp.

3. Popular; such as is known or admitted in the general business of life.

We have found it, with a moral certainty, the
seat of the Mosaical abyss. Burnet's Theory of the Earth.

Mathematical things are capable of the
strictest demonstration; conclusions in natural
philosophy are capable of proof by an
induction of experiments; things of a moral
nature by moral arguments, and matters
of fact by credible testimony.
Tillotson's Sermons.

A moral universality, is when the predicate
agrees to the greatest part of the particulars
which are contained under the universal
subject. Watts's Logick.

morígerous adj. [*morigerus,* Lat.] Obedient; obsequious.

mórmo n.s. [η μορμω.] Bugbear; false terrour.

mórris, mórris-dance n.s. [that is *moorish* or *morisco-dance*.]

1. A dance in which bells are gingled, or staves or swords clashed, which was learned by the Moors, and was probably a kind of Pyrrhick or military dance.

The queen stood in some doubt of a Spanish invasion, though it proved but a morris-dance upon our waves. Wotton.

One in his catalogue of a feigned library, sets down this title of a book, The morris-dance of hereticks. Bacon.

The sounds and seas, with all their finny drove, Now to the moon in wavering morrice move. Milton.

I took delight in pieces that shewed a country village, morrice-dancing, and peasants together by the ears. Peacham.

Four reapers danced a morrice to oaten pipes. Spectator.

2. Nine mens morris. A kind of play with nine holes in the ground.

The folds stand empty in the drowned field, And crows are fatted with the murrain flock; The nine mens morris is filled up with mud. Shakespeare.

mórtal adj. [*mortalis*, Lat. *mortel*, Fr.]

1. Subject to death; doomed sometime to die.

*Nature does require
Her times of preservation, which, perforce,
I her frail son amongst my breth'ren mortal
Must give my attendance to.* Shakesp. Henry VIII.

This corruptible must put on incorruption, and this mortal must put on immortality. 1 Cor. xv. 53.

*Heav'nly powers, where shall we find such love!
Which of ye will be mortal to redeem
Man's mortal crime; and just, th' unjust
to save.* Milton.

*Know,
The day thou eat'st thereof, my sole command
Transgrest, inevitably thou shalt die;
From that day mortal: and this happy state
Shalt lose.* Milton's Par. Lost, b. viii.

2. Deadly; destructive; procuring death.

*Come all you spirits
That tend on mortal thoughts, unsex me here,
And fill me from the crown to th' toe, top full
Of cruelty.* Shakespeare's Macbeth.

The mortalest poisons practised by the West Indians, have some mixture of the blood, fat, or flesh of man. Bacon.

*The fruit
Of that forbidden tree, whose mortal taste
Brought death into the world, and all our
woe.* Milton.

Some circumstances have been great discouragers of trade, and others are absolutely mortal to it. Temple.

*Hope not, base man! unquestion'd hence to go,
For I am Palamon, thy mortal foe.* Dryden.

3. Bringing death.

*Safe in the hand of one disposing pow'r,
Or in the natal, or the mortal hour.* Pope's Essay on Man.

4. Human; belonging to man.

They met me in the day of success; and I have learned by the perfected report, they have more in them than mortal knowledge. Shakespeare's Macbeth.

*Macbeth
Shall live the lease of nature, pay his breath
To time and mortal custom.* Shakespeare's Macbeth.

*The voice of God
To mortal ear is dreadful; They beseech,
That Moses might report to them his will,
And terror cease.* Milton's Par. Lost, b. xii.

*Success, the mark no mortal wit,
Or surest hand can always hit.* Butler.

No one enjoyment but is liable to be lost by ten thousand accidents, out of all mortal power to prevent. South's Serm.

5. Extreme; violent. A low word.

The birds were in a mortal apprehension of the beetles, till the sparrow reasoned them into understanding. L'Estrange.

The nymph grew pale and in a mortal fright,
Spent with the labour of so long a flight;
And now despairing, cast a mournful look
Upon the streams. Dryden.

mórtress n.s. [from *mortier de sagesse.* Skinner.] A dish of meat of various kinds beaten together.

A mortress made with the brawn of capons, stamped, strained, and mingled with like quantity of almond butter, is excellent to nourish the weak. Bacon's Nat. Hist.

mosque n.s. [*mosquée*, French; *moschit*, Turkish.] A Mahometan temple.

motátion n.s. Act of moving. Dict.

móther n.s. [*moðor*, Saxon; *moder*, Danish; *moeder*, Dutch.]

1. A woman that has born a child; correlative to son or daughter.

Let thy mother rather feel thy pride, than fear
Thy dangerous stoutness. Shakespeare's Coriolanus.

Come sit down every mother's son,
And rehearse your parts. Shakespeare.

I had not so much of man in me,
But all my mother came into mine eyes,
And gave me up to tears. Shakesp. Henry V.

2. That which has produced any thing.

   Alas, poor country! It cannot
Be call'd our mother, but our grave.
Shakespeare.

The resemblance of the constitution and diet of the inhabitants to those of their mother country, occasion a great affinity in the popular diseases. Arbuthnot on Air.

The strongest branch leave for a standard, cutting off the rest close to the body of the mother plant. Mortimer's Husb.

3. That which has preceded in time: as, a mother church to chapels.

4. That which requires reverence and obedience.

The good of mother church, as well as that of civil society, renders a judicial practice necessary. Ayliffe's Parergon.

5. Hysterical passion; so called, as being imagined peculiar to women.

This stopping of the stomach might be the mother; forasmuch as many were troubled with mother fits, although few returned to have died of them. Graunt's Bills.

6. A familiar term of address to an old woman; or to a woman dedicated to religious austerities.

7. Mother in law. A husband's or wife's mother. Ains.

I am come to set at variance the daughter in law against the mother in law. Matth. x. 35.

8. [*Moeder*, Dutch, from *modder*, mud.] A thick substance concreting in liquors; the lees or scum concreted.

If the body be liquid, and not apt to putrefy totally, it will cast up a mother, as the mothers of distilled waters. Bacon.

Potted fowl, and fish come in so fast,
That ere the first is out the second stinks,
And mouldy mother gathers on the brinks.
Dryden.

9. [More properly *modder; modde*, Dutch.] A young girl. Now totally obsolete.

A sling for a mother, a bow for a boy,
A whip for a carter. Tusser's Husbandry.

móthery adj. [from *mother.*] Concreted; full of concretions; dreggy; feculent; used of liquors.

mótto n.s. [*motto*, Italian.] A sentence added to a device, or prefixed to any thing written.

It may be said to be the motto of human nature, rather to suffer than to die.
L'Estrange's Fables.

We ought to be meek-spirited, till we are assured of the honesty of our ancestors; for covetousness and circumvention make no good motto for a coat. Collier.

It was the motto of a bishop eminent for his piety and good works in king Charles the second's reign, Inservi Deo & lætare, *Serve God and be chearful.* Addison's Freeholder.

móuntainet n.s. [from *mountain.*] A hillock; a small mount. Elegant, but not in use.

Her breasts sweetly rose up like two fair mountainets in the pleasant vale of Tempe. Sidney.

móuntebank n.s. [*montare* in *banco,* Italian.]

1. A doctor that mounts a bench in the market, and boasts his infallible remedies and cures.

*I bought an unction of a mountebank
So mortal, that but dip a knife in it,
Where it draws blood, no cataplasm so rare,
Can save the thing from death.* Shakesp. Hamlet.

*She, like a mountebank, did wound
And stab herself with doubts profound,
Only to shew with how small pain
The sores of faith are cur'd again.* Hudibras, p. i.

*But Æschylus, says Horace in some page,
Was the first mountebank that trod the stage.* Dryden.

It looks so like a mountebank to boast of infallible cures. Baker's Reflections on Learning.

2. Any boastful and false pretender.

*As nimble jugglers, that deceive the eye,
Disguised cheaters, prating mountebanks,
And many such like libertines of sin.* Shakespeare.

There are mountebanks, and smatterers in state. L'Estrange.

Nothing so impossible in nature but mountebanks will undertake. Arbuthnot's Hist. of John Bull.

mouse plural mice. n.s. [*mus,* Saxon; *mus,* Latin.] The smallest of all beasts; a little animal haunting houses and corn fields, destroyed by cats.

*The eagle England being in prey,
To her unguarded nest the weazel Scot
Comes sneaking, and so sucks her princely eggs;
Playing the mouse in absence of the cat.* Shakespeare.

These shall be unclean; the weasle, the mouse, and the tortoise. Lev. xi. 29.

*Where mice and rats devour'd poetick bread,
And with heroick verse luxuriously were fed.* Dryden.

This structure of hair I have observed in the hair of cats, rats, and mice. Derham's Physico-Theol.

múckender n.s. [*mouchoir,* French; *mocadero,* Spanish; *muccinium,* low Latin.] A handkerchief.

*For thy dull fancy a muckender is fit,
To wipe the slabberings of thy snotty wit.* Dorset.

to múcker v.n. [from *muck.*] To scramble for money; to hoard up; to get or save meanly: a word used by Chaucer, and still retained in conversation.

múcksweat n.s. [*muck* and *sweat*: in this low word, *muck* signifies wet, moist.] Profuse sweat.

mufti n.s. [a Turkish word.] The high priest of the Mahometans.

múghouse n.s. [*mug* and *house.*] An alehouse; a low house of entertainment.

*Our sex has dar'd the mughouse chiefs to meet,
And purchas'd fame in many a well fought street.* Tickell.

to mulct v.a. [*mulcto,* Lat. *mulcter,* Fr.] To punish with fine or forfeiture.

Marriage without consent of parents they do not make void, but they mulct it in the inheritors; for the children of such marriages are not admitted to inherit above a third part of their parents inheritance. Bacon's New Atlantis.

muliébrity n.s. [*muliebris,* Lat.] Womanhood; the contrary to virility; the manners and character of woman.

múllgrubs n.s. Twisting of the guts. Ains.

mulse n.s. Wine boiled and mingled with honey. Dict.

multíscious adj. [*multiscius*, Latin.] Having variety of knowledge.

multísonous adj. [*multisonus*, Lat.] Having many sounds. Dict.

mum interject. [Of this word I know not the original: it may be observed, that when it is pronounced it leaves the lips closed.] A word denoting prohibition to speak, or resolution not to speak; silence; hush.

Mum then, and no more proceed. Shakesp. Tempest.

Well said, master; mum! and gaze your fill. Shakesp.

The citizens are mum, say not a word. Shak. Rich. III.

Intrust it under solemn vows
Of mum, and silence, and the rose. Hudibras, p. iii.

mum n.s. [*mumme*, German.] Ale brewed with wheat.

In Shenibank, upon the river Elbe, is
a storehouse for the wheat of which mum
is made at Brunswick. Mortimer.

Sedulous and stout
With bowls of fat'ning mum. Philips.

The clam'rous crowd is hush'd with mugs of mum,
Till all tun'd equal send a general hum. Pope.

múmmer n.s. [*mumme*, Danish.] A masker; one who performs frolicks in a personated dress.

If you chance to be pinch'd with the colick,
you make faces like mummers. Shakesp. Coriolanus.

Jugglers and dancers, anticks, mummers. Milton.

I began to smoke that they were a parcel of mummers. Add.

Peel'd, patch'd and pyebald, linsey-woolsey brothers;
Grave mummers! Pope's Dunciad, b. iii.

múmmy n.s. [*mumie*, Fr. *mumia*, Lat. derived by Salmasius from *amomum*, by Bochart from the Arabick.]

1. A dead body preserved by the Egyptian art of embalming.

We have two different substances preserved for medicinal use under the name of mummy: one is the dried flesh of human bodies embalmed with myrrh and spice; the other is the liquor running from such mummies when newly prepared, or when affected by great heat, or by damps: this is sometimes of a liquid, sometimes of a solid form, as it is preserved in vials well stopped, or suffered to dry and harden in the air: the first kind is brought to us in large pieces, of a lax and friable texture, light and spungy, of a blackish brown colour, and often black and clammy on the surface; it is of a strong but not agreeable smell: the second sort, in its liquid state, is a thick, opake, and viscous fluid, of a blackish and a strong, but not disagreeable smell: in its indurated state it is a dry, solid substance, of a fine shining black colour and close texture, easily broken, and of a good smell: this sort is extremely dear, and the first sort so cheap, that as all kinds of mummy are brought from Egypt we are not to imagine it to be the ancient Egyptian mummy. What our druggists are supplied with is the flesh of executed criminals, or of any other bodies the Jews can get, who fill them with the common bitumen so plentiful in that part of the world, and adding aloes, and some other cheap ingredients, send them to be baked in an oven till the juices are exhaled, and the embalming matter has penetrated so thoroughly that the flesh will keep. Mummy has been esteemed resolvent and balsamick; and besides it, the skull, and even the moss growing on the skulls of human skeletons, have been celebrated for antiepileptick virtues; the fat also of the human body has been recommended in rheumatisms, and every other part or humour have been in repute for the cure of some disease: at present we are wise enough to know, that the virtues ascribed to the parts of the human body are all either imaginary, or such as may be found in other animal substances: the mummy and the skull alone of all these horrid medicines retain their places in the shops. Hill's Mat. Med.

*The silk
Was dy'd in mummy, which the skilful
Conserv'd of maidens hearts.* Shakesp. Othello.

It is strange how long carcases have continued uncorrupt, as appeareth in the mummies of Egypt, having lasted some of them three thousand years. Bacon's Nat. Hist. N⁰ 771.

*Sav'd by spice, like mummies, many a year,
Old bodies of philosophy appear.*
Dunciad, b. i.

2. Mummy is used among gardeners for a sort of wax used in the planting and grafting of trees. Chambers.

3. To beat to a mummy. To beat soundly. Ains.

múmper n.s. [In cant language.] A beggar.

mumps n.s. [*mompelen*, Dutch.] Sullenness; silent anger. Skinner.

mundátory adj. [from *mundus*, Lat.] Having the power to cleanse.

mundívagant adj. [*mundivagus*, Lat.] Wandering through the world. Dict.

mundúngus n.s. Stinking tobacco. Bailey.

muse n.s. [from the verb.]

1. Deep thought; close attention; absence of mind; brown study.

*The tidings strange did him abashed make,
That still he sat long time astonished
As in great muse, ne word to creature spake.*
Fa. Queen.

*He was fill'd
With admiration and deep muse, to hear
Of things so high and strange.* Milton.

2. The power of poetry.

Begin my muse. Cowley.

*The muse-inspired train
Triumph, and raise their drooping
heads again.* Waller.

*Lodona's fate, in long oblivion cast,
The muse shall sing.* Pope.

múseum n.s. [μουσειον.] A repository of learned curiosities.

músick n.s. [μουσικη; *musique*, Fr.]

1. The science of harmonical sounds.

*The man that hath no musick in himself,
Nor is not mov'd with concord of sweet sounds,
Is fit for treasons.* Shakesp. Merchant of Venice.

*Now look into the musick-master's gains,
Where noble youth at vast expence is taught,
But eloquence not valu'd at a groat.*
Dryden's Juvenal.

2. Instrumental or vocal harmony.

*When she spake,
Sweet words, like droping honey, she did shed;
And 'twixt the pearls and rubies softly brake
A silver sound, that heavenly musick seem'd
to make.* F. Qu.

*Such musick
Before was never made,
But when of old the sons of morning sung.*
Milton.

*By musick minds an equal temper know,
Nor swell too high, nor sink too low;
Warriours she fires with animated sounds,
Pours balm into the bleeding lover's wounds.*
Pope.

We have dancing-masters and musick-masters. Arb. and Pope.

músket n.s. [*mousquet*, Fr. *mosquetto*, Italian, a small hawk. Many of the fire-arms are named from animals.]

1. A soldier's handgun.

*Thou
Wast shot at with fair eyes, to be the mark
Of smoky muskets.* Shakesp. All's well that ends well.

Practise to make swifter motions than any you have out of your muskets. Bacon.

*They charge their muskets, and with hot desire
Of full revenge, renew the fight with fire.*
Waller.

He perceived a body of their horse within musket-shot of him, and advancing upon him. Clarendon.

One was brought to us, shot with a musket-ball on the right side of his head. Wiseman's Surgery.

2. A male hawk of a small kind, the female of which is the sparrow hawk; so that eyas musket is a young unfledged male hawk of that kind. Hanmer.

Here comes little Robin.—
—How now my eyas musket, what news with you. Shak.

The musket and the coystrel were too weak,
Too fierce the falcon; but above the rest,
The noble buzzard ever pleas'd me best. Dryden.

musketoón n.s. [*mousqueton*, Fr.] A blunderbuss; a short gun of a large bore. Dict.

múslin n.s. A fine stuff made of cotton.

By the use of certain attire made of cambrick or muslin upon her head, she attained to such an evil art in the motion of her eyes. Tatler, Nº 110.

In half-whipt muslin needles useless lie,
And shuttle-cocks across the counter fly. Gay.

mussitátion n.s. [*mussito*, Lat.] Murmur; grumble.

Mússulman n.s. A Mahometan believer.

mynchen n.s. [*mynchen*, Saxon.] A nun. Dict.

myopy n.s. Shortness of sight.

myrópolist n.s. [μυρον and πωλεω.] One who sells unguents.

mystagógue n.s. [μυσταγωγος; *mystagogus*, Latin.] One who interprets divine mysteries; also one who keeps church relicks, and shews them to strangers. Bailey.

mystery n.s. [μυστηριος; *mystere*, Fr.]

1. Something above human intelligence; something awfully obscure.

They can judge as fitly of his worth,
As I can of those mysteries which heav'n
Will not have earth to know. Shakespeare's Coriolanus.

Upon holy days, let the matter of your meditations be according to the mystery of the day; and to your ordinary devotions of every day, add the prayer which is fitted to the mystery. Taylor.

If God should please to reveal unto us this great mystery of the trinity, or some other mysteries in our holy religion, we should not be able to understand them, unless he would bestow on us some new faculties of the mind. Swift's Serm.

2. An enigma; any thing artfully made difficult.

To thy great comfort in this mystery of ill opinions, here's the twin brother of thy letter. Shak. Mer. Wives of Windsor.

Important truths still let your fables hold,
And moral mysteries with art unfold. Granville.

3. A trade; a calling: in this sense it should, according to Warburton, be written *mistery*, from *mestiere*, French, a trade.

And that which is the noblest mysterie,
Brings to reproach and common infamy. Hubberd's Tale.

Instruction, manners, mysteries and trades,
Degrees, observances, customs and laws,
Decline to your confounding contraries. Shakespeare.

mystical, mystick adj. [*mysticus*, Latin.]

1. Sacredly obscure.

Let God himself that made me, let not man that knows not himself, be my instructor concerning the mystical way to heaven. Hooker, b. i.

From salvation all flesh being excluded this way, God hath revealed a way mystical and supernatural. Hooker, b. i.

2. Involving some secret meaning; emblematical.

Ye five other wand'ring fires! that move
In mystick dance not without song, resound
His praise, who out of darkness call'd up light. Milton.

It is Christ's body in the sacrament and out of it; but in the sacrament not the natural truth, but the spiritual and mystical. Taylor's Worthy Communicant.

It is plain from the Apocalypse, that mystical Babylon is to be consumed by fire. Burnet's Theory of the Earth.

3. Obscure; secret.

Lest new fears disturb the happy state,
Know, I have search'd the mystick rolls of fate.
Dryden.

mythólogy n.s. [μυθος and λογος; *mythologie*, French.] System of fables; explication of the fabulous history of the gods of the heathen world.

The modesty of mythology deserves to be commended: the scenes there are laid at a distance; it is once upon a time, in the days of yore, and in the land of Utopia. Bentley.

N, a semivowel, has in English an invariable sound; as, *no*, *name*, *net*; it is sometimes after *m* almost lost; as, *condemn*, *contemn*.

to nab v.a. [*nappa*, Swedish.] To catch unexpectedly; to seize without warning. A word seldom used but in low language.

naff n.s. A kind of tufted sea-bird.

nápery n.s. [*naperia*, Italian.] Table-linen. Dict.

narcótick adj. [ναρκοω; *narcotique*, Fr.] Producing torpor, or stupefaction.

Narcotick includes all that part of the materia medica, *which any way produces sleep, whether called by this name, or hypnoticks, or opiates.* Quincy.

The ancients esteemed it narcotick or stupefactive, and it is to be found in the list of poisons by Dioscorides. Brown's Vulgar Errours, b. vi.

nárrate v.a. [*narro*, Latin.] To relate; to tell; a word only used in Scotland.

narrátor n.s. [*narrateur*, French; from *narro*, Latin.] A teller; a relater.

Consider whether the narrator be honest and faithful, as well as skilful; whether he hath no peculiar gain or profit by believing or reporting it. Watts's Logick.

násicornous adj. [*nasus* and *cornu*.] Having the horn on the nose.

Some unicorns are among insects; as those four kinds of nasicornous beetles described by Muffetus. Brown's V. Err.

nástiness n.s. [from *nasty*.]

1. Dirt; filth.

This caused the seditious to remain within their station, which by reason of the nastiness of the beastly multitude, might more fitly be termed a kennel than a camp. Hayward.

Haughty and huge, as high Dutch bride,
Such nastiness and so much pride
Are oddly join'd by fate. Swift.

2. Obscenity; grossness of ideas.

Their nastiness, their dull obscene talk and ribauldry, cannot but be very nauseous and offensive to any who does not baulk his own reason, out of love to their vice. South.

A divine might have employed his pains to better purpose, than in the nastiness of Plautus and Aristophanes. Dry.

natátion n.s. [*natatio*, Latin.] The act of swimming.

In progressive motion, the arms and legs move successively, but in natation both together. Brown's Vulgar Errours.

nátion n.s. [*nation*, Fr. *natio*, Latin.] A people distinguished from another people; generally by their language, original, or government.

If Edward III. had prospered in his French wars, and peopled with English the towns which he won, as he began at Calais driving out the French, his successors holding the same course, would have filled all France with our nation. Ral.

A nation properly signifies a great number of families derived from the same blood, born in the same country, and living under the same government. Temple.

nátional adj. [*national*, Fr. from *nation*.]

1. Publick; general; not private; not particular.

They in their earthly Canaan plac'd,
Long time shall dwell and prosper: but when sins
National interrupt their public peace.
Milton's P. Lost.

Such a national devotion inspires men with sentiments of religious gratitude, and swells their hearts with joy and exultation. Addison's Freeholder, Nº 49.

The astonishing victories our armies have been crowned with, were in some measure the blessings returned upon that national charity which has been so conspicuous. Addison.

God, in the execution of his judgments, never visits a people with public and general calamities, but where their sins are public and national too. Rogers's Sermons.

2. Bigotted to one's own country.

nátive adj. [*nativus*, Latin; *natif-ve*, Fr.] Produced by nature; natural, not artificial.

She more sweet than any bird on bough,

Would oftentimes amongst them bear a part,
And strive to pass, as she could well enough,
Their native musick by her skilful art.
Fairy Q. b. ii.

This doctrine doth not enter by the ear,
But of itself is native in the breast. Davies.

2. Natural; such as is according to nature.

The members retired to their homes, reassume
the native sedateness of their temper. Swift.

3. Conferred by birth.

But ours is a privilege ancient and native,
Hangs not on an ordinance, or power legislative;
And first, 'tis to speak whatever we please.
Denham.

4. Relating to the birth; pertaining to the
time or place of birth.

If these men have defeated the law, and
outrun native punishment; though they can
outstrip men they have no wings to fly from
God. Shakespeare's Henry V.

Many of our bodies shall, no doubt,
Find native graves. Shakes. Hen. V.

5. Original; natural.

Have I now seen death? is this the way
I must return to native dust? O sight
Of terror, foul, and ugly to behold.
Milt. Par. Lost.

nátural adj. [*naturel*, French, from *nature*.]

1. Produced or effected by nature.

There is no natural motion of any particular
heavy body, which is perpetual, yet it is
possible from them to contrive such an
artificial revolution as shall constantly be
the cause of itself. Wilkins's Dedalus.

2. Illegitimate.

This would turn the vein of that we call
natural, to that of legal propagation; which
has ever been encouraged as the other has been
disfavoured by all institutions. Temple.

3. Bestowed by nature.

If there be any difference in natural parts, it
should seem that the advantage lies on the side
of children born from noble and wealthy
parents. Swift.

4. Not forced; not farfetched; dictated
by nature.

I will now deliver a few of the properest and
naturallest considerations that belong to this
piece. Wotton's Arch.

5. Consonant to natural notions.

Such unnatural connections become, by
custom, as natural to the mind as sun and
light: fire and warmth go together, and so
seem to carry with them as natural an
evidence as self-evident truths themselves.
Locke.

6. Tender; affectionate by nature.

To leave his wife, to leave his babes,
He wants the nat'ral touch. Shakespeare's
Macbeth.

7. Unaffected; according to truth
and reality.

What can be more natural than the
circumstances in the behaviour of those
women who had lost their husbands on
this fatal day. Addison.

8. Opposed to violent; as, a natural death.

nátural n.s. [from *nature*.]

1. An idiot; one whom nature debars from
understanding; a fool.

That a monster should be such a natural.
Shakespeare.

Take the thoughts of one out of that narrow
compass he has been all his life confined to, you
will find him no more capable of reasoning
than a perfect natural. Locke.

2. Native; original inhabitant.

The inhabitants and naturals of the place,
should be in a state of freemen. Abbot's
Description of the World.

Oppression, in many places, wears the robes of
justice, which domineering over the naturals
may not spare strangers, and strangers will
not endure it. Raleigh's Essays.

3. Gift of nature; nature; quality.

The wretcheder are the contemners of all helps;
such as presuming on their own naturals,
deride diligence, and mock at terms when they
understand not things. Ben. Johnson.

To consider them in their pure naturals, the earl's intellectual faculties were his stronger part, and the duke, his practical. Wotton.

náturalist n.s. [from *natural.*] A student in physicks, or natural philosophy.

Admirable artifice! wherewith Galen, tho' a mere naturalist, was so taken, that he could not but adjudge the honour of a hymn to the wise creator. More.

It is not credible, that the naturalist could be deceived in his account of a place that lay in the neighbourhood of Rome. Addison on Italy.

to náturalize v.a. [from *natural.*]

1. To adopt into a community; to invest with the privileges of native subjects.

The great lords informed the king, that the Irish might not be naturalized without damage to themselves or the crown. Davies on Ireland.

2. To make natural; to make easy like things natural.

He rises fresh to his hammer and anvil; custom has naturalized his labour to him. South's Sermons.

náture n.s. [*natura*, Latin; *nature*, French.]

1. An imaginary being supposed to preside over the material and animal world.

Thou, nature, art my goddess; to thy law My services are bound. Shakespeare's K. Lear.

When it was said to Anaxagoras, the Athenians have condemned you to die; he said again, and nature them. Bacon.

Let the postilion nature mount, and let The coachman art be set. Cowley.

*Heav'n bestows
At home all riches that wise nature needs.* Cowley.

Simple nature to his hope has giv'n, Beyond the cloud-topt hill an humbler heav'n. Pope.

2. The native state or properties of any thing, by which it is discriminated from others.

Between the animal and rational province, some animals have a dark resemblance of the influxes of reason: so between the corporeal and intellectual world, there is man participating much of both natures. Hale's Orig. of Mankind.

3. The constitution of an animated body.

Nature, as it grows again tow'rd earth, Is fashion'd for the journey, dull and heavy. Shakes.

*We're not ourselves,
When nature, being opprest, commands the mind To suffer with the body.* Shakespeare's King Lear.

4. Disposition of mind; temper.

Nothing could have subdu'd nature To such a lowness but his unkind daughters. Shakes.

A credulous father, and a brother noble, Whose nature is so far from doing harms, That he suspects none; on whose foolish honesty My practices ride easy. Shakespeare's King Lear.

5. The regular course of things.

*My end
Was wrought by nature, not by vile offence.* Shakes.

6. The compass of natural existence.

If their dam may be judge, the young apes are the most beautiful things in nature. Glanv.

7. Natural affection, or reverence; native sensations.

*Have we not seen
The murd'ring son ascend his parent's bed, Thro' violated nature force his way, And stain the sacred womb where once he lay?* Pope.

8. The state or operation of the material world.

He binding nature fast in fate, Left conscience free and will. Pope.

9. Sort; species.

A dispute of this nature caused mischief in abundance betwixt a king and an archbishop. Dryden.

10. Sentiments or images adapted to nature, or conformable to truth and reality.

Only nature can please those tastes which are unprejudiced and refined. Addison.

Nature and Homer were he found the same. Pope.

11. Physics; the science which teaches the qualities of things.

Nature and nature's laws lay hid in night,
God said, let Newton be, and all was light. Pope.

naúmachy n.s. [*naumachie*, Fr. *naumachia*, Latin.] A mock sea fight.

naútilus n.s. [Latin; *nautile*, Fr.] A shell fish furnished with something analogous to oars and a sail.

Learn of the little nautilus to sail,
Spread the thin oar and catch the driving
   gale. Pope.

neaf n.s. [*nefi*, Islandick.] A fist. It is retained in Scotland; and in the plural neaves.

Give me thy neaf, Monsieur Mustardseed. Shakespeare.

nécklace n.s. [*neck* and *lace*.] An ornamental string of beads or precious stones, worn by women on their neck.

Ladies, as well then as now, wore estates in their ears. Both men and women wore torques, chains, or necklaces of silver and gold set with precious stones. Arbuthnot on Coins.

Or lose her heart, or necklace, at a ball. Pope.

nécromancy n.s. [νεκρος and μαντις; *necromance*, Fr.]

1. The art of revealing future events, by communication with the dead.

The resurrection of Samuel is nothing but delusion in the practice of necromancy and popular conception of ghosts. Brown's Vulgar Errours, b. i.

2. Enchantment; conjuration.

He did it partly by necromancy, wherein he was much skilled. Abbot's Description of the World.

This palace standeth in the air,
By necromancy placed there,
That it no tempests needs to fear. Drayt. Nym.

néctarine n.s. [*nectarine*, French.] A fruit of the plum kind. This fruit differs from a peach in having a smooth rind and the flesh firmer. Miller.

The only nectarines are the murry and the French; of the last there are two sorts, one, which is the best, very round, and the other something long; of the murry there are several sorts. Temple.

to neese v.n. [*nyse*, Danish; *niesen*, Dutch.] To sneese; to discharge flatulencies by the nose. Retained in Scotland.

He went up and stretched himself upon him; and the child neesed seven times, and opened his eyes. 2 Kings iv. 35.

By his neesings a light doth shine, and his eyes are like the eye-lids of the morning. Job xli. 18.

neóphyte n.s. [*neophyte*, Fr. νεος and φυω.] One regenerated; a convert.

neotérick adj. [*neotericus*, Latin.] Modern; novel; late.

We are not to be guided either by the misreports of some ancients, or the capricio's of one or two neotericks. Grew.

népenthe n.s. [νη and πενθος.] A drug that drives away all pains.

There where no passion, pride, or shame
   transport,
Lull'd with the sweet nepenthe of a court;
There where no fathers, brothers, friends disgrace,
Once break their rest nor stir them from their
   place. Pope.

nerve n.s. [*nervus*, Latin; *nerf*, Fr.]

1. The organs of sensation passing from the brain to all parts of the body.

The nerves do ordinarily accompany the arteries through all the body; they have also blood-vessels, as the other parts of the body. Wherever any nerve sends out a branch, or receives one from another, or where two nerves join together, there is generally a ganglio or plexus. Quincy.

What man dare, I dare:
Approach thou like the rugged Russian bear;
Take any shape but that, and my firm nerves
Shall never tremble. Shakespeare's Macbeth.

2. It is used by the poets for sinew or tendon.

Strong Tharysmed discharged a speeding blow
Full on his neck, and cut the nerves in two.
Pope's Odyss.

nérvous adj. [*nervosus*, Latin.]

1. Well strung; strong; vigorous.

What nervous arms he boasts, how
  firm his tread,
His limbs how turn'd. Pope's Odyssey, b. viii.

2. Relating to the nerves; having the seat in the nerves.

3. [In medical cant.] Having weak or diseased nerves.

Poor, weak, nervous creatures. Cheyne.

néscience n.s. [from *nescio*, Latin.] Ignorance; the state of not knowing.

Many of the most accomplished wits of all ages, have resolved their knowledge into Socrates his sum total, and after all their pains in quest of science, have sat down in a professed nescience. Glanv. Sceps. c. ii.

nétwork n.s. [*net* and *work*.] Any thing reticulated or decussated, at equal distances, with interstices between the intersections.†

Nor any skill'd in workmanship emboss'd;
Nor any skill'd in loops of fing'ring fine;
Might in their diverse cunning ever dare,
With this so curious network to compare.
Spenser.

A large cavity in the sinciput was filled with ribbons, lace, and embroidery, wrought together in a curious piece of network. Addison's Spectator.

newfángled adj. [*new* and *fangle*.] Formed with vain or foolish love of novelty.

At Christmas I no more desire a rose,
Than wish a snow in May's newfangled shows;
But like of each thing, that in season grows.
Shakes.

Those charities are not newfangled devices of yesterday, but are most of them as old as the reformation. Atterbury.

news n.s. without the singular. [from *new*, *nouvelles*, Fr.]

1. Fresh account of any thing; something not heard before.

As he was ready to be greatly advanced for some noble pieces of service which he did, he heard news of me. Sidney.

When Rhea heard these news, she fled from her husband to her brother Saturn. Raleigh's Hist. of the World.

Evil news rides fast, while good news baits. Milt. Agonist.

With such amazement as weak mothers use,
And frantick gesture, he receives the news.
Waller.

Now the books, and now the bells,
And now our act the preacher tells,
To edify the people;
All our divinity is news,
And we have made of equal use
The pulpit and the steeple. Denham.

The amazing news of Charles at once
  was spread,
At once the general voice declared
Our gracious prince was dead. Dryden.

It is no news for the weak and poor to be a prey to the strong and rich. L'Estrange.

They have news-gatherers and intelligencers distributed into their several walks, who bring in their respective quotas, and make them acquainted with the discourse of the whole kingdom. Spectator, Nº 439.

2. Papers which give an account of the transactions of the present times.

Their papers, filled with a different party spirit, divide the people into different sentiments, who generally consider rather the principles than the truth of the news-writer. Addis.

Advertise both in every news-paper; and let it not be your fault or mine, if our country-men will not take warning. Swift's Drapiers Letters.

Wood is generally his own news-writer. I cannot but observe from that paragraph, that this public enemy treats this kingdom with contempt. Swift's Drapiers Letters.

Pamphlets and news-papers have been full of me. Pope.

nice adj. [*nese*, Saxon, soft.]†

1. Accurate in judgment to minute exactness; superfluously exact. It is often used to express a culpable delicacy.

Such a man was Argalus, as hardly the nicest eye can find a spot in. Sidney.

He that stands upon a slipp'ry place,
Makes nice of no vile hold to stay him up.
Sha. K. John.

Nor be so nice in taste myself to know,
If what I swallow be a thrush or no.
Dryd. Persius.

Thus critics, of less judgment than caprice,
Curious, not knowing, not exact, but nice,
Form short ideas, and offend in arts,
As most in manners, by a love to parts.
Pope on Crit.

Our author, happy in a judge so nice,
Produc'd his play, and begg'd the knight's
   advice. Pope.

2. Delicate; scrupulously and minutely cautious.

The letter was not nice, but full of charge
Of dear import. Shakes. Romeo and Juliet.

Dear love! continue nice and chaste;
For if you yield, you do me wrong;
Let duller wits to love's end haste,
I have enough to woo thee long. Donne.

Of honour men at first like women nice,
Raise maiden scruples at unpractis'd vice.
E. Hallifax.

Having been compiled by Gratian, in an ignorant age, we ought not to be too nice in examining it. Baker.

3. Fastidious; squeamish.

   God hath here
Varied his bounty so with new delights,
As may compare with heaven; and to taste,
Think not I shall be nice. Milt. Par. Lost.

4. Easily injured; delicate.

With how much ease is a young muse betray'd?
How nice the reputation of the maid?
Roscommon.

5. Formed with minute exactness.

Indulge me but in love, my other passions
Shall rise and fall by virtue's nicest rules.
Addison's Cato.

6. Requiring scrupulous exactness.

Supposing an injury done, it is a nice point to proportion the reparation to the degree of the indignity. L'Estrange.

My progress in making this nice and troublesome experiment, I have set down more at large. Newton's Opt.

7. Refined.

A nice and subtile happiness I see
Thou to thyself proposest, in the choice
Of thy associates, Adam; and wilt taste
No pleasure, tho' in pleasure solitary.
Milt. P. Lost.

8. Having lucky hits. This signification is not in use.

   When my hours
Were nice and lucky, men did ransom lives
Of me for jests. Shakes. Ant. and Cleopatra.

nicknáme n.s. [*nom de nique*, French.] A name given in scoff or contempt; a term of derision; an opprobrious or contemptuous appellation.

The time was when men were had in price for learning; now letters only make men vile. He is upbraidingly called a poet, as if it were a contemptible nickname. Ben. Johnson.

My mortal enemy hath not only falsely surmised me to be a feigned person, giving me nicknames, but also hath offered large sums of money to corrupt the princes with whom I have been retained. Bacon's Hen. VII.

So long as her tongue was at liberty, there was not a word to be got from her, but the same nickname in derision. L'Estrange.

to níctate v.a. [*nicto*, Latin.] To wink.

There are several parts peculiar to brutes, which are wanting in man; as the seventh or suspensory muscle of the eye, the nictating membrane, and the strong aponeuroses on the sides of the neck. Ray.

nídget n.s. [corrupted from *nithing* or *niding*. The opprobrious term with which the man was anciently branded who refused to come to the royal standard in times of exigency.] A coward; a dastard.

There was one true English word of greater force than them all, now out of all use; it signifieth no more than abject, baseminded, false-hearted, coward, or nidget. Camden.

nidificátion n.s. [*nidificatio*, Latin.] The act of building nests.

That place, and that method of nidification, doth abundantly answer the creature's occasions. Derham.

níghtmare n.s. [*night*, and according to Temple, *mara*, a spirit that, in the heathen mythology, was related to torment or suffocate sleepers.] A morbid oppression in the night, resembling the pressure of weight upon the breast.

Saint Withold footed thrice the would,
He met the nightmare, and her name he told;
Bid her alight, and her troth plight. Shakes. K. Lear.

The forerunners of an apoplexy are, dulness, drowsiness, vertigoes, tremblings, oppressions in sleep, and night-mares. Arbuthnot on Aliments.

nihílity n.s. [*nihilité*, Fr. *nihilum*, Latin.] Nothingness; the state of being nothing.

Not being is considered as excluding all substance, and then all modes are also necessarily excluded; and this we call pure nihility, or mere nothing. Watts's Logick.

to nim v.a. [*nemen*, Dutch, to take.] To take. In cant, to steal.

They'll question Mars, and by his look
Detect who 'twas that nimm'd a cloak.
Hudibras, p. i.

They could not keep themselves honest of their fingers, but would be nimming something or other for the love of thieving. L'Estrange, Fable 241.

nímiety n.s. [*nimietas*, school Latin.] The state of being too much.

níncompoop n.s. [A corruption of the Latin *non compos*.] A fool; a trifler.

An old ninnyhammer, a dotard, a nincompoop, is the best language she can afford me. Addison.

nínepins n.s. [*nine* and *pin*.] A play where nine pieces of wood are set up on the ground to be thrown down by a bowl.

A painter made blossoms upon the trees in December, and school-boys playing at nine-pins upon the ice in July. Peacham on Drawing.

For as when merchants break, o'erthrown
Like nine-pins, they strike others down.
Hud. p. ii.

nínnyhammer n.s. [from *ninny*.] A simpleton.

Another vents her passion in scurrilous terms; an old ninny-hammer, a dotard, a nincompoop, is the best language she can afford me. Addison's Guardian, Nº 109.

Have you no more manners than to rail at Hocus, that has saved that clod-pated, numskull'd, ninny-hammer of yours from ruin, and all his family. Arbuth. John Bull.

níthing n.s. A coward, dastard, poltroon.

níveous adj. [*niveus*, Latin.] Snowy; resembling snow.

Cinabar becomes red by the acid exhalation of sulphur, which otherways presents a pure and niveous white. Brown.

nízy n.s. A dunce; a simpleton. A low word.

nobílity n.s. [*nobilitas*, Latin.]

1. Antiquity of family joined with splendour.

When I took up Boccace unawares, I fell on the same argument of preferring virtue to nobility of blood, and titles, in the story of Sigismunda. Dryden, Fab. Pref.

   Long galleries of ancestors,
Challenge, nor wonder, or esteem from me,
"Virtue alone is true nobility." Dryden.

2. Rank or dignity of several degrees, conferred by sovereigns. Nobility in England is extended to five ranks; duke, marquis, earl, viscount, baron.

3. The persons of high rank; the persons who are exalted above the commons.

   It is a purpos'd thing,
To curb the will of the nobility.
Shakes. Coriolanus.

4. Dignity; grandeur; greatness.

Though she hated Ampialus, yet the nobility of her courage prevailed over it; and she desired he might be pardoned that youthful errour; considering the reputation he had to be the best knight in the world; so as hereafter he governed himself, as one remembering his fault. Sidney, b. ii.

But ah, my muse, I would thou hadst facility
To work my goddess so by thy invention,
On me to cast those eyes where shine nobility.
Sidney.

Base men, being in love, have then a nobility in their natures more than is native to them. Shakespeare's Othello.

They thought it great their sov'reign to controul,
And nam'd their pride, nobility of soul.
Dryden.

nócent adj. [*nocens*, Latin.]

1. Guilty; criminal.

The earl of Devonshire being interested in the blood of York, that was rather feared than nocent; yet as one, that might be the object of others plots, remained prisoner in the Tower during the king's life. Bacon's Henry VII.

2. Hurtful; mischievous.

His head, well-stor'd with subtile wiles:
Not yet in horrid shade, or dismal den,
Nor nocent yet; but on the grassy herb,
Fearless unfear'd he slept. Milton's Paradise Lost, b. ix.

   The warm limbec draws
Salubrious waters from the nocent brood.
Philips.

They meditate whether the virtues of the one will exalt or diminish the force of the other, or correct any of its nocent qualities. Watts's Improvement of the Mind.

noctívagant adj. [*noctivagus*, Latin.] Wandering in the night. Dict.

nóddy n.s. [from *naudin*, French.] A simpleton; an idiot.

The whole race of bawling, fluttering noddies, by what title soever dignified, are a-kin to the ass in this fable. L'Estrange, Fable 150.

nolítion n.s. [*nolitio*, Latin.] Unwillingness; opposed to volition.

The proper acts of the will are, volition, nolition, choice, resolution, and command, in relation to subordinate faculties. Hale's Origin of Mankind.

nómbles n.s. The entrails of a deer.

nonconfórmity n.s. [*non* and *conformity*.]

1. Refusal of compliance.

The will of our maker, whether discovered by reason or revelation, carries the highest authority with it; a conformity or nonconformity to it, determines their actions to be morally good or evil. Watts's Logick.

2. Refusal to join in the established religion.

Since the liturgy, rites, and ceremonies of our church, are so much struck at, and all upon a plea of conscience, it will concern us to examine the force of this plea, which our adversaries are still setting up as the grand pillar and butteress of nonconformity. South's Sermons.

The lady will plead the toleration which allows her nonconformity in this particular. Addison's Spectator.

nonjúring adj. [*non* and *juro*, Latin.] Belonging to those who will not swear allegiance to the Hanoverian family.†

This objection was offered me by a very pious, learned, and worthy gentleman of the nonjuring party. Swift.

nonjúror n.s. [from *non* and *juror*.] One who conceiving James II. unjustly deposed, refuses to swear allegiance to those who have succeeded him.

nonparéil n.s. [*non* and *pareil*, French.]

1. Excellence unequalled.

My lord and master loves you: O such love Could be but recompens'd tho' you were crown'd The nonpareil of beauty. Shakes. Twelfth Night.

2. A kind of apple.

3. Printers letter of a small size, on which small Bibles and Common Prayers are printed.

noódle n.s. [from *noddle* or *noddy*.] A fool; a simpleton.

nósology n.s. [νοσος and λογος.] Doctrine of diseases.

nosopoétick adj. [νοσος and ποιεω.] Producing diseases.

The qualities of the air are nosopoetick; that is, have a pow'r of producing diseases. Arbuthnot on Air.

nóstrum n.s. [Latin.] A medicine not yet made publick, but remaining in some single hand.

Very extraordinary, and one of his nostrums, let it be writ upon his monument, Hic jacet auctor hujus argumenti; *for no body ever used it before.* Stillingfleet.†

What drop or nostrum can this plague remove? Pope.

noun n.s. [*nom*, French; *nomen*, Latin.] The name of any thing in grammar.

A noun is the name of a thing, whether substance, mode or relation, which in speech is used to signify the same when there is occasion to affirm or deny any thing about it, or to express any relation it has in discourse to any other thing. Clarke's Lat. Grammar.

Thou hast men about thee, that usually talk of a noun and a verb, and such abominable words as no christian ear can endure to hear. Shakespeare's Henry VI.

The boy, who scarce has paid his entrance down, To his proud pedant, or declin'd a noun. Dryden.

novátor n.s. [Latin.] The introducer of something new.

nóvel n.s. [*nouvelle*, French.]

1. A small tale, generally of love.

Nothing of a foreign nature; like the trifling novels which Ariosto inserted in his poems. Dryden.

Her mangl'd fame in barb'rous pastime lost, The coxcomb's novel and the drunkard's toast. Prior.

2. A law annexed to the code.

By the civil law, no one was to be ordained a presbyter till he was thirty-five years of age: though by a later novel it was sufficient, if he was above thirty. Ayliffe's Par.

nózle n.s. [from *nose*.] The nose; the snout; the end.

It is nothing but a paultry old sconce, with the nozle broke off. Arbuthnot and Pope's Mart. Scrib.

to núbble v.a. To bruise with handy cuffs. Ains.

to núbilate v.a. [*nubilo*, Latin.] To cloud. Dict.

núciferous adj. [*nuces* and *fero*, Latin.] Nutbearing. Dict.

nugácity n.s. [*nugacis*, Latin.] Futility; trifling talk or behaviour.

nullibíety n.s. [from *nullibi*, Latin.] The state of being nowhere.

númber n.s. [*nombre*, French; *numerus*, Latin.]

1. The species of quantity by which it is computed how many.

Hye thee, from this slaughter-house,
Lest thou increase the number of the dead.
Sha. Rich. III.

The silver, the gold, and the vessels, were weighed by number and by weight.
Ezra viii. 34.

Thou shalt take a few in number, and bind them in thy skirts. Ezek. v. 3.

There is but one gate for strangers to enter at, that it may be known what numbers of them are in the town. Addison.

2. Any particular aggregate of units, as *even* or *odd.*

This is the third time; I hope good luck lies in odd numbers: they say there is divinity in odd numbers, either in nativity, chance, or death.
Shakesp. M. W. of Wind.

3. Many; more than one.

Much of that we are to speak may seem to a number perhaps tedious, perhaps obscure, dark, and intricate. Hooker.

Water lilly hath a root in the ground; and so have a number of other herbs that grow in ponds. Bacon.

Ladies are always of great use to the party they espouse, and never fail to win over numbers. Addison.

4. Multitude that may be counted.

Of him came nations and tribes out of number. 2 Esd. iii. 7.

Loud as from numbers without number.
Milton.

5. Comparative multitude.

Number itself importeth not much in armies, where the people are of weak courage: for, as Virgil says, it never troubles a wolf how many the sheep be. Bacon.

6. Aggregated multitude.

If you will, some few of you shall see the place; and then you may send for your sick, and the rest of your number, which ye will bring on land. Bacon's N. Atlantis.

7. Harmony; proportions calculated by number.

They, as they move
Their starry dance in numbers that compute
Days, months, and years, tow'rds his
all-chearing lamp,
Turn swift. Milton.

8. Verses; poetry.

Should the muses bid my numbers roll
Strong as their charms. Pope.

9. [In grammar.]

In the noun is the variation or change of termination to signify a number more than one. When men first invented names, their application was to single things; but soon finding it necessary to speak of several things of the same kind together, they found it likewise necessary to vary or alter the noun.
Clark's Lat. Grammar.

How many numbers is in nouns?—
—Two. Shakesp. Merry W. of Windsor.

númmary adj. [from *nummus*, Latin.] Relating to money.

The money drachma in process of time decreased; but all the while the ponderal drachma continued the same, just as our ponderal libra remains as it was, though the nummary hath much decreased. Arbuthnot on Coins.

númskull n.s. [Probably from *numb*, dull, torpid, insensible, and *skull*.]

1. A dullard; a dunce; a dolt; a blockhead.

Or toes and fingers, in this case,
Of Numskulls self should take the place. Prior.

2. The head. In burlesque.

They have talked like numskulls.
Arb. and Pope.

nuncupátive, nuncupátory adj. [*nuncupatus*, Lat. *nuncupatif*, Fr.] Publickly or solemnly declaratory; verbally pronounced.

núnnery n.s. [from *nun*.] A house of nuns; of women under a vow of chastity, dedicated to the severer duties of religion.

I put your sister into a nunnery, with a strict command not to see you, for fear you should have wrought upon her to have taken the habit. Dryden's Spanish Friar.

O has in English a long sound; as, *drone, groan, stone, alone, cloke, broke, coal, droll*; or short, *got, knot, shot, prong, long*. It is usually denoted long by a servile *a* subjoined; as, *moan*, or by *e* at the end of the syllable; as, *bone*: when these vowels are not appended, it is generally short, except before *ll*; as, *droll, scroll*, and even then sometimes short; as, *loll*.

oaf n.s. [This word is variously written; *auff*, *ofe*, and *oph;* it seems a corruption of *ouph*, a demon or fairy, in German *alf*, from which *elf*: and means properly the same with *changeling;* a foolish child left by malevolent *ouphs* or *fairies*, in the place of one more witty, which they steal away.]

1. A changeling; a foolish child left by the fairies.

These, when a child haps to be got,
Which after proves an idiot,
When folk perceives it thriveth not,
The fault therein to smother:
Some silly doating brainless calf,
That understands things by the half,
Says that the fairy left this oaf,
And took away the other. Drayt. Nymphid.

2. A dolt; a blockhead; an idiot.

oak n.s. [*ac*, *æc*, Saxon; which, says Skinner, to shew how easy it is to play the fool, under a shew of literature and deep researches, I will, for the diversion of my reader, derive from οικος, a house; the oak being the best timber for building. Skinner seems to have had Junius in his thoughts, who on this very word has shewn his usual fondness for Greek etymology, by a derivation more ridiculous than that by which Skinner has ridiculed him. *Ac* or *oak*, says the grave critick, signified among the Saxons, like *robur* among the Latins, not only an *oak* but *strength*, and may be well enough derived, *non incommode deduci potest*, from αλκη, strength; by taking the three first letters and then sinking the λ, as is not uncommon.] The oak-tree hath male flowers, or katkins, which consist of a great number of small slender threads. The embryos, which produced at remote distances from these on the same tree, do afterwards become acorns, which are produced in hard scaly cups: the leaves are sinuated. The species are five. Miller.

He return'd with his brows bound with oak.
Shakesp.

    He lay along
Under an oak, whose antique root peeps out
Upon the brook that brawls along this wood.
Shakesp.

No tree beareth so many bastard fruits as the oak: for besides the acorns, it beareth galls, oak apples, oak nuts, which are inflammable, and oak berries, sticking close to the body of the tree without stalk. Bacon's Nat. History.

The monarch oak, the patriarch of the trees,
Shoots rising up and spreads by slow degrees:
Three centuries he grows, and three he stays
Supreme in state; and in three more decays.
Dry.

An oak growing from a plant to a great tree, and then lopped, is still the same oak. Locke.

A light earthy, stony, and sparry matter, incrusted and affixed to oak leaves.
Woodward on Foss.

In the days of Homer every grove, river, fountain, and oak tree, were thought to have their peculiar deities. Odyss.

Let India boast her plants, nor envy we
The weeping amber and the balmy tree,
While by our oaks the precious loads are born,
And realms commanded which those trees
    adorn. Pope.

oath n.s. [*aith*, Gothick; *að*, Saxon. The distance between the noun *oath*, and the verb *swear*, is very observable, as it may shew that our oldest dialect is formed from different languages.] An affirmation, negation, or promise, corroborated by the attestation of the Divine Being.

Read over Julia's heart, thy first best love,
For whose dear sake thou then did'st rend
    thy faith
Into a thousand oaths; and all those oaths
Descended into perjury to love me.
Shakespeare.

He that strikes the first stroke, I'll run him up to the hilts as I am a soldier.
—An oath of mickle might; and fury shall abate. Sha.

We have consultations, which inventions shall be published, which not: and take an oath of secrecy for the concealing of those which we think fit to keep secret. Bacon.

Those called to any office of trust, are bound by an oath to the faithful discharge of it: but an oath is an appeal to God, and therefore can have no influence, except upon those who believe that he is. Swift.

oats n.s. [*aten*, Saxon.] A grain, which in England is generally given to horses, but in Scotland supports the people.†

It is of the grass leaved tribe; the flowers have no petals, and are disposed in a loose panicle: the grain is eatable. The meal makes tolerable good bread. Miller.

The oats have eaten the horses. Shakespeare.

It is bare mechanism, no otherwise produced than the turning of a wild oatbeard, by the insinuation of the particles of moisture. Locke.

For your lean cattle, fodder them with barley straw first, and the oat straw last. Mortimer's Husbandry.

His horse's allowance of oats and beans, was greater than the journey required. Swift.

obambulátion n.s. [*obambulatio*, from *obambulo*, Latin.] The act of walking about. Dict.

óbelisk n.s. [*obeliscus*, Latin.]

1. A magnificent high piece of solid marble, or other fine stone, having usually four faces, and lessening upwards by degrees, till it ends in a point like a pyramid. Harris.

Between the statues obelisks were plac'd, And the learn'd walls with hieroglyphicks grac'd. Pope.

2. A mark of censure in the margin of a book, in the form of a dagger [†].

He published the translation of the Septuagint, having compared it with the Hebrew, and noted by asterisks what was defective, and by obelisks what redundant. Grew.

obequitátion n.s. [from *obequito*, Latin.] The act of riding about.

obése adj. [*obesus*, Latin.] Fat; loaden with flesh.

to objúrgate v.a. [*objurgo*, Latin.] To chide; to reprove.

óbloquy n.s. [*obloquor*, Lat.]

1. Censorious speech; blame; slander; reproach.

Reasonable moderation hath freed us from being deservedly subject unto that bitter kind of obloquy, whereby as the church of Rome doth, under the colour of love towards those things which be harmless, maintain extremely most hurtful corruptions; so we peradventure might be upbraided, that under colour of hatred towards those things that are corrupt, we are on the other side as extreme, even against most harmless ordinances. Hooker, b. iv. s. 14.

Here new aspersions, with new obloquies, Are laid on old deserts. Daniel's Civil War.

Canst thou with impious obloquy condemn The just decree of God, pronounc'd and sworn? Milton.

Shall names that made your city the glory of the earth, be mentioned with obloquy and detraction? Addison.

Every age might perhaps produce one or two true genius, if they were not sunk under the censure and obloquy of plodding, servile, imitating pedants. Swift.

2. Cause of reproach; disgrace. Not proper.

My chastity's the jewel of our house, Bequeathed down from many ancestors; Which were the greatest obloquy i' th' world In me to lose. Shakespeare's All's well that ends well.

obmutéscence n.s. [from *obmutesco*, Latin.] Loss of speech.

A vehement fear often produceth obmutescence. Brown.

obréption n.s. [*obreptio*, Latin.] The act of creeping on.

obscéne adj. [*obscene*, Fr. *obscænus*, Latin.]

1. Immodest; not agreeable to chastity of mind; causing lewd ideas.

Chemos th' obscene dread of Moab's sons. Milton.

Words that were once chaste, by frequent use grow obscene and uncleanly. Watts's Logick.

2. Offensive; disgusting.

A girdle foul with grease binds his obscene attire. Dryden.

Home as they went, the sad discourse renew'd,
Of the relentless dame to death pursu'd,
And of the sight obscene so lately view'd.
Dryden.

3. Inauspicious; ill omined.

Care shuns thy walks, as at the chearful light
The groaning ghosts, and birds obscene take
  flight. Dryd.

It is the sun's fate like your's, to be displeasing to owls and obscene animals, who cannot bear his lustre. Pope's Lett.

obsérvatory n.s. [*observatoire*, French.] A place built for astronomical observations.

Another was found near the observatory in Greenwich Park. Woodward on Fossils.

obséssion n.s. [*obsessio*, Latin.]

1. The act of besieging.

2. The first attack of Satan, antecedent to possession.

obstétrick adj. [from *obstetrix*, Lat.] Midwifish; befitting a midwife; doing the midwife's office.

There all the learn'd shall at the labour stand,
And Douglas lend his soft obstetrick hand.
Dunciad, b. iv.

obstupefáctive adj. [from *obstupefacio*, Lat.] Obstructing the mental powers; stupifying.

The force of it is obstupefactive, and no other. Abbot.

óccident n.s. [from *occidens*, Latin.] The west.

The envious clouds are bent
To dim his glory, and to stain the tract
Of his bright passage to the occident.
Shakes. R. II.

occísion n.s. [from *occisio*, Latin.] The act of killing.

océllated adj. [*ocellatus*, Latin.] Resembling the eye.

The white butterfly lays its offspring on cabbage leaves; a very beautiful reddish ocellated one. Derham's Physico. Theol.

octáve n.s. [*octave*, Fr. *octavus*, Lat.]

1. The eighth day after some peculiar festival.

2. [In musick.] An eighth or an interval of eight sounds.

3. Eight days together after a festival. Ains.

octávo [Lat.] A book is said to be in octavo when a sheet is folded into eight leaves. Dict.

They now accompany the second edition of the original experiments, which were printed first in English in octavo. Boyle.

octonócular adj. [*octo* and *occulus*.] Having eight eyes.

Most animals are binocular; spiders for the most part octonocular, and some senocular. Derham's Physico-Theol.

ode n.s. [ωδη.] A poem written to be sung to musick; a lyrick poem; the ode is either of the greater or less kind. The less is characterised by sweetness and ease; the greater by sublimity, rapture, and quickness of transition.

A man haunts the forest that abuses our young plants with carving Rosalind on their barks; hangs odes upon hawthorns, and elegies on brambles, all forsooth deifying the name of Rosalind. Shakesp. As you like it.

O run, prevent them with thy humble ode,
And lay it lowly at his blessed feet.
Milt. Poems.

What work among you scholar Gods!
Phœbus must write him am'rous odes;
And thou, poor cousin, must compose
His letters in submissive prose. Prior.

odontálgick adj. [οδων and αλγος.] Pertaining to the tooth-ach.

OE This combination of vowels does not properly belong to our language, nor is ever found but in words derived from the Greek, and not yet wholly conformed to our manner of writing: oe has in such words the sound of E.

óffice n.s. [*office*, Fr. *officium*, Latin.]

1. A publick charge or employment.

You have contriv'd to take
From Rome all season'd office, and to wind
Yourself into a power tyrannical. Shakesp. Coriolanus.

Methought this staff, mine office-badge in court,
Was broke in twain. Shakesp. Henry VI. p. ii.

The insolence of office. Shakespeare.

2. Agency; peculiar use.

All things that you should use to do me wrong,
Deny their office. Shakesp. King Lear.

In this experiment the several intervals of the teeth of the comb do the office of so many prisms, every interval producing the phenomenon of one prism. Newt. Opt.

3. Business; particular employment.

The sun was sunk, and after him the star
Of Hesperus, whose office is to bring
Twilight upon the earth.
Milt. Par. Lost, b. ix.

4. Act of good or ill voluntarily tendered.

Wolves and bears
Casting their savageness aside, have done
Like offices of pity. Shakesp. Winter's Tale.

Mrs. Ford, I see you are obsequious in your love, and I profess requital to a hair's breadth; not only in the simple office of love, but in all the accoustrement, complement, and ceremony of it. Shakesp. Merry W. of Windsor.

I would I could do a good office between you. Shakesp.

The wolf took this occasion to do the fox a good office. L'Estrange.

You who your pious offices employ
To save the reliques of abandon'd Troy.
Dryd. Virg.

5. Act of worship.

This gate
Instructs you how t' adore the heavens,
and bows you
To morning's holy office.
Shakesp. Cymbeline.

6. Formulary of devotions.

Whosoever hath children or servants, let him take care that they say their prayers before they begin their work: the Lord's prayer, the ten commandments, and the creed, is a very good office for them, if they are not fitted for more regular offices. Taylor's Devotion.

7. Rooms in a house appropriated to particular business.

What do we but draw anew the model
In fewer offices? at least desist
To build at all. Shakesp. Henry IV. p. ii.

Let offices stand at distance, with some low galleries to pass from them to the palace itself. Bacon.

8. Place where business is transacted. [*Officina*, Lat.]

What shall good old York see there,
But empty lodgings and unfurnish'd walls,
Unpeopled offices, untroden stones?
Sha. Rich. II.

Empson and Dudley, though they could not but hear of these scruples in the king's conscience, yet as if the king's soul and his money were in several offices, that the one was not to intermeddle with the other, went on with as great rage as ever. Bacon's Henry VII.

óglio n.s. [from *olla*, Spanish.] A dish made by mingling different kinds of meat; a medley; a hotchpotch.

These general motives of the common good, I will not so much as once offer up to your lordship, though they have still the upper end; yet, like great oglio's, they rather make a shew than provoke appetite. Suckling.

Where is there such an oglio or medley of various opinions in the world again, as those men entertain in their service, without any scruple as to the diversity of their sects and opinions? King Charles.

He that keeps an open house, should consider that there are oglio's of guests, as well as of dishes, and that the liberty of a common table is as good as a tacit invitation to all sorts of intruders. L'Estrange.

oílman n.s. [*oil* and *man.*] One who trades in oils and pickles.

oleáginous adj. [*oleaginus*, Lat. from *oleum*, *oleagineux*, Fr.] Oily; unctuous.

The sap when it first enters the root, is earthy, watery, poor, and scarce oleaginous.
Arbuthnot on Aliments.

ómbre n.s. [*hombre*, Spanish.] A game of cards played by three.[†]

He would willingly carry her to the play; but she had rather go to lady Centaure's and play at ombre. Tatler.

ómelet n.s. [*omelette*, Fr.] A kind of pancake made with eggs.

omnífick adj. [*omnis* and *facio*, Lat.] All-creating.

Silence, ye troubled waves, and thou deep, peace! Said then th' omnific word, your discord end. Milton.

omnípotent adj. [*omnipotens*, Lat.] Almighty; powerful without limit.

You were also Jupiter, a swan, for the love of Leda: oh omnipotent love! how near the god drew to the complexion of a goose? Shakesp. Merry Wives of Wind.

The perfect being must needs be omnipotent; both as self-existent and as immense: for he that is self-existent, having the power of being, hath the power of allbeing; equal to the cause of all being, which is to be omnipotent. Grew's Cosmol. b. i. c. 1.

omníscience, omnísciency n.s. [*omnis* and *scientia*, Lat.] Boundless knowledge; infinite wisdom.

In all this misconstruction of my actions, as I have no judge but God above me, so I can have comfort to appeal to his omniscience. King Charles.

Thinking by this retirement to obscure himself from God, he infringed the omnisciency and essential ubiquity of his maker, who as he created all things, so is he beyond and in them all. Brown's Vulgar Errours, b. i.

An immense being does strangely fill the soul; and omnipotency, omnisciency, and infinite goodness, enlarge the spirit while it fixtly looks upon them. Burnet.

Since thou boast'st th' omniscience of a God, Say in what cranny of Sebastian's soul, Unknown to me, so loath'd a crime is lodg'd? Dryden.

oneirocrítical adj. [ονειροκριτικος, Gr. *onirocritique*, Fr. It should therefore according to analogy be written onirocritical and onirocritick.] Interpretative of dreams.

If a man has no mind to pass by abruptly from his imagined to his real circumstances, he may employ himself in that new kind of observation which my oneirocritical correspondent has directed him to make. Addison's Spectator.

ontólogy n.s. [οντα and λογος.] The science of the affections of being in general; metaphysicks.

The modes, accidents and relations that belong to various beings, are copiously treated of in metaphysicks, or more properly ontology. Watts's Logick.

ópera n.s. [Italian.] An opera is a poetical tale or fiction, represented by vocal and instrumental musick, adorned with scenes, machines, and dancing. Dryden's Pref. to Albion.

operóse adj. [*operosus*, Latin.] Laborious; full of trouble and tediousness.

Such an explication is purely imaginary, and also very operose, and would affect a great part of the universe; they would be as hard put to it to get rid of this water, when the deluge was to cease, as they were at first to procure it. Burnet's Theory of the Earth.

Written language, as it is more operous, so it is more digested, and is permanent. Holder.

ophióphagous adj. [οφις and φαγω.] Serpenteating. Not used.

All snakes are not of such poisonous qualities as common opinion presumeth; as is confirmable from ophiophagous nations, and such as feed upon serpents. Brown's V. Err.

ópiate n.s. A medicine that causes sleep.

They chose atheism as an opiate, to still those frightning apprehensions of hell, by inducing a dulness and lethargy of mind, rather than to make use of that native and salutary medicine, a hearty repentance.
Bentley's Serm.

opínionist n.s. [*opinioniste*, Fr. from *opinion.*] One fond of his own notions.

Every conceited opinionist sets up an infallible chair in his own brain.
Glanv. to Albius.

ópium n.s. A juice, partly of the resinous, partly of the gummy kind. It is brought to us in flat cakes or masses, usually of a roundish figure, very heavy and of a dense texture, not perfectly dry: its colour is a dark brownish yellow; its smell is very unpleasant, of a dead faint kind; and its taste very bitter and very acrid. It is brought from Natolia, from Egypt, and from the East-Indies, where it is produced from the white garden poppy; a plant of which every part is full of a milky juice, and with which the fields of Asia-Minor are in many places sown as ours are with corn. When the heads grow to maturity, but are yet soft, green and full of juice, incisions are made in them, and from every one of these a few drops flow of a milky juice, which soon hardens into a solid consistence. These drops are gathered with great care, and the finest opium proceeds from the first incisions. In the countries where opium is produced, multitudes are employed in preparing it with water, honey and spices, and working it up into cakes; but what we generally have is the mere crude juice, or at most worked up with water, or a small quantity of honey sufficient to bring it into form. The ancients were greatly divided about the virtues and use of opium; some calling it a poison, and others the greatest of all medicines. At present it is in high esteem, and externally applied it is emollient, relaxing and discutient, and greatly promotes suppuration. A moderate dose of opium taken internally, is generally under a grain, yet custom will make people bear a dram as a moderate dose; but in that case nature is vitiated. Its first effect is the making the patient cheerful, as if he had drank moderately of wine; it removes melancholy, excites boldness, and dissipates the dread of danger; and for this reason the Turks always take it when they are going to battle in a larger dose than ordinary: it afterward quiets the spirits, eases pain, and disposes to sleep. After the effect of a dose of opium is over, the pain generally returns in a more violent manner; the spirits, which had been elevated by it, become lower than before, and the pulse languid. An immoderate dose of opium brings on a sort of drunkenness, cheerfulness and loud laughter, at first, and, after many terrible symptoms, death itself. Those who have accustomed themselves to an immoderate use of opium, are subject to relaxations and weaknesses of all the parts of the body; they are apt to be faint, idle and thoughtless; and are generally in a stupid and uncomfortable state, except just after they have taken a fresh dose: they lose their appetite, and in fine grow old before their time. Hill.

Sleep hath forsook and giv'n me o'er
To death's benumbing opium as my only cure.
Milton.

The colour and taste of opium are, as well as its soporific or anodyne virtues, mere powers depending on its primary qualities, whereby it is fitted to produce different operations on different parts of our bodies. Locke.

opsímathy n.s. [οψιμαθια.] Late education; late erudition.

óptick n.s. [οπτικη.] The science of the nature and laws of vision.

No spherical body of what bigness soever illuminates the whole sphere of another, although it illuminate something more than half of a lesser, according unto the doctrine of opticks. Brown's Vulgar Err. b. vi.

Those who desire satisfaction in the appearance, must go to the admirable treatise of opticks by Sir Isaac Newton. Cheyne's Phil. Prin.

optimity n.s. [from *optimus.*] The state of being best.

óratory n.s. [*oratoria, ars,* Lat.]

1. Eloquence; rhetorical skill.

Each pasture stored with sheep feeding with sober security, while the pretty lambs with bleating oratory craved the dams comfort. Sidney.

When a world of men
Could not prevail with all their oratory,
Yet hath a woman's kindness over-rul'd. Shakespeare.

When my oratory grew tow'rd end,
I bid them that did love their country's good,
Cry, God save Richard. Shakesp. Rich. III.

Sighs now breath'd
Unutterable, which the spirit of pray'r
Inspir'd, and wing'd for heav'n with
speedier flight
Than loudest oratory. Milton's Paradise Lost, b. xi.

By this kind of oratory and professing to decline their own inclinations and wishes, purely for peace and unity, they prevailed over those who were still surprised. Clarend.

The former who had to deal with a people of much more politeness, learning, and wit, laid the greatest weight of his oratory upon the strength of his arguments. Swift.

Come harmless characters, that no one hit,
Come Henley's oratory, Osborn's wit. Pope.

2. Exercise of eloquence.

The Romans had seised upon the fleet of the Antiates, among which there were six armed with rostra, with which the consul Menenius adorned the publick place of oratory. Arb.

3. [*Oratoire,* French.] *Oratory* signifies a private place, which is deputed and allotted for prayer alone, and not for the general celebration of divine service. Ayliffe's Parergon.

They began to erect to themselves oratories not in any sumptuous or stately manner, which neither was possible by reason of the poor estate of the church, and had been perilous in regard of the world's envy towards them. Hooker.

Do not omit thy prayers for want of a good oratory or place to pray in; nor thy duty for want of temporal encouragements. Taylor's Guide to Devotion.

órbity n.s. [*orbus,* Latin.] Loss, or want of parents or children.

órchestre n.s. [French. ορχηστρα.] The place where the musicians are set at a publick show.

órdinary n.s.

1. Established judge of ecclesiastical causes.

The evil will
Of all their parishioners they had constrain'd,
Who to the ordinary of them complain'd. Hubberd.

If fault be in these things any where justly found, law hath refered the whole disposition and redress thereof to the ordinary of the place. Hooker, b. v. s. 12.

2. Settled establishment.

Spain had no other wars save those which were grown into an ordinary; now they have coupled therewith the extraordinary of the Valtoline and Palatinate. Bacon.

3. Actual and constant office.

Villiers had an intimation of the king's pleasure to be his cup-bearer at large; and the summer following he was admitted in ordinary. Wott.

4. Regular price of a meal.

Our courteous Antony,
Being barber'd ten times o'er, goes to the feast;
And for his ordinary pays his heart
For what his eyes eat only. Shakesp. Ant. and Cleopat.

5. A place of eating established at a certain price.

They reckon all their errors for accomplishments; and all the odd words they have picked up in a coffee-house, or a gaming ordinary, are produced as flowers of style. Swift.

órgan n.s. [*organe*, Fr. οργανον.]

1. Natural instrument; as the tongue is the organ of speech, the lungs of respiration.

When he shall hear she died upon his words,
The ever lovely organ of her life
Shall come apparell'd in more precious habit,
Than when she liv'd indeed. Shakespeare.

For a mean and organ, by which this operative virtue might be continued, God appointed the light to be united, and gave it also motion and heat. Raleigh.

The aptness of birds is not so much in the conformity of the organs of speech, as in their attention. Bacon.

　Wit and will
Can judge and chuse, without the body's aid;
Tho' on such objects they are working still,
As thro' the body's organs are convey'd.
Davies.

2. An instrument of musick consisting of pipes filled with wind and of stops, touched by the hand. [*Orgue*, Fr.]

A hand of a vast extension, and a prodigious number of fingers playing upon all the organ pipes in the world, and making every one sound a particular note. Keil.

While in more lengthen'd notes and slow,
The deep, majestick, solemn organs blow.
Pope.

orgánical, orgánick adj. [*organique*, Fr. *organicus*, Lat.]

1. Consisting of various parts co-operating with each other.

He rounds the air, and breaks the hymnick notes
In birds, heav'n's choristers, organick throats;
Which, if they did not die, might seem to be
A tenth rank in the heavenly hierarchy.
Donne.

He with serpent tongue
Organick, or impulse of vocal air,
His fraudulent temptation thus began.
Milt. P. Lost.

The organical structure of human bodies, whereby they live and move and are vitally informed by the soul, is the workmanship of a most wise, powerful, and beneficent being. Bentley's Sermons.

2. Instrumental; acting as instruments of nature or art, to a certain end.

Read with them those organick arts which enable men to discourse and write perspicuously, elegantly, and according to the fittest style of lofty, mean, or lowly. Milton.

3. Respecting organs.

She could not produce a monster of any thing that hath more vital and organical parts than a rock of marble. Ray.

They who want the sense of discipline, or hearing, are also by consequence deprived of speech, not by any immediate, organical indisposition, but for want of discipline. Holder's Elements of Speech.

orgásm n.s. [*orgasme*, Fr. οργασμος.] Sudden vehemence.

By means of the curious lodgment and inosculation of the auditory nerves, the orgasms of the spirits should be allayed, and perturbations of the mind quieted. Derham's Physico-Theol.

órgies n.s. [*orgies*, Fr. *orgia*, Lat.] Mad rites of Bacchus; frantick revels.

　These are nights
Solemn to the shining rites,
Of the fairy prince and knights,
While the moon their orgies lights.
Ben. Johnson.

She feign'd nocturnal orgies; left my bed,
And, mix'd with Trojan dames, the dances led.
Dryd.

orgíllous adj. [*orgueilleux*, French.] Proud; haughty.

From isles of Greece
The princes orgillous, their high blood chafed,
Have to the port of Athens sent their ships.
Shakesp.

oriéntal n.s. An inhabitant of the eastern parts of the world.

They have been of that great use to following ages, as to be imitated by the Arabians and other orientals. Grew.

oriéntalism n.s. [from *oriental.*] An idiom of the eastern languages; an eastern mode of speech.

oríginal adj. [*originel*, Fr. *originalis*, Latin.] Primitive; pristine; first.[†]

The original question was, whether God by this law hath forbidden the giving any worship to himself by an image? Stillingfleet on Idolatry.

Had Adam obeyed God, his original perfection, the knowledge and ability God at first gave him, would still have continued. Wake's Prep. for Death.

You still, fair mother, in your offspring trace
The stock of beauty destin'd for the race;
Kind nature, forming them the pattern took,
From heav'n's first work, and Eve's original
    look. Prior.

órisons n.s. [*oraison*, French: this word is variously accented; Shakespeare has the accent both on the first and second syllables; Milton and Crashaw on the first, others on the second.] A prayer; a supplication.

Nymph, in thy orisons
Be all thy sins remember'd. Shakesp. Hamlet.

Alas! your too much love and care of me,
Are heavy orisons 'gainst this poor wretch. Shakesp.

He went into St. Paul's church, where he had orisons and Te Deum sung. Bacon's Henry VII.

   My wakeful lay shall knock
At th' oriental gates, and duly mock
The early larks shrill orisons, to be
An anthem at the day's nativity. Crashaw.

His daily orisons attract our ears. Sandys on Job.

Lowly they bow'd, adoring, and began
Their orisons, each morning duly paid. Milton.

So went he on with his orisons,
Which, if you mark them well, were wise ones. Cotton.

   Here at dead of night
The hermit oft, mid his orisons, hears
Aghast the voice of time disparting tow'rs. Dyer.

orníscopist n.s. [ορνις and εσκοπα.] One who examines the flight of birds in order to foretel futurity.

orphánotrophy n.s. [ορφανος and τροφη.] An hospital for orphans.

órrery n.s. An instrument which by many complicated movements represents the revolutions of the heavenly bodies. It was first made by Mr. Rowley, a mathematician born at Litchfield, and so named from his patron the earl of Orrery: by one or other of this family almost every art has been encouraged or improved.

órthodox adj. [ορθος and δοκεω; *orthodox*, Fr.] Sound in opinion and doctrine; not heretical.

Be you persuaded and settled in the true protestant religion professed by the church of England; which is as sound and orthodox in the doctrine thereof, as any Christian church in the world. Bacon.

Eternal bliss is not immediately superstructed on the most orthodox beliefs; but as our Saviour saith, if ye know these things, happy are ye if ye do them; the doing must be first superstructed on the knowing or believing, before any happiness can be built on it. Hammond.

órtolan n.s. [French.] A small bird accounted very delicious.

Nor ortolans nor godwits. Cowley.

oscitancy n.s. [*oscitantia*, Lat.]

1. The act of yawning.

2. Unusual sleepiness; carelessness.

If persons of so circumspect a piety, have been thus overtaken, what security can there be for our wreckless oscitancy? Government of the Tongue.

It might proceed from the oscitancy of transcribers, who, to dispatch their work the sooner, used to write all numbers in cyphers. Addison's Spectator, Nᵒ 470.

óssuary n.s. [*ossuarium*, Lat.] A charnel house; a place where the bones of dead people are kept. Dict.

óstler n.s. [*hostelier*, French.] The man who takes care of horses at an inn.

The smith, the ostler, and the boot-catcher, ought to partake. Swift's Direct. to the Groom.

óstrich n.s. [*autruche*, Fr. *struthio*, Lat.] Ostrich is ranged among birds. It is very large, its wings very short, and the neck about four or five spans. The feathers of its wings are in great esteem, and are used as an ornament for hats, beds, canopies: they are stained of several colours, and made into pretty tufts. They are hunted by way of course, for they never fly; but use their wings to assist them in running more swiftly. The ostrich swallows bits of iron or brass, in the same manner as other birds will swallow small stones or gravel, to assist in digesting or comminuting their food. It lays its eggs upon the ground, hides them under the sand, and the sun hatches them. Calmet.

I'll make thee eat iron like an ostrich, and swallow my sword like a great pin, ere thou and I part. Shakesp.

Gavest thou the goodly wings unto the peacock? or wings and feathers unto the ostrich. Job xxxix. 13.

The Scots errant fight, and fight to eat,
Their ostrich stomachs make their swords their
  meat. Cleav.

Modern ostriches are dwindled to meer larks, in comparison with those of the ancients. Arbuthnot.

óthergates adv. [*other* and *gate*, for way.] In another manner.

If sir Toby had not been in drink, he would have tickled you othergates than he did. Shakesp. Twelfth Night.

ótter n.s. [*oter*, Saxon.] An amphibious animal that preys upon fish.

The toes of the otter's hinder feet, for the better swimming, are joined together with a membrane, as in the bevir; from which he differs principally in his teeth, which are canin; and in his tail, which is felin, or a long taper: so that he may not be unfitly called putoreus aquaticus, *or the water pole-cat. He makes himself burrows on the water side, as a bevir; is sometimes tamed and taught, by nimbly surrounding the fishes to drive them into the net.* Grew.

At the lower end of the hall is a large otter's skin stuffed with hay. Addison's Spectator, Nᵒ 115.

Would you preserve a num'rous finny race?
Let your fierce dogs the rav'nous otter chase;
Th' amphibious monster ranges all the shores,
Darts thro' the waves, and ev'ry haunt
  explores. Gay.

ounce n.s. [*once*, French; *onza*, Spanish.] A lynx; a panther.

The ounce,
The libbard, and the tiger, as the mole
Rising, the crumbled earth above them threw
In hillocks. Milton's Par. Lost, b. vii.

ovárious adj. [from *ovum*.] Consisting of eggs.

He to the rocks
Dire clinging gathers his ovarious food. Thomson.

to óver-dress v.a. [*over* and *dress*.] To adorn lavishly.

In all, let nature never be forgot;
But treat the goddess like a modest fair,
Nor over-dress, nor leave her wholly bare. Pope.

to own v.a. [from the noun.]

1. To acknowledge; to avow for one's own.

When you come, find me out,
And own me for your son. Dryden's
Cleomenes.

2. To possess; to claim; to hold by right.

Tell me, ye Trojans, for that name you own;
Nor is your course upon our coasts unknown.
Dryden.

Others on earth o'er human race preside,
Of these the chief, the care of nations own,
And guard with arms divine the British
    throne. Pope.

3. To avow.

I'll venture out alone,
Since you, fair princess, my protection own.
Dryden.

4. To confess; not to deny.

Make this truth so evident, that those who
are unwilling to own it may yet be ashamed
to deny it. Tillotson.

Others will own their weakness of
understanding. Locke.

óxymel n.s. [οξυμελι, οξυς and μελι.]
A mixture of vinegar and honey.

In fevers, the aliments prescribed by
Hippocrates, were ptisans and decoctions of
some vegetables, with oxymel or the mixture
of honey and vinegar. Arbuthnot.

oxymóron n.s. [οξυμωρος.] A rhetorical
figure, in which an epithet of a quite contrary
signification is added to any word. Dict.

óyer n.s. [*oyer*, old French, to hear.] A court
of oyer and terminer, is a judicature where
causes are heard and determined.

oyés n.s. [*oyez*, *hear ye*, French.] Is the
introduction to any proclamation or
advertisement given by the publick
criers both in England and Scotland. It is
thrice repeated.

Fairies, black, grey, green, and white,
Attend your office and your quality.
Crier hobgoblin make the fairy O yes. Shakesp.

O yes! if any happy eye
This roving wanton shall descry;
Let the finder surely know
Mine is the wag. Crashaw.

ozæna n.s. [οζαινα, from οζω; *ozene*, Fr.]
An ulcer in the inside of the nostrils that
gives an ill stench. Quincy.

P is a labial consonant, formed by a slight compression of the anterior part of the lips; as, *pull*, *pelt*. It is confounded by the Germans and Welsh with *b*: it has an uniform sound: it is sometimes mute before *t*; as, *accompt*, *receipt*; but the mute *p* is in modern orthography commonly omitted.

págan n.s. [*paganisc*, Saxon; *paganus*, Latin; from *pagus*, a village; the villages continuing heathen after the cities were christian.] A Heathen; one not a Christian.

págod n.s. [probably an Indian word.]

1. An Indian idol.

They worship idols called pagods, after such a terrible representation as we make of devils. Stillingfleet.

2. The temple of the idol.

See thronging millions to the pagod run,
And offer country, parent, wife, or son. Pope.

paígles n.s. Flowers; also called cowslips. Dict.

to paint v.n. To lay colours on the face.

Such a sin to paint. Pope.

palánquin n.s. Is a kind of covered carriage used in the eastern countries that is supported on the shoulders of slaves, and wherein persons of distinction are carried.

pálfrey n.s. [*palefroy*, French.] A small horse fit for ladies: it is always distinguished in the old books from a war horse.

Her wanton palfrey all was overspread
With tinsel trappings, woven like a wave. Fa. Queen.

The damsel is mounted on a white palfrey, as an emblem of her innocence. Addison's Spectator, No 99.

The smiths and armorers on palfreys ride. Dryden.

pálindrome n.s. [παλινδρομια, παλιν and δρομεω.] A word or sentence which is the same read backward or forwards: as, *madam;* or this sentence, *Subi dura a rudibus.*

pallmáll n.s. [*pila* and *malleus*, Lat. *pale maille*, French] A play in which the ball is struck with a mallet through an iron ring.

pálliardise n.s. [*pailliardise*, Fr.] Fornication; whoring. Obsolete.

pálmer n.s. [from *palm*.] A pilgrim: they who returned from the holy land carried branches of palm.

My sceptre, for a palmer's walking staff. Shakesp.

Behold yon isle, by palmers, pilgrims trod,
Men bearded, bald, cowl'd, uncowl'd, shod, unshod. Pope.

palmétto n.s. A species of the palm-tree: It grows in the West-Indies to be a very large tree; with the leaves the inhabitants thatch their houses. These leaves, before they are expanded, are cut and brought into England to make womens plaited hats; and the berries of these trees were formerly much used for buttons.

Broad o'er my head the verdant cedars wave,
And high palmettos lift their graceful shade. Thomson.

pálmipede adj. [*palma* and *pes*, Lat.] Webfooted; having the toes joined by a membrane.

It is described like fissipedes, whereas it is a palmipede or fin-footed like swans. Brown's Vulgar Err. b. v.

Water-fowl which are palmipede, are whole footed, have very long necks, and yet but short legs, as swans. Ray.

to pálpitate v.a. [*palpito*, Latin; *palpiter*, Fr.] To beat as the heart; to flutter; to go pit a pat.

pam n.s. [probably from *palm*, victory; as *trump* from *triumph*.] The knave of clubs.

Ev'n mighty pam that kings and queens o'erthrew,
And mow'd down armies in the fights of lu. Pope.

pamphletéer n.s. [from *pamphlet*.] A scribbler of small books.

The squibs are those who in the common phrase are called libellers, lampooners, and pamphleteers. Tatler.

With great injustice I have been pelted by pamphleteers. Swift.

páncake n.s. [*pan* and *cake*.] Thin pudding baked in the frying-pan.

A certain knight swore by his honour they were good pancakes, and swore by his honour the mustard was naught. Shak.

The flour makes a very good pancake, mixed with a little wheat flour. Mortimer's Husbandry.

pándect n.s. [*pandecta*, Latin.]

1. A treatise that comprehends the whole of any science.

It were to be wished, that the commons would form a pandect of their power and privileges, to be confirmed by the entire legislative authority. Swift.

2. The digest of the civil law.

pánder n.s. [This word is derived from *Pandarus*, the pimp in the story of Troilus and Cressida; it was therefore originally written *pandar*, till its etymology was forgotten.] A pimp; a male bawd; a procurer.

 Let him with his cap in hand,
Like a base pander, hold the chamber door
Whilst by a slave
His fairest daughter is contaminated.
Shakesp. Hen. V.

If thou fear to strike, and to make me certain it is done, thou art the pander to her dishonour, and equally to me disloyal. Shakesp. Cymbeline.

If ever you prove false to one another, since I have taken such pains to bring you together, let all pitiful goers-between be call'd panders after my name. Shakesp. Troil and Cressida.

Camillo was his help in this, his pander, There is a plot against my life. Shakesp. Wint. Tale.

The sons of happy Punks, the pander's heir, Are privileged To clap the first, and rule the theatre. Dryden.

Thou hast confess'd thyself the conscious pandar Of that pretended passion; A single witness infamously known, Against two persons of unquestion'd fame. Dryden.

My obedient honesty was made The pander to thy lust and black ambition. Rowe.

pántofle n.s. [*pantoufle*, French; *pantofula*, Italian.] A slipper.

Melpomene has on her feet, her high cothurn or tragick pantofles of red velvet and gold, beset with pearls. Peacham.

papácy n.s. [*papat, papauté*, Fr. from *papa*, the pope.] Popedom; office and dignity of bishops of Rome.

Now there is ascended to the papacy a personage, that through he loves the chair of the papacy well, yet he loveth the carpet above the chair. Bacon.

páper n.s. [*papier*, French; *papyrus*, Latin.]

1. Substance on which men write and print; made by macerating linen rags in water, and then spreading them in thin sheets.
I have seen her unlock her closet, take forth paper. Shake.

2. Piece of paper.
'Tis as impossible to draw regular characters on a trembling mind, as on a shaking paper. Locke on Education.

3. Single sheet printed, or written. It is used particularly of essays or journals, or any thing printed on a sheet. [*Feuille volante.*]

What see you in those papers, that you lose So much complexion? look ye how they change! Their cheeks are paper. Shakespear's Hen. V.

Nothing is of more credit or request, than a petulant paper, or scoffing verses. Ben Johnson.

They brought a paper to me to be sign'd. Dryden.

Do the prints and papers lie? Swift.

papilionáceous adj. [from *papilio*, Latin.] The flowers of some plants are called *papilionaceous* by botanists, which represent something of the figure of a butterfly, with its wings displayed: and here the petala, or flower leaves, are always of a diform figure: they are four in number, but joined together at the extremities; one of these is usually larger than the rest, and is erected in the middle of the flower, and by some called vexillum: the plants, that have this flower, are of the leguminous kind; as pease, vetches, &c. Quincy.

páradigm n.s. [παραδειγμα.] Example.

páradox n.s. [*paradoxe*, Fr. παραδοξος.] A tenet contrary to received opinion; an assertion contrary to appearance; a position in appearance absurd.

A glosse there is to colour that paradox, and make it appear in shew not to be altogether unreasonable. Hooker.

You undergo too strict a paradox,
Striving to make an ugly deed look fair.
Shakesp.

In their love of God, men can never be too affectionate: it is as true, though it may seem a paradox, that in their hatred of sin, men may be sometimes too passionate. Sprat.

páragraph n.s. [*paragraphe*, Fr. παραγραφη.] A distinct part of a discourse.

Of his last paragraph, I have transcribed the most important parts. Swift.

párallax n.s. [παραλαξις.] The distance between the true and apparent place of the sun, or any star viewed from the surface of the earth.

By what strange parallax or optick skill
Of vision multiply'd. Milton's Paradise Regained.

Light moves from the sun to us in about seven or eight minutes time, which distance is about 70,000,000 English miles, supposing the horizontal parallax of the sun to be about twelve seconds. Newton's Optics.

paraphernália n.s. [Lat. *paraphernaux*, Fr.] Goods in the wife's disposal.

páraphrase n.s. [παραφρασις; *paraphrase*, Fr.] A loose interpretation; an explanation in many words.

All the laws of nations were but a paraphrase upon this standing rectitude of nature, that was ready to enlarge itself into suitable determinations, upon all emergent objects and occasions. South's Sermons.

In paraphrase, or translation with latitude, the author's words are not so strictly followed as his sense, and that too amplified, but not altered: such is Mr. Waller's translation of Virgil's fourth Æneid. Dryden.

párasite n.s. [*parasite*, Fr. *parasita*, Latin.] One that frequents rich tables, and earns his welcome by flattery.

He is a flatterer,
A parasite, a keeper back of death,
Who gently would dissolve the bands of life,
Which false hopes linger. Shakespeare.

Most smiling, smooth, detested parasites,
Courteous destroyers, affable wolves, meek bears,
You fools of fortune. Shakespeare.

Come, you parasite, answer me
Directly to this question. Shakespeare.†

Diogenes, when mice came about him, as he was eating, said, I see, that even Diogenes nourisheth parasites. Bacon.

Thou, with trembling fear,
Or like a fawning parasite, obeyed;
Then to thyself ascrib'st the truth foretold.
Milton.

The people sweat not for their king's delight,
T' enrich a pimp, or raise a parasite. Dryden.

párasol n.s. A small sort of canopy or umbrello carried over the head, to shelter from rain and the heat of the sun. Dict.

párbreak n.s. [from the verb.] Vomit.

Her filthy parbreak all the place defiled has.
Fa. Queen.

parchment n.s. [*parchemin*, French; *pergamena*, Latin.] Skins dressed for the writer. Among traders, the skins of sheep are called parchment, those of calves vellum.

Is not this a lamentable thing, that the skin of an innocent lamb should be made parchment; that parchment, being scribbled o'er, should undo a man? Shakesp. Hen. VI.

In the coffin, that had the books, they were
found as fresh as if newly written, being
written in parchment, and covered with
watch candles of wax. Bacon.

Like flying shades before the clouds we shew,
We shrink like parchment in consuming flame.
Dryden.

pard, párdale n.s. [*pardus, pardalis,* Latin.]
The leopard; in poetry, any of the spotted
beasts.

parentátion n.s. [from *parento,* Latin.]
Something done or said in honour of the
dead.

paríetal adj. [from *paries,* Latin.]
Constituting the sides or walls.

The lower part of the parietal and upper
part of the temporal bones were fractured.
Sharp's Surgery.

párliament n.s. [*parliamentum,* low Lat.
parlement, Fr.] In England, is the assembly
of the king and three estates of the realm;
namely, the lords spiritual, the lords
temporal, and commons, for the debating
of matters touching the common wealth,
especially the making and correcting of
laws; which assembly or court is, of all
others, the highest, and of greatest
authority. Cowel.

The king is fled to London,
To call a present court of parliament.
Shakesp.

Far be the thought of this from Henry's heart,
To make a shambles of the parliament house.
Shakesp.

The true use of parliaments is very excellent;
and be often called, and continued as long as
is necessary. Bacon.

I thought the right way of parliaments, the
most safe for my crown, as best pleasing to my
people. King Charles.

These are mob readers: if Virgil and Martial
stood for parliament-men, we know who
would carry it. Dryden.

párlous adj. [This might seem to come
from *parler,* Fr. to speak; but Junius derives

it, I think, rightly, from *perilous,* in which
sense it answers to the Latin *improbus.*]
Keen; sprightly; waggish.

Midas durst communicate
To none but to his wife his ears of state;
One must be trusted, and he thought her fit,
As passing prudent, and a parlous wit.
Dryden.

párnel n.s. [the diminutive of *petronella.*]
A punk; a slut. Obsolete. Skinner.

párody n.s. [*parodie,* Fr. παρωδια.] A kind
of writing, in which the words of an author
or his thoughts are taken, and by a slight
change adapted to some new purpose.

The imitations of the ancients are added
together with some of the parodies and
allusions to the most excellent of the moderns.
Pope's Dunciad.

pároxysm [παροξυσμος; *paroxysme,* Fr.]
A fit; periodical exacerbation of a disease.

I fancied to myself a kind of ease, in the
change of the paroxysm. Dryden.

Amorous girls, through the fury of an hysteric
paroxysm, are cast into a trance for an hour.
Harvey.

The greater distance of time there is between
the paroxysms, the fever is less dangerous, but
more obstinate. Arbuthnot.

párterre n.s. [*parterre,* Fr.] A level division
of ground, that, for the most part, faces the
south and best front of an house, and is
generally furnished with greens, flowers,
&c. Miller.

There are as many kinds of gardening, as of
poetry; your makers of parterres and flower
gardens are epigramatists and sonneteers.
Spectator, N° 477.

The vast parterres a thousand hands shall make;
Lo! Cobham comes, and floats them with
a lake. Pope.

párty n.s. [*partié,* French.]

1. A number of persons confederated
   by similiarity of designs or opinions
   in opposition to others; a faction.

When any of these combatants strips his terms of ambiguity, I shall think him a champion for truth, and not the slave of vain glory or a party. Locke.

This account of party patches will appear improbable to those, who live at a distance from the fashionable world. Addis.

Party writers are so sensible of the secret virtue of an innuendo, that they never mention the q—n at length. Spectat.†

This party rage in women only serves to aggravate animosities that reign among them. Addis. Spect. N° 81.

As he never leads the conversation into the violence and rage of party disputes, I listened to him with pleasure. Tatler.

Division between those of the same party, exposes them to their enemies. Pope.

The most violent party men are such, as, in the conduct of their lives, have discovered least sense of religion or morality. Swift.

2. One of two litigants.

When you are hearing a matter between party and party, if pinched with the cholick, you make faces like mummers, and dismiss the controversy more entangled by your hearing: all the peace you make in their cause, is calling both parties knaves. Shakesp.

The cause of both parties shall come before the judges. Exodus xxii. 9.

If a bishop be a party to a suit, and excommunicates his adversary; such excommunication shall not bar his adversary from his action. Ayliffe's Parergon.

3. One concerned in any affair.

The child was prisoner to the womb, and is Free'd and enfranchis'd; not a party to The anger of the king, nor guilty of The trespass of the queen. Shakesp.

I do suspect this trash To be a party in this injury. Shakesp.

4. Side; persons engaged against each other.

Our Foes compell'd by need, have peace embrac'd: The peace, both parties want, is like to last. Dryden.

5. Cause; side.

Ægle came in, to make their party good. Dryden.

6. A select assembly.

Let me extol a cat, on oysters fed, I'll have a party at the Bedford-head. Pope.

If the clergy would a little study the arts of conversation, they might be welcome at every party, where there was the least regard for politeness or good sense. Swift.

7. Particular person; a person distinct from, or opposed to, another.

As she paced on, she was stopped with a number of trees, so thickly placed together, that she was afraid she should, with rushing through, stop the speech of the lamentable party, which she was so desirous to understand. Sidney.

The minister of justice may, for publick example, virtuously will the execution of that party, whose pardon another, for consanguinity's sake, as virtuously may desire. Hooker.

If the jury found, that the party slain was of English race, it had been adjudged felony. Davies on Ireland.

How shall this be compast? canst thou bring me to the party? Shakespear's Tempest.

The smoke received into the nostrils, causes the party to lie as if he were drunk. Abbot's Descript. of the World.

The imagination of the party to be cured, is not needful to concur; for it may be done without the knowledge of the party wounded. Bacon's Natural History.

He that confesses his sin, and prays for pardon, hath punished his fault; and then there is nothing left to be done by the offended party, but to return to charity. Taylor.

Though there is a real difference between one man and another, yet the party, who has the advantage, usually magnifies the inequality. Collier on Pride.

8. A detachment of soldiers: as, he
commanded that party sent thither.

párty-man n.s. [*party* and *man*.] A factious
person; an abettor of a party.

párvity n.s. [from *parvus*, Lat.] Littleness;
minuteness.

What are these for fineness and parvity,
to those minute animalcula discovered in
pepper-water. Ray.

pash n.s. [*pox*, Spanish.] A kiss. Hanmer.

Thou want'st a rough pash, and the shoots
*   that I have,*
To be full like me. Shakesp. Winter's Tale.

pásquil, pásquin, pásquinade n.s. [from
pasquino, a statue at Rome, to which they
affix any lampoon or paper of satirical
observation.] A lampoon.

He never valued any pasquils that were
dropped up and down, to think them worthy
of his revenge. Howel.

The pasquils, lampoons, and libels, we meet
with now-a-days, are a sort of playing with
the four and twenty letters, without sense,
truth, or wit. Tatler, Nº 92.

pássion n.s. [*passion*, French; *passio*, Latin.]

1. Any effect caused by external agency.

The differences of mouldable and not
mouldable, scissible and not scissible, and
many other passions of matter are plebeian
notions, applied to the instruments men
ordinarily practise. Bacon.

A body at rest affords us no idea of any active
power to move, and when, set in motion, it is
rather a passion than an action in it. Locke.

2. Violent commotion of the mind.

All the other passions fleet to air,
As doubtful thoughts and rash embrac'd
*   despair.* Shakesp.

Thee every thing becomes, to chide, to laugh,
To weep: whose every passion fully strives
To make itself in thee fair and admired.
Shakespeare.

*   Vex'd I am*
Of late, with passions of some difference.
Shakespeare.

*   I am doubtful, lest*
You break into some merry passion,
And so offend him:
If you should smile, he grows impatient.
Shakesp.

In loving thou do'st well, in passion not;
Wherein true love consists not. Milton's
Par. Lost.

*   Cruel his eye, but cast*
Signs of remorse and passion, to behold
The fellows of his crime condemn'd
For ever now to have their lot in pain.
Milton's Par. Lost.

Passion's too fierce to be in fetters bound,
And nature flies him like enchanted ground.
Dryden.

All the art of rhetorick, besides order and
perspicuity, only moves the passions, and
thereby misleads the judgment. Locke.

3. Anger.

The word passion signifies the receiving any
action in a large philosophical sense; in a more
limited philosophical sense, it signifies any of
the affections of human nature; as love, fear,
joy, sorrow: but the common people confine it
only to anger. Watts.

4. Zeal; ardour.

Where statesmen are ruled by faction and
interest, they can have no passion for the glory
of their country, nor any concern for the figure
it will make. Addison on Medals.

5. Love.

*   For your love,*
You kill'd her father: you confess'd you drew
A mighty argument to prove your passion for
the daughter. Dryden and Lee's Oedipus.

*   He, to grate me more,*
Publickly own'd his passion for Amestris.
Rowe.

Survey yourself, and then forgive your slave,
Think what a passion such a form must have.
Granvil.

6. Eagerness.

Abate a little of that violent passion for fine
cloaths, so predominant in your sex. Swift.

7. Emphatically. The last suffering of the redeemer of the world.

He shewed himself alive after his passion, by many infallible proofs. Acts i. 3.

pástern n.s. [*pasturon*, French.]

1. The knee of an horse.†

I will not change my horse with any that treads on four pasterns. Shakespeare's Henry V.

The colt that for a stallion is design'd, Upright he walks on pasterns firm and straight, His motions easy, prancing in his gait. Dryden.

Being heavy, he should not tread stiff, but have a pastern made him, to break the force of his weight: by this his body hangs on the hoof, as a coach doth by the leathers. Grew.

2. The legs of an human creature in contempt.

So straight she walk'd, and on her pasterns high: If seeing her behind, he lik'd her pace, Now turning short, he better lik'd her face. Dryden.

pástoral n.s. A poem in which any action or passion is represented by its effects upon a country life; or according to the common practice in which speakers take upon them the character of shepherds; an idyl; a bucolick.

Pastoral is an imitation of the action of a shepherd, the form of this imitation is dramatick or narrative, or mixed of both, the fable simple, the manners not too polite nor too rustick. Pope.

The best actors in the world, for tragedy, comedy, history, pastoral. Shakesp. Hamlet.

There ought to be the same difference between pastorals and elegies, as between the life of the country and the court; the latter should be smooth, clean, tender and passionate: the thoughts may be bold, more gay, and more elevated than in pastoral. Walsh.

pat adj. [from *pas*, Dutch. Skinner.] Fit; convenient; exactly suitable either as to time or place. This is a low word, and should not be used but in burlesque writings.

Pat pat; and here's a marvellous convenient place for our rehearsal. Shakespeare's Midsummer Night's Dream.

Now I might do it pat, now he is praying. Shakesp.

They never saw two things so pat, In all respects, as this and that. Hudibras, p. ii.

Zuinglius dreamed of a text, which he found very pat to his doctrine of the Eucharist. Atterbury.

He was surely put to 't at the end of a verse, Because he could find no word to come pat in. Swift.

pathétical, pathétick [παθητικος; *pathetique*, Fr.] Affecting the passions; passionate; moving.

His page that handful of wit; 'Tis a most pathetical neat. Shakesp.

How pathetick is that expostulation of Job, when, for the trial of his patience, he was made to look upon himself in this deplorable condition. Spectator, No 571.

Tully considered the dispositions of a sincere and less mercurial nation, by dwelling on the pathetick part. Swift.

While thus pathetick to the prince he spoke, From the brave youth the streaming passion broke. Pope.

pátible adj. [from *patior*, Lat.] Sufferable; tolerable. Dict.

pátibulary adj. [*patibulaire*, Fr. from *patibulum*, Latin.] Belonging to the gallows. Dict.

pátriot n.s. One whose ruling passion is the love of his country.†

Patriots who for sacred freedom stood. Tickel.

The firm patriot there, Who made the welfare of mankind his care, Shall know he conquer'd. Addison's Cato.

Here tears shall flow from a more gen'rous cause, Such tears as patriots shed for dying laws. Pope.

pátron n.s. [*patron*, Fr. *patronus*, Latin.]

1. One who countenances, supports or protects. Commonly a wretch who supports with insolence, and is paid with flattery.

I'll plead for you, as for my patron. Shakesp.

Ne'er let me pass in silence Dorset's name;
Ne'er cease to mention the continu'd debt,
Which the great patron only would forget.
Prior.

2. A guardian saint.

Thou amongst those saints, whom thou do'st see,
Shall be a saint, and thine own nation's friend
And patron. Fairy Queen, b. i.

St. Michael is mentioned as the patron of the Jews, and is now taken by the Christians, as the protector general of our religion. Dryden.

3. Advocate; defender; vindicator.

We are no patrons of those things; the best defence whereof is speedy redress and amendment. Hooker, b. ii. s. 1.

Whether the minds of men have naturally imprinted on them the ideas of extension and number, I leave to those who are the patrons of innate principles. Locke.

4. One who has donation of ecclesiastical preferment.

pávan, pávin n.s. A kind of light tripping dance. Ains.

paúciloquy n.s. [*pauciloquium*, Lat.] Sparing and rare speech. Dict.

to peach v.n. [Corrupted from *impeach*.] To accuse of some crime.

If you talk of peaching, I'll peach first, and see whose oath will be believed; I'll trounce you. Dryden.

péccant adj. [*peccant*, Fr. *peccans*, Latin.]

1. Guilty; criminal.

From them I will not hide
My judgments, how with mankind I proceed;
As how with peccant angels late they saw.
Milton.

That such a peccant creature should disapprove and repent of every violation of the rules of just and honest, this right reason could not but infer. South's Sermons.

2. Ill disposed; corrupt; bad; offensive to the body; injurious to health. It is chiefly used in medical writers.

With laxatives preserve your body sound,
And purge the peccant humours that abound.
Dryden.

Such as have the bile peccant or deficient are relieved by bitters, which are a sort of subsidiary gall. Arbuthnot.

3. Wrong; bad; deficient; unformal.

Nor is the party cited bound to appear, if the citation be peccant in form or matter. Ayliffe's Parergon.

pedáneous adj. [*pedaneus*, Lat.] Going on foot. Dict.

pédant n.s. [*pedant*, French.]

1. A schoolmaster.

A pedant that keeps a school i' th' church. Shakesp.

The boy who scarce has paid his entrance down
To his proud pedant, or declin'd a noun.
Dryden.

2. A man vain of low knowledge; a man awkwardly ostentatious of his literature.

The pedant can hear nothing but in favour of the conceits he is amorous of. Glanville.

The preface has so much of the pedant, and so little of the conversation of men in it, that I shall pass it over. Addison.

In learning let a nymph delight,
The pedant gets a mistress by 't. Swift.

pélican n.s. [*pelicanus*, low Lat. *pellican*, Fr.] There are two sorts of pelicans; one lives upon the water and feeds upon fish; the other keeps in deserts, and feeds upon serpents and other reptiles: the pelican has a peculiar tenderness for its young; it generally places its nest upon a craggy rock: the pelican is supposed to admit its young to suck blood from its breast. Calmet.

Should discarded fathers
Have this little mercy on their flesh;
'Twas this flesh begot those pelican daughters.
Shakesp.

The pelican hath a beak broad and flat,
like the slice of apothecaries. Hakewill
on Providence.

pen n.s. [*penna*, Latin.]

1. An instrument of writing.

Never durst poet touch a pen to write,
Until his ink were temper'd with love's sighs.
Shakesp.

Eternal deities!
Who write whatever time shall bring to pass,
With pens of Adamant on plates of brass.
Dryden.

He takes the papers, lays them down again;
And, with unwilling fingers, tries the pen.
Dryden.

I can, by designing the letters, tell what new
idea it shall exhibit the next moment, barely
by drawing my pen over it, which will
neither appear, if my hands stand still; or
though I move my pen, if my eyes be shut.
Locke.

2. Feather.

The pens that did his pinnions bind,
Were like main-yards with flying canvas lin'd.
Fairy Queen.

3. Wing; though even here it may mean
feather.

Feather'd soon and fledg'd,
They summ'd their pens; and soaring
th' air sublime,
With clang despis'd the ground.
Milton's Paradise Lost.

4. [From *pennan*, Saxon.] A small
inclosure; a coop.

My father stole two geese out of a pen.
Shakesp.

The cook was ordered to dress capons for
supper, and take the best in the pen.
L'Estrange.

She in pens his flocks will fold. Dryden's
Horace.

Ducks in thy ponds, and chickens in thy pens,
And be thy turkeys num'rous as thy hens.
King.

The gather'd flocks
Are in the wattled pen innumerous press'd,
Head above head. Thomson's Summer.

péncil n.s. [*penicillum*, Latin.]

1. A small brush of hair which painters dip
in their colours.

Pencils can by one slight touch restore
Smiles to that changed face, that wept before.
Dryden.

For thee the groves green liv'ries wear,
For thee the graces lead the dancing hours,
And nature's ready pencil paints the flow'rs.
Dryden.

A sort of pictures there is, wherein the colours,
as laid by the pencil on the table, mark out
very odd figures. Locke.

The faithful pencil has design'd
Some bright idea of the master's mind,
Where a new world leaps out at his command,
And ready nature waits upon his hand. Pope.

One dips the pencil, t' other strings the lyre.
Pope.

2. A black lead pen, with which cut to
a point they write without ink.

Mark with a pen or pencil the most
considerable things in the books you desire
to remember. Watts.

3. Any instrument of writing without ink.

pénguin n.s. [*anser magellanicus*, Latin.]

1. A bird. This bird was found with this
name, as is supposed, by the first
discoverers of America; and penguin
signifying in Welsh a white head, and
the head of this fowl being white, it has
been imagined, that America was
peopled from Wales; whence *Hudibras*:

British Indians nam'd from penguins.

Grew gives another account of the
name, deriving it from *pinguis*, Lat. *fat*;
but is, I believe, mistaken.

The penguin is so called from his extraordinary fatness: for though he be no higher than a large goose, yet he weighs sometimes sixteen pounds: his wings are extreme short and little, altogether unuseful for flight, but by the help whereof he swims very swiftly. Grew's Musæum.

2. A fruit.

The penguin is very common in the West Indies, where the juice of its fruit is often put into punch, being of a sharp acid flavour: there is also a wine made of the juice of this fruit, but it will not keep good long. Miller.

pénman n.s. [*pen* and *man*.]

1. One who professes the act of writing.

2. An author; a writer.

The four evangelists, within fifty years after our Saviour's death, consigned to writing that history, which had been published only by the apostles and disciples: the further consideration of these holy penmen will fall under another part of this discourse. Addison on the Christian Religion.

The descriptions which the evangelists give, shew that both our blessed Lord and the holy penmen of his story were deeply affected. Atterbury.

pénsion n.s. [*pension*, Fr.] An allowance made to any one without an equivalent. In England it is generally understood to mean pay given to a state hireling for treason to his country.†

A charity bestowed on the education of her young subjects has more merit than a thousand pensions to those of a higher fortune. Addison's Guardian, N° 105.

He has liv'd with the great without flattery, and been a friend to men in power without pensions. Pope.

péony n.s. [*pæonia*, Latin.] The peony hath a flower composed of several leaves, which are placed orbicularly, and expand in form of a rose, out of whose empalement rises the pointal, which afterwards becomes a fruit, in which several little horns bent downwards are gathered, as it were, into a little head covered with down opening lengthways, containing many globular seeds. Miller.

A physician had often tried the peony root unseasonably gathered without success; but having gathered it when the decreasing moon passes under Aries and tied the slit root about the necks of his patients, he had freed more than one from epileptical fits. Boyle.

péppercorn n.s. [*pepper* and *corn*.] Any thing of inconsiderable value.

Our performances, though dues, are like those peppercorns which freeholders pay their landlord to acknowledge that they hold all from him. Boyle.

Folks from mud-wall'd tenement
Bring landlords peppercorn for rent. Prior.

péppermint n.s. [*pepper* and *mint*.] Mint eminently hot.

to péregrinate v.n. [*peregrinus*, Lat.] To travel; to live in foreign countries. Dict.

pérfect adj. [*perfectus*, Lat. *parfait*, Fr.]

1. Complete; consummate; finished; neither defective nor redundant.

We count those things perfect, which want nothing requisite for the end, whereto they were instituted. Hooker.

2. Fully informed; fully skilful.

   Within a ken our army lies;
Our men more perfect in the use of arms,
Our armour all as strong, our cause the best;
Then reason wills our hearts should be as
   good. Shakesp.

   Fair dame! I am not to you known,
Though in your state of honour I am perfect.
Shakespeare.

I do not take myself to be so perfect in the privileges of Bohemia, as to handle that part; and will not offer at that I cannot master. Bacon.

3. Pure; blameless; clear; immaculate. This is a sense chiefly theological.

My parts, my title, and my perfect soul
Shall manifest me rightly. Shakesp. Othello.

Thou shalt be perfect with the Lord thy God.
Deutr. xviii.

4. Safe; Out of danger.

Thou art perfect then, our ship hath touch'd upon
The deserts of Bohemia. Shakespeare's
Winter's Tale.

périod n.s. [*periode*, Fr. περιοδος.]

1. A circuit.

2. Time in which any thing is performed,
so as to begin again in the same manner.

Tell these, that the sun is fixed in the centre,
that the earth with all the planets roll round
the sun in their several periods they cannot
admit a syllable of this new doctrine. Watts.

3. A stated number of years; a round of
time, at the end of which the things
comprised within the calculation shall
return to the state in which they were
at beginning.

A cycle or period is an account of years that
has a beginning and end too, and then begins
again as often as it ends. Holder on Time.

We stile a lesser space a cycle, and a greater
by the name of period; and you may not
improperly call the beginning of a large period
the epocha thereof. Holder on Time.

4. The end or conclusion.

If my death might make this island happy,
And prove the period of their tyranny,
I would expend it with all willingness;
But mine is made the prologue to their play.
Shakesp.

There is nothing so secret that shall not be
brought to light within the compass of our
world; whatsoever concerns this sublunary
world in the whole extent of its duration,
from the chaos to the last period. Burnet's
Theory of the Earth.

What anxious moments pass between
The birth of plots and their last fatal periods.
Oh! 'tis a dreadful interval of time. Addison.

5. The state at which any thing terminates.

Beauty's empires, like to greater states,
Have certain periods set, and hidden fates.
Suckling.

Light-conserving stones must be set in the sun
before they retain light, and the light will
appear greater or lesser, until they come to
their utmost period. Digby.

6. Length of duration.

Some experiment would be made how by art
to make plants more lasting than their
ordinary period; as to make a stalk of wheat
last a whole year. Bacon's Natural History.

7. A complete sentence from one full stop
to another.

Periods are beautiful, when they are not too
long: for so they have their strength too as in
a pike or javelin. B. Johns.

Is this the confidence you gave me,
Lean on it safely, not a period
Shall be unsaid for me. Milton.

Syllogism is made use of to discover a fallacy,
cunningly wrapt up in a smooth period.
Locke.

For the assistance of weak memories, the
first words of every period in every page may
be written in distinct colours. Watts's
Improvement of the Mind.

From the tongue
Th' unfinish'd period falls. Thomson's Spring.

périwig n.s. [*perruque*, Fr.] Adscititious
hair; hair not natural, worn by way of
ornament or concealment of baldness.

Her hair is auburn, mine is perfect yellow;
If that be all the difference in his love,
I'll get me such a colour'd periwig. Shakesp.

It offends me to hear a robusteous periwig-
pated fellow tear a passion to tatters, to split
the ears of the groundlings. Shakespeare.

The sun's
Dishevel'd beams and scatter'd fires
Serve but for ladies periwigs and tires
In lovers sonnets. Donne.

Madam time, be ever bald,
I'll not thy periwig be call'd. Cleaveland.

For vailing of their visages his highness and
the marquis bought each a periwig, somewhat
to overshadow their foreheads. Wotton.

They used false hair or periwigs. Arbuthnot
on Coins.

From her own head Megara takes
A periwig of twisted snakes,
Which in the nicest fashion curl'd,
Like toupets. Swift's Miscellanies.

perpotátion n.s. [*per* and *poto*, Latin.] The
act of drinking largely.

pervicácious adj. [*pervicax*, Lat.] Spitefully
obstinate; peevishly contumacious.

May private devotions be efficacious upon the
mind of one of the most pervicacious young
creatures! Clarissa.

perúke n.s. [*peruque*, Fr.] A cap of false
hair; a periwig

I put him on a linen cap, and his peruke over
that. Wiseman.

pésthouse n.s. [from *pest* and *house*.] An
hospital for persons infected with the
plague.

péstilent adj. [*pestiltnt*, Fr. *pestilens*, Lat.]

1. Producing plagues; malignant.

Great ringing of bells in populous cities
dissipated pestilent air, which may be from the
concussion of the air, and not from the sound.
Bacon's Natural History.

To those people that dwell under or near
the equator, a perpetual spring would be a
most pestilent and insupportable summer.
Bentley's Sermons.

2. Mischievous; destructive.

There is nothing more contagious and
pestilent than some kinds of harmony; than
some nothing more strong and potent unto
good. Hooker, b. v. s. 38.

Hoary moulded bread the soldiers thrusting
upon their spears railed against king
Ferdinand, who with such corrupt and
pestilent bread would feed them. Knolles.

Which president, of pestilent import,
Against thee, Henry, had been brought.
Daniel.

The world abounds with pestilent books,
written against this doctrine. Swift's
Miscellanies.

3. In ludicrous language, it is used to
exaggerate the meaning of another
word.

One pestilent fine,
His beard no bigger though than thine,
Walked on before the rest. Suckling.

pet n.s. [This word is of doubtful
etymology; from *despit*, Fr. or *impetus*, Lat.
Perhaps it may be derived some way from
petit, as it implies only a little fume or fret.]

1. A slight passion; a slight fit of anger.

If all the world
Should in a pet of temperance feed on pulse,
Drink the clear stream, and nothing
wear but freeze,
Th' all-giver would be unthankt, would
be unprais'd. Milton.

If we cannot obtain every vain thing we ask,
our next business is to take pet at the refusal.
L'Estrange.

Life, given for noble purposes, must not be
thrown up in a pet, nor whined away in love.
Collier.

They cause the proud their visits to delay,
And send the godly in a pet to pray. Pope.

2. A lamb taken into the house, and
brought up by hand. A cade lamb.
[Probably from *petit*, little.] Hanmer.

pétar, pétard n.s. [*petard*, Fr. *petardo*,
Italian.] A petard is an engine of metal,
almost in the shape of an hat, about seven
inches deep, and about five inches over at
the mouth: when charged with fine powder
well beaten, it is covered with a madrier or
plank, bound down fast with ropes, running
through handles, which are round the rim
near the mouth of it: this petard is applied
to gates or barriers of such places as are
designed to be surprized, to blow them up:

they are also used in countermines to break through into the enemies galleries. Military Dict.

'Tis the sport to have the engineer
Hoist with his own petar. Shakespeare's Hamlet.

Find all his having and his holding,
Reduc'd t' eternal noise and scolding;
The conjugal petard that tears
Down all portcullices of ears. Hudibras.

petról, petróleum n.s. [*petrole*, Fr.] Petrol or petroleum is a liquid bitumen, black, floating on the water of springs. Woodward.

pétticoat n.s. [*petit* and *coat*.] The lower part of a woman's dress.

What trade art thou, Feeble?
—A woman's taylor, sir.
—Wilt thou make as many holes in an
enemy's battle, as thou hast done in a woman's
petticoat? Shakespeare.

Her feet beneath her petticoat,
Like little mice, stole in and out,
As if they fear'd the light. Suckling.

It is a great compliment to the sex, that the
virtues are generally shewn in petticoats.
Addison.

To fifty chosen sylphs, of special note,
We trust th' important charge, the petticoat;
Oft have we known that sevenfold fence to fail,
Though stiff with hoops, and arm'd with ribs
*   of whale.* Pope's Rape of the Lock.

pettifógger n.s. [corrupted from *pettivoguer; petit* and *voguer*, Fr.] A petty small-rate lawyer.

The worst conditioned and least cliented
petivoguers get, under the sweet bait of
revenge, more plentiful prosecution of actions.
Carew's Survey of Cornwall.

Your pettifoggers damn their souls
To share with knaves in cheating fools.
Hudibras.

Consider, my dear, how indecent it is to
abandon your shop and follow pettifoggers;
there is hardly a plea between two country

esquires about a barren acre, but you draw
yourself in as bail, surety or solicitor.
Arbuthnot's Hist. of J. Bull.

Physicians are apt to despise empiricks,
lawyers, pettifoggers, merchants and pedlars.
Swift.

pharisáical adj. [from *pharisee.*] Ritual; externally religious, from the sect of the Pharisees, whose religion consisted almost wholly in ceremonies.

The causes of superstition are pleasing
and sensual rites, excess of outward and
pharisaical holiness, over-great reverence of
traditions, which cannot but load the church.
Bacon.

Suffer us not to be deluded with pharisaical
washings instead of christian reformings.
King Charles.

pharmacopoeía n.s. [φαρμακον and ποιεω; *pharmacopée*, Fr.] A dispensatory; a book containing rules for the composition of medicines.

philáctery n.s. [φιλακτηριον; *phylactere*, Fr.] A bandage on which was inscribed some memorable sentence.

The philacteries on their wrists and foreheads
were looked on as spells, which would yield
them impunity for their disobedience.
Hammond.

*   Golden sayings*
On large phylacteries expressive writ,
Were to the foreheads of the Rabbins ty'd.
Prior.

philánthropy n.s. [φιλεω and ανθρωπος.] Love of mankind; good nature.

Such a transient temporary good nature is not
that philanthropy, that love of mankind,
which deserves the title of a moral virtue.
Addison's Spectator, Nᵒ 177.

philóloger n.s. [φιλολογος.] One whose chief study is language; a grammarian; a critick.

Philologers and critical discoursers, who look
beyond the shell and obvious exteriors of
things, will not be angry with our narrower
explorations. Brown.

You expect, that I should discourse of this matter like a naturalist, not a philologer. Boyle.

The best philologers say, that the original word does not only signify domestick, as opposed to foreign, but also private, as opposed to common. Sprat's Sermons.

phílomel, philoméla n.s. [from *Philomela,* changed into a bird.] The nightingale.

Time drives the flocks from field to fold,
When rivers rage, and rocks grow cold,
And philomel becometh dumb. Shakesp.†

Hears the hawk, when philomela sings? Pope.

   Listening philomela deigns
To let them joy. Thomson.

philósopheme n.s. [φιλοσοφημα.] Principle of reasoning; theorem. An unusual word.

You will learn how to address yourself to children for their benefit, and derive some useful philosophemes for your own entertainment. Watts.

philosophers stone n.s. A stone dreamed of by alchemists, which, by its touch, converts base metals into gold.

philosophy n.s. [*philosophie,* Fr. *philosophia,* Latin.]

1. Knowledge natural or moral.

I had never read, heard nor seen any thing, I had never any taste of philosophy nor inward feeling in myself, which for a while I did not call to my succour. Sidney.

   Hang up philosophy;
Unless philosophy can make a Juliet,
Displant a town, reverse a prince's doom,
It helps not. Shakesp.

The progress you have made in philosophy, hath enabled you to benefit yourself with what I have written. Digby.

2. Hypothesis or system upon which natural effects are explained.

We shall in vain interpret their words by the notions of our philosophy, and the doctrines in our schools. Locke.

3. Reasoning; argumentation.

Of good and evil much they argu'd then
Vain wisdom all and false philosophy. Milton.

His decisions are the judgment of his passions and not of his reason, the philosophy of the sinner and not of the man. Rogers's Sermons.

4. The course of sciences read in the schools.

phiz n.s. [This word is formed by a ridiculous contraction from *physiognomy,* and should therefore, if it be written at all, be written *phyz.*] The face, in a sense of contempt.

His air was too proud, and his features amiss,
As if being a traitor had alter'd his phiz. Stepney.

phlebótomy n.s. [φλεβοτομια, φλεψ, φλεβος, vena, and τεμνω, *phlebotomie,* Fr.] Bloodletting; the act or practice of opening a vein for medical intentions.

Although in indispositions of the liver or spleen, considerations are made in phlebotomy to their situation, yet, when the heart is affected, it is thought as effectual to bleed on the right as the left. Brown's Vulgar Errours.

Pains for the spending of the spirits, come nearest to the copious and swift loss of spirits by phlebotomy. Harvey.

phlogíston n.s. [φλογιστος, from φλεγω.]

1. A chemical liquor extremely inflammable.

2. The inflammable part of any body.

phthísick n.s. [φθισις; *phtysie,* Fr.] A consumption.

His disease was a phthisick or asthma oft incurring to an orthopnea. Harvey on Consumptions.

physick n.s. [φυσικη, which, originally signifying natural philosophy, has been transferred in many modern languages to medicine.]

1. The science of healing.

Were it my business to understand physick, would not the safer way be to consult nature herself in the history of diseases and their cures, than espouse the principles of the dogmatists, methodists or chymists. Locke.

2. Medicines; remedies.

In itself we desire health, physick only for health's sake. Hooker, b. v. s. 48.

Use physick or ever thou be sick. Ecclus. xviii. 19.

Prayer is the best physick for many melancholy diseases. Peacham.

He 'scapes the best, who nature to repair Draws physick from the fields in draughts of vital air. Dryd.

3. [In common phrase.] A purge.

The people use physick to purge themselves of humours. Abbot's Description of the World.

physiógnomy n.s. [for *physiognomony;* φυσιογνωμονια; *physionomie,* Fr.]

1. The act of discovering the temper, and foreknowing the fortune by the features of the face.

In all physiognomy, the lineaments of the body will discover those natural inclinations of the mind which dissimulation will conceal, or discipline will suppress. Bacon's Nat. Hist.

2. The face; the cast of the look.

The astrologer, who spells the stars, Mistakes his globes and in her brighter eye Interprets heaven's physiognomy. Cleaveland.

They'll find i' th' physiognomies O' th' planets all men's destinies. Hudibras.

The end of portraits consists in expressing the true temper of those persons which it represents, and to make known their physiognomy. Dryden's Dufresnoy.

The distinguishing characters of the face, and the lineaments of the body, grow more plain and visible with time and age; but the peculiar physiognomy of the mind is most discernible in children. Locke.

phytívorous adj. [φυτον and *voro,* Lat.] That eats grass or any vegetable.

Hairy animals with only two large foreteeth, are all phytivorous, and called the hare-kind. Ray.

pica n.s. Among printers, a particular size of their types or letters. This dictionary is in small pica.[†]

píckleherring n.s. [*pickle* and *herring.*] A jack-pudding; a merry-andrew; a zany; a buffoon.

Another branch of pretenders to this art, without horse or pickleherring, lie snug in a garret. Spectator, Nº 572.

The pickleherring found the way to shake him, for upon his whistling a country jig, this unlucky wag danced to it with such a variety of grimaces, that the countryman could not forbear smiling, and lost the prize. Addis. Spect.

picktóoth n.s. [*pick* and *tooth.*] An instrument by which the teeth are cleaned.

If a gentleman leaves a picktooth case on the table after dinner, look upon it as part of your vails. Swift.

pickthánk n.s. [*pick* and *thank.*] An officious fellow, who does what he is not desired; a whispering parasite.

With pleasing tales his lord's vain ears he fed, A flatterer, a pickthank, and a lyer. Fairfax.

Many tales devis'd, Oft the ear of greatness needs must hear, By smiling pickthanks and base newsmongers. Shakesp.

The business of a pickthank is the basest of offices. L'Estrange.

If he be great and powerful, spies and pickthanks generally provoke him to persecute and tyrannize over the innocent and the just. South's Sermons.

pict n.s. [*pictus,* Lat.] A painted person.

Your neighbours would not look on you as men, But think the nations all turn'd picts again. Lee.

pictórial adj. [from *pictor*, Lat.] Produced by a painter. A word not adopted by other writers, but elegant and useful.

Sea horses are but grotesco delineations, which fill up empty spaces in maps, as many pictorial inventions, not any physical shapes. Brown's Vulgar Errours.

to piddle v.n. [This word is obscure in its etymology; Skinner derives it from *picciolo*, Italian; or *petit*, Fr. little; Mr. Lye thinks the diminutive of the Welsh *breyta*, to eat; perhaps it comes from *peddle*, for Skinner gives for its primitive signification, to deal in little things.]

1. To pick at table; to feed squeamishly, and without appetite.

From stomach sharp, and hearty feeding,
To piddle like a lady breeding. Swift's Miscellanies.

2. To trifle; to attend to small parts rather than to the main. Ains.

pie n.s. [This word is derived by Skinner from *biezan*, to build, that is to build of paste; by Junius derived by contraction from *pasty;* if pasties, doubled together without walls, were the first pies, the derivation is easy from *pie*, a foot; as in some provinces, an apple pasty is still called an apple foot.]

1. Any crust baked with something in it.

    No man's pie is freed
From his ambitious finger. Shakesp. Henry VIII.

Mincing of meat in pies saveth the grinding of the teeth, and therefore more nourishing to them that have weak teeth. Bacon's Natural History.

He is the very Withers of the city; they have bought more editions of his works, than would serve to lay under all their pies at a lord mayor's Christmas. Dryden.

    Chuse your materials right;
From thence of course the figure will arise,
And elegance adorn the surface of your pies. King.

Eat beef or pie-crust, if you'd serious be. King.

2. [*Pica*, Lat.] A magpie; a particoloured bird.

The pie will discharge thee for pulling the rest. Tusser.

The raven croak'd hoarse on the chimney's top,
And chattering pies in dismal discords sung. Shakesp.

Who taught the parrot human notes to try,
Or with a voice endu'd the chatt'ring pie?
'Twas witty want. Dryden.

3. The old popish service book, so called, as is supposed, from the different colour of the text and rubrick.

4. Cock and pie was a slight expression in Shakespeare's time, of which I know not the meaning.

Mr. Slender, come; we stay for you.—
—I'll eat nothing, I thank you, Sir.—
—By cock and pie, you shall not chuse,
Sir; come, come. Shakesp. Merry Wives of Windsor.

pígmy n.s. [*pigmée*, Fr. *pigmæus*, Lat.] A small nation, fabled to be devoured by the cranes; thence any thing mean or inconsiderable.

When cranes invade, his little sword and shield
The pigmy takes. Dryden's Juvenal.

The criticks of a more exalted taste, may discover such beauties in the antient poetry, as may escape the comprehension of us pigmies of a more limited genius. Garth.

    But that it wanted room,
It might have been a pigmy's tomb. Swift.

pígsney n.s. [*piga*, Sax. a girl.] A word of endearment to a girl. It is used by Butler for the eye of a woman, I believe, improperly.

Shine upon me but benignly
With that one, and that other pigsney. Hudibras.

pigwídgeon n.s. This word is used by Drayton as the name of a fairy, and is a kind of cant word for any thing petty or small.

Where's the Stoick can his wrath appease,
To see his country sick of Pym's disease;

By Scotch invasion to be made a prey
To such pigwidgeon myrmidons as they?
Cleaveland.

pile n.s. [*pile*, Fr. *pyle*, Dutch.]

1. A strong piece of wood driven into the ground to make firm a foundation.

The bridge the Turks before broke, by plucking up of certain piles, and taking away of the planks. Knolles.

If the ground be hollow or weak, he strengthens it by driving in piles. Moxon.

The foundation of the church of Harlem is supported by wooden piles, as the houses in Amsterdam are. Locke.

2. A heap; an accumulation.

That is the way to lay the city flat,
And bury all which yet distinctly ranges
In heaps and piles of ruin. Shakesp.

What piles of wealth hath he accumulated
To his own portion! what expence by th' hour
Seems to flow from him! how i' th' name of thrift,
Does he rake this together. Shakesp.

By the water passing through the stone to its perpendicular intervals, was brought thither all the metallic matter now lodged therein, as well as that which lies only in an undigested and confused pile. Woodward.

3. Any thing heaped together to be burned.

I'll bear your logs the while; pray give me it,
I'll carry 't to the pile. Shakesp. Tempest.

Woe to the bloody city, I will even make the pile for fire great. Ezekiel xxiv. 9.

In Alexander's time, the Indian philosophers, when weary of living, lay down upon their funeral pile without any visible concern. Collier on the Value of Life.

The wife, and counsellor or priest,
Prepare and light his fun'ral fire,
And cheerful on the pile expire. Prior.

4. An edifice; a building.

Th' ascending pile stood fix'd her stately height. Milt.

Not to look back so far, to whom this isle
Owes the first glory of so brave a pile.
Denham.

The pile o'erlook'd the town, and drew the sight. Dryd.

Fancy brings the vanish'd piles to view,
And builds imaginary Rome anew.
Pope's Miscellanies.

No longer shall forsaken Thames
Lament his old Whitehall in flames;
A pile shall from its ashes rise,
Fit to invade or prop the skies.
Swift's Miscellanies.

5. A hair. [*pilus*, Lat.]

Yonder's my lord, with a patch of velvet on 's face; his left cheek is a cheek of two pile and a half, but his right cheek is worn bare. Shakesp. All's well that ends well.

6. Hairy surface; nap.

Many other sorts of stones are regularly figured; the amianthus of parallel threads, as in the pile of velvet. Grew.

7. [*Pilum*, Lat.] The head of an arrow.

His spear a bent,
The pile was of a horse fly's tongue,
Whose sharpness nought revers'd.
Drayton's Nymph.

8. [*Pile*, Fr. *pila*, Italian.] One side of a coin; the reverse of cross.

Other men have been, and are of the same opinion, a man may more justifiably throw up cross and pile for his opinions, than take them up so. Locke.

9. [In the plural, piles.] The hæmorrhoids.

Wherever there is any uneasiness, solicit the humours towards that part, to procure the piles, which seldom miss to relieve the head. Arbuthnot.

pílser n.s. The moth or fly that runs into a candle flame. Ains.

to pimp v.a. [from the noun.] To provide gratifications for the lust of others; to pander; to procure.

But he's possest with a thousand imps,
To work whose ends his madness pimps.
Swift.

Yet bards like these aspir'd to lasting praise,
And proudly hop'd to pimp in future days.
Anonymous.†

pímple n.s. [*pompette*, Fr.] A small red pustule.

If Rosalinda is unfortunate in her mole,
Nigranilla is as unhappy in a pimple.
Addison's Spect.

If e'er thy gnome could spoil a grace,
Or raise a pimple on a beauteous face. Pope.

píneal adj. [*pineale*, Fr.] Resembling a pineapple. An epithet given by Des Cartes from the form, to the gland which he imagined the seat of the soul.

Courtiers and spaniels exactly resemble one another in the pineal gland. Arbuthnot and Pope.

píneapple n.s. The pineapple hath a flower consisting of one leaf, divided into three parts, and is funnel-shaped: the embryos are produced in the tubercles: these become a fleshy fruit full of juice: the seeds, which are lodged in the tubercles, are very small and almost kidney-shaped. Miller.

Try if any words can give the taste of a pineapple, and make one have the true idea of its relish. Locke.

If a child were kept where he never saw but black and white, he would have no more ideas of scarlet, than he that never tasted a pineapple, has of that particular relish. Locke.

pínguid adj. [*pinguis*, Lat.] Fat; unctuous. Little used.

Some clays are more pinguid, and other more slippery; yet all of them are very tenacious of water on the surface. Mortimer's Husbandry.

to pink v.n. [*pincken*, Dutch; from the noun.] To wink with the eyes.

A hungry fox lay winking and pinking, as if he had sore eyes. L'Estrange's Fables.

pírate n.s. [πειρατης; *pirata*, Lat. *pirate*, Fr.]

1. A sea-robber.

Wrangling pirates that fall out
In sharing that which you have pill'd from
me. Shakesp.

Pirates all nations are to prosecute, not so much in the right of their own fears, as upon the band of human society. Bacon.

Relate, if business or the thirst of gain
Engage your journey o'er the pathless main,
Where savage pirates seek through seas unknown
The lives of others, vent'rous of their own.
Pope.

2. Any robber; particularly a bookseller who seizes the copies of other men.

piscátion n.s. [*piscatio*, Lat.] The act or practice of fishing.

There are extant four books of cynegeticks, or venation; five of halieuticks, or piscation, commented by Ritterhusius. Brown's Vulgar Errours.

pish interj. A contemptuous exclamation. This is sometimes spoken and written *pshaw*. I know not their etymology, and imagine them formed by chance.

There was never yet philosopher
That could endure the toothach patiently;
However they have writ,
And made a pish at chance or sufferance.
Shakesp.

She frowned and cried pish, when I said a thing that I stole. Spectator, N° 268.

písmire n.s. [*mysra*, Sax. *pismiere*, Dutch.] An ant; an emmet.

His cloaths, as atoms might prevail,
Might fit a pismire or a whale. Prior.

Prejudicial to fruit are pismires, caterpillars and mice. Mort.

to piss v.n. [*pisser*, Fr. *pissen*, Dutch.] To make water.

I charge the pissing conduit run nothing but claret. Shakesp.

One ass pisses, the rest piss for company.
L'Estrange.

Once possess'd of what with care you save,
The wanton boys would piss upon your grave.
Dryden.

píssburnt adj. Stained with urine.

pístole n.s. [*pistole*, Fr.] A coin of many countries and many degrees of value.

I shall disburden him of many hundred pistoles, to make him lighter for the journey. Dryden's Spanish Fryar.

pízzle n.s. [quasi *pissle*. Minshew.] The pizzle in animals is official to urine and generation. Brown's Vulgar Errours, b. iii.

plágiary n.s. [from *plagium*, Lat.]

1. A thief in literature; one who steals the thoughts or writings of another.

The ensuing discourse, lest I chance to be traduced for a plagiary by him who has played the thief, was one of those that, by a worthy hand, were stolen from me. South.

Without invention, a painter is but a copier, and a poet but a plagiary of others; both are allowed sometimes to copy and translate. Dryden's Dufresnoy.

2. The crime of literary theft. Not used.

Plagiary had not its nativity with printing, but began when the paucity of books scarce wanted that invention. Brown.

pláguy adj. [from *plague*.] Vexatious; troublesome. A low word.

Of heats,
Add one more to the plaguy bill. Donne.

What perils do environ
The man that meddles with cold iron,
What plaguy mischiefs and mishaps
Do dog him still with after-claps. Hudibras.

plaid n.s. A striped or variegated cloth; an outer loose weed worn much by the highlanders in Scotland: there is a particular kind worn too by the women; but both these modes seem now nearly extirpated among them; the one by act of parliament, and the other by adopting the English dresses of the sex.†

pláinwork n.s. [*plain* and *work*.] Needlework as distinguished from embroidery; the common practice of sewing or making linen garments.

She went to plainwork, and to purling brooks. Pope.

plánet n.s. [*planeta*, Lat. πλαναω; *planette*, Fr.] Planets are the erratick or wandering stars, and which are not like the fixt ones always in the same position to one another: we now number the earth among the primary planets, because we know it moves round the sun, as Saturn, Jupiter, Mars, Venus and Mercury do, and that in a path or circle between Mars and Venus: and the moon is accounted among the secondary planets or satellites of the primary, since she moves round the earth: all the planets have, besides their motion round the sun, which makes their year, also a motion round their own axes, which makes their day; as the earth's revolving so makes our day and night: it is more than probable, that the diameters of all the planets are longer than their axes: we know 'tis so in our earth; and Flamsteed and Cassini found it to be so in Jupiter: Sir Isaac Newton asserts our earth's equatorial diameter to exceed the other about thirty-four miles; and indeed else the motion of the earth would make the sea rise so high at the equator, as to drown all the parts thereabouts. Harris.†

Barbarous villains! hath this lovely face
Rul'd like a wand'ring planet over me,
And could it not inforce them to relent. Shakesp.

And planets, planet-struck, real eclipse
Then suffer'd. Milton's Paradise Lost, b. x.

There are seven planets or errant stars in the lower orbs of heaven. Brown's Vulgar Errours, b. iv.

plant n.s. [*plant*, Fr. *planta*, Latin.]

1. Any thing produced from seed; any vegetable production.

What comes under this denomination, Ray has distributed under twenty-seven genders or kinds: **1.** The imperfect plants, which do either totally want both flower and seed, or else seem to do so. **2.** Plants producing either no flower at all, or an imperfect one, whose seed is so small as not to be discernible by the naked eye. **3.** Those whose seeds are not so small, as singly to be invisible, but yet have an imperfect or staminous flower; i.e. such a one, as is without the petala, having only the stamina and the perianthium. **4.** Such as have a compound flower, and emit a kind of white juice or milk when their stalks are cut off or their branches broken off. **5.** Such as have a compound flower of a discous figure, the seed pappous, or winged with downe, but emit no milk. **6.** The herbæ capitatæ, or such whose flower is composed of many small, long, fistulous or hollow flowers gathered round together in a round button or head, which is usually covered with a squamous or scaly coat. **7.** Such as have their leaves entire and undivided into jags. **8.** The corymbiferous plants, which have a compound discous flower, but the seeds have no downe adhering to them. **9.** Plants with a perfect flower, and having only one single seed belonging to each single flower. **10.** Such as have rough, hairy or bristly seeds. **11.** The umbelliferous plants, which have a pentapetalous flower, and belonging to each single flower are two seeds, lying naked and joining together; they are called umbelliferous, because the plant, with its branches and flowers, hath an head like a lady's umbrella:

> Such as have a broad flat seed almost of the figure of a leaf, which are encompassed round about with something like leaves.
>
> Such as have a longish seed, swelling out in the middle, and larger than the former.
>
> Such as have a shorter seed.
>
> Such as have a tuberose root.
>
> Such as have a wrinkled, channelated or striated seed.

12. The stellate plants, which are so called, because their leaves grow on their stalks at certain intervals or distances in the form of a radiant star: their flowers are really monopetalous, divided into four segments, which look like so many petala; and each flower is succeeded by two seeds at the bottom of it. **13.** The asperifolia, or rough leaved plants: they have their leaves placed alternately, or in no certain order on their stalks; they have a monopetalous flower cut or divided into five partitions, and after every flower there succeed usually four seeds. **14.** The suffrutices, or verticilate plants: their leaves grow by pairs on their stalks, one leaf right against another; their leaf is monopetalous, and usually in form of an helmet. **15.** Such as have naked seeds, more than four, succeeding their flowers, which therefore they call *polyspermæ plantæ semine nudo;* by naked seeds, they mean such as are not included in any seed pod. **16.** Bacciferous plants, or such as bear berries. **17.** Multisiliquous, or corniculate plants, or such as have, after each flower, many distinct, long, slender, and many times crooked cases or siliquae, in which their seed is contained, and which, when they are ripe, open themselves and let the seeds drop out. **18.** Such as have a monopetalous flower, either uniform or difform, and after each flower a peculiar seed-case containing the seed, and this often divided into many distinct cells. **19.** Such as have an uniform tetrapetalous flower, but bear these seeds in oblong siliquous cases. **20.** Vasculiferous plants, with a tetrapetalous flower, but often anomalous. **21.** Leguminous plants, or such as bear pulse, with a papilionaceous flower. **22.** Vasculiferous plants, with a pentapetalous flower; these have, besides the common calix, a peculiar case containing their seed, and their flower consisting of five leaves. **23.** Plants with a true bulbous root, which consists but of one round ball or head, out of whose lower part go many fibres to keep it firm in the earth: the plants of this kind come up but with one leaf; they have no foot stalk, and are long and slender: the seed vessels are divided into three partitions: their flower is sexapetalous. **24.** Such as have their fruits approaching to a bulbous form: these emit, at first coming up, but one leaf, and in leaves, flowers and roots resemble the true bulbous plant. **25.** Culmiferous plants, with a grassy leaf, are such as have a smooth hollow-jointed stalk, with one sharp-pointed leaf at each joint, encompassing the stalk, and set out without any foot stalk: their seed is contained within a chaffy husk. **26.** Plants with a grassy leaf, but not culmiferous, with an imperfect or staminous flower. **27.** Plants whose place of growth is uncertain and various, chiefly water plants.

> *Butchers and villains,*
> *How sweet a plant have you untimely cropt.*
> Shakesp.

Between the vegetable and sensitive province there are plant-animals and some kind of insects arising from vegetables, that seem to participate of both. Hale's Origin of Mankind.

The next species of life above the vegetable, is that of sense; wherewith some of those productions, which we call plant-animals, are endowed. Grew's Cosmol.

It continues to be the same plant, as long as it partakes of the same life, though that life be communicated to new particles of matter, vitally united to the living plant, in a like continued organization, conformable to that sort of plants. Locke.

> *Once I was skill'd in ev'ry herb that grew,*
> *And ev'ry plant that drinks the morning dew.*
> Pope.

2. A sapling.

A man haunts the forest, that abuses our young plants with carving Rosalind on their barks. Shakesp. As You like it.

> *Take a plant of stubborn oak,*
> *And labour him with many a stubborn stroke.*
> Dryden.

3. [*Planta*, Lat.] The sole of the foot. Ainsworth.

plástick adj. [πλαστικος.] Having the power to give form.

> *Benign creator! let thy plastick hand*
> *Dispose its own effect.* Prior.

There is not any thing strange in the production of the said formed metals, nor other plastick virtue concerned in shaping them into those figures, than merely the configuration of the particles. Woodward's Natural History.

play n.s.

1. Action not imposed; not work; dismission from work.

2. Amusement; sport.

> *My dearling and my joy;*
> *For love of me leave off this dreadful play.*
> Fa. Queen.

Two gentle fawns at play. Milton.

3. A drama; a comedy or tragedy, or any thing in which characters are represented by dialogue and action.

> *Only they,*
> *That come to hear a merry play,*
> *Will be deceiv'd.* Shakesp. Henry VIII.

A play ought to be a just image of human nature, representing its humours and the changes of fortune to which it is subject, for the delight and instruction of mankind. Dryden.

Visits, plays and powder'd beaux. Swift.

4. Game; practice of gaming; contest at a game.

> *I will play no more, my mind's not on 't;*
> *I did never win of you,*
> *Nor shall not when my fancy's on my play.*
> Shakesp.

5. Practice in any contest.

When they can make nothing else on 't, they find it the best of their play to put it off with a jest. L'Estrange.

He was resolved not to speak distinctly, knowing his best play to be in the dark, and that all his safety lay in the confusion of his talk. Tillotson.

In arguing the opponent uses comprehensive and equivocal terms, to involve his adversary in the doubtfulness of his expression, and therefore the answer on his side makes it his play to distinguish as much as he can. Locke.

Bull's friends advised to gentler methods with the young lord; but John naturally lov'd rough play. Arbuthnot.

6. Action; employment; office.

The senseless plea of right by providence Can last no longer than the present sway; But justifies the next who comes in play. Dryden.

7. Practice; action; manner of acting.

Determinining, as after I knew, in secret manner, not to be far from the place where we appointed to meet, to prevent any foul play that might be offered unto me. Sidney, b. ii.

8. Act of touching an instrument.

9. Irregular and wanton motion.

10. A state of agitation or ventilation.

Many have been sav'd, and many may, Who never heard this question brought in play. Dryden.

11. Room for motion.

The joints are let exactly into one another, that they have no play between them, lest they shake upwards or downwards. Moxon's Mechanical Exercises.

12. Liberty of acting; swing.

Should a writer give the full play to his mirth, without regard to decency, he might please readers; but must be a very ill man, if he could please himself. Addison's Freeholder.

plebeían n.s. [*plebeïen*, Fr. *plebeius*, Lat.] One of the lower people.

Let him Hoist thee up to the shouting plebeians. Shakespeare.

You're plebeians, if they be senators. Shakespeare.

Upon the least intervals of peace, the quarrels between the nobles and the plebeians would revive. Swift.

plédget n.s. [*plagghe*, Dutch.] A small mass of lint.

I applied a pledget of basilicon. Wiseman's Surgery.

pléonasm n.s. [*pleonasme*, Fr. *pleonasmus*, Lat.] A figure of rhetorick, by which more words are used than are necessary.

pleurisy n.s. [πλευριτις; *pleuresie*, Fr. *pleuritis*, Lat.] Pleurisy is an inflammation of the pleura, though it is hardly distinguishable from an inflammation of any other part of the breast, which are all from the same cause, a stagnated blood; and are to be remedied by evacuation, suppuration or expectoration, or all together. Quincy.

plícature, plicátion n.s. [*plicatura*, from *plico*, Lat.] Fold; double. Plication is used somewhere in Clarissa.

plum n.s. [*plum*, *plumtreow*, Sax. *blumme*, Danish. A custom has prevailed of writing *plumb*, but improperly.]

1. A fruit.

The flower consists of five leaves, which are placed in a circular order, and expand in form of a rose, from whose flower-cup rises the pointal, which afterwards becomes an oval or globular fruit, having a soft fleshy pulp, surrounding an hard oblong stone, for the most part pointed; to which should be added, the footstalks are long and slender, and have but a single fruit upon each: the species are; 1. The jeanhâtive, or white primordian. 2. The early black damask, commonly called the Morocco plum. 3. The little black damask plum. 4. The great damask violet of Tours. 5. The Orleans plum. 6. The Fotheringham plum. 7. The Perdrigon plum. 8. The violet Perdrigon plum. 9. The white Perdrigon plum. 10. The red imperial plum, sometimes called the red bonum magnum. 11. The white imperial bonum magnum; white Holland or Mogul plum. 12. The Cheston plum. 13. The apricot plum. 14. The maitre claude. 15. La roche-courbon, or diaper rouge; the red diaper plum. 16. Queen Claudia. 17. Myrobalan plum. 18. The green gage plum. 19. The cloth of gold plum. 20. St. Catharine plum. 21. The royal plum. 22. La mirabelle. 23. The Brignole plum. 24. The empress. 25. The monsieur plum: this is sometimes called the Wentworth plum, both resembling the bonum magnum. 26. The cherry plum. 27. The white pear plum. 28. The muscle plum. 29. The St. Julian plum. 30. The black bullace-tree plum. 31. The white bullace-tree plum. 32. The black thorn or sloe-tree plum. Miller.

Philosophers in vain enquired, whether the summum bonum consisted in riches, bodily delights, virtue or contemplation: they might as reasonably have disputed, whether the best relish were in apples, plums or nuts. Locke.

2. Raisin; grape dried in the sun.

I will dance, and eat plums at your wedding. Shakesp.

3. [In the cant of the city.] The sum of one hundred thousand pounds.

By the present edict, many a man in France will swell into a plum, who fell several thousand pounds short of it the day before. Addison.

The miser must make up his plum,
And dares not touch the hoarded sum. Prior.

By fair dealing John had acquired some plums, which he might have kept, had it not been for his law-suit. Arbuth.

Ask you,
Why she and Sappho raise that monstrous sum?
Alas! they fear a man will cost a plum. Pope.

4. A kind of play, called how many plums for a penny. Ains.

plúmber n.s. [*plombier*, Fr.] One who works upon lead. Commonly written and pronounced plummer.

plúmipede n.s. [*pluma* and *pes*, Lat.] A fowl that has feathers on the foot. Dict.

plúnket n.s. A kind of blue colour. Ainsworth.

plúralist n.s. [*pluraliste*, Fr. from *plural*.] One that holds more ecclesiastical benefices than one with cure of souls.

If the pluralists would do their best to suppress curates, their number might be so retrenched, that they would not be in the least formidable. Collier on Pride.

plúvial, plúvious adj. [from *pluvia*, Latin.] Rainy; relating to rain.

The fungous parcels about the wicks of candles only signifieth a moist and pluvious air about them. Brown.

pneumatólogy n.s. [πνευματολογια.] The doctrine of spiritual existence.

pócketbook n.s. [*pocket* and *book*.] A paper book carried in the pocket for hasty notes.

Licinius let out the offals of his meat to interest, and kept a register of such debtors in his pocketbook. Arbuthnot.

Note down the matters of doubt in some pocketbook, and take the first opportunity to get them resolved. Watts.

póckhole n.s. [*pock* and *hole*.] Pit or scar made by the smallpox.

Are these but warts and pockholes in the face O' th' earth? Donne.

póem n.s. [*poema*, Lat. ποιημα.] The work of a poet; a metrical composition.

A poem is not alone any work, or composition of the poets in many or few verses; but even one alone verse sometimes makes a perfect poem. Benj. Johnson.

The lady Anne of Bretaigne, passing through the presence of France, and espying Chartier, a famous poet, fast asleep, kissing him, said, we must honour the mouth whence so many golden poems have proceeded. Peacham on Poetry.

To you the promis'd poem I will pay. Dryden.

póesy n.s. [*poesie*, Fr. *poesis*, Lat. ποιησις.]

1. The art of writing poems.

*A poem is the work of the poet; poesy is
his skill or craft of making; the very fiction
itself, the reason or form of the work.*
Benj. Johnson.

> *How far have we
> Prophan'd thy heav'nly gift of poesy?
> Made prostitute and profligate the muse,
> Whose harmony was first ordain'd above
> For tongues of angels.* Dryden.

2. Poem; metrical composition; poetry.

Musick and poesy use to quicken you.
Shakesp.

*There is an hymn, for they have excellent
poesy; the subject is always the praises of
Adam, Noah and Abraham, concluding ever
with a thanksgiving for the nativity of our
Saviour.* Bacon's New Atlantis.

*They apprehend a veritable history in an
emblem or piece of christian poesy.* Brown's
Vulgar Errours.

3. A short conceit engraved on a ring or
other thing.

*A paltry ring, whose poesy was,
For all the world like cutler's poetry
Upon a knife; love me, and leave me not.*
Shakesp.

póet n.s. [*poete*, Fr. *poeta*, Lat. ποιητης.]
An inventor; an author of fiction; a writer of
poems; one who writes in measure.

*The poet's eye in a fine frenzy rowling,
Doth glance from heav'n to earth, from
    earth to heav'n;
And, as imagination bodies forth
The forms of things unknown, the poet's pen
Turns them to shape, and gives to ev'ry thing
A local habitation and a name.* Shakesp.

*Our poet ape, who would be thought the chief,
His works become the frippery of wit,
From brocage he is grown so bold a thief,
While we the robb'd despise, and pity it.*
B. Johnson.

> *'Tis not vain or fabulous
> What the sage poets taught by the heav'nly muse
> Story'd of old in high immortal verse,
> Of dire chimeras and enchanted isles.* Milton.

*A poet is a maker, as the word signifies; and
he who cannot make, that is invent, hath his
name for nothing.* Dryden.

poetáster n.s. [Latin.] A vile petty poet.

*Let no poetaster command or intreat
Another extempore verses to make.*
Benj. Johnson.

*Begin not as th' old poetaster did,
Troy's famous war, and Priam's fate I sing.*
Roscommon.

*Horace hath exposed those trifling poetasters,
that spend themselves in glaring descriptions,
and sewing here and there some cloth of gold
on their sackcloth.* Felton.

póetry n.s. [ποιητρια; from *poet*.]

1. Metrical composition; the art or practice
of writing poems.†

*Strike the best invention dead,
Till baffled poetry hangs down the head.*
Cleaveland.

*Although in poetry it be necessary that the
unities of time, place and action should be
explained, there is still something that gives
a greatness of mind to the reader, which few
of the criticks have considered.* Addison's
Spectator, Nº 409.

2. Poems; poetical pieces.

> *She taketh most delight
> In musick, instruments and poetry.* Shakesp.

pólecat n.s. [*Pole* or *Polish* cat, because they
abound in Poland.] The fitchew; a stinking
animal.

Polecats? there are fairer things than polecats.
Shakesp.

*Out of my door, you witch! you hag, you
polecat! out, out, out; I'll conjure you.*
Shakesp. Merry Wives of Windsor.

*She, at a pin in the wall, hung like a polecat
in a warren, to amuse them.* L'Estrange.

> *How should he, harmless youth,
> Who kill'd but polecats, learn to murder men.*
Gay.

pólice n.s. [French.] The regulation and
government of a city or country, so far as
regards the inhabitants.†

to pólish v.a. [*polio*, Lat. *polir*, Fr.]

1. To smooth; to brighten by attrition; to gloss.

He setteth to finish his work, and polisheth it perfectly. Eccl.

Pygmalion, with fatal art,
Polish'd the form that stung his heart.
Granvil.

2. To make elegant of manners.

Studious they appear
Of arts that polish life, inventors rare.
Milton.

Bid soft science polish Britain's heroes. Irene.

políte adj. [*politus*, Latin.]

1. Glossy; smooth.

Some of them are diaphanous, shining and polite; others not polite, but as if powder'd over with fine iron dust. Woodw.

If any sort of rays, falling on the polite surface of any pellucid medium, be reflected back, the fits of easy reflexion, which they have at the point of reflexion, shall still continue to return. Newton's Opticks.

The edges of the sand holes, being worn away, there are left all over the glass a numberless company of very little convex polite risings like waves. Newton's Opticks.

2. Elegant of manners.

A nymph of quality admires our knight,
He marries, bows at court, and grows polite.
Pope.

politicáster n.s. A petty ignorant pretender to politicks.

There are quacks of all sorts; as bullies, pedants, hypocrites, empiricks, law jobbers and politicasters. L'Estrange.

politícian n.s. [*politicien*, Fr.]

1. One versed in the arts of government; one skilled in politicks.

Get thee glass eyes,
And, like a scurvy politician, seem
To see things thou dost not. Shakesp.
King Lear.

And 't be any way, it must be with valour; for policy I hate: I had as lief be a Brownist as a politician. Shakespeare.

Although I may seem less a politician to men, yet I need no secret distinctions nor evasions before God. King Charles.

While emp'rick politicians use deceit,
Hide what they give, and cure but by a cheat,
You boldly show that skill, which they pretend,
And work by means as noble as your end.
Dryden.

Coffee, which makes the politician wise,
And see through all things with his half-
*   shut eyes,*
Sent up in vapours to the baron's brain
New stratagems, the radiant lock to gain.
Pope.

2. A man of artifice; one of deep contrivance.

Your ill-meaning politician lords,
Under pretence of bridal friends and guests,
Appointed to await me thirty spies. Milton.

If a man succeeds in any attempt, though undertook with never so much rashness, his success shall vouch him a politician, and good luck shall pass for deep contrivance; for give any one fortune, and he shall be thought a wise man. South.

póliticks n.s. [*politique*, Fr. πολιτικη.] The science of government; the art or practice of administring publick affairs.

Be pleas'd your politicks to spare,
I'm old enough, and can myself take care.
Dryden.

It would be an everlasting reproach to politicks, should such men overturn an establishment formed by the wisest laws, and supported by the ablest heads. Addison.

Of crooked counsels and dark politicks. Pope.

to pollúte v.a. [*polluo*, Lat. *polluer*, Fr.]

1. To make unclean, in a religious sense; to defile.

Hot and peevish vows
Are polluted offerings, more abhorr'd
Than spotted livers in the sacrifice. Shakesp.

2. To taint with guilt.

She woos the gentle air,
To hide her guilty front with innocent snow,
And on her naked shame,
Pollute with sinful blame,
The saintly veil of maiden white to throw.
Milton.

3. To corrupt by mixtures of ill.

Envy you my praise, and would destroy
With grief my pleasures, and pollute my joy?
Dryden.

4. Milton uses this word in an uncommon construction.

Polluted from the end of his creation. Milton.

polygraphy n.s. [πολυς and γραφη; *polygraphie*, Fr.] The art of writing in several unusual manners or cyphers; as also decyphering the same. Dict.

polymathy n.s. [πολυς and μανθανω.] The knowledge of many arts and sciences; also an acquaintance with many different subjects. Dict.

polythéism n.s. [πολυς and θεος; *polytheïsme*, Fr.] The doctrine of plurality of gods.

The first author of polytheism, Orpheus, did plainly assert one supreme God. Stillingfleet.

pómpous adj. [*pompeux*, Fr.] Splendid; magnificent; grand.

What flatt'ring scenes our wand'ring fancy
  wrought,
Rome's pompous glories rising to our thought.
Pope.

An inscription in the ancient way,
plain, pompous, yet modest, will be best.
Atterbury to Pope.

pópery n.s. [from *pope*.] The religion of the church of Rome.

Popery for corruptions in doctrine and discipline, I look upon to be the most absurd system of christianity. Swift.

pópgun n.s. [*pop* and *gun*.] A gun with which children play, that only makes a noise.

Life is not weak enough to be destroyed by this popgun artillery of tea and coffee. Cheyne.

pórpoise, pórpus n.s. [*pore poisson*, Fr.] The sea-hog.

Amphibious animals link the terrestrial and aquatick together; seals live at land and at sea, and porpoises have the warm blood and entrails of a hog. Locke.

Parch'd with unextinguish'd thirst,
Small beer I guzzle till I burst;
And then I drag a bloated corpus
Swell'd with a dropsy like a porpus. Swift.

pósset n.s. [*posca*, Lat.] Milk curdled with wine or any acid.

We'll have a posset at the latter end of a seacoal fire. Shak.

In came the bridemaids with the posset,
The bridegroom eat in spight. Suckling.

I allowed him medicated broths, posset ale and pearl julep. Wiseman's Surgery.

A sparing diet did her health assure;
Or sick, a pepper posset was her cure. Dryden.

The cure of the stone consists in vomiting with posset drink, in which althea roots are boiled. Floyer on the Humours.

Increase the milk when it is diminished by the too great use of flesh meats, by gruels and posset drink. Arbuthnot.

posturemáster n.s. [*posture* and *master*.] One who teaches or practises artificial contortions of the body.

When the students have accomplished themselves in this part, they are to be delivered into the hands of a kind of posturemaster. Spectator, Nº 305.

potáto n.s. [I suppose an American word.] An esculent root.

The red and white potatoes are the most common esculent roots now in use, and were originally brought from Virginia into Europe. Miller.

On choicest melons and sweet grapes they dine,
And with potatoes fat their wanton swine.
Waller.

The families of farmers live in filth and nastiness upon butter-milk and potatoes. Swift.

Leek to the Welch, to Dutchmen butter's dear,
Of Irish swains potatoe is the chear;
Oats for their feasts the Scottish shepherds grind,
Sweet turnips are the food of Blouzelind;
While she loves turnips, butter I'll despise,
Nor leeks, nor oatmeal, nor potatoe prize.
Gay.

póttle n.s. [from *pot.*] Liquid measure containing four pints.

He drinks you with facility your Dane dead drunk, ere the next pottle can be filled. Shakesp. Othello.

Roderigo hath to-night carous'd
Potations pottle deep. Shakesp.

The oracle of Apollo
Here speaks out of his pottle,
Or the Tripos his tower bottle.
Benj. Johnson.

potváliant adj. [*pot* and *valiant.*] Heated with courage by strong drink.

poúpicts n.s. In cookery, a mess of victuals made of veal stakes and slices of bacon. Bailey.

powdering-tub n.s. [*powder* and *tub.*]

1. The vessel in which meat is salted.

When we view those large bodies of oxen, what can we better conceit them to be, than so many living and walking powdering-tubs, and that they have animam salis. More.

2. The place in which an infected lecher is physicked to preserve him from putrefaction.

To the spital go,
And from the powd'ring-tub of infamy
Fetch forth the lazar kite Doll Tearsheet.
Shakesp.

pragmátick, pragmátical adj. [πραγματα; *pragmatique,* Fr.] Meddling; impertinently busy; assuming business without leave or invitation.

No sham so gross, but it will pass upon a weak man that is pragmatical and inquisitive. L'Estrange.

Common estimation puts an ill character upon pragmatick meddling people. Government of the Tongue.

He understands no more of his own affairs, than a child; he has got a sort of a pragmatical silly jade of a wife, that pretends to take him out of my hands. Arbuthnot.

The fellow grew so pragmatical, that he took upon him the government of my whole family. Arbuthnot.

Such a backwardness there was among good men to engage with an usurping people, and pragmatical ambitious orators. Swift.

They are pragmatical enough to stand on the watch tower, but who assigned them the post? Swift.

to prate v.n. [*praten,* Dutch.] To talk carelessly and without weight; to chatter; to tattle; to be loquacious; to prattle.

His knowledge or skill is in prating too much. Tusser.

Behold me, which owe
A moiety of the throne, here standing
To prate and talk for life and honour, 'fore
Who please to hear. Shakesp. Winter's Tale.

This starved justice hath prated to me of the wildness of his youth, and the feats he hath done about Turnbal-street; and every third word a lie. Shakesp. Henry IV. p. ii.

After Flammock and the blacksmith had, by joint and several pratings, found tokens of consent in the multitude, they offered themselves to lead them. Bacon's Henry VII.

Oh listen with attentive sight
To what my prating eyes indite! Cleaveland.

What nonsense would the fool thy master prate,
When thou, his knave, can'st talk at such
a rate. Dryden.

She first did wit's prerogative remove,
And made a fool presume to prate of love.
Dryden.

This is the way of the world; the deaf will prate of discords in musick. Watts.

to prefígure v.a. [*præ* and *figuro*, Lat.] To exhibit by antecedent representation.

What the Old Testament hath, the very same the New containeth; but that which lieth there, as under a shadow, is here brought forth into the open sun; things there prefigured, are here performed. Hooker.

Such piety, so chaste use of God's day, That what we turn to feast, she turn'd to pray, And did prefigure here in devout taste, The rest of her high sabbath, which shall last. Donne.

If shame superadded to loss, and both met together, as the sinners portion here, perfectly prefiguring the two saddest ingredients in hell, deprivation of the blissful vision, and confusion of face, cannot prove efficacious to the mortifying of vice, the church doth give over the patient. Hammond.

préjudice n.s. [*prejudice*, Fr. *prejudicium*, Lat.]

1. Prepossession; judgment formed beforehand without examination. It is used for prepossession in favour of any thing or against it. It is sometimes used with *to* before that which the prejudice is against, but not properly.

The king himself frequently considered more the person who spoke, as he was in his prejudice, than the counsel itself that was given. Clarendon, b. viii.

My comfort is, that their manifest prejudice to my cause will render their judgment of less authority. Dryden.

There is an unaccountable prejudice to projectors of all kinds, for which reason, when I talk of practising to fly, silly people think me an owl for my pains. Addison.

2. Mischief; detriment; hurt; injury. This sense is only accidental or consequential; a bad thing being called a prejudice, only because prejudice is commonly a bad thing, and is not derived from the original or etymology of the word:

it were therefore better to use it less; perhaps prejudice ought never to be applied to any mischief, which does not imply some partiality or prepossession. In some of the following examples its impropriety will be discovered.

I have not spake one the least word, That might be prejudice of her present state, Or touch of her good person. Shakesp. Henry VIII.

England and France might, through their amity, Breed him some prejudice; for from this league Peep'd harms that menac'd him. Shakesp. Henry VIII.

Factions carried too high and too violently, is a sign of weakness in princes, and much to the prejudice of their authority and business. Bacon.

How plain this abuse is, and what prejudice it does to the understanding of the sacred scriptures. Locke.

A prince of this character will instruct us by his example, to fix the unsteadiness of our politicks; or by his conduct hinder it from doing us any prejudice. Addison.

presbytérian adj. [πρεσβυτερος.] Consisting of elders; a term for a modern form of ecclesiastical government.

Chiefly was urged the abolition of episcopal, and the establishing of presbyterian government. King Charles.

prescríption n.s. [*prescription*, Fr. *præscriptio*, Lat. from *præscribo*, Lat.]

1. Rules produced and authorised by long custom; custom continued till it has the force of law.

You tell a pedigree Of threescore and two years, a silly time To make prescription for a kingdom's worth. Shakesp.

Use such as have prevailed before in things you have employed them; for that breeds confidence, and they will strive to maintain their prescription. Bacon's Essays.

It will be found a work of no small difficulty, to dispossess a vice from that heart, where long possession begins to plead prescription. South's Sermons.

Our poet bade us hope this grace to find, To whom by long prescription you are kind. Dryden.

The Lucquese plead prescription, for hunting in one of the duke's forests, that lies upon their frontiers. Addison.

2. Medical receipt.

My father left me some prescriptions Of rare and prov'd effects; such as his reading And manifest experience had collected For general sov'reignty. Shakesp.

Approving of my obstinacy against all common prescriptions, he asked me, whether I had never heard the Indian way of curing the gout by moxa. Temple.

préssgang n.s. [*press* and *gang*.] A crew that strols about the streets to force men into naval service.

préssman n.s. [*press* and *man*.]

1. One who forces another into service; one who forces away.

One only path to all; by which the pressmen came. Chap.

2. One who makes the impression of print by the press: distinct from the compositor, who ranges the types.

préssmoney n.s. [*press* and *money*.] Money given to a soldier when he is taken or forced into the service.

Here Peascod, take my pouch, 'tis all I own, 'Tis my pressmoney.—Can this silver fail? Gay.

prestigátion n.s. [*prestigatio*, Lat.] A deceiving; a juggling; a playing legerdemain. Dict.

présto n.s. [*presto*, Italian.] Quick; at once. A word used by those that show legerdemain.

Presto! begone! 'tis here again; There's ev'ry piece as big as ten. Swift.

preténder n.s. [from *pretend*.] One who lays claim to any thing.

The prize was disputed only till you were seen; now all pretenders have withdrawn their claims. Dryden.

Whatever victories the several pretenders to the empire obtained over one another, they are recorded on coins without the least reflection. Addison on Ancient Medals.

The numerous pretenders to places would never have been kept in order, if expectation had been cut off. Swift.

To just contempt ye vain pretenders fall, The people's fable and the scorn of all. Pope.

Pretenders to philosophy or good sense grow fond of this sort of learning. Watts.

priápism n.s. [*priapismus*, Lat. *priapisme*, Fr.] A preternatural tension.

Lust causeth a flagrancy in the eyes and priapism. Bacon.

The person every night has a priapism in his sleep. Floyer.

pride n.s. [*prit* or *pryd*, Saxon.]

1. Inordinate and unreasonable self-esteem.

I can see his pride Peep through each part of him. Shakesp. Henry VIII.

Pride hath no other glass To shew itself, but pride; for supple knees Feed arrogance, and are the proud man's fees. Shakesp.

He his wonted pride soon recollects. Milton.

Vain aims, inordinate desires Blown up with high conceits engend'ring pride. Milton.

2. Insolence; rude treatment of others; insolent exultation.

That witch Hath wrought this hellish mischief unawares; That hardly we escap'd the pride of France. Shakesp.

They undergo This annual humbling certain number'd days, To dash their pride and joy for man seduc'd. Milton.

Wantonness and pride
Raise out of friendship, hostile deeds in peace.
Milton.

3. Dignity of manner; loftiness of air.

4. Generous elation of heart.

The honest pride of conscious virtue. Smith.

5. Elevation; dignity.

A falcon, tow'ring in her pride of place,
Was by a mousing owl hawkt at and kill'd.
Shakesp.

6. Ornament; show; decoration.

Whose lofty trees, yclad with summer's pride,
Did spread so broad, that heavens light did
        hide. F. Qu.

    Smallest lineaments exact,
In all the liveries deck'd of summer's pride.
Milton.

    Be his this sword,
Whose ivory sheath, inwrought with
        curious pride,
Adds graceful terror to the wearer's side.
Pope.

7. Splendour; ostentation.

In this array the war of either side,
Through Athens pass'd with military pride.
Dryden.

8. The state of a female beast soliciting
    the male.

It is impossible you should see this,
Were they as salt as wolves in pride. Shakesp.

priestcraft n.s. [*priest* and *craft*.] Religious
frauds; management of wicked priests to
gain power.

Puzzle has half a dozen common-place
topicks; though the debate be about Doway,
his discourse runs upon bigotry and
priestcraft. Spectator.

From priestcraft happily set free,
Lo! ev'ry finish'd son returns to thee. Pope.

priestess n.s. [from *priest*.] A woman who
officiated in heathen rites.

Then too, our mighty sire, thou stood'st disarm'd,
When thy rapt soul the lovely priestess charm'd,
That Rome's high founder bore. Addison.

These two, being the sons of a lady who was
priestess to Juno, drew their mother's chariot
to the temple. Spectator.

She as priestess knows the rites,
Wherein the God of earth delights.
Swift's Miscel.

Th' inferior priestess, at her altar's side,
Trembling, begins the sacred rites of pride.
Pope.

priestridden adj. [*priest* and *ridden*.]
Managed or governed by priests.

Such a cant of high-church and persecution,
and being priestridden. Swift.

prig n.s. [A cant word derived perhaps
from *prick*, as he *pricks* up, he is *pert*; or from
prickeared, an epithet of reproach bestowed
upon the presbyterian teachers.] A pert,
conceited, saucy, pragmatical, little fellow.

The little man concluded, with calling
monsieur Mesnager an insignificant prig.
Spectator, Nº 482.

There have I seen some active prig,
To shew his parts, bestride a twig.
Swift's Miscel.

primero n.s. [Spanish.] A game at cards.

    I left him at primero
With the duke of Suffolk. Shakesp.
Henry VIII.

to prink v.n. [*pronken*, Dutch.] To prank; to
deck for show.

Hold a good wager she was every day longer
prinking in the glass than you was. Art of
Tormenting.

to print v.a. [*imprimer, empreint*, Fr.]

1. To mark by pressing any thing upon
    another.

On his fiery steed betimes he rode,
That scarcely prints the turf on which he trod.
Dryden.

2. To impress any thing, so as to leave
    its form.

3. To form by impression.

Your mother was most true to wedlock, prince,
For she did print your royal father off,
Conceiving you. Shakesp. Winter's Tale.

*Ye shall not make any cuttings in your flesh
for the dead, nor print any marks upon you.*
Lev. ix. 28.

*Perhaps some footsteps printed in the clay,
Will to my love direct your wand'ring way.*
Roscommon.

*His royal bounty brought its own reward;
And in their minds so deep did print the sense,
That if their ruins sadly they regard,
'Tis but with fear.* Dryden.

4. To impress words or make books, not
   by the pen, but the press.

*Thou hast caused printing to be used; and,
contrary to the king, his crown and dignity,
built a paper-mill.* Shakesp.

*This nonsense got in by a mistake of the stage
editors, who printed from the piecemeal
written parts.* Pope.

*Is it probable, that a promiscuous jumble of
printing letter should often fall into a method,
which should stamp on paper a coherent
discourse.* Locke.

*As soon as he begins to spell, pictures of
animals should be got him, with the printed
names to them.* Locke.

prism n.s. [*prisme*, Fr. πρισμα.] A prism of
glass is a glass bounded with two equal and
parallel triangular ends, and three plain and
well polished sides, which meet in three
parallel lines, running from the three angles
of one end, to the three angles of the other
end. Newton's Opticks.

*Here, aweful Newton, the dissolving clouds
Form fronting, on the sun, thy showery prism.*
Thomson.

prisonbase n.s. A kind of rural play,
commonly called prisonbars.

*The spachies of the court play every friday
at ciocho di canni, which is no other than
prisonbase upon horseback, hiting one another
with darts, as the others do with their hands.*
Sandys's Travels.

privateer n.s. [from *private*.] A ship fitted
out by private men to plunder enemies.

*He is at no charge for a fleet, further than
providing privateers, wherewith his subjects
carry on a pyratical war at their own expence.*
Swift's Miscellanies.

privy n.s. Place of retirement; necessary
house.

  *Your fancy
Would still the same ideas give ye,
As when you spy'd her on the privy.* Swift.

prizefighter n.s. [*prize* and *fighter*.] One
that fights publickly for a reward.

*Martin and Crambe engaged like
prizefighters.* Arb. and Po.

In Fig the prizefighter by day delight.
Bramston.

probóscis n.s. [*proboscis*, Lat.] A snout; the
trunk of an elephant; but it is used also for
the same part in every creature, that bears
any resemblance thereunto.

*The elephant wreath'd to make them sport
His lithe proboscis.* Milton.

procúress n.s. [from *procure*.] A bawd.

*I saw the most artful procuress in town,
seducing a young girl.* Spectator.

pródigy n.s. [*prodige*, Fr. *prodigium*, Lat.]

1. Any thing out of the ordinary process of
   nature, from which omens are drawn;
   portent.

*Be no more an exhal'd meteor,
A prodigy of fear, and a portent
Of broached mischief, to the unborn times.*
Shakesp.

*The party opposite to our settlement, seem to
be driven out of all human methods, and are
reduced to the poor comfort of prodigies and
old womens fables.* Addison.

2. Monster.

*Most of mankind, through their own
sluggishness, become nature's prodigies, not
her children.* Benj. Johnson.

3. Any thing astonishing for good or bad.

They would seem prodigies of learning.
Spectator.

próditor n.s. [Latin.] A traytor. Not in use.

Piel'd priest, dost thou command me be shut out?
—I do, thou most usurping proditor.
Shakesp.

proféssor n.s. [*professeur*, Fr. from *profess.*]

1. One who declares himself of any
opinion or party.

When the holiness of the professors of religion
is decayed you may doubt the springing up of
a new sect. Bacon's Essays.

2. One who publickly practises or teaches
an art.

Professors in most sciences, are generally the
worst qualified to explain their meanings
to those who are not of their tribes. Swift.

3. One who is visibly religious.

Ordinary illiterate people, who were
professors, that shewed a concern for religion,
seemed much conversant in St. Paul's Epistles.
Locke.

prófligate n.s. An abandoned shameless
wretch.

It is pleasant to see a notorious profligate
seized with a concern for his religion, and
converting his spleen into zeal. Add.

I have heard a profligate offer much stronger
arguments against paying his debts, than ever
he was known to do against christianity;
because he happened to be closer pressed by the
bailiff than the parson. Swift's Miscellanies.

How could such a profligate as Antony, or
a boy of eighteen, like Octavius, ever dare to
dream of giving the law to such an empire
and people. Swift.

to prog v.n.

1. To rob; to steal.

2. To shift meanly for provisions. A low
word.

She went out progging for provisions as
before. L'Estr.

prognóstick n.s. [from the adj.]

1. The skill of foretelling diseases or the
event of diseases.

Hippocrates's prognostick is generally true,
that it is very hard to resolve a small
apoplexy. Arbuthnot.

2. A prediction.

Though your prognosticks run too fast,
They must be verify'd at last. Swift.

3. A token forerunning.

Whatsoever you are or shall be, has been but
an easy prognostick from what you were.
South.

    Careful observers
By sure prognosticks may foretell a show'r.
Swift.

projéctor n.s. [from *project.*]

1. One who forms schemes or designs.

The following comes from a projector, a
correspondent as diverting as a traveller; his
subject having the same grace of novelty to
recommend it. Addison.

Among all the projectors in this attempt, none
have met with so general a success, as they
who apply themselves to soften the rigour of
the precept. Rogers's Sermons.

2. One who forms wild impracticable
schemes.

Chymists, and other projectors, propose to
themselves things utterly impracticable.
L'Estrange.

Astrologers that future fates foreshew,
Projectors, quacks, and lawyers not a few.
Pope.

proletárian adj. Mean; wretched; vile;
vulgar.

Like speculators should foresee,
From pharos of authority,
Portended mischiefs farther than
Low proletarian tything-men. Hudibras, p. i.

promíscuous adj. [*promiscuus*, Lat.]
Mingled; confused; undistinguished.

Glory he requires, and glory he receives,
Promiscuous from all nations. Milton's
Par. Lost.

Promiscuous love by marriage was restrain'd.
Roscom.

In rush'd at once a rude promiscuous crowd;
The guards, and then each other overbear,
And in a moment throng the theatre.
Dryden.

No man, that considers the promiscuous
dispensations of God's providence in this
world, can think it unreasonable to conclude,
that after this life good men shall be rewarded,
and sinners punished. Tillotson's Sermons.

The earth was formed out of that promiscuous
mass of sand, earth, shells, subsiding from the
water. Woodward.

Clubs, diamonds, hearts, in wild disorder seen,
With throngs promiscuous strow the level
green. Pope.

A wild, where weeds and flow'rs promiscuous
shoot. Pope.

próperty n.s. [from *proper.*]

1. Peculiar quality.

What special property or quality is that,
which being no where found but in sermons,
maketh them effectual to save souls?
Hooker, b. v. s. 22.

A secondary essential mode, is any attribute
of a thing, which is not of primary
consideration, and is called a property. Watts.

2. Quality; disposition.

'Tis conviction, not force, that must induce
assent; and sure the logick of a conquering
sword has no great property that way; silence
it may, but convince it cannot. D. of Piet.

It is the property of an old sinner to find
delight in reviewing his own villanies
in others. South's Sermons.

3. Right of possession.

Some have been deceived into an opinion,
that the inheritance of rule over men, and
property in things, sprung from the same
original, and were to descend by the same
rules. Locke.

Property, whose original is from the right a
man has to use any of the inferior creatures,
for subsistence and comfort, is for the sole
advantage of the proprietor, so that he may
even destroy the thing that he has property in.
Locke.

4. Possession held in one's own right.

For numerous blessings yearly show'r'd,
And property with plenty crown'd,
Accept our pious praise. Dryden.

5. The thing possessed.

'Tis a thing impossible
I should love thee but as a property. Shakesp.

No wonder such men are true to a
government, where liberty runs so high,
where property is so well secured. Swift.

6. Nearness or right. I know not which
is the sense in the following lines.

Here I disclaim all my paternal care,
Propinquity, and property of blood,
And as a stranger to my heart and me,
Hold thee. Shakesp. King Lear.

7. Something useful; an appendage.

I will draw a bill of properties, such as our
play wants. Shakesp. Midsummer's
Night's Dream.

The purple garments raise the lawyer's fees,
High pomp and state are useful properties.
Dryden.

Greenfield was the name of the property man
in that time, who furnished implements for
the actors. Pope.

8. Property for propriety. Any thing
peculiarly adapted.

Our poets excel in grandity and gravity,
smoothness and property, in quickness and
briefness. Camden.

próphet n.s. [*prophete*, Fr. προφητης.]

1. One who tells future events; a predicter;
a foreteller.

Ev'ry flower
Did as a prophet weep what it foresaw,
In Hector's wrath. Shakesp. Troilus
and Cressida.

Jesters oft prove prophets. Shakesp.
King Lear.

O prophet of glad tidings! finisher
Of utmost hope! Milton.

He lov'd so fast,
As if he fear'd each day wou'd be her last;
Too true a prophet to foresee the fate,
That should so soon divide their happy state.
Dryden.

God, when he makes the prophet, does not
unmake the man. Locke.

2. One of the sacred writers empowered by
   God to foretell futurity.

His champions are the prophets and apostles.
Shakesp.

prophyláctick adj. [προφυλακτικος, from
προφυλασσω.] Preventive; preservative.

Medicine is distributed into prophylactick, or
the art of preserving health; and therapeutick,
or the art of restoring health. Watts's Logick.

to prorógue v.a. [*prorogo*, Lat. *proroger*, Fr.]

1. To protract; to prolong.

He prorogued his government, still threatning
to dismiss himself from publick cares. Dryden.

2. To put off; to delay.

My life were better ended by their hate,
Than death prorogued, wanting of thy love.
Shakesp.

3. To interrupt the session of parliament to
   a distant time.

By the king's authority alone, they are
assembled, and by him alone are they
prorogued and dissolved, but each house
may adjourn itself. Bacon.

prose n.s. [*prose*, Fr. *prosa*, Lat.] Language
not restrained to harmonick sounds or set
number of syllables; discourse not metrical.

Things unattempted yet in prose or rhime.
Milton.

The reformation of prose was owing to
Boccace, who is the standard of purity in the
Italian tongue, though many of his phrases
are become obsolete. Dryden.

A poet lets you into the knowledge of a device
better than a prose writer; as his descriptions
are often more diffuse. Add.

Prose men alone for private ends,
I thought, forsook their ancient friends. Prior.

I will be still your friend in prose:
Esteem and friendship to express,
Will not require poetick dress. Swift.

My head and heart thus flowing through
my quill,
Verse man and prose man, term me which
you will. Pope.

prosódian n.s. [from *prosody*.] One skilled
in metre or prosody.

Some have been so bad prosodians, as from
thence to derive malum, *because that fruit*
was the first occasion of evil. Brown.[†]

prósody n.s. [*prosodie*, Fr. προσωδια.] The
part of grammar which teaches the sound
and quantity of syllables, and the measures
of verse.

prosopopoéia n.s. [προσωποποιια;
prosopopée, Fr.] Personification; figure by
which things are made persons.

These reasons are pathetically urged, and
admirably raised by the prosopopœia of nature
speaking to her children. Dryden.

próstitute n.s. [from the verb.]

1. A hireling; a mercenary; one who is set
   to sale.

At open fulsome bawdry they rejoice,
Base prostitute! thus dost thou gain thy bread.
Dryden.

No hireling she, no prostitute to praise. Pope.

2. [*Prostibula*, Lat.] A publick strumpet.

*   From every point they come,*
Then dread no dearth of prostitutes at Rome.
Dryden.

prótestant n.s. [*protestant*, Fr. from *protest*.]
One of those who adhere to them, who, at
the beginning of the reformation, protested
against the errours of the church of Rome.

This is the first example of any protestant
subjects, that have taken up arms against
their king a protestant. K. Charles.

prótoplast n.s. [πρωτος and πλαστος.]
Original; thing first formed as a copy to be
followed afterwards.

The consumption was the primitive disease,
which put a period to our protoplasts, Adam
and Eve. Harvey.

próvender n.s. [*provande*, Dutch; *provende*,
Fr.] Dry food for brutes; hay and corn.

Good provender labouring horses would have.
Tusser.

I do appoint him store of provender;
It is a creature that I teach to fight. Shakesp.

Many a duteous and knee-crooking knave
Wears out his time, much like his master's ass,
For nought but provender. Shakesp. Othello.

Whene'er he chanc'd his hands to lay
On magazines of corn or hay,
Gold ready coin'd appear'd, instead
Of paultry provender and bread.
Swift's Miscel.

For a fortnight before you kill them, feed them
with hay or other provender. Mortimer.

provérbial adj. [*proverbial*, Fr. from
proverb.]

1. Mentioned in a proverb.

In case of excesses, I take the German
proverbial cure, by a hair of the same beast,
to be the worst in the world; and the best, the
monks diet, to eat till you are sick, and fast till
you are well again. Temple's Miscel.

Despis'd and curs'd Leontius must descend
Through hissing ages, a proverbial coward.
Irene.

2. Resembling a proverb; suitable to
   a proverb.

This river's head being unknown, and drawn
to a proverbial obscurity, the opinion thereof
became without bounds. Brown's Vulgar
Errours.

3. Comprised in a proverb.

Moral sentences and proverbial speeches are
numerous in this poet. Pope.

to prowl v.n. To wander for prey; to prey;
to plunder.

The champion robbeth by night,
And prowleth and filcheth by daie. Tusser.

Nor do they bear so quietly the loss of some
parcels confiscated abroad, as the great
detriment which they suffer by some prowling
vice-admiral or publick minister. Raleigh.

As when a prowling wolf,
Whom hunger drives to seek new haunt
    for prey. Milton.

Shall he, who looks erect on heav'n,
E'er stoop to mingle with the prowling herd,
And dip his tongue in gore. Thomson.

And here the fell attorney prowls for prey.
Anon.†

prude n.s. [*prude*, Fr.] A woman over nice
and scrupulous, and with false affectation.

The graver prude sinks downward to a gnome,
In search of mischief, still on earth to roam.
Pope.

Not one careless thought intrudes,
Less modest than the speech of prudes. Swift.

prúrience, prúriency n.s. [from *prurio*,
Lat.] An itching or a great desire or
appetite to any thing. Swift.

pseúdo n.s. [from ψευδος.] A prefix,
which, being put before words, signifies
false or counterfeit: as, pseudapostle, a
counterfeit apostle.

pseúdology n.s. [pseudologia.] Falsehood
of speech.

It is not according to the sound rules of
pseudology, to report of a pious prince, that
he neglects his devotion, but you may report
of a merciful prince, that he has pardoned
a criminal who did not deserve it. Arbuthnot.

ptísan n.s. [*ptisanne*, Fr. πτισσανη.]
A medical drink made of barley decocted
with raisins and liquorice.

Thrice happy were those golden days of old,
When dear as Burgundy the ptisans sold;
When patients chose to die with better will,
Than breathe and pay the apothecary's bill.
Garth.

In fevers the aliments prescribed by
Hippocrates, were ptisans and cream of barley.
Arbuthnot.

ptysmagogue n.s. [πτυσμα and αγω.] A medicine which discharges spittle. Dict.

pubérty n.s. [*puberté*, Fr. *pubertas*, Lat.] The time of life in which the two sexes begin first to be acquainted.

The cause of changing the voice at the years of puberty seemeth to be, for that when much of the moisture of the body, which did before irrigate the parts, is drawn down to the spermatical vessels, it leaveth the body more hot than it was, whence cometh the dilatation of the pipes. Bacon.

All the carnivorous animals would have multiplied exceedingly, before these children that escaped could come to the age of puberty. Bentley's Sermons.

públican n.s. [from *publicus*, Lat.]

1. A toll gatherer.

As Jesus sat at meat, many publicans and sinners came and sat down with him. Matth. ix. 10.

2. A man that keeps a house of general entertainment. In low language.

públick adj. [*public*, *publique*, Fr. *publicus*, Lat.]

1. Belonging to a state or nation; not private.

By following the law of private reason, where the law of publick should take place, they breed disturbance. Hooker.

*Of royal maids how wretched is the fate,
Born only to be victims of the state;
Our hopes, our wishes, all our passions try'd
For publick use, the slaves of others pride.* Granvil.

Have we not able counsellors, hourly watching over the publick weal. Swift.

2. Open; notorious; generally known.

Joseph being a just man, and not willing to make her a publick example, was minded to put her away privily. Matth.

3. General; done by many.

*A dismal universal hiss, the sound
Of publick scorn.* Milton.

4. Regarding not private interest, but the good of the community.

They were publick hearted men, as they paid all taxes, so they gave up all their time to their country's service, without any reward. Clarendon.

All nations that grew great out of little or nothing, did so merely by the publick mindedness of particular persons. South.

A good magistrate must be endued with a publick spirit, that is with such an excellent temper, as sets him loose from all selfish views, and makes him endeavour towards promoting the common good. Atterbury.

5. Open for general entertainment.

The income of the commonwealth is raised on such as have money to spend at taverns and publick houses. Addison.

to públish v.a. [*publier*, Fr. *publico*, Lat.]

1. To discover to mankind; to make generally and openly known; to proclaim; to divulge.

*How will this grieve you,
When you shall come to clearer knowledge, that
You thus have published me.* Shakesp. Winter's Tale.

His commission from God and his doctrine tend to the impressing the necessity of that reformation, which he came to publish. Hammond's Fundamentals.

*Suppose he should relent,
And publish grace to all.* Milton.

*Th' unwearied sun, from day to day,
Does his Creator's pow'r display,
And publishes to every land
The work of an almighty hand.* Addison's Spectator.

2. To put forth a book into the world.

If I had not unwarily too far engaged myself for the present publishing it, I should have kept it by me. Digby.

pucélage n.s. [French.] A state of virginity. Dict.

puck n.s. [perhaps the same with *pug*.] Some sprite among the fairies, common in romances.

O gentle puck, take this transformed scalp
From off the head of this Athenian swain.
Shakesp.

    Turn your cloaks,
Quoth he, for puck is busy in these oaks,
And this is fairy ground. Corbet.

púdding n.s. [*potten*, Welsh, an intestine;
boudin, French; *puding*, Swedish.]

1. A kind of food very variously
    compounded, but generally made
    of meal, milk, and eggs.

Sallads, and eggs, and lighter fare
Tune the Italian spark's guitar;
And if I take Dan Congreve right,
Pudding and beef make Britons fight. Prior.

2. The gut of an animal.

He'll yield the crow a pudding one of
these days; the king has kill'd his heart.
Shakesp. Henry V.

As sure as his guts are made of puddings.
Shakesp.

3. A bowel stuffed with certain mixtures of
    meal and other ingredients.

Mind neither good nor bad, nor right nor wrong,
But eat your pudding, slave, and hold your
tongue. Prior.

to puff v.a.

1. To swell as with wind.

Let him fall by his own greatness,
And puff him up with glory, till it swell
And break him. Denham's Sophy.

Flattering of others, and boasting of ourselves,
may be referred to lying; the one to please
others, and puff them up with self-conceit;
the other to gain more honour than is due to
ourselves. Ray on the Creation.

2. To drive or agitate with blasts of wind.

    I have seen the cannon,
When it has blown his ranks into the air,
And from his arm pufft his own brother.
Shakesp.

Have I not heard the sea, puff'd up with winds,
Rage like an angry boar chafed with sweat?
Shakesp.

Th' unerring sun by certain signs declares,
When the South projects a stormy day,
And when the clearing North will puff the
    clouds away. Dryden's Virgil's Georgicks.

Why must the winds all hold their tongue?
If they a little breath should raise,
Would that have spoil'd the poet's song,
Or puff'd away the monarch's praise? Prior.

I have been endeavouring very busily to raise
a friendship, which the first breath of any
ill-natured by-stander could puff away. Pope.

3. To drive with a blast of breath
    scornfully.

    When she dances in the wind,
And shakes her wings, and will not stay,
I puff the prostitute away;
The little or the much she gave is quietly
    resign'd. Dryd.

4. To swell or blow up with praise.

The attendants of courts engage them in
quarrels of jurisdiction, being truly parasiti
curiæ, *in puffing a court up beyond her*
bounds for their own advantage. Bacon.[†]

5. To swell or elate with pride.

His looke like a coxcombe up puffed with
pride. Tusser.

This army, led by a tender prince,
Whose spirit with divine ambition pufft,
Makes mouths at the invisible event.
Shakesp. Hamlet.

Think not of men above that which is
written, that no one of you be puffed up
one against another. 1 Cor. iv. 6.

Your ancestors, who puff your mind with pride,
Did not your honour, but their own advance.
Dryden.

Who stands safest; tell me, is it he
That spreads and swells in puff'd posterity?
Pope.

The Phæacians were so puffed up with their
constant felicity, that they thought nothing
impossible. Broome.

pug n.s. [*piga*, Saxon, a girl. Skinner.] A
kind name of a monkey, or any thing
tenderly loved.

Upon setting him down, and calling him pug,
I found him to be her favourite monkey.
Addison's Spectator.

pugh interj. [corrupted from *puff,* or borrowed from the sound.] A word of contempt.

to puke v.n. To spew; to vomit.

    The infant
Mewling and puking in the nurse's arms.
Shakesp.

pulícose adj. [*pulicosus, pulex,* Latin.] Abounding with fleas. Dict.

to púlvil v.a. [from the noun.] To sprinkle with perfumes in powder.

Have you pulvilled the coachman and
postilion, that they may not stink of the stable.
Congreve's Way of the World.

pun n.s. [I know not whence this word is to be deduced: to pun, is to grind or beat with a pestle; can pun mean an empty sound, like that of a mortar beaten, as clench, the old word for pun, seems only a corruption of clink?] An equivocation; a quibble; an expression where a word has at once different meanings.

It is not the word, but the figure that appears
on the medal: cuniculus *may stand for a*
rabbit or a mine, but the picture of a rabbit
is not the picture of a mine: a pun can be no
more engraven, than it can be translated.
Addison.

But fill their purse, our poet's work is done,
Alike to them by pathos, or by pun. Pope.

punch n.s. [from the verb.]

1. A pointed instrument, which, driven by a blow, perforates bodies.

The shank of a key the punch cannot strike,
because the shank is not forged with substance
sufficient; but the drill cuts a true round hole.
Moxon's Mechanical Exercises.

2. [Cant word.] A liquour made by mixing spirit with water, sugar, and the juice of lemons.

The West India dry gripes are occasioned
by lime juice in punch. Arbuthnot on Aliments.

No brute can endure the taste of strong liquor,
and consequently it is against all the rules of
hieroglyph to assign those animals as patrons
of punch. Swift.

3. [*Punchinello,* Italian.] The buffoon or harlequin of the puppet-show.

Of rareeshows he sung and punch's feats. Gay.

4. Punch is a horse that is well set and well knit, having a short back and thin shoulders, with a broad neck, and well lined with flesh. Farrier's Dict.

5. [*Punctilio obesus,* Lat.] In contempt or ridicule, a short fat fellow.

punctílio n.s. A small nicety of behaviour; a nice point of exactness.

Common people are much astonished, when
they hear of those solemn contests which are
made among the great, upon the punctilios
of a publick ceremony. Addison.

Punctilio is out of doors, the moment a
daughter clandestinely quits her father's house.
Clarissa.

púndle n.s. [*mulier pumila & obesa,* Lat.] A short and fat woman. Ainsworth.

puníceous adj. [*puniceus,* Lat.] Purple. Dict.

punk n.s. A whore; a common prostitute; a strumpet.

She may be a punk; for many of them are
neither maid, widow, nor wife. Shakesp. Measure for Measure.

And made them fight, like mad or drunk,
For dame religion as for punk. Hudibras.

Near these a nursery erects its head,
Where unfledg'd actors learn to laugh and cry,
Where infant punks their tender voices try.
Dryden.

púnster n.s. [from *pun.*] A quibbler; a low wit who endeavours at reputation by double meaning.[†]

His mother was cousin to Mr. Swan, gamester and punster of London. Arbuthnot and Pope.

púrgatory n.s. [*purgatoire*, Fr. *purgatorium*, Lat.] A place in which souls are supposed by the papists to be purged by fire from carnal impurities, before they are received into heaven.

Thou thy folk, through pains of purgatory,
Dost bear unto thy bliss. Spenser's Hymn
on Love.

In this age, there may be as great instances produced of real charity, as when men thought to get souls out of purgatory. Stillingfleet.

purge n.s. [from the verb.] A cathartick medicine; a medicine that evacuates the body by stool.

Meet we the med'cine of the sickly weal,
And with him pour we in our country's purge
Each drop of us. Shakesp.

  Pills nor laxatives I like;
Of these his gain the sharp physician makes,
And often gives a purge, but seldom takes.
Dryden.

He was no great friend to purging and clisters; he was for mixing aloes with all purges. Arbuthnot.

púrist n.s. [*puriste*, Fr.] One superstitiously nice in the use of words.

púritan n.s. [from *pure.*] A sectary pretending to eminent purity of religion.[†]

The schism which the papists on the one hand, and the superstition which the puritan on the other, lay to our charge, are very justly chargeable upon themselves. Sanderson.

to purr v.a. To murmur as a cat or leopard in pleasure.

púrsy adj. [*poussif,* Fr.] Shortbreathed and fat.

In the fatness of these pursy times,
Virtue itself of vice must pardon beg,
Yea courb and woo for leave to do it good.
Shakesp.

  Now breathless wrong
Shall sit and pant in your great chairs of ease,
And pursy insolence shall break his wind
With fear and horrid flight. Shakesp. Timon
of Atheus.

  By these, the Medes
Perfume their breaths, and cure old
  pursy men. Temple.

  An hostess dowager,
Grown fat and pursy by retail
Of pots of beer and bottl'd ale. Hudibras, p. iii.

puss n.s. [I know not whence derived; *pusio,* Lat. is a dwarf.]

1. The fondling name of a cat.

A young fellow, in love with a cat, made it his humble suit to Venus to turn puss into a woman. L'Estrange.

Let puss practise what nature teaches.
Watts.

I will permit my son to play at apodidrascinda, which can be no other than our puss in a corner. Arbuth. and Pope.

2. The sportsman's term for a hare.

  Poor honest puss,
It grieves my heart to see thee thus;
But hounds eat sheep as well as hares. Gay.

pútage n.s. [*putain,* Fr.] In law, prostitution on the woman's part.

pyrrhonism n.s. [from *Pyrrho,* the founder of the scepticks.] Scepticism; universal doubt.

Q , is a consonant borrowed from the Latin or French, for which, though *q* is commonly placed in the Saxon alphabet, the Saxons generally used *cw*; as *cwellan*, to quell: *qu* is, in English, pronounced as by the Italians and Spaniards *cw*; as *quail*, *quench*, except *quoit*, which is spoken, according to the manner of the French, *coit*: the name of this letter is *cue*, from *queue*, French, tail; its form being that of an *O* with a tail.

quack n.s. [from the verb.]

1. A boastful pretender to arts which he does not understand.

The change, schools and pulpits are full of quacks, jugglers and plagiaries. L'Estrange.

Some quacks in the art of teaching, pretend to make young gentlemen masters of the languages, before they can be masters of common sense. Felton on the Classicks.

2. A vain boastful pretender to physick; one who proclaims his own medical abilities in publick places.

At the first appearance that a French quack made in Paris: a little boy walked before him, publishing with a shrill voice, "My father cures all sorts of distempers"; to which the doctor added in a grave manner, "The child says true." Addison.

3. An artful tricking practitioner in physick.

Despairing quacks with curses fled the place, And vile attorneys, now an useless race. Pope.

quadragésimal adj. [*quadragesimal*, Fr. *quadragesima*, Latin.] Lenten; belonging to Lent; used in Lent.

I have composed prayers out of the church collects, adventual, quadragesimal, paschal, or pentecostal. Sanderson.

quadratick equations In algebra, are such as retain, on the unknown side, the square of the root or the number sought: and are of two sorts; first, simple quadraticks, where the square of the unknown root is equal to the absolute number given; secondly, affected quadraticks, which are such as have, between the highest power of the unknown number and the absolute number given, some intermediate power of the unknown number. Harris.

quádrille n.s. A game at cards. Dict.

quággy adj. [from *quagmire*.] Boggy; soft; not solid. Ains. This word is somewhere too in Clarissa.

quaint adj. [*coint*, Fr. *comptus*, Lat.]

1. Nice; scrupulously, minutely, superfluously exact; having petty elegance.

Each ear sucks up the words a true love scattereth, And plain speech oft, than quaint phrase framed is. Sidney.

You were glad to be employ'd, To shew how quaint an orator you are. Shakesp.

He spends some pages about two similitudes; one of mine, and another quainter of his own. Stillingfleet.

2. Subtle; artful. Obsolete.

As clerkes been full subtle and queint. Chaucer.

3. Neat; pretty; exact.

But for a fine, quaint, graceful and excellent fashion, yours is worth ten on 't. Shakesp.

Her mother hath intended, That, quaint in green, she shall be loose enrob'd With ribbands pendent, flaring 'bout her head. Shakesp.

I never saw a better fashion'd gown, More quaint, more pleasing, nor more commendable. Sha.

4. Subtly excogitated; finespun.

I'll speak of frays, Like a fine bragging youth, and tell quaint lies, How honourable ladies sought my love, Which I denying they fell sick and died. Shakesp.

He his fabrick of the heav'ns Hath left to their disputes, perhaps to move His laughter at their quaint opinions wide Hereafter. Milton's Par. Lost, b. viii.

5. Quaint is, in Spenser, quailed; depressed. I believe by a very licentious irregularity.

With such fair slight him Guyon fail'd: Till at the last, all breathless, weary and faint, Him spying, with fresh onset he assail'd, And kindling new his courage, seeming quaint,

Struck him so hugely, that through
*   great constraint,*
He made him stoop. Fairy Queen, b. ii.

6. Affected; foppish. This is not the true
   idea of the word, which Swift seems
   not to have well understood.

To this we owe those monstrous productions,
which under the name of trips, spies,
amusements, and other conceited appellations,
have overrun us; and I wish I could say, those
quaint fopperies were wholly absent from
graver subjects. Sw.

quálity n.s. [*qualitas*, Lat. *qualité*, Fr.]

1. Nature relatively considered.

These, being of a far other nature and quality,
are not so strictly or everlastingly commanded
in scripture. Hooker.

Other creatures have not judgment to examine
the quality of that which is done by them, and
therefore in that they do, they neither can
accuse nor approve themselves. Hooker.

Since the event of an action usually follows
the nature or quality of it, and the quality
follows the rule directing it, it concerns a
man, in the framing of his actions, not to be
deceived in the rule. South.

The power to produce any idea in our mind,
I call quality of the subject, wherein that
power is. Locke.

2. Property; accident.

In the division of the kingdom, it appears
not which of the dukes he values most; for
qualities are so weighed, that curiosity in
neither can make choice of either's moiety.
Shak.

No sensible qualities, as light and colour, heat
and sound, can be subsistent in the bodies
themselves absolutely considered, without a
relation to our eyes and ears, and other organs
of sense: these qualities are only the effects of
our sensation, which arise from the different
motions upon our nerves from objects without,
according to their various modification and
position. Bentley.

3. Particular efficacy.

O, mickle is the powerful grace, that lies
In plants, herbs, stones, and their true
*   qualities.* Shakesp.

4. Disposition; temper.

To-night we'll wander through the streets,
*   and note*
The qualities of people. Shakesp. Ant.
and Cleopatra.

5. Virtue or vice.

One doubt remains, said I, the dames in green,
What were their qualities, and who their
*   queen?* Dryden.

6. Accomplishment; qualification.

He had those qualities of horsemanship,
dancing and fencing, which accompany
a good breeding. Clarendon.

7. Character.

The attorney of the dutchy of Lancaster
partakes of both qualities, partly of a judge in
that court, and partly of an attorney general.
Bacon's Advice to Villiers.

We, who are hearers, may be allowed some
opportunities in the quality of standers-by.
Swift.

8. Comparative or relative rank.

It is with the clergy, if their persons be
respected, even as it is with other men; their
quality many times far beneath that which
the dignity of their place requireth. Hooker.

We lived most joyful, obtaining acquaintance
with many of the city, not of the meanest
quality. Bacon.

The masters of these horses may be admitted
to dine with the lord lieutenant: this is to be
done, what quality soever the persons are of.
Temple.

9. Rank; superiority of birth or station.

Let him be so entertained, as suits with
gentlemen of your knowing to a stranger
of his quality. Shakesp. Cymbeline.

10. Persons of high rank. Collectively.

I shall appear at the masquerade dressed up
in my feathers, that the quality may see how
pretty they will look in their travelling habits.
Addison's Guardian, Nº 112.

Of all the servile herd, the worst is he,
That in proud dullness joins with quality,
A constant critick at the great man's board,
To fetch and carry nonsense for my lord.
Pope.

quárantain, quárantine n.s. [*quarantain*, Fr.] The space of forty days, being the time which a ship, suspected of infection, is obliged to forbear intercourse or commerce.

Pass your quarantine among some of the churches round this town, where you may learn to speak before you venture to expose your parts in a city congregation. Swift.

quárto n.s. [*quartus*, Lat.] A book in which every sheet, being twice doubled, makes four leaves.

Our fathers had a just value for regularity and systems; then folio's and quarto's were the fashionable sizes, as volumes in octavo are now. Watts.

quátrain n.s. [*quatrain*, Fr.] A stanza of four lines rhyming alternately: as,

> *Say, Stella, what is love, whose*
> > *fatal pow'r*
> *Robs virtue of content, and youth of joy?*
> > *What nymph or goddess in a luckless hour*
> *Disclos'd to light the mischief-making boy.*
Mrs. Mulso.†

I have writ my poem in quatrains or stanza's of four in alternate rhyme, because I have ever judged them of greater dignity for the sound and number, than any other verse in use. Dryden.

quean n.s. [*cwean*, Saxon, a barren cow; *Horcwen*, in the laws of Canute, a strumpet.] A worthless woman, generally a strumpet.

As fit as the nail to his hole, or as a scolding quean to a wrangling knave. Shakesp.

This well they understand like cunning queans, And hide their nastiness behind the scenes. Dryden.

Such is that sprinkling, which some careless quean Flirts on you from her mop. Swift.

to queck v.n. To shrink; to show pain; perhaps to complain.

The lads of Sparta were accustomed to be whipped at altars, without so much as quecking. Bacon.

queer adj. [of this word the original is not known: a correspondent supposes a queer man to be one who has a *quære* to his name in a list.]† Odd; strange; original; particular.

He never went to bed till two in the morning, because he would not be a queer fellow; and was every now and then knocked down by a constable, to signalize his vivacity. Spect.

to queme v.n. [*cweman*, Saxon.] To please. An old word. Skinner.

quérpo n.s. [corrupted from *cuerpo*, Spanish.] A dress close to the body; a waistcoat.

I would fain see him walk in querpo, like a cased rabbit, without his holy furr upon his back. Dryden.

quíbble n.s. [from *quidlibet*, Latin.] A low conceit depending on the sound of words; a pun.

This may be of great use to immortalize puns and quibbles, and to let posterity see their forefathers were blockheads. Add.

Quirks or quibbles have no place in the search after truth. Watts.

quíddany n.s. [*cydonium, cydoniatum*, Lat. *quidden*, German, a quince.] Marmalade; confection of quinces made with sugar.

quíddit n.s. [corrupted from *quidlibet*, Lat. or from *que dit*, Fr.] A subtilty; an equivocation. A low word.

Why may not that be the skull of a lawyer? where be his quiddits now? his quillets? his cases? and his tricks? Shak.

quíncunx n.s. [Latin.] Quincunx order is a plantation of trees, disposed originally in a square, consisting of five trees, one at each corner, and a fifth in the middle, which disposition, repeated again and again, forms a regular grove, wood or wilderness; and, when viewed by an angle of the square or paralellogram, presents equal or parallel alleys. Brown produces several examples in his discourse about the quincunx. Ray on the Creation.

He whose light'ning pierc'd th' Iberian lines,
Now forms my quincunx, and now ranks
   my vines. Pope.

quínsy n.s. [corrupted from *squinancy.*]
A tumid inflammation in the throat, which
sometimes produces suffocation.

The throttling quinsey 'tis my star appoints,
And rheumatisms I send to rack the joints.
Dryden.

Great heat and cold, succeeding one another,
occasion pleurisies and quinsies. Arbuthnot
on Air.

quintéssence n.s. [*quinta essentia,* Lat.]

1. A fifth being.

From their gross matter she abstracts the forms,
And draws a kind of quintessence from things.
Davies.

The ethereal quintessence of heav'n
Flew upward, spirited with various forms,
That rowl'd orbicular, and turn'd to stars.
Milton.

They made fire, air, earth, and water, to be
the four elements, of which all earthly things
were compounded, and supposed the heavens
to be a quintessence or fifth sort of body
distinct from all these. Watts's Logick.

2. An extract from any thing, containing
all its virtues in a small quantity.

To me what is this quintessence of dust?
man delights not me, nor woman neither.
Shakesp. Hamlet.

Who can in memory, or wit, or will,
Or air, or fire, or earth, or water find?
What alchymist can draw, with all his skill,
The quintessence of these out of the mind.
Davies.

For I am a very dead thing,
In whom love wrought new alchymy,
For by his art he did express
A quintessence even from nothingness,
From dull privations and lean emptiness.
Donne.

Paracelsus, by the help of an intense cold,
teaches to separate the quintessence of wine.
Boyle.

Let there be light! said God; and forthwith light
Ethereal, first of things, quintessence pure,
Sprung from the deep. Milton's Paradise
Lost, b. vii.

When the supreme faculties move regularly,
the inferior passions and affections following,
there arises a serenity and complacency upon
the whole soul, infinitely beyond the greatest
bodily pleasures, the highest quintessence and
elixir of worldly delights. South's Sermons.

to quip v.a. To rally with bitter sarcasms.
Ainsworth.

quits interj. [from *quit.*] An exclamation
used when any thing is repayed and the
parties become even.

to quob v.n. [a low word.] To move as the
embrio does in the womb; to move as the
heart does when throbbing.

quodlibetárian n.s. [*quodlibet,* Lat.] One
who talks or disputes on any subject. Dict.

quoit n.s. [*coete,* Dutch.]

1. Something thrown to a great distance to
a certain point.

He plays at quoits well. Shakesp. Henry IV.

When he played at quoits, he was allowed his
breeches and stockings. Arbuthnot and Pope.

2. The discus of the ancients is sometimes
called in English *quoit,* but improperly;
the game of *quoits* is a game of skill; the
discus was only a trial of strength, as
among us to throw the hammer.

quóndam [Latin.] Having been formerly.
A ludicrous word.

This is the quondam king, let's seize upon
him. Shakesp.

What lands and lordships for their owner know
My quondam barber, but his worship now.
Dryden.

quotídian n.s. [*febris quotidiana,* Lat.]
A quotidian fever; a fever which returns
every day.

If I could meet that fancymonger, I would
give him some good counsel; for he seems to
have the quotidian of love. Shakespeare.

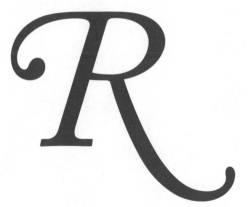

R, is called the canine letter, because it is uttered with some resemblance to the growl or snarl of a cur: it has one constant sound in English, such as it has in other languages; as *red, rose, more, muriatick*: in words derived from the Greek, it is followed by an *h*, *rhapsody*: *r* is never mute, unless the second *r* may be accounted mute, where two *rr* are used; as *myrrh*.

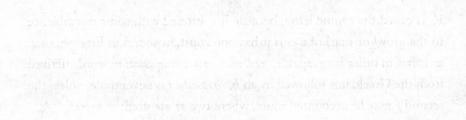

rábbi, rábbin n.s. A doctor among the Jews.

The Hebrew rabbins say, that nature hath given man, for the pronouncing of all letters, the lips, the teeth, the tongue, the palate and throat. Camden's Remains.

Be not ye called rabbi; for one is your master, even Christ, and all ye are brethren. Mat. xxiii. 8.

race n.s. [*race*, Fr. from *radice*, Lat.]

1. A family ascending.

2. Family descending.

He in a moment will create
Another world; out of man, a race
Of men innumerable, there to dwell. Milton.

Male he created thee, but thy consort
Female for race. Milton.

High as the mother of the gods in place,
And proud like her of an immortal race. Dryden.

Hence the long race of Alban fathers come. Dryden.

3. A generation; a collective family.†

A race of youthful and unhandled colts,
Fetching mad bounds. Shakesp. Merchant of Venice.

4. A particular breed.

Instead
Of spirits malign, a better race to bring
Into their vacant room. Milton.

In the races of mankind and families of the world, there remains not to one above another the least pretence to have the right of inheritance. Locke.

5. Race of ginger. [*rayz de gengibre*, Spanish.] A root or sprig of ginger.

6. A particular strength or taste of wine, applied by Temple to any extraordinary natural force of intellect.

Of gardens there may be forms wholly irregular, that may have more beauty than of others; but they must owe it to some extraordinary dispositions of nature in the seat, or some great race of fancy or judgment in contrivance. Temple.

7. [*Ras*, Islandick.] Contest in running.

To describe races and games
Or tilting furniture. Milton.

8. Course on the feet.

The flight of many birds is swifter than the race of any beasts. Bacon.

9. Progress; course.

It suddenly fell from an excess of favour, which many examples having taught them, never stopt his race till it came to a headlong overthrow. Sidney.

My race of glory run, and race of shame. Milton.

Their ministry perform'd, and race well run. Milton.

The great light of day yet wants to run Much of his race though steep. Milton.

He safe return'd, the race of glory past, New to his friends embrace. Pope's Odyssey.

10. Train; process.

An offensive war is made, which is unjust in the aggressor; the prosecution and race of the war carrieth the defendant to invade the ancient patrimony of the first aggressor, who is now turned defendant; shall he sit down, and not put himself in defence? Bacon.

The race of this war fell upon the loss of Urbin, which he re-obtained. Bacon.

racemíferous adj. [*racemus* and *fera*, Latin.] Bearing clusters.

ráckoon n.s. The rackoon is a New England animal, like a badger, having a tail like a fox, being cloathed with a thick and deep furr: it sleeps in the day time in a hollow tree, and goes out a-nights, when the moon shines, to feed on the sea side, where it is hunted by dogs. Bailey.

ragamúffin n.s. [from *rag* and I know not what else.] A paltry mean fellow.

I have led my ragamuffins where they were pepper'd; there's not three of my hundred and fifty left alive; and they are for the town's end to beg during life. Shakesp. Henry IV.

Shall we brook that paltry ass
And feeble scoundrel, Hudibras,
With that more paltry ragamuffin,
Ralpho, vapouring and huffing.
Hudibras, p. i.

Attended with a crew of ragamuffins, she
broke into his house, turned all things
topsy-turvy, and then set it on fire. Swift.

ragoût n.s. [French] Meat stewed and
highly seasoned.

To the stage permit
Ragouts for Tereus or Thyestes drest,
'Tis task enough for thee t' expose a Roman
feast. Dryden.

No fish they reckon comparable to a ragout
of snails. Add.

When art and nature join, th' effect will be
Some nice ragout, or charming fricasy.
King's Cookery.

to rail v.n. [railler, Fr. rallen, Dutch.] To use
insolent and reproachful language; to speak
to, or to mention in opprobrious terms.

Your husband is in his old lunes again; he so
rails against all married mankind, curses all
Eve's daughters. Shakesp.

What a monstrous fellow art thou? thus to
rail on one, that is neither known of thee,
nor knows thee. Shakesp.

'Till thou can'st rail the seals from off my bond,
Thou but offend'st thy lungs to speak so loud.
Shakesp.

He tript me behind; being down, insulted, rail'd,
And put upon him such a deal of man,
That worthied him. Shakesp. King Lear.

Of words cometh railings and evil surmisings.
1 Tim. vi.

Angels bring not railing accusation against
them. 2 Pet. ii.

If any is angry, and rails at it, he may
securely. Locke.

Thou art my blood, where Johnson has no part;
Where did his wit on learning fix a brand,
And rail at arts he did not understand?
Dryden.

Lesbia for ever on me rails,
To talk of me she never fails. Swift.

raíllery n.s. [raillerie, Fr.] Slight satire;
satirical merriment.

Let raillery be without malice or heat.
Benj. Johnson.

A quotation out of Hudibras shall make them
treat with levity an obligation wherein their
welfare is concerned as to this world and
the next: raillery of this nature is enough to
make the hearer tremble. Addison's
Freeholder, N° 6.

Studies employed on low objects; the very
naming of them is almost sufficient to
turn them into raillery. Addison on
Ancient Medals.

To these we are solicited by the arguments of
the subtile, and the railleries of the prophane.
Rogers's Sermons.

rainbow n.s. [rain and bow.] The iris; the
semicircle of various colours which appears
in showery weather.

Casting of the water in a most cunning
manner, makes a perfect rainbow, not more
pleasant to the eye than to the mind, so
sensibly to see the proof of the heavenly iris.
Sidney.

To add another hue unto the rainbow.
Shakesp.

The rainbow is drawn like a nymph with
large wings dispread in the form of a
semicircle, the feathers of sundry colours.
Peach.

They could not be ignorant of the promise
of God never to drown the world, and the
rainbow before their eyes to put them in
mind of it. Brown's Vulgar Errours.

This rainbow never appears but where it
rains in the sunshine, and may be made
artificially by spouting up water, which may
break aloft, and scatter into drops, and fall
down like rain; for the sun, shining upon these
drops, certainly causes the bow to appear to
a spectator standing in a true position to the
rain and sun: this bow is made by refraction
of the sun's light in drops of falling rain.
Newton's Opticks.

The dome's high arch reflects the mingled blaze,
And forms a rainbow of alternate rays. Pope.

raíndeer [*hranas*, Saxon; *rangifer*, Latin.] A deer with large horns, which, in the northern regions, draws sledges through the snow.

rake n.s. [*rastrum*, Lat. *race*, Sax. *racche*, Dutch.]

1. An instrument with teeth, by which the ground is divided, or light bodies are gathered up.

At Midsummer down with the brembles and brakes,
And after abroad with thy forkes and thy rakes. Tusser.

O that thy bounteous deity wou'd please
To guide my rake upon the chinking sound
Of some vast treasure hidden under grouud. Dryden.

He examines his face in the stream, combs his ruful locks with a rake. Garth.

2. [*Racaille*, Fr. the low rabble; or *rekel*, Dutch, a worthless cur dog.] A loose, disorderly, vicious, wild, gay, thoughtless fellow; a man addicted to pleasure.

The next came with her son, who was the greatest rake in the place, but so much the mother's darling, that she left her husband for the sake of this graceless youth. Addison.

Rakes hate sober grave gentlewomen. Arbuthnot.

Men, some to bus'ness, some to pleasure take;
But ev'ry woman is at heart a rake. Pope.

The sire saw smiling his own virtues wake;
The mother begg'd the blessing of a rake. Pope.

rákehel n.s. [of this word the etymology is doubtful: as it is now written, it is apparently derived from *rake* and *hell*, and may aptly represent a wretch whose life is passed in places of lewdness and wickedness: Skinner derives it from *racaille*, French, the rabble; Junius, from *rekel*, Dutch, a mongrel dog.] A wild, worthless, dissolute, debauched, sorry fellow.

Out of the frie of these rakehell horse-boys, growing up in knavery and villainy, are their kern supplied. Spenser.

The king, when he heard of Perkins's siege of Exeter, said in sport, that the king of rakehells was landed in the West, and that he hoped now to see him. Bacon.

A rakehell of the town, whose character is set off with excessive prodigality, prophaneness, intemperance and lust, is rewarded with a lady of great fortune to repair his own, which his vices had almost ruined. Swift.

to rálly v.a. [*rallier*, Fr.]

1. To put disordered or dispersed forces into order.

With rallied arms to try what may be yet Regain'd in heav'n. Milton.

Publick arguing serves to whet the wits of hereticks, and by shewing weak parts of their doctrines, prompts them to rally all their sophistry to fortify them with fallacy. D. of Pie.

Luther deters men from solitariness; but he does not mean from a sober solitude, that rallies our scattered strengths, and prepares us against any new encounters from without. Atterb.

2. [*Railler*, Fr.] To treat with slight contempt; to treat with satirical merriment.

Honeycomb has not lived a month, for these forty years, out of the smoke of London, and rallies me upon a country life. Addison's Spectator.

If after the reading of this letter, you find yourself in a humour rather to rally and ridicule, than to comfort me, I desire you would throw it into the fire. Addison.

Strephon had long confess'd his am'rous pain, Which gay Corinna rally'd with disdain. Gay.

to rámble v.n. [*rammelen*, Dutch, to rove loosely in lust; *ramb*, Swedish, to rove.] To rove loosely and irregularly; to wander.

Shame contracts the spirits, fixes the ramblings of fancy, and gathers the man into himself. South.

He that is at liberty to ramble in perfect darkness, what is his liberty better than if driven up and down as a bubble by the wind. Locke.

Chapman has taken advantage of an immeasurable length of verse, notwithstanding which, there is scarce any paraphrase so loose and rambling as his. Pope.

Never ask leave to go abroad, for you will be thought an idle rambling fellow. Swift's Directions to Footmen.

O'er his ample sides the rambling sprays Luxuriant shoot. Thomson's Spring.

rámbler n.s. [from *ramble*.] Rover; wanderer.

Says the rambler, we must e'en beat it out. L'Estrange.

rámbooze, rámbuse n.s. A drink made of wine, ale, eggs and sugar in the winter time; or of wine, milk, sugar and rosewater in the summer time. Bailey.

rampállian n.s. A mean wretch. Not in use.

Away you scullion, you rampallian, you fustilarian. Shak.

rántipole adj. [this word is wantonly formed from *rant*.] Wild; roving; rakish. A low word.

What at years of discretion, and comport yourself at this rantipole rate! Congreve's Way of the World.

rape n.s. [*rapt*, Fr. *raptus*, Latin.]

1. Violent defloration of chastity.

You are both decypher'd For villains mark'd with rape. Shakesp. Titus Andronicus.

Rape call you it, to seize my own, My true betrothed love. Shakesp. Titus Andronicus.

The parliament conceived, that the obtaining of women by force into possession, howsoever afterwards assent might follow by allurements, was but a rape drawn forth in length, because the first force drew on all the rest. Bacon's Henry VII.

Witness that night In Gibeah, when the hospitable door Expos'd a matron, to avoid worse rape. Milton.

The haughty fair, Who not the rape ev'n of a god could bear. Dryden.

Tell Thracian tyrant's alter'd shape, And dire revenge of Philomela's rape. Roscommon.

2. Privation; act of taking away.

Pear grew after pear, Fig after fig came; time made never rape Of any dainty there. Chapman's Odyssey.

3. Something snatched away.

Sad widows by thee rifled, weep in vain, And ruin'd orphans of thy rapes complain. Sandys.

Where now are all my hopes? oh never more Shall they revive! nor death her rapes restore! Sandys.

4. The juice of grapes is drawn as well from the rape, or whole grapes pluck'd from the cluster, and wine pour'd upon them in a vessel, as from a vat, where they are bruised. Ray.

5. A plant, from the seed of which oil is expressed.

rápper n.s. [from *rap*.] One who strikes.

rápture n.s.

1. Ecstasy; transport; violence of any pleasing passion; enthusiasm; uncommon heat of imagination.

Musick, when thus applied, raises in the mind of the hearer great conceptions; it strengthens devotion, and advances praise into rapture. Addison's Spectator, Nº 406.

You grow correct, that once with rapture writ. Pope.

2. Rapidity; haste.

The wat'ry throng, Wave rowling after wave, where way they found,

If steep, with torrent rapture; if through plain
Soft-ebbing; nor withstood them rock or hill.
Milton.

ráreeshow n.s. [this word is formed in imitation of the foreign way of pronouncing *rare show*.] A show carried in a box.

The fashions of the town affect us just like
a rareeshow, we have the curiosity to peep
at them, and nothing more. Pope.

Of rareeshows he sung, and Punch's feats.
Gay.

rasp n.s. [*raspo*, Italian.] A delicious berry that grows on a species of the bramble; a raspberry.

Sorrel set amongst rasps, and the rasps will
be the smaller. Bacon's Natural History.

Now will the corinths, now the rasps supply
Delicious draughts, when prest to wines.
Philips.

rat n.s. [*ratte*, Dutch; *rat*, Fr. *ratta*, Spanish.] An animal of the mouse kind that infests houses and ships.

Our natures do pursue,
Like rats that ravin down their proper bane.
Shakesp.

Make you ready your stiff bats and clubs,
Rome and her rats are at the point of battle.
Shakesp.

I have seen the time, with my long sword I
would have made you four tall fellows skip
like rats. Shakesp.

Thus horses will knable at walls, and rats
will gnaw iron. Brown's Vulgar Errours.

If in despair he goes out of the way like a rat
with a dose of arsenick, why he dies nobly.
Dennis.

to smell a rat To be put on the watch by suspicion as the cat by the scent of a rat; to suspect danger.

Quoth Hudibras, I smell a rat,
Ralpho, thou dost prevaricate. Hudibras, p. i.

ratáfia n.s. A fine liquor, prepared from the kernels of apricots and spirits. Bailey.

re Is an inseparable particle used by the Latins, and from them borrowed by us to denote iteration or backward action: as, return, to come back; to revive, to live again; repercussion, the act of driving back.

to read v.a. pret. read, part. pass. read. [*ræd*, Saxon.]

1. To peruse any thing written.

I have seen her take forth paper, write
upon 't, read it, and afterwards seal it.
Shakesp. Macbeth.

The passage you must have read, though since
slipt out of your memory. Pope.

If we have not leisure to read over the book
itself regularly, then by the titles of chapters
we may be directed to peruse several sections.
Watts's Improvement of the Mind.

2. To discover by characters or marks.

An armed corse did lye,
In whose dead face he read great
magnanimity. Spenser.

3. To learn by observation.

Those about her
From her shall read the perfect ways
of honour. Shakesp.

4. To know fully.

O most delicate fiend!
Who is 't can read a woman?
Shakesp. Cymbeline.

réal adj. [*reel*, Fr. *realis*, Latin.]

1. Relating to things not persons; not personal.

Many are perfect in men's humours, that are
not greatly capable of the real part of business;
which is the constitution of one that hath
studied men more than books. Bacon.

2. Not fictitious; not imaginary; true; genuine.

We do but describe an imaginary world,
that is but little a-kin to the real one.
Glanvill's Sceps.

When I place an imaginary name at the head
of a character, I examine every letter of it,
that it may not bear any resemblance to one
that is real. Addison.

3. In law, consisting of things immoveable, as land.

I am hastening to convert my small estate, that is personal, into real. Child's Discourse of Trade.

reálity n.s. [*realité*, Fr. from *real.*]

1. Truth; verity; what is, not what merely seems.

I would have them well versed in the Greek and Latin poets, without which a man fancies that he understands a critic, when in reality he does not comprehend his meaning. Addison's Spectator, Nº 291.

The best accounts of the appearances of nature in any single instance human penetration can reach, comes infinitely short of its reality and internal constitution; for who can search out the Almighty's works to perfection? Cheyne.

2. Something intrinsically important; not merely matter of show.

   Of that skill the more thou know'st,
The more she will acknowledge thee her head,
And to realities yield all her shows,
Made so adorn for thy delight the more.
Milton.

reáson n.s. [*raison*, Fr. *ratio*, Lat.]

1. The power by which man deduces one proposition from another, or proceeds from premises to consequences; the rational faculty.

Reason is the director of man's will, discovering in action what is good; for the laws of well-doing are the dictates of right reason. Hooker, b. i. s. 7.

Though brutish that contest and foul,
When reason hath to deal with force; yet so
Most reason is that reason overcome. Milton.

Dim, as the borrow'd beams of moon and stars
To lonely, weary, wand'ring travellers,
Is reason to the soul: and as on high,
Those rowling fires discover but the sky,
Not light us here; so reason's glimmering ray
Was lent, not to assure our doubtful way,
But guide us upward to a better day. Dryden.

It would be well, if people would not lay so much weight on their own reason in matters of religion, as to think every thing impossible and absurd, which they cannot conceive: how often do we contradict the right rules of reason in the whole course of our lives? reason itself is true and just, but the reason of every particular man is weak and wavering, perpetually swayed and turn'd by his interests, his passions and his vices. Swift's Miscellanies.

2. Cause; ground or principle.

Virtue and vice are not arbitrary things, but there is a natural and eternal reason for that goodness and virtue, and against vice and wickedness. Tillotson.

3. Cause efficient.

Spain is thin sown of people, partly by reason of the sterility of the soil, and partly their natives are exhausted by so many employments in such vast territories as they possess. Bac.

The reason of the motion of the balance in a wheel watch, is by the motion of the next wheel. Hale.

By reason of the sickness of a reverend prelate, I have been overruled to approach this place. Sprat.

I have not observed equality of numbers in my verse; partly by reason of my haste, but more especially because I would not have my sense a slave to syllables. Dryden.

4. Final cause.

Reason, in the English language, sometimes is taken for true and clear principles; sometimes for clear and fair deductions; sometimes for the cause, particularly the final cause: but here for a faculty in man. Locke.

5. Argument; ground of persuasion; motive.

I mask the business from the common eye For sundry weighty reasons. Shakesp. Macbeth.

If it be natural, ought we not rather to conclude, that there is some ground and reason for these fears, and that nature hath not planted them in us to no purpose. Tillotson.

6. Ratiocination; discursive power.

When she rates things, and moves from
    ground to ground,
The name of reason she obtains by this;
But when by reason she the truth hath found,
And standeth fixt, she understanding is.
Davies.

7. Clearness of faculties.

Lovers and madmen have their seething brains,
Such shaping fantasies that apprehend
More than cool reason ever comprehends.
Shakesp.

When valour preys on reason,
It eats the sword it fights with.
Shakesp. Ant. and Cleop.

8. Right, justice.

I was promis'd on a time,
To have reason for my rhyme:
From that time unto this season,
I receiv'd nor rhyme nor reason. Spenser.

Are you in earnest?
—Ay, and resolv'd withal
To do myself this reason and this right.
Shakesp.

The papists ought in reason to allow them all the excuses they make use of for themselves; such as an invincible ignorance, oral tradition and authority. Stillingfleet.

Let it drink deep in thy most vital part;
Strike home, and do me reason in thy heart.
Dryden.

9. Reasonable claim; just practice.

God brings good out of evil; and therefore it were but reason we should trust God to govern his own world, and wait till the change cometh, or the reason be discovered. Taylor.

Conscience, not acting by law, is a boundless presumptuous thing; and, for any one by virtue thereof, to challenge himself a privilege of doing what he will, and of being

unaccountable, is in all reason too much, either for man or angel. South.

A severe reflection Montaigne has made on princes, that we ought not in reason to have any expectatious of favour from them. Dryden's Dedication to Aurengzebe.

We have as great assurance that there is a God, as the nature of the thing to be proved is capable of, and as we could in reason expect to have. Tillotson's Preface.

When any thing is proved by as good arguments as a thing of that kind is capable of, we ought not in reason to doubt of its existence. Tillotson.

10. Rationale; just account.

To render a reason of an effect or phenomenon, is to deduce it from something else more known than itself. Boyle.

11. Moderation; moderate demands.

The most probable way of bringing France to reason, would be by the making an attempt upon the Spanish West Indies, and by that means to cut off all communication with this great source of riches. Addison.

to reáson v.n. [*raisonner*, Fr.]

1. To argue rationally; to deduce consequences justly from premises.

No man, in the strength of the first grace, can merit the second; for reason they do not, who think so; unless a beggar, by receiving one alms, can merit another. South.

Ideas, as ranked under names, are those, that for the most part men reason of within themselves, and always those which they commune about with others. Locke.

Every man's reasoning and knowledge is only about the ideas existing in his own mind; and our knowledge and reasoning about other things is only as they correspond with those our particular ideas. Locke.

Love is not to be reason'd down, or lost
In high ambition. Addison.

   In the lonely grove,
'Twas there just and good he reason'd strong,
Clear'd some great truth. Tickell.

2. To debate; to discourse; to talk; to take or give an account. Not in use.

Reason with the fellow,
Before you punish him, where he heard this.
Shakesp.

I reason'd with a Frenchman yesterday,
Who told me in the narrow seas,
There miscarried a vessel of our country.
Shakesp.

Stand still, that I may reason with you of all
the righteous acts of the Lord. 1 Sam. xii. 7.

3. To raise disquisitions; to make enquiries.

Jesus, perceiving their thoughts, said, what
reason ye in your hearts? Luke v. 22.

They reason'd high
Of providence, foreknowledge, will and fate.
Milton.

Already by thy reasoning this I guess,
Who art to lead thy offspring; and supposest,
That bodies bright and greater should not serve
The less not bright. Milton.

Down reason then, at least vain reasoning
down. Milt.

to reáson v.a. To examine rationally. This is a French mode of speech.

When they are clearly discovered, well
digested, and well reasoned in every part,
there is beauty in such a theory. Burn.

rébeck n.s. [*rebec*, Fr. *ribecca*, Italian.]
A three stringed fiddle.

When the merry bells ring round,
And the jocund rebecks sound,
To many a youth and many a maid,
Dancing in the checker'd shade. Milton.

rébel n.s. [*rebelle*, Fr. *rebellis*, Lat.] One who opposes lawful authority.

The merciless Macdonel
Worthy to be a rebel; for to that
The multiplying villanies of nature
Do swarm upon him. Shakesp. Macbeth.

The rebels there are up,
And put the Englishmen unto the sword.
Shakesp.

Shall man from nature's sanction stray,
A rebel to her rightful sway. Fenton.

rébus n.s. [*rebus*, Latin.] A word represented by a picture.

Some citizens, wanting arms, have coined
themselves certain devices alluding to their
names, which we call rebus: Master Jugge the
printer, in many of his books, took, to express
his name, a nightingale sitting in a bush with
a scrole in her mouth, wherein was written
jugge, jugge, jugge. Peac.

receípt n.s. [*receptum*, Latin.]

1. The act of receiving.

Villain, thou did'st deny the gold's receipt,
And told me of a mistress. Shakesp.
Com. of Err.

It must be done upon the receit of the wound,
before the patient's spirits be overheated.
Wiseman's Surgery.

The joy of a monarch for the news of a victory
must not be expressed like the ecstasy of a
harlequin, on the receipt of a letter from his
mistress. Dryden.

2. The place of receiving.

Jesus saw Matthew sitting at the receipt
of custom. Matt.

3. [*Recepte*, Fr.] A note given, by which money is acknowledged to have been received.

4. Reception; admission.

It is of things heavenly an universal
declaration, working in them, whose hearts
God inspireth with the due consideration
thereof, an habit or disposition of mind,
whereby they are made fit vessels, both for the
receipt and delivery of whatsoever spiritual
perfection. Hooker, b. v. s. 37.

5. Reception; welcome.

The same words in my lady Philoclea's mouth
might have had a better grace, and perchance
have found a gentler receipt. Sidney.

6. [From *recipe*.] Prescription of ingredients for any composition.

On 's bed of death
Many receipts he gave me, chiefly one
Of his old experience th' only darling.
Shakesp.

That Medea could make old men young
again, was nothing else, but that, from
knowledge of simples, she had a receipt
to make white hair black. Brown's
Vulgar Errours.

Wise leeches will not vain receipts obtrude,
While growing pains pronounce the humours
	crude. Dryd.

Some dryly plain, without invention's aid,
Write dull receipts how poems may be made.
Pope.

Scribonius found the receipt in a letter wrote
to Tiberius, and was never able to procure the
receipt during the emperor's life. Arbuthnot
on Coins.

récipe n.s. [*recipe*, Lat. the term used by
physicians, when they direct ingredients.]
A medical prescription.

I should enjoin you travel; for absence doth
in a kind remove the cause, and answers the
physicians first recipe, vomiting and purging;
but this would be too harsh. Suckling.

Th' apothecary train is wholly blind,
From files a random recipe they take,
And many deaths of one prescription make.
Dryden.

récitative, recitatívo n.s. [from *recite*.] A
kind of tuneful pronunciation, more
musical than common speech, and less
than song; chaunt.

He introduced the examples of moral virtue,
writ in verse, and performed in recitative
musick. Dryden.

By singing peers upheld on either hand,
Then thus in quaint recitativo spoke.
Dunciad, b. iv.

rédcoat n.s. A name of contempt for
a soldier.

The fearful passenger, who travels late,
Shakes at the moon-shine shadow of a rush,
And sees a redcoat rise from ev'ry bush.
Dryden.

reformátion n.s. [*reformation*, Fr. from
reform.]

1. Change from worse to better.

Never came reformation in a flood
With such a heady current, scow'ring faults;
Nor ever Hydra-headed wilfulness
So soon did lose his seat, as in this king.
Shakesp. Henry V.

Satire lashes vice into reformation. Dryden.

The pagan converts mention this great
reformation of those who had been the greatest
sinners, with that sudden and surprising
change, which the christian religion made in
the lives of the most profligate. Addison.

2. The change of religion from the
corruptions of popery to its primitive
state.

The burden of the reformation lay on Luther's
shoulders. Atterbury.

refráction n.s. [*refraction*, Fr.] Refraction,
in general, is the incurvation or change of
determination in the body moved, which
happens to it whilst it enters or penetrates
any medium: in dioptricks, it is the
variation of a ray of light from that right
line, which it would have passed on in, had
not the density of the medium turned it
aside. Harris.

Refraction, out of the rarer medium into the
denser, is made towards the perpendicular.
Newton's Opticks.

régicide n.s. [*regicida*, Lat.]

1. Murderer of his king.

I through the mazes of the bloody field,
Hunted your sacred life; which that I miss'd
Was the propitious error of my fate,
Not of my soul; my soul's a regicide. Dryden.

2. [*Regicidium*, Lat.] Murder of his king.

Were it not for this amulet, how were it
possible for any to think they may venture
upon perjury, sacrilege, murder, regicide,
without impeachment to their saintship.
D. of Piety.

Did fate or we, when great Atrides dy'd,
Urge the bold traitor to the regicide.
Pope's Odyssey.

réglet n.s. [*reglette*, from *regle*, Fr.] Ledge of wood exactly planed, by which printers separate their lines in pages widely printed.

régular n.s. [*regulier*, Fr.] In the Romish church, all persons are said to be *regulars*, that do profess and follow a certain rule of life, in Latin stiled *regula;* and do likewise observe the three approved vows of poverty, chastity and obedience. Ayliffe's Parergon.

to reláx v.a. [*relaxo*, Lat.]

1. To slacken; to make less tense.

The sinews, when the southern wind bloweth,
are more relax. Bacon's Natural History.

2. To remit; to make less severe or rigorous.

The statute of mortmain was at several times
relaxed by the legislature. Swift.

3. To make less attentive or laborious.

Nor praise relax, nor difficulty fright.
Vanity of Wishes.

4. To ease; to divert.

5. To open; to loose.

It serv'd not to relax their serried files.
Milton.

religion n.s. [*religion*, Fr. *religio*, Lat.]

1. Virtue, as founded upon reverence of God, and expectation of future rewards and punishments.

He that is void of fear, may soon be just,
And no religion binds men to be traitors.
Benj. Johnson.

One spake much of right and wrong,
Of justice, of religion, truth and peace
And judgment from above. Milton.

If we consider it as directed against God,
it is a breach of religion; if as to men, it is
an offence against morality. South.

By her inform'd, we best religion learn,
Its glorious object by her aid discern.
Blackmore.

Religion or virtue, in a large sense, includes
duty to God and our neighbour; but in a
proper sense, virtue signifies duty towards
men, and religion duty to God. Watts.

2. A system of divine faith and worship as opposite to others.

The image of a brute, adorn'd
With gay religions, full of pomp and gold.
Milton.

The christian religion, rightly understood, is
the deepest and choicest piece of philosophy
that is. More.

The doctrine of the gospel proposes to men
such glorious rewards and such terrible
punishments as no religion ever did, and gives
us far greater assurance of their reality and
certainty than ever the world had. Tillotson.

religionist n.s. [from *religion.*] A bigot to any religious persuasion.

The lawfulness of taking oaths may be
revealed to the quakers, who then will stand
upon as good a foot for preferment as any
other subject; under such a motly
administration, what pullings and hawlings,
what a zeal and biass there will be in each
religionist to advance his own tribe, and
depress the others. Swift.

religious adj. [*religieux*, Fr. *religiosus*, Lat.]

1. Pious; disposed to the duties of religion.

It is a matter of sound consequence, that all
duties are by so much the better performed, by
how much the men are more religious, from
whose habilities the same proceed. Hook.

When holy and devout religious christians
Are at their beads, 'tis hard to draw them
from thence;
So sweet is zealous contemplation! Shakesp.

Their lives
Religious titled them the sons of God. Milton.

2. Teaching religion.

He God doth late and early pray,
More of his grace than gifts to lend;
And entertains the harmless day
With a religious book or friend. Wotton.

3. Among the Romanists, bound by the vows of poverty, chastity and obedience.

Certain fryars and religious men were moved with some zeal, to draw the people to the christian faith. Abbot.

France has vast numbers of ecclesiasticks, secular and religious. Addison's State of the War.

What the protestants would call a fanatick, is in the Roman church a religious of such an order; as an English merchant in Lisbon, after some great disappointments in the world, resolved to turn capuchin. Addison.

4. Exact; strict.

Renárd n.s. [*renard*, a fox, Fr.] The name of a fox in fable.

> *Before the break of day,*
> *Renard through the hedge had made his way.*
> Dryden.

renáscent adj. [*renascens*, Lat.] Produced again; rising again into being.

to repaír v.n. [*repairer*, Fr.] To go to; to betake himself.

May all to Athens back again repair. Shakesp.

> *Depart from hence in peace,*
> *Search the wide world, and where you*
>   *please repair.* Dryd.

'Tis fix'd; th' irrevocable doom of Jove:
Haste then, Cyllenius, through the liquid air,
Go mount the winds, and to the shades repair.
Pope.

represéntative n.s.

1. One exhibiting the likeness of another.

A statue of rumour whispering an idiot in the ear, who was the representative of credulity. Addison's Freeholder.

2. One exercising the vicarious power given by another.

I wish the welfare of my country; and my morals and politicks teach me to leave all that to be adjusted by our representatives above, and to divine providence. Blount to Pope.

3. That by which any thing is shown.

Difficulty must cumber this doctrine, which supposes that the perfections of God are the representatives to us, of whatever we perceive in the creatures. Locke.

reptíle n.s. An animal that creeps upon many feet.

Terrestial animals may be divided into quadrupeds or reptiles, which have many feet, and serpents which have no feet. Locke's Elements of Natural Philosophy.

Holy retreat! sithence no female hither,
Conscious of social love and nature's rites,
Must dare approach, from the inferior reptile,
To woman, form divine. Prior.

repúblican n.s. [from *republick*.] One who thinks a commonwealth without monarchy the best government.†

These people are more happy in imagination than the rest of their neighbours, because they think themselves so; though such a chimerical happiness is not peculiar to republicans. Add.

repúblick n.s. [*respublica*, Lat. *republique*, Fr.] Commonwealth; state in which the power is lodged in more than one.

> *Those that by their deeds will make it known,*
>   *Whose dignity they do sustain;*
>   *And life, state, glory, all they gain,*
> *Count the republick's, not their own.*
> Benj. Johnson.

They are indebted many millions more than their whole republick is worth. Addison's State of the War.

réremouse n.s. [*hreremus*, Saxon.] A bat.

rescíssory adj. [*rescissoire*, Fr. *rescissus*, Lat.] Having the power to cut off.

restauratión n.s. [*restauro*, Lat.] The act of recovering to the former state.

Adam is in us an original cause of our nature, and of that corruption of nature which causeth death; Christ as the cause original of restauration to life. Hooker, b. v. s. 56.

O my dear father! restauration hang
Thy medicine on my lips; and let this kiss
Repair those violent harms, that my two sisters
Have in thy reverence made. Shakesp.
King Lear.

Spermatical parts will not admit a regeneration, much less will they receive an integral restauration. Brown.

restórative n.s. [from *restore*.] A medicine that has the power of recruiting life.

I will kiss thy lips;
Haply some poison yet doth hang on them,
To make me die with a restorative. Shakesp. Rom. and Jul.

God saw it necessary by such mortifications to quench the boundless rage of an insatiable intemperance, to make the weakness of the flesh, the physick and restorative of the spirit. South's Sermons.

Asses milk is an excellent restorative in consumptions. Mort.

He prescribes an English gallon of asses milk, especially as a restorative. Arbuthnot.

resurréction n.s. [*resurrection*, Fr. *resurrectum*, Lat.] Revival from the dead; return from the grave.

The Sadduces were grieved, that they taught, and preached through Jesus the resurrection from the dead. Acts iv. 2.

Nor after resurrection shall he stay
Longer on earth, than certain times t' appear
To his disciples. Milton.

He triumphs in his agonies, whilst the soul springs forward to the great object which she has always had in view, and leaves the body with an expectation of being remitted to her in a glorious and joyful resurrection. Addison's Spectator.

Perhaps there was nothing ever done in all past ages, and which was not a publick fact, so well attested as the resurrection of Christ. Watts.

to retíre v.n. [*retirer*, Fr.]

1. To retreat; to withdraw; to go to a place of privacy.

The mind contracts herself, and shrinketh in,
And to herself she gladly doth retire. Davies.

The less I may be blest with her company, the more I will retire to God and my own heart. King Charles.

Thou open'st wisdom's way,
And giv'st access, though secret she retire. Milton.

The parliament dissolved, and gentlemen charged to retire to their country habitations. Hayward.

2. To retreat from danger.

Set up the standard towards Zion,
retire, stay not. Jer.

Set Uriah in the fore front of the hottest battle, and retire ye from him, that he may die. 2 Sam. xi. 15.

From each hand with speed retir'd,
Where erst was thickest th' angelick throng. Milton.

3. To go from a publick station.

He, that had driven many out of their country, perished in a strange land, retiring to the Lacedemonians. 2 Mac. v.

4. To go off from company.

The old fellow skuttled out of the room, and retired. Arb.

revelátion n.s. [from *revelation*, Fr.] Discovery; communication; communication of sacred and mysterious truths by a teacher from heaven.

When the divine revelations were committed to writing, the Jews were such scrupulous reverers of them, that they numbered even the letters of the Old Testament. D. of Pie.

As the gospel appears in respect of the law to be a clearer revelation of the mystical part, so it is a far more benign dispensation of the practical part. Sprat.

revolútion n.s. [*revolution*, Fr. *revolutus*, Lat.]

1. Course of any thing which returns to the point at which it began to move.

On their orbs impose
Such restless revolution, day by day
Repeated. Milton's Paradise Lost, b. viii.

They will be taught by the diurnal revolution of the heavens. Watts's Improvement of the Mind.

2. Space measured by some revolution.

At certain revolutions are they brought,
And feel by turns the bitter change. Milton.

Meteors have no more time allowed them for their mounting, than the short revolution of a day. Dryden.

The Persian wept over his army, that within the revolution of a single age, not a man would be left alive. Wake.

3. Change in the state of a government or country. It is used among us κατα εξοχην, for the change produced by the admission of king William and queen Mary.†

4. Rotation in general; returning motion.

    Fear
Comes thund'ring back with dreadful revolution
On my defenseless head. Milton.

rhabárbarate adj. [from *rhabarbara,* Lat.] Impregnated or tinctured with rhubarb.

The salt humours must be evacuated by the sennate, rhabarbarate, and sweet manna purgers, with acids added, or the purging waters. Floyer on the Humours.

rhápsody n.s. [ραψωδια; ραπτω, to sew, and ωδη, a song.] Any number of parts joined together, without necessary dependence or natural connection.

Such a deed, as sweet religion makes
A rhapsody of words. Shakesp. Hamlet.

This confusion and rhapsody of difficulties was not to be supposed in each single sinner. Hammond.

He, that makes no reflexions on what he reads, only loads his mind with a rhapsody of tales fit for the entertainment of others. Locke.

The words slide over the ears, and vanish like a rhapsody of evening tales. Watts's Improvement of the Mind.

rhétorick n.s. [ρητορικη; *rhetorique,* Fr.]

1. The act of speaking not merely with propriety, but with art and elegance.

We could not allow him an orator, who had the best thoughts, and who knew all the rules of rhetorique, if he had not acquired the art of using them. Dryden's Dufresnoy.

Of the passions, and how they are moved, Aristotle, in his second book of rhetorick, hath admirably discoursed in a little compass. Locke's Thoughts on Reading.

Grammar teacheth us to speak properly, rhetorick instructs to speak elegantly. Baker's Reflections on Learning.

2. The power of persuasion; oratory.

The heart's still rhetorick, disclos'd with eyes. Shakesp.

His sober lips then did he softly part, Whence of pure rhetorick whole streams outflow. Fairfax.

Enjoy your dear wit and gay rhetorick, That hath so well been taught her dazling fence. Milton.

rheum n.s. [ρευμα; *rheume,* Fr.] A thin watery matter oozing through the glands, chiefly about the mouth. Quincy.

Trust not those cunning waters of his eyes; For villainy is not without such a rheum; And he long traded in it, makes it seem Like rivers of remorse. Shakesp.

You did void your rheum upon my beard. Shakesp.

Why holds thine eye that lamentable rheum, Like a proud river peering o'er his bounds. Shakesp.

Each changing season does its poison bring, Rheums chill the winter, agues blast the spring. Prior.

rhinóceros n.s. [ριν and κερας; *rhinocerot,* Fr.] A vast beast in the East Indies armed with a horn in his front.

Approach thou like the rugged Russian bear, The arm'd rhinoceros, or Hyrcanian tyger; Take any shape but that, and my firm nerves Shall never tremble. Shakesp. Macbeth.

If you draw your beast in an emblem, shew a landscape of the country natural to the beast; as to the rhinoceros an East Indian landscape, the crocodile, an Egyptian. Peacham.

rhyme n.s. [ρυθμος; *rhythme,* Fr.]

1. A harmonical succession of sounds.

2. The consonance of verses; the correspondence of the last sound of one verse to the last sound or syllable of another.

The youth with songs and rhimes:
Some dance, some hale the rope. Denham.

For rhyme the rudder is of verses,
With which like ships they steer their courses.
Hudibras.

Such was the news, indeed, but songs and rhymes
Prevail as much in these hard iron times;
As would a plump of trembling fowl, that rise
Against an eagle sousing from the skies.
Dryden.

If Cupid throws a single dart,
We make him wound the lover's heart;
But if he takes his bow and quiver,
'Tis sure he must transfix the liver;
For rhime with reason may dispense,
And sound has right to govern sense. Prior.

3. Poetry; a poem.

All his manly power it did disperse,
As he were warmed with inchanted rhimes,
That oftentimes he quak'd. Fairy Queen, b. i.

Who would not sing for Lycidas? he knew
Himself to sing, and build the lofty rhyme.
Milton.

　　Now sportive youth,
Carol incondite rhythms with suiting notes,
And quaver inharmonious. Philips.

rhyme or reason Number or sense.

I was promis'd on a time,
To have reason for my rhyme;
But from that time unto this season,
I had neither rhyme nor reason. Spenser.

The guiltiness of my mind drove the grossness
of the foppery into a received belief, in
despight of the teeth of all rhime and reason,
that they were fairies. Shakesp.

rhymer, rhymster n.s. [from *rhyme*.] One who makes rhymes; a versifier; a poet in contempt.

Scall'd rhimers will ballad us out o' tune.
Shakesp.

It was made penal to the English, to permit
the Irish to graze upon their lands, to
entertain any of their ministrels, rhimers,
or news-tellers. Davies on Ireland.

Rhymer come on, and do the worst you can;
I fear not you, nor yet a better man. Dryden.

His rhime is constrained at an age, when the
passion of love makes every man a rhimer,
though not a poet. Dryden.

I speak of those who are only rhimsters.
Dennis.

So modern rhimers wisely blast
The poetry of ages past,
And from its ruin build their own. Shakesp.†

rhythmical adj. [ρυθμικος; *rythmique*, Fr. from *rhyme* or *rhythm*.] Harmonical; having proportion of one sound to another.

ríbald n.s. [*ribauld*, Fr. *ribaldo*, Italian.] A loose, rough, mean, brutal wretch.

That lewd ribbald, with vile lust advanced,
Laid first his filthy hands on virgin clean,
To spoil her dainty corse so fair and sheen.
Fairy Queen.

　　Your ribauld nag of Egypt,
The breeze upon her, like a cow in June,
Hoists sails, and flies. Shakesp. Antony and Cleopatra.

　　The busy day,
Wak'd by the lark, has rous'd the ribald crows,
And dreaming night will hide our joys no
　　longer. Shakesp.

Ne'er one sprig of laurel grac'd these ribbalds,
From slashing Bentley down to pidling
　　Tibbalds. Pope.†

ríband n.s. [*rubande, ruban*, Fr.] A filet of silk; a narrow web of silk, which is worn for ornament.

Quaint in green, she shall be loose enrob'd,
With ribbands pendent, flaring 'bout her
　　head. Shakesp.

A ribband did the braided tresses bind,
The rest was loose. Dryden's Knight's Tale.

See! in the lists they wait the trumpets sound;
Some love device is wrought on ev'ry sword,

And ev'ry riband bears some mystick word.
Granville.

to ríbroast v.n. [*rib* and *roast.*] To beat
soundly. A burlesque word.

That done, he rises, humbly bows,
And gives thanks for the princely blows;
Departs not meanly proud, and boasting
Of his magnificent ribroasting. Butler.

I have been pinched in flesh, and well
ribroasted under my former masters; but
I'm in now for skin and all. L'Estrange.

rice n.s. [*oryza*, Lat.] One of the esculent
grains: it hath its grains disposed into a
panicle, which are almost of an oval figure,
and are covered with a thick husk,
somewhat like barley: this grain is greatly
cultivated in most of the Eastern countries.
Miller.

Rice is the food of two thirds of mankind; it
is kindly to human constitutions, proper for
the consumptive, and those subject to
hæmorrhages. Arbuthnot.

If the snuff get out of the snuffers, it may fall
into a dish of rice milk. Swift's Directions
to the Butler.

rídicule n.s. [*ridicule*, Fr. *ridiculum*, Lat.]
Wit of that species that provokes laughter.

Sacred to ridicule his whole life long,
And the sad burthen of some merry song.
Pope.

Touch'd and sham'd by ridicule alone. Pope.

Those, who aim at ridicule,
Should fix upon some certain rule,
Which fairly hints they are in jest.
Swift's Miscellanies.

rigadóon n.s. [*rigadon*, French.] A dance.

rigátion n.s. [*rigatio*, Lat.] The act of
watering. Dict.

right n.s.

1. Justice; not wrong.

Persons of noble blood are less envied in their
rising; for it seemeth but right done to their
birth. Bacon.

In the midst of your invectives, do the Turks
this right, as to remember that they are no
idolaters. Bacon.

One rising, eminent
In wise deport, spake much of right and wrong,
Of justice, of religion, truth, and peace,
And judgement from above. Milton's
Par. Lost.

Long love to her has borne the faithful knight,
And well deserv'd, had fortune done him
right. Dryden.

He, that would do right to religion, cannot
take a more effectual course, than by
reconciling it with the happiness of mankind.
Tillotson.

2. Freedom from errour.

Seldom your opinions err;
Your eyes are always in the right. Prior.

3. Just claim.

The Roman citizens were, by the sword,
taught to acknowledge the pope their lord,
though they knew not by what right.
Raleigh's Essays.

The proud tyrant would many times say, that
whatsoever belonged unto the empire of
Rome, was of right his, for as much as he was
possessed of the imperial scepter, which his
great grandfather Mahomet had by law of
arms won from Constantine. Knolles's
History of the Turks.

Subdue by force, all who refuse
Right reason for their law; and for their king
Messiah, who by right of merit reigns.
Milton.

My right to it appears,
By long possession of eight hundred years.
Dryden.

Might and right are inseparable in the
opinion of the world. L'Estrange's Fables.

Descriptions, figures, and fables must be in all
heroick poems; every poet hath as much right
to them, as every man hath to air. Dryden.

Judah pronounced sentence of death against
Thamar: our author thinks it is very good
proof, that because he did it, therefore he had
a right to do it. Locke.

Agrippa is generally ranged in sets of medals among the the emperors; as some among the empresses have no other right. Addison.

4. That which justly belongs to one.

To thee doth the right of her appertain, seeing thou only art of her kindred. Tob. vi. 11.

The custom of employing these great persons in all great offices, passes for a right. Temple.

The pris'ner freed himself by nature's laws, Born free, he sought his right. Dryden's Knight's Tale.

5. Property; interest.

A subject in his prince may claim a right, Nor suffer him with strength impair'd to fight. Dryden.

6. Power; prerogative.

God hath a sovereign right over us, as we are his creatures, and by virtue of this right, he might, without injustice, have imposed difficult tasks: but in making laws, he hath not made use of this right. Tillotson.

7. Immunity; privilege.

*The citizens,
Let them but have their rights, are ever forward
In celebration of this day with shews.*
Shakesp.

Their only thoughts and hope was to defend their own rights and liberties, due to them by the law. Clarendon.

8. The side not left.

*On his right
The radiant image of his glory sat,
His only son.* Milton.

9. To rights. In a direct line; straight.

These strata failing, the whole tract sinks down to rights into the abyss, and is swallowed up by it. Woodward.

10. To rights. Deliverance from errour.

Several have gone about to inform them, and set them to rights; but for want of that knowledge of the present system of nature, have not given the satisfaction expected. Woodw.

ringleáder n.s. [*ring* and *leader.*] The head of a riotous body.

He caused to be executed some of the ringleaders of the Cornish men, in sacrifice to the citizens. Bacon's Henry VII.

The nobility escaped; the poor people, who had been deluded by these ringleaders, were executed. Addison.

ríot n.s. [*riotte*, old Fr. *riotto*, Italian.]

1. Wild and loose festivity.

*When his headstrong riot hath no curb,
When rage and hot blood are his counsellors,
When means and lavish manners meet together,
Oh! with what wings shall his affection fly
Tow'rd fronting peril and oppos'd decay.*
Shakesp. Hen. IV.

*So senseless of expence,
That he will neither know how to maintain it,
Nor cease his flow of riot.* Shakesp. Timon of Athens.

*All now was turn'd to jollity and game,
To luxury and riot, feast and dance.* Milton.

2. A sedition; an uproar.

*Transform'd to serpents all, as accessories
To his bold riot.* Milton.

3. To run riot. To move or act without controll or restraint.

One man's head runs riot upon hawks and dice. L'Estr.

*You never can defend his breeding,
Who, in his satyre's running riot,
Could never leave the world in quiet.*
Swift's Miscel.

rite n.s. [*rit*, Fr. *ritus*, Lat.] Solemn act of religion; external observance.

The ceremonies, we have taken from such as were before us, are not things that belong to this or that sect, but they are the ancient rites and customs of the church. Hooker.

It is by God consecrated into a sacrament, a holy rite, a means of conveying to the worthy receiver the benefits of the body and blood of Christ. Hammond's Fundamentals.

When the prince her fun'ral rites had paid,
He plow'd the Tyrrhene seas. Dryden.

rítual adj. [*rituel*, Fr.] Solemnly ceremonious; done according to some religious institution.

Instant I bade the priests prepare
The ritual sacrifice, and solemn pray'r. Prior.

If to tradition were added, certain constant ritual and emblematical observances, as the emblems were expressive, the memory of the thing recorded would remain. Forbes.

rixdóllar n.s. A German coin, worth about four shillings and six-pence sterling. Dict.

robóreous adj. [*robur*, Lat.] Made of oak. Dict.

rócket n.s. [*rocchetto*, Italian.] An artificial firework, being a cylindrical case of paper filled with nitre, charcoal, and sulphur, and which mounts in the air to a considerable height, and there bursts.

Every rocket ended in a constellation, strowing the air with a shower of silver spangles. Addison.

When bonefires blaze, your vagrant works shall rise
In rockets, till they reach the wond'ring skies. Garth.

to rodomontáde v.n. [from the noun.] To brag thrasonically; to boast like Rodomonte.†

rogue n.s. [of uncertain etymology.]

1. A wandering beggar; a vagrant; a vagabond.

For fear lest we, like rogues, should be reputed,
And for ear-marked beasts abroad be bruited. Hubberd.

The sheriff and the marshal may do the more good, and more terrify the idle rogue. Spenser on Ireland.

The scum of people and wicked condemned men spoileth the plantation; for they will ever live like rogues, and not fall to work, but be lazy and do mischief. Bacon's Essays.

The troops are all scattered, and the commanders very poor rogues. Shakesp. All's well that ends well.

2. A knave; a dishonest fellow; a villain; a thief.

Thou kill'st me like a rogue and a villain. Shakesp.

A rogue upon the highway may have as strong an arm, and take off a man's head as cleverly as the executioner; but then there is a vast disparity, when one action is murther, and the other justice. South.

If he call rogue and rascal from the garret,
He means you no more mischief than a parrot. Dryden.

The rogue and fool by fits is fair and wise,
And ev'n the best, by fits, what they despise. Pope.

3. A name of slight tenderness and endearment.

Oh, what a rogue and pleasant slave am I! Shakesp.

I never knew a woman love man so.
—Alas, poor rogue, I think indeed she loves. Shakesp.

4. A wag.

roíster, or **roisterer** n.s. [from the verb.] A turbulent, brutal, lawless, blustering fellow.

róllypooly n.s. A sort of game, in which, when a ball rolls into a certain place, it wins. A corruption of roll ball into the pool.

Let us begin some diversion; what d' ye think of roulypouly or a country dance? Arbuthnot's History of John Bull.

románce n.s. [*roman*, Fr. *romanza*, Italian.]

1. A military fable of the middle ages; a tale of wild adventures in war and love.

What resounds
In fable or romance of Uther's son. Milton.

A brave romance who would exactly frame,
First brings his knight from some immortal dame. Waller.

Some romances entertain the genius; and strengthen it by the noble ideas which they give of things; but they corrupt the truth of history. Dryden's Dufresnoy.

2. A lie; a fiction. In common speech.

to románce v.n. [from the noun.] To lie; to forge.

This is strange romancing. Pamela.

to rómanize v.a. [from *roman*, Fr.] To latinize; to fill with modes of the Roman speech.

He did too much romanize our tongue, leaving the words, he translated, almost as much Latin as he found them. Dryd.

romántick adj. [from *romance*.]

1. Resembling the tales of romances; wild.

Philosophers have maintained opinions, more absurd than any of the most fabulous poets or romantick writers. Keil.

Zeal for the good of one's country a party of men have represented, as chimerical and romantick. Addison.

2. Improbable; false.

3. Fanciful; full of wild scenery.

The dun umbrage, o'er the falling stream, Romantick hangs. Thomson's Spring.

Rómish adj. [from *Rome*.] Popish.

Bulls or letters of election only serve in the Romish countries. Ayliffe's Parergon.

romp n.s.

1. A rude, awkward, boisterous, untaught girl.

She was in the due mean between one of your affected courtesying pieces of formality, and your romps that have no regard to the common rules of civility. Arbuthnot.

2. Rough rude play.

Romp loving miss Is haul'd about in gallantry robust. Thomson.

rónion n.s. [I know not the etymology, nor certainly the meaning of this word.] A fat bulky woman.

Give me, quoth I, Aroint the witch! the rump fed ronyon cries. Shakesp.

rópedancer n.s. [*rope* and *dancer*.] An artist who dances on a rope.

Salvian, amongst other publick shews, mentions the Petaminarii; probably derived from the Greek πιτασθαι, which signifies to fly, and may refer to such kind of ropedancers. Wilkins's Mathemaitcal Magick.

Statius, posted on the highest of the two summits, the people regarded with the same terror, as they look upon a daring ropedancer, whom they expect to fall every moment. Addison's Guardian.

Nic bounced up with a spring equal to that of one of your nimblest tumblers or ropedancers, and fell foul upon John Bull, to snatch the cudgel he had in his hand. Arbuthnot.

rópetrick n.s. [*rope* and *trick*.] Probably rogue's tricks; tricks that deserve the halter.

She may perhaps call him half a score knaves, or so: an he begin once, he'll rail in his ropetricks. Shakespeare.

rorífluent adj. [*ros* and *fluo*, Lat.] Flowing with dew. Dict.

rósary n.s. [*rosarium*, Lat.] A bunch of beads, on which the Romanists number their prayers.

No rosary this votress needs, Her very syllables are beads. Cleaveland.

Every day propound to yourself a rosary or a chaplet of good works, to present to God at night. Taylor.

rose n.s. [*rose*, Fr. *rosa*, Lat.] A flower.

The flower of the rose is composed of several leaves, which are placed circularly, and expand in a beautiful order, whose leafy flower-cup afterward becomes a roundish or oblong fleshy fruit inclosing several angular hairy seeds; to which may be added, it is a weak pithy shrub, for the most part beset with prickles, and hath pinnated leaves: the species are, 1. The wild briar, dog rose, or hep-tree. 2. Wild briar or dog rose, with large prickly heps. 3. The greater English apple-bearing rose. 4. The dwarf wild Burnet-leaved rose. 5. The dwarf wild Burnet-leaved rose, with variegated leaves. 6. The striped Scotch rose. 7. The sweet briar or eglantine. 8. Sweet briar, with a double flower. All the other sorts of roses are originally of foreign growth, but are hardy enough to endure the cold of our climate in the open air, and produce beautiful and fragrant flowers. Miller.

Make use of thy salt hours, season the slaves
For tubs and baths, bring down the rose
   cheek'd youth
To th' tub fast and the diet. Shakesp.
Timon of Athens.

Patience thou young and rose lipp'd cherubin. Shakesp.

Let us crown ourselves with rose buds, before they be withered. Wisdom ii. 8.

This way of procuring autumnal roses will, in most rose bushes, fail; but, in some good bearers, it will succeed. Boyle.

Here without thorn the rose. Milton.

For her th' unfading rose of Eden blooms. Pope.

to speak under the rose To speak any thing with safety, so as not afterwards to be discovered.

By desiring a secrecy to words spoke under the rose, we mean, in society and compotation, from the ancient custom in symposiack meetings, to wear chaplets of roses about their heads. Brown's Vulgar Errours.

rótgut n.s. [*rot* and *gut*.] Bad beer.

They overwhelm their panch daily with a kind of flat rotgut, we with a bitter dreggish small liquor. Harvey.

rotúndifolious adj. [*rotundus* and *folium*, Lat.] Having round leaves.

roúndel, roúndelay n.s.

1. [*Rondelet*, French.] A kind of ancient poetry, which commonly consists of thirteen verses, of which eight are of one kind of rhyme and five of another: it is divided into three couplets; and at the end of the second and third, the beginning of the roundel is repeated in an equivocal sense, if possible. Trevoux.

Siker, sike a roundle never heard I none,
Little lacketh Perigot of the best,

And Willie is not greatly over-gone,
So weren his under-songs well addrest.
Spenser's Past.

To hear thy rimes and roundelays,
Which thou wert wont in wastful hills to sing,
I more delight than lark in summer days,
Whose echo made the neighb'ring groves to
   ring. Spenser.

Come now a roundel and a fairy song.
Shakesp.

They list'ning heard him, while he search'd
   the grove,
And loudly sung his roundelay of love,
But on the sudden stop'd. Dryden's
Knight's Tale.

2. [*Rondelle*, Fr.] A round form or figure.

The Spaniards, casting themselves into roundels, and their strongest ships walling in the rest, made a flying march to Calais. Bacon.

The muses and graces made festivals; the fawns, satyrs, and nymphs did dance their roundelays. Howel.

roúndhead n.s. [*round* and *head*.] A puritan, so named from the practice once prevalent among them of cropping their hair round.

Your petitioner always kept hospitality, and drank confusion to the roundheads.
Spectator, No 629.

roúndhouse n.s. [*round* and *house*.] The constable's prison, in which disorderly persons, found in the street, are confined.

They march'd to some fam'd roundhouse.
Pope.

rouse n.s. [*rusch*, German, half drunk.] A dose of liquor rather too large.

They have given me a rouse already.
—Not past a pint as I am a soldier.
Shakesp. Othello.

No jocund health that Denmark drinks to-day,
But the great cannon to the clouds shall tell;
And the king's rouse shall bruit it back again,
Respeaking earthly thunder. Shakesp.

róyalist n.s. [from *royal*.] Adherent to a king.

Where Candish fought, the royalists prevail'd,
Neither his courage nor his judgment fail'd.
Waller.

The old church of England royalists, another
name for a man who prefers his conscience
before his interests, are the most meritorious
subjects in the world, as having passed all
those terrible tests, which domineering malice
could put them to, and carried their credit
and their conscience clear. South.

róyalty n.s. [*roialté*, Fr.]

1. Kingship; character or office of a king.

Suppose, that you have seen
The well appointed king at Hampton peer,
Embark his royalty. Shakesp. Henry V.

Draw, you rascal; you come with letters
against the king, and take vanity the puppet's
part against the royalty of her father.
Shakesp. King Lear.

He will lose his head, ere give consent,
His master's son, as worshipfully he terms it,
Shall lose the royalty of England's throne.
Shakesp.

If they had held their royalties by this title,
either there must have been but one sovereign,
or else every father of a family had as good
a claim to royalty as these. Locke.

2. State of a king.

I will, alas! be wretched to be great,
And sigh in royalty, and grieve in state.
Prior.

3. Emblems of royalty.

Wherefore do I assume
These royalties, and not refuse to reign.
Milton.

to royne v.a. [*rogner*, Fr.] To gnaw; to bite.
Spenser.

róynish adj. [*rogneux*, Fr. mangy, paltry.]
Paltry; sorry; mean; rude.

The roynish clown, at whom so oft
Your grace was wont to laugh, is also missing.
Shakesp.

rubífick adj. [*ruber* and *facio*, Lat.]
Making red.

While the several species of rays, as the
rubifick, are by refraction separated one from
another, they retain those motions proper to
each. Grew's Cosmol.

rúbrick n.s. [*rubrique*, Fr. *rubrica*, Lat.]
Directions printed in books of law and in
prayer books; so termed, because they were
originally distinguished by being in red ink.

No date prefix'd,
Directs me in the starry rubrick set.
Milton's Par. Reg.

They had their particular prayers according to
the several days and months; and their tables
or rubricks to instruct them. Stillingfleet.

rude adj. [*rede*, Saxon; *rudis*, Lat.]

1. Rough; savage; coarse of manners;
   uncivil; brutal.

Ruffian, let go that rude uncivil touch;
Thou friend of an ill fashion. Shakesp.

Vane's bold answers, termed rude and
ruffian–like, furthered his condemnation.
Hayward.

You can with single look inflame
The coldest breast, the rudest tame. Waller.

It has been so usual to write prefaces, that a
man is thought rude to his reader, who does
not give him some account beforehand.
Walsh.

2. Violent; tumultuous; boisterous;
   turbulent.

Clouds push'd with winds rude in their shock.
Milton.

The water appears white near the shore,
and a ship; because the rude agitation breaks
it into foam. Boyle.

3. Harsh; inclement.

Spring does to flow'ry meadows bring,
What the rude winter from them tore. Waller.

4. Ignorant; raw; untaught.

Though I be rude in speech, yet not in
knowledge. 2 Cor.

He was yet but rude in the profession of
arms, though greedy of honour. Wotton's
Buckingham.

Such tools as art yet rude had form'd. Milton.

5. [*Rude*, Fr.] Rugged; uneven; shapeless.

It was the custom to worship rude and unpolished stones. Stillingfleet.

6. Artless; inelegant.

I would know what ancient ground of authority he hath for such a senseless fable; and if he have any of the rude Irish books. Spenser.

One example may serve, till you review the Æneis in the original, unblemished by my rude translation. Dryden.

7. Such as may be done with strength without art.

To his country farm the fool confin'd;
Rude work well suited with a rustick mind.
Dryden.

rúderary adj. [*rudera*, Lat.] Belonging to rubbish. Dict.

rule n.s. [*regula*, Lat.]

1. Government; empire; sway; supreme command.

I am asham'd, that women
Should seek for rule, supremacy, or sway,
When they are bound to serve, love, and obey.
Shakesp.

May he live
Ever belov'd, and loving may his rule be!
Shakesp.

A wise servant shall have rule over a son that causeth shame. Proverbs xvii. 2.

There being no law of nature nor positive law of God, that determines which is the positive heir, the right of succession; and consequently of bearing rule, could not have been determined. Locke.

This makes them apprehensive of every tendency, to endanger that form of rule established by the law of their country. Addison's Freeholder, Nº 52.

Instruct me whence this uproar;
And wherefore Vanoe, the sworn friend to Rome,
Should spurn against our rule, and stir
The tributary provinces to war.
A. Philips's Briton.

Sev'n years the traytor rich Mycenæ sway'd,
And his stern rule the groaning land obey'd.
Pope.

2. An instrument by which lines are drawn.

If your influence be quite dam'd up
With black usurping mists, some gentle taper,
Though a rush-candle from the wicker hole
Of some clay habitation, visit us
With thy long levell'd rule of streaming light.
Milton.

A judicious artist will use his eye, but he will trust only to his rule. South's Sermons.

3. Canon; precept by which the thoughts or actions are directed.

Adam's sin did not deprive him of his rule, but left the creatures to a reluctation. Bacon.

This little treatise will furnish you with infallible rules of judging truly. Dryden's Dufresnoy.

Know'st with an equal hand to hold the scale;
See'st where the reasons pinch, and where they fail,
And where exceptions o'er the general rule prevail. Dry.

We profess to have embraced a religion, which contains the most exact rules for the government of our lives. Tillots.

We owe to christianity the discovery of the most certain and perfect rule of life. Tillotson.

4. Regularity; propriety of behaviour.

Some say he's mad; others, that lesser hate him,
Do call it valiant fury; but for certain,
He cannot buckle his distemper'd cause
Within the belt of rule. Shakesp. Macbeth.

rum n.s.

1. A country parson. A cant word.

I'm grown a mere mopus; no company comes,
But a rabble of tenants and rusty dull rums.
Swift.

2. A kind of spirits distilled from molosses.

rúmour n.s. [*rumeur*, Fr. *rumor*, Lat.]
Flying or popular report; bruit; fame.

We hold rumour from what we fear. Shakesp.

    There ran a rumour
Of many worthy fellows that were out.
Shakesp. Macbeth.

Great is the rumour of this dreadful knight,
And his atchievements of no less account.
Shakesp.

This rumour of him went forth throughout
all Judea. Luke.

    Rumour next and chance
And tumult and confusion all embroil'd.
Milton.

She heard an ancient rumour fly,
That times to come should see the Trojan race
Her Carthage ruin. Dryden's Æneis.

rúnnion n.s. [*rognant*, Fr. scrubbing.] A
paltry scurvy wretch.

You witch! you poulcat! you runnion!
Shakesp.

rúricolist n.s. [*ruricola*, Lat.] An inhabitant
of the country. Dict.

ruse n.s. [French.] Cunning; artifice; little
stratagem; trick; wile; fraud; deceit. A
French word neither elegant nor necessary.

I might here add much concerning the wiles
and ruses, which these timid creatures use
to save themselves. Ray.

to rústicate v.a. To banish into the country.

I was deeply in love with a milliner, upon
which I was sent away, or, in the university
phrase, rusticated for ever. Spect.

rústick adj. [*rusticus*, Lat.]

1. Rural; country.

By Lelius willing missing was the odds of the
Iberian side, and continued so in the next by
the excellent running of a knight, though
fostered so by the muses, as many times the
very rustick people left both their delights and
profits to harken to his songs. Sidney, b. ii.

2. Rude; untaught; inelegant.

An ignorant clown cannot learn fine language
or a courtly behaviour, when his rustick airs
have grown up with him till the age of forty.
Watts's Logick.

3. Brutal; savage.

My soul foreboded I should find the bow'r
Of some fell monster, fierce with barb'rous pow'r;
Some rustick wretch, who liv'd in heav'n's
    despight,
Contemning laws, and trampling on
    the right. Pope.

4. Artless; honest; simple.

5. Plain; unadorned.

An altar stood, rustick, of grassy ford. Milton.

With unguents smooth the polish'd marble shone,
Where ancient Neleus sat, a rustick throne.
Pope.

rústick n.s. A clown; a swain; an inhabitant
of the country.

As nothing is so rude and insolent as a wealthy
rustick, all this his kindness is overlooked, and
his person most unworthily railed at. South.

rúttish adj. [from *rut*.] Wanton; libidinous;
salacious; lustful; lecherous.

That is an advertisement to one Diana, to
take heed of the allurement of count Rousillon,
a foolish idle boy; but for all that very ruttish.
Shakesp. All's well that ends well.

S, has in English the same hissing sound as in other languages, and unhappily prevails in so many of our words that it produces in the ear of a foreigner a continued sibilation.

In the beginning of words it has invariably its natural and genuine sound: in the middle it is sometimes uttered with a stronger appulse of the tongue to the palate, like *z*; as *rose, roseate, rosy, osier, nosel, resident, busy, business*. It sometimes keeps its natural sound; as *loose, designation*; for which I know not whether any rules can be given.

In the end of monosyllables it is sometimes *s*, as in *this*; and sometimes *z*, as in *as, has*; and generally where *es* stands in verbs for *eth*, as *gives*. It seems to be established as a rule, that no noun singular should end with *s* single: therefore in words written with diphthongs, and naturally long, an *e* is nevertheless added at the end, as *goose, house*; and where the syllable is short the *s* is doubled, and was once *sse*, as *ass*, anciently *asse*; *wilderness*, anciently *wildernesse*; *distress*, anciently *distresse*.

sabbátical adj. [*sabbaticus*, Lat. *sabbatique*, Fr. from *sabbath*.] Resembling the sabbath; enjoying or bringing intermission of labour.

The appointment and observance of the sabbatical year, and after the seventh sabbatical year, a year of jubilee, is a circumstance of great moment. Forbes.

sábbatism n.s. [from *sabbatum*, Latin.] Observance of the sabbath superstitiously rigid.

sábulous adj. [*sabulum*, Latin.] Gritty; sandy.

sack n.s. [שק, Hebrew; σακκος; *saccus*, Latin; *sæc*, Sax. It is observable of this word, that it is found in all languages, and it is therefore conceived to be antediluvian.]†

1. A bag; a pouch; commonly a large bag.

Our sacks shall be a mean to sack the city,
And we be lords and rulers over Roan.
Shak. Henry VI.

Vastius caused the authors of that mutiny to be thrust into sacks, and in the sight of the fleet cast into the sea. Knolles.

2. The measure of three bushels.

3. A woman's loose robe.

sácrilege n.s. [*sacrilege*, Fr. *sacrilegium*, Lat.] The crime of appropriating to himself what is devoted to religion; the crime of robbing heaven; the crime of violating or profaning things sacred.

By what eclipse shall that sun be defac'd,
What mine hath erst thrown down so fair
*   a tower!*
What sacrilege hath such a saint disgrac'd?
Sidney.

Then 'gan a cursed hand the quiet womb
Of his great grandmother with steel to wound,
And the hid treasures in her sacred tomb
With sacrilege to dig. Fairy Queen.

We need not go many ages back to see the vengeance of God upon some families, raised upon the ruins of churches, and enriched with the spoils of sacrilege. South's Sermons.

sálad n.s. [*salade*, Fr. *salaet*, Germ.] Food of raw herbs.

I climbed into this garden to pick a salad,
which is not amiss to cool a man's stomach.
Shakesp. Henry VI.

*   My sallet days,*
When I was green in judgment, cold in blood.
Shakespeare.

You have, to rectify your palate,
An olive, capers, or some better salad,
Ush'ring the mutton. Ben. Johnson.

Some coarse cold salad is before thee set;
Fall on. Dryden's Pers. Sat.

The happy old Coricyan's fruits and salads, on which he lived contented, were all of his own growth. Dryden.

Leaves, eaten raw, are termed salad: if boiled, they become potherbs; and some of those plants which are potherbs in one family, are sallad in another. Watts.

salamánder n.s. [*salamandre*, Fr. *salamandra*, Lat.] An animal supposed to live in the fire, and imagined to be very poisonous. Ambrose Parey has a picture of the salamander, with a receipt for her bite; but there is no such creature, the name being now given to a poor harmless insect.

The salamander liveth in the fire, and hath force also to extinguish it. Bacon's Natural History.

According to this hypothesis the whole lunar world is a torrid zone, and may be supposed uninhabitable, except they are salamanders which dwell therein. Glanv. Sceps.

Whereas it is commonly said that a salamander extinguisheth fire, we have found by experience, that on hot coals it dieth immediately. Brown's Vulgar Errours.

The artist was so encompassed with fire and smoke, that one would have thought nothing but a salamander could have been safe in such a situation. Addison's Guardian.

sálmagundi n.s. [It is said to be corrupted from *selon mon gout*, or *sale à mon goût*.] A mixture of chopped meat and pickled herrings with oil, vinegar, pepper, and onions.

salsamentárious adj. [*salsamentarius*, Latin.] Belonging to salt things. Dict.

salt n.s. [*salt*, Gothick; *sealt*, Saxon; *sal*, Latin; *sel*, French.]

1. Salt is a body whose two essential properties seem to be dissolubility in water, and a pungent sapor: it is an active incombustible substance: it gives all bodies consistence, and preserves them from corruption, and occasions all the variety of tastes. There are three kinds of salts, fixed, volatile, and essential: fixed salt is drawn by calcining the matter, then boiling the ashes in a good deal of water: after this the solution is filtrated, and all the moisture evaporated, when the salt remains in a dry form at the bottom: this is called a lixivious salt. Essential salt is that drawn chiefly from the parts of animals, and some putrified parts of vegetables: it rises easily, and is the most volatile of any. The essential salt is drawn from the juice of plants by crystalization. Harris.

Is not discourse, manhood, learning, gentleness, virtue and liberality, the spice and salt that seasons a man? Shakesp.

He perfidiously has given up, For certain drops of salt, your city Rome, To his wife and mother. Shak. Coriolanus.

Since salts differ much, some being fixt, some volatile, some acid, and some urinous, the two qualities wherein they agree are, that it is easily dissoluble in water, and affects the palate with a sapour, good or evil. Boyle.

A particle of salt may be compared to a chaos, being dense, hard, dry, and earthy in the centre, and rare, soft, and moist in the circumference. Newton's Opt.

Salts are bodies friable and brittle, in some degree pellucid, sharp or pungent to the taste, and dissoluble in water; but after that is evaporated, incorporating, crystalizing, and forming themselves into angular figures. Woodward.

2. Taste; smack.

Though we are justices and doctors, and churchmen, Mr. Page, we have some salt of our youth in us; we are the sons of women. Shakesp. Merry Wives of Windsor.

3. Wit; merriment.

sáltant adj. [*saltans*, Latin.] Jumping; dancing.

saltinbánco n.s. [*saltare in banco*, to climb on a bench, as a mountebank mounts a bank.] A quack or mountebank.

Saltinbancoes, quacksalvers, and charlatans deceive them: were Æsop alive, the Piazza and Pont-neuf could not speak their fallacies. Brown's Vulgar Errours.

He play'd the saltinbanco's part, Transform'd t' a Frenchman by my art. Hudibras.

to salúte v.a. [*saluto*, Latin; *saluer*, French.]

1. To greet; to hail.

The golden sun salutes the morn, And, having gilt the ocean with his beams, Gallops the zodiack in his glist'ring coach. Shakes. Tit. And.

One hour hence Shall salute your grace of York as mother. Shak. R. III.

2. To please; to gratify.

Would I had no being, If this salute my blood a jot: it faints me, To think what follows. Shakesp. Henry VIII.

3. To kiss.

salutíferous adj. [*salutifer*, Latin.] Healthy; bringing health.

The king commanded him to go to the south of France, believing that nothing would contribute more to the restoring of his former vigour than the gentle salutiferous air of Montpelier. Dennis's Letters.

sane adj. [*sanus*, Latin.] Sound; healthy. Baynard wrote a poem on preserving the body in a sane and sound state.

sánhedrim n.s. [*synedrium*, Latin.] The chief council among the Jews, consisting of seventy elders, over whom the high priest presided.

saponáceous, sáponary adj [from *sapo*, Latin, soap.] Sopy; resembling soap; having the qualities of soap.

By digesting a solution of salt of tartar with oil of almonds, I could reduce them to a soft saponary substance. Boyle.

Any mixture of an oily substance with salt, may be called a soap: bodies of this nature are called saponaceous. Arbuthnot.

sárcasm n.s. [*sarcasme*, Fr. *sarcasmus*, Latin.] A keen reproach; a taunt; a gibe.

Sarcasms of wit are transmitted in story. Gov. of the Tongue.

Rejoice, O young man, says Solomon, in a severe sarcasm, in the days of thy youth, and walk in the ways of thy heart; but know that for these things God will bring thee into judgment. Rogers's Sermons.

When an angry master says to his servant it is bravely done, it is one way of giving a severe reproach; for the words are spoken by way of sarcasm, or irony. Watts.

sarcocéle n.s. [σαρξ and κηλη; *sarcocele*, Fr.] A fleshy excrescence of the testicles, which sometimes grow so large as to stretch the scrotum much beyond its natural size. Quincy.†

sarcóphagous adj. [σαρξ and φαγω.] Flesh-eating; feeding on flesh.

sarculátion n.s. [*sarculus*, Latin.] The act of weeding; plucking up weeds. Dict.

sarn n.s. A British word for pavement, or stepping stones, still used in the same sense in Berkshire and Hampshire.

sássafras n.s. A tree: one of the species of the cornelian cherry. The wood is medicinal.

Sátan n.s. [שטן *Satanas*, Latin.] The prince of hell; the devil; any wicked spirit.

I beheld Satan as lightning fall from heaven. Lu. x. 18.

They are much increased by the false suggestions of Satan. Sanderson's Judgment in one View.

The despiteful act
Of Satan done in Paradise. Milton.

sátire n.s. [*satira*, anciently *satura*, Lat. not from *satyrus*, a satyr; *satire*, Fr.]† A poem in which wickedness or folly is censured. Proper satire is distinguished, by the generality of the reflections, from a lampoon which is aimed against a particular person; but they are too frequently confounded.

He dares to sing thy praises in a clime
Where vice triumphs, and virtue is a crime;
Where ev'n to draw the picture of thy mind,
Is satyr on the most of human kind. Dryden.

satírical, satírick adj. [*satiricus*, Latin; *satirique*, French; from *satire*.]

1. Belonging to satire; employed in writing of invective.

You must not think, that a satyrick style
Allows of scandalous and brutish words. Roscommon.

What human kind desires, and what they shun,
Rage, passions, pleasures, impotence of will,
Shall this satirical collection fill. Dryden's Juvenal.

2. Censorious; severe in language.

Slanders, sir; for the satirical slave says here, that old men have grey beards; that their faces are wrinkled. Shak. Hamlet.

He that hath a satirical vein, as he maketh others afraid of his wit, so he had need be afraid of others memory. Bacon.

On me when dunces are satirick,
I take it for a panegyrick. Swift.

Sáturn n.s. [*saturne*, French; *saturnus*, Latin.]

1. The remotest planet of the solar system: supposed by astrologers to impress melancholy, dulness, or severity of temper.

The smallest planets are placed nearest the sun and each other; whereas Jupiter and Saturn, that are vastly greater, are wisely removed to the extreme regions. Bentley.

From the far bounds
Of utmost Saturn, wheeling wide his round. Thomson.

2. [In chemistry.] Lead.

satúrnian adj. [*saturnius*, Latin.] Happy; golden: used by poets for times of felicity, such as are feigned to have been in the reign of Saturn.

Th' Augustus, born to bring Saturnian times. Pope.

sáturnine adj. [*saturninus*, Lat. *saturnien*, Fr. from *Saturn*.] Not light; not volatile; gloomy; grave; melancholy; severe of temper: supposed to be born under the dominion of Saturn.

I may cast my readers under two divisions, the mercurial and saturnine: the first are the gay part, the others are of a more sober and solemn turn. Addison.

sátyr n.s. [*satyrus*, Latin.] A sylvan god: supposed among the ancients to be rude and lecherous.

Satyrs, as Pliny testifies, were found in times past in the eastern mountains of India. Peacham on Drawing.

sáucebox n.s. [from *sauce*, or rather from *saucy*.] An impertinent or petulant fellow.

The foolish old poet says, that the souls of some women are made of sea-water: this has encouraged my saucebox to be witty upon me. Addison's Spectator.

sáusage n.s. [*saucisse*, French; *salsum*, Latin.] A roll or ball made commonly of pork or veal, and sometimes of beef, minced very small, with salt and spice; sometimes it is stuffed into the guts of fowls, and sometimes only rolled in flower.

sávage n.s. [from the adjective.] A man untaught and uncivilized; a barbarian.

Long after these times were they but savages. Raleigh.

The seditious lived by rapine and ruin of all the country, omitting nothing of that which savages, enraged in the height of their unruly behaviour, do commit. Hayward.

To deprive us of metals is to make us mere savages; to change our corn for the old Arcadian diet, our houses and cities for dens and caves, and our clothing for skins of beasts: 'tis to bereave us of all arts and sciences, nay, of revealed religion. Bentley.

savánna n.s. [Spanish, according to Bailey.] An open meadow without wood; pasture ground in America.

He that rides post through a country may tell how, in general, the parts lie; here a morass, and there a river; woodland in one part, and savanna's in another. Locke.

   Plains immense,
And vast savanna's, where the wand'ring eye, Unfix'd, is in a verdant ocean lost. Thomson's Summer.

sáveall n.s. [*save* and *all*.] A small pan inserted into a candlestick to save the ends of candles.

Sáviour n.s. [*sauveur*, Latin.] Redeemer; he that has saved mankind from eternal death.

So judg'd he man, both judge and Saviour sent. Milton.

However consonant to reason his precepts appeared, nothing could have tempted men to acknowledge him as their God and Saviour, but their being firmly persuaded of the miracles he wrought. Addison.

scale n.s. [*scale*, Saxon; *schael*, Dutch; *skal*, Islandick.]

1. A balance; a vessel suspended by a beam against another vessel.

   If thou tak'st more
Or less than just a pound, if the scale turn But in the estimation of a hair, Thou diest. Shak. Merchant of Venice.

Your vows to her and me, put in two scales, Will even weigh, and both as light as tales. Shakespeare.

Here's an equivocator, that could swear, in both the scales, against either scale; who committed treason enough for God's sake, yet could not equivocate to heaven. Shakesp. Macbeth.

   Long time in even scale
The battle hung. Milton's Parad. Lost, b. vi.

The world's scales are even; what the main
In one place gets, another quits again.
Cleaveland.

The scales are turn'd, her kindness weighs
    no more
Now than my vows. Waller.

In full assemblies let the crowd prevail;
I weigh no merit by the common scale,
The conscience is the test. Dryden.

If we consider the dignity of an intelligent
being, and put that in the scales against brute
inanimate matter, we may affirm, without
overvaluing human nature, that the soul of
one virtuous and religious man is of greater
worth and excellency than the sun and his
planets. Bentley's Sermons.

2. The sign Libra in the Zodiack.

Juno pours out the urn, and Vulcan claims
The scales, as the just product of his flames.
Creech.

3. [*Escaille*, French; *squama*, Latin.] The
    small shells or crusts which lying one
    over another make the coats of fishes.

He puts him on a coat of mail,
Which was made of a fish's scale. Drayton.

Standing aloof, with lead they bruise the scales,
And tear the flesh of the incensed whales.
Waller.

4. Any thing exfoliated or desquamated;
    a thin lamina.

Take jet and the scales of iron, and with a wet
feather, when the smith hath taken an heat,
take up the scales that fly from the iron, and
those scales you shall grind upon your painter's
stone. Peacham.

When a scale of bone is taken out of a
wound, burning retards the separation.
Sharp's Surgery.

5. [*Scala*, a ladder, Latin.] Ladder; means
    of ascent.

    Love refines
The thoughts, and heart enlarges; hath his seat
In reason, and is judicious; is the scale
By which to heav'nly love thou may'st ascend.
Milton.

On the bendings of these mountains the marks
of several ancient scales of stairs may be seen,
by which they used to ascend them. Addison
on Italy.

6. The act of storming by ladders.

    Others to a city strong
Lay siege, encamp'd; by batt'ry, scale, and mine
Assaulting. Milt. Parad. Lost.

7. Regular gradation; a regular series rising
    like a ladder.

Well hast thou the scale of nature set,
From centre to circumference; whereon
In contemplation of created things,
By steps we may ascend to God.
Milt. Par. Lost.

The scale of the creatures is a matter of high
speculation. Grew.

The higher nature still advances, and
preserves his superiority in the scale of being.
Addison.

All the integral parts of nature have a
beautiful analogy to one another, and to their
mighty original, whose images are more or
less expressive, according to their several
gradations in the scale of beings. Cheyne's
Phil. Princ.

We believe an invisible world, and a scale of
spiritual beings all nobler than ourselves.
Bentley's Sermons.

Far as creation's ample range extends,
The scale of sensual mental pow'rs ascends.
Pope.

In contemplation's scale I'll soar,
And be enraptur'd more and more;
Whilst thus new matter of surprise
In each gradation shall arise. Macbean.[†]

8. A figure subdivided by lines like the
    steps of a ladder, which is used to
    measure proportions between pictures
    and the thing represented.

The map of London was set out in the year
1658 by Mr. Newcourt, drawn by a scale
of yards. Graunt.

9. The series of harmonick or musical proportions.

The bent of his thoughts and reasonings run up and down this scale, that no people can be happy but under good governments. Temple.

10. Any thing marked at equal distances.

    They take the flow o' th' Nile
By certain scale i' th' pyramid: they know
By th' height, the lowness, or the mean, if dearth
Or foizon follow. Shak. Ant. and Cleopatra.

scálpel n.s. [Fr. *scalpellum*, Latin.] An instrument used to scrape a bone by chirurgeons.

to scámble v.n. [This word, which is scarcely in use, has much exercised the etymological sagacity of Meric Casaubon; but, as is usual, to no purpose.]

1. To be turbulent and rapacious; to scramble; to get by struggling with others.

    Have fresh chaff in the bin,
And somewhat to scamble for hog and for hen.
Tusser.

Scambling, out-facing, fashion-mong'ring boys,
That lie, and cog, and flout, deprave and
    slander. Shakesp.

That self bill is urg'd, and had against us past,
But that the scambling and unquiet time
Did push it out of further question.
Shakes. Henry V.

He was no sooner entered into the town but a scambling soldier clapt hold of his bridle, which he thought was in a begging or a drunken fashion. Wotton.

2. To shift aukwardly.

Some scambling shifts may be made without them. More.

scámbler n.s. [Scottish.] A bold intruder upon one's generosity or table.

to scan v.a. [*scandre*, French; *scando*, Latin.]

1. To examine a verse by counting the feet.

Harry, whose tuneful and well measur'd song
First taught our English musick how to span

Words with just note and accent, not to scan
With Midas' ears, committing short and long.
Milton.

They scan their verses upon their fingers, run after conceits and glaring thoughts. Walsh.

2. To examine nicely.

    So he goes to heav'n,
And so am I reveng'd: that would be scann'd.
Shakes. Ham.

    The rest the great architect
Did wisely to conceal; and not divulge
His secrets to be scann'd by them, who ought
Rather admire. Milton's Paradise
Lost, b. viii.

Every man has some guilts, which he desires should not be rigorously scanned; and therefore, by the rule of charity and justice, ought not to do that which he would not suffer. Government of the Tongue.

At the final reckoning, when all mens actions shall be scanned and judged, the great king shall pass his sentence, according to the good men have done, or neglected to do. Calam.

Sir Roger exposing his palm, they crumpled it into all shapes, and diligently scanned every wrinkle that could be made in it. Addison.

The actions of men in high stations are all conspicuous, and liable to be scanned and sifted. Atterbury.

In full fruition of successful pow'r,
One moment and one thought might let him scan
The various turns of life, and fickle state of
    man. Prior.

scáramouch n.s. [*escarmouche*, Fr.] A buffoon in motly dress.

It makes the solemnities of justice pageantry, and the bench reverend poppets, or scaramouches in scarlet. Collier.

scátches n.s. [*chasses*, French.] Stilts to put the feet in to walk in dirty places. Bailey.

scaturíginous adj. [from *scaturigo*, Latin.] Full of springs or fountains. Dict.

scélerat n.s. [French; *sceleratus*, Latin.] A villain; a wicked wretch. A word introduced unnecessarily from the French by a Scottish author.

Scelerats can by no arts stifle the cries of a wounded conscience. Cheyne.

scénick adj. [*scenique*, Fr. from *scene*.] Dramatick; theatrical.

With scenick virtue charm the rising age. Anonym.†

scheme n.s. [σχημα]

1. A plan; a combination of various things into one view, design, or purpose; a system.

Were our senses made much quicker, the appearance and outward scheme of things would have quite another face to us, and be inconsistent with our well being. Locke.

We shall never be able to give ourselves a satisfactory account of the divine conduct, without forming such a scheme of things as shall at once take in time and eternity. Atterbury.

2. A project; a contrivance; a design.

The haughty monarch was laying schemes for suppressing the ancient liberties, and removing the ancient boundaries of kingdoms. Atterbury's Sermons.

He forms the well-concerted scheme of mischief; 'Tis fix'd, 'tis done, and both are doom'd to death. Rowe.

The stoical scheme of supplying our wants by lopping of our desires, is like cutting off our feet when we want shoes. Swift.

3. A representation of the aspects of the celestial bodies; any lineal or mathematical diagram.

It hath embroiled the endeavours of astrology in the erection of schemes, and the judgment of death and diseases. Brown's Vulgar Errours.

It is a scheme and face of heaven, As th' aspects are dispos'd this even. Hudibras.

schism n.s. [σχισμα; *schisme*, Fr.] A separation or division in the church of God.

Set bounds to our passions by reason, to our errours by truth, and to our schisms by charity. King Charles.

Oppose schisms by unity, hypocrisy by sober piety, and debauchery by temperance. Spratt's Sermons.

When a schism is once spread, there grows at length a dispute which are the schismaticks: in the sense of the law the schism lies on that side which opposes itself to the religion of the state. Swift.

schólar n.s. [*scholaris*, Latin; *ecolier*, French.]

1. One who learns of a master; a disciple.

Many times that which deserveth approbation would hardly find favour, if they which propose it were not to profess themselves scholars, and followers of the ancients. Hooker.

The scholars of the Stagyrite, Who for the old opinion fight, Would make their modern friends confess The diff'rence but from more to less. Prior.

2. A man of letters.

This same scholar's fate, res angusta domi, hinders the promoting of learning. Wilkins's Math. Magic.†

To watch occasions to correct others in their discourse, and not slip any opportunity of shewing their talents, scholars are most blamed for. Locke.

3. A pedant; a man of books.

To spend too much time in studies, is sloth; to make judgment wholly by their rules, is the humour of a scholar: they perfect nature, and are perfected by experience. Bacon.

4. One who has a lettered education.

My cousin William is become a good scholar: he is at Oxford still, is he not? Shakesp. Henry IV.

schólastick adj. [from *schola*, Latin; *scholastique*, French.]

1. Pertaining to the school, practised in schools.

I would render this intelligible to every rational man, however little versed in scholastick learning. Digby on Bodies.

Scholastick education, like a trade, does so fix a man in a particular way, that he is not fit to judge of any thing that lies out of that way. Burnet's Theory of the Earth.

2. Befitting the school; suitable to the school; pedantick; needlessly subtle.

The favour of proposing there, in convenient sort, whatsoever ye can object, which thing I have known them to grant of scholastick courtesy unto strangers, never hath nor ever will be denied you. Hooker.

Sir Francis Bacon was wont to say, that those who left useful studies for useless scholastick speculations, were like the Olympick gamesters, who abstained from necessary labours, that they might be fit for such as were not so. Bacon.

Both sides charge the other with idolatry, and that is a matter of conscience, and not a scholastick nicety. Stillingfleet.

schóliast n.s. [*scholiaste*, French; *scholiastes*, Latin.] A writer of explanatory notes.

The title of this satyr, in some ancient manuscripts, was the reproach of idleness; though in others of the scholiasts 'tis inscribed against the luxury of the rich. Dryden.

What Gellius or Stobæus cook'd before, Or chew'd by blind old scholiasts o'er and o'er. Dunciad.

schólion, schólium n.s. [Latin.] A note; an explanatory observation.

Hereunto have I added a certain gloss or scholion, for the exposition of old words, and harder phrases, which manner of glossing and commenting will seem strange in our language. Spenser.

Some cast all their metaphysical and moral learning into the method of mathematicians, and bring every thing relating to those abstracted or practical sciences under theorems, problems, postulates, scholiums, and corollaries. Watts.

schóly n.s. [*scholie*, Fr. *scholium*, Latin.] An explanatory note. This word, with the verb following, is, I fancy, peculiar to the learned Hooker.

He therefore, which made us to live, hath also taught us to pray, to the end, that speaking unto the Father in the Son's own prescript form, without scholy or gloss of ours, we may be sure that we utter nothing which God will deny. Hooker.

That scholy had need of a very favourable reader, and a tractable, that should think it plain construction, when to be commanded in the word, and grounded upon the word, are made all one. Hooker.

to schóly v.n. [from the noun.] To write expositions.

The preacher should want a text, whereupon to scholy. Hooker.

school n.s. [*schola*, Latin; *ecole*, French.]

1. A house of discipline and instruction.

Their age the same, their inclinations too, And bred together in one school they grew. Dryden.

2. A place of literary education.

My end being private, I have not expressed my conceptions in the language of the schools. Digby.

Writers on that subject have turned it into a composition of hard words, trifles, and subtilties, for the mere use of the schools, and that only to amuse men with empty sounds. Watts.

3. A state of instruction.

The calf breed to the rural trade, Set him betimes to school, and let him be Instructed there in rules of husbandry. Dryden.

4. System of doctrine as delivered by particular teachers.

No craz'd brain could ever yet propound, Touching the soul, so vain and fond a thought; But some among these masters have been found, Which in their schools the self-same thing had taught. Davies.

Let no man be less confident in his faith, concerning the great blessings God designs in these divine mysteries, by reason of any difference in the several schools of Christians, concerning the consequent blessings thereof. Taylor.

5. The age of the church, and form of theology succeeding that of the fathers.

The first principles of Christian religion should not be farced with school points and private tenets. Sanderson.

A man may find an infinite number of propositions in books of metaphysicks, school divinity, and natural philosophy, and know as little of God, spirits, or bodies, as he did before. Locke.

schóolman n.s. [*school* and *man.*]

1. One versed in the niceties and subtilties of academical disputation.

The king, though no good schoolman, converted one of them by dispute. Bacon.

Unlearn'd, he knew no schoolman's subtle art; No language, but the language of the heart. Pope.

2. One skilled in the divinity of the school.

If a man's wit be not apt to distinguish or find differences, let him study the schoolmen. Bacon.

To schoolmen I bequeath my doubtfulness, My sickness to physicians. Donne.

Men of nice palates could not relish Aristotle, as he was drest up by the schoolmen. Baker.

Let subtle schoolmen teach these fiends to fight, More studious to divide than to unite. Pope.

science n.s. [*science*, French; *scientia*, Latin.]

1. Knowledge.

If we conceive God's sight or science, before the creation of the world, to be extended to all and every part of the world, seeing every thing as it is, his prescience or foresight of any action of mine, or rather his science or sight, from all eternity, lays no necessity on any thing to come to pass, any more than my seeing the sun move hath to do in the moving of it. Hamm.

2. Certainty grounded on demonstration.

So you arrive at truth, though not at science. Berkley.[†]

3. Art attained by precepts, or built on principles.

Science perfects genius, and moderates that fury of the fancy which cannot contain itself within the bounds of reason. Dryd.

4. Any art or species of knowledge.[†]

No science doth make known the first principles, whereon it buildeth; but they are always taken as plain and manifest in themselves, or as proved and granted already, some former knowledge having made them evident. Hooker.

Whatsoever we may learn by them, we only attain according to the manner of natural sciences, which mere discourse of wit and reason findeth out. Hooker.

   I present you with a man Cunning in musick and the mathematicks, To instruct her fully in those sciences. Shakespeare.

The indisputable mathematicks, the only science heaven hath yet vouchsafed humanity, have but few votaries among the slaves of the Stagirite. Glanv. Sceps.

5. One of the seven liberal arts, grammar, rhetorick, logick, arithmetick, musick, geometry, astronomy.

Good sense, which only is the gift of heav'n, And though no science, fairly worth the sev'n. Pope.

scientifical, **scientifick** adj. [*scientifique*, Fr. *scientia* and *facio*, Lat.] Producing demonstrative knowledge; producing certainty.

Natural philosophy proceeding from settled principles, therein is expected a satisfaction from scientifical progressions, and such as beget a sure or rational belief. Brown's Vulg. Err.

No where are there more quick, inventive, and penetrating capacities, fraught with all kind of scientifical knowledge. Howel.

No man, who first trafficks into a foreign country, has any scientifick evidence that there is such a country, but by report, which can produce no more than a moral certainty;

that is, a very high probability, and such as there can be no reason to except against. South's Sermons.

The systems of natural philosophy that have obtained, are to be read more to know the hypotheses, than with hopes to gain there a comprehensive, scientifical, and satisfactory knowledge of the works of nature. Locke.

sciólist n.s. [*sciolus*, Latin.] One who knows many things superficially.

'Twas this vain idolizing of authors which gave birth to that silly vanity of impertinent citations: these ridiculous fooleries signify nothing to the more generous discerners, but the pedantry of the affected sciolists. Glanv. Sceps.

These passages, in that book, were enough to humble the presumption of our modern sciolists, if their pride were not as great as their ignorance. Temple.

sciómachy n.s. [*schiamachie*, Fr. σκια and μαχη.] Battle with a shadow. This should be written *skiamachy*.

To avoid this sciomachy, or imaginary combat of words, let me know, sir, what you mean by the name of tyrant? Cowley.

scold n.s. [from the verb.] A clamourous, rude, mean, low, foul-mouthed woman.

A shrew in domestick life, is now become a scold in politicks. Addison's Freeholder.

Sun-burnt matrons mending old nets;
Now singing shrill, and scolding oft between;
Scolds answer foul-mouth'd scolds. Swift.

scomm n.s. [Perhaps from *scomma*, Latin.] A buffoon. A word out of use, and unworthy of revival.

The scomms, or buffoons of quality, are wolvish in conversation. L'Estrange.

to sconce v.a. [A word used in the universities, and derived plausibly by Skinner, whose etymologies are generally rational, from *sconce*, as it signifies the head; to sconce being to fix a fine on any one's head.] To mulct; to fine. A low word which ought not to be retained.[†]

scópulous adj. [*scopulosus*, Latin.] Full of rocks. Dict.

scorbútical, scorbútick n.s. [*scorbutique*, Fr. from *scorbutus*, Latin.] Diseased with the scurvy.

A person about forty, of a full and scorbutical body, having broke her skin, endeavoured the curing of it; but observing the ulcer sanious, I proposed digestion. Wiseman.

Violent purging hurts scorbutick constitutions; lenitive substances relieve. Arbuthnot.

scotch collops, or **scotched collops** n.s. [from *To scotch*, or cut.] Veal cut into small pieces.

scotch hoppers n.s. A play in which boys hop over lines or scotches in the ground.

Children being indifferent to any thing they can do, dancing and scotch hoppers would be the same thing to them. Locke.

scótomy n.s. [σκοτωμα.] A dizziness or swimming in the head, causing dimness of sight, wherein external objects seem to turn round. Ains. and Bailey.

scóttering A provincial word which denotes, in Herefordshire, a custom among the boys of burning a wad of pease-straw at the end of harvest. Bailey.

scóvel n.s. [*scopa*, Latin.] A sort of mop of clouts for sweeping an oven; a maulkin. Ains. and Bailey.

scrag n.s. [*scraghe*, Dutch.] Any thing thin or lean.

to scranch v.a. [*schrantzer*, Dutch.] To grind somewhat crackling between the teeth. The Scots retain it.

scránnel adj. [Of this word I know not the etymology, nor any other example.] Vile; worthless. Perhaps grating by the sound.

When they list, their lean and flashy songs
Grate on their scrannel pipes of wretched
*   straw.* Milton.

scrat n.s. [*scritta*, Saxon.] An hermaphrodite. Skinner and Junius.

scréable adj. [*screabilis*, Latin.] That which may be spit out. Bailey.

scríbbler n.s. [from *scribble*.] A petty author; a writer without worth.

The most copious writers are the arrantest scribblers, and in so much talking the tongue runs before the wit. L'Estrange.

The actors represent such things as they are capable, by which they and the scribbler may get their living. Dryden.

The scribbler, pinch'd with hunger, writes to dine, And to your genius must conform his line. Granv.

To affirm he had cause to apprehend the same treatment with his father, is an improbable scandal flung upon the nation by a few bigotted French scribblers. Swift.

No body was concerned or surprised, if this or that scribbler was proved a dunce. Letter to Pope's Dunciad.

scrófula n.s. [from *scrofa*, Latin, a sow, as χοιρας.] A depravation of the humours of the body, which breaks out in sores commonly called the king's evil.[†]

If matter in the milk dispose to coagulation, it produces a scrofula. Wiseman of Tumours.

scroyle n.s. [This word I remember only in Shakespeare: it seems derived from *escrouelle*, French, a scrofulous swelling; as he calls a mean fellow a *scab* from his itch, or a *patch* from his raggedness.] A mean fellow; a rascal; a wretch.

The scroyles of Angiers flout you kings, And stand securely on their battlements, As in a theatre. Shakespeare's King John.

to scrúple v.n. [from the noun.] To doubt; to hesitate.

He scrupled not to eat Against his better knowledge; not deceiv'd, But fondly overcome with female charms. Milt. Par. Lost.

scrutátion n.s. [*scrutor*, Latin.] Search; examination; inquiry. Dict.

scrutóire n.s. [for *scritoire*, or *escritoire*.] A case of drawers for writings.

I locked up these papers in my scrutoire, and my scrutoire came to be unlocked. Prior.

to scúddle v.n. [from *scud*.] To run with a kind of affected haste or precipitation. A low word.

scúllion n.s. [from *escueille*, French, a dish.] The lowest domestick servant, that washes the kettles and the dishes in the kitchen.

I must, like a whore, unpack my heart with words, And fall a cursing like a very drab, A scullion, fye upon 't! foh! about my brain. Shak. Hamlet.

If the gentleman hath lain there, get the cook, the stablemen, and the scullion, to stand in his way. Swift.

scútiform adj. [*scutiformis*. Latin.] Shaped like a shield.

sea n.s. [*sæ*, Saxon; *see*, or *zee*, Dutch.][†]

1. The ocean; the water opposed to the land.

Will all great Neptune's ocean wash this blood Clean from my hand? No, this my hand will rather Thy multitudinous sea incarnardine, Making the green one red. Shakesp. Macbeth.

The rivers run into the sea. Carew.

He made the sea, and all that is therein. Ex. xx. 11.

So do the winds and thunders cleanse the air, So working seas settle and purge the wine. Davies.

Amphibious between sea and land The river horse. Milton.

Some leviathan, Haply slumb'ring on the Norway foam, The pilot of some small night-founder'd skiff Deeming some island, oft as seamen tell, With fixed anchor in his scaly rind, Moors by his side under the lee, while night Invests the sea. Milton.

Small fragments of shells, broken by storms on some shores, are used for manuring of sea land. Woodward.

They put to sea with a fleet of three hundred sail. Arbuthn.

Sea racing dolphins are train'd for our motion,
Moony tides swelling to roll us ashore.
Dryden's Albion.

But like a rock unmov'd, a rock that braves
The raging tempest, and the rising waves,
Propp'd on himself he stands: his solid sides
Wash off the sea weeds, and the sounding
tides. Dryden.

The sea could not be much narrower than it is, without a great loss to the world. Bentley.

So when the first bold vessel dar'd the seas,
High on the stern the Thracian rais'd his strain,
While Argo saw her kindred trees
Descend from Pelion to the main. Pope.

2. A collection of water; a lake.

Jesus walking by the sea of Galilee, saw two brethren. Mat. iv. 18.

3. Proverbially for any large quantity.

That sea of blood which hath in Ireland
been barbarously shed, is enough to drown
in eternal infamy and misery the malicious
author and instigator of its effusion.
King Charles.

4. Any thing rough and tempestuous.

To sorrow abandon'd, but worse felt within,
And in a troubled sea of passion tost. Milton.

5. Half seas over. Half drunk.

The whole magistracy was pretty well
disguised before I gave 'em the slip: our friend
the alderman was half seas over before the
bonfire was out. Spectator.

Sea is often used in composition, as will appear in the following examples.

séacow n.s. [*sea* and *cow*.] The manatee.

The seacow is a very bulky animal, of the
cetaceous kind. It grows to fifteen feet long,
and to seven or eight in circumference: its
head is like that of a hog, but longer, and more
cylindrick: its eyes are small, and it has no
external ears, but only two little apertures in
the place of them; yet its sense of hearing is
very quick. Its lips are thick, and it has two

long tusks standing out. It has two fins, which
stand forward on the breast like hands,
whence the Spaniards first called it manatee.
The female has two round breasts placed
between the pectoral fins. The skin is very
thick and hard, and not scaly, but hairy. This
creature lives principally about the mouths of
the large rivers in Africa, the East Indies, and
America, and feeds upon vegetables. Its flesh
is white like veal, and very well tasted. The
lapis manati, *which is of a fine clean white*
colour, and bony texture, is properly the os
petrosum *of this animal. This stone has been*
supposed to be a powerful amulet, but is now
neglected. Hill's Mat. Med.

seadóg n.s. [*sea* and *dog*.] Perhaps the shark.

Fierce seadogs devour the mangl'd friends.
Roscommon.

When, stung with hunger, she embroils the flood,
The seadog and the dolphin are her food.
Pope's Odyssey.

séahog n.s. [*sea* and *hog*.] The porpus.

séahorse n.s. [*sea* and *horse*.]

1. The seahorse is a fish of a very singular form, as we see it dried, and of the needlefish kind. It is about four or five inches in length, and nearly half an inch in diameter in the broadest part. Its colour, as we see it dried, is a deep reddish brown; and its tail is turned round under the belly. It is found about the Mediterranean, and has been celebrated for medicinal virtues; but is at present wholly neglected. Hill's Materia Med.

2. The morse.

Part of a large tooth, round and tapering:
a tusk of the morse, or waltrons, called by
some the seahorse. Woodward.

3. The medical and the poetical seahorse seem very different. By the seahorse Dryden means probably the hippopotamus.

By 'em
Seahorses, flound'ring in the slimy mud,
Toss'd up their heads, and dash'd the ooze
about 'em. Dry.

séamonster n.s. [*sea* and *monster.*] Strange animal of the sea.

Seamonsters give suck to their young. La. iv. 3.

Where luxury once reign'd, seamonsters whelp. Milton.

searóver n.s. [*sea* and *rove.*] A pirate.

séaserpent n.s. [*sea* and *serpent.*] Serpent generated in the water.

seasérvice n.s. [*sea* and *service*] Naval war.

You were pressed for the seaservice, and got off with much ado. Swift's Direct. to Servants.

to secéde v.n. [*secedo*, Latin.] To withdraw from fellowship in any affair.

sécond sight n.s. The power of seeing things future, or things distant: supposed inherent in some of the Scottish islanders.†

As he was going out to steal a sheep, he was seised with a fit of second sight: the face of the country presented him with a wide prospect of new scenes, which he had never seen before. Addison's Freeholder.

séctary n.s. [*sectaire*, French; from *sect.*]

1. One who divides from publick establishment, and joins with those distinguished by some particular whims.

My lord, you are a sectary,
That's the plain truth. Shakes.

Romish catholick tenets are inconsistent, on the one hand, with the truth of religion professed and protested by the church of England, whence we are called protestants; and the anabaptists, and separatists, and sectaries, on the other hand, whose tenets are full of schism, and inconsistent with monarchy. Bac.

The number of sectaries does not concern the clergy in point of interest or conscience. Swift.

2. A follower; a pupil.

The sectaries of my celestial skill,
That wont to be the world's chief ornament,
And learned imps that wont to shoot up still,
They under keep. Spenser.

sedán n.s. [from *sedes*, Latin.] A kind of portable coach; a chair.

Some beg for absent persons, feign them sick,
Close mew'd in their sedans for want of air,
And for their wives produce an empty chair. Dryden.

By a tax of Cato's it was provided, that women's wearing cloaths, ornament and sedan, exceeding 121l. 1s. 10d. halfpenny, should pay 30s. in the hundred pound value. Arbuthn.

to sedúce v.a. [*seduco*, Latin; *seduire*, French.] To draw aside from the right; to tempt; to corrupt; to deprave; to mislead; to deceive.

'Tis meet
That noble minds keep ever with their likes;
For who so firm that cannot be seduc'd? Shakesp. Jul. Cæs.

Me the gold of France did not seduce,
Although I did admit it as a motive,
The sooner to effect what I intended. Shakesp. H. V.

A beauty-waining and distressed widow,
Seduc'd the pitch and height of all his thoughts
To base declension. Shakesp. R. III.

In the latter times some shall depart from the faith, giving heed to seducing spirits. 1 Tim. iv. 1.

I shall never gratify the spightfulness of a few with any sinister thoughts of all their allegiance, whom pious frauds have seduced. King Charles.

Subtle he needs must be who could seduce Angels. Milton.

Nor let false friends seduce thy mind to fame,
By arrogating Johnson's hostile name;
Let father Flecknoe fire thy mind with praise,
And uncle Ogleby thy envy raise. Dryden.

séeksorrow n.s. [*seek* and *sorrow.*] One who contrives to give himself vexation.

Afield they go, where many lookers be,
And thou seeksorrow, Klaius, them among:
Indeed thou saidst it was thy friend to see,
Strephon, whose absence seem'd unto thee long. Sidney.

ségnity n.s. [from *segnis*, Latin.] Sluggishness; inactivity. Dict.

selénography n.s. [*selenographie*, Fr. σεληνη and γραφω.] A description of the moon.

Hevetius, in his accurate selenography, or description of the moon, hath well translated the known appellations of regions, seas, and mountains, unto the parts of that luminary. Brown.

semicólon n.s. [*semi* and κωλον.] Half a colon; a point made thus [;] to note a greater pause than that of a comma.

semitóne n.s. [*semiton*, French.] In musick, one of the degrees of concinuous intervals of concords. Bailey.

sénary adj. [*senarius, seni*, Latin.] Belonging to the number six; containing six.

sénate n.s. [*senatus*, Latin; *senat*, French.] An assembly of counsellors; a body of men set apart to consult for the publick good.

We debase
The nature of our seats, which will
* in time break ope*
The locks o' th' senate, and bring in the crows
To peck the eagles. Shak. Coriolanus.

There they shall found
Their government, and their great senate
* chuse.* Milton.

He had not us'd excursions, spears, or darts,
But counsel, order, and such aged arts;
Which, if our ancestors had not retain'd,
The senate's name our council had not gain'd.
Denham.

Gallus was welcom'd to the sacred strand,
The senate rising to salute their guest.
Dryden.

sénile adj. [*senilis*, Latin.] Belonging to old age; consequent on old age.

My green youth made me very unripe for a task of that nature, whose difficulty requires that it should be handled by a person in whom nature, education, and time have happily matched a senile maturity of judgment with youthful vigour of fancy. Boyle on Colours.

sense n.s. [*sens*, French; *sensus*, Latin.]

1. Faculty or power by which external objects are perceived; the sight; touch; hearing; smell; taste.

This pow'r is sense, which from abroad
* doth bring*
The colour, taste, and touch, and scent,
* and sound,*
* The quantity and shape of ev'ry thing*
Within earth's centre, or heav'n's circle found:
* And though things sensible be numberless,*
But only five the sense's organs be;
* And in those five, all things their forms*
*   express,*
Which we can touch, taste, feel, or hear or see.
Davies.

Then is the soul a nature, which contains
The pow'r of sense within a greater pow'r,
* Which doth employ and use the sense's pains;*
But sits and rules within her private bow'r.
Davies.

Both contain
Within them ev'ry lower faculty
Of sense, whereby they hear, see, smell,
* touch, taste.* Milt.

Of the five senses, two are usually and most properly called the senses of learning, as being most capable of receiving communication of thought and notions by selected signs; and these are hearing and seeing. Holder's Elements of Speech.

2. Perception by the senses; sensation.

In a living creature, though never so great, the sense and the affects of any one part of the body instantly make a transcursion throughout the whole. Bacon's Natural History.

If we had nought but sense, then only they
Should have sound minds which have their
* senses sound;*
* But wisdom grows when senses do decay,*
And folly most in quickest sense is found.
Davies.

Such is the mighty swiftness of your mind,
That, like the earth's, it leaves the sense
* behind.* Dryden.

3. Perception of intellect; apprehension of mind.

*This Basilius, having the quick sense of a
lover, took as though his mistress had given
him a secret reprehension.* Sidn.

*God, to remove his ways from human sense,
Plac'd heav'n from earth so far.* Milton.

Why hast thou added sense of endless woes?
Milton.

4. Sensibility; quickness or keenness of
perception.

*He should have liv'd,
Save that his riotous youth, with dangerous sense,
Might in the times to come have ta'en
revenge.* Shakesp.

5. Understanding; soundness of faculties;
strength of natural reason.

*Opprest nature sleeps:
This rest might yet have balm'd thy broken
senses.* Shakes.

*God hath endued mankind with powers and
abilities, which we call natural light and
reason, and common sense.* Bentley.

*There's something previous ev'n to taste; 'tis sense,
Good sense, which only is the gift of heav'n,
And, though no science, fairly worth the sev'n:
A light within yourself you must perceive;
Jones and Le Nôtre have it not to give.* Pope.

6. Reason; reasonable meaning.

*He raves; his words are loose
As heaps of sand, and scattering wide from sense:
You see he knows not me, his natural father;
That now the wind is got into his head,
And turns his brains to frenzy.* Dryd.
Spanish Fryar.

7. Opinion; notion; judgment.

*I speak my private but impartial sense
With freedom, and, I hope, without offence.*
Roscommon.

8. Consciousness; conviction.

*In the due sense of my want of learning,
I only make a confession of my own faith.*
Dryden.

9. Moral perception.

*Some are so hardened in wickedness, as to
have no sense of the most friendly offices.*
L'Estrange.

10. Meaning; import.

*In this sense to be preserved from all sin is
not impossible.* Hooker, b. v.

*My hearty friends,
You take me in too dolorous a sense.*
Shakespeare.

*This comes out of a haughty presumption, that
because we are encouraged to believe that
in some sense all things are made for man,
that therefore they are not made at all for
themselves.* More's Antidote against
Atheism.

*All before Richard I. is before time of memory;
and what is since, is, in a legal sense, within
the time of memory.* Hale.

*In one sense it is, indeed, a building of
gold and silver upon the foundation
of Christianity.* Tillotson.

*When a word has been used in two or three
senses, and has made a great inroad for error,
drop one or two of those senses, and leave it
only one remaining, and affix the other senses
or ideas to other words.* Watts's Logick.

sensibílity n.s. [*sensibilité*, French.]

1. Quickness of sensation.

*Modesty is a kind of quick and delicate feeling
in the soul: it is such an exquisite sensibility,
as warns a woman to shun the first
appearance of every thing hurtful.*
Addison's Spectator.

2. Quickness of perception.

sénsible adj. [*sensible*, French; *sensilis*, Latin.]

1. Having the power of perceiving by
the senses.

*Would your cambrick were as sensible as your
finger, that you might leave pricking it for
pity.* Shakespeare.

*These be those discourses of God, whose effects
those that live witness in themselves; the
sensible in their sensible natures, the
reasonable in their reasonable souls.* Raleigh.

*A blind man conceives not colours, but under
the notion of some other sensible faculty.*
Glanv. Sceps.

2. Perceptible by the senses.

By reason man attaineth unto the knowledge of things that are and are not sensible: it resteth, therefore, that we search how man attaineth unto the knowledge of such things unsensible as are to be known. Hooker.

Is this a dagger which I see before me,
The handle tow'rd my hand? Come, let
  me clutch thee:
I have thee not, and yet I see thee still:
Art thou not, fatal vision, sensible
To feeling as to sight? Shakesp. Macbeth.

The space left and acquired in every sensible moment in such slow progressions, is so inconsiderable, that it cannot possibly move the sense. Glanv. Sceps.

It is manifest that the heavens are void of all sensible resistance, and by consequence of all sensible matter. Newton.

The far greater part of men are no otherwise moved than by sense, and have neither leisure nor ability so far to improve their power of reflection, as to be capable of conceiving the divine perfections, without the assistance of sensible objects. Rogers's Sermons.

Air is sensible to the touch by its motion, and by its resistance to bodies moved in it. Arbuthnot on Air.

3. Perceived by the mind.

Idleness was punished by so many stripes in publick, and the disgrace was more sensible than the pain. Temple.

4. Perceiving by either mind or senses; having perception by the mind or senses.

  This must needs remove
The sensible of pain. Milton.

I saw you in the East at your first arising: I was as soon sensible as any of that light, when just shooting out, and beginning to travel upwards to the meridian. Dryden.

I do not say there is no soul in man, because he is not sensible of it in his sleep; but I do say, he cannot think at any time, waking or sleeping, without being sensible of it. Locke.

The versification is as beautiful as the description complete; every ear must be sensible of it. Broome's Notes on the Odyss.

5. Having moral perception; having the quality of being affected by moral good or ill.

If thou wert sensible of courtesy,
I should not make so great a shew of zeal.
Shakespeare.

6. Having quick intellectual feeling; being easily or strongly affected.

Even I, the bold, the sensible of wrong,
Restrain'd by shame, was forc'd to hold
  my tongue. Dryd.

7. Convinced; persuaded. A low use.

They are very sensible that they had better have pushed their conquests on the other side of the Adriatick; for then their territories would have lain together. Addison.

8. In low conversation it has sometimes the sense of reasonable; judicious; wise.

I have been tired with accounts from sensible men, furnished with matters of fact, which have happened within their own knowledge. Addison.

sénsitive adj. [*sensitif*, French.] Having sense or perception, but not reason.

The sensitive faculty may have a sensitive love of some sensitive objects, which though moderated so as not to fall into sin; yet, through the nature of man's sense, may express itself more sensitively towards that inferior object than towards God: this is a piece of human frailty. Hammond.

All the actions of the sensitive appetite are in painting called passions, because the soul is agitated by them, and because the body suffers and is sensibly altered. Dryden.

Bodies are such as are endued with a vegetative soul, as plants; a sensitive soul, as animals; or a rational soul, as the body of man. Ray.

séntence n.s. [*sentence*, French; *sententia*, Latin.]

1. Determination or decision, as of a judge civil or criminal.

The rule of voluntary agents on earth is the sentence that reason giveth, concerning the goodness of those things which they are to do. Hooker.

If we have neither voice from heaven, that so pronounceth of them, neither sentence of men grounded upon such manifest and clear proof, that they, in whose hands it is to alter them, may likewise infallibly, even in heart and conscience, judge them so; upon necessity to urge alteration, is to trouble and disturb without necessity. Hooker.

How will I give sentence against them. Jer. iv. 12.

If matter of fact breaks out with too great an evidence to be denied, why, still there are other lenitives, that friendship will apply, before it will be brought to the decretory rigours of a condemning sentence. South's Sermons.

Let him set out some of Luther's works, that by them we may pass sentence upon his doctrines. Atterbury.

2. It is usually spoken of condemnation pronounced by the judge; doom.

By the consent of all laws, in capital causes, the evidence must be full and clear; and if so, where one man's life is in question, what say we to a war, which is ever the sentence of death upon many? Bacon's holy War.

What rests but that the mortal sentence pass? Milton.

3. A maxim; an axiom, generally moral.

A sentence may be defined a moral instruction couched in a few words. Broome's Notes on the Odyssey.

4. A short paragraph; a period in writing.

An excellent spirit, knowledge, understanding, and shewing of hard sentences were found in Daniel. Dan. v. 12.

séntiment n.s. [*sentiment*, French.]

1. Thought; notion; opinion.

The consideration of the reason, why they are annexed to so many other ideas, serving to give us due sentiments of the wisdom and goodness of the sovereign Disposer of all things, may not be unsuitable to the main end of these enquiries. Loc.

Alike to council or th' assembly came,
With equal souls and sentiments the same.
Pope.

2. The sense considered distinctly from the language or things; a striking sentence in a composition.

sépilible adj. [*sepio*, Lat.] That may be buried. Bailey.

septénnial adj. [*septennis*, Latin.]

1. Lasting seven years.

2. Happening once in seven years.

Being once dispensed with for his septennial visit, by a holy instrument from Petropolis, he resolved to govern them by subaltern ministers. Howel's Vocal Forest.

With weekly libels and septennial ale,
Their wish is full, to riot and to rail.
Anonym.†

seráglio n.s. [Italian, perhaps of Oriental original. The *g* is lost in the pronunciation.] A house of women kept for debauchery.

There is a great deal more solid content to be found in a constant course of well living, than in the voluptuousness of a seraglio. Norris.

séraphim n.s. [This is properly the plural of seraph, and therefore cannot have s added; yet, in compliance with our language, seraphims is sometimes written.] Angels of one of the heavenly orders.

To thee cherubim and seraphim continually do cry. Com. Pr.

Then flew one of the seraphims unto me, having a live coal in his hand. Is. vi. 6.

Of seraphim another row. Milton.

sermocinátion n.s. [*sermocinatio*, Latin.] The act or practice of making speeches.

sésquipedal,   **sesquipedálian** adj. [*sesquipedalis*, Latin.] Containing a foot and a half.

As for my own part, I am but a sesquipedal, having only six foot and a half of stature. Addis. Guard.

Hast thou ever measured the gigantick Ethiopian, whose stature is above eight cubits high, or the sesquipedalian pigmey? Arbuth. and Pope's Mart. Scrib.

sesquitértian [in mathematicks.] Having such a ratio, as that one quantity or number contains another once and one third part more; as between 6 and 8. Dict.

settée n.s. A large long seat with a back to it.

sex n.s. [*sexe*, French; *sexus*, Latin.]

1. The property by which any animal is male or female.

These two great sexes animate the world. Milton.

Under his forming hands a creature grew, Manlike, but different sex. Milton.

2. Womankind; by way of emphasis.

Unhappy sex! whose beauty is your snare; Expos'd to trials; made too frail to bear. Dryd.

Shame is hard to be overcome; but if the sex once get the better of it, it gives them afterwards no more trouble. Garth.

to shab v.n. To play mean tricks; a low barbarous cant word.

shábby adj. [A word that has crept into conversation and low writing; but ought not to be admitted into the language.] Mean; paltry.

The dean was so shabby, and look'd like a ninny, That the captain suppos'd he was curate to Jenny. Swift.

to shail v.n. To walk sideways; a low word.

Child, you must walk strait, without skiewing and shailing to every step you set. L'Estrange.

shall v. defective. [*sceal*, Sax. is originally I owe, or I ought. In Chaucer, *the faithe I shall to God*, means *the faith I owe to God*: thence it became a sign of the future tense. The French use *devoir, dois, doit*, in the same manner, with a kind of future signification; and the Swedes have *skall*, and the Islanders *skal*, in the same sense. It has no tenses but shall future, and should imperfect. The explanation of shall, which foreigners and provincials confound with will, is not easy; and the difficulty is increased by the poets, who sometimes give to shall an emphatical sense of will: but I shall endeavour, *crassa Minervâ*, to show the meaning of shall in the future tense.]†

1. I shall love. It will so happen that I must love; I am resolved to love.

2. Shall I love? Will it be permitted me to love? Will you permit me to love? Will it happen that I must love?

3. Thou shalt love. I command thee to love; it is permitted thee to love: [in poetry or solemn diction] it will happen that thou must love.

4. Shalt thou love? Will it happen that thou must love? Will it be permitted to thee to love?

5. He shall love. It will happen that he must love; it is commanded him that he love.

It is a mind, that shall remain a poison where it is.
——Shall remain!
Hear you this triton of the minnows? Mark you His absolute shall? Shakesp. Coriolanus.

    See Romulus the great:
This prince a priestess of your blood shall bear, And like his sire in arms he shall appear. Dryden's Æn.

That he shall receive no benefit from Christ, is the affirmation whereon all his despair is founded; and the one way of removing this dismal apprehension, is to convince him that Christ's death, and the benefits thereof, either do, or, if he perform the condition required of him, shall certainly belong to him. Hammond's Fundamentals.

6. Shall he love? Is it permitted him to love? In solemn language, Will it happen that he must love?

7. The plural persons follow the signification of the singulars.

sháveling n.s. [from *shave*.] A man shaved; a friar, or religious. Used in contempt.

Of elfes, there be no such things; only by bald fryars and knavish shavelings so feigned. Spenser.

shékel n.s. [שקל.] An ancient Jewish coin equal to four Attick drachms, or four Roman denarii, in value about 2s. 6d. sterling. Dict.

The Jews, albeit they detested images, yet imprinted upon their sheckle on one side the golden pot which had the manna, and on the other Aaron's rod. Camden.

The huge iron head six hundred shekels weighed, And of whole bodies but one wound it made, Able death's worst command to overdoe Destroying life at once and carcase too. Cowley.

This coat of mail weighed five thousand shekels of brass. Broome.

shérbet n.s. [*sharbat*, Arabick.] The juice of lemons or oranges mixed with water and sugar. Dict.

They prefer our beer above all other drinks; and considering that water is with the rarest, especially in this clime, the dearest of sherbets, and plenty of barley, it would prove infinitely profitable to such as should bring in the use thereof. Sand.

sherris, shérris sack, shérry [from *Xeres*, a town of Andalusia in Spain.] A kind of sweet Spanish wine.

Your sherris warms the blood, which before, cold and settled, left the liver white, which is the badge of pusilanimity; but the sherris makes it course from the inwards to the parts extreme. Shakespeare.

Good sherris sack ascends me into the brain, dries me there all the foolish dull vapours, and makes it apprehensive. Shak.

shílling n.s. [*scylling*, Sax. and Erse; *schelling*, Dut.] A coin of various value in different times. It is now twelve pence.

Five of these pence made their shilling, which they called scilling, *probably from* scilingus, *which the Romans used for the fourth part of an ounce; and forty-eight of these scillings made their pound, and four hundred of these pounds were a legacy for a king's daughter, as appeareth by the last will of king Alfred.* Camden's Remains.

The very same shilling may at one time pay twenty men in twenty days, and at another rest in the same hands one hundred days. Locke.

shill-I-shall-I A corrupt reduplication of shall I? The question of a man hesitating. To stand shill-I-shall-I, is to continue hesitating and procrastinating.

I am somewhat dainty in making a resolution, because when I make it, I keep it: I don't stand shill-I shall-I then; if I say 't, I'll do 't. Congreve's Way of the World.

shíngles n.s. Wants singul. [*cingulum*, Latin; *zona morbus*, Plinio.] A kind of tetter or herpes that spreads itself round the loins.

Such are used successfully in erysipelas and shingles, by a slender diet of decoctions of farinaceous vegetables, and copious drinking of cooling liquors. Arbuthnot on Diet.

shirt n.s. [*shiert*, Danish; *scyrc*, *scyric*, Saxon.] The under linen garment of a man.

Shift a shirt: the violence of action hath made you reek as a sacrifice. Shakesp. Cymbeline.

I take but two shirts out with me, and I mean not to sweat extraordinarily. Shakesp. Henry IV.

When we lay next us what we hold most dear, Like Hercules, envenom'd shirts we wear, And cleaving mischiefs. Dryden.

Several persons in December had nothing over their shoulders but their shirts. Addison on Italy.

shíttlecock n.s. [Commonly and perhaps as properly *shuttlecock*. Of *shittle* or *shuttle* the etymology is doubtful: Skinner derives it from *schutteln*, German, to shake; or *sceafan*, Saxon, to throw. He thinks it is called a cock from its feathers. Perhaps it is properly *shuttlecork*, a cork driven to and fro, as the instrument in weaving, and softened by frequent and rapid utterance from *cork* to *cock*.] A cork stuck with feathers, and driven by players from one to another with battledoors.

You need not discharge a cannon to break the chain of his thoughts: the pat of a shittlecock, or the creaking of a jack, will do his business. Collier.

shrew n.s. [*schreyen*, German, to clamour.] A peevish, malignant, clamorous, spiteful, vexatious, turbulent woman. [It appears in Robert of Gloucester, that this word signified anciently any one perverse or obstinate of either sex.]

There dede of hem vor hunger a thousand and mo,
And yat nolde the screwen to none pes go. Robert of Gloucester.

   Be merry, my wife has all;
For women are shrews both short and tall. Shak. H. IV.

By this reckoning he is more shrew than she. Shakespeare.

A man had got a shrew to his wife, and there could be no quiet in the house for her. L'Estrange.

Her sallow cheeks her envious mind did shew, And ev'ry feature spoke aloud the shrew. Dryden.

Every one of them, who is a shrew in domestick life, is now become a scold in politicks. Addis. Freeholder.

shúfflecap n.s. [*shuffle* and *cap*.] A play at which money is shaken in a hat.

He lost his money at chuck farthing, shufflecap, and allfours. Arbuthnot's Hist of John Bull.

sídebox n.s. [*side* and *box*.] Seat for the ladies on the side of the theatre.

Why round our coaches crowd the white-glov'd beaus?
Why bows the sidebox from its inmost rows? Pope.

sign n.s. [*signe*, French; *signum*, Latin.]

1. A token of any thing; that by which any thing is shown.

Signs must resemble the things they signify. Hooker.

Signs for communication may be contrived from any variety of objects of one kind appertaining to either sense. Holder.

To express the passions which are seated in the heart by outward signs, is one great precept of the painters, and very difficult to perform. Dryden's Dufresnoy.

When any one uses any term, he may have in his mind a determined idea which he makes it the sign of, and to which he should keep it steadily annexed. Locke.

2. A wonder; a miracle.

If they will not hearken to the voice of the first sign, they will not believe the latter sign. Ex. iv. 8.

Cover thy face that thou see not; for I have set thee for a sign unto Israel. Ezek. xii. 6.

Compell'd by signs and judgments dire. Milton.

3. A picture hung at a door, to give notice what is sold within.

I found my miss, struck hands, and pray'd him tell,
To hold acquaintance still, where he did dwell;
He barely nam'd the street, promis'd the wine;
But his kind wife gave me the very sign. Donne.

Underneath an alehouse' paltry sign. Shakesp. H. VI.

   True sorrow's like to wine,
That which is good does never need a sign. Suckling.

Wit and fancy are not employed in any one article so much as that of contriving signs to hang over houses. Swift.

4. A monument; a memorial.

The fire devoured two hundred and fifty men, and they became a sign. Num. xxvi. 10.

5. A constellation in the zodiack.

There stay until the twelve celestial signs Have brought about their annual reckoning. Shakespeare.

Now did the sign reign, and the constellation was come, under which Perkin should appear. Bacon's Henry VII.

After ev'ry foe subdu'd, the sun Thrice through the signs his annual race shall run. Dryden.

6. Note of resemblance.

7. Ensign.

The ensign of Messiah blaz'd, Aloft by angels borne, his sign in heaven. Milton.

8. Typical representation; symbol.

The holy symbols or signs are not barely significative; but what they represent is as certainly delivered to us as the symbols themselves. Brerewood.

9. A subscription of one's name: as, a sign manual.

to signify v.a. [*signifier*, French; *significe*, Latin.]

1. To declare by some token or sign.

The maid from that ill omen turn'd her eyes, Nor knew what signify'd the boding sign, But found the pow'rs displeas'd. Dryden.

Those parts of nature, into which the chaos was divided, they signified by dark and obscure names; as the night, tartarus, and oceanus. Burnet's Theory of the Earth.

2. To mean; to express.

Life's but a walking shadow; a poor player, That struts and frets his hour upon the stage, And then is heard no more! It is a tale, Told by an ideot, full of sound and fury, Signifying nothing! Shakespeare's Macbeth.

Stephano, signify Within the house your mistress is at hand. Shakespeare.

3. To import; to weight. This is seldom used but interrogatively, what signifies? or with much, little, or nothing.

Though he that sins frequently, and repents frequently, gives reason to believe his repentances before God signify nothing; yet that is nothing to us. Taylor.

What signifies the splendor of courts, considering the slavish attendances that go along with it? L'Estrange.

He hath one way more, which although it signify little to men of sober reason, yet unhappily hits the suspicious humour of men, that governors have a design to impose. Tillotson.

If the first of these fail, the power of Adam, were it never so great, will signify nothing to the present societies in the world. Locke.

What signifies the people's consent in making and repealing laws, if the person who administers hath no tie. Swift.

4. To make known.

I'll to the king, and signify to him, That thus I have resign'd to you my charge. Shakes. R. III.

He sent and signified it by his angel unto John. Rev. i. 1.

The government should signify to the protestants of Ireland, that want of silver is not to be remedied. Swift.

siker adv. The old word for sure, or surely. Spenser.

siliginose adj. [*siliginosus*, Latin.] Made of fine wheat. Dict.

sillabub n.s. [This word has exercised the etymologists. Minshew thinks it corrupted from *swillingbubbles*. Junius omits it. Henshaw, whom Skinner follows, deduces it from the Dutch *sulle*, a pipe, and *buyck*, a paunch; because *sillabubs* are commonly drunk through a spout, out of a jug with a large belly. It seems more probably derived from *esil*, in old English vinegar, *esil a bouc*, vinegar for the mouth, vinegar made pleasant.] Curds made by milking upon vinegar.

Joan takes her neat rubb'd pail, and now
She trips to milk the sand-red cow;
Where, for some sturdy foot-ball swain,
Joan strokes a sillabub or twain. Wotton.

A feast,
By some rich farmer's wife and sister drest,
Might be resembled to a sick man's dream,
Where all ideas huddling run so fast,
That sillabubs come first, and soups the last.
King.

silly adj. [*selig*, German. Skinner.]

1. Harmless; innocent; inoffensive;
   plain; artless.

2. Weak; helpless.

After long storms,
In dread of death and dangerous dismay,
With which my silly bark was tossed sore,
I do at length descry the happy shore. Spenser.

3. Foolish; witless.

Perhaps their loves, or else their sheep,
Was that did their silly thoughts so busy keep.
Milton.

The meanest subjects censure the actions of
the greatest prince; the silliest servants, of
the wisest master. Temple.

I have no discontent at living here; besides
what arises from a silly spirit of liberty, which
I resolve to throw off. Swift.

Such parts of writings as are stupid or silly,
false or mistaken, should become subjects
of occasional criticism. Watts.

simpleton n.s. [from *simple.*] A silly mortal;
a trifler; a foolish fellow. A low word.

A country farmer sent his man to look after an
ox; the simpleton went hunting up and down
till he found him in a wood. L'Estrange.

Those letters may prove a discredit, as lasting
as mercenary scribblers, or curious simpletons
can make it. Pope.

sin n.s. [*syn*, Saxon.]

1. An act against the laws of God;
   a violation of the laws of religion.

How hast thou the heart,
Being a divine, a ghostly confessor,
A sin absolver, and my friend profest,
To mangle me with that word banishment.
Shakespeare.

But those that sleep, and think not on their sins,
Pinch them. Shakespeare's Merry Wives
of Windsor.

Thou knowest, Lord, that I am pure from
all sin with man. Tob. iii. 14.

2. Habitual negligence of religion.

Sin, death, and hell, have set their
   marks upon him,
And all their ministers attend on him.
Shakespeare.

Dishonest shame
Of nature's works: honour dishonourable!
Sin-bred! how have ye troubled all mankind?
Milton.

Is there no means, but that a sin-sick land
Should be let blood with such a boist'rous
   hand? Daniel.

Vice or virtue chiefly imply the relation of our
actions to men in this world: sin and holiness
rather imply their relation to God and the
other world. Watts's Logick.

Light from her thought, as summer's careless robe,
Fell each affection of this sin-worn globe.
Brooke.

3. It is used by Shakespeare emphatically
   for a man enormously wicked.

Thy ambition,
Thou scarlet sin, robb'd this bewailing land
Of noble Buckingham. Shakespeare's
Henry VIII.

singult n.s. [*singultus*, Latin.] A sigh.
Spenser.

sinworm n.s. [*sin* and *worm.*] A vile sinful
creature.

I would not soil these pure ambrosial weeds,
With the rank vapours of the sin-worm
   mould. Milton.

sirrah n.s. [*sir, ha!* Minshew.] A
compellation of reproach and insult.

Go, sirrah, to my cell;
Take with you your companions: as you look
To have my pardon, trim it handsomely.
Shakes. Tempest.

Sirrah, there's no room for faith, troth,
or honesty in this bosom of thine.
Shakespeare's Henry IV.

It runs in the blood of your whole race, sirrah,
to hate our family. L'Estrange.

Guess how the goddess greets her son,
Come hither, sirrah; no, begone. Prior.

sízer, or *servitor* n.s. A certain rank of students in the universities.[†]

They make a scramble for degree.
Masters of all sorts and of all ages,
Keepers, sub-sisers, lackeys, pages.
Bp. Corbet.

skáddons n.s. The embryos of bees. Bailey.

sképtick n.s. [σκεπτικος, Gr. *sceptique,* French.] One who doubts, or pretends to doubt of every thing.

Bring the cause unto the bar; whose authority
none must disclaim, and least of all those
scepticks in religion. Dec. of Piety.

Survey
Nature's extended face, then scepticks say,
In this wide field of wonders can you find
No art. Blackmore.

With too much knowledge for the scepticks side,
With too much weakness for the stoicks pride,
Man hangs between. Pope's Essay on Man.

The dogmatist is sure of every thing, and the
sceptick believes nothing. Watts's Logick.

skilt n.s. [A word used by Cleaveland, of which I know not either the etymology or meaning.][†]

Smectymnus! ha! what art?
Syriack? Or Arabick? Or Welsh? What skilt?
Ape all the bricklayers that Babel built.
Cleaveland.

skímbleskamble adj. [A cant word formed by reduplication from *scamble.*] Wandering; wild.

A couching lion and a ramping cat,
And such a deal of skimbleskamble stuff,
As puts me from my faith. Shakespeare.

to skink v.n. [*scencan,* Saxon.] To serve drink. Both noun and verb are wholly obsolete.

skípjack n.s. [*skip* and *jack.*] An upstart.

The want of shame or brains does not
presently entitle every little skipjack to
the board's-end in the cabinet. L'Estr.

skípkennel n.s. [*skip* and *kennel.*] A lackey; a footboy.

sleazy adj. [often written *sleezy.*] Weak; wanting substance. This seems to be of the same race with *sleave,* or from to *sley.*

slíppy adv. [from *slip.*] Slippery; easily sliding. A barbarous provincial word.

The white of an egg is ropy, slippy, and
nutritious. Floyer.

slípslop n.s. Bad liquor. A low word formed by reduplication of *slop.*

slop n.s. [from the verb.] Mean and vile liquor of any kind. Generally some nauseous or useless medicinal liquor.

The sick husband here wanted for neither slops
nor doctors. L'Estrange.

But thou, whatever slops she will have bought,
Be thankful. Dryden's Juvenal.

slúbberdegullion n.s. [I suppose a cant word without derivation.] A paltry, dirty, sorry wretch.

Quoth she, although thou hast deserv'd,
Base slubberdegullion, to be serv'd
As thou did'st vow to deal with me,
If thou had'st got the victory. Hudibras.

smart n.s. A fellow affecting briskness and vivacity. A cant word.

sméllfeast n.s. [*smell* and *feast.*] A parasite; one who haunts good tables.

The ant lives upon her own, honestly gotten;
whereas the fly is an intruder, and a common
smellfeast that spunges upon other people's
trenchers. L'Estrange.

to smerk v.a. [*smercian*, Saxon.] To smile wantonly.

Certain gentlemen of the gown, whose aukward, spruce, prim, sneering, and smirking countenances have got good preferment by force of cringing. Swift.

smícket n.s. [Diminutive of *smock, smocket, smicket.*] The under garment of a woman.

smóker n.s. [from *smoke.*]

1. One that dries or perfumes by smoke.

2. One that uses tobacco.

smug adj. [*smuck*, dress, *smucken*, to dress, Dutch.] Nice; spruce; dressed with affectation of niceness, but without elegance.

There I have a bankrupt for a prodigal, who dares scarce shew his head on the Rialto;
a beggar, that used to come so smug upon the mart. Shak. Merchant of Venice.

He who can make your visage less horrid, and your person more smug, is worthy some good reception. Spectator.

smúggler n.s. [from *smuggle.*] A wretch, who, in defiance of justice and the laws, imports or exports goods either contraband or without payment of the customs.

smut n.s. [*smitta*, Saxon; *smette*, Dutch.]

1. A spot made with soot or coal.

2. Must or blackness gathered on corn; mildew.

Farmers have suffered by smutty wheat, when such will not sell for above five shillings a bushel; whereas that which is free from smut will sell for ten. Mortimer's Husbandry.

3. Obscenity.

snack n.s. [from *snatch.*] A share; a part taken by compact.

If the master gets the better on 't, they come in for their snack. L'Estrange.

For four times talking, if one piece thou take, That must be cantled, and the judge go snack. Dryden.

All my demurs but double his attacks;
At last he whispers, "Do, and we go snacks."
Pope.

snéaker n.s. A large vessel of drink.

I have just left the right worshipful and his myrmidons about a sneaker of five gallons. Spectator.

snew The old preterite of to snow. Dict.

snick and snee n.s. A combat with knives.

Among the Dunkirkers, where snick and snee was in fashion, a boatswain with some of our men drinking together, became quarrelsome: one of our men beat him down; then kneeling upon his breast, he drew out a knife, sticking in his sash, and cut him from the ear towards the mouth. Wiseman's Surgery.

snípsnap n.s. [A cant word formed by reduplication of *snap.*] Tart dialogue.

Dennis and dissonance, and captious art, And snipsnap short, and interruption smart. Pope's Dunciad.

snot n.s. [*snote*, Saxon; *snot*, Dutch.] The mucus of the nose.

Thus, when a greedy sloven once has thrown His snot into the mess, 'tis all his own. Swift.

to snudge v.n. [*sniger*, Danish.] To lie idle, close, or snug.

Now he will fight it out, and to the wars; Now eat his bread in peace, And snudge in quiet; now he scorns increase; Now all day spares. Herbert.

snuff n.s. [*snuf*, Dutch, snot.]

1. Snot. In this sense it is not used.

2. The useless excrescence of a candle: whence *moucher la chandelle.*

   My great affliction, If I could bear longer, and not fall To quarrel with your opposeless wills, My snuff and loathed part of nature should Burn itself out. Shakesp. King Lear.

But dearest heart, and dearer image, stay! Alas! true joys at best are dreams enough: Though you stay here, you pass too fast away; For even at first life's taper is a snuff. Donne.

The snuff-dishes shall be of pure gold.
Ex. xxv. 38.

*If the liquor be of a close and glutinous
consistency, it may burn without any snuff,
as we see in camphire, and some other
bituminous substances; and most of the
ancient lamps were of this kind, because none
have been found with such wicks.* Wilk.

3. A candle almost burnt out.

   Lamentable!
*To hide me from the radiant sun, and solace
I' th' dungeon by a snuff.* Shakesp.
Cymbeline.

4. The fired wick of a candle remaining
   after the flame.

*A torch, snuff and all, goes out in a moment,
when dipped into the vapour.* Addison
on Italy.

5. Resentment expressed by snifting;
   perverse resentment.

   *What hath been seen
Either in snuffs or packings of the duke's,
Or the hard rein which both of them have borne
Against the old kind king.* Shakesp.
King Lear.

*Jupiter took snuff at the contempt, and
punished him: he sent him home again.*
L'Estrange.

6. Powdered tobacco taken by the nose.

*Just where the breath of life his nostrils drew,
A charge of snuff the wily virgin threw;
The gnomes direct to ev'ry atom just
The pungent grains of titillating dust.* Pope.

to snúggle v.n. [from *snug*.] To lie close; to
lie warm.

sock n.s. [*soccus*, Latin; *socc*, Saxon; *socke*,
Dutch.]

1. Something put between the foot
   and shoe.

*Ere I lead this life long, I'll sow nether socks,
and mend them, and foot them too.*
Shakespeare's Henry IV.

*A physician, that would be mystical,
prescribeth for the rheum to walk continually*

*upon a camomile alley; meaning he should
put camomile within his socks.* Bacon.

2. The shoe of the ancient comick actors,
   taken in poems for comedy, and
   opposed to buskin or tragedy.

*Then to the well trod stage anon,
If Johnson's learned sock be on,
Or sweetest Shakespeare, fancy's child,
Warble his native wood-notes wild.* Milton.

*Great Fletcher never treads in buskins here,
Nor greater Johnson dares in socks appear;
But gentle Simkin just reception finds
Amidst the monument of vanish'd minds.*
Dryden.

*On two figures of actors in the villa Mathei
at Rome, we see the fashion of the old sock
and larva.* Addison.

sófa n.s. [I believe an eastern word.] A
splendid seat covered with carpets.

*The king leaped off from the sofa on which he
sat, and cried out, 'tis my Abdallah!* Guardian.

sóldan n.s. [for *sultan*.] The emperor of
the Turks.

They at the soldan's chair defy'd the best.
Milton.

sólecism n.s. [σολοικισμος.] Unfitness of
one word to another; impropriety in
language. A barbarism may be in one word,
a solecism must be of more.

*There is scarce a solecism in writing which the
best author is not guilty of, if we be at liberty
to read him in the words of some manuscript.*
Addison.

solifidian n.s. [*solus* and *fides*, Latin.] One
who supposes only faith, not works,
necessary to justification.

*It may be justly feared, that the title of
fundamentals, being ordinarily confined to the
doctrines of faith, hath occasioned that great
scandal in the church of God, at which so
many myriads of solifidians have stumbled,
and fallen irreversibly, by conceiving heaven
a reward of true opinions.* Hammond.

solitáire n.s. [*solitaire*, French.]

1. A recluse; a hermit.

Often have I been going to take possession
of tranquillity, when your conversation has
spoiled me for a solitaire. Pope.

2. An ornament for the neck.

sólo n.s. [Italian.] A tune played by a single
instrument.

sonáta n.s. [Italian.] A tune.

He whistled a Scotch tune, and an Italian
sonata. Addison.

Could Pedro, think you, make no trial
Of a sonata on his viol,
Unless he had the total gut,
Whence every string at first was cut. Prior.

song n.s. [from *gesungen*, Saxon.]

1. Any thing modulated in the utterance.

Noise other than the sound of dance and song.
Milton.

He first thinks fit no sonnetter advance
His censure farther than the song or dance.
Dryden.

2. A poem to be modulated by the voice;
a ballad.

Pardon, goddess of the night,
Those that slew thy virgin knight;
For the which, with songs of woe,
Round about his tomb they go! Shakespeare.

   In her days ev'ry man shall sing
The merry songs of peace to all his neighbours.
Sh. H. VIII.

3. A poem; lay; strain.

The bard that first adorn'd our native tongue,
Tun'd to his British lyre this ancient song.
Dryden.

4. Poetry; poesy.

This subject for heroick song pleas'd me.
Milton.

   Names memorable long,
If there be force in virtue, or in song. Pope.

5. Notes of birds.

   The lark, the messenger of day,
Saluted in her song the morning grey.
Dryden.

6. An old song. A trifle.

I do not intend to be thus put off with an
old song. More.

A hopeful youth, newly advanced to great
honour, was forced by a cobler to resign all
for an old song. Addison.

sónnet n.s. [*sonnet*, French; *sonnetto*, Italian.]

1. A short poem consisting of fourteen
lines, of which the rhymes are adjusted
by a particular rule. It is not very
suitable to the English language, and
has not been used by any man of
eminence since Milton.[†]

A book was writ of late call'd Tetrachordon,
And woven close, both matter, form, and stile;
The subject new: it walk'd the town a-while,
Numb'ring good intellects, now seldom por'd on:
Cries the stall-reader, Bless us, what a word on
A title-page is this! and some in file
Stand spelling false, while one might walk to
   Mile-End-green.
Why is it harder, sirs, than Gordon,
Colkitto, or Macdonnel, or Galasp?
Those rugged names to our like mouths
   grow sleek,
That would have made Quintilian stare
   and gasp:
Thy age like ours, soul of sir John Cheek,
Hated not learning worse than toad or asp,
When thou taught'st Cambridge and king
   Edward Greek. Milton.

2. A small poem.

Let us into the city presently,
To sort some gentlemen well skill'd in musick;
I have a sonnet that will serve the turn.
Shakespeare.

soph n.s. [from *sophista*, Latin.] A young
man who has been two years at the
university.

Three Cambridge sophs, and three pert
   templars came,
The same their talents, and their tastes the same;
Each prompt to query, answer and debate,
And smit with love of poesy and prate.
Pope's Dunciad.

sóphi n.s. [Persian.] The emperor of Persia.

By this scimitar
That slew the sophi and a Persian prince.
Shakespeare.

A fig for the sultan and sophi. Congreve.

sóphist n.s. [*sophista*, Latin.] A professor of philosophy.

The court of Crœsus is said to have been much resorted by the sophists of Greece in the happy beginning of his reign. Tem.

to sophísticate v.a. [*sophistiquer*, Fr. from *sophist*] To adulterate; to corrupt with something spurious.

If the passions of the mind be strong, they easily sophisticate the understanding, they make it apt to believe upon every slender warrant, and to imagine infallible truth, where scarce any probable shew appeareth. Hooker.

Here's three of us are sophisticated. Shakespeare.

Divers experiments succeeded not, because they were at one time tried with genuine materials, and at another time with sophisticated ones. Boyle.

The only persons amongst the heathens, who sophisticated nature and philosophy, were the Stoicks; who affirmed a fatal, unchangeable concatenation of causes, reaching even to the elicite acts of man's will. South's Sermons.

Yet the rich cullies may their boasting spare;
They purchase but sophisticated ware:
'Tis prodigality that buys deceit,
Where both the giver and the taker cheat.
Dryden.

The eye hath its coats and humours transparent and colourless, lest it should tinge and sophisticate the light that it lets in by a natural jaundice. Bentley.

soporíferous adj. [*sopor* and *fero*.] Productive of sleep; causing sleep; narcotick; opiate; dormitive; somniferous; anodyne; sleepy.

The particular ingredients of those magical ointments are opiate and soporiferous; for anointing of the forehead, neck, feet, and back-bone, procures dead sleeps. Bacon.

While the whole operation was performing,
I lay in a profound sleep, by the force of that soporiferous medicine infused into my liquor. Gulliver's Travels.

soróricide n.s. [*soror* and *cædo*.] The murder of a sister.

to sot v.n. To tipple to stupidity.

soul n.s. [*sawel*, Sax. *sael*, Dan. *sual*, Islandick; *siel*, Dutch.]

1. The immaterial and immortal spirit of man.

When death was overcome, he opened heaven as well to the believing Gentiles as Jews: heaven till then was no receptacle to the souls of either. Hooker.

Fie, fie, unreverent tongue! to call her bad,
Whose sov'reignty so oft thou hast preferr'd
With twenty thousand soul-confirming oaths.
Shakespeare.

Perhaps, for want of food, the soul may pine;
But that were strange, since all things bad
*   and good;*
Since all God's creatures, mortal and divine;
Since God himself is her eternal food. Davies.

He remembered them of the promises, seals and oaths, which by publick authority had passed for concluding this marriage, that these being religious bonds betwixt God and their souls, could not by any politick act of state be dissolved. Hayward.

Eloquence the soul, song charms the sense. Milton.

2. Vital principle.

They say this town is full of cozenage,
Drug-working sorcerers that change the mind;
Soul-killing witches that deform the body;
And many such like libertines of sin.
Shakespeare.

Thou almost mak'st me waver in my faith,
To hold opinion with Pythagoras,
That souls of animals infuse themselves
Into the trunks of men. Shakesp. Merch. of Venice.

Thou sun, of this great world both eye and soul. Milton.

Join voices all ye living souls! ye birds,
That singing up to heav'n-gate ascend,
Bear on your wings, and in your notes
    his praise. Milton.

In common discourse and writing, we leave
out the words vegetative, sensitive, and
rational; and make the word soul serve for
all these principles. Watts.

3. Spirit; essence; quintessence; principal
    part.

He has the very soul of bounty. Shakespeare.

Charity the soul of all the rest. Milton.

4. Interiour power.

There is some soul of goodness in things evil,
Would men observingly distil it out.
Shakespeare.

5. A familiar appellation expressing
    the qualities of the mind.

Three wenches where I stood, cry'd:
"Alas, good soul!" Shakespeare's
Julius Cæsar.

This is a poor mad soul; and she says up and
down the town, that her eldest son is like you.
Shakesp. Hen. IV.

The poor soul sat singing by a sycamore tree,
Sing all a green willow:
Her hand on her bosom, her head on her knee.
Shakesp.

Unenlarged souls are disgusted with the
wonders of the microscope, discovering
animals which equal not a peppercorn. Watts.

6. Human being.

The moral is the case of every soul of us.
L'Estrange.

Keep the poor soul no longer in suspense,
Your change is such as does not need defence.
Dryden.

It is a republick; there are in it a hundred
burgeois, and about a thousand souls.
Addison's Italy.

My state of health none care to learn;
My life is here no soul's concern. Swift.

7. Active power.

Earth, air and seas, through empty space
    would rowl,
And heav'n would fly before the driving soul.
Dryden.

8. Spirit; fire; grandeur of mind.

9. Intelligent being in general.

Every soul in heav'n shall bend the knee.
Milton.

soúlshot n.s. [*soul* and *shot*.] Something
paid for a soul's requiem among the
Romanists.

In the Saxon times there was a funeral duty
to be paid, called pecunia sepulchralis &
symbolum animæ, *and in Saxon soulshot.*
Ayliffe's Parergon.†

soup n.s. [*soupe*, French.] Strong decoction
of flesh for the table.

Spongy morells in strong ragousts are found,
And in the soup the slimy snail is drown'd.
Gay's Trivia.

Let the cook daub the back of the footman's
new livery, or, when he is going up with a
dish of soup, let her follow him softly with
a ladle-full. Swift.

spadílle n.s. [*spadille*, or *espadille*, French.]
The ace of spades at ombre.

spark n.s. [*spearca*, Saxon; *sparke*, Dutch.]

1. A small particle of fire, or kindled
    matter.

If any marvel how a thing, in itself so weak,
could import any great danger, they must
consider not so much how small the spark is
that flieth up, as how apt things about it are
to take fire. Hooker.

I am about to weep; but thinking that
We are a queen, my drops of tears I'll turn
To sparks of fire. Shakespeare.

I was not forgetful of the sparks which some
mens distempers formerly studied to kindle
in parliaments. K. Charles.

In this deep quiet, from what source unknown,
Those seeds of fire that fatal birth disclose:
And first, few scatt'ring sparks about
    were blown,

Big with the flames that to our ruin rose.
Dryden.

Oh, may some spark of your celestial fire
The last, the meanest of your sons inspire.
Pope.

2. Any thing shining.

We have, here and there, a little clear light,
some sparks of bright knowledge. Locke.

3. Any thing vivid or active.

If any spark of life be yet remaining,
Down, down to hell, and say, I sent thee
*   thither.* Shakesp.

4. A lively, showy, splendid, gay man. It is
commonly used in contempt.

How many huffing sparks have we seen, that
in the same day have been both the idols and
the scorn of the same slaves? L'Estrange.

A spark like thee, of the mankilling trade
Fell sick. Dryden.

As for the disputes of sharpers, we don't read
of any provisions made for the honours of such
sparks. Collier.

The finest sparks, and cleanest beaux
Drip from the shoulders to the toes. Prior.

I who have been the poet's spark to day,
Will now become the champion of his play.
Granville.

Unlucky as Fungoso in the play,
These sparks with aukward vanity display
What the fine gentlemen wore yesterday.
Pope.

spectátor n.s. [*spectateur*, Fr. *spectator*,
Latin.] A looker on; a beholder.

    More
Than history can pattern, though devis'd
And play'd, to take spectators. Shakespeare.

If it proves a good repast to the spectators, the
dish pays the shot. Shakespeare's Cymbeline.

An old gentleman mounting on horseback got
up heavily; but desired the spectators that they
would count fourscore and eight before they
judged him. Dryden.

He mourns his former vigour lost so far,
To make him now spectator of a war.
Dryden.

What pleasure hath the owner more than the
spectator? Seed.

spéctrum n.s. [Latin.] An image; a visible
form.

This prism had some veins running along
within the glass, from the one end to the other,
which scattered some of the sun's light
irregularly, but had no sensible effect in
encreasing the length of the coloured spectrum.
Newton's Opticks.

spéculum n.s. [Latin.] A mirrour; a
looking-glass; that in which representations
are formed by reflection.

A rough and coloured object may serve for
a speculum, to reflect the artificial rainbow.
Boyle on Colours.

spermólogist n.s. [σπερμολογος.] One
who gathers or treats of seeds. Dict.

spick and span [This word I should not
have expected to have found authorised by
a polite writer. *Span-new* is used by
Chaucer, and is supposed to come from
spannan, to stretch, Sax. *expandere*, Lat.
whence *span*. *Span-new* is therefore
originally used of cloath new extended or
dressed at the clothiers, and *spick and span*
is newly extended on the *spikes* or tenters:
it is however a low word.] Quite new; now
first used.

    While the honour, thou hast got,
Is spick and span new, piping hot,
Strike her up bravely. Butler.

They would have these reduced to nothing,
and then others treated spick and span new
out of nothing. Burnet.

I keep no antiquated stuff;
But spick and span I have enough. Swift.

spíder n.s. [Skinner thinks this word
softened from *spinder*, or *spinner*, from *spin*:
Junius, with his usual felicity, dreams that
it comes from σπιζειν, to extend; for the
spider extends his web. Perhaps it comes
from *spieden*, Dutch; *Speyden*, Danish, to
spy, to lye upon the catch. *Dor, dora*, Saxon,
is a beetle, or properly an humble bee, or
stingless bee. May not *spider* be *spy dor*, the
insect that watches the *dor*?]† The animal
that spins a web for flies.

More direful hap betide that hated wretch,
Than I can wish to adders, spiders, toads.
Shakespeare.

    The spider's web to watch we'll stand,
And when it takes the bee,
    We'll help out of the tyrant's hand
The innocent to free. Drayton.

    Insidious, restless, watchful spider,
Fear no officious damsel's broom;
    Extend thy artful fabrick wider,
And spread thy banners round my room:
    While I thy curious fabrick stare at,
And think on hapless poet's fate,
    Like thee confin'd to noisome garret,
And rudely banish'd rooms of state.
Dr. Littleton.

The spider's touch how exquisitely fine!
Feels at each thread, and lives along the line.
Pope.

spindleshánked adj. [*spindle* and *shank*.]
Having small legs.

Her lawyer is a little rivelled, spindleshanked
gentleman. Addis.

spínet n.s. [*espinette*, French.] A small
harpsichord, an instrument with keys.

When miss delights in her spinnet,
A fiddler may his fortune get. Swift.

spínny adj. I suppose small, slender. A
barbarous word.

They plow it early in the year, and then
there will come some spinny grass that will
keep it from scalding in summer.
Mortimer's Husbandry.

spírit n.s. [*spiritus*, Latin.]

1. Breath; wind in motion.

All purges have in them a raw spirit or wind,
which is the principal cause of tension in the
stomach. Bacon.

The balmy spirit of the western breeze.
Anon.[†]

2. [*Esprit*, Fr.] An immaterial substance.

Spirit is a substance wherein thinking,
knowing, doubting, and a power of moving
do subsist. Locke.

I shall depend upon your constant friendship;
like the trust we have in benevolent spirits,
who, though we never see or hear them, we
think are constantly praying for us. Pope.

She is a spirit; yet not like air, or wind;
Nor like the spirits about the heart, or brain;
Nor like those spirits which alchymists do find,
When they in ev'ry thing seek gold in vain;
For she all natures under heav'n doth pass,
Being like those spirits which God's bright
    face do see,
Or like himself whose image once she was,
Though now, alas! she scarce his shadow be;
For of all forms she holds the first degree,
That are to gross material bodies knit;
Yet she herself is bodyless and free;
And though confin'd is almost infinite.
Davies.

If we seclude space, there will remain in the
world but matter and mind, or body and
spirit. Watts's Logick.

3. The soul of man.

The spirit shall return unto God that gave it.
Bible.

Look, who comes here! a grave unto a soul,
Holding th' eternal spirit 'gainst her will
In the vile prison of afflicted breath.
Shakespeare's K. John.

4. An apparition.

They were terrified, and supposed that they
had seen a spirit. Luke xxiv. 37.

Perhaps you might see the image, and not the
glass; the former appearing like a spirit in
the air. Bacon.

Whilst young, preserve his tender mind from
all impressions of spirits and goblins in
the dark. Locke.

5. Temper; habitual disposition of mind.

    He sits
Upon their tongues a various spirit, to rase
Quite out their native language. Milton.

That peculiar law of christianity which
forbids revenge, no man can think it grievous
who considers the restless torment of a
malicious and revengeful spirit. Tillotson.

Nor once disturb their heav'nly spirits
With Scapin's cheats, or Cæsar's merits. Prior.

6. Ardour; courage; elevation; vehemence
of mind.

'Tis well blown, lads;
This morning, like the spirit of a youth
That means to be of note, begins betimes.
Shakespeare.

Farewel the big war,
The spirit stirring drum, th' ear piercing fife.
Shakespeare.

7. Genius; vigour of mind.

More ample spirit than hitherto was wont,
Here needs me, whiles the famous ancestors
Of my most dreaded sovereign I recount,
By which all earthly princes she doth far
*   surmount.* Fa. Q.

To a mighty work thou goest, O king,
That equal spirits and equal pow'rs shall
*   bring.* Daniel.

A wild Tartar, when he spies
A man that's handsome, valiant, wise,
If he can kill him, thinks t' inherit
His wit, his beauty, and his spirit. Butler.

The noblest spirit or genius cannot deserve
enough of mankind, to pretend to the esteem
of heroick virtue. Temple.

A perfect judge will read each work of wit,
With the same spirit that its author writ:
Survey the whole, nor seek slight fault to find,
Where nature moves, and rapture warms the
*   mind.* Pope.

8. Turn of mind; power of mind moral or
intellectual.

*   You were us'd*
To say extremity was the trier of spirits,
That common chances common men could
*   bear.* Shakesp.

I ask but half thy mighty spirit for me.
Cowley.

9. Intellectual powers distinct from
the body.

These discourses made so deep impression upon
the mind and spirit of the prince, whose

nature was inclined to adventures, that
he was transported with the thought of it.
Clarendon.

*   In spirit perhaps he also saw*
Rich Mexico, the seat of Montezume. Milton.

10. Sentiment; perception.

You are too great to be by me gainsaid:
Your spirit is too true, your fears too certain.
Shakespeare.

11. Eagerness; desire.

God has changed mens tempers with the
times, and made a spirit of building succeed
a spirit of pulling down. South.

12. Man of activity; man of life, fire and
enterprise.

*   The watry kingdom is no bar*
To stop the foreign spirits, but they come.
Shakespeare.

13. Persons distinguished by qualities of
the mind. A French word, happily
growing obsolete.

Such spirits as he desired to please, such would
I chuse for my judges. Dryden.

14. That which gives vigour or
cheerfulness to the mind; the purest
part of the body bordering, says
Sydenham, on immaterialty. In this
meaning it is commonly written with
the plural termination.

*   Though thou didst but jest:*
With my vex'd spirits I cannot take a truce,
But they will quake. Shakespeare's
King John.

*   When I sit and tell*
The warlike feats I've done, his spirits fly out
Into my story. Shakespeare's Cymbeline.

*   Alas! when all our lamps are burn'd,*
Our bodies wasted, and our spirits spent,
*   When we have all the learned volumes*
*   turn'd,*
Which yield men's wits both help and ornament;
What can we know, or what can we discern?
Davies.

To sing thy praise, wou'd heav'n my
*   breath prolong,*

Infusing spirits worthy such a song,
Not Thracian Orpheus should transcend my
   lays. Dryden.

By means of the curious lodgment and
inosculation of the auditory nerves, the
orgasms of the spirits should be allayed.
Derham.

In some fair body thus the secret soul
With spirits feeds, with vigour fills the whole;
Each motion guides, and ev'ry nerve sustains,
Itself unseen, but in the effects remains. Pope.

The king's party, called the cavaliers, began to
recover their spirits. Swift.

15. The likeness; essential qualities.

Italian pieces will appear best in a room
where the windows are high, because they are
commonly made to a descending light, which
of all other doth set off mens faces in their
truest spirit. Wotton.

16. Any thing eminently pure and refined.

   Nor doth the eye itself,
That most pure spirit of sense, behold itself.
Shakespeare.

17. That which hath power or energy.

All bodies have spirits and pneumatical parts
within them; but the main difference between
animate and inanimate are, that the spirits of
things animate are all continued within
themselves, and branched in veins as blood is;
and the spirits have also certain feats where
the principal do reside, and whereunto the rest
do resort; but the spirits in things inanimate
are shut in and cut off by the tangible parts,
as air in snow. Bacon's Natural History.

18. An inflammable liquour raised by
   distillation.

What the chymists call spirit, they apply the
name to so many differing things, that they
seem to have no settled notion of the thing. In
general, they give the name of spirit to any
distilled volatile liquour. Boyle.

All spirits, by frequent use, destroy, and at last
extinguish the natural heat of the stomach.
Temple.

In distillations, what trickles down the sides
of the receiver, if it will not mix with water,
is oil; if it will, it is spirit. Arbuthnot
on Aliments.

19. It may be observed, that in the old
   poets spirit was commonly a
   monosyllable, being written spright or
   sprite.

The charge thereof unto a courteous spright
Commanded was. Spenser.

spittal n.s. [Corrupted from *hospital.*]
A charitable foundation. In use only in the
phrases, a spittal sermon, and rob not
the spittal.

to spitchcock v.a. To cut an eel in pieces
and roast him. Of this word I find no good
etymology.

No man lards salt pork with orange peel,
Or garnishes his lamb with spitchcockt eel.
King.

spleen n.s. [*splen*, Latin.]

1. The milt; one of the viscera, of which
   the use is scarcely known. It is supposed
   the seat of anger and melancholy.

If the wound be on the left hypochondrium,
under the short ribs, you may conclude the
spleen wounded. Wiseman.

2. Anger; spite; ill-humour.

   If she must teem,
Create her child of spleen, that it may live
And be a thwart disnatured torment to her.
Shakespeare.

Charge not in your spleen a noble person,
And spoil your nobler soul. Shakespeare.

Kind pity checks my spleen; brave scorn forbids
Those tears to issue, which swell my eye-lids.
Donne.

All envy'd; but the Thestyan brethren show'd
The least respect; and thus they vent their
   spleen aloud:
Lay down those honour'd spoils. Dryden.

   In noble minds some dregs remain,
Not yet purg'd off, of spleen and sour disdain.
Pope.

3. A fit of anger.

Brief as the lightning in the collied night,
That, in a spleen, unfolds both heav'n and earth;
And, ere a man hath power to say, behold!
The jaws of darkness do devour it up.
Shakespeare.

4. Melancholy; hypochondriacal vapours.

Spleen, vapours, and small-pox above them
all. Pope.

Bodies chang'd to recent forms by spleen.
Pope.

sponk n.s. A word in Edinburgh which
denotes a match, or any thing dipt in
sulphur that takes fire: as, any sponks will ye
buy? Touchwood.

spóonmeat n.s. [*spoon* and *meat.*] Liquid
food; nourishment taken with a spoon.

We prescribed a slender diet, allowing only
spoonmeats. Wise.

    Wretched
Are mortals born to sleep their lives away!
Go back to what thy infancy began,
Eat pap and spoonmeat; for thy gugaws cry,
Be sullen, and refuse the lullaby.
Dryden's Pers.

Diet most upon spoonmeats, as veal, or
cock-broths. Harv.

sport n.s. [*sport*, a make-game, Islandick.]

1. Play; diversion; game; frolick and
   tumultuous merriment.

Her sports were such as carried riches of
knowledge upon the stream of delight. Sidney.

As flies to wanton boys, are we to th' gods;
They kill us for their sport. Shakespeare's
K. Lear.

If I suspect without cause, why then make
sport at me; then let me be your jest.
Shakespeare.

When their hearts were merry, they said, call
for Samson, that he may make us sport; and
they called for him, and he made them sport.
Judg. xvi. 25.

As a mad-man who casteth fire-brands,

arrows and death; so is the man that deceiveth
his neighbour, and saith, am not I in sport?
Prov. xxvi. 19.

The discourse of fools is irksome, and their
sport is in the wantonness of sin. Ecclus.
xxvii. 13.

2. Mock; contemptuous mirth.

They had his messengers in derision and made
a sport of his prophets. I Esdr. i. 51.

To make sport with his word, and to
endeavour to render it ridiculous, by turning
that holy book into raillery, is a direct affront
to God. Tillotson's Sermons.

3. That with which one plays.

Each on his rock transfix'd, the sport and prey
Of wrecking whirlwinds. Milton.

Commit not thy prophetick mind
To flitting leaves, the sport of every wind,
Lest they disperse in air. Dryden.

4. Play; idle gingle.

An author who should introduce such a sport
of words upon our stage, would meet with
small applause. Broome.

5. Diversion of the field, as of fowling,
   hunting, fishing.

Now for our mountain sport, up to yon hill,
Your legs are young. Shakespeare's
Cymbeline.

The king, who was excessively affected to
hunting, and the sports of the field, had a
great desire to make a great park for red as
well as fallow deer, between Richmond and
Hampton court. Clarendon.

spraints n.s. The dung of an otter. Dict.

springe n.s. [from *spring.*] A gin; a noose
which fastened to any elastick body catches
by a spring or jerk.

As a woodcock to my own springe, Osrick,
I'm justly kill'd with mine own treachery.
Shakespeare's Hamlet.

Let goats for food their loaded udders lend;
But neither springes, nets, nor snares employ.
Dryden.

With hairy springes we the birds betray,
Slight lines of hair surprize the finny prey.
Pope.

spud n.s. A short knife.

My love to Sheelah is more firmly fixt,
Than strongest weeds that grow these
    stones betwixt:
My spud these nettles from the stones can part,
No knife so keen to weed thee from my heart.
Swift.

spúnginghouse n.s. [*spunge* and *house.*] A
house to which debtors are taken before
commitment to prison, where the bailiffs
sponge upon them, or riot at their cost.

A bailiff kept you the whole evening in
a spunginghouse. Sw.

sputátion n.s. [*sputum*, Latin.] The act of
spitting.

A moist consumption receives its nomenclature
from a moist sputation, or expectoration: a dry
one is known by its dry cough. Harvey on
Consumptions.

squintifégo adj. Squinting. A cant word.

The timbrel and the squintifego maid
Of Isis awe thee; lest the gods for sin,
Should, with a swelling dropsy stuff thy skin.
Dryden.

stágnant adj. [*stagnans*, Latin.] Motionless;
still; not agitated; not flowing; not running.

What does the flood from putrefaction keep?
Should it be stagnant in its ample seat,
The sun would through it spread destructive
    heat. Blackm.

'Twas owing to this hurry and action of the
water that the sand now was cast into layers,
and not to a regular settlement, from a water
quiet and stagnant. Woodward.

Immur'd and busied in perpetual sloth,
That gloomy slumber of the stagnant soul.
Irene.

stámmel n.s. Of this word I know not the
meaning.†

Reedhood, the first that doth appear
In stammel: scarlet is too dear. Ben. Johnson.

stándish n.s. [*stand* and *dish.*] A case for
pen and ink.

A grubstreet patriot does not write to secure,
but get something: should the government be
overturned he has nothing to lose but an old
standish. Addison.

I bequeath to Dean Swift esq; my large silver
standish, consisting of a large silver plate, an
ink-pot, and a sand-box. Swift.

stánza n.s. [*stanza*, Ital. *stance*, Fr.] A
number of lines regularly adjusted to each
other; so much of a poem as contains every
variation of measure or relation of rhyme.
Stanza is originally a room of a house, and
came to signify a subdivision of a poem;
a staff.

Horace confines himself strictly to one sort of
verse or stanza in every ode. Dryden.

In quatrains, the last line of the stanza is to
be considered in the composition of the first.
Dryden.

Before his sacred name flies ev'ry fault,
And each exalted stanza teems with thought.
Pope.

státesman n.s. [*state* and *man.*]

1. A politician; one versed in the arts of
   government.

    It looks grave enough
To seem a statesman. Ben. Johnson's Epigr.

The corruption of a poet is the generation of
a statesman. Pope.

2. One employed in publick affairs.

If such actions may have passage free,
Bond-slaves and pagans shall our statesmen
    be. Shak. Othello.

It is a weakness which attends high and low;
the statesman who holds the helm, as well
as the peasant who holds the plough.
South's Sermons.

A British minister must expect to see many
friends fall off, whom he cannot gratify, since,
to use the phrase of a late statesman, the
pasture is not large enough. Addison.

Here Britain's statesmen oft the fall foredoom
Of foreign tyrants, and of nymphs at home.
Pope.

státeswoman n.s. [*state* and *woman.*] A
woman who meddles with publick affairs.
In contempt.

How she was in debt, and where she meant
To raise fresh sums: she's a great stateswoman!
B. Johnson.

Several objects may innocently be ridiculed, as
the passions of our stateswomen. Addison.

stays n.s. Without singular.

1. Boddice; a kind of stiff waistcoat made
   of whalebone, worn by ladies.

2. Ropes in a ship to keep the mast from
   falling aft. All masts, topmasts, and
   flagstaves have stays, except the spritsail
   topmast: the mainmast, foremast, with
   the masts belonging to them, have also
   back stays, which help to keep the mast
   from pitching forward or overboard.
   Harris.

They were come upon the stays, when one
of the sailors descried a galley. Sidney.

3. Any support; any thing that keeps
   another extended.

Weavers stretch your stays upon the weft.
Dryden.

steak n.s. [*styck*, Islandick and Erse, a piece;
steka, Swedish, to boil.] A slice of flesh
broiled or fried; a collop.

The surgeon protested he had cured him very
well, and offered to eat the first stake of him.
Tatler.

    Fair ladies who contrive
To feast on ale and steaks. Swift.

steganógraphy n.s. [στεγανος and γραφω.]
The art of secret writing by characters or
cyphers, intelligible only to the persons who
correspond one with another. Bailey.

stentorophónick adj. [from *Stentor*, the
Homerical herald, whose voice was as loud
as that of fifty men, and φωνη, a voice.]
Loudly speaking or sounding.

Of this stentorophonick horn of Alexander
there is a figure preserved in the Vatican.
Derham's Physico-Theology.

sternutátion n.s. [*sternutatio*, Latin.] The
act of sneezing.

Sternutation is a convulsive shaking of the
nerves and muscles, first occasioned by an
irritation of those in the nostrils. Quincy.

Concerning sternutation, or sneezing, and
the custom of saluting upon that motion, it is
generally believed to derive its original from
a disease wherein sternutation proved mortal,
and such as sneezed died. Brown's Vulgar
Errours.

stew n.s. [*estuve*, French; *stufa*, Italian;
estufa, Spanish.]

1. A bagnio; a hot-house.

As burning Ætna from his boiling stew
Doth belch out flames, and rocks in pieces broke,
And ragged ribs of mountains molten new,
Enwrapt in coal-black clouds and filthy
    smoke. Fa. Queen.

The Lydians were inhibited by Cyrus to use
any armour, and give themselves to baths
and stews. Abbot.

2. A brothel; a house of prostitution. [This
   signification is by some imputed to this,
   that there were licensed brothels near
   the stews or fishponds in Southwark;
   but probably stew, like bagnio, took
   a bad signification from bad use.]

There be that hate harlots, and never were
at the stews; that abhor falshood, and never
brake promise. Ascham.

    My business in this state
Made me a looker-on here in Vienna,
Where I have seen corruption boil and bubble,
'Till it o'er-run the stew. Shakespeare.

With them there are no stews, no dissolute
houses, no curtesans. Bacon's New Atlantis.

Her, though seven years she in the stews had laid,
A nunnery durst receive and think a maid
And though in childbirth's labour she did lie,
Midwives would swear 'twere but a
    tympany. Donne.

What mod'rate fop would rake the park or stews,
Who among troops of faultless nymphs can
chuse? Roscom.

Making his own house a stews, a bordel, and
a school of lewdness, to instill the rudiments of
vice into the unwary flexible years of his poor
children. South's Sermons.

3. [*Stowen*, Dutch, to store.] A storepond;
   a small pond where fish are kept for
   the table.

stígma n.s. [*stigma*, Latin.]

1. A brand; a mark with a hot iron.

2. A mark of infamy.

stíngo n.s. [from the sharpness of the
taste.] Old beer. A cant word.

stínkard n.s. [from *stink*.] A mean stinking
paltry fellow.

stínkpot n.s. [*stink* and *pot*.] An artificial
composition offensive to the smell.

The air may be purified by fires of pitch-
barrels, especially in close places, by burning
of stinkpots. Harvey.

stírious adj. [from *stiria*, Latin.]
Resembling icicles.

Chrystal is found sometimes in rocks, and in
some places not much unlike the stirious or
stillicidious dependencies of ice. Brown's
Vulgar Errours.

stoat n.s. A small stinking animal.

stóckjobber n.s. [*stock* and *job*.] A low
wretch who gets money by buying and
selling shares in the funds.

The stockjobber thus from 'Change-alley
    goes down,
And tips you the freeman a wink;
Let me have but your vote to serve for the town,
And here is a guinea to drink. Swift.

stóick n.s. [στωικος; *stoique*, Fr.] A
philosopher who followed the sect of Zeno;
holding the neutrality of external things.[†]

   While we admire
This virtue, and this moral discipline,
Let's be no stoicks, nor no stocks, I pray.
Shakespeare.

stórmy adj. [from *storm*.]

1. Tempestuous.

Bellowing clouds burst with a stormy sound,
And with an armed winter strew the ground.
Addison's Italy.

The tender apples from their parents rent
By stormy shocks, must not neglected lie.
Philips.

2. Violent; passionate.

The stormy sultan rages at our stay. Irene.

stríngury n.s. [στραγγυρια; *strangurie*,
French.] A difficulty of urine attended
with pain.

stráppado n.s. Chastisement by blows.[†]

Were I at the strappado, or all the racks in the
world, I would not tell you on compulsion.
Shakespeare.

strápping adj. Vast; large; bulky. Used of
large men or women in contempt.

strídulous adj. [*stridulus*, Latin.] Making
a small noise.

It arises from a small and stridulous noise,
which, being firmly rooted, maketh a
divulsion of parts. Brown.

stripe n.s. [*strepe*, Dutch.]

1. A lineary variation of colour. This seems
   to be the original notion of the word.

Gardeners may have three roots among
an hundred that are rare, as purple and
carnation of several stripes. Bacon.

2. A shred of a different colour.

One of the most valuable trimmings of their
cloaths was a long stripe sowed upon the
garment, called latus clavus. Arbuth.

3. A weal; or discolouration made by a lash
   or blow.

Cruelty marked him with inglorious stripes.
Thomson.

4. A blow; a lash.

A body cannot be so torn with stripes, as a
mind with remembrance of wicked actions.
Hayward.

*To those that are yet within the reach of the
stripes and reproofs of their own conscience;
I would address that they would not seek to
remove themselves from that wholsome
discipline.* Decay of Piety.

strophe n.s. [*strophe*, Fr. στροφη.] A stanza.

strúmpet n.s. A whore; a prostitute. Of
doubtful original. *Stropo vieux mot palliardise.
Stuprum*, Lat. Trevoux.†

*How like a younker or a prodigal
The skarfed bark puts from her native bay,
Hugg'd and embraced by the strumpet wind!
How like a prodigal doth she return,
Lean, rent, and beggar'd by the strumpet
    wind.* Shakesp.

   *Ne'er could the strumpet,
With all her double vigour, art and nature,
Once stir my temper, but this virtuous maid
Subdues me quite.* Shakesp. Measure
for Measure.

*If to preserve this vessel for my lord
From any other, foul, unlawful touch,
Be not to be a strumpet, I am none.*
Shakespeare's Othello.

*Common fame is as false and impudent
as a common strumpet.* L'Estrange.

   *Honour had his due;
Before the holy priest my vows were ty'd:
So came I not a strumpet but a bride.*
Dryden.

stúdious adj. [*studieux*, French; *studiosus*,
Latin.]

1. Given to books and contemplation;
   given to learning.

*A proper remedy for wandering thoughts,
he that shall propose, would do great service
to the studious and contemplative part of
mankind.* Locke.

2. Diligent; busy.

Studious to find new friends, and new allies.
Tickell.

3. Attentive to; careful.

   *The people made
Stout for the war, and studious of their trade.*
Dryden.

*There are who, fondly studious of increase,
Rich foreign mold on their ill-natur'd land
Induce.* Philips.

4. Contemplative; suitable to meditation.

*Let my due feet never fail
To walk the studious cloister's pale.* Milton.

   *Him for the studious shade
Kind nature form'd.* Thomson's Summer.

stúdy n.s. [*estude*, French; *studium*, Latin.]

1. Application of mind to books and
   learning.

*Study gives strength to the mind;
conversation, grace.* Temp.

*Engage the mind in study by a consideration
of the divine pleasures of truth and
knowledge.* Watts.

2. Perplexity; deep cogitation.

*Th' idea of her life shall sweetly creep
Into his study of imagination.* Shak.
Much Ado about Nothing.

*The king of Castile, a little confused, and in a
study, said, that can I not do with my honour.*
Bacon's Henry VII.

3. Attention; meditation; contrivance.

   *What can happen
To me above this wretchedness? All your studies
Make me a curse like this.* Shakesp.
Henry VIII.

*Just men they seem'd, and all their study bent
To worship God aright, and know his works.*
Milton.

4. Any particular kind of learning.

*Studies serve for delight in privateness and
retiring, for ornament in discourse, and for
ability in the judgment and disposition of
business.* Bacon's Essays.

5. Apartment set off for literary
   employment.

Get me a taper in my study, Lucius.
Shakes. Jul. Cæs.

*Knock at the study, where, they say, he keeps,
To ruminate strange plots.* Shakesp. Titus
Andronicus.

Let all studies and libraries be towards the East. Wotton.

Some servants of the king visited the lodgings of the accused members, and sealed up their studies and trunks. Clarendon.

    Both adorn'd their age;
One for the study, t' other for the stage.
Dryden.

stuff n.s. [*stoffe*, Dutch; *estoffe*, French.]

1. Any matter or body.

Let Phidias have rude and obstinate stuff to carve: though his art do that it should, his work will lack that beauty, which otherwise in fitter matter it might have had. Hooker.

The workman on his stuff his skill doth show, And yet the stuff gives not the man his skill. Davies.

Of brick, and of that stuff, they cast to build A city and tow'r. Milton.

Pierce an hole near the inner edge, because the triangle hath there most substance of stuff. Moxon's Mech. Exer.

2. Materials out of which any thing is made.

Thy verse swells with stuff so fine and smooth, That thou art even natural in thine art. Shakesp. Timon.

    Cæsar hath wept;
Ambition should be made of sterner stuff. Shakesp. Jul. Cæs.

Success or loss, what is or is not, serves As stuff for these two to make paradoxes. Shakespeare.

    Thy father, that poor rag,
Must be thy subject, who in spight put stuff To some she-beggar, and compounded thee Poor rogue hereditary. Shakespeare's Timon.

Degrading prose explains his meaning ill, And shews the stuff, and not the workman's skill. Roscom.

3. Furniture; goods.

Fare away to get our stuff aboard. Shakespeare.

He took away locks, and gave away the king's stuff. Hayw.

Groaning waggons loaded high With stuff. Cowley's Davideis.

4. That which fills any thing.

With some sweet oblivious antidote Cleanse the stuff'd bosom of that perilous stuff Which weighs upon the heart. Shakespeare.

5. Essence; elemental part.

Though in the trade of war I have slain men, Yet do I hold it very stuff o' th' conscience To do no contriv'd murther. Shakesp. Othello.

6. Any mixture or medicine.

    I did compound for her A certain stuff, which, being ta'en, would seize The present power of life. Shakesp. Cymbeline.

7. Cloth or texture of any kind.

8. Textures of wool thinner and slighter than cloath.

Let us turn the wools of the land into cloaths and stuffs of our own growth, and the hemp and flax growing here into linen cloth and cordage. Bacon's Advice to Villiers.

9. Matter or thing. In contempt.

    O proper stuff!
This is the very painting of your fear. Shakes. Macbeth.

    Such stuff as madmen Tongue and brain not. Shakespeare.

    At this fusty stuff The large Achilles, on his prest bed lolling, From his deep chest laughs out a loud applause. Shakesp.

Please not thyself the flatt'ring crowd to hear, 'Tis fulsome stuff to feed thy itching ear. Dryden's Pers.

    Anger would indite Such woful stuff as I or Shadwell write. Dryden's Juven.

To-morrow will be time enough To hear such mortifying stuff. Swift.

The free things that among rakes pass for wit and spirit, must be shocking stuff to the ears of persons of delicacy. Clariss.

10. It is now seldom used in any sense but in contempt or dislike.

stultíloquence n.s. [*stultus* and *loquentia*, Lat.] Foolish talk. Dict.

style n.s. [*stylus*, Latin.]

1. Manner of writing with regard to language.

Happy
That can translate the stubbornness of fortune
Into so quiet, and so sweet a style.
Shakespeare.

Their beauty I will rather leave to poets, than venture upon so tender and nice a subject with my severer style. More.

Proper words in proper places, make the true definition of a stile. Swift.

*   Let some lord but own the happy lines,*
How the wit brightens, and the style refines.
Pope.

2. Manner of speaking appropriate to particular characters.

No style is held for base, where love well named is. Sidney.

*   There was never yet philosopher,*
That could endure the toothach patiently,
However they have writ the style of gods,
And make a pish at chance and sufferance.
Shakespeare.

3. Title; appellation.

Ford's a knave, and I will aggravate his stile; thou shalt know him for knave and cuckold.
Shakespeare.

The king gave them in his commission the style and appellation which belonged to them.
Clarendon.

O virgin! or what other name you bear
Above that style; O more than mortal fair!
Let not an humble suppliant sue in vain.
Dryden's Æn.

*   Propitious hear our pray'r,*
Whether the style of Titan please thee more,

Whose purple rays th' Achæmenes adore.
Pope's Statius.

4. Course of writing. Unusual.

While his thoughts the ling'ring day beguile,
To gentle Arcite let us turn our style. Dryden.

5. A pointed iron used anciently in writing on tables of wax.

6. Any thing with a sharp point, as a graver; the pin of a dial.

Placing two stiles or needles of the same steel, touched with the same loadstone, when the one is removed but half a span, the other would stand like Hercules's pillars. Brown.

7. The stalk which rises from amid the leaves of a flower.

Style is the middle prominent part of the flower of a plant, which adheres to the fruit or seed: 'tis usually slender and long, whence it has its name. Quincy.

The figure of the flower-leaves, stamina, apices, stile, and seed-vessel. Ray.

8. Style of Court, is properly the practice observed by any court in its way of proceeding. Ayliffe's Parergon.

súblapsary adj. [*sub* and *lapsus*, Latin.] Done after the fall of man.

sublíme adj. [*sublimis*, Latin.]

1. High in place; exalted aloft.

They sum'd their pens, and soaring th' air sublime
With clang despis'd the ground. Milton.

Sublime on these a tow'r of steel is rear'd,
And dire Tisiphone there keeps the ward.
Dryden.

2. High in excellence; exalted by nature.

My earthly strained to the height
In that celestial colloquy sublime. Milton.

*   Can it be, that souls sublime*
Return to visit our terrestrial clime;
And that the gen'rous mind releas'd by death,
Can cover lazy limbs? Dryden.

3. High in stile or sentiment; lofty; grand.

Easy in stile, thy work in sense sublime.
Prior.

4. Elevated by joy.

All yet left of that revolted rout,
Heav'n-fall'n, in station stood or just array,
Sublime with expectation. Milton.

Their hearts were jocund and sublime,
Drunk with idolatry, drunk with wine.
Milton.

5. Haughty; proud.

He was sublime, and almost tumorous in his
looks and gestures. Wotton.

sublíme n.s. The grand or lofty stile. *The*
sublime is a Gallicism, but now naturalized.

    Longinus strengthens all his laws,
And is himself the great sublime he draws.
Pope.

The sublime rises from the nobleness of
thoughts, the magnificence of the words, or the
harmonious and lively turn of the phrase; the
perfect sublime arises from all three together.
Addis.

súbmarine adj. [*sub* and *mare.*] Lying or
acting under the sea.

This contrivance may seem difficult, because
these submarine navigators will want winds
and tides for motion, and the sight of the
heavens for direction. Wilkins.

Not only the herbaceous and woody submarine
plants, but also the lithophyta affect this
manner of growing, as I observed in corals.
Ray on the Creation.

submérsion n.s. [*submersion*, Fr. from
submersus, Latin.] The act of drowning;
state of being drowned.

The great Atlantick island is mentioned
in Plato's Timæus, almost contiguous to the
western parts of Spain and Africa, yet wholly
swallowed up by that ocean: which if true,
might afford a passage from Africa to America
by land before that submersion. Hale's
Origination of Mankind.

subordinátion n.s. [*subordination*, Fr. from
subordinate.]

1. The state of being inferior to another.

Nor can a council national decide,
But with subordination to her guide.
Dryden.

2. A series regularly descending.

If we would suppose a ministry, where every
single person was of distinguished piety, and
all great officers of state and law diligent
in chusing persons, who in their several
subordinations would be obliged to follow the
examples of their superiors, the empire of
irreligion would be soon destroyed. Swift.

to subtílize v.n. To talk with too much
refinement.

Qualities and moods some modern
philosophers have subtilized on. Digby
on Bodies.

súburb n.s. [*suburbium*, Latin.]

1. Building without the walls of a city.

There's a trim rabble let in: are all these your
faithful friends o' th' suburbs? Shakespeare's
Henry VIII.

What can be more to the disvaluation of the
power of the Spaniard, than to have marched
seven days in the heart of his countries, and
lodged three nights in the suburbs of his
principal city? Bacon's War with Spain.

2. The confines; the outpart.

The suburbs of my jacket are so gone,
I have not left one skirt to sit upon.
Cleaveland.

    They on the smoothed plank,
The suburb of their strawbuilt citadel,
Expatiate. Milton.

When our fortunes are violently changed, our
spirits are unchanged, if they always stood
in the suburbs and expectation of sorrows.
Taylor.

súcket n.s. [from *suck.*] A sweet meat.

Nature's confectioner, the bee,
Whose suckets are moist alchimy;
The still of his refining mold,
Minting the garden into gold. Cleaveland.

súckingbottle n.s. [*suck* and *bottle.*] A
bottle which to children supplies the want
of a pap.

He that will say, children join these general abstract speculations with their suckingbottles, has more zeal for his opinion, but less sincerity. Locke.

sudorifick [*sudorifique,* Fr. *sudor* and *facio,* Latin.] Provoking or causing sweat.

Physicians may do well when they provoke sweat in bed by bottles, with a decoction of sudorifick herbs in hot water. Bacon.

Exhaling the most liquid parts of the blood by sudorifick or watery evaporations brings it into a morbid state. Arbuthnot.

súicide n.s. [*suicidium,* Latin.] Self-murder; the horrid crime of destroying one's self.

Child of despair, and suicide my name. Savage.

To be cut off by the sword of injured friendship is the most dreadful of all deaths, next to suicide. Clarissa.

súltana, súltaness n.s. [from *sultan.*] The queen of an Eastern emperour.

Turn the sultana's chambermaid. Cleaveland.

Lay the tow'ring sultaness aside. Irene.

superstítion n.s. [*superstition,* Fr. *superstitio,* Latin.]

1. Unnecessary fear or scruples in religion; observance of unnecessary and uncommanded rites or practices; religion without morality.

They the truth
With superstitions and traditions taint. Milton.

A rev'rent fear, such superstition reigns
Among the rude, ev'n then possess'd the swains. Dryden.

2. False religion; reverence of beings not proper objects of reverence; false worship.

They had certain questions against him of their own superstition. Acts xxv. 19.

3. Over-nicety; exactness too scrupulous.

supervacáneousness n.s. [from the adjective.] Needlessness. Bailey.

suppositítious adj. [from *suppositus, supposititius,* Lat.] Not genuine; put by a trick into the place or character belonging to another.

The destruction of Mustapha was so fatal to Solyman's line, as the succession of the Turks from Solyman is suspected to be of strange blood; for that Selymus II. was thought to be supposititious. Bacon.

It is their opinion that no man ever killed his father; but that, if it should ever happen, the reputed son must have been illegitimate, supposititious, or begotten in adultery. Addison.

Some alterations in the globe tend rather to the benefit of the earth, and its productions, than their destruction, as all these supposititious ones manifestly would do. Woodward.

surd adj. [*surdus,* Latin.]

1. Deaf; wanting the sense of hearing.

2. Unheard; not perceived by the ear.

3. Not expressed by any term.

surtoút n.s. [French.] A large coat worn over all the rest.

The surtout if abroad you wear,
Repels the rigour of the air;
Would you be warmer, if at home
You had the fabrick, and the loom? Prior.

Sir Roger she mortally hated, and used to hire fellows to squirt kennel-water upon him, so that he was forced to wear a surtout of oiled cloth, by which means he came home pretty clean, except where the surtout was a little scanty. Arbuthnot.

swain n.s. [*swein,* Saxon and Runick.]

1. A young man.

That good knight would not so nigh repair,
Himself estranging from their joyance vain,
Whose fellowship seem'd far unfit for warlike swain. F. Q.

2. A country servant employed in husbandry.

It were a happy life
To be no better than a homely swain.
Shak. Henry VI.

3. A pastoral youth.

Blest swains! whose nymphs in ev'ry grace excel;
Blest nymphs! whose swains those graces sing
so well. Pope.

sway n.s. [from the verb.]

1. The swing or sweep of a weapon.

To strike with huge two-handed sway.
Milton.

2. Any thing moving with bulk and power.

Are not you mov'd, when all the sway of earth
Shakes like a thing unfirm? Shak.
Julius Cæsar.

Expert
When to advance, or stand, or turn the sway
Of battle. Milton.

3. Power; rule; dominion.

This sort had some fear that the filling up the
seats in the consistory, with so great number
of laymen, was but to please the minds of the
people, to the end they might think their own
sway somewhat. Hooker.

In the end, very few excepted, all became
subject to the sway of time: other odds there
was none, saving that some fell sooner, and
some later, from the soundness of belief.
Hook.

Only retain
The name and all th' addition to a king;
The sway, revenue, execution of th' hest,
Beloved sons, be yours. Shakes. King Lear.

Her father counts it dangerous
That she should give her sorrow so much sway,
And in his wisdom hastes our marriage,
To stop the inundation of her tears.
Shakespeare.

Too truly Tamerlane's successors they;
Each thinks a world too little for his sway.
Dryd. Aurengz.

When vice prevails, and impious men bear sway,
The post of honour is a private station.
Addison's Cato.

4. Influence; direction.

An evil mind in authority doth not only
follow the sway of the desires already within
it, but frames to itself new desires, not before
thought of. Sidney.

They rush along, the rattling woods give way,
The branches bend before their sweepy sway.
Dryden.

sweepstake n.s. [*sweep* and *stake*.] A man
that wins all.

Is 't writ in your revenge,
That sweepstake you will draw both
friend and foe,
Winner and loser. Shakespeare.

swingebuckler n.s. [*swinge* and *buckler*.] A
bully; a man who pretends to feats of arms.

You had not four such swingebucklers in all
the inns of court again. Shakesp. Henry IV.

to swink v.n. [*swincan*, Saxon.] To labour;
to toil; to drudge. Obsolete.

Riches, renown, and principality,
For which men swink and sweat incessantly.
Fairy Queen.

For they do swink and sweat to feed the other,
Who live like lords of that which they do
gather. Hub. Tale.

swordlaw n.s. Violence; the law by which
all is yielded to the stronger.

So violence
Proceeded, and oppression, and swordlaw,
Through all the plain, and refuge none was
found. Milton.

syllable n.s. [συλλαβη; *syllabe*, French.]

1. As much of a word as is uttered by the
help of one vowel, or one articulation.

I heard
Each syllable that breath made up between
them. Shakesp.

There is that property in all letters of aptness
to be conjoined in syllables and words, through
the voluble motions of the organs from one stop
or figure to another, that they modify and
discriminate the voice without appearing to
discontinue it. Holder's Elements of Speech.

2. Any thing proverbially concise.

Abraham, Job, and the rest that lived before any syllable of the law of God was written, did they not sin as much as we do in every action not commanded? Hooker.

To-morrow, and to-morrow, and to-morrow, Creeps in this petty pace from day to day, To the last syllable of recorded time; And all our yesterdays have lighted fools The way to dusty death. Shakes. Macbeth.

He hath told so many melancholy stories, without one syllable of truth, that he hath blunted the edge of my fears. Swift.

syllabus n.s. [συλλαβος.] An abstract; a compendium containing the heads of a discourse.

sympathy n.s. [*sympathie*, French; συμπαθεια.] Fellowfeeling; mutual sensibility; the quality of being affected by the affection of another.

A world of earthly blessings to my soul, If sympathy of love unite our thoughts. Shakesp. H. VI.

You are not young; no more am I: go to, then, there's sympathy: you are merry, so am I; ha! ha! then there's more sympathy: you love sack, and so do I; would you desire better sympathy? Shakesp. Merry Wives of Windsor.

> *But what it is, The action of my life is like it, which I'll keep, If but for sympathy.* Shakes. Cymbeline.

> *If there was a sympathy in choice, War, death, or sickness did lay siege to it.* Shakespeare.

> *I started back; It started back: but pleas'd I soon return'd; Pleas'd it return'd as soon, with answering looks Of sympathy and love.* Milton's Paradise Lost.

They saw, but other sight instead, a crowd Of ugly serpents: horror on them fell, And horrid sympathy. Milton.

Or sympathy, or some connat'ral force, Pow'rful at greatest distance to unite, With secret amity, things of like kind, By secretest conveyance. Milt. Paradise Lost.

There never was any heart truly great and generous, that was not also tender and compassionate: it is this noble quality that makes all men to be of one kind; for every man would be a distinct species to himself, were there no sympathy among individuals. South's Sermons.

Can kindness to desert, like your's, be strange? Kindness by secret sympathy is ty'd; For noble souls in nature are ally'd. Dryden.

There are such associations made in the minds of most men, and to this might be attributed most of the sympathies and antipathies observable in them. Locke.

system n.s. [*systeme*, Fr. συστημα.]

1. Any complexure or combination of many things acting together.

2. A scheme which reduces many things to regular dependence or co-operation.

3. A scheme which unites many things in order.

Aristotle brings morality into system, by treating of happiness under heads, and ranges it in classes according to its different objects, distinguishing virtues into their several kinds which had not been handled systematically before. Baker.

The best way to learn any science is to begin with a regular system, or a short and plain scheme of that science well drawn up into a narrow compass. Watts.

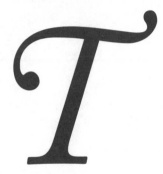

T, a consonant, which, at the beginning and end of words, has always the same sound nearly approaching to the *d*; but before an *i*, when followed by a vowel, has the sound of an obscure *s*: as, *nation, salvation*, except when *s* precedes *t*: as, *Christian, question*.

to tábefy v.n. [*tabefacio*, Latin.] To waste; to be extenuated by disease. In the following example it is improperly a verb active.

Meat eaten in greater quantity than is convenient tabefies the body. Harvey on Consumptions.

tábour n.s. [*tabourin, tabour,* old French.] A small drum; a drum beaten with one stick to accompany a pipe.

If you did but hear the pedlar at door, you would never dance again after a tabour and pipe. Shakesp. Winter's Tale.

The shepherd knows not thunder from a tabour, More than I know the sound of Marcius' tongue From every meaner man. Shakesp. Coriolanus.

Morrice-dancers danced a maid marian, and a tabour and pipe. Temple.

táchygraphy n.s. [ταχυς and γραφω.] The art or practice of quick writing.

tádpole n.s. [*tad, toad,* and *pola, a young one,* Saxon.] A young shapeless frog or toad, consisting only of a body and a tail; a porwiggle.

I'll broach the tadpole on my rapier's point. Shakespeare.

Poor Tom eats the toad and the tadpole. Shakespeare.

The result is not a perfect frog but a tadpole, without any feet, and having a long tail to swim with. Ray.

A black and round substance began to dilate, and after awhile the head, the eyes, the tail to be discernable, and at last become what the ancients called gyrinus, *we a porwigle or tadpole.* Brown's Vulgar Errours, b. iii.

tálent n.s. [*talentum,* Lat.]

1. A talent signified so much weight, or a sum of money, the value differing according to the different ages and countries. Arbuthnot.

    Five talents in his debt,
His means most short, his creditors most straight. Shakesp.

Two tripods cast in antick mould, With two great talents of the finest gold. Dryden.

2. Faculty; power; gift of nature.
    A metaphor borrowed from the talents mentioned in the holy writ.

Many who knew the treasurer's talent in removing prejudice, and reconciling himself to wavering affections, believed the loss of the duke was unseasonable. Clarendon.

He is chiefly to be considered in his three different talents, as a critick, satyrist, and writer of odes. Dryden.

'Tis not my talent to conceal my thoughts, Or carry smiles and sunshine in my face, When discontent sits heavy at my heart. Addison's Cato.

They are out of their element, and logick is none of their talent. Baker's Reflections on Learning.

Persons who possess the true talent of raillery are like comets; they are seldom seen, and all at once admired and feared. Female Quixote.†

3. Quality; nature. An improper and mistaken use.

Though the nation generally was without any ill talent to the church in doctrine or discipline, yet they were not without a jealousy that popery was not enough discountenanced. Clarendon.

It is the talent of human nature to run from one extreme to another. Swift.

Tálmud, Thálmud n.s. The book containing the Jewish traditions, the rabbinical constitutions and explications of the law.

táminy n.s. A woollen stuff.

táper n.s. [*taper,* Saxon.] A wax candle; a light.

Get me a taper in my study, Lucius: When it is lighted come and call me. Shakespeare.

My daughter and little son we'll dress With rounds of waxen tapers on their heads, And rattles in their hands. Shakespeare.

If any snatch the pure taper from my hand,
and hold it to the devil, he will only burn
his own fingers, but shall not rob me of the
reward of my good intention. Taylor.

  There the fair light,
Like hero's taper in the window plac'd,
Such fate from the malignant air did find,
As that exposed to the boist'rous wind.
Waller.

  To see this fleet
Heav'n, as if there wanted lights above,
For tapers made two glaring comets rise.
Dryden.

tápster n.s. [from *tap*.] One whose business
is to draw beer in an alehouse.

The oath of a lover is no stronger than the
word of a tapster; they are both the confirmers
of false reckonings. Shak.

Though you change your place, you need not
change your trade: I'll be your tapster still.
Shakespeare.

The world is come now to that pass, that the
vintner and tapster may broach what religion
they please; and the apothecary may mingle
her as he pleases. Howel.

Though the painting grows decay'd,
The house will never lose its trade;
Nay, though the treacherous tapster Thomas
Hangs a new angel two doors from us,
In hopes that strangers may mistake it. Swift.

tarántula n.s. [Italian; *tarentule*, French.]
An insect whose bite is only cured by
musick.

This word, lover, did no less pierce poor
Pyrocles than the right tune of musick
toucheth him that is sick of the tarantula.
Sidney.

He that uses the word tarantula, without
having any idea of what it stands for, means
nothing at all by it. Locke.

Tárgum n.s. [תרגום.] A paraphrase on the
pentateuch in the Chaldee language.[†]

taste n.s. [from the verb.]

1. The act of tasting; gustation.

Best of fruits, whose taste gave elocution.
Milton.

2. The sense by which the relish of any
   thing on the palate is perceived.

Bees delight more in one flower than another,
and therefore have taste. Bacon's Nat. Hist.

Delicacies of taste, sight, smell. Milton.

The tardy plants in our cold orchards plac'd,
Reserve their fruit for the next age's taste.
Waller.

3. Sensibility; perception.

I have almost forgot the taste of fears:
The time has been, my senses would have cool'd
To hear a night shriek. Shakesp. Macbeth.

  Musick in the close,
As the last taste of sweets is sweetest last.
Shakesp. R. II.

4. That sensation which all things taken
   into the mouth give particularly to the
   tongue, the papillæ of which are the
   principal instruments hereof. Quincy.

Manna was like coriander seed, white; and
the taste of it was like wafers made with
honey. Exod. xvi. 31.

Though there be a great variety of tastes, yet,
as in smells, they have only some few general
names. Locke.

5. Intellectual relish or discernment.

Seeing they pretend no quarrel at other psalms
which are in like manner appointed to be
daily read, why do these so much offend and
displease their tastes? Hooker.

Sion's songs to all true tastes excelling,
Where God is prais'd aright. Milton.

  I have no taste
Of popular applause. Dryden's Spanish Friar.

As he had no taste of true glory, we see him
equipped like an Hercules, with a club and
a lion's skin. Addison.

This metaphor would not have been so
general, had there not been a conformity
between the mental taste and that sensitive
taste which gives us a relish of every flavour.
Addison.

Your way of life, in my taste, will be the best. Pope.

I see how ill a taste for wit and sense prevails in the world. Swift.

Pleasure results from a sense to discern, and a taste to be affected with beauty. Seed's Sermons.

6. An essay; a trial; an experiment. Not in use.

I hope, for my brother's justification, he wrote as an essay or taste of my virtue. Shakespeare.

7. A small portion given as a specimen.

They thought it not safe to resolve, till they had a taste of the people's inclination. Bacon's Henry VII.

Besides the prayers mentioned, I shall give only a taste of some few recommended to devout persons in the manuals and offices. Stillingfleet.

tatterdemálion n.s. [*tatter* and I know not what.] A ragged fellow.

As a poor fellow was trudging along in a bitter cold morning with never a rag, a spark that was warm clad called to this tatterdemalion, how he could endure this weather? L'Estrange.

to táttle v.n. [*tateren*, Dutch.] To prate; to talk idly; to use many words with little meaning.

He stands on terms of honourable mind, Ne will be carried with every common wind Of court's inconstant mutability, Ne after every tattling fable fly. Hubberd's Tale.

The one is too like an image, and says nothing; and the other too like my lady's eldest son, evermore tattling. Shak.

Excuse it by the tattling quality of age, which is always narrative. Dryden.

The world is forward enough to tattle of them. Locke.

Their language is extremely proper to tattle in; it is made up of so much repetition and compliment. Addison.

táttler n.s. [from *tattle*.] An idle talker; a prater.

Going from house to house, tatlers, busy bodies, which are the canker and rust of idleness, as idleness is the rust of time, are reproved by the apostle. Taylor.

tattóo n.s. [perhaps from *tapotez tous*, Fr. to strike.] The beat of drum by which soldiers are warned to their quarters.

All those whose hearts are loose and low, Start if they hear but the tatto. Prior.

tauricórnous adj. [*taurus* and *cornu*, Latin.] Having horns like a bull.

Their descriptions must be relative, or the tauricornous picture of the one the same with the other. Brown.

taw n.s. A marble to play with.

   Trembling I've seen thee Mix with children as they play'd at taw; Nor fear the marbles as they bounding flew, Marbles to them, but rolling rocks to you. Swift.

tea n.s. [a word, I suppose, Chinese; *thé*, Fr.] A Chinese plant, of which the infusion has lately been much drunk in Europe.[†]

The muses friend, tea, does our fancy aid, Repress those vapours which the head invade. Waller.

One has a design of keeping an open tea table. Addison.

I have filled a tea pot, and received a dish of it. Addison.

He swept down a dozen tea dishes. Spectator.

Nor will you encourage the common tea table talk. Spect.

Green leaves of tea contain a narcotick juice, which exudes by roasting: this is performed with great care before it is exposed to sale. Arbuthnot on Aliments.

Here living tea pot stands; one arm held out, One bent; the handle this, and that the spout. Pope.

The mistress of the tea shop may give half an ounce. Sw.

The fear of being thought pedants hath taken many young divines off from their severer studies, which they have exchanged for plays, in order to qualify them for tea tables. Swift.

When you sweep, never stay to pick up tea spoons. Swift.

teague n.s. A name of contempt used for an Irishman.

teens n.s. [from *teen* for *ten*.] The years reckoned by the termination teen; as, thirteen, fourteen.

Our author would excuse these youthful scenes,
Begotten at his entrance, in his teens;
Some childish fancies may approve the toy,
Some like the muse the more for being a boy.
Granville.

télescope n.s. [*telescope*, Fr. τελος and σκοπεω.] A long glass by which distant objects are viewed.

The telescope discovers to us distant wonders in the heavens, and shews the milky way, and the bright cloudy spots, in a very dark sky, to be a collection of little stars. Watts.

témplar n.s. [from the *Temple*, an house near the Thames, anciently belonging to the knights *templars*, originally from the temple of Jerusalem.] A student in the law.

Wits and templars ev'ry sentence raise,
And wonder with a foolish face of praise.
Pope's Epist.

témulent adj. [*temulentus*, Lat.] Inebriated; intoxicated as with strong liquors.

tenébricose, ténebrous adj. [*tenebricosus, tenebrosus*, Latin.] Dark; gloomy.

ténnis n.s. [this play is supposed by Skinner to be so named from the word *tenez*, take it, hold it, or there it goes, used by the French when they drive the ball.] A play at which a ball is driven with a racket.

The barber's man hath been seen with him, and the old ornament of his cheek hath already stuffed tennis balls. Shak.

There was he gaming, there o'ertook in 's rowse, There falling out at tennis. Shakesp. Hamlet.

A prince, by a hard destiny, became a tennis ball long to the blind goddess. Howel's Vocal Forest.

It can be no more disgrace to a great lord to draw a fair picture, than to play at tennis with his page. Peacham.

The inside of the uvea is blacked like the walls of a tennis court, that the rays falling upon the retina may not, by being rebounded thence upon the uvea, be returned again; for such a repercussion would make the sight more confused. More's Antidote against Atheism.

We conceive not a tennis ball to think, and consequently not to have any volition, or preference of motion to rest. Locke.

We have no exedra for the philosophers adjoining to our tennis court, but there are alehouses. Arbuthnot and Pope.

tentíginous adj. [*tentiginis*, Lat.] Stiff; stretched.

tepefáction n.s. [*tepefacio*, Latin.] The act of warming to a small degree.

teratólogy n.s. [τερατος and λεγω.] Bombast, affectation of false sublimity. Bailey.

tergiversátion n.s. [*tergum* and *verso*, Lat.]

1. Shift; subterfuge; evasion.

Writing is to be preferred before verbal conferences, as being freer from passions and tergiversations. Bishop Bramhall.

2. Change; fickleness.

The colonel, after all his tergiversations, lost his life in the king's service. Clarendon.

térmagant adj. [*tyr* and *magan*, Saxon, eminently powerful.]

1. Tumultuous; turbulent.

'Twas time to counterfeit, or that hot termagant Scot had paid me scot and lot too. Shakesp. Henry IV. p. i.

2. Quarrelsome; scolding; furious.

The eldest was a termagant, imperious, prodigal, profligate wench. Arbuthnot's Hist. of John Bull.

terráqueous adj. [*terra* and *aqua*, Latin.] Composed of land and water.

The terraqueous globe is, to this day, nearly in the same condition that the universal deluge left it. Woodward.

terrífick adj. [*terrificus*, Latin.] Dreadful; causing terrour.

The serpent, subtlest beast of all the field,
Of huge extent sometimes, with brazen eyes
And hairy mane terrifick. Milton's
Par. Lost, b. vii.

The British navy through ocean vast
Shall wave her double cross, t' extremest climes
Terrifick. Philips.

térrour n.s. [*terror*, Lat. *terreur*, Fr.]

1. Fear communicated.

Amaze and terrour seiz'd the rebel host.
Milton.

The thunder when to roll
With terrour through the dark aerial hall.
Milton.

2. Fear received.

It is the cowish terrour of his spirit
That dares not undertake. Shakesp.
King Lear.

They shot thorough both the walls of the town and the bulwark also, to the great terrour of the defendants. Knolles.

They with conscious terrours vex me round.
Milton.

O sight
Of terrour, foul and ugly to behold,
Horrid to think, how horrible to feel. Milton.

The pleasures and terrours of the main.
Blackmore.

3. The cause of fear.

Lords of the street, and terrours of the way.
Anonym.†

Those enormous terrours of the Nile. Prior.

So spake the griesly terrour. Milton.

tértian n.s. [*tertiana*, Lat.] Is an ague intermitting but one day, so that there are two fits in three days.

Tertians of a long continuance do most menace this symptom. Harvey on Consumptions.

tésticle n.s. [*testiculus*, Lat.] Stone.

That a bever, to escape the hunter, bites off his testicles or stones, is a tenent very antient. Brown's Vulg. Err.

The more certain sign from the pains reaching to the groins and testicles. Wiseman's Surgery.

testudíneous adj. [*testudo*, Lat.] Resembling the shell of a tortoise.

tête à tête n.s. [French.] Cheek by jowl.

Long before the squire and dame
Are tête à tête. Prior.

Deluded mortals, whom the great
Chuse for companions tête à tête;
Who at their dinners, en famille,
Get leave to sit whene'er you will.
Swift's Miscel.

téxtman n.s. [*text* and *man*.] A man ready in quotation of texts.

Mens daily occasions require the doing of a thousand things, which it would puzzle the best textman readily to bethink himself of a sentence in the Bible, clear enough to satisfy a scrupulous conscience of the lawfulness of. Sanderson.

thane n.s. [ðegn, Saxon.] An old title of honour, perhaps equivalent to baron.

By Sinel's death I know I'm thane of Glamis;
But how of Cawdor? the thane of Cawdor
lives. Shakesp.

théatre n.s. [*theatre*, Fr. *theatrum*, Lat.]

1. A place in which shews are exhibited; a playhouse.

This wise and universal theatre,
Presents more woful pageants than the scene
Wherein we play. Shakesp. As you like it.

When the boats came within sixty yards of the pillar, they found themselves all bound, yet so as they might go about, so as they all stood as in a theatre beholding this light. Bacon.

2. A place rising by steps like a theatre.

Shade above shade, a woody theatre
Of stateliest view. Milton.

In the midst of this fair valley stood
A native theatre, which rising slow,
By just degrees o'erlook'd the ground below.
Dryden.

√**theocracy** n.s. [*theocratie*, Fr. θεος and κρατεω.] Government immediately superintended by God.

The characters of the reign of Christ are chiefly justice, peace, and divine presence or conduct, which is called theocracy. Burnet's Theory of the Earth.

theogony n.s. [*theogonie*, Fr. θεογονια.] The generation of the gods. Bailey.

theology n.s. [*theologie*, Fr. θεολογια.] Divinity.

The whole drift of the scripture of God, what is it but only to teach theology? Theology, what is it but the science of things divine? Hooker, b. iii.

She was most dear to the king in regard of her knowledge in languages, in theology, and in philosophy. Hayward.

The oldest writers of theology were of this mind. Tillotson.

theomachy n.s. [θεος and μαχη.] The fight against the gods by the giants. Bailey.

theory n.s. [*theorie*, Fr. θηωρια.] Speculation; not practice; scheme; plan or system yet subsisting only in the mind.

If they had been themselves to execute their own theory in this church, they would have seen being nearer at hand. Hooker, b. v.

In making gold, the means hitherto propounded to effect it are in the practice full of errour, and in the theory full of unsound imagination. Bacon's Nat. Hist. No 326.

Practice alone divides the world into virtuous and vicious; but as to the theory and speculation of virtue and vice, mankind are much the same. South's Sermons.

thésmothete n.s. [*thesmothete*, Fr. θεσμοθετης, θεσμος and τιθημι.] A lawgiver.

théurgy n.s. [θεουργια.] The power of doing supernatural things by lawful means, as by prayer to God. Bailey.

to think v.n. preter. thought. [*thankgan*, Gothick; ðencean, Saxon; *dencken*, Dutch.]

1. To have ideas; to compare terms or things; to reason; to cogitate; to perform any mental operation.

Thinking, in the propriety of the English tongue, signifies that sort of operation of the mind about its ideas, wherein the mind is active; where it, with some degree of voluntary attention, considers any thing. Locke.

What am I? or from whence? for that I am I know, because I think; but whence I came, Or how this frame of mine began to be, What other being can disclose to me? Dryden.

Those who perceive dully, or retain ideas in their minds ill, will have little matter to think on. Locke.

It is an opinion that the soul always thinks, and that it has the actual perception of ideas in itself constantly, and that actual thinking is as inseparable from the soul, as actual extension is from the body. Locke.

These are not matters to be slightly and superficially thought upon. Tillotson's Sermons.

His experience of a good prince must give great satisfaction to every thinking man. Addison's Freeholder.

2. To judge; to conclude; to determine.

Let them marry to whom they think best; only to their father's tribe shall they marry. Num. xxxvi. 6.

I fear we shall not find This long desired king such as was thought. Daniel.

3. To intend.

Thou thought'st to help me, and such thanks
  I give,
As one near death to those that wish him live.
Shakespeare.

4. To imagine; to fancy.

Something since his coming forth is thought
  of, which
Imports the kingdom so much fear and danger,
That his return was most requir'd. Shakesp.
King Lear.

  Edmund, I think, is gone,
In pity of his misery, to dispatch
His nighted life. Shakesp. King Lear.

We may not be startled at the breaking of the
exterior earth; for the face of nature hath
provoked men to think of and observe such
a thing. Burnet's Theory of the Earth.

Those who love to live in gardens, have
never thought of contriving a winter garden.
Spectator, Nº 477.

5. To muse; to meditate.

You pine, you languish, love to be alone,
Think much, speak little, and in speaking
  sigh. Dryden.

6. To recollect; to observe.

We are come to have the warrant.
—Well thought upon; I have it here about me.
Shakesp.

Think upon me, my God, for good, according
to all that I have done. Neh. v. 19.

7. To judge; to conclude.

If your general acquaintance be among ladies,
provided they have no ill reputation, you
think you are safe. Swift.

Still the work was not complete,
When Venus thought on a deceit.
Swift's Miscel.

The opinions of others whom we know and
think well of are no ground of assent. Locke.

8. To consider; to doubt.

Any one may think with himself, how then
can any thing live in Mercury and Saturn.
Bentley's Sermons.

thou n.s. [þu, Saxon; du, Dutch; in the
oblique cases singular *thee*, þe, Saxon; in the
plural *ye*, Saxon; in the oblique cases plural
you, *eow*, Saxon.]

1. The second pronoun personal.

Is this a dagger which I see before me,
The handle tow'rd my hand? Come let
  me clutch thee.
I have thee not, and yet I see thee still.
Art thou not, fatal vision, sensible
To feeling as to sight. Shakesp. Macbeth.

I am as like to call thee so again,
To spit on thee again, to spurn thee too,
If thou wilt lend this money lend it not
As to thy friend. Shakesp. Merchant
of Venice.

Thou, if there be a thou in this base town,
Who dares with angry Eupolis to frown;
Who at enormous villany turns pale,
And steers against it with a full-blown sail.
Dryden.

2. It is used only in very familiar or very
   solemn language. When we speak to
   equals or superiors we say you; but in
   solemn language, and in addresses of
   worship, we say thou.

to thou v.a. [from *thou*.] To treat with
familiarity.

Taunt him with the licence of ink; if thou
thou'st him some thrice, it shall not be amiss.
Shakespeare.

thrápple n.s. The windpipe of any animal.
They still retain it in the Scottish dialect.

thrasónical adj. [from *Thraso*, a boaster in
old comedy.]† Boastful; bragging.

His humour is lofty, his discourse peremptory,
his general behaviour vain, ridiculous, and
thrasonical. Shakespeare.

There never was any thing so sudden but the
fight of two rams, and Cæsar's thrasonical
brag of, I came, saw, and overcame. Shakesp.
As you like it.

to threap v.a. A country word denoting to
argue much or contend. Ains.

thréepenny adj. [*triobolaris*, Lat.] Vulgar;
mean.

threnódy n.s. [θρηνωδια.] A song of lamentation.

thro' Contracted by barbarians from through.

What thanks can wretched fugitives return,
Who scatter'd thro' the world in exile mourn.
Dryden.

thúnderstone n.s. [*thunder* and *stone.*] A stone fabulously supposed to be emitted by thunder; thunderbolt.

Fear no more the light'ning flash,
Nor th' all-dreaded thunderstone.
Shakesp. Cymbeline.

thurificátion n.s. [*thuris* and *facio*, Latin.] The act of fuming with incense; the act of burning incense.

The several acts of worship which were
required to be performed to images are
processions, genuflections, thurifications,
deosculations, and oblations. Stillingfleet.

to tíckle v.a. [*titillo*, Lat.]

1. To affect with a prurient sensation by slight touches.

Dissembling courtesy! How fine this tyrant
Can tickle where she wounds. Shakesp.
Cymbeline.

The mind is moved in great vehemency only
by tickling some parts of the body. Bacon.

There is a sweetness in good verse, which
tickles even while it hurts; and no man can
be heartily angry with him who pleases him
against his will. Dryden.

It is a good thing to laugh at any rate; and if
a straw can tickle a man, it is an instrument
of happiness. Dryden.

2. To please by slight gratifications.

Dametas, that of all manners of stile could
best conceive of golden eloquence, being withal
tickled by Musidorus's praises, had his brain so
turned, that he became slave to that which he
that sued to be his servant offered to give him.
Sidney.

Expectation tickling skittish spirits
Sets all on hazard. Shakespeare.

Such a nature
Tickled with good success, disdains the shadow
Which it treads on at noon. Shakesp.
Coriolanus.

I cannot rule my spleen;
My scorn rebels, and tickles me within.
Dryden.

Dunce at the best; in streets but scarce allow'd
To tickle, on thy straw, the stupid crowd.
Dryden.

A drunkard, the habitual thirst after his cups,
drives to the tavern, though he has in his
view the loss of health, and perhaps of the
joys of another life, the least of which is such
a good as he confesses is far greater than the
tickling of his palate with a glass of wine.
Locke.

tícktack n.s. [*trictac*, Fr.] A game at tables.
Bailey.

tiff n.s. [A low word, I suppose without etymology.]

1. Liquor; drink.

I, whom griping penury surrounds,
And hunger, sure attendant upon want,
With scanty offals, and small acid tiff,
Wretched repast! my meagre corps sustain.
Phillips.

2. A fit of peevishness or sullenness; a pet.

tíger n.s. [*tigre*, Fr. *tigris*, Latin.] A fierce beast of the leonine kind.

When the blast of war blows in your ear,
Then imitate the action of the tiger:
Stiffen the sinews, summon up the blood.
Shakesp. H. V.

Approach thou like the rugged Russian bear,
The arm'd rhinoceros, or Hyrcanian tiger;
Take any shape but that, and my firm nerves
Shall never tremble. Shakesp. Macbeth.

This tiger-footed rage, when it shall find
The harm of unskain'd swiftness will, too late,
Tie leaden pounds to 's heels. Shakesp.
Coriolanus.

Tigris, in the medals of Trajan, is drawn
like an old man, and by his side a tiger.
Peacham on Drawing.

Has the steer,
At whose strong chest the deadly tiger hangs,
E'er plow'd for him. Thomson's Spring.

tillyfally, tillyvalley adj. A word used formerly when any thing said was rejected as trifling or impertinent.

Am not I consanguinious? am not I of her blood? tillyvalley lady. Shakesp. Twelfth Night.

Tillyfally, sir John, never tell me; your ancient swaggerer comes not in my doors. Shakesp. Henry IV. p. ii.

time n.s. [*tima*, Saxon; *tym*, Erse.]

1. The measure of duration.

This consideration of duration, as set out by certain periods, and marked by certain measures or epochas, is that which most properly we call time. Locke.

*Time is like a fashionable host,
That slightly shakes his parting guest by th' hand,
But with his arms out-stretch'd, as he would fly,
Grasps the incomer.* Shakesp. Troilus and Cressida.

*Come what come may,
Time and the hour runs through the roughest day.* Shakesp.

Nor will polished amber, although it send forth a gross exhalement, be found a long time defective upon the exactest scale. Brown's Vulgar Errours, b. ii.

Time, which consisteth of parts, can be no part of infinite duration, or of eternity; for then there would be infinite time past to day, which to morrow will be more than infinite. Time is therefore one thing, and infinite duration is another. Grew's Cosmol. b. i.

2. Space of time.

Daniel desired that he would give him time, and that he would shew him the interpretation. Dan. ii. 16.

He for the time remain'd stupidly good. Milton.

No time is allowed for digressions. Swift.

3. Interval.

Pomanders, and knots of powders, you may have continually in your hand; whereas perfumes you can take but at times. Bacon's Nat. Hist. Nº 929.

4. Season; proper time.

To every thing there is a season, and a time to every purpose. Ecclus. iii. 1.

They were cut down out of time, whose foundation was overflown with a flood. Job xxii. 16.

He found nothing but leaves on it; for the time of figs was not yet. Mar. xi. 13.

Knowing the time, that it is high time to awake out of sleep. Rom. xiii. 11.

Short were her marriage joys; for in the prime Of youth her lord expir'd before his time. Dryden.

*I hope I come in time, if not to make,
At least, to save your fortune and your honour:
Take heed you steer your vessel right.* Dryden.

The time will come when we shall be forced to bring our evil ways to remembrance, and then consideration will do us little good. Calamy's Sermons.

5. A considerable space of duration; continuance; process of time.

*Fight under him, there's plunder to be had;
A captain is a very gainful trade:
And when in service your best days are spent,
In time you may command a regiment.* Dryden's Juvenal.

In time the mind reflects on its own operations about the ideas got by sensation, and thereby stores itself with a new set of ideas, ideas of reflection. Locke.

One imagines, that the terrestrial matter which is showered down along with rain enlarges the bulk of the earth, and that it will in time bury all things under-ground. Woodward.

I have resolved to take time, and, in spite of all misfortunes, to write you, at intervals, a long letter. Swift.

6. Age; particular part of time.

When that company died, what time the
fire devoured two hundred and fifty men.
Num. xxvi. 10.

They shall be given into his hand until a time
and times. Dan. vii. 25.

If we should impute the heat of the season
unto the cooperation of any stars with the sun,
it seems more favourable for our times to
ascribe the same unto the constellation of leo.
Brown's Vulgar Errours, b. iv.

The way to please being to imitate nature, the
poets and the painters, in ancient times, and
in the best ages, have studied her. Dryden's
Dufresnoy.

7. Past time.

I was the man in th' moon when time was.
Shakespeare.

8. Early time.

Stanley at Bosworth field, though he came
time enough to save his life, yet he staid long
enough to endanger it. Bacon.

If they acknowledge repentance and a more
strict obedience to be one time or other
necessary, they imagine it is time enough
yet to set about these duties. Rogers.

9. Time considered as affording
    opportunity.

The earl lost no time, but marched day
and night. Clarend.

He continued his delights till all the enemies
horse were passed through his quarters; nor
did then pursue them in any time.
Clarendon, b. viii.

Time is lost, which never will renew,
While we too far the pleasing path pursue,
Surveying nature. Dryden's Virgil.

10. Particular quality of the present.

Comets, importing change of times and states,
Brandish your crystal tresses in the sky.
Shakespeare.

All the prophets in their age, the times
Of great Messiah sing. Milton's
Par. Lost, b. xii.

If any reply, that the times and manners
of men will not bear such a practice, that is
an answer from the mouth of a professed
time-server. South's Sermons.

11. Particular time.

Give order, that no sort of person
Have, any time, recourse unto the princes.
Shakespeare.

The worst on me must light, when time
 shall be. Milt.

A time will come when my maturer muse,
In Cæsar's wars a nobler theme shall chuse.
Dryden.

These reservoirs of snow they cut, distributing
them to several shops, that from time to time
supply Naples. Addison.

12. Hour of childbirth.

She intended to stay till delivered; for she was
within one month of her time. Clarendon.

The first time I saw a lady dressed in one
of these petticoats, I blamed her for walking
abroad when she was so near her time; but
soon I found all the modish part of the sex as
far gone as herself. Addison's Spect. Nº 127.

13. Repetition of any thing, or mention
    with reference to repetition.

Four times he cross'd the car of night. Milton.

Every single particle would have a sphere of
void space around it many hundred thousand
million million times bigger than the
dimensions of that particle. Bentley.

Lord Oxford I have now the third time
mentioned in this letter expects you. Swift.

14. Musical measure.

Musick do I hear!
Ha, ha! keep time. How sour sweet musick is
When time is broke and no proportion kept.
Shakespeare.

You by the help of tune and time
Can make that song which was but rime.
Waller.

On their exalted wings
To the cœlestial orbs they climb,
And with th' harmonious spheres keep time.
Denham.

Heroes who o'ercome, or die,
Have their hearts hung extremely high;
The strings of which in battle's heat
Against their very corslets beat;
Keep time with their own trumpet's measure,
And yield them most excessive pleasure. Prior.

to tink v.n. [*tinnio*, Latin; *tingian*, Welsh]
To make a sharp shrill noise.

típple n.s. [from the verb.] Drink; liquor.

While the tipple was paid for, all went
merrily on. L'Estr.

tírewoman n.s. [*tire* and *woman*.] A woman
whose business is to make dresses for
the head.

Why should they not value themselves for this
outside fashionableness of the tirewoman's
making, when their parents have so early
instructed them to do so. Locke on
Education.

tíringhouse, tíringroom n.s. [*tire* and
house, or *room*.] The room in which players
dress for the stage.

This green plot shall be our stage, this hawthorn
brake our tiringhouse. Shakespeare.

Man's life's a tragedy; his mother's womb,
From which he enters, is the tiringroom;
This spacious earth the theatre, and the stage
That country which he lives in; passions, rage,
Folly, and vice, are actors. Wotton.

tit n.s.

1. A small horse: generally in contempt.

No storing of pasture with baggagely tit,
With ragged, with aged, and evil at hit.
Tusser.

Thou might'st have ta'en example
From what thou read'st in story;
*   Being as worthy to sit*
*   On an ambling tit,*
As thy predecessor Dory. Denham.

2. A woman: in contempt.

What does this envious tit, but away to
her father with a tale. L'Estrange.

A willing tit that will venture her corps
with you. Dryden.

Short pains for thee, for me a son and heir.
Girls cost as many throes in bringing forth;
Beside, when born, the tits are little worth.
Dryden.

3. A titmouse or tomtit. A bird.

titubátion n.s. [*titubo*, Lat.] The act of
stumbling.

toast n.s. [from the verb.]

1. Bread dried before the fire.

You are both as rheumatick as two dry toasts;
you cannot one bear with another's
confirmities. Shakesp. Henry IV.

Every third day take a small toast of manchet,
dipped in oil of sweet almonds new drawn,
and sprinkled with loaf sugar. Bacon's
Physical Remains.

2. Bread dried and put into liquor.

*   Where's then the saucy boat*
Co-rival'd greatness? or to harbour fled,
Or made a toast for Neptune? Shakesp.
Troil. and Cressida.

Some squire, perhaps, you take delight to rack;
Whose game is whisk, whose treat a toast in
*   sack.* Pope.

3. A celebrated woman whose health
   is often drunk.

I shall likewise mark out every toast, the club
in which she was elected, and the number of
votes that were on her side. Addison's
Guard. Nº 107.

Say, why are beauties prais'd
*   and honour'd most,*
The wise man's passion, and the
*   vain man's toast?*
Why deck'd with all that land and sea afford,
Why angels call'd, and angel-like ador'd?
Pope.

tobácco n.s. [from *Tobaco* or *Tobago* in
America.] The flower of the tobacco
consists of one leaf, is funnelshaped, and
divided at the top into five deep segments,
which expand like a star; the ovary becomes
an oblong roundish membranaceous fruit,
which is divided into two cells by an
intermediate partition, and is filled with
small roundish seeds. Miller.

It is a planet now I see;
And, if I err not, by his proper
Figure, that's like a tobacco-stopper.
Hudibras, p. ii.

Bread or tobacco may be neglected; but reason
at first recommends their trial, and custom
makes them pleasant. Locke.

Salts are to be drained out of the clay by
water, before it be fit for the making tobacco-
pipes or bricks. Woodward.

tóilet n.s. [*toilette*, Fr.] A dressing table.

The merchant from the exchange returns in peace,
And the long labours of the toilet cease. Pope.

tóllbooth n.s. [*toll* and *booth*.] A prison.
Ains.

tómboy n.s. [*Tom* a diminutive of *Thomas*,
and *boy*.] A mean fellow; sometimes a wild
coarse girl.

    A lady
Fasten'd to an empery, to be partner'd
With tomboys, hir'd with that self-exhibition
Which your own coffers yield! Shakesp.
Cymbeline.

tónguepad n.s. [*tongue* and *pad*.] A great
talker.

She who was a celebrated wit at London
is, in that dull part of the world, called a
tonguepad. Tatler.

to toot v.n. [Of this word, in this sense,
I know not the derivation: perhaps *totan*,
Saxon, contracted from *towetan*, to know
or examine.] To pry; to peep; to search
narrowly and slily. It is still used in the
provinces, otherwise obsolete.

I cast to go a shooting,
Long wand'ring up and down the land,
With bow and bolts on either hand,
For birds and bushes tooting. Spenser's Past.

tóothdrawer n.s. [*tooth* and *draw*.] One
whose business is to extract painful teeth.

Nature with Scots, as toothdrawers, hath dealt,
Who use to string their teeth upon their belt.
Cleaveland.

When the teeth are to be dislocated,
a toothdrawer is consulted.
Wiseman's Surgery.

tóper n.s. [from *tope*.] A drunkard.

topógraphy n.s. [*topographie*, Fr. τοπος and
γραφω.] Description of particular places.

That philosophy gives the exactest topography
of the extramundane spaces. Glanville's Scep.

The topography of Sulmo in the Latin makes
but an aukward figure in the version.
Cromwell.

topsytúrvy adv. [This Skinner fancies to *top*
in *turf*.] With the bottom upward.

All suddenly was turned topsyturvy, the noble
lord eftsoons was blamed, the wretched people
pitied, and new counsels plotted. Spenser
on Ireland.

If we without his help can make a head
To push against the kingdom; with his help
We shall o'erturn it topsyturvy down.
Shakesp. Henry IV.

God told man what was good, but the devil
surnamed it evil, and thereby turned the
world topsy-turvy, and brought a new chaos
upon the whole creation. South's Sermons.

Man is but a topsyturvy creature; his head
where his heels should be, grovelling on the
earth. Swift.

torpédo n.s. [Lat.] A fish which while
alive, if touched even with a long stick,
benumbs the hand that so touches it, but
when dead is eaten safely.

tórvous adj. [*torvus*, Lat.] Sour of aspect;
stern; severe of countenance.

That torvous sour look produced by anger, and
that gay and pleasing countenance
accompanying love. Derham.

tóry n.s. [A cant term, derived, I suppose,
from an Irish word signifying a savage.]
One who adheres to the antient
constitution of the state, and the apostolical
hierarchy of the church of England,
opposed to a whig.†

The knight is more a tory in the country
than the town, because it more advances his
interest. Addison.

To confound his hated coin, all parties and
religions join whigs, tories. Swift.

toupét n.s. [Fr.] A curl; an artificial lock of hair.

Remember second-hand toupees and repaired ruffles. Swift.

tóuchy adj. [from *touch*.] Peevish; irritable; irascible; apt to take fire. A low word.

You are upon a touchy point, and therefore treat so nice a subject with proportionable caution. Collier on Pride.

You are so touchy, and take things so hotly, I am sure there must be some mistake in this. Arbuthnot's Hist. of J. Bull.

tówntalk n.s. [*town* and *talk*.] Common prattle of a place.

If you tell the secret, in twelve hours it shall be towntalk. L'Estrange.

toy n.s. [*toyen, tooghen*, to dress with many ornaments, Dutch.]

1. A petty commodity; a trifle; a thing of no value.

Might I make acceptable unto her that toy which I had found, following an acquaintance of mine at the plough. Sidn.

They exchange for knives, glasses and such toys, great abundance of gold and pearl. Abbot.

*Because of old
Thou thyself doat'dst on womankind, admiring
Their shape, their colour, and attractive grace:
None are, thou think'st, but taken with such
    toys.* Milton.

*O virtue! virtue! what art thou become,
That men should leave thee for that toy
    a woman.* Dryden.

2. A plaything; a bauble.

*To dally thus with death is no fit toy,
Go find some other play-fellows, mine own
    sweet boy.* Fairy Queen, b. i.

What a profusion of wealth laid out in coaches, trappings, tables, cabinets, and the like precious toys. Addison.

*In Delia's hand this toy is fatal found,
Nor could that fabled dart more surely wound.* Pope.

3. Matter of no importance.

*'Tis a cockle or a walnut shell,
A knack, a toy, a trick, a baby's cap.* Shakespeare.

4. Folly; trifling practice; silly opinion.

The things which so long experience of all ages hath confirmed and made profitable, let us not presume to condemn as follies and toys, because we sometime know not the cause and reason of them. Hooker, b. iv.

5. Play; sport; amorous dalliance.

*Ye sons of Venus, play your sports at will;
For greedy pleasure, careless of your toys,
Thinks more upon her paradise of joys.* Spenser's Epithal.

*So said he, and forbore not glance or toy
Of amorous intent.* Milton.

6. Odd story; silly tale.

*I never may believe
These antick fables, nor these fairy toys.* Shakespeare.

7. Frolick; humour; odd fancy.

Shall that which hath always received this construction, be now disguised with a toy of novelty. Hooker, b. v.

*The very place puts toys of desperation,
Without more motive, into every brain,
That looks so many fathoms to the sea,
And hears it roar beneath.* Shakesp. Hamlet.

to toy v.n. [from the noun.] To trifle; to dally amorously; to play.

tóyshop n.s. [*toy* and *shop*.] A shop where playthings and little nice manufactures are sold.

Fans, silks, ribbands, laces, and gewgaws, lay so thick together, that the heart was nothing else but a toyshop. Add.

*With varying vanities from every part,
They shift the moving toyshop of their heart.* Pope.

trade n.s. [*tratta*, Italian.]

1. Traffick; commerce; exchange of goods for other goods, or for money.

Whosoever commands the sea, commands the trade; whosoever commands the trade of the world, commands the riches of the world, and consequently the world itself. Ral.

Trade increases in one place and decays in another. Temple.

2. Occupation; particular employment whether manual or mercantile, distinguished from the liberal arts or learned professions.

Appoint to every one that is not able to live of his freehold a certain trade of life; the which trade he shall be bound to follow. Spenser on Ireland.

> *How dizzy! half way down*
> *Hangs one that gathers samphire, dreadful trade.* Shakesp.

I'll mountebank their loves, and come home belov'd
Of all the trades in Rome. Shakesp. Coriolanus.

> *Fear and piety,*
> *Instruction, manners, mysteries, and trades,*
> *Decline to your confounding contraries.*
> Shakespeare.

> *The rude Equicolæ*
> *Hunting their sport, and plund'ring was their trade.* Dryd.

Fight under him; there's plunder to be had;
A captain is a very gainful trade.
Dryden's Juv.

The whole division that to Mars pertains,
All trades of death, that deal in steel for gains.
Dryden.

The emperor Pertinax applied himself in his youth to a gainful trade; his father, judging him fit for a better employment, had a mind to turn his education another way; the son was obstinate in pursuing so profitable a trade, a sort of merchandise of wood.
Arbuthnot on Coins.

3. Instruments of any occupation.

> *The shepherd bears*
> *His house and houshold gods, his trade of war,*
> *His bow and quiver, and his trusty cur.*
> Dryden's Virgil.

4. Any employment not manual; habitual exercise.

Call some of young years to train them up in that trade; and so fit them for weighty affairs. Bacon.

tráffick n.s. [*trafique*, Fr. *traffico*, Italian.]

1. Commerce; merchandising; large trade; exchange of commodities.

Traffick's thy god. Shakesp. Timon of Athens.

> *My father*
> *A merchant of great traffick through the world.* Shakesp.

As the first of these was, for his great wisdom, stiled the English Solomon, he followed the example of that wise king in nothing more than by advancing the traffick of his people. Addison's Freeholder, Nº 41.

2. Commodities; subject of traffick.

You'll see a draggled damsel
From Billingsgate her fishy traffick hear. Gay.

trágedy n.s. [*tragedie*, Fr. *tragœdia*, Lat.]

1. A dramatick representation of a serious action.

Thousands more, that yet suspect no peril,
Will now conclude their plotted tragedy.
Shakespeare.

All our tragedies are of kings and princes; but you never see a poor man have a part unless it be as a chorus, or to fill up the scenes, to dance, or to be derided. Taylor's holy living.

Imitate the sister of painting, tragedy; which employs the whole forces of her art in the main action. Dryden.

An anthem to their god Dionysus, whilst the goat stood at his altar to be sacrificed, was called the goat-song or tragedy. Rymer's Tragedies of the last Age.

There to her heart sad tragedy addrest
The dagger, wont to pierce the tyrant's breast.
Pope.

2. Any mournful or dreadful event.

> *I shall laugh at this,*
> *That they, who brought me in my master's hate,*
> *I live to look upon their tragedy.* Shakesp. Rich. III.

I look upon this now done in England as another act of the same tragedy which was lately begun in Scotland. K. Ch.

tragicómedy n.s. [*tragicomedie*, Fr. from *tragedy* and *comedy*.] A drama compounded of merry and serious events.†

On the world's stage, when our
applause grows high,
For acting here life's tragi-comedy,
The lookers-on will say we act not well,
Unless the last the former scenes excel.
Denham.

The faults of that drama are in the kind of it, which is tragi-comedy; but it was given to the people. Dryden.

We have often had tragi-comedies upon the English theatre with success: but in that sort of composition the tragedy and comedy are in distinct scenes. Gay.

trainbánds n.s. [*train* and *band:* I suppose for *trained band*.] The militia; the part of a community trained to martial exercise.

He directed the trainbands of Westminster and Middlesex, which consisted of the most substantial housholders, to attend. Clarendon.

Give commission
To some bold man, whose loyalty you trust,
And let him raise the trainbands of the city. Dryden.

A council of war was called, wherein we agreed to retreat: but before we could give the word, the trainbands, taking advantage of our delay, fled first. Addison's Freeholder.

trait n.s. [*trait*, Fr.] A stroke; a touch. Scarce English.

By this single trait Homer marks an essential difference between the Iliad and Odyssey; that in the former the people perished by the folly of their kings; in this by their own folly. Broome's Notes on the Odyssey.

tralatítious adj. [from *translatus*, Lat.] Metaphorical; not literal.

trángram n.s. [A cant word.] An odd intricately contrived thing.

What's the meaning of all these trangrams and gimcracks? what are you going about, jumping over my master's hedges, and running your lines cross his grounds? Arbuthnot.

to transláte v.n. [*translatus*, Lat.]

1. To transport; to remove.

Since our father is translated unto the gods, our will is that they that are in our realm live quietly. 2 Mac. xi. 23.

By faith Enoch was translated that he should not see death. Heb. xi. 5.

Those argent fields
Translated saints or middle spirits hold. Milton.

Of the same soil their nursery prepare
With that of their plantation, left the tree
Translated should not with the soil agree. Dryden.

The gods their shapes to winter birds translate,
But both obnoxious to their former fate. Dryden.

To go to heaven is to be translated to that kingdom you have longed for; to enjoy the glories of eternity. Wake.

2. It is particularly used of the removal of a bishop from one see to another.

Fisher, bishop of Rochester, when the king would have translated him from that poor bishoprick to a better, he refused, saying, he would not forsake his poor little old wife, with whom he had so long lived. Camden's Remains.

3. To transfer from one to another; to convey.

I will translate the kingdom from the house of Saul, and set up the throne of David. 2 Sam. iii. 10.

Because of unrighteous dealings the kingdom is translated from one people to another. Ecclus. x. 8.

Lucian affirms the souls of usurers, after their death, to be metempsychosed, or translated into the bodies of asses, there to remain for

poor men to take their pennyworths out of
their bones and sides with the cudgel and spur.
Peacham.

As there are apoplexies from inveterate gouts,
the regimen must be to translate the morbifick
matter upon the extremities of the body.
Arbuthnot.

Perverse mankind! whose wills, created free,
Charge all their woes on absolute decree;
All to the dooming gods their guilt translate,
And follies are miscall'd the crimes of fate.
Pope.

4. To change.

One do I personate of Timon's frame,
Whom fortune with her iv'ry hand wafts to her,
Whose present grace to present slaves
 and servants
Translates his rivals. Shakesp. Timon
of Athens.

 Happy is your grace,
That can translate the stubbornness of fortune
Into so quiet and so sweet a style. Shakesp.
As you like it.

5. [*Translater*, old Fr.] To interpret in
   another language; to change into
   another language retaining the sense.

I can construe the action of her familiar stile,
and the hardest voice of her behaviour, to be
englished right, is, I am Sir John Falstaff's.
—He hath studied her well, and translated
her out of honesty into English. Shakesp.
Merry Wives of Windsor.

Nor word for word too faithfully translate.
Roscommon.

Read this ere you translate one bit
Of books of high renown. Swift.

 Were it meant that in despite
Of art and nature such dull clods should write,
Bavius and Mævius had been sav'd by fate
For Settle and for Shadwell to translate.
Duke.

6. To explain. A low colloquial use.

There's matter in these sighs, these
 profound heaves

You must translate; 'tis fit we understand
 them. Shakesp.

transpícuous adj. [*trans* and *specio*, Latin.]
Transparent; pervious to the sight.

 What if that light,
Sent from her through the wide transpicuous air,
To the terrestrial moon be as a star. Milton.

Now thy wine's transpicuous, purg'd from all
Its earthy gross, yet let it feed awhile
On the fat refuse. Philips.

transportátion n.s. [from *transport.*]

1. Removal; conveyance; carriage.

Sir Francis Cottington and Mr. Endymion
Porter had been sent before to provide a vessel
for their transportation. Wotton's Life of
Buckingham.

Some were not so solicitous to provide against
the plague, as to know whether we had it
from the malignity of our own air, or by
transportation. Dryden.

2. Banishment for felony.

3. Ecstatick violence of passion.

All pleasures that affect the body must needs
weary, because they transport, and all
transportation is a violence; and no violence
can be lasting but determines upon the falling
of the spirits. South.

transubstantiátion n.s. [*transubstantiation*,
Fr.] A miraculous operation believed in the
Romish church, in which the elements of
the eucharist are supposed to be changed
into the real body and blood of Christ.

How is a Romanist prepared easily to
swallow, not only against all probability,
but even the clear evidence of his senses, the
doctrine of transubstantiation? Locke.

to trape v.a. [commonly written *to traipse*:
probably of the same original with *drab*.] To
run idly and sluttishly about. It is used only
of women.

tránters n.s. Men who carry fish from the
sea-coasts to sell in the inland countries.
Bailey.

trápstick n.s. [*trap* and *stick.*] A stick with which boys drive a wooden ball.

A foolish swoop between a couple of thick bandy legs and two long trapsticks that had no calfs. Spect. Nº 559.

trávesty adj. [*travesti*, Fr.] Dressed so as to be made ridiculous; burlesqued.

tráytrip n.s. A kind of play, I know not of what kind.†

Shall I play my freedom at traytrip, and become thy bond slave. Shakespeare's Twelfth Night.

tréason n.s. [*trahison*, French.] An offence committed against the dignity and majesty of the commonwealth: it is divided into high treason and petit treason. High treason is an offence against the security of the commonwealth, or of the king's majesty, whether by imagination, word, or deed; as to compass or imagine treason, or the death of the prince, or the queen consort, or his son and heir-apparent; or to deflower the king's wife, or his eldest daughter unmarried, or his eldest son's wife; or levy war against the king in his realm, or to adhere to his enemies by aiding them; or to counterfeit the king's great seal, privy seal, or money; or knowingly to bring false money into this realm counterfeited like the money of England, and to utter the same; or to kill the king's chancellor, treasurer, justice of the one bench, or of the other; justices in Eyre, justices of assize, justices of oyer and terminer, when in their place and doing their duty; or forging the king's seal manual, or privy signet; or diminishing or impairing the current money: and, in such treason, a man forfeits his lands and goods to the king: and it is called treason paramount. Petit treason is when a servant kills his master, a wife her husband; secular or religious kills his prelate: this treason gives forfeiture to every lord within his own fee: both treasons are capital. Cowel.

Man disobeying,
Disloyal breaks his fealty, and sins
Against the high supremacy of heaven:
To expiate his treason hath nought left.
Milton.

He made the overture of thy treasons to us. Shakespeare.

Athaliah cried, treason, treason. 2 Kings xi. 14.

tréble n.s. A sharp sound.

The treble cutteth the air so sharp, as it returneth too swift to make the sound equal; and therefore a mean or tenor is the sweetest. Bacon.

The lute still trembles underneath thy nail:
At thy well-sharpen'd thumb from shore to shore,
The trebles squeak for fear, the bases roar. Dryden.

tree n.s. [*trie*, Islandick; *tree*, Danish.]

1. A large vegetable rising, with one woody stem, to a considerable height.

Trees and shrubs, of our native growth in England, are distinguished by Ray.

Such as have their flowers disjointed and remote from the fruit; and these are,

Nuciferous ones; as, the walnut tree, the hazel-nut tree, the beach, the chesnut, and the common oak.

Coniferous ones; of this kind are the Scotch firs, male and female; the pine, the common alder tree, and the birch tree.

Bacciferous; as, the juniper and yew trees.

Lanigerous ones; as, the black, white, and trembling poplar, willows, and osiers of all kinds.

Such as bear their seeds, having an imperfect flower, in leafy membranes; as, the horse-bean.

Such as have their fruits and flowers contiguous; of these some are pomiferous; as, apples and pears: and some bacciferous; as, the sorb or service tree, the white or hawthorn, the wild rose, sweet brier, currants, the great bilbery bush, honeysuckle, joy.

Pruniferous ones, whose fruit is pretty large and soft, with a stone in the middle; as, the black-thorn or sloe tree, the black and white bullace tree, the black cherry, &c.

Bacciferous ones; as, the strawberry tree in the west of Ireland, misletoe, water elder, the dwarf, a large laurel, the viburnum or way-fairing tree, the dog-berry tree, the sea black thorn, the berry-bearing elder, the privet barberry, common elder, the holy, the buckthorn, the berry-bearing heath, the bramble, and spindle tree or prickwood.

Such as have their fruit dry when ripe; as, the bladder nut tree, the box tree, the common elm and ash, the maple, the gaule or sweet willow, common heath, broom, dyers wood, furze or gorse, the lime tree, &c. Miller.

Sometime we see a cloud that's dragonish,
A forked mountain, or blue promontory
With trees upon 't, that nod unto the world,
And mock our eyes with air. Shakesp.
Ant. and Cleopatra.

Who can bid the tree unfix his earth-bound root. Shak.

It is pleasant to look upon a tree in Summer covered with green leaves, decked with blossoms, or laden with fruit, and casting a pleasant shade: but to consider how this tree sprang from a little seed, how nature shaped and fed it till it came to this greatness, is a more rational pleasure. Burnet.

Trees shoot up in one great stem, and at a good distance from the earth, spread into branches: thus gooseberries are shrubs, and oaks are trees. Locke.

2. Any thing branched out.

Vain are their hopes who fancy to inherit,
By trees of pedigrees, or fame or merit:
Though plodding heralds through each
*   branch may trace*
Old captains and dictators of their race.
Dryden.

tree of life n.s. [*lignum vitæ*, Latin.] An evergreen: the wood is esteemed by turners. Miller.

treméndous adj. [*tremendus*, Latin.] Dreadful; horrible; astonishingly terrible.

There stands an altar where the priest celebrates some mysteries sacred and tremendous. Tatler, Nº 57.

In that portal shou'd the chief appear,
Each hand tremendous with a brazen spear.
Pope's Odyssey.

trepán n.s. [*trepan*, Fr.]

1. An instrument by which chirurgeons cut out round pieces of the skull.

2. A snare; a stratagem by which any one is ensnared. [Of this signification Skinner assigns for the reason, that some English ships in queen Elizabeth's reign being invited, with great shew of friendship, into *Trapani*, a part of Sicily, were there detained.]

But what a thoughtless animal is man,
How very active in his own trepan.
Roscommon.

Can there be any thing of friendship in snares, hooks, and trepans. South's Sermons.

During the commotion of the blood and spirits, in which passion consists, whatsoever is offered to the imagination in favour of it, tends only to deceive the reason: it is indeed a real trepan upon it, feeding it with colours and appearances instead of arguments.
South's Sermons.

tricksy adj. [from *trick*.] Pretty. This is a word of endearment.

The fool hath planted in his memory
An army of good words; and I do know
A many fools that stand in better place,
Garnish'd like him, that for a tricksy word
Defy the matter. Shakesp. Merchant of Venice.

All this service have I done since I went.
—My tricksy spirit! Shakespeare's Tempest.

trigonómetry n.s. [*trigonometrie*, Fr.] Trigonometry is the art of measuring triangles, or of calculating the sides of any triangle sought, and this is plain or spherical. Harris.

On a discovery of Pythagoras all trigonometry, and consequently all navigation, is founded.
Guardian.

tríllion n.s. [A word invented by Locke: *trilion*, Fr.] A million of millions of millions; a million twice multiplied by a million.

trímmer n.s. [from *trim*.]

1. One who changes sides to balance parties; a turncoat.

The same bat taken after by a weazel begged for mercy: no, says the weazle, no mercy to a mouse: well, says t' other, but you may see by my wings that I am a bird; and so the bat 'scaped in both by playing the trimmer. L'Estrange's Fab.

To confound his hated coin,
All parties and religions join,
Whigs, tories, trimmers. Swift.

2. A piece of wood inserted.

Before they pin up the frame of ground-plates, they must fit in the summer and the girders, and all the joists and the trimmers for the stair-case. Moxon's Mech. Exercise.

trínity n.s. [*trinitas*, Lat. *trinité*, Fr.] The incomprehensible union of the three persons in the Godhead.

Touching the picture of the trinity, I hold it blasphemous and utterly unlawful. Peacham.

In my whole essay there is not any thing like an objection against the trinity. Locke.

tripudiátion n.s. [*tripudium*, Lat.] Act of dancing.

triséction n.s. [*tres* and *sectio*, Lat.] Division into three equal parts: the trisection of an angle is one of the desiderata of geometry.

trívial n.s. [*trivial*, Fr. *trivialis*, Lat.]

1. Vile; worthless; vulgar; such as may be picked up in the highway.

Be subjects great, and worth a poet's voice,
For men of sense despise a trivial choice. Roscommon.

2. Light; trifling; unimportant; inconsiderable. This use is more frequent, though less just.

This argues conscience in your grace,
But the respects thereof are nice and trivial,
All circumstances well considered. Shakesp. Rich. III.

See yon mad fools, who, for some trivial right,
For love, or for mistaken honour, fight. Dryden.

Were they only some slight and trivial indiscretions, to which the example of the

world exposed us, it might perhaps not much concern our religion. Rogers's Serm.

In ev'ry work regard the writer's end;
And if the means be just, the conduct true,
Applause, in spite of trivial faults, is due. Pope.

The ancient poets are like many modern ladies: let an action be never so trivial in itself, they always make it appear of the utmost importance. Pope.

trócar n.s. [*trocar* corrupted from *trois quart*, French.] A chirurgical instrument.

The handle of the trocar is of wood, the canula of silver, and the perforator of steel. Sharp's Surgery.

tróchee n.s. [*trochæus*, Lat. *trochée*, Fr. τροχαιος.] A foot used in Latin poetry, consisting of a long and short syllable.

tróchings n.s. The branches on a deer's head. Ains.

tróllop n.s. [A low word, I know not whence derived.] A slatternly, loose woman.

trólmydames n.s. [Of this word I know not the meaning.]†

A fellow I have known to go about with trolmydames: I knew him once a servant of the prince. Shak. Winter's Tale.

trope n.s. [τροπος; *trope*, Fr. *tropus*, Lat.] A change of a word from its original signification; as, the clouds *foretel* rain for *foreshew*.

For rhetorick he could not ope
His mouth, but out there flew a trope. Hudibras.

If this licence be included in a single word, it admits of tropes; if in a sentence, of figures. Dryden.

to trow v.n. [*treoðian*, Saxon; *troe*, Danish.] To think; to imagine; to conceive. A word now disused, and rarely used in ancient writers but in familiar language.

What handsomeness, trow you, can be observed in that speech, which is made one knows not to whom? Sidney.

Is there any reasonable man, trow you, but will judge it meeter that our ceremonies of Christian religion should be Popish than Turkish or Heathenish. Hooker, b. iv.

Lend less than thou owest.
Learn more than thou trowest.
Shakesp. King Lear.

To-morrow next
We will for Ireland; and 'tis time, I trow.
Shakespeare.

O rueful day! rueful indeed, I trow. Gay.

trúbtail n.s. A short squat woman. Ainsworth.

truepénny n.s. [*true* and *penny*.] A familiar phrase for an honest fellow.

Say'st thou so? art thou there, truepenny?
Come on. Shakespeare.

trúffle n.s. [*trufle, truffe*, French.] In Italy, the usual method for the finding of truffles, or subterraneous mushrooms, called by the Italians *tartutali*, and in Latin *tubera terræ*, is by tying a cord to the hind leg of a pig, and driving him, observing where he begins to root. Ray.

trull n.s. [*trulla*, Italian.]

1. A low whore; a vagrant strumpet.

I'm sure, I scar'd the dauphin and his trull.
Shakespeare.

A trull who sits
By the town wall, and for her living knits.
Dryden.

So Mævius, when he drain'd his skull,
To celebrate some suburb trull;
His similies in order set,
And ev'ry crambo he cou'd get;
Before he could his poem close,
The lovely nymph had lost her nose. Swift.

2. It seems to have had first at least a neutral sense: a girl; a lass; a wench.

Among the rest of all the route
A passing proper lasse,
A white-hair'd trull, of twenty years,
Or neere about there was:
In stature passing all the rest,
A gallant girl for hewe;

To be compar'd with townish nymphs,
So fair she was to viewe. Turberville.

trúmpet n.s. [*trompette*, French and Dutch.]

1. An instrument of martial musick sounded by the breath.

What's the business?
That such a hideous trumpet calls to parley
The sleepers of the house. Shakespeare.

If any man of quality will maintain upon Edmund earl of Gloster, that he is a manifold traitor, let him appear by the third sound of the trumpet. Shakesp. King Lear.

He blew
His trumpet, heard in Oreb since perhaps
When God descended, and perhaps once more
To sound at gen'ral doom. Th' angelick blast
Filled all the regions. Milton.

The last loud trumpet's wond'rous sound
Shall through the rending tombs rebound,
And wake the nations under ground.
Roscommon.

Things of deep sense we may in prose unfold,
But they move more in lofty numbers told;
By the loud trumpet which our courage aids,
We learn that sound, as well as sense,
   persuades. Waller.

The trumpet's loud clangor
Excites us to arms,
   With shrill notes of anger,
And mortal alarms. Dryden.

Every man is the maker of his own fortune, and must be in some measure the trumpet of his fame. Tatler.

No more the drum
Provokes to arms, or trumpet's clangor shrill
Affrights the wives. Philips.

Let the loud trumpet sound,
Till the roofs all around,
The shrill echoes rebound. Pope.

2. In military stile, a trumpeter.

He wisely desired, that a trumpet might be first sent for a pass. Clarendon, b. viii.

Among our forefathers, the enemy, when there was a king in the field, demanded by a trumpet in what part he resided, that they might avoid firing upon the royal pavilion. Addison.

3. One who celebrates; one who praises.

Glorious followers, who make themselves as trumpets of the commendation of those they follow, taint business for want of secrecy, and export honour from a man, and make him a return in envy. Bacon.

That great politician was pleased to have the greatest wit of those times in his interests, and to be the trumpet of his praises. Dryden.

truth n.s. [*treowða*, Saxon.]

1. The contrary to falsehood; conformity of notions to things.

Truth is the joining or separating of signs, as the things signified agree or disagree. Locke.

That men are pubescent at the year of twice seven is accounted a punctual truth. Brown.

 *Persuasive words, impregn'd
With reason to her seeming and with truth.* Milton.

This clue leads them through the mizmaze of opinions and authors to truth and certainty. Locke.

2. Conformity of words to thoughts.

Shall truth fail to keep her word? Milton.

And lend a lie the confidence of truth. Anonymous.†

3. Purity from falsehood.

*So young and so untender?
—So young, my lord, and true.
—Let it be so, thy truth then be thy dower.* Shakesp.

4. Fidelity; constancy.

*The thoughts of past pleasure and truth,
The best of all blessings below.* Song.

5. Honesty; virtue.

*The money I tender for him in the court;
If this will not suffice, it must appear
That malice bears down truth.* Shakespeare.

6. It is used sometimes by way of concession.

She said, truth, Lord: yet the dogs eat of the crumbs which fall. Matth. xv. 27.

7. Exactness; conformity to rule.

Ploughs to go true depend much upon the truth of the iron work. Mortimer's Husbandry.

8. Reality.

In truth, what should any prayer, framed to the minister's hand, require, but only so to be read as behoveth. Hooker.

9. Of a truth, or in truth. In reality.

Of a truth, Lord, the kings of Assyria have destroyed the nations. 2 Kings xix. 17.

túcker n.s. A small piece of linen that shades the breast of women.

A female ornament by some called a tucker, and by others the neck-piece, being a slip of fine linen or muslin, used to run in a small kind of ruffle round the uppermost verge of the stays. Addison's Guardian.

túel n.s. [*tuyeau*, French.] The anus. Skinner.

túfty adj. [from *tuft*.] Adorned with tufts. A word of no authority.

*Let me strip thee of thy tufty coat,
Spread thy ambrosial stores.* Thomson's Summer.

túlip n.s. [*tulipe*, Fr. *tulipa*, Lat.] A flower.

It hath a lilly flower, composed of six leaves, shaped somewhat like a pitcher; the pointal rising in the middle of the flower is surrounded with stamina, and afterwards becomes an oblong fruit, which opens into three parts, and is divided into three cells, full of plain seeds, resting upon one another in a double row. To these may be added a coated root, with fibres on the lower part. The properties of a good tulip, according to the characteristicks of the best florists of the present age, are, 1. It should have a tall stem. 2. The flower should consist of six leaves, three within, and three without, the former being larger than the latter. 3. Their bottom should be proportioned to their top; their upper part should be rounded off, and not terminate in a point. 4. The leaves when opened should neither turn inward nor bend outward, but rather stand erect; the flower should be of a middling size, neither over large nor too small. **5.** *The stripes should be small and regular, arising quite from the bottom of the flower. The chives should not be yellow, but of a brown colour. They are generally divided into three classes, viz.* præcoces, *or early flowers;* media's, *or middling flowers; and* serotines, *or late flowers. The early blowing tulips are not near so fair, nor rise half so high as the late ones, but are chiefly valued for appearing so early in the spring. Their roots should be taken up and spread upon mats in a shady place to dry; after which they should be cleared from their filth, and put up in a dry place until the season for planting.* Miller.

The tulip opens with the rising, and shuts with the setting sun. Hakewill.

Why tulips of one colour produce some of another, and running thro' all, still escape a blue. Brown's Vulgar Errours.

túmbrel n.s. [*tombereau,* Freuch.] A dungcart.

Twifallow once ended, get tumbrel and man, And compass that fallow as soon as ye can. Tuss. Husb.

My corps is in a tumbril laid, among The filth and ordure, and inclos'd with dung; That cart arrest, and raise a common cry, For sacred hunger of my gold I die. Dryden.

What shall I do with this beastly tumbril? go lie down and sleep, you sot. Congreve.

To convince the present little race how unequal all their measures were to an antediluvian, in respect of the insects which now appear for men, he sometimes rode in an open tumbril. Tatler.

túmour n.s. [*tumor,* Latin.]

1. A morbid swelling.

Tumour is a disease, in which the parts recede from their natural state by an undue encrease of their bigness. Wiseman.

Having dissected this swelling vice, and seen what it is that feeds the tumour, if the disease be founded in pride, the abating that is the most

natural remedy. Govern. of the Tongue.

2. Affected pomp; false magnificence; puffy grandeur; swelling mien; unsubstantial greatness.

His stile was rich of phrase, but seldom in bold metaphors; and so far from the tumour, that it rather wants a little elevation. Wotton.

It is not the power of tumour and bold looks upon the passions of the multitude. L'Estrange.

túmulose adj. [*tumulosus,* Lat.] Full of hills. Bailey.

to tup v.n. To but like a ram.

túrban, túrbant, túrband n.s. [A Turkish word.] The cover worn by the Turks on their heads.

Gates of monarchs Arch'd are so high, that giants may jet through, And keep their impious turbands on, without Good morrow to the sun. Shakespeare.

His hat was in the form of a turban, not so huge as the Turkish turbans. Bacon.

From utmost Indian isle, Taprobane, Dusk faces with white silken turbants wreath'd. Milton.

I see the Turk nodding with his turbant. Howel.

Some for the pride of Turkish courts design'd, For folded turbants finest Holland bear. Dryden.

turbinátion n.s. [from *turbinated.*] The art of spinning like a top.

túrcism n.s. [*turcismus,* low Latin.] The religion of the Turks.

Methinks I am at Mecca, and hear a piece of turcism preached to me by one of Mahomet's priests. Dr. Maine.

He is condemned immediately, as preferring Turcism to Christianity. Atterbury.

turd n.s. [*turd,* Saxon.] Excrement.

túrncoat n.s. [*turn* and *coat.*] One who forsakes his party or principles; a renegade.

Courtesy itself must turn to disdain, if you
come in her presence—
Then is courtesy a turncoat. Shakesp.

túrtle, túrtledove *n.s.* [*turtle*, Saxon;
tortorelle, French; *tortarella*, Italian; *turtur*,
Latin.]

1. A species of dove.

When shepherds pipe on oaten straws,
And merry larks are ploughmens clocks:
When turtles tread. Shak. Love's Lab. Lost.

We'll teach him to know turtles from jays.
Shak.

Take me an heifer and a turtle dove.
Gen. xv. 9.

Galen propos'd the blood of turtles dropt warm
from their wings. Wiseman.

2. It is used among sailors and gluttons for
a tortoise.

tuz *n.s.* [I know not whether it is not a
word merely of cant.] A lock or tuft of hair.

With odorous oil thy head and hair are sleek;
And then thou kemp'st the tuzzes on thy cheek;
Of these thy barbers take a costly care.
Dryden.

to twáttle *v.n.* [*schwatzen*, German.] To
prate; to gabble; to chatter.

It is not for every twattling gossip to
undertake. L'Estrange.

twíster *n.s.* [from *twist*.] One who twists;
a ropemaker. To this word I have annexed
some remarkable lines, which explain twist
in all its senses.

When a twister a-twisting will twist
*   him a twist,*
For the twisting of his twist, he three twines
*   doth intwist;*
But if one of the twines of the twist do untwist,
The twine that untwisteth untwisteth the twist.
Untwirling the twine that untwisteth between,
He twirls with his twister the two in a twine;
Then twice having twisted the twines
*   of the twine,*
He twitcheth the twine he had twined in twain.

The twain that in twining before in the twine,
As twins were intwisted, he now doth untwine,
'Twixt the twain intertwisting a twine
*   more between,*
He, twirling his twister, makes a twist of
*   the twine.* Wallis.

twittletwáttle *n.s.* [A ludicrous reduplication
of *twattle*.] Tattle; gabble. A vile word.

Insipid twittletwatles, frothy jests, and
jingling witticisms, inure us to a
misunderstanding of things. L'Estrange.

type *n.s.* [*type*, Fr. *typus*, Lat. τυπος.]

1. Emblem; mark of something.

*   Clean renouncing*
The faith they have in tennis, and tall stockings,
Short bolster'd breeches, and those types of travel,
And understanding again the honest men.
Shakespeare.

Thy emblem, gracious queen, the British rose,
Type of sweet rule, and gentle majesty. Prior.

2. That by which something future
is prefigured.

*   Informing them by types*
And shadows of that destin'd seed to bruise
The serpent, by what means he shall atchieve
Mankind's deliverance. Milton.

The Apostle shews the Christian religion
to be in truth and substance what the Jewish
was only in type and shadow.
Tillotson's Sermons.

3. A stamp; a mark. Not in use.

Thy father bears the type of King of Naples,
Yet not so wealthy as an English yeoman.
Shakespeare.

What good is cover'd with the face of heav'n
To be discovered, that can do me good?
—Th' advancement of your children, gentle lady,
—Up to some scaffold, there to lose their heads;
—No, to the dignity and height of fortune,
The high imperial type of this earth's glory.
Shakespeare.

4. A printing letter.

typógraphy n.s. [*typographie*, Fr. *typographia*, Lat.]

1. Emblematical, figurative, or hieroglyphical representation.

Those diminutive and pamphlet treatises daily published amongst us, are pieces containing rather typography than verity. Brown's Vulgar Errours.

2. The art of printing.

tyránt n.s. [τυραννος; *tyrannus*, Latin. Rowland contends that this word, with the correspondent Greek and Latin, is derived from *tir*, Welch and Erse, land, and *rhanner*, Welch, to share, *q.d. tirhanner*, a sharer, or divider of and among his vassals.]

1. An absolute monarch governing imperiously.

2. A cruel despotick and severe master; an oppressor.

Love to a yielding heart is a king, but to a resisting is a tyrant. Sidney, b. i.

I would not be the villain that thou think'st, For the whole space that's in the tyrant's grasp, And the rich east to boot. Shakespeare's Macbeth.

Dissembling courtesy! how fine this tyrant Can tickle where she wounds! Shakesp. Cymb.

The house of woe, and dungeon of our tyrant. Milton.

Consider those grand agents and lieutenants of the devil, by whom he scourges and plagues the world under him, to wit, tyrants; and was there ever any tyrant who was not also false and perfidious! South's Sermons.

Thou meant'st to kill a tyrant, not a king. Dryden.

When tyrant custom had not shackl'd man, But free to follow nature was the mode. Thomson.

U

U, the vowel, has two sounds; one clear, expressed at other times by *eu*, as *obtuse*; the other close, and approaching to the Italian *u*, or English *oo*, as *obtund*.

V, has two powers, expressed in modern English by two characters, *V* consonant and *U* vowel, which ought to be considered as two letters; but as they were long confounded while the two uses were annexed to one form, the old custom still continues to be followed.

V, the consonant, has a sound nearly approaching to those of *b* and *f*. With *b* it is by the Spaniards and Gascons always confounded, and in the Runick alphabet is expressed by the same character with *f*, distinguished only by a diacritical point. Its sound in English is uniform. It is never mute.

úberty n.s. [*ubertas*, Latin.] Abundance; fruitfulness.

ubicátion, ubíety n.s. [from *ubi*, Latin.] Local relation; whereness. A scholastick term.

Relations, ubications, duration, the vulgar philosophy admits to be something; and yet to enquire in what place they are, were gross. Glanville.

ulíginous adj. [*uliginosus*, Latin.] Slimy; muddy.

The uliginous lacteous matter taken notice of in the coral fishings upon the coast of Italy, was only a collection of the corallin particles. Woodward.

ultróneous adj. [*ultro*, Lat.] Spontaneous; voluntary.

úmbles n.s. [*umbles*, Fr.] A deer's entrails. Dict.

umbrágeous adj. [*ombragieux*, Fr.] Shady; yielding shade.

Umbrageous grots and caves of cool recess. Milton.

Walk daily in a pleasant, airy, and umbrageous garden. Harvey.

The stealing shower is scarce to patter heard, Beneath th' umbrageous multitude of leaves. Thomson.

umbrél, umbrélla n.s. [from *umbra*, Lat.] A skreen used in hot countries to keep off the sun, and in others to bear off the rain.†

I can carry your umbrella, and fan your ladyship. Dryden.

*Good housewives
Defended by th' umbrella's oily shed,
Safe through the wet on clinking pattens
    tread.* Gay.

uncónquered adj.

1. Not subdued; not overcome.

*To die so tamely,
O'ercome by passion and misfortune,
And still unconquer'd by my foes, sounds ill.* Denham.

*Unconquer'd yet, in that forlorn estate,
His manly courage overcame his fate.* Dryden.

2. Insuperable; invincible.

These brothers had a-while served the king of Pontus; and in all his affairs, especially of war, whereunto they were only apt, they had shewed as unconquered courage, so rude a faithfulness. Sidney.

What was that snaky-headed gorgon shield, That wise Minerva wore, unconquer'd virgin! Wherewith she freez'd her foes to congeal'd stone, But rigid looks, and chaste austerity, And noble grace, that dash'd brute violence, With sudden adoration and blank awe? Milton.

Unconquer'd lord of pleasure and of pain. Johnson.

uncóuth adj. [*uncuð*, Saxon.] Odd; strange; unusual.

*A very uncouth sight was to behold, How he did fashion his untoward pace; For as he forward mov'd his footing old, So backward still was turn'd his wrinkled
    face.* Fairy Queen.

The lovers standing in this doleful wise, A warrior bold unwares approached near, Uncouth in arms yclad, and strange disguise. Fairfax.

I am surprized with an uncouth fear; A chilling sweat o'erruns my trembling joints; My heart suspects more than mine eye can see. Shakesp.

The trouble of thy thoughts this night Affects me equally; nor can I like This uncouth dream, of evil sprung, I fear. Milton.

*Say on;
For I that day was absent, as befel,
Bound on a voyage uncouth, and obscure,
Far on excursion toward the gates of hell.* Milton.

It was so uncouth a sight, for a fox to appear without a tail, that the very thought made him weary of his life. L'Estrange.

The secret ceremonies I conceal, Uncouth, perhaps unlawful to reveal. Dryden.

I am more in danger to misunderstand his true meaning, than if I had come to him with a mind unpossessed by doctors of my sect, whose reasonings will of course make all chime that way, and make the genuine meaning of the author seem harsh, strained, and uncouth to me. Locke.

He made that a pleasant study, which, in the hands of Bartolus and Baldus, was uncouth and rugged. Baker.

to undermíne v.a. [*under* and *mine*.]

1. To dig cavities under any thing, so that it may fall, or be blown up; to sap.

Though the foundation on a rock were laid, The church was undermin'd and then betray'd. Denham.

An injudicious endeavour to exalt Virgil, is much the same, as if one should think to raise the superstructure by undermining the foundation. Pope's Preface to the Iliad.

2. To excavate under.

A vast rock undermin'd from one end to the other, and a highway running through it, as long and as broad as the mall. Addison's Remarks on Italy.

3. To injure by clandestine means.

Making the king's sword strike whom they hated, the king's purse reward whom they loved; and, which is worst of all, making the royal countenance serve to undermine the royal sovereignty. Sidney.

They, knowing Eleanor's aspiring humour, Have hir'd me to undermine the dutchess. Shakesp.

   The father secure, Ventures his filial virtue, Against whate'er may tempt, whate'er seduce, Allure or terrify, or undermine. Milton.

The undermining smile becomes habitual; and the drift of his plausible conversation, is only to flatter one, that he may betray another. Dryden.

He should be warn'd who are like to undermine him, and who to serve him. Locke on Education.

únderplot n.s. [*under* and *plot*.]

1. A series of events proceeding collaterally with the main story of a play, and subservient to it.

In a tragi-comedy, there is to be but one main design; and though there be an underplot, yet it is subservient to the chief fable. Dryden's Dedication to Juvenal.

2. A clandestine scheme.

The husband is so misled by tricks, and so lost in a crooked intrigue, that he still suspects an underplot. Addison.

understánding n.s. [from *understand*.]

1. Intellectual powers; faculties of the mind, especially those of knowledge and judgment.

I speak as my understanding instructs me, and as mine honesty puts it to utterance. Shakesp. Winter Tale.

Make him of quick understanding in the fear of the Lord. Isaiah.

It maketh day-light understanding, out of darkness. Bacon.

When she rates things, and moves from ground to ground, The name of reason she obtains by this: But when by reason she the truth hath found, And standeth fix'd, she understanding is. Davies.

   Life and sense, Fancy and understanding: whence the soul Reason receives, and reason is her being. Milton.

God is to the understanding of man, as the light of the sun is to our eyes, its first and most glorious object. Tillotson.

2. Skill.

The understandings of a senate are often enslaved by three or four leaders. Swift.

Right understanding consists in the perception of the visible or probable agreement or disagreement of ideas. Locke.

Very mean people have raised their minds to a great sense and understanding of religion. Locke.

3. Intelligence; terms of communication.

He hoped the loyalty of his subjects would concur with him in the preserving of a good understanding between him and his people. Clarendon.

We have got into some understanding with the enemy, by means of Don Diego. Arbuthnot.

underwríter n.s. [from *underwrite*.] An insurer; so called from writing his name under the conditions.

to undó v.a. preterite undid; participle passive undone. [from *do*.]

1. To ruin; to bring to destruction.

As this immoderate favour of the multitude did him no good, so will it undo so many as shall trust unto it. Hayward.

Subdued, undone, they did at last obey, And change their own for their invader's way. Roscommon.

Where, with like haste, though several ways they run, Some to undo, and some to be undone. Denham.

Hither ye come, dislike, and so undo The players, and disgrace the poet too. Denham.

When I behold the charming maid, I'm ten times more undone; while hope and fear, With variety of pain distract me. Addison's Cato.

2. To loose; to open what is shut or fastened; to unravel.

They false and fearful do their hands undo; Brother, his brother; friend doth friend forsake. Sidney.

Pray undo this button. Shakespeare's K. Lear.

We implore thy powerful hand, To undo the charmed band Of true virgin here distress'd. Milton.

Were men so dull, they cou'd not see That Lyce painted, should they flee, Like simple birds, into a net, So grossly woven and ill-set;

Her own teeth would undo the knot, And let all go that she had got. Waller.

3. To change any thing done to its former state; to recall, or annul any action.

They may know, that we are far from presuming to think that men can better any thing which God hath done, even as we are from thinking, that men should presume to undo some things of men, which God doth know they cannot better. Hooker.

It was a torment To lay upon the damn'd, which Sycorax Could not again undo. Shakespeare's Tempest.

We seem ambitious God's whole work t' undo; Of nothing he made us, and we strive too, To bring ourselves to nothing back. Donne.

They make the Deity do and undo, go forward and backwards. Burnet's Theory of the Earth.

By granting me so soon, He has the merit of the gift undone. Dryden.

Without this our repentance is not real, because we have not done what we can to undo our fault. Tillotson.

Now will this woman, with a single glance, Undo what I've been labouring all this while. Addison.

When in time the martial maid Found out the trick that Venus play'd, She shakes her helm; she knits her brows, And, fir'd with indignation, vows, Tomorrow e'er the setting sun, She'd all undo, that she had done. Swift.

to ungód v.a. To divest of divinity.

Were we wak'ned by this tyranny, T' ungod this child again, it could not be I should love her, who loves not me. Donne.

Thus men ungodded may to places rise, And sects may be preferr'd without disguise. Dryden.

únity n.s. [*unitas*, Lat.]

1. The state of being one.

Those hereticks introduced a plurality of Gods; and so made the profession of the unity part of the symbolum, that should discriminate the orthodox from them. Hammond.

The production of one being the destruction of another, although they generate, they increase not; and must not be said to multiply, who do not transcend an unity. Brown.

> *Man is to beget*
> *Like of his like; his image multiply'd:*
> *In unity defective; which requires*
> *Collateral love, and dearest amity.*
> Milton's Par. Lost.

Whatever we can consider as one thing, suggests to the understanding the idea of unity. Locke.

2. Concord; conjunction.

> *That which you hear, you'll swear*
> *You see, there is such unity in the proofs.*
> Shakespeare.

We, of all christians, ought to promote unity among ourselves and others. Sprat's Sermons.

3. Agreement; uniformity.

To the avoiding of dissension, it availeth much, that there be amongst them an unity, as well in ceremonies as in doctrine. Hooker, b. iv.

4. Principle of dramatick writing, by which the tenour of the story, and propriety of representation is preserved.[†]

The unities of time, place, and action, are exactly observed. Dryden's Pref. to All for Love.

Although in poetry it be absolutely necessary that the unities of time, place, and action should be thoroughly understood, there is still something more essential, that elevates and astonishes the fancy. Addison.

5. [In law.] Unity of possession is a joint possession of two rights by several titles. For example, I take a lease of land from one upon a certain rent; afterwards I buy the fee-simple. This is an unity of possession, whereby the lease is

extinguished; by reason that I, who had before the occupation only for my rent, am become lord of the same, and am to pay my rent to none. Cowel.

úniverse n.s. [*univers*, Fr. *universum*, Lat.] The general system of things.

> *Creeping mumur, and the poring dark,*
> *Fills the wide vessel of the universe.*
> Shakespeare.

God here sums up all into man; the whole into a part; the universe into an individual. South's Sermons.

> *Father of heav'n!*
> *Whose work call'd out this universe to birth.*
> Prior.

univérsity n.s. [*universitas*, Lat.] A school, where all the arts and faculties are taught and studied.

While I play the good husband at home, my son and servants spend all at the university. Shakesp. Taming of the Shrew.

The universities, especially Aberdeen, flourished under many excellent scholars, and very learned men. Clarendon.

unmánlike, unmánly adj.

1. Unbecoming a human being.

It is strange to see the unmanlike cruelty of mankind, who, not content with their tyrannous ambition, to have brought the others virtuous patience under them, think their masterhood nothing, without doing injury to them. Sidney.

Where the act is unmanly, or the expectation contradictious to the attributes of God, our hopes we ought never to entertain. Collier against Despair.

2. Unsuitable to a man; effeminate.

By the greatness of the cry, it was the voice of man; though it were a very unmanlike voice, so to cry. Sidney.

> *New customs,*
> *Though never so ridiculous,*
> *Nay, let them be unmanly, yet are follow'd.*
> Shakespeare.

This is in thee a nature but affected;
A poor unmanly melancholy, sprung
From change of fortune. Shakesp.
Timon of Athens.

My servitude, ignoble,
Unmanly, ignominious, infamous. Milton's
Agonistes.

Think not thy friend can ever feel the soft
Unmanly warmth, and tenderness of love.
Addison.

Unmanly dread invades the French astony'd,
And streight their useless arms they quit.
Philips.

unórthodox adj. Not holding pure doctrine.

A fat benefice became a crime against its
incumbent; and he was sure to be unorthodox,
that was worth the plundering. Decay
of Piety.

to unphilósophize v.a. To degrade from the
character of a philosopher. A word made by
Pope.

Our passions, our interests flow in upon us,
and unphilosophize us into mere mortals.
Pope.

urbánity n.s. [*urbanité,* Fr. *urbanitas,* Lat.]
Civility; elegance; politeness; merriment;
facetiousness.

A rustical severity banishes all urbanity,
whose harmless condition is consistent with
religion. Brown's Vulg. Errours.

Raillery is the sauce of civil entertainment;
and without some such tincture of urbanity,
good humour falters. L'Estr.

Moral doctrine, and urbanity, or well-
mannered wit, constitute the Roman satire.
Dryden.

úrim n.s. Urim and thummim were
something in Aaron's breastplate; but what,
criticks and commentators are by no means
agreed. The word urim signifies light, and
thummim perfection. It is most probable
that they were only names given to signify
the clearness and certainty of the divine
answers which were obtained by the high
priest consulting God with his breast-plate

on, in contradistinction to the obscure,
enigmatical, uncertain, and imperfect
answers of the heathen oracles. Newton's
Notes on Milton.

He in cœlestial panoply, all arm'd
Of radiant urim, work divinely wrought.
Milton.

úrinal n.s. [*urinal,* Fr. from *urine.*] A bottle,
in which water is kept for inspection.

These follies shine through you, like the water
in an urinal. Shakespeare's Two Gentlemen
of Verona.

A candle out of a musket will pierce through
an inch board, or an urinal force a nail
though a plank. Brown.

This hand, when glory calls,
Can brandish arms, as well as urinals.
Garth.

Some with scymitars in their hands,
and others with urinals, ran to and fro.
Spectator, Nº 159.

urinátor n.s. [*urinateur,* Fr. *urinator,* Lat.]
A diver; one who searches under water.

The precious things that grow there, as pearl,
may be much more easily fetched up by the
help of this, than by any other way of the
urinators. Wilkins's Math. Magic.

Those relations of urinators belong only to
those places where they have dived, which
are always rocky. Ray.

úsage n.s. [*usage,* Fr.]

1. Treatment.

Which way
Might'st thou deserve, or they impose this usage,
Coming from us? Shakesp. K. Lear.

The lustre in your eye, heav'n in your check,
Plead you fair usage. Shakesp. Troil. and
Cressida.

My brother
Is prisoner to the bishop, at whose hands
He hath good usage, and great liberty.
Shakesp. Hen. VI.

What usage have I met with from this
adversary, who passes by the very words

I translated, and produces other passages; and then hectors and cries out of my disingenuity. Stil.

Are not hawks brought to the hand, and to the lure; and lions reclaimed by good usage? L'Estrange.

Neptune took unkindly to be bound,
And Eurus never such hard usage found
In his Æolian prison. Dryden.

2. Custom; practice long continued.

Of things once received and confirmed by use, long usage is a law sufficient. In civil affairs, when there is no other law, custom itself doth stand for law. Hooker, b. ii.

3. Manners; behaviour. Obsolete.

A gentle nymph was found,
Hight Astery, excelling all the crew,
In courteous usage, and unstained hue.
Spenser.

usquebáugh n.s. [An Irish and Erse word, which signifies the water of life.] It is a compounded distilled spirit, being drawn on aromaticks; and the Irish sort is particularly distinguished for its pleasant and mild flavour. The Highland sort is somewhat hotter; and, by corruption, in Scottish they call it whisky.

ústion n.s. [*ustion*, Fr. *ustus*, Lat.] The act of burning; the state of being burned.

usufrúct n.s. [*usufruit*, Fr. *usus* and *fructus*, Lat.] The temporary use; enjoyment of the profits, without power to alienate.

The persons receiving the same, have only the usufruct thereof, and not any fee or inheritance therein. Ayliffe.

úsury [*usuré*, Fr. *usura*, Lat.]

1. Money paid for the use of money; interest.

He that high does sit, and all things see,
With equal eyes, their merits to restore;
Behold, what ye this day have done for me,
And what I cannot quit, requite with usury.
Fairy Queen.

The wished day is come at last,
That shall, for all the pains and sorrows past,
Pay to her usury of long delight. Spenser.

Our angles are like money put to usury; they may thrive, though we sit still and do nothing. Walton's Angler.

What he borrows from the antients, he repays with usury of his own; in coin as good, and almost as universally valuable. Dryden's Dedication to Juvenal.

2. The practice of taking interest. It is commonly used with some reproach.

Usury bringeth the treasure of a realm into few hands: for the usurer being at certainties, and others at uncertainties, at the end, most of the money will be in the box. Bacon.

útis n.s. A word which probably is corrupted, at least, is not now understood.[†]

Then here will be old utis: it will be an excellent stratagem. Shakespeare's Hen. IV.

uvúla n.s. [*uvula*, Lat.] In anatomy, a round soft spongeous body, suspended from the palate near the foramina of the nostrils over the glottis. Dict.

By an instrument bended up at one end, I got up behind the uvula. Wiseman's Surgery.

uxórious adj. [*uxorius*, Lat.] Submissively fond of a wife; infected with connubial dotage.

Towards his queen he was nothing uxorious, nor scarce indulgent; but companionable and respective. Bacon.

That uxorious king, whose heart, though large,
Beguil'd by fair idolatresses, fell
To idols foul. Milton's Paradise Lost.

How would'st thou insult,
When I must live uxorious to thy will
In perfect thraldom, how again betray me?
Milton.

vacátion n.s. [*vacation*, Fr. *vacatio*, Latin.]

1. Intermission of juridical proceedings, or any other stated employments; recess of courts or senates.

Vacation is all that time which passes between term and term, at London. Cowel.

As these clerks want not their full task of labour during the open term, so there is for them whereupon to be occupied in the vacation only. Bacon Off. of Alienat.

2. Leisure; freedom from trouble or perplexity.

Benefit of peace, quiet, and vacation for piety, have rendered it necessary in every christian commonwealth, by laws to secure propriety. Hammond's Fundamentals.

vacúity n.s. [*vacuitas*, from *vacuus*, Lat. *vacuité*, Fr.]

1. Emptiness; state of being unfilled.

Hunger is such a state of vacuity, as to require a fresh supply of aliment. Arbuthnot.

2. Space unfilled; space unoccupied.

In filling up vacuities, turning out shadows and ceremonies, by explicit prescription of substantial duties, which those shadows did obscurely represent. Hammond's Fund.

*He, that seat soon failing, meets
A vast vacuity.* Milton.

Body and space are quite different things, and a vacuity is interspersed among the particles of matter. Bentley.

God, who alone can answer all our longings, and fill every vacuity of our soul, should intirely possess our heart. Rogers.

3. Inanity; want of reality.

The soul is seen, like other things, in the mirror of its effects: but if they'll run behind the glass to catch at it, their expectations will meet with vacuity and emptiness. Glanv.

vágrant n.s. [*vagant*, Fr.] A sturdy beggar; wanderer; vagabond; man unsettled in habitation. In an ill sense.

Vagrants and outlaws shall offend thy view, Train'd to assault, and disciplin'd to kill. Prior.

You'll not the progress of your atoms stay, Nor to collect the vagrants find a way. Blackmore.

To relieve the helpless poor; to make sturdy vagrants relieve themselves; to hinder idle hands from being mischievous, are things of evident use. F. Atterbury.

*Ye vagrants of the sky,
To right or left, unheeded, take your way.* Pope.

valedíction n.s. [*valedico*, Lat.] A farewel. Ainsw.

A valediction forbidding to weep. Donne.

válentine n.s. A sweetheart, chosen on Valentine's day.

*Now all nature seem'd in love,
And birds had drawn their valentines.* Wotton.

válet n.s. [*valet*, French.] A waiting servant.

Giving cast-clothes to be worn by valets, has a very ill effect upon little minds. Addison.

valetudinárian,   valetúdinary   adj. [*valetudinaire*, Fr. *valetudo*, Lat.] Weakly; sickly; infirm of health.

Physic, by purging noxious humours, prevents sickness in the healthy, or recourse thereof in the valetudinary. Browne.

Shifting from the warmer vallies, to the colder hills, or from the hills to the vales, is a great benefit to the valetudinarian, feeble part of mankind. Derham.

Cold of winter, by stopping the pores of perspiration, keeps the warmth more within; whereby there is a greater quantity of spirits generated in healthful animals, for the case is quite otherwise in valetudinary ones. Cheyne's Phil. Prin.

Valetudinarians must live where they can command and scold. Swift.

to vamp v.a. [This is supposed probably enough by Skinner to be derived from *avant*, Fr. *before;* and to mean laying on a new outside.] To piece an old thing with some new part.

*You wish
To vamp a body with a dangerous physick,
That's sure of death without.* Shakesp. Coriolanus.

This opinion hath been vamped up by Cardan. Bentley.

I had never much hopes of your vampt play. Swift.

vanílla n.s. [*vanille*, French.] A plant. It hath an anomalous flower, consisting of six leaves, five of which are placed in a circular order, and the middle one is concave: the empalement becomes an horned, soft, fleshy fruit, filled with very small seeds. The fruit of those plants is used to scent chocolate. Miller.

When mixed with vanillios, or spices, it acquires the good and bad qualities of aromatic oils. Arbuthnot on Aliments.

vánity n.s. [*vanitas*, Lat. *vanité*, Fr.]

1. Emptiness; uncertainty; inanity.

2. Fruitless desire; fruitless endeavour.

Vanity possesseth many, who are desirous to know the certainty of things to come. Sidney.

   Thy pride,
And wand'ring vanity, when least was safe,
Rejected my forewarning. Milton.

3. Trifling labour.

To use long discourse against those things which are both against scripture and reason, might rightly be judged a vanity in the answerer, not much inferior to that of the inventor. Raleigh's Hist. of the World.

4. Falshood; untruth.

Here I may well shew the vanity of that which is reported in the story of Walsingham. Sir J. Davies.

5. Empty pleasure; vain pursuit; idle shew; unsubstantial enjoyment; petty object of pride.

Were it not strange if God should have made such store of glorious creatures on earth, and leave them all to be consumed in secular vanity, allowing none but the baser sort to be employed in his own service. Hooker.

   I must
Bestow upon the eyes of this young couple
Some vanity of mine art. Shakespeare's Tempest.

Cast not her serious wit on idle things;
Make her free will slave to vanity. Davies.

Sin, with vanity, had fill'd the works of men. Milton.

The eldest equal the youngest in the vanity of their dress; and no other reason can be given of it, but that they equal, if not surpass them, in the vanity of their desires. South.

Think not when woman's transient breath is fled,
That all her vanities at once are dead;
Succeeding vanities she still regards,
And though she plays no more, o'erlooks
   the cards. Pope.

6. Ostentation; arrogance.

The ground-work thereof is true, however they, through vanity, whilst they would not seem to be ignorant, do thereupon build many forged histories of their own antiquity. Spenser.

Whether it were out of the same vanity, which possessed all those learned philosophers and poets, that Plato also published, not under the right authors names, those things which he had read in the scriptures; or fearing the severity of the Areopagite, and the example of his master Socrates, I cannot judge. Raleigh's Hist. of the World.

7. Petty pride; pride exerted upon slight grounds; pride operating on small occasions.

Can you add guilt to vanity, and take
A pride to hear the conquests which you make. Dryden.

'Tis an old maxim in the schools,
That vanity's the food of fools;
Yet now and then your men of wit
Will condescend to take a bit. Swift's Miscel.

vápour n.s. [*vapeur*, Fr. *vapor*, Latin.]

1. Any thing exhalable; any thing that mingles with the air.

Vapour, and mist, and exhalation hot. Milton.

When first the sun too pow'rful beams displays,
It draws up vapours which obscure its rays:
But ev'n those clouds at last adorn its way,

Reflect new glories, and augment the day.
Pope.

2. Wind; flatulence.

In the Thessalian witches, and the meetings of witches that have been recorded, great wonders they tell, of carrying in the air, transforming themselves into other bodies. These fables are the effects of imagination: for ointments, if laid on any thing thick, by stopping of the pores, shut in the vapours, and send them to the head extremely. Bacon.

3. Fume; steam.

The morning is the best, because the imagination is not clouded by the vapours of meat. Dryden.

In distilling hot spirits, if the head of the still be taken off, the vapour which ascends out of the still will take fire at the flame of a candle, and the flame will run along the vapour from the candle to the still. Newton's Optics.

For the imposthume, the vapour of vinegar, and any thing which creates a cough, are proper. Arbuthnot on Diet.

4. Mental fume; vain imagination; fancy unreal.

If his sorrow bring forth amendment, he hath the grace of hope, though it be clouded over with a melancholy vapour, that it be not discernible even to himself. Hammond.

5. [In the plural.] Diseases caused by flatulence, or by diseased nerves; hypochondriacal maladies; melancholy; spleen.

To this we must ascribe the spleen, so frequent in studious men, as well as the vapours to which the other sex are so often subject. Addison's Spectator, Nº 115.

to váriegate v.a. [*variegatus*, school Latin.] To diversify; to stain with different colours.

The shells are filled with a white spar, which variegates and adds to the beauty of the stone. Woodward on Fossils.

They had fountains of variegated marble in their rooms. Arb.

Ladies like variegated tulips show;
'Tis to the changes half the charms we owe:
Such happy spots the nice admirers take,
Fine by defect, and delicately weak.
Pope's Epist.

varíety n.s. [*varieté*, Fr. *varietas*, Latin.]

1. Change; succession of one thing to another; intermixture of one thing with another.

All sorts are here that all th' earth yields;
Variety without end. Milton's Par. Lost.

Variety is nothing else but a continued novelty. South.

If the sun's light consisted of but one sort of rays, there would be but one colour in the whole world, nor would it be possible to produce any new colour by reflections or refractions; and by consequence that the variety of colours depends upon the composition of light. Newton's Opticks.

2. One thing of many by which variety is made. In this sense it has a plural.

The inclosed warmth, which the earth hath in itself, stirred up by the heat of the sun, assisteth nature in the speedier procreation of those varieties, which the earth bringeth forth. Raleigh's Hist. of the World.

3. Difference; dissimilitude.

There is a variety in the tempers of good men, with relation to the different impressions they receive from different objects of charity. F. Atterbury.

4. Variation; deviation; change from a former state.

It were a great vanity to reject those reasons drawn from the nature of things, or to go about to answer those reasons by suppositions of a variety in things, from what they now appear. Hale's Origin. of Mankind.

várvels n.s. [*vervelles*, Fr.] Silver rings about the leg of a hawk, on which the owner's name is engraved. Dict.

vastídity n.s. [*vastitas*, Lat. from *vasty*.] Wideness; immensity. A barbarous word.

Perpetual durance,
Through all the world's vastidity.
Shakespeare.

váticide n.s. [*vates* and *cædo*, Latin.] A
murderer of poets.

The caitiff vaticide conceiv'd a prayer.
Pope's Dunciad.

váudevil n.s. [*vaudeville*, Fr.] A song
common among the vulgar, and sung about
the streets. Trev. A ballad; a trivial strain.

váulty adj. [from *vault*.] Arched; concave.
A bad word.

I will kiss thy detestable bones,
And put my eye-balls in thy vaulty brows,
And ring these fingers with thy houshold
    worms. Shakesp.

I'll say that is not the lark, whose notes do beat
The vaulty heav'ns so high above our heads.
Shakesp.

to vaunt v.n.

1. To play the braggart; to talk with
   ostentation; to make vain show;
   to boast.

   You say, you are a better soldier;
Let it appear so; make your vaunting true.
Shakesp.

The illusions of magick were put down, and
their vaunting in wisdom reproved with
disgrace. Wisdom xvii. 7.

So spake th' apostate angel, though in pain;
Vaunting aloud, but rack'd with deep despair.
Milton.

Pride which prompts a man to vaunt and
overvalue what he is, does incline him to
disvalue what he has. Gov. of Tongue.

2. I scarcely know in what sense Dryden
   has used this word, unless it be
   miswritten for vaults.

'Tis he: I feel him now in ev'ry part;
Like a new world he vaunts about my heart.
Dryden.

vávasour n.s. [*vavasseur*, Fr.] One who
himself holding of a superior lord, has
others holding under him.

Names have been taken of civil honours, as
king, knight, valvasor, or vavasor, squire.
Camden.

végetable n.s. [*vegetabilis*, school Lat.
vegetabile, Fr.] Any thing that has growth
without sensation, as plants.

Vegetables are organized bodies consisting of
various parts, containing vessels furnished
with different juices; and taking in their
nourishment from without, usually by means
of a root, by which they are fixed to the earth,
or to some other body, as in the generality
of plants; sometimes by means of pores
distributed over the whole surface, as in
sub-marine plants. Hill's Materia Medica.

Let brutes and vegetables that cannot drink,
So far as drought and nature urges, think.
Waller.

In vegetables it is the shape, and in bodies, not
propagated by seed, it is the colour we most fix
on. Locke.

Other animated substances are called
vegetables, which have within themselves the
principle of another sort of life and growth,
and of various productions of leaves, flowers
and fruit, such as we see in plants, herbs, trees.
Watts.

velléity n.s. [*velleïté*, Fr. *velleitas*, from *velle*,
Latin.] Velleity is the school-term used to
signify the lowest degree of desire. Locke.

The wishing of a thing is not properly the
willing of it; but it is that which is called
by the schools an imperfect velleity, and
imports no more than an idle, un-operative
complacency in, and desire of the end, without
any consideration of the means. South.

to véllicate v.a. [*vellico*, Latin.] To twitch;
to pluck; to act by stimulation.

Those smells are all strong, and do pull and
vellicate the sense. Bacon.

Convulsions arising from something
vellicating a nerve in its extremity, are
not very dangerous. Arbuthnot.

véllum n.s. [*velin*, Fr. *velamen*, Latin; rather
vitulinum, low Latin.] The skin of a calf
dressed for the writer.

The skull was very thin, yielding to the least pressure of my finger, as a piece of vellum. Wiseman.

venéreal adj. [*venereus*, Latin.]

1. Relating to love.

These are no venereal signs;
Vengeance is in my heart, death in my hand.
Shakes.

Then swol'n with pride, into the snare I fell,
Of fair fallacious looks, venereal trains,
Soften'd with pleasure and voluptuous life.
Milton.

They are averse to venereal pleasure.
Addison.

2. Consisting of copper, called venus by chemists.

Blue vitriol, how venereal and unsophisticated soever, rubbed upon the whetted blade of a knife, will not impart its latent colour. Boyle.

veneficiously adv. [from *veneficium*, Latin.] By poison or witchcraft.

Lest witches should draw or prick their names therein, and veneficiously mischief their persons, they broke the shell. Brown's Vulgar Errours.

veneséction n.s. [*vena* and *sectio*, Latin.] Blood-letting; the act of opening a vein; phlebotomy.

If the inflammation be sudden, after evacuation by lenient purgatives, or a clyster and venesection, have recourse to anodynes. Wiseman's Surgery.

ventríloquist n.s. [*ventriloque*, Fr. *venter* and *loquor*, Lat.] One who speaks in such a manner as that the sound seems to issue from his belly.

verb n.s. [*verbe*, Fr. *verbum*, Lat.] A part of speech signifying existence, or some modification thereof, as action, passion. And withal some disposition or intention of the mind relating thereto, as of affirming, denying, interrogating, commanding. Clarke's Latin Grammar.

Men usually talk of a noun and a verb. Shakes.

vérbal adj. [*verbal*, Fr. *verbalis*, Latin.]

1. Spoken, not written.

2. Oral; uttered by mouth.

Made she no verbal quest?—
—Yes; once or twice she heav'd the name of father
Pantingly forth, as if it prest her heart.
Shakespeare.

3. Consisting in mere words.

If young African for fame,
His wasted country freed from Punick rage,
The deed becomes unprais'd, the man at least;
And loses, though but verbal, his reward.
Milton.

Being at first out of the way to science, in the progress of their inquiries they must lose themselves, and the truth, in a verbal labyrinth. Glanville.

It was such a denial or confession of him as would appear in preaching: but this is managed in words and verbal profession. South.

4. Verbose; full of words. Out of use.

I am sorry
You put me to forget a lady's manners,
By being so verbal. Shakesp.

5. Minutely exact in words.

6. Literal, having word answering to word.

Neglect the rules each verbal critick lays,
For not to know some trifles is a praise. Pope.

Whosoever offers at verbal translation, shall have the misfortune of that young traveller, who lost his own language abroad, and brought home no other instead of it. Denham.

The verbal copier is incumber'd with so many difficulties at once, that he can never disentangle himself from all. Dryden.

7. [*verbal*, Fr. in grammar.] A verbal noun is a noun derived from a verb.

verecúnd adj. [*verecond*, old French; *verecundus*, Latin.] Modest; bashful. Dict.

verídical adj [*veridicus*, Latin.] Telling truth. Dict.

vermicélli n.s. [Italian.] A paste rolled and broken in the form of worms.

With oysters, eggs, and vermicelli,
She let him almost burst his belly. Prior.

vermiculátion n.s. [from *vermiculate.*] Continuation of motion from one part to another.

My heart moves naturally by the motion
of palpitation; my guts by the motion of
vermiculation. Hale.

vermículous adj. [*vermiculosus*, Lat.] Full of grubs.

vérmiform adj. [*vermiforme*, Fr. *vermis* and *formo*, Lat.] Having the shape of a worm.

vernácular adj. [*vernaculus*, Latin.] Native; of one's own country.

London weekly bills number deep in
consumptions; the same likewise proving
inseparable accidents to most other diseases;
which instances do evidently bring a
consumption under the notion of a vernacular
disease to England. Harvey.

The histories of all our former wars are
transmitted to us in our vernacular idiom.
I do not find in any of our chronicles, that
Edward the third ever reconnoiter'd the
enemy, though he often discovered the posture
of the French, and as often vanquished them.
Addison.

verse n.s. [*vers*, Fr. *versus*, Latin.]

1. A line consisting of a certain succession of sounds, and number of syllables.

Thou hast by moonlight at her window sung,
With feigning voice, verses of feigning love.
Shakesp.

2. [*verset*, Fr.] A section or paragraph of a book.

Thus far the questions proceed upon the
construction of the first earth; in the following
verses they proceed upon the demolition of that
earth. Burnet.

3. Poetry; lays; metrical language.

Verse embalms virtue: and tombs and thrones
of rhymes
Preserve frail transitory fame as much
As spice doth body from air's corrupt touch.
Donne.

If envious eyes their hurtful rays have cast,
More pow'rful verse shall free thee from the
blast. Dryden.

Whilst she did her various pow'r dispose;
Virtue was taught in verse, and Athens' glory
rose. Prior.

You compose
In splay-foot verse, or hobbling prose. Prior.

4. A piece of poetry.

Let this verse, my friend, be thine. Pope.

to be vérsed v.n. [*versor*, Lat.] To be skilled in; to be acquainted with.

She might be ignorant of their nations, who
was not versed in their names, as not being
present at the general survey of animals,
when Adam assigned unto every one a name
concordant unto its nature. Brown's
Vulgar Errours.

This, vers'd in death, th' infernal knight relates,
And then for proof fulfill'd their common fates.
Dryden.

vérsicle n.s. [*versiculus*, Lat.] A little verse.

versificátion n.s. [*versification*, Fr. from *versify.*] The art or practice of making verses.

Donne alone had your talent, but was not
happy to arrive at your versification.
Dryden.

Some object to his versification; which is
in poetry, what colouring is in painting, a
beautiful ornament. But if the proportions are
just, though the colours should happen to be
rough, the piece may be of inestimable value.
Granville.

vert n.s. [*vert*, Fr.] Vert, in the laws of the forest, signifies every thing that grows, and bears a green leaf within the forest, that may cover and hide a deer. Cowel.

I find no mention in all the records of Ireland,
of a park or free warren, notwithstanding
the great plenty of vert and venison.
Sir J. Davies.

vésper n.s. [Latin.] The evening star; the evening.

These signs are black Vesper's pageants.
Shakesp.

véspers n.s. [without the singular, from *vesperus*, Latin.] The evening service of the Romish church.

veterinárian n.s. [*veterinarius*, Lat.] One skilled in the diseases of cattle.

That a horse has no gall, is not only
swallowed by common farriers, but also
receiv'd by good veterinarians, and some who
have laudably discoursed upon horses. Brown.

víand n.s. [*viande*, Fr. *vivanda*, Ital.] Food; meat dressed.

The belly only like a gulf remain'd,
I' th' midst of the body idle and unactive,
Still cupboarding the viand. Shakesp.

No matter, since
They've left their viands behind, for
we have stomachs.
Wilt please you taste of what is here?
Shakesp.

These are not fruits forbidden; no interdict
Defends the touching of these viands pure;
Their taste no knowledge works, at least of
evil. Milton.

From some sorts of food less pleasant to the
taste, persons in health, and in no necessity of
using such viands, had better to abstain. Ray.

The tables in fair order spread;
Viands of various kinds allure the taste,
Of choicest sort and savour; rich repast! Pope.

viáticum n.s. [Latin.]

1. Provision for a journey.

2. The last rites used to prepare the passing soul for its departure.

vice n.s. [*vitium*, Latin.]

1. The course of action opposite to virtue; depravity of manners; inordinate life.

No spirit more gross to love
Vice for itself. Milton.

The foundation of error will lie in wrong
measures of probability; as the foundation of
vice in wrong measures of good. Locke.

2. A fault; an offence. It is generally used for an habitual fault, not for a single enormity.

No vice, so simple, but assumes
Some mark of virtue on its outward parts.
Shakesp.

Yet my poor country
Shall have more vices than it had before;
More suffer by him that shall succeed.
Shakesp.

Ungovern'd appetite, a brutish vice. Milton.

I cannot blame him for inveighing so sharply
against the vices of the clergy in his age.
Dryden.

3. The fool, or punchinello of old shows.

I'll be with you again
In a trice, like to the old vice,
Your need to sustain;
Who with dagger of lath, in his rage
and his wrath,
Cries, ah, ha! to the devil. Shakespeare.

His face made of brass, like a vice in a game.
Tusser.

4. [*Vijs*, Dutch.] A kind of small iron press with screws, used by workmen.

He found that marbles taught him percussion;
bottle-screws, the vice; whirligigs, the axis in
peritrochio. Arbuth. and Pope.

5. Gripe; grasp.

If I but fist him once; if he come but within
my vice. Shakespeare.

6. [*Vice*, Latin.] It is used in composition for one, *qui vicem gerit*, who performs, in his stead, the office of a superiour, or who has the second rank in command: as a viceroy; vice-chancellor.

vícenary adj. [*vicenarius*, Lat.] Belonging to twenty. Bailey.

vidúity n.s. [from *viduus*, Lat.] Widowhood.

vigesimátion n.s. [*vegesimus*, Latin.] The act of putting to death every twentieth man. Bailey.

vine n.s. [*vinea*, Latin.] The plant that bears the grape.

The flower consists of many leaves placed in a regular order, and expanding in form of a rose: the ovary, which is situated in the bottom of the flower, becomes a round fruit, full of juice, and contains many small stones in each. The tree is climbing, sending forth claspers at the joints, by which it fastens itself to what plant stands near it, and the fruit is produced in bunches. The species are, 1. The wild vine, commonly called the claret grape. 2. The July grape. 3. The Corinth grape, vulgarly called the currant grape. 4. The parsley leav'd grape. 5. The miller's grape. This is called the Burgundy in England: the leaves of this sort are very much powdered with white in the spring, from whence it had the name of miller's grape. 6. Is what is called in Burgundy Pineau, and at Orleans, Auverna: it makes very good wine. 7. The white chasselas, or royal muscadine: it is a large white grape; the juice is very rich. 8. The black chasselas, or black muscadine; the juice is very rich. 9. The red chasselas, or red muscadine. 10. The burlake grape. 11. The white mustat, or white Frontiniac. 12. The red Frontiniac. 13. The black Frontiniac. 14. The damask grape. 15. The white sweet water. 16. The black sweet water. 17. The white muscadine. 18. The raisin grape. 19. The Greek grape. 20. The pearl grape. 21. The St. Peter's grape, or hesperian. 22. The malmsey grape. 23. The malmsey muscadine. 24. The red Hamburgh grape. 25. The black Hamburgh, or warmer grape. 26. The Switzerland grape. 27. The white muscat, or Frontiniac of Alexandria; called also the Jerusalem muscat and gross muscat. 28. The red muscat, or Frontiniac of Alexandria. 29. The white melie grape. 30. The white morillon. 31. The Alicant grape. 32. The white Auvernat. 33. The grey Auvernat. 34. The raisin muscat. The late duke of Tuscany, who was very curious in collecting all the sorts of Italian and Greek grapes into his vineyards, was possessed of upwards of three hundred several varieties. Miller.

The vine-prop elm, the poplar never dry. Fairy Queen.

In her days every man shall eat in safety, Under his own vine, what he plants. Shakes.

The captain left of the poor to be vine-dressers. 2 Kings xxv.

Depending vines the shelving cavern screen, With purple clusters blushing through the green. Pope.

víol n.s. [*violle*, Fr. *viola*, Ital.] A stringed instrument of musick.

My tongue's use is to me no more, Than an unstringed viol, or a harp. Shakesp.

To strain a string, stop it with the finger, as in the necks of lutes and viols. Bacon.

Loud o'er the rest Cremona's trump doth sound; Me softer airs befit, and softer strings Of lute, or viol, still more apt for mournful things. Milton.

violoncéllo n.s. [Italian.] A stringed instrument of musick.

virágo n.s. [Latin.]

1. A female warriour; a woman with the qualities of a man.

Melpomene represented like a virago or manly lady, with a majestick and grave countenance. Peacham.

To arms! to arms! the fierce virago cries, And swift as lightening to the combat flies. Pope.

2. It is commonly used in detestation for an impudent turbulent woman.

vírgin n.s. [*vierge*, Fr. *virgo*, Lat.]

1. A maid; a woman unacquainted with men.

This aspect of mine hath fear'd the valiant; The best regarded virgins of our clime Have lov'd it too. Shakesp.

Senseless bauble!
Art thou a fœdary for this act, and look'st
So virgin-like without? Shakesp. Cymbeline.

The damsel was very fair, and a virgin.
Gen. xxiv. 16.

Angelo is an adult'rous thief,
An hypocrite, a virgin violator. Shakespeare.

Much less can that have any place,
At which a virgin hides her face. Cowley.

2. A woman not a mother. Unusual.

Likest to Ceres in her prime,
Yet virgin of Proserpina from Jove. Milton.

3. Any thing untouched or unmingled.

Tapers of white wax, commonly called virgin
wax, burn with less smoke than common
yellow wax. Boyle.

I have found virgin earth in the peat-marshes
of Cheshire. Woodward.

Below the upper was a deep bed of sand only,
which I weighed, together with the virgin-
mould. Derham.

4. The sign of the zodiack in which the
sun is in August.

Thence down amain by Leo and the Virgin.
Milton.

virginal n.s. [more usually *virginals*.] A
musical instrument so called, because
commonly used by young ladies.

The musician hath produced two means of
straining strings. The one is stopping them
with the finger, as in the necks of lutes and
viols; the other is the shortness of the string,
as in harps and virginals. Bacon.

virility n.s. [*virilité*, Fr. *virilitas*, Lat. from
virile.]

1. Manhood; character of man.

The lady made generous advances to
the borders of virility. Rambler.

2. Power of procreation.

The great climacterical was past, before they
begat children, or gave any testimony of their
virility; for none begat children before the age
of sixty-five. Brown.

virtue n.s. [*virtus*, Lat.]

1. Moral goodness.

Either I'm mistaken, or there is virtue in that
Falstaff. Shakes.

If there's a power above us,
And that there is, all nature cries aloud
Through all her works, he must delight in virtue,
And that which he delights in must be happy.
Addison.

Virtue only makes our bliss below. Pope.

The character of prince Henry is improved by
Shakespear; and through the veil of his vices
and irregularities, we see a dawn of greatness
and virtue. Shakesp. illustrated.

2. A particular moral excellence.

In Belmont is a lady,
And she is fair, and, fairer than that word,
Of wond'rous virtues. Shakesp. Merchant
of Venice.

Remember all his virtues,
And shew mankind that goodness is your care.
Addison.

3. Medicinal quality.

All blest secrets,
All you unpublish'd virtues of the earth,
Be aidant and remediate. Shakesp. K. Lear.

The virtuous bezoar is taken from the beast
that feedeth upon the mountains; and that
without virtue from those that feed in the
vallies. Bacon.

4. Medicinal efficacy.

An essay writer must practise the chymical
method, and give the virtue of a full draught
in a few drops. Addison.

5. Efficacy; power.

If neither words, nor herbs will do, I'll
try stones; for there's a virtue in them.
L'Estrange.

Where there is a full purpose to please God,
there, what a man can do, shall, by virtue
thereof, be accepted. South.

They are not sure, by virtue of syllogism, that
the conclusion certainly follows from the
premises. Locke.

This they shall attain, partly in virtue of the promise made by God; and partly in virtue of piety. Atterbury.

He used to travel through Greece, by virtue of this fable, which procured him reception in all the towns. Addison.

6. Acting power.

Jesus knowing that virtue had gone out of him, turned him about. Mark v. 30.

7. Secret agency; efficacy, without visible or material action.

She moves the body, which she doth possess;
Yet no part toucheth, but by virtue's touch.
Davies.

8. Bravery; valour.

Trust to thy single virtue; for thy soldiers
Took their discharge. Shakesp. K. Lear.

The conquest of Palestine, with singular virtue they performed, and held that kingdom some few generations. Raleigh.

9. Excellence; that which gives excellence.

In the Greek poets, as also in Plautus, the oeconomy of poems is better observed than in Terence; who thought the sole grace and virtue of their fable, the sticking in of sentences, as ours do the forcing in of jests. B. Johnson.

10. One of the orders of the celestial hierarchy.

Thrones, domination, princedoms, virtues, pow'rs. Milt.

A winged virtue through th' etherial sky,
From orb to orb unwearied dost thou fly.
Tickell.

virtuóso n.s. [Italian.] A man skilled in antique or natural curiosities; a man studious of painting, statuary, or architecture.

Methinks those generous virtuosi dwell in a higher region than other mortals. Glanville.

Virtuoso, the Italians call a man who loves the noble arts, and is a critick in them. And amongst our French painters, the word vertueux *is understood in the same signification.* Dryd.

This building was beheld with admiration by the virtuosi of that time. Tatler, Nº 52.

Showers of rain are now met with in every water-work; and the virtuoso's of France covered a little vault with artificial snow. Addison.

vísion n.s. [*vision*, Fr. *visio*, Latin.]

1. Sight; the faculty of seeing.

Anatomists, when they have taken off from the bottom of the eye that outward and most thick coat called the dura mater, *can then see through the thinner coats, the pictures of objects lively painted thereon. And these pictures, propagated by motion along the fibres of the optick nerves into the brain, are the cause of vision.* Newton's Opticks.

These theorems being admitted into optics, there would be scope enough of handling that science voluminously, after a new manner; not only by teaching those things which tend to the perfection of vision, but also by determining mathematically all kinds of phenomena of colours which could be produced by refractions. Newton's Opticks.

2. The act of seeing.

Vision in the next life is the perfecting of faith in this; or faith here is turned into vision there, as hope into enjoying. Hammond's Pract. Catechism.

3. A supernatural appearance; a spectre; a phantom.

The day seems long, but night is odious;
No sleep, but dreams; no dreams, but visions strange. Sidney.

Last night the very gods shew'd me a vision. Shakesp.

God's mother deigned to appear to me;
And, in a vision, full of majesty,
Will'd me to leave my base vocation.
Shakesp. Hen. VI.

    Him God vouchsaf'd,
To call by vision, from his father's house,
Into a land which he will shew him.
Milton's Par. Lost.

4. A dream; something shewn in a dream. A dream happens to a sleeping, a vision may happen to a waking man. A dream is supposed natural, a vision miraculous; but they are confounded.

His dream returns; his friend appears again:
The murd'rers come; now help, or I am slain!
'Twas but a vision still, and visions are but
*   vain.* Dryden.

The idea of any thing in our mind, no more
proves the existence of that thing, than the
visions of a dream make a true history.
Locke.

visionary, visionist n.s. [*visionaire*, Fr.] One whose imagination is disturbed.

The lovely visionary gave him perpetual
uneasiness. Fem. Quix.

vitious adj. [*vicieux*, Fr. *vitiosus*, Latin.]

1. Corrupt; wicked; opposite to virtuous. It is rather applied to habitual faults, than criminal actions.

*   Make known*
It is no vitious blot, murder, or foulness
That hath depriv'd me of your grace.
Shakesp. K. Lear.

*   Witness th' irreverent son*
Of him who built the ark; who, for the shame
Done to his father, heard his heavy curse,
"Servant of servants," on his vitious race.
Milton.

Wit's what the vitious fear, the virtuous shun;
By fools 'tis hated, and by knaves undone.
Pope.

No troops abroad are so ill disciplin'd as the
English; which cannot well be otherwise,
while the common soldiers have before their
eyes the vitious example of their leaders.
Swift.

2. Corrupt; having physical ill qualities.

When vitious language contends to be high,
it is full of rock, mountain, and pointedness.
B. Johnson.

Here from the vicious air and sickly skies,
A plague did on the dumb creation rise.
Dryden.

vituline adj. [*vitulinus*, Lat.] Belonging to a calf, or to veal. Bailey.

viz. n.s. [This word is *videlicet*, written with a contraction.] To wit; that is. A barbarous form of an unnecessary word.

That which so oft by sundry writers
Has been apply'd t' almost all fighters,
More justly may b' ascrib'd to this,
Than any other warrior, viz.
None ever acted both parts bolder,
Both of a chieftain and a soldier. Hudibras.

The chief of all signs which the Almighty
endued man with, is humane voice, and the
several modifications thereof by the organs of
speech, viz. the letters of the alphabet, form'd
by the several motions of the mouth. Holder.

Let this be done relatively, viz. one thing
greater or stronger, casting the rest behind,
and rendering it less sensible by its opposition.
Dryden's Dufresnoy.

vizier n.s. [properly *Wazir.*] The prime minister of the Turkish empire.

He made him vizier, which is the chief of all
the bassa's. Knolles's Hist. of the Turks.

This grand vizier presuming to invest
The chief imperial city of the west;
With the first charge compell'd in haste to rise,
His treasure, tents and cannon left a prize.
Waller.

vocabulary n.s. [*vocabularium*, Lat. *vocabulaire*, Fr.] A dictionary; a lexicon; a word-book.

Some have delivered the polity of spirits, and
that they stand in awe of conjurations, which
signify nothing, not only in the dictionary of
man, but in the subtiler vocabulary of Satan.
Brown's Vulg. Errours.

Among other books, we should be furnished
with vocabularies and dictionaries of several
sorts. Watts.

vogue n.s. [*vogue*, Fr. from *voguer*, to float, or fly at large.] Fashion; mode.

It is not more absurd to undertake to tell the
name of an unknown person by his looks, than
to vouch a man's saintship from the vogue of
the world. South.

Use may revive the obsoletest words,
And banish those that now are most in vogue.
Roscommon.

What factions th' have, and what they drive at
In publick vogue, or what in private.
Hudibras.

In the vogue of the world, it passes for an
exploit of honour, for kings to run away with
whole countries that they have no pretence to.
L'Estrange.

No periodical writer, who always maintains
his gravity, and does not sometimes sacrifice
to the graces, must expect to keep in vogue for
any time. Addison.

At one time they keep their patients so close
and warm, as almost to stifle them; and all
on a sudden the cold regimen is in vogue.
Baker's Reflections on Learning.

vólant adj. [*volans*, Lat. *volant*, Fr.]

1. Flying; passing through the air.

The volant, or flying automata, are such
mechanical contrivances as have a self-
motion, whereby they are carried aloft in the
air, like birds. Wilkins's Math. Magick.†

2. Nimble; active.

   His volant touch
Instinct through all proportions, low, and high,
Fled, and pursu'd transverse the resonant
   fugue. Milton.

   Blind British bards, with volant touch,
Traverse loquacious strings, whose solemn notes
Provoke to harmless revels. Philips.

vole n.s. [*vole*, Fr.] A deal at cards, that
draws the whole tricks.

Past six, and not a living soul!
I might by this have won a vole. Swift.

volcáno n.s. [Italian, from *Vulcan*.] A
burning mountain.

Navigators tell us there is a burning
mountain in an island, and many volcano's
and fiery hills. Brown.

When the Cyclops o'er their anvils sweat,
From the volcano's gross eruptions rise,
And curling sheets of smoke obscure the skies.
Garth.

Subterraneous minerals ferment, and cause
earthquakes, and cause furious eruptions of
volcano's, and tumble down broken rocks.
Bentley's Sermons.

voluntéer n.s. [*voluntaire*, Fr.] A soldier who
enters into the service of his own accord.

Congreve, and the author of the Relapse,
being the principals in the dispute, I satisfy
them; as for the volunteers, they will find
themselves affected with the misfortune of
their friends. Collier.†

All Asia now was by the ears;
And Gods beat up for volunteers
To Greece and Troy. Prior.

volúptuary n.s. [*voluptuaire*, Fr. *voluptuarius*,
Lat.] A man given up to pleasure and luxury.

Does not the voluptuary understand in all the
liberties of a loose and a lewd conversation,
that he runs the risk of body and soul?
L'Estrange.

The parable was intended against the
voluptuaries; men who liv'd like heathens,
dissolutely, without regarding any of the
restraints of religion. Atterbury.

vówel n.s. [*voyelle*, Fr. *vocalis*, Lat.] A letter
which can be uttered by itself.

I distinguish letters into vowels and
consonants, yet not wholly upon their
reason, that a vowel may be sounded alone,
a consonant not without a vowel; which
will not be found all true; for many of the
consonants may be sounded alone, and some
joined together without a vowel, as bl. st. *and*
as we pronounce the latter syllable of people,
riffle. Holder.

Virgil makes the two vowels meet without an
elision. Broome.

vúlgar adj. [*vulgaire*, Fr. *vulgaris*, Lat.]

1. Plebeian; suiting to the common people;
   practised among the common people.

Men who have passed all their time in low
and vulgar life, cannot have a suitable idea
of the several beauties and blemishes in the
actions of great men. Addison.

2. Mean; low; being of the common rate.

It requiring too great a sagacity for vulgar minds to draw the line between virtue and vice, no wonder if most men attempt not a laborious scrutiny into things themselves, but only take names and words, and so rest in them. South.

Now wasting years my former strength confound,

And added woes have bow'd me to the ground:
Yet by the stubble you may guess the grain,
And mark the ruins of no vulgar man.
Broome.

3. Publick; commonly bruited.

Do you hear aught of a battle toward?—
—Most sure, and vulgar; every one hears
that. Shakesp.

W, is a letter of which the form is not to be found in the alphabets of the learned languages; though it is not improbable that by our *w* is expressed the sound of the Roman *v*, and the Eolick *f*. Both the form and sound are excluded from the languages derived from the Latin.

W is sometimes improperly used in diphthongs as a vowel, for *u, view; strew:* the sound of *w* consonant is uniform.

X is a letter, which, though found in Saxon words, begins no word in the English language.[†]

wag n.s. [*wagian*, Saxon, to cheat.] Any one ludicrously mischievous; a merry droll.

Cupid the wag, that lately conquer'd had
Wise counsellors, stout captains puissant;
And ty'd them fast to lead his triumphs bad,
Glutted with them, now plays with meanest
   things. Sidney.

Was not my lord the verier wag o' th' two?
Shakesp.

   We wink at wags, when they offend,
And spare the boy, in hopes the man may
   mend. Dryden.

A counsellor never pleaded without a piece of
packthread in his hand, which he used to twist
about a finger all the while he was speaking:
the wags used to call it the thread of his
discourse. Addison.

to wággle v.n. [*wagghelen*, German.] To waddle; to move from side to side.

The sport Basilius would shew to Zelmane,
was the mounting of his hawk at a heron,
which getting up on his waggling wings with
pain, as though the air next to the earth were
not fit for his great body to fly through, was
now grown to diminish the sight of himself.
Sidney.

Why do you go nodding and waggling so, as
if hip-shot? says the goose to her gosseling.
L'Estrange.

wair n.s. [In carpentry.] A piece of timber two yards long, and a foot broad. Bailey.

wállet n.s. [*weallian*, to travel, Saxon.]

1. A bag, in which the necessaries of a traveller are put; a knapsack.

Having entered into a long gallery, he laid
down his wallet, and spread his carpet, in
order to repose himself upon it. Add.

2. Any thing protuberant and swagging.

Who would believe, that there were
   mountaineers
Dew-lapt like bulls, whose throats had
   hanging at them
Wallets of flesh. Shakespeare.

to wámble v.n. [*wemmelen*, Dutch.] To roll with nausea and sickness. It is used of the stomach.

A covetous man deliberated betwixt the
qualms of a wambling stomach, and an
unsettled mind. L'Estrange.

to want v.a. [*wana*, Saxon.]

1. To be without something fit or necessary.

Want no money, Sir John; you shall want
none. Shakesp.

A man to whom God hath given riches, so
that he wanteth nothing for his soul of all
that he desireth, yet God giveth him not
power to eat thereof. Eccl. vi. 2.

2. To be defective in something.

Smells do most of them want names. Locke.

   Nor can this be,
But by fulfilling that which thou didst want,
Obedience to the law. Milton.

3. To fall short of; not to contain.

   Nor think, though men were none,
That heav'n wou'd want spectators, God
want praise. Milt.

4. To be without; not to have.

By descending from the thrones above,
Those happy places, thou hast deign'd a-while
To want, and honour these. Milton's
Par. Lost.

How loth I am to have recourse to rites
So full of horror, that I once rejoice
I want the use of sight. Dryden and
Lee's Oedipus.

The unhappy never want enemies. Clarissa.

5. To need; to have need of; to lack.

It hath caused a great irregularity in our
calendar, and wants to be reformed, and the
equinox to be rightly computed. Holder.

God, who sees all things intuitively, does not
want helps; he neither stands in need of logick,
nor uses it. Baker.

6. To wish for; to long for.

Down I come, like glist'ring Phæton,
Wanting the manage of unruly jades.
Shakespeare.

The sylvans to their shades retire,
Those very shades and streams new shades
   and streams require,
And want a cooling breeze of wind to fan
   the raging fire. Dry.

What wants my son? for know
My son thou art, and I must call thee so.
Addison's Ovid.

Men who want to get a woman into their
power, seldom scruple the means. Clarissa.

wánton n.s. [This word is derived by
Minshew from *want one*, a man or woman
that wants a companion. This etymology,
however odd, Junius silently adopts.
Skinner, who had more acuteness, cannot
forbear to doubt it, but offers nothing
better.]

1. Lascivious; libidinous; letcherous; lustful.

Thou art froward by nature, enemy to peace,
Lascivious, wanton; more than well beseems
A man of thy profession. Shakesp. Hen. VI.

Entic'd to do him wanton rites. Milton.

2. Licentious; dissolute.

   My plenteous joys,
Wanton in fulness, seek to hide themselves
In drops of sorrow. Shakesp. Macbeth.

Men grown wanton by prosperity,
Study'd new arts of luxury and ease.
Roscommon.

3. Frolicksome; gay; sportive; airy.

As flies to wanton boys, we are to th' gods:
They kill us for their sport. Shakesp. K. Lear.

   Note a wild and wanton herd,
Or race of youthful and unhandled colts,
Fetching mad bounds. Shakesp. Merch.
of Venice.

Time drives the flocks from field to fold;
The flow'rs do fade, and wanton fields
To wayward winter reckoning yields.
Raleigh.

How eagerly ye follow my disgrace,
As if it fed ye; and how sleek and wanton
Y' appear, in every thing may bring my ruin.
Shakespeare.

4. Loose; unrestrained.

How does your tongue grow wanton in
her praise! Addis.

5. Quick, and irregular of motion.

6. Luxuriant; superfluous.

   What we by day lop overgrown,
One night or two, with wanton growth derides,
Tending to wild. Milton.

Women richly gay in gems and wanton dress.
Milton.

7. Not regular; turned fortuitously.

The quaint mazes in the wanton green,
For want of tread are undistinguishable.
Milton.

wántwit n.s. [*want* and *wit*.] A fool; an idiot.

Such a wantwit sadness makes of me,
That I have much ado to know myself.
Shakespeare.

war n.s. [*werre*, old Dutch; *guerre*, Fr.]

1. War may be defined as the exercise of
violence under sovereign command
against withstanders; force, authority,
and resistance being the essential parts
thereof. Violence, limited by authority, is
sufficiently distinguished from robbery,
and the like outrages; yet consisting in
relation towards others, it necessarily
requires a supposition of resistance,
whereby the force of war becomes
different from the violence inflicted upon
slaves or yielding malefactors. Raleigh.[†]

   On, you noblest English,
Whose blood is fetcht from fathers of war
   proof. Shakesp.

After a denunciation or indiction of war,
the war is no more confined to the place of
the quarrel, but left at large. Bacon.

I saw the figure and armour of him, that
headed the peasants in the war upon Bern,
with the several weapons found on his
followers. Addison.

2. The instruments of war, in poetical
language.

The god of love inhabits there,
With all his rage, and dread, and grief, and care;
His complement of stores, and total war.
Prior.

3. Forces; army. Poetically.

On th' embattled ranks the waves return,
And overwhelm the war. Milton's
Par. Lost, b. xii.

4. The profession of arms.

Thine almighty word leapt down from
heaven, as a fierce man of war into the midst
of a land of destruction. Wisdom.

5. Hostility; state of opposition; act of
opposition.

   Duncan's horses
Turn'd wild in nature, broke their stalls,
   flung out,
Contending 'gainst obedience, as they would
Make war with man. Shakespeare's
Macbeth.

wárling n.s. [from *war.*] This word is I believe
only found in the following adage, and seems
to mean, one often quarrelled with.

Better be an old man's darling than a young
man's warling. Camden's Remains.

wárlock, wárluck n.s. [*vardlookr*, Islandick,
a charm; *werlog*, Saxon, an evil spirit. This
etymology was communicated by Mr.
Wise.] A male witch; a wizzard. *Warluck* in
Scotland is applied to a man whom the
vulgar suppose to be conversant with spirits,
as a woman who carries on the same
commerce is called a witch: he is supposed
to have the invulnerable quality which
Dryden mentions, who did not understand
the word.

He was no warluck, as the Scots commonly
call such men, who they say are iron free or
lead free. Dryden.

warm adj. [*warm*, Gothick; *wearm*, Sax.
warm, Dutch.]

1. Not cold, though not hot; heated to
a small degree.

He stretched himself upon the child, and the
flesh of the child waxed warm. 2 Kings iv. 34.

Main ocean flow'd, not idle, but with warm
Prolifick humour, soft'ning all her globe.
Milton.

2. Zealous; ardent.

I never thought myself so warm in any party's
cause as to deserve their money. Pope.

Scaliger in his poetics is very warm against it.
Broome's Notes on the Odyssey.

3. Violent; furious; vehement.

Welcome day-light; we shall have
   warm work on 't:
The Moor will 'gage
His utmost forces on his next assault,
To win a queen and kingdom. Dryden's
Spanish Friar.

4. Busy in action.

I hate the ling'ring summons to attend,
Death all at once would be a nobler end;
Fate is unkind: methinks a general
Should warm, and at the head of armies fall.
Dryden.

5. Fanciful; enthusiastick.

If there be a sober and a wise man, what
difference will there be between his knowledge
and that of the most extravagant fancy in the
world? If there be any difference between
them, the advantage will be on the warm-
headed man's side, as having the more ideas,
and the more lively. Locke.

wássail n.s. [from *wæs hæl*, your health,
Saxon.]

1. A liquour made of apples, sugar, and
ale, anciently much used by English
goodfellows.

2. A drunken bout.

The king doth wake to-night, and takes his rouse,
Keeps wassail, and the swagg'ring upspring
   reels. Shakesp.

wáterman n.s. [*water* and *man.*] A
ferryman; a boatman.

Having blocked up the passage to Greenwich,
they ordered the watermen to let fall their oars
more gently. Dryden.

Bubbles of air working upward from the very
bottom of the lake, the watermen told us that
they are observed always to rise in the same
places. Addison on Italy.

The waterman forlorn, along the shore,
Pensive reclines upon his useless oar. Gay.

wátermelon n.s. A plant. It hath trailing
branches, as the cucumber or melon, and is
distinguished from other cucurbitaceous
plants, by its leaf deeply cut and jagged, and
by its producing uneatable fruit. Miller.

wélaway interj. [This I once believed a
corruption of *weal away*, that is, happiness
is gone: so Junius explained it; but the
Saxon exclamation is *walawa*, woe on woe:
from *welaway*, is formed by corruption
weladay.] Alas.

Harrow now out, and wealaway, he cried,
What dismal day hath sent this cursed light!
Spenser.

Ah, welaway! most noble lords, how can
Your cruel eyes endure so piteous light?
Fairy Queen.

Welaway, the while I was so fond,
To leave the good that I had in hond.
Spenser.

wélkin n.s. [from *wealcan*, to roll, or *welcen*,
clouds, Sax.]

1. The visible regions of the air. Out of
use, except in poetry.

Ne in all the welkin was no cloud. Chaucer.

He leaves the welkin way most beaten plain,
And rapt with whirling wheels inflames
    the skyen,
With fire not made to burn, but fairly for
    to shine. Fa. Qu.

The swallow peeps out of her nest,
And cloudy welkin cleareth. Spenser's
Pastorals.

Spur your proud horses hard, and ride in blood:
Amaze the welkin with your broken staves.
Shak. R. III.

  With feats of arms
From either end of heav'n the welkin burns.
Milton.

Now my task is smoothly done,
I can fly, or I can run
Quickly to the green earth's end,
Where the bow'd welkin slow doth bend.
Milton.

  Their hideous yells
Rend the dark welkin. Philips.

2. Welkin eye, is, I suppose, blue eye;
skycoloured eye.

  Yet were it true
To say this boy were like me! Come, sir page,
Look on me with your welkin eye, sweet
    villain. Shakespeare.

wench n.s. [*wencle*, Saxon.]

1. A young woman.

What do I, silly wench, know what love hath
prepared for me? Sidney, b. ii.

Now—how dost thou look now? Oh ill-
    starr'd wench!
Pale as thy smock! when we shall meet at compt,
This look of thine will hurl my soul from heav'n,
And fiends will snatch at it. Cold, cold, my girl,
Ev'n like thy chastity. Shakesp. Othello.

Thou wouldst perswade her to a worse offence
Than that, whereof thou didst accuse her
    wench. Donne.

2. A young woman in contempt; a strumpet.

But the rude wench her answer'd nought
at all. Spenser.

Do not play in wench-like words with that
Which is so serious. Shakesp. Cymbeline.

Men have these ambitious fancies,
And wanton wenches read romances. Prior.

3. A strumpet.

It is not a digression to talk of bawds in a
discourse upon wenches. Spectator, Nº 266.

whale n.s. [*hwale*, Saxon.] The largest of
fish; the largest of the animals that inhabit
this globe.

God created the great whales. Genesis.

Barr'd up with ribs of whale-bone, she did leese
None of the whale's length, for it reach'd her
    knees. Bp. Corbet.

The greatest whale that swims the sea,
Does instantly my pow'r obey. Swift.

whelp n.s. [*welp*, Dutch; *huolpar*, Islandick; *hwalp*, Swedish.]

1. The young of a dog; a puppy.

They call'd us, for our fierceness, English dogs,
Now, like their whelps, we crying run away.
Shakespeare.

Whelps come to their growth within three
quarters of a year. Bacon's Natural History.

Whelps are blind nine days, and then begin
to see as generally believed; but as we have
elsewhere declared, it is rare that their eye-lids
open until the twelfth day. Brown.

2. The young of any beast of prey.

The lion's whelp shall be to himself unknown.
Shakespeare.

Those unlickt bear whelps. Donne.

3. A son. In contempt.

The young whelp of Talbot's raging brood
Did flesh his puny sword in Frenchmens
blood. Shakespeare.

4. A young man. In contempt.

Slave, I will strike your soul out with my foot,
Let me but find you again with such a face:
You whelp. Ben. Johnson's Catiline.

That aukward whelp, with his money-bags,
would have made his entrance. Addison's
Guardian.

to whérret v.a. [Corrupted, I suppose, from
ferret.]

1. To hurry; to trouble; to teaze. A low
colloquial word.

2. To give a box on the ear. Ainsworth.

whérry n.s. [Of uncertain derivation.]
A light boat used on rivers.

And falling down into a lake,
Which him up to the neck doth take,
His fury somewhat it doth slake,
He calleth for a ferry;
What was his club he made his boat,
And in his oaken cup doth float,
As safe as in a wherry. Drayton's Nymphid.

Let the vessel split on shelves,
With the freight enrich themselves:
Safe within my little wherry,
All their madness makes me merry. Swift.

whig n.s. [*hwæg*, Saxon.]

1. Whey.

2. The name of a faction.[†]

The southwest counties of Scotland have
seldom corn enough to serve them round the
year; and the northern parts producing more
than they need, those in the west come in the
Summer to buy at Leith the stores that come
from the north; and from a word, whiggam,
used in driving their horses, all that drove
were called the whiggamors, *and shorter the*
whiggs. *Now in that year before the news*
came down of duke Hamilton's defeat, the
ministers animated their people to rise and
march to Edinburgh; and they came up
marching on the head of their parishes with
an unheard-of fury, praying and preaching all
the way as they came. The marquis of Argyle
and his party came and headed them, they
being about six thousand. This was called the
whiggamor's inroad; and ever after that, all
that opposed the court came in contempt to be
called whigs: and from Scotland the word was
brought into England, where it is now one of
our unhappy terms of disunion. Burnet.

Whoever has a true value for church and state,
should avoid the extremes of whig for the sake
of the former, and the extremes of tory on the
account of the latter. Swift.

whíggism n.s. [from *whig*.] The notions
of a whig.

I could quote passages from fifty pamphlets,
wholly made up of whiggism and atheism.
Swift.

whíphand n.s. [*whip* and *hand*.] Advantage
over.

The archangel, when discord was restive and
would not be drawn from her beloved
monastry with fair words, has the whiphand
of her, and drags her out with many stripes.
Dryd.

whírligig n.s. [*whirl* and *gig*.] A toy which
children spin round.

He found that marbles taught him percussion,
and whirligigs the axis in peritrochio.
Arbuthn. and Pope's Mart. Scribl.

That since they gave things their beginning,
And set this whirligig a spinning. Prior.

whist n.s. A game at cards, requiring close attention and silence.

The clergyman used to play at whist and swobbers. Swift.

   Whist awhile
Walks his grave round, beneath a cloud of smoke,
Wreath'd fragrant from the pipe. Thomson's Autumn.

whitemeat n.s. [*white* and *meat*.] Food made of milk.

Much saltness in whitemeat is ill for the stone. Tusser.

The Irish banished into the mountains, lived only upon whitemeats. Spenser.

whóreson n.s. [*whore* and *son*.] A bastard. It is generally used in a ludicrous dislike.

Whoreson, mad compound of majesty, thou art welcome. Shakespeare's Henry IV.

Thou whoreson Zed! thou unnecessary letter. Shakespeare.

   How now, you whoreson peasant,
Where have you been these two days loitering? Shakesp.

Frog was a cunning, sly whoreson, quite the reverse of John. Arbuthnot's History of John Bull.

to whurr v.n. To pronounce the letter *r* with too much force. Dict.

widowhúnter n.s. [*widow* and *hunter*.] One who courts widows for a jointure.

The widowhunters about town often afford them great diversion. Addison's Spectator.

wife n.s. Plural wives [*wif*, Saxon; *wiff*, Dutch.]

1. A woman that has a husband.

   Your claim, fair sister,
I bar it in the interest of my wife.
Shakespeare's King Lear.

   There's no bottom, none
In my voluptuousness: your wives,
   your daughters,
Your matrons and your maids could not fill up
The cistern of my lust. Shakespeare's Macbeth.

Why saidst thou, she is my sister? so I might have taken her to me to wife. Gen. xii: 19.

The wife, where danger or dishonour lurks,
Safest and seemliest by her husband stays. Milton.

The wife her husband murders, he the wife. Dryden.

Fond of his friend, and civil to his wife. Pope.

2. It is used for a woman of low employment.

Strawberry wives lay two or three great strawberries at the mouth of their pot, and all the rest are little ones. Bacon.

wight n.s. [*wiht*, Saxon.] A person; a being. Obsolete.

Beshrew the witch! with venomous wights
   she stays,
Tedious as hell; but flies the grasps of love,
With wings more momentary swift than
   thought. Shakesp.

This world below did need one wight,
Which might thereof distinguish ev'ry part. Davies.

This meaner wights, of trust and credit bare,
Not so respected, could not look t' effect. Daniel.

A wight he was, whose very sight wou'd
Entitle him mirror of knighthood. Hudibras.

The water flies all taste of living wight. Milton.

How could'st thou suffer thy devoted knight,
On thy own day, to fall by foe oppress'd,
The wight of all the world who lov'd thee
   best. Dryden.

His station he yielded up to a wight as disagreeable as himself. Addison's Guardian.

will n.s. [*willa*, Saxon; *wille*, Dutch.]

1. Choice; arbitrary determination.

Will is the power, which the mind has to order the consideration of any idea, or the forbearing to consider it, or to prefer the motion of any part of the body to its rest, and vice versa. Locke's Works.

Two principal fountains there are of human actions, knowledge and will; which will, in things tending towards any end, is termed choice. Hooker, b. i.

Is it her nature, or is it her will,
To be so cruel to an humble foe?
If nature, then she may it mend with skill;
If will, then she at will may will forego.
Spenser.

These things have a shew of wisdom in will worship and humility. Col. ii. 23.

Will holds the sceptre in the soul,
And on the passions of the heart doth reign.
Sir J. Dav.

The truth is, such a man understands by his will, and believes a thing true or false, merely as it agrees or disagrees with a violent inclination; and therefore, whilst that inclination lasts in its strength, he discovers nothing of the different degrees of evidence. Atterbury.

2. Discretion; choice.

Go then the guilty at thy will chastize. Pope.

3. Command; direction.

At his first sight the mountains are shaken, and at his will the south wind bloweth. Eccles. xliii. 16.

4. Disposition; inclination; desire.

I make bold to press upon you with
so little preparation.
You're welcome; what's your will?
Shakespeare.

He hath a will, he hath a power to perform. Drummond.

He said, and with so good a will to die,
Did to his breast the fatal point apply,
It found his heart. Dryden.

5. Power; government.

Deliver me not over unto the will of mine enemies. Psal.

He had the will of his maid before he could go; he had the mastery of his parents ever since he could prattle; and why, now he is grown up, must he be restrained? Locke.

6. Divine determination.

I would give a thousand furlongs of sea for an acre of barren ground. The wills above be done; but I would fain die a dry death. Shakespeare.

7. Testament; disposition of a dying man's effects.

Another branch of their revenue still
Remains, beyond their boundless right to kill,
Their father yet alive, impower'd to make
a will. Dryd.

Do men make their last wills by word of mouth only? Stephen's Sermons.

8. Good-will. Favour; kindness.

I'll to the doctor, he hath my good-will,
And none but he to marry with Nan Page.
Shakesp.

9. Good-will. Right intention.

Some preach Christ of envy, and some of good will. Phil. i. 15.

10. Ill-will. Malice; malignity.

11. [Contracted from William.] Will with a wisp, Jack with a lanthorn.

Will with the wisp is of a round figure, in bigness like the flame of a candle; but sometimes broader, and like a bundle of twigs set on fire. It sometimes gives a brighter light than that of a wax-candle; at other times more obscure, and of a purple colour. When viewed near at hand, it shines less than at a distance. They wander about in the air, not far from the surface of the earth; and are more frequent in places that are unctuous, mouldy, marshy, and abounding with reeds. They haunt burying places, places of execution, dunghills. They commonly appear in summer, and at the beginning of autumn, and are generally at the height of about six feet from the ground. Now they dilate themselves, and now contract. Now they go on like waves, and rain as it were sparks of fire; but they burn nothing. *They follow those that run away, and fly from those that follow them. Some that have been catched were observed to consist of a shining, viscous, and gelatinous matter, like the spawn of frogs, not hot or burning, but only shining; so that the matter seems to be phosphorus, prepared and raised from putrified plants or carcasses by the heat of the sun; which is condensed by the cold of the evening, and then shines.* Musch.

Will-a wisp misleads night-faring clowns, O'er hills and sinking bogs. Gay.

wíndward *adv.* [from *wind.*] Towards the wind.†

wiseácre n.s. [It was antiently written *wisesegger*, as the Dutch *wiseggher*, a soothsayer.]

1. A wise, or sententious man. Obsolete.

2. A fool; a dunce.

Why, says a wiseacre that sat by him, were I as the king of France, I would scorn to take part with footmen. Addison.

wísket n.s. A basket. Ainsworth.

wit n.s. [*sgewit*, Saxon; from *witan*, to know.]

1. The powers of the mind; the mental faculties; the intellects. This is the original signification.

Who would set his wit to so foolish a bird? Shakespeare.

The king your father was reputed for A prince most prudent, of an excellent And unmatch'd wit and judgment. Shakesp. Hen. VIII.

Will puts in practice what the wit deviseth: Will ever acts, and wit contemplates still: And as from wit the power of wisdom riseth, All other virtues daughters are of will. Will is the prince, and wit the counsellor, Which doth for common good in council sit; And when wit is resolv'd, will lends her power To execute what is advis'd by wit. Davies's Ireland.

For wit and pow'r, their last endeavours bend T' outshine each other. Dryden.

2. Imagination; quickness of fancy.

They never meet, but there's a skirmish of wit between them.—

—Alas, in our last conflict four of his five wits went halting off, and now is the whole man govern'd by one. Shakesp.

Lewd, shallow, hair-brain'd huffs, make atheism and contempt of religion, the only badge and character of wit. South.

And though a tun in thy large bulk be writ, Yet thou art but a kilderkin of wit. Dryden.

Wit lying most in the assemblage of ideas, and putting those together with quickness and variety, wherein can be found any resemblance, or congruity, thereby to make up pleasant pictures in the fancy. Judgment, on the contrary, lies in separating carefully one from another, ideas, wherein can be found the least difference, thereby to avoid being misled by similitude. Locke.

Cou'd any but a knowing prudent cause Begin such motions, and assign such laws? If the great mind had form'd a different frame, Might not your wanton wit the system blame? Blackmore.

3. Sentiments produced by quickness of fancy.

All sorts of men take a pleasure to gird at me. The brain of this foolish compounded clay, man, is not able to invent any thing that tends more to laughter, than what I invent, and is invented on me. I am not only witty in myself, but the cause that wit is in other men. Shakespeare.

His works become the frippery of wit. B. Johnson.

The Romans made those times the standard of their wit, when they subdu'd the world. Sprat.

The definition of wit is only this; that it is a propriety of thoughts and words; or, in other terms, thoughts and words elegantly adapted to the subject. Dryden.

Let a lord once but own the happy lines; How the wit brightens, and the style refines! Pope.

4. A man of fancy.

Intemperate wits will spare neither friend nor foe; and make themselves the common enemies of mankind. L'Estr.

A poet, being too witty himself, could draw nothing but wits in a comedy: even his fools were infected with the disease of their author. Dryden.

To tell them wou'd a hundred tongues require;
Or one vain wit's, that might a hundred tire. Pope.

5. A man of genius.

Searching wits, of more mechanick parts;
Who grac'd their age with new-invented arts:
Those who to worth their bounty did extend,
And those who knew that bounty to
  commend. Dryden.

How vain that second life in others breath?
Th' estate which wits inherit after death;
Ease, health, and life, for this they must resign,
Unsure the tenure, but how vast the fine!
The great man's curse, without the gain endure;
Be envy'd, wretched; and be flatter'd, poor. Pope.

6. Sense; judgment.

  Strong was their plot,
Their practice close, their faith suspected not;
Their states far off, and they of wary wit. Daniel.

Come, leave the loathed stage,
And this more loathsome age;
Where pride and impudence in faction knit,
Usurp the chair of wit. B. Johnson.

Though his youthful blood be fir'd with wine,
He wants not wit the danger to decline. Dryden.

7. In the plural. Sound mind; intellect not crazed.

If our wits run the wild-goose chace, I have done: for thou hast more of the wild-goose in one of thy wits, than I have in my whole five. Shakesp. Romeo and Juliet.

  I had a son,
Now outlaw'd from my blood; he sought my life:
The grief hath craz'd my wits. Shakesp. K. Lear.

Are his wits safe? is he not light of brain? Shakespeare.

Sound sleep cometh of moderate eating; he riseth early, and his wits are with him: but the pain of watching, and choler, and pangs of the belly, are with an unsatiable man. Ecclus. xxxi. 20.

Wickedness is voluntary frenzy, and every sinner does more extravagant things than any man that is crazed, and out of his wits, only that he knows better what he does. Tillotson.

No man in his wits can seriously think that his own soul hath existed from all eternity. Bentley.

8. Contrivance; stratagem; power of expedients.

How can it chuse but bring the simple to their wits end? how can it chuse but vex and amaze them? Hooker.

I was like to be apprehended for the witch of Brainford; but that my admirable dexterity of wit, counterfeiting the action of an old woman, delivered me. Shakespeare.

Sleights from his wit and subtlety proceed. Milton.

The neighbourhood were at their wits end, to consider what would be the issue. L'Estrange.

witcracker n.s. [*wit* and *cracker*.] A joker; one who breaks a jest.

A college of witcrackers cannot flout me out of my humour; dost thou think I care for a satire or an epigram? Shak.

witling n.s. [Diminutive of *wit*.] A pretender to wit; a man of petty smartness.

You have taken off the senseless ridicule, which for many years the witlings of the town have turned upon their fathers and mothers. Addison's Spectator.

Those half-learn'd witlings num'rous in our isle,
As half-form'd insects on the banks of Nile. Pope.

A beau and witling perish'd in the throng,
One dy'd in metaphor, and one in song. Pope.

witticism n.s. [from *witty*.] A mean attempt at wit.

We have a libertine fooling even in his last agonies, with a witticism between his teeth, without any regard to sobriety and conscience. L'Estrange.

He is full of conceptions, points of epigram and witticisms, all which are below the dignity of heroick verse. Addison.

wittol n.s. [*wittol*, Sax.] A man who knows the falsehood of his wife and seems contented; a tame cuckold.

O Mars, for what doth serve thy armed ax?
To let that witold beast consume in flames
Thy Venus child. Sidney.

Amaimon sounds well; Lucifer well; yet they are the names of fiends: but cuckold, wittol, the devil himself hath not such a name. Shakespeare's Merry Wives of Windsor.

The Theban wittal, when he once descries
Jove is his rival, falls to sacrifice. Cleaveland.

witty adj. [from *wit*.]

1. Judicious; ingenious.

The deep-revolving, witty Buckingham
No more shall be the neighbour to my counsels. Shakesp.

Thou art beautiful in thy countenance, and witty in thy words. Judith xi. 23.

2. Full of imagination.

Histories make men wise, poets witty, the mathematick subtile. Bacon.

Where there is a real stock of wit, yet the wittiest sayings will be found in a great measure the issues of chance. South.

In gentle verse the witty told their flame,
And grac'd their choicest songs with Emma's name. Prior.

3. Sarcastick; full of taunts.

Honeycomb, who was so unmercifully witty upon the women, has given the ladies ample satisfaction by marrying a farmer's daughter. Addison's Spectator.

witworm n.s. [*wit* and *worm*.] One that feeds on wit; a canker of wit.

Thus to come forth so suddenly a witworm. B. Johnson.

wóman [*wifman*, *wimman*, Saxon; whence we yet pronounce women in the plural, *wimmen*, Skinner.]

1. The female of the human race.

That man who hath a tongue is no man,
If with his tongue he cannot win a woman. Shakespeare.

Thou dotard, thou art woman-tir'd, unroosted
By thy dame Parlet here. Shakespeare's Winter's Tale.

Women are soft, mild, pitiful and flexible;
Thou stern, obdurate, flinty, rough,
   remorseless. Shakesp.

And Abimelech took men-servants and women-servants. Gen.

O woman, lovely woman, nature form'd thee
To temper man: we had been brutes without
   thee. Otway.

Ceneus a woman once and once a man;
But ending in the sex she first began. Dryden's Æn.

Women are made as they themselves
   would choose,
Too proud to ask, too humble to refuse. Garth.

Women in their nature are much more gay and joyous than men; whether it be that their blood is more refined, their fibres more delicate, and their animal spirits more light; vivacity is the gift of women, gravity that of men. Addison.

2. A female attendant on a person of rank.

I could not personally deliver to her
What you commanded me; but by her woman
I sent your message. Shakespeare's Henry VIII.

to womaníse v.a. [from *woman*.] To emasculate; to effeminate; to soften. Proper, but not used.

This effeminate love of a woman doth womanize a man. Sid.

wóndrous adj. [This is contracted from *wonderous*, of *wonder*.]

1. Admirable; marvellous; strange; surprising.

The credit of whose virtue rest with thee;
Wondrous indeed, if cause of such effects.
Milton.

In such charities she pass'd the day;
'Twas wond'rous how she found an hour
    to pray. Dryden.

Researches into the springs of natural bodies,
and their motions, should awaken us to
admire the wondrous wisdom of our Creator
in all the works of nature. Watts.

2. [Wondrous is barbarously used for an
    adverb.] In a strange degree.

From that part where Moses remembereth the
giants, begotten by the sons of good men upon
the daughters of the wicked; did they steal
those wondrous great acts of their ancient
kings and powerful giants. Raleigh.

    To shun th' allurement is not hard
To minds resolv'd, forewarn'd and
    well-prepar'd;
But wond'rous difficult, when once beset,
To struggle through the straits, and break th'
    involving net. Dryden.

    You are so beautiful,
So wondrous fair, you justify rebellion.
Dryden.

Sylphs, yet mindful of their ancient race,
Are, as when women, wond'rous fond of place.
Pope.

to wont, to be wont v.n. [Preterite and
participle wont; *wunian*, Saxon; *gewoonen*,
Dutch.] To be accustomed; to use; to be
used.

A yearly solemn feast she wont to make
The day that first doth lead the year around.
Fairy Queen.

Through power of that, his cunning thieveries
He wonts to work, that none the same espies.
Hubberd.

Jason the Thessalian was wont to say, that
some things must be done unjustly, that many
things may be done justly. Bacon.

    I this night have dream'd;
If dream'd, not as I oft am wont, of thee,
But of offence and trouble. Milton's
Paradise Lost.

The eagle's fate and mine are one,
Which on the shaft that made him die
Espy'd a feather of his own,
Wherewith he wont to soar so high. Waller.

A mother was wont always to indulge her
daughters, when any of them desired squirrels
or birds, but then they must keep them well.
Locke.

Another sort of sophism is wont to be called
an imperfect enumeration or false induction,
when from a few experiments men infer
general theorems. Watts's Logick.

wood adj. [*wods*, Gothick; *wod*, Saxon;
woed, Dutch.] Mad; furious; raging.
Obsolete.

Winds do rage, as winds were wood,
And cause spring tides to raise great flood.
Tusser.

Coal-black steeds yborn of hellish brood,
That on their rusty bits did champ as they
    were wood. Fairy Queen.

Calm the tempest of his passion wood;
The banks are overflown, when stopped is
    the flood. Fa. Q.

wóodnote n.s. Wild musick.

Then to the well-trod stage anon,
If Johnson's learned sock be on,
Or sweetest Shakespear, fancy's child,
Warble his native woodnotes wild. Milton.

word n.s. [*word*, Saxon; *woord*, Dutch.]

1. A single part of speech.

If you speak three words, it will three times
report you the three words. Bacon.

As conceptions are the images of things to the
mind within itself, so are words or names the
marks of those conceptions to the minds of
them we converse with. South's Sermons.

Amongst men who confound their ideas
with words, there must be endless disputes,
wrangling, and jargon. Locke.

Each wight who reads not, and but
    scans and spells,
Each word catcher that lives on syllables.
Pope.

2. A short discourse.

*Shall I vouchsafe your worship a word or two?
—Two thousand, and I'll vouchsafe thee the
hearing.* Shak.

   *A word, Lucilius,
How he receiv'd you.* Shakesp. Julius Cæsar.

*A friend who shall own thee in thy lowest
condition, answer all thy wants, and, in
a word, never leave thee.* South.

*In a word, the Gospel describes God to us in
all respects such a one as we would wish him
to be.* Tillotson.

3. Talk; discourse.

*Why should calamity be full of words?
—Windy attorneys to their client woes!
Let them have scope, though what they
   do impart
Help nothing else, yet they do ease the heart.*
Shak. R. III.

   *If you dislike the play,
Pray make no words on 't 'till the second day,
Or third be past; for we would have you know it,
The loss will fall on us, not on the poet.*
Denham.

*Cease this contention: be thy words severe,
Sharp as he merits; but the sword forbear.*
Dryden.

*If words are sometimes to be used, they ought
to be grave, kind, and sober, representing the
ill, or unbecomingness of the faults.* Locke.

*If I appear a little word-bound in my first
solutions, I hope it will be imputed to the long
disuse of speech.* Spectator.

4. Dispute; verbal contention.

   *In argument upon a case,
Some words there grew 'twixt Somerset and
me.* Shakesp.

5. Language.

*Found you no displeasure by word or
countenance?* Shakesp.

*I'll write thee a challenge, or I'll deliver thy
indignation to him by word of mouth.*
Shakes. Twelfth Night.

*He commanded the men to be ranged in
battalions, and rid to every squadron, giving
them such words as were proper to the
occasion.* Clarendon.

*An easy way, by word of mouth
communicated to me.* Boyle.

6. Promise.

*Obey thy parents, keep thy word justly, swear
not.* Shakes.

*I take your princely word for these redresses.
—I give it you, and will maintain my word.*
Shak. H. IV.

*The duke shall wield his conqu'ring sword,
The king shall pass his honest word.* Dryden.

7. Signal; token.

   *Every soldier, kill his prisoners;
Give the word through.* Shak. Henry V.

8. Account; tydings; message.

   *Bring me word thither
How the world goes, that to the pace of it
I may spur on my journey.* Shakesp.
Coriolanus.

*Why should she write to Edmund?
Might not you
Transport her purposes by word?*
Shakesp. King Lear.

   *Two optick nerves she ties,
Like spectacles across the eyes;
By which the spirits bring her word,
Whene'er the balls are fix'd or stirr'd.* Prior.

9. Declaration.

*I know you brave, and take you at your word;
That present service which you vaunt, afford.*
Dryden.

10. Affirmation.

*Every person has enough to do to work out his
own salvation; which, if we will take the
apostle's word, is to be done with fear and
trembling.* Decay of Piety.

*I desire not the reader should take my word,
and therefore I will set two of their discourses
in the same light for every man to judge.*
Dryden.

11. Scripture; word of God.

They say this church of England neither hath the word purely preached, nor the sacraments sincerely ministred. Whitg.

12. The second person of the ever adorable Trinity. A scripture term.

Thou my Word, begotten son, by thee This I perform. Milton.

work n.s. [*weorc*, Saxon; *werk*, Dutch.]

1. Toil; labour; employment.

Bread, correction, and work for a servant. Ecclus. xxxiii.

In the bottom of some mines in Germany there grow vegetables, which the work-folks say have magical virtue. Bac.

The ground, unbid, gives more than we can ask; But work is pleasure, when we chuse our task. Dryden.

2. A state of labour.

All the world is perpetually at work, only that our poor mortal lives should pass the happier for that little time we possess them, or else end the better when we lose them: upon this occasion riches came to be coveted, honours esteemed, friendship pursued, and virtues admired. Temple.

3. Bungling attempt.

It is pleasant to see what work our adversaries make with this innocent canon: sometimes 'tis a mere forgery of hereticks, and sometimes the bishops that met there were not so wise as they should have been. Stillingfleet.

4. Flowers or embroidery of the needle.

Round her work she did empale, With a fair border wrought of sundry flowers, Inwoven with an ivy-winding trail. Spenser.

That handkerchief, you gave me: I must take out the work: a likely piece of work, that you should find it in your chamber, and know not who left it there. This is some minx's token, and I must take out the work? There, give it your hobbyhorse: wheresoever you had it, I'll take out no work on 't. Shakesp. Othello.

5. Any fabrick or compages of art.

Nor was the work impair'd by storms alone, But felt th' approaches of too warm a sun. Pope.

6. Action; feat; deed.

The instrumentalness of riches to works of charity, have rendered it necessary in every Christian commonwealth by laws to secure propriety. Hammond.

As to the composition or dissolution of mixt bodies, which is the chief work of elements, and requires an intire application of the agents, water hath the principality and excess over earth. Digby.

Nothing lovelier can be found in woman, Than good works in her husband to promote. Milton.

While as the works of bloody Mars employ'd, The wanton youth inglorious peace enjoy'd. Pope.

7. Any thing made.

Where is that holy fire, which verse is said To have? Is that enchanting force decay'd? Verse, that draws nature's works from nature's law, Thee, her best work, to her work cannot draw. Donne.

O fairest of creation! last and best Of all God's works! creature, in whom excels Whatever can to sight or thought be form'd; Holy, divine, good, amiable, or sweet, How art thou lost! Milton's Paradise Lost.

8. Management; treatment.

Let him alone; I'll go another way to work with him. Shak.

9. To set on work. To employ; to engage.

It setteth those wits on work in better things, which would be else employed in worse. Hooker.

wórkhouse, wórkinghouse n.s. [from *work* and *house*.]

1. A place in which any manufacture is carried on.

The quick forge and workinghouse of thought. Shak. H. V.

Protogenes had his workhouse in a garden out of town, where he was daily finishing those pieces he begun. Dryden.

2. A place where idlers and vagabonds are condemned to labour.

Hast thou suffered at any time by vagabonds and pilferers? Esteem and promote those useful charities which remove such pests into prisons and workhouses. Atterbury.

wórkyday n.s. [Corrupted from *workingday*.] The day not the sabbath.

Tell her but a workyday fortune. Shakespeare.

The other days, and thou
Make up one man; whose face thou art,
The workydays are the back part;
The burden of the week lies there. Herbert.

Holydays, if haply she were gone,
Like workydays, I wish would soon be done.
Gay.

world n.s. [*world*, Saxon; *wereld*, Dutch.]

1. World is the great collective idea of all bodies whatever. Loc.

2. System of beings.

Begotten before all worlds. Nicene Creed.

God hath in these last days spoken unto us by his son, by whom he made the worlds.
Hebr. i. 2.

 Know how this world
Of heav'n and earth conspicuous first began.
Milton.

3. The earth; the terraqueous globe.

 He the world
Built on circumfluous waters. Milton's Paradise Lost.

4. Present state of existence.

I'm in this earthly world, where to do harm
Is often laudable; to do good sometime
Accounted dangerous folly. Shakesp.
Macbeth.

I was not come into the world then.
L'Estrange.

He wittingly brought evil into the world.
More.

Christian fortitude consists in suffering for the love of God, whatever hardships can befal in the world. Dryden.

5. A secular life.

Happy is she that from the world retires,
And carries with her what the world admires.
Thrice happy she, whose young thoughts
 fixt above,
While she is lovely, does to heav'n make love;
I need not urge your promise, ere you find
An entrance here, to leave the world behind?
Waller.

By the world, we sometimes understand the things of this world; the variety of pleasures and interests which steal away our affections from God. Sometimes we are to understand the men of the world, with whose solicitations we are so apt to comply. Rogers's Sermons.

6. Publick life.

Hence banished, is banish'd from the world;
And world exil'd is death. Shakesp.
Romeo and Juliet.

7. Business of life; trouble of life.

Here I'll set up my everlasting rest,
And shake the yoke of man's suspicious stars
From this world-wearied flesh. Shakesp.
Romeo and Juliet.

8. Great multitude.

 You a world of curses undergo,
Being the agents, or base second means.
Shakespeare.

Nor doth this wood lack worlds of company;
For you in my respect are all the world.
Shakespeare.

I leave to speak of a world of other attempts furnished by kings. Raleigh's Apology.

What a world of contradictions would follow upon the contrary opinion, and what a world of confusions upon the contrary practice.
Bp. Sanderson.

Just so romances are, for what else
Is in them all, but love and battles?
O' th' first of these we have no great matter
To treat of, but a world o' th' latter.
Hudibras.

It brought into this world a world of woe.
Milton.

There were a world of paintings, and among the rest the picture of a lion. L'Estrange.

Marriage draws a world of business on our hands, subjects us to law-suits, and loads us with domestick cares. Dryden.

From thy corporeal prison freed,
Soon hast thou reach'd the goal with mended pace;
A world of woes dispatch'd in little space.
Dryden.

Why will you fight against so sweet a passion,
And steel your heart to such a world of charms? Addison.

9. Mankind; an hyperbolical expression for many.

This hath bred high terms of separation between such and the rest of the world, whereby the one sort are named the brethren, the godly; the other worldlings, time-servers, pleasers of men more than of God. Hooker.

'Tis the duke's pleasure,
Whose disposition, all the world well knows,
Will not be rubb'd nor stopp'd. Shakesp.
K. Lear.

Why dost thou shew me thus to th' world?
Bear me to prison. Shakesp. Measure
for Measure.

He was willing to declare to all the world, that, as he had been brought up in that religion established in the church of England, so he could maintain the same by unanswerable reasons. Clarendon.

10. Course of life.

Persons of conscience will be afraid to begin the world unjustly. Clarissa.

11. Universal empire.

Rome was to sway the world. Milton.

This through the east just vengeance hurl'd,
And lost poor Antony the world. Prior.

12. The manners of men.

Children should not know any wickedness.
Old folks have discretion, and know the world. Shakespeare.

What start at this! when sixty years have spread
Their grey experience o'er thy hoary head?
Is this the all observing age could gain?
Or hast thou known the world so long in vain? Dryden.

If knowledge of the world makes man perfidious,
May Juba ever live in ignorance.
Addison's Cato.

The girl might pass, if we could get her
To know the world a little better;
To know the world! a modern phrase
For visits, ombre, balls and plays. Swift.

13. A collection of wonders; a wonder.
Obsolete.

The bassa having recommended Barbarussa, it was a world to see, how the court was changed upon him. Knolles.

14. Time. A sense originally Saxon; now only used in World without end.

15. In the world. In Possibility.

All the precautions in the world were taken for the marriage of his younger brother.
Addison.

16. For all the world. Exactly. A ludicrous sense; now little used.

He had a pair of horns like a bull, his feet cloven, as many eyes upon his body as my grey mare hath dapples, and for all the world so placed. Sidney, b. ii.

wórsted n.s. [from *Worsted*, a town in Norfolk famous for the woolen manufacture.] Woolen yarn; wool spun.

A base, proud, shallow, beggarly three suited, hundred pound, filthy worsted-stocking knave. Shakespeare's King Lear.

There Ridpath, Roper cudgel'd might ye view;
The very worsted still look'd black and blue.
Pope.

to wot v.n. [*witan*, Saxon; whence weet, to know; of which the preterite was wot, knew; which by degrees was mistaken for the present tense.] To know; to be aware.
Obsolete.

*The salve of reformation they mightily call
for, but where, and what the sores are which
need it, as they wot full little, so they think
not greatly material to search.* Hooker.

*Well I wot, compar'd to all the rest
Of each degree, that beggar's life is best.*
Hubberd.

*More water glideth by the mill
Than wots the miller of.* Shakespeare.

    *Wot you, what I found?
Forsooth, an inventory, thus importing.*
Shakespeare.

woúndy adj. Excessive. A low bad word.

*We have a world of holydays; that 'tis a
woundy hindrance to a poor man that lives
by his labour.* L'Estrange.

*These stockings of Susan's cost a woundy
deal of pains the pulling on.* Gay.

wretch n.s. [*wrecca*, Saxon.]

1. A miserable mortal.

When I loved, I was a wretch. Accidence.

*She weeps, and says her Henry is depos'd;
He smiles, and says his Edward is install'd;
That she, poor wretch, for grief can speak
    no more.* Shak.

*The butcher takes away the calf,
And binds the wretch, and beats it when
    it strives.* Shakesp.

*Illustrious wretch! repine not, nor reply:
View not what heav'n ordains, with reason's eye;
For bright the object is, the distance is too
    high.* Prior.

2. A worthless sorry creature.

*Base-minded wretches, are your thoughts
so deeply bemired in the trade of ordinary
worldlings, as for respect of gain some paultry
wool may yield you, to let so much time pass
without knowing perfectly her estate?* Sidney.

    *He now
Has these poor men in question: never saw I
Wretches so quake; they kneel, they kiss the earth,
Forswear themselves as often as they speak.*
Shakespeare.

*Title of honour, worth and virtue's right,
Should not be given to a wretch so vile.*
Daniel's Civil War.

*When they are gone, a company of starved
hungry wretches shall take their places.*
L'Estrange.

3. It is used by way of slight, or ironical
    pity, or contempt.

*When soon away the wasp doth go;
Poor wretch was never frighted so:
He thought his wings were much too slow,
O'erjoy'd they so were parted.* Drayton's
Nymphid.

*Then, if the spider find him fast beset,
She issues forth, and runs along her loom:
She joys to touch the captive in her net,
And drags the little wretch in triumph home.*
Dryden.

4. It is sometimes a word of tenderness,
    as we now say poor thing.

*Chastened but thus, and thus his lesson taught,
The happy wretch she put into her breast.*
Sidney.

writative A word of Pope's coining: not to
be imitated.

*Increase of years makes men more talkative,
but less writative; to that degree, that I now
write no letters but of plain how d'ye's.*
Pope to Swift.

to write v.n.

1. To perform the act of writing.

*I have seen her rise from her bed, take forth
paper, fold it, and write upon 't.* Shakesp.
Macbeth.

    *Bassanio gave his ring away
Unto the judge that begg'd it; and his clerk,
That took some pains in writing, he begg'd
    mine.* Shakesp.

2. To play the authour.

*Hearts, tongues, figures, scribes, bards,
    poets, cannot
Think, speak, cast, write, sing, number
His love to Antony.* Shakes. Ant. and
Cleopatra.

There is not a more melancholy object in the learned world than a man who has written himself down. Addison.

3. To tell in books.

I past the melancholy flood,
With that grim ferryman which poets write
of. Shak. R. III.

4. To send letters.

He wrote for all the Jews, concerning their freedom. 1 Esdr.

5. To call one's self; to be entitled; to use the stile of.

About it, and write happy when thou'st done. Shakesp.

Let it not your wonder move,
Less your laughter that I love;
Though I now write fifty years,
I have had, and have my peers.
Ben. Johnson.

He writes himself divina providentia, *whereas other bishops only use* divina permissione. Ayliffe.[†]

6. To compose; to form compositions.

Chaste moral writing we may learn from hence,
Neglect of which no wit can recompence;
The fountain which from Helicon proceeds,
That sacred stream, should never water
  weeds. Waller.

They can write up to the dignity and character of their authors. Felton on the Classicks.

writer n.s. [from *write.*]

1. One who practises the art of writing.

2. An authour.

All three were ruined by justice and sentence, as delinquents; and all three famous writers. Bacon.

Peaceable times are the best to live in, though not so proper to furnish materials for a writer. Addison's Freeholder.

Writers are often more influenced by a desire of fame, than a regard to the publick good. Addison's Freeholder.

Would a writer know how to behave himself with relation to posterity, let him consider in old books what he finds that he is glad to know, and what omissions he most laments. Swift.

Y, at the beginning of words, is a consonant; at the end, and when it follows a consonant, is a vowel, and has the sound of *i*. It is used at the end of words, and whenever two *i i*'s would come together; and in words derived from the Greek, to express the *v*. *Y* was much used by the Saxons, whence *y* is found for *i* in the old English writers.

Z, is found in the Saxon alphabets, set down by Grammarians, but is read in no word originally Teutonick: its sound is uniformly that of an hard *S*.

yare adj. [*gearwe*, Saxon.] Ready; dextrous; eager.

Yare, yare, good Iros, quick;—methinks I hear Antony call. Shakesp. Ant. and Cleopatra.

I do desire to learn, Sir; and I hope, if you have occasion to use me for your turn, you shall find me yare. Shakespeare.

to yarr v.n. [from the sound, *hirrio*, Lat.] To growl, or snarl like a dog. Ainsworth.

ycleped [The participle passive of clepe, to call; *clepan*, Saxon; with the increasing particle *y*, which was used in the old English in the preterites and participles, from the Saxon *ge*.] Called; termed; named.

But come, thou goddess, fair and free,
In heav'n yclep'd Euphrosine,
And by men, heart-easing mirth. Milton.

year n.s. [*gear*, Saxon.]

1. If one by the word year mean twelve months of thirty days each, i.e. three hundred and sixty days; another intend a solar year of three hundred sixty-five days; and a third mean a lunar year, or twelve lunar months, i.e. three hundred fifty-four days, there will be a great variation and error in their account of things, unless they are well apprized of each other's meaning. Watts's Logick.

See the minutes, how they run:
How many makes the hour full compleat,
How many hours bring about the day,
How many days will finish up the year,
How many years a mortal man may live.
Shakespeare.

With the year
Seasons return, but not to me returns
Day, or the sweet approach of morn. Milton.

Oviparous creatures have eggs enough at first conceived in them, to serve them for many years laying, allowing such a proportion for every year, as will serve for one or two incubations. Ray on the Creation.

He accepted a curacy of thirty pounds a year. Swift.

2. It it often used plurally, without a plural termination.

I fight not once in forty year. Shakespeare.

3. In the plural old age.

Some mumble-news,
That smiles his cheek in years, and knows the trick
To make my lady laugh when she's dispos'd,
Told our intents. Shakesp. Love's Labour Lost.

There died also Cecile, mother to king Edward IV. being of extreme years, and who had lived to see three princes of her body crowned, and four murthered. Bacon's Hen. VII.

He look'd in years, yet in his years were seen,
A youthful vigour, and autumnal green. Dryden.

yéarling adj. [from *year*.] Being a year old.

A yearling bullock to thy name shall smoke;
Untam'd, unconscious of the galling yoke. Pope.

yéllowboy n.s. A gold coin. A very low word.

John did not starve the cause; there wanted not yellowboys to see council. Arbuthnot's John Bull.

yéoman n.s. [Of this word the original is much doubted: the true etymology seems to be that of Junius, who derives it from *geman*, Frisick, a villager.]

1. A man of a small estate in land; a farmer; a gentleman farmer.

Gentlemen should use their children as the honest farmers and substantial yeomen do theirs. Locke.

He that has a spaniel by his side is a yeoman of about one hundred pounds a year, an honest man: he is just qualified to kill an hare. Addison.

2. It seems to have been anciently a kind of ceremonious title given to soldiers: whence we have still yeomen of the guard.

Tall yeomen seemed they, and of great might,
And were enranged ready still for fight. Fairy Queen.

You, good yeomen,
Whose limbs were made in England,
   shew us here
The mettle of your pasture. Shakesp.
Henry V.

He instituted, for the security of his person,
a band of fifty archers, under a captain, to
attend him, by the name of yeomen of his
guard. Bacon's Henry VII.

Th' appointment for th' ensuing night he heard;
And therefore in the cavern had prepar'd
Two brawny yeomen of his trusty guard.
Dryden.

At Windsor St. John whispers me i' th' ear;
The waiters stand in ranks, the yeomen cry
Make way for the dean, as if a duke pass'd by.
Swift.

3. It was probably a freeholder not
   advanced to the rank of a gentleman.

His grandfather was Lyonel duke of Clarence,
Third son to the third Edward king of England;
Spring crestless yeomen from so deep a root?
Shak. H. VI.

4. It seems to have had likewise the notion
   of a gentleman servant.

A jolly yeoman, marshal of the hall,
Whose name was appetite, he did bestow
Both guests and meats. Spenser.

youngth n.s. [from *young.*] Youth. Obsolete.

The mournful muse in mirth now list ne mask,
As she was wont in youngth and summer
   days. Spenser.

yuck n.s. [*jocken,* Dutch.] Itch.

yule n.s. [*geol, yeol, yehul,* Saxon.] The time
of Christmas.

yux n.s. [*yeox,* Saxon.] The hiccough.

zány n.s. [Probably of *zanei.* The
contraction of Giovanni or sanna, a scoff,
according to Skinner.] One employed to
raise laughter by his gestures, actions and
speeches; a merry Andrew; a buffoon.

Some carrytale, some pleaseman,
   some slight zany,
Some mumblenews, some trencher
   knight, some Dick,
Told our intents before. Shakespeare.

Then write that I may follow, and so be
Thy echo, thy debtor, thy foil, thy zany,
I shall be thought, if mine like thine I shape,
All the world's lion, though I be thy ape.
Donne.

Oh, great restorer of the good old stage,
Preacher at once, and zany of thy age.
Pope's Dunciad.

zeal n.s. [ζηλος, *zelus,* Latin.] Passionate
ardour for any person or cause.

This present age, wherein zeal hath drowned
charity and skill; meekness will not now suffer
any man to marvel, whatsoever he shall hear
reproved by whomsoever. Hooker.

If I had had time to have made new liveries,
I would have bestowed the thousand pound I
borrowed of you: but it is no matter, this poor
show doth better; this doth infer the zeal I had
to see him. Shakespeare's Henry IV.

   O Cromwell, Cromwell!
Had I but serv'd my God with half the zeal
I serv'd my king, he would not in mine age
Have left me naked to mine enemies.
Shakespeare.

   Among the seraphims
Abdiel, than whom none with more zeal ador'd
The Deity, and divine commands obey'd,
Stood up, and in a flame of zeal severe,
The current of his fury thus oppos'd. Milton's
Parad. Lost.

Zeal, the blind conductor of the will. Dryden.

She with such a zeal the cause embrac'd,
As women, where they will, are all in haste;
The father, mother, and the kin beside,
Were overborne by the fury of the tide.
Dryden.

The princes applaud with a furious joy,
And the king seiz'd a flambeau with zeal
   to destroy. Dryden.

Seriousness and zeal in religion is natural
to the English. Tillotson's Sermons.

Good men often blemish the reputation of
their piety by over-acting some things in their
religion; by an indiscreet zeal about things
wherein religion is not concerned. Tillotson.

True zeal seems not to be any one single affection of the soul; but rather a strong mixture of many holy affections; rather a gracious constitution of the whole mind, than any one particular grace, swaying a devout heart, and filling it with all pious intentions; all not only uncounterfeit, but most fervent. Sprat's Sermons.

When the sins of a nation have provoked God to forsake it, he suffers those to concur in the most pernicious counsels for enslaving conscience, who pretend to the greatest zeal for the liberty of it. Stillingfleet.

This rebellion has discovered to his majesty, who have espoused his interests with zeal or indifference. Addison's Freeh.

A scorn of flattery and a zeal for truth. Pope.

zeálot n.s. [*zeloteur*, French; ζηλοτης.] One passionately ardent in any cause. Generally used in dispraise.

The fury of zealots, intestine bitterness and division were the greatest occasion of the last fatal destruction of Jerusalem. King Charles.

Are not those men too often the greatest zealots who are most notoriously ignorant? true zeal should always begin with true knowledge, and thence proceed to an unwearied passion, for what it once knows to be worthy of such passion. Sprat.

No wonder that so many of these deluded zealots have been engaged in a cause which they at first abhorred, and have wished or acted for the success of an enterprize, that might have ended in the extirpation of the protestant religion. Addison.

zed n.s. The name of the letter z.

Thou whoreson zed, thou unnecessary letter. Shakespeare.

zéphyr, zéphyrus n.s. [*zephyrus*, Latin.] The west wind; and poetically any calm soft wind.

They are as gentle
As zephyrs blowing blow the violet.
Shakespeare's Cymbeline.

Zephyr, you shall see a youth with a merry countenance, holding in his hand a swan with

wings displayed, as about to sing. Peacham on Drawing.

Forth rush the levent and the ponent winds, Eurus and Zephyr. Milton.

Mild as when Zephyrus on Flora breathes. Milton.

Their every musick wakes,
Whence blending all the sweeten'd zephyr springs. Thomson.

zest n.s.

1. The peel of an orange squeezed into wine.

2. A relish; a taste added.

zetétick adj. [from ζειτεω.] Proceeding by enquiry.

zeúgma n.s. [from ζευγμα.] A figure in Grammar, when a verb agreeing with divers nouns, or an adjective with divers substantives, is referred to one expresly, and to the other by supplement, as lust overcame shame, boldness fear, and madness reason.

zócle n.s. [In architecture.] A small sort of stand or pedestal, being a low square piece or member, serving to support a busto, statue, or the like, that needs to be raised; also a low square member serving to support a column, instead of a pedestal, base, or plinth. Dict.

zoógraphy n.s. [of ζωη and γραφω.] A description of the forms, natures, and properties of animals.

If we contemplate the end of the effect, its principal final cause being the glory of its maker, this leads us into divinity; and for its subordinate, as it is designed for alimental sustenance to living creatures, and medicinal uses to man, we are thereby conducted into zoography. Glanv. Sceps.

zoólogy n.s. [of ζωον and λογος.] A treatise concerning living creatures.

zoóphyte n.s. [ζωοφυτον, of ζωος and φυτον.] Certain vegetables or substances which partake of the nature both of vegetables and animals.

THE PLAN OF A DICTIONARY
OF THE ENGLISH LANGUAGE;
Addressed to the Right Honourable
PHILIP DORMER, Earl of CHESTERFIELD,
One of His Majesty's Principal Secretaries of State.

My LORD,

WHEN first I undertook to write an English Dictionary, I had no expectation of any higher patronage than that of the proprietors of the copy, nor prospect of any other advantage than the price of my labour; I knew, that the work in which I engaged is generally considered as drudgery for the blind, as the proper toil of artless industry, a task that requires neither the light of learning, nor the activity of genius, but may be successfully performed without any higher quality than that of bearing burthens with dull patience, and beating the track of the alphabet with sluggish resolution.

WHETHER this opinion, so long transmitted and so widely propagated, had its beginning from truth and nature, or from accident and prejudice, whether it be decreed by the authority of reason, or the tyranny of ignorance, that of all the candidates for literary praise, the unhappy lexicographer holds the lowest place, neither vanity nor interest incited me to enquire. It appeared that the province allotted me was of all the regions of learning generally confessed to be the least delightful, that it was believed to produce neither fruits nor flowers, and that after a long and laborious cultivation, not even the barren laurel had been found upon it.

YET on this province, my Lord, I enter'd with the pleasing hope, that as it was low, it likewise would be safe. I was drawn forward with the prospect of employment, which, tho' not splendid, would be useful, and which tho' it could not make my life envied, would keep it innocent, which would awaken no passion, engage me in no contention, nor throw in my way any temptation to disturb the quiet of others by censure, or my own by flattery.

I HAD read indeed of times, in which princes and statesmen thought it part of their honour to promote the improvement of their native tongues, and in which dictionaries were written under the protection of greatness. To the patrons of such undertakings, I willingly paid the homage of believing that they, who were thus solicitous for the perpetuity of their language, had reason to expect that their actions would be celebrated by posterity, and that the eloquence which they promoted would be employed in their praise. But I considered such acts of beneficence as prodigies, recorded rather to raise wonder than expectation; and content with the terms that I had stipulated, had not suffer'd my imagination to flatter me with any other encouragement, when I found that my design had been thought by your Lordship of importance sufficient to attract your favour.

Of all the candidates for literary praise, the unhappy lexicographer holds the lowest place.... It appeared that the province allotted me was of all the regions of learning generally confessed to be the least delightful, that it was believed to produce neither fruits nor flowers, and that after a long and laborious cultivation, not even the barren laurel had been found upon it.

In lexicography, as in other arts, naked science is too delicate for the purposes of life. The value of a work must be estimated by its use: it is not enough that a dictionary delights the critic, unless at the same time it instructs the learner....

How far this unexpected distinction can be rated among the happy incidents of life, I am not yet able to determine. Its first effect has been to make me anxious lest it should fix the attention of the public too much upon me, and as it once happened to an epic poet of France, by raising the reputation of the attempt, obstruct the reception of the work. I imagine what the world will expect from a scheme, prosecuted under your Lordship's influence, and I know that expectation, when her wings are once expanded, easily reaches heights which performance never will attain, and when she has mounted the summit of perfection, derides her follower, who dies in the pursuit.

Not therefore to raise expectation, but to repress it, I here lay before your Lordship the plan of my undertaking, that more may not be demanded than I intend, and that before it is too far advanced to be thrown into a new method, I may be advertised of its defects or superfluities. Such informations I may justly hope from the emulation with which those who desire the praise of elegance or discernment must contend in the promotion of a design that you, my Lord, have not thought unworthy to share your attention with treaties and with wars.

In the first attempt to methodise my ideas, I found a difficulty which extended itself to the whole work. It was not easy to determine by what rule of distinction the words of this dictionary were to be chosen. The chief intent of it is to preserve the purity and ascertain the meaning of our English idiom; and this seems to require nothing more than that our language be considered so far as it is our own; that the words and phrases used in the general intercourse of life, or found in the works of those whom we commonly stile polite writers, be selected, without including the terms of particular professions, since, with the arts to which they relate, they are generally derived from other nations, and are very often the same in all the languages of this part of the world. This is perhaps the exact and pure idea of a grammatical dictionary; but in lexicography, as in other arts, naked science is too delicate for the purposes of life. The value of a work must be estimated by its use: it is not enough that a dictionary delights the critic, unless at the same time it instructs the learner; as it is to little purpose, that an engine amuses the philosopher by the subtilty of its mechanism, if it requires so much knowledge in its application, as to be of no advantage to the common workman.

The title which I prefix to my work has long conveyed a very miscellaneous idea, and they that take a dictionary into their hands have been accustomed to expect from it a solution of almost every difficulty. If foreign words therefore were rejected, it could be little regarded, except by critics, or those who aspire to criticism; and however it might enlighten those that write, would be all darkness to them that only read. The unlearned much oftener consult their dictionaries, for the meaning of words, than for their structures or formations; and the words that most want explanation, are generally terms of art, which therefore experience has taught my predecessors to spread with a kind of pompous luxuriance over their productions.

THE academicians of France, indeed, rejected terms of science in their first essay, but found afterwards a necessity of relaxing the rigour of their determination; and, though they would not naturalize them at once by a single act, permitted them by degrees to settle themselves among the natives, with little opposition, and it would surely be no proof of judgment to imitate them in an error which they have now retracted, and deprive the book of its chief use by scrupulous distinctions.

OF such words, however, all are not equally to be considered as parts of our language, for some of them are naturalized and incorporated, but others still continue aliens, and are rather auxiliaries than subjects. This naturalization is produced either by an admission into common speech in some metaphorical signification, which is the acquisition of a kind of property among us, as we say the *zenith* of advancement, the *meridian* of life, the †*cynosure* of neighbouring eyes; or it is the consequence of long intermixture and frequent use, by which the ear is accustomed to the sound of words till their original is forgotten, as in *equator, satellites*; or of the change of a foreign to an English termination, and a conformity to the laws of the speech into which they are adopted, as in *category, cachexy, peripneumony*.

OF those which yet continue in the state of aliens, and have made no approaches towards assimilation, some seem necessary to be retained, because the purchasers of the dictionary will expect to find them. Such are many words in the common law, as *capias, habeas corpus, præmunire, nisi prius*: such are some terms of controversial divinity, as *hypostasis*; and of physick, as the names of diseases; and in general all terms which can be found in books not written professedly upon particular arts, or can be supposed necessary to those who do not regularly study them. Thus when a reader not skilled in physick happens in Milton upon this line,

> ————pining atrophy,
> *Marasmus*, and wide-wasting pestilence.

he will with equal expectation look into his dictionary for the word *marasmus*, as for *atrophy*, or *pestilence*, and will have reason to complain if he does not find it.

IT seems necessary to the completion of a dictionary designed not merely for critics but for popular use, that it should comprise, in some degree, the peculiar words of every profession; that the terms of war and navigation should be inserted so far as they can be required by readers of travels, and of history; and those of law, merchandise and mechanical trades, so far as they can be supposed useful in the occurrences of common life.

BUT there ought, however, to be some distinction made between the different classes of words, and therefore it will be proper to print

It seems necessary to the completion of a dictionary designed not merely for critics but for popular use, that it should comprise, in some degree, the peculiar words of every profession; that the terms of war and navigation should be inserted...and those of law, merchandise and mechanical trades....But there ought, however, to be some distinction made between the different classes of words....

---

† Milton.

those which are incorporated into the language in the usual character, and those which are still to be considered as foreign in the Italick letter.

ANOTHER question may arise, with regard to appellatives, or the names of species. It seems of no great use to set down the words *horse*, *dog*, *cat*, *willow*, *alder*, *daisy*, *rose*, and a thousand others, of which it will be hard to give an explanation not more obscure than the word itself. Yet it is to be considered, that, if the names of animals be inserted, we must admit those which are more known, as well as those with which we are, by accident, less acquainted; and if they are all rejected, how will the reader be relieved from difficulties produced by allusions to the crocodile, the camæleon, the ichneumon, and the hyæna? If no plants are to be mentioned, the most pleasing part of nature will be excluded, and many beautiful epithets be unexplained. If only those which are less known are to be mentioned, who shall fix the limits of the reader's learning? The importance of such explications appears from the mistakes which the want of them has occasioned. Had Shakespear had a dictionary of this kind, he had not made the *woodbine* entwine the *honeysuckle*; nor would Milton, with such assistance, have disposed so improperly of his *ellops* and his *scorpion*.

Had Shakespear had a dictionary of this kind, he had not made the woodbine entwine the honeysuckle; nor would Milton, with such assistance, have disposed so improperly of his ellops and his scorpion.

BESIDES, as such words, like others, require that their accents should be settled, their sounds ascertained, and their etymologies deduced, they cannot be properly omitted in the dictionary. And though the explanations of some may be censured as trivial, because they are almost universally understood, and those of others as unnecessary, because they will seldom occur, yet it seems not proper to omit them, since it is rather to be wished that many readers should find more than they expect, than that one should miss what he might hope to find.

WHEN all the words are selected and arranged, the first part of the work to be considered is the ORTHOGRAPHY, which was long vague and uncertain, which at last, when its fluctuation ceased, was in many cases settled but by accident, and in which, according to your Lordship's observation, there is still great uncertainty among the best critics; nor is it easy to state a rule by which we may decide between custom and reason, or between the equiponderant authorities of writers alike eminent for judgment and accuracy.

THE great orthographical contest has long subsisted between etymology and pronunciation. It has been demanded, on one hand, that men should write as they speak; but as it has been shewn, that this conformity never was attained in any language, and that it is not more easy to persuade men to agree exactly in speaking than in writing, it may be asked with equal propriety, why men do not rather speak as they write. In France, where this controversy was at its greatest height, neither party, however ardent, durst adhere steadily to their own rule; the etymologist was often forced to spell with the people; and the advocate for the authority of pronunciation, found it sometimes deviating capriciously from the received use of writing, that he was constrained to comply with the rule of his adversaries, lest he should lose the end by the means, and be left alone by following the crowd.

WHEN a question of orthography is dubious, that practice has, in my opinion, a claim to preference, which preserves the greatest number of radical letters, or seems most to comply with the general custom of our language. But the chief rule which I propose to follow, is to make no innovation, without a reason sufficient to balance the inconvenience of change; and such reasons I do not expect often to find. All change is of itself an evil, which ought not to be hazarded but for evident advantage; and as inconstancy is in every case a mark of weakness, it will add nothing to the reputation of our tongue. There are, indeed, some who despise the inconveniencies of confusion, who seem to take pleasure in departing from custom, and to think alteration desirable for its own sake; and the reformation of our orthography, which these writers have attempted, should not pass without its due honours, but that I suppose they hold singularity its own reward, or may dread the fascination of lavish praise.

THE present usage of spelling, where the present usage can be distinguished, will therefore in this work be generally followed, yet there will be often occasion to observe, that it is in itself inaccurate, and tolerated rather than chosen; particularly, when by the change of one letter, or more, the meaning of a word is obscured, as in *farrier*, for *ferrier*, as it was formerly written, from *ferrum* or *fer*, in *gibberish* for *gebrish*, the jargon of Geber and his chymical followers, understood by none but their own tribe. It will be likewise sometimes proper to trace back the orthography of different ages, and shew by what gradations the word departed from its original.

CLOSELY connected with orthography is PRONUNCIATION, the stability of which is of great importance to the duration of a language, because the first change will naturally begin by corruptions in the living speech. The want of certain rules for the pronunciation of former ages, has made us wholly ignorant of the metrical art of our ancient poets; and since those who study their sentiments regret the loss of their numbers, it is surely time to provide that the harmony of the moderns may be more permanent.

A NEW pronunciation will make almost a new speech, and therefore since one great end of this undertaking is to fix the English language, care will be taken to determine the accentuation of all polysyllables by proper authorities, as it is one of those capricious phænomena which cannot be easily reduced to rules. Thus there is no antecedent reason for difference of accent in the two words *dolorous* and *sonorous*, yet of the one Milton gives the sound in this line,

He pass'd o'er many a region *dolorous*,

The want of certain rules for the pronunciation of former ages, has made us wholly ignorant of the metrical art of our ancient poets; and since those who study their sentiments regret the loss of their numbers, it is surely time to provide that the harmony of the moderns may be more permanent.

and that of the other in this,

Sonorous metal blowing martial sounds.

The care of such minute particulars may be censured as trifling, but these particulars have not been thought unworthy of attention in more polished languages.

IT may be likewise proper to remark metrical licenses, such as contractions, *generous, gen'rous, reverend, rev'rend;* and coalitions, as *region, question.*

BUT it is still more necessary to fix the pronunciation of monosyllables, by placing with them words of correspondent sound, that one may guard the other against the danger of that variation, which to some of the most common has already happened, so that the words *wound*, and *wind*, as they are now frequently pronounced, will not rhyme to *sound*, and *mind*. It is to be remarked that many words written alike are differently pronounc'd, as *flow*, and *brow*, which may be thus registered *flow, woe, brow, now*, or of which the exemplification may be generally given by a distich. Thus the words *tear* or lacerate, and *tear* the water of the eye, have the same letters, but may be distinguished thus, *tear, dare; tear, peer.*

SOME words have two sounds, which may be equally admitted, as being equally defensible by authority. Thus *great* is differently used.

> For Swift and him despis'd the farce of state,
> The sober follies of the wise and *great*. POPE.

> As if misfortune made the throne her seat,
> And none could be unhappy but the *great*.
> 　　　　　　　　　　　ROWE.

The care of such minute particulars may be censured as trifling, but these particulars have not been thought unworthy of attention in more polished languages.

THE accuracy of the French, in stating the sounds of their letters, is well known; and, among the Italians, Crescembeni has not thought it unnecessary to inform his countrymen of the words, which, in compliance with different rhymes, are allowed to be differently spelt, and of which the number is now so fixed, that no modern poet is suffered to encrease it.

WHEN the orthography and pronunciation are adjusted, the ETYMOLOGY or DERIVATION is next to be considered, and the words are to be distinguished according to the different classes, whether simple, as *day, light*, or compound as *day-light*; whether primitive, as, to *act*, or derivative, as *action, actionable, active, activity*. This will much facilitate the attainment of our language, which now stands in our dictionaries a confused heap of words without dependence, and without relation.

WHEN this part of the work is performed, it will be necessary to inquire how our primitives are to be deduced from foreign languages, which may be often very successfully performed by the assistance of our own etymologists. This search will give occasion to many curious disquisitions, and sometimes perhaps to conjectures, which, to readers unacquainted with this kind of study, cannot but appear improbable and capricious. But it may be reasonably imagined, that what is so much in the power of men as language, will very often be capriciously conducted. Nor are these disquisitions and conjectures to be considered altogether as wanton sports of wit, or vain shews of learning; our language is well known not to be primitive or self-originated, but to have adopted words of every generation, and either for the supply of its necessities, or the encrease of its copiousness, to have received additions from very distant regions; so that in search of the progenitors of our speech, we may wander from the tropic to the frozen zone, and find some in the valleys of Palestine and some upon the rocks of Norway.

BESIDE the derivation of particular words, there is likewise an etymology of phrases. Expressions are often taken from other languages, some apparently, as to *run a risque*, *courir un risque*; and some even when we do not seem to borrow their words; thus, to *bring about* or accomplish, appears an English phrase, but in reality our native word *about* has no such import, and it is only a French expression, of which we have an example in the common phrase, *venir à bout d' une affaire*.

IN exhibiting the descent of our language, our etymologists seem to have been too lavish of their learning, having traced almost every word through various tongues, only to shew what was shewn sufficiently by the first derivation. This practice is of great use in synoptical lexicons, where mutilated and doubtful languages are explained by their affinity to others more certain and extensive, but is generally superfluous in English etymologies. When the word is easily deduced from a Saxon original, I shall not often inquire further, since we know not the parent of the Saxon dialect, but when it is borrowed from the French, I shall shew whence the French is apparently derived. Where a Saxon root cannot be found, the defect may be supplied from kindred languages, which will be generally furnished with much liberality by the writers of our glossaries; writers who deserve often the highest praise, both of judgment and industry, and may expect at least to be mentioned with honour by me, whom they have freed from the greatest part of a very laborious work, and on whom they have imposed, at worst, only the easy task of rejecting superfluities.

BY tracing in this manner every word to its original, and not admitting, but with great caution, any of which no original can be found, we shall secure our language from being over-run with *cant*, from being crouded with low terms, the spawn of folly or affectation, which arise from no just principles of speech, and of which therefore no legitimate derivation can be shewn.

To bring about *or accomplish, appears an English phrase, but in reality our native word* about *has no such import, and it is only a French expression, of which we have an example in the common phrase,* venir à bout d' une affaire.

Speech was not formed by an analogy sent from heaven. It did not descend to us in a state of uniformity and perfection, but was produced by necessity and enlarged by accident, and is therefore composed of dissimilar parts, thrown together by negligence, by affectation, by learning, or by ignorance.

WHEN the etymology is thus adjusted, the ANALOGY of our language is next to be considered; when we have discovered whence our words are derived, we are to examine by what rules they are governed, and how they are inflected through their various terminations. The terminations of the English are few, but those few have hitherto remained unregarded by the writers of our dictionaries. Our substantives are declined only by the plural termination, our adjectives admit no variation but in the degrees of comparison, and our verbs are conjugated by auxiliary words, and are only changed in the preter tense.

TO our language may be with great justness applied the observation of *Quintilian*, that speech was not formed by an analogy sent from heaven. It did not descend to us in a state of uniformity and perfection, but was produced by necessity and enlarged by accident, and is therefore composed of dissimilar parts, thrown together by negligence, by affectation, by learning, or by ignorance.

OUR inflections therefore are by no means constant, but admit of numberless irregularities, which in this dictionary will be diligently noted. Thus *fox* makes in the plural *foxes*, but *ox* makes *oxen*. *Sheep* is the same in both numbers. Adjectives are sometimes compared by changing the last syllable, as *proud, prouder, proudest*; and sometimes by particles prefixed, as *ambitious, more* ambitious, *most* ambitious. The forms of our verbs are subject to great variety; some end their preter tense in *ed*, as I *love*, I *loved*, I have *loved*, which may be called the regular form, and is followed by most of our verbs of southern original. But many depart from this rule, without agreeing in any other, as I *shake*, I *shook*, I have *shaken*, or *shook* as it is sometimes written in poetry; I *make*, I *made*, I have *made*; I *bring*, I *brought*; I *wring*, I *wrung*; and many others, which, as they cannot be reduced to rules, must be learned from the dictionary rather than the grammar.

THE verbs are likewise to be distinguished according to their qualities, as actives from neuters; the neglect of which has already introduced some barbarities in our conversation, which, if not obviated by just animadversions, may in time creep into our writings.

THUS, my Lord, will our language be laid down, distinct in its minutest subdivisions, and resolved into its elemental principles. And who upon this survey can forbear to wish, that these fundamental atoms of our speech might obtain the firmness and immutability of the primogenial and constituent particles of matter, that they might retain their substance while they alter their appearance, and be varied and compounded, yet not destroyed.

BUT this is a privilege which words are scarcely to expect; for, like their author, when they are not gaining strength, they are generally losing it. Though art may sometimes prolong their duration, it will rarely give them perpetuity, and their changes will be almost always informing us, that language is the work of man, of a being from whom permanence and stability cannot be derived.

WORDS having been hitherto considered as separate and unconnected, are now to be likewise examined as they are ranged in their various relations to others by the rules of SYNTAX or construction, to which I do not know that any regard has been yet shewn in English dictionaries, and in which the grammarians can give little assistance. The syntax of this language is too inconstant to be reduced to rules, and can be only learned by the distinct consideration of particular words as they are used by the best authors. Thus, we say according to the present modes of speech, the soldier died *of* his wounds, and the sailor perished *with* hunger; and every man acquainted with our language would be offended with a change of these particles, which yet seem originally assigned by chance, there being no reason to be drawn from grammar why a man may not, with equal propriety, be said to dye *with* a wound or perish *of* hunger.

OUR syntax therefore is not to be taught by general rules, but by special precedents; and in examining whether Addison has been with justice accused of a solecism in this passage,

> The poor inhabitant——
> Starves in the midst of nature's bounty curst,
> And in the loaden vineyard *dies for thirst,*

it is not in our power to have recourse to any established laws of speech, but we must remark how the writers of former ages have used the same word, and consider whether he can be acquitted of impropriety, upon the testimony of Davies, given in his favour by a similar passage.

> She loaths the watry glass wherein she gaz'd,
> And shuns it still, although *for thirst she dye.*

WHEN the construction of a word is explained, it is necessary to pursue it through its train of PHRASEOLOGY, through those forms where it is used in a manner peculiar to our language, or in senses not to be comprised in the general explanations; as from the verb *make*, arise these phrases, to *make love*, to *make an end*, to *make way*, as he *made way* for his followers, the ship *made way* before the wind; to *make a bed*, to *make merry*, to *make a mock*, to *make presents*, to *make a doubt*, to *make out an assertion*, to *make good* a breach, to *make good* a cause, to *make nothing* of an attempt, to *make lamentation*, to *make a merit*, and many others which will occur in reading with that view, and which only their frequency hinders from being generally remarked.

THE great labour is yet to come, the labour of interpreting these words and phrases with brevity, fulness and perspicuity; a task of which the extent and intricacy is sufficiently shewn by the miscarriage of those who have generally attempted it. This difficulty is increased by the necessity of explaining the words in the same language, for there is often only one word for one idea; and though it be easy to translate the

The great labour is yet to come, the labour of interpreting these words and phrases with brevity, fulness and perspicuity; a task of which the extent and intricacy is sufficiently shewn by the miscarriage of those who have generally attempted it.

words *bright, sweet, salt, bitter,* into another language, it is not easy to explain them.

WITH regard to the INTERPRETATION many other questions have required consideration. It was some time doubted whether it be necessary to explain the things implied by particular words. As under the term *baronet,* whether instead of this explanation, *a title of honour next in degree to that of baron,* it would be better to mention more particularly the creation, privileges and rank of baronets; and whether under the word *barometer,* instead of being satisfied with observing that it is *an instrument to discover the weight of the air,* it would be fit to spend a few lines upon its invention, construction and principles. It is not to be expected that with the explanation of the one the herald should be satisfied, or the philosopher with that of the other; but since it will be required by common readers, that the explications should be sufficient for common use, and since without some attention to such demands the dictionary cannot become generally valuable, I have determined to consult the best writers for explanations real as well as verbal, and perhaps I may at last have reason to say, after one of the augmenters of Furetier, that my book is more learned than its author.

I have determined to consult the best writers for explanations real as well as verbal, and perhaps I may at last have reason to say, after one of the augmenters of Furetier, that my book is more learned than its author.

IN explaining the general and popular language, it seems necessary to sort the several senses of each word, and to exhibit first its natural and primitive signification, as

> TO *arrive,* to reach the shore in a voyage. He *arrived* at a safe harbour.

THEN to give its consequential meaning, *to arrive,* to reach any place whether by land or sea; as, he *arrived* at his country seat.

THEN its metaphorical sense, to obtain any thing desired; as, he *arrived* at a peerage.

THEN to mention any observation that arises from the comparison of one meaning with another; as, it may be remarked of the word *arrive,* that in consequence of its original and etymological sense, it cannot be properly applied but to words signifying something desirable; thus, we say a man *arrived* at happiness, but cannot say, without a mixture of irony, he *arrived* at misery.

> *Ground,* the earth, generally as opposed to the air or water. He swam till he reached *ground.* The bird fell to the *ground.*

THEN follows the accidental or consequential signification, in which *ground* implies any thing that lies under another; as, he laid colours upon a rough *ground.* The silk had blue flowers on a red *ground.*

THEN the remoter or metaphorical signification; as, the *ground* of his opinion was a false computation. The *ground* of his work was his father's manuscript.

AFTER having gone through the natural and figurative senses, it will be proper to subjoin the poetical sense of each word, where it differs from that which is in common use; as, *wanton* applied to any thing of which the motion is irregular without terrour, as

> In *wanton* ringlets curl'd her hair.

To the poetical sense may succeed the familiar; as of *toast*, used to imply the person whose health is drunk.

> The wise man's passion, and the vain man's *toast*. POPE.

THE familiar may be followed by the burlesque; as of *mellow*, applied to good fellowship.

> In all thy humours whether grave, or *mellow*. ADDISON.

OR of *bite* used for *cheat*.

> ——More a dupe than wit,
> Sappho can tell you, how this man was *bit*. POPE.

AND lastly, may be produced the peculiar sense, in which a word is found in any great author. As *faculties* in Shakespeare signifies the powers of authority.

> ——This Duncan
> Has born his *faculties* so meek, has been
> So clear in his great office, that *&c.*

THE signification of adjectives, may be often ascertained by uniting them to substantives, as *simple swain, simple sheep*; sometimes the sense of a substantive may be elucidated by the epithets annexed to it in good authors, as the *boundless ocean*, the *open lawns*, and where such advantage can be gained by a short quotation it is not to be omitted.

THE difference of signification in words generally accounted synonimous, ought to be carefully observed; as in *pride, haughtiness, arrogance*: and the strict and critical meaning ought to be distinguished from that which is loose and popular; as in the word *perfection*, which though in its philosophical and exact sense, it can be of little use among human beings, is often so much degraded from its original signification, that the academicians have inserted in their work *the perfection of a language*, and with a little more licentiousness might have prevailed on themselves to have added *the perfection of a dictionary*.

THERE are many other characters of words which it will be of use to mention. Some have both an active and passive signification, as *fearful*, that which gives or which feels terror, a *fearful prodigy*, a *fearful hare*. Some have a personal, some a real meaning, as in opposition to *old* we use the adjective *young* of animated beings, and *new* of other things. Some are restrained to the sense of praise, and others to that of disapprobation, so commonly, though not always, we *exhort* to good

We use the adjective young of animated beings, and new of other things...we exhort to good actions, we instigate to ill; we animate, incite and encourage indifferently to good or bad. So we usually ascribe good, but impute evil; yet neither the use of these words, nor perhaps of any other in our licentious language, is so established as not to be often reversed by the correctest writers.

actions, we *instigate* to ill; we *animate, incite* and *encourage* indifferently to good or bad. So we usually *ascribe* good, but *impute* evil; yet neither the use of these words, nor perhaps of any other in our licentious language, is so established as not to be often reversed by the correctest writers. I shall therefore, since the rules of stile, like those of law, arise from precedents often repeated, collect the testimonies on both sides, and endeavour to discover and promulgate the decrees of custom, who has so long possessed, whether by right or by usurpation, the sovereignty of words.

IT is necessary likewise to explain many words by their opposition to others; for contraries are best seen when they stand together. Thus the verb *stand* has one sense as opposed to *fall*, and another as opposed to *fly*; for want of attending to which distinction, obvious as it is, the learned Dr. Bentley has squandered his criticism to no purpose, on these lines of Paradise Lost.

> ——In heaps
> Chariot and charioteer lay over-turn'd,
> And fiery foaming steeds. What *stood, recoil'd*,
> O'erwearied, through the faint Satanic host,
> Defensive scarce, or with pale fear surpris'd
> *Fled* ignominious——

"Here," says the critic, "as the sentence is now read, we find that what *stood, fled*," and therefore he proposes an alteration, which he might have spared if he had consulted a dictionary, and found that nothing more was affirmed than that those *fled* who did *not fall*.

IN explaining such meanings as seem accidental and adventitious, I shall endeavour to give an account of the means by which they were introduced. Thus to *eke out* any thing, signifies to lengthen it beyond its just dimensions by some low artifice, because the word *eke* was the usual refuge of our old writers when they wanted a syllable. And *buxom*, which means only *obedient*, is now made, in familiar phrases, to stand for *wanton*, because in an antient form of marriage, before the reformation, the bride promised complaisance and obedience in these terms, "I will be bonair and *buxom* in bed and at board."

I KNOW well, my Lord, how trifling many of these remarks will appear separately considered, and how easily they may give occasion to the contemptuous merriment of sportive idleness, and the gloomy censures of arrogant stupidity; but dulness it is easy to despise, and laughter it is easy to repay. I shall not be sollicitous what is thought of my work by such as know not the difficulty or importance of philological studies, nor shall think those that have done nothing qualified to condemn me for doing little. It may not, however, be improper to remind them, that no terrestrial greatness is more than an aggregate of little things, and to inculcate after the Arabian proverb, that drops added to drops constitute the ocean.

Buxom, which means only obedient, *is now made, in familiar phrases, to stand for* wanton, *because in an antient form of marriage, before the reformation, the bride promised complaisance and obedience in these terms, "I will be* bonair and buxom *in bed and at board."*

THERE remains yet to be considered the DISTRIBUTION of words into their proper classes, or that part of lexicography which is strictly critical.

THE popular part of the language, which includes all words not appropriated to particular sciences, admits of many distinctions and subdivisions; as, into words of general use; words employed chiefly in poetry; words obsolete; words which are admitted only by particular writers, yet not in themselves improper; words used only in burlesque writing; and words impure and barbarous.

WORDS of general use will be known by having no sign of particularity, and their various senses will be supported by authorities of all ages.

THE words appropriated to poetry will be distinguished by some mark prefixed, or will be known by having no authorities but those of poets.

OF antiquated or obsolete words, none will be inserted but such as are to be found in authors who wrote since the accession of Elizabeth, from which we date the golden age of our language; and of these many might be omitted, but that the reader may require, with an appearance of reason, that no difficulty should be left unresolved in books which he finds himself invited to read, as confessed and established models of stile. These will be likewise pointed out by some note of exclusion, but not of disgrace.

THE words which are found only in particular books, will be known by the single name of him that has used them; but such will be omitted, unless either their propriety, elegance, or force, or the reputation of their authors affords some extraordinary reason for their reception.

WORDS used in burlesque and familiar compositions, will be likewise mentioned with their proper authorities, such as *dudgeon* from Butler, and *leasing* from Prior, and will be diligently characterised by marks of distinction.

BARBAROUS or impure words and expressions, may be branded with some note of infamy, as they are carefully to be eradicated wherever they are found; and they occur too frequently even in the best writers. As in Pope,

> ——*in* endless error *hurl'd.*

> *'Tis these* that early taint the female soul.

In Addison,

> Attend to what a *lesser* muse indites.

And in Dryden,

> A dreadful quiet felt, and *worser* far
> Than arms——

If this part of the work can be well performed, it will be equivalent to the proposal made by Boileau to the academicians, that they should review all their polite writers, and correct such impurities as might be

Of antiquated or obsolete words, none will be inserted but such as are to be found in authors who wrote since the accession of Elizabeth, from which we date the golden age of our language…. Barbarous or impure words and expressions, may be branded with some note of infamy, as they are carefully to be eradicated wherever they are found; and they occur too frequently even in the best writers.

found in them, that their authority might not contribute, at any distant time, to the depravation of the language.

Many of the writers whose testimonies will be alledged, were selected by Mr. Pope, of whom I may be justified in affirming, that were he still alive, solicitous as he was for the success of this work, he would not be displeased that I have undertaken it.

WITH regard to questions of purity, or propriety, I was once in doubt whether I should not attribute too much to myself in attempting to decide them, and whether my province was to extend beyond the proposition of the question, and the display of the suffrages on each side; but I have been since determined by your Lordship's opinion, to interpose my own judgment, and shall therefore endeavour to support what appears to me most consonant to grammar and reason. Ausonius thought that modesty forbad him to plead inability for a task to which Cæsar had judged him equal.

Cur me posse negem posse quod ille putat?

And I may hope, my Lord, that since you, whose authority in our language is so generally acknowledged, have commissioned me to declare my own opinion, I shall be considered as exercising a kind of vicarious jurisdiction, and that the power which might have been denied to my own claim, will be readily allowed me as the delegate of your Lordship.

IN citing authorities, on which the credit of every part of this work must depend, it will be proper to observe some obvious rules, such as of preferring writers of the first reputation to those of an inferior rank, of noting the quotations with accuracy, and of selecting, when it can be conveniently done, such sentences, as, besides their immediate use, may give pleasure or instruction by conveying some elegance of language, or some precept of prudence, or piety.

IT has been asked, on some occasions, who shall judge the judges? And since with regard to this design, a question may arise by what authority the authorities are selected, it is necessary to obviate it, by declaring that many of the writers whose testimonies will be alledged, were selected by Mr. Pope, of whom I may be justified in affirming, that were he still alive, solicitous as he was for the success of this work, he would not be displeased that I have undertaken it.

IT will be proper that the quotations be ranged according to the ages of their authors, and it will afford an agreeable amusement, if to the words and phrases which are not of our own growth, the name of the writer who first introduced them can be affixed, and if, to words which are now antiquated, the authority be subjoined of him who last admitted them. Thus for *scathe* and *buxom*, now obsolete, Milton may be cited.

——The mountain oak
Stands *scath'd* to heaven——
——He with broad sails
Winnow'd the *buxom* air——

By this method every word will have its history, and the reader will be informed of the gradual changes of the language, and have before his eyes the rise of some words, and the fall of others. But observations so minute and accurate are to be desired rather than expected, and if use be carefully supplied, curiosity must sometimes bear its disappointments.

THIS, my Lord, is my idea of an English dictionary, a dictionary by which the pronunciation of our language may be fixed, and its attainment facilitated; by which its purity may be preserved, its use ascertained, and its duration lengthened. And though, perhaps, to correct the language of nations by books of grammar, and amend their manners by discourses of morality, may be tasks equally difficult; yet as it is unavoidable to wish, it is natural likewise to hope, that your Lordship's patronage may not be wholly lost; that it may contribute to the preservation of antient, and the improvement of modern writers; that it may promote the reformation of those translators, who for want of understanding the characteristical difference of tongues, have formed a chaotic dialect of heterogeneous phrases; and awaken to the care of purer diction, some men of genius, whose attention to argument makes them negligent of stile, or whose rapid imagination, like the Peruvian torrents, when it brings down gold, mingles it with sand.

WHEN I survey the Plan which I have laid before you, I cannot, my Lord, but confess, that I am frighted at its extent, and, like the soldiers of Cæsar, look on Britain as a new world, which it is almost madness to invade. But I hope, that though I should not complete the conquest, I shall at least discover the coast, civilize part of the inhabitants, and make it easy for some other adventurer to proceed farther, to reduce them wholly to subjection, and settle them under laws.

WE are taught by the great Roman orator, that every man should propose to himself the highest degree of excellence, but that he may stop with honour at the second or third: though therefore my performance should fall below the excellence of other dictionaries, I may obtain, at least, the praise of having endeavoured well, nor shall I think it any reproach to my diligence, that I have retired without a triumph from a contest with united academies and long successions of learned compilers. I cannot hope in the warmest moments, to preserve so much caution through so long a work, as not often to sink into negligence, or to obtain so much knowledge of all its parts, as not frequently to fail by ignorance. I expect that sometimes the desire of accuracy will urge me to superfluities, and sometimes the fear of prolixity betray me to omissions; that in the extent of such variety I shall be often bewildered, and in the mazes of such intricacy be frequently entangled; that in one part refinement will be subtilised beyond exactness, and evidence dilated in another beyond perspicuity. Yet I do not despair of approbation from those who knowing the uncertainty of conjecture, the scantiness of knowledge, the fallibility of memory, and the unsteadiness of attention, can compare the causes of error with the means of avoiding it, and the extent of art with the capacity of man; and whatever be the event of my endeavours, I shall

When I survey the Plan which I have laid before you, I cannot, my Lord, but confess, that I am frighted at its extent, and, like the soldiers of Cæsar, look on Britain as a new world, which it is almost madness to invade. But I hope, that though I should not complete the conquest, I shall at least discover the coast, civilize part of the inhabitants, and make it easy for some other adventurer to proceed farther....

not easily regret an attempt which has procured me the honour of appearing thus publickly,

My Lord,

Your Lordship's

Most Obedient

and

Most Humble Servant,

S A M. J O H N S O N.

NOTES

A

academy
Plato set up his famous philosophical school near Athens in an olive grove sacred to the legendary Academus. It was called the Academy after the name of the grove.

allegro
Johnson refers to "L'Allegro," the companion piece to "Il Penseroso," two of Milton's most famous short poems.

amphibology
Depending on the placement of the comma, the Latin *Noli regem occidere timere bonum est* can mean either "Don't kill the king, it's good to be afraid" or "Don't be afraid to kill the king, it's a good thing." According to tradition, when Bishop Orleton was holding Edward II in prison in 1327, he sent that ambiguous note to his jailer. The most famous telling of the story is in Christopher Marlowe's *Edward II*, Act V, Scene iv.

The Latin *captare lepores* can mean either "striving to be urbane" (reading *lepores* as the plural of *lepos*: pleasantry, wit, humor) or "hunting rabbits" (with *lepores* as the plural of *lepus*: a hare).

amulet
As a child, Johnson suffered from scrofula (see the notes for **scrofula** and **kingsevil**). When he was three years old, his mother brought him to London to be "touched" by the queen (according to legend, the royal touch would cure the disease), and he was given a golden amulet, a "touchpiece." He wore it for the rest of his life.

ana
Scaligerana and *Thuaniana* were collections of "table-talk," the conversations of the great scholars Joseph Scaliger and Jacques-Auguste de Thou. The most famous English ana is James Boswell's *Life of Samuel Johnson*, which began a flood of Johnsoniana.

ancient
Ancient (or Ensign) Pistol is Falstaff's companion in Shakespeare's *2 Henry IV*, *Henry V* and *The Merry Wives of Windsor*.

antithesis
The verses from Sir John Denham's poem of 1642, *Cooper's Hill*—"Though deep, yet clear; though gentle, yet not dull;/Strong without rage, without o'erflowing, full"—were among the best-known lines in the eighteenth century. Johnson said in his *Life of Denham* that "almost every writer for a century past has imitated" them, and with good reason: "So much meaning is comprised in so few words…that the passage however celebrated has not been praised above its merit."

B

baron
Hac vice tantum is Latin for "on this occasion only," the opening words of a legal writ.

boghouse
A "house of office" is a euphemism for a privy or outhouse.

bum
The identity of "W—n" has never been determined. It may be Philip Wharton, Duke of Wharton (1698-1731), who wrote poetry in that vein.

C

caitiff

The Greek passage (slightly abridged from Homer's *Odyssey*, book 17) means "Half a man's virtue is taken away the day he becomes a slave"—or, as it appeared in Pope's translation, "Jove fix'd it certain, that whatever day/Makes man a slave, takes half his worth away."

chronogram

Gloria lausque Deo, *sæ*CL*or*VM *in sæc*V*la sunt* is Latin for "Glory and praise to God forever and ever." The capital letters D, C, L, V (twice) and M all have values in Roman numerals. Added together, they make 1660.

cit

The lines come from Alexander Pope's imitation of Horace's *Epistle* 1.1. The identity of "D—l" is not certain; Pope's editors suggest Francis Scott, the Earl of Delorain. The second line as originally published read "But wretched Bug, his *Honour*, and so forth."

club

Johnson was the center of a famous "assembly of good fellows" formed in London in 1764, known as The Club or The Literary Club. Members included the painter Sir Joshua Reynolds, the politician Edmund Burke (author of *Reflections on the Revolution in France*), the novelist and playwright Oliver Goldsmith (*She Stoops to Conquer*), the playwright Richard Brinsley Sheridan (*The School for Scandal*), the actor David Garrick, the economist Adam Smith (*The Wealth of Nations*), the historian Edward Gibbon (*The Decline and Fall of the Roman Empire*), the antiquarians Thomas Warton (*A History of English Poetry*) and his brother Joseph (*An Essay on the Writings and Genius of Pope*), the musicologist Charles Burney, the scholar Edmund Malone, Bishop Thomas Percy (*Reliques of Ancient English Poetry*), Johnson's friends Topham Beauclerk and Bennet Langton, and eventually Johnson's biographer, James Boswell. The Club met weekly. For a twentieth-century equivalent, Paul Fussell suggests we imagine Winston Churchill, Samuel Beckett, Harold Pinter, Laurence Olivier, D. Nichol Smith, John Kenneth Galbraith, Ezra Pound, A. J. P. Taylor, Sir George Grove, Louis MacNeice, R. W. Chapman and Ben Nicholson gathering "to listen to a man each one recognizes as his intellectual superior."

coffee

Coffee first arrived in Europe in 1615 and soon became fashionable in Italy, Holland and France. The first commercial coffeehouse in England opened in Oxford in 1650, and within fifty years there were two thousand in London alone. They became important cultural centers where men met to discuss politics, poetry and the latest news. There were also chocolate houses and tea houses, both centered on hot beverages recently introduced into Europe from the wider world. See the note for **tea**.

crack-hemp

Furcifer is Latin for "rascal" or "someone bound for the gallows."

curmudgeon

Cœur mechant is French for "bitter heart," a suggestion Johnson received from "an unknown correspondent." In 1775, a lexicographer named John Ash misread the entry and blundered by giving the etymology as "from the French *cœur*, unknown, and *mechant*, a correspondent."

D

dad

Mammas atque tatas habet Afra is Latin for "Afra has mamas and papas." The line is from the poet Martial's *Epigrams*, 1.100.

December

The calendar Julius Caesar devised began the new year on 25 March. Counting March as the first month, then, the Latin names of the later months—September, "seventh"; October, "eighth"; November, "ninth"; and December, "tenth"—make more sense. As Johnson was working on the *Dictionary*, Britain abandoned the old Julian calendar for the Gregorian calendar, which Catholic Europe had used since 1582 (and which we still use today). The change required more than a different New Year's Day. Because of the way the two systems counted leap years, by the middle of the eighteenth century the Julian calendar had fallen eleven days behind the true date. When it was 1 July 1750 in England, it was 12 July 1750 in France; and because of the different New Year's Day, when it was 1 February 1751 in England, it was 12 February 1752 in France. The resulting confusion is easy to imagine. Lord Chesterfield (the would-be patron of the *Dictionary*) pushed through the legislation bringing Britain in line with the rest of Europe. In 1752, Britons went to bed on Wednesday, 2 September, and woke up on Thursday, 14 September. Russia kept the Julian calendar until 1923, by which time it was thirteen days behind the rest of the world.

differential method

Sir Isaac Newton and Gottfried Wilhelm von Leibniz (or Leibnitz) independently developed the differential method—known today as calculus—at the end of the seventeenth century. Johnson was interested in mathematics throughout his life and would often calm his mind by performing laborious calculations, although there is no evidence he ever learned calculus.

dissipate

"Savage's Life" is Johnson's own *Life of Savage*, first published in 1744. The impoverished poet Richard Savage was among Johnson's first friends in London, where the two passed many nights wandering the streets together. This quotation comes from Johnson's final summing up of Savage's character: "An irregular and dissipated Manner of Life had made him the Slave of every Passion that happened to be excited by the Presence of its Object, and that Slavery to his Passions reciprocally produced a Life irregular and dissipated. He was not Master of his own Motions, nor could promise any Thing for the next Day." Savage died in debtor's prison in 1743.

doctor

Though it's now normal to refer to a physician as doctor, it was still controversial in the eighteenth century. A Scottish physician, Dr. Memis, offended at being called a "doctor of medicine" rather than a "physician" in the Royal Infirmary's charter, sued for damages in 1775. Boswell, a lawyer, was involved in the case.

dream

The lines come from *The Greek Anthology*, a collection of more than six thousand lyric poems from the seventh century B.C. through the tenth century A.D. This poem, number 10.72, means, "All of life is a stage and a plaything: either put aside seriousness and learn to play, or endure your afflictions." Johnson, an insomniac, translated these poems into Latin to steady his mind during sleepless nights. As he wrote to Hester Thrale about a year before he died, "I used to drive the night along, by turning Greek epigrams into Latin. I know not if I have turned a hundred."

dropsy

In a dropsy—known today as edema—lymph collects in the organs, producing painful swelling. Johnson suffered from this condition at the end of his life, probably as a result of congestive heart failure. In February 1784, he wrote to Boswell, "My legs and thighs are very much swollen with water…. My nights are very sleepless and very tedious. And yet I am extremely afraid of dying." Two weeks later he wrote to Lucy Porter, his step-daughter, that he "received, by the mercy of GOD, sudden and unexpected relief last Thursday, by the discharge of twenty pints of water." In his final months, the swelling in his legs was so bad, says his friend John Hawkins, that "he got at a pair of scissars that lay in a drawer by him, and plunged them deep in the calf of each leg…. He looked upon himself as a bloated carcase; and, to attain the power of easy respiration, would have undergone any degree of temporary pain."

E

electricity
The most important "philosopher" Johnson refers to is Benjamin Franklin, the first part of whose *Experiments and Observations on Electricity* appeared in 1751. Though Johnson and Franklin traveled in the same circles in London for years, it seems they met only once, five years after the *Dictionary* was published.

element
Scientists had not seriously believed in the four elements—earth, air, fire and water—for a long time, but neither had they worked out the modern system of chemical elements. That had to wait for Antoine Laurent Lavoisier, who in his *Traité élémentaire de chimie* (1789) spelled out the rudiments of atomic theory.

etch
The *Oxford English Dictionary* offers a definition of the word under a variant spelling, *eddish*: "An aftergrowth of grass after mowing...stubble."

excise
Johnson's definition nearly got him into serious trouble. "The Commissioners of Excise," noted Boswell, "being offended by this severe reflection, consulted Mr. Murray, then Attorney General, to know whether redress could be legally obtained." They determined that "the passage might be considered as actionable; but that it would be more prudent in the board not to prosecute."

F

factotum
Scrub is a servant in George Farquhar's play *The Beaux' Stratagem* (1707).

faith
In defining faith as "Belief of the revealed truths of religion," Johnson was taking a polemical stand. Advocates of "natural religion" argued that all the essential religious truths could be deduced from our experience of the world, without resorting to the "revealed truth" of the Bible. For Johnson, those who ignored the revelation lacked faith.

fortnight
Non dierum numerum ut nos, sed noctium computant is Latin for "They don't count the number of days like us, but the nights."

G

galligaskins
The *Oxford English Dictionary* is a little more thorough: "A kind of wide hose or breeches worn in the 16th and 17th centuries; later, a more or less ludicrous term for loose breeches in general."

to ganch
Smith's *Pocockius* is Edmund Smith's *Thales: A Monody Sacred to the Memory of Dr. Pococke, in Imitation of Spenser*. Johnson makes a passing reference to it in his *Life of Smith*.

garnish
Pensiuncula carceraria means "prison payment." Prisoners were expected to bribe their jailers to get the best treatment. As the jailer tells Macheath when he arrives in the prison in John Gay's *Beggar's Opera*, "You know the custom, Sir. Garnish, captain, Garnish."

geneva
The "distilled spirituous water of juniper" called geneva was later shortened to gin. The "wonder" that "any people could accustom themselves to drink with pleasure" was warranted. Since the sale of gin was unregulated, it was produced under abysmal conditions, often adulterated with poisonous ingredients. Some who drank it went blind or even died. In *The Beggar's Opera*, when Lucy Lockit plans to poison her rival, Polly Peachum, she explains, "I run no Risque; for I can lay her Death upon the Ginn, and so many dye of that naturally that I shall never be call'd in question." It was the crack cocaine of its day, blamed for poverty and crime. Henry Fielding, a magistrate as well as a novelist, worried about the countless "Wretches...who swallow Pints of this Poison."

girdle
The lines are not Shakespeare's at all, but from Christopher Marlowe's "Passionate Shepherd to His Love." Johnson used William Warburton's edition of Shakespeare (1747); Warburton had inserted lines from Marlowe's "Passionate Shepherd" and Sir Walter Raleigh's "Nymph's Reply to the Shepherd" into *The Merry Wives of Windsor*, Act III, Scene i. When Johnson edited Shakespeare's plays in 1765, he corrected his predecessor: "These two Poems, which Dr. *Warburton* gives to *Shakespeare*, are, by writers nearer that time, disposed of, one to *Marlow*, the other to *Raleigh*." Marlowe, now considered one of Shakespeare's greatest contemporaries, was almost completely forgotten in Johnson's day. In *The History of English Poetry*, Johnson's friend Thomas Warton called Marlowe's *Dr. Faustus* "proof of the credulous ignorance which still prevailed," the sort of thing that "now only frightens children at a puppet-show in a country-town."

glossary
Stillingfleet refers to Marcus Varro (116-27 B.C.), who said that a *delubrum* (a temple or shrine) was a place "in which the image of a god was consecrated."

gold
Χρυση αφροδιτη is Greek for "golden Aphrodite." *Animamque moresque aureos educit in astra* comes (slightly modified) from Horace's *Ode* 4.2; it means "He raises his spirit and his golden virtue to the stars."

goujeres
"The French disease" is venereal disease.

gout
Johnson later suffered from gout; it was one of many conditions that plagued him throughout his life. See the notes for **dropsy, kingsevil, sarcocele** and **scrofula**.

grammar
Varium & mutabile semper femina is Latin for "Woman is always changing and changeable." The "satire" consists in the fact that *varium* and *mutabile* are neuter adjectives, not feminine, like *femina*. The sentence is grammatical only if you read it as "The female *animal* is always changing and changeable."

green
Sappho, the ancient lyric poet from Lesbos, lived in the second half of the seventh century B.C. Χλωροτερη ποιας, "greener than grass," comes from her most famous poem, fragment 31.

grubstreet
Grub Street was a section of London in which poor writers tried to eke out a living. As Wall Street means finance and Fleet Street means journalism, Grub Street came to stand for the whole milieu of hack writing. Johnson spent his early years in London turning out translations, reviews and poems for the new magazines that had sprung up (see the note for **magazine**). The

lines (from the *Greek Anthology* 9.458—see the note for **dream**) mean, "Hail, Ithaca! After pains and bitter hardships, I happily reach your soil." Johnson jokingly likens himself to Odysseus, returning to his homeland after years of wandering. The literal Grub Street no longer exists; the Barbican Centre swallowed up the entire area in the twentieth century.

H

hautboy
The hautboy is better known today as the oboe.

hieroglyph
Egyptian hieroglyphics were not understood at all until 1821, when Jean-François Champollion, working with the Rosetta stone, finally discovered the principles underlying the ancient writing system. The eighteenth century was filled with bizarre attempts to decode the mysterious symbols.

hocus pocus
Johnson admits ignorance of the word's origin: "It is corrupted from some words that had once a meaning, and which perhaps cannot be discovered." The word is actually a "corrupt" pronunciation of *hoc est corpus*, "This is [my] body." It comes from Protestant satires on the Catholic doctrine of transubstantiation, in which the Eucharist was believed to be the literal body of Christ. Protestants seized on what they considered a preposterous notion and ridiculed it by playing with the words. *Hocus pocus* came to mean any cheap magic trick.

huggermugger
Johnson complained about this word in his edition of *Hamlet* but resisted other editors' decision to replace *in huggermugger* with *in private*. "That the words now replaced are better, I do not undertake to prove; it is sufficient that they are Shakespeare's: if phraseology is to be changed as words grow uncouth by disuse, or gross by vulgarity, the history of every language will be lost; we shall no longer have the words of any authour; and, as these alterations will be often unskilfully made, we shall in time have very little of his meaning."

I–J

idoneous
De jure is Latin for "by right" or "according to law"; *de facto* means "in fact" or "the reality, regardless of what the law says."

imposture
Ubi is Latin for "where."

irony
The reference is to Henry St. John, Viscount Bolingbroke, a politician who died in 1751. Johnson had few kind words for Bolingbroke's principles, though he admitted to his friend Charles Burney, "I have never read Bolingbroke's impiety."

island
The couplet is not by Johnson at all but by Alexander Pope. Why he attributed it to himself is a mystery.

jakes
As in **boghouse**, a "house of office" is a privy or outhouse.

K

kingsevil
Scrofula was called kingsevil because, according to legend, a touch from the king could cure the disease. Johnson suffered from scrofula in his infancy, and the results were with him for his whole life. See the notes for **amulet** and **scrofula**.

L

lady
In attributing the passage to "Shakespeare's Merch. of Verona," Johnson's mind seems to have wandered, conflating *The Merchant of Venice* with *Two Gentlemen of Verona*. The quotation is from *The Merchant of Venice*, Act I, Scene ii.

latitudinarian
Beginning in the 1660s, Latitudinarians hoped to reduce the importance of religious doctrine, ecclesiastical hierarchy and liturgical forms in favor of a more liberal and tolerant theology. Johnson, a firm believer in orthodoxy, did not like the Latitudinarians' Low Church principles or Whiggish leanings. But he admired a number of liberal theologians, including John Tillotson and Edward Stillingfleet.

to learn
Although Johnson's quotations are often inexact, he rarely distorts them this severely. Rather than "my profit on 't/Is, I know not how to curse," Shakespeare actually wrote "I know how to curse."

leeward
Boswell writes of Johnson, "A few of his definitions must be admitted to be erroneous. Thus, *Windward* and *Leeward*, though directly of opposite meaning, are defined identically the same way."

liberty
The Latin *jura regalia* means "kingly prerogatives," a term from medieval law.

lich
Salve magna parens means "Hail, great mother." Johnson was born in Lichfield, a town in the English Midlands. This Latin tag is a facetious tribute to his hometown.

L.L.D.
Boswell writes that in 1765, Trinity College, Dublin "surprised Johnson with a spontaneous compliment of the highest academical honours, by creating him Doctor of Laws." From then on, he was widely known as "Doctor Johnson." He was honored to receive the degree but never warmed to the title. "It is remarkable," writes Boswell, "that he never, so far as I know, assumed his title of *Doctor*, but called himself *Mr.* Johnson."

luxurious
Like several of the "anonymous" quotations, this one comes from Johnson's *Vanity of Human Wishes*.

M

magazine
Johnson refers to *The Gentleman's Magazine*, the first publication to use the word *magazine* in its title. Edward Cave began publishing it in 1731, and it became one of the most popular periodicals of the century. In 1734, Johnson wrote to Cave offering "not only poems, inscriptions, &c. never printed before…but likewise short literary dissertations in Latin or English, critical remarks on authours ancient or modern, forgotten poems that deserve revival, or loose pieces." Nothing came of it. Persistence paid off, though, and Johnson became a regular contributor in 1738. "When he first saw St. John's Gate," wrote Boswell, "the place where that deservedly popular miscellany was originally printed, he 'beheld it with reverence.'" Much of his work involved the "emendation and improvement of the productions of other contributors," but in 1741 he began reporting on the debates in Parliament. Because it was illegal to publish the debates, Cave printed them under the title "Debates in the Senate of Magna Lilliputia," giving them a thin veneer of fiction to avoid prosecution.

martyr

In quoting King Charles here, Johnson seems to invite a political interpretation. Charles was executed in 1649 and was known to royalists as "Charles the Martyr." Johnson aligns himself with those who revered the king.

meeting-house

Dissenters were the more radical Protestants in seventeenth- and eighteenth-century England, those who did not belong to the Church of England. Although Johnson was friendly with many Dissenters, he remained a firm supporter of the established Church. Hester Thrale Piozzi records some of his more biting comments on Dissenting preachers: "Their religion, he frequently said, was too worldly, too political, too restless and ambitious.... He knew that a wild democracy had overturned King, Lords, and Commons; and that a set of Republican Fanatics, who would not bow at the name of JESUS, had taken possession of all the livings and all the parishes in the kingdom."

megrim

A megrim is better known today as a migraine.

melancholy

Melancholy in eighteenth-century medical parlance meant more than feeling a little blue. It was an oppressive mental and physical condition, akin to what we would term clinical depression. Johnson had his first severe bout of melancholy in 1729, when he left Oxford and suffered what we might now call a nervous breakdown. From then on, he always feared he might be on the verge of insanity. As he told Boswell, another chronic melancholic, "I inherited...a vile melancholy from my father, which has made me mad all my life, at least not sober." In 1777, he complained of "disturbances of the mind very near to madness." The need to stave off melancholy led him to seek company and to keep his mind active. "Against melancholy," says Boswell, "he recommended constant occupation of mind, a great deal of exercise, moderation in eating and drinking, and especially to shun drinking at night."

metaphrase

In his edition of Ovid's *Epistles* (1680), John Dryden distinguished three kinds of translation: "Metaphrase, or turning an author word by word, and line by line, from one language to another.... Paraphrase, or translation with latitude, where the author is kept in view by the translator, so as never to be lost, but his words are not so strictly followed as his sense.... Imitation, where the translator (if now he has not lost that name) assumes the liberty, not only to vary from the words and sense, but to forsake them both as he sees occasion." Johnson's two most famous poems, *London* and *The Vanity of Human Wishes*, are imitations of Juvenal's Latin satires.

methodist

The "new kind of puritans" arose in the 1730s in Oxford's Holy Club, led by John and Charles Wesley. Johnson admired John Wesley but objected to many points of methodist theology, especially its "enthusiasm." "Speaking of the *inward light*, to which some methodists pretended," Boswell records, "he said, it was a principle utterly incompatible with social or civil security."

millennium

The "doubtful text in the Apocalypse" is Revelation 20:1-11, one of the most hotly debated passages in the Bible. The verses seem to describe the prospect of a thousand-year reign of Christ on earth before the end of the world, but critics have argued for centuries over their exact interpretation.

mimick

The "anonymous" line comes from Johnson's poem *London* (1737), in his description of England's decline after Edward III's triumphs at Crecy: "Behold the Warriour dwindled to a Beau;/Sense, Freedom, Piety, refin'd away,/Of FRANCE the Mimic, and of SPAIN the Prey."

minim

In his satire of unthinking literary criticism in *Idler* 60 and 61, Johnson gave the name Dick Minim to his dimwitted critic, a mere parroter of critical commonplaces.

modern

Vel potius ab adverbio mado, *modernus, ut a* die *diurnus* is Latin for "Perhaps *modern*, from the adverb *mado*, as *daily* comes from *day*."

moderns

The "battle of the ancients and moderns" was an important episode in seventeenth-century intellectual history. On one side were those who insisted that the learning of ancient Greece and Rome had never been surpassed; on the other, those who argued that poetry, statecraft and science had reached their heights only in the last few centuries. Jonathan Swift's *Battle of the Books* is the most lasting English product of the conflict. Johnson, as usual, refused to take a simple stance and advised, "No man ought severely to ape either the ancients or the moderns."

to modulate

The "anonymous" quotation is from one of Johnson's minor poems, "To Miss —— on Her Playing upon the Harpsicord in a Room Hung with Some Flower-Pieces of Her Own Painting."

money

Johnson refers only to metal money because paper currency was a relatively new development. The first European paper money was issued in Sweden in 1661, and it was controversial for decades. Many experiments with paper money had proved disastrous, as when banks issued more paper currency than they had "real" money on hand, precipitating crises in confidence.

N

network

This definition, "Any thing reticulated or decussated, at equal distances, with interstices between the intersections," is often singled out as an example of Johnson's preposterously latinate diction. The definition seems to have been inspired by Sir Thomas Browne's *Garden of Cyrus*, chapter 3: "This Reticulate or Net-work was also considerable in the inward parts of man, not only from the first *subtegmen* or warp of his formation, but in the netty *fibres* of the veins and vessels of life; wherein according to common Anatomy the right and transverse *fibres* are decussated, by the oblique *fibres*."

nice

The etymology deriving nice from the Saxon *nese*, "soft," is wrong; it's actually from the Latin *nescire*, "not to know." The long entry in the *Oxford English Dictionary* traces its complicated history. In the thirteenth century, nice meant "foolish; stupid; senseless," and over the years it picked up other derogatory meanings ("lascivious," "lazy," "effeminate"). In the sixteenth century, it came to mean "fastidious," which could also have a positive spin: "particular, precise, strict, careful." In the seventeenth century, it meant "punctilious, scrupulous, sensitive," terms applied to one who could settle a "nice" question ("Not obvious or readily apprehended; difficult to decide or settle; demanding close consideration or thought; intricate"). Only after Johnson's *Dictionary* did it pick up the meaning "Agreeable; that one derives pleasure or satisfaction from; delightful." Jane Austen alludes to this entry in *Northanger Abbey*, chapter 14.

nonjuring

Johnson refers to the complicated politics of the late seventeenth and early eighteenth centuries. In 1688, James II of the House of Stuart was forced to flee the country, and William of Orange was brought from Holland to rule the country with his wife, Queen Mary. James's supporters—known as Jacobites, from the Latin *Jacobus*, "James"—hoped for his eventual return. In 1714,

George, Elector of Hanover and a German prince, became George I of England, excluding the Stuart line from the throne. On several occasions, most notably in 1715, 1719 and 1745, the Stuarts and their Jacobite partisans mounted failed invasions of England, hoping to take the country back from the Hanoverians. Those who refused to swear allegiance to George I and George II were known as Nonjurors, from the Latin for "not swearing."

nostrum

Hic jacet auctor hujus argumenti is Latin for "Here lies the author of this argument."

O

oats

This is perhaps the most famous definition in the *Dictionary*. Johnson was notorious for being prejudiced against the Scots, and his enemies pointed to this definition as evidence of his bigotry. To be fair, though, many of his friends were Scottish—including James Boswell—and he made a tour of the Western Islands of Scotland with Boswell in 1773. The definition, moreover, was borrowed from other dictionaries. In any case, the jest seems harmless. Hester Thrale Piozzi wrote in her diary, "We all know well he loved to abuse the Scotch, & indeed to be abused by them in return." He jokingly admitted as much to Boswell: "Boswell. 'You set out with attacking the Scotch; so you got a whole nation for your enemies.' Johnson. 'Why, I own, that by my definition of *oats* I meant to vex them.'"

ombre

This popular card game dominates Canto III of Pope's *Rape of the Lock*. The rules appeared in Richard Seymour's *Court Gamester* (1719). The eighteenth century was a great age of card and board games, and saw some of the first printed collections of rules. The most famous were by Edmond Hoyle, who began publishing them in 1743. "Hoyle's" is still in print, having gone through many dozens of editions.

original

Notice that original in our day does not mean the same thing as in Johnson's. Edward Young's *Conjectures on Original Composition* (1759) was influential in shifting the word from "going back to the origins" to "being its own origin." Originality in the modern sense becomes increasingly prized in the literary criticism of the 1760s and later.

P

parasite

Johnson misquotes *1 Henry IV* and mistakes the very word he is illustrating: not "Come, you parasite," but "Come, you Paraquito" (parakeet).

party

"They never mention the q—n" was a sly way of avoiding charges of treason for speaking ill of the queen or other members of the royal family. No one was fooled. Johnson resorted to the same trick in his poem *London*: "Lest Ropes be wanting in the tempting Spring,/To rig another Convoy for the K—g."

pastern

Johnson's most famous mistake: the pastern is, in fact, the part of a horse's leg between the fetlock and the hoof. According to Boswell (although the story may well be apocryphal), "A lady once asked him how he came to define Pastern the knee of a horse. Instead of making an elaborate defence, as she expected, he at once answered, 'Ignorance, Madam, pure ignorance.'"

patriot
In the fourth edition of his *Dictionary* (1773), Johnson added a second, more bitter definition: "It is sometimes used for a factious disturber of the government." Boswell records his more famous comment: "Patriotism is the last refuge of a scoundrel."

pension
When Johnson received a government pension of £300 a year in 1762, his enemies were quick to quote this definition and accuse him of hypocrisy. He expected as much, and even hesitated before taking it, but Lord Bute assured him that "the pension was granted to Johnson solely as the reward of his literary merit, without any stipulation whatever." Johnson insisted "I am the same man in every respect that I have ever been." Boswell, eager to defend his friend, wrote, "There was nothing inconsistent or humiliating in Johnson's accepting of a pension so unconditionally and so honourably offered to him."

philomel
The supposed Shakespeare quotation actually comes from Sir Walter Raleigh. See also the note for **girdle**.

pica
Johnson's *Dictionary* was originally set in small pica. More precisely, the Preface and the column headers were in a 4.6mm English font and the text was in 3.5mm pica. This Levenger edition is in Adobe Caslon and the headers are in Colmcille. Adobe Caslon is based on the work of William Caslon (1692-1766), an English typefounder whose typefaces were hugely popular in England and America. They were used in the first settings of the Declaration of Independence.

to pimp
The "anonymous" quotation is from Johnson's poem, "Prologue Spoken at the Opening of the Theatre in Drury-Lane, 1747."

plaid
Men's wearing of plaid was "extirpated" by "act of parliament" after the failed Jacobite invasion of Britain in 1745 and '46 (see the note for **nonjuring**). Since Scottish Highlanders played a prominent part in the rebellion, the British Parliament punished them in a series of measures designed to crush their spirits and eradicate their culture. Scots were not permitted to carry weapons; their native language, Scots Gaelic, was outlawed; and they were forbidden to wear their traditional plaid kilts. A passage in Tobias Smollett's novel, *Humphry Clinker* (1771), describes the plight of the defeated Highlanders: they were "deprived of their ancient garb, which was both graceful and convenient; and what is a greater hardship still, they are compelled to wear breeches; a restraint which they cannot bear with any degree of patience....They are even debarred the use of their striped stuff, called Tartane, which was their own manufacture, prized by them above all the velvets, brocards, and tissues of Europe and Asia."

planet
Harris lists only six planets: Mercury, Venus, Earth, Mars, Jupiter and Saturn. Uranus was discovered in 1781, Neptune in 1846 and Pluto only in 1930.

poetry
Boswell once asked Johnson, "What is poetry?" "Why, Sir," replied Johnson, "it is much easier to say what it is not. We all *know* what light is; but it is not easy to *tell* what it is."

police
The word is set in italics, meaning Johnson didn't consider it a fully naturalized English word, and it is far from our sense of police. There was nothing akin to a modern police force in Great Britain until 1750, when John Fielding and his half-brother Henry Fielding (the novelist) formed

the Bow Street Runners, the first paid force in England. Sir Robert Peel professionalized the police in 1829, when he established a metropolitan force based in London's Scotland Yard.

prosodian

The line depends on a pun on the Latin word *malum*, which can mean "apple" or "evil." But only "bad prosodians" would derive one from the other, because in *malum*, "apple," the *a* is long, and in *malum*, "evil," it is short.

prowl

The "anonymous" quotation is from Johnson's *London*: "Their Ambush here relentless Ruffians lay,/And here the fell Attorney prowls for Prey;/Here falling Houses thunder on your Head,/And here a female Atheist talks you dead."

to puff

Parasiti curiæ is Latin for "parasites of the court."

punster

Johnson wasn't alone in attacking puns: many eighteenth-century critics considered such wordplay "false wit." Johnson levels some of his sharpest criticism at Shakespeare for his fondness for puns (known at the time as quibbles): "A quibble is to Shakespeare, what luminous vapours are to the traveller; he follows it at all adventures, it is sure to lead him out of his way, and sure to engulf him in the mire. It has some malignant power over his mind…. A quibble, poor and barren as it is, gave him such delight, that he was content to purchase it, by the sacrifice of reason, propriety and truth. A quibble was to him the fatal Cleopatra for which he lost the world, and was content to lose it."

puritan

The Puritans arose in the sixteenth century, as England was caught up in the Protestant Reformation. The Church of England, which Henry VIII founded, sought a middle way between Catholicism and radical Protestantism. Some were unsatisfied with this "leaden mean." Those who hoped to strip English Christianity of all its Catholic "impurities" were therefore known as Puritans. Johnson greatly admired the theologian Richard Hooker, whose *Laws of Ecclesiastical Polity* defended the Anglican Church from Puritan attacks in the 1590s.

Q

quatrain

Johnson knew Hester Mulso Chapone through Samuel Richardson. She was one of the learned women known as the Bluestockings and contributed to two of Johnson's projects, *The Rambler* and *The Adventurer*. Johnson was very fond of this poem and, according to Frances Reynolds, he "used to repeat [it], with very apparent delight." The admiration wasn't entirely mutual. Mulso thought Johnson "ought to be ashamed of publishing such an ill-contrived, unfinished, unnatural, and uninstructive tale" as *Rasselas* and complained of the "shocking pictures of human nature…speaking of envy and malice as universal passions" in *The Rambler*. Many women writers received support from Johnson, who, said Reynolds, "set a higher value upon female friendship than, perhaps, most men."

queer

The Latin *quære* is related to the English *query*, and in this context means much the same thing: "ask about it."

R

race
Our modern notion of race is not to be found here, though this third definition probably comes closest. Scientists (and pseudo-scientists) began to categorize human beings into classes based on characteristics such as skin color and facial structure only in the late eighteenth century.

republican
Certainly Johnson, a firm supporter of monarchy, did not think a "commonwealth without monarchy" the best government. In his *Life of Milton*, he criticizes Milton as an "acrimonious and surly republican" whose "republicanism was, I am afraid, founded in an envious hatred of greatness, and a sullen desire of independence; in petulance impatient of controul, and pride disdainful of superiority."

revolution
The Greek κατα εξοχην means "especially" or "above all." Johnson here refers to the Glorious Revolution of 1688-89, when James II was removed from the throne and the Dutch William of Orange came to England and ruled the country with Queen Mary. See the note for **nonjuring** for more details.

rhymer
The quotation attributed to Shakespeare is actually from Jonathan Swift's "Vanbrug's House," slightly misquoted.

ribald
The "slashing Bentley" and "pidling Tibbalds" refer to the scholars Richard Bentley and Lewis Theobald. Both were among Pope's many enemies. Bentley had argued with Pope's friend Swift, and Theobald's *Shakespeare Restored* is a harsh and extended criticism of Pope's edition of Shakespeare. Pope responded by making Bentley and Theobald two of the "heroes" in his mock epic poem, *The Dunciad*.

to rodomontade
Rodomonte was a character in Matteo Boiardo's *Orlando Innamorato* and Ludovico Ariosto's *Orlando Furioso*, two romantic epics of the Italian Renaissance.

S

sack
In suggesting the word sack is "antediluvian" (from before Noah's flood), Johnson enters into some of the contemporary debates over the origins of language. For centuries scholars had tried to account for the variety of languages in the world. Encounters with ever more exotic languages as Europe expanded its empire only exacerbated the problem. Many believed in the scattering of tongues after the fall of the Tower of Babel (see Gen. 10:8-10), in which a single language, given by God in Eden, had been replaced by many mutually unintelligible languages. Johnson's friend Sir William Jones, a poet, jurist and orientalist, was the first to offer a coherent scientific theory for the relationships between languages. In his *Third Anniversary Discourse* (1786), Jones argued for the existence of a Proto-Indo-European tongue, an extinct ancestor to languages as diverse as Sanskrit, Greek, Latin, Russian and German. The hypothesis was developed over the course of the next century and is the basis of subsequent historical linguistics.

sarcocele
Near the end of his life, Johnson suffered from this painful condition. As his friend John Hawkins records, "He was alarmed by a tumour, [which] surgeons termed a sarcocele, that, as it increased, gave him great pain, and, at length, hurried him to town, with a resolution to submit, if it should

be thought necessary, to a dreadful chirurgical operation." (Boswell calls it "a painful chirurgical operation, from which most men would shrink.") He was fortunate that a "less severe" treatment "restored him to a state of perfect ease in the part affected."

satire

Johnson's etymology alludes to the debates over the origin of the word satire: some proposed it came from *satura lanx*, "a mixed platter"; others from *satyrus*, "a satyr play." John Dryden famously discusses the two in his "Discourse on the Original and Progress of Satire."

scale

The poem was by one of Johnson's amanuenses, the Scotsman Alexander Macbean. Johnson relied on him for information on many Scottish words and expressions. Macbean later went on to write his own *Dictionary of Ancient Geography* in 1773, to which Johnson contributed a preface. In later life he faced poverty, and Johnson worked to find him a means of support. After Macbean's death in 1784, Johnson wrote, "He was very pious; he was very innocent; he did no ill; and of doing good a continual tenour of distress allowed him few opportunities."

scenick

The "anonymous" quotation is from Johnson's poem, "Prologue Spoken at the Opening of the Theatre in Drury-Lane, 1747."

scholar

Res angusta domi comes from the Latin poet Juvenal's third satire: *Haud facile emergunt quorum virtutibus obstat/Res angusta domi*, "Those whose talents are blocked by poverty at home don't easily rise out of obscurity." When Johnson imitated this poem in 1738 as *London*, he rendered this passage in small capital letters: "SLOW RISES WORTH, BY POVERTY DEPRESS'D."

science 2

"Berkley" here is Bishop George Berkeley, a philosopher famous for the adage *Esse est percipi*, "To be is to be perceived"—that is, things exist only insofar as they are observed. Boswell records Johnson's famous reply: "We stood talking for some time together of Bishop Berkeley's ingenious sophistry to prove the non-existence of matter, and that every thing in the universe is merely ideal. I observed, that though we are satisfied his doctrine is not true, it is impossible to refute it. I never shall forget the alacrity with which Johnson answered, striking his foot with mighty force against a large stone, till he rebounded from it, 'I refute it *thus.*'"

science 4

Our modern sense of science, confined to disciplines such as chemistry, biology and physics, is nowhere to be found in the middle of the eighteenth century. It wasn't until the nineteenth century that the word began to narrow in meaning from "Any art or species of knowledge" to only those that proceed by hypothesis and experiment.

to sconce

Although Johnson dismisses sconce as "A low word which ought not to be retained," he apparently used it himself. When a student at Oxford, Johnson often skipped lectures, including those of Jordan, his tutor (the rough equivalent of a major professor). According to Sir John Hawkins, Johnson's friend and first biographer, Johnson "would oftener risque the payment of a small fine than attend his lectures.... Upon occasion of one such imposition, he said to Jordan, 'Sir, you have sconced me two-pence for nonattendance at a lecture not worth a penny.'"

scrofula

Scrofula is a tubercular infection of the lymph nodes in the neck. Johnson was afflicted with it in infancy, perhaps infected by his wetnurse. The effects remained with him for life, and Hester Thrale wrote that it "left such marks as greatly disfigured a countenance naturally harsh and rugged, beside doing irreparable damage to the auricular organs, which never could perform their functions since I knew him; and it was owing to that horrible disorder, too, that one eye was perfectly useless to him." See the entries for **kingsevil** and **amulet**.

sea

This word almost didn't make it into the *Dictionary*. As Johnson writes in the Preface, "It is remarkable that, in reviewing my collection, I found the word SEA unexemplified."

second sight

Johnson investigated the possibility that the Scottish Highlanders might have this supernatural ability during his tour of the Western Islands in 1773. Boswell records that he asked a minister in Slate whether "there were any remains of the second sight." The minister said "he was *resolved* not to believe it, because it was founded on no principle.—*Johnson*. 'There are many things then, which we are sure are true, that you will not believe. What principle is there, why a loadstone attracts iron? why an egg produces a chicken by heat? why a tree grows upwards, when the natural tendency of all things is downwards? Sir, it depends upon the degree of evidence that you have.' " In the end, though, the "degree of evidence" wasn't enough, and Johnson remained a skeptic. He wrote to Boswell in 1775, "The notion of the second sight I consider as a remnant of superstitious ignorance and credulity, which a philosopher will set down as such, till the contrary is clearly proved, and then it will be classed among the other certain, though unaccountable, parts of our nature, like dreams, and—I do not know what."

septennial

The "anonymous" quotation is from Johnson's *Vanity of Human Wishes*. He alludes to the feasts held before elections, when the candidates would hope to bribe their constituents with food and drink. According to a law of 1716, a parliamentary election had to be held at least every seven years.

shall

"Crassa Minervâ," a proverbial expression for homespun wit, comes from Horace's *Satire* 2.2.

sizer

A sizer, or sizar, was a poor university student who paid for his education by working as a servant for the other scholars. John Hawkins writes that the young Johnson "could not…divest himself of an opinion, that poverty was disgraceful; and was very severe in his censures of that œconomy in both our universities, which exacted at meals the attendance of poor scholars, under the several denominations of servitors in the one [Oxford], and sizers in the other [Cambridge]: he thought that the scholar's, like the christian life, levelled all distinctions of rank and worldly pre-eminence; but in this he was mistaken." Later his opinion seems to have softened, and he helped the son of a friend to get a servitorship at Oxford.

skilt

Johnson confesses he does not know the meaning and neither, apparently, does the *Oxford English Dictionary*, which omits the word. The editors of Cleveland's poetry, however, suggest it means "signify," and interpret "What skilt?" as "What does it matter?"

sonnet

The assertion that the sonnet is "not very suitable to the English language" seems odd when we think about the great examples by Shakespeare, Donne and others. But Johnson's judgment wasn't perverse by the standards of his day, since many critics complained that English wasn't rich enough in rhymes to pull off such a complicated form. And his claim that it "has not been used by any man of eminence since Milton" is correct. There were some scattered minor efforts by Thomas Edwards, Thomas Warton and Thomas Gray, but the first important collection of sonnets after Milton's was published by Charlotte Smith in 1784, the year Johnson died.

soulshot

Pecunia sepulchralis & symbolum animæ is Latin for "funeral money and contribution for the soul."

spider

Spider comes from the Middle English *spither*, from Old English *spinnan*, "to spin." Given the ironic tone of his reference to Junius, Johnson's fanciful etymology may be facetious.

spirit

The "anonymous" quotation is apparently from one of Johnson's earliest poems, "On a Daffodil," probably quoted from memory: "May lambent zephyrs gently wave thy head,/And balmy spirits thro' thy foliage play."

stammel

The *Oxford English Dictionary* defines stammel as "A coarse woolen cloth" or "The shade of red in which the cloth was commonly dyed."

stoick

Stoics never come off well in Johnson's works. In *Rambler* 32 he said their "wild enthusiastick virtue pretended to an exemption from the sensibilities of unenlightened mortals." Such an "exemption," he insisted, was impossible. The most famous example is the philosopher in chapter 18 of *Rasselas*, who strove for "the conquest of passion…after which man is no longer the slave of fear, nor the fool of hope…but walks on calmly through the tumults or the privacies of life." Young Rasselas, impressed by these Stoic principles, declares, "This man shall be my future guide: I will learn his doctrines, and imitate his life." The older and wiser Imlac, though, warns him that "teachers of morality…discourse like angels, but they live like men." When the philosopher's daughter dies, all his precepts are forgotten: " 'What comfort,' said the mourner, 'can truth and reason afford me? of what effect are they now, but to tell me, that my daughter will not be restored?' "

strappado

Wrong: strappado is "A form of punishment or of torture to extort confession in which the victim's hands were tied across his back and secured to a pulley; he was then hoisted from the ground and let down half way with a jerk" (*Oxford English Dictionary*).

strumpet

The French quotation from Trevoux's dictionary means "*Stropo*, an old word [for] *palliardise*." Johnson defines palliardise as "Fornication; whoring."

T

talent

The Female Quixote was a novel by Johnson's friend Charlotte Lennox. Johnson wrote the Dedication and may have contributed a chapter.

Targum

The Targum is a set of translations and paraphrases of the Hebrew Bible, including the first five books—the pentateuch—into Aramaic (known in Johnson's day as Chaldee or Chaldaic).

tea

Tea was indeed "lately…much drunk in Europe." It first arrived in Europe in the sixteenth century, but was little known outside Portugal and Holland until the seventeenth. Thomas Garway offered it for sale in London in 1657, and in the next year, an advertisement appeared in the *Mercurius Politicus* for "China Tcha, Tay or Tee." Soon tea houses sprang up across London. It was Johnson's favorite drink. Boswell supposed "No person ever enjoyed with more relish the infusion of that fragrant leaf than Johnson. The quantities which he drank of it at all hours were so great, that his nerves must have been uncommonly strong." A friend recollected that "when Sir

Joshua Reynolds…reminded Dr. Johnson that he had drank eleven cups, he replied:—'Sir, I did not count your glasses of wine, why should you number up my cups of tea?' " But calculating his prodigious consumption was a common sport. A woman remembered that she "had herself helped Dr. Johnson one evening to fifteen cups." In 1757, he wrote a review of Jonas Hanway's *Journal of Eight Days' Journey,* a work that "endeavours to show, that the consumption of tea is injurious to the interest of our country." Johnson would have none of it. "He is to expect little justice from the author of this extract, a hardened and shameless tea-drinker, who has, for twenty years, diluted his meals with only the infusion of this fascinating plant; whose kettle has scarcely time to cool; who with tea amuses the evening, with tea solaces the midnight, and, with tea, welcomes the morning."

terrour
The "anonymous" quotation comes from Johnson's poem *London:* "Yet ev'n these Heroes, mischievously gay,/Lords of the Street, and Terrors of the Way;/Flush'd as they are with Folly, Youth and Wine,/Their prudent Insults to the Poor confine;/Afar they mark the Flambeau's bright Approach,/And shun the shining Train, and golden Coach."

thrasonical
Thraso is a boastful soldier in Terence's play, *Eunuchus.*

tory
Tories and Whigs were the two major political parties in eighteenth-century England, and Johnson was famous for his Tory principles. It has been common to contrast this definition— "One who adheres to the antient constitution of the state, and the apostolical hierarchy of the church of England"—with that of whig, "The name of a faction." But the long and sympathetic quotation under *whig* from Gilbert Burnet, well known for his Whiggism, made a fuller definition unnecessary. Besides, Johnson is kinder than many lexicographers: *A New World of Words* defines whig as "A Fanatick; a Factious Fellow." In spite of the occasional dig (such as "The first Whig was the Devil"), Johnson respected a great many Whigs, observing, "A wise Tory and a wise Whig, I believe, will agree."

tragicomedy
The mixing of tragedy and comedy bothered many eighteenth-century critics, who wanted to keep their genres distinct. Johnson, though, was uncommonly tolerant of Shakespeare's "mixing [of] comick and tragick scenes," arguing that "Shakespeare's plays are not in the rigorous and critical sense either tragedies or comedies, but compositions of a distinct kind…. Shakespeare has united the powers of exciting laughter and sorrow…. That this is a practice contrary to the rules of criticism will be readily allowed; but there is always an appeal open from criticism to nature."

traytrip
The *Oxford English Dictionary* offers only a little help: "A game at dice, or with dice, in which success probably depended on the casting of a trey or three."

trolmydames
The *Oxford English Dictionary* defines *troll-madam* as "A game played by ladies, resembling bagatelle." It in turn defines bagatelle as "A game played on a table having a semi-circular end at which are nine holes. The balls used are struck from the opposite end of the board with a cue."

truth
Another "anonymous" quotation from Johnson's *London:* "Here let those reign, whom Pensions can incite/To vote a Patriot black, a Courtier white;/Explain their Country's dear-bought Rights away,/And plead for Pirates in the Face of Day;/With slavish Tenets taint our poison'd Youth,/And lend a Lye the confidence of Truth."

U–V

umbrel

The men's umbrella was brand-new when Johnson was writing the *Dictionary*. Only women had carried them in England. Jonas Hanway (1712-86), a travel writer, was the first man publicly to carry an umbrella in London, beginning in 1750. Men's umbrellas were long known as "Hanways." For Johnson's quarrel with Hanway, see the note on **tea**.

unity

The three unities of time, place and action were central to Renaissance criticism. Claiming to derive the rules from Aristotle's *Poetics* (but in fact distorting what he wrote), critics insisted that the action of a play must happen within twenty-four hours; that it must be confined to one place; and that it must have only one plot. Shakespeare made mincemeat of these rules. Many commentators chastised him for it, but Johnson defended Shakespeare in his edition of the plays in 1765: "To the unities of time and place he has shewn no regard.... I cannot think it much to be lamented, that they were not known by him, or not observed.... The unities of time and place are not essential to a just drama, that though they may sometimes conduce to pleasure, they are always to be sacrificed to the nobler beauties of variety and instruction."

utis

"Old utis" seems to mean "a high old time." The *Oxford English Dictionary* suggests utis can mean either "noise, confusion, din" or "jollification, period of festivity."

volant

Johnson was fascinated by flying machines, even though he died more than a century before the Wright Brothers' flight at Kitty Hawk in 1903. In his philosophical romance *Rasselas* (1759), he satirizes a "projector" for building a flying machine, and he draws on this passage from Wilkins's *Mathematical Magic*. He was also fascinated by the news of Joseph Michel and Jacques Etienne Montgolfier, the brothers who in June 1783 constructed the first practical hot-air balloons. Johnson wrote in December of that year, "The air ballon...has taken full possession, with a very good claim, of every philosophical mind and mouth. Do you not wish for the flying coach?"

volunteer
The Relapse was a play by Sir John Vanbrugh (1664-1726).

W–X

war

This definition was introduced into the proceedings of a recent federal lawsuit (*Campbell* v. *Clinton*, 2000), challenging the President's authority to order airstrikes in Yugoslavia. Since the U.S. Constitution gives Congress sole power to declare war, Congress turned to the dictionary written closest to the Constitution in 1787 to clarify what *war* meant to its Framers. The *Dictionary* has often been cited in debates over the Constitution in the U.S. courts. In *U.S.* v. *Weisenbaker* (1994), the judge invoked Johnson's notorious definition of *excise* before finding the defendant guilty of tax evasion. In *Kohler* v. *Bank of Bermuda (New York) Ltd.* (2000), the definition of *subject* was introduced to clarify the distinction between subjects and citizens. Then again, not all the legal citations have been complimentary. In *State* v. *Stroupe* (1953), the North Carolina court cited the definition of *network* as an example of how "a thing in itself very plain is obscured."

whig
See the note for **tory**.

windward
See the note for **leeward**.

write

"He writes himself *divina providentia* [by divine providence], whereas other bishops only use *divina permissione* [by divine permission]."

X

We might think we have caught Johnson in an error when he notes that X "begins no word in the English language," but he wasn't far wrong. All the familiar words beginning with X entered the language after the *Dictionary* was published. These include *xenophobia* (first used in 1909), *X-ray* (1896) and *xylophone* (1866). The *Oxford English Dictionary* lists only nine words beginning with X (other than proper names) that were in use in 1755, all of them very rare: *xenium* ("A present given to a guest or stranger"), first used in 1706; *xeonodochium* ("A house of reception for strangers and pilgrims"), 1612; *xerophagy* ("The eating of dry food"), 1656; *xerophthalmia* ("An ophthlamia without discharge"), 1656; *xilinous* ("Of cotton"), 1656; *xiphoid* ("Sword-shaped"), 1746; *xoanon* ("A primitive rudely carved image or statue"), 1706; *xylobalsamum* ("The fragrant wood of the tree *Balsamodendron gileadense*"), 1398; and *xystus* ("Among the ancient Greeks, a long covered portico or court used for athletic exercises"), 1664.

SUGGESTED READING

Dictionaries

Johnson's *Dictionary* gets a chapter to itself in Jonathon Green's *Chasing the Sun*, an entertaining (but not always reliable) introduction to dictionaries from ancient Sumeria to Silicon Valley. Sidney Landau's *Dictionaries* is also valuable. DeWitt T. Starnes and Gertrude E. Noyes survey Johnson's English predecessors in their scholarly work, *The English Dictionary from Cawdrey to Johnson*. K. M. Elisabeth Murray's *Caught in the Web of Words* is a lively biography of her grandfather, James Murray, the first editor of the *Oxford English Dictionary*. Simon Winchester's *Professor and the Madman* tells the fascinating story of one of the volunteer contributors to that project.

Samuel Johnson

The classic biography is James Boswell's *Life of Samuel Johnson*, published seven years after Johnson's death. The *Life* cannot be taken at face value—Boswell's stories, reported decades after the fact (and sometimes third-hand), are not always accurate—but his portrait of Johnson and his age remains indispensable. The most useful edition for general readers is one edited by R. W. Chapman, although scholars rely on the massive six-volume edition edited by G. B. Hill and L. F. Powell. More recent and more reliable biographies abound. Walter Jackson Bate's *Samuel Johnson* and James L. Clifford's two volumes, *Young Sam Johnson* and *Dictionary Johnson: Samuel Johnson's Middle Years*, are authoritative and accessible. Robert DeMaria's biography of Johnson focuses on his frustrated desires to be a Latin scholar and poet, and Thomas Kaminski's *Early Career of Samuel Johnson* meticulously describes Johnson's labors after his arrival in London.

Although Johnson's own writings have sometimes been crowded out by the work of his biographers, most of his works are still available, and all are worth reading. The standard scholarly edition is the Yale Edition of the Works of Samuel Johnson, in thirteen volumes to date. The volume of *Philological Writings*, edited by Gwin J. Kolb and Robert DeMaria, should appear shortly. Individual titles are available in more affordable paperback editions, and selections such as Donald J. Greene's volume of *Oxford Authors* show the remarkable range of his writing.

Hundreds of books and articles on Johnson appear every year. The best short introductions are Paul Fussell's *Samuel Johnson and the Life of Writing*, Donald J. Greene's *Samuel Johnson* and Thomas Woodman's *Preface to Samuel Johnson*. In *The Cambridge Companion to Samuel Johnson*, Greg Clingham collects essays by fifteen distinguished Johnsonians. *The Samuel Johnson Encyclopedia* by Pat Rogers is an invaluable overview of Johnson's life and works. For a thorough survey of other studies, see the bibliographies by Clifford and Greene, Greene and Vance, and Lynch.

Johnson's Dictionary

The best complete text is *A Dictionary of the English Language on CD-ROM*, edited by Anne McDermott. This remarkable project contains not only transcriptions of the first and fourth editions but also images of every page.

Many hundreds of studies of the *Dictionary* have been published, including important articles by Kolb, Reddick, DeMaria, McDermott, Nagashima and Hedrick. Three books, however, are especially worth reading. James H. Sledd and Gwin J. Kolb's *Dr. Johnson's Dictionary: Essays in the Biography of a Book* was tremendously influential when it first appeared in 1955. Scholars since then have provided more details. Allen Reddick's *Making of Johnson's* Dictionary is a painstaking account of Johnson's composition and revision of his work. Robert DeMaria, in *Johnson's Dictionary and the Language of Learning*, gives a challenging reading of the quotations. For a comprehensive list of studies of the *Dictionary* from its appearance to the early 1980s, see J. E. and Elizabeth C. Congleton, *Johnson's Dictionary: Bibliographical Survey, 1746-1984, with Excerpts for All Entries.*

Johnson's Age

Richard B. Schwartz's *Daily Life in Johnson's London* is a readable introduction to the world of the eighteenth century. In *Johnson's England*, A. S. Turberville describes "the life and manners of his age" in a series of essays. Jeremy Black and Roy Porter edited *The Penguin Dictionary of Eighteenth-Century History*, a convenient one-volume companion to the age in which Johnson lived.

BIBLIOGRAPHY

Aarsleff, Hans. *The Study of Language in England, 1780-1860*. Princeton: Princeton Univ. Press, 1967.

Ainsworth, Robert. *Thesaurus Linguæ Latinæ Compendiarius; or, A Compendious Dictionary of the Latin Tongue, Designed for the Use of the British Nations*. London, 1736.

Alston, Robin C. *The English Dictionary*. Leeds: E. J. Arnold and Son, 1966.

Atkinson, A. D. "Dr. Johnson and Newton's *Opticks*." *Review of English Studies*, n.s. 2 (July 1951): 226-37.

Bailey, Nathan. *An Universal Etymological English Dictionary*. London, 1721.

————. *Dictionarium Britannicum; or, A More Compleat Universal Etymological English Dictionary than Any Extant*. London, 1730.

Barrell, John. "The Language Properly So-Called: Johnson's Language and Politics." In *English Literature in History, 1730-1780: An Equal, Wide Survey*, 189-205. London: Hutchinson, 1983.

Bate, W. Jackson. *Samuel Johnson*. Washington, D.C.: Counterpoint, 1998.

Black, Jeremy, and Roy Porter. *The Penguin Dictionary of Eighteenth-Century History*. London: Penguin, 1996. Originally published as *A Dictionary of Eighteenth-Century World History* (Oxford: Blackwell, 1994).

Blount, Thomas. *Glossographia; or, A Dictionary, Interpreting All Such Hard Words, Whether Hebrew, Greek, Latin, Italian, Spanish, French, Teutonick, Belgick, British or Saxon; as Are Now Used in Our Refined English Tongue*. London, 1656.

Boswell, James. *The Life of Samuel Johnson*. Ed. G. B. Hill, rev. L. F. Powell. 6 vols. Oxford: Clarendon Press, 1934-64.

————. *Boswell's Journal of a Tour to the Hebrides with Samuel Johnson, LL.D., Now First Published from the Original Manuscript*. Ed. Frederick A. Pottle and Charles H. Bennett. London: William Heinemann, 1936.

————. *The Life of Samuel Johnson*. Ed. R. W. Chapman. Oxford: Clarendon Press, 1950.

Boulton, James T. *Johnson: The Critical Heritage*. New York: Barnes & Noble, 1971.

Browne, Sir Thomas. *The Works of Sir Thomas Browne*. Ed. Geoffrey Keynes. 4 vols. 2d ed. London: Faber & Faber, 1964.

Butt, John. *The Mid-Eighteenth Century*. Vol. 8 of *The Oxford History of English Literature*. Oxford: Clarendon Press, 1979.

Campbell, Archibald. *Lexiphanes: A Dialogue, Imitated from Lucian, and Suited to the Present Times, Being an Attempt to Restore the English Tongue to Its Ancient Purity, and to Correct, as Well as Expose, the Affected Style, Hard Words, and Absurd Phraseology of Many Late Writers, and Particularly of Our English Lexiphanes, the Rambler*. 2d ed. London, 1767.

Cawdrey, Robert. *A Table Alphabeticall, Conteyning and Teaching the True Writing, and Understanding of Hard Usuall English Words, Borrowed from the Hebrew, Greeke, Latine, or French, &c. with the Interpretation thereof by Plaine English Words*. London, 1604.

Chapman, Robert William. "Johnson's *Plan of a Dictionary*." *Review of English Studies* 2 (April 1926): 216-18.

Cleveland, John. *The Poems of John Cleveland*. Ed. Brian Morris and Eleanor Withington. Oxford: Clarendon Press, 1967.

Clifford, James L. *Young Sam Johnson*. New York: McGraw-Hill, 1955.

———. *Dictionary Johnson: Samuel Johnson's Middle Years*. New York: McGraw-Hill, 1979.

Clifford, James L., and Donald J. Greene. *Samuel Johnson: A Survey and Bibliography of Critical Studies*. Minneapolis: Univ. of Minnesota Press, 1970.

Clingham, Greg, ed. *The Cambridge Companion to Samuel Johnson*. Cambridge: Cambridge Univ. Press, 1997.

Cockeram, Henry. *The English Dictionarie; or, An Interpreter of Hard English Words*. London, 1623.

Coleridge, Samuel Taylor. *Biographia Literaria*. Ed. James Engell and Walter Jackson Bate. 2 vols. Princeton: Princeton Univ. Press, 1983.

Congleton, J. E. "Pronunciation in Johnson's *Dictionary*." In *Papers on Lexicography in Honor of Warren N. Cordell*, ed. J. E. Congleton, J. Edward Gates, and Donald Hobar, 59-91. Terre Haute, Ind.: Dictionary Society of North America, 1979.

Congleton, J. E., and Elizabeth C. Congleton. *Johnson's "Dictionary": Bibliographical Survey, 1746-1984, with Excerpts for All Entries*. Terre Haute: Dictionary Society of North America, 1984.

Cooper, Lane. "Dr. Johnson on Oats and Other Grains." *PMLA* 52 (Sept. 1937): 785-802.

DeMaria, Robert, Jr. *Johnson's* Dictionary *and the Language of Learning*. Chapel Hill: Univ. of North Carolina Press, 1986.

———. "The Theory of Language in Johnson's *Dictionary*." In *Johnson after Two Hundred Years*, ed. Paul J. Korshin, 159-74. Philadelphia: Univ. of Pennsylvania Press, 1986.

———. "The Politics of Johnson's *Dictionary*." *PMLA* 104, no. 1 (Jan. 1989): 64-74.

———. *The Life of Samuel Johnson: A Critical Biography*. Oxford: Blackwell, 1993.

———. "Johnson's *Dictionary*." In *The Cambridge Companion to Samuel Johnson*, ed. Greg Clingham, 85-101. Cambridge: Cambridge Univ. Press, 1997.

———. *Samuel Johnson and the Life of Reading*. Baltimore: Johns Hopkins Univ. Press, 1997.

DeMaria, Robert, Jr., and Gwin J. Kolb. "Johnson's *Dictionary* and Dictionary Johnson." *Yearbook of English Studies* 28 (1998): 19-43.

Dryden, John. *The Works of John Dryden*. Ed. Edward Niles Hooker and H. T. Swedenborg Jr. 20 vols. Berkeley: Univ. of California Press, 1956-.

Elyot, Thomas. *The Dictionary of Syr Thomas Eliot Knyght*. London, 1538.

Fielding, Henry. *An Enquiry into the Causes of the Late Increase of Robbers*. London, 1751.

Fleeman, J. D. *A Bibliography of the Works of Samuel Johnson: Treating His Published Works from the Beginnings to 1984*. 2 vols. Oxford: Clarendon Press, 2000.

Fussell, Paul. *Samuel Johnson and the Life of Writing*. New York: Norton, 1970.

Gay, John. *Dramatic Works*. 2 vols. Oxford: Clarendon Press, 1983.

Gilmore, Thomas B., Jr. "Johnson's Attitudes toward French Influence on the English Language." *Modern Philology* 78 (1981): 243-60.

Green, Jonathon. *Chasing the Sun: Dictionary Makers and the Dictionaries They Made*. New York: Henry Holt, 1996.

Greene, Donald J. "Johnson's Definition of 'Network.'" *Notes & Queries* 194 (10 Dec. 1949): 538-39.

———. *Samuel Johnson*. Updated edition. Boston: Twayne, 1989.

Greene, Donald J., and John A. Vance. *A Bibliography of Johnsonian Studies, 1970-1985*. Victoria, B.C.: Univ. of Victoria, 1987.

Griffith, Philip Mahone. "Samuel Johnson and King Charles the Martyr: Veneration in the *Dictionary*." *The Age of Johnson: A Scholarly Annual* 2 (1989): 235-61.

Gunn, Daniel P. "The Lexicographer's Task: Language, Reason, and Idealism in Johnson's *Dictionary* Preface." *The Age of Johnson: A Scholarly Annual* 11 (2000): 105-24.

Harp, Richard L., ed. *Dr. Johnson's Critical Vocabulary: A Selection from His Dictionary*. Lanham, Md.: Univ. Press of America, 1986.

Hedrick, Elizabeth. "Locke's Theory of Language and Johnson's *Dictionary*." *Eighteenth-Century Studies* 20, no. 4 (Summer 1987): 422-44.

———. "Fixing the Language: Johnson, Chesterfield, and *The Plan of a Dictionary*." *English Literary History* 55, no. 2 (Summer 1988): 421-42.

Hill, G. B., ed. *Johnsonian Miscellanies*. 2 vols. Oxford: Clarendon Press, 1897.

Hooker, Richard. *The Folger Library Edition of the Works of Richard Hooker*. Ed. W. Speed Hill et al. 6 vols. in 7. Cambridge: Harvard Univ. Press; Binghamton, N.Y.: Medieval & Renaissance Texts & Studies, 1977-93.

Hudson, Nicholas. "Johnson's *Dictionary* and the Politics of Standard English." *Yearbook of English Studies* 28 (1998): 77-93.

Johnson, Samuel. *A Dictionary of the English Language*. 2 vols. London, 1755.

———. *Lives of the English Poets*. Ed. G. B. Hill. 3 vols. Oxford: Clarendon Press, 1905.

———. *The Yale Edition of the Works of Samuel Johnson*. 13 vols. to date. New Haven: Yale Univ. Press, 1958-.

———. *The Oxford Authors: Samuel Johnson*. Ed. Donald J. Greene. Oxford: Oxford Univ. Press, 1984.

———. *The Letters of Samuel Johnson*. Ed. Bruce Redford. 5 vols. Princeton: Princeton Univ. Press, 1992-94.

———. *A Dictionary of the English Language on CD-ROM*. Ed. Anne McDermott. Cambridge: Cambridge Univ. Press, 1996.

Junius, Francis. *Francisci Junii Francisci filii Etymologicum anglicanum, ex autographo descripsit & accessionibus permultis auctum edidit Edwardus Lye*. Oxford, 1743.

Kahane, Henry, and Renée Kahane. "Dr. Johnson's *Dictionary*: From Classical Learning to the National Language." *Lexicographia* 41 (1992): 50-53.

Kaminski, Thomas. *The Early Career of Samuel Johnson*. New York: Oxford Univ. Press, 1987.

Keast, W. R. "Self-Quotation in Johnson's *Dictionary*." *Notes & Queries*, Sept. 1955, 392-93.

Kernan, Alvin B. *Printing Technology, Letters, and Samuel Johnson*. Princeton: Princeton Univ. Press, 1987.

Kersey, John. *A New English Dictionary; or, A Compleat Collection of the Most Proper and Significant Words, Commonly Used in the Language*. London, 1702.

Kezar, Dennis Dean, Jr. "Radical Letters and Male Genealogies in Johnson's *Dictionary*." *Studies in English Literature 1500-1900* 35, no. 3 (Summer 1995): 493-517.

Kolb, Gwin J. "Studies of Johnson's *Dictionary*." *Dictionaries* 2 (1990): 113-26.

Kolb, Gwin J., and Ruth A. Kolb. "The Selection and Use of the Illustrative Quotations in Dr. Johnson's *Dictionary*." In *New Aspects of Lexicography: Literary Criticism, Intellectual History, and Social Change*, ed. Howard D. Weinbrot, 61-72. Carbondale: Southern Illinois Univ. Press, 1972.

Kolb, Gwin J., and James H. Sledd. "The Reynolds Copy of Johnson's *Dictionary*." *Bulletin of the John Rylands Library* 37 (March 1955): 446-75.

Korshin, Paul J. "Johnson and the Renaissance Dictionary." *Journal of the History of Ideas* 35 (1974): 300-12.

Landau, Sidney I. *Dictionaries: The Art and Craft of Lexicography*. 2d ed. Cambridge: Cambridge Univ. Press, 2001.

Long, Percy W. "English Dictionaries before Webster." *Bibliographical Society of America Papers* 4 (1910): 25-43.

Lynch, Jack. *A Bibliography of Johnsonian Studies, 1986-1998*. New York: AMS Press, 2000.

———. *The Age of Elizabeth in the Age of Johnson*. Cambridge: Cambridge Univ. Press, 2003.

Macaulay, Thomas Babington, Lord Macaulay. *Miscellaneous Works*. London, 1871.

McAdam, E. L., Jr. "Inkhorn Words before Dr. Johnson." In *Eighteenth-Century Studies in Honor of Donald F. Hyde*, ed. W.H. Bond. New York: Grolier Club, 1970.

McAdam, E. L., Jr., and George Milne, eds. *Johnson's Dictionary: A Modern Selection*. New York: Pantheon Books, 1963.

McArthur, Tom. *Worlds of Reference: Lexicography, Learning, and Language from the Clay Tablet to the Computer*. Cambridge: Cambridge Univ. Press, 1986.

McCracken, David. "The Drudgery of Defining: Johnson's Debt to Bailey's *Dictionarium Britannicum*." *Modern Philology* 66 (May 1969): 338-41.

McCue, George S. "Sam Johnson's Word-Hoard." *Modern Language Notes* 63 (Jan. 1948): 43-45

McDermott, Anne. "Johnson's Use of Shakespeare in the Dictionary." *New Rambler* D:5 (1989-90): 7-16.

———. "The Reynolds Copy of Johnson's *Dictionary*: A Re-Examination." *Bulletin of the John Rylands University Library of Manchester* 74, no. 1 (Spring 1992): 29-38.

———. "The Defining Language: Johnson's *Dictionary* and *Macbeth*." *Review of English Studies* 44, no. 176 (Nov. 1993): 521-38.

———. "Preparing the *Dictionary* for CD-ROM." *New Rambler* D:12 (1996-97): 17-25.

———. "Johnson's *Dictionary* and the Canon: Authors and Authority." *Yearbook of English Studies* 28 (1998): 44-65.

McDermott, Anne, and Marcus Walsh. "Editing Johnson's *Dictionary*: Some Editorial and Textual Considerations." In *The Theory and Practices of Text-Editing: Essays in Honour of James T. Boulton*, ed. Ian Small and Marcus Walsh, 35-61. Cambridge: Cambridge Univ. Press, 1991.

McLaverty, James. "From Definition to Explanation: Locke's Influence on Johnson's *Dictionary*." *Journal of the History of Ideas* 47, no. 3 (July-Sept. 1986): 377-94.

Mencken, H. L. *The American Language: An Inquiry into the Development of English in the United States.* 2d ed. New York: Knopf, 1921.

Mulcaster, Richard. *The First Part of the Elementarie Which Entreateth Chefelie of the Right Writing of Our English Tung, Set Forth by Richard Mulcaster.* London, 1582.

Murray, James A. H., et al. *A New English Dictionary on Historical Principles: Founded Mainly on the Materials Collected by the Philological Society.* 10 vols. Oxford: Oxford Univ. Press, 1888-1928. Second edition, *The Oxford English Dictionary*, ed. J. A. Simpson et al. 20 vols. Oxford: Oxford Univ. Press, 1989.

———. *The Evolution of English Lexicography.* Oxford: Clarendon Press, 1900.

Murray, Katharine Maud Elisabeth. *Caught in the Web of Words: James A. H. Murray and the Oxford English Dictionary.* New Haven: Yale Univ. Press, 1977.

Nagashima, Daisuke. "Johnson's Use of Skinner and Junius." In *Fresh Reflections on Samuel Johnson*, ed. Prem Nath, 283-98. Troy, N.Y.: Whitston, 1987.

———. *Johnson the Philologist.* Hirakata: Intercultural Research Inst., Kansai Univ. of Foreign Studies, 1988.

———. "Johnson's Revisions of His Etymologies." *Yearbook of English Studies* 28 (1998): 94-105.

———. "The Biblical Quotations in Johnson's *Dictionary*." *The Age of Johnson: A Scholarly Annual* 10 (1999): 89-126.

Newton, A. Edward. "The Pathos and Humor of Dr. Johnson's Dictionary." *Atlantic Monthly* 139 (April 1927): 502-11.

Noyes, Gertrude E. "The Critical Reception of Johnson's *Dictionary* in the Latter Eighteenth Century." *Modern Philology* 52 (Feb. 1955): 175-91.

Phillips, Edward. *The New World of English Words; or, A General Dictionary: Containing the Interpretations of Such Hard Words as Are Derived from Other Languages; Whether Hebrew, Arabick, Syriack, Greek, Latin, Italian, French, Spanish, British, Dutch, Saxon, &c.* London, 1658.

Pope, Alexander. *The Twickenham Edition of the Poems of Alexander Pope.* Ed. John Butt et al. 11 vols. in 12. New Haven: Yale Univ. Press, 1939-69.

Read, Allen Walker. "The History of Dr. Johnson's Definition of Oats." *Agricultural History* 8 (July 1934): 81-94.

———. "The Contemporary Quotations in Johnson's Dictionary." *English Literary History* 2 (Nov. 1935): 246-51.

Reddick, Allen. "Teaching the *Dictionary*." In *Approaches to Teaching the Works of Samuel Johnson*, ed. David R. Anderson and Gwin J. Kolb, 84-91. New York: MLA, 1993.

———. *The Making of Johnson's Dictionary, 1746-1773.* 2d ed. Cambridge: Cambridge Univ. Press, 1996.

———. "Johnson's *Dictionary of the English Language* and Its Texts: Quotation, Context, Anti-Thematics." *Yearbook of English Studies* 28 (1998): 66-76.

Reed, Joseph W., Jr. "Noah Webster's Debt to Samuel Johnson." *American Speech* 37 (May 1962): 95-105.

Rogers, Pat. *Grub Street: Studies in a Subculture.* London: Methuen, 1972.

———. *The Samuel Johnson Encyclopedia.* Westport, Conn.: Greenwood Press, 1996.

Rypins, Stanley. "Johnson's Dictionary Reviewed by His Contemporaries." *Philological Quarterly* 4 (July 1925): 281-86.

Schwartz, Richard B. *Daily Life in Johnson's London*. Madison: Univ. of Wisconsin Press, 1983.

Segar, Mary. "Dictionary Making in the Early Eighteenth Century." *Review of English Studies* 7 (April 1931): 210-13.

Sherbo, Arthur. "Dr. Johnson Quotes One of His Amanuenses." *Notes & Queries*, 21 June 1952: 276.

Siebert, Donald T. *"Bubbled, Bamboozled,* and *Bit*: Low Bad Words in Johnson's *Dictionary.*" *Studies in English Literature 1500-1900* 26 (1986): 485-96.

Skeat, Walter W. "Dr. Johnson's Definition of Oats." *Notes & Queries*, 4th series, 10 (19 Oct. 1872): 309.

Skinner, Stephen. *Etymologicon linguæ Anglicanæ, seu Explicatio vocum Anglicarum etymologica ex propriis fontibus, scil. ex linguis duodecim*. London, 1671.

Sledd, James H., and Gwin J. Kolb. "Johnson's Definitions of *Whig* and *Tory*." *PMLA* 67 (Sept. 1952): 882-85.

———. *Dr. Johnson's* Dictionary: *Essays in the Biography of a Book*. Chicago: Univ. of Chicago Press, 1955.

Smollett, Tobias. *The Expedition of Humphry Clinker*. Ed. Thomas R. Preston. Athens: Univ. of Georgia Press, 1990.

Starnes, DeWitt T., and Gertrude E. Noyes. *The English Dictionary from Cawdrey to Johnson, 1604-1755*. 2d ed. Amsterdam and Philadelphia: J. Benjamin, 1991.

Thompson, G. H. "Dr. Johnson and Oats." *Notes & Queries*, 7th series, 3 (8 Jan. 1887): 26.

Trench, Richard Chevenix. *On Some Deficiencies in Our English Dictionaries*. London, 1857.

Turberville, A. S., ed. *Johnson's England: An Account of the Life and Manners of His Age*. 2 vols. Oxford: Clarendon Press, 1933.

Tyers, Thomas. *A Biographical Sketch of Dr. Samuel Johnson*. In *The Early Biographies of Samuel Johnson*. Ed. O. M. Brack Jr. and Robert E. Kelley. Iowa City: Univ. of Iowa Press, 1974.

Warton, Thomas. *The History of English Poetry*. 4 vols. London, 1775-81.

Weinbrot, Howard D. "Samuel Johnson's *Plan* and *Preface* to the *Dictionary*: The Growth of a Lexicographer's Mind." In *New Aspects of Lexicography: Literary Criticism, Intellectual History, and Social Change*, ed. Howard D. Weinbrot, 73-94. Carbondale: Southern Illinois Univ. Press, 1972.

Wimsatt, W. K. "Johnson and Scots." *TLS*, 9 March 1946, 115.

———. "Johnson on Electricity." *Review of English Studies* 23 (July 1947): 257-60.

———. *Philosophic Words: A Study of Style and Meaning in the* Rambler *and* Dictionary *of Samuel Johnson*. New Haven: Yale Univ. Press, 1948.

Wimsatt, W. K., and Margaret H. Wimsatt. "Self-Quotations and Anonymous Quotations in Johnson's Dictionary." *English Literary History* 15 (March 1948): 60-68.

Winchester, Simon. *The Professor and the Madman: A Tale of Murder, Insanity, and the Making of the Oxford English Dictionary*. New York: HarperCollins, 1998.

Withals, John. *A Shorte Dictionarie for Yonge Begynners: Gathered of Good Authours, Specially of Columell, Grapald, and Plini*. London, 1553.

Wood, Nigel. "The Tract and Tenor of the Sentence: Conversing, Connection, and Johnson's *Dictionary*." *Yearbook of English Studies* 28 (1998): 110-27.

Woodman, Thomas M. *A Preface to Samuel Johnson*. London: Longman, 1993.

INDEX OF
SHAKESPEAREAN CITATIONS

In his Dictionary, *Johnson frequently cited Shakespeare without indicating the work. This index makes amends for that.*

The two plays, or parts, of Henry IV *and the three of* Henry VI *are identified by the respective Arabic numeral.*

For words that feature more than one definition, the number of the applicable definition is noted. Abbreviations of parts of speech, such as n.s. and adj., are noted only when needed for clarification.

All's Well that Ends Well

coxcomb 3, dog v.a., gamester 4, kicksy-wicksey, modern adj. 2, musket 1, obloquy 2, pile 5, prescription 2, quean, receipt 6, rogue 1, ruttish, think 3

Antony and Cleopatra

author 2, billiards, cup 1, darkling, *decorum*, dislimn, distraction 1, domestick 4, element 2, empire 2, estrich, fear 4, figure 8, formal 7, green 7, heart 18, holy 4, immoment, judgment 6, lady 3, lethe, levity 5, license 1, magick 1, modern adj. 2, monarch 1, monarch 3, nice 8, ordinary 4, passion 2, plebeian, quality 4, reason n.s. 7, rhymer, ribald, salad, scale 10, sense 10, spirit 6, tree 1, *vesper*, workday, write 2, yare

As You Like It

age 1, ape 1, atom 2, caper, December, dog n.s. 5, dull 1, elegy 1, flux 5, flux 6, formal 1, Frenchify, giant, housewife 2, hyen, incontinent 1, irk, justice 12, limn, love 1, lunacy, melancholy 2, modern adj. 2, monkey 1, oak, ode, pancake, plant 2, puke, quotidian, roynish, style 1, tapster, theatre 1, thrasonical, translate 4

The Comedy of Errors

anatomy 5, burden 3, dalliance 3, diamond, diet 1, dote 1, elm 2, fashion 4, female, football, formal 7, fortuneteller, fraughtage, gossip 1, handwriting, libertine 3, licentious 1, mome, mountebank 2, nature 5, receipt 1, soul 2, stuff 3

Coriolanus

apoplexy, arithmetick, author 1, barbarian 2, bastard 2, bisson, blockhead, bowels 2, burden 1, buss, cat, chair 2, choler 3, citizen 2, diet 1, dissemble, dragon 1, empirical 2, entertainment 5, epitome, fond 1, forehead 1, garlickeater, *gratis*, harlot, heart 13, heaven 4, humorous 2, it 2, it 7, jack 1, judgment 10, larum 1, law 2, law 4, mean 2, mechanick, million 1, mother 1, mummer, mystery 1, nobility 3, oak, office 1, party 2, pile 2, plebeian, rat, reason v.n. 2, salt 1, senate, sensible 1, shall 5, spirit 8, tabour, tickle 2, tiger, trade 2, vamp, viand, word 8

Cymbeline

book 3, brogue 1, character 2, clotpoll 2, December, diamond, doctor 3, doubt 2, dragon 1, egregious 2, geck, giant, giglet, gout 1, heaven 4, holy 1, honour 6, interpret, jack 1, ken, lady 2, law 2, law 5, learn 2, lust 1, mercurial 1, *monsieur*, office 5, pander, quality 9, read 4, shirt, snuff 3, spectator, spirit 14, sport 5, stuff 6, stuff 9, sympathy, thunderstone, tickle 1, tomboy, turban, tyrant 2, verbal 4, virgin 1, vision 3, wench 2, whelp 2, zephyr

Hamlet

asshead, beetle, bisson, brothel, compass 7, disaster 1, drab, ecstasy 5, eisel, fardel, favourite 2, gender 1, gentry 4, goblin 1, heaven 1, journeyman, loggats, matin, moble, mope, mountebank 1, office 1, orisons,

INDEX OF
ADDITIONAL LITERARY CITATIONS

With four exceptions (the Bible; Musæ Anglicanæ; Prayers, Proverbs, Songs and Oral Tradition; and Trevoux), citations are listed by author. In instances where Johnson frequently cites the work but not the author, as with Spenser's Faerie Queene, *there is a cross-reference. (Note: Johnson did not distinguish between the two Burnets, but this index does.)*

Johnson used the spellings of authors' names that were common in his day. Thus John Minsheu appears as Minshew; Sir Thomas Browne usually lacks the final e, and Robert Grosseteste is also Grosthead. This index uses the spellings preferred in our day.

For words that feature more than one definition, the number of the applicable definition is noted. Abbreviations of parts of speech, such as n.s. and adj., are noted only when needed for clarification.

Abbot, George (1562-1633), author of *A Briefe Description of the Whole Worlde*: heart 3, letter 2, lust 1, natural n.s. 2, necromancy 2, obstupefactive, party 7, physick 3, religious 3, stew 1, toy n.s. 1

Addison, Joseph (1672-1719), essayist and poet, best known for *The Spectator* (with Sir Richard Steele) and *The Guardian*; Johnson wrote his *Life*: afford 3, afterages, air 11, air 12, air 13, allow 7, amour, antick, antiquity 1, baboon, baggage 1, baggage 3, barbarian 1, beauty 2, biographer, book 4, bookish, bookworm 1, bowels 2, Bridewell, bubble, burlesque adj, business 4, cabal 2, cancer 3, cant n.s. 2, catcal, character 5, character 6, chitchat, chop-house, classical 1, clown 2, compass 2, compass 3, confoundedly, cotquean, countenance 4, crisis 2, criticism 2, critick n.s. 2, cup 2, curtain-lecture, daisy, death 7, dedication 1, dervis, discipline 6, distraction 2, diversion 3, dogmatical, domestical 3, dote 1, doublet 1, dowager 1, dumbfound, earthquake, editor, egotism, ell 1, emblem 2, enigmatist, enlighten 2, episode, escargatoire, etymology 1, exercise 3, exercise 6, expatiate 1, fable n.s. 1, fable n.s. 4, fabulous, fain, fame 1, fancy 3, fantastical 5, father 8, favourite 1, fiddlefaddle, figure 3, figure 4, figure 5, fin, firework, flagitious, *flambeau*, flirt 1, flirt 3, fond 3, freak 2, freethinker, fribbler, fury 4, gabel, gallant 2, gamester 1, gamut, genius 2, georgick, giant, gipsy 1, gloss 3, glum, government 2, gravity 3, habit 2, hallucination, heart 9, heathen, Hebraism, hecatomb, hoary 1, honeymoon, hospital 1, housewife 2, housewife 3, humorist 1, humorous 1, humour 3, hunks, idle 3, impeach 2, impertinence 4, implex, incendiary 2, incog, independence, inspire 2, intelligencer, it 1, it 5, jack pudding, journeyman, judgment 3, judgment 9, knight 2, lachrymary, lady 2, lady 3, Latinism, law 3, lawn 1, lecture 1, legend 1, legend 4, legislature, letter 5, liberty 1, license 2, light 5, linguist, *literati*, literature, loo, lord 1, love 1, loveletter, man 6, man 7, march 3, martyr, mask 1, medly, meeting-house, memory 1, memory 4, *menage*, mental, merchant, merry-andrew, milksop, minuet, mispel, mistress 3, modesty-piece, modish, money, morris 1, motto, mummer, national 1, natural adj. 7, naturalist, nature 10, network, news 1, news 2, nice 5, nincompoop, ninnyhammer, nonconformity 2, number 1, number 3, obloquy 1, oneirocritical, oscitancy 2, otter, palfrey, parterre, party 1, passion 4, pathetical, patriot, pedant 2, penman 2, pension, period 4, petticoat, philanthropy, pickleherring, pimple, pish, play 12,

orthodox, papacy, parasite, parchment, parliament, party 7, passion 1, perfect 2, period 6, pestilent 1, pharisaical, physiognomy 1, pie 1, pirate 1, poesy 2, prate, prejudice 2, prescription 1, priapism, professor 1, prorogue 3, puberty, puff 4, quality 7, quality 8, queck, race 8, race 10, rakehel, rape 1, rasp, real 1, reason 3, relax 1, right 1, ringleader, rogue 1, roundel 2, rule 3, salamander, satirical 2, scholar 3, scholastick 2, schoolman 1, schoolman 2, sectary 1, sense 2, sentence 2, sign 5, sock 1, soporiferous, spirit 1, spirit 4, spirit 17, stew 2, stripe 1, study 2, study 4, stuff 8, suburb 1, sudorifick, supposititious, taste 2, taste 7, theatre 1, theory, tickle 1, time 3, time 8, toast 1, trade 4, treble, trumpet 3, turban, understanding 1, usury 2, uxorious, vacation 1, vapour 2, vellicate, viol, virginal, virtue 3, war 1, whelp 1, wife 2, witty 2, wont, word 1, work 1, writer 2, year 3, yeoman 2

Bailey, Nathan (d. 1742), lexicographer: dapatical, ereptation, ereption, fream, gip, Lammas, lampoon, minum 2, mundungus, mystagogue, poupicts, rackoon, rambooze, ratafia, savanna, scatches, scotomy, scottering, scovel, screable, semitone, sepilible, skaddons, steganography, supervacaneousness, teratology, theogony, theomachy, theurgy, ticktack, tranters, tumulose, vicenary, vigesimation, vituline, wair

Baker, Thomas (1656-1740), author of *Reflections upon Learning*: doubt 4, element 3, gloss 1, glossary, kind 2, law 2, mountebank 1, nice 2, rhetorick 1, schoolman 2, system 3, talent 2, uncouth, *vogue*, want 5

Bentley, Richard (1662-1742), classical scholar and clergyman: airpump, atheist, business 8, cannibal, conceit 7, constitution 2, ethicks, formal 6, galaxy, gospel n.s. 1, highwayman, horoscope, incendiary 2, instincted, institution 4, intelligence 1, it 1, jack 7,

learning 1, legend 3, levity 1, microscope, miracle 2, mythology, opiate, organical 1, pestilent 1, puberty, quality 2, Saturn 1, savage, scale 1, scale 7, sea 1, sense 5, sophisticate, think 8, time 13, vacuity 2, vamp, *volcano*, wit 7

Berkeley, George (1685-1753), bishop of Cloyne and philosopher: science 2

Bible, in the Authorized Version (King James Version) of 1611: addict 1, age 1, allow 3, amaze 1, *amen*, ancient adj. 2, author 3, baggage 1, black 1, black 2, bowels 1, business 7, chaste 4, college 3, conceit 2, conceit 4, conceive 1, conceive 2, death 1, death 4, death 7, discord 1, discover 1, discover 2, dissemble, doctor 1, doctrine 2, dog n.s. 3, dominion 5, dote 1, dower 3, dull 4, element 2, element 6, evil 2, evil 3, evil 4, fable n.s. 3, faction 1, faith 1, faith 2, faith 8, fame 1, fame 2, fashion 1, father 2, father 5, father 7, father 11, fear 1, fear 2, fear 3, fear 5, fear 6, female, figure 10, fool 2, fury 2, gay 2, gentile 1, gentle 2, god 1, god 2, god 3, greaves, heart 7, heart 11, heathen, hell 2, hell 3, hope n.s. 1, hope n.s. 2, hope v.n. 2, imagination 3, incontinent 1, inspire 1, interpret, judgment 3, judgment 7, judgment 8, judgment 10, judgment 11, justice 1, justice 2, justice 4, knowledge 5, leaf 3, learn 1, learn 2, leprosy, letter 1, letter 4, *leviathan*, license 2, license 3, light 4, light 7, living 1, locust, love 3, love 5, lust 2, maid 3, man 2, man 8, mandrake, mean 6, medicine, melody, merchant, money, mortal 1, mother 7, mouse, neese, number 1, number 4, ostrich, party 2, passion 7, perfect 3, physick 2, pile 3, polish 1, print 3, publican 1, publick 2, puff 5, rabbi, rail, reason v.n. 2, reason v.n. 3, receipt 2, resurrection, retire 2, retire 3, right 4, rose, rude 4, rule 1, rumour, Satan, sea 1, sea 2, seamonster, seduce, sentence 1, sentence 4, seraphim, sign 2, sign 4,

reason 3, reason 8, reason 9, receipt 1, receipt 6, recipe, recitative, redcoat, reformation 1, regicide 1, Renard, repair, revolution 2, rhetorick 1, rhyme 2, rhymer, riband, right 1, right 3, right 5, rite, rogue 2, romance n.s. 1, romanize, roundel 1, rude 6, rude 7, rule 3, rumour, salad, satire, satirical 1, scale 1, scholiast, school 1, school 3, science 3, scribbler, sea 1, seahorse 3, sedan, seduce, senate, sense 2, sense 6, sense 8, sensible 4, sensible 6, sensitive, sex 2, shall 5, shirt, shrew, sign 1, sign 5, signify 1, slop, snack, sock 2, song 1, song 3, song 5, sophisticate, soul 6, soul 7, spark 1, spark 4, spectator, spirit 13, spirit 14, spleen 2, spoonmeat, sport 3, springe, squintifego, stanza, stays 3, strumpet, studious 3, study 5, stuff 9, style 3, style 4, sublime adj. 1, sublime adj. 2, subordination 1, superstition 1, sway 3, sway 4, sympathy, talent 1, talent 2, taper, taste 5, tattle, theatre 2, think 1, think 5, thou n.s. 1, thro', tickle 1, tickle 2, time 4, time 5, time 6, time 9, time 11, tit 2, toy n.s. 1, trade 2, trade 3, tragedy 1, tragicomedy, trainbands, translate 1, transportation 1, treble, tree 2, trivial 2, trope, trull 1, trumpet 1, trumpet 3, tumbrel, turban, tuz, tyrant 2, umbrel, unconquered 1, uncouth, undermine 3, underplot 1, undo 3, ungod, unity 4, urbanity, usage 1, usury 1, vanity 7, vapour 3, vaunt 2, verbal 6, verse 3, versed, versification, vice 2, *virtuoso*, vision 4, vitious 2, viz, wag, want 4, want 6, warlock, warm 3, warm 4, waterman, whiphand, wife 1, wight, will 4, will 7, wit 1, wit 2, wit 3, wit 4, wit 5, wit 6, woman 1, wondrous 1, wondrous 2, word 3, word 6, word 9, word 10, work 1, workhouse 1, world 4, world 8, world 12, wretch 3, year 3, yeoman 2, zeal

Duke, Richard (1658-1711), poet; Johnson wrote his *Life*: **translate 5**

Dunciad See **Pope, Alexander**

Duppa, Brian (1588-1662), bishop and author of *Holy Rules and Helps to Devotion*: **engine 5, fortuneteller**

Dyer, John (c. 1700-58), poet; Johnson wrote his *Life*: **orisons**

Eachard, John (c. 1639-97), author of *The Ground and Occasions of the Contempt of the Clergy and Religion*: **merrythought**

Evelyn, John (1620-1706), author of *Kalendarium Hortense; or, The Gard'ner's Almanac*: **exotick, impertinence 4, imposture**

Fairfax, Edward (d. 1635), poet and translator: **distaff 1, eame, eath, engine 2, gentle 2, hierarchy 1, humour 4, idea, legend 2, pickthank, rhetorick 2, uncouth**

Fairy Queen See **Spenser, Edmund**

Felton, Henry (1679-1740), classical scholar, author of *A Dissertation on Reading the Classics*: **annotator, classical 1, flux 2, Gallicism, illuminator 2,** *Poetaster,* **quack 1, write 6**

Female Quixote See **Lennox, Charlotte**

Fenton, Elijah (1683-1730), poet; Johnson wrote his *Life*: **kickshaw 2, rebel**

Flatman, Thomas (1637-88), poet: **it 1**

Floyer, Sir John (1649-1734), physician: **caseous, epilepsy, febrifuge, hysterical 1, incubus, posset, priapism, rhabarbarate, slippy**

Forbes, Duncan (1685-1747), religious writer: **institution 3, ritual, sabbatical**

F.Q. See **Spenser, Edmund**

Garth, Sir Samuel (1661-1719), physician and poet, best known for *The Dispensary*; Johnson wrote his *Life*: **alligator, fautress, gipsy 1, glebe, glout, green 2, grocer, pigmy, ptisan, rake 1, rocket, sex 2, urinal,** *volcano,* **woman 1**

Gay, John (1685-1732), poet and satirist, best known for *The Beggar's Opera*; Johnson wrote his *Life*: **ballad, base-born, bat, bravo, cricket 1, dad, dowdy,**

compass 6, compass 9, complex,
conceit 3, consumer, criticise 2,
critick n.s. 1, critick n.s. 2,
curmudgeon, decimal, democracy,
dibstone, dog n.s. 1, dominion 2, dull 3,
ecstasy 1, ectype, effeminate,
enthusiasm 1, epitome, epoch,
essay v.a. 3, essay n.s. 3, ether 1, evil 4,
exercise 7, exist, faculty 2, faculty 4,
fancy 2, fashion 7, father 1, fear 1,
figure 1, figure 11, flummery, flux 2,
foetus, fool 1, fool 6, goblin 1, gold 1,
grammar 1, grammar school, guinea,
habit 3, happiness 1, heart 11, heathen,
heterodox, hope n.s. 1, husband 1,
hypotenuse, idea, idle 3, imagination 2,
inane, infancy 1, insect 1, intermundane,
it 1, it 5, jig, judgment 1, justice 1, ken,
knowledge 1, larum 2, Latin, learned 1,
learned 3, lecture 1, liberty 2, liberty 5,
license 1, license 2, lie 2, light 2, light 6,
lord 1, madness 1, magazine 1, magnet,
male, man 1, man 6, memory 1,
mental, million 2, money, monkey 1,
monster 1, natural adj. 5, natural n.s. 1,
oak, oats, opium, own 4, paper 2,
party 1, passion 1, passion 2, patron 3,
pen 1, pencil 1, period 7, philosophy 2,
physick 1, physiognomy, pile 1, pile 8,
pineapple, plant 1, play 5, plum 1,
porpoise, prejudice 2, press 4,
professor 3, property 3, prophet 1,
quality 1, race 4, rail, ramble, reason 4,
reason v.n. 1, representative 3, reptile,
rhapsody, rhetorick 1, right 3, royalty 1,
rule 1, savanna, scheme 1, scholar 2,
school 5, scientifical, scotch hoppers,
sensible 4, sentiment 1, shilling, sign 1,
signify 3, spark 2, spirit 2, spirit 4,
studious 1, suckingbottle, sympathy,
tarantula, taste 4, tattle, tennis, think 1,
think 7, tickle 2, time 1, time 5,
tirewoman, tobacco, transubstantiation,
tree 1, trillion, trinity, truth 1, uncouth,
undermine 3, understanding 2,
unity 1, vegetable, velleity, vice 1,
virtue 5, vision 4, want 2, warm 5,
will 1, will 5, wit 2, wont, word 1,
word 3, world 1, yeoman 1

Lye, Edward (1694-1767), author of a
*Dictionarium Saxonico et Gothico-
Latinum* (*Saxon- and Gothic-Latin
Dictionary*): **gun, jilt, piddle**

MacBean, Alexander (d. 1784), one of
Johnson's amanuenses: **scale 7**

Mackenzie, George (1669-1725), author
of *The Lives and Characters of the Most
Eminent Writers of the Scots Nation*: **fag**

Marlowe, Christopher (1564-93), poet
and playwright: **girdle 1**

Marvel, Andrew (1621-78), poet: **excise**

Mayne, Jasper (1604-72), religious writer:
turcism

Ménage, Gilles (1613-92), author of
*Dictionnaire etymologique de la langue
françoise* (*Etymological Dictionary of
the French Language*): **algebra, baron,
donjon, harlequin**

Miller, Philip (1691-1771), gardening
writer: **chocolate 1, coffee, daffodil,
daisy, elm 1, garlick, licorice, lime tree 1,
maize, mandrake, nectarine, oak, oats,
penguin 2, peony, pineapple, plum 1,
potato, rice, rose, tobacco, tree 1, tree
of life, tulip, vanilla, vine, watermelon**

Milton, John (1608-74), poet, best known
for *Paradise Lost*; Johnson wrote his
Life: **accident 3, adamant 1, aerial 1,
aerial 3, age 2, aggravate 1, air 3, air 10,
air 12, alchymy 2, *allegro, amphisbæna*,
anarch, anarchy, answerable 4,
answerable 5, apocalypse, appetence,
arms 4, atheist, author 1, awful 1,
beauty 4, beldam 1, bosky, brake,
brevier, brinded, burden 2, cataphract,
cates, character 1, civil 1, civil 11,
compass 4, compass 8, condescend 3,
countenance 1, cricket 1, curfew 1,
daffodil, dalliance 1, dalliance 2,
darkling, descant 1, diet 1, divan 2,
dominion 1, drop serene, dulcet 1,
dulcet 2, dwarf 1, ecstasy 3, element 3,
elixir 4, empirical 1, empyreal,
empyrean, equipage 2, eremite,
exercise 8, experiment, faculty 2, faith 6,**

Milton, John *(continued)*

fancy 1, father 1, fond 1, fool 4, forgery 2, galaxy, genius 1, gentle 1, giant, gin 1, glebe 1, gloss 2, gloze 1, goblin 1, government 2, grotesque, hallelujah, harmony 3, heart 5, heart 7, heaven 2, heaven 3, hell 1, hierarchy 1, honour 8, hope n.s. 1, humour 2, idea, idle 3, idle 4, imagination 1, inly, insect 1, inspire 1, inspire 2, intellectual 4, intelligence 3, intercourse 1, interpret, invention 5, judgment 7, ken, kickshaw, kickshaw 1, kind 1, lawn 1, lay, lazar-house, lethe, levant, levity 3, lexicon, liberal 3, license 1, light 2, light 7, linguist, lion, liquor 1, list, livery 6, lord 1, lubber, luxurious 4, luxurious 6, lyrical, magazine 1, mask 4, mean 5, memory 3, mental, mickle, minim 1, mistress 1, moonstruck, mope, morris 1, mortal 1, mortal 2, mortal 4, mummer, muse 1, musick 2, mystical 2, national 1, native 5, news 1, nice 3, nice 7, nocent 2, number 4, number 7, obloquy 1, obscene 1, ode, office 3, omnifick, opium, oratory 1, organical 1, organical 2, orisons, ounce, parallax, parasite, passion 2, peccant 1, pen 3, period 7, pet 1, philosophy 3, pile 4, planet, play 2, poet, polish 2, politician 2, pollute 2, pollute 4, pride 1, pride 2, pride 6, proboscis, promiscuous, prophet 1, prose, prowl, publick 3, publish 1, quaint 4, quintessence 1, quintessence 2, race 2, race 4, race 7, race 9, rally 1, rape 1, rapture 2, reality 2, reason 1, reason v.n. 3, rebeck, relax 5, religion 1, religion 2, religious 1, resurrection, retire 1, retire 2, revolution 1, revolution 2, revolution 4, rhetorick 2, rhyme 3, right 1, right 3, right 8, riot 1, riot 2, romance n.s. 1, rose, royalty 3, rubrick, rude 2, rude 4, rule 2, rumour, rustick adj. 5, Satan, Saviour, scale 1, scale 5, scale 6, scale 7, scan 1, scan 2, scrannel, scruple, sea 1, sea 4, seamonster, seduce, senate, sense 1, sense 3, sensible 4, sentence 2, seraphim, sex 1, sign 2, sign 7, silly 3, sin 2, sinworm, sock 2, soldan, song 1, song 4, sonnet 1, soul 1, soul 2, soul 3, soul 9, spirit 5, spirit 9, sport 3, studious 4, study 3, stuff 1, sublime adj. 1, sublime adj. 2, sublime adj. 4, suburb 2, superstition 1, sway 1, sway 2, swordlaw, sympathy, taste 1, taste 2, taste 5, terrifick, terrour 1, terrour 2, terrour 3, theatre 2, time 2, time 10, time 11, time 13, toy n.s. 1, toy n.s. 5, translate 1, transpicuous, treason, trumpet 1, truth 1, truth 2, turban, type 2, tyrant 2, umbrageous, unconquered 2, uncouth, undermine 3, understanding 1, undo 2, unity 1, unmanlike 2, urim, uxorious, vacuity 2, vanity 2, vanity 5, vapour 1, variety 1, vaunt 1, venereal 1, verbal 3, viand, vice 1, vice 2, viol, virgin 2, virgin 4, virtue 10, vision 3, vitious 1, volant 2, want 2, want 3, want 4, wanton 1, wanton 6, wanton 7, war 3, warm 1, welkin 1, wife 1, wight, wit 8, wondrous 1, wont, woodnote, word 12, work 6, work 7, world 2, world 3, world 8, world 11, ycleped, year 1, zeal, zephyr

Minsheu, John (fl. c. 1617), etymologist and scholar: caterpillar, chitterlings, girl, lunch, pizzle, sillabub, sirrah, wanton

Moore, Edward (1712-57), poet: fun

More, Henry (1614-87), religious writer and author of *An Antidote against Atheism*: egregious 1, evolution 2, excogitate, exemptitious, fin, flagelet, illaqueate, indigitation, linkboy, man 6, naturalist, powdering-tub 1, religion 2, scamble 2, sense 10, song 6, style 1, tennis, world 4

More, Sir Thomas (1478-1535), author of *Utopia*: huggermugger

Mortimer, John (c. 1656-1736), agricultural writer: cony, dwarf 2, etch, fancy 8, green 5, green 7, headgargle, heart 17, hydromel, jack 4, mango, mother 2, mum n.s., oats, pancake, pinguid, pismire, provender, restorative, smut 2, spinny, truth 7

Moxon, Joseph (1627-91), mathematician and physicist: **heart 3, jack 3, letter 6, pile 1, play 11, punch 1, stuff 1, trimmer 2**

Mulso, Hester (later Hester Chapone; 1727-1801), poet and author of *Letters on the Improvement of the Mind*: **quatrain**

Musæ Anglicanæ, a collection of poetry from 1692: **ganch**

Musschenbroek, Pieter van (1692-1761), Dutch scientist: **will 11**

Newton, Sir Isaac (1642-1727), physicist and mathematician: **aerial 1, analysis 2, artist 1, author 1, constitution 2, ether 1, gravity 1,** *ignis fatuus*, **lens, light 1, nice 6, office 2, parallax, polite 1, prism, rainbow, refraction, salt 1, sensible 2, spectrum, vapour 3, variety 1, vision 1**

Newton, Thomas (1704-82), clergyman and editor of Milton's *Paradise Lost*: **urim**

Norris, John (1657-1711), religious writer: **seraglio**

Otway, Thomas (1652-85), playwright and poet; Johnson wrote his *Life*: **doubt 4, fulsome 1, jilt 1, lumber, lusty, woman 1**

Pamela See **Richardson, Samuel**

Paradise Lost See **Milton, John**

Paré, Ambroise (c. 1510-90), physician: **salamander**

Peacham, Henry (c. 1579-c. 1643), author of *Graphice; or, The Most Auncient and Excellent Art of Drawing and Limning*: **allegory, bungler, cat, caterpillar, conservative, discord 3, emblem 2, epigram, eschutcheon, football, goat, gold, limn, lion, lust 2, mask 5, metaphysick, morris 1, ninepins, pantofle, physick 2, poem, rainbow, rebus, rhinoceros, satyr, scale 4, tennis, tiger, translate 3, trinity,** *virago* **1, zephyr**

Philips, Ambrose (1674-1749), poet and playwright; Johnson wrote his *Life*: **aerial 5, author 2, barbarian 3, cates, defecate 1, ecstasy 2, egregious 1, falchion, galligaskins, gloze 1, kern, lazar, learn 1, lion, mean 3, medly, million, mum n.s., nocent 2, rasp, rhyme 3, rule 1, stormy 1, studious 3, terrifick, tiff 1, transpicuous, trumpet 1, unmanlike 2, volant 2, welkin 1**

Phillips, Edward (1630-c. 1696), nephew of John Milton, lexicographer and author of *The New World of Words*: **caudebeck, king 4**

Pope, Alexander (1688-1744), poet and author of *The Dunciad*; Johnson wrote his *Life*: **adept, aerial 4, air 3, air 8, air 11, air 12, air 13, air 14, alexandrine, allow 2, anatomy 1, ancient n.s., antiquary,** *antithesis*, **arms 1, arms 3, art 1, atom 1, barbecue, bead 1, beauty 1, bilingsgate, blockhead, bodkin 2, bodkin 3, bohea, bookful, bookworm 2, brain v.a., bug, candid 2, catcal,** *cento*, **chair 1, chair 3, character 7, chicanery, china, chocolate 3, chymist, cipher 3, cit, climacterick, clinch 1, club 2, codille, coffee, comedy, compass 3, conceit 6, contract 1, coquette, coxcomb 3, crack-brained, cricket 2, criticise 1, critick n.s. 1, critick n.s. 2, cup 2, daisy, death 8, death 9, dedication 2, devil 4, disaster 2, discord 2, discover 3, divan 2, dog n.s. 5, dog v.a., doublet 1, dower 1, drab, dragon 1,** *duenna*, **eclogue, editor, egregious 2, elegant 1, elegant 2, empyreal, enchant 3, encomium, engine 3, epic, equipage 3, essay v.a. 1, expatiate 1, expatiate 2, fame 1, fashion 6, favourite 1, favourite 2, fib, fibre 1, flagitious, flirt 1, fool 1, fool 7, football, formal 5, frank 2, frippery 2, furbelow, gavot, gay 1, generous 2, genius 4, genius 5, gentle 1, giant, gin 4, gloss 1, green 1, grot, grotesque, gymnastick, hackney 3, hackney 4, handydandy, happiness 3, heart 1, heart 6, heart 8, heart 11, hebetate,**

INDEX OF
PIQUANT TERMS

For words that feature more than one definition, the number of the applicable definition is noted.
Abbreviations of parts of speech, such as n.s. and adj., are noted only when needed for clarification.

For definitions of "cant," "low and bad" and "ludicrous" words, see How to Read Johnson's Dictionary.

Animals

alligator, *amphisbæna*, animal n.s.,
animal adj., animalcule, antler, ape,
baboon, bat, bitch 1, brach, bug,
camelopard, cancer 1, cat, caterpillar,
cony, cow-leech, crocodile, dog n.s. 1,
dog n.s. 5, *dracunculus*, dragon 1, elk,
emmet, ephemera 2, escargatoire,
estrich, farcy, feline, feuterer, fin, fizgig,
fleam, flittermouse, gare, gibcat, goat,
gregarious, guineapig, headgargle,
hedge-pig, hippopotamus, humblebee,
husband 2, hyen, ichneumon, insect,
jack 9, kine, kitten, *leviathan*, lion,
lizard, lob 3, locust, lomp, mantiger,
menage, minim 2, monkey, moose,
mouse, musket 2, naff, *nautilus*,
ortolan, ostrich, otter, ounce, pard,
pastern, pelican, penguin 1, pet 2,
philomel, phytivorous, pie 2, pilser,
pismire, polecat, porpoise, proboscis,
provender, pudding 2, pug, purr, puss,
rackoon, raindeer, rat, Renard, reptile,
reremouse, rhinoceros, salamander,
seacow, seadog, seahog, seahorse,
seaserpent, spider, stoat, tadpole,
tarantula, tiger, torpedo, trochings,
turtle, veterinarian, whale, whelp,
zoography, zoology, zoophyte

Art and Theatre

architecture, art, artist, beauty, cartoon,
catcal, crayon, dislimn, drama,
entertainment 8, factitious, figure,
grotesque, histrionical, icon,
illuminator 2, japan, light 3, limn,
lithography, mask 5, *mezzotinto*,
pencil 1, pictorial, play 3, rebus,
scenick, sidebox, sock 2, theatre,
tiringhouse, *virtuoso*, zocle

Books and Writing

abc, abridgment, acrostick, *amanuensis*,

ana, annotator, anthology, apocrypha,
aqua fortis, author, autography, Bible,
book, bookful, bookish, bookworm,
brachygraphy, breviary, brevier, canon 8,
catchword, character, chronogram,
cipher, compositor, crossrow,
cryptography, cryptology, dictionary,
ectype, editor, element 5, encyclopedia,
epitome, errata, escritoir, expurgatory,
exscript, fescue, *folio*, glaire, gloss 1,
glossary, gloze 2, grubstreet,
handwriting, hieroglyph, holograph,
hyphen, illuminator 2, inkhorn, leaf 2,
lection, legend 4, letter, lexicographer,
lexicon, librarian, magazine 2,
manuscript, mercury 3, minum 1,
monogram, motto, news 2, nonpareil 3,
obelisk 2, *octavo*, pamphleteer, pandect,
paper, paraphrase, parchment, patron,
pen 1, pencil, penman, philactery, pica,
pie 3, pirate 2, plagiary, pocketbook,
polygraphy, pressman 2, print, publish,
quarto, read, rebus, *reglet*, rubrick,
scribbler, scrutoire, semicolon, sign 9,
standish, style 5, tachygraphy, type,
typography, vellum, verse 2, writative,
write, writer

Cant Words

bamboozle, belch 2, belswagger, betty,
bilingsgate, bishop, brogue 2, bub,
bubble, bucaniers, cabbage, conycatch,
crambo, crincum, doodle, fap, fib,
fiddlefaddle, fig 2, flam, flipp, fulham,
fun, gambler, gibberish, glum, *gout*,
heart-breaker, *hiccius doccius*, higgledy-
piggeldy, jiggumbob, laudanum, *lingo*,
mercury 4, monstrous, mopus,
mumper, nervous 3, nim, pigwidgeon,
plum 3, prig, punch 2, rum 1, shab,
skimbleskamble, slubberdegullion,

abligurition, abnormous, absinthiated, absonous, absterge, abstorted, acclivous, accubation, acephalous, acervose, actitation, aculeate, addulce, adiaphory, adipous, adjutrix, agalaxy, agminal, agnation, agnomination, agrestick, algid, allubescency, alluvious, alogy, altiloquence, altivolant, amaritude, amatorculist, amnicolist, amygdaline, anatiferous, androtomy, anhelose, anileness, anorexy, appropinquate, apricate, arenation, argillaceous, armigerous, armisonous, arrision, arrode, artuate, ascii, astrigerous, aurioation, baccated, baccivorous, balbucinate, bellipotent, bibacious, bibacity, blatteration, bombycinous, botryoid, brait, brontology, bulimy, cachinnation, cacuminate, calceated, calefactive, caliginous, cecity, cenatory, cephalalgy, cerulifick, cibarious, ciliary, circumforaneous, concinnity, conglaciation, consopiation, cornute, crebritude, crepitate, cretated, crinigerous, crispisculant, cruentate, cubation, dapatical, deaureate, debacchation, debarb, debullition, decacuminated, decempedal, deglutition, delirate, deosculation, depucelate, desidiose, despumation, desquamation, dicacity, digladiation, disard, discalceation, dislimb, dodecatemorion, *dracunculus*, draffy, ebriety, echinate, edacious, edulcorate, effigiate, effossion, elumbated, emulge, enatation, enecate, enubilate, enucleate, epulation, ereptation, ereption, errhine, erubescent, esurient, eventerate, exanimous, excarnate, excubation, exemptitious, eximious, exomphalos, exossated, expugn, exspuition, exsudation, fabaceous, facinorous, famosity, farinaceous, fatiferous, feateous, febricitate, febrifuge, feriation, ferity, festinate, figulate, flabile, flammivomous, flexanimous, flosculous, fluviatick, fructiferous, fulgid, fulguration, fungosity, furacious,

fuscation, fustigate, fustilarian, galericulate, gemelliparous, geminate, gemmosity, genethliacks, geniculation, glabrity, gracile, gracilent, grandevity, grandinous, gregal, gremial, gry, gulosity, halituous, hamated, hamble, hebdomad, hebetate, hederaceous, helminthick, heptacapsular, herbescent, hodiernal, horrisonous, humicubation, ignivomous, ignoscible, illachrymable, illaeqeuate, immarcessible, impetiginous, impignorate, impinguate, inceration, increpate, inescation, infundibuliform, infuscation, ingannation, ingurgitate, inopinate, insulse, insusurration, knubble

Inkhorn Terms, L-Z

labefy, labent, laciniated, lamm, lancinate, languet, lanigerous, lapicide, lapidate, lascivient, latitation, lentiform, lentiginous, leporine, libral, limitaneous, linguacious, logomachy, luciferous, lucrifick, luctation, ludification, lusk, lusorious, lutarious, lymphated, macilent, mactation, maculate, madefy, maffle, malefick, malvaceous, malversation, mammiform, manducate, manubial, maritated, marmorean, melliferous, meracious, mimographer, minacious, moidered, moky, morigerous, *mormo*, motation, muliebrity, multiscious, multisonous, mumps, mundivagant, mundungus, mussitation, mynchen, nasicornous, natation, nictate, nidification, nimiety, niveous, noctivagant, nombles, nosology, nosopoetick, nubble, nubilate, nuciferous, nullibiety, nummary, nuncupative, obambulation, obequitation, objurgate, obmutescence, obreption, obstupefactive, occision, ocellated, octonocular, odontalgick, omnifick, ophiophagous, opsimathy, optimity, orbity, orgillous, orphanotrophy, oscitancy, ossuary, papilionaceous, parentation, parietal, parvity, pash, patible, patibulary,

Inkhorn Terms, L-Z *(continued)*

pauciloquy, pedaneous, perpotation, pervicacious, phytivorous, pilser, piscation, pledget, plumipede, plunket, pluvial, pneumatology, poupicts, prestigation, pulicose, pulvil, puniceous, racemiferous, rescissory, rhabarbarate, rigation, roboreous, rorifluent, rotundifolious, royne, rubifick, ruderary, ruricolist, sabulous, salsamentarious, salutiferous, saponaceous, sarculation, sarn, scatches, scaturiginous, sciomachy, scopulous, screable, scrutation, scutiform, segnity, sepilible, sermocination, sesquipedal, sesquitertian, siliginose, skaddons, soporiferous, sororicide, spraints, steganography, stentorophonick, sternutation, stirious, stridulous, stultiloquence, sudorifick, supervacaneousness, tauricornous, tenebricose, tentiginous, tepefaction, teratology, testudineous, thesmothete, thrapple, thrasonical, thurification, titubation, torvous, tralatitious, trangram, transpicuous, tripudiation, tumulose, turbination, uberty, ubication, uliginous, ultroneous, umbles, ustion, varvels, vellicate, verecund, veridical, vermiculation, vermiculous, vermiform, vicenary, viduity, vituline, yarr, zetetick, zocle

Insults

airling, asshead, backbiter, backfriend, barbarian 3, bedpresser, bellygod, bitch 2, blockhead, blowze, blunderhead, booby, *borachio*, buffleheaded, bumpkin, bungler, caitiff, callat, churl, cit, clodpate, clotpoll, clown, coxcomb 3, crack-brained, crack-hemp, crack-rope, craver, cudden, cully, curmudgeon, cynick, dam, dandiprat, disard, dizzard, dog 3, dolt, doodle, dotard, double-dealer, dowdy, doxy, drab, dull, dunce, empiric, erke, errant 2, fashionist, fatwitted, *fico*, fig, finical,

flagitious, flasher, fleer, fool, footlicker, fop, fopdoodle, foutra, fren, Frenchify, fribbler, fub, fustilarian, garlickeater, geck, glassgazing, glike, gorbelly, gormand, *grammaticaster*, half-scholar, half-wit, harlot, harridan, hatchet-face, hector, hoiden n.s., hunks, idler, jack 1, jack pudding, jackalent, jilt, jobbernowl, jogger, jolthead, knave 3, knuff, lackbrain, lewdster, linseywoolsey, lob 1, looby, lordling, losel, lown, lubber, lumpish, lusk, macaroon 1, madcap, malapert, man 5, meacock, merry-andrew, milksop, mimick 2, minx, mome, moon-calf 2, mope, mopus, nidget, nincompoop, ninnyhammer, nithing, nizy, noddy, noodle, numskull, oaf 2, pedant, pettifogger, pickleherring, pickthank, *poetaster*, politicaster, prig, profligate, punch 5, pundle, punk, pursy, quaint 6, quean, ragamuffin, rake 2, rakehel, rampallian, rantipole, redcoat, rhymer, ribald, rogue, roister, ronion, roynish, runnion, saucebox, scambler, *scelerat*, scold, scomm, scroyle, seeksorrow, shaveling, shrew, silly, simpleton, sirrah, skipjack, slubberdegullion, smellfeast, spark 4, stateswoman, stinkard, strapping, tatterdemalion, teague, tomboy, trollop, trubtail, trull, *virago*, wantwit, whelp 4, whoreson, wiseacre, witling, wittol, witworm, zany, zealot

Law and Crime

abannition, age, *alias*, alimony, animadversion, anomy, antinomy, attaint, baron 4, base-born, bastard, betty, black-mail, Bridewell, bucaniers, cabbage, cadi, chancery, citizen, civilian, contract, *corsair*, crack-hemp, crack-rope, cuckingstool, disannul, doomsday 2, dowager, dower, entail, felo-de-se, felony, forgery 1, gallowtree, gaol, garnish 3, garnish 4, gibbet 1, glebe 2, highwayman, holograph, *ignoramus* 1, impeach, incendiary, infancy 2, jailbird, jointure,

narcotick, nepenthe, nerve, nervous 3,
nightmare, nosology, nosopoetick,
nostrum, odontalgick, opiate, opium,
organ 1, orgasm, ozæna, parbreak,
paroxysm, peccant 2, pesthouse,
pestilent, pharmacopoeia, philactery,
phlebotomy, phthisick, physick,
physiognomy, picktooth, pile 9, pimple,
pineal, piss, pizzle, pleurisy, pockhole,
powdering-tub 2, prescription 2,
priapism, prognostick 1, prophylactick,
ptisan, ptysmagogue, puke, purge,
quack, quarantain, quinsy, quob,
quotidian, receipt 6, recipe, restorative,
rheum, saltinbanco, salutiferous, sane,
sarcocele, sarcophagous, sassafras,
scalpel, scorbutical, scotomy, scrofula,
seahorse, shingles, slop, snot, snuff 1,
soporiferous, spleen 1, strangury,
tabefy, tertian, testicle, thrapple,
toothdrawer, trepan 1, trocar, tuel,
tumour 1, urinal, uvula, valetudinarian,
vapour 5, venesection, veterinarian,
virtue 3, virtue 4, wamble, yux

Money and Business

business, cadger, clicker, commerce,
corsair, dollar, *doublon*, ducat, economy,
excise, factory, frank 3, gabel, gold,
grocer, guinea, haggle, higgle,
intercourse, landfall, landjobber, leaf 4,
Lewis d'or, *livre*, lucrifick, *mammon*,
mendicant, merchant, moidore, money,
monopoly, nummary, office, pile 8,
pirate, pistole, plum 3, pressmoney,
property, publican 1, rixdollar, searover,
shekel, shilling, stockjobber, talent 1,
trade, traffick, underwriter, usury,
workhouse, yellowboy

Music and Dance

adagio, air, *allegro*, *aria*, ballad, ballette,
boree, burden 4, *cantata*, cantation,
castanet, compass 7, *coupée*, crowder,
da capo, dance, descant 1, diatonick,
discord 3, dulcet 2, flagelet, galliard 2,
gamut, gavot, gleek, guitar, harmony,
harpsichord, hautboy, jack 8, jig,
lavolta, lyrical, maidmarian, melody,
minuet, minum 2, morris 1, musick,

octave 2, *opera*, *orchestre*, organ 2,
pavan, play 8, rebeck, recitative,
rhythmical, rigadoon, scale 9,
semitone, solo, *sonata*, song, spinet,
tabour, tattoo, time 14, treble,
tripudiation, trumpet, viol, *violoncello*,
virginal, woodnote

Philosophy and Psychology

antinomy, beauty, bigot, brain n.s.,
complex, conceit, cynick, dialectick,
doctrine, dogmatical, doubt, empirical 2,
empiricism, ethicks, faculty, fancy,
fantastical, fascinate, fear, flexanimous,
fury, genius, hallucination, happiness,
heterodox, hope n.s., hope v.n., idea,
ideal, imagination, inspire, intellect,
intellectual, intelligence, judgment 1,
knowledge, liberty 2, logick, lunacy,
lunatick, madhouse, madness,
materialist, melancholy, memory,
mental, metaphysick, mnemonicks,
moonstruck, moral, muse 1, nihility,
nolition, oneirocritical, ontology,
paradox, passion, pathetical,
philosopheme, philosophy, pineal,
pneumatology, property, pyrrhonism,
quality, quintessence, rapture, real,
reality, reason n.s., reason v.n.,
reason v.a., right, sane, sense,
sensibility, sensible, sensitive,
sentiment, skeptick, sophist, soul,
spirit, stoick, sublime, sympathy,
talent 2, taste, terrifick, terrour, theory,
think, time, transportation 3, truth,
ubication, understanding, universe,
vacuity, vanity, vapour 4, velleity, vision,
visionary, warm, will, wit, witty, wood,
zeal, zealot

Plants

agnus castus, daffodil, daisy,
dendrology, dwarf 4, elm, flosculous,
garlick, gramineous, gymnospermous,
hederaceous, heliotrope, herbescent,
insemination, ironwood, leaf 1, lime
tree, maize, mandrake, mummy 2,
nectarine, nonpareil 2, oak, paigles,
palmetto, papilionaceous, penguin 2,
peony, pineapple, plant, plum, rape 5,

Uncommon Books for Serious Readers

Levenger Press is the publishing arm of

LEVENGER®
TOOLS FOR SERIOUS READERS

www.Levenger.com   **800-544-0880**

**Eight or Nine Wise Words
About Letter-Writing**
by Lewis Carroll

Feeding the Mind
by Lewis Carroll

Painting as a Pastime
by Winston S. Churchill

Rare Words
and ways to master their meanings
by Jan Leighton and Hallie Leighton

Samuel Johnson's Dictionary
Selections from the 1755 work
that defined the English language
edited by Jack Lynch

The Silverado Squatters
Six selected chapters
by Robert Louis Stevenson

Words That Make a Difference
and how to use them
in a masterly way
by Robert Greenman